The law relating to actionable non-disclosure : and other breaches of duty in relations of confidence and influence.

George Spencer Bower

The Making of Modern Law collection of legal archives constitutes a genuine revolution in historical legal research because it opens up a wealth of rare and previously inaccessible sources in legal, constitutional, administrative, political, cultural, intellectual, and social history. This unique collection consists of three extensive archives that provide insight into more than 300 years of American and British history. These collections include:

Legal Treatises, 1800-1926: over 20,000 legal treatises provide a comprehensive collection in legal history, business and economics, politics and government.

Trials, 1600-1926: nearly 10,000 titles reveal the drama of famous, infamous, and obscure courtroom cases in America and the British Empire across three centuries.

Primary Sources, 1620-1926: includes reports, statutes and regulations in American history, including early state codes, municipal ordinances, constitutional conventions and compilations, and law dictionaries.

These archives provide a unique research tool for tracking the development of our modern legal system and how it has affected our culture, government, business – nearly every aspect of our everyday life. For the first time, these high-quality digital scans of original works are available via print-on-demand, making them readily accessible to libraries, students, independent scholars, and readers of all ages.

THE LAW RELATING TO
ACTIONABLE NON-DISCLOSURE

THE LAW
RELATING TO
ACTIONABLE
NON-DISCLOSURE

AND OTHER BREACHES OF DUTY
IN RELATIONS OF
CONFIDENCE AND INFLUENCE

BY

GEORGE SPENCER BOWER

ONE OF HIS MAJESTY'S COUNSEL, A MASTER OF THE BENCH OF THE INNER TEMPLE,
AUTHOR OF "A CODE OF THE LAW OF ACTIONABLE DEFAMATION,"
"THE LAW OF ACTIONABLE MISREPRESENTATION,"
ETC , ETC

"ἆ Ζεῦ, τί δράσω; δεύτερον ληφθῶ κακός,
κρύπτων θ᾽ ἃ μὴ δεῖ, καὶ λέγων αἴσχιστ᾽ ἐπῶν,"

SOPH , *Philoct.* 908, 909.

"Justitiæ soror
Incorrupta Fides, nudaque Veritas."

HOR., *Carm* I xxiv

LONDON
BUTTERWORTH & CO, BELL YARD, TEMPLE BAR
Law Publishers.

SYDNEY	BUTTERWORTH & CO. (AUSTRALIA), LTD
CALCUTTA	BUTTERWORTH & CO. (INDIA), LTD
WINNIPEG	BUTTERWORTH & CO (CANADA), LTD
WELLINGTON (N Z)	BUTTERWORTH & CO. (AUSTRALIA), LTD.

1915

PRINTED BY
WILLIAM CLOWES AND SONS, LIMITED,
LONDON AND BECCLES

PREFACE.

EACH of the quotations appearing on the title-page of this book emphasizes the two aspects of the general duty of honesty in the use of speech between man and man. "Nuda veritas," and its contravention by the "λέγων αἴσχιστ᾽ ἐπῶν," formed the subject of my former work on Actionable Misrepresentation. The present treatise is devoted to "incorrupta fides," and its violation by the "κρύπτων ἃ μὴ δεῖ." The two books, therefore, may be regarded as, in a sense, the counterparts and complements of one another.

The close alliance between these two branches of what is really one great jural department, with the necessary result that at many points they intersect and overlap one another, is not without embarrassment and inconvenience to the writer who essays to treat them separately and successively. The specialist is prone to regard every phenomenon as in some way connected with his subject. Accordingly, when specializing on misrepresentation, I was assailed by the strong temptation to regard certain species of non-disclosure as merely so many forms of implied misrepresentation, just as, in dealing with non-disclosure, I have often been sensible of the converse temptation, though not nearly in the same degree. The result has been that in some parts of the present work I have retraversed ground already covered by its predecessor. This, however, I venture to think, was unavoidable. Where an actionable wrong may reasonably be regarded in either of two lights, it is rightly the subject of double treatment. The "δεύτερον κακός," whether in jurisprudence or in ethics, is necessarily exposed to cross fires.

The several matters with which the present treatise is concerned are classified, and the scheme and arrangement of each chapter is set forth and fully explained, in the First or introductory Chapter; and it is unnecessary to repeat here what is said there

To my Commentary on Misrepresentation I prefixed a statement of the law in a codified form. The present work contains no such code. I made an attempt in this direction; but the result was not at all satisfactory, and I was soon convinced that the subject does not lend itself to this mode of treatment. The concepts and principles involved are too fluid and delicate to justify the Procrustean extension or compression which would be necessary to fit them into the rigid frame-work of a code. The requisite propositions must either be drawn out to a length sufficient to comprehend the infinite developments, and possibilities of development, of the various doctrines— which would be to reproduce the very "wilderness of single instances" which it is the function of a good code to get rid of,—or else they must be expressed in terms of such blank and naked universality as to afford no guidance or instruction, the result being (as Bacon said "of all rules that are very general") a mere "sound in the air,"—a series of statements *lucifera*, perhaps, but not *fructifera*,— tenuity, if not obscurity. As Aristotle wisely observed with reference to similar generalities in the domain of ethics, "ἔστι τὸ μὲν εἰπεῖν οὕτως ἀληθὲς μὲν, οὐθὲν δὲ σαφές" (*Eth.* vi. 1, 2).

It has been no easy matter to devise a title for the present work which shall at once accurately and completely indicate its intended scope. "Actionable Non-Disclosure," without more, would be a correct designation of the contents of the greater part of the work, but it would not perhaps be considered adequate as a description of the important subjects dealt with in the Fourth and Fifth Chapters, since these include certain obligations of good faith in relations of confidence, and of influence, which are regarded by most lawyers as additional to that of disclosure, though (as will be seen) there is some reason for deeming them either forms, or species, or offshoots of the one primary duty of disclosure in its largest sense (see §§ 316, 366, 473–9). "Actionable Abuses of Confidence, and of Influence," would, no doubt, cover the whole ground, but it would include a good deal more ; and, in any case, the phrase lacks terminological precision. On the whole, the title selected seemed the least open to objection of any which suggested themselves.

These are not propitious times for the bringing out of a jurisprudential treatise. Amid the clash of arms, not laws only, but law books are silenced. The thunder of legions over the face of the earth may seem for the moment to have drowned the pure voice of Justice, and the fumes of smouldering cathedrals to have clouded her august features. We have seen the criminal violation in the international arena of all those duties of good faith in relations of confidence and influence which, as established in British jurisprudence between individuals, it has been the object of this work to expound,— we have seen a trustee and guardian State ravishing the honour and independence and devastating the possessions of the State which was its *cestui que trust* and ward Nay, more,—we have heard those crimes justified by a commandeered philosophy which has not scrupled to "push beyond her mark, and be Procuress to the lords of Hell." It remains to be seen whether those "armed opinions" are to subjugate mankind, or mankind them. Only one who despairs of the moral order of the universe can doubt the ultimate result, or hesitate to acknowledge the existence and sovereignty in human affairs of international Duty and Honour; not, indeed, in the narrow Austinian aspect, but in that higher sense in which Hooker hymns the majesty of Law at the close of the First Book of his *Ecclesiastical Polity*. "Of Law there can be no less acknowledged than that her seat is the bosom of God, her voice the harmony of the world, all things in heaven and on earth do her homage, the very least as feeling her care, and the greatest as not exempting her power." This is that immutable, absolute, and universal Duty to whose beauty and sanctity the German philosopher of other and better times paid as lively a homage as the English poet of a later day. Wordsworth's superb apostrophe is but the translation into poetry of Kant's "categorical imperative."

> "Thou dost preserve the stars from wrong;
> And the most ancient heavens through Thee are fresh and strong"

There is no longer any Amphictyonic Council, or College of Fetiales, to enforce the observance of this Duty on nations in the œcumenical convulsion now raging around us. But it is our pride to know that by land, by sea, by air,—in the heights and in the depths,—as near to our shores as the trenches in Flanders, and as far away overseas as the Falkland Islands,—the British Empire is unweariedly upholding in arms against delinquent States those same principles of good faith, honour, and justice which for centuries past she has enforced in her Courts upon her own subjects.

And now, inauspicious as the moment of its birth may be, without more ado I leave my offspring on the doorstep of public hospitality, addressing to it the language of "Herrick to his Book":—

> "Go thou forth, my book, though late,
> Yet be timely fortunate
> It may chance good luck may send
> Thee a kinsman, or a friend,
> That may harbour thee, when I
> With my fates neglected lie.
> If thou know'st not where to dwell,
> See, the fire's by farewell"

G. SPENCER BOWER.

2, HARE COURT, TEMPLE.
February, 1915.

TABLE OF CONTENTS.

TABLE OF CASES.

A.

TABLE OF CASES.

H.

L.

N.

S.

TABLE OF STATUTES.

THE LAW RELATING TO
ACTIONABLE NON-DISCLOSURE
AND OTHER BREACHES OF DUTY IN
RELATIONS OF
CONFIDENCE AND INFLUENCE.

CHAPTER I.

INTRODUCTORY

SECT 1   SCOPE OF THE TREATISE.

1. IN all transactions and relations of which the law takes cognizance there is a general duty of veracity owed by the parties to one another, in the sense and to the extent that any departure from this duty constitutes, under certain conditions (a), a misrepresentation which is actionable at the suit of the party misled   But there are also certain defined types of transaction and relation (b), in which the parties are under an obligation not merely to state truly whatever is stated, but to divulge with candour and completeness facts which, in transactions and relations not falling within the recognized classes, there is no obligation to disclose at all.   In the former description of case, the law requires no more from the party than to speak the truth, if he speaks at all, in the latter, it exacts not merely a deliverance of "the truth and nothing but the truth," but a full revelation of "the whole truth" (c).   This has been occasionally, though perhaps not very felicitously, expressed by the proposition that, whereas in all contracts and relations good faith is required, a superlative degree of good faith, extending to duties of disclosure and others, is demanded in negotiations for contracts, or during the subsistence of relations, which fall within the special classes above referred to (d).   In other words, whilst *bona fides* only need characterize the one, *uberrima fides* must characterize the other   It may be doubted whether these terms are judiciously

---

(a) Such as materiality, inducement, and, in certain cases, fraud and damage

(b) The statement of BULLER, J , sitting in Chancery, at p 389 of *Pearson* v *Morgan* (1788), 2 Brown C C 388—"it is *always* considered a constructive *fraud* when the party knows the truth and conceals it, and such constructive fraud *always* makes the party liable "—is quite incorrect, unless this proposition is to be taken as limited to those transactions and relations which are described in the text

(c) See the observations of FRY, J., at p 136 of *Re Banister* (1879), 12 C. D 131, C A. ("it must be the truth, and the whole truth "), and again at p 17 of *Re Marsh and Earl Granville* (1883), 24 C D 11, C A ("he must tell the truth, and all the truth ").

(d) See the expressions of Lord MANSFIELD, C J , and Lord ABINGER, C B , as cited in notes (a) and (b) to § 87, *post*, and those of TURNER, V C , cited in note (r) to § 82, *post*.

chosen, and whether it was wise to introduce, and encourage, the idea of comparative degree of honesty at all (e), but they now occupy too firm a place in the gloss ries of our jurisprudence to be easily dislodged. Indeed, the English equivalent of *uberrima fides* has latterly been accorded the express recognition and *imprimatur* of the legislature (f).

2. Apart from relations of the above character, involving confidence only, and giving rise to a purely fiduciary duty of disclosure, there are relations from which the law presumes the existence and exercise of domination and influence by the one party over the other. Here it is not merely a case of the one party necessarily trusting to the other for full information as to those matters which, from the nature of the contract, transaction, or relation, he cannot ordinarily be supposed to know himself; it is a case where one of the two parties is not only superior in knowledge, but also in will and moral strength, and therefore comes into the arena with a double advantage and inequality, involving a correspondingly double duty on his part, before entering upon any transaction with the other party during the subsistence of the relationship and the influence resulting from it, to see that the other's mind is fully instructed, and his will completely emancipated, and that, in these and other respects, the "inequality" is removed or neutralized.

3. This treatise is concerned with the duties of disclosure and otherwise which arise out of the transactions and relations indicated, and the civil rights and liabilities occasioned by the violation of those duties.

SECT. 2 CLASSIFICATION OF THE TRANSACTIONS AND RELATIONS GIVING RISE TO THE DUTY OF DISCLOSURE AND KINDRED DUTIES.

4. There are five *genera*, divisible in each case into various species, of the transactions and relations in question, all of which involve the duty of disclosure, and some of which involve other duties as well.

5. The first of these classes consists of cases where, in negotiating for contracts of certain kinds, the one party must necessarily, from the nature of the contemplated transaction, be cognisant of facts of which the other party must be presumed ignorant, and for the disclosure of which the latter must rely on the good faith of the former, to enable him to form a judgment as to the expediency of entering into the contract on the terms proposed The one knows, and is trusted : the other does not know, and trusts The first is therefore, under a duty, down to the moment when the contract is concluded,

---

(e) It seems somewhat ridiculous to apply the Aristotelian μέσον to such a subject-matter as this, and to suggest the possibility of a distinction between conduct which is "indifferent honest," and excessively honest—between faith and super-faith. The Roman law distinguishes between actions *bonæ fidei*, that is, actions in respect of contracts and relations of a fiduciary character, and actions which are not *bonæ fidei*, it does not erect into a third and superlative class, with a special name, such transactions and relations as English law designates *uberrimæ fidei* See App C, § 672, *post*

(f) In the Marine Insurance Act, 1906 (6 Edw. 7, c 41), s 17 · "a contract of marine insurance is a contract based upon the utmost good faith, and, if the utmost good faith be not observed by either party, the contract may be avoided by the other party" At p 792 of *Seaton v Heath*, [1899] 1 Q B 782, C A , ROMER, L J , describes the phrase as "short and convenient"

to disclose all such material facts as are within his actual or presumptive knowledge, and are not within the actual or presumptive knowledge of the other. This class comprises negotiations preliminary to contracts of insurance, sale, suretyship, releases and compromises, and the like. The extent and degree of the required disclosure vary considerably according to the species of contract which is in contemplation, but in all cases alike there is an obligation to disclose material facts, though in the character and nature of the facts deemed material in the several species there is the widest difference (g).

6. In the second class, it is no longer a question of disclosure of matters likely to affect the judgment of one of the parties to a negotiation or treaty. It is here assumed that a relation has already been established, whether by express contract or by conduct and circumstances, which implies a fiduciary bond between the persons so related, and a consequent duty on the party in whom confidence is placed to observe good faith towards the party reposing that confidence, when entering into any transaction, either with him or with third persons, during the continuance of the relation. The relations referred to are those of trustee and *cestui que trust*, promoter and company, and principal and agent (including partner and firm). The duty here is on the trustee, promoter, or agent, to disclose to his *cestui que trust*, to the company promoted by him, or to his principal, as the case may be, the nature and particulars of any transaction with a third person whereby he has obtained, or is promised, a personal profit or advantage; and, in the case of a transaction direct with the *cestui que trust*, company, or principal, his duty is to divulge all material information acquired or possessed by him during his trusteeship, promotership, or agency, with the added duty of refraining from the transaction altogether, unless the *cestui que trust*, company, or principal is independently advised, or he (the trustee, &c.) has given the *cestui que trust*, &c., exactly the same advice and protection against himself as he would have given him against a stranger, and (in certain cases of purchase) unless he has given full value (h)

7. The third class consists of all those relations in which there is either presumed in law, or proved in fact, to have existed on the one side supremacy, and, on the other, subjection; in which (to adopt the phraseology of the law of easements) the will of the one party is " dominant," and the will of the other is " servient " These include domestic relations, such as those of parent and child, or guardian and ward, and relations between persons in *loco parentis*, or standing in the position of guardians, though not so in strict technicality, and the persons committed to, or in fact under, their charge and protection; professional relations such as those between solicitor and client, between medical man and patient, and between priest, or spiritual director, and penitent, or disciple; and such relations of influence and domination as, in any particular case, may be proved to have existed in fact. In all these cases the duty of the dominant party, whilst the relation exists, and further whilst the influence arising from the relation endures, is not to accept any gift from,

(g) Ch. III, *post*, deals with this class.   (h) See Ch. IV, *post*.

or make any contract with, the servient party, unless he has not only put him
in possession of all material circumstances, but also has honestly and fully
informed him as to his rights and interests, and further (in cases of gifts) has
procured for him the independent and competent advice of a third person, and
(in certain cases of contract) has given full value and consideration (*i*).

8. All cases of a positive statutory duty of disclosure, for the violation
of which a party aggrieved has a civil remedy, are included in the fourth class(*j*).
It is obvious that, in such cases, in order to determine the nature and limits of
the duty, the precise matters to be disclosed, the parties entitled and liable,
and the form and mode of relief, resort must be had to the express provisions
of the particular statute or enactment. The most important of these enactments are certain sections of the Companies (Consolidation) Act, 1908, with
reference to prospectuses of companies (*k*).

9. The fifth, and last, class consists of cases in which a person is injuriously
affected by, and has a right of complaint and relief in respect of, another
person's breach of a duty of disclosure owed by him, primarily or immediately
to the Court, the State, or a class of third persons, and not, except indirectly,
to the party complaining (*l*).

SECT. 3. TOPICS INCLUDED. ORDER OF TREATMENT

10. In this Commentary, it is intended, after a preliminary discussion of
certain leading principles and conceptions which underlie the whole law of the
subject (*m*), to discuss separately and *seriatim* the duty of disclosure and other
analogous duties of good faith, in their civil aspect, arising out of the five
classes of transactions and relations above enumerated (*n*), and to add a
chapter on jurisdiction and procedure (*o*), followed by four Appendices, dealing
with terminology, the ethical (as compared with the juridical) treatment of
the subject, Roman law, and Scottish law, respectively (*p*)

11. The Chapters (*q*) on the first three of the five classes above enumerated
are all constructed on the same plan, and divided into the same number of
Sections, which, in each case, deal with the subject of the chapter, in the
following (which is conceived to be the logical) order of treatment. Sect. 1
is devoted to a short statement of the theory and principle on which the duty
is based, and a general description of the nature and limits of the duty.
Sect. 2 deals successively with the various species of the class, and with
the kinds of matters required to be disclosed, and the other duties (if
any) to be discharged, in transactions and relations belonging to each
particular species. Sect. 3 treats of the burden of proof which rests on the

(*i*) This class is the subject of Ch. V, *post*
(*j*) See Ch VI, *post*.
(*k*) See Ch. VI, *post*
(*l*) See Ch. VII, *post*
(*m*) These are expounded in Ch II, *post*
(*n*) In §§ 4-9, *sup.*
(*o*) Ch. VIII, *post*
(*p*) Appendices A, B, C, and D, respectively, *post*.
(*q*) Chs III, IV, V, *post*

party to whom the duty is owed ; Sect. 4, of the affirmative defences by which, and (in many cases) by which alone, the *primâ facie* case established against him can be rebutted by the party owing the duty ; Sect. 5, of remedies and relief , Sect. 6, of questions of law and fact ; and Sect. 7, of the parties to the duty, and to the proceedings arising out of an alleged violation of such duty. Each of the last two of the five classes obviously demands a separate and special mode of treatment (r).

12. Throughout this treatise, whenever it seems desirable for the purpose of avoiding troublesome reduplication of language and involution of sentences, the party who is entitled to insist on the observance of a duty of disclosure or other duty of good faith is termed " the party complaining," and the party who owes the duty is described as " the party charged." It may be said that these expressions are inapt, because the one party may never complain, and the other party may never be charged, and that the duty will none the less have existed all the time. To this the answer is that, until the one complains, and the other is charged, the law of *actionable* non-disclosure is not concerned with either. Except as actual or potential litigants, the parties have no interest for a treatise which is devoted to the dynamics, and not the statics, of the subject Duties and rights, abstracted from their amenability to legal process, and contemplated as in a state of rest, are the concern of ethics rather than of jurisprudence. It may then be objected that, in that case, there is no reason why the parties should not be called plaintiff and defendant respectively There is, however, this very important reason—viz that the right of the party complaining is, as regards most of the transactions and relations to be considered, asserted quite as often by affirmative defence, as in the form of active proceedings for rescission or otherwise (s), and, in one very important and extensive type of transaction, namely, insurance, it is almost invariably so asserted (t).

SECT 4 TOPICS EXCLUDED.

13. Where the parties to any transaction have made an express " contract for the truth " (u), or for full disclosure of all material facts, as is frequently the case in life or health insurance business (v), the sole question is whether the express term, condition, or warranty (as the case may be) has, or has not, been complied with This question, so far, belongs strictly to the domain of contract law, and not to that of non-disclosure · but, inasmuch as the existence of such a contractual engagement does not necessarily exclude the possibility of a co-existing obligation to disclose material facts not provided for by the warranty or condition, the subject demands, and receives, special consideration in its proper place (w)

(r) See Chs VI, and VII, *post*
(s) See Ch III, Sect 3, Ch IV, Sect 3, and Ch V, Sect 3, *post*.
(t) See Ch. III, Sect 3, *post*.
(u) The expression of MOULTON, L J., at p. 885 of *Joel* v. *Law Union and Crown Insurance Co* , [1908] 2 K B 863, C A.
(v) See §§ 169-171, *post*.
(w) *Ibid.*

14. " Non-disclosure " excludes " mistake," which, in its strict and proper sense, imports a self-induced misapprehension, either on the part of both the parties to a transaction, or on the part of one of them, arising from ignorance of some fact in the case, but not of any fact which it was the duty of one of the parties to reveal to the other. Of course every case of non-disclosure, or indeed of misrepresentation, does produce " mistake " in one sense of the word, but not in the sense in which that term is understood by lawyers.

15. *Ex vi termini*, non-disclosure has no concern with pure misrepresentation, *as such*. But those types of implied misrepresentation which consist of the omission or suppression of qualifying facts, or facts which the circumstances of the individual case raise a duty to divulge, fall within the limits of this work (*x*), as well as within those of the law relating to misrepresentation (*y*).

16. There are several legal consequences of non-disclosure besides civil liability That form of estoppel *in pais* which results from inaction and negligence is one (*z*) , criminal responsibility, where non-disclosure of specified matters is made an offence by the express provisions of a statute (*a*), or where, with other circumstances, it amounts to a "false pretence," is another. But since neither of these constitutes, or confers, as such, a cause of *action*, neither of them comes within the scope of *actionable* non-disclosure.

(*x*) See Ch III, Sect 2, Sub s. (8), *post*

(*y*) And, as such, this topic is dealt with in §§ 82-92, and §§ 103-106, of the author's *Law of Actionable Misrepresentation*.

(*z*) Estoppel is a rule of evidence, not a cause of action The same facts which establish the estoppel may of course be ground for relief in proceedings for non disclosure , but this is only an accident. Estoppel, as such, merely removes a barrier in the way of, or interposes an obstacle to, a cause of action which would otherwise fail or succeed respectively

(*a*) Many such statutory offences are created by the Companies (Consolidation) Act, 1908 (8 Edw 7, c. 69).

CHAPTER II.

GENERAL PROPOSITIONS AND DEFINITIONS IN RELATION TO DISCLOSURE, MATERIALITY, AND KNOWLEDGE.

17. IN all the classes of transactions and relations which form the subject of this work, there is a duty on one, or sometimes on each, of the parties to disclose to the other, or to one another, as the case may be, all material facts which are within the knowledge, actual or presumed, of the person who owes the duty, and are not within the knowledge, actual or presumed, of the person to whom the duty is owed. In some of the relations, there are other, and very important, coexisting duties, which must be discharged in addition to that of disclosure, but this latter obligation is a feature common to all of them

18. The mere enunciation of the above general rule instantly provokes the following inquiries. (1) what is the kind and degree of disclosure which satisfies the requirements of the rule? (2) what is the legal meaning of materiality? and (3) when is a party proved or presumed in law to know a fact? It is essential, therefore, that an analysis of these three leading concepts, Disclosure, Materiality, and Knowledge, should be entered upon at the outset, before commencing to deal with the several classes of matters to all of which alike the general principle is applied.

SECT 1. DISCLOSURE.

19. The only kind of disclosure which satisfies the requirements of the law is a disclosure which is both (i) exact and complete, and also (ii) explicit and unambiguous Any communication which falls short of the above whether the failure to divulge the whole truth in clear language arose from intellectual incapacity, or mere carelessness, or, on the other hand, from a preconceived and fraudulent design, is in law no disclosure at all

20. First, as to the requirement of precision and completeness, the rule, and the reason for it, have never been more clearly and succinctly stated than in a sentence taken from the work of a moral philosopher whose statements of the root principles and the theory of law are always admirable, and have rarely been improved upon by professed lawyers (b) "In insurances," says Paley—and insurances may be taken as typical of all the transactions comprised in the first of the classes already enumerated (c)—" in which the

(b) On the peculiar qualifications (natural and acquired) of Paley to speak with authority on matters of jurisprudence, and the justification for the frequent citation of his views in these pages, see § 650, *post*

(c) See § 5, *ante.*

underwriter computes his risk entirely from the account given by the person insured, it is absolutely necessary to the justice and validity of the contract that this account be exact and complete " (d)   To adopt another form of words, frequently used by judges, which bears precisely the same meaning, the disclosure must be " full and fair " (e)   A " partial or imperfect " revelation of the facts (f), or " a half-disclosure " (g), will not do   Indeed, a " half-disclosure " may be worse than no disclosure at all, because of its greater tendency to mislead, just as, in the provinces of misrepresentation or defamation, " the lie which is half the truth " has a more insidious potency of deception or denigration, as the case may be, than " a lie which is all a lie " (h). So, in relation to contracts for the sale of land, it has been well observed that " it is not for him "—the vendor—" just to tell what is not actually untrue, leaving out a great deal that is true, and leaving it to the purchaser to inquire whether there is any . . . omission in the description or not " (i)

21. Several instances of the recognition and strict application of the rule that incomplete and inexact disclosure is in law no disclosure at all, are to be found amongst the decisions relating to each of the different kinds of transaction in respect of which disclosure is obligatory (j), such as marine insurances (k),

(d) *Principles of Moral and Political Philosophy*, Bk. III, Part I, Ch viii (" Contracts of Hazard ").

(e) See, for example, *Bowles* v *Stewart* (1803), 1 Sch & Lefr. 209, *per* Lord REDFSDALE, L.C. (Ir), at p 226.

(f) *Greenwood* v *Greenwood* (1863), 2 De G J & S 28, *per* TURNER, L J , at pp 42, 43.

(g) The expression of COLLINS, M R , at p 359 of *Bartram & Sons* v *Lloyd* (1904), 90 L. T 357, C. A   Cp *Walker* v *Symonds* (1818), 3 Swanst 1 (*per* Lord ELDON, L.C., at p 73. "he who . . gives but *half information*, in the doctrine of this Court, conceals ")

(h) See the author's *Law of Actionable Misrepresentation*, Ch. IV, Sect 4, Sub s (2), as to the half truths which amount to misrepresentation.

(i) *Per* KINDERSLLY, V. C., at p. 430 of *Brandling* v *Plummer* (1854), 2 Dr 427 ; 100 R. R 209.

(j) It will be understood here that the common type of case, where the party charged makes no disclosure at all, examples of which are cited in the notes to Chapters III, IV, and V, *passim*, is not now under examination.   It is only cases where the party charged is shown to have revealed *something*, but not *everything*, or not to have been sufficiently precise and clear in his disclosure, which concern the present discussion.

(k) See *Rickards* v *Murdock* (1830), 10 B & C 527 (where the plaintiff sued on a policy on goods on board the " Cumberland," which he had effected as agent for one Campbell, a Sydney merchant, and the defendant set up non disclosure   It was proved that Campbell had written to the plaintiff, after the vessel had started, instructing him, in the event of the letter arriving before the ship, to wait thirty days to give her a chance of arriving, and, if not arrived at the end of that period, to insure   The plaintiff waited the thirty days, and the ship not having arrived, instructed his broker to insure   The broker did so, at the same time giving the defendant the following " partial " information, viz (i) the date when the " Cumberland " sailed, (ii) the date when Campbell's letter was written, (iii) a portion of the contents of such letter, which he read out , but he did not disclose, (iv) when the letter was received, or (v) the important part of such letter, viz the instructions to wait thirty days, and, if the vessel had not then arrived, to insure. Held, an inadequate disclosure, and therefore no disclosure at all) , *Westbury* v. *Aberdein* (1837), 2 M & W. 267 (where the material facts were—(i) that the " King George " on which a policy had been effected from Malaga to London, and another vessel, the " Fruiter," had sailed from Malaga on the 9th and 10th October, respectively, (ii) that the " Fruiter " arrived without the " King George," and (iii) that the captain of the " Fruiter " had parted company with the " King George " in a gale off Oporto on the 21st October.   The plaintiff disclosed (i), and the defendant was apprised of (ii) by Lloyd's Lists, but no disclosure was made to the defendant, nor had he any knowledge *aliunde* of, (iii)   Held that if

contracts between vendor and purchaser (*l*), releases and compromises (*m*), contracts of waiver (*n*), transactions between promoter and company (*o*), or between principal and agent, or partners (*p*), or contracts and gifts induced by undue influence (*q*).

(iii) was material, as to which there was some doubt, there had been a failure to make *complete* disclosure, and the defendant would be entitled to succeed); *Ionides* v. *Pender* (1874), L. R. 9 Q. B 531 (where the party charged, the plaintiff, had disclosed that the spirits on board the vessel had been valued with anticipated or imaginary profits, but not that they had been valued with an addition of profit to an amount greater than could possibly be expected under any normal circumstances. This was a communication of *something*, but not of *everything*, material, and the party complaining, the defendant, was held entitled to the verdict)

(*l*) *Re Banister* (1879), 12 C. D 131, C. A. (*per* FRY, J., at p. 136 : " the statement of fact must be an honest and fair one , it must not for the purpose in hand be a part of the truth only , it must, so far as that purpose is concerned, be the truth, *and the whole truth* ") ; *Re Marsh and Earl Granville* (1883), 24 C. D 11, C A (*per* FRY, J , again, at p 17 " he must tell the truth, *and all the truth*, which is relevant to the matter in hand ") ; *Heywood* v *Mallalieu* (1883), 25 C D 357, *per* BACON, V -C , at pp 361, 364, 365, where the party charged (plaintiff and defendant to counterclaim) was held not to have discharged his duty of disclosure, by a mere communication, through his solicitor, of the fact that certain privileges and rights over the property being sold had been vaguely asserted by third persons, without also divulging the fact that those claims had assumed a definite and precise form to his knowledge, and that it was at least possible, if not probable, that they were well founded. See also the cases cited in note (*x*) to § 24, *post*

(*m*) *Bowles* v. *Stewart* (1803), 1 Sch & Lefr 209, 227, *Gordon* v. *Gordon* (1821), 30 Swanst 400 , 19 R R. 230 (*per* Lord ELDON, L C , at p. 173 " in contracts of this sort, *full and complete* communication of all material circumstances is what the Court must insist on "). *Greenwood* v. *Greenwood* (1863), 2 De G J & S 28 (*per* TURNER, L J , at p 42 " now I take the rule of law to be that in order to support a transaction not otherwise valid, upon the footing of a family arrangement, the parties must be upon an equal footing, and there must be a *full and fair communication of all the circumstances* affecting the question which forms the subject of the arrangement ") On reference to the above cases, it will be seen that in all of them *some* disclosure was made, but not enough

(*n*) *Jenkins* v *Hales* (1802), 6 Ves 646, *per* Lord ELDON, L C , at p. 655 where the vendor is plaintiff, if the rule is founded on a principle of conscience, and requiring all possible security to be given to a purchaser, the Court will at least take care that, when it is contended that the defendant has waived his right . it shall be clear that . . there has been a *full and fair representation* as to the title on the part of the plaintiff " See also generally, the cases referred to in some of the notes to § 371, and to § 562, *post*.

(*o*) *Re Madrid Bank, Ex p Williams* (1866), L R. 2 Eq 216, *per* Lord ROMILLY, M R , at pp 218, 219 (where part of the material agreement was disclosed by the promoters, but not the whole), *Gluckstein* v *Barnes*, [1900] A C 240, H L , *per* Lord HALSBURY, L.C., at p. 246, Lord MACNAGHTEN, at p 249, and Lord ROBERTSON, at pp. 256–8

(*p*) *Selsey (Lord)* v *Rhoades* (1824), 2 Sim & St 41, 25 R R. 150, affirmed, on other grounds, (1827) 1 Bligh N S 1 ; 30 R R 1 (*per* LEACH, V -C , at pp. 49, 50 · " the steward is bound to make out that the employer was *fully* informed of *every* circumstance respecting the property which was either within the knowledge of the steward, or ought to have been within his knowledge, which would tend to demonstrate the value of the property "—so far as the transaction was a purchase—"and the *precise measure and extent* of the bounty of the employer "—so far as the transaction was " united with motives of bounty "). In *Dunne* v. *English* (1872), L R 18 Eq 524 (*per* JESSEL, M R , at pp. 533, 535, 536), *Imperial Mercantile Credit Association* v *Coleman* (1873), L R 6 H. L 189 (*per* Lord CHELMSFORD, at p 200, and Lord CAIRNS, at p. 205), and *Costa Rica Railway Co* v. *Forwood*, [1900] 1 Ch 746, C A (*per* RIGBY, L J , at p 756, VAUGHAN WILLIAMS, L J , at p. 761, and STIRLING, L.J , at p 766), the distinction was clearly drawn between the mere declaration of the existence of *an* interest, and the disclosure of the exact character and extent of that interest, and it was held that the partner in the first case, and the

(*q*) *Groves* v. *Perkins* (1834), 6 Sim 576, *per* SHADWELL, V C , at p 583 (mere statement of fact that the intestate's property was " considerable " was not enough, without full disclosure of the extent, nature, and particulars of the property), *Wright* v *Carter*, [1903] 1 Ch 27, C A (*per* VAUGHAN WILLIAMS, L J , at pp 54–56, and STIRLING, L.J , at p. 60)

22. Where it is a question of a transaction (whether contract or gift) which cannot be entered into without disclosure of all material circumstances bearing upon it, the party upon whom the duty of disclosure lies does not acquit himself of his duty by merely stating the terms of the transaction, and the facts upon which it is based and is intended to operate. He must also explain with precision and in detail the legal effect of the transaction upon the other party's rights and interests (r), and, further, must make it clear in certain cases that the other party has the right to revoke the gift or avoid the contract, if he so pleases (s)

23. When it is said that disclosure must be exact and complete, exactitude and completeness in all material particulars is meant. The law does not require more than a substantial disclosure. If this be made, it does not signify that immaterial details are omitted (t). Conversely, the most precise and punctilious disclosure of unimportant *minutiæ* will not avail to render the disclosure valid, if it is incomplete in essential matters (u) The

director in the other two, in communicating merely the former, without the latter, information, had not made that disclosure which the law requires in order to validate the transaction Lord CAIRNS, at p 205 of *Imperial Mercantile Credit Association v Coleman, ubi sup*, states the principle very convincingly as follows " Now was it material that Mr Coleman's co-directors should know *what* his interest was ? In my opinion, it was most material No better instance of the materiality of such a declaration could be found than in the present case . . Did he then declare *what* his interest was ? Certainly he did not A man declares his opinion or his intentions when he states what his opinion is, or what his intentions are, not that he has an opinion, or that he has intentions , and so . . a man declares his interest, not when he states that he has an interest, but when he states what his interest is " See also *Bartram & Sons v Lloyd* (1904), 90 L T 357, C A., where, in the plaintiff's action for damages for breach of contract, the defendant pleaded that the plaintiff had made a secret arrangement with his (the defendant's) agent, one Campbell, in the nature of a bribe, and it was held by the C. A , reversing BRUCE, J , that though the defendant was told by the plaintiff, or knew from other sources, (i) that a commission was being paid by the plaintiff to Campbell, and (ii) the nature of the dealings of the plaintiff with Campbell for this purpose, he was not informed of (iii) the fact that the commission had been promised by the plaintiff during the negotiations for the contract which was the subject of the action, and with the intention and result of procuring such contract, and that this " half disclosure " was not a compliance with his duty by the party charged (*per* COLLINS, M R , at p 339)

(r) *Bennett v Vade* (1742), 2 Atk 324 (*per* Lord HARDWICKE, L C., at p 327); *Cutts v. Salmon* (1852), 21 L J (Ch.) 750 (*per* Lord ST LEONARDS, L C , at p. 751); *Savery v King* (1856), 5 H. L. C 627 , *Coulson v. Allison* (1860), 2 De G. F & J 521 (*per* Lord CAMPBELL, L C , at p 525—see the citation in note (z) to § 24, *post*); *Sharp v. Leach* (1862), 31 Beav 491 (*per* ROMILLY, M R , at pp 494–501), *Clarke v Malpas* (1862), 4 De G F & J 401 (*per* KNIGHT-BRUCE, L J., at p 404), *Moxon* v. *Payne* (1873), 8 Ch App. 881 (*per* JAMES, L J , at p 885), *Howley* v. *Cook* (1873), Ir R. 8 Eq. 370 (as to the duty to explain the effect of unprecedented clauses in a mortgage), *Willis* v. *Barron*, [1902] A C. 271, H. L (*per* Lord HALSBURY, L.C , at p 276, and Lord MACNAGHTEN, at pp. 280, 281), *Re Haslam & Hier-Evans*, [1902] 1 Ch 765, C A (*per* VAUGHAN WILLIAMS, L J , at p. 769) , *Harris* v. *Clarson* (1910), 27 T L R. 30 (where CHANNELL, J , held that it was the duty of a moneylender to explain very clearly to the borrower the *effect* of a clause in the contract whereby the whole of the money became due on failure to pay any one instalment), *London & Westminster Loan & Discount Co* v *Bilton* (1911), 27 T. L R 184 (the like); *Stirling* v *Rose* (1913), 30 T L R 67 (the like)

(s) *Savery* v. *King, sup*, per Lord CRANWORTH, L C , at pp 603, 664 , *Procter v. Robinson* (1867), 15 L T. 431, per TURNER, L J , at pp. 431, 432, and CAIRNS, L J , at pp. 432, 433. Cp. *Re Webb*, [1894] 1 Ch 73, C. A. (*per* LINDLEY, L J , at p 79, as to the duty of a solicitor to inform the party complaining that his bill may be taxed)

(t) *Asjar & Co* v *Blundell*, [1896] 1 Q B 123, C. A. (*per* Lord ESHER, M R , at pp 129, 130).

(u) A corresponding rule prevails in the law of misrepresentation See § 71 of the

disclosure may be made in any form, or by any means, unless it be expressly agreed between the parties that it shall not be deemed such, unless made in a particular specified manner, as, for instance, in the form of answers to be given by the assured in writing to specific questions contained in documents tendered by the insurers (*uu*).

24. Besides being exact and complete, the disclosure must be made in terms which are clear and unambiguous. The party on whom the obligation lies must not leave the other party to put two and two together. He must put them together himself, and call them four Though $x + y = z$, that is, though facts x and y lead to a reasonable inference of fact z, the duty is nevertheless to disclose z, and not $x + y$, or not merely $x + y$. When the shorter and simpler course is not adopted, there must be some reason for not doing so, and that reason is almost invariably that the party on the one hand hopes that z will not be inferred from $x + y$, and, on the other, has the fraudulent intention of setting up the revelation of $x + y$ as a defence in the event of a case of concealment being afterwards made against him It is idle to urge that something tantamount to disclosure was done. In business of this kind, the artist's claim,—"piece out our imperfections with your thoughts,"—has no place. These "doubtful equivalents" are not disclosure in law, but non-disclosure (*v*), and non-disclosure of a particularly disingenuous type (*w*) Illustrations are frequent of the failure of such expedients for the purpose of withholding material facts, whilst insuring in advance against the consequences of so doing, as "catching" conditions and particulars

author's *Law of Actionable Misrepresentation* "where the entirety of a representation forms a faithful picture or transcript of the facts, its truth is established, and is not affected by any number of inaccuracies in unimportant details. On the other hand, if the general impression conveyed is false, the utmost precision and the most punctual and scrupulous accuracy in a number of immaterial minutiæ will not avail to stamp the misrepresentation with the sign of truth."

(*uu*) As in *Levy* v. *Scottish Employers Insurance Co* (1901), 17 T. L R. 229, Div Ct (*per* WILLS, J , at p 230)

(*v*) *Bates* v. *Hewitt* (1867), L R 2 Q B 595, a marine insurance case, where the defendant set up non disclosure of the fact that the vessel insured, the S S "Georgia," had been a Confederate cruiser, and was therefore liable to capture by the United States, and it was held that the mere communication by the plaintiff of certain particulars which, together with what the defendant already knew as to the past history of the Confederate "Georgia," might have led to the truth, was not enough, it not being proved that the plaintiff had in plain terms informed the defendant that the "Georgia" insured was identical with the Confederate cruiser of that name This amounted to no more than "partial information" (*per* COCKBURN, C J , at p 608), or the use of "doubtful equivalents in lieu of actual and plain communications" (*per* MELLOR, J , at p 610), *Gandy* v *Adelaide Marine Insurance Co* (1871), L.R. 6 Q B 746 (where, at p 758, COCKBURN, C.J , said that the duty of disclosure is not excused "where a material fact is matter of *positive knowledge* to the party proposing the insurance, and only matter of *possible infer-ence*, from very imperfect materials, to the underwriter ") The two cases of *Nicholson* v. *Power* (1869), 20 L T 580, and *Leigh* v *Adams* (1871), 25 L T. 566, are both excellent illustrations of the futility of the pretence that leaving the party to put two and two together amounts to a discharge of the duty of disclosure For the facts of these two cases see note (*k*) to § 43, *post*

(*w*) *Greenwood* v *Greenwood* (1863), 2 De G J & S 28, *per* TURNER, L J , at pp 42, 43 "this Court . . expects and requires in such cases the most perfect *bona fides*, and it is not, in my opinion, consistent with *bona fides* that partial and imperfect statements should be made on the one side, the party making them taking the chance whether a full and perfect explanation will be required on the other side " Cf *Gluckstein* v *Barnes*, [1900] A C 240, H. L (*per* Lord HALSBURY, L C , at pp 246, 247).

of sale in contracts between vendor and purchaser (x), " tricky " waiver clauses in prospectuses of companies (y), and other like subdolous pretences of candour without its reality (z).

SECT. 2. MATERIALITY.

25. The full and clear disclosure required by the law, as already explained, is a full and clear disclosure of such facts and circumstances (a) only as are

(x) See *Brandling* v *Plummer* (1854), 2 Drew. 427, 100 R. R. 209, *per* KINDERSLEY, V C, at pp 430-3, *Smith* v. *Harrison* (1857), 26 L. J. (Ch.) 412, where " the chattel interest, *if any*," of a certain person in the stock fixtures and effects of his late firm, and in a certain lease, was put up for sale by a vendor who knew that in fact the person in question had no saleable interest whatever in the property, the whole assets of the firm being insufficient to pay its creditors, and where PAGE WOOD, V C., at p. 414, draws particular attention to the misleading ambiguity—which, with inexplicable generosity, he hesitates to call fraudulent—of the expression " if any," used as it was by the vendor in the secret sense of " if any, which there is not," but intended at the same time to convey to the purchaser the possibility of the interest in question having some value, however slight or remote, *Re Banister* (1879), 12 C. D. 131, C A (*per* FRY, J, at p 136 : " it is, therefore "—*i.e* because the one party knows, and the other trusts—" fair that the person who does know should explain his meaning so as to be *perfectly intelligible* to the person who does not know "), *Re Marsh and Earl Granville* (1882), 24 C D. 11, C A, *per* FRY, J, at p 17 (" explicit and plain conditions "), BAGGALLAY, L J, at pp 22, 23, and COTTON, L.J, at p 24, *Nottingham Patent Brick & Tile Co* v *Butler* (1886), 16 Q B D 778, C A (*per* LINDLEY, L J, at p 788).

(y) See the prospectus cases of *Greenwood* v *Leather Shod Wheel Co*, [1900] 1 Ch. 421, 431, C A, *Cackett* v *Keswick*, [1902] 2 Ch 456, 467, 476-8, C A, *Watts* v *Bucknall*, [1903] 1 Ch. 766, 775, 778, C A., as to the designedly equivocal phrase, " there *may be* contracts," &c.

(z) Such as *Coulson* v *Allison* (1860), 2 De G. F. & J 521, where, a widower, one Nicholson, having married his deceased wife's sister, it was held by Lord CAMPBELL, L C, affirming STUART, V. C, that it was incumbent upon him, when claiming the benefit of a marriage settlement made upon him by the lady, to prove that she had been " fully and duly and truly informed of all the circumstances of the case, and of the possible consequences of what she was about to do " (p 524),—to which he adds, at p 525   " I am of opinion that   . there is an entire absence of evidence that she was fully, fairly, and truly informed of the situation in which she stood   It was represented to her as a matter of *some doubt* whether the alleged marriage was valid or not, whereas at that time it had solemnly been adjudged that the marriage of a widower with a sister of his deceased wife was illegal, and absolutely null and void   She ought to have been informed of that, and not left in a state of uncertainty as to the consequences which might result from a continuation of her cohabitation with Nicholson   Again it is not made to appear that Mrs Welbank was duly informed of the risk she ran in executing a deed conveying away all her property, except her small annuity, to Nicholson, of being abandoned at any moment and left without any other resource than her annuity   The moving consideration for the deed was clearly the notion of a valid subsisting marriage   This is shown by the wording of the deed, every syllable of which proceeds upon the footing of a supposed subsisting marriage, and it is further shown by her executing and acknowledging it in the character of a married woman "   In other words, Nicholson vainly hoped that the above ambidextrous phraseology and devices would serve as an immediate inducement to the lady to believe that she was validly married, and at the same time as a prophylactic against any charge of non disclosure in the future   Cp *Gluckstein* v *Barnes*, [1900] A. C 240, H L, and the caustic observations of Lord MACNAGHTEN, at p 249, as to the attempt—described by him as " almost a stroke of genius "—to make out that the lavish use of the phrase " interim investments " amounted to a fair and unambiguous disclosure of the promoter's secret operations and profits   See, also, *Oelkers* v *Ellis*, [1914] 2 K B 139, for an excellent example of a fraudulent semi-disclosure (*per* HORRIDGE, J, at pp 147, 148).   A number of these *amphibologiæ*, as they are termed in theological casuistry, are collected in § 82, and the notes thereto, of the author's *Law of Actionable Misrepresentation*

(a) " Fact " and " circumstance " are used here as convertible terms   The latter expression has the advantage over the former of suggesting the idea of relevancy to the material in the particular case (b). This statement involves the preliminary question as to what undisclosed matters are in contemplation of law facts or circumstances; for nothing can carry with it the possibility even of materiality which is not a fact or circumstance at all.

Sub-s. (1) *What are deemed Facts or Circumstances.*

26. For the purpose of the rules relating to disclosure, a fact or circumstance has the same juridical connotation as it has for the purpose of the law relating to misrepresentation (c). That is to say, the expression includes any event or thing, present or past (d); and the present or past qualities, attributes, state, condition, or incidents, of any such event or thing.

27. It has long been settled, chiefly in reference to marine insurance, that reports, instructions, advices, information, intelligence, and even, in certain cases, rumours, are circumstances or facts which, if material, must be divulged (e) This means that the receipt of the information or intelligence

transaction in hand, *circumstantia* being neither more nor less than "surrounding facts." "Circumstances," rather than "facts," are referred to in many of the judgments relating to the duty of disclosure, e.g in those of Lord MANSFIELD, C.J., in *Carter v Boehm* (1766), 3 Burr 1905, Lord ELLENBOROUGH, C J, at p. 18 of *Bridges v. Hunter* (1813), 1 M. & S 15, Lord ELDON, L C, at p 473 of *Gordon v Gordon* (1821), 3 Swanst 400, LEACH, V C., at pp 49, 50 of *Selsey (Lord) v Rhoades* (1824), 2 Sim. & St 41, Lord CAMPBELL, L.C., at p. 524 of *Coulson v. Allison* (1860), 2 De G F. & J. 521, and TURNER, L J, at p 42 of *Greenwood v. Greenwood* (1863), 2 De G J & S 28, not to mention numerous others And the statute which codifies the law relating to marine insurance—the Marine Insurance Act, 1906—prescribes disclosure of "every material *circumstance* known to the assured" in s 18, sub s (1), and, in sub s (5) of the same section, states what "*the term* ' *circumstance*' includes " It will be noticed that the phrase "surrounding circumstances" —in very common use—is as glaring a pleonasm as ' a round circle," or a "rectangular square," would be.

(b) This is clearly stated or assumed in all the authorities Where a general and summary form of words is used which omits this qualification, as, for instance, by Lord ST LEONARDS, who, when SIR EDWARD SUGDEN, L C (h), at p 425 of *Murphy v. O'Shea* (1845), 2 Jo & Lat 422, spoke of "a full disclosure of all that he "—the agent, when dealing with his principal—" knows with respect to the property," the qualification must be supplied, as was pointed out by JESSEL, M R , at p 534 of *Dunne v. English* (1872), L R. 18 Eq 524, where, after citing the above expression, he added,—" that of course means everything *material* which he knows " As regards marine insurance, see the judgment of the Court of Q B at p 539 of *Ionides v Pender* (1874), L R 9 Q B 531 "we agree that it would be too much to put on the assured the duty of disclosing *everything* which might influence the mind of an underwriter Business could hardly be carried on if this were required", and *The Bedouin*, [1894] P. 1 , C A (per Lord ESHER, M R , at p 12 "the assured is bound to tell him "—i e the underwriter—" not every fact, but the material facts ")

(c) See §§ 15-18, 28-44, of the author's *Law of Actionable Misrepresentation*

(d) Whether a past event is material or not in the particular case is another question altogether This depends on the degree of proximity in time, and the closeness of connection from other points of view, between the past event and the transaction in which the duty of disclosure arises See *Carter v. Boehm* (1766), 3 Burr 1905 (where it was held that a design which the French had upon Fort Marlborough the year before, and which had been laid aside, was of no importance), *Haywood v. Rogers* (1804), 4 East, 590 (per Lord ELLENBOROUGH, C J , at pp 596, 597, as to what circumstances in the past history of a vessel are, and what are not, required to be disclosed in contracts of marine insurance), *Freeland v. Glover* (1806), 7 East, 457 (per GROSE, J , and LAWRENCE, J , at p. 463,—the like), *Blackburn, Low & Co v. Vigors* (1887), 12 A C 531, H L. (per Lord HALSBURY, L C , at pp 536, 537)

(e) *Durrell v Bederley* (1816), Holt N P 283 ; 17 R R 639, where, to an action on a policy of marine insurance on a vessel which had been captured, the defendant set

is in itself a fact which may be material, apart altogether from the question whether its subject-matter, in the sense of having, or having had, a real existence, is a fact or not. However ill founded the report, communication, or rumour, may subsequently turn out to have been, the existence of it is a " circumstance " which, if within the knowledge of the party subject to the duty of disclosure, must be revealed to the party to whom that duty is owed, if it is of a nature to affect the latter's judgment in considering whether or not to enter into the contract or transaction in question on the terms proposed (*f*). Still less is the party's duty of disclosure affected by the mere fact that he *bonâ fide* believed the information or rumour to be untrue (*ff*).

28. It is equally well established that a person's existing mental condition is a " circumstance " which has the capacity of materiality, and, as such, may have to be disclosed. "The state of a man's mind is as much a fact as the state of his digestion," according to Bowen, L J. "It is true," he adds, " that it is very difficult to prove what the state of a man's mind at a particular time is, but if it can be substantiated, it is as much fact as anything else " (*g*) A man's mental state may mean the state of his will, or the state

up non-disclosure by the plaintiff of *reports* current in Jersey some weeks back, of captures effected by a French frigate in those waters, and where Gibbs, C J , directed the jury, at p 285, that " *intelligence*, properly so called, and as it is understood by mercantile men, ought to be disclosed when known If the concealment be of a material fact, whether *a rumour, report*, or an article of intelligence, it ought to be communicated," and, at p. 286, that " he "—the plaintiff—" knew the *current knowledge of Jersey* on this subject, the underwriters could know nothing of it ", *Friere* v *Woodhouse* (1816), Holt N. P. 572 ; 17 R R 679, where it was again recognized that an " article of intelligence " is a " fact," though in this case the party complaining failed, because he had presumptive knowledge of the fact , *Gordon* v *Gordon* (1821), 3 Swanst 400 , 19 R. R. 230, a compromise case, in which Lord Eldon, L C , set aside an agreement between two brothers for the division of family estates which proceeded on the basis of the elder brother's legitimacy being at least doubtful, the ground of his decision being that the younger had not disclosed to the elder certain *information* which he had received from two persons, and also the currency, known to him, of *rumours*, to the effect that a private ceremony of marriage between the parents had taken place (p 473) , *Ionides* v *Pender* (1874), L R 9 Q B 531, *per Cur* at p 538, approving an American case, abstracted in note (*w*) to § 104, *post*, where again " information " was treated as a fact to be disclosed.

(*f*) *Lynch* v. *Dunsford* (1811), 14 East, 494, *per* Lord Ellenborough, ('J , at p 497 . " the duty . . must attach at the time of effecting the insurance, and cannot depend upon the subsequent event," and, therefore (pp 497, 498) the proved falsity of the rumour or intelligence in that case was not allowed to affect the result

(*ff*) *Gordon* v. *Gordon, sup* , where Lord Eldon, L C , at pp 463, 464, pointed out that though the defendant honestly believed that the reported ceremony was not a marriage *de jure*, he ought none the less to have communicated to the plaintiff the fact that it had been so reported, and left the plaintiff to form his own judgment as to the weight to be attached to the report. So also in respect of information which he had personally received from certain persons as to the ceremony, "although he might not have believed that statement, still he was bound to communicate it to his brother " (p 474). On the same principle, if an assured party has a report or opinion of an expert as to the condition of a vessel " though he thinks it erroneous, he must disclose his unfavourable report " *per* Scrutton, J , at p 116 of *Cantiniere Meccanico Brialisino* v *Janson*, [1912] 2 K. B. 112, cited and approved by Vaughan Williams, L J , at pp 461, 462 of the report of the case on appeal, [1912] 3 K B 452, C A

(*g*) At p 483 of *Edgington* v *Fitzmaurice* (1885), 29 C. D 459, C A Cp. his observations to the same effect at p. 470 of *Angus* v. *Clifford*, [1891] 2 Ch. 449, C A Both these were misrepresentation cases, but since a representation is a statement of fact, it became necessary in each of them to consider whether, and in what sense, a man's mental state is a fact.

of his belief, whether as to the past, the present, or the future. Consequently, the present intention (h), or the opinion, whether professional or otherwise, as to any existing or past matter (i), or the expectations (j), or apprehensions (k) as to the future, whether of an individual, or of a class, or body of persons, are all "facts," to which the obligation of disclosure may attach ; and here again the existence of the intention, opinion, hope, or fear is not the less a fact merely because the intention may not materialize, or merely because the opinion, hope, or fear, may prove to have been groundless, or the party charged may at the time have thought it to be so (kk).

29. Similarly the making of an agreement is a fact, which may be subject

(h) *Carter* v. *Boehm* (1766), 3 Burr. 1905 (a marine insurance case, in which Lord MANSFIELD, C J , recognized that a *design* of the French upon Fort Marlborough was a fact which *might* be material, though in the circumstances of that case, the design having been entertained and abandoned a year previously, it was held not to be so) , *Bridges* v *Hunter* (1813), 1 M &. S. 15 (also a marine insurance case, in which the *intention* of the captain to sail on a certain date was clearly considered a "fact") , *Evans* v. *Edmonds* (1853), 13 C B. 777 (as to the undisclosed intention of a trustee of a separation deed to use his position as trustee for the purpose of facilitating the continuance of an adulterous intercourse with the wife) , *Evans* v *Carrington* (1860), 2 De F G & J 481, a similar case ; *Traill* v *Baring* (1864), 4 De G J & S 318 (in which it was the basis of the decision that the alteration in the originally expressed intention of the party to take a third of the life insurance risk was a fact); *Gandy* v. *Adelaide Marine Insurance Co* (1871), L. R 6 Q B 746 (a marine insurance case, in which the *resolution* of the plaintiff not to continue the ship on Lloyd's register was, in one of the questions left to the jury, described as a "fact") , *Leigh* v. *Adams* (1871), 25 L. T 566 (the *intention* to ship a cargo on a certain vessel for the assured , also the *intention* of the owners of the vessel to lose her on her next voyage) ; *Glasgow Assurance Corporation* v *William Symondson & Co* (1911), 104 L T 254, where, at p 258, SCRUTTON, J., obviously considered the "intention" of the defendant to declare his own underwriting partners as assured, was a fact, capable of being, though in this case it was not, material. Cp. the misrepresentation cases cited in the notes to § 17, and in note (q) to § 90, of the author's *Law of Actionable Misrepresentation*, all of which are illustrations of intention being regarded as a fact

(i) Opinions of the party charged, or of third persons, as to matters of law, were held to be facts which, being material, ought to have been disclosed, in *Bowles* v *Stewart* (1803), 1 Sch & Lefr 209, *per* Lord REDESDALE, L C (Ir), at p 226 (a case where a deed of release executed by one from whom counsel's opinion had been withheld was set aside) , *Reynell* v *Sprye* (1852), 1 De G M & G. 660 (*per* Lord CRANWORTH, L J , at pp 703-705, a similar case of imperfect disclosure of counsel's opinion); *Davies* v *London and Provincial Marine Insurance Co.* (1878), 8 C. D. 469 (suppression of counsel's opinion that no criminal offence had been committed *per* FRY, J , at p ¯¯7) , *Re Roberts*, [1905] 1 Ch 704, C A (at p. 710) The same views have been ex   l in respect of opinions on other matters, e g., valuations, as in *Brooke* v. *Lord   n* (1865), 3 De G J & S 373 , *Dougan* v *Macpherson*, [1902] A C 197, H L   medical opinion as to a person's expectation of life, as in *Coaks* v. *Boswell* (1886), 11 App Cas 232, H L ; or "the opinion of the neighbourhood" as to a woman's character, as in *Foulkes* v *Sellway* (1800), 3 Esp 235 (as to which case see note (s) to § 148, *post*) Cp the misrepresentation cases in the notes to §§ 32-35 of the author's *Law of Actionable Misrepresentation*, as to a statement of an opinion being a statement of the fact that the opinion is entertained by the person to whom it is attributed

(j) *Willes* v *Glover* (1804), 1 B. & P. (N. R) 14 , 8 R R. 739 (*per* Sir JAMES MANS-FIELD, C.J , at p 16).

(k) *Court* v *Martineau* (1782), 3 Dougl (K. B) 161 (fears of the owner of two prizes that one of them may have been retaken) , *Rickards* v *Murdock* (1830), 10 B & C. 527 (fears of the owner of the vessel as to her arrival) In *Bell* v *Bell* (1810), 2 Campb 475 the remark of Lord ELLENBOROUGH, C J , that the "sensation and apprehensions at Riga" as to the effect of an order of the Russian Government upon the safety of the vessel did not constitute "facts" was made *per incuriam* It must be supposed that he meant no more than that the facts in question were probably not material.

(kk) See the last of the cases cited in note (ff) to § 27, *ante*

to the rules of disclosure, whether the agreement so made be valid and enforceable or not (*l*).

Sub-s. (2). *The Meaning of Materiality.*

30. Any fact or circumstance is deemed "material to be disclosed," which, if disclosed, would influence the mind of a reasonable person in determining whether to enter into the proposed contract or transaction at all, or in deciding upon the terms of such contract or transaction, *having regard to its class and character* (*ll*). This definition has been expressed in various forms of words, as applied to the different classes of transactions and relations giving rise to the duty of disclosure (*m*), but the substance of it is as above stated

31. It will be observed that in each case the question to be determined, in accordance with the above proposition, is not so much whether the undisclosed fact was material to the contract itself or (in the case of insurance) to the precise risk undertaken, as whether it was material to the inducement, that is, whether it was of a nature to affect the judgment of the party from

(*l*) See *Thames and Mersey Marine Insurance Co* v *Gunford Ship Co*, [1911] A C 529, H L, *per* Lord ALVERSTONE, at pp 537, 538, as to "honour" policies of marine insurance, which are facts, and material facts, though not legally enforceable contracts.

(*ll*) This is a vital consideration for, as will be seen from an abundance of illustrations appearing hereafter—see §§ 84, 85, 92, 93, 95, 96, 99, 117, 120, 122, 123, 137, 141, 147, note (*p*), 148, 150—there are many circumstances which, though material in the sense of being important for the party to know, are yet not "material to be disclosed," that is to say not such that, from the nature of the contract or business, the party is entitled to assume their non-existence.

(*m*) As to marine insurance, see the expressions used by Sir JAMES MANSFIELD, C J, at p 16 of *Willes* v *Glover* (1804), 1 B & P (N R) 14 ("an opportunity of exercising their judgment in settling the premium"), by GIBBS, C J, at p 286 of *Durrell* v *Bederley* (1816) Holt N P 283, by HOLROYD, J, at p 259 of *Berthon* v *Loughman* (1817), 2 Stark 259 ("whether particular facts, if disclosed to an underwriter would . . make a difference as to the amount of premium"), by Lord TENTERDEN, C J, at p 540 of *Rickards* v *Murdock* (1830), 10 B & C. 527 (' would have influenced the mind of the underwriter in deciding upon what terms he would accept the risk"), by ROLFE, B, at pp 243, 244 of *Dalglish* v *Jarvie* (1850), 2 Macn & G 231 ("anything that may affect the rate of premium which the underwriter may require"), by COCKBURN, C J, at pp. 604, 605 of *Bates* v *Hewitt* (1867), L R 2 Q B 595 ("all matters which will enable him to determine the extent of the risk against which he undertakes to guarantee the assured"), by the Court of Queen's Bench at p 539 of *Ionides* v *Pender* (1874), L. R 9 Q B 531 ("the rule laid down in Parsons on Insurance, vol 1 p 495, that all should be disclosed which would affect the judgment of a rational underwriter governing himself by the principles and calculations on which underwriters do in practice act, seems to us a sound one"), and by the legislature in the Marine Insurance Act, 1906 (6 Edw. 7, c 41), s. 18, sub s (2) "every circumstance is material which would influence the judgment of a prudent insurer in fixing the premium, or determining whether he will take the risk" As regards partnership, Lord CRANWORTH, L C, at p 188 of *Clements* v *Hall* (1858), 2 De G & J. 173, said that a surviving partner is bound to divulge "every fact which may enable the representative"—*i e* of the deceased partner—"to exercise a sound discretion as to the course he ought to pursue." Generally, for illustrations of the application of the definition to the several classes of transactions and relations dealt with in this treatise, see Ch. III, Sect 2, Ch IV, Sect 2, and Ch V, Sect. 2, *post*. As to what materiality means as applied to a representation, see § 126 of the author's *Law of Actionable Misrepresentation*

whom the fact is withheld (n)   The same distinction is to be noted in cases of misrepresentation (o).

32. Another observation which it is proper to make in this connexion is that, in order to establish materiality, it is not necessary to show that the disclosure of the uncommunicated fact would inevitably have deterred the party from entering into the contract or transaction on any terms, or on the terms proposed : it is enough to show that it might possibly have had such a deterrent effect, and would certainly have had some effect upon his judgment, in the sense that it would have presented something for him to weigh and take into consideration, and would have " given him pause " (p).

33. The belief of any of the parties to a contract or transaction as to the materiality or non-materiality of any undisclosed fact is quite unimportant. On the one hand, if the fact is not shown by evidence or otherwise to have been material, the opinion entertained at the time, or professed at the trial, by the party complaining cannot make it so (q)   on the other hand, if the fact undisclosed is proved to have been material, such materiality cannot be affected by any allegation (even if believed) of the party charged that he did not at the time, or does not at the trial, consider it to have been material (r)   But, where the matter is *in dubio*, words or acts of the party

(n) *Ionides* v *Pender, sup , per Cur* at p 538   " it was argued before us that the nature of the risks (that is to say, the strength and seaworthy qualities of the Da Capo, and the probability of encountering storms on the voyage, and so forth) was not in the least affected by the amount at which the goods were valued   which is no doubt true " but, said the Court (see pp 538, 539), it was enough that the over valuation, though strictly extraneous to the risk, would, as had been proved by evidence, affect an underwriter's mind, *Tate & Sons* v *Hyslop* (1885), 15 Q B D 368, C A , another marine insurance case (*per* BRETT, M R , at p 376   " the authorities show that the materiality is not as to the risk, but as to whether it would influence the underwriters in entering upon the insurance or the terms on which they would insure ")

(o) Thus in *Sibbald* v *Hill* (1814), 2 Dow H L 263, Lord ELDON, L C , decided in favour of the underwriters, " not on the ground that the misrepresentation affected the *nature* of the risk, but because it induced a confidence without which the party would not have acted " (p 267)   And cp § 129 of the author's *Law of Actionable Misrepresentation*, and the authorities there cited

(p) See *Smith* v *Pincombe* (1852), 2 Macn & G. 653, *per* Lord TRURO, L C , at pp 658, 659 (" calculated to influence the judgment in the adoption of the compromise "), *Green- wood* v *Greenwood* (1863), 2 De G J & S 28, *per* TURNER, L J , at p 43 (" a full and fair communication   would, or at least might, have materially influenced the other parties in determining the question whether they would have entered into the agreement "), *Traill* v *Baring* (1864), 4 De G J & S 318 (*per* TURNER, L J , at p 330   " it is impossible to say what course the plaintiffs might have pursued, whether they would or would not have accepted the policy   They might have done so, but it is equally clear that they might not, and we cannot say whether they would or would not , but it was to them that the communication should have been made, in order that they might exercise their option upon the subject), *Brooke* v. *Lord Mostyn* (1865), 2 De G J & S 373 , *William Pickersgill & Sons, Ltd* v *London and Provincial Marine and General Insurance Co ,* [1912] 3 K B 614 (*per* HAMILTON, J , at p 619)

(q) *Haywood* v. *Rodgers* (1804), 4 East, 590 (*per* Lord ELLENBOROUGH, C J , who, at p. 597, speaks of the " almost absolute impossibility for the assured to state . . every- thing which, if stated, might have been deemed, *in the judgment of the underwriter*, material to the question "), *Beachey* v *Brown* (1860), E B & E 796 (*per* CROMPTON, J , at p 803 · " I do not think that non disclosure of a fact which is material *in the mind of the defendant* " —who in that case was setting up non-disclosure as an answer to an action for breach of promise of marriage—" is enough ")

(r) *Lindenau* v. *Desborough* (1828), 8 B & C 586, a life insurance case, *per* BAYLEY, J , at p 592 (" the proper question is, whether any particular circumstance was in fact material,

charged, or of the party complaining, which indicate a belief or consciousness on his part that the withheld fact was, or was not, material, as the case may be, may be sufficient to turn the scale against him (s). The mere individual views of a witness as to the materiality of a fact, as distinguished from his evidence as to the general belief and practice of men engaged in the trade to which the transaction in question belongs, is equally without significance (t).

and not whether the party believed it to be so   The contrary doctrine would lead to frequent suppression of information, and it would often be extremely difficult to show that the party neglecting to give the information thought it material "), and *per* LITTLEDALE, J, at p. 593 ("the question on such a policy is not whether a certain individual thought a particular fact material, but whether it was in fact material, and of that the jury are by law constituted the judges "), *Railton* v. *Mathews and Leonard* (1844), 10 Cl & F 934 (a suretyship case), *per* LORD CAMPBELL, at p 944, *Dalglish* v. *Jarvie* (1850), 2 Maen & G 231, *per* ROLFE, B, at p 243 (" in cases of insurance, a party is required not only to state all matters within his knowledge which he believes to be material to the question of insurance, but all which in point of fact are so "), *Bates* v *Hewitt* (1867), L. R 2 Q. B. 595, a marine insurance case, *per* COCKBURN, C J., at p 607 (" it is immaterial whether the omission to communicate a material fact arose from . its not being present to the mind of the assured that the fact was one which it was material to be made known "); *Imperial Mercantile Credit Association* v *Coleman* (1873), L R 6 H. L 189, a principal and agent case (*per* Lord CAIRNS at pp 209, 210), *London Assurance Co* v *Mansel* (1879), 11 C D. 363, a life insurance case (*per* JESSEL, M.R, at p 368), *Brownlie* v *Campbell* (1880), 5 App Cas. 925, H L, *per* Lord BLACKBURN at p. 954 (" the concealment of a material circumstance known to you, whether you thought it material or not, avoids the policy "), *Grant* v *Gold Exploration and Development Syndicate*, [1900] 1 Q B 233, C A, a principal and agent case (*per* COLLINS, L J, at pp. 248–250); *Joel* v *Law Union and Crown Insurance Co.*, [1908] 2 K. B 863, C A, a life insurance case (*per* MOULTON, L J, at p 885)

(s) In the following cases, acts and conduct of the party charged, evidencing a consciousness or suspicion on his part of materiality, were held to conclude the issue of materiality in fact (which otherwise might have been doubtful) against such party   *Ellard* v *Lord Llandaff* (1810), 1 Ball & Beatty, 241, 12 R R 22, where Lord MANNERS, L C (Ir), at pp. 248, 249, refers to a variety of expressions used by the party charged, and his conduct generally, and, at p. 149, concludes   "is not this decisive to show that *in the opinion of the plaintiff* this was a material fact ?", the plaintiff being the party charged, and on this consciousness he founds his decision that the undisclosed circumstances were in point of fact material, a decision at which he would not probably have otherwise arrived, and which, indeed, even so, has not escaped much adverse criticism, *Bufe* v *Turner* (1815), 6 Taunt 338, a fire insurance case, which is abstracted in note (w) to § 104, *post*, in which the assured by his mode of dealing with the situation evinced a keen sense of the materiality of a fire in neighbouring premises to his own, and of the force and applicability of *tua res agitur, paries cum proximus ardet*, *Russell* v *Thornton* (1859), 4 H & N 788, a marine insurance case, *per* CHANNELL, B, at pp 802, 803 (' the plaintiff himself, in communicating and sending a copy of it to his own agents   thought the information most material "), *British Equitable Insurance Co* v *G W Ry Co* (1869), 38 L J Ch 314 (a life insurance case, where the fact that the assured took, and believed, the opinion of a specialist in preference to that of the general practitioner, was evidence of his own sense of the gravity of the disease), *London Assurance Co* v *Mansel, sup*, *per* JESSEL, M R, at pp 371, 372, *Tate & Sons* v *Hyslop* (1885), 15 Q B D 368, C A, *per* BRETT, M R, at pp 375–377, *Laing* v *Union Marine Insurance Co* (1895), 1 Comm Cas 11 *per* MATHEW, J, at pp 17, 18   Conversely, in *Seaton* v *Burnand*, [1900] A C 135, H L, the fact that the party complaining had shown by his conduct that he did not regard the undisclosed circumstances as material, and had directed his inquiries to, and concerned himself with, circumstances of a different nature, which had been duly disclosed, was held to be of considerable importance in arriving at the decision, which was adverse to the party complaining (see the observations of Lord HALSBURY, L C, at pp 139, 141, 142, Lord SHAND at pp 146, 147, and Lord BRAMPTON at p 148), *Broome* v *Speak*, [1903] 1 Ch. 586, C A. (*per* COLLINS, M R, at p 614), as to a prospectus

(t) See *Berthon* v *Loughman* (1817), 2 Stark 258, a marine insurance case, where HOLROYD, J, at p 259, in directing the jury, said   "whether particular facts, if disclosed to an underwriter, would, in the opinion of a witness, or as a matter of judgment, make a difference in the amount of premium is, I think, admissible evidence," but was

Similar rules prevail in the law of misrepresentation, with regard to the views of parties as to the materiality of a statement (u), and in the law of defamation, with regard to the views of parties and witnesses as to the meaning of the alleged defamatory matter (v).

34. As will be explained hereafter in detail, materiality is a question of fact (w), the burden of establishing which is on the party complaining (x).

SECT. 3. KNOWLEDGE

35. The question of the knowledge (actual or presumptive) possessed by either of the parties to a contract or transaction involving a duty of disclosure, as to the existence of the facts which in the particular case are the subject of the duty, is of obvious and vital importance. In a treatise of high merit and authority (y), concealment or non-disclosure is said to exist " where one party suppresses or neglects to communicate to the other a material fact which, if communicated, would tend directly to prevent the other from entering into the contract, or to induce him to demand terms more favourable to himself, and which is known, or presumed to be so, to the party not disclosing it, and is not known, or presumed to be so, to the other " This definition involves three propositions :—(i) that non-disclosure of what is known to the party complaining is not actionable, for *scientia utrinque par pares contrahentes facit*, (ii) that non-disclosure of what is not known to the party charged is equally devoid of legal consequences, for *ignorantia utrinque par pares contrahentes facit* (z), and (iii) that knowledge may be actual or presumed. In every case, therefore, it must appear that the material fact undisclosed was within the knowledge of the one party, and without the knowledge of the other Further, in cases where express or implied waiver is set up as an answer to an allegation of non-disclosure, or where affirmation or confirmation is suggested as a bar to relief (a), knowledge of all material facts on the part of the party alleged to have waived the disclosure, or to have affirmed or confirmed the contract or transaction, must

careful to add " the question is not what the private opinion of the individual may be as to the probable course of his conduct in a particular case, but what in his judgment the general opinion would be amongst those conversant with such matters " So also, in *Glasgow Assurance Corporation v William Symondson & Co* (1911), 104 L T 254, SCRUTTON, J , points out that, in marine insurance, it is the opinion of the prudent insurer which counts, and not that of the general public (p 257) See also *Traill v Baring* (1864), 4 De G J & S 318 (*per* TURNER, L J , at p 330)

(u) See §§ 127, 128 of the author's *Law of Actionable Misrepresentation*
(v) See Article 17 (5) of the author's *Code of the Law of Actionable Defamation*
(w) This topic is dealt with in Ch III, Sect 6, Sub s (1), and in Ch IV, Sect 6, *post*.
(x) See § 174, *post*
(y) Phillips on Insurance, § 531. The proposition cited in the text, though intended to be applied immediately to cases of insurance, is so worded as to admit of a general application to all classes of case which involve the duty of disclosure Vid note (a) to § 629, *post*, as to Lord ESHER'S high opinion of Phillips as a clear and precise expounder of legal principles
(z) See the observation of BRAMWELL, L J , at p 464 of *Bradford v Symondson* (1881), 7 Q B D 456, C A · " if it is true "—i e that the party is not liable for non-disclosure —' when both parties know, it is equally true when they do not "
(a) See Ch. III, Sect 4, Sub ss. (2) and (4), Ch IV, Sect 4, Sub s (3) and (4), and Ch V, Sect 4, Sub s (3), *post*

be clearly established. Again, where it is a question of the rights and liabilities of an assignee of a contract alleged to be voidable for non-disclosure, the assignee's notice, or want of notice, of the non-disclosure set up as a ground for such voidability may be, or become, of the utmost materiality (b) From all these points of view, knowledge or notice must always be a subject of vital concern in every transaction or relation giving rise to a duty of disclosure, and, as such, demands special examination at the outset.

Sub-s (1). *Actual and Presumptive Knowledge.*

36. Knowledge may be either a fact, to be established by evidence, like any other fact, or it may be deemed in law to have existed, without proof as a fact. The former class of knowledge is usually called " actual " knowledge or notice, though the epithet has been extended by some authorities to certain species of the other class : the latter has been termed " constructive," " imputed," or " presumed," knowledge or notice. These expressions, however, have been used in so many different senses, and have been so variously distinguished from one another, at different times and by different judges and jurists—as will be indicated hereafter (c)—that it is necessary to state at once the terminology intended to be adopted and adhered to in this treatise, which is as follows Wherever the term " actual " knowledge is used in this work, it means actual and personal knowledge Every other kind of knowledge will be comprised under the general name of " presumptive " knowledge, of which there are the several species enumerated below (d).

37. Actual knowledge or notice, in the above sense, when alleged, must be strictly proved as a fact by evidence. That is to say, the fact of which the actual knowledge is set up must be shown to have been personally, and not vicariously, known to the person to whom it is attributed (e), and actually present to his mind at the material date (f).

38. Presumptive knowledge consists of five species, which may be stated broadly and summarily as follows —

(b) See Ch III, Sect 7, Ch IV, Sect 7, and Ch V, Sect 7, *post*
(c) §§ 644, 645, App A, Sect 4, *post*
(d) See § 38, *inf.*
(e) *Saffron Walden Second Benefit Building Society* v. *Rayner* (1880), 14 C. D 406, C A (*per* JAMES, L.J., at pp 410–412, BAGGALLAY, L.J , at p 414, and BRAMWELL, I J , at pp 417, 418) Cp what is said by Lord COTTENHAM, L C , at pp 623, 624 of *Wilde* v *Gibson* (1848), 1 H L. C. 605, as to the irrelevance of a suggested case of constructive notice, where personal notice is distinctly alleged, and made the sole foundation of the claim to relief
(f) In *Bates* v *Hewitt* (1867), L R 2 Q B 595, it was pointed out by COCKBURN, C J., at p 605, that the party charged had failed to prove that the party complaining knew that the S S " Georgia," the subject of the policy, had been the notorious Confederate cruiser of that name, it appearing that though he had at one time known the history of the Confederate " Georgia," he had, at the date of the insurance, forgotten it, so that the knowledge in question was *not then present to his mind*, and it was the duty of the party charged to bring home to him such information as would enable him to identify the vessel, in which duty he had failed Cp. *Ellis* v. *Rogers* (1885), 29 C D 661, C A , a vendor and purchaser case, where the purchaser knew of the restrictive covenants, the suppression of which he complained of, but did not know or believe that they were operative at the time *per* COTTON, L J , at p 671 ; *Nocton* v *Lord Ashburton*, [1914] A C 932, H L (*per* Lord DUNEDIN at p. 962), a solicitor and client case

(i) Facts of public notoriety, and rules and principles of general application in ordinary life, are presumed without proof to be within the knowledge of both parties ·

(ii) The law presumes, without proof, knowledge of all facts which, in the course of his business, the party ought to be acquainted with

(iii) From the proved actual knowledge of a fact by an agent, if he be "an agent to know," the law infers, without proof, a knowledge of that fact on the part of his principal .

(iv) From the proved actual knowledge by a party of a fact, the law infers, without proof, a knowledge by that party of any further fact to which the actual knowledge of the first fact would naturally have led, or which such inquiries as were reasonable under the circumstances would have elicited :

(v) By virtue of certain enactments, the legislature imputes knowledge of certain facts to the persons, and under the conditions, prescribed

These several species form the subject of separate and successive treatment in the next five sub-sections (g)

Sub-s. (2). *Presumptive Knowledge of Matters of General Notoriety*

39. For the purposes of the duty of disclosure, any party to a contract or transaction is presumed to be acquainted with all matters of general notoriety (h), whether the notoriety extends to the entire community, or only to a class or section of the public, if the class or section is one to which the party to whom the knowledge is imputed belongs (i), or to a locality or district, if it is one in which the party to whom the local knowledge is ascribed either carries on business or resides, as the case may be (ii).

(g) The two first of these classes, in relation to marine insurance, are dealt with in the famous judgment of Lord MANSFIELD, C J , in *Carter* v *Boehm* (1766), 3 Burr 1905, at pp 1910, 1911 , also by COCKBURN, C J , at pp 605, 607, MELLOR, J , at pp 609, 610, and SHEE, J , at pp 610, 611 of *Bates* v *Hewitt*, *sup* , by COCKBURN, C J , at p 757 of *Gandy* v *Adelaide Marine Insurance Co* (1871), L R 6 Q B 746, and in s 18 of the Marine Insurance Act, 1906 The third and fourth are summarily described by Lord ELDON, L C , at p 120 of *Hiern* v *Mill* (1806), 13 Ves 114

(h) See the citations from the marine insurance cases cited in the last note, and s 18, sub s (3) (b) of the Marine Insurance Act, 1906, whereby it is provided that "the *insurer* is presumed to know matters of common notoriety or knowledge " It is true that in the corresponding provision in this Act relating to the presumed knowledge of the *assured*— s 18, sub s (1)—there is no express mention of such matters, but they are probably intended to be included in the general phrase "every circumstance which, in the ordinary course of business, ought to be known to him "

(i) Thus in *Durrell* v *Bederley* (1816), Holt N P 283 , 17 R R 639, a marine insurance case, " the current knowledge of Jersey " as to a French frigate which had made captures on that coast, was imputed to the plaintiff who was the party charged (for he carried on his business there), but was not imputed to the party complaining, the underwriter in London, for ' the underwriters could know nothing of it " (*per* GIBBS, C J , at p. 286) See also *Harrower* v *Hutchinson* (1870), L R 5 Q B 584, Exch Ch , *per* KELLY, C B , at pp 591–593, as to the presumption of an underwriter's knowledge of the local regulations of foreign States Again, in *Edwards* v *Meyrick* (1842), 2 Hare, 60, a solicitor and client case, WIGRAM, V -C , at pp 73–75, pointed out that the solicitor was not bound to call his client's attention to the speculative possibility that a railway, which in the district where the parties resided was known to be in contemplation, might improve the value of the land which was the subject of the action

(ii) Thus, in vendor and purchaser cases, the purchaser is presumed to know, if resident

40. Amongst matters of such general notoriety that every person of average education and ordinary intelligence is deemed to be cognizant of them, and of which no person can be heard to assert his ignorance, whether such ignorance actually exists or not, are "general topics of speculation, as, for instance," in cases of marine insurance, "the underwriter is bound to know every cause which may occasion natural perils, as the difficulty of the voyages—the kind of seasons—the probability of lightning, hurricanes, earthquakes, etc. He is bound to know every cause which may occasion political perils, from war, and the various operations of it . . . Men argue differently from natural phenomena and political appearances: . . . but the means of information are open to both. each professes to act from his own skill and capacity; and, therefore, neither needs to communicate to the other " (*j*). And, in addition to the ordinary physical laws and phenomena above referred to, a knowledge would probably be imputed to either party of all such elementary and general rules of mathematical and other sciences, as may be supposed to be within the limits of the ordinary education of a normal person but not of any method of calculation or scientific principle going a step beyond these limits. Thus the borrower of money from a money-lender is not presumed to appreciate, without explanation, the effect on the rate of interest charged of a clause in the contract providing for the whole amount becoming due on failure to pay any one instalment, and the money-lender has no right to assume that the borrower is mathematician enough to make the necessary calculation (*k*), and probably, though the two ancient authorities on the point do not offer much guidance, an appreciation of the

---

in the locality, all those features of the property sold which are within the physical cognizance of the neighbourhood see *Boules* v *Round* (1800), 5 Ves 508, where to an action for specific performance of an agreement to purchase a meadow the defence was non disclosure of the fact that there was a way round it, and a footpath across it, which Lord LOUGHBOROUGH, L C, disposed of by the observation, at p 509 " certainly the meadow is very much the worse for a road going through it, but I cannot help the care lessness of the purchaser, who does not choose to enquire *It is not a latent defect* " But it must be remembered that, in such cases, no more knowledge is imputed even to a resident than " what any person going over the property would acquire from ocular inspection ": *per* KINDERSLEY, V C, at p 431 of *Brandling* v *Plummer* (1854), 2 Drew 427, 100 R R 209 See also *Pimm* v *Lewis* (1862), 2 F & F 778, where one party was presumed to know that the other party was in the habit of grinding rice chaff in his mill (which was the undisclosed fact), since the practice was public and open, and the parties were neighbours. CHITTY, J, at pp 408, 409 of *Ashburner* v *Sewell*, [1891] 3 Ch 405, states very clearly the rule as to ' patent defects " of which knowledge is presumed, and " latent defects " of which no knowledge is presumed, in particular reference to rights of way. The case before him was one of latent defect. With the above may be usefully contrasted those " objects of sense " cases where a positive misrepresentation has been made, and where therefore the presumption is excluded, or at least is much less readily made See note (*l*) to § 209 of the author's *Law of Actionable Misrepresentation*. Cp also the " latent defect " cases cited in notes (*t*) and (*v*) to § 118, *post*.

(*j*) *Carter* v *Boehm* (1766), 3 Burr 1905, *per* Lord MANSFIELD, C J, at pp 1910, 1911 Cp. *Bates* v *Hewitt* (1867), L R 2 Q. B 595, and *Harrower* v. *Hutchinson* (1870), L R 5 Q B 584, Exch Ch, *per* KELLY, C B, at pp 591–593, as to the presumption that underwriters are acquainted with (*inter alia*) matters of political, geographical, and marine information *in general*

(*k*) *Harris* v *Clarson* (1910), 27 T L R 30 (*per* CHANNELL, J), *London and West-minster Loan and Discount Co* v *Bilton* (1911), 27 T L R 184 (*per* JOICE, J.), *Stirling* v. *Rose* (1913), 30 T. L. R. 67.

terrific results of applying to an everyday transaction even such a simple mathematical law as that of geometrical progression is not to be attributed to the ordinary or normal person (*l*). This "normal person" whose capacity is made the standard of the kind of presumptive knowledge now under consideration, is neither an idiot nor a genius, he is "the man in the street," the average citizen, "the prudent man" in business, the Aristotelian "φρόνιμος" (*m*). In the Digest the rule as to the normal person is thus stated: "Facti ignorantia ita demum cuique non nocet si non ei summa negligentia objiciatur. Quid enim si omnes in civitate sciant quod ille solus ignorat? Et recte Labeo definit scientiam neque curiosissimi neque negligentissimi hominis accipiendam" (*n*).

41. The general principles of the *corpus juris* are presumed to be within the cognizance of every citizen, not because they form part of his ordinary education, but on grounds of public policy (*o*) This, however, does not mean that a party is deemed to know and appreciate questions relating to particular titles, estates, and interests, or the rights and liabilities flowing from a particular contract or transaction (*p*). Indeed it is the non-disclosure of such matters which forms one of the most important and frequent grounds for avoiding releases, compromises (*q*), contracts or transactions between trustee and *cestui que trust* (*r*), between principal and agent (*s*), and, generally, between parties standing in a fiduciary relation to one another (*t*), and for refusing to give effect to pleas of waiver (*u*) or affirmation (*v*)

(*l*) The two authorities referred to are *James* v *Morgan* (1674), 1 Lev 111 , 1 Keb 569, and *Thornborow* v *Whitacre* (1705), 2 Ld. Raym 1164 , 6 Mod 305. They are abstracted and discussed in Ch III , Sect. 8, Sub s (1), *post*

(*m*) See the Ethics, *passim*. As to the like characteristics of the "normal person," for the purpose of determining questions as to the meaning of alleged defamatory matter, see the author's *Code of the Law of Actionable Defamation*, Article 15, note (*m*), and App VI, Sect 1

(*n*) Dig 22. 6 9 2 The passage is cited by KNIGHT BRUCE, L J , at p. 687 of *Reynell* v *Sprye* (1852), 1 De G. M & G 660

(*o*) *Cooper* v *Phibbs* (1867), L R 2 H L 149, *per* Lord WESTBURY, at p 170 , *The Bedouin*, [1894] P 1 (*per* Lord ESHER, M R , at p 12 " the assured is not bound to tell the underwriter what the law is ") A party has thus been presumed to be acquainted with even the general principles of local government law see *Re Leyland and Taylor's Contract*, [1900] 2 Ch 625, C A (*per* Lord ALVERSTONE, M R , at p 630) The rule of Roman jurisprudence was that knowledge of law was imputed to one who had access to a jurisconsult, or was one himself see Dig 22. 6. 9. 3 ("sed juris ignorantiam non prodesse Labeo ita accipiendum existimat, si juris consulti copiam haberet, vel suâ prudentiâ instructus sit, ut cui facile sit scire, ei detrimento sit juris ignorantia , quod rarô accipiendum est")—a passage which is also cited by KNIGHT BRUCE, L J , in *Reynell* v. *Sprye*, *ubi sup* It should be noted here that an ambassador or diplomatic agent is excepted from the presumption, and no knowledge even of the general law of this country can be imputed to him *Re Republic of Bolivia Exploration Syndicate*, [1914] 1 Ch 139 (*per* ASTBURY, J , at p 156).

(*p*) *Reynell* v. *Sprye*, *sup* , *per* KNIGHT BRUCE, L J , at p 687, and Lord CRANWORTH, L J , at p 710 , *Cooper* v *Phibbs*, *sup* , with which compare §§ 41, 42 of the author's *Law of Actionable Misrepresentation*, as to misstatements of law

(*q*) See Ch III , Sect 2, Sub s (5), *post*

(*r*) See Ch IV , Sect 2, Sub-s (1), *post*

(*s*) See Ch. IV, Sect. 2, Sub s (3), *post*

(*t*) See Ch. V, *post*

(*u*) See §§ 201–208, *post*

(*v*) See §§ 209–215, 372, 373, 480, 481, *post*.

Sub-s. (3). *Presumptive Knowledge of Facts and Usages peculiar to the Business or Transaction*

42. Apart from matters of general notoriety, the parties to any contract or transaction as to which a duty of disclosure exists are presumed in law to be acquainted with all such facts, circumstances, practices, and usages as form part of the common stock of knowledge, or are current in the particular business which either of them carries on, and to have all such notice as is, so to speak, inherent in the nature of the contract or transaction in which they are engaged, or contemplate being engaged (*w*). Thus, in the department of marine insurance, which is the most fruitful in illustrations of the species of presumptive knowledge now under discussion, the underwriter is " presumed to know .. matters which an insurer, in the ordinary course of his business, as such, ought to know " (*x*) ; and amongst such matters are the practices and customs of the trade or business of the assured in relation to the subject of the insurance (*y*), the situation and local usages of ports (*z*), the ordinary

(*w*) *Carter* v *Boehm* (1766), 3 Burr 1905, *per* Lord MANSFIELD, C J , at pp. 1010, 1011 (" if an underwriter insures private ships of war,   he needs not to be told the secret enterprises they are destined upon, because he knows some expedition must be in view, and *from the nature of the contract*, without being told, he waives the information ") , *Hiern* v *Mill* (1806), 13 Ves 114, *per* Lord ERSKINE, L.C , who dealing with instances of constructive notice, says at p 120 " another case is where the law imputes that notice which, from the nature of the transaction, every person of ordinary prudence must necessarily have " , *Wythes* v *Labouchere* (1859), 3 De G & J. 593, *per* Lord CHELMSFORD, L C , at p. 610

(*x*) Marine Insurance Act, 1906, s 18, sub s (3) (b)

(*y*) " Every underwriter is presumed to be acquainted with the practice of the trade he insures, and that whether it is established or not   If he does not know it, he ought to inform himself "   *per* Lord MANSFIELD, C J , at p 512 of *Noble* v *Kennaway* (1780), 2 Dougl (K B) 510   If, however, Lord Mansfield intended by the words " whether established or not " to lay down that an underwriter has presumptive knowledge of every usage or practice, however recent, he was to this extent in conflict with later authority (see note (*h*) to § 43, *post*), and was certainly wrong   The usage or practice of which knowledge was imputed in that case was one which prevailed in the Newfoundland fishing trade, and so also in *Ougier* v *Jennings* (1800), 1 Campb 504 n , *per* LORD ELDON, C J , and in *Vallance* v *Dewar* (1808), 1 Campb 503, *per* Lord ELLENBOROUGH, C J , at p 506 (" the broker must communicate what is in the special knowledge of the assured, not what is in the middle between them and the underwriters "   the usage there, which was ' in the middle between " the parties was the custom of employing the ship in " banking ' or fishing on the bank of Newfoundland)   In *Salvador* v *Hopkins* (1765), 3 Burr 1707, Lord MANSFIELD, C J , at p 1715, characterized " the usage of the East India Company s trade, and the course of their voyages " as " a fact notorious, and so well known both to the insurers and the insured that they must be supposed fully apprized and sufficiently conversant of it " , in *Foley* v *Tabor* (1861), 2 F & F 106, the underwriter was deemed to have presumptive notice of the fact that railways were then being constructed in India, and that most trading ships going to Kurrachee carried cargoes of iron for that purpose For other practices of which a knowledge was imputed to the underwriter, see *Da Costa* v *Edwards* (1815), 4 Campb 142 (mode of loading and stowing carboys of vitriol) , *Stewart* v. *Bell* (1821), 5 B & Ald 238, *per Cur* at p. 239 (" the underwriter is presumed to be acquainted with the usual course of the voyage," and " should enquire, therefore, what is the usual mode of landing the goods insured   Here it appears to have been the usage to tranship the goods into shallops "), *Tate & Sons* v *Hyslop* (1885), 15 Q B D 368, C. A , where, *per* BRETT, M R , at p 378, it was recognized that if it had been proved which it had not, that there was a general practice amongst sugar refiners to employ lightermen on terms of restricted liability, the underwriters would have been presumed cognizant thereof

(*z*) See *Kingston* v *Knibbs* (1809), 1 Campb 508 n (custom to take in part of the cargo inside, and the remainder outside, the bar of Oporto) , *Stewart* v *Bell, sup* (practice in

clauses and provisions of charter-parties and other commercial instruments used for purposes of marine adventures, or in the particular trade of the vessel insured (a), as well as the rules and practice of underwriters generally (b), and all such facts as may be gleaned from the usual sources of information available to an underwriter in his business; such as Lloyd's Shipping Lists and Registers, and the like (c). So also, in principal and agent cases, the principal

Jamaica, for vessels drawing a certain amount of water to discharge their cargo at Port Morant into shallops, and tranship to the place required); *Harrower* v. *Hutchinson* (1870), L. R. 5 Q. B. 584, Exch. Ch. (*per* KELLY, C.B , at pp 591-593, as to an underwriter's presumptive acquaintance with the situation of recognized ports generally, and local regulations, &c.)

(a) See *Salvador* v. *Hopkins* (1765), 3 Burr. 1707 (charter-party in a well-known printed form—*per* Lord MANSFIELD, C J., at p 1715), *The Bedouin*, [1894] P. 1, C. A (the common " 24 hours " clause in a time charter . *per* Lord ESHER, M.R , at pp 12, 13), *Charlesworth* v. *Faber* (1900), 5 Comm. Cas. 408 (*per* BIGHAM, J., at pp. 411, 412, as to Clause 7 of the " Elder Dempster & Co.'s Clauses," which was proved to be in common use).

(b) See *Bates* v *Hewitt* (1867), L. R. 2 Q. B 595 (*per* SHEE, J , at p. 610 . " he is not bound to communicate facts or circumstances which are within the ordinary professional knowledge of an underwriter "); *Gandy* v. *Adelaide Marine Insurance Co* (1871), L. R. 6 Q. B. 746 (rules of Lloyd's as to classification of ships ; *per* MELLOR, J , delivering the judgment of the majority of the Court, at p. 755 " *primâ facie* we should think that every underwriter who relies upon the classification of a ship in Lloyd's Register, as determining the rate of insurance, ought to be acquainted with the rules and practice which give the classification its value ")

(c) It was laid down generally in *Friere* v. *Woodhouse* (1816), Holt N P 572 , 17 R. R. 670, *per* BURROUGH, J , at p 573, that " what the underwriters by fair inquiry or due diligence may learn from the ordinary sources of information need not be disclosed," and, as regards the similarly presumed knowledge of the assured, by the Court of Q B , at pp 521, 522 of *Proudfoot* v. *Montefiore* (1867), L R 2 Q. B. 511, that " the insurer is entitled to assume, as the basis of the contract between him and the assured, that . . . the latter will take the necessary measures . . to obtain, through the ordinary channels of intelligence in use in the mercantile world, all due information as to the subject matter of the insurance," and by Lord HALSBURY, L C , at pp. 536, 537 of *Blackburn, Low & Co.* v *Vigors* (1877), 12 App Cas 531, H L , that " when a man comes for insurance on his ship, he may be expected to know both the then condition and the history of the ship he seeks to insure " As to Lloyd's Lists and Registers, and the knowledge of their contents which is imputed to underwriters, see *Friere* v *Woodhouse, sup* , *Mackintosh & Dreyer* v *Marshall* (1843), 11 M & W. 116 (where it was recognized that, but for the positive mis- representation which was proved there, the knowledge in question would have been presumed, *per* Lord ABINGER, C B , at p 127 " the materiality of such a document at Lloyd's depends entirely on the silence of all parties respecting the date of the vessel's sailing When there is no wrong representation about it, no communication calculated to mislead, then the document at Lloyd's is competent evidence where the means of know- ledge are common to both These are the only cases in which that document concludes the underwriter ") , *Foley* v *Tabor* (1861), 2 F & F 663 (*per* ERLE, C J , at p 672, as to the imputed knowledge of the nature of cargoes of vessels from a book for that purpose kept at Lloyd's) , *Nicholson* v *Power* (1869), 20 L T 580, Exch Ch , where the rule was recognized, though it was held inapplicable to the circumstances of that case see note (*l*) to § 43, *post* , *Leigh* v *Adams* (1871), 25 L T 566, *per* COCKBURN, C J , at p 569 (" it has been laid down that the lists at Lloyd's are within the knowledge that every underwriter is presumed to possess ") , *Gandy* v *Adelaide Marine Insurance Co* (1871), L R 6 Q B. 746 (Lloyd's Register of classification of ships) In *Morrison* v *Universal Marine Insurance Co* (1872), L R 8 Exch 40, it was said by the Court of Exchequer, *per* MARTIN, B , at pp 52, 53, that no one is presumed, as a matter of law, to carry in his head the whole contents of Lloyd's Lists, and *per* BRAMWELL, B , at p 54, that the only matters of which a knowledge is imputed to the underwriter from those lists are " matters of general knowledge, not matters relating to any particular ship " These pronouncements are certainly not law The decision itself was reversed by the Exchequer Chamber (1873), L R 8 Exch 197, but the point in question was not there debated, there having been no leave reserved to raise it If it had been discussed, it can hardly be doubted that the Exchequer Chamber would have disagreed with the Court of Exchequer on this question, as well as on the others

is presumed to be cognizant of the well-known and established customs and practices of the business in which the agent is employed as to discounts, rebates, allowances, bonuses, and the like, and, where such presumptive knowledge exists, he is unable to establish against the agent a case of secret profit or advantage (d)

43. The above rule, like all others emanating from the doctrine of constructive notice, is cautiously applied, and is hedged round with many and stringent limitations. Thus, no knowledge is imputed of a custom which, if given effect to, would alter the whole contractual relation between the parties, and turn, for instance, an agent or broker into a vendor or purchaser (e), nor of a practice or usage which is not honest (f). Again, there is no presumed knowledge of a practice which is not clearly proved to have existed, or which is only one of two or more general practices, and not *the* general practice set up (g), nor of a usage which is of recent growth, and not established (h), nor of unusual and novel clauses in mercantile instruments (hh), nor of occasional and temporary regulations of foreign States in relation to marine commerce (i). And, in cases of marine insurance, though the underwriter is presumed to know the situation of foreign ports, he is not expected to know of the existence or locality or dangers of places not established as

(d) *Great Western Insurance Co.* v. *Cunliffe* (1874), 9 Ch. App 525, *per* JAMES, L.J , at pp 537, 538, and MELLISH, L J., at pp 539, 540, *Baring* v. *Stanton* (1876), 3 C D. 502, (A. (*per* JAMES, L.J , at p 506, MELLISH, L J., at p. 506, and BAGGALLAY, L J , at p 507); *Williamson* v *Hine Brothers*, [1891] 1 Ch 390, C.A (as to the practice of paying commissions on insurance premiums and apprentices' fees, *per* KEKEWICH, J., affirmed by the C A , at p 391) ; *Re White and Smith's Contract*, [1896] 1 Ch 637 (*per* STIRLING, J., at p 642 no presumptive notice of custom in City of London to deposit leases with solicitors on sales of leaseholds) , *Stubbs* v *Slater*, [1910] 1 Ch 632, C A (as to stockholder's charges, *per* COZENS-HARDY, M R , at p 642, and JOYCE, J , at p 648) , *Aston* v. *Kelsey*, [1913] 3 K. B. 314, C A (the like) , *Blaker* v *Hawes* (1913), 100 L T. 320 (the like).
(e) *Brookman* v *Rothschild* (1831), 5 Bligh (N S) 165 , *Robinson* v *Mollett* (1875), L R. 7 H L. 802. See also, generally, many of the cases cited in the notes to Ch. IV, Sect 2, Sub s (3), *post* As to the reluctance of the Courts to extend the doctrine of constructive notice, see §§ 77, 78, *post*
(f) *Brookman* v *Rothschild*, *ubi sup* , *per* LORD WYNFORD, at pp 190, 201, 202 , *Robinson* v *Mollett*, *ubi sup* , *per* Lord CHELMSFORD at pp 837, 838, adopting the views of the Judges who had been summoned to a *concilium*, and particularly those of BRETT, J , at pp 817–819, and 825 , *Hippisley* v *Knee Brothers*, [1905] 1 K B 1, Div Ct , *per* Lord ALVERSTONE, C J , at p 7, and KENNEDY, J , at p 9 Here again, see several of the cases cited in the notes to Ch IV, Sect 2, Sub s (3), *post*
(g) *Tate & Sons* v *Hyslop* (1885), 15 Q B D 368, C A , *per* BRETT, M R , at p 378 , *Williamson* v *Hine Brothers*, [1891] 1 Ch 390, C.A , where the alleged custom of which it was sought to impute knowledge to the party complaining (viz a custom for the managing owners of a vessel to retain for themselves brokerage on freights and charters procured by them, as against the other owners) was not proved *per* KEKEWICH, J , at pp 393, 394)
(h) *Harrower* v *Hutchinson* (1870), L R 5 Q B. 584, Exch Ch , *per* KELLY, C B , at p 591 (' usages of trade can only exist in a known and established trade, and all the analogies seem to show that the usages of trade mentioned are confined to owners of a known and established trade ") The dictum of Lord MANSFIELD, C J , to the contrary —see note (y) to § 42, *ante*—must be considered incorrect
(hh) See *Mercantile Steamship Co* v *Tyser* (1881), 7 Q B D 73 (*per* COLERIDGE, C J , at p 77), *Cockburn* v. *Edwards* (1881), 18 C D 449, 455, 462, C A
(i) *Harrower* v *Hutchinson*, *sup* , *per* KELLY, C B , at p 591 (" a recent foreign trade law . not known or presumed from its publicity or otherwise to be so to the underwriter "), and again at p 592 (" new and shifting regulations of foreign states by which the property is exposed to seizure . cannot be presumed to be necessarily within the knowledge of the underwriter ")

ports in general use (j). Nor is a party deemed to be acquainted with more than the actual contents of any mercantile register, book, or instrument in general use in the particular business, and such further facts as ought reasonably to be inferred therefrom by one carrying on that business : and in any case where there is any undisclosed circumstance or detail, or unsupplied information, which was necessary to give materiality and significance to such contents, no knowledge is imputed to the party to whom the duty of making the disclosure was owed, in favour of the party who was subject to the obligation, and left it undischarged (k).

Sub-s. (4). *Presumptive Knowledge through Agents*

44. For purposes of the law of disclosure, as for other purposes, it may be stated generally, though perhaps somewhat elliptically (l), that the

(j) *Harrower* v *Hutchinson, sup.,* where the plaintiff effected a policy of marine insurance on bone and bone ash on board a vessel " at and from Buenos Ayres and port or ports of loading in the province of Buenos Ayres, to a port or ports of call and discharge in the United Kingdom " The vessel sailed from Buenos Ayres to a place called Laguna de los Padres, in the province of Buenos Ayres, but being unable to get a cargo there, she returned to Buenos Ayres, and was lost on her way. There was no artificial port at the place in question, which was merely a slaughter-house with a wooden jetty or pier, and a roadstead in a bay formed by natural headlands. It was unknown to underwriters in general as a place of loading, and there was no trade between it and Europe, though there was a purely local trade between it and Buenos Ayres in hides, bones, &c. (p. 388). The Exchequer Chamber, reversing the Q. B , held that though the defendant, as an underwriter, was bound to know the situation of ports known to underwriters in general, or in the trade generally, he was not presumed to know the situation or existence, or dangerous character, of such a place as this (*per* KELLY, C B , at pp 592, 593, delivering the judgment of himself, CHANNELL and PIGOTT, BB , and BYLES and BRETT, JJ) See also *Laing* v. *Union Marine Insurance Co* (1895), 1 Com Cas 11, *per* MATHEW, J , at pp 17, 18, as to the underwriter in that case not being affected with presumptive notice of the dangers and difficulties of the port of Hongay in Japan

(k) See *Nicholson* v *Power* (1869), 20 L T 580, Exch Ch (where COCKBURN, C J , at p. 580, points out that, assuming that the underwriter had constructive notice of whatever was shown by the announcement in Lloyd's Lists, all he could have learned from it was that " a British barque with copper ore " was aground , no knowledge could be imputed to him of the identity of that barque with the " Pedro Ferrar," whose freight was the subject of the policy, since the information required to enable this identification to be made ought to have, but had not, been supplied by the assured) , *Leigh* v *Adams* (1871), 25 L T. 566, where the plaintiff's practice was to insure at Lloyd's cargoes of cochineal shipped by him from the Canaries on floating policies, and to declare the name of the ship upon receipt of each bill of lading When effecting a policy on one of these shipments he knew two facts, neither of which he disclosed, first, the existence of an anonymous letter stating that the owners intended to lose a vessel called the " Candida " on her next voyage, and secondly, that a cargo was to be shipped for him on board the " Candida," though " he did not at that time know that this policy would apply to, or that he should be able to declare the policy upon, the ' Candida ' " (*per* COCKBURN, C J , at p 569) The anonymous letter was posted up on a board at Lloyd's, but it was held that, assuming the underwriter to have had presumptive knowledge of the contents of the letter from the announcement so made, which was evidently thought a matter of considerable doubt in the case of ' a notice of this extraordinary and exceptional nature," such knowledge was utterly meaningless and valueless to him without the disclosure of the second of the two undisclosed facts above mentioned , and he was therefore held to have had no presumptive knowledge of the material circumstances, and succeeded in his defence (*per* COCKBURN, C J , at the same page) Cp *Laing* v *Union Marine Insurance Co* (1895), 1 Comm Cas 11 (*per* MATHEW, J , at p 18, as to a statement in Lloyd's Shipping Index that two vessels had sailed to Hongay, in Japan, not affecting the underwriter with constructive knowledge of the character of that port)

(l) See § 646, *post,* as to the misleading character of these elliptical maxims and formulæ

knowledge of the agent is the knowledge of the principal. This means that, with certain qualifications and exceptions to be discussed presently (m), the law imputes to any party to a contract or transaction knowledge of all facts and circumstances of which any agent of his *for that purpose* (n), *and in that contract or transaction* (o), is actually or presumptively cognizant. The same rule of course applies to partnership which is mutual agency (p)

45. Every legal presumption of the existence of a thing which is not proved as a fact demands justification. The presumption now under discussion is based upon, and justified by, three theories, viz. (1) fairness as between the parties, (2) public necessity and convenience, and (3) the strong probability that, in the great majority of cases, the presumption is in accordance with the fact

46. In the first place, the imputation of the agent's knowledge to the principal is said to be just and reasonable as between the parties, because the principal selects the agent, and, for his own convenience and advantage, puts his *alter ego* in a position to perform acts which may affect the interests of third parties   *Qui sentit commodum, sentire debet et onus.* "It would be a monstrous injustice," in any such case, "that I should have the advantage of what he knows without the disadvantage " (q).

47. The second justification for the presumption is public policy, both in the sense of mercantile convenience amounting almost to an absolute necessity, and also in the sense of public morality   " Mankind," said Lord HATHERLEY, L C , " would not be safe if it was held that, under such circumstances, a man had not notice of that which his agent has actual notice of . . It cannot be left to the possibility or impossibility of the man who seeks to affect you with notice being able to prove that your solicitor "— the agent in the case which elicited the proposition happened to be a solicitor—" did his duty in communicating that which, according to the terms of your employment of him, was the very thing which you employed him to ascertain " (r)

(m) In § 57, *post*
(n) See §§ 49, 50, *post*
(o) See §§ 53–56, *post.*
(p) See *Sadler* v *Lee* (1843), 6 Beav 324, 351 (the passage cited in note (r), *infra*), and *Williamson* v *Barber* (1877), 9 C D 529 (*per* JESSEL, M R , at p 535)   The rule is codified, as regards partnership, in s 16 of the Partnership Act, 1890 (53 & 54 Vict c 39) " notice to any partner who habitually acts in the partnership business of any matter relating to the partnership affairs, operates as notice to the firm, except in the case of a fraud on the firm committed by, or with the consent of, that partner "
(q) *Boursot* v *Savage* (1866), L R 2 Eq 134, *per* KINDERSLEY, V C , at p 142   Cp *Barwick* v *English Joint Stock Bank* (1867), L R 2 Exch 259, 266, Exch Ch
(r) *Rolland* v *Hart* (1871), 6 Ch App 678, at pp 681, 682   Lord BROUGHAM, L C , also rests the doctrine on the ground of public policy at p 719 of *Kennedy* v *Green* (1834), 3 My & K 699 (' policy, and the safety of the public, forbids a person to deny knowledge while he is so dealing as to keep himself ignorant,   and yet all the while let his agent know, and himself perhaps profit by that knowledge "). Cp *Sadler* v *Lee, sup* , per Lord LANGDALE, M R , at p 351 ("courts of justice, for the protection of those who deal with partnerships, *must* impute the knowledge which the partners, acting in their interests and in the discharge of their plain duty, might and ought to have obtained " , *Sharpe* v *Foy* (1868), 4 Ch App 35, where PAGE-WOOD, L J , at p 40, speaks of "the rule of notice " as having been " established for the safety of mankind ")   See also, in illustration of the similar rule and theory in the law of misrepresentation, the cases cited in note (k) to § 163 of the author's *Law of Actionable Misrepresentation.*

On the other hand, the requirements of public policy, in the strict sense of public morals, are also insisted upon in certain weighty judgments, where it is pointed out that, if the presumption in question be not made, and made irrebuttably, the law would pander to perjury and fraud, and its ministers would be continually engaged in the onerous and odious operation of unravelling it by evidence (s). Public policy, however, in the latter sense does not seem so convincing a foundation of the doctrine, as it does in the former; and, indeed, some of the forms which this ethical justification (t) has assumed may appear a little strained and grotesque (u)

48. The third ground on which the rule is based is that the conditions " beget a presumption so strong of actual knowledge, that the law holds the knowledge to exist, because it is highly improbable it should not " (v), or, as it has otherwise been expressed, that " the Court imputes " the knowledge " to a party upon a presumption, so strong that it cannot be allowed to be rebutted, that the knowledge must have been communicated " (w)

49. The presumption is made against either the party to whom the duty of disclosure is owed (x), or to the party who owes the duty (y), as the case

(s) See *Kennedy* v. *Green, sup.,* per Lord BROUGHAM, L C , at p 719 " in such a case it would be most iniquitous, and most dangerous, and give shelter and encouragement to all kinds of fraud, were the law not to consider the knowledge of one as common to both, whether it be so in fact or not " So FRY, J , at p. 705 of *Kettlewell* v. *Watson* (1882), 21 C D 685, said that where it is the duty of an agent to communicate a fact to his principal, " the Court always holds that he did communicate it, not because, in many cases he did communicate it, but because, as I understand it, it would be too dangerous to inquire whether the communication was really made ; it would open the door to perjury "

(t) See the language used by Lord ELLENBOROUGH, C J , at p 38 of *Gladstone* v *King* (1813), 1 M & S 35 (" if the captain might be permitted to wink at these circumstances without hazard to the owners, the latter would in all such cases instruct their captain to remain silent , by which means the underwriter, at the time of subscribing the policy, would incur a certainty of being liable ") , by the Court of Q B at p 522 of *Proudfoot* v *Montefiore* (1847), L R 2 Q B 511 (" by thus holding, we shall prevent the tendency to fraudulent concealment on the part of masters of vessels and agents at a distance, in matters on which they ought to communicate information to their principals, as also any tendency on the part of principals to encourage their servants and agents so to act ") , and by LINDLEY, L J , at p 576, and LOPES, L J , at p 584, of *Blackburn, Low & Co* v *Vigors* (1886), 17 Q B D 553, C A

(u) And they were emphatically repudiated by Lord ESHER, M R , at pp 570, 571, of *Blackburn, Low & Co* v *Vigors, sup* , in a judgment which was approved by the H L , (1887), 12 App Cas 531, H. L (see, particularly, the observations of Lord MACNAGHTEN at p. 543), reversing the decision of the majority of the C A

(v) *Per* Lord BROUGHAM, L C , at p 719 of *Kennedy* v *Green* (1834), 3 My & K 699

(w) *Per* TURNER, V C , at p 455 of *Hewitt* v *Loosemoore* (1851), 9 Hare, 449 Cp KINDERSLEY, V C , at p 142 of *Boursot* v *Savage* (1866), L R 2 Eq 134

(x) Out of many illustrations, the following may be selected Insurance —*Maynard* v *Rhodes* (1824), 5 Dowl & Ry 266 , 27 R R 526 , *Wing* v *Harvey* (1854), 5 De G M & G 265 (*per* KNIGHT-BRUCE, L J , at p 270, and TURNER, L J , at p 271) , *Bawden* v *London, Edinburgh and Glasgow Assurance Co* , [1893] 2 Q B 534, C A , *Hough* v *Guardian Fire & Life Assurance Co* (1902), 18 T L R 273 , *Holdsworth* v *Lancashire & Yorkshire Insurance Co* (1907), 23 T L R 521 (*per* BRAY, J , at pp 523, 524) , *Thornton-Smith* v *Motor Union Insurance Co* (1913), 30 T L R 139 Transactions relating to land —*Brotherton* v *Hatt* (1706), 2 Vern 574 , *Toulmin* v *Steere* (1817), 3 Mer 210 (*per* GRANT, M.R , at pp 222, 224) , Conveyancing Act, 1882 (45 & 46 Vict c 39), as cited in § 66, *post* Generally, see the cases cited in the notes to this Subsection.

(y) See, for illustrations—in marine insurance, *Foley* v *Tabor* (1861), 2 F & F 663 (*per* ERLE, C J , at p 673, where knowledge was imputed to a partner) , *Proudfoot* v. *Montefiore* (1867), L R 2 Q B 511 , *Morrison* v *Universal Marine Insurance Co* (1873),

may require; provided that the agent through whom the knowledge is
imparted be an "agent to know," that is to say, an agent to communicate to
his principal such information as he either acquires or receives on his behalf
in the discharge of the duties of the agency (z). It is in this sense that,
notwithstanding Lord ESHER's objection to the expression in any sense, it
is correct to say that the knowledge of the agent is the knowledge of the
principal (a)   but, in the case of a person who is not an agent to receive and
impart information, but merely to make the contract for his principal, the
phrase is not scientifically exact, since the doctrine of presumptive knowledge does not strictly apply to this class of agency, as such, at all.   The
result, it is true, is precisely the same : that is to say, the party who is under
an obligation to disclose all material facts, is held to have failed in his duty
when the agent to whom he has committed the negotiation of the contract
has not made due disclosure, as much as when he has himself omitted to
disclose material facts within the knowledge of one who is his "agent to
know"   but the liability in the former case arises from the application of the

L. R 8 Exch. 197, Exch Ch. ,—in life insurance, *Everett* v *Desborough* (1829), 5 Bing 503
(*per* BEST, C J, at pp 515, 516, and PARKE, J, at p. 518),—in sales and mortgages of
land, *Gibson* v *D'Este* (1843), 2 Y & C (CH) 542 (*per* KNIGHT-BRUCE, V C, at pp. 570,
571), *Hepworth* v *Pickles*, [1900] 1 Ch 108 (presumptive knowledge of solicitor through
possession of title deeds deemed the knowledge of his client, *per* FARWELL, J , at p 111),
Dixon v *Winch*, [1900] 1 Ch 736, C A (*per* LINDLEY, M.R., at p 745)   And, generally,
see the cases cited in the notes to this Sub section.
    (z) For illustrations of this class of agent, and of the imputation of his knowledge to
the principal, see *Brotherton* v *Hall* (1708), 2 Vern 574 (" all the securities being transacted
at the shop of . . the scriveners, who were . . in the nature of agents to all the several
lenders , notice to the agent is good notice to the party, and consequently they that lend
last must come last, having notice of what was before lent ." *per* Lord Keeper NORTH, at
pp 573, 574), and the marine insurance cases of *Fitzherbert* v *Mather* (1785), 1 Term Rep
12 (consignor and shipper of goods), *Gladstone* v *King* (1813), 1 M & S 35 (captain of
the vessel), *Proudfoot* v *Montefiore* (1867), L R. 2 Q B. 511 (local business representative
of the assured)   At pp 537, 538 of *Blackburn, Low & Co* v *Vigors* (1887), 12 App Cas 531,
Lord HALSBURY, L C, referring to the above illustrations, observes . " I cannot but think
that the somewhat vague use of the word 'agent' leads to confusion   Some agents
so far represent the principal that in all respects their acts and their intentions and their
knowledge may be said to be the acts, intentions, and knowledge of the principal.   Other
agents may have so limited and narrow an authority both in fact and in the common
understanding of their form of employment that it would be quite inaccurate to say that
such an agent's knowledge or intentions are the knowledge or intentions of his principal."
For examples of failure to prove an agency of the former kind, and therefore to establish
presumptive knowledge, see *Saffron Walden Second Benefit Building Society* v *Rayner* (1880),
14 C. D 406, C A (where it was held that the solicitor of trustees for certain purposes
is not the kind of agent whose knowledge of general matters will affect such trustees),
Tate & Sons v *Hyslop* (1885), 15 Q B. D 368, C A (*per* BRETT, M R, at p 374 ' a
solicitor is not a standing agent for one who has been, or may be, his client, to receive a
mercantile notice in respect of mercantile business "), *Wilson* v *Salamandra Assurance Co
of St Petersburg* (1903), 8 Comm Cas 129 (an action by underwriters at Lloyd's on a
policy of reinsurance of a cargo of sugar with the defendants, where the actual knowledge
of Lloyd's agents at Gibraltar that the sugar was damaged was in vain sought to be imputed to the plaintiffs)   Cp the life insurance case of *Levy* v *Scottish Employers' Insurance Co* (1901), 17 T L R 229, Div Ct
    (a) Lord ESHER's criticism is to be found at pp 556–560 of *Blackburn, Low & Co* v
Vigors (1886), 17 Q B D 553, C A, and the observations of Lord HALSBURY, L C., are
at p 537 of the same case in the H L (1887), 12 App Cas 531 (" I am unable to accept the
criticism of the Master of the Rolls upon the proposition that the knowledge of the agent
is the knowledge of the principal   Where a person is *the agent to know*, his knowledge does
bind the principal ")

rule " that a man cannot by delegating to an agent to do what he might do himself, obtain greater rights than if he did the thing himself " (b), rather than from any theory of constructive notice. The distinction between the two classes of case has nowhere been more lucidly explained than by Lord MACNAGHTEN in relation to marine insurance (c). " There is," he says, " nothing unreasonable in imputing to a shipowner who effects an insurance on his vessel the information with regard to his own property which the agent to whom the management of that property is committed possessed at the time, and might in the ordinary course of things have communicated to his employer. In such a case it may be said without impropriety that the knowledge of the agent is the knowledge of the principal. But the case is different when the agent whose knowledge it is sought to impute to the principal is not the agent to whom the principal looked for information, but an agent employed for the special purpose of effecting the insurance. It is quite true that the insurance would be vitiated by concealment on the part of such an agent, just as it would be by concealment on the part of the principal. But that is not because the knowledge of the agent is to be imputed to the principal, but because the agent of the assured is bound, as the principal is bound, to communicate to the underwriters all material facts within his knowledge Concealment of these facts is a breach of duty on his part to those with whom his principal has placed him in communication "

50. For the purposes of the rule relating to presumptive knowledge through agents, a sub-agent, if acting as such with the assent of the ultimate principal, may be an " agent to know " (d) For the like purpose, there may also be an agency by adoption and ratification (e) In the case of statutory corpora-

(b) Per Lord ESHER, M R , at p 559 of *Blackburn, Low & Co* v *Vigors* (1886), 17 Q B D 553, C A In relation to marine insurance the rule is codified in s 19 of the Marine Insurance Act, 1906 (" the agent must disclose to the insurer   every material circumstance which the assured is bound to disclose ") Cp *Arnot* v *Biscoe* (1748), 1 Ves Sr 94 (where Lord HARDWICKE, L.C , said that the agent or attorney of the vendor has the same duty of disclosure to the purchaser as the vendor himself) , *Stevens* v *Adamson* (1818), 2 Stark 422 (another vendor and purchaser case where ABBOTT, C J , at pp 422, 423, lays down, and applies, the same rule—" the vendor, or *his agent*, was bound to communicate to the vendee " . .), *Berwick & Co* v *Price*, [1905] 1 Ch 632 (*per* JOYCE, J at p 639 " no one, by delegating his authority to an agent, can put himself in a better position than he would be in himself If this were the rule, anyone could escape by employing agents ")

(c) At pp 542, 543 of *Blackburn, Low & Co* v *Vigors* (1887), 12 App Cas 531, H L To these observations, add those of Lord WATSON in the same case, who, after stating, at p 539, that, in the case of agents to effect the insurance, " the ordinary rule of law applies, and non disclosure of material facts will affect the principal, and give the insurer good ground for avoiding the contract," proceeds, at p 541, to distinguish this class of agency from the other   the decisions which relate to captains and ship agents   do not appear to me to have any analogy to the case of agents employed to effect a policy   The one class is specially employed for the purpose of communicating to him "— the employer—" the very facts which the law requires him "—the employer—" to divulge to his insurer , the other is employed, not to procure or furnish information respecting the ship, but to effect an insurance   . It cannot reasonably be supposed that the insurer relies to any extent upon the private information possessed by persons of whose existence he presumably knows nothing "

(d) *Brewin* v *Briscoe* (1859), 2 E & E 116 (*per* CROMPTON, J , at p 132) In a later case of *Re Ashton, Ex p. McGowan* (1891), 64 L T 28, the above principle was recognized, but the necessary facts were not proved (*per* CAVE, J , at p 29)

(e) *Jennings* v. *Moore* (1708), 2 Vern. 609 (*per* Lord COWPER, L C)

tions, the particular statute and the statutory instrument of constitution must be carefully examined in order to ascertain who are the officials whose knowledge can properly be said to be that of the corporation : since no such knowledge can be imputed through any other persons Where it is the case of a limited company, such company is ordinarily deemed to have knowledge or notice of those matters only of which its directors, sitting together as a board, have knowledge or notice. Any other person, though he may be the company's agent for other purposes, such as a secretary or auditor, or an individual director acting unofficially, is not a person whose knowledge, affects the company with notice (f)

51. One of the grounds, already indicated (g), on which the presumption in question has been based, is the strong probability, amounting to a practical certainty, that the agent will in the ordinary course communicate to his principal the knowledge which the law imputes to the latter   The same reasoning, where there is the like probability, justifies the converse proposition that the knowledge of the principal is the presumed knowledge of the agent (h)   It also justifies, in certain cases, the imputation of knowledge to one person from the actual knowledge of another who is not, in the fullest sense of the word, or for all purposes, either his principal or agent   Thus notice to a husband has been deemed notice to the wife (i) , infants may be affected by notice to their ancestor (j) : and it has been decided that a *cestui que trust* has no better equity, and is in no better position, as regards the doctrine of constructive notice, than his trustee (k).

52. It has already been stated (l) that it is not only the actual, but the presumptive, knowledge of the agent which may be imputed to the principal Thus, an agent may, in virtue of his actual notice of a fact or document, be affected with presumptive notice of another fact or document to which, if the proper inquiries were made, the first fact or document would point (m), and in that event, as much as if the agent had direct and express notice, his presumptive notice is, by a further presumption, imputed to his principal (n)

(f) *Metropolitan Bank v Heiron* (1880), 5 Ex D 319, C A (*per* BRETT L J , at p. 325, and COTTON, L J , at p 326) , *Société Générale de Paris v Tramways Union Co* (1884), 14 Q B D 424, C A (*per* LINDLEY, L.J , at p 450) , *Swale v Ipswich Tannery, Ltd* (1906), 11 Comm Cas 88 (*per* KENNEDY, J , at p 96)   Cp the cases cited in the notes to § 393, *post*

(g) See § 48, *ante*

(h) *Mayhew v Eames* (1825), 3 B & C 601 , *Willis v Bank of England* (1835), 4 A & E 21 (*per* Lord DENMAN, C J , delivering the judgment of the Court, at p 39   "the general rule of law is that notice to the principal is notice to all his agents , at any rate if there be reasonable time, as there was here, for the principal to communicate that knowledge to his agents before the event which raises the question happens ")

(i) *Le Neve v Le Neve* (1747), Ambl 436 (*per* Lord HARDWICKE, L C)

(j) *Toulmin v Steere* (1817), 3 Mer 210 (*per* GRANT, M R , at pp 222, 223   "were it otherwise a man would only have to purchase on behalf of infants to free an estate from all equitable incumbrances to which it might be subject ")

(k) *Lloyds Banking Co v Jones* (1885), 29 C D 221 (*per* PEARSON, J , at pp 227, 228) , *Walker v Lynom*, [1907] 2 Ch 104 (*per* PARKER, J , at pp 115–119)   On the other hand, notice to one of several trustees is not presumptive notice to the others   *Low v Bouverie*, [1891] 3 Ch 82, C A (*per* LINDLEY, L J , at p 104)

(l) See § 44, *ante*

(m) This is the class of presumptive knowledge discussed in the next Sub-section.

(n) In *Kennedy v. Green* (1834), 3 My & K 699, Lord BROUGHAM, L C., after expressing

53. It has been laid down that the agent's knowledge is only deemed that of the principal "if the agent comes to the knowledge of the fact while he is concerned for the principal, and in the course of the very transaction which becomes the subject of the suit" (*o*). This statement involves three propositions : (i) that the knowledge of the agent affects with constructive notice no other person than the particular principal for whom he is acting ; (ii) that it affects the principal with notice of no other matters than those of which the agent acquires knowledge when acting in his character as an agent of the particular kind alleged ; (iii) that it affects the principal with notice of no other matters than those of which the agent acquires knowledge when acting in the particular transaction alleged, or, as it is frequently expressed, *in hâc re*

54. It results from the first of the above propositions that, where a solicitor or other agent is acting for A., in a transaction between A. and B., and B. chooses not to employ any solicitor or agent, it cannot be presumed from that fact alone that the knowledge of the solicitor or agent is the knowledge of B., as well as of A., as regards any matters coming to the solicitor's or agent's notice in the course of his agency for the latter (*p*) ; and that, where there is a common officer of two companies, the knowledge acquired by him as officer of company A. will not be imputed to company B., unless it was his duty, as the officer of company A. to communicate it to company B, and also his duty, as officer of company B., to receive such a communication (*q*)   In former times there was a curious and subtle theory that, where a solicitor is acting for both parties to a transaction, the constructive notice which he acquires as solicitor for the one party is somehow imputable to the other party for whom he is also acting : that is to say, that the latter party, as principal, is fixed with constructive possession of the knowledge which the solicitor

his disagreement with LEACH, M R , as to the possibility of imputing the solicitor s knowledge to the client, on the assumption that the solicitor was intending to commit a fraud on his client—see note (*f*) to § 57, *post*—proceeds, at pp 720–724, to point out that, on the hypothesis of the solicitor's innocence, the client would still be affected with notice, because the former, in virtue of a number of "suspicious appearances " on the face of a certain deed, had been put upon inquiry which, if pursued, would have led to the discovery of further documents and facts, and that the latter was, in contemplation of law, put upon the same inquiry, and affected by the same presumptive knowledge as the former   A similar opinion on somewhat similar facts was expressed by Lord ST LEONARDS, when Sir EDW SUGDEN, L C (Ir), at p 22 of *Roddy* v *Williams* (1845), 3 Jo & Lat 1 , 72 R R. 1 See also *Hepworth* v *Pickles*, [1900] 1 Ch 108, where the constructive knowledge of the solicitor in virtue of his possession or control of documents of title—he admittedly had no actual knowledge—was imputed to the client (*per* FARWELL, J , at p 111), *Berwick & Co* v *Price*, [1905] 1 Ch 632 (*per* JOYCE, J , at p 639, who imputed to the client the constructive knowledge of his solicitor as to the existence of a sub mortgage)

(*o*) *Per* ERSKINE, L C , at p 120 of *Hiern* v *Mill* (1806), 13 Ves 114

(*p*) *Kennedy* v *Green* (1834), 3 My & K 699 (*per* LEACH, M R , at pp 712, 713, and Lord BROUGHAM, L C , at pp 720–724), *Espin* v *Pemberton* (1859), 3 De G & J 547 (*per* Lord CHELMSFORD, L C , at pp 554, 555), *Perry* v *Holl* (1860), 2 De G F & J 38

(*q*) *Re Hampshire Land Co* , [1896] 2 Ch 743 , *Re Fenwick, Stobart & Co , Ltd* , [1902] 1 Ch 507 , *Re David Payne & Co , Ltd* , [1904] 2 Ch 608, C A (*per* VAUGHAN WILLIAMS, L J , at pp 616, 617, ROMER, L J , at pp 618, 619, and COZENS HARDY, L J , at p. 620).

presumptively acquired as agent for the former party (r)   This doctrine is now exploded by an express provision of the Conveyancing Act, 1882 (s).

55. The second proposition is equally well established, viz. that, where the person through whom it is sought to impute knowledge to another, though proved to have been the agent for certain purposes of that other, is yet not proved to have been acting in his capacity as such agent, and for those purposes (t), at the precise time (u) when he received the notice or obtained the information, the principal is not affected with such notice.

56. Lastly, notwithstanding that the agent be proved to have been acting at the material date in his capacity as agent, and as an agent of the particular kind, and for the particular purposes, alleged, his knowledge is still not imputable to the principal, unless it was acquired in the course of the identical transaction or business which gives rise to the question of notice (v) ; and, further, the

(r) *Nixon* v *Hamilton* (1838), 2 Dr & Wall. 364 , 56 R R. 246 , *Roddy* v *Williams* (1845), 3 Jo. & Lat 1, *per* SUGDEN, L C (Ir), at p 16 , *Spencer v. Topham* (1856), 22 Beav. 573.

(s) See s. 3, sub s. (1), (ii). That the enactment in question, which is set out in § 66, *post*, has superseded the old rule, if indeed that rule was ever good law, is clear from *Re Cousins* (1886), 31 C D 671 (*per* CHITTY, J , at pp 676, 677), and *Taylor v London & County Banking Co* , [1901] 2 Ch 231, C. A. (*per* CHITTY, L J , at pp 258, 259).

(t) *Wilde* v. *Gibson* (1848), 1 H L C 605 (knowledge acquired by agent otherwise than as agent for sale not imputed to the principal, in a vendor and purchaser case *per* Lord COTTENHAM, L C , at pp 624, 625, and Lord CAMPBELL, at pp 634, 635) , *Saffron Walden Second Benefit Building Society v Rayner* (1880), 14 C D 406, C A., where it was held that notice to solicitors employed by trustees merely for the purpose of effecting a particular investment of the trust funds upon mortgage could not be imputed to the trustees (*per* JAMES, L J , at pp 409, 410, and BRAMWELL, L J , at pp 414–416), nor could personal notice given to them at the close of a meeting called upon other business (*per* JAMES, L.J , at pp 410–412, BAGGALLAY, L J , at p 414, and BRAMWELL, L.J , at pp 417, 418) , *Société Générale de Paris v Tramways Union Co* (1884), 14 Q B D 424, C A (*per* LINDLEY, L J , at p 450   " the secretary was in no way representing the company at the funeral   no notice was given to him as the agent of the company , nor did he acquire any knowledge of the defendant's security whilst transacting the company's business, or in any way for or on behalf of the company ") , *Lagunas Nitrate Co v Lagunas Syndicate*, [1899] 2 Ch 392, C A (*per* LINDLEY, M R , at p 431   " to impute to the Nitrate Company the knowledge which the directors had acquired in another capacity , and which knowledge they did not disclose to any one, is neither law nor sense ")

(u) *Mountford* v *Scott* (1818), 3 Madd 34 (*per* LEACH, V-C,   40   " the agent stands in place of the principal, and notice, therefore, to the agent is   to the principal , but he cannot stand in place of the principal until the relation of principal and agent is constituted ") , *Williamson v. Barber* (1877), 9 C D 529 (*per* JESSEL, M R , at p 535. " as I understand the doctrine of partnership, which for this purpose is a branch of the law of agency, notice to a partner in a partnership matter during the continuance of the partnership is as a general rule notice to the firm   It has not, so far as I know, been held that notice to a man who afterwards becomes a partner is notice to the firm ") See, now, s 16 of the Partnership Act, 1890

(v) *Hiern v Mill* (1806), 13 Ves 114 (*per* Lord ERSKINE, L C , at p 120) , *Kennedy v. Green* (1834), 3 My & K 699 (*per* Lord BROUGHAM, L C , at p 720) , *Nixon v Hamilton* (1838), 2 Drew & Wall 364 (*per* Lord PLUNKET, L C (Ir), at p 392) , *Thompson v Cartwright* (1863), 33 Beav 178 (*per* ROMILLY, M R , at p 185) , *Wyllie v Pollen* (1863), 3 De G J & S 596, 601 , *Williamson v Barber*, *sup* (*per* JESSEL, M R , at p. 535), *Bradley v Riches* (1878), 9 C D 189 (*per* FRY, J , at p 195) , *Saffron Walden Second Benefit Building Society v Rayner* (1880), 14 C D 406, C A (as to which see note (t), *sup*), *Blackburn, Low & Co v Vigors* (1887), 12 App Cas 531, H. L (*per* Lord HALSBURY, L C , at p 535 " neither the plaintiff, nor the agent through whom the policy was effected, had any knowledge of the material fact, the concealment or non disclosure of which is relied upon as vitiating the policy , but an agent, who did not effect the policy, at an earlier period received information admitted to be material, while he was acting as agent to effect an insurance "—*i e* another insurance, and a different transaction—" for the plaintiff," knowledge possessed is, even then, only a knowledge of such matters as are material, and which, therefore, it was the duty of the agent to communicate to his principal (w). Again, there is no sufficient ground for presuming knowledge, if the alleged agent who had notice in the course of the transaction, turns out to have been introduced into the business merely for the purposes of some isolated step or ceremony or act, and not to have been employed throughout the transaction and for all its purposes (x) Conversely however, if the alleged agent is shown to have been employed for the general purposes of the transaction in question, the knowledge coming to him in the execution of such agency will not the less be imputed to his principal, merely because the latter, whether with a fraudulent object or not, chose to employ a stranger to the business to perform some single act or formality in connection with it (y). It has been occasionally suggested by such high authorities as Lord ELDON, L C, and JESSEL, M R, that the principal is presumed to have notice of facts of which the agent was apprised when acting *in alia re*, if the *alia res* was so closely bound up with the *haec res* as to suggest that the agent must have had the facts present to his mind when acting *in hâc re*, or, in other words, had presumptive, though not actual, notice of them, when so acting, and that his presumptive notice may thereupon be imputed to the principal (z) But the doctrine seems a loose and dangerous one, since the

and, again, at p 538 "where the employment of the agent is such that in respect of the particular matter in question, he really does represen[t] [p]rincipal, the formula that the knowledge of the agent is his knowledge, is, I think [ ]); *Taylor* v. *Yorkshire Insurance Co*, [1913] 2 Ir R 1 (*per* PALLES, C B, a. p[ ] 4, a case of insurance of a horse, where the agent of the company acquired the [ ] [kn]wledge previously to the commencement of his agency, when acting for another compa[ ]) See also the Conveyancing Act, 1881 s 3, sub ss (1), (i) and (ii), and § 66, *post*, and, is to partnership, s 16 of the Partnership Act, 1890

(w) *Wyllie* v. *Pollen*, *sup* (*per* Lord WESTBURY, L C, at p 601)

(x) *Huckman* v *Fernie* (1838), 3 M & W. 505 (a life insurance case, in which it was pointed out by Lord ABINGER, C B, delivering the judgment of the Court of Exchequer, at pp 517, 518, that the defendants had not even pleaded, much less proved, that the deceased was the agent of the plaintiff for the purposes of the entire transaction, but only that he was the agent of the plaintiff for the purpose of answering certain specific questions, none of which bore upon the matters alleged to have been concealed, and, therefore, the knowledge of the deceased was not the knowledge of the plaintiff), *Kettlewell* v *Watson* (1882), 21 C D 685, in which a purchaser's solicitor, as a matter of convenience, prepared a conveyance from such purchaser to a sub-purchaser, but was not otherwise the agent of the sub purchaser, and FRY, J, at pp 707, 708, contrasting the case of *Brotherton* v. *Hatt*—*vid* note (z) to § 49, *ante*—held that the knowledge of certain facts which the solicitor had acquired when acting for the original purchaser could not be imputed to the sub-purchaser

(y) *Rolland* v. *Hart* (1871), 6 Ch App 678 (*per* Lord HATHERLEY, L C, at p 683)

(z) *Mountford* v *Scott* (1823), T & Russ 274, where Lord ELDON, L C, at pp 279, 280, criticized, as too broad, the view of LEACH, V-C, in the Court below—at p 40 of (1818), 3 Madd 34, as to which see note (u), *sup*—that there *never* could be an imputation of knowledge to the principal, unless the transaction in question was the very transaction in which the agent acquired the knowledge, for a solicitor could not be allowed to say that he had forgotten in the evening what he knew in the morning, *Nixon* v *Hamilton* (1838), 2 Dr & Wall 364, where Lord PLUNKET, L C (Ir), at pp 392–394, pointed out that, in the case last cited, Lord ELDON, L C, had no intention of frittering away the *in hâc re* rule, but merely wished to correct the too absolute form in which LEACH, V C, had expressed it, and to admit, as a possible exception, the case of a transaction so closely, in point of time and subject matter, connected with the transaction in question, as to lead to the inference that, though not literally identical, it was substantially one with it), *Boursot* v.

so-called presumptive notice of the agent is not really based upon any warrantable presumption of law, but on an assumption of fact, which ought not to be made without evidence ; and, when evidence is imported, all questions of presumption disappear It is quite clear, however, that the theory except in a rigidly qualified sense, has now been put an end to by express statutory enactment (a).

57. The presumption in question, as it requires no evidence of actual knowledge to support it, so also does not admit of any evidence of absence of actual knowledge to negative it. To this extent, and in this sense, it is irrebuttable (b) Indeed, it would be of very little practical value, were this not so. The imputation which the law makes "assumes a [knowledge], if you had it not "; consequently it is no answer to say "I had it not," when the assumption starts with this very hypothesis. But, though the mere allegation or proof of actual ignorance is wholly inefficacious, the presumption may still be rebutted by allegation and proof of such ignorance in fact, and also of matters calculated to destroy any of the foundations on which the presumption rests : *cessante ratione cessat lex*. Now, as has been indicated, one of these foundations is the strong probability that the agent will, pursuant to his duty, and in the ordinary course of business, impart his knowledge to his principal (c) : and another is the justice and fairness, as between the parties, that he who resorts to an agent and selects him, and benefits by his knowledge, should suffer the burdensome, as well as enjoy the beneficial, consequences of so doing (d). Where, therefore, neither of these conditions is present, as, for instance, where it can be established by evidence not only that the principal was in fact ignorant of the matters of which knowledge is sought to be imputed to him, but also that at the material date his agent was perpetrating a fraud upon him, the presumption is not made, because, on the one hand, it is displaced by the much onger presumption that, in the particular circumstances of the case, there is no probability that the agent will communicate the matter to his principal, but on the contrary a probability, amounting to a moral certainty, that he will not and,

Savage (1866), L R 2 Eq 134 (*per* KINDERSLEY, V C , at p 142) , *Williamson* v *Barber* (1877), 9 C D 529 (*per* JESSEL, M R , at p 535 ' notice to a solicitor in the same transaction, or *in any connected transaction*, while he is acting for the same client, is also notice to the client, but notice to him, *even prior to his acting for the client*, may be constructive notice to the client, *when it is clear he must have had it present to his mind, that is, he could not be supposed to have forgotten it when he was transacting the business of the client* ")

(a) See s 3, sub s (1), (11), of the Conveyancing Act, 1882 (45 & 46 Vict c 49), as set out in § 66, *post*, and *Re Cousins* (1886), 31 C D 671 (*per* CHITTY, J , at p 674) The rule, as laid wn by Lord ELDON, L C , and Lord PLUNKET, L C (Ir), in the first two of the cases cited in the last note, may possibly be unaffected by the above enactment, for a transaction of the kind there mentioned might perhaps be deemed part and parcel of the *haec res*, and not an *alia res* at all, but the ruling of KINDERSLEY, V C , and the italicized observations of JESSEL, M R , in the other two cases cited in the same note, certainly cannot be now regarded as law

(b) *Bradley* v *Riches* (1878), 9 C D 189 (*per* FRY, J., at p 196 " it appears to me to be clear that that presumption or imputation is a thing which the client cannot be allowed to rebut If it could be rebutted, it was amply rebutted in *Le Neve* v. *Le Neve* If it could be rebutted, the language of Lord HATHERLEY in *Rolland* v *Hart* could not be up held ") , *Berwick & Co* v. *Price*, [1905] 1 Ch 632 (*per* JOYCE, J , at p 639)

(c) See § 48, *ante*

(d) See § 46, *ante*

on the other hand, it must yield to the further legal presumption that, in selecting and employing his agent, the principal did not select or employ him to commit a fraud upon himself (e). This exception to the general rule, or rather to the irrebuttability of the general rule, as to the presumptive knowledge of a principal, has been laid down and recognized in a series of authorities from 1834 downwards (f). Similarly, the ordinary presumption may be rebutted by proof of the expressed intention of the agent not to communicate the facts in question to his principal, with the complicity and collusion of the party invoking the aid of the general rule (g). Whether the

(e) *Espin* v. *Pemberton* (1859), 3 De G. & J 547, where Lord CHELMSFORD, L.C., mentions the two grounds on which the exception may be justified, viz. (i) that the agent "was committing a fraud in the transaction which he could not be presumed to communicate," and (ii) "that the commission of the fraud broke off the relation of principal and agent, or was beyond the scope of his authority," at the same time expressing his preference for the latter theory. So, at pp 642, 643 of *Cave* v. *Cave* (1880), 15 C. D. 639, FRY, J, observes: "there is undoubtedly an exception to the construction or imputation of notice from the agent to the principal, that exception arising in the case of such conduct by the agent as raises a conclusive presumption that he would not communicate the fact in controversy This exception has been put in two ways. . In the one view, notice is not imputed because the circumstances are such as not to raise the conclusion of law which does ordinarily arise from the mere existence of notice to the agent, in the other view—that of Lord CHELMSFORD and Lord HATHERLEY—the act done by the agent is such as cannot be said to be done by him in his character of agent, but is done by him in the character of a party to an independent fraud on the principal, and that is not to be imputed to the principal as an act done by his agent."
(f) *Kennedy* v. *Green* (1834), 3 My. & K. 699 (per Lord BROUGHAM, L C, at p 720,—the leading decision on the exception in question), *Hewitt* v *Loosemoore* (1851), 9 Hare 449 (per TURNER, V -C, who, at pp 455, 456, refers to "the well founded and wholesome limitation upon the doctrine of constructive notice established by *Kennedy* v *Green*"), *Thompson* v *Cartwright* (1863), 33 Beav. 178 (per ROMILLY, M R., at p 185 "in this state of things, is it to be presumed that Mr Montriou *must* have concealed the fact of that mortgage from his client Mr Downes ? The case of *Kennedy* v *Green*, which is always cited on these occasions, establishes a very important principle, but one which must be very cautiously applied to the case of notice of facts given to the solicitor employed by the client . . I take the rule to be, generally, that the client must be treated as having had notice of all the facts which in the same transaction have come to the knowledge of the solicitor, and that the burden of proof lies on him (the client) to show that there is a probability, amounting almost to a moral certainty, that the solicitor would not have communicated those facts to his client "), *Rolland* v *Hart* (1871), 6 Ch App 678 (per Lord HATHERLEY, L C, at p 683), *Waldy* v *Gray* (1875), L R 20 Eq 238 (per BACON, V C, at pp. 251, 252, at p 251 he says that '*Kennedy* v *Green* lays down a principle which must commend itself to everybody's sense of justice "), *Cave* v *Cave*, sup (see the passage cited in the last note), *Kettlewell* v. *Watson* (1882), 21 C D 685 (per FRY, J, who, at p 707, recognizing the exception established by *Kennedy* v *Green*, points out at the same time its limitations), *Re Fitzroy Bessemer Steel Co* (1884), 50 L T 144, *Berwick & Co* v. *Price*, [1905] 1 Ch 632 (per JOYCE, J, at pp 640, 641)
(g) *Sharp* v. *Foy* (1868), 4 Ch App 35, where a solicitor acted for the mortgagors (husband and wife) and also for the mortgagee in respect of a mortgage The mortgagors informed the mortgagee that there was a marriage settlement, and the solicitor thereupon, with the silent acquiescence and concurrence of the mortgagors, announced to them that he should not reveal the existence of the marriage settlement to the mortgagee, "because it might make him nervous about his security " Held that no knowledge of the settlement could be imputed to the mortgagee, per PAGE WOOD, L J, at p 40 ("it would be an encouragement of fraud to apply the rule of notice, which was established for the safety of mankind, to a transaction like this , it would be sanctioning a scheme to rob a man by colluding with his solicitor "), and SELWYN, L J, at pp 41, 42 Cp *Biggar* v *Rock Life Assurance Co*, [1902] 1 K B 516, where WRIGHT, J, held that no knowledge could be imputed to the insurance company by reason of the personal knowledge of their agent who, in collusion with the assured, had fraudulently "invented " untrue answers to the questions in the proposal form

circumstances exist which are necessary to rebut the presumption is a question of fact, and the burden of proving them lies on the party who seeks to escape from the operation of the rule, and bring his case within the exception (h). Mere proof of the agent's having had an interest in not making the communication which he was under a duty to make is not sufficient of itself to negative the presumption where no actual fraud by the agent is proved, or at least is not conclusively or necessarily so (i). The agent's fraud must be shown to have been directed against the principal   it is of no avail to establish mere general dishonesty on his part whereby other persons are defrauded (j). Further, to bring the case within the exception, it must be shown that the agent's fraud was committed at the time of, and in relation to, the very transaction which raises the question of notice (k).

Sub-s (5)   Knowledge of Facts or Documents presumed from Actual Knowledge of other Facts or Documents

98. Besides imputing to one person the knowledge of facts actually possessed by another under the conditions already discussed, the law presumes from proved actual notice of any fact or document knowledge of connected facts or documents in all cases where the former, would have inevitably led to the latter, knowledge if such further steps had been taken by the party to whom the knowledge is imputed as, under the circumstances of the case, ought

(h) See *Thompson v Cartwright* (1863), 33 Beav 178, *per* ROMILLY, M R , who at p 185, after stating the rule as to burden of proof—see the end of the citation from his judgment in note (f), *sup*—proceeds as follows   "the question here is, whether the applicant, Mr Downes, discharges the burden so imposed on him   Upon the whole, I think that he does " So, in *Care v Care* (1880), 15 C D 369, FRY, J , after stating the rule and theory of the exception—see the passage cited in note (e), *sup.*—continues, at p 644   "these being the principles applicable, . .   I must ask myself what are the circumstances," and, at p 645, after reviewing these circumstances, finds that the burden of establishing that they brought the case outside the rule, and within the exception, had been abundantly discharged   Similarly most of the other cases cited in note (f), *sup*, were brought within the exception   On the other hand, the burden was not sustained, and the rule accordingly prevailed, in *Spaight v Cowne*, (1863), 1 H & M 359 (*per* WOOD, V -C , at pp 365, 366), and in *Rolland v Hart* (1871), 6 Ch App 678 (*per* Lord HATHERLEY, L C , at p 683, for the agent in that case, a solicitor, "does not," he said, " appear to have been concerned in any fraud which would render concealment necessary, so as to bring the case within *Kennedy v Green* ")

(i) So FRY, J , held at p 196 of *Bradley v Riches* (1878), 9 C D 189 ("I will not lay down as a rule that where a solicitor owes a duty on the one side, and has an interest on the other side, the presumption arises that he follows his interest, and not his duty   I shall on the contrary presume that *in this case* he performed his duty, though it was against his interest "), and was followed by JOYCE, J , at pp 640, 641 of *Berwick & Co v Price*, [1905] 1 Ch 632

(j) *Boursot v Savage* (1866), L R 2 Eq 134, *per* KINDERSLEY, V-C , at p 142   On this ground the general rule prevailed, and not the exception, in *Attorbury v Wallis* (1856), 8 De G M & G 454 (*per* KNIGHT BRUCE and TURNER, LL JJ), and in *Spencer v Topham* (1856), 22 Beav 573 (*per* ROMILLY, M R , at p 575)

(k) *Rolland v Hart, sup , per* Lord HATHERLEY, L C , at p 683   "I was anxious to ascertain whether there was any evidence that Robinson was *at the time* in a position in which he could be fixed with any such fraud   But I cannot find evidence of anything of the kind *at that time*   The circumstance that, six months after he had improperly borrowed money for Hall, he fell into difficulties and fled the country, cannot affect the state of things *at the time of these transactions* ")

reasonably to have been taken by him (*l*). No catalogue of cases falling within, or without, the rule can be drawn up *a priori*, for what will affect with constructive notice one man, situated in one way, and under one set of circumstances, will not so affect another man, under a different set of circumstances, and differently situated (*ll*) ; but the above may be taken to be an accurate, though a very broad and general, description of the species of presumptive knowledge now to be considered. It has sometimes been said that the abstention from inquiry must amount to a "fraudulent blindness," or a "wilful shutting of the eyes to the truth," or to "diligence in ignorance," or again that it must be accompanied by such gross negligence as ought to be considered tantamount to fraud, or evidence of fraud ; and the above have often been contradistinguished from one another, as two separate species of presumptive notice. But neither a fraudulent motive, nor a remissness or want of care, is in the least necessary as a condition precedent to the presumption, as will be abundantly shown hereafter (*m*) ; nor, therefore, can there be two such species as above suggested. The law is absolutely unconcerned with the reasons or motives (if any) which actuated the party not to acquire the knowledge which he might have acquired : it is enough that it *assumes* the fact that it was not acquired actually, and then *presumes*, on grounds of general convenience, that it existed nevertheless. To impose on the Courts the troublesome and delicate duty o sifting the motives, and searching the conscience, of the party, before the presumption can be made, would destroy its utility altogether, and defeat the very object with which the rule has been established , for the inquiry embarked upon would involve an issue of fact quite as difficult to determine as, and in most cases a great deal more so than, the issue of fact which would be involved if there were no presumption at all, viz whether or not the party had actual knowledge. The rule, as above stated, independently of, and unhampered by, any such condition or qualifications as above mentioned, has been applied in the form of a variety of subordinate rules, adapted to the nature of the respective subject-matters, which it is now proposed to examine

59. From the proved actual knowledge of the existence of a document, or of a part of its contents, the law in general presumes notice of the contents, or of the residue of the contents, as the case may be, of that document (*n*)

(*l*) ' Where a person has actual notice of any matter of fact, there can be no danger of doing injustice if he is held to be bound by all the consequences of that which he knows to exist " *per* Lord CRANWORTH, L C , at p 473 of *Ware* v *Lord Egmont* (1854), 4 De G. M & G 460

(*ll*) *Jones* v *Smith* (1841), 1 Hare 43 (*per* WIGRAM, V C , at p. 55)

(*m*) See App A, Sect 2, Sub ss (2) and (3), *post*

(*n*) *Hill* v *Sampson* (1801), 7 Ves 152 (bankers, to whom part of estate of deceased was transferred by his executors to secure a loan, having actual notice from one of the executors of the existence of a will, held to have constructive notice of the contents of such will, and of the rights of legatees thereunder) , *Eyre* v *Dolphin* (1813), 2 Ball & B 290 , 12 R R 94 (mortgagee, having express notice of a settlement by the mortgagor, held to have presumptive notice of its contents and provisions) , *Taylor* v *Baker* (1818), 5 Price 306 , *Penny* v *Watts* (1849), 1 Macn & G 150 (*per* Lord COTTENHAM, L C., at pp 166, 167) , *Smith* v *Capron* (1849), 7 Hare 185 (*per* WIGRAM, V C , at pp 192, 193 "in this case Mr Capron saw the indorsement on the lease, and by that indorsement it appeared that the licence to assign was necessary It is also admitted that he looked into the body of

If the document is in a foreign language, the law presumes that the party is acquainted with its English meaning, or has provided himself with a translation (o). But possession of a security lodged with a bank, such as a debenture, by one customer, is not constructive notice on the part of the bank, as against another customer, of the terms and contents of such security (p). Where a man is entering upon a transaction which necessarily involves the existence of an instrument at the back of it, and therefore his knowledge of that existence, as, for instance, where he proposes to purchase or accept from another a sublease of property, which of course presupposes the existence of an original or head lease, or where, in contracts of marine insurance, the subject of the insurance is chartered freight, or profit on charter, or the policy is one of reinsurance subject to the terms of the original policy, or where the party is engaging in a transaction in relation to a company which, to his knowledge, has issued debentures, the person in question is presumed to have knowledge of all the usual, ordinary, and typical terms, conditions, and clauses of such superior lease (q), charter (r), original policy (s), or debentures (t) respectively: but not of any unusual or extraordinary restriction, condition, clause, or stipulation therein (u), unless and until, having been

the lease, and therefore he had actual notice of . . . such parts of the contents as he thought it useful or material to read. The presumption therefore would be that he had made himself acquainted with the whole of the instrument. I do not think that I ought to allow the presumption to be rebutted by the averment of the defendant that he looked into the other parts of the lease, and did not observe the covenants upon which his objection is founded "); *New Brunswick & Canada Railway & Land Co* v. *Conybeare* (1862), 9 H. L 711 (*per* Lord WESTBURY, L.C., at p. 734,—presumed notice of contents of a company's deed of association). *Farrant* v *Blanchford* (1863), 32 L. J. (CH.) 237 (*per* Lord WESTBURY, L.C., at p 239 actual receipt, and immediate deposit with bankers, of a bundle of deeds, without opening the bundle : held that the party had presumptive knowledge of the content of all the deeds).

(o) *Ionides* v *Pender* (1874), L R 9 Q B 531 (*per Cur*, at p 537).

(p) *Re Castell & Brown, Ltd.,* [1898] 1 Ch 315, *Re Valletort Sanitary Steam Laundry Co.,* [1903] 2 Ch 654 (*per* SWINFEN EADY, J, at pp 659-662).

(q) This was either stated (as in *Cosser* v *Collinge, inf*, by LEACH, M R., at p 287 · " prima facie a man who agrees to take an underlease must know that he is bound by the covenants contained in the original lease "), or assumed, in all the cases relating to sub leases which are cited in note (*u*), *inf*

(r) *The Bedouin,* [1894] P 1, C A (where it was proved by evidence that the " 24 hours' clause " in a time charter was in common use *per* GORELL BARNES, J, at p 7, and Lord ESHER, M R , at pp 12, 13), *Asfar & Co* v *Blundell,* [1896] 1 Q B 123, C A, where also the clause in question was considered usual one in a charter party *per* KAY, L J , at pp. 133, 134)

(s) *Charlesworth* v *Faber* (1900), 5 Comm Cas 408 (where one of " the Elder Dempster & Co 's clauses " was proved by evidence to be a usual term in a policy of insurance *per* BIGHAM, J , at pp 411, 412).

(t) This was assumed in the cases relating to debenture transactions cited in the next note.

(u) In the following cases relating to subleases, the restrictive and onerous conditions in the head lease were held unusual, and such, therefore, as to raise no presumption of knowledge against the party complaining *Cosser* v *Collinge* (1832), 3 My & K 283, *Wilbraham* v *Livesey,* (1854), 18 Beav 206 (*per* ROMILLY, M R , at pp. 209, 210), *Hyde* v *Warden* (1877), 3 Ex D 72, C A (*per Cur*, at pp 80, 81), *Reeve* v. *Berridge* (1888), 20 Q. B D 523, C A (*per Cur* at pp 527, 528), *Re White and Smith's Contract,* [1896] 1 Ch 637 (*per* STIRLING, J , at p 643), *Re Haedicke and Lipski's Contract,* [1901] 2 Ch 666 (*per* BYRNE, J , at p 668), *Molyneux* v *Hawtrey,* [1903] 2 K B 487, C A (*per* COLLINS, M.R , at pp 491-494, and COZENS HARDY, L J , at p 497) In the following cases, clauses and conditions in debentures were considered unusual, and the Court refused to impute knowledge of them to the party complaining *English & Scottish Mercantile Investment Co* v.

given " a fair opportunity " of inspecting the instrument, he has neglected to avail himself of it, in which event the presumption, which down to the date of such neglected opportunity has not operated, immediately arises (v). Notice of the existence of a document, which expressly refers to, and incorporates provisions in, a second document, which again has the like reference to, and incorporation of, a third, is presumptive notice of the existence and contents of both the two latter instruments (w). So also, notice of a memorial of a deed, is constructive notice of the contents of such deeds (x). But a mere reference in a bill of lading to a charterparty does not affect the holder with presumptive notice of all the terms of such charterparty (y). Possession by a solicitor of the title-deeds generally relating to a property is presumptive notice of the existence and contents of a deed to which a predecessor in title was a party containing covenants restrictive of the user of the property (z). Notice of one of several incumbrances on a property is not necessarily notice of others, at all events where there has been a definite misrepresentation (a) ; though, ordinarily, from notice of specified incumbrances the party is not entitled to infer that they are the sole incumbrances (b) An intending purchaser or mortgagee of, or other person contemplating a transaction with reference to, land or any estate or interest therein, who is entitled to delivery, or to production, as the case may be, of title deeds, is bound to insist on such delivery, or production, and in case of non-delivery, or non-production, to demand an explanation ; and if he neglects either to insist on the delivery, or production, as the case may be, in the first instance, or to prosecute further inquiries, if the documents are withheld, he does so at the peril of notice of their contents being imputed to him, either in a question of non-disclosure, or (where the point, as regards land, is most frequently raised)

Brunton, [1892] 2 Q B 700 C. A , *Re Valletort Sanitary Steam Laundry Co* , [1903] 2 Ch. 654 (per SWINFEN EADY, J , at pp 659, 660) For an example of an unusual term in an original policy, subject to which a marine re insurance contract was made, see *Property Insurance Co* v *National Protector Insurance Co* (1913), 108 L T 104 , and for the like in a charter party, where the insurance was on chartered freight, see *Mercantile S & Co.* v. *Tyser* (1881), 7 Q B D 73 (at p 77)

(v) See the cases as to subleases cited in the preceding note In none of them was "the fair opportunity of inspection " established, except in *Cosser* v *Collinge, sup* As to whether actual knowledge of similarly onerous restrictions in leases of adjoining properties in the same estate would be a ground for imputing knowledge of the restrictions complained of in the lease the subject of the action, see § 64, note (w), *post*

(w) *Davies* v *Thomas* (1830), 2 Y & C (Eq Exch) 234, per ALDERSON, B . at p 244, in the case of one who had actual notice of a marriage settlement which recited a conveyance, which again referred to a will), *Re Childe and Hodgson's Contract* (1906), 54 W R 234, where a contract for sale provided that the sale was to be subject to the conditions contained in deed A , which in its turn provided that it was to be subject to conditions contained in deed B , and WARRINGTON, J , held that the party had presumptive knowledge of the contents of both deeds

(x) *Rochard* v *Fulton* (1844), 1 Jo. & Lat 413 , 68 R R 265, per SUGDEN, L C (Ir), at pp 441–444

(y) *Manchester Trust* v *Furness*, [1895] 2 Q B 539, C A (per LINDLEY, L.J , at pp 544–546, LOPES, L J., at p 547, and RIGBY, L J , at p 549)

(z) *Hepworth* v *Pickles*, [1900] 1 Ch. 108 (per FARWELL, J , at p 111)

(a) *Jones* v *Smith* (1841), 1 Hare 43 (per WIGRAM, V -C , at pp 68–70)

(b) *Ibid.*, per WIGRAM V C , at pp 66, 67 see also *Jones* v *Williams* (1857), 24 Beav 47 (per ROMILLY, M.R , at pp 57, 58) in a question of priorities (o). Where he has no right to such production or delivery, he is under no such obligation to inquire : thus, the purchaser of a sublease, though affected with notice of the existence and contents of the superior lease on the principle of another rule (already stated), is under no duty to inquire " what has become of the original lease," or in whose custody or possession it is, and " there is no imputation on him for not so inquiring," since " such an inquiry is not usual in transactions of this nature " (cc). And, in any case, the party is only affected with presumptive notice of such instruments or facts as reasonable and proper inquiries under the circumstances would have revealed, not of instruments or facts which such inquiries would not have elicited, or, as it has been otherwise expressed, the knowledge imputed to him is the knowledge which a sensible man—neither over-suspicious nor foolishly sanguine—ought to have acquired, starting from the instrument or fact of which he has express notice and pursuing a rational course of investigation on that basis, but not the knowledge which he might, or might not, have so acquired (d). " When it is said that a person is put on inquiry,

(c) *Birch* v. *Ellames* (1794), 2 Anstr. 427 , *Hiern* v. *Mill* (1806), 13 Ves. 114 (*per* Lord ERSKINE, L C., at p 122 actual knowledge by purchaser that title-deeds are in possession of equitable mortgagee is constructive notice of the incumbrance); *Dryden* v. *Frost* (1838), 3 My & Cr. 670, 673 (the like, as to a third person's interest), *Jones* v. *Smith* (1841), 1 Hare 43 (*per* WIGRAM, V. C), and (1843), 1 Ph 244 (*per* Lord LYNDHURST, L C, who held that a purchaser having notice of the existence of a deed, instrument, or fact affecting his property, is fixed with constructive notice of the contents of such deed, or *the nature and details of such incumbrances or facts as reasonable inquiry would have revealed*), *Worthington* v *Morgan* (1849), 6 Sim. 547, 551 (unpaid vendor's lien) , *Jones* v *Williams* (1857), 24 Beav. 47, 57, 58 , *Peto* v. *Hammond* (1861), 30 Beav 495 (*per* ROMILLY, M R , at p 510 " if the purchaser had inquired for the deed, he would have found that it was not in the vendor's possession, and, if he had inquired why it was not, he would have ascertained that it was not in his possession because the purchase money had not been paid "), *Wilson* v *Hart* (1866), 1 Ch. App 463 (where TURNER, L J , held that the rule applies to the purchase of a yearly tenancy as much as to that of a larger interest) , *Maxfield* v *Burton* (1873), L R. 17 Eq 15 (*per* JESSEL, M.R , at pp. 18, 19 a case of a marriage settlement) , *Northern Counties of England Fire Insurance Co* v *Whipp* (1884), 26 C D. 482, C. A (*per* FRY, L J , delivering the judgment of the Court, at pp. 491, 492, as to absence of inquiry for title-deeds, and leaving such deeds in the hands of a mortgagor to raise money), *Gainsborough (Earl of)* v *Watcombe Terra Cotta Clay Co* (1885), 54 L J (CH) 991 (*per* NORTH, J , at pp 994, 995) , *Berwick & Co* v *Price*, [1905] 1 Ch 632 (*per* JOYCE, J , at p 639) , *Walker* v *Lynom*, [1907] 2 Ch 104 (*per* PARKER, J , at pp 110-114), *Re Greer*, [1907] 1 Ir R 57 , *Re Heniger's Policy*, [1910] 2 Ch 291 (*per* PARKER, J , at pp 295, 296) The rule is codified in s 3, (1), (i) of the Conveyancing Act, 1882 (45 & 46 Vict c 39), which is set out in § 66, *post*

(cc) *Per* LEACH, V -C , at p 40 of *Mountford* v *Scott* (1818), 3 Madd 34

(d) *Jones* v *Smith*, *sup* (*per* WIGRAM, V -C , at pp 60 61 a purchaser from an heir at law, with actual notice of a will by the ancestor under whom the heir claims, is not necessarily affected with notice of the contents of the will it depends on the circumstances , and, in any case—at p 61, the V -C adds—' it would by no means follow that the same reasoning would apply to a marriage settlement A will imports the disposition by the testator of his property I am not aware of any legal or equitable presumption that a man makes a settlement of his landed estate upon his marriage "), *West* v. *Reid* (1843), 2 Hare 249, where, at p 259, WIGRAM, V -C , speaks of a " disregard of some facts known to a purchaser, which at least indicated the existence of these facts notice of which the Court imputes to the purchaser," as an essential element in the doctrine, and adds at pp 260, 261 " a purchaser may be presumed to investigate the title of the property he purchases, and may therefore be presumed to have examined every instrument forming a link, directly or by inference, in that title, and that presumption I take to be the foundation of the whole doctrine *But it is impossible to presume that a purchaser examines instruments not directly nor presumptively connected with the title, only because they may*

the result in point of law is that he is deemed to know the facts which he would have ascertained if he had made inquiry. He cannot better his position by abstaining from so doing. On the other hand, his position cannot be worse than it would have been had he made inquiry and been in possession of the result of it " (e)

60. If the deeds or instruments in respect of which it is suggested that the party ought to have made inquiry, or further or more diligent inquiry, are of such a character that they *may, or may not*, relate to the property which is the subject of the transaction, no imputation of knowledge is made against him, whether any statement has or has not been made to him by the opposite party as to the contents of such deeds ; *a fortiori* is the party free of any such imputation where a positive misrepresentation has been made to him, whether in words, or by acts and conduct (such as the delivery of part only of title-deeds, as and for the whole), with the object and result of misleading him : but, if the instrument is one that *must* relate to the property, the imputation is made, even though he has been deceived by a direct falsehood as to its provisions and terms (f) On the other hand, where the instrument in question forms no part of the title which is the subject of the transaction, no presumption can possibly be made against a party abstaining from investigation, since the instrument obviously *cannot* relate to the property (g).

by possibility affect it "), *Sadler* v *Lee* (1843), 6 Beav 324 (per Lord LANGDALE, M R., at pp 350, 351—"might, and *must*, have discovered," &c), *Barnhart* v. *Greenshields* (1853), 9 Moore P C 18, 32, 33 , *Ware* v. *Lord Egmont* (1854), 4 De G M & G 460 (per Lord CRANWORTH, L C , at p. 473 . " he ought not to be treated as if he had notice, unless the circumstances are such as to enable the Court to say, not only that he might have acquired, but also that he ought to have acquired, the notice with which it is sought to affect him "), *Gainsborough* (*Earl of*) v. *Watcombe Terra Cotta Clay Co* (1885), 54 L J (c r.) 991 (per NORTH, J , at pp 994, 995 a purchaser or mortgagee who takes without investigation of title is not affected with notice of such matters as he could not have ascertained without going behind the documents of title, but only of such facts as the usual investigation of title would disclose), *Lloyds Banking Co* v *Jones* (1885), 29 C D 221 (per PEARSON, J , at p 230 . notice of mere fact of marriage of mortgagor is not notice of the existence or contents of a marriage settlement , cp *Jones* v *Smith, sup*) , *Bailey* v. *Barnes*, [1894] 1 Ch 25, C A (per Cur at pp 34, 35) , *Hunt* v. *Luck*, [1902] 1 Ch 428, C A (per VAUGHAN WILLIAMS, L J , who, at p 434, points out that the inquiries which it was contended that the mortgagee ought to have made of the tenants would have revealed nothing as to the equitable title notice of which was sought to be imputed to him). The opinion to the contrary of the above rulings expressed by ROMILLY, M R , at p 62 of *Jones* v *Williams*, (1857), 24 Beav 47, is clearly erroneous

(e) Per Lord HERSCHELL, at p 220 of *London Joint Stock Bank* v. *Simmons*, [1892] A C 201, H. L , an estoppel case

(f) *Jones* v *Smith* (1841), 1 Hare 43, per WIGRAM, V -C , at pp 68–70, and per Lord LYNDHURST, L C , on appeal (1843), 1 Ph 244, at pp 253, 254 , *Hunt* v *Elmes* (1860), 2 De G F & J 578 , *Wilson* v *Hart* (1866), 1 Ch App. 463 (per TURNER, L J , at p 468) , *Ratcliffe* v *Barnard* (1871), 6 Ch App 652 (per JAMES, L J , at p 654) , *Patman* v *Harland* (1881), 17 C D 353 (per JESSEL, M R , at pp 356–358) , *Northern Counties, &c , Co* v *Whipp* (1884), 26 C D 482, C. A (per Cur at p 492) , *English & Scottish Mercantile Investment Co.* v *Brunton*, [1892] 2 Q. B 700, C A (per Lord ESHER, M R , at p 711, and BOWEN, L J , at p 717, who there point out that there is no presumptive notice, whether a misstatement is made to the party or not, of the contents of an indorsement which may or may not relate to the property) , *Re Valletort Sanitary Steam Laundry Co* , [1903] 2 Ch 654 (per SWINFEN EADY, J , at pp 659, 660)

(g) *Wilkes* v *Spooner*, [1911] 2 K. B. 473, C A (where the party was held not to have constructive notice of an instrument which formed no part of the title of the surrenderor

61. In such transactions and circumstances as are above referred to, the party to whom notice would otherwise be imputed, is free from such imputation, if, having duly made his demand for the delivery or production, as the case may be, of the deed or other instrument, he is met with a reasonable excuse for non-delivery or non-production, and he honestly believes that the excuse is based on facts truly stated (h) ; but not of course if the statement made by way of excuse is obviously frivolous or fraudulent, or if, without being so, the party does not in fact believe in its truth or *bona fides*, or if it takes such a form as to suggest and invite further inquiry, capable of being at once and easily set on foot, in which case the party may still be affected with notice, if he fails to prosecute such further inquiry, and if the inquiry would have revealed the falsity of the representation as to the nature of the instrument (hh), or as to the purpose for which it was lodged or deposited with a third person (i). And when a party is put on inquiry, the question of whether the answer he receives from the person of whom he inquires is one with which he might reasonably be satisfied depends in some cases on the question whether he made the proper kind of inquiry Thus, where a party entitled to production of a document demands, not production, but delivery, and receives a statement which would constitute a reasonable excuse for withholding delivery, but not for withholding production, he may be affected with constructive notice of the contents of the document (j)

62. In the case of sales of real property, a purchaser who has actual notice that a tenant is in possession or occupation of the property is presumed, as against that tenant or occupier, to have notice of his title and rights (k),

to the particular surrendered lease which was in question, and therefore not to be chargeable with having failed to make " such reasonable inquiries as ought to have been made " per VAUGHAN WILLIAMS, L J , at pp 484, 485, and FARWELL, L J , at pp 486, 487)

(h) *Hewitt v. Loosemoore* (1851), 9 Hare 449 (per TURNER, V -C., at p 458) , *Barnhart v Greenshields* (1853), 9 Moore P C 18 (at pp 33 *sqq*) , *Jones v Williams* (1857), 24 Beav 47 (per ROMILLY, M R , whose statement of the law, at p 62, is correct, if the addition referred to in note (d), *sup* , be eliminated) , *Espin v Pemberton* (1859), 3 De G & J 547 (per Lord CHELMSFORD, L C , at p 556) , *Agra Bank, Ltd. v Barry* (1874), L R 7 H L 135 (per Lord CAIRNS, L C , at pp 147, 149, and Lord HATHERLEY at pp 154, 155) , *Northern Counties of England Fire Insurance Co v Whipp* (1884), 26 C D 482, C. A. (per Cur at p 492)

(hh) *Taylor v Baker* (1818), 5 Price 306

(i) *Maxfield v Burton* (1873), L R 17 Eq 15 (per JESSEL, M R , at pp 18, 19 · " a man on his marriage has a freehold estate , he tells the solicitor for the lady with whom he is about to be married, on being asked for his deeds, ' they are deposited at my bankers' for safe custody ' The solicitor does nothing more, and it turns out that they are pledged to the bankers I hold that it was the duty of the solicitor to make further inquiry of the bankers, and to ask for the deeds If he had done so, he would have been told that the representation made to him of their being deposited for safe custody, which of course means safe custody only , was incorrect , inasmuch as they were deposited by way of mortgage, and on that mortgage a considerable sum of money was then due I consider that that was constructive notice, and bound the lady who was about to be married ") , *Spencer v Clarke* (1878), 9 C D 137 (per HALL, V -C , at pp. 141, 142, following the case last cited) , *Hunt v Luck, ubi inf*

(j) Per RIGBY, L J , at pp 275, 276 of *Oliver v Hinton,* [1899] 2 Ch 264, C A. See also *Hunt v Luck,* [1902] 1 Ch 428, C A (per VAUGHAN WILLIAMS, L J , at p 434)

(k) *Taylor v Stibbert* (1794), 2 Ves 437 (per Lord LOUGHBOROUGH, L C , at p 440) . *Daniels v Davison* (1811), 16 Ves 249 (per Lord ELDON, L C , at p 254) . *Allen v Anthony* (1816), 1 Mer 282 (per Lord ELDON, L C , at pp 284, 285), *Bailey v Richardson* (1852), 9 Hare 734 , *Barnhart v Greenshields* (1853), 9 Moore P C 18, at pp 32, 33 , *Knight v Bouyer* (1858), 2 De G. & J 421 , *Hunt v Luck, sup* (per FARWELL, J , at p 51) but not, as against the vendor, to have notice of *his* title and rights or of any limitation thereon created by such tenancy. "There is no pretence," as is clearly laid down by JAMES, L.J. (though at one time it seems to have been thought otherwise), for the doctrine "that a person who wants to buy such property, and has notice of the occupation of a tenant, is bound to inquire of the tenant what is the nature of his tenancy. For this purpose *James* v. *Litchfield* was cited as an authority. In that case there were certainly some dicta which nearly go to that extent, and which support the notion that the doctrine of *Daniels* v. *Davison* applies as between vendor and purchaser, and whilst the matter still rests in contract. It is not necessary now to deal with that case, but I am not prepared to assent to any such proposition. The doctrine in question seems to me to refer to equities between the purchaser and the tenant, when the legal estate has passed, and to have nothing to do with the rights and liabilities of vendors and purchasers If there is anything in the nature of the tenancies which affects the property sold, the vendor is bound to tell the purchaser, and to let him know what it is which is being sold, and the vendor cannot afterwards say to the purchaser, 'If you had gone to the tenant and inquired, you would have found out all about it '" (*l*) But actual knowledge that the rents of the property are paid to, and received by, a person whose receipts are *inconsistent with the vendor's title* is presumptive knowledge of that person's right, though no such knowledge is presumed from the mere fact that the party had actual notice that the rent was paid to local agents, and nothing more, where, if he had inquired of those agents, he would have discovered nothing as to the inconsistent right of any such third person (*ll*). Where the property, though not in possession of the vendor, is not in the possession of any other person either, the purchaser is not put on inquiry as to the title of the last occupier of the vacant land, nor fixed with notice of his title, if he refrains from such inquiry (*m*).

63. A person dealing with a limited company, though not a shareholder, is bound to take notice of what Lord HATHERLEY called its "external position," that is to say, he has presumptive knowledge of the contents of all such constitutive and other instruments relating to its status and powers as are accessible to the public (*n*) *A fortiori* is such notice imputed to him,

(*l*) *Caballero* v *Henty* (1874), 9 Ch App 447 (*per* JAMES, L J, at pp 449, 450) The opinion there expressed was adopted in *Hunt* v *Luck*, [1902] 1 Ch 428, C A, by FAR WELL, J, at the trial, and, on appeal, by VAUGHAN WILLIAMS, L J, at pp 432, 433, and COZENS HARDY, L J, at p 435, emphatically disapproving the incautious expression used by JESSEL, M R, at p 562 of *Mumford* v *Stohwasso* (1874), L R 18 Eq 556, which seems to imply a contrary view The dicta in *James* v *Litchfield* (1869), L R 9 Eq 51, which were disapproved of by JAMES, L J, in the passage from his judgment which is cited in the text, are those of ROMILLY, M R, at pp 54, 55 *Daniels* v *Davison* is cited in the last note
(*ll*) *Hunt* v *Luck*, *sup*, *per* FARWELL, J, at the trial, and VAUGHAN WILLIAMS, L J, at p 434, on appeal
(*m*) *Miles* v *Langley* (1831), 2 Russ & M 626
(*n*) *Mahony* v *East Holyford Mining Co* (1875), L R 7 H L 869 (*per* Lord HATHERLEY at p 893 · "those who deal with joint stock companies are bound to take notice of that which I may call the external position of the company. Every joint stock company has its memorandum and articles of association . or its partnership deed under

where he has become a member of the company (o) · indeed, s. 14 (1) of
the Companies (Consolidation Act, 1908 (which is a reproduction of corresponding sections in a succession of previous Companies Acts) expressly
provides that "the memorandum and articles shall, when registered, bind
the company and the members thereof to the same extent as if they
respectively had been signed and sealed by each member, and contained
covenants on the part of each member, his heirs, executors, and administrators, to observe all the provisions of the memorandum and of the
articles, subject to the provisions of this Act." But a stranger entering
into a transaction with a company is not deemed to have notice of the " indoor
management " of the company, or of anything beyond what may be gleaned
from instruments of the type above mentioned, or from statutes relating to
companies in general. Thus, where the articles of a company provided
that the board of directors might by resolution fix the number who were to
constitute a quorum, the party was held not to be fixed with notice of the
fact that the directors had exercised their power by resolving that three
should constitute a quorum, or of the fact that the instruction to enter into
the mortgage of which he was seeking foreclosure had been given at a meeting
of two directors only (p); and a *bond fide* holder of a debenture in the form
prescribed by the constitution of the company was similarly deemed free
from the imputation of knowledge of the fact that no directors had ever
been appointed, and no resolution, therefore, to issue debentures had ever
been passed (q).

64. Miscellaneous illustrations of presumptive knowledge are the following.
Where a solicitor, knowing that an order for an injunction is about to be
pronounced on the hearing of a motion, goes out of court for the purpose of
qualifying himself to assert afterwards with literal accuracy that he had no
actual knowledge of the terms of the order, he is nevertheless presumed to
have had all such knowledge thereof as he would have acquired if he had
stayed to hear it made (r). It was said, in another case (s), of a partner in
a business who set up actual ignorance of certain facts, that " if he had used

which it acts   Those articles of association and that partnership deed are open to all
who are minded to have any dealings whatsoever with the company, and those who
so deal with them must be affected with notice of all that is contained in those two documents ")

(o) *New Brunswick & Canada Railway & Land Co.* v *Conybeare* (1862), 9 H L C
711 (*per* Lord WESTBURY, L C, at p. 734)   For this reason it was always held, and with
particular insistence and emphasis by Lord CAIRNS, L.J , that it is for the shareholder
seeking revocation of his contract to take shares, on the ground of misrepresentation of
the objects of the company, to move with more than ordinary promptitude, if he wishes
to protect himself against a plea of presumptive knowledge and affirmation · see his
observations at pp. 423, 424 of *Lawrence's Case* (1867), 2 Ch App 412 , pp. 426, 427 of
Kincaid's Case (1867), 2 Ch App 420 , pp. 540, 541 of *Wilkinson's Case* (1867), 2 Ch.
App. 536 ; and p 684 of *Peel's Case* (1867), 2 Ch App 674

(p) *County of Gloucester Bank* v. *Rudry Merthyr Steam & House Coal Colliery Co* ,
[1895] 1 Ch 629, C A (*per* Lord HALSBURY at pp. 632, 633, and LINDLEY, L.J., at pp 635,
636).

(q) *Duck* v. *Tower Galvanizing Co* , [1901] 2 K B 314 (*per* Lord ALVERSTONE, C.J.,
at p 318)

(r) *Hearn* v. *Thomas* (1807), 14 Ves 136.

(s) *Sadler* v. *Lee* (1843), 6 Beav. 324

ordinary diligence and attention in the management of his business, he might and must have discovered all the facts which are material to this case ; the means of knowledge appear to have been in his power ; he would, with very little trouble, have found confusion and irregularity in the accounts, and a proper investigation of the sources of such confusion and irregularity would have led to the disc ery of all that had been done   In such a case as this, and under such circumstances, Courts of Justice . .   must impute the knowledge which the partners, acting in their interests and in the plain discharge of their duty, might and ought to have obtained " (t)   A party seeking to set aside a deed whereby he had compromised his liability under a previous deed of suretyship, on the ground that, unknown to him, certain events had happened between the dates of the two deeds in virtue of which he had become discharged from his guarantee under the earlier deed, was held disentitled to relief, inasmuch as, the burden being on him of proving ignorance of the above-mentioned events at the date of the compromise, he had failed to sustain the burden, it being proved that, three years previously to that date, he had made inquiries as to the circumstances in question, and had been furnished with the names and addresses of all the persons who could and would have informed him, if asked (and who in fact eventually did so), and yet took no steps whatever to ascertain the truth from any of those persons till after the compromise ; and the party was accordingly deemed affected with constructive notice of the whole of the facts (u). It has been laid down that " when a person purchases property where a visible state of things exists which could not legally exist "—or even which is " very unlikely to exist "—" without the property being subject to some burden, he is taken to have notice of that burden," but the conditions stated are not present when the only " visible state of things " is the existence of windows in an adjoining house, from which no knowledge of an agreement giving a right to access of light to them can be imputed to the purchaser (v). In cases of purchasing, or taking, subleases, it has been thrown out, as a suggestion, that the party so purchasing or taking may possibly be affected with presumptive knowledge of unusual restrictive covenants in the head lease if he has acquired actual knowledge of similar covenants in leases of adjoining portions of the same estate ; but the precise point has never been actually decided (w)

(t) *Sadler* v. *Lee* (1843), 6 Beav 324, *per* Lord LANGDALE, M R , at pp 350. 351
(u) *Wason* v. *Wareing* (1852), 15 Beav 151 (*per* ROMILLY, M R , at p 155)
(v) *Allen* v *Seckham* (1879), 11 C D. 790, C. A , *per* BRETT, L J , at pp 795, 796
(w) *Re White and Smith's Contract*, [1896] 1 Ch 637 (*per* STIRLING, J , at pp 642, 643 : " I can imagine cases in which the Court might hold that a purchaser had failed to take reasonable precautions if he did not avail himself of an opportunity, or even a possible opportunity, of examining a lease ; as, for example, where knowledge was brought home to him of the existence of similar covenants in leases of adjoining portions of the same estate ")   In this case, however, that which STIRLING, J , " imagined," as a possible ground for the inference of the knowledge referred to, was not proved, or even alleged. In *Molyneux* v *Hawtrey*, [1903] 2 K B 487, C A , the plaintiff, excusing himself from producing the head lease itself, had tendered for inspection a document which he stated to be a copy of a lease of some adjoining property with the same kind of covenants, but which the defendant's solicitor was unable to, and did not in fact, peruse, by reason of the pressure of other engagements ; and it was contended for the plaintiff that this

Sub-s (6). Statutory Presumptions of Knowledge.

65. There are various statutes and enactments whereby, in different branches of the law, it is provided that certain presumptions of knowledge shall, or shall not, be made in the circumstances and under the conditions respectively prescribed. These may be divided into two main classes: the one consisting of those codifying statutes or enactments, the principal object of which is merely to declare, in a succinct and summary form, with or without extensions or restrictions in this or that particular, the substance of the existing common law rules relating to constructive notice, and the other comprising all those statutory provisions which abolish or curtail old, or introduce new, presumptions of notice.

66. By far the most important example of the former class of enactment is s. 3, sub-s. (1) of the Conveyancing Act, 1882 (x), which is in the following terms :—

"A purchaser shall not be prejudicially affected by notice of any instrument, fact, or thing unless—

(i) It is within his own knowledge, or would have come to his knowledge, if such inquiries or inspections had been made as ought reasonably to have been made by him ; or

(ii) In the same transaction with respect to which a question of notice to the purchaser arises, it has come to the knowledge of his counsel, as such, or of his solicitor or other agent, as such, or would have come to the knowledge of his solicitor or other agent, as such, if such inquiries and inspections had been made as ought reasonably to have been made by the solicitor or other agent "

67. The scope of the above statutory rules is, by force of the statute itself, extended far beyond that which would appear to be indicated by the literal language of the section, or the short title of the Act: that is to say, it is not confined to sales of real property, or to conveyancing transactions in their strictest sense (though these, no doubt, are the kind of transactions which are most fertile in illustrations of the doctrine of presumptive knowledge), for by the interpretation clause of the statute the term " purchaser " is defined as including " a lessee, a mortgagee, or an intending purchaser, lessee, or mortgagee, or other *person who, for valuable consideration, takes or deals for property* " (y), whilst " ' property ' includes real and personal property,

---

constituted " a fair opportunity " to the defendant's solicitor to acquaint himself with the nature of the onerous restrictions there in question, and that the defendant consequently had presumptive knowledge of those restrictions, but the C A, affirming WRIGHT, J, considered that " fair opportunity " was a question of fact, and that the plaintiff had not discharged the burden on him of proving this fact (*per* COLLINS, M R, at pp 491, 492, MATHEW, L J., at p 496 ; COZENS-HARDY, L J, at p. 497). The case, therefore, suggested by STIRLING, J, did not arise It would have arisen if the defendant's solicitor had in fact perused the document produced to him, but admittedly he had not, and consequently no " knowledge was brought home to him of the existence of similar covenants," such as would be required to raise the question.

(x) 45 & 46 Vict. c. 39

(y) *Ibid*, s 1, sub-s (4), (n)   See also s 1, (2), of the Money-Lenders Act, 1911, cited at the end of § 72, *post*, for a further statutory application of the term " purchaser."

and any debt, and any thing in action, and any other right or interest in the nature of property, whether in possession or not " (z). In other words the rules in question are to be applied to every species of transaction for valuable consideration in relation to property of every description known to the law, and, in the light of the above statutory definitions, the section would run as follows · " A person taking, or dealing for, or intending to take, or deal for, property of any description whatever, for valuable consideration, shall not be prejudicially affected by notice of any instrument, fact, or thing unless—
(i) it is within his own knowledge or would have come to his knowledge, if such inquiries or inspections had been made as ought reasonably to have been made by him ; or (ii) in the same transaction with regard to which a question of notice to such person arises, it has come to the knowledge of his agent, as such, or would have come to the knowledge of his agent, as such, if such inquiries and inspections had been made as ought reasonably to have been made by the agent."

68. It will be seen that the doctrine, as so stated, is a substantial reproduction and declaration, in most lucid and apt phraseology, of the pre-existing judicially declared rules as to the knowledge imputed to a person from the actual knowledge of his agent, or from his own actual knowledge of an instrument or fact putting him upon inquiry as to other instruments or facts (a). It is true that there is no reference in the section to the supposed requirements of "fraud," or "gross negligence," in cases where knowledge of one fact is imputed to a person from his proved actual knowledge of another , but neither is there, in general, any such condition precedent to the presumption at common law, as will be hereafter explained (b) , at all events, if and in so far as any judicial expositions of the doctrine may be deemed to have lent countenance to such a view, they are now replaced by the clear and precise provisions of this enactment (c) In fact, generally, as has been pointed out in more than one case (d), it is clear from the strictly negative form in which it is expressed (e) that the section was intended to operate rather by way

(z) Conveyancing Act, 1882, s. 1, sub-s (4), (1)

(a) Being the rules discussed in Sub ss (4) and (5) of this Section, *ante* Several references are made in those Sub sections to the enactment in question see note (x) to § 49, note (s) to § 54, notes (v) and (a) to § 56, and note (c) to § 59. Eminent authorities have always regarded the statutory provision as reflecting common law principles, and, further, as expressing those principles in more terse, definite, and correct language than that which had been used by some of the judges . see the observations of LINDLEY, L.J , delivering the judgment of the Court, at p 35 of *Bailey v. Barnes*, [1894] 1 Ch 25, C A , of ROMER, J , at p 269 of *Oliver v. Hinton*, [1899] 2 Ch 264, C A ; of VAUGHAN WILLIAMS, L.J , at p 435 of *Hunt v Luck*, [1902] 1 Ch 428, C A , of COLLINS, M R., at p. 493, MATHEW, L.J , at pp 495, 496, and COZENS-HARDY, L.J , at p 497, of *Molyneux v. Hawtrey*, [1903] 2 K B 487, C. A , in which last case the preference of the Court for the plain and direct language of the statute over previous judicial refinements was most marked.

(b) See App. A, Sect. 2, Sub-ss (3), (4), *post*

(c) See the passages from *Molyneux* v. *Hawtrey*, cited in note (a), *sup*

(d) See *Bailey* v. *Barnes, sup., per Cur.*, at p 35 "the Conveyancing Act, 1882, really does no more than state the law as it was before, but its negative form shows that a restriction rather than an extension of the doctrine of notice was intended by the legis lature" To the same effect SWINFEN EADY, J , at p. 663 of *Re Valletort Sanitary Steam Laundry Co* , [1903] 2 Ch 654, and JOYCE, J., at pp. 640, 641 of *Berwick & Co* v. *Price*, [1905] 1 Ch 632

(e) See the opening words of s 3, sub s. (1), (i), as cited in § 66, *ante* . "a purchaser

of restriction on. than extension of, the existing rules of law   Thus it has given the quietus, as has already been indicated, to at least two propositions of a somewhat heretical character, which, but for the intervention of the legislature, might possibly by this time have been accepted as sound doctrine (*f*).

69. Other declaratory or codifying enactments, with reference to presumptive knowledge, which have already been noticed, are s 16 of the Partnership Act, 1890 (*g*), and ss 18, 19 of the Marine Insurance Act, 1906 (*h*).

70. Besides the above, there are various statutes and statutory provisions which, without purporting to declare or codify any of the established rules of common law as to presumptive knowledge, relate to "notice" of certain facts in such a way as to presuppose and incorporate such rules   How far, in each case, the term "notice" includes knowledge other than actual, must depend upon the language and intention of the particular statute   Thus (to take a few examples only out of many) in the various enactments providing that "notice of an act of bankruptcy" shall entail certain consequences on the position of any person having such notice, it has been held that "notice" means knowledge (*notitia*), and is not confined to its popular meaning as a formal document "giving notice," and that it includes that species of knowledge which is presumed from wilful and fraudulent blindness and abstention from inquiry, but not that which is presumed from mere abstention in fact, unaccompanied by any want of good faith (*i*)   So also in enactments relating to the "holder in due course" of a negotiable instrument, the same meaning is given to the "notice of a defect in the title" of a previous party to the instrument which invalidates the claim of any person to be considered such a holder (*j*)   A like limited construction has been placed upon the expression in question as used in s 55 (1) of the Conveyancing and Law of Property Act, 1881 (44 & 45 Vict c 41), which provides that "a receipt for consideration money or other consideration in the body of a deed, or endorsed thereon, shall in favour of a subsequent purchaser, not having notice that the money or other consideration thereby acknowledged to be

shall *not* be prejudicially affected .   *unless*   " (not—"a purchaser *shall* be prejudicially affected,   *if* .."), and, in order that there might be no possible mistake about the meaning and object of the enactment, the further restrictive provision in sub s (3) that "a purchaser shall not by reason of anything in this section be affected by notice in any case where he would not have been so affected if this section had not been enacted "

(*f*) See § 54, note (*s*), and § 56, note (*a*), *ante*.

(*g*) See § 44, note (*s*), § 55, note (*u*), and § 56, note (*v*), *ante*.

(*h*) See § 38, note (*g*), § 39, note (*h*), § 42, note (*x*), and § 49, note (*b*), *ante*

(*i*) As to notice of an act of bankruptcy within the meaning of 2 & 3 Vict c 29, see *Bird v Bass* (1843), 6 M. & G 143, at pp 147, 148   As to such notice within the meaning of a similar provision in the Bankruptcy Act, 1869, s 20, see *Ex p Snowball* (1872), 7 Ch App 534, *per Cur*, at p 549 ("he is not allowed to escape from the effects of having had notice by saying he has not read it, when he ought to have read it," or " by saying that he did not draw the natural inference from the fact ")   The corresponding sections of the Bankruptcy Act, 1883, are ss. 45, 49, as to which, generally, see Lord Halsbury's *Laws of England*, title *Bankruptcy and Insolvency*, vol ii, pp 288–291

(*j*) See s 29 of the Bills of Exchange Act, 1882 (45 & 46 Vict. c 61), and the cases on the meaning of " notice " in that section which are cited in the notes thereto in Chalmers' Digest.

received was not in fact paid or given, wholly or in part, be sufficient evidence of the payment or giving of the whole amount thereof " (*jj*). Again, with reference to notice of the existence or determination of the authority of a mercantile agent to make a disposition of goods, within the meaning of ss 2 and 4 of 6 Geo. 4, c. 94, s 4 of 5 & 6 Vict c. 39, and s. 2 of the Factors Act, 1877 (40 & 41 Vict. c. 39), all of which sections are now reproduced in s. 2 of the Factors Act, 1889 (52 & 53 Vict. c. 45), it has been held by Lord St. Leonards, dealing with the Act of 1842, that a pledgee, if his title is to be invalidated, must be fixed with actual knowledge that the agent pledging the goods was acting *malâ fide*, and beyond his authority, in so doing, and that mere suspicion is not enough , and by Lord Herschell, with reference to the Factors Acts generally, that their effect is " to attach some of the elements of negotiability to documents of title to goods, and render the mere possession of them evidence of authority to deal with them in the ordinary course of business, and to preclude the necessity of any further inquiry " (*zz*). The meaning of " knowingly issuing," and " notice of contracts," in company legislation, will be dealt with hereafter in its proper place (*k*). It is very rarely indeed that an enactment distinguishes between "actual" and "constructive notice" in express terms, but there is at least one instance of this being done and, when it is, the expressions in question must of course be taken in their established technical meanings (*l*)

71. The second class of enactments has now to be considered, viz. those which either curtail the effect and range of common law presumptions of knowledge—this is by far the more common case—or ordain new presumptions which the common law would not, or might not, otherwise make

72. Of the former species, examples are to be found in (besides those just mentioned) the enactments which expressly relieve certain classes of persons from the necessity of making inquiry as to certain facts (which means of course that knowledge of those facts is not to be imputed to them if they omit to make such inquiry), such as the provision, with reference to settled lands, that " a person dealing in good faith with the tenant for life is *not concerned to inquire respecting* the giving of any such notice as is required by this section " (*m*) ; the provision, with reference to conveyancing transactions, that upon a sale made in professed exercise of the power conferred on mortgagees by the Conveyancing and Law of Property Act, 1881, " a purchaser *is not, and never has been, concerned to see or inquire* whether a case has arisen to authorize the sale, or due notice has been given, or the power

(*jj*) See *Lloyds Bank* v *Bullock*, [1896] 2 Ch 192, *per* Chitty, J , at p 197 , *Powell* v *Browne* (1907), 97 L T 854, C A , *per* Cozens Hardy, M R., and Moulton, L.J , at p 856 , *Capell* v *Winter*, [1907] 2 Ch. 376, *per* Parker, J., at p 392

(*zz*) The cases containing the opinions of Lord St. Leonards and Lord Herschell, referred to in the text, are respectively *Navulshaw* v *Brownrigg* (1852), 2 De G M. & G. 441, 451, and *London Joint Stock Bank* v. *Simmons*, [1892] A C 201, 218, H. L.

(*k*) In Ch VI, § 556, *post*

(*l*) See note (z) to § 73, *post*

(*m*) Settled Land Act, 1882 (45 & 46 Vict c 38), s 45 As to " dealing in good faith," see *Mogridge* v. *Clapp*, [1892] 3 Ch. 382, 395, 399, C.A.

is otherwise properly and regularly exercised " (n), and the provision of the Moneylenders Act, 1911, in relation to moneylenders, that " a person shall not be deemed to have had notice of a defect in an agreement or security by reason only that a search in the register established under the Money-lenders Act, 1900, would have disclosed the defect or shown that the agreement or security was effected with a moneylender, and, for the purposes of this Act and the Moneylenders Act, 1900, the provisions of section three of the Conveyancing Act, 1882, shall apply and be deemed always to have applied as if the expression ' purchaser ' included a person making any such payment or transfer as aforesaid," i e. "any payment or transfer of money or property made *bonâ fide* by any person, whether acting in a fiduciary capacity or otherwise, on the faith of the validity of any agreement with, or security taken by a moneylender " (o).

73. The second species of this class finds illustration in a variety of miscellaneous enactments (oo), but principally in those which provide for compulsory registration of the matters therein mentioned Of these, the most important, in the sense that they have given rise to the greatest number of decisions on the canons of interpretation to be applied to the legislative creation or restriction of presumptions of knowledge, are the Acts requiring registration of titles to, and incumbrances upon, estates and interests in land, in Middlesex (p), Yorkshire (q), Ireland (r), Scotland (s), and certain of the

(n) Conveyancing Act, 1911 (1 & 2 Geo. 5, c. 37), s 5 (1), which has now replaced, and enlarged, s 21 (2) of the Conveyancing Act, 1881, as to the construction of which see *Bailey* v *Barnes*, [1894] 1 Ch 25, C A (at pp 30, 34, 36)

(o) Moneylenders Act, 1911 (1 & 2 Geo 5, c. 38), s 1, sub s. (2)   For an instance of an enactment which renders void any condition purporting to fix a party with notice, see s 81 (4) of the Companies (Consolidation) Act, 1908, which is the subject of § 562, *post*.

(oo) These are scattered over the whole field of the statute law   Useful illustrations may be gleaned from legislative repression or restriction of dangerous trades and occupations, *e g.* s. 2, sub s (2), and s 3, of the Betting and Loans (Infants) Act, 1892 (55 Vict. c. 4), and s 3 of the Moneylenders Act, 1900 (63 & 64 Vict. c 51), where *primâ facie* presumptions are made in certain cases against money-lenders of knowledge of the minority of persons solicited and circularized by them

(p) The statute here is the Middlesex Registry Act, 1708 (7 Anne, c 20), by s 1 of which it is provided that the deed or conveyance " shall be adjudged fraudulent and void against any subsequent purchaser or mortgagee for valuable consideration, unless such memorial thereof be registered as by this Act is directed before the registering of the memorial of the deed or conveyance under which such subsequent purchaser or mortgagee shall claim."   For decisions on this section, see *Hine* v. *Dodd* (1741), 2 Atk 275, *Le Neve* v. *Le Neve* (1747), Ambl 436, 3 Atk 346, 1 Ves. 64, *Jolland* v. *Stainbridge* (1797), 3 Ves 478 ; *Wyatt* v *Barwell* (1815), 19 Ves 345, *Sumpter* v *Cooper* (1831), 2 B. & Ad 223, *Robinson* v. *Woodward* (1851), 4 De G & Sm 562, *Rolland* v *Hart* (1871), 6 Ch App 678

(q) The statutes as to Yorkshire are the following. 2 & 3 Anne, c 4, and 6 Anne, c 2 (as to the West Riding), 6 Anne, c 35, 6 Anne, c 62, and 8 Geo 2, c 6 (as to the East Riding) ; and the Yorkshire Registries Act, 1884 (47 & 48 Vict c 54), and the Yorkshire Registries Amendment Act, 1885 (48 & 49 Vict c 26), on which see note (z), *post* (as to the North, East, and West Ridings)   For the construction of the earlier statutes, now repealed, see *Chadwick* v *Turner* (1866), 1 Ch. App 310, *Kettlewell* v *Watson* (1882), 21 C. D 685   for that of the Acts of 1884 and 1885, see *Battison* v *Hobson*, [1896] 2 Ch 403, *Manks* v. *Whiteley*, [1912] 1 Ch 735, C A.

(r) The Irish registry statute was 6 Anne, c 2, now repealed. See the following decisions thereon · *Nixon* v. *Hamilton* (1838), 2 Dr & Wall 364 ; 56 R. R 246, *Rochard* v *Fulton* (1844), 1 Jo. & Lat 413, 68 R R 265, *Agra Bank, Ltd* v. *Barry* (1874), L R. 7 H. L 135

(s) See, as to the effect of registration in the Register of Sasines, *Gordon-Cumming* v. *Houldsworth*, [1901] A C 537, H. L

colonies (*t*), and providing that unregistered deeds and conveyances shall
be deemed fraudulent and void against subsequent purchasers or mortgagees
for valuable consideration. This involves two things : (i) the creation of a
statutory presumption of knowledge on the part of every one of what is
entered on the register, for compulsory registration is peremptory notice to
all the world of all matters so recorded (*u*), in the absence of any express
proviso in the statute to the contrary (*uu*) ; and (ii) a statutory dispensation
to all parties having transactions relating to registered lands from instituting
those inquiries and investigations as to matters not on the register which
otherwise they would be expected to institute, and of which, in the absence
of such inquiry, they would be affected with constructive notice That is
to say, a person who has duly registered his deed is not to be fixed with
presumptive knowledge of the existence or contents of, or submit to have
his deed postponed to, a prior unregistered deed by reason only of his
having such notice of related facts as would, but for the statute, have raised
a presumption against him of the knowledge in question This, however,
does not mean that, if he has *actual* notice of the unregistered conveyance,
he is protected by the registration. It was, indeed at one time " much
doubted whether the Courts ought ever to have suffered the question of
notice "—that is, *any* kind of notice—" to be agitated against a party who
has duly registered his conveyance : but they have said ' we cannot permit
fraud to prevail ; and it shall only be in cases where the notice is so clearly
proved as to make it fraudulent in the purchaser to take and register a conveyance in prejudice to the known title of another, that we will suffer the
registered deed to be affected ' " (*v*)   Bad faith cannot be allowed to shelter
itself under the protection of even the most express and uncompromising
statutory language, or, putting it on another ground, the one object of the
statute is to secure notoriety of titles, and, in the case of proved knowledge in fact, that purpose is effected in the particular case, though by other
means but, whichever theory be adopted, it is well established that
only the clearest and most incontrovertible proof of express and direct notice
is sufficient to deprive a party of his statutory right to rely upon his registration (*w*). Mere suspicion—even strong suspicion—that the party had actual
knowledge, or wilfully shut his eyes to the truth, will not, as it might in
ordinary cases, suffice for this purpose (*x*)   On the other hand, if the actual

(*t*) See *Crowly* v *Bergtheil*, [1899] A C 374, P C (Natal)
(*u*) *Hine* v *Dodd*, *sup*, per Lord HARDWICKE, L C, at p 275
(*uu*) As there is in s. 1 (2) of the Moneylenders Act, 1911, cited in § 72, *ante*
(*v*) *Wyatt* v *Barwell*, *sup*, per GRANT, M R, at p 438.
(*w*) *Hine* v *Dodd*, *sup*, where Lord HARDWICKE, L C, at p 276, says that either clear
and undoubted notice, or fraud, must be shown, *Le Neve* v. *Le Neve* (1747), Ambl 436
(per Lord HARDWICKE, L C, at pp. 441–447), *Jolland* v *Stainbridge*, *sup* (per ARDEN, M R,
at p 485), *Nixon* v. *Hamilton*, *sup* (per Lord PLUNKET, L C (Ir), at pp 390, 391),
Rolland v *Hart*, *sup* (per Lord HATHERLEY, L C, at p 681)
(*x*) *Hine* v *Dodd*, *sup* (per Lord HARDWICKE, L C, at p 276 " suspicion of notice,
though a strong suspicion, is not sufficient to justify the Court in breaking in upon the
Act of Parliament "), *Robinson* v *Woodward*, *sup*, *Chadwick* v *Turner*, *sup* (per
TURNER, L J., at p 319 " that the facts . . . raise a strong suspicion of notice cannot
be denied, but I think they fall short of what is required to affect a registered title, for

knowledge be clearly proved, it does not signify whether it was the knowledge of the party himself, or his agent, for where fraud is proved principal and agent are, for this purpose, one (y). In one of the Registry Acts, the legislature has *ex abundanti cautelâ*, gone so far as to enact that no notice, even " actual notice," shall deprive a party of the benefit of registration, unless there has been also " actual fraud " (z).

74. The statutory presumption of knowledge of course only operates upon such instruments as are required by the particular statute to be, and are, registered, and those of which the existence is implied by such registration. Thus, on the one hand, it has been held that a memorial of a deed which purported, on the face of the memorial, to relate to all the estate of the grantor in the lands thereby conveyed, was notice of an assignment of a partial interest in the same lands made in trust for the same grantee by the same deed, sufficient to avoid the effect of a subsequent registered assignment of such partial interest (a) : but, on the other hand, the ordinary type of registry enactment, which relates only to transactions contained in deeds or other instruments in writing, has been held not to apply to equitable mortgages by deposit unaccompanied by a memorandum (b), or to a vendor's lien for unpaid purchase

which purpose the notice must be clear and distinct, and amounting in fact to fraud "), *Rolland* v *Hart, sup (per* Lord HATHERLEY, L.C , at p 681 there must be " actual notice implying fraud "), *Agra Bank, Ltd.* v *Barry, sup (per* Lord CAIRNS, L C , at pp 148-150, —the whole of this passage deserves careful perusal,—Lord HATHERLEY at pp 155, 156, and Lord SELBORNE at p. 158, at p 149 Lord CAIRNS expresses some doubt whether even wilful blindness, or, as it has elsewhere been called, " fraudulent ignorance," would be sufficient to get rid of the effect of registration), *Kettlewell* v *Watson, sup (per* FRY, J , at p. 704), *Crowly* v. *Bergtheil, sup.* (at p 382)

(y) *Le Neve* v. *Le Neve* (1747), Ambl 436 (*per* Lord HARDWICKE, L C , at p 447 " fraud, or *mala fides*, is the true ground on which the Court is governed in cases of notice and it is in consequence of the decision of the former question that notice to the agent is sufficient ; for if the ground is the fraud or *mala fides* of the party, then it is all one whether by the party himself or his agent , still it is a *machinatio ad circumveniendum* "), *Nixon* v *Hamilton* (1838), 2 Dr & Wall 364, *per* Lord PLUNKET, L C (Ir.), at pp 391, 392 (" notice to the agent, if in the same transaction, clearly affects the principal, and for this reason, because in such cases it is a fraud in the agent, and his fraud makes the principal cease to be a purchaser for valuable consideration, within the meaning of the Registry Act, and this is the ground on which Lord HARDWICKE founds his opinion in *Le Neve* v *Le Neve* "), *Agra Bank, Ltd* v *Barry* (1874), L R 7 H L 135 (*per* Lord CAIRNS, L C , at p. 148 " these cases depend, and depend entirely, upon the question of actual notice, either to the principal, *or to the agent,* whose knowledge is that of the principal ")

(z) The Yorkshire Registries Act, 1884 (47 & 48 Vict c 54), which, in s 14, provides that " all priorities given by this Act shall have full effect in all Courts, *except in cases of actual fraud,* and all persons claiming thereunder any legal or equitable interests shall be entitled to corresponding priorities, and no such person shall lose any such priority *merely in consequence of his having been affected with actual or constructive notice, except in cases of actual fraud.*" This is reinforced by s 15. One would have supposed that the above language was absolutely proof against any possible misconstruction, but we are favoured with the report of a case—*Battison* v. *Hobson*, [1896] 2 Ch 403, in which STIRLING, J , was invited to, and did, at p 412, solemnly pronounce that the statute meant what it had so clearly said See also *Whiteley* v *Delaney*, [1914] A C 132, H L (*per* Lord HALDANE, L.C , at p 147, as to s 15 of this Act).

(a) *Rochard* v *Fulton* (1844), 1 Jo & Lat 413 , 68 R R. 265 (*per* SUGDEN, L C (Ir), at pp. 441-444).

(b) *Sumpster* v *Cooper* (1831), 2 B & Ad 223 (*per* Lord TENTERDEN, C J , at p 225 · " it cannot be held to apply to the case of an equitable mortgage. It refers only to the registration of deeds , and where there is only a legal or equitable mortgage executed by deposit of deeds, there is no instrument to be registered ") money (o). *Secus*, in the case of any enactment—there appears to be only one—which expressly provides otherwise (d)

75. It is provided by the statutes enabling (not requiring) registration of patents, designs, and trade marks that the person for the time being entered on the register as the proprietor shall, subject to any rights appearing from such register to be vested in any other person, have power to assign the same, and give effectual receipts for any consideration for such assignment, but this is followed by a proviso (which, like that contained in s. 57 of the Merchant Shipping Act, 1894, with reference to the registry of ships, has the effect of almost neutralizing the statutory protection) that any equities in respect of such patent, design, or trade mark, may be enforced in like manner as in respect of any other personal property This proviso has been held to cover unregistered, as well as registered, equities, because the latter are already provided for in the earlier part of the enactment : so that a person who registers with notice of an unregistered equity derives no benefit by his registration as against the person entitled to enforce the equity but it has also been held, in analogy to the decisions on the statutes relating to the registration of title to land, that the statutory registration of a patent, design, or trade mark is of value to the registered proprietor to the extent that the notice of such equity must be actual notice, so as to render it unconscionable and fraudulent in the party to rely upon his registration as against the known rights of another (e).

76. There are a variety of other statutes and enactments requiring registration of instruments and facts, or insertion or entry of matters in books or documents accessible to the public, to some of which the rules above indicated as to statutory presumptions of notice have been, or may be, applied (f). but it is sufficient, perhaps, for purposes of illustration, to have selected the two types of enactment which have been already discussed.

Sub-s (7)   *Judicial Observations on the Doctrine of Presumptive Knowledge.*

77. For upwards of half a century, indeed almost from the time when the rules as to presumptive knowledge began to assume a definite shape and form, the judges who had invented and established these rules began to

(c) *Kettlewell* v *Watson* (1882), 21 C D 685 (*per* FRY, J , at p. 702)

(d) By s 7 of the Yorkshire Registries Act, 1884 (47 & 48 Vict c 54), it is enacted that "where any lien or charge on any lands within any of the three Ridings is claimed in respect of any unpaid purchase money, or by reason of any deposit of title deeds, a memorandum of such lien or charge may be registered " Effect was given to this provision in *Battison* v. *Hobson, sup.* (*per* STIRLING, J , at pp 411, 412)

(e) The section which was the subject of the decision referred to in the text is s 87 of the Patents Designs and Trade Marks Act, 1883, reproduced, as regards patents and designs, in s 71 (3) of the Patents and Designs Act, 1907 (7 Edw 7, c 29), and, as regards trademarks, in s 38 of the Trade Marks Act, 1905 (5 Edw. 7, c 15)   The decision is *New Ixion Tyre & Cycle Co* v. *Spilsbury*, [1898] 2 Ch 484, C A , at pp 488, 490 as to the first, and p 489 as to the second, point mentioned in the text

(f) See (but only as illustrations selected from an enormous number of such statutes) the Acts providing for the registration of bills of sale, judgments, Crown debts, *lites pendentes*, and mortgages and charges on the property of limited companies , trade unions, friendly and building societies, and their rules ; moneylenders, &c , and see the various treatises on these respective branches of the law

discern their perilous possibilities and potency. Though here and there we find intermittent protests against any attempt to emasculate them (g), the main current of judicial authority soon set in favour of an attitude of vigilance and jealous restriction , and reiterated warnings have been thrown out by a series of eminent judges (h) against the slightest extension of a doctrine which, even admitting it to be " based on good sense " (i), is now recognized as being, to say the least of it, " subtle and difficult " (j), " very refined " (k), and to be applied with the utmost caution.

78. Particularly has this distrust and revolt been manifested by that unbending opponent of everything in the nature of a " fiction," or an " oracular phrase," Lord ESHER (l), in relation to all kinds of transactions, whether

(g) Thus TURNER, L J , at p 467 of *Wilson* v *Hart* (1866), 1 Ch App 463, says . " I am not by any means inclined to extend the doctrine of constructive notice ; but, on the other hand, I am as little inclined to fritter away the principles of the Court by refusing to apply them to cases to which they properly extend " To the same effect are the observations of KEKEWICH, J , at p 361 of *Davis* v *Hutchings*, [1907] 2 Ch 356 (" non extension is quite a different thing from frittering away ") And see those of LINDLEY, L J , in *Bailey* v. *Barnes*, as cited in the next note.

(h) Such as Lord ST LEONARDS, when Sir EDW SUGDEN, L C (Ir), at p. 29 of *Roddy* v *Williams* (1845), 3 Jo & Lat 1 , 72 R R 1 , Lord CRANWORTH, L C , at p 473 of *Ware* v. *Lord Egmont* (1854), 4 De G M. & G. 460 (" I must not part with this case without expressing my entire concurrence in what has on many occasions of late years fallen from Judges of great eminence on the subject of constructive notice, namely, that it is highly inexpedient for Courts of equity to extend this doctrine, and to attempt to apply it to cases to which it has not hitherto been held applicable ") , Lord WESTBURY, L C , who, at p 601 of *Wyllie* v *Pollen* (1863), 3 De G J & S 596, " said that he concurred with those Judges who thought that the doctrine of constructive notice ought not to be extended, but ought to be reduced within clear and definite principles " Cp *Allen* v *Seckham* (1879), 11 C D. 790, C A (*per* BRETT, L J , at p 795 " the doctrine of constructive notice ought to be narrowly watched, and not enlarged. Indeed anything 'constructive' ought to be narrowly watched, because it depends on a fiction "); *Re Ashton, Ex p McGowan* (1891), 64 L T 28, 29 , *English & Scottish Mercantile Investment Co* v *Brunton*, [1892] 2 Q B 700, C A (*per* Lord ESHER, M.R , at p 708 " of late years, after the doctrine had been invented and put into form, the Chancery Judges saw that it was being carried much further than had been intended, and they declined to carry it further In a series of cases Lords COTTENHAM, LYNDHURST, and CRANWORTH, Lord Justice TURNER, and the late Master of the Rolls, Sir GEORGE JESSEL, have said that the doctrine ought not to be extended one bit further ; all the Judges seem to have agreed upon that. In *Allen* v *Seckham*, I pointed out that the doctrine is a dangerous one . " &c), *Bailey* v *Barnes*, [1894] 1 Ch 25, C A (*per Cur* , at p. 34 " the doctrine of constructive notice is based on good sense, and is designed to prevent frauds on owners of property , but the doctrine must not be carried to such an extent as to defeat honest purchasers , and although this limitation has sometimes been lost sight of, still the limitation is as important and as well known as the doctrine itself ") , *Molyneux* v *Hawtrey*, [1903] 2 K B 487, C. A , *Powell* v *Browne* (1908), 97 L T 854, C A (*per* FARWELL, L J , at p 856 " the Courts have of late years refused to extend the doctrine of constructive notice which has been put forward here—a doctrine which rests on imputing to a person knowledge which it is admitted he never had I am speaking of constructive notice of the sort which is suggested here, where there is no imputation of want of good faith ").

(i) See the passage cited in the last note from *Bailey* v. *Barnes*, *sup.*

(j) By FRY, J , at p 704 of *Kettlewell* v *Watson* (1882), 21 C D 685.

(k) By CHITTY, J , at p 676 of *Re Cousins* (1886), 31 C D 671, where he says that s 3 of the Conveyancing Act, 1882, was " clearly intended for the protection of purchasers to some extent—the question is to what extent—against that refined doctrine of imputed notice which was found very very grievous injustice to honest men, the notice being implied in a very refined manner, and brought home to a man who knew nothing about the matter, and who found that, though he had acted perfectly honestly, he was postponed by reason of the doctrine of the Court " See also the observations of CAVE, J , at p 29 of *Re Ashton, Ex p McGowan* (1891), 64 L. T. 28.

(l) See his observations, cited in note (h), *sup* , in *Allen* v *Seckham*, *sup.*, and his still

mercantile or not, though the attempts made to extend the doctrine to the principles of commercial law moved his especial abhorrence. Indeed, not he only, but the Courts generally, for a reason given by Lord LINDLEY (m), which will be readily appreciated, have shown themselves more disinclined to extend the presumptions in question to mercantile contracts than to others (n)

79. It is needless to add that the natural repugnance of judges to impute knowledge by a fiction to a person who admittedly has none, only operates where that person's ignorance is honest; and that the very same motive which encourages, in such a case, a tendency to confine the rules within the narrowest limits, promotes a contrary desire to enlarge them to the most liberal extent, where the party's actual ignorance is proved to have been fraudulent (o).

more vigorous and trenchant language, at a later date, at p 707 of *English & Scottish Mercantile Investment Co* v. *Brunton*, [1892] 2 Q. B. 700, C A., where he contemptuously repudiates any kinship between this theory and the principles of common law, and fathers it entirely upon equity ("the doctrine of constructive notice is wholly *equitable*, *it is not known to the common law*"), and then, after mentioning the common law rule as to wilful blindness for a fraudulent purpose, and stating that such rule is really not one of constructive notice at all—see note (o), *inf.*—he proceeds, in the passage cited in note (h), *sup*, to show how even the Chancery Frankensteins have become afraid of their artificial creation.

(m) In *Manchester Trust* v *Furness*, [1895] 2 Q B 539, C A, where, after citing authorities against the extension of the doctrine to commercial transactions, he concludes, at p 545 "the Courts have always set their faces resolutely against it," and adds (later on the same page) "in dealing with estates in land, title is everything, and it can be leisurely investigated; in commercial transactions possession is everything, and there is no time to investigate title, and, if we were to extend the doctrine of constructive notice to commercial transactions, we should be doing infinite mischief, and paralyzing the trade of the country"

(n) For instance, this special disinclination has been manifested in relation to the following transactions and instruments.—marine insurance, as in *Blackburn, Low & Co.* v *Vigors* (1887), 12 App. Cas 531, H L (where, at p. 542, after stating that the doctrine of constructive notice is one which "eminent judges have frequently said ought not to be extended," Lord MACNAGHTEN goes on to show that "the decision under appeal involves a great and dangerous extension of that doctrine"), debentures, as in *English & Scottish Mercantile Investment Co* v *Brunton*, *sup*, *Manchester Trust* v *Furness*, *sup*, and *Re Valletort Sanitary Steam Laundry Co*, [1903] 2 Ch. 654 (where SWINFEN EADY, J, at p 662, observes "it has frequently been said that the doctrine of constructive notice is not to be extended, and in my opinion it would be extending it to hold that the banks were affected with notice, and that their security was postponed to that of the debenture holders"), negotiable securities, as in *London Joint Stock Bank* v *Simmons*, [1892] A C 201, H L (*per* Lord HERSCHELL, at p 221 "I should be very sorry to see the doctrine of constructive notice introduced into the law of negotiable instruments"), admiralty transactions as in *The Birnam Wood*, [1907] P. 1, C A, where COZENS HARDY, L.J, at p 13, says "I think that really would be carrying the doctrine of implied notice to an extent which would be quite shocking, and must interfere with honest and legitimate business dealings," and FARWELL, L J, at p 14 "the Courts have of late years been unwilling to apply the principle of constructive notice so as to fix companies and persons with knowledge of facts of which they had no knowledge whatever")

(o) Thus Lord ESHER, M R, at pp 707, 708 of *English & Scottish Mercantile Investment Co* v. *Brunton*, [1892] 2 Q B 700, C A, is careful to explain how readily and liberally, though he refuses to allow that "constructive notice" is the right term to be applied to the process, an inference of knowledge may be drawn from proved *fraudulent* abstention from inquiry "There is," he there says, "an inference of fact known to common lawyers which comes somewhat near to it When a man has statements made to him of something which is against him, and he abstains from making further inquiry because he knows what the result would be—or, as the phrase is, he 'wilfully shuts his eyes'—then judges are in the habit of telling juries that they may infer that he did know what was against him. There is no question of constructive notice, or constructive knowledge in that inference, it is actual knowledge which is inferred" Cp the similar distinction drawn by FARWELL, L J, at p 856 of *Powell* v. *Browne* (1908), 97 L T 854, C A, in the passage cited in note (h) to § 77, *ante*.

CHAPTER III.

THE DUTY OF DISCLOSURE IN NEGOTIATIONS FOR CERTAIN CONTRACTS TERMED *UBERRIMÆ FIDEI*

80. THE first main class of transactions in respect of which a duty of disclosure arises comprises all those contracts in the negotiation for which one of the parties must, from the very nature of the transaction, have either actual or presumptive knowledge of circumstances which ordinarily are not within the actual or presumptive knowledge of the other party, and the knowledge of which is, or may be, of importance to that other party to enable him to judge of the expediency of entering into the particular contract proposed. Such contracts (of which the typical, or "prerogative example," as BACON would term it, is the contract of insurance, though there are several others) are usually, whether with strict accuracy or not (*p*), described as contracts *uberrimæ fidei.*

SECT. 1. GENERAL STATEMENT AND THEORY.

81. The governing proposition or rule, in the class of case now being dealt with, is as follows : where two parties are negotiating with reference to a contemplated contract of the above description, the party who has the private or special knowledge must disclose (in the sense and to the extent mentioned in Ch. II, Sect 1) to the party who, from the nature of the case, must necessarily depend upon him for information and instruction, all such facts as are material (in the sense described in Ch. II, Sect. 2) to the particular contract or transaction, and are within his actual or presumed knowledge (see Ch. II, Sect. 3), except such as the law presumes, and he, therefore, has a right to presume, that the other party is acquainted with, or such as he is in a position to prove by evidence that the other party was cognizant of in fact.   The duty of voluntary disclosure, in the present class of case, endures no longer than the conclusion of the contract, and only relates to such matters as come to his actual or constructive notice before that date (*pp*).   Any obligation of disclosure, as between the parties to a concluded contract, must arise, if at all, from the express or implied terms of the contract itself, or from the relation (such as that of principal and agent, partnership, trustee-ship, and the like) thereby constituted (*q*), and does not fall within the scope of the particular kind of duty now being considered

(*p*) See § 1, and note (*e*) thereto, *ante*
(*pp*) See §§ 181, 189, *post*
(*q*) See Chapter IV, *post*

82. It is now firmly established that this duty of disclosure before the conclusion of the contract is special to contracts of the nature indicated, and of which the several species are dealt with in the present chapter, and does not exist in relation to other contracts, though here and there, no doubt, there are to be found incautious judicial pronouncements (r) which, unless taken in a more restricted sense than the language used would by itself justify, or unless qualified by reference to the context or subject-matter, would seem to be in conflict with this proposition.

83. The rule is founded on the *necessitas rei*, the nature of the contract which is in course of negotiation, and the relation to one another of the parties negotiating, where the one *must* know, and the other *must* confide (s) Where two persons are treating with one another in contemplation of contracts not *uberrimæ fidei*, there is no such necessity : there is no certainty or probability, inherent in the nature of the case, that either party knows more than the other, or that either is specially dependent on the other · the conditions, so far as the law can predict, are equal : and each of the parties must suffer for his own ignorance, and is entitled to profit by his own knowledge, assuming of course that the one is not produced, and the other is not acquired, by fraud   But, where the contract is one *uberrimæ fidei*, the rule in question is a peremptory demand of elementary justice, since, without such a rule, the parties cannot be placed upon equal terms, that is to say (for, in one sense of the word, the terms can never be equal) upon such a parity as the law has the power, and is under the duty, to secure   It is the province of jurisprudence to see that a confidence which the circumstances of the case, and not his own want of care or caution, have forced upon one of the parties, shall not be defeated, and that for this purpose the knowledge which these circumstances have in the first instance placed within the exclusive possession of the other party shall be made common to both   It is in this aspect of the matter that disclosure has been often judicially characterized as a condition essential or precedent to the validity of the contract or transaction itself (t),

(r) As in *Blisset* v *Daniel* (1853), 10 Hare 493 (*per* TURNER, V-C, at p 522   "good faith is unquestionably of the essence of all contracts . . The Court presupposes in every contract, and if there can be a difference, more especially in every contract of partnership, a basis of good faith "), and in *British Equitable Insurance Co* v. *Great Western Railway Co* (1868), 38 L J (CH) 132 (*per* MALINS, V-C, at p 135 . ' in *all* matters of contract, it is the duty of *either* one of two contracting parties to communicate to the other all material facts within his knowledge *relating to the subject-matter of the contract*, and, if any such material facts be concealed, the opposite party will not be bound ").   The proposition of TURNER, V-C, though somewhat unguarded and misleading, may, if construed in a certain sense, be sound enough   but that of MALINS, V-C, is radically and hopelessly erroneous. Indeed it would be difficult to pack within the compass of a single sentence a richer collection of mistakes—see the three italicized expressions, in each of which the absence of qualification is quite contrary to both principle and authority

(s) See *Wainwright* v. *Bland* (1836), 1 M & W 32, a life insurance case, *per* PARKE, B, at p. 35 . "*from the nature of the contract*, a suppression of any material fact . .   *must* avoid the policy "), cp, as to marine insurance, *Robinson* v *Mollett* (1875), L R. 7 H L 802 (*per* BRETT, J., one of the judges summoned to assist the House, at p 817 : " when shipowners and underwriters disputed upon the effect of concealing certain facts, the Courts, finding that the contract of maritime insurance *must* be one of confidence, because the knowledge of many material facts *must of necessity be confined to the shipowner*, applied the principle of *uberrima fides* ").

(t) *Moens* v *Heyworth* (1842), 10 M. & W 147, *per* PARKE, B, at pp 157, 158, see

and, in philosophy, as amounting even to a necessity of social life. "Some may imagine," says a very acute moralist, "that, if this obligation were suspended, a general caution and mutual distrust would ensue which might do as well ; but this is imagined without considering how every hour of our lives we trust to, and depend upon others ; and how impossible it is to stir a step or, which is worse, to sit still a moment without some trust and dependence " (u).

SECT. 2. THE VARIOUS SPECIES OF CONTRACTS AND TRANSACTIONS TO WHICH THE RULE APPLIES

Sub-s. (1).   General Description.

84. The kinds of contract in the negotiation for which a duty of disclosure arises of the nature already indicated are those relating to insurance (in all its branches), sales and purchases, suretyship, releases and compromises, partnership, marriage, and the like   In all of these there are *some* material matters which must ordinarily be within the exclusive knowledge of one of the negotiating parties, and as to which the other must necessarily trust to the former, and to all of them, therefore, the duty applies alike.   There is, of course, in the case of these different species of contract, the widest possible variety both as regards the quantity and kind of matters deemed to be within the exclusive cognizance of the parties affected, and also as regards the quantity and kind of matters deemed material to be disclosed ; but this does not negative the proposition that the rule, as above stated, which operates on this varying material is one and the same rule, nor (it is submitted) does it justify the views which have occasionally been expressed that some of the contracts enumerated, such as those of vendor and purchaser, or of suretyship, are not strictly subject to the doctrine (uu), any more than the fact that a physical law operates upon different materials in a different manner ("limus ut hæc durescit, et hæc ut cera liquescit Uno eodemque igni ") prevents that law from being identically the same.   The electrical energy which expresses itself at

the citation in note (c) to § 87, *post* ; *Blackburn, Low & Co* v *Vigors* (1886), 17 Q B D. 553, C A , *per* Lord ESHER, M R , at pp 560 562, citing and approving Phillips's treatise, and (1887), 12 App Cas 531, H L , *per* Lord WATSON at p 539 (" it is, in my opinion, a *condition precedent* of every contract of marine insurance, that the insured shall make a full disclosure of all facts materially affecting the risk which are within his personal knowledge when the contract is made "), *William Pickersgill & Sons, Ltd* v *London & Provincial Marine & General Insurance Co* , [1912] 3 K B 614 (*per* HAMILTON, J , at p 621   " an implied condition contained in the contract itself, precedent to the liability of the underwriter to pay." Similarly, COCKBURN, CJ , at pp 802, 803, of *Beachey* v *Brown* (1860), E. B & E 796, observed, in the case of a contract to marry, " where it turns out that a woman is of unchaste conduct, *which goes to the very root of the contract of marriage,* there *from the . .   necessity of the case,* the man is released from the contract." At p 663 of *Elkin* v *Janson* (1845), 13 M & W 655, PARKE, B , says that the duty rests " either upon the principle that every policy is based upon the supposed existence of a certain state of facts, or on the ground that insurance" (the case happened to be one of insurance) " is a contract *uberrimæ fidei* "

(u) Paley's *Principles of Moral and Political Philosophy*, Book III, Part I, Ch. v.

(uu) See §§ 106–109, and §§ 120, 121, *post*.

one moment as light, at another as heat, at another as sound, at another as power, is not, in these various manifestations, a different, but the same force. It is the same Nasmyth's hammer which beats out a ton of metal, or puts a head on a pin

85. It is probably the use, or rather the misuse, of the perhaps unfortunately chosen term "uberrimæ fidei," which has encouraged these dubious forms of expression, as it has undoubtedly encouraged barren logomachies as to whether a particular transaction should be labelled thus or thus, with the underlying suggestion that, if one of two possible designations is correct, it falls within the *uberrimæ fidei* class, and, if the other is correct, does not ; the true view being, as has lately been held (v), that the sole questions to be asked and solved in every case are whether the nature and circumstances of the particular contract or transaction are such as (by reason of the necessarily or probably exclusive knowledge of one of the parties) to call for the application of the doctrine , and, if they are, whether the withheld facts are such as, having regard again to the nature of the particular contract, are material to be disclosed. Each of these inquiries is essential; facts of the utmost importance for one of the parties to know, if not of the kind deemed to be within the private knowledge of the other, and, conversely, facts within the exclusive cognizance of that other, if not material to the transaction, are alike exempt from the duty of disclosure. But both inquiries may be successfully pursued without affixing any name or title whatever to the contract under consideration, or deciding whether it is, or is not, proper to call it a contract *uberrimæ fidei*, or whether it has, or has not, been so denominated in the past. In the development of mercantile affairs, new types of agreement between business men are daily being invented, which it may be difficult to bring under any one of the hitherto recognized denominations , and the application of the rule to these new types might be seriously hampered by any attempt to impart an artificial rigidity to the flexible Lesbian rule of the law, or to canton out the territory on which that rule operates into defined and named provinces.

Sub-s. (2). Insurance.

86. More obviously and clearly than in the case of any other of the species to be considered, the contract of insurance invites the application of the doctrine now under consideration "In insurances, in which the underwriter computes his risk entirely from the account given by the person insured, it is absolutely necessary to the justice and validity of the contract that this account be exact and complete " (w) The contract, indeed, is a kind of wager, or a " contract of hazard," as it has been called by moralists (x),

(v) *Seaton* v *Heath*, [1899] 1 Q B. 782, C. A (*per* ROMER, L.J , at p 792 · " whether the contract be one requiring *uberrima fides* or not, must depend upon its substantial character, and how it came to be effected ")

(w) Paley, *Principles of Moral and Political Philosophy*, Book III, Part I, Ch viii.

(x) Thus Paley begins his chapter on " Contracts of Hazard " (*Principles of Moral and Political Philosophy*, Book III, Part I, Ch viii) by announcing that " by contracts of hazard or a "contract upon speculation" (y), or an "aleatory contract" (z), to use the language of judges and jurists; and, in such transactions, it has always been considered by the world that "betting on a certainty" renders the wager invalid.

87. Notwithstanding certain expressions made use of by Lord MANS-FIELD, C.J (a), and Lord ABINGER, C B. (b), which, unless duly qualified, would seem to indicate a different view, contracts of insurance (and, generally, the various types of contract to be considered in this Chapter) are distinctly marked off from all other contracts, in respect of the duty of disclosure during the negotiations preceding the conclusion of the contract (c). It is not a case of good faith being required in all contracts, and an extra or special degree of good faith being required in the contracts under discussion the law is that, whereas one duty of good faith, namely veracity, is required in negotiation for all contracts, this, and another duty of good faith, viz. candid disclosure of material facts, is demanded in negotiating for contracts of insurance, and the like.

I mean gaming and insurance," and then proceeds to illustrate the exact analogy between wagers and insurance policies in respect of the matters which ought to be, and need not be, disclosed respectively

(y) See the observations of Lord MANSFIELD, C J , at pp. 1909, 1910 of *Carter v. Boehm* (1766), 3 Burr. 1905 · "*Insurance is a contract upon speculation* The special facts upon which the contingent chance is to be computed lie most commonly in the knowledge of the insured only; the underwriter trusts to his representation, and proceeds upon con fidence that he does not keep back any circumstance in his knowledge to mislead the underwriter into the belief that the circumstance does not exist " So ROMER, L J , at p 793 of *Seaton* v. *Heath,* [1899] 1 Q B 782, C A (" contracts of insurance are generally matters of speculation, where the person desiring to be insured has means of knowledge as to the risk, and the insurer has not the means, or not the same means ")

(z) Bunyon's *Law of Life Assurance,* pp. 3, 4, in reference to one kind of life insurance (" a wager, or more aleatory contract, the premium being put at hazard upon the chance of the contingency happening or, according to Johnson's definition of a wager, ' a thing pledged upon a chance ' ")

(a) In *Carter v. Boehm,* sup , where, shortly after the passage cited in note (y), sup , he says . "the governing principle is applicable to all contracts and dealings Good faith forbids either party, by concealing what he privately knows, to draw the other into a bargain from his ignorance of that fact and his believing the contrary." This propo-sition, however,—obviously too wide as it stands,—is immediately qualified by his reference to the Ciceronian definition of culpable reticence (" aliud est celare," &c. , see § 675, post), and his further observation that " this definition of concealment, restrained to the efficient motives and precise subject of any contract, will generally hold to make it void, in favour of the party misled by his ignorance of the thing concealed."

(b) In *Cornfoot* v *Fowke* (1840), 6 M & W 358, at p 379 "a policy of insurance is a contract, and is to be governed by the same principles as govern other contracts. When it is said to be a contract *uberrimæ fidei,* this only means that the good faith, which is the basis of other contracts, is more especially required in that species of contract in which one of the parties is necessarily less acquainted with the details of the subject of the con tract than the other." This is a clearly defective statement, in that it makes the dis tinction between the class of contract referred to and all other classes to depend solely on a difference in the *degree* of good faith which is required ; whereas the difference is in *kind,* the *bona fides* essential to ordinary contracts being limited to abstention from direct and implied misrepresentation, whilst, in contracts of insurance, good faith includes full voluntary disclosure, and its requirements in such cases are not satisfied by mere veracity

(c) *Per* PARKE, B , at pp 157, 158, of *Moens* v. *Heyworth* (1842), 10 M & W 147 " the case of a policy of insurance does not seem to me analogous to the present " (which was a case of a contract for the sale of goods alleged to have been induced by misrepre-sentation) , " *those* instruments are made upon an implied contract between the parties, that everything material known to the assured shall be disclosed by them That is the

88. On the other hand, it is now well settled that the duty of disclosure equally arises whether the insurance be marine, life and health, fire, accident, or any of the innumerable varieties which the growing intricacy of human affairs and risks are continually adding to the list (*d*), and, again, as was pointed out by JESSEL, M.R (*e*), the obvious fact that what is material in one class of insurance may not be of importance in another, and that the duty attaches to different subject-matters in the several cases, does not in the least negative the fact that the rule is the same, and the duty the same, in all of them.

89. Though the rule is commonly stated in a form which assumes that the assured must always be the party on whom the duty of disclosure lies, and not the insurer, and though this mode of expressing the proposition works no harm in practice, since it is almost invariably the assured who has the exclusive knowledge, yet it must not be forgotten that, in theory and strictness, the rule is that the party who has this exclusive knowledge, *whichever party it may be*, is subject to the duty, and that party, as has been judicially recognized, may, in quite conceivable circumstances, be the insurer, and not the assured (*f*)

basis upon which the contract proceeds ; . . . In this case the plaintiff must prove a representation by words or acts . . " So BLACKBURN, J , delivering the judgment of the Q.B , says, at p 537 of *Ionides* v *Pender* (1874), L R 9 Q. B. 531 "it is perfectly well established that the law as to a contract of insurance differs from that as to other contracts "—a statement which, as Lord BLACKBURN, he repeated at p 954 of *Brownlie* v. *Campbell* (1880), 5 App. Cas. 925, H L

(*d*) *Newcastle Fire Insurance Co.* v. *Macmorran & Co* (1815), 3 Dow. App Cas 255 (per Lord ELDON, L C , at p 262), *Lindenau* v. *Desborough* (1828), 8 B & C 586 (per BAYLEY, J., at p. 592 · "in all cases of insurance, whether on ship, houses, or lives, the underwriter should be informed of every material circumstance within the knowledge of the assured "), *Jones* v *Provincial Insurance Co* (1857), 3 C B (N S) 65 (per *Cur.*, at p 86), *Wheelton* v *Hardisty* (1858), 8 E & B 232, Exch Ch (per Lord CAMPBELL, C J , at pp. 269, 270), *Brownlie* v. *Campbell*, sup (per Lord BLACKBURN at p 954 · "in policies of insurance, whether marine insurance or life insurance "), *Thomson* v *Weems* (1884), 9 App. Cas 671, H L (per Lord BLACKBURN at p 684 · "I think that on the balance of authority the same principles of insurance law apply to all insurances, whether marine, life, or fire "), *Seaton* v *Heath*, [1899] 1 Q B. 782, C A. (per ROMER, L J., at p 792) And see the citations in the next note

(*e*) In *London Assurance Co* v *Mansel* (1879), 11 C D 363, at p 367 " As regards the general principle, I am not prepared to lay down the law as making any difference in substance between one contract of insurance and another. Whether it is life, or fire, or marine assurance, I take it good faith is required in all cases, and though there may be certain circumstances from the peculiar nature of marine insurance which require to be disclosed, and which do not apply to other contracts of insurance, that is rather in my opinion an illustration of the application of the principle than a distinction in principle " To the same effect are the observations of VAUGHAN WILLIAMS, L J , at pp. 878-880 of *Joel* v *Law Union & Crown Insurance Co* , [1908] 2 K B 863, C A. For an example of the above mentioned difference in the application of the rule, see the observations of SCRUTTON, J , at p 257 of *Glasgow Assurance Corporation* v *William Symondson & Co* (1911), 104 L T 254, where he points out that the question whether the assured has previously been insured, and with whom, which is so vital in life insurance cases, has no importance in marine insurance, and need not be disclosed

(*f*) Lord MANSFIELD, C J , at p 1909 of *Carter* v *Boehm* (1766) 3 Burr 1905, is careful to point out that " the policy would be equally void against the underwriter, if *he* concealed ; as if he insured a ship on her voyage, which he privately knew to be arrived, and an action would lie to recover the premium " In *Bradford* v. *Symondson* (1881), 7 Q. B. D 456, C A , where the vessel insured had arrived before the policy was effected it was fully recognized that, if the underwriter had been aware of the arrival, the assured

90. In cases of insurance, the right to have the contract treated as void by reason of non-disclosure, where it exists, is for obvious practical reasons usually asserted by way of defence to an action for recovery of the assured sum but, in theory, it may be, and in a few cases has been, asserted by the insurer in the form of active proceedings for rescission (g)

91. The most important branch of insurance, from a juridical point of view, and the richest in illustrations of the principles of disclosure, is marine insurance. A contract of marine insurance is now defined by enactments codifying the common law of the subject (h). So also are the rules as to what must, and what need not, be disclosed, but in such exceedingly general and abstract terms as to be of little practical use (i). For the purpose of ascertaining the particular topics as to which disclosure is, or is not, essential, resort must still be had to the authorities. From these may be extracted materials for the rough classification which follows

92. In the first place, the assured must communicate to the underwriter all such actual or presumptive knowledge (see Ch. II, Sect 3, *ante*) as he has with reference to the condition and history of the vessel insured, as, for instance, the fact—this is the most obvious illustration—that she is lost, wrecked, stranded, or aground or that she is " missing," or the date of her sailing and the time which has elapsed since that date, or the storms, bad weather, accidents, or injuries she has encountered during the voyage, or while in port, or the receipt of intelligence, whether true or false, as to any of such matters (j) · but such facts as the condition of goods insured, when put

would not have been bound, and no exception was taken by the Court to this proposition when advanced in argument, at p 459, on the authority of *Carter v Boehm*, *sup*, and the leading treatises on marine insurance. It was only because admittedly the underwriter had no such knowledge that, following *Natusch v Henderson* (1871), 7 Q B D 460 n, it was held otherwise The statement in the text is involved in s 17 of the Marine Insurance Act, 1906 (6 Edw 7, c 41) "if the utmost good faith be not observed by *either party*, the contract may be avoided by the other party "

(g) See § 249, *post*.

(h) See ss 1, 2, 3 of the Marine Insurance Act, 1906, which define " a contract of marine insurance," " mixed sea and land risks," and " maritime adventure " and " maritime perils," respectively *Carter v Boehm*, *sup*, though regarded by Lord MANSFIELD, C J., and dealt with in his judgment, as a case of marine insurance, was hardly even " a mixed sea and land risk," since the subject of insurance was not a vessel at all, but a fort in the island of Sumatra, though no doubt it was exposed to, and insured against, capture by naval forces.

(i) Marine Insurance Act, 1906, ss 17, 18, 19, 21.

(j) See the following cases, in each of which the undisclosed fact is stated within brackets after the reference to the report · *Fitzherbert v Mather* (1785), 1 Term Rep. 12 (loss of ship) ; *Willes v Glover* (1804), 1 B & P. (N R) 14, 8 R R 739 (letter received by the assured from shipper of goods " I think the captain will sail to-morrow, but if the ship has not arrived when you receive this, insure as low as possible ") , *Lynch v Durnford* (1811), 14 East 494 (*intelligence* that a vessel had fallen in with the vessel insured, and had parted company with her, she being then in a leaky and perilous condition . it was held here by Lord ELLENBOROUGH, C J, at p. 497, that it made no difference to the materiality of this item of intelligence that in fact it was afterwards shown to have been false); *Bridges v. Hunter* (1813), 1 M & S 15 (date of sailing with convoy, and arrival of convoy without the ship *per* Lord ELLENBOROUGH, C J, at p. 18, and LE BLANC, J, at p 19 " it has always been considered that the time of the ship's sailing, if known to the assured, is a material fact to be communicated to the underwriter ") , *Gladstone v. King* (1813), 1 M. & S 35 (fact that the ship had been driven from her moorings by a storm in the harbour, and had struck on a rock, though she had got off again without substantial

on board, or the date of the ship's sailing, if it has no bearing on the question whether she is missing, or out of time, are not material (*h*). Where, however, machinery is insured against breakage by perils of the sea, it may be material to disclose the fact that the machinery is second-hand (*kk*)

93. Secondly, the assured must reveal all such matters within his exclusive knowledge (actual or presumed) as bear upon the war risks of the subject of the insurance, as, for example, facts showing the probability, or reasonable apprehension, of the capture of a vessel, or the recapture of a prize, or orders of foreign States affecting the safety of the ship, or the prevalence of rumours and reports as to the activity of foreign naval forces and captures of other vessels, or the identity of a dismantled and refitted vessel with a cruiser liable to capture, or the fact that the vessel insured is carrying articles which are contraband of war, and the like (*l*), but not such matters as a past and

damage but see, as to this curious case, § 249, *post*), *Sawtell v Loudon* (1814), 5 Taunt 359 (fact that the insured vessel was at sea without a convoy), *Friere v Woodhouse* (1816), Holt N P. 572, 17 R R 679 (fact that other vessels which had sailed in company with the ship insured had arrived at their destination before her, but in this case the underwriter failed, because he was presumed to have had knowledge of the fact through Lloyd's Lists), *Kirby v. Smith* (1818), 1 B & Ald 672 (fact that the assured, who was the owner of the vessel, had sailed six hours after her in another vessel, and had arrived first, after experiencing rough weather), *Rickards v Murdock* (1830), 10 B & C 527 (instructions in letter to wait 30 days to give the ship a chance of arriving, and then, if not arrived, to insure, and the date when the letter was received, though the dates when the letter was sent, and when the ship sailed, were disclosed), *Westbury v. Aberdein* (1837), 2 M. & W 267 (fact that another ship had seen the insured vessel off Oporto in a gale, having sailed from Malaga one day before her, and had parted company with her), *Elkin v Janson* (1845), 13 M & W. 655 (date, far back, of ship's sailing, and fact that, when policy effected, she was a missing ship), *Anderson v Thornton* (1853), 8 Exch 425 (true date of sailing), *Russell v Thornton* (1859), 4 H & N 788 (letter from the captain of the ship that she had been aground, and had received some very heavy blows, and had made her way in a sinking condition to the port where she then lay); *Proudfoot v Montefiore* (1867), L R 2 Q B 511 (stranding and wreck of vessel); *Nicholson v Power* (1869), 20 L T 580, Exch. Ch (vessel reported by another ship to be aground), *Cory v Patton* (1872), L R 7 Q B 304 (accident to ship, with insured goods on board, on voyage); *Morrison v Universal Marine Insurance Co* (1873), L. R 8 Exch 197, Exch Ch (intelligence that vessel aground); *Stribley v Imperial Marine Insurance Co.* (1876), 1 Q B. D. 507 (letter from the captain stating that ship had arrived at a certain port, and that he was loading, but could not say when he would be able to finish, the weather being very bad on the coast · and the *date* of this letter, and the *fact that it was the last letter from the ship*), *Blackburn, Low & Co v Vigors* (1887), 12 App Cas 531, H L, and *Same v Haslam* (1888), 21 Q B D 144 (fact, common to both cases, that a certain steamer had seen a vessel having on board some of the shipwrecked crew of the vessel insured in the former case, however, the party complaining failed, because presumptive knowledge of the undisclosed fact was not brought home to the party charged; in the latter, he succeeded, because it was) See as to the materiality of facts affecting the condition of the vessel, *Cantiniere Meccanico Brindisino v Janson*, [1912] 3 K B 452, C A, *per* VAUGHAN WILLIAMS, L J, at p 461

(*k*) As to the condition of goods, see *Boyd v. Dubois* (1811), 3 Camb 132, where Lord ELLENBOROUGH, C J, directed the jury that the assured was emphatically bound to disclose the damaged state of the cargo of hemp insured, and its liability in consequence to ferment and take fire As to the date of ship's sailing, see *Littledale v. Kenyon* (1805), 1 B. & P (N R) 151, *Beckwith v. Sydebotham* (1807), 1 Campb 115, *Foley v. Moline* (1814), 5 Taunt 430

(*kk*) *Hewitt Bros v Wilson* (1914), 30 T. L R. 619

(*l*) In *Court v Martineau* (1782), 3 Dougl. (K B) 161, it was not doubted that it was the duty of the assured to communicate to the underwriter the fact that, of two prizes insured, a brig and a ship, the brig had arrived without the ship, and that he entertained, and had expressed to his agent in London, a fear that the ship might have been recaptured, but the party complaining failed, because in this case he was shown to have presumptive knowledge of the undisclosed fact. In *Bell v. Bell* (1810), 2 Campb 475, where the

B N D   F

abandoned design of the enemy, or an edict of a foreign State which has never been acted on, and has always been treated as a dead letter (m)

94. Next, exclusive knowledge of facts relating to places of loading or discharge must be communicated ; as, for example, that the vessel insured is proceeding to a place which is not known as a port, or to a port of a specially dangerous character (n)

95. Further, the assured must divulge any " over-insurance, so large as to be material to be considered by a prudent underwriter " (nn) ; and, in cases of valued policies, he must disclose the real value of the subject of the insurance, where such real value is so greatly below the agreed value as to lead to a reasonable suspicion in the mind of the underwriter that the insurance was intended as a mere cloak for illegal gaming, or was part of a fraudulent design, but not otherwise (o)

---

plaintiff had effected a policy on ship and freight from Riga to the United Kingdom, the alleged undisclosed facts, which had been communicated to him in a letter from his Riga correspondent, were (i) that there had been an order to send the ship's papers to Petersburg, (ii) that the ship's papers had been so sent, and (iii) that the order had created a great sensation at Riga, and the writer himself entertained grave apprehensions as to the ship's safety. No one doubted the materiality of facts (i) and (ii), but they were shown to have been both duly disclosed, and in view of the disclosure of these two, which were the really important matters, Lord ELLENBOROUGH, C J , invited the jury not to pay much regard to the non disclosure of (iii) In *Durrell* v *Bederley* (1816), Holt N P 283 , 17 R. R 639, where the policy was on a ship having letters of marque as a privateer, the material undisclosed fact was the prevalence in Jersey, for some weeks past, of reports that a French frigate had been seen about the coast, and had effected a capture *Bates* v. *Hewitt* (1867), L R 2 Q. B 595, was a case of non disclosure of the fact that the vessel insured, lately dismantled and turned into a merchant vessel, had originally been a Confederate cruiser, and, as such, was liable to capture by the United States. In *London & Provincial Insurance Co* v *Seymour* (1873), L R 17 Eq. 85, the fact withheld, and the suppression of which BACON, V C , at p 89, characterized as grossly fraudulent, was " that the shippers had contracted with the Confederate Government to send articles contraband of war in the ship which was insured."

(m) Thus, in *Carter* v *Boehm* (1766), 3 Burr 1905, Lord MANSFIELD, C J , held that there was no duty on the assured to disclose the fact that, a year previously, a design of the French upon Fort Marlborough, the subject of the insurance, had been entertained, and abandoned , and in *Fracis, Times & Co* v *Sea Insurance Co.* (1898), 79 L. T 28, where the action was brought in respect of a total loss of arms and ammunition by capture, BIGHAM, J , considered that the assured was not bound to communicate the fact that by an edict of the Persian Government in 1881, which had never been acted upon, and had ever since been generally regarded as a *brutum fulmen*, the importation of arms and ammunition into Persia had been prohibited.

(n) *Harrower* v. *Hutchison* (1870), L R 5 Q B. 584, Exch. Ch , where the undisclosed fact was that the vessel was going to Laguna de Los Padres, in the Province of Buenos Ayres, a place not known or recognized as a port of loading or discharge ; *Laing* v. *Union Marine Insurance Co* (1895), 1 Comm Cas 11, where the assured withheld the fact that a certain port in Japan was one of special difficulty and danger

(nn) *William Pickersgill & Sons, Ltd* v *London & Provincial Marine Insurance Co.,* [1912] 3 K B 614 (*per* HAMILTON, J., at p 619). Cp. *Gooding* v *White* (1913), 29 T L R 312

(o) *Herring* v *Jackson* (1895), 1 Comm Cas 177, an action on a valued policy at £5000 on the plaintiff's yacht "Mohican," to which the defendant pleaded (i) *fraudulent* concealment of the real cost and value of the yacht, which was much less than £5000, and alternatively (ii) innocent non-disclosure of the above. The jury negatived (i), and as to (ii), MATHEW, J , at pp 178, 179, laid down the rule as stated in the text, relying for this purpose on the opinion expressed by WILLES, J , in his " Memorandum on Over Insurance, Valued Policy, &c " (1867), used by the Commission on Unseaworthy Ships which sat in 1874, and on Phillips's *Law of Insurance* (Boston, 1853), § 1183, cited and approved by WILLES, J , in this Memorandum The jury found, in answer to two questions directed to the point, and applying the principles laid down by MATHEW, J , that the valuation in this case was *not* " excessive," and that it was *not* ' material to the underwriters to know

96. Where the insurance is on chartered freight, or is a reinsurance on the terms of the original policy, it is the duty of the assured to communicate to the underwriter any unusual clause or condition in the charter-party, or in the original policy, as the case may be (p); but not any terms or clauses which are in common use and established, for of these the underwriter has presumptive notice (q).

97. Where there are two facts within the knowledge of the assured, one of which is wholly meaningless and unimportant to the underwriter except in the light of the other, the assured does not discharge his duty of disclosure by revealing the first, without the second, or excuse his non-performance of such duty by proof that the underwriter had notice of the first fact only (r).

what the vessel had cost the insured" On the other hand, in *Ionides* v *Pender* (1874), L. R. 9 Q. B 531, where the assured had not revealed to the underwriters the fact that "insurances were made by him, and others in concert with him, on interests alleged to be at risk in the vessel, at values greatly exceeding the actual values of those interests" (per Cur., at p 533), "so that the assured stood to receive a very large profit if their venture was lost" (pp. 534, 535), the jury in answer to questions left to them by HANNEN, J , at the trial, of the same character as those addressed to the jury in the case last cited, found that the valuations *were* excessive, and that, whether fraudulent or not (as to which they could not agree), it *was* material to the underwriters to know that they were; and the Court refused to disturb these findings, pointing out (pp. 538, 539) that "the excessive valuation may lead to the suspicion of foul play," which was of itself sufficient to render over valuation conceivably material, and to support the "distinct and uncontradicted evidence" (p 539) which underwriters had given at the trial that it was so in fact in this case So, in *Thames & Mersey Marine Insurance Co* v. *Gunford Ship Co*, [1911] A C 529, H L , it was held by the House of Lords, reversing the Court of Session, that a double insurance of freight, wages, &c , to the extent of £35,000, whereas the risk was only £14,000, amounted to an over-valuation which, in the circumstances, was a direct incentive and temptation to nefarious conduct, being, in fact, "an insurance *for* loss, and *not against* loss," as one of the witnesses had pithily expressed it, and, therefore, a matter essential to be disclosed (Lord ALVERSTONE at pp 534–540 , Lord SHAW at pp 542–547, and Lord ROBSON at pp. 550, 551)

(p) *Mercantile Steamship Co* v. *Tyser* (1881), 7 Q. B D 73, where the policy was on chartered freight, and there was a clause in the charter party giving the charterers an option to cancel it if the vessel did not arrive at New York by a specified date, and where, after evidence on the point, Lord COLERIDGE, C J (see p 77), expressed the view that this clause was "of recent introduction," as to which there was no uniform practice, and therefore constituted "a fact which the assured was bound to disclose to the underwriter" Cp *Property Insurance Co* v. *National Protector Insurance Co* (1913), 108 L T. 104

(q) The following were considered to be usual clauses and provisions, and, as such, not subject to the duty of disclosure .—the "24 hours" clause in a time charter, in *The Bedouin*, [1894] P 1, C A (per GORELL BARNES, J , at p 9, and Lord ESHER, M R , at pp 12, 13) , a condition in a charter party for a lump sum that all freight earned by the ship should be for the account of the charterers, in *Asgar & Co.* v *Blundell*, [1896] 1 Q B. 123, C. A (per KAY, L.J , at pp 133, 134) , a clause in an original policy—the action being on a policy of reinsurance—that "should the vessel be at sea or abroad on the expiration of this policy, it is agreed to hold her covered till her arrival at her final port of destination . at a *pro ratâ* daily premium," in *Charlesworth* v *Faber* (1900), 5 Comm Cas 408 (per BIGHAM, J , who, after hearing evidence, at pp 411, 412, came to the conclusion that the clause, which was one of those known as "Elder Dempster & Co.'s clauses," was in common knowledge and use).

(r) Thus, in *Lynch* v. *Dunsford* (1811), 14 East 494, which was an action on a valued policy on goods on board a *ship or ships*, at and from the Canary Islands to London, the defendants had presumptive knowledge, through a notice stuck up on a board at Lloyd's, that a certain ship had fallen in with a vessel called "The President" from Lanzarette, and had left her in a distressed and leaky condition, but this announcement conveyed nothing whatever to them without the knowledge, which the plaintiff omitted to impart to them, that "The President" was one of the unnamed "ships" referred to in the policy, and Lord ELLENBOROUGH, C J , at p 497, who was affirmed by the Exchequer Chamber, held that the plaintiff, having failed in his duty to disclose the fact which alone gave

98. The following are miscellaneous examples, not strictly falling under any of the foregoing heads, of matters which juries, or judges sitting without juries, have found to be material, and, as such, subject to the duty of disclosure, unless the underwriter is presumed in law to be cognizant of them. Where policies had been effected on sugar on boats and lighters, while loading and unloading, and until finally delivered at the assured's sugar refinery, the jury found that an agreement made by the assured with a certain lighterman whereby the latter was to be liable for negligence only, and to that extent was to be exempt from his common law liability as a common carrier, was a fact material to be disclosed (s)   In the case of a policy upon the freight of (inter alia) frozen apples, it was considered that an agreement whereby the freight on these apples was liable to be lost if the steamer did not arrive at Hobart by a certain date was material, and ought to have been disclosed (t). Where four open policies had been underwritten at successive dates for certain sums on fruit and produce from Greece to London or Liverpool by any steamers on which such goods might be shipped from time to time, which shipments were to be declared and valued as interest might appear, it was held, in an action on the later policies, that the non-disclosure of the full value of the shipments under the earlier policies was such a concealment as was sufficient to avoid the policies sued upon (tt)   So, also, as to the concealment of the fact that the policy sued upon was intended as a mere bet on the arrival of the vessel at a certain place within a certain time (ttt).   In other cases, the materiality of such circumstances as an agreement for the detention of the vessel insured or her employment at other places and times

---

significance to the known fact, failed in his action also   Similarly, in *Leigh* v *Adams* (1871), 25 L T 566, where the plaintiff having insured quantities of cochineal shipped from the Canaries on a floating policy, on terms of declaring the name of the ship upon receipt of each bill of lading, failed to communicate either of the following facts,—(i) an anonymous letter stating that the owners intended to lose a certain vessel called " The Candida " on her next voyage, (ii) the fact that a cargo of cochineal was to be shipped for him on board this vessel   It was assumed by the Court of Queen's Bench (COCKBURN, C J , and LUSH and HANNEN, JJ) , though COCKBURN, C J , appears to have been of a different opinion, that the defendants had constructive notice of (i), the letter having been posted up at Lloyd's, but it was held that, the plaintiff, not having disclosed (ii), had failed to reveal the fact in conjunction with and in the light of which alone the defendants' knowledge of the other fact could have been of any use to them
    (s) *Tate & Sons* v *Hyslop* (1885), 15 Q B D 368, C A.
    (t) *Scottish Shire Line, Ltd* v *London & Provincial Marine & General Insurance Co* , [1912] 3 K B 51.   At pp 70, 71, HAMILTON, J., explains how, on the evidence before him, the materiality is made out to his satisfaction . " the risk, if there was no date in this contract, would merely be that when the vessel arrived at Hobart there would be no apples, in which case she could not earn freight by carrying them, and that she might be prevented from arriving at Hobart while there were apples to ship by perils of the sea. Considering that she was about to leave English waters at the end of the year, and considering that the apple season at Hobart appears to extend for about two months, the underwriter would have a very considerable time in which the vessel might arrive and save her freight   If the time is to be about the 20th March, the risk is materially altered, and the likelihood of the underwriter being called upon to pay in the event of accident is considerably increased "
    (tt) *Rivaz* v. *Gerussi Bros & Co* (1880), 6 Q B D. 222, C A
    (ttt) *Gedge* v. *Royal Exchange Assurance Corpn* , [1900] 2 Q B 214, *per* KENNEDY, J , at pp. 222, 223, who there so held, independently of the other ground of his decision, which was that the policy was illegal (p 219).

and for other purposes than those which were immediately contemplated, or an unusual mode or place of taking in, or loading, or stowing, her cargo, has been judicially recognized, though the underwriter in each case failed to make good his defence by reason of his presumptive knowledge of the undisclosed facts (u).

99. Generally, it may be stated that it is not all matters even of importance, or which would affect the mind of some underwriters, which must be disclosed; but only those which have a direct relation to, and bearing upon, the subject-matter of a marine policy (v), or which, whether strictly so related or not, "would affect the judgment of a rational underwriter governing himself by the principles and calculations on which underwriters do in practice act" (vv). Whenever one or other of these conditions has not been present, the underwriter has failed in his defence of non-disclosure (w).

(u) See *Salvador* v. *Hopkins* (1765), 3 Burr 1707 (an agreement to detain the insured vessel—an East India ship—for a year longer in India than the enlarged time provided for by the charter party), *Ougier* v *Jennings* (1800), 1 Campb 504 n (trip of insured vessel to Sydney in ballast to take in a cargo of coals, the insurance being on fish at and from Newfoundland to a port in Portugal); *Vallance* v *Dewar* (1808), 1 Campb 503 (employment of ship in "banking" or fishing on the "bank" of Newfoundland, whereby the voyage home was, it was urged, turned from a summer voyage into a winter one); *Kingston* v *Knibbs* (1809), 1 Campb 508 n. (fact that the ship took in part of her cargo inside, and part outside the bar of Oporto), *Da Costa* v *Edwards* (1815), 4 Campb 142 (the fact that the 40 carboys of vitriol, the subject of the insurance, were carried on deck, and loaded and stored in a manner alleged to be dangerous) In none of the above cases was it suggested that the undisclosed facts were not material but in all of them it was decided that the several facts were in accordance with well-known practices and usages of the trade or locality to which the insurance related, and that consequently the underwriters had presumptive notice thereof

(v) Per SCRUTTON, J, at p 257 of *Glasgow Assurance Corporation* v *William Symondson & Co* (1911), 104 L. T. 254

(vv) *Ionides* v. *Pender* (1874), L R 9 Q B 531, *per Cur*, at p 539 It was here considered that over-valuation, though in one sense extraneous to the risk, comes within this second principle. Cp the American fire insurance case cited in note (w) to § 104, *post*.

(w) In *Gandy* v *Adelaide Marine Insurance Co* (1871), L R 6 Q B 746, where the policy, the ship of which was initialled in November, 1869, was on a bark which had been classed A1 in Lloyd's Register for 7 years in November, 1865, the assured omitted to communicate to the underwriter the fact that, when the vessel was due for the usual "half-time survey" in the 4th year, he had expressed his intention of not undergoing the survey, the effect of which would be that she would be struck off the register BRETT, J, at the trial, left to the jury the question whether this fact was material or not They answered the question in the negative, and the Court of Q B discharged the rule which had been obtained for a new trial In *Lebon & Co* v. *Straits Insurance Co* (1894), 10 T L R 517, C A, the C. A. agreed with CHARLES, J, as to the immateriality of the undisclosed fact that the plaintiff, having previously insured goods on board the same vessel with the Globe Insurance Co, had been told by their representative three or four months afterwards that "they would like to be off the risk," Lord ESHER, M R, observing at p 518 "it was admitted that, as a rule, the assured was not bound to state what another underwriter had said, as that he had refused to take the risk, or even that, a week after he had accepted the insurance, he had expressed a wish to be released, but it was suggested that, where an underwriter had expressed a wish three or four months after he had taken the risk, this was a fact that the assured was bound to disclose, because it indicated a belief that some evil had happened to the ship It was clear, however, that it did not amount to a statement that the ship had probably sustained some injury, but it merely showed that the underwriter, perhaps because he had been insuring too much, did not wish to run the particular risk any longer " In *Thames & Mersey Marine Insurance Co.* v *Gunford Ship Co.*, [1911] A C 529, H L, one of the alleged undisclosed facts, viz the master's very bad record,—he had not been to sea for 22 years, had lost his last ship, and his certificate had been suspended for six months,—was held both by the Court of

100. Second only in importance to contracts of marine insurance are
life and health policies. A contract of life insurance has been defined as a
contract " in which one party agrees to pay a given sum upon the happening
of a particular event contingent upon the duration of human life, in consideration of the immediate payment of a smaller sum, or certain equivalent
periodical payments, by another " (x) ; but, having regard to the modern
endowment policies, and innumerable other new forms of assurance, the
introduction of which is mainly due to the business ingenuity and inventive-
ness of the United States, it cannot be said that the above definition is now
adequate Its connotation is too wide, and its denotation too narrow. It
is submitted that every agreement by one person to pay a sum, or series of
sums, of money to another person on the happening of an event contingent
upon the duration of human life in consideration of the payment by the
other person of a sum, or series of sums, certain, at a date or dates prior to
the happening of such event, is a contract of life assurance. For the purposes
of a modern statute dealing with assurance business of various kinds, a
" policy upon human life " means " any instrument by which the payment
of money is assured on death (except death by accident only) or the happening
of any contingency dependent on human life, or any instrument evidencing
a contract which is subject to the payment of premiums for a term dependent
upon human life " (y)

101. Whichever of the above may be taken as the correct definition of a
contract of life insurance, it is clear that the uncertain event upon which
the wager is made is the duration of the life which is the subject of the insurance, and, therefore, that in every such contract, and also in contracts of
insurance against disease, the matters to be disclosed by the assured must
be all those, but those only, which, being within his exclusive knowledge,
have a bearing upon the assured person's chances of life or health This is
the effect of the authorities, though the number of actual cases decided on
the pure question of what amount and kind of disclosure is sufficient to satisfy
the common law duty is exceedingly small, for the simple reason that it has
long become the almost universal practice of insurance companies for their

Session and the House of Lords (somewhat strangely, it may be thought,—indeed, at p 541,
Lord SHAW expressed grave doubts) to be immaterial In *Glasgow Assurance Corporation
v. William Symondson & Co* (1911), 104 L T 254, the plaintiffs, who had by a general
" treaty " with the defendants undertaken to reinsure marine risks to be selected by them,
sued for rescission of this " treaty," and also of certain policies which, pursuant thereto,
they had underwritten by way of reinsurance, when tendered to them by the defendants
for that purpose, on the ground (amongst others) that the defendants had not disclosed
the following facts   (i) that similar " treaties " to the above had previously resulted in
loss to the underwriters, (ii) that the defendants knew that *this* " treaty " must so result
in loss to the plaintiffs, and (iii) that the defendants had a system whereby some of the
risks selected and tendered for reinsurance were risks which they themselves undertook.
SCRUTTON, J , at pp 257, 258, expressed his opinion that none of the above facts were
material He had some little doubt as to (iii), but, after noting that the defendants had
called no evidence of underwriters on the point, which, if capable of being adduced, would
obviously have been of the utmost importance, concluded (p 258)   " I find that the
intention of the broker to declare his own underwriting partners as assured, who would
make a profit by difference of premiums, was not a fact material to be disclosed "
    (x) Bunyon's *Law of Life Assurance*, p. 1
    (y) Assurance Companies Act, 1909 (9 Edw 7, c. 49), s 30

own supposed protection—though whether they have derived any real advantage from so doing, is extremely doubtful (z)—to exact "contracts for the truth" by asking a number of specific questions, and making the accuracy of the answers to these questions, and also the complete disclosure of everything material as to which no specific inquiry has been made, the "basis" and foundation of the contract itself. From this it results that nearly all the authorities on life insurance law are merely so many decisions on the construction of these express warranties, conditions, or contracts for disclosure, the only question in each case being whether the contract, properly construed, has been performed or not. No question of the obligation of the assured to communicate material facts which are not the subject of his agreement usually arises, though in contemplation of law that obligation still exists (a), because, in most of such cases the attention of the Court is naturally diverted to, and concentrated upon, the contract itself, and, as regards the materiality of facts which *are* the subject of the specific inquiries, and of the warranted answers and declarations, there can be no discussion whatever, since it is the very office and effect of a warranty or condition to preclude the possibility of any such discussion (b). Still, after excluding all reported cases relating *solely* to non-compliance with a term or warranty in a contract which expressly provides that such non-compliance shall render it void, there remains a small *fasciculus* of authorities in which are to be found either decisions, or judicial propositions (other than mere *obiter dicta*), as to the non-contractual obligation of disclosure, and the classes of facts required by the law, apart from any agreement between the parties, to be divulged in order to comply with such obligation. Amongst these may be included decisions as to the truth of an affirmative answer to a completely general question, such as—"Do you know of any other circumstances which the directors ought to be acquainted with?" (c), or as to whether there has been a satisfaction of some equally general condition in the contract, such as a condition that "if any . information necessary to be made known to the company has been withheld, . the assurance shall be absolutely null and void" (d); because the only effect of such a question is to inquire whether the common law duty of disclosure has been performed, and the only effect

(z) As to this, see § 171, *post*
(a) *Joel* v *Law Union & Crown Insurance Co*, [1908] 2 K B 863, C A, *per* VAUGHAN WILLIAMS, L J, at pp 876–878, and MOULTON, L J, at pp 892, 893.
(b) See § 170, *post*
(c) As in *Lindenau* v *Desborough* (1828), 8 B & C 586 (*per* Lord TENTERDEN, C.J, at pp 591, 592 "admitting this not to fall within any of the specific questions, still the general question put by the office requires information of every fact which any reasonable man would think material"), and in *Hutton* v *Waterloo Life Assurance Co* (1859), 1 F & F. 735 In *Jones* v *Provincial Insurance Co* (1857), 3 C B (N S) 65, the general question was—"are you aware of any disorder or circumstance tending to shorten life, or to render an insurance on your [his] life more than ordinarily hazardous?" So also in *Swete* v. *Fairlie* (1833), 6 C & P. 1. In a horse insurance case of *Taylor* v *Yorkshire Insurance Co*, [1910] 2 Ir R 1, there was a warranty that no "important information" had been withheld.
(d) See *Thomson* v *Weems* (1884), 9 App Cas 671, at p 680 Cp the similar condition in the fire insurance case of *Pimm* v. *Lewis* (1862), 2 F. & F 778, cited in note (w) to § 104, *post*

of such a condition is to stipulate that the common law duty shall be performed, whence it follows that any decision that the question has not been truthfully answered, or the condition not duly complied with, must necessarily be a decision that the party has not revealed some material fact within his knowledge that it was " necessary " for the insurers to know, and " ought " not to have been withheld from them,—in other words, has failed to discharge the obligation of disclosure which, without such question or express condition, would have been incumbent on him, and would have been a condition in law of the validity of the contract. And where a specific question is not answered at all, the case becomes of course one of non-disclosure, pure and simple (e). Further, some of the cases as to misrepresentation inducing a contract of life insurance, other than cases of misrepresentation in answer to a question where the truth of the answer is warranted, are relevant in so far as it was either decided, or assumed on the basis of the decision, that the facts alleged to have been misrepresented were material ; for any fact of which a misrepresentation is material may also (though it need not necessarily) be a fact which it is material to disclose (f)

102. It being well established, as has already been pointed out (g), that the assured is under a duty of disclosure in life assurances as much as in marine, or in any other, the difference being only in the application of the rules and the kind of matters deemed material in the several branches, it only remains to give illustrations of the circumstances which have been found or held or assumed to be necessary and proper subjects of disclosure in the branch now under discussion These comprise the following :—existing or past disease, if of such a character as substantially to affect the expectation of life (h), but not otherwise (i), and if known to the person whose life is insured both to exist and to answer to the above description, which is often not the case (j), the habits and manner of living of the assured, or other person

(e) See *London Assurance Co* v. *Mansel* (1879), 11 C D 363, *per* JESSEL, M R, at p 369. Cp *Re General Provincial Life Assurance Co, Ex p Daintree* (1870), 18 W R 396
(f) See generally, for these cases, Lord Halsbury's *Laws of England,* title " Insurance," vol xvii, pp. 550–554
(g) In § 88, and notes (d) and (e) thereto, *ante*
(h) *Maynard* v *Rhodes* (1824), 5 Dowl & Ry 266, 27 R R 526 (disorder of long standing), *Morrison* v *Muspratt* (1827), 4 Bing 60 (severe pulmonary complaint), *Lindenau* v *Desborough,* *sup* (tumour in brain, and impairment of mental faculties, &c), *Duckett* v *Williams* (1834), 2 C & K 348 (" a disease which tended to shorten life "—not stated what—*per Cur,* at p 350) ; *Foster* v *Mentor Life Assurance Co* (1854), 3 E & B. 48 ; *Joel* v *Law Union & Crown Insurance Co, inf* (mental and nervous breakdown)
(i) Thus in *Watson* v *Mainwaring* (1813), 4 Taunt 763, it was held that a disease which does not *generally* result in shortening life is not one which " tends " to do so, though in fact the assured died of it This was assumed also in *Geach* v *Ingall* (1845), 14 M & W 95, but the insurers succeeded in that case because, in addition to general questions they had framed a specific question—" have you had any spitting of blood ? "—which was falsely answered in the negative, and it was held that the question and answer were directed to the *fact,* and not the disease, because the *fact* might, to the expert, though not to the assured, be symptomatic of disease Even here, however, it was pointed out that only such " spitting of blood " was material to be disclosed as was *capable* of being regarded by a medical man as a symptom, not every spitting of blood, such as (*e.g*) would follow the extraction of a tooth
(g) *Per* MOULTON, L J, at pp 884, 885, of *Joel* v *Law Union & Crown Insurance Co,* [1908] 2 K B 863, C A. For illustrations of questions put to the jury in such a form as to leave it open to them to find for the plaintiff, if they thought that the assured *bona fide*

whose life is the subject of the insurance, in so far as those habits tend to injure health (*k*); the fact of "the life" having been previously insured by other offices (*l*); the person for whose benefit the insurance is effected (*m*), and other matters "tending to increase the hazard, or to affect the question of the life being an eligible or proper object of insurance" (*mm*), and which the prudent insurer would take into consideration before accepting the risk (*n*). As to the name of the usual family doctor, or the most recent medical attendant, of "the life," it may be doubted whether it would be considered a duty on the part of the assured to communicate such facts in the absence of contract or express inquiry, though of course a misrepresentation as to the matter in answer to a specific question, where the truth of every answer is warranted, would render the policy void (*o*): and, even when there is no such warranty, the concealment of the name of the physician or surgeon who treated or operated on "the life" for a serious disorder or injury, where that disorder or injury has also been concealed, may be considered the suppression of a material fact (*p*).

did not realize that his experiences constituted a disease, see *Swete* v. *Fairlie* (1833), 6 C & P. 1 (at p. 8), *Jones* v. *Provincial Insurance Co* (1857), 3 C B (N s.) 65 (at p 86), *Fowkes* v. *Manchester & London Life Insurance Co*, No. 1 (1862), 3 F & F 440 (*per* COCKBURN, C J., at pp 443, 444) In all the above, the jury found that the "life" was not aware of the disease in the sense indicated On the other hand, in *Hutton* v. *Waterloo Life Assurance Co* (1859), 1 F. & F 735, they found that he was so aware

(*k*) *Everett* v *Desborough* (1829), 5 Bing 503 (habits of intoxication), *Hutton* v *Waterloo Life Assurance Co*, *sup* (the like, followed by delirium tremens), *Thomson* v *Weems* (1884), 9 App Cas 671, H L (habitual and heavy drinking, followed by hepatitis)

(*l*) *Wainwright* v *Bland* (1836), 1 M & W 32 (where the jury found, in answer to questions left to them by the judge, that certain representations as to insurances with other offices, and also as to the person for whose benefit the policy sued upon had been effected, were material), *London Assurance Co* v *Mansel* (1879), 11 C D 363 (*per* JESSEL, M R, who, at pp 369–372, expressed a very decided opinion as to the materiality of the undisclosed fact that the life of the assured had been declined by other offices) The view of MALINS, V-C, to the contrary, at p 307 of *Re General Provincial Life Assurance Co.*, *Ex p Daintree* (1870), 18 W R 396, is incorrect.

(*m*) *Wainwright* v *Bland*, *sup*

(*mm*) *Per* Lord DENMAN, C J, at p 333 of *Rawlins* v *Desborough* (1840), 2 M. & Rob. 328

(*n*) In *Huguenin* v. *Rayley* (1815), 6 Taunt 186, the fact suppressed was that the woman whose life was insured had been confined in the county gaol for debt, and the Court considered that, as this fact may have affected her health, it was capable of being found material by the jury, though they held that the trial judge was quite wrong in taking upon himself to hold, as matter of law, that the fact *must* be material, and in nonsuiting the plaintiff on that view In *Traill* v *Baring* (1864), 4 De G J & S 318, one life assurance society successfully sued another for rescission of a policy of reinsurance on a certain life, on the ground of (*inter alia*) non-disclosure by the defendant society of the fact that, before the policy was effected, they had abandoned their professed intention, upon the basis of which the negotiations had been instituted, to join with the plaintiffs and a third society in the transaction on the terms of the three societies taking the risk in equal shares (*per* KNIGHT-BRUCE, L J, at p 326, and TURNER, L J, at pp 329, 330) See also *Rawlins* v *Desborough*, *sup* (non-disclosure of certificate as to health by medical officer of insurance company whose risk the plaintiffs were reinsuring)

(*o*) As in *Everett* v *Desborough* (1829), 5 Bing. 503 See also *Hutton* v *Waterloo Life Assurance Co* (1859), 1 F & F 735

(*p*) It was held by the Court of C P in *Morrison* v *Muspratt* (1827), 4 Bing 60, that a circumstance so withheld might well be thought by the jury, and probably was, material, and the judge at the trial having ignored the question of non disclosure, directing the jury to find merely whether there had been misrepresentation or not, a new trial was ordered (*per* BEST, C J, at p 62 "whether or not it was material for the defendants to have been made acquainted with the fact which has been withheld from their knowledge,

103. Insurances against destruction of, or injury to, property by fire, lightning, hail, tempest, or otherwise arising from the action of the elements, are, like marine insurances, contracts of indemnity (q), differing herein from life insurances (r), and most forms of insurance against disease, or loss of or injury to a limb by accident, and the like, in which the contract is to pay a specific sum of money, whether the payment of such sum operates as more, or less, than full compensation to the assured in the circumstances of the case   On the other hand, they have this feature in common with life insurances, that the contract is usually expressed to be for a year, but automatically renewable for further terms of one year, so long as the annual premiums are paid at the stipulated dates, or within the agreed or customary period " of grace " (s).

104. To fire and the other insurances above enumerated, and indeed to all the many different forms of insurance which mercantile prudence has sought for, and speculative ingenuity has offered, the same rule of *uberrima fides* is applied which obtains in marine and life assurances ; though the facts considered material are of course relative in each case to the character and subject-matter of the contract in question   But, here again, the required disclosure is so habitually provided for by the contract itself, or made the subject of question and answer, or complicated with issues of misrepresentation, that these last-mentioned branches of insurance are even more unproductive

is a question for the jury.   It is probable, however, it would be esteemed material, because all insurance offices are desirous to consult with the medical man who has been last in attendance on the life insured ")   In *Cazenove* v *British Equitable Assurance Co* (1860), 29 L. J (c p) 160, Exch. Ch , it was recognized that it was quite open to the jury to find, if they thought fit to do so, that the names of the doctors specially consulted as to a grave malady were material to be disclosed, but in this case the jury found otherwise, and their verdict could not be disturbed   it is true that the Exchequer Chamber held that the insurance company was entitled to succeed, but this was solely on the separate and distinct ground of non-compliance with an express condition as to the truth of answers to questions   In *British Equitable Insurance Co* v *G W Ry Co* (1869), 38 L J (ch) 314, it was decided that the suppression of a grave disorder, and the fact that the assured had consulted a specialist for it, was fraudulent   In *Joel* v *Law Union & Crown Insurance Co* , [1908] 2 K B 863, C A , it was found by the jury (*inter alia*) that the fact that the deceased had consulted a certain doctor for a nervous breakdown in the year 1894 was material for the company to know in considering whether they could insure her life ; and it was not attempted in the Court of Appeal to disturb this finding, though a new trial was ordered on other grounds   And, since the C A had held that, on the true construction of the documents, there was no term that the answers of the assured should be the basis of the contract, this, like the former case, was one of pure non disclosure. As to matters considered material in miscellaneous cases of insurance, see cases cited in note (t), *inf* (refusal to renew insurance, malformation of animal, &c.)

(q) *Dalby* v *India & London Life Assurance Co* (1854), 15 C B 365, *per* PARKE, B , at p 387 ·   " policies of assurance against fire and against marine risks are both properly contracts of indemnity "

(r) *Ibid* , *per* PARKE, B., at the same page   " this species of insurance "—he is dealing with life insurance—" in no way resembles a contract of indemnity."

(s) Unless, it is expressly, or, as in *Stokell* v. *Heywood*, [1897] 1 Ch. 459, impliedly agreed otherwise, and it is made clear that only one contract for one year is intended, with liberty to the parties to make a fresh contract on the expiration of that year for a further year, or a succession of yearly contracts at the expiration of each succeeding year.   But, even in the ordinary type of contract, it seems to have been thought by CRESSWELL, J —see p 25 of *Pim & Rogers* v *Reid* (1843), 6 M & G 1—that each renewal by payment of the premium, though no fresh proposal is required, may possibly be regarded as constituting a new contract

than life insurances have been shown to be (t), of authority in illustration of the pure non-contractual duty of disclosure. After eliminating all cases of breach of contractual liability to give information of specified kinds of circumstances before the conclusion of the contract, or of altered circumstances during the currency of the policy (u), and all cases amounting to neither more nor less than misrepresentation (v), there scarcely remains a single decision on the question of what is, or is not, considered material to be disclosed by the assured to the insurer, pursuant solely to the general duty of disclosure, in cases of insurances other than marine and life insurance (w).

(t) See § 101, ante. Miscellaneous cases of this class are *Taylor* v *Yorkshire Insurance Co*, [1913] 2 Ir R. 1 (a stallion), *Thornton Smith* v *Motor Union Insurance Co.* (1913), 30 T. L. R 139 (a motor car).

(u) Such as *Pim & Rogers* v. *Reid*, sup, and *Sillem* v. *Thornton* (1854), 3 E & B 868, according to the view of that case taken by POLLOCK, C B, at p. 337 of *Stokes* v. *Cox* (1856), 1 H & N 320

(v) Such as *Dobson* v *Sotheby* (1827), M & M 90 (alleged misdescription of the character of the building insured)

(w) The writer has only been able to discover the following (that is, amongst British authorities). In *Bufe* v. *Turner* (1815), 6 Taunt 338, the plaintiff was the owner of two warehouses, one of which was next but one to a boat builder's shop On the 11th July, 1814, a fire broke out in this shop, but was extinguished in half an hour, and the plaintiff, in his capacity of magistrate in that district, employed men to watch and guard those premises. On the same day, he sent instructions by special conveyance (the mail having left) to his London agent to insure that one of his two warehouses which was near the boatbuilder's shop, *but not the other* The letter reached London on the 24th, and the policy was effected on the 25th On the morning of the 13th, another fire broke out in the boatbuilder's shop, and the plaintiff's insured warehouse was burnt down At the trial of an action on the policy, to which the defendants pleaded non-disclosure of the above facts in relation to the boat builder's shop, "the jury acquitted the plaintiff of any fraud or dishonest design, but thought that the circumstance of the fire on the 11th ought to have been communicated to the defendants who, without this information, did not engage on fair grounds with the plaintiff, and for whom under those circumstances they gave their verdict" (p 340), and this verdict the Court declined to disturb In *Pimm* v *Lewis* (1862), 2 F & F 778, which was an action on a fire policy on the stock in-trade in a water cornmill, there was, it is true, an express condition that if the assured should (inter alia) "omit to communicate any matter material to be made known to the company in order to enable them to judge of the risk, the policy should be void" but, inasmuch as this condition was nothing but an exact and complete expression of the duty of disclosure imposed by the general law, and of the consequences of violating it, the case may be properly cited as an illustration of that general law Of several defences, the only one which MARTIN, B, at the trial, considered of any substance was the non-disclosure by the plaintiff of the fact that he was in the habit of grinding rice chaff in his mill, which substance was said to increase the danger of fire The plaintiff succeeded, but solely on the ground that the defendants were proved to have had presumptive, if not actual, knowledge of the fact alleged to have been suppressed, it not being disputed that the fact was one which it was material to disclose Lastly, in *Yager* v *Guardian Assurance Co* (1912), 108 L T 38, where an arbitrator having found that the refusal of another office to renew their insurance of certain premises of the assured was a material fact to be disclosed, the Court declined to disturb the finding Besides the above, there are American cases on the duty of disclosure in fire insurances, irrespective of contract, but of these it is only necessary to cite one, viz *New York Bowery Fire Insurance Co* v *New York Fire Insurance* (1837), 17 Wend (N. Y) 359, which was referred to with approval by BLACKBURN, J, delivering the judgment of the Court, at p 538 of *Ionides* v *Pender* (1874), L R 9 Q B 531 "In that case," it is there said, "the plaintiffs had insured certain property against fire, and the president of the company heard that the person insuring with them, or at least some one of the same name, had been so unlucky as to have had several fires, in each of which he was heavily insured The plaintiffs reinsured with the defendants, but did not inform them of this A fire did take place, the insured came upon the plaintiffs, who came upon the defendants The judge directed the jury that if this information given to the president of the plaintiffs was intentionally kept back, it would vitiate the policy of reinsurance.

105. All questions in insurance cases as to the burden of proof on "the party complaining," and the affirmation defences available to "the party charged" (x), as to relief and remedy, as to matters of law and issues of fact, and as to parties (whether parties to the duty of disclosure, or to proceedings instituted in respect of the omission of such duty), are left over for discussion in their proper places (y).

Sub-s (3)   Contracts between Vendor and Purchaser.

106. If a student of our jurisprudence were suddenly let loose amongst the reports of cases on the law of vendor and purchaser, without any guiding hand, and without any clear direction as to the meaning and limits of that somewhat delusive phrase, *uberrima fides*, and were then asked to find out from the authorities whether the relation in question is, or is not, one in which the law requires from the parties disclosure of material facts, he would find it impossible to give a clear, or at any rate a confident, answer, for he would hear "the sages of the law" speaking to him in two voices, which, without the means of harmonizing their discord, would greatly puzzle his unschooled ear. He would learn from Lord CAMPBELL, L C, in the plainest terms, that there is "*no fiduciary relation* between vendor and purchaser in *the negotiation*" (z) ; but ABBOTT, C J , would tell him that "in such transactions good faith is most essential" (a), TURNER and CAIRNS, LL JJ, that "the Court requires good faith in conditions of sale" (b), and KINDERSLEY, V.-C, "that it is the obvious duty of a vendor . . to describe everything which it is material to know of the nature and value of the property" (c) , whilst Lord HATHERLEY, L C, would instruct him, in still more unqualified and uncompromising language, that "this Court requires *the utmost good faith* between buyer and seller" (d)   And if our ingenuous student were then to apply his (again unassisted) intelligence to the question of what is deemed to be comprised in the expressions, "everything which it is material to know," and "the nature and value of the property," he would meet with further bewildering divergences of judicial statement.

107. The above discrepancies will vanish on closer examination, or will be seen to be no more than variations in expression, arising from the fact that in using these apparently discordant forms of words, the several judges were applying their minds and observations in each case to some particular

The jury found for the plaintiffs, but the Court, on appeal, directed a new trial on the ground that the concealment was of a material fact, and, whether intentional or not, it vitiated the insurance "
   (x) For the meaning intended to be placed on the expressions "the party complaining," and "the party charged," whenever they are used, in this work, and the reasons for using them, see § 12, *ante*
   (y) Namely, in Sections 3, 4, 5, 6, and 7 of this Chapter respectively
   (z) *Walters* v *Morgan* (1861), 3 De G J & F 718, at p. 723   LEACH, M R , at pp. 71, 72 of *Adamson* v *Evitt* (1830), 2 Russ & M 66, had previously made use of similar expressions
   (a) *Stevens* v *Adamson* (1818), 2 Stark 422, at p. 423.
   (b) *Dimmock* v *Hallett* (1866), 2 Ch App. 21, at pp. 28 and 31
   (c) *Brandling* v *Plummer* (1854), 2 Drew 427, at p 430
   (d) *Phillips* v *Homfray, No* 1 (1871), 6 Ch App 770, at p 778.

feature in the general proposition as to disclosure in negotiations preliminary to a contract between vendor and purchaser, to the exclusion, for the moment, of other features.

108. The general proposition referred to is no other than the general proposition which has already been stated (*e*), and the theory on which it is applied to contracts of the species now under consideration is precisely the same as that on which it is applied to insurance and all the other species dealt with in this Chapter. That is to say, here, as there, one of the parties to the negotiation must ordinarily be supposed to have exclusive cognizance of certain matters material to the contract (*f*), this person being usually the vendor or lessor. For information on these matters the other party must therefore ordinarily trust to him. It follows, almost as a matter of course, that the law must impose on the first party the duty of communicating to the other all such material matters as are, or come within, his actual or presumptive knowledge before the conclusion of the contract (*g*), and are not, or do not before that date, come within the actual or presumptive knowledge (*h*) of the other party. The imposition of this obligation has been based sometimes upon " a principle of conscience " (*i*), sometimes, and far more frequently, upon a principle of convenience,—convenience so obvious as to amount almost to a necessity,—or, in other words, policy and practical reasonableness (*j*). If the former aspect of the matter be regarded by itself, it justifies the above judicial conception of the relation of vendor and purchaser as one of good faith : if the latter be regarded alone, it is easy to understand how the seemingly contrary statement that the relation is not a fiduciary one came to be made. The difficulty in basing the doctrine entirely " upon a principle of conscience " is that, on that view, there is no intelligible reason

(*e*) See § 81, *ante*

(*f*) See the cases cited in note (*j*), *inf*

(*g*) As to the time during which the duty exists, see §§ 181, 182, *post*

(*h*) As to " actual " and " presumptive knowledge," see Ch II, Sect 3, *ante*

(*i*) As by Lord ELDON, L C , at p. 655 of *Jenkins* v *Hales* (1802), 6 Ves 646 " the rule is founded upon a principle of conscience, and requiring all possible security to be given to a purchaser "

(*j*) This was the view expressed in the following —*Re Banister* (1879), 12 C D 131, C A (*per* FRY, J , whose decision was upheld in the C A , at p 136 " one of the main reasons why the Courts have treated conditions of sale in this way is, that the vendor is a person who knows, and he is stipulating with a purchaser, a person who does not know ") *Re Marsh and Earl Granville* (1882), 24 C D 11 (*per* FRY, J , again, who adds a second reason which, however, seems to be only an amplification of the first, at pp 17, 18 "in the first place, as I observed in *In re Banister*, the vendor knows the condition of the title, and the purchaser does not, . In the next place, the descriptions in the contract, or conditions of sale, are the only materials which the purchaser has for deliberating upon before he enters into the purchase He knows as much as is told him, and no more, and, therefore, he ought to be put into possession of everything, so far as it is touched upon by the conditions of sale, which is likely to influence his mind in determining whether he will buy or not "), *Reeve* v *Berridge* (1888), 20 Q B D. 523, C. A (*per* FRY, L.J , delivering the judgment of Lord ESHER, M R , himself, and LOPES, L J , at p 528 : " we cannot but observe that there is *great practical convenience* in requiring the vendor, who knows his own title, to disclose all that is necessary to protect himself, rather than in requiring the purchaser to demand an inspection of the vendor's title deeds, *before entering into the contract*, a demand which the owners of property will in many cases be unwilling to concede, and which is not, in our opinion, in accordance with the usual course of business in sales by private contract ") for stopping short of the ethical rules laid down by such moralists as Paley (k) in relation to the duty of disclosure, which far transcend the limits within which, on the other basis of policy and practicability, jurisprudence is compelled to confine herself   The true view may, perhaps, be stated thus   On grounds of " convenience," the law declares the duty , and then, having declared it, operates upon the " conscience " of the party subject to it, and makes it a matter of " good faith " with him to observe it.   Policy is the origin and motive of the rule, and " good faith " is the name by which obedience to that rule is characterized.

109. Another explanation of the apparent discrepancy in the two forms of expression is that the area of material upon which the doctrine operates is, in cases of vendor and purchaser, unlike cases of insurance, and particularly marine insurance (where the ratio is the other way), much smaller than that of the material to which it has no application, inasmuch as the facts and circumstances which are within the *exclusive* and private cognizance of the vendor or lessor are much less than the numerous other facts and circumstances which, not being within his exclusive knowledge, though material in one sense (viz that they might, if disclosed, affect the judgment of a reasonable purchaser or lessee), need not be communicated ;   and, when observing that the relation of the negotiating parties is not fiduciary, the authors of the proposition must have been directing their attention to this larger domain with which the rule has no concern, whilst those judges who have laid down that the relation *is* fiduciary, must have had present to their minds,—indeed they have in most cases said so,—the more restricted area in which alone the principle comes into play (l)

110. The transactions, often roughly classed as " vendor and purchaser " cases, in the negotiations leading to which a duty of disclosure arises, are by no means confined to contracts for the sale and purchase of land.   They include not only contracts for the sale of land, or any estate or interest in, or right or claim in relation to real property or chattels real, of any description (m), but also contracts for the demise, surrender, exchange, or settlement, of any such property (n), and contracts for the assignment of, or otherwise dealing with, choses in action (o) : the above being the kind of transactions

(k) Who goes the length of assigning to a vendor's non-disclosure of the known faults and defects, the same degree of moral culpability, in *all* cases, as attaches to a fraudulent misrepresentation of the merits and qualities, of the property which is the subject of the sale   See the passage cited in note (u) to § 667, *post*

(l) The limits of this restricted area are defined in §§ 112–118, *post*

(m) See, generally, the cases cited in the notes to this Sub section, for illustrations of the ordinary type of contract for the sale of land, or the sale of a leasehold interest in land   As to others, the subject of the contract was an exchange, by mutual surrenders, of land in *Ellard* v. *Lord Llandaff* (1810), 1 Ball & B 241 ; a sale of an advowson, in *Edwards Woods* v *Majoribanks* (1860), 7 H L C 806 , a grant of a right to dig for and get clay, with an option of a lease, in *Walters* v *Morgan* (1861), 3 De G F. & J. 718 . a life interest in a trust fund, in *Coaks* v *Boswell* (1886), 11 App Cas. 232, H L.

(n) The rule was applied in cases where a lessee complained of the lessor's non-disclosure in *Cosser* v. *Collinge* (1832), 3 My. & K 283 , *Keates* v *Cadogan* (1851), 10 B & C 591 , *Mostyn* (*Lord*) v. *West Mostyn Coke & Iron Co* (1876), 1 C P D 145

(o) See *Maddeford* v *Austwick* (1826), 1 Sim 89 (sale of a share in a partnership), *Law* v. *Law*, [1905] 1 Ch 140, C A (tho like).   For illustrations of contracts for the sale

in which title is everything, and possession counts for very little (*p*), and in which the facts relating to such title must ordinarily be within the knowledge of the vendor or lessor, and not within that of the purchaser or lessee (*q*). In sales of chattels, where possession counts for much more than title, there is now, by statute, deemed to be an implied condition that the seller has a good title, and an implied warranty that the thing sold is free from incumbrances (*r*). These, and certain other statutory provisions (*s*), being in ordinary cases quite adequate protection to the buyer, there is now no occasion to invoke the application of any common law rule of disclosure during the negotiations for the contract

111. The rule of disclosure in this class of case, which (it may be noted) applies to sales by private treaty as much as to sales by public auction (*t*) and to sales by order or direction of the Court no less than to other sales (*u*), is that the party who presumably alone knows the facts relating to his title to the subject of the sale, or lease, or other transaction,—such person being usually the vendor, or lessor (*v*), though circumstances are conceivable in which the purchaser or lessee may be the party having the exclusive knowledge (*vv*)—must disclose such facts fully (*w*), and clearly (*x*), to the other party And this duty is either the same duty as, or, if not, must be deemed additional to, and independent of, the vendor's agreement to make a good title which is, in one view, to be implied in the contract itself (*y*), and, in another, is assumed by the law to exist, as something outside the contract, but collateral to it (*z*).

112. The facts which have been considered to have a bearing, direct or indirect, on the question of title, and which, as such, the vendor, lessor, or

of an annuity, see *Coverley* v. *Burrell* (1821), 5 B & Ald 257, and *Adamson* v. *Evitt* (1830), 2 Russ. & M 66

(*p*) See the observations of LINDLEY, L J , at p. 545 of *Manchester Trust* v *Furness*, [1895] 2 Q B 539, C A

(*q*) See the cases cited in note (*j*) to § 108, *ante*

(*r*) Sale of Goods Act, 1893 (56 & 57 Vict c 71), s. 12.

(*s*) *Ibid.*, s. 21, and the Factors Acts therein referred to

(*t*) *Re White and Smith's Contract* (1896), 1 Ch 637, *per* STIRLING, J , at p 641 ; *Re Hœdicke and Lipski's Contract*, [1901] 2 Ch. 666, *per* BYRNE, J., at pp 668, 669

(*u*) See § 252, *post*.

(*v*) See *Coaks* v. *Boswell* (1886), 11 App Cas. 232, H L (*per* Lord SELBORNE, L.C , at pp 235, 236 (" a purchaser is generally speaking under no obligation to communicate to his vendor "   &c) , and cp what is said by Lord CAMPBELL, L C , to the same effect at p 723 of *Walters* v *Morgan* (1861), 3 De G F & J. 718.

(*vv*) No such case has yet come up for decision , in all those cases in which a vendor has succeeded against a non-disclosing purchaser, referred to in § 154 and § 156, *post*, the circumstances were very special, and fraud, as well as the mere fact of non disclosure, was established.

(*w*) See §§ 20-23, *ante*.

(*x*) See § 24, *ante*

(*y*) This was the view expressed by PARKE, B , at p 701 of *Gray* v *Stanion* (1836), 1 M. & W 695, and implied in the observations of JESSEL, M.R , at p 891 of *Ungley* v *Ungley* (1877), 5 C. D 887, C. A. (" it is clear that if you once prove that a man has made an agreement to sell a house, it must be taken that he means to sell it free from incumbrances, without his saying so   So, if a man agrees to settle a house in consideration of marriage, he must be taken to mean free from incumbrances ")

(*z*) This, and the view referred to in the last note, were mentioned by COTTON, L J (without expressing any preference for either), at pp 670, 671 of *Ellis* v *Rogers* (1885), 29 C. D 661, C A

other person in the like position, is required to divulge, may be classified as follows

113. The first, and most obvious, kind of matter to be disclosed is the absence, or circumstances indicating the absence, or grave doubts as to the existence, of any title at all to the property sold (*a*), or to some particular portion of it (*b*)

114. Next, disclosure is demanded of all facts showing that the title is of a different nature in any material respect to that which the purchaser or lessee was entitled from the terms or conditions of the contract to expect (*c*).

115. Thirdly, the vendor or lessor must communicate to the purchaser or lessee the existence and the nature of all mortgages, charges, liens, easements, and incumbrances of every sort on the property sold (*d*) ; also of any previous deeds or instruments binding the property, and restricting

(*a*) *Edwards* v *M'Leay* (1815), G Cooper 308, a decision by GRANT, M R , affirmed by Lord ELDON, L C (1818), 2 Swanst. 287, was a case of this description

(*b*) As in *Mostyn (Lord)* v. *West Mostyn Coke & Iron Co* (1876), 1 C. P. D. 145 See *Re Brewer and Hankin's Contract* (1899), 80 L T 127, C A

(*c*) *Coverley* v *Burrell* (1821), 5 B & Ald 257 (where the undisclosed fact was the liability of the annuity purchased to redemption in five years) , *James* v *Litchfield* (1869), L R. 9 Eq 51, as to which see note (*g*) to § 115, *post* ; *Re Banister* (1879), 12 C. D. 131, C A (where the suppressed fact was that the vendor was not sei sd in fee, but was "a mortgagee remaining in possession after the mortgaged estate had come to an end," and " simply and solely as a person whose title was not challenged by the true owner, whoever he was " JESSEL, M R , at p 144), *Re Marsh and Earl Granville* (1882), 24 C D 11, C. A (where the vendor had omitted to disclose the fact that the instrument constituting the root of title, *quoad* the freehold lands, was a voluntary one, and that power was reserved thereby to the grantor to revoke the trusts therein declared, which would include the trust for sale see the observations of COTTON, L J , at p 25 " in my opinion it is most material for enabling a purchaser to decide whether he will enter into such a contract that he should know whether the deed was upon a transaction in which ordinarily there would be an investigation of the title, and if the vendor knows that the deed was on a transaction where there would be no investigation, and does not disclose that fact, the purchaser, in my opinion, has a right to complain that this fact was not disclosed in the contract ") , *Nottingham Patent Brick & Tile Co* v *Butler* (1886), 16 Q B D 778, C A (where the vendor had suppressed not only the restrictive covenants in a predecessor's deed of title, as mentioned in note (*e*), *inf* .but also the fact that, though without notice of these restrictions when he purchased, he knew of them when he sold, and to that extent had a title which might be questioned afterwards) , *Re Ward and Jordan's Contract*, [1902] 1 Ir R 73 (where, on the sale of a licensed public house, the purchaser complained that the vendor had suppressed the fact that a conviction of the vendor had been endorsed on the licence, and it was recognized by the Court that if the indorsement had been such as to imperil the qualification of *the premises* for a licence, it would have been material to be disclosed , but it was held that, on the true construction of the licensing statute applicable to the case, the indorsement would not have this effect : pp 76–78)

(*d*) For illustrations generally, see the following decisions (the undisclosed incumbrance in each case being stated within brackets after the citation) —*Arnot* v *Biscoe* (1748), 1 Ves Sr 94 (a mortgage, and decree of foreclosure) , *Martin* v *Cooper* (1846), 3 Jo. & Lat. 496 , 72 R R 100 (property subject to certain reservations of rights to limestone, and of turbary) , *Shackleton* v *Sutcliffe* (1847), 1 De G & Sm 609 (numerous easements and water-rights in favour of lower lands) , *Wilde* v *Gibson* (1848), 1 H L C 605 (a public right of way, or footpath , though ultimately the party complaining failed on other grounds, which are discussed in Sect. 8, Sub s (2), *post*) , *Smith* v *Harrison* (1857), 26 L J. (CH) 412 (claims of creditors largely in excess of the value of the chattel interest of a certain bankrupt in a lease and partnership effects of his late firm then being sold by auction) , *Torrance* v *Bolton* (1872), L R 14 Eq. 124 (mortgages) ; *Jones* v *Rimmer* (1880), 14 C D 588, C A. (ground rent) ; *Heywood* v *Mallalieu* (1883), 25 C D 357 (right of owner of adjoining premises to use for certain purposes the kitchen of the house which was the subject of the sale) , *Mahomed Kala Mea* v *Harperink* (1908), 25 T L R 180, P. C (incumbrances to an amount in excess of the utmost value of the land)

its user in the hands of successors in title (e), and where he is an intending assignor of a lease, or an intending sub-lessor, any and every unusual covenant contained in the original or superior lease which operates as a burden on the property or a restriction upon its use for either general purposes, or the particular purposes declared in the contract, or, to his knowledge, in fact contemplated by the intended assignee or sub-lessee (f). He must also divulge the exact nature of any tenancy which affects the property (g),

(e) See *Andrew* v. *Aitken* (1883), 31 W. R. 425 (unusually restrictive covenants and provisos in previous deed of conveyance), *Ellis* v *Rogers* (1885), 29 C D. 661, C A. (where the vendor of an interest in a building agreement was held to have been wrong in not disclosing restrictive covenants therein), *Nottingham Patent Brick & Tile Co* v. *Butler* (1886), 16 Q B D. 778, C A (suppression of covenants against brick-making contained in a previous conveyance of the land); *Re Cox and Neve's Contract*, [1891] 2 Ch. 109 (non disclosure of a deed of exchange between the vendor and a third person, containing covenants restrictive of building: *per* NORTH, J, at pp 116, 117); *Hepworth* v *Pickles*, [1900] 1 Ch 108 (non-disclosures of a deed of 1874 whereby the land was conveyed to the vendor's predecessor in title, containing restrictions against the use of any houses built thereon as an inn, tavern, or beerhouse, for which purpose the purchaser, to the knowledge of the vendor, was taking the premises. *per* FARWELL, J, at p 112 The party complaining, however, failed here on another ground)

(f) *Cosser* v *Collinge* (1832), 3 My & K 283 (a case of a contract to grant an under-lease, where it was held by LEACH, M R., that the party charged had failed in his duty of disclosure in that he had not communicated covenants in the head lease which prohibited the carrying on of certain trades on the demised premises, though the party complaining failed in the action because he was proved to have had a "fair opportunity" of inspecting this head lease, and so was fixed with constructive notice of its contents), *Flight* v *Booth* (1834), 1 Bing (N C) 370 (non disclosure of covenants in the original lease prohibiting the use of the premises for the purposes of certain inoffensive trades), *Smith* v. *Capron* (1849), 7 Hare 185 (non disclosure of covenant in original lease against assignment without consent of landlord held to be non compliance on part of the vendor of the leasehold premises, but the purchaser failed here, because he had constructive notice, see note (o) to § 59, *ante*), *Wilbraham* v *Livesey* (1854), 18 Beav 206 (where the plaintiff sued for specific performance of an agreement to sell to the defendant leasehold premises in the Strand, and which, therefore, he must have known would be required for some trade purposes—in fact, the defendant required them for printing and publishing a newspaper—and ROMILLY, M.R , refused to order specific performance, at all events until after further inquiries which he directed, on the ground that the plaintiff had not divulged covenants in the head lease restrictive of the user of the premises for trade purposes—pp 209, 210), *Hyde* v. *Warden* (1877), 3 Ch. D 72, C A (a case of a contract to accept a sub-lease, where the intending sub lessor had not disclosed the existence of covenants in the original lease empowering the owner to re enter if the lessor should become insolvent, or have an execution levied against him), *Reeve* v *Berridge* (1888), 20 Q B D 523, C A (non disclosure of covenant in the original lease against trade user of the leasehold premises which were the subject of the sale), *Re Davis and Cavey* (1888), 40 C D 601 (where the circumstances were similar), *Re White and Smith's Contract*, [1898] 1 Ch 637 (non-disclosure of admittedly onerous and unusual covenants, the nature of which the report does not state), *Re Summerson*, [1900] 1 Ch 112 n (covenants in head lease prohibiting the use of the leasehold premises as an alehouse or spirit shop, though here the party complaining failed on other grounds), *Re Hœdicke and Lipski's Contract*, [1901] 2 Ch 666 (covenants against erecting or altering buildings without the licence of the lessor, and against carrying on trades, with proviso for re entry, &c.), *Molyneux* v. *Hawtrey*, [1903] 2 K B 487, C A (an action for damages for breach of a contract to purchase leasehold premises, in which WRIGHT, J , whose decision was affirmed by the C. A , gave judgment for the defendant on the ground that the plaintiff had not disclosed to the defendant, or given her a "fair opportunity ' of making herself acquainted with, certain specially onerous and unusual covenants in the head lease, obliging the lessee to submit to interference with the access of light during and after the building of Westminster Cathedral, and the ringing of bells for divine service at any hour, and not to exercise a number of innocent and inoffensive professions, or to keep any animals, or play music, &c, &c)

(g) *Brandling* v *Plummer* (1854), 2 Drew 447, where, amongst other lots sold by auction by direction of the Court, was a certain lot consisting of 88 cottages, and described as

though the purchaser may have actual notice of the occupation of the tenant, for the old heresy that such actual notice is constructive notice to a purchaser, as between him and a vendor, of all the terms and conditions of the tenancy, is now completely exploded (h).

110. Lastly, if any notice or order has been served upon the vendor, pursuant to lawful authority, which, if not complied with, will affect the title to the property, and will in any case constitute a burden on it, the vendor must communicate this circumstance. The rule of disclosure has been applied in this way to the case of a sale of leasehold premises in a very dilapidated condition, where the vendor's landlord had, only a day before the conclusion of the contract, served a notice of re-entry, unless the necessary repairs should be executed in three months, and "ABBOTT, C.J., was of opinion that a person putting up premises for sale was bound to know how the premises were circumstanced; and whether notice of re-entry had been given by the landlord, in case the premises should not be put into repair In such transactions good faith was most essential, and the vendor, or his agent, was bound to communicate to the vendee the fact of such notice" (i). So, in the case of a notice served by the local authority to pave the street facing the premises, it has been held that such a fact might be material to the title (j); and a prohibition by a local authority, under its bye-laws, of any building on the land sold until all the refuse with which certain excavations had been filled up should have been removed (k), as also a party-wall statutory award, made two days before the contract, ordering the vendors to contribute a portion of the cost of certain works to be executed by the adjoining owner (l), have been held facts material to be disclosed

being "in the occupation of the owners of Sedghill Colliery, or their undertenants or workmen," and the fact which was held to have been improperly suppressed by the vendor was the peculiar nature of the tenancy referred to, in that none of the 88 cottages paid any rent, and, further, the owners "had a right to build cottages for the use of their workmen, and not to a limited number, but as many as they liked, and not to pay any rent for them, but merely to pay for the damage done to the tenants of the soil" *per* KINDERSLEY, V.-C, at pp 431, 432, *Dimmock* v *Hallett* (1866), 2 Ch App 21, where the tenants of certain farms had given notice to quit, and the vendor omitted to disclose this fact, an "omission" which CAIRNS, L J, at p 20 pronounced to be "very material": see also TURNER, L.J, at pp 28, 29; *James* v *Latchfield* (1869), L R 9 Eq 51, where the vendor, having sold five houses and some vacant adjoining land for building purposes, withheld the fact that one of the houses and most of the adjoining land was in the occupation of a certain person not as a yearly tenant merely (as, to his knowledge, the purchaser supposed), but under a lease for 21 years, *Caballero* v. *Henty* (1874), 9 Ch App 447, a case of a contract to sell a public house, the purchasers being browers who, to the knowledge of the vendor, intended to sell their own beer on the premises, where the vendor was held not to have complied with his duty of disclosure, in that he had omitted to divulge the fact that the premises were in the occupation of another brewer under a lease from the plaintiff which still had eight years to run

    (h) See § 62 and note (l) thereto, *ante*
    (i) At pp 423, 433 of *Stevens* v *Adamson* (1818), 2 Stark 422
    (j) *Re Leyland and Taylor's Contract*, [1900] 2 Ch 625, C. A, where Lord ALVERSTONE, M.R, at p 630, and RIGBY, L J, at p 632, expressed an opinion that the undisclosed fact might very well have been material to a case of rescission since, however, the purchaser did not ask for rescission, but on the contrary had elected to affirm the contract, and prayed compensation only, he failed, the circumstance in question not being considered by the C A. to have any substantial bearing on *that* issue
    (k) *Baker* v. *Moss* (1902), 66 J P 360 (*per* JOYCE, J)
    (l) *Carlish* v. *Salt*, [1906] 1 Ch 335 (*per* JOYCE, J, at p 340 "I hold that the party

117. All the above species of facts, it will be seen, immediately and obviously in some cases, and indirectly and inferentially in others, affect the title to the property sold. It is probably correct to say that no circumstances need be disclosed which relate *solely* to matters having no bearing, direct or indirect, on the question of title; for such matters cannot be supposed to be necessarily within the exclusive knowledge of the vendor or lessor, or material to be disclosed in the sense that they have a vital bearing on the contract, though they may be of the most obvious materiality in another sense, and though, consequently, any misrepresentation of such circumstances would clearly be actionable. Thus, to take first a few typical illustrations about which there has never been any doubt or controversy, there is no obligation to divulge the ruinous or unsafe condition of a lessor's premises (m), or the fact that the grantor of an annuity offered for sale is in embarrassed circumstances (n), or a deed acknowledging that the vendor is not entitled, as against an adjoining owner, to access of light over his land (o), or the indorsement of a conviction on the licence of the vendor of a public house, not being of a nature to imperil the qualification *of the premises* for a renewal of the licence (p), or, in the absence of any such relation between the parties as that which is the subject of investigation in the next Chapter (q), the price which the vendor gave for the property which he is contracting to sell (r). And it is further to be observed that in order to establish a breach of a duty to disclose, it must be shown that the undisclosed fact not only affects title, but affects the title to the particular property which is the subject of the contract. Thus, in the case of a contract for the sale of an *advowson*, the vendor is not required to reveal the existence of a charge on *the living* (s).

118. It is frequently stated, or assumed, that the duty of disclosure is not limited, as above submitted, to matters affecting title, but extends to matters affecting the quality, condition, or value of the property which is the subject of the contract: but, on examination of the authorities which are

wall notice, and the award, constituted a material fact affecting the price to be paid, and in so far as they imposed a liability of uncertain amount at some future time on the owner of the premises, I am of opinion that they constituted a latent defect, not in the quality of, but in the title to the property, and ought to have been disclosed ") In this case the award was made under s. 98 of the London Building Act, 1894, s 99 whereof vests the entire ownership of the party wall in the party to whom the contribution awarded is to be paid, until the payment is duly made

(m) *Keates* v *Cadogan* (1851), 10 B & C 591, *Ryall* v *Kidwell*, [1914] 3 K. B 135.

(n) *Adamson* v. *Evitt* (1830), 2 Russ & M 66 Nor would the grantor himself have come under any such obligation (per LEACH, M.R , at pp. 71, 72)

(o) *Greenhalgh* v. *Brindley*, [1901] 2 Ch 324, per FARWELL, J , at p 328, *Smith* v *Colbourne*, [1914] 2 Ch 533, 539, 542, 545, C A

(p) *Re Ward and Jordan's Contract*, [1902] 1 Ir R 73, at pp. 77, 78

(q) Which deals with the obligations of trustees, promoters, and agents to disclose all profits, benefits, advantages, &c , derived from any transaction in which they may be engaged during the continuance of the relationship

(r) Per Lord HATHERLEY at p 1244 of *Erlanger* v. *New Sombrero Co* (1878), 3 App Cas. 1218, H L (" a vendor need not do what at one time was asserted by this bill, namely, disclose what he has paid in effecting his own anterior purchase before asking an enhanced price from him to whom he seeks to sell the property ")

(s) *Edwards Woods* v. *Majoribanks* (1860), 7 H L C 806

supposed to support this proposition, it will be found that in all of them either title was involved, though indirectly, or the cause of action was express or implied misrepresentation, and not non disclosure, except as contributing to establish a case of misrepresentation. Thus the "latent defect" cases are said to presuppose a duty on the part of the vendor to disclose to the purchaser the existence of drains, culverts, and the like, running under the property, which constitute defects in its quality or condition ; but such matters are also defects in title, and, wherever the party complaining has succeeded, his right to succeed has been put on this ground, though expressions may have also been used indicating that (as was the fact) the physical quality of the property was at the same time affected (t), or else on the ground that there had been an express or implied misdescription of the property (u) Where neither of these conditions was present, the party complaining has always failed (v), unless he has succeeded in bringing his case within some

(t) In *Ashburner* v *Sewell*, [1891] 3 Ch 405, CHITTY, J., at p 108, distinctly hold that a purchaser's objection that the vendor had not disclosed a right of way over a road in the property enjoyed by owners and servants of adjoining lands was an objection *to title*, and not merely an omission in the description of the property, though it was that as well In *Re Puckett and Smith's Contract*, [1902] 2 Ch 258, C A., the purchaser of land sold to him by private treaty incorporating the conditions of a previous abortive auction sale, complained of the non-disclosure of the fact that a culvert ran underneath what, until after the execution of the contract, he supposed, not unreasonably, to be a dry ditch The vendors thereupon took out a summons under the Vendor and Purchaser Act, 1874, asking for a declaration that they had made out a good *title*, the purchaser contending that his objections to *title*, and his requisition on the vendor to divert the culvert, or pay compensation, had not been sufficiently answered KEKEWICH, J , dismissed the vendors' application, and agreed with the purchaser's contention, and the C A affirmed his decision. This case, therefore, clearly proceeded on the ground of non disclosure of a circumstance affecting title ; and, though STIRLING, L.J , at p 265, expresses his personal view that " the question which remains is not really one of title," he goes on to say that it is rather " whether the case falls within the rule laid down by TINDAL, C J , in *Flight* v *Booth*," and founds his judgment on that case Now *Flight* v. *Booth* (1834), 1 Bing (N C) 370— see note (f) to § 115, *ante*—was certainly either a case of non disclosure of a matter affecting title, as was thought in *Shepherd* v *Croft*, cited in note (v), *inf* , or else it was not a case of non-disclosure at all, but rather of misrepresentation See also *Re Brewer and Hankins' Contract*, cited in note (v), *inf*

(u) *Re Puckett and Smith's Contract*, *sup* , may be regarded as a case of misrepresentation of the nature and character of the premises as fit for building, since the vendor knew that the purchaser was buying the land solely for that purpose, and the negotiations, as COLLINS, M R , points out at p 263, and also STIRLING, L J , at p 265, proceeded upon that basis , and further, the vendor had described the property as having " a valuable prospective building element," and being " suitable for development," and with " no restrictions as to the class of houses to be erected " (*per* COLLINS, M R , at p 264) More over, the above-mentioned references—see the last note—to *Flight* v. *Booth*, which is usually regarded and cited as a case of implied misrepresentation by omission of qualifying facts, as it certainly was, though it may be regarded as involving non disclosure as well, suggest that the C. A. considered the case from that point of view, as well as from the other, and so far as STIRLING, L.J , was concerned, in preference to it

(v) See *Re Brewer and Hankins' Contract* (1899), 80 L T 127, C A , where the undisclosed matters were the existence of a public sewer running underground at the rear of the estate, and the fact that under the Public Health Act, 1875, the corporation of Bristol was entitled to enter upon the land, whenever they thought fit, for purposes of repairing and cleaning the sewer, which was not discoverable except by excavation Here STIRLING, J., and the C A , affirming him, held that, as the land had not been sold for building purposes, and as there was no substantial difference in character between what was promised and what was tendered, the purchaser was not entitled to relief So far, it would seem that the case was regarded as one of misdescription, where, however, the proof of the alleged representation failed At p 265 of *Re Puckett and Smith's Contract*, *sup* , STIRLING, L.J , points to this as constituting the essential distinction between the two cases ' there,"

other rule of disclosure, such as the "fraudulent silence" principle discussed hereafter (w). So also, there are judicial observations, in some of the cases, as to the undisclosed facts being such as would impair the value of the property : but the true ground of the decision in each of them was that the matters withheld were such as had a bearing on the question of title ; though, in prejudicially affecting the title, they would also necessarily depreciate the value of the property (x).

119. The topics of the burden of proof on the party complaining, the affirmative pleas available to the party charged, the proper relief and remedy, matters of law and fact, parties, &c , in relation to negotiations for transactions of the character indicated in this Sub-section, are examined in detail hereafter (y).

Sub s. (4). Contracts of Suretyship.

120. It is now agreed that contracts of suretyship or guarantee belong to the class of transactions in the negotiation of which a duty of disclosure arises, whatever the extent of that duty may be (which is another question,

he says—that is, in the earlier case —" it was quite clear that the property was not offered for building purposes," whereas in the later case it was equally clear that it was The earlier case was, however, also put as one of omission to disclose a want of title to a part of the premises (per STIRLING, J , at p. 128), but the complaint, put in this way, failed by reason of the express terms of certain of the conditions of sale In *Shepherd* v *Croft*, [1911] 1 Ch 521, where the property sold was described in the particulars of sale as " desirable residential property " with " building advantages," &c , the purchaser refused to complete on the ground of the vendor's non disclosure of a natural underground watercourse in a culvert or piping constructed by the owners of the various properties, and PARKER, J , at p 528, held that the case was within the principle of *Re Brewer and Hankins' Contract*, and not within *Re Puckett and Smith's Contract*, *sup* , and that the purchaser was getting a property not differing in character from that which it had been represented to be, since it was still " desirable residential property," and had " building advantages " . in other words, that there had been no misdescription of the premises, or no such substantial misdescription as, having regard to the conditions of sale, would entitle her to relief.

(w) See Sub-s (8), *post*.

(x) Thus, in *Re Ward and Jordan's Contract*, [1902] 1 Ir R 73, which is cited in note (p) to § 117, *ante*, as an illustration of non-disclosure of matters affecting title, the M R (Ir) at p. 76, observes that " the omission to disclose a material circumstance, affecting the value of the property, known to the vendor, and not known to the purchaser would in this Court entitle the plaintiff to relief," where the dictum must be taken to be limited to the circumstances of that case, in which it was obvious that the undisclosed fact affected the value by affecting the title So in *Carlish* v *Salt*, [1906] 1 Ch 335, cited in note (l) to § 116, *ante*, as a case of non disclosure of an award and order of a competent authority affecting the title, it will be seen that JOYCE, J , at p 340, in the passage from his judgment which is transcribed in that note, speaks of the above as " a material fact *affecting the price to be paid*," and again, at p 341, as " a fact which was *material to the value of the property*," but what he means by this is clear from his definite statement that the making of the award and order " constituted a latent defect "—the phrase seems more than usually inept in this connection—" not in the quality of, but in the title to the property " It must be admitted, however, that JOCYE, J , does not seem very sure of his ground in this case At p 341, he seems by the use of the phrase " material defect in the title, or in the subject of the sale," to be still halting between two opinions , whilst, at pp. 340, 341, he cites in support of his conclusion several of the " fraudulent silence " cases,—see Sub s (8), *post*,—a resort to which is only necessary when the case is not within any of those recognized types in which the duty of disclosure arises by reason only of the transaction being what it is.

(y) See Sects 3–7, *post*.

to be considered presently), and whether such contracts are, or are not, properly and strictly styled *uberrimæ fidei* (z). It has, indeed, from time to time been asserted, or expressions have been used which clearly imply, that, for purposes of the rules relating to disclosure, there is a vital and essential distinction between contracts of guarantee and the other species of contract which form the subject of this Chapter, particularly policies of insurance. Thus, the view has been taken that, unlike a policy of insurance, a contract of suretyship is " one in which there is no *universal* obligation to make disclosure " (a), and again, still more pointedly, that non-disclosure will not vitiate a guarantee unless the undisclosed circumstance was " fraudulently kept back " (b), or " unless there be," in the course of the negotiation, either " fraud or misrepresentation," it being understood that " misrepresentation might undoubtedly be made by concealment " (c). But, unless the above propositions be understood in the sense that the duty of disclosure operates in cases of suretyship within far narrower limits than in other cases, and, in particular, than in those of insurance (d), or unless the " fraud " which is there stated to be essential be taken to mean no more than the non-performance of a duty to disclose, on which supposition the existence of such a duty is plainly recognized (e), it seems clear on principle, supported by authority (f),

(z) See § 1, note (e), *ante*, as to the unsatisfactory nature of this expression   and, as to the comparative unimportance of the particular designation of the transaction, see *Seaton* v. *Heath*, [1899] 1 Q B 782, C. A , *per* ROMER, L J , at p 792.

(a) *Per* FRY, J , at p 475 of *Davies* v. *London & Provincial Marine Insurance Co* (1878), 8 C. D 469   See also what is said by Lord CHELMSFORD, L C , at pp 608–610 of *Wythes* v. *Labouchere* (1859), 3 De G & J. 593.

(b) *Per* POLLOCK, C B , delivering the judgment of the Court of Exchequer, at p 535 of *North British Insurance Co* v *Lloyd* (1854), 10 Exch 523   See also *Wythes* v *Labouchere, sup*, *per* Lord CHELMSFORD, L C , at p 609

(c) *Per* ROMER, L.J , at p 792 of *Seaton* v *Heath, sup*

(d) Thus, in *North British Insurance Co* v *Lloyd, sup*, ALDERSON, B , during the argument, at p 529, recognizes, on the authority of *Smith* v. *Bank of Scotland*—see note (yy) to § 126, *post*—that " a case may exist where a bond of suretyship may be invalidated by the mere non-communication of existing facts "

(e) This appears to have been the view of PARKE, B   see p 527 of *North British Insurance Co* v. *Lloyd, sup*, where, in the argument, he observes · " if a fact ought to be mentioned by the creditor to the surety, the omission to communicate it may amount to a fraud "   Cp the observations of FRY, J , in *Davies* v *London & Provincial Marine Insurance Co*, *sup*, who, at p 475, after drawing the distinction between contracts of suretyship and others which has been already referred to—see note (a), *sup* —is careful to add   " but I do think that the contract of suretyship is, as expressed by Lord WESTBURY, one which should be based upon the free and voluntary agency of the individual who enters into it   I think, to use the language of Lord ELDON   it is a contract in respect of which a very little is sufficient   Very little said which ought not to have been said, and very little not said which ought to have been said, will be sufficient to prevent the contract being valid "

(f) For instance, VAUGHAN WILLIAMS, L J , at p 80 of *London General Omnibus Co* v *Holloway*, [1912] 2 K B 72, C A , says · " I think it right to say that I find it difficult to understand what POLLOCK, C B , in *North British Insurance Co* v *Lloyd* means when he concludes his judgment with these words · "—he then cites the passage in which the necessity of fraud being established is insisted on, and which is referred to in note (b), *sup*   And the whole of the Lord Justice's judgment (pp 76–80) is a careful and clear exposition (with reference to the authorities which at first sight seem to suggest the contrary) of the true doctrine that innocent non disclosure of material facts in suretyship cases may be actionable, though the facts deemed material are of a much more limited character than in other cases   Cp the passage from the judgment of FARWELL, L J , which is cited in note (h), *inf* that these propositions are incorrect, and that the true view is that expressed by Lord TRURO, L.C , in one of the earlier decisions (g), and by the Court of Appeal in a very recent case (h), viz. that the same rule of disclosure governs suretyship transactions as governs those of insurance or any other type of transaction belonging to the class now under consideration, but that the application of the rule differs widely according to the character of the particular species of transaction on which it operates. The principle is identical, but, like the leaden rule of the Lesbians, it is flexible and plastic, and bends itself into a variety of shapes so as to conform to the angles and curves of the material to which for the moment it is being applied, as has already been observed in discussing its application to contracts between vendor and purchaser (i) That principle is, that where the nature of the contract or transaction is such that, as to certain material facts, one of the parties must necessarily have exclusive knowledge, and such material facts are not amongst those which the other party, having regard again to the essence and object of the transaction, *must necessarily be supposed to take the risk of not knowing*, the first party is required to divulge to the other those facts, be they many or few, *and those facts only* (j)

121. Now, keeping again to the supposed distinction between guarantees and insurance policies, it is manifest, on close examination, that, for the purposes of the duty of disclosure, there is no such distinction *in principle* at all, and that the only difference is in the kind of matters of the existence of which the insurer in the one class of case, and the surety, in the other, is supposed to take the risk It is obvious—so much, indeed, is declared by the very terms "insurance" and "suretyship"—that the purpose of the transaction in each case is to make a person "sure," or secure, against the chance of loss from some defined contingency : and it is quite immaterial to the question of the object of the contract what the contingency is in the particular case. There is no reason, as has been pointed out (k), "why,

(g) At pp 396, 397 of *Owen* v *Homan* (1851), 3 Macn & G 378, where he points out the want of a distinct definition of the nature of the creditor's obligation of disclosure to the surety (p 396), and (at p 397) concludes that, at all events, " where communication does take place between the creditor and the surety, the *duty of the creditor cannot be better illustrated than by the case of the assured*," and that " the same principle," i e as that which governs insurances, " is applicable to the case of sureties "

(h) *London General Omnibus Co* v *Holloway*, *sup*, where FARWELL, L J , at p 81 says that " although the doctrine by which *uberrima fides* is required in insurance cases is *not applicable to the same extent* in suretyship cases, still the surety is entitled to relief on the ground of non disclosure of matters which ought to have been communicated to him, whether the non communication was or was not innocent," and where VAUGHAN WILLIAMS, L.J , convincingly establishes that in all the previous cases in which expressions had been used indicating that non-disclosure in suretyship cases amounts to fraudulent misrepresentation or concealment, it so happened that in the arguments, or the judgments, or both, it was put in this way, dishonesty being in *fact* established in all of them, as well as a mere violation of the duty of disclosure , but that in none of them, except *North British Insurance Co* v *Lloyd*, *sup*, was it necessary for the Court to pronounce, nor did any Court pronounce, the opinion that, in *all* cases of suretyship, disclosure is not obligatory, as such, that is to say, is not required unless it constitutes, or contributes to constitute, misrepresentation or fraud (pp 76–80)

(i) See § 109, *ante*, For the Lesbian rule, see § 649, *post*, and note (*f*) thereto

(j) See §§ 84, 85, *ante*.

(k) *Per* A L SMITH, L J , at p 790 of *Seaton* v *Heath*, [1899] 1 Q. B 782, C A. See

when a person insures his ship, or his house, or his life, he should be bound to disclose material facts of which he is cognizant and the underwriter is not, and yet not be bound to disclose such facts when an underwriter is asked to take a risk upon, say, the soundness of a racehorse," and, on the same reasoning, there is no reason why a creditor "should not be under the same obligation when a surety is asked to take a risk upon the financial soundness of a debtor : indeed, in some kinds of suretyship, those to which the name of " guarantee policy " is now commonly applied, the contract, as the name itself indicates, not only has the same purpose and effect as, but is identical with, a contract of insurance. " The difference between these two classes of contract does not depend upon any essential difference between the word ' insurance ' and the word ' guarantee.' There is no magic in the use of those words. The words, to a great extent, have the same meaning and effect ; and many contracts . . . may with equal propriety be called contracts of insurance or contracts of guarantee. Whether the contract be one requiring *uberrima fides* or not must depend upon its substantial character and how it came to be effected " (*l*)

122. But, though the governing rule is the same, its application to the two species of transaction necessarily results in a much less heavy burden of disclosure being imposed on the creditor, employer, or other person to whom a guarantee is given, than on an assured person. For, in the first place, the " exclusive knowledge " of the material facts, which is one of the conditions essential to the existence of the duty, is ordinarily not possessed by the person to whom a guarantee is given, whereas, in contracts of insurance, " in general, the assured knows, and the underwriter does not know, the circumstances of the voyage, or the state of health " (*m*). But " in general, contracts of guarantee are between persons who occupy, or ultimately assume, the positions of creditor, debtor, and surety, and thereby the surety becomes bound to pay the debt or make good the default of the debtor. In general, the creditor does not himself go to the surety, or represent or explain to the surety the risk to be run. The surety often takes the position from motives of friendship to the debtor, and generally not as the result of any direct bargaining between him and the creditor, or in consideration of any remuneration passing to him from the creditor. The risk undertaken is generally known to the surety, and the circumstances generally point to the view that,

Dane v *Mortgage Insurance Corporation*, [1894] 1 Q B 54, C A (*per* Lord ESHER, M.R., at p 60), and *Re Law Guarantee Trust & Accident Society* (1914), 30 T. L. R 616, C. A , as to the difference between suretyship and insurance for other purposes

(*l*) *Per* ROMER, L.J , at p 792 of *Seaton* v. *Heath, sup* The contract in that case was pronounced to be one of those which could equally be described by either name The decision of the C. A. was reversed by the House of Lords, *sub nom* , *Seaton* v. *Burnand*, [1900] A. C. 135, on certain grounds, but without the slightest expression of dissent from the above view, or from any view of the Lords Justices as to the nature of the two classes of contracts, or the duty of disclosure existing in the respective cases. NEVILLE, J , at pp. 611, 612 of *Re Law Guarantee Trust and Accidental Society*, [1913] 2 Ch. 604, took one view of the nature of the transaction in that case, and the Court of Appeal), *ubi supra cit.*—see the last note—took the other, but both Courts dealt with the question as one of substance and fact, and not of names

(*m*) *North British Insurance Co* v *Lloyd* (1854), 10 Exch. 523, *per Cur.* at p. 533.

as between the creditor and the surety, it was contemplated and intended that the surety should take upon himself to ascertain exactly what risk he was taking upon himself " (n). Secondly, the general rule being that the party having exclusive knowledge of facts which are material in one sense is still not bound to divulge any fact of the existence or non-existence of which the other party is, by the very nature of the contract, professing to undertake the risk, it follows that a creditor or other guaranteed person is under no obligation to disclose such financial difficulties in the debtor's affairs as the surety ought to assume to exist in one shape or another, since their existence is the whole foundation and motive of the suretyship which he is invited to take upon himself (nn) The surety must be intending to undertake *some* risk, and, if such matters as are above indicated have to be fully revealed to him, he would be converting a speculation into a certainty, and insuring against loss, not the party supposed to be protected, but himself. " I think," said BLACKBURN, J, in the Exchequer Chamber, "that great practical mischief would ensue if the creditor were by law required to disclose everything material known to him . . If it were so, no creditor could rely on a contract of guarantie, unless he communicated to the proposed sureties everything relating to his dealings with the principal, to an extent which would in the ordinary course of things be so vexatious and annoying to the principal and his friends, the intended sureties, that such a rule of law would practically prohibit the obtaining of contracts of suretyship in matters of business " (o).

123. On the other hand, where the undisclosed matters within the exclusive knowledge of the party to whom the guarantee is given are not such as also form part of the normal risk of the surety, they must be disclosed. For this purpose the nature of the contract,—for there are several well-defined types of suretyship,—must be examined in each individual case. And, on such examination, " the criterion whether the disclosure ought to be made voluntarily " has been laid down by Lord CAMPBELL, in a celebrated passage which has always been considered the *locus classicus* on this topic (p), as being " whether there is anything that might not naturally be expected to take

(n) Per ROMER, L.J, at p. 793 of *Seaton v. Heath, sup* Cp the observations of BLACKBURN, J., to the same effect at p. 503 of *Lee v. Jones* (1864), 17 C. B (N s) 482, Exch Ch

(nn) At p 120 of *Hamilton v. Watson, inf*, Lord CAMPBELL points out a variety of circumstances which are " extremely material for the surety to know "—that is, in the sense that a knowledge of them would affect his judgment—and points out that they are nevertheless not required to be disclosed, or material in that sense.

(o) At pp. 503, 504 of *Lee v Jones, sup.*

(p) At p 119 of *Hamilton v. Watson* (1845), 12 Cl & F 109 The proposition may be expressed a little more broadly, as is pointed out by VAUGHAN WILLIAMS, L.J, at p 79 of *London General Omnibus Co v. Holloway,* [1912] 2 K B. 72, C A . " Lord CAMPBELL, it is true, takes as his example of what might not naturally be expected an unusual contract between creditor and debtor whose debt the surety guarantees, but I take it this is only an example of the general proposition that a creditor must reveal to the surety every fact which under the circumstances the surety would expect not to exist, for the omission to mention that such a fact does exist is an implied representation that it does not." Cp. *National Provincial Bank of England v Glanusk,* [1913] 3 K B. 335 (per HORRIDGE, J, at p. 338)

place between the parties who are concerned in the transaction ; " and it is
on this theory that the suppression of such circumstances has been regarded
as an implied misrepresentation (q), at all events, in all cases where there
has been direct bargaining or communication between the creditor and the
surety (r)

124. The existence of a duty of disclosure in the negotiation preliminary
to a contract of suretyship, but limited and varying as above stated according
to the nature of the particular kind of guarantee which raises the question,
is best established by examining the several modes in which the doctrine has
been applied to the respective classes of suretyship, of which there may be
said to be three main types   first, where the surety guarantees a debt, or an
indebtedness to be incurred for money lent, goods supplied, or other consideration , secondly, where he guarantees the future honesty or fidelity of
a person employed, or to be employed, by the person to whom the guarantee
is given   lastly, where he guarantees the due performance of a particular
transaction or the carrying out of a particular enterprise or adventure by a
person with whom the party to whom the guarantee is given has contracted
or is associated   The first two classes embrace normal and ordinary cases of
suretyship . the last includes contracts of a kind which, in many instances,
are scarcely distinguished from contracts of insurance (s).

125. In contracts of the first type, that is, where a person's credit is guaranteed, the creditor, when treating with the proposed surety, must reveal to
him such material circumstances in relation to the past conduct of the principal debtor as are within his knowledge, and are not within either the actual
or presumptive knowledge of the surety, and a circumstance is not deemed
to be within the surety's presumptive knowledge unless it is one of the existence or possibility of which he is invited by the nature of the transaction
itself to take notice   Thus, in the case of a guarantee of the debtor's liability
to the intending creditors for iron to be supplied, the creditors were held to
be under a duty to disclose to the surety the fact that the debtor had applied
to them to supply him with the iron on credit, on the terms that he was to
pay them 10s. on every ton of iron sold in liquidation of an old debt (t) ;
and, in the case of a guarantee given to coal merchants of the future liability
of their agent for the sale of coal on commission, the creditors, in suppressing
the fact that in the course of his past duties as recited in the agreement of
suretyship the agent had been a heavy defaulter, and was then indebted to
them in a very large aggregate sum in respect of those defaults, were held to have

<hr>

(q) As it was by the majority of the Exchequer Chamber in *Lee* v *Jones, sup* (*per*
SHEE, J , at p 500, and BLACKBURN, J , at pp 503, 504)   Cp the observations of BLACK-
BURN, J , at p 679 of *Phillips* v *Foxall* (1872), L. R 7 Q B 666 (" I still adhere to the
opinion that I expressed in *Lee* v *Jones*, that if such a transaction as is alleged in the plea
had taken place before the defendant entered into the contract of suretyship, and had been
concealed from him, it would have furnished evidence of a false representation to the surety
that no such thing existed "), and those of VAUGHAN WILLIAMS, L J , cited at the end of
the last note.

(r) See the view expressed by Lord TRURO, L C , as cited in note (g) to § 120, *ante.*

(s) See § 121, *ante.*

(t) *Pidcock* v. *Bishop* (1825), 3 B & C 605

violated a plain duty of disclosure, and, in the circumstances, to have also been guilty of gross fraud (u). On the other hand, where the undisclosed fact is, unlike those in the above illustrations, incidental to, and a natural feature of, the situation which calls for the protection of a suretyship contract, and therefore one which the surety is bound to contemplate as not only possible, but highly probable, the creditor is under no liability for not volunteering information, for instance, to take the typical case of a guarantee given to a bank of a customer's overdraft, the bank is not bound to disclose the condition of the customer's old account, or any matters tending to show his existing or previous embarrassment (v), because the person who has assumed the character of guarantor must know that the customer's bad credit was the only reason of his being asked to do so (w); nor are bankers required to communicate the existence of a *mere intention* on their part, before the conclusion of the contract of suretyship, to employ the cash credit to be given to the customer in paying off an old debt due from him to themselves (x), though, in the authority for this illustration, it was acknowledged that, if there had been an agreement to the effect stated, as distinguished from a mere purpose (even if afterwards accomplished), the fact would have been a proper subject of disclosure (y) Nor, in this class of guarantee, as distinguished from that next to be discussed, is the previous misconduct, or strongly suspected criminality even, of the customer, a fact which the bank is under any obligation to disclose to the surety (yy)

126. In the second class of suretyship contract, consisting of what are commonly called "fidelity bonds," the burden of disclosure is heavier than in either of the two other classes, for the area of relevant matters of which the surety in this class cannot be expected to have either knowledge or suspicion obviously extends further. Where the surety guarantees merely the credit of a person who is about to be trusted, he knows that his financial record must have become dubious, for otherwise there would be no necessity to resort to the credit of another person. but where he is guaranteeing the future honesty or fidelity of a servant, official, or agent, he is not in the least bound to suspect that he is

(u) *Lee* v *Jones* (1864), 17 C B (N S) 482, Exch Ch
(v) *Wythes* v *Labouchere* (1859), 3 De G & J 593, *per* Lord CHELMSFORD, L C, at pp 608–610
(w) *Hamilton* v *Watson, sup*, *per* Lord CAMPBELL at p 120, and *London General Omnibus Co* v *Holloway, sup*, *per* FARWELL, L J, at p 82 "guarantees for overdrafts are required for the purpose, and not on the chance, of being used it is perfectly legitimate and usual for a man to carry on his business on borrowed money, including money borrowed from his bankers by way of overdraft, and the surety knows this, and becomes surety for the very purpose of enabling him to do so There is nothing in such a case which the surety does not know as well as any other member of the community," and again at p. 83 (after citing the passage above referred to from Lord CAMPBELL's speech in *Hamilton* v *Watson*) "no surety asked to guarantee a banking account is entitled to assume that the customer of the bank has not been in the habit of overdrawing, the proper presumption in most instances is that he has been doing so, and wishes to do so again."
(x) *Hamilton* v *Watson, sup*, *per* Lord LYNDHURST, L C, at p 118, and Lord CAMPBELL, at pp 119, 120
(y) *Ibid*, *per* Lord LYNDHURST, L C, at p 118, and Lord CAMPBELL, at p 119
(yy) *Bank of Scotland* v *Morrison*, [1911] Ct. of Sess Cas 593, *National Provincial Bank of England* v *Glanusk*, [1913] 3 K B 335 (*per* HORRIDGE, J., at pp 338, 339).

being asked to make himself liable for the future defaults and delinquencies of one who is already a professed or proved knave, since it is not an unusual, but a natural thing, and quite in the normal course of business, for an intending employer, and particularly if he is a public officer or authority, and the proposed servant is to be entrusted with public moneys, to insure himself against loss from the contingency of a man of good reputation yielding to temptation . whereas it is positively fraudulent (z), and therefore presumably unusual, to invite another to take the like risk in respect of one whose past conduct is known to the employer, or even suspected by him, to have been dishonest or criminal · and no surety is bound to presume that either the employer has a dishonest intention in proposing the suretyship, or that the servant whose future conduct is to be guaranteed has a dishonest past (zz). In accordance with this principle, it has been held that the duty of the employer, in the case of fidelity bonds, is to divulge, during the treaty for the suretyship, even facts tending to raise a strong suspicion of previous misconduct on the part of a person employed as agent to a bank (a) , a fortiori, facts positively establishing previous irregularity and misconduct on the part of a person whilst acting in partnership with another as commission agents for the employers, in a case where this person's future individual conduct in the same capacity (the partnership having been dissolved) was guaranteed (b) , and facts establishing previous embezzlements on the part of a tea-merchant's van-man (c), or previous defalcations and embezzlements on the part of a

(z) This was the view expressed by Lord ELDON, L C., at p 292 of *Smith* v *Bank of Scotland* (1813), 1 Dow App Cas 272 " if a man found that his agent had betrayed his trust, that he owed him a sum of money, or that it was likely he was in his debt ; if under such circumstances he required sureties for his fidelity, holding him out as a trustworthy person, knowing, or having ground to believe, that he was not so . then it was agreeable to the doctrines of equity, at least in England, that no one should be permitted to take advantage of such conduct, even with a view to security against future transactions of the agent."

(zz) See *London General Omnibus Co* v. *Holloway*, *sup* , *per* FARWELL, L J , at p 82 " a surety may well be willing to guarantee an employer against defalcations by a servant believed to be honest . it is quite another matter, if the servant has already been found guilty of defalcations The surety believes that he is making himself answerable for a presumably honest man, not for a known thief " And, later on the same page, in explaining the essential distinction between fidelity and other guarantees, he observes ' the surety may well complain ' I did not know that your servant was a thief '; but he cannot be heard to complain ' I did not know your customer had been overdrawing his account or what the nature of his business was ' " This vital difference between the two types of case is also insisted on by the Lord Justice Clerk at p 602 of *Bank of Scotland* v *Morrison*, *sup* , as it had been in the Court below by Lord MACKENZIE (at p 601 n), who also points out that, when guaranteeing honesty and fidelity, the surety is helpless he cannot make the guaranteed person be honest, or rid himself of his liability , whereas, where he is only guaranteeing a debt, he can at any moment pay the debt, with recourse against the debtor. The Lord Ordinary puts this forward as an additional ground for requiring a further measure of disclosure in the former case

(a) *Smith* v *Bank of Scotland*, *sup*., *per* Lord ELDON, L C , at pp 291–295, and Lord REDESDALE at p 297

(b) *Railton* v *Mathews & Leonard* (1844), 10 Cl & F. 934, *per* Lord COTTENHAM, L C , at pp 940, 941, and Lord CAMPBELL at p 943

(c) *Phillips* v *Foxall* (1872), L. R 7 Q B 666. This was a case, not of non disclosure of the servant's misconduct during the proposals for the suretyship, but of suppression of that fact during the currency of a continuing guarantee, and, therefore, the actual decision belongs to the class of cases referred to in § 129, note (l), *post*, as not strictly relevant to the subject now being considered The joint judgment, however, of COCKBURN, C.J , and

clerk to an omnibus company (d) On the other hand, there is no obligation to communicate any circumstances not showing, or giving rise to a reasonable suspicion of, moral delinquency, such as the mere fact that the collector of a municipal corporation has been in the habit, during his past service, of rendering his accounts at irregular intervals, contrary to an express resolution of the corporation, where there is no suggestion or suspicion of dishonesty (e).

127. In the third type of suretyship, where the surety assumes a secondary liability in the event of the person primarily liable making default in the performance of a particular bargain or transaction, the nature both of this bargain or transaction, and of the contract of suretyship, must first be examined, and then the governing rule must be applied; the question being whether, in the individual case, the undisclosed fact was such as would reasonably be within the contemplation of the surety as part of the risk which he was undertaking, or whether, on the contrary, it was something that he would not naturally expect to exist, or to have taken place The application of this rule has resulted in the following illustrative decisions Where the surety guaranteed the due execution by another person of a contract whereby that person covenanted with the party to whom the guarantee was given for the payment to him of certain annuities in consideration of the conveyance of property described as being subject to certain charges, the last-named party was held to have failed in his duty of disclosure in suppressing the fact that there was a mortgage on the property apart from the specified charges (f). So, where certain persons became sureties for the due performance by another person of his obligations under a contract for sewerage which he had entered into with a local authority, whereby he was to be paid on the certificate of a named firm, described as the local authority's surveyors, it was held that the fact that the local authority had entered into an agreement with the landowner that the work was to be done under the joint superintendence and control of the local authority's named surveyors *and the landowner's surveyor*, was a fact which ought to have been communicated to the sureties (g). On the other hand, where the surety had guaranteed a certain loan, it was held that the fact that there had been a previous guarantor of the same loan, and that, at his request, and on the terms of his finding another guarantor, he had been released by the lenders, was not a fact which was necessarily material to be disclosed, and the jury having found that in that case it was not, the Court refused to disturb their finding (h). So, where two persons had joined as sureties with a third person as principal in a bond for the repayment

LUSH and QUAIN, JJ., is prefaced by a discussion of what would have been the legal consequences if the non-disclosure in question had been a non-disclosure *before* the execution of the contract of suretyship (p 671), and the conclusion arrived at is that the contract would clearly have been vitiated

(d) *London General Omnibus Co* v. *Holloway*, [1912] 2 K B 72, C A

(e) *Durham Corporation* v *Fowler* (1889), 22 Q B D 394, *per* CHARLES, J , at p 404, and *per* DENMAN and STEPHEN, JJ , affirming him, at p 415. It was recognized by the Court that, if the irregularity there had amounted to dishonesty, the result would have been different

(f) *Willis* v *Willis* (1850), 17 Sim 218 (*per* SHADWELL, V C)

(g) *Stiff* v *Local Board of Eastbourne* (1868), 19 L T 408 (*per* STUART, V C)

(h) *North British Insurance Co* v. *Lloyd* (1854), 10 Exch 523, *per Cur.* at pp. 532, 533.

of a certain loan to a life insurance company, it was held that there was no obligation on one of the two sureties to disclose to his co-surety (because there would have been none on either of the sureties to disclose to the creditor) the fact that the first surety had agreed with the principal debtor that the latter, out of the money to be lent by the insurance company, should pay to the former a certain sum in discharge of an old debt ; and it was said that to hold otherwise would be " to invent new equities to enable people to escape from mercantile obligations " (i). And where certain underwriters at Lloyd's had entered into an agreement with a lady who had lent money to one B , in respect of which she held his promissory note for £15,000, by which agreement they guaranteed, not the repayment of the note, but the solvency of one H. in respect of a guarantee which he had given to the lady for the repayment of it, it was held by the House of Lords, in this respect reversing the C. A , that, whether this curious contract (which was in the form of a policy, but contained stipulations proper to a transaction of surety-ship) was to be regarded as one of insurance or guarantee, there was no duty on the lady to disclose to the underwriters the fact that £2625 of the £15,000 represented interest, or the fact that she had refused to lend any money to B at less than 40 per cent interest, and that neither of these facts was in the least material, or could, as the Court of Appeal thought possible, be properly so found by a jury (j)   They might have been material to the risk of the non-payment of the note by B , but this was not the risk which the under-writers undertook, whether as insurers or guarantors, which was solely the risk of H 's insolvency, and to this the facts in question obviously had no sort of relevance

128. It should be added that in negotiating for contracts of suretyship, it has been laid down by Lord St Leonards, L C , that a creditor may be under a duty of investigation, even though he is not in direct treaty with the surety, under certain circumstances which he describes as follows " without saying that in every case a creditor is bound to inquire under what circumstances his debtor has obtained the concurrence of a surety, it may

(i) *Mackreth* v *Walmsley* (1884), 51 L T 19 (*per* Kay, J)
(j) *Seaton* v *Burnand*, [1900] A C. 135, H L. This case, *sub nom Seaton* v *Heath*, was tried before Bigham, J , and a jury, the lady being the plaintiff, and the defendants, the underwriters, setting up (*inter alia*) non disclosure of the facts stated in the text On the jury answering in the negative a general question left to them by the judge, " whether the transaction was one of exceptional risk," Bigham, J , entered judgment for the plaintiff   The C A (A L Smith, Collins, and Romer, LL.JJ) directed a new trial—*Seaton* v. *Heath*, [1899] 1 Q B 782, C A —on the ground that the minds of the jury had not been directed to the real issues, and that the undisclosed facts were at least capable of being considered material by the jury, if asked specifically whether they were or were not, which Bigham, J , had not done   The House of Lords, without disagreeing with any of the rules and propositions of law laid down by the Court of Appeal, reversed their decision, and restored the judgment of Bigham, J , solely on the ground stated in the text, namely, that the particular withheld facts were not capable of being considered material to the particular risk undertaken (*per* Lord Halsbury, L C , at p 139, and Lord Brampton at p 148), or, putting it another way, there was no evidence of any withholding of any fact which was material to the risk, that is, of any fact having a bearing on the solvency of H (*per* Lord Halsbury, L.C , at pp 139, 140, and Lord Robertson at p 149), the result being that the defendants had not established that anything undisclosed was material, or that anything material was undisclosed.

safely be stated that if the dealings are such as fairly to lead a reasonable man to believe that fraud must have been used in order to obtain such concurrence, he is bound to make inquiry, and cannot shelter himself under the plea that he was not called on to ask, and did not ask, any question on the subject " (*k*).

129. It is to be observed that the duty of disclosure with which alone this Chapter is concerned is a duty which, *as such*, comes to an end on the conclusion of the contract. In the case of continuing guarantees, the creditor still owes a duty to the surety after this date, but a contractual duty only, arising under and out of the suretyship itself, and such that mere disclosure is not a discharge of, or strictly speaking, relevant to, such duty The obligation of the creditor, in all such cases, is to abstain during the currency of the suretyship, from varying in the slightest degree (whether a normal person would consider the variation material or immaterial, for not he, but the surety is to be judge of this matter) the contractual relations which existed between himself and the principal debtor at the date of the commencement of the suretyship, without the *consent* of the surety. If the creditor violates this contractual obligation, the surety has a good contractual defence to any action on the guarantee, for he never agreed to make good the default of the principal debtor in respect of such altered relation, be it in ever so minute a particular, but only in respect of the relation which existed when he gave the guarantee, and to which alone that guarantee was expressed to apply He is entitled to set up the plea of *non hæc in fœdera veni* ; or, in other words, the law discharges him altogether from the liability as surety to which he would otherwise have been subject (*l*). If, however, the creditor can establish the *assent* of the surety to the alteration in the principal contract, he establishes at the same time his implied assent to a corresponding modification of the suretyship contract, and an enlargement to that extent of his liability thereunder. But nothing short of consent will suffice (*m*)· and,

(*k*) *Owen* v *Homan* (1853), 4 H L C 997, at pp 1034, 1035

(*l*) It follows, therefore, that the authorities on this topic are, strictly considered, irrelevant to this treatise It will be sufficient to give here the references to the principal decisions (some of which, however, will be again cited in the notes immediately following, for the purpose of discriminating the two kinds of obligation) They are as follows .— *Whitcher* v *Hall* (1826), 5 B & C 269 , *Mactaggart* v *Wilson* (1835), 3 Cl & F. 525 , *Bonar* v *Macdonald* (1850), 3 H L C 226 , *Dawson* v *Lawes* (1854), 23 L J (CH) 434 , *Small* v *Currie* (1854), 23 L. J (CH) 746 ; *North Western Railway Co* v *Whinray* (1854), 10 Exch 77 , *Stewart* v *M'Kean* (1855), 10 Exch 655 , *Berwick Corporation* v *Oswald* (1855), 5 H L C 856 , *Pybus* v *Gibb* (1856), 6 E & B 902 , *Blest* v *Brown* (1862), 4 De G F & J. 367 , *Tayleur* v *Wildin* (1868), L R 3 Exch 303 , *Phillips* v *Foxall* (1872), L R. 7 Q B 666 , *Polak* v *Everett* (1876), 1 Q B D 669 , *Holme* v *Brunskill* (1878), 3 Q B D 495, C. A (*per* CHARLES, J , at p 394, and DENMAN and STEPHEN, JJ , at pp 421-423, as to variation of the contract between the employer and the servant during the currency of the suretyship there was also a defence of non disclosure before the suretyship was entered upon, as to which see § 126, note (*c*), *ante*) , *Caxton and Accrington Union* v *Dew* (1899), 68 L J (Q B) 380 ; *Snaddon* v *London, Edinburgh & Glasgow Assurance Co* (1902), 5 F 182

(*m*) At p 239 of *Bonar* v *Macdonald*, *sup.*, a Scotch case, the following passage from Bell's " Principles " was cited and approved by the House of Lords as being a correct statement of both the Scottish and the English law on the question " the cautioner is freed by any essential change, consented to by the creditor, in the principal obligation or transaction, without the knowledge *or assent* of the cautioner " So, in *Phillips* v *Foxall*, *sup* , after stating the effect of non disclosure before the conclusion of the contract of suretyship, as to which see note (*c*) to § 126, *ante*, the joint judgment of COCKBURN, C J ,

though of course consent is inefficacious without full and exact knowledge of that which is consented to, and such knowledge, if established at all, is usually made out by proof of direct disclosure on the part of the creditor to the surety, this only means that communication and consultation with the surety is ordinarily an essential preliminary to the obtaining of the consent. But, if no consent results from this communication and consultation, the creditor has no answer to the surety's claim to be discharged ; the latter is entitled, if he pleases, to stand still and mutely watch the process of striking off his shackles ; and the fullest knowledge, by disclosure or otherwise, of all the facts which, unless he gives his assent, will effect his liberation, is not a substitute for, or the equivalent, of such assent (n) · which shews that, *per se*, disclosure is immaterial to the question of the creditor's obligations to the surety after the conclusion of the contract of suretyship

130. The questions of the burden of proof on the party complaining (the surety), the affirmative pleas available to the party charged (the creditor, employer, or other person to whom the guarantee is given), the appropriate remedy and relief, matters of law and fact, and parties, are discussed in other sections of this Chapter (o)

Sub-s (5). *Releases, Waivers, Compromises, and Compositions*

131. Where parties are in treaty with one another with a view to a release or waiver on one side, or a compromise on both sides, of rights or claims, the rules of good faith, in the matter of disclosure, apply but the application, as will be seen, varies according to the nature of the transaction contemplated, that is to say, accordingly as it is a release or waiver of a particular specified right, or of all rights and claims, or a compromise of disputed claims, and, if a compromise, accordingly as it is, or is not, of the character of a family arrangement.

132. First, as to releases and waivers A release or waiver may either be of a particular defined right or claim, or it may be expressed in general terms so as to purport to surrender all claims of every sort or kind in relation to a certain subject-matter. In the former case, the party obtaining the

and LUSH and QUAIN, JJ , proceeds (at p. 674) : " we think that in the case of a continuing guarantee a similar concealment made during the progress of the contract ought to have a similar effect as regards the future liability of the surety *unless his assent has been obtained, after knowledge of the dishonesty, that his guarantee shall hold good during the subsequent service*," and, at p. 677, the necessity of obtaining the surety's " assent " is insisted upon And, at pp 505, 506 of *Holme v Brunskill, sup* , COTTON, L.J., states " the true rule " to be " that if there is any agreement between the principals with reference to the matter guaranteed, the surety ought to be consulted, and that, if he has not consented to the alteration, . . . the Court will . . hold that in such a case the surety himself must be the *sole judge whether he will consent* to remain liable notwithstanding the alteration, and that, if he has never consented, he will be discharged "

(n) This was clearly and emphatically laid down by BLACKBURN, J., at p 672 of *Polak v Everett, sup.*, as follows · " we must take it to be the fact that though the defendant was well aware of the release being executed, he was not an assenting party to it. Then it is argued that knowledge on the part of the surety that there is going to be a release of a part of the security is enough without assent. I cannot see any authority for that . . To say that a person who, being a surety, becomes aware that a creditor is going to give time, or do something else which, if done without his assent, may discharge him, is bound to warn the creditor against doing it, is a thing for which no authority whatever has been cited "

(o) See Sects 3–7 respectively, *post.*

release or waiver, must disclose during the negotiation all such matters affecting the specified right or claim as are within his knowledge, and of which, to his knowledge, the other party is ignorant (p) In the latter case, his duty of disclosure is much wider. the party in whose favour the general release or waiver is made must divulge to the other party any particular right of the class purporting to be released or waived which he knows, but the other party does not know, to be enforceable against himself by that other,—every right, in fact, the renunciation of which, as being literally within the general terms, he intends afterwards to assert and rely upon, but which the other party does not know that he possesses, and does not believe, therefore, to be included in such general terms, or to be the subject of the release or waiver. This rule has been rigidly applied not only to releases, strictly so called (q), but to "catching conditions of sale" (r), and "tricky" waiver clauses in prospectuses of companies (s)

(p) Thus, in *M'Carthy* v *Decaix* (1831), 2 Russ & M 614, an action brought by the personal representative of one T against the personal representatives of T's wife for arrears of an annuity to which T. had become entitled under a marriage settlement, to which the defendants pleaded a renunciation by T of his rights under the settlement in favour of his wife's family, and the plaintiff replied that the renunciation was of no effect on the ground of the suppression from T. of (*inter alia*) the true amount and value of his wife's property when she died, T being, in the absence of information as to these matters, under the impression that his wife had died a pauper, Lord BROUGHAM, L C , reversing LEACH, V C., held that the "renunciation" could not stand, and gave judgment for the plaintiff

(q) See *Hylton* v *Hylton* (1754), 2 Ves Sr 547, where the plaintiff sued to set aside various grants which he had made to the defendant by way of gift, and, *inter alia*, the grant of a certain release in general terms, and Lord HARDWICKE, L.C , held, as to this release, that it could not stand, for the reason, amongst others, that no account had been rendered to the plaintiff of the matters which, in general terms, he had purported to release Cp. *Bowles* v *Stewart* (1803), 1 Sch & Lefr 209, an action for a similar purpose, where Lord REDESDALE, L C (Ir), set aside a release given by the plaintiff, framed in the most general terms, and extending far beyond the matters in contest, on the ground that the nature and extent of the rights which the plaintiff was purporting to renounce had never been explained to him, and an opinion of counsel as to these matters, and various deeds and facts indicating that the value of these rights was much larger than he supposed, had been withheld from him, and that there had been an absence of "full and fair disclosure" (p. 226), and the release had been "unfairly obtained under a suppression of the plaintiff's rights" (p 227), *Lloyd* v *Attwood* (1859), 3 De G & J 614 (*per* TURNER, L J , at p 649 general release of trustees), *Farrant* v *Blanchford* (1863), 32 L J (CH) 237 (*per* Lord WESTBURY, L C , at p 240 the like) Cp *Lyall* v *Edwards* (1861), 6 H & N 337 (*per* POLLOCK, C B , and MARTIN, B , at p 347), and the observations of Lord WESTBURY at p 623 of *London & South Western Railway Co* v *Blackmore* (1870), L R. 4 H L 610, and of SWINFEN EADY, J , in *Re Joint Stock Trust & Finance Corporation* (1912), 56 Sol J. 272 And see, further, the observations as to general releases cited in note (s), *inf*

(r) In *Nottingham Patent Brick & Tile Co* v *Butler* (1886), 16 Q B D 778, C A , there was a condition of sale that "the property is sold subject to . any matter or thing affecting the same, whether disclosed at the time of sale or not," and it was held that, the vendor not having divulged the facts that in a predecessor's deed of title there were restrictions against brickmaking, and that, though he purchased without notice of those restrictions, he sold with notice of them, so that he was conferring a title which might conceivably be impeached afterwards, the general waiver sought to be put upon the purchaser by the above condition was entirely inefficacious, LINDLEY, L J , observing, at p 789 "assuming that he was a *bonâ fide* purchaser for value without notice, but at the time of the sale to the plaintiffs he was aware of the restrictions, if he intended to cover that blot in his title, and to say to a purchaser, You must take such title as I have got, I am a *bonâ fide* purchaser for value, without notice of any restrictions , you must buy upon this condition ,—he ought to have used a condition pointing to the blot much more specifically than the actual conditions have done " Cp the judicial expressions as to "catching conditions of sale" which are cited in the next note

(s) See *Greenwood* v. *Leather Shod Wheel Co* , [1900] 1 Ch 421, C A , *per* LINDLEY, M R ,

133. Compromises and settlements of disputed claims, which form the other of the two above-mentioned classes of transaction whereby rights are surrendered, stand on a very different footing from releases and waivers; though, as will be shown presently, it is going too far to say that no duty of disclosure in the former type of case exists at all unless the circumstances amount to or suggest something more than a mere omission to convey information. A party giving a release in general terms has a right to complain if he is not fully informed as to specific rights which, known to the other party, but unknown to himself, are supposed to be included in the comprehensive formula to which he has subscribed : whereas, in cases of compromise, as the name itself imports, the very consideration and essence of the transaction is a mutual surrender of claims *bonâ fide* asserted, however ill-founded they may subsequently prove to have been (*t*), as to the validity, value, and details of which neither party has, or desires to have, any exact knowledge or information, the object on both sides being to put an end to past, and still more to avoid the possibility of future, contest or litigation, and, by striking a rough guesswork balance once for all, on the principle of "give and take," to escape the time, worry, and expense involved in production, inspection, calculation, and verification of accounts, vouchers, and other documentary evidence, and in the elucidation of facts by means of

---

at p 437   "if a company's prospectus is fraudulent   .   , and an applicant for shares signs a contract which is intended to deprive him of redress, he is not bound in equity by what he signs *unless his attention is called to the existence of facts which render the prospectus fraudulent* The introduction of a stipulation that an applicant for shares is to be deemed to have notice of what is in fact concealed from him, is simply part of the trick . . The principle of refusing to give effect to parts of documents so as to prevent successful deception by means of them is quite familiar in its application to general words in releases, and to catching conditions of sale," and again, at pp 437, 438   "general waiver clauses in prospectuses, applications for shares, articles of association, or other documents addressed to large numbers of persons are always suspicious, and require careful scrutiny", *Cackett v Keswick*, [1902] 2 Ch 456, C A , *per* FARWELL, J , whose decision was affirmed by the C A , at pp 467, 468 ("a man who desires to take advantage of a waiver clause must state the facts fairly . . . if the element of unfairness is requisite, it is found when he insists that its effect is to make the other contracting party give up something of the existence of which the asserter knew, and the other contracting party was ignorant As I read the judgments in *Greenwood* v *Leather Shod Wheel Co* , the decision, and the reasons given for it, involve the proposition that   . the person said to have waived must have sufficient information of what he was waiving , and that, apart from fraud, the same principles apply to waiver clauses as are applicable to ambiguous and misleading state ments in conditions of sale or releases "), *per* ROMER, L.J , at p 476 ("no fair or sufficient notice "), and *per* STIRLING, L J., at p 477 (such as   . fairly to convey to the mind of the intending shareholder the nature of the contracts which have been excluded "), *Watts* v. *Bucknall*, [1903] 1 Ch 766, C A., *per* COLLINS, M R , at p 776, citing and adopting the above statement of FARWELL, J , in *Cackett v Keswick*, *sup* , and at pp 776, 777, citing and approving similar language used by the same judge in the Court below in the case then under appeal ("it is a true statement of the law to say that no protection can be afforded to those responsible for the issue of a prospectus, under a waiver clause which they invite subscribers to submit themselves to, *unless they fairly disclose what is the nature of the rights which they ask should be released or waived* "), and *per* COZENS-HARDY, L J., at p 780 ("I doubt whether a waiver clause of this nature ought ever to be allowed to operate, except under such conditions as would enable the defendant '—who in that case was the party relying upon the waiver—"to rely upon a release in general terms " Waiver clauses in prospectuses of companies are now, as to a large number of matters, rendered absolutely void by statute (see § 562, *post*), but this fact is no way affects the relevancy of the above propositions in their application to releases and waivers in general.

   (*t*) See § 138, *post*, and note (*x*) thereto.

difficult and tedious researches amongst persons, and in places, perhaps not easily accessible. Neither party, therefore, starts with the intention of giving, or with the expectation of receiving, any precise disclosure : for it is the basis of the transaction that neither has any precise knowledge to impart to the other (u). On this principle, whenever the party charged has been guilty of no such active concealment or obliquity of conduct or other breach of duty as is mentioned below (v), the compromise has been supported, and the party complaining has failed (w). And, where litigated claims are the subject

(u) *Per* Lord MANNERS, L C. (Ir.), at p 180 of *Leonard* v. *Leonard* (1812), 2 Ball & B. 171 (" between a mere release and a deed of compromise . there is this distinction ; that in the former, the parties know their respective rights, and the one surrenders his right to the other : in the latter, both parties are ignorant of their rights, and the agreement is founded on that ignorance "). See also the observations of Lord COTTENHAM, L C., at p. 970 of *Stewart* v. *Stewart* (1839), 6 Cl & F 911 , and of the C A (Lord HALSBURY, L.C , and VAUGHAN WILLIAMS and STIRLING, LL JJ.) at p 710 of *Re Roberts* , *Roberts* v *Roberts*, [1905] 1 Ch 704, C A (" generally, the very object of the compromise is to avoid the necessity of having the exact relative legal rights determined by litigation ")

(v) See § 136-138, *post*

(w) As in *Naylor* v. *Winch* (1824), 1 Sim & St 555 , *Watt* v *Assets Co* , [1905] A. C. 317, H L (as to which see note (r) to § 137, *post*), and *Law* v *Law*,[1905] 1 Ch 140, C A In the last cited case, which is a very useful illustration of the principles on which the Courts will uphold a compromise, and reject a plea of non disclosure, the facts were these It was agreed between two brothers, James and William Law, partners in a certain business, that William should sell his share in the business to James for £21,000, which sum was to be paid as to £10,500 at once, and as to the remaining £10,500, in six months' time, the latter payment being secured by James's bond William afterwards discovered that, in the course of the negotiations for the above sale, James had concealed the existence of partnership assets to a very considerable amount, which concealment of course gave him a right to relief by way of rescission—see § 149, and note (d) thereto, *post*,—and, if the concealment amounted to fraud, damages He elected to sue for damages in the K B D for fraudulent misrepresentation After the issue of the writ, he discovered still further suppression of assets on the part of James, and suspected (not without reason, as appeared afterwards) that he had not yet got to the bottom of James's concealments With that knowledge and suspicion, however, during the progress of the action, he agreed to a compromise, embodied in a written agreement, followed by a consent order, whereby he, withdrawing all charges of fraud, was to receive £3550 from James " in discharge of every claim relating to any matter whatever between the plaintiff and the defendant, and to be accepted in full satisfaction thereof " After this compromise, William discovered, as he anticipated he would, that James had suppressed yet further partnership assets, to the amount of no less than £80,000, and thereupon sued (*inter alios*) the executors of James (who had died in the meantime) for rescission of the compromise, and for taking of the partnership accounts Pending suit, William died, and the action was continued by William's executors KEKEWICH, J , held, and was affirmed by the C A in so doing, that, under these circumstances, the case set up of non-disclosure failed, and that the compromise could not be disturbed, observing, at p 147, that " with that knowledge, and with the knowledge that he could obtain full discovery in the action, he chose to take £3550 in settlement of all claims. He was prepared to take that sum to settle the litigation, put an end to disputes, and avoid the troublesome taking of accounts, and going into all the matters in question," and, therefore, " it would be against common sense and common honesty that the plaintiff should be allowed to say that he accepted that sum only in settlement of his claim in respect of the non-disclosure of certain assets, and now to claim to go into the question of the non disclosure of other assets " The C A (*per* COZENS-HARDY, LJ), at p 158, expressed their agreement with this view in these terms " before this settlement was arrived at, William had ascertained that there were still further partnership assets not disclosed by James, and he surmised and believed that there might be others, though he was not aware of their particulars or amount. Under these circumstances it was, of course, open to William, if he chose, not to insist on his full rights, and, in particular, not to obtain disclosure of what the assets consisted, and to come to a settlement or compromise with James on that footing And this is what he did What his reasons were for so doing concerned himself alone, and it would be idle to speculate whether he was influenced by fraternal affection, . . . or by some other reason. But after the

of settlement, however seriously the party charged may have violated some
other duty of disclosure in respect of which violation the litigation is instituted,
that duty, as such, ceases on the commencement of the proceedings, when
the parties are at arm's length, and thenceforth is superseded by such duty
of disclosure, if any, as under the circumstances may be incumbent on them
as parties to a negotiation for a compromise (x)   More especially, of course,
are the Courts disposed to uphold a compromise where the party seeking to
set it aside is shown to have entered into it, not merely with that general
intention to waive all exact information which characterizes the ordinary
type of compromise, but with a strong inkling or suspicion of all or some of
the facts of the suppression of which he afterwards complains, and with the
secret and unconscientious design of first taking the present benefit of the
compromise, and then, at a convenient subsequent date, seeking relief in
respect of the alleged non-disclosure of facts which at the time he suspected,
or vaguely believed, to exist (y)

134. It must be remembered that, as in other departments of law (z),
the Court looks to the substance, object, and effect of the transaction, rather
than to the phraseology employed by the parties, or appearing on the face
of the instrument itself, for the purpose of determining whether it is a release
or a compromise, and which, accordingly, of the above different degrees of
disclosure should be required in the particular case (a)

settlement so come to, in our opinion it was not possible for William to reopen the transaction "
   (x) *Law v Law, sup*, *per Cur*, at p 159 (" it has been strenuously argued that the
duty resting on the purchasing partner continued in full force and effect up to and after
the settlement of the action, so that James could not rely on a binding election by William
unless and until a full disclosure had been made   We know of no authority which supports
this proposition, and it seems to us to be contrary to principle ")
   (y) *Law v Law, sup*, *per Cur*, at p 150, where, after referring to the facts proved in
evidence, which they stated to be highly important, that William had assigned James's
bond for the second £10,500—see note (w), *sup*.—to trustees, and had joined with those
trustees in suing for, and obtaining in the action, that amount with interest and costs,
pursuant to a consent order, the Court observes   " this was four days before the writ
in the action "—that is the action for damages in the K B D—" was issued   In point of
fact, William, with knowledge that the sale might be upset or damages recovered, de
liberately postponed proceedings with that view until after he had obtained payment of
the balance of the purchase money, to which he had no title except upon the footing that
the sale was not to be set aside.   It is now too late for William to repudiate the contract
of which he has thus deliberately secured the benefits "
   (z) For instance, what is called a " warranty " may be treated as a " condition," and
vice versâ, in contracts of sale, if the real nature of the transaction has been misdescribed
or mislabelled by the parties   and similarly, as to " penalties " and " liquidated damages ",
and as to insurances and guarantees—see §§ 120, 121, *ante*   So also the character in law
of a particular society, *e g* whether it is a " trade union " or not, does not depend on the
name given to it in its constitution or rules   And there are numerous other illustrations
   (a) Thus, in *Leonard v. Leonard* (1812), 1 Ball & B 171, where the plaintiff sued to set
aside a deed " by which he conveyed and *released* all his right and interest as heir at law,
and one of the next of kin, of Samuel Leonard, in consideration of an annuity of £100 to
be paid to him by the defendant, during his, the plaintiff's, life " (p 176), Lord MANNERS,
L.C (Ir), at p 180, said   " this deed has been treated as a release   now that is not the
precise description of it," and he then proceeds to deal with it as a compromise, and he
emphasizes the importance of so doing by a careful discrimination between " a mere
release and a deed of compromise *of this nature* "   see note (u) to § 133, *ante*   So also
Lord MACCLESFIELD, L.C, in *Cann v Cann* (1721), 1 P Wms 723, seems to have treated
the question before him as one of compromise, rather than release, though the parties

135. If, on the principle of *interest reipublicæ ut sit finis litium*, it is the practice of the Courts to support and effectuate all honest compromises, of whatever kind, the object of which is to settle litigation, or to adjust disputed claims before resort to litigation, and so effect the "prevention" which is proverbially "better than cure," still more cordially is this judicial favour extended, in the absence of any counterbalancing considerations, to the particular kind of compromise which is usually denominated a "family arrangement," *i e* an agreement between kindred for the compromise of domestic differences, or the settlement or division of family estates, which is calculated to prevent the institution, or the recurrence, of family litigation, or to preserve the family property, peace, security, or honour (*b*). In such

had described the transaction as a release, and, indeed, the Lord Chancellor himself freely uses that term. But the propositions which he enunciates, and the reasoning by which they are supported, at p 727, are such as to show that he is directing his attention to agreements of compromise, and not to releases except so far as they are entered into for the purpose of effecting such an agreement, and it is evident from the language subsequently used by Lord HARDWICKE, L.C, at p 10 of *Stapilton v Stapilton* (1739), 1 Atk 2, when referring to and adopting the above propositions, that he so understood his predecessor And PLUMER, M R, at pp 151, 152 of *Dunnage v White* (1818), 1 Swanst 137 ; 18 R R. 33, takes the same view of Lord MACCLESFIELD's meaning

(*b*) This leaning of the Courts in favour of family arrangements is recognized in the following *Leonard v Leonard, sup*, *per* Lord MANNERS, L C (Ir), at p 179 (" to avoid litigation, the expenses and the uncertainty of it, was, according to the evidence .   the object of the arrangement .   . and it would be to defeat an object, in itself perfectly rational and just, and the more so, as between two brothers, an object which this Court would be disposed rather to promote than discountenance, were the Court to set aside a fair dealing upon a doubtful right, because it should afterwards appear that one of the parties had not got full value"), *Stockley v. Stockley* (1812), 1 V & B. 23 (*per* Lord ELDON, L.C. at pp 30, 31), *Dunnage v. White, sup*, *per* PLUMER, M R, at pp 151, 152 (" it is then insisted that the deed may be supported as a family arrangement, according to the doctrine of *Stapilton v Stapilton*, and *Cann v Cann* Undoubtedly parties entitled in different events may, while the uncertainty exists, effect a valid compromise. In *Stapilton v. Stapilton*, the legitimacy of the eldest son was doubtful, that was a question proper to be settled," &c), *Gordon v Gordon* (1821), 3 Swanst 400, 19 R R 230, which was also a case of doubtful legitimacy (*per* Lord ELDON, L C, at pp 463, 470, 476, 477 see the passages cited verbatim in the discussion of this case in Sect 8, Sub-s [1], §§ 307, 308, *post*), *Hoghton v Hoghton* (1852), 15 Beav 278 (*per* ROMILLY, M R, who, at p 298, discriminates between two classes of domestic influence, one " where one person, by *undue* influence, obtains an advantage over another," and the other "when arrangements are entered into for the peace of families and the security of the family property," in which latter class there is, as he explains at pp 301–304, a judicial presumption not against, but in favour of, the domestic influence, as being, in such circumstances, proper and praiseworthy), *Williams v Williams* (1867), 2 Ch App 294 (*per* TURNER, L J, at p 304, who there says that the doctrine applies " not merely to cases in which arrangements are made between members of a family for the preservation of its peace, but to cases in which arrangements are made between them for the preservation of its property "), *Fane v Fane* (1875), L R 20 Eq 689 (*per* HALL, V -C, who, at p 706, speaking of re-settlements by father and son, observes that " they are not to be interfered with lightly   for the Court has thought such re settlements desirable, and has favoured them "); *Hoblyn v. Hoblyn* (1889), 41 C D 200, another " re-settlement " case (*per* KEKEWICH, J, at p 204 " this settlement belongs to that class of settlements usually styled family arrangements. . . . In regarding settlements of this character, claims to upset them, and the rights of the parties thereunder, the Court gives weight to considerations which on other occasions would scarcely be allowed in the scale The duty to preserve in the family property hitherto held by it is recognized, so is also the duty of providing for those members of the family who are not intended to succeed to the property, and the harmony which may thus be expected to be established is respected There are frequently other considerations, such as the preservation of the honour of the family ") It so happens that, though in all the above cases the judicial leaning in favour of family arrangements is declared, in none of them was this leaning given effect to (by reason of countervailing and neutralizing

cases, the law will not be "extreme to mark what is done amiss," and circumstances in the conduct of the parties which might imperil the validity of an ordinary compromise, may be overlooked in consideration of the higher general good to be achieved by encouraging transactions of the class in question. But, in order to lay claim to this favourable consideration, it must appear beyond doubt that the sole object of the transaction was as above stated, and not some other and sinister object, such as the obtaining by one party of an advantage to himself by the exercise of improper domestic influence, without surrendering anything to the other party (c). The objects or intentions of the parties may be obvious from the nature of the transaction, or they may be proved by evidence (d). Further, whatever the intention may have been, the Court must be convinced that the result will in all probability be as stated, and that the transaction is really calculated to preclude future disputes, and not rather to invite them (e). It should also be remembered that compromises and settlements between members of a family, when one of them is in a position of domination and superiority as regards the others, are not only not regarded with the leniency and favour shown to other family arrangements, but are subjected to a specially vigilant and critical investigation, with the view of determining whether they are obnoxious to the doctrine (to be discussed hereafter in its proper place) of undue influence, and the very kinship which ordinarily is the reason for encouraging the arrangement is, in such cases, the ground on which it may be impeached (f).

considerations, such as misrepresentation or suppression of facts, or undue influence), except in *Hoblyn* v *Hoblyn*, *sup*, and then only on the party charged giving up the objectionable parts of the instrument on which he relied

(c) For an illustration of this kind of case, where the alleged "family settlement" was held not to fall within that description at all, see *Turner* v. *Collins* (1871), 7 Ch App 329 (per Lord HATHERLEY, L.C., reversing MALINS, V.-C, at pp. 338, 339 . "the Vice Chancellor seems to have been struck with the expressions about re settlements and family arrangements, and with the cases on that subject. . . This case does not in the least partake of the character of a re-settlement of family estates or family property The son is giving back to the father what had come from the father, but he also gives his mother s property, and as the deed now stands, if there should be a third marriage, the son may take no interest whatever in that property It is not a re settlement, but an absolute sweeping of it away from the son, and handing it over to the step-mother and half sister This is not a re-settlement, and the question is, under what circumstances it was made ")

(d) As it was in *Leonard* v *Leonard* (1812), 1 Ball & B 171 (per Lord MANNERS, L.C. (Ir), at p 179, where he finds that "the object of the arrangement" was, "*according to the evidence*, . . to avoid litigation," &c).

(e) In *Dunnage* v *White* (1818), 1 Swanst. 137, 18 R R 33, PLUMER, M.R., was not so satisfied, and accordingly declined to treat the transaction as a family arrangement, the reason for upholding such arrangements being conspicuously absent in that case At p 152, he observes. "by this instrument he covenants that two-sixths of the personalty shall belong to Dunnage and Atwell and their wives; but under the will their children had fixed interests in the event of survivorship. What power had the parents to dispose of the property in their own favour ? . . . *Instead of ending litigation, the deed creates it*. as soon as the children become of age, they must be advised to assert the rights of which it sought to deprive them."

(f) This topic belongs, not to this Chapter, but to Chapter V, Sect 2, Sub-s (1), which deals with domestic relations raising a presumption of "influence." See accordingly § 410, *post*, and the cases cited in the notes thereto, and particularly *Hoghton* v *Hoghton*, *Fane* v *Fane*, *Hoblyn* v *Hoblyn*, which are also referred to in note (b), *sup*, and *Turner* v *Collins*, which is also cited in note (c), *sup*. In *Tennent* v. *Tennent* (1870), L R 2 H L (Sc) 6, Lord WESTBURY, L C. (p 10), speaks of family arrangements of any kind as requiring "*uberrima fides* on all sides."

136. But whilst it is true to say that family arrangements, where no breach of duty on either side is established, have always, and even more readily than ordinary agreements of compromise, been supported (g), it is equally true that neither compromises, nor even family arrangements, will stand in any case in which such a breach is alleged and proved. The question at once arises,—what is this duty ? What is the theory of it, and what are its limits ? It is no easy matter to reconcile the conflicting opinions expressed at various times and by various courts on this topic, or to assign a definite meaning to the vague and unscientific phrases (such as " fairness " and " equality ") most unfortunately applied to conceptions which above all stand in need of precision in statement and clarity in exposition, or, therefore, to formulate with any confidence an answer to the question propounded which shall be at once comprehensive and exact   It has never been doubted that where either of the parties to a compromise (whether family arrangement or not) has been guilty of actual fraud (h), or of misrepresentation (i), even when innocent (j), or of suppression, or wilful and industrious concealment of material facts, amounting to what has been called " fraudulent silence " (k), the compromise will be upset, or treated as a nullity   The question is whether, when there has been no misconduct of any of the above kinds on either side, an agreement for compromise can be successfully impeached on the ground of mere honest non-disclosure, and, if so, of what nature must that non-disclosure be, in order to constitute an invalidating cause

137. Two extreme views have been advanced ; one, that any innocent non-disclosure will invalidate even a family arrangement, and a fortiori a compromise which does not partake of this nature (l) ; the other, that no

(g) As in *Cann* v *Cann* (1721) 1 P Wms 723 ; *Stapilton* v *Stapilton* (1739), 1 Atk 2 ; *Stewart* v *Stewart* (1839), 6 Cl & F 911 ; *Bellamy* v *Sabine* (1847), 2 Ph 425 (as to one of the two agreements there in question) ; *Tennent* v *Tennent, sup*

(h) See *Lloyd* v. *Passingham* (1815), G Cooper, 152 ; 14 R R 228 (fraudulent tampering with the Fleet book of marriages, and register of baptisms, whereby compromise of certain proceedings in ejectment was procured) ; *Bellamy* v *Sabine, sup* (as to one of the two transactions impeached, but not the other, which was upheld,—see the last note) ; *Moxon* v *Payne* (1873), 8 Ch App 881.

(i) As in *Leonard* v. *Leonard, sup* (incorrect statement of the effect of counsel's opinion that there had been a severance of a certain joint tenancy) *Re Roberts*, [1905] 1 Ch. 704, C. A. (a similar case).

(j) As in *Fane* v *Fane* (1875), L R 20 Eq 698

(k) " Fraudulent silence " was the expression used in the argument for the defendant in *Turner* v *Green*, [1895] 2 Ch. 205 (at p. 206) ; in many of the cases cited in the following notes the non-disclosure was variously described as " concealment," " active concealment," " suppression," or " industrious " reticence

(l) There are some scattered dicta in *Leonard* v *Leonard, inf* —see note (s), *inf* —and also in the judgment, or rather in the series of judgments, delivered by Lord ELDON, L.C., in *Gordon* v *Gordon* (1821), 3 Swanst. 400 ; 19 R R 230, which, if taken by themselves, might seem to point in this direction ; but, if the whole of the judgments in these cases are carefully considered—see § 307, *post*, for a close examination of the latter authority— it will be seen that Lord ELDON's final opinion, after long deliberation, was as stated in the text In *Gibbons* v *Caunt* (1799), 4 Ves 839, Lord ALVANEY, M R , at p 848a, undoubtedly commits himself to the wholly unqualified proposition " that this Court will *never* hold parties " to a compromise of doubtful rights " to be bound, unless they act with full knowledge of all the doubts and differences that arise,"—but this statement is evidently dissented from by Lord COTTENHAM, L C , at p 970 of *Stewart* v *Stewart* (1839), 6 Cl & F 911 See also some observations of the like dubious generality in the judgment of Lord MANNERS, L C (Ir), at pp. 180, and 182, of *Leonard* v. *Leonard* (1812), 1 Ball & B 171.

species or amount of *mere* non-disclosure can vitiate even an ordinary agreement of compromise,—much less a family arrangement (*m*). It is submitted that each of these absolute propositions is incorrect (*n*), and that the true rule which emerges from the mists of oracular phraseology (" inequality," " unfairness," " hardship," " mistake," and the like) behind which judges have veiled their curious disinclination to state any proposition on this subject in clear and direct terms, may be stated thus. There is undoubtedly a duty of disclosure on parties negotiating for a compromise, even where the compromise comes within the class of " family arrangements " : any compromise, whatever its nature, may be set aside, or treated as void, on proof of the breach of that duty, without establishing fraud, misrepresentation, " fraudulent silence," or other obliquity of conduct, except in the sense that any breach of an equitable rule is often called misconduct by equity lawyers (*o*) . and, in order to establish a breach of such duty, or, in other words, actionable non-disclosure, it is on the one hand necessary for the party complaining to prove as much as, but, on the other hand, it is sufficient for him to prove no more than, the following —(i) the existence of a fact which, besides being material in the sense that, if divulged to the party complaining, it would have influenced his judgment in determining whether to agree to the compromise or not, was also material to be disclosed in the sense that it was a fact which the party charged had no right to assume, from the nature of the transaction or the other circumstance of the case, that the party complaining is taking the risk of not knowing, and has no desire to know (*p*), and is impliedly waiving information about (*q*) , (ii) knowledge by the party charged, during the negotiation, of such fact , (iii) ignorance thereof, during the like period, on the part of the party complaining ; and, perhaps also (iv), knowledge on the part of the party charged that the party complaining is ignorant of the fact, and is compromising in the belief, and on the basis, of its non-existence, and not irrespective and regardless of the question whether or not the fact exists, or the event has happened.   It will be seen that the above proposition represents, with the exception of the fourth (possible) requirement, merely an application to agreements of compromise of the general rules of disclosure applicable to the negotiation of all contracts where such a duty exists at all.

(*m*) There are expressions used by Lord ELDON, L C , in *Gordon* v *Gordon, sup* , which (isolated from the context) verge upon this other extreme view, so much so, indeed, that those who argued for the party charged in *Fane* v *Fane, sup* , felt themselves encouraged thereby, as HALL, V -C , notes with some surprise, to cite *Gordon* v *Gordon* as an authority in their favour, not recognizing that, taken as a whole, the series of judgments in that case constituted the most weighty authority that could possibly be cited against their contention that family arrangements could never be upset for mere non disclosure

(*n*) The former of the two propositions need only be mentioned to be put aside   It is obvious that non-disclosure of anything in the world, or even of any material fact, unless materiality is understood with the limitation indicated in the text, will not do   The latter would appear to, but really does not, derive countenance from *Turner* v *Green, sup*   The grounds on which the author has ventured to challenge the soundness of that decision (for the purposes of which it was *assumed without argument* that no duty of disclosure exists at all in the first instance) are set forth in detail in Sect 8, Sub-s (3), *post*.

(*o*) See the cases cited in notes (*r*) and (*s*), *inf*.

(*p*) See Sub-s (1) of this Section, *ante*.

(*q*) See § 99, and the cases cited in notes (*v*) and (*w*) thereto, *ante*.

The authority for the proposition that all the above are necessary elements in the burden of proof incumbent on a party who seeks to have a compromise set aside or disregarded on the ground of non-disclosure, and also for the statement that nothing more need be shown in order to establish this right, is to be found not only in the decided cases in which the party setting up the non-disclosure succeeded, contrasted with those in which he failed, relating to ordinary compromises (r), but also, and even more clearly, on a like

(r) The following are cases of compromise between strangers, in which it was held, on the principles stated in the text, that a duty of disclosure existed, and had not been discharged, and in which the compromise was accordingly invalidated, or would have been so but for the establishment of some affirmative answer. *Wason* v *Wareing* (1852), 15 Beav 151 (*per* ROMILLY, M.R , at p. 155 here the plaintiff compromised certain claims which the defendant apparently had against him as a surety, the defendant not disclosing to the plaintiff the fact that, by certain transactions between himself and the principal debtor, the plaintiff had been released from his suretyship obligations . the action, however, failed, but only because the plaintiff had presumptive knowledge of the fact withheld) : *Moxon* v. *Payne* (1873), 8 Ch App. 881 (where, amongst other things, it was held that a certain compromise set up by the defendant was ineffectual, because the plaintiff withheld the fact that the rights he was supposed to be compromising had themselves been obtained by fraud, and where JAMES, L J., at p 885, lays down in the most general terms,—perhaps a little too general, as applied to compromises,—that " to make a confirmation or com-promise of any value in this Court the parties must be at arm's length, on equal terms, *with equal knowledge*, and with sufficient advice and protection ") , *Gilbert* v. *Endean* (1878), 9 C. D 259, C. A (where the plaintiff agreed with the defendant, in the course of the trial of an action between them, to compromise the matters in dispute, which agreement was embodied in a consent decree, whereby the defendant was ordered to give a bond to the plaintiff for payment of the agreed sum Thereupon, the defendant neglecting either to pay this sum or give the bond, being absolutely penniless, and it being supposed by all parties, and indeed represented by the defendant's solicitor, that the father of the defendant, a man of reputed means, had refused to assist the defendant in any way, a second compromise was entered into by the solicitors to the parties, whereby the plaintiff agreed to reduce his claims to a considerable extent During the imparlance leading to this second arrangement, the defendant's father died intestate, leaving a widow and the defendant to share his estate, and putting the latter in a position of ample ability to satisfy the terms of the first compromise This fact was known to the defendant's solicitor and not communicated to the plaintiff, or his solicitor, and, though the other members of the Court thought that the concealment of the supervening fact amounted to positive, though implied, misrepresentation, JESSEL, M R , puts the decision plainly on the ground of a violated duty of disclosure, the breach of that duty consisting in the knowledge of the fact on the part of the defendant's solicitor, the ignorance of it on the part of the plaintiff's solicitor, and the former's knowledge of, and trading on, the latter's ignorance " the real question," he says at p 267, " appears to be whether the death of the father was so obviously a material circumstance that the defendant's solicitor ought to have com-municated it to the other side It appears to me that the fact was material, and ought to have been known by Mr Gregory to have been material to be communicated, and that the compromise was allowed to be signed when Mr Gregory knew, or ought to have known, that Mr Greenip was ignorant of the fact of the death of the father , and it appears to me that the compromise cannot be supported ") It is submitted that the above authori-ties, and particularly the last cited passage from the judgment of JESSEL, M R —which was not a mere passing reflection, but a statement of "*the* real question," and indeed constituted the whole of his judgment on what he describes as "the merits "—justify every part of the proposition in the text And there is nothing in any of the cases in which compromises between strangers have been supported which in the slightest degree con-troverts that proposition, not even, for the reasons stated in Sect. 8, Sub-s (3), *post*, excepting *Turner* v. *Green*, [1905] 2 Ch 205 It will be noticed that in all the above cases the undisclosed fact was regarded as one which it could not be supposed that the party complaining was not concerned in knowing, or took the risk of not knowing In *Law* v. *Law*, [1905] 1 Ch 140, C A , which, though brothers were the disputants, was a case of a compromise of business, and not of domestic, disputes, there were, as in *Moxon* v *Payne* sup , two "imparlances" and two successive transactions, first, an arrangement by which William agreed to sell his share in the partnership to James for £21,000, and then an action by William in respect of assets undisclosed by James at the time of the former arrangement,

comparison and contrast, in the cases which are concerned with family arrangements (s).

which action was itself compromised by terms embodied in a consent order, and this latter compromise the C A refused to disturb, not on the ground that there is no duty of disclosure in negotiations for compromises, but solely on the grounds stated fully in notes (w) and (y) to § 133, ante, i e affirmation, estoppel, election, and a not very conscientious course of conduct on the part of William, completely disentitling him to that relief which there is nothing in the case to suggest that he would not have otherwise obtained. So also, in *Watt* v *Assets Co* , [1905] A C 317, H. L., in the first place, the company failed to prove non-disclosure of any kind ; secondly, there was an express agreement between the parties that, in effect, only concealment of certain facts known or believed by the contributory to exist should vitiate the compromise, which of course at once put the burden on the company of proving, *in that case*, fraud, a burden which they utterly failed in sustaining ; and, lastly, the company had waited for over twenty years, until all the persons were dead who could have thrown light on the transaction (*per* Lord HALSBURY, L C., at pp. 329, 330, 333) it was on these grounds that the House refused to rescind the compromise, and not on the ground that, apart from the above circumstances, there was no duty to communicate the facts : on the contrary, the first of the three grounds indicated presupposes that there is in such cases generally, and was even in that case, a *primâ facie* obligation of disclosure.

(s) In the following cases " family arrangements " were successfully impeached on the principles stated in the text   *Leonard* v. *Leonard* (1812), 2 Ball & B 171—see note (a) to § 132, *ante*—where the undisclosed fact was that there had been circumstances which, as counsel had advised, operated as a severance of a joint tenancy, and where Lord MANNERS, L C (Ir), at p 182, held that " the compromise is deficient in that which is *essential to its validity*, that both parties were in *equal ignorance*," having previously recognized, at p 180, that " if both parties are in the same ignorance, the fairness of the compromise cannot be affected by a subsequent investigation and result " , *Gordon* v *Gordon* (1821), 3 Swanst 400 , 19 R R. 230, where, in an arrangement between two brothers, the legitimacy of whom was doubtful, James (the defendant) had innocently (as, for the purposes of his final opinion, Lord ELDON, L C , assumed) withheld from Harry (the plaintiff) the fact that he had been informed that a private ceremony of marriage had taken place before the birth of the children, though (as was again assumed) he did not believe that any valid marriage was constituted thereby , and on the ground of this innocent non-disclosure, the arrangement, though a family one, and though 19 years had elapsed before it was challenged, was set aside (see § 307, *post*, where it is shown, by citations from Lord ELDON's successive judgments that, without fraud or imposition, though those terms are freely used in the earlier expressions of his views, the mere omission to communicate a material fact of which, to the knowledge of the party charged, the party complaining is ignorant, is sufficient of itself to invalidate even a family arrangement) , *Greenwood* v *Greenwood* (1863), 2 De G J & S 28, where KNIGHT BRUCE and TURNER, LL.JJ , affirmed the decision of KINDERSLEY, V -C , who had set aside an agreement, a deed, an award, and other instruments constituting, or carrying into effect, a family arrangement of disputed claims under a will, on the ground that one of the parties had failed to disclose facts relating to the testator's property and business in New Zealand which were within his *exclusive* knowledge. he having been partner with the testator in the colony, and the other parties being in England , TURNER, L J , at p 42, distinctly stating " the rule of law to be that in order to support a transaction not otherwise valid, *upon the footing of a family arrangement*, the parties must be on an equal footing, and there must be *a full and fair communication of all the circumstances affecting the question which forms the subject of the arrangement*," and the meaning of " full and fair communication " being, in his opinion (p 43), a communication of everything which " would, *or at least might*, have materially influenced the other parties in determining the question whether they would have entered into the agreement " , *Re Roberts*, [1905] 1 Ch 704, C A , where the full effect of counsel's opinion was not disclosed or explained, or (as it was also put) was " inaccurately stated " by the family solicitor to one of the parties   The above, and particularly *Gordon* v *Gordon*, *sup* , and *Greenwood* v *Greenwood*, *sup* , bear out, and even go beyond, the proposition in the text   It will be observed that in none of them was the undisclosed fact held to be one which the party charged had any right to assume that the party complaining was content to be ignorant of ; indeed it was not so pretended in any of them, except in *Re Roberts*, where, after it had been recognized that in compromises there are usually a number of facts which the parties deliberately take the risk of not knowing, and as to which, therefore, no disclosure is to be expected—see note (u) to § 133, *ante*,—the contention was thus disposed of by the C A (*per* VAUGHAN WILLIAMS, L.J), at p 711 · " we find it, however, very difficult to draw the inference in this case that Mrs

138. Since the persistent, and most misleading, terminology already referred to has undoubtedly encouraged, at least in earlier times, the notion that something less than non-disclosure might, under such conveniently ambiguous phrases as "inequality," "unfairness," "hardship," "mistake," and the like, suffice to undo a compromise, it becomes (what it otherwise would scarcely be) necessary to point out here that the only "inequality" and "unfairness" which is adequate for that purpose is the "inequality" which results from the party charged not having observed such duty of disclosure, if any, as in the circumstances of the case, and in conformity with the rules stated, was incumbent on him; that the only "hardship" recognized by the law as a relevant element in the discussion of such cases is that which consists in the "hard" conduct of the party charged, and that, again, the only hard conduct which is entitled to any judicial consideration in this connection is non-disclosure of the nature already indicated (*t*); lastly, that the only "mistake"—or, rather, the only unilateral mistake—which can upset a compromise is a mistake induced by a misrepresentation or actionable non-disclosure of the party charged, or to which he is otherwise accessory (*u*).

Roberts intended to make the agreement of compromise irrespective of her legal rights. That Mrs. Roberts wished to avoid litigation we believe, but that she was willing to compromise irrespective of her legal rights, if the solicitor advised her that such a compromise would be a good thing, we do not believe. The very object of taking counsel's opinion was to ascertain what the respective rights of herself and William Roberts and the pecuniary legatees were." There is nothing in any of the cases cited in note (*x*) *inf*, where the family arrangement was supported, which militates in any way against the proposition that, in family arrangements as well as in compromises between strangers, a duty of disclosure arises during the "imparlance" under the conditions, within the limits, and of the nature, stated in the text. for in all those cases non disclosure was not even alleged, but merely "hardship," "inequality," misconception of rights, or disappointing results, so that it was quite unnecessary to pronounce whether, and under what conditions, the parties are bound to communicate material facts to one another, though in many of them the Court went out of its way to express an opinion that such an obligation exists, and to a wider extent even than has been suggested in the text. There is one case, indeed, *Brooke* v *Lord Mostyn* (1865), 33 Beav. 457 (ROMILLY, M R.), (1865), 2 De G J & S 373 (KNIGHT-BRUCE and TURNER, LL.JJ.), and, in the House of Lords, *sub nom Mostyn* (*Lord*) v *Brooke* (1866), L R 4 H. L 304, where the House of Lords reversed the decision of the Lords Justices that a family compromise, sanctioned by the Court, was invalidated by the non disclosure to the Court of a certain material valuation, and restored that of ROMILLY, M R., who had upheld the compromise; but it appears from the short note of the House of Lords decision—there is no report of the judgments, or any report at all in the proper sense of the word—that the sole ground of that decision was that non-disclosure had not been proved, and no disagreement whatever was expressed with the view of the Lords Justices that a duty to disclose the document rested on the party charged

(*t*) Of course, the "hardship," "inequality," and "unfairness" which may be said to characterize transactions in which an unconscientious advantage is taken of another's distress, or the influence presumed from certain relations is abused, as to which see Ch V, *post*, is another matter altogether, and is not now under consideration.

(*u*) In *Gordon* v *Gordon* (1821), 3 Swanst. 400, at p 467, Lord ELDON, L C, speaks of the party charged being "accessory to the mistake of the other,"—an expression used in some other of the cases. An excellent statement of the necessary elements in conduct "accessory to the mistake" is to be found in *Smith* v *Hughes* (1871), L R 6 Q B. 597, where the plaintiff was suing on a contract for the sale of oats by sample, which he knew to be new oats, and which the defendant, to the plaintiff's knowledge, believed to be old oats, and where, the oats being according to the sample, and the plaintiff having made no representation of any kind to the defendant, the Court refused to relieve the defendant, for (as was said by HANNEN, J, at p 611) "in order to relieve the defendant, it was necessary to find not merely that the plaintiff believed the defendant to believe that he was buying old oats, but that he believed the defendant to believe that he, the plaintiff, was contracting to sell old oats"

It is only because the expressions in question are *ancipitis sensus*, having (like other phrases taken from the *vulgare eloquium*, and fathered by jurisprudence) both a popular and a scientific meaning, that it has been possible to raise, with some show of plausibility, the contention that " inequality " of a nature to invalidate a compromise may include that sort of inequality which subsequent events prove to have existed at the time of the negotiation ; that " unfairness " may reasonably comprehend conduct which *in foro conscientiæ* would be considered indelicate, or would not be approved by the *arbitrium boni viri* (*v*) , that " hardship " may mean no more than " hard luck " ; and that " mistake " may be predicated of a compromising party who has merely misconceived the nature of the doubtful and contested right which, by the settlement, he has agreed to surrender, acquire, exchange, or define   These and similar contentions have always failed.   It is well established that the abandonment of a claim honestly asserted is a good consideration for an agreement of compromise, though a judicial decision, or subsequent discovery or investigation, may show that at the date of the compromise there was, in fact and in law, no sort of foundation for the claim (*w*)   and it is quite hopeless, therefore, in the absence of any suggestion of such non-disclosure as the law declares to be actionable, or of dishonesty, for a party to a compromise, " wise after the event," to invoke the assistance of the Court on no other ground than that he was not wise before it.   At that rate, no compromise would be possible, or at least none would have any certainty, or even probability, of enduring, since its existence and validity would be at the mercy of the belated resipiscence of any party to it who might be able to show that the bargain had turned out a disastrous one for him, and that supervening events had given him great cause for repenting of it (*x*).

(*v*) As to the similar havoc and confusion created in another department of jurisprudence, viz defamation, by the use of the same word " fair " as applied to comment, see the author's *Code of the Law of Actionable Defamation*, App XII, Sect 4
(*w*) *Frank* v *Frank* (1668), 1 Ch Cas 84 , *Cann* v *Cann* (1721), 1 P Wms 723 (see the next note) , *Stockley* v *Stockley* (1812), 1 V & B 23 , *Cook* v *Wright* (1861), 1 B & S 559 (*per* BLACKBURN, J , delivering the judgment of the Court of Q B , at pp 568–570) , *Callisher* v *Bischoffsheim* (1870), L R 5 Q B 449 (*per* COCKBURN, C J , at pp 451, 452, and BLACKBURN, J at p 452) , *Ockford* v *Barrett* (1871), 20 W R 116 (*per* CHANNELL, B , delivering the judgment of the Court of Exchequer, at p 117) , *Miles* v *New Zealand Alford Estate Co* (1886), 32 C D 266, C A (*per* COTTON, L J , at pp 283, 284, BOWEN, L.J., at pp 291, 292, and FRY, L J , at pp 297, 298)
(*x*) In *Frank* v *Frank*, *sup* , the Court acceded to the argument for the defendant that " here is enough to justify and execute " (in modern language, " consideration to support ") " the agreement," which was one of compromise of litigated claims in respect of certain estates, " and thereupon the bill of review was dismissed with costs , for *modus et contentio vincunt legem*   So that in this case the agreement of the party, upon conceit he had not (when in truth he had) a title to permit another to enjoy lands, shall for ever bind him , and yet this agreement doth appear to be upon no valuable consideration " (that is to say, there is consideration sufficient to support such an agreement, though there is no valuable consideration in the narrowest sense of that term, i e no delivery or promise of anything of then ascertained cash value).   Other illustrations are   *Cann* v. *Cann* (1721), 1 P Wms 723 (*per* Lord MACCLESFIELD, L C , at p 727   " nothing like this had ever been attempted by any person "—the Court was here asked to ignore a release and compromise without any suggestion even of non-disclosure or ignorance, much less of fraud —" where two parties are contending in this Court, and one releases his pretensions to the other, there can be no colour to set this release aside, because the man that made it had a right , every release supposes the party making it to have a right , but this can be no reason for

139. There is a class of arrangements, viz. compositions made by an insolvent with his creditors, which would fall to be considered here but for the fact that, in such cases, the person entitled to complain of the non-disclosure is, ordinarily, not one of the parties to the arrangement sought to be avoided or treated as void It seems preferable, therefore, to discuss this type of compromise, and the duty of disclosure which arises in relation to it, in the Chapter devoted to the topic of Concealment from Third Persons (y).

140. In the subsequent Sections of this Chapter (z), the questions of burden of proof, affirmative defences, remedy and relief, matters of law and fact, and parties, are discussed in relation to releases and compromises, as well as the other types of transaction which form the subject of this Chapter, except in so far as questions of burden of proof in respect of the last-named species have already been dealt with (a).

its being set aside, for then every release might be avoided · . . . solemn conveyances, releases, and agreements made by the parties are not slightly to be blown off and set aside) , *Stapilton* v *Stapilton* (1739), 1 Atk 2 (*per* Lord HARDWICKE, L C, at p. 10 " in the case of *Cann* v. *Cann*, it was laid down by Lord MACCLESFIELD that an agreement entered into upon a supposition of a right, or of a doubtful right, though it after comes out that the right was on the other side, shall be binding, and the right shall not prevail against the agreement of the parties, for the right must always be on one side or the other, and therefore the compromise of a doubtful right is a sufficient foundation of an agreement "); *Pullen* v *Ready* (1743), 2 Atk 587 (*per* Lord HARDWICKE, L C, at p 591, again citing and applying *Cann* v *Cann*); *Gibbons* v *Caunt* (1799), 4 Ves 839 (*per* Lord ALVANLEY, M R, at p 848A), *Stockley* v *Stockley* (1812), 1 V. & B. 23 (where Lord ELDON, L C, adopts the principle laid down in *Cann* v *Cann*, and *Stapilton* v *Stapilton*, to its full extent, and, though he confesses to having entertained at first some doubts as to whether in the former case Lord MACCLESFIELD, L C, intended to go as far as he appeared to have gone, those doubts, he says at p. 13, had been removed " I had a doubt whether what is in *Stapilton* v *Stapilton* represented as falling from Lord MACCLESFIELD in *Cann* v *Cann* could have been his language If a doubt is raised between parties as to their rights, and adverting to that doubt they come to an agreement . . . in family matters, the Court goes a long way to carry it into execution but my difficulty was that there might be a supposition of right without a doubt upon it , that it would be too much to execute an agreement entered into upon such a supposition, if unfounded , and the words of Lord MACCLESFIELD, instead of 'a supposition of right' might have been 'a doubtful right' but I observe, in a manuscript note that I have, the same words are represented as those of Lord MACCLESFIELD " It will be observed that, as in so many other cases where " the Chancellor said, 'I doubt,' " Lord ELDON's difficulty was self created that is to say, it would never have arisen if he had not allowed his reason to be cheated by his own ambiguous phraseology, for obviously the expression " a supposition of a right without a doubt upon it " may mean eith hat the party asserting the right had no doubt *in his own mind* that he had no such i o that he honestly thought there was some doubt about the matter, though in law, in the judgment of any skilled professional adviser, there was absolutely none In the former case, the compromise clearly cannot stand, being vitiated by fraud in the latter, it is equally clear that it cannot be disturbed), *Leonard* v *Leonard* (1812), 1 Ball & B. 171 (*per* Lord MANNERS, L C (Ir), at p 179 " if the validity of a deed of compromise is to depend on a subsequent decision on those rights which were the subject of the agreement, no disputed or disputable title could be compromised ", and, at p. 180, " the party surrendering may in truth have nothing to surrender," but " if both parties are in the same ignorance, the fairness of the compromise cannot be affected by a subsequent investigation and result "), *Gordon* v. *Gordon* (1821), 3 Swanst 400 (*per* Lord ELDON, L C, at p 476 see § 307, *post*, as to this case), *Naylor* v *Winch* (1824), 1 Sim & St 555 (*per* LEACH, V -C, at pp 565, 566), *Stewart* v *Stewart* (1839), 6 Cl & F 911 (*per* Lord COTTENHAM, L C, at p 970), *Law* v *Law*, [1905] 1 Ch 140, C. A (*per Cur*, at p 156 · " it cannot be sufficient to allege and prove that, if the action had been fought out, the plaintiff would have recovered damages greatly in excess of £3550," which was the sum he had compromised for)

(y) See Ch VII, §§ 587-602, *post*.
(z) Sects 3–7, *post*, respectively
(a) See § 138, *ante*.

Sub-s. (6).　Contracts for Partnership.

141. When parties are in treaty with one another with a view to the formation of a partnership between them, or to the purchase or sale of a share or interest in, or the dissolution or termination of, a subsisting partnership, and where one of such parties is already carrying on the business which is the subject of the proposed partnership, or is the active or managing partner in the conduct of it, and the other party is either an entire stranger to the business which he is invited to join, or is a mere dormant member of, or a successor by operation of law to an interest in, an established firm his partnership share in which is the subject of the negotiation, it is obvious that the first-named of the above parties, in the ordinary course of things and in every normal type of case, must have not only knowledge, but exclusive knowledge, of all or most of the facts on a consideration of which the other party is to exercise his judgment as to the policy of acquiring, purchasing, selling, or extinguishing (as the case may be), on the terms proposed, the share or interest in the partnership which is the subject of the dealing , and that this other party is therefore dependent upon the first for information as to all such facts, and can in no sense be said to take upon himself the risk of whether they exist or not　If so, all the conditions already indicated (b) as conditions required to constitute a fiduciary relation between two persons negotiating with a view to a contract or transaction, are present in this class of case , and there is accordingly a duty on the party who presumably has the exclusive knowledge to communicate to the party who presumably has none, or not so much, all such matters as are actually or constructively within his cognizance, and, in their nature, must have a bearing upon the contemplated transaction.

142. Thus, to take first the simplest case, a person carrying on a business who proposes to a stranger to join him as a partner in that business on certain terms is bound to impart to him all information which he has, or ought to have, acquired as to the property, income, outgoings, and dealings of the business, its books and other commercial documents, and, generally, the past and existing conduct and state of its affairs (c).　Further, where persons who are already partners are negotiating for the sale and purchase of the share of one of them to the other, if one of them has exclusive or superior knowledge of the affairs of the partnership, the other being either a dormant partner, or the "outdoor" partner who does not keep the books or accounts, or has not access to all of them, a like duty is incumbent on the first to communicate to the second, before the conclusion of the contract, all the private information which he possesses, and which, to his knowledge, the other does not possess (d)　" It is clear law that in a transaction between co-partners

(b) Vid Sect 1, ante
(c) There is no reported case of *pure* non disclosure in this particular species of negotiation, unless it be *Andrewes* v *Garstin* (1861). 10 C B (N S) 444, where the party complaining failed for the reasons stated in note (h) to § 143, *post*　But the principle is assumed in all the authorities, and stated in all the treatises on partnership, and is obviously an *a fortiori* application of the rule laid down in the authorities cited in the next four notes
(d) *Maddeford* v. *Austwick* (1826), 1 Sim. 89, where LEACH, V.-C , affirmed (1833), 2

for a sale by one to the other of a share in the partnership business, there is a duty resting upon the purchaser (e) who knows, and is aware that he knows, more about the partnership accounts than the vendor, to put the vendor into possession of all material facts with reference to the partnership assets, and not to conceal what he alone knows ; and that, unless such information has been furnished, the sale is voidable and may be set aside " (f). Lastly, where one of two partners dies, and his representative accordingly becomes entitled, if the survivor continues to carry on the business, to elect whether to take the deceased's share of profits, and be treated as a partner, or to charge the survivor with interest on the capital of the deceased retained or used by him, it is the duty of the survivor, who has the exclusive knowledge of the partnership affairs, when in treaty with the deceased's representative, who presumably has little or no knowledge of them, "to disclose *uberrimâ fide* every fact which may enable the representative to exercise a sound discretion as to the course he ought to pursue " (g).

143. It must be remembered that, as in all the other classes of negotiation mentioned in this Chapter, the duty of disclosure lies on the party who has the exclusive or superior acquaintance with the facts. There is no duty on the other party. This is so obvious that the caution being given may seem somewhat superfluous . but it has been interjected because at least one attempt

My & K. 279, by Lord BROUGHAM, L.C , rescinded an agreement whereby the plaintiff had agreed to accept £1000 in full discharge of his share (down to 1817) of the profits of the business of carriers which he and the defendant had been carrying on in partnership, on the ground of the non disclosure by the defendant of entries in his *private* book (he being the partner who attended to the accounts, and the plaintiff being the " outdoor " partner) showing that this sum was many hundred pounds less than a fair price to pay , and where, at p 96, LEACH, V.-C , concluded "the defendant, being the partner whose business it was to keep the whole accounts of the concern, could not, in fairness, deal with the plaintiff for his share of the profits of the concern, without putting him into possession of all the information which he himself had with respect to the state of the accounts between them The defendant knew, from the accounts in his possession, that the £1000 was not an adequate consideration for the plaintiff's share of the profits The supposed account . up to the end of 1817 necessarily formed the basis of the plaintiff's calculation of profits for the ensuing three years , and, being misled in that respect, he is entitled to avoid the whole agreement," &c In *Law v Law*, [1905] 1 Ch 140, C A , where, in negotiating for the sale by one partner of his share to the other, the purchasing party, who knew a great deal more about the accounts and the business than the selling party, had concealed from him the existence of assets to a very large amount, the C A , whose joint judgment was delivered by COZENS-HARDY, L.J , adopted the principle of *Maddeford v Austwick, sup* , and would on that principle have set aside the agreement, but for the fact that the plaintiff had chosen, with full knowledge, to compromise his claim (as to which see note (w) to § 133, *ante*)

(e) It so happened that in this case, as well as in *Maddeford v Austwick, sup* , the party charged was the purchaser But of course the same principle would apply to a vendor withholding information as to the losses in a business as applies to a purchaser withholding information as to its assets and profits

(f) *Law v Law, sup.,* at p 157.

(g) *Per* Lord CRANWORTH, L C , at p 188 of *Clements v Hall* (1858), 2 De G & J 173 The epithet "sound" is not well chosen What was meant was an "informed" or "instructed " judgment. The partnership interest which was the subject of the decision was an interest in the lease of a mine, and it was established to the satisfaction of the Court (*per* Lord CRANWORTH, L C , on the same page) that " Alfred "—the survivor—" up to a period long subsequent to the renewed lease, refused to furnish her "—the representative of the deceased partner—" with any accounts of the mine, and so kept her in ignorance of all which might be necessary to enable her to decide on the propriety of her insisting on her equitable right to be treated as a partner " has been gravely made, though it failed, to establish, under cover of hazy generalizations as to the fiduciary element in the jural concept of *societas*, the existence of an obligation of unlimited disclosure on both sides, irrespective of the relative knowledge of the parties, in any negotiation whatsoever for a contract of partnership (*h*)

144. It should also be borne in mind that the duty of disclosure now being dealt with is the duty which arises during a treaty for a contract of partnership, and must not be confused with the other and quite distinct duty which is incidental to the contract itself, and to the relation thereby established, and which lasts during the subsistence of such relation (*i*). This latter is dealt with hereafter in its proper place (*j*).

Sub-s. (7). *Contracts to Marry and Separation Deeds*

145. Mutual promises of two persons to marry one another involve an obligation on each of the parties to reveal to the other during the treaty or communications leading up to the contract all matters which (1) may be presumed to be within his, or her, exclusive knowledge, and (2) are material to be disclosed · and " material to be disclosed " means, in this as in the other classes of case which form the subject of this Chapter, that which, having regard to its peculiar nature and objects (*k*), has a vital bearing on the matrimonial relation contracted for, and which the promisee cannot be expected to take the risk of not knowing.

146. First among the facts which are undoubtedly and obviously vital, and which must therefore be disclosed, is unchastity or incontinence on the part of the woman, for this " goes to the very root of the contract of marriage," and where, therefore, this fact is not communicated, " from the excess " [*sic*, *qy* " stress " ?] " and necessity of the case, the man is released from the contract " (*l*).

(*h*) This attempt was made in *Andrewes* v. *Garstin* (1861), 10 C B (N s) 444, where, to an action for damages for breach of his agreement to take the plaintiff into partnership, as a jobmaster, which business the defendant was then carrying on, the defendant set up that the plaintiff who, so far as appears knew nothing of the defendant's business, or even of that class of business, had failed to divulge his past misconduct when in partnership with another person in another business (that of iron and tinplate workers)   The strange " argument urged so emphatically by Mr Manisty," as ERLE, C J , said at p 452, was founded on a supposed analogy between contracts of partnership and contracts of marriage —though not much support was added to the contention by this analogy, as was pointed out by the Court, even supposing it to exist—and on a confusion between relations of marriage or partnership and negotiations with a view to contracts *for* marriage or partnership, followed by a fallacious application to the latter of the general principles correctly applied by the civilians, and in such treatises as Collier on Partnership, to the former (see the argument of Manisty, Q C , at pp 450–452)

(*i*) This confusion vitiated the argument for the defendant in the case last cited. It may be said that, in some of the illustrations given in § 142, *sup* , the parties were already partners.   This is true, but the duty of non-disclosure which is stated in the text in respect to such parties is not a duty incumbent on them *quâ* partners, but *quâ* negotiators for a fresh contract altering their pre-existing partnership relations

(*j*) See § 341, in Chap IV, Sect 2, Sub s (3), *post*

(*k*) *Andrewes* v. *Garstin* (1861), 10 C B (N s) 444, *per* ERLE, C.J , at p 449

(*l*) *Per* Lord CAMPBELL, C J , at p 759 of *Hall* v *Wright* (1858), E B & E 746, COCK-BURN, C J., at pp 802, 803, and HILL, J., at p. 805, of *Beachey* v. *Brown* (1860), E B & E.

147. On the other hand, it has been decided that a *previous* attack of insanity, and confinement in a lunatic asylum, need not be divulged (*m*) : also that a *previous* engagement of the woman to another person is not a matter which goes to the very root of the contract, or such that the concealment of it will release the man from his promise, for (putting it in another way) it cannot be said that in such cases "there is an implied warranty of the virginity, not only of the person, but of the affections " (*n*). It has also been judicially suggested, though there is no actual decision to that effect, that the mere fact that a woman habitually resorts to the appliances of art, to supplement the deficiencies or repair the ravages of nature, is not material to be disclosed (*o*) , and, generally, it has been stated by COCKBURN, C J., that "there are many things which a man might desire to have communicated to him, if they existed, at the time of making the contract, such as that the plaintiff is in debt, or subject to other liabilities, or some circumstances relating to her person, her temper, her disposition, the discovery of which would yet not entitle the defendant to refuse to fulfil his engagement. It might be right to disclose such things ; and yet it has never been held that the discovery of them justified a party in breaking his contract " (*p*). In other words, there are many things which an affianced man or woman cannot claim as of right to be disclosed to him or her before the contract, though he or she may well expect such a disclosure as a matter of honour, delicacy, or decency, —many aleatory hazards which, when venturing upon what proverbial cynicism has styled "the lottery of marriage," he or she must be supposed to take upon himself or herself. But even a gamester is entitled to expect that the gaming be fair, that the dice be not clogged, that the lots be drawn honestly, and that nothing shall be hidden from him tending to show the contrary, or that the proposed prize or stake is something totally different in character from that which it purported to be It is on this principle that the decisions above referred to, on the one side or the other, have been founded , and it is this principle which must guide the decision of the many conceivable cases which may arise in the future, and which are untouched as yet in the very scanty field of express authority available

148. There is undoubtedly a very large debateable territory intermediate between the class of case where disclosure is clearly obligatory, and that in

796, and ERIE, C J , at p 127 of *Baker v Cartwright* (1861), 10 C. B (N S) 124 See also the *nisi prius* cases of *Irving v Greenwood* (1824), 1 C & P 350 (ABBOTT, C J.), and *Bench v Merrick* (1844), 1 C & K 463.

(*m*) *Baker v Cartwright, sup*

(*n*) *Beachey v Brown, sup , per* COCKBURN, C J , at p 800

(*o*) *Per* CROMPTON, J , who, at p. 803 of *Beachey v Brown, sup ,* says, by way of *reductio ad absurdum*, that, on the theory contended for, a man " might complain that what he took to be a beautiful head of hair turned out to be a wig."

(*p*) At p 802 of *Beachey v Brown, sup* So also (though, before the passing of the Married Women's Property Acts, non disclosure of property on the part of the wife would have been held a fraud on the *jus mariti*) there is now no longer any duty on either spouse to communicate to the other his or her pecuniary position or circumstances But of course if he or she chooses to make a statement on such or similar matters which is false, or not completely true, he or she at once becomes liable for misrepresentation, for the purposes of which the fact misstated is material, though not material to be disclosed See *Wharton v Lewis* (1824), 1 C & P. 529 , *Foote v. Hayne* (1824), 1 C & P 545

B N D I

which it clearly is not : and the opinion of ERLE, C.J , who, in denying that any fact need be disclosed except unchastity on the part of the woman (q), would exclude the possibility of any such debateable territory, is manifestly unsound in principle, and, to some extent, is also in conflict with other judicial pronouncements.   There are direct decisions and dicta that other matters than actual incontinence and positive acts of misconduct on the part of the woman must be divulged, such as a *permanent* and serious disease or physical infirmity on the part of either of the parties (r), or a general loose character or reputation on the part of the woman (s), or alcoholic intemperance on the part of either party (ss), or dishonest and criminal behaviour on the part of the man (t), or " moral turpitude, or an incompetency for the purposes of the marriage " on the part of either (u), or *permanent* intellectual disease (v) ; and the very authority on which ERLE, C J , relied for the statement which he incautiously made does not in the least support it, but, on the contrary, contains judicial observations distinctly at variance with it including, strange to say, those of the learned Chief Justice himself, then ERLE, J , who had there cited and approved all the decisions above mentioned (w)   Many other illustrations are conceivable.   It can hardly be doubted

(q) At p 127 of *Baker* v *Cartwright, sup* (" the general doctrine laid down by the Exchequer Chamber in the case referred to is that the contract binds, and that want of chastity is the only exception ")

(r) *Aitchison* v. *Baker* (1797), 1 Peake 103, where Lord KENYON, C J , held that non disclosure of a cancer by a man suing for breach of promise of marriage constituted a good defence to the action, and (at p 105), in reference to an unreported case in which Lord MANSFIELD, C.J , had held that bad character on the part of either party, if concealed, was a valid answer, observed that " whether the infirmity was bodily or mental, the reason was the same "

(s) See the case before Lord MANSFIELD, C.J , referred to in the last note, and *Foulkes* v *Sellway* (1800), 3 Esp 235, where Lord KENYON, C J , admitted evidence of the lady's bad character and reputation, for " character here was the only point in issue   That was public opinion founded on the conduct of the party."   There was also, however, in this case, evidence of one act of gross misconduct on the woman's part   See also *Irving* v *Greenwood*, and *Bench* v *Merrick*, cited in note (l), *sup*   Even a past lapse from virtue, according to *Bench* v *Merrick*, notwithstanding the intervention of a considerable period of uninterrupted good conduct, may be material to be disclosed.   But this view would perhaps not be adopted, at all events universally, at the present day   It would depend upon all the circumstances

(ss) *Herbert* v *Edgington* (1844), 1 C & K 464 n , where PARKE, B , considered that concealment of drunkenness on the woman's part would be a good defence, for he left this issue to the jury, who, however, found that it was not established

(t) *Baddeley* v *Mortlock* (1816), Holt N P 151, per GIBBS, C J., who, at p 152, directed the jury that " if a woman improvidently promises to marry a man who turns out upon inquiry to be of bad character, she is not bound to perform her promise   But it must appear that the plaintiff *is* of bad character   The accusation is not enough   The existence of the rumour is not sufficient to discharge her from her promise   Without proof that the charges were well founded, she is not absolved from her contract   But it affects the damages "   In this case the charges (viz of dishonesty and perjury in certain business transactions) were not proved to the satisfaction of the jury, but acting on the hint thrown out at the end of the judge's summing up, they awarded the plaintiff nominal damages only

(u) Per CROMPTON, J , at p 803 of *Beachey* v. *Brown* (1860), E B & E 796.

(v) Per ERLE, J , at p 755 of *Hall* v *Wright* (1858), E B & E 746, Exch Ch

(w) *Hall* v *Wright, sup* , is the authority relied upon by ERLE, C J , in his observations cited in note (q), *sup*   The defence raised by the man there was that, *after* the conclusion of the contract, he had contracted a severe pulmonary disease, which rendered the performance of his marital obligations impossible without danger to life, and it was contended that, at the present day, if either of the parties were to complain of the suppression by the other, before the making of the contract, of any permanent disease or physical disability which would endanger his or her life or health, or, by reason of its contagious character, the life or health of both, or any pernicious habit which had so enslaved and enfeebled the victim's will and resolution as to destroy all reasonable hope of emancipation or cure, such as the morphia or like drug habit, effect would be given to the complaint, and the contract held voidable. It would be otherwise if, at the time of the contract, the disease had been cured, or was curable, or if the habit and tendency had been overcome. So also even the case put, " pour rire," by CROMPTON, J., of a lady's concealment of the fact that her tresses are borrowed (x) is not, or, with other concealments, would not be, so ridiculous as he seems to have thought. It is a question of degree, and also of the relative situation of the parties Assume the matrimonial proposal to emanate from some gross plutocrat, whose object in offering marriage, to the knowledge of the lady when accepting the offer, was to buy a wife at a heavy price for the mere gratification of his sensual propensities, or love of display · and assume that, after the contract, some accident, or the treachery of some confidant of his fiancée, reveals to him, not merely the innocent secrets of the toilet, but the falsity of all the features and seemingly natural attractions of her person, so that the entire outward form of his divinity is shown to be the mere product of " the adulteries of art," and a whited sepulchre,—would not such a person, if he chose to invo   the jurisdiction of the Courts, have a right to be relieved of his contract ?   ould he not be in the position, if the expression be not considered too ungallant, of the purchaser of land or goods who complains of the vendor not having disclosed matters negativing or prejudicing his title, and who insists that he is being asked to take a conveyance of property differing in substance and nature from that which it purported to be, or of the

(though unsuccessfully) that this being a fact supervening, without the fault of either party, each of them was excused thenceforth from any further obligation under the contract The case, therefore, was not strictly one of non disclosure at all But the principles upon which the decision was grounded are precisely the same as those which regulate the duty of disclosure in such cases for, obviously, any fact which, if arising *after* the contract, would excuse either party from further performance would be of sufficient materiality to entitle either party to have it divulged, if arising, and known to the other party, *before* the contract The point, however, which distinguishes, and vitally distinguishes, this authority (treating it as tantamount to a non disclosure case) from all other non disclosure cases of this description is that the party complaining was *the person who had contracted the disease*, and not the lady who, if it had been a non disclosure case, would have been the person to elect whether she would or would not exercise her right to avoid the contract She, however, elected to insist on the performance of the contract It was this peculiar feature in the case which principally influenced the decision of the majority in the Exchequer Chamber, and, indeed, is the only ground on which at the present day that much canvassed decision would be supported or applied Neither the Q B, nor the Exchequer Chamber, said a word to indicate that " want of chastity is *the only* exception," and Sir WILLIAM ERLE, then ERLE, J , in the course of his powerful dissentient judgment, at pp 764, 765, took pains to show, by reference to the non-disclosure authorities referred to in the text, in what a number and variety of cases promises to marry had been held unenforceable, where information as to matters other than incontinence, but of a nature to frustrate one of the purposes of matrimony, viz " comfort in cohabitation," had been withheld

(x) See note (o), *sup*

purchaser of a chattel, the defects in which had been covered up or hidden away by fraudulent devices or positive means? (xx). On the other hand, this reasoning would not apply to a case where the relative position of the betrothed persons, instead of being, as in the illustration given, such that the one party is not expected to anticipate the undisclosed facts, is, on the contrary, one in which, as in the case of the betrothal of an actor to an actress, each party has presumptive knowledge of their probable existence, or takes the risk of ignorance, and cannot affect to be surprised or disappointed by subsequent revelations of "beauty" not quite "unadorned." The test would seem to be whether the suppressed moral, mental, or physical defects are, or are not, of such a permanent and substantial character as to preclude the reasonable possibility and expectation of safety, decency, or comfort in cohabitation (y).

149. The rules of disclosure under consideration are of course applied only to contracts *to marry*, not to any contracts *of marriage*, as the *matrimonium* itself is frequently, though very inaptly, called   Marriage is a relation or a status, not a contract (yy). and the ceremony of marriage is the act of conveyance, or *traditio*, whereby the betrothal, which, in modern times at least (z), has the only real title to the name of "contract," is completed or satisfied (a).   By terming the act of marriage a contract, a misnomer has been perpetrated, to which JEUNE, P., has said that "the English Courts have not taken a pedantic objection" (aa). It is submitted, however, that the objection, if taken, as it ought to have been, is by no means pedantic, but substantial. Could an objection to call by the name of contract a conveyance of land, or the delivery of a horse, be deemed pedantic?   This terminological error, like most others, has had results   It has not only led to the invention of cumbrous forms of language by which to distinguish from marriage the promise to marry, such as "not a contract of marriage, but a promise to make such a contract" (b), *quod est absurdum*, for no such promise is enforceable by

(xx) These acts might indeed be regarded as not mere non disclosure, but as so many fraudulent falsehoods by silent impersonation   Tertullian took this view, when he denounced the feminine practices of his day—" oculos circumducto nigrore fucare, et genas mendacio ruboris inficere, et mutare *adulterinis coloribus* crinem, et *expugnare omnem oris et capitis veritatem* '

(y) Still further cases suggest themselves   Ordinarily neither of the spouses could be expected to reveal to the other, unless interrogated on the subject, the nature of his or her religious belief   but would not a minister of the Established Church be entitled to be relieved of his promise to marry a lady who at the time of the contract was secretly a Roman Catholic, or a deist, or an atheist? Or a statesman (say, a royalist in the time of Charles I), who should discover that his fiancee had never divulged to him that she was an influential adherent and supporter of the Parliament against the King?

(yy) Per HANNEN, P, at p 101 of *Sottomayer* v *De Barros* (1879), 5 P D 94

(z) In our early history, that is, from the reign of Edw VI to Geo II, the betrothal, or "pre-contract," as it was then styled, had the same effect as the actual marriage *in facie ecclesiæ*   This state of the law was impliedly abolished by 26 Geo 2, c 33, s 13, and 4 Geo 4, c 76, s 27   See the observations of COCKBURN, C J , at p 802, and HILL, J , at p 805, of *Beachey* v *Brown* (1860), E. B. & E 796

(a) The reason for *matrimonium* having acquired the name of contract is probably that all the formal declarations made by the spouses in the marriage ceremony are based upon the *sponsiones* and *responsiones* of the Roman contract of *stipulatio*, as is clearly shown by Dr W E. Ball, at pp. 46–49 of his *St Paul and the Roman Law*

(aa) At p 268 of *Moss* v *Moss*, *inf*

(b) The expression of CROMPTON, J , at p. 804 of *Beachey* v *Brown*, *sup.*

the law of England (c), but it has also, within recent times, encouraged grave heresies in the substance of the law. It is now, however, well established that no amount of misrepresentation, much less non-disclosure or suppression, however fraudulent, of facts, however material, will render a marriage voidable at the option of the party deceived. The marriage may, indeed, be the subject of statutory annulment in the Divorce Court if it was procured by misrepresentation or concealment of such a character, and relating to such matters (e g. the identity of the spouses, or the nature of the ceremony), as is sufficient to show that, in the so-called marriage, there was the mere appearance without the reality of consent, and that, notwithstanding the outward forms of solemnization, there never was, in truth or in law, any marriage at all (d); but for no other cause is marriage dissoluble in the Divorce Court, or elsewhere (e). Nor can a marriage settlement, any more than the marriage which is its consideration, be nullified for any non-disclosure, or other cause, or in any event (f), except of the character above stated, as, for instance, in a case where the party relying upon the settlement is proved to have procured it by the fraudulent suppression of the fact that the marriage was illegal (g) And, where any licence is required to validate a marriage according to the ecclesiastical law of the country where it is solemnized, there is no more jurisdiction to set aside or ignore such licence, on the mere ground of

(c) See *Loftus* v. *Roberts* (1902), 18 T L R 582, C A
(d) As in *Ford* v *Sher.* [1896] P 1, and *Hall* v *Hall* (1908), 24 T L R 756, where JEUNE, P , and GORELL BARNES, P , respectively decreed nullity, on the ground that the woman had been kept in ignorance of the fact that the ceremony was one of marriage
(e) *Swift* v *Kelly* (1835), 3 Knapp 257 , 40 R R 22 , *Ford* v *Sher.* [1896] P 1 , *Moss* v *Moss*, [1897] P 263 The caution in the text may seem rather unnecessary, but is not so, having regard to the fact that in a quite modern case, *Scbright* v *Scbright* (1886), 12 P D 21, we have the solemnly recorded opinion of BUTT, J , to the contrary (at pp 23, 24) The gross inaccuracy of this dictum is, though in very delicate terms, exposed by JEUNE, J , at pp 270, 271 of *Moss* v *Moss, sup* Indeed Sir CHARLES BUTT himself, when President, apparently unconscious of his heresy of two years back, stated the true proposition in unimpeachable terms, at p 15 of *Andrews* v *Ross* (1888), 14 P. D 15 (" the principles prevailing in contracts of marriage differ from those prevailing in other contracts known to the law " he had in the earlier case said that they were " precisely the same ").
(f) *Evans* v *Carrington* (1860), 2 De G F & J 481, which was an action brought to set aside both a marriage settlement on the ground of the wife's misconduct before the marriage, and a subsequent separation deed, on the grounds stated in note (o) to § 150. *post* WOOD, V. C , refused relief as to both deeds Lord CAMPBELL, L C , as to the former, affirmed this decision, on the ground that the settlement could no more be impeached than the marriage itself could, in a court of equity (pp 488, 489), and that whatever relief the plaintiff might be entitled to he must obtain in the only Court which, according to the then recent legislation, could dissolve the marriage itself (pp 489–491) See also *J.* v *J* (1884), 53 L J (CH) 1014, *per* PEARSON, J , at pp 1015, 1016
(g) *Coulson* v *Allison* (1860), 2 De G F & J 521, where a widower, having married his deceased wife's sister (at that time an illegal marriage), claimed the benefit of a marriage settlement made on him by the lady, without having " fully and duly and truly informed her of all the circumstances of the case, and of the possible consequences of what she was about to do " (p 524), and Lord CAMPBELL, L C , on that ground affirmed the decision of STUART, V C , who had set aside the deed of settlement, holding (p 525) that it was the husband's duty to have made the most clear and ample disclosure of the illegality, and that the burden was on him of adducing evidence establishing that he had done so, and that, there being " an entire absence " of such evidence, though there was " no proof of threats, or pressure, or solicitation having been used," the plaintiff was entitled to the relief prayed.

misrepresentation to, or suppression from, the ecclesiastical authority empowered to grant it, than there is to annul the marriage itself (h)

150. But, though a marriage settlement is in the same position as the
marriage with respect to non-voidability for non-disclosure, or any fraud or
coercion whatsoever, inducing a real consent, a deed of separation, on the other
hand, is voidable for material non-disclosure, just as much as any promise
to marry, for the object and effect of such a deed is, not to destroy or affect
the matrimonial relation or status of the parties, but merely to terminate or
suspend cohabitation, and the exercise of certain other mutual rights derived
from the relation, on specified conditions ; and such a deed may be likened
to a contract for the termination or readjustment of partnership interests,
which, as we have seen, involves a duty on the parties to disclose material
facts before the conclusion of the contract, just as much, and on the same
principle, as a contract to enter into partnership (i). It follows that parties
negotiating for a deed of separation, as in the case of any other special type
of contract dealt with in this Chapter (j), are entitled to assume that no
circumstances exist which would tend to show that the object and office of
the contemplated contract is different from its normal and usual purpose ;
and the normal purpose of deeds of separation is to provide, on equitable
terms, facilities for the spouses living apart, and avoiding the misery which,
owing to " unhappy differences " and to those alone, they are both agreed
in foreseeing will be the inevitable result of continued cohabitation.
Accordingly, if there be any circumstances, to the knowledge of one of the
spouses, indicating that the deed has a wholly different character and purpose,
the other has a right to a full disclosure of them before the contract is concluded Now every deed of separation, or at any rate every deed which
contains provisions for the maintenance of the wife, is based on the assumption that the husband is liable to maintain her, which of course he is
not, if she has broken her marriage vows Consequently an adulterous
intercourse carried on by the wife before the execution of the deed,
being a fact which the husband certainly " would not naturally expect "
to have taken place (k), having regard to the nature of the contract contemplated, is a fact which must be disclosed, and the suppression of which will
entitle the husband to have the deed rescinded or treated as a nullity (l).

(h) See *Swift* v *Kelly* (1835), 3 Knapp 257, where, to a suit for restitution of conjugal
rights, one of the pleas was that the licence for the marriage—which was a Roman Catholic
one—had been obtained by " a fraud upon the Holy See " (*per* PARKE, B , at p 282), and
the plea was held bad, Lord BROUGHAM, who delivered the judgment of the Privy Council,
at p 293, observing, first, that the marriage itself could not be dissolved on the ground
set up, and proceeding —" if such be the law touching consent to the marriage itself,
and the fraud whereby true consent was obtained, it would be extraordinary indeed if
another rule were allowed to govern the case where fraud has been practised upon a third
party "
   (i) See § 142, *ante.*
   (j) *Vid. ante,* § 99 (marine insurance), § 101 (life insurance), § 117 (vendor and purchaser), §§ 120, 122, 123 (suretyship), § 137 (compromise), and § 141 (partnership)
   (k) Lord CAMPBELL's criterion, applied to a suretyship case, for determining whether
a fact is material to be disclosed, or not . see § 122, and notes (n) and (p) thereto, *ante*
   (l) *Evans* v *Edmonds* (1853), 13 C B 777, where the trustee of the separation deed
sued the husband for arrears of an annuity payable by him thereunder, to which the

And, further, even if the evidence only goes to prove misconduct on the part of the wife after the conclusion of the contract, and there is no strict proof of infidelity before that date, in which event ordinarily the party complaining would not be entitled to relief (*m*), yet, if it can be shown that, before the above material date, the wife had the then present intention—and intention is "a fact" in contemplation of law (*n*)—of renewing her former liaison, and of using the deed as an instrument under cover of which she would enjoy greater facilities for so doing in secrecy and security, the non-disclosure of such intention will invalidate the deed (*o*).

husband pleaded two separate pleas, one of fraudulent misrepresentation, and the other a plea which the Court construed as a separate and distinct defence of fraudulent non-disclosure, and he succeeded on both. The observations as to the plea of non disclosure, dealt with separately from the other (which does not concern the present discussion), are those of JERVIS, C J, at p 784 ("if there had been criminal intercourse between the plaintiff and the defendant's wife before the separation"—for it so happened that "l'autre" in this case was actually the trustee of the deed—"and the plaintiff at the time of such intercourse knew that she was the defendant's wife, and concealed her criminality from the defendant, with a view to induce him to execute the deed—all which the jury must be assumed to have found—that was such a suppression of a material fact as will support a general plea of fraud"), and those of MAULE, J , at pp. 786, 787, and CRESSWELL, J., at p 787

(*m*) See Sect 3, Sub s (2), §§ 180, 181, *post*

(*n*) As explained in § 28, *ante*.

(*o*) *Evans v Carrington* (1860), 2 De G F & J 481, a very curious and interesting case, which neatly illustrates the distinction adverted to in the text between marriage settlements and deeds of separation The action there was brought by the husband against the wife in her maiden name of Carrington (she having been divorced), and the trustees of the respective deeds, for rescission both of a settlement in contemplation of marriage, and also of a subsequent deed of separation, and Lord CAMPBELL, L C , whilst agreeing with WOOD, V -C , as stated in note (*f*) to § 119, *ante*, that there was jurisdiction to set aside the settlement, on the ground of the undisclosed liaison of the lady with one Robinson before the execution of such settlement, disagreed with him in his view that the Court had no power to set aside the deed of separation It was established to the satisfaction of the Court that the lady had misconducted herself with Robinson, unknown to the plaintiff, before the execution of the marriage settlement, which was on the 12th November, 1850, followed by her marriage to the plaintiff two days afterwards There was no proof, though a very strong suspicion, that the lady had committed adultery with Robinson after the marriage, and before the separation deed which was executed on the 10th May, 1851, but it was proved that she executed such deed with the secret intention stated in the text After the separation deed, she committed adultery with Robinson, whom the plaintiff sued for criminal conversation in 1854, recovering against him, on a second trial (the verdict given for Robinson on the first trial having been set aside) £500 damages In January, 1859, the plaintiff took advantage of the then recently introduced divorce legislation, and obtained a decree of divorce On the 20th October of the same year, the trustees of the separation deed sued the plaintiff at law for arrears of annuity under the separation deed, whereupon the plaintiff filed his bill for the purposes above stated In these circumstances Lord CAMPBELL, L C , whilst agreeing with WOOD, V -C , that proof of the wife's actual adultery after the marriage, but before the separation deed, unknown to the plaintiff, would have been clearly enough to invalidate that instrument (pp 491, 492), and also that such adultery had not been strictly proved (p 492), and that, in order to avoid the deed it was necessary that the principle of *Evans v Edmonds*— see note (*l*), *sup* —should be extended, or rather applied to a fresh subject matter, dissented from the decision under appeal, the difference between the two views being that the V C was not, and Lord CAMPBELL was, prepared to make this fresh application, for the reasons stated by him at pp 492, 493 . " I am of opinion that the deed of separation was fraudulent and void in its inception, on the ground that the wife, having before the marriage had illicit intercourse with Robinson, induced the plaintiff to execute the deed in contemplation of a renewal of that illicit intercourse, and that she might carry it on with more facility If there be evidence reasonably to support such inferences, I cannot doubt that the deed ought to be set aside. *Evans v Edmonds* is not an exact authority

Sub s (8).   *Cases, not within any of the foregoing Classes, where nevertheless one of the negotiating parties may be, or become, subject to a duty of disclosure.*

151. Putting aside entirely all cases of concealment, suppression, or omission of qualifying facts or conditions whereby a statement made is rendered false and fallacious, and which, except in that character, are not actionable at all—for these belong solely to the province of misrepresentation (*p*), and in no way concern that of non-disclosure—there are a large number of cases, not falling within any of the classes hitherto discussed, in which nevertheless one of the negotiating parties is, or becomes, during the negotiation under a duty to divulge material facts to the other party. It is necessary now to examine closely the principles upon which such a duty may be created by the circumstances, though not ordinarily existing at all, or not ordinarily existing at the commencement of the negotiation, and to classify the conditions under which the duty arises.

152. Broadly, there are three, and only three, classes of cases in which an obligation of disclosure which does not ordinarily arise at all, or which does not originally arise, may be created by circumstances occurring before or during the negotiation. These are as follows :—

(A) Where one of the negotiating parties enters upon the negotiation laden with the duty of revealing his own previous fraud in relation to the subject of the contemplated contract or transaction :

(B) Where, during the negotiation, one of the negotiating parties says or does something, or something happens which, having regard to his previous declarations or acts, requires him to speak, in order to correct or remove a delusion in the mind of the other party for the creation of which he is responsible .

(C) Where one of such parties is in the course of negotiation asked a question by the other party in respect of any matter, whereupon a duty is incumbent on the first party, if he answers the question at all, to answer it truthfully and fully.

It is proposed to consider these three classes *seriatim* (*q*), and then to establish (*r*) that, except in any case falling within some one or more of them, no duty of disclosure whatever can either exist originally, or arise incidentally, in negotiations for contracts other than contracts of the six types already dealt with (*s*)

153. Most of the illustrations of the first of the above classes are to be found in cases of vendor and purchaser. When contemplating a transaction of this description, the vendor, as has been already stated (*t*), ordinarily

for this position, as here there is no sufficient evidence of an act of adultery having been committed prior to the execution of the deed of separation But I think that both cases rest upon the same principles of morality, justice and expediency "

(*p*) And, as such, form the subject of Ch IV. Sect 4, Sub s. (2), §§ 83–86 of the author's *Law of Actionable Misrepresentation,* where all the authorities are collected.

(*q*) Class (A) is the subject of §§ 153, 154 , Class (B), of §§ 155–158 , Class (C), of §§ 159–161, *post*

(*r*) See §§ 163–167, *post.*

(*s*) In Sub-s (2)–(7), respectively, *ante.*

(*t*) See § 117, *ante*

enters upon the negotiation with no duty whatever to reveal any defects in the quality of the thing sold (whether land or a chattel) which have no relation, direct or indirect, to any question of title. But if the property which he is offering for sale has a defect which, before the negotiation, he has carefully covered up or hidden away by means of positive devices, he is under a duty at the outset to reveal the defect, for not to do so would be to perpetuate his dishonesty. *Fraus est celare fraudem* (u). He commences the bargaining, therefore, laden with a duty which his own misconduct has placed on his shoulders, and of which he would otherwise be free. Examples of the application of this doctrine to negotiations for the sale and purchase of chattels are abundant (v). Similarly, in a curious case where the party charged, being manager for a firm of publishers, acquired by dishonest means a large partnership interest in the business and its copyrights, then sold this interest for a dishonest consideration to his partners, and, lastly, arranged a compromise of his rights under the sale, based on an admission that the price was excessive, it was held that he had violated the duty of honest disclosure which, by reason of his previous fraudulent acquisition of the property sold, lay upon him at the outset of the negotiations for the sale, and also the further and double duty of disclosure which both the fraudulent acquisition and the fraudulent sale had imposed on him, and with which he was saddled at the threshold of the subsequent negotiations for the compromise (w). And not only is full disclosure incumbent on a vendor under such circumstances, so as to entitle the party complaining to avoid the sale, but, inasmuch as a past fraud created the duty, and another fraud, or a perpetuation of the first, is constituted by the violation of that duty, the party complaining is entitled to all the additional relief (such as the right to recover damages) which is available in any action of deceit, and the party charged is subject to all those additional disabilities to which, if it were a question of mere non-disclosure, he would not be subject, such as, for instance, an incapacity to take advantage of an express agreement or condition to purchase "at all risks" or "with all faults" (x), or of an agreement

(u) A felicitous adaptation by Dr Story (*Eq Jurispr.*, vol 1 §§ 384, 390) of a well-known artistic canon.

(v) See *Jones* v *Bowden* (1813), 4 Taunt 847 (concealment of sea damage to pimento by repacking, and so preventing the purchaser from discovering the damage, as he would have done on seeing the stained bags in which they had originally been packed, the jury expressly found that the defendant ought to have communicated the fact, and the Court refused to disturb the finding), *Ormrod* v *Huth* (1845), 14 M & W 651 ("false packing of cotton"), *Horsfall* v. *Thomas* (1862), 1 H & C 90 (covering up defects in a cannon). In the two last cases the party charged escaped, because the facts proved were not sufficient to bring home to him the fraudulent stratagem alleged But the duty was recognized in all the cases Cp the common devices of salted mines, or faked furniture

(w) *Moxon* v *Payne* (1873), 8 Ch App 881. The situation is caustically summed up at p 885 by James, L J, in these terms —"A man fraudulently appropriates another man's property He then sells it to him for a fraudulent price He then agrees that there was a mistake as to the price, and that the real value should be ascertained and the property taken at that ascertained value, and then says to a court of equity ' now I can hold fast what I so got Giving up the benefit of the second fraud in the sale I have had my first fraud in the acquisition of the property condoned, and my right confirmed and established, so that you cannot deprive me of it '" Cp *Crowe* v *Ballard* (1790), 1 Ves Jr. 215 (*per* Lord Thurlow, L C, at pp 219, 220 a similar attempt "to double hatch the fraud").

(x) An express agreement to sell with all faults protects the seller from liability, even for any fault known to him, but is no protection whatever in the circumstances stated in

to accept compensation in lieu of rescission for omissions in the particulars of sale (y), and, generally, an incapacity to take the benefit of any express or implied contract of waiver (z), or of the fact that the sale has been completed by conveyance (a).

154. Conversely, if a purchaser who is not ordinarily subject to any duty of disclosure whatever (b), paves the way for a cheap purchase by fraudulent manœuvres designed to conceal or depreciate the merits or value of that which is the matter of the negotiation, he enters upon that negotiation subject to the like duty, and, if he violates it, to the like disabilities, as a vendor who has employed similar stratagems and artifices for the purpose of hiding the defects and worthlessness of that which he offers for sale. The principle has been applied to purchasers in such cases as the following :—the case of an intending buyer of shares who, previously to the negotiation, had manipulated certain accounts over which he had control so as to make it appear that the shares were of much less than their real value (c) ; the case of two solvent partners in the business of working a certain colliery who, before negotiating for the purchase from the sheriff of their insolvent partner's interest in the colliery which had been taken in execution, removed the gear, and prevented access to the coal-mine through the shaft, and hid away a quantity of iron-stone recently raised, as so to conceal from the vendor the fact that the seam of coal had nearly been reached (d), and the case of a mine-owner who, before treating for the purchase of an adjoining mine, had for some time past been surreptitiously abstracting coal from it, where it was held that this conduct cast upon the purchaser a duty of disclosure to the vendor which otherwise would not have arisen (e), and this though the vendor, being

the text as was held in *Baglehole* v *Walters* (1811), 3 Campb 154 (*per* Lord ELLENBOROUGH, C J , at p 157 " unless the seller by positive means renders it impossible for the purchaser to detect secret faults "), *Schneider* v. *Heath* (1813), 3 Campb 506 (where the vendor had removed the vessel which was to be taken with all faults from the ways in which she lay, so that, throughout the negotiation, her bottom and keel were concealed, and their defective condition was only discovered when the vessel was delivered), and *Ward* v *Hobbs* (1878), 4 App Cas 13, H L (where, at p 27, Lord O'HAGAN refers to, and adopts, the proposition of Lord ELLENBOROUGH, C J , cited *sup*) In the first and third of the above cases, the resort to contrivances to disguise or cover up defects was not proved, or, in the third case, even alleged In the second, it was proved.

(y) See §§ 206–208, *post*.

(z) See § 202, *post*

(a) See § 230, *post*

(b) *Vid* note (i) to § 111, *ante*. Cp also the latter part of § 165, *post*

(c) *Walsham* v *Stainton* (1863), 1 De G J & S 678 (*per* TURNER, L J , at pp 689, 690)

(d) *Perens* v *Johnson* (1857), 3 Sm & G 419 (*per* STUART, V C , at p 425)

(e) *Phillips* v *Homfray* (1871), 6 Ch App. 770, where Lord HATHERLEY, L C , grounds his decision on the fact that the purchaser was under a duty to divulge facts having a bearing on the value of the property which, besides being within his own exclusive knowledge—this alone would clearly not give rise to any duty—were also the issue of his own volition and wrongful conduct " If a man," he says at p 770, " knows that he has committed a trespass of a very serious character upon his own neighbour's property, and finding it convenient to screen himself from the consequences, makes a proposal for the purchase of that property, he certainly ought to communicate to the person with whom he is dealing the exact state of the case . . . The proposal which he makes is not in reality a simple proposal for the purchase of the property , it involves a buying up of rights which the owner has acquired against him, and of which the owner is not aware He is therefore ignorant of these trespasses, was selling at a price based on the assumption that no coal had been taken : the reason being that the trespasses gave the adjoining landowner rights against the trespasser of a different nature from, and of a larger pecuniary value than, a mere vendor's right to the price of the coal (f).

155. The second of the three classes above mentioned comprises all those cases in which the party starts the negotiation with a clean bill of health, there being no duty of disclosure laid upon him by reason of the nature of the transaction contemplated, and either no representation at all having been made by him beforehand, or none which was false ; but where, during the progress of the negotiation, he says or does something, or something happens, which immediately casts upon him the duty of breaking the silence which till then he has legitimately observed, and which otherwise he need never have broken (g). So acutely does our jurisprudence appreciate the importance and desirability of "justifying its ways" to the moral sense of the community, whenever it is possible, that it habitually casts a powerful searchlight over the entire *res gestæ* of a case to see whether anything is to be found in them indicating that the limits of excusable reticence have b on exceeded After laying down the general principle that silence is not actionable where there is no duty to disclose, Lord ELDON, L C., is careful to add   "but a very little is sufficient to affect the application of that principle If a word, if a single word, is dropped which tends to mislead , the principle will not be allowed to operate " (h). And to this "single word" Lord CAMPBELL, L C., in a later case, adds "a nod, or a wink, or a shake of the head, or a smile " (i), as facts which may make all the difference. A third Lord Chancellor, Lord SELBORNE L C, in a case which related (as did also the two cases before Lord ELDON and Lord CAMPBELL) to the duties of a purchaser, puts the proposition thus . "inasmuch as a purchaser is (generally speaking) under

. not at liberty to enter into a contract without disclosing his commission of an act which has rendered him liable to certain consequences, and of which act the person with whom he is dealing has the right to be informed, in order to know what course to adopt "

(f) *Ibid.*, *per* Lord HATHERLEY, L C , at pp 780, who there points out the distinction between the purchase price of a coal mine which would be based on the value of the coal ungotten, or (which is the same thing) its market price at the pit's head, less the cost of severing and raising it, and the measure of damages against a trespasser, which would be the value of the coal gotten without any deduction whatever for the expense of severing and raising it, because, as against the trespasser, those acts are in law simply part of the trespass So that the analogy suggested in argument on behalf of the purchaser, at p. 777 (viz. "buying a box of gold from which the purchaser, unknown to the vendor, has sub tracted some pieces. The vendor puts his price upon it on the footing that all the gold is there, so he cannot be damnified ") is no analogy at all

(g) "In ordinary contracts," i e contracts other than those described in the foregoing Sub sections, which, from their nature, involve a duty of disclosure, " the duty may arise from circumstances which occur during the negotiation"   *per* FRY, J , at p 475 of *Davies* v *London and Provincial Marine Insurance Co* (1878), 8 C D 469   Cp the observations of the same authority at pp 310, 311 of *Arkwright* v *Newbold* (1881) 17 C D 301, C A ("a question has been considerably argued before me with regard to the question how far silence is fraudulent. Undoubtedly, as a general rule, when there are two contracting parties, each may hold his tongue, but, if one says something, it may create an obligation to say something more ")

(h) At p 178 of *Turner* v *Harvey* (1821), Jacob 169 ; 23 R R 15

(i) *Walters* v *Morgan* (1861), 3 De G. F & J 718, at p 724

no antecedent obligation to communicate to his vendor facts which may influence his own conduct or judgment when bargaining for his own interest, no deceit can be implied from his mere silence as to such facts, unless he undertakes or proposes to communicate them. This, however, he may be held to do, if he makes some other communication which, without the addition of those facts would be necessarily, or naturally and probably, misleading" (j). In short, though the party need not say anything at all, if he does say anything, he must say everything, that is, everything material to the topic in question : by breaking silence he impliedly " undertakes " a duty which otherwise the law would not have prescribed

156. Thus, a purchaser, who ordinarily enters upon the negotiation in absolute freedom from any duty of disclosure whatever (k), may nevertheless by deceptive acts and conduct during the bargaining become subject to such an obligation (l), and, if he obtains knowledge of a material event happening in the course of the negotiation which the vendor is ignorant of, though he is still entitled to keep this knowledge to himself, he ceases to be so if, and as soon as, he uses ambidextrous language with the express object and result of quieting the vendor, putting him off inquiry, and lulling him into a false security, or lets fall something which, whether he so intended or not at the moment, he soon perceives to be having a delusive effect on the mind of the vendor, whereupon he becomes bound at once to remove the delusion by full revelation of the truth (m). So also, the vendor of a patented invention, who ordinarily is not deemed to warrant its commercial value, and is not therefore under any duty to disclose circumstances which may affect such value, puts himself in a very different position if, in the progress of the negotiation, he voluntarily exhibits to the proposed purchaser, and allows him to make, " fallacious experiments " under special conditions secretly arranged beforehand so as to make the invention appear

(j) *Coaks* v. *Boswell* (1886), 11 App Cas. 252, H L , at pp 235, 236

(k) See the citation in the last note, and § 165, *post*

(l) See *Walters* v. *Morgan, sup* , where the purchaser failed in his suit for specific performance on the ground (*per* Lord CAMPBELL, L C , at p 723) that " by the *contrivance* of the plaintiff the defendant was *surprised* and induced to sign the agreement in ignorance of the value of his property "

(m) In *Turner* v *Harvey, sup* , the vendor sued for rescission of a contract for the sale of certain property, on the ground that the purchaser knew of the death of a certain person (a circumstance which greatly increased the value of the property), and kept the knowledge of it to himself, knowing and trading on the vendor's ignorance   On these grounds alone Lord ELDON, L C , would not have granted the relief prayed, but did grant it on proof that at the outset the purchaser had by designed ambiguity of language encouraged a delusion in the vendors' minds as to the nature of the interest in the property held by the bankrupt whose assignees they were, speaking of it as " a supposed interest," when to his knowledge it was an absolute interest subject to the life-interest of his wife, and afterwards, hearing of the wife's death, did nothing to remove, but everything to foster, the vendors' delusion, carefully suppressing both the fact of the death, and the vital bearing of that fact on the value of the bankrupt's interest in the property. Cp *Thompson* v *Lambert* (1868), 17 W. R. 111, where it was held that one who was in treaty with another for the purchase of a policy on the life of a third person, and during the negotiation was apprised of an accident t hat person, was entitled to keep silence as to the fact, but that, if he had in any man r insinuated afterwards that the health of the assured remained as before, his continued silence from that point would have been wholly unjustifiable (*per* WALSH, M.R. (Ir), at p 113).

to accomplish that which under the conditions named in the specification it is, to the vendor's knowledge, quite incapable of accomplishing (*n*). And, in cases of marine insurance, the party proposing to insure his vessel, though he may be entitled to observe silence as to certain matters which are presumed to lie within the common knowledge of both parties, is not entitled to maintain that silence after he has once broken it by positive, though indirect, suggestion of the non-existence of any such matter which is known by him to exist (*o*).

157. Similarly, where A. and B. are the negotiating parties, and, in the course of the bargaining, A. perceives that B. is labouring under a mistake as to some matter vital to the contract or transaction, he may come under an obligation to correct the mistake, at all events if the circumstances are such that his omission to do so must inevitably foster and perpetuate the delusion   In such cases silence is actionable, for it is in effect a misrepresentation, and has in many of the authorities been so regarded ard dealt with. This state of things arises when B , or a third person in his presence or to his knowledge, states or does something which indicates to A that B is being, or will be, misled, unless the necessary correction be made   Silence on the part of A may, in such circumstances, amount either to a tacit adoption of another's incorrect statement as his own, or a tacit confirmation of another's error as truth   Thus, where the plaintiff called for orders at the office of a firm of Gandell & Co , packers, and one Edward Gandell, who was managing the business as clerk to Thomas Gandell, the sole member of that firm, presented himself in answer to his inquiry, and handed to him a card of " Thomas Gandell & Co ," and then ordered goods to be invoiced and sent to " Edward Gandell & Co ," knowing that the firm with which the plaintiff was desirous of, and thought he was, doing business, was the Gandell & Co at whose office the interview was taking place, and withheld the fact that he was carrying on a separate and distinct business with one Todd at another place, where he and Todd intended to obtain delivery and possession of the goods ordered, this suppression was held to constitute fraud, and (since it induced *error personæ*) fraud of such a vital character as to render the alleged contract not merely voidable but void (*p*)   And so also was the conduct of a party

(*n*) *Lovell* v *Hicks* (1836), 2 Y. & C (Exch) 46, *per* ALDERSON, B , who, after finding that " this invention purported to be one for obtaining spirits by means of a patent apparatus for baking bread of the ordinary description fermented in the ordinary method " (p. 53), and recognizing that, if the bread actually baked had really been ordinary bread, *or if the attention of the purchaser had been called to the fact of its not being prepared in the ordinary way, either before or during the early experiments* " (p 56), the defendant would have violated no duty but, this not having been done, " every experiment became of itself a fraudulent misrepresentation " (p 55), and the agreement was accordingly set aside

(*o*) *Harrower* v *Hutchinson* (1870), L R 5 Q B 584, Exch Ch , *per* CLEASBY, B , at p 595 " this rule"—*i e* the rule that the assured need not disclose any fact which is in the presumptive knowledge of the underwriter—" would, however, I think, be subject to the qualification, that the assured had not by any contrivance in the wording of the proposal or policy intentionally hid from the underwriters what was the real risk intended to be covered . .   Silence as to certain material particulars is one thing ; but hiding and covering them up is another , and in such a contract as this, .   avoids the policy " MARTIN, B , at p 594, uses more vigorous language " that is a concealment at the best. I should say it is something more , in my judgment it is a fraud "

(*p*) *Hardman* v *Booth* (1863), 1 H & C 803

m leaving uncorrected the form in which letters were addressed to him, as and for a person of somewhat similar name to his own in the same street, for whom he knew he was being mistaken by the party on whom, by means of this fraudulent reticence, he was seeking to foist the contract (q). The above may be regarded as cases of personation by silence. But the rule is not confined to *error personæ*. Thus, where proposals were being made for a policy of marine insurance on a cargo on board a vessel " at and from Buenos Ayres and port or ports of loading in the province of Buenos Ayres to port or ports of call and discharge in the United Kingdom," and the underwriters, by making out the policy as " at and from Buenos Ayres " only, made it clear to the assured, if it was not clear to him before (as it was, or ought to have been), that they knew of no other port in the Province of Buenos Ayres than the port of Buenos Ayres, it became, from that moment at any rate, the duty of the assured to break silence by revealing the fact that there was a certain dangerous place, not regarded generally as a port at all, which he was nevertheless in his own secret mind meaning by the general expression " port or ports of loading in the Province of Buenos Ayres," and so to dispel the underwriters' delusion (r). And when, in the course of negotiations for the purchase of land, the purchaser's solicitors made a note on the margin of the draft agreement that they assumed that the covenants referred to " contained nothing unusually restrictive," it was held that it was the vendor's duty to immediately correct this false assumption, and that having failed to discharge it, he was not only disentitled to specific performance, but was also subject to a counter-claim for rescission (s). Further, where one of the parties to the negotiation stands by and allows in silence an erroneous statement made by a third person to, or in the presence or hearing of, the other party, he may be violating a duty of disclosure created by the circumstances (t)

(q) *Cundy* v *Lindsay* (1878), 3 App Cas 459, H L, *per* Lord CAIRNS, L C, at p 465 " they"—the jurors—" have found that by the form of the signatures which were written by Blenkarn . and *by the way in which he left uncorrected the mode and form in which, in turn, he was addressed by the respondents* , that by all these means he led and intended the respondents to believe that the person with whom they were communicating was not Blenkarn, the dishonest and irresponsible man, but was a well-known and solvent house of Blenkiron & Co, doing business in the same street "

(r) *Harrower* v *Hutchinson, sup*, *per* CLEASBY, B, at pp 595, 596

(s) *Andrew* v *Aitken* (1883), 31 W R 425 (*per* FRY, J, at p 426)

(t) For illustrations of this contingent and incidental duty to correct a third person s misleading statement addressed to the other party to the negotiation, see *Pilmore* v *Hood* (1838), 5 Bing (N C.) 97 (*per* TINDAL, C.J, and VAUGHAN, J, at p 107), *Nottingham Patent Brick and Tile Co* v *Butler* (1886), 16 Q B D 778, C A (*per* Lord ESHER, M R . at p 788 : a case of a party confirming by his silence his solicitor's false correction of his own accurate statement, in the presence and hearing of the other party), *Marnham* v. *Weaver* (1899), 80 L T 412 The existence of the duty is recognized by ALDERSON, B, at p 529 of *North British Insurance Co* v *Lloyd* (1854), 10 Exch 523, and by JOYCE, J, at pp 334, 335 of *Seddon* v *North Eastern Salt Co*, [1905] 1 Ch 326 Cp Story's *Equity Jurispr*, vol 1, §§ 384 385, 389, 390 The doctrine is further illustrated by the analogous cases of partnership by estoppel (as to which see Lord Lindley's and Sir Frederick Pollock's treatises) See also the observations of BLACKBURN, J, at p 673 of *Polak* v *Everett* (1876), 1 Q B D 669, in relation to the estoppel rule that " if a man stands by and allows another to act without objecting when, from the usage of trade or otherwise, there is a duty to speak, his silence would preclude him as much as if he proposed the act himself " The rule enunciated in the Digest is the same *qui tacet, consentire videtur, qui potest et debet vetare, jubet si non vetat* This answers to the moral canon stated in

158. A very important type of case in which a duty of disclosure springs into being in the course of the negotiations is where, the party charged having made a representation in the first instance, facts supervene before the conclusion of the contract which have an effect on either the veracity, or the verity, of the original statement. During the above-mentioned intervening period the situation may be altered in two ways : and, in both cases, a duty of disclosure is created by the change. The rule, as to both, is well stated by FRY, J., in a memorable judgment, where, after dealing with the initial and absolute duty of disclosure in contracts and relations *uberrimæ fidei*, he proceeds : " again, in *ordinary* contracts, the duty may arise from circumstances which occur during the negotiations. Thus, for instance, if one of the negotiating parties has made a statement which is false in fact, but which he believes to be true, and which is material to the contract, and during the course of the negotiations he discovers the falsity of that statement, he is under an obligation to correct his erroneous statement ; although, if he had said nothing, he very likely might have been entitled to hold his tongue throughout. So, again, if a statement has been made which was true at the time, but which in the course of the negotiations becomes untrue, then the person who knows that it has become untrue is under an obligation to disclose to the other the change of circumstances " (*u*) In the former type of case, the duty is obvious (*v*) what was originally false remains false, but the

Arist Eth iv. 8 8 (" ἃ γὰρ ὑπομένει ἀκούων, ταῦτα καὶ ποιεῖν δοκεῖ "), and to the proverbial " silence gives consent " Of course, where there never was any duty to speak in the first instance, and none has arisen out of supervening circumstances, reticence constitutes neither an actionable breach of duty, nor an estoppel, and is therefore absolutely innocuous in law, whatever it may be in morals See *Russell* v *Thornton* (1859), 4 H & N. 788, *per* BRAMWELL, B , at p 798 (" Mr Honyman says silence gives consent In some cases it may , for instance, where there is a duty to speak, and the party does not, an assent may be inferred from his silence " he then goes on to show that in that case there was no such duty, and therefore no such implied assent), *Marnham* v *Weaver*, sup , per ROMER, J (" though a person may be deceived by another with the knowledge of a third person, if that third person is not a party to the deceit, and owes no legal duty or obligation to the party deceived, and does nothing but preserve silence, however morally blameworthy he cannot be held liable at the instance of the party deceived," but where the party is, as he was held to be in that case, not a mere " passive spectator," but one who " actively assists in the deceit " by silence under circumstances creating a duty to speak, he is liable) , *British Linen Co* v *Cowan* (1906), 8 F 704 (where a party was held not to be estopped from denying the genuineness of his signature to a bill of exchange, merely because he had observed an unbroken silence on receipt of letters from the party setting up the estoppel, in which it was alleged or assumed that he was the acceptor for there was no duty to answer such letters, or to assert the true facts On the same principle it has been held that no admission of a promise is to be inferred from the mere fact of not answering a communication from the supposed promisee in which such promise is asserted or implied : *Richards* v *Gellatly* (1872), L R 7 C P 127 (*per* WILLES, J , at p 131), and *Wiedemann* v *Walpole*, [1891] 2 Q B 534, C A

(*u*) *Davies* v *London and Provincial Marine Insurance Co* (1878), 8 C D 469, at p 475.

(*v*) See *Edwards* v *M'Leay* (1815), G Cooper 308 (GRANT, M R), affirmed by Lord ELDON, L.C (1818), 2 Swanst 287 (where it was held that a vendor who, having represented himself to be an owner in fee simple, subsequently received information which showed that his representation was inaccurate, and yet allowed the purchaser to complete in ignorance of the information, was liable to have the sale set aside as a *fraudulent* concealment, even after completion) , *Jarrett* v *Kennedy* (1848), 6 C B 319, *per* WILDE, C J , at p 323 (where directors of a company, having discovered, before allotment, that all the statements in the prospectus were false when made, withheld this fact from the allottees, and were accordingly held guilty of a fraudulent suppression and misrepresentation, entitling the

importance of any failure to observe the plain duty of correcting an innocent misrepresentation immediately on discovery that it was false *when made* is that from that point what has hitherto been innocent becomes fraudulent ; and the non-disclosing party becomes liable not only to rescission and analogous relief, on the theory of a mere breach of a duty to disclose, but to damages also, on the theory of fraud, which alone justifies the granting of that form of relief (*w*).   In the latter type of case, where the statement made in the first instance was *in fact* true when made, that is to say, in substantial accord with the material facts then existing, but, by reason of supervening events *becomes* false before the contract is concluded, that is to say, becomes in substantial disaccord with the complete facts existing at the later date, it is no less clear and well established that the party charged, if and when he acquires knowledge of the supervening facts, comes at once under an obligation to reveal them to the other party, by way of correction or modification of his original statement, and, if he fails to discharge this obligation, is liable at least to the extent to which a non-disclosing party is ordinarily liable (*x*),

---

plaintiff to damages), *Reynell* v *Sprye* (1852), 1 De G M & G 660, *per* Lord CRANWORTH, L J , at p 709 (" this, from the date of the discovery "—i e of the fact that the plaintiff's interest under a will was much larger than the defendant had originally represented or supposed—" becomes, in the contemplation of this Court, a fraudulent misrepresentation, even though it was not so originally "), *Arnison* v *Smith* (1888), 41 C D 358, C A, a prospectus case of the same type as *Jarrett* v *Kennedy*, *sup* , and with the same result of rendering the defendant liable in damages on the footing of fraud   Contrast with the above the case of *Golding* v *Royal London Auxiliary Insurance Co* (1914), 30 T L R. 350, where the accused, having incorrectly stated, in answer to a question, that he had never had a fire before, realized his mistake and corrected it almost immediately, and was accordingly held entitled to succeed in his claim for the insurance moneys (*per* BAILHACHE, J , at p 351)

(*w*) See the cases cited in the last note, and the first part of the passage cited in note (*z*), *inf* , from the speech of Lord BLACKBURN at p 950 of *Brownlie* v *Campbell* (1880), 5 App. Cas. 925, H. L

(*x*) See the following illustrations   In *Turner* v *Harvey* (1821), Jac 169 ; 23 R R 15, a purchaser of a bankrupt s interest in certain property at the outset described it (so far, with literal accuracy) as then subject to the life interests of the bankrupt's parents and of his wife   before the completion of the contract the wife died, and the purchaser was apprised of this fact, and kept it secret from the vendors, the bankrupt's assignees   It was held by Lord ELDON, L C (p 174) that the language which he had originally used, assuming it to have been true at the time, " he could not use when the wife was dead," and that, having violated the duty of disclosure which attached immediately on his acquiring knowledge of the supervening fact which made his original statement false, he was liable in a suit by the vendors for rescission (p 178)   In *Adamson* v *Jervis* (1827), 4 Bing 66, an auctioneer had stated before the auction sale had commenced that he had the authority of the owner to sell   This statement was true when made, but at the time of the sale it had ceased to be so   In an action for damages for *fraudulent* misrepresentation, not for mere breach of warranty of authority, it was held by BEST, C J , at p 74, delivering the judgment of the Court of C P , that " for this injury the plaintiff is entitled to compensation, *whether the affirmation was false or true at the time it was made*   If the defendant had authority to sell at the time he employed the plaintiff, but ceased to have that authority at the time of the sale, he should have informed the plaintiff of this change in his s tuation," and his silence under the circumstances was not only actionable, but fraudulent, for only on the hypothesis of fraud could he have been made to pay damages, having regard to the form of action   Similar omissions to correct a statement, true in fact when made, but rendered untrue by supervening circumstances, were considered not only breaches of duty but tantamount to fraudulent concealment, in *Denton* v *Great Northern Railway Co* (1856), 5 E & B 860 (failure to correct a time table), *per* Lord CAMPBELL, C J., at pp 866, 867, and WIGHTMAN, J , at p 867 , *Traill* v *Baring* (1864), 4 De G J & S 318 (concealment of subsequent change of intention truly represented to exist in the first instance) ; *British*

that is, to have the contract avoided, or, if he sues upon it, treated as void (*y*). It seems also that on principle, and in accordance with the general current of authority, this second species of concealment, though not morally as censurable, is deemed in law to be equally fraudulent with the first species, and renders the party guilty of it equally liable to an action of deceit, and to all other civil consequences of any proceeding where fraud is alleged and proved (*z*)   Of

Equitable Insurance Co. v *Great Western Railway Co.* (1869), 38 L. J. (CH) 314 (where the assured, having correctly stated in answer to a question, when signing the proposal form, that he had no medical adviser, subsequently, and before the policy was effected, consulted a specialist, who diagnosed his case as one of Bright's disease, without divulging this fact to the insurance company, and it was held that the policy was void (*per* GIFFARD, L.J ; at p. 318 : "there cannot be a doubt that the suppression of that fact was *fraudulent*"); *Gilbert* v. *Endean* (1878), 9 C. D. 259, C. A (representation by the solicitor of an impecunious person negotiating for the compromise of litigation that this person's father, though a man of property, refused to assist him, followed by death of the father intestate, leaving his estate to be shared between his widow and son, which fact, known to the party charged before the compromise was effected, was suppressed . *per* BRETT, L.J., at p 268); *Davies* v. *London & Provincial Marine Insurance Co.* (1878), 8 C D. 469 (where one of the parties had, impliedly at least, represented to the other that a certain person was liable to a criminal prosecution; at a subsequent interview, no disclosure was made of the fact that in the meantime the advice of counsel had been obtained to the effect that the success of criminal proceedings was very doubtful, and FRY, J., accordingly ordered the contract of compromise entered into on the faith of the original and uncorrected statement to be set aside), *Re Scottish Petroleum Co , Anderson's Case* (1881), 17 C. D 373 (*per* MALINS, V. C , at p 377), and *Re Same, Wallace's Case* (1883), 23 C. D 413, C A (*per* BAGGALLAY, L.J., at p 432, LINDLEY, L.J , at p 435, and FRY, L J , at p 438), cases as to retirement of directors (truly described in the prospectus as being so at that date) after the issue of the prospectus, and before allotment ; *Re Marshall and ___ Employers Liability and General Insurance Co.* (1902), 85 L T 757 (statement by ___ when made, that he was not insured in any other office, rendered false, before ___ licy was granted, by his subsequently effecting such an insurance), *Whurr v Dev ___ 904), 20 T L R 385 (where the vendor of a horse by auction correctly described it as ___ s property, before the sale commenced   While it was proceeding, however, the horse was sold privately, and the vendor authorized the sale to continue, without divulging the supervening fact   The sale was rescinded), *Harrington v Pearl Life Assurance Co* (1914), 30 T L T 613, C A (alteration in state of assured's health)   Op the authorities on the liability, as a partner by estoppel, of a person who retires from a firm without notifying his retirement, which are collected in the various treatises on partnership, and particularly *Goode and Bennion* v *Harrison* (1821), 5 B & Ald 147, a case of an infant partner omitting to give notice of his retirement from the firm on his becoming of age (*per* BAYLEY, J , at p 158, who speaks of the partner "having done nothing to correct the mistake," and of his "suffering that delusion to continue," and points out his duty and interest, if he wished to prevent the operation of estoppel, to "protect himself from the consequences of that misrepresentation by giving notice")

   (*y*) See Sect 5, *post*
   (*z*) At p 950 of *Brownlie* v *Campbell* (1880), 5 App Cas 925, H. L , Lord BLACKBURN seems to be of opinion that each of the two species of omission to disclose supervening facts which are discussed in the text constitutes fraud, for, after first dealing with the case of a direct lie, he proceeds   "I further agree in this "—which is the first of the above two propositions—"that when a statement or representation has been made in the *bona fide* belief that it is true, and the party who has made it afterwards comes to find out that it is untrue, and discovers what he should have said, he can no longer honestly keep up that silence on the subject after that has come to his knowledge   That would be fraud, too, I should say, as at present advised   And I go on further still to say, which is perhaps not so clear, but certainly it is my opinion"—and here he is dealing with the second, or a class which includes the second, of the above types of omission, viz omission to correct a statement which, when made, was believed to be true, and *was true in fact*, but which subsequent events have rendered false—"where there is a duty and an obligation to speak, and a man in breach of that duty or obligation, holds his tongue and does not speak, and does not say the thing he was bound to say, if that was done with the intention of inducing the other party to act upon the belief that the reason why he did not speak was because he had nothing to say, I should be inclined myself to hold that that was fraud also " It is true that in the following year, JAMES, L J , at p 329 of *Arkwright* v *Newbold* (1881),

course, it is vital for the party complaining to make out that the party charged has made a representation of some kind in the first instance: unless this is shown, it is idle to prove a change of circumstances, of however material a nature (a), for under such conditions the party is free " to hold his tongue throughout." On the other hand, when once the fact of the original statement is established against him, and the fact that such statement was false when made, or became false before the contract was concluded, the burden lies heavily on the party charged to establish that he has observed the duty of disclosure referred to, and this burden he discharges, not by pointing to some ambidextrous and sub dolous communication, designed to disguise the truth under a vesture of words which may be afterwards claimed as a revelation of it (b), but only by proof of having made a correction at once timely, complete, and unambiguous (c).

17 C D 301, C A, in a supplementary statement made by him after the judgments of himself and the other members of the Court had been delivered, takes upon himself to express his personal view (quite unnecessary to the decision, which was in favour of the defendant on other grounds) that persons issuing a prospectus would not be liable to an action of *deceit*, though they would be to proceedings for rescission, merely " because they do not mention a fact coming to their knowledge before the allotment of shares, which falsifies a statement in the prospectus " (meaning, of course, a statement which was in fact true when made) This dictum, however, for it is only a dictum, is not only opposed to all principle (JAMES, L.J, himself gives no reasons whatever for his opinion), but is inconsistent with at least the first five of the authorities cited in note (x), *sup*, two of which were common law actions of *deceit*, and in the other three of which the equity judges who decided them went out of their way to characterize the silence of the party as *fraudulent* suppression, and, further, it was impliedly, but emphatically, repudiated and dissented from, five years later, by LINDLEY, L J, at p. 733 of *Canning* v. *Farquhar* (1886), 16 Q B D. 727, C A · " if he had paid the money without disclosing to the office the fact that his statements, *which were true when he made them*, were so no longer, he would have done that which would have been *plainly dishonest*."

(a) *Thompson* v *Lambert* (1868), 17 W R 111, is a good illustration of this In that case, where a vendor of a policy of assurance on the life of a certain person sued the purchaser for rescission, there had been no initial misrepresentation, and no insinuation of a falsehood, or any positive fraud, in the course of the negotiations, on the part of the defendant and though to his knowledge, a very important change in the health of the assured person occurred before the contract was entered into, WALSH, M R (Ir), held, at p 112, that there was no principle on which the defendant could be held liable by reason of this fact alone, though he is careful to observe (p 113) that, if the defendant had been guilty of any of the above acts, the concealment would have been fraudulent, and relief would have been given to the plaintiff.

(b) As was the ambiguous circular issued by the directors of a company, on ascertaining the falsity of the prospectus, in *Arnison* v *Smith* (1888), 41 C. D 358, C A, which was so framed as " to avoid bringing to the mind of the plaintiffs the real facts of the case, whilst stating enough to enable the defendant to say that the plaintiffs were informed of those facts (*per* Lord HALSBURY, L C, at p 370, after laying down that " it obviously lies on those who rely on a subsequent explanation to show that such explanation was quite clear ")

(c) See §§ 19-24, *ante* For instances of proper corrections of previous misstatements in the particulars of sale made orally during the progress of the auction sale, see *Edwards to Daniel Sykes & Co*, Ltd (1890), 62 L T 445, and *Re Hare and O'More's Contract*, [1901] 1 Ch 93 The party charged must establish not only the explicit character of such oral correction, but also the fact that the party complaining heard and understood it In the former of the two cases cited, CHITTY, J., found that the purchaser (or rather his manager, who attended the sale) had heard the correction, in the latter JOYCE, J, seems not to have been satisfied on the point, since he granted the purchaser rescission, though he refused the particular form of relief prayed, which was specific performance with compensation *Torrance* v *Bolton* (1872), 8 Ch App 118. was a case in which the reversion offered for sale was misdescribed in newspaper advertisements as " absolute," when in fact it was subject to three mortgages the necessary correction was made, not in the particulars of sale (which was the proper place for it), but in one of the conditions The vendor never circulated any printed or written copies of the conditions, but they were read from a manuscript at the sale In those circumstances, the onus was held to be on the vendor of

159. The third and last class of case in which a qualified duty of disclosure may be incidentally created by special circumstances is where, in the course of the negotiation, one of the parties asks a direct question of the other as to some fact or matter of which that other was never under any obligation to make any voluntary and unsolicited communication. Of course, where such a duty exists *ab initio*, the party on whom it lies is not allowed to wait till an inquiry is made, and cannot excuse himself by pointing to the absence of such inquiry(d): but, where there is either no such original duty at all, or none in relation to the particular matter in question, the party who seeks to render the other liable must, if he is to establish such liability, begin by putting a question as to the existence, or non-existence, or the circumstances, of the particular fact, event, or matter. Several other conditions must then be fulfilled before he can make out his right to ....ess : but this first step must at least be taken , otherwise he fails *in limine*. The duty, on the one side, to inquire, where there is no duty of volunt y disclosure on the other, is insisted upon in a large number of the authorit s, particularly those relating to marine insurance (e), life insurance (*f*), contracts between vendor and purchaser (g), and suretyship (h).

proving that the correction was in this way brought to the actual notice of the purchaser Not only did the vendor not discharge this onus, but the purchaser established that, being very deaf, he did not hear what was read out, and rescission was accordingly decreed (per JAMES, L.J , at pp. 123, 124)

(d) See *Turner* v *Harvey* (1821). Jac. 169, 23 R. R. 15, where Lord ELDON, L C , at p 177, refers to the carelessness of the plaintiff in not making any inquiry of the defendant whether the bankrupt's wife was alive or dead, but adds (p 178) that this was no answer to the claim, for it was the duty of the defendant to give the information without waiting to be asked, and "the Court would not permit the party to take advantage of that negligence" So, at pp 42, 43 of *Greenwood* v. *Greenwood* (1863), 2 De G J & S 28, TURNER, L.J , disposes of the contention "that it was competent to the other parties to have asked for the particulars not communicated, and that they did not do so," by pointing out that "this Court does not deal with cases of family arrangement on any such footing. It expects and requires, as I think, in such cases, a full and complete disclosure   . whether inquiries be made or not   It expects and requires, in such cases, the most perfect *bona fides*, and it is not in my opinion consistent with *bona fides* that partial and imperfect statements should be made on the one side, the *party making them taking the chance whether a full and perfect explanation will be required on the other side*"

(e) See *Carter* v *Boehm* (1766), 3 Burr 1905 (per Lord MANSFIELD, C J , at pp 1918, 1919), *Haywood* v *Rogers* (1804), 4 East 590 (per Lord ELLENBOROUGH, C J , at p 596), *Harrower* v *Hutchinson* (1870), L. R. 5 Q B 584, Exch Ch (per CLEASBY, B , at p 594), *The Bedouin*, [1894] P 1, C. A (per Lord ESHER, M R , at p 12) ; *Glasgow Assurance Corporation* v. *William Symondson & Co* (1911), 104 L T 254 (per SCRUTTON, J , at p 257. "if the underwriter wants to know who is the assured"—this was a case of re-insurance—" he must ask"), *Cantiere Meccanico Brindisino* v *Janson*, [1912] 3 K B 452, C A (per VAUGHAN WILLIAMS, L.J , at p 462, citing s 18, sub s (3) of the Marine Insurance Act, 1906)

(*f*) Re *General Provincial Life Assurance Co , Ltd , Ex p Daintree* (1870), 18 W R 396 (per MALINS, V C , who, at p 397, after stating that "he did not think that this Court would oblige a person to say, without being questioned, by what offices he had been refused," points out that, in that case, there *had* been a question, and a false answer, which made all the difference) And see the cases cited in the notes to §§ 101, 102, ante

(g) *Adamson* v *Evitt* (1830), 2 Russ & M 66 (per LEACH, M R , at pp 71, 72) , *Jones* v *Keene* (1841) 2 M & Rob 348 (where the party charged had made a positive misrepresentation in answer to a question, and was held liable on this ground, apart from non disclosure), *Nelthorpe* v *Holgate* (1844), 1 Coll 203 (per KNIGHT BRUCE, V -C, at pp 220, 221), *Ex p Burrell, Re Robinson* (1875), 1 C D 537, C A (per BAGGALLAY, L J , at p 553 · "it was perfectly competent to any of the creditors who were present to have inquired of him whether there was any charge affecting the assets," and, having failed to do so, they could not complain of the bankrupt's non disclosure, there being no duty on him to make such disclosure except in answer to a question), *Coaks* v *Boswell* (1886), 11 App Cas 232, H L (per Lord SELBORNE at p 240)

(h) *Hamilton* v *Watson* (1845), 12 Cl & F 109 , *Wythes* v *Labouchere* (1859), 3 De G &

160. Having put the question, assuming it to be a proper one (*i*), the party who seeks to make the other responsible, and who (since there is *ex hypothesi* no original duty of disclosure on that other) can only do so on the basis of misrepresentation, must get an answer to this inquiry. If he receives none he is not in a position to establish any failure of duty, either to divulge the facts (for the other party has never come under any such obligation), or to state them truly (for he has made no statement at all). Having no right to an answer, he has no ground of complaint. There are no doubt, here and there, loose dicta to be found containing an assertion, or involving an assumption, of the existence of such a right (*j*) but these dicta are demonstrably erroneous; for at that rate a party to whom no duty of disclosure is owed could at his own will and pleasure, as if he were a statutory or official inquisitor armed with special authority for that purpose, impose a duty on the other party, and confer ·ht upon himself, which is wholly unrecognized by the law The true rul   that the party interrogated is entitled to use his discretion as to whether he will answer the question or not (*k*) He is under no duty to answe   all, and no inference can be drawn from his refusal or neglect to do so (*l*) but if he elects to answer, assuming again that the question is a proper one (*i*), he is under a duty to answer truthfully, honestly, and fully (*m*),

J 593 (*per* Lord CHELMSFORD, L C, at p 610 "if he meant to act cautiously and prudently, he should, according to the case of *Hamilton* v *Watson*, have put the questions and obtained the information which he required"), *Mackreth* v *Walmsley* (1884), 51 L T 19 (*per* KAY, J), *Seaton* v *Burnand*, [1900] A C 135, H L (*per* Lord HALSBURY, L.C., at pp 141, 142, and Lord SHAND at pp 146, 147)

(*i*) In the sense mentioned in § 161, and note (*p*) thereto, *inf*

(*j*) Several of the expressions used in *Cantiere Meccanico Brindisino* v *Janson*, *sup*, to the effect that there is no duty to disclose "till asked" or "without his — *e* the underwriter's—" asking for it" (see p 162, *per* VAUGHAN WILLIAMS, L J), as also the first words of s 18, sub s (3) of the Marine Insurance Act, 1906 (" in the absence of inquiry"), would seem to suggest that, when asked the question, the duty does arise   though this is not really a legitimate inference   It was, however, undoubtedly said in plain terms by that singularly inaccurate judge (particularly in marine insurance law), Lord ELLENBOROUGH, C J , at p 596 of *Haywood* v *Rogers* (1804), 4 East 590, that if, in the case of a marine policy, a question is put which " may be very proper and convenient for an underwriter to be informed of before he undertakes the risk," and which therefore " may be asked of the assured," and if, thereupon, the assured " should withhold, on being asked for it, any material part of such required information, his policy could not be sustained for a moment"

(*k*) *Coaks* v *Boswell* (1886), 11 App Cas 232, H L (*per* Lord SELBORNE at p 240 " he "—the respondent—" asked no question on that subject , *if he had done so, it would then have been for M, Coaks to exercise his discretion as to answering or not* ")

(*l*) Except, of course, in a case where the truth and completeness of answers to specific questions are made the basis of the contract, as in most life insurance transactions, and where, therefore, the assured cannot escape by leaving the space for the answer blank · see the observations of JESSEL, M R , at p 369 of *London Assurance Co.* v *Mansel* (1879), 11 C D 363

(*m*) *Harrower* v *Hutchinson* (1870), L R 5 Q B 584, Exch Ch. (*per* CLEASBY, B., at p 594 " it was for them "—the underwriters—" to ask such questions as they deemed material, and then they would have been entitled to true answers") , *The Bedouin*, [1894] P 1, C A (*per* Lord ESHER, M R , at p 12 " his other obligation "—the first being the original duty to communicate facts material to be disclosed—" is this, that if he is asked a question   he must answer truly If he answers it falsely with intent to deceive, though it may not be a material fact, it ' vitiate the policy The underwriter has a right to have his question truly answered   The above are marine insurance cases An instance of the application of the same rule to a case of life insurance is to be found in

and any violation of *this* duty exposes him at once to all the consequences of misrepresentation. But, though he is under no legal obligation to reply to the inquiry, he has an obvious interest in doing so, and in this highly metaphorical sense, but in no other, he may be said to be "bound" to answer (n) : for silence, under such conditions, must almost inevitably have the effect of closing the negotiations at once, and killing the business (o), the assumption being that no statement in response to the invitation can truthfully be made which would not have a deterrent operation upon the mind of the person inviting it.

161. Assuming that the questioner has elicited an answer, and that the answer is false, he is still not in a position to fix responsibility upon the answerer, unless he can establish the other elements of proof necessary to constitute a good cause of action for misrepresentation. These other elements are inducement and materiality. In most cases, there is no difficulty whatever in proving the former ; but it is not always so easy to prove materiality, by which is meant, not materiality to be disclosed (for the discussion begins with the assumption that the fact about which the inquiry s made is not a fact required to be disclosed), but materiality in the sense in which that term is applied to a misrepresentation of a nature to induce a person to act on the faith of it (p). This latter kind of materiality he must prove (q), though, no doubt, the mere fact that the question is asked at all goes a long

Re General Provincial Life Assurance Co , Ex p Daintree (1870), 18 W. R 396 (per MALINS, V. C , at p 397), and of its application to a suretyship case, in *Mackreth* v. *Walmsley* (1884), 51 L T 19

(n) A similar use, or misuse, of the word "duty" is made in connection with the doctrine of presumptive knowledge, whenever it is said that a person "put upon inquiry" is "bound" to investigate, nothing more being meant than that, in his own interest, he must do so   See App. A, § 638, *post*.

(o) This was well put by KNIGHT BRUCE, V C , at p 221 of *Nelthorpe v Holgate* (1844), 1 Coll 203   " the answer to which "—i e the question which the vendor ought to have asked of the purchaser, but did not—" if false, might possibly have given a defence against the contract , if true or evasive might possibly have stopped the progress of the transaction '   It will be observed that the V C applies the word "possibly" to both the events which he is contemplating, instead of " inevitably " or " probably," which, as stated in the text, would be the term applicable to the normal type of case   but this was because the inquiry in the particular case before him would have relat d to a fact of extremely doubtful materiality even in the narrower sense of the term   see note (u), *inf*   It must also be remembered that if, on a question being left unanswered (e g in a proposal form for insurance), the insurer goes on with the negotiations and ultimately issues the policy, this fact alone may be some evidence that he never thought the question of any importance, or will at all events strengthen any other evidence there may be that he knew the facts *aliunde*, as in *Thornton Smith v Motor Union Insurance Co.* (1913), 30 T. L. R. 139

(p) As to what materiality means for the purposes of the law of misrepresentation, see Ch VI, Sect 2 of the author's *Law of Actionable Misrepresentation*   For illustrations of circumstances which, though material in the sense that any misstatement of them might give a cause of action to a person in fact induced thereby to alter his position, are yet not material to be disclosed, see *ante*, § 85 (general), § 99 (marine insurance), § 101 (life insurance), § 117 (vendor and purchaser) §§ 120, 122, 123 (suretyship), § 137 (compromises), § 141 (partnership), §§ 147, 148 (contracts to marry), § 150 (deeds of separation), and the cases cited in the notes thereto respectively

(q) When, at p 12 of *The Bedouin*, [1894] P 1, C A., Lord ESHER, M R —see the citation in note (m), *sup*.—says, " though it may not be a material fact," he must mean that it is not necessary to show that the fact was *material to be disclosed*   If he meant anything else, the statement is quite contrary to all the authorities

way to prove that the questioner at least regarded it as material (r), and that the party of whom the question is asked knew that the questioner so regarded it, and thus to establish materiality as between the parties, or " materiality to the inducement " (as it has been called), which is enough (s) : just as, conversely, the fact that the party complaining has made no inquiry as to a particular point, especially if he has prosecuted diligent researches in some other and distinct direction, is almost conclusive evidence that he never considered it of any importance or materiality (t). If, however, it appears that, though a question was put as to a certain fact, it was nevertheless not regarded by the questioner as of any importance, or was so obviously unimportant that it could not have been so regarded, but must have been put in mere idleness, there may be much difficulty in obtaining relief on the basis of actionable misrepresentation (u) . whilst, if the question is wholly officious and improper (v), the party putting it not only is not entitled to have an answer—to that he has no right in any case—but he has not even a right to a truthful answer (w).

162. To sum up :—the party who asks a question as to a matter which there was no duty on the other party to reveal voluntarily, has no ground of complaint, unless his inquiry elicits an answer. He has no ground of complaint in respect of this answer, unless it s false. And he has no cause of action in respect of a false answer, unless it induced him to enter into the contract or transaction contemplated, and was such that its tendency, or its natural and probable result, was to so induce him

163. Except under the condit already stated, no duty of disclosure whatever exists or can arise during negotiations preliminary to contracts and transactions other than those already specified (x)   Put shortly, where the contract contemplated by the negotiating parties is not such as to raise an original duty of disclosure, no such duty can be created afterwards, except by circumstances which make non-disclosure a " fraudulent silence," as it has been termed (y), or which constitute fraudulent misrepresentation, or

(r) As was observed by JESSEL, M R , at p 371 of Lo lon Assurance Co v Mansel (1879), 11 C D 363, and by BAILHACHE, J , at p 351 of Golding v Royal London Auxiliary Insurance Co (1914), 30 T L R 350

(s) See § 129 of the author's Law of Actionable Misrepresentation

(t) This was the case in Seaton v Burnand, [1900] A C 135, H L , where Lord HALS BURY, L C , at p 139, and Lord BRAMPTON at p 148, point out that though persistent inquiries were made as to a certain person's solvency, which was what the defendants had guaranteed or insured, none were instituted as to the circumstances of the loan made by the plaintiff which the defendants were held not to have guaranteed

(u) See Nelthorpe v Holgate (1844), 1 Coll 203, where a vendor suing for specific performance, complained that the purchaser had not divulged to him that he had an arrangement to resell to a third party, and where KNIGHT-BRUCE, V -C , thinking that, even if a question had been put by the vendor, which it was not, and had elicited a false answer, the misrepresentation would have been of very doubtful materiality, used the cautious expression " possibly " referred to in note (o), sup

(v) As was the requisition made in Ford v Hill (1879), 10 C D 365, C A.

(w) This is discussed in § 119 of the author s Law of Actionable Misrepresentation   See the cases cited in the notes thereto

(x) See Sub-s (2)-(7) of this Section, ante

(y) " Fraudulent silence " is the expression used by FRY, J , at pp 310, 311 of Arkwright v Newbold (1881), 17 C D 301, C A., as cited in note (g) to § 155, ante, and pertinaciously otherwise establish an intention to deceive. The proposition, in its widest application, as laid down by the Exchequer Chamber (z), is that "if *dolus* . . . can exist independently of evil intention, it cannot so exist without either the violation of some duty independent of contract, or the breach of a contract, express or implied, between the parties (a). To recognize in a Court of justice *dolus*, or wrong, or misconduct, as a ground of action or defence, apart from these conditions, would be to confound all certainty in the law." It may now be said to be firmly established that silence as to matters which there is no duty, original or supervening, to divulge, however actionable a positive misrepresentation of such matters may be (b), and however censurable *in foro conscientiœ* even the withholding of them may be (c), subjects the party observing silence to no legal liability whatever: and the Courts have, on the whole, steadily refused to accede to the invitations, again and again addressed to them, to pronounce that reticence, except under the conditions stated, can, under the seductive designations of "fraudulent silence," "sharp practice," "hardship," "oppression," and the like, ever be deemed equivalent to fraud or even misrepresentation (d) "Concealment" or *suppressio veri*, which is often said to be actionable, imports the existence of a duty. A man cannot be said to conceal what he is not bound to reveal, suppress what he need not express, or keep back what he is not bound to put forward. No doubt there are scattered dicta to be found in the reports (e), and even one or two actual decisions (f), which may be said

clung to in the argument for the defendant in *Turner* v *Green*, [1895] 2 Ch. 205, as to which case see Sect 8, Sub s (3), *post*. Cp. the expression "fraudulent blindness" (in relation to presumptive knowledge) which is discussed in § 634, *post*.

(z) At p 1049 of *Thompson* v *Hopper* (1858), E B & E 1038, Exch Ch   A similar rule applies in cases of estoppel by "omission" to speak, which only arises "where there is a duty cast upon a person, by usage of trade or otherwise, to disclose the truth," per PARKE, B , at p 663 of *Freeman* v *Cooke* (1848), 2 Exch 654

(a) See Sub s. (9) of this Section, *post*, as to "contracts for the truth"

(b) See the illustrations given of matters which there is no obligation to disclose, in §§ 92, 93, 95, 96, 99, *ante* (marine insurance) , § 117, *ante*, and § 165, *post* (vendor and purchaser) , §§ 120, 122, 123, *ante* (suretyship) , § 141, *ante* (agreements for partnership) , § 147, and note (p) thereto, *ante* (promises to marry) , § 150, *post* (deeds of separation) ; § 167, and note (o) thereto, *post* (infancy) , § 167, and notes (q), (r), (s), (t), (u) thereto, *post* (miscellaneous)   It is clear that misrepresentation of these matters, as is pointed out in the several places cited, would be actionable.

(c) See App B, § 667, *post*

(d) *Horsfall* v *Thomas* (1862), 1 H & C 90 (per BRAMWELL, B , at p 100 · "there must be   the suppression of that which is true, and *which it was his duty to communicate*"), *Walters* v *Morgan* (1861) 3 De G F & J 718 (per Lord CAMPBELL, L C , at pp. 723, 724 "simple reticence d   not amount to legal fraud, however it may be viewed by moralists "), *Davies* v *London Provincial Marine Insurance Co* (1878), 8 C D 469 (per FRY, J , at p 474   "wh s parties are negotiating with one another, each may, *unless there is a duty to disclose*, observe silence," &c), *Brownlie* v *Campbell* (1880), 5 App Cas 925, H L. (per Lord BLACKBURN at p 950   "*where there is a duty and an obligation to speak*, and a man in breach of that duty or obligation holds his tongue and does not speak," &c), *Seddon* v *North Eastern Salt Co* , [1905] 1 Ch 326 (per JOYCE, J , at p 335 "as far as I know, silence has never yet been held to amount to misrepresentation,"— meaning, of course, *mere* silence)

(e) See, for instance, the amazing deliverance of BULLER, J 'sitting in Chancery for

(f) These are *Ellard* v *Lord Llandaff* (1810), 1 Ball & B 241 , 12 R R 22 a case which is abstracted and fully discussed in Sect. 8, Sub s. (4), *post*, and *Hill* v *Gray* (1816), 1 Stark 434

to have adopted, or encouraged, the heresy in question : but the dicta must now be regarded as quite unsound (g), and the decisions, if not in terms overruled, have been so plainly dissented from in later judicial deliverances (h) as to divest them entirely of any authority they may have ever possessed.

164. The most attractive form in which this erroneous doctrine has been presented is the following. It has been frequently urged that, assuming a negotiation between A. and B. in contemplation of some contract or transaction not falling within any of the special classes already indicated, and admitting that in any such case the mere knowledge by A. of some fact having an important bearing on the subject of the negotiation, coupled with B.'s ignorance of that fact, raises no duty of disclosure on the part of A.,— indeed, it would be hopeless to contend otherwise (i),—yet, if the additional

Lord Thurlow), which is cited in § 1, note (b), *ante* ; also that portion of Rolfe, B's direction to the jury in *Jones* v *Keene* (1841), 2 M & Rob 348, in which he laid down that, apart from the misrepresentation there proved, it was open to the jury to find for the plaintiff on the mere ground that the defendant had not communicated a certain fact, which (it being a case of vendor and purchaser, and the fact in question not being one relating to title) there was no duty to disclose, and, lastly, a pious suggestion, rather than a definite expression of opinion emanating from Fry, J, at p 311 of *Arkwright* v. *Newbold*, *sup.*, as to the duty of prospectus framers extending so far as to comprise an obligation to make full disclosure to the public of material facts, in addition to the obligation not to expressly or impliedly misrepresent them, following some similarly wide observations at pp. 381, 382 of *New Brunswick & Canada Railway & Land Co* v. *Muggeridge* (1860), 1 Dr & Sm 363 Sir Francis Buller, above referred to, though an excellent common law judge, and so much in Lord Mansfield's confidence that during the last few years of the latter's judicial life he practically presided over the King's Bench, was not very successful when called away from his normal sphere to intermittent exercises in Chancery, and of his " knowledge of equity, Lord Thurlow," as Hamilton, LJ, observes at p 139 of *Baylis* v *Bishop of London*, [1913] 1 Ch 127, C A , "spoke disrespectfully"

(g) See notes (z) and (d), *sup*, and *Turner* v *Green*, [1895] 2 Ch. 205, where, though reasons are given in Sect 8, Sub s (3), *post*, for considering the decision itself to be incorrect, the principles laid down which repudiate the errors mentioned in the text are quite sound

(h) The decision of Lord Manners, L C (Ir), in *Elland* v *Llandaff* (1810), 1 Ball & B 241, in so far as it proceeded on the impugned doctrine, cannot be supported see Sect 8, Sub s (4), *post* The summing up of Lord Ellenborough, C J , in *Hill* v *Gray*, *sup*, which contains still more extraordinary views of the duty of disclosure, was distinctly disapproved of, if not formally overruled, by Jervis, C J , at p 600 of *Keates* v *Cadogan* (1851), 10 C B 591, and by Lord Chelmsford, L C , at pp 390, 391 of *Peek* v *Gurney* (1873), L R 6 H L 377 A full abstract and criticism of *Hill* v *Gray* is to be found in § 92 of the author's *Law of Actionable Misrepresentation*

(i) See the passage which is cited in § 165, *post*, from the judgment of Lord Thurlow, L C , in *Fox* v *Mackreth* (1788), 2 Cox 320 , also the judgment of Knight Bruce, V C , in *St. Leman* v *Dawson* (1847), 1 De G & Sm 90, a case in which the plaintiff propounded " the notion of charging a man in equity after his majority upon a contract made during his minority, merely because, without any false assertion by him, the other party believed he was not a minor " (p 116), or, put more in detail, " the contention that, on the assumption of the young man's acquaintance with his minority, and also of the broker's belief, during their dealings with him that he was not a minor, as well as of his omission to communicate to them the fact that he was a minor, there was a fraud on his part, for which he became or was after his majority, and is, answerable in a court of equity " (pp 108, 109) This 'contention,' and "general proposition" (p 113), the V C, at p 116, pronounces to be "contrary to principle, of dangerous consequence, and not established by authority " So Williams, J , at p 780 of *Smith* v *Scott* (1859), 6 C B (N S) 771 ("the allegation of knowledge in the plaintiff, and absence of knowledge in the defendant, does not amount to an allegation of fraud'), and Walsh, M R (Ir), at p 112 of *Thompson* v *Lambert* (1868), 17 W R 111 ("I cannot hold that the mere knowledge of a fact which had some influence on the conduct of the one

element be present that A. knows or believes that B. is ignorant of the fact and is negotiating in that ignorance, A. at once comes under an obligation of disclosure to which, but for the presence of this additional element, he would admittedly never have been subject. This contention, though it derives some encouragement from a careful selection, and detachment from their context, of passages containing individual expressions of judicial opinion or suggestions thrown out *en passant* (*j*), is utterly and obviously unsound in principle One starts with the hypothesis that A. is under no duty to divulge what he knows to B., who has no knowledge How can the added fact that A. knows that B is ignorant create an obligation on A.'s part which did not previously exist ? If under the conditions stated (viz. his own knowledge and B.'s ignorance) A. has a legal right to observe silence, that right cannot possibly be extinguished or affected by the mere circumstance that A. is conscious of the existence of these conditions, any more than any other legal right ceases to be so merely because it is exercised in a spirit of personal malevolence, hostility, or oppression towards the person over whom the right exists (*k*). The dicta referred to will be found either in cases where the actual decision was against the party complaining, and where, therefore, they can only be regarded as gratuitous and supererogatory suggestions of elements which, if established, might conceivably, in the view of the particular judge at the moment, have constituted a ground of complaint (*l*), or in cases where, though the judgment containing the dictum was in favour of the party complaining, it was not based on the contention in question, but on some other ground (*m*), or where (as in one case which, so far as the decision

party, and which the other was ignorant of, is sufficient to invalidate a contract "), and see *Smith* v *Hughes* (1871), L R 6 Q B 597, where it was held to be no defence to an action for the price of new oats sold by sample that the purchaser believed them to be old oats, and, as such, commanding a higher price, whereas the seller knew that they were not

(*j*) See the language used by Lord MANNERS, L C (Ir.), at p 250 of *Ellard* v *Lord Llandaff, sup.* (" the plaintiff must not be allowed to deal on a lease as a good and subsisting one, when at the time he was conscious that it was worth nothing, and *that the other party was ignorant of that fact* "), by Lord ELDON, L C, at pp 463, 464 of *Gordon* v *Gordon* (1821), 3 Swanst 400 (" I suppose the most prominent mode of putting the fact of imposition is this that James Gordon knew that there had been a marriage *de facto* . and *knew that Harry was not aware of it*, and kept from him the knowledge of that fact "), and, again, at p 178 of *Turner* v *Harvey* (1821), Jac 169 (" this case goes further, for it is a case where the defendant knew the fact of the wife's death, and *where he must have known*, before he could get the contract completed, *that they* "—the assignees—" *did not know it* "), by BYLES, J, at p 783 of *Smith* v *Scott, sup* (" the plea omits to add that the plaintiff was aware of the defendant's want of knowledge "), implying that, if this addition had been made, the plea would have been good, by JERVIS, C J, at p 784 of *Evans* v *Edmonds* (1853), 13 C B 777, by HILL, J, at p 797 of *Beachey* v *Brown* (1860), E B & E 796 (" it is not averred that the plaintiff knew that the defendant did not know of the first contract "), and by HANNEN, J, at p 611 of *Smith* v *Hughes, sup*, who there lays down that if the seller believed that the purchaser believed that the oats were old, and that he (the seller) was contracting to sell them as old, there would have been a defence to the action

(*k*) *Allen* v *Flood*, [1898] A C 1, H L

(*l*) This was the case in *Smith* v *Scott, Beachey* v *Brown*, and *Smith* v *Hughes, sup*

(*m*) As in *Gordon* v *Gordon, sup*, where the decision was based on the duty of disclosure arising out of negotiations for a compromise, *Turner* v *Harvey, sup*, where the real ground of the judgment was fraud and misrepresentation, *Evans* v *Edmonds, sup*, as to which see note (*l*) to § 150, *ante*

rests upon such contention, is now regarded as of no authority) the judgment proceeded upon two distinct lines of reasoning, one of which (not being the heresy now under discussion) was quite sound, and sufficient to support the decision (n). Wherever the point has been definitely raised as a proposition necessary, or conceived by the party advancing it to be necessary, to success in the action, it has failed (o).

165. Illustrations of the rigid application of the above principles and of the steady refusal of the courts to invent, or to countenance the introduction of, new equities or new common law duties, in the province of disclosure, are abundant Thus, it has been held that the owner of land who is proposing to sell or demise it to another may, without entailing any legal consequences, observe and maintain absolute silence as to its physical condition or defects (p) , the vendor of a chattel need not, in the absence of any express or implied warranty, reveal, though he must not by positive contrivances cover up or hide away, any of its imperfections (q), or divulge the absence of a quality which the buyer believed it to possess, for " even if the vendor was aware that the purchaser thought that the article possessed that quality, and would not have entered into the contract unless he had so thought, still the purchaser is bound, unless the vendor was guilty of some fraud or deceit upon him, and . . . a mere abstinence from disabusing the purchaser of that impression is not fraud or deceit, for, whatever may be the case in a court of morals, there is no legal obligation to inform the purchaser that he is under a mistake not induced by the misrepresentation of the vendor " (r), and " the passive acquiescence of the seller in the self-deception of the buyer " will not " entitle the latter to avoid the contract " (s) ; the re-seller of property, *as such*, need not disclose to the purchaser what he paid to acquire it, or what profit he is making on the re-sale (t) , nor is a patentee who is negotiating for the grant of a licence to work the patented invention bound to communicate to the intending licensee the fact that the patent has no value, or even validity (u) and a director of a company, when in treaty with an

(n) This was *Ellard* v *Lord Llandaff* (1810), 1 Ball & B 241, as to which case see Sect 8, Sub s (4), *post*

(o) See, especially, *Turner* v *Green*, [1895] 2 Ch 205 (as to so much of the judgment of CHITTY, J , as deals with, and disposes of, the contention in question), and the discussion of this case in Sect 8, Sub s (3), *post*

(p) See, as to a lease of premises known by the lessor, and not known by the lessee, to be ruinous or unsafe, *Keates* v *Cadogan* (1851), 10 C B 591 , *Cavalier* v *Pope*, [1906] A C 428, H L (*per* Lord MACNAGHTEN at p 430), *Ryall* v *Kidwell & Son*, [1914] 3 K B 135   And see, generally, the cases cited in the notes to § 117, *ante*

(q) *Horsfall* v *Thomas* (1862), 1 H & C 90

(r) *Smith* v *Hughes* (1871), L R 6 Q B 597 (the oats case referred to in note (i) to § 164, *sup*), per BLACKBURN, J , at p 607

(s) *Ibid* , *per* COCKBURN, C J , at p 603

(t) Per Lord HATHERLEY, L C , at p 1244 of *Erlanger* v *New Sombrero Co* (1878), 3 App Cas 1218, H. L , as cited in note (r) to § 117, *ante*   *Secus*, if the vendor is not merely a vendor, but stands also in some relation to the purchaser other than that of mere vendor, such as is described in Chapters IV and V, *post*   In the case cited, the vendor was also promoter of the company to whom he was reselling, and there was therefore, in virtue of this added relation, a duty of disclosure which would not have been incumbent on him as a vendor and nothing else   As to this distinction, see § 330, *post*

(u) *Smith* v *Scott* (1859), 6 C B (N S) 771 (at pp 780, 782, 783)

individual shareholder (t), *a fortiori* when he is dealing with a member of the outside public, is free from any obligation to communicate any knowledge he may have acquired in his office as to losses incurred by the company in the ordinary course of management. Conversely, the negotiating purchaser is under no legal duty to communicate facts, unknown to the vendor, which are calculated to enhance the value of the property. The typical case selected by judges to illustrate this side of the proposition is the case of a mine known to the intending buyer to exist under the property, but of which the vendor has no knowledge or suspicion. "Let me put this case," says Lord THURLOW, L.C., in a famous judgment (w):—"Suppose A., knowing of a mine on the estate of B., and knowing at the same time that B. was ignorant of it, should treat and contract with B. for the purchase of that estate at only half its real value, can a court of equity set aside this bargain? No; but why is it impossible? Not because the one party is not aware of the unreasonable advantage taken by the other of this knowledge, but because there is no contract existing between them by which the one party is bound to disclose to the other the circumstances which had come within his knowledge. . . . It is therefore not only necessary that great advantage should be taken in such a contract, and that such an advantage should arise from a superiority of skill or information, but it is also necessary to show some obligation binding the party to make such a disclosure. Therefore, the question is, not whether the transaction be such as a man of honour would disclaim and disdain, but it must fall within some settled definition of wrong recognized by this Court." Similarly, Lord ELDON, L.C., in a later case, in order to enforce his proposition that "the purchaser may use his own knowledge, and is not bound to give the vendor information of the value of his property," employs the same illustration. "If an estate is offered for sale, and I treat for it, knowing that there is a mine under it, and the other party makes no inquiry, I am not bound to give him any information of it; he acts for himself, and exercises his own sense and knowledge." (x) To the same effect, COCKBURN, C.J., observes that "the question is not what a man of scrupulous morality or nice honour would do under such circumstances. The case put of a purchaser of an estate, in which there is a mine under the surface, but the fact is unknown to the seller, is one in which a man of tender conscience or high honour would be unwilling to take advantage of the ignorance of the seller; but there can be no doubt that the contract for the sale of the estate would be binding." (y) It is scarcely necessary, except *ex abundanti cautelâ*, to enter a caveat here against the application of the above illustrations to any case in which the intended purchaser of the

---

(v) For though he stands in a certain fiduciary relation to the company, he stands in none towards any of the shareholders, as explained by SWINFEN EADY, J., at p 426 of *Percival* v *Wright*, [1902] 2 Ch 421, in the absence of special circumstances, such as existed in, for instance, *Allen* v *Hyatt* (1914), 30 T L R 144, P. C, and this, whether he is proposing to sell, or to purchase see note (f). *inf*

(w) *Fox* v *Mackreth* (1788), 2 Cox 320, at p 322

(x) At p 178 of *Turner* v *Harvey* (1821) Jac 169, 23 R R 15

(y) At pp 603, 604 of *Smith* v *Hughes* (1871), L. R. 6 Q B. 597

mine is something more than a negotiator for such purchase, that is to say, stands to the other party in a relation which disables him from contracting at all with such party except under very stringent conditions, one of which is full disclosure (z), or to any case of the type already discussed in which the purchaser has been guilty of active fraud in the course of the negotiations or before their commencement (a). Another familiar example is the case of a purchase of a valuable picture by a skilled person from one who thinks it rubbish, and sells it as such   After observing that " it would be an error to say generally that you cannot enforce a contract in this court where the one party knows more of the value than the other does," Lord HATHERLEY, L C , adds—' it happens frequently in the purchase of pictures, for instance, that one party knows more of the value than the other, yet the bargain is perfectly good " (b).   But here, again, there is an exception which proves the rule, viz. when the party proposing the purchase has acquired his peculiar and exclusive knowledge in the course and exercise of fiduciary duties ; to take the instance put by Lord HATHERLEY himself in the very passage above cited,—if " a picture-dealer, employed to clean a picture, scrapes off a part of the picture to see if he can discover a mark which will tell him who is the artist, and then finds a mark showing it to be the mark of a great artist , that would not be a legitimate mode of acquiring knowledge for the purpose of enabling him to buy the picture at a lower price than the owner would have sold it for had he known it to be the work of that artist " (c)   and so, if the party charged makes the discovery when agent for the sale of the picture (d).   Similarly, an intending purchaser is not required by any rule of law to communicate to the proposed vendor the fact, previously ascertained by him, that a railway authorized by Parliament is intended to pass through the property proposed to be bought, or (even if he is also the vendor's solicitor) the speculative possibility that a railway known to be in contemplation will improve the value of such property (e) , or, if he is a director of a company proposing to buy shares from a shareholder, " a large casual profit, the discovery of a new vein, or the prospect of a good dividend in the immediate future " (f) ; or any of the motives or considerations which " may influence

(z) See the distinction which is drawn between the two classes of case, in reference to this illustration of undisclosed mines, in note (b) to § 318, post
(a) See the cases cited in notes (d), (e), and (f) to § 154, ante
(b) At p 779 of *Phillips* v *Homfray* (1871), 6 Ch App 770
(c) Ibid., p 780.
(d) *Lowther* v *Lord Lowther* (1806), 13 Ves. 95, where the agent to sell a " Mars and Venus " found out, in the course of his agency, that it was a Titian, and as such worth about £5000, and at once proceeded to negotiate and effect a purchase of the picture from his principal for £300 (*per* Lord ERSKINE, L.C., at p 103)   This case may have been in Lord HATHERLEY's mind when he gave the illustration mentioned in the text.
(e) *Edwards* v. *Meyrick* (1842), 2 Hare 60 (*per* WIGRAM, V.-C., at pp 73–75).
(f) *Per* SWINFEN EADY, J , at p 426 of *Percival* v. *Wright*, [1902] 2 Ch 421, in the same passage—see note (v), *sup* —in which he insists on the like absence of duty to disclose information as to circumstances likely to depreciate the shares in the converse case of the director proposing to sell   Still less is such a director called upon to divulge the receipt of news from the seat of the company's operations to Stock Exchange brokers who improperly pester him with questions and seek to worm confidential secrets out of him for their own purposes see *Tackey* v *McBain*, [1912] A. C. 186, 192, P. C

his own conduct or judgment when bargaining for his own interest " (g), e.g. a contract to resell the property, when acquired, to a third person at a profit (h), or the use to which he intends to put the property after completion of his purchase (i), or the fact that he is buying for a principal, or, if he is so buying, the name of such principal (j) : though, if any of the above matters be actually misrepresented, in answer to an inquiry or otherwise, such misrepresentation may be " material to the inducement," if not to the contract, and so become actionable (k), unless it is a mere case of general belittling and depreciation, which is no more actionable than the laudatory generalities and exaggerations of the vendor ; for, as has been said, " a stranger bargaining for himself . . might say, Your house is not a good one ; he might say it was valueless. . . . Such has been the course of business for at least 3000 years ; 'It is naught, it is naught, saith the buyer, but when he has gone his way, then he boasteth ' " (kk). So also, the silence of one who is purchasing the services of another as to the difficulties which may be encountered by the contractor in the execution of the specific work is quite innocuous (l), though an express or implied denial of their existence, or misdescription of their nature, is clearly actionable (m).

166. In all the above instances, assuming that no single word has been let fall which might mislead, and no device of any sort employed, and further that the parties, when negotiating, stand in no other relation to one another than that of persons so negotiating, reticence is unamenable to the law. It is often simply a case of one man bringing his knowledge, experience, skill, or sagacity (native or trained), to bear upon the transaction, and so using

(g) Per Lord SELBORNE at pp 235, 236 of Coaks v Boswell (1886), 11 App Cas. 232, H L To the same effect, ROMILLY, M R , observed at p 407 of Dolman v Nokes, inf : " it is not generally the duty of a purchaser to inform a vendor of any of the circumstances he may be acquainted with which may make it desirable for him to purchase any property "

(h) Nelthorpe v. Holgate (1844), 1 Coll. 203 , Dolman v Nokes (1850), 22 Beav 402

(i) Ex p Burrell, Re Robinson (1875), 1 C D 537, C A (per JAMES, L J , at p 551)

(j) Nelthorpe v Holgate, sup (per KNIGHT-BRUCE, V -C, at p 220), Nash v Dix (1898), 78 L T 445

(k) All the cases in which a misrepresentation of these and other like matters has been held material, and the cases in which it has not been so held, are abstracted and fully discussed in the author's Law of Actionable Misrepresentation, § 129 See, particularly, as to the identity or personality of the purchaser's principal, Smith v Wheatcroft (1878), 9 C D. 223, and Archer v Stone (1898), 78 L. T 34 , as to the personality of the vendor's principal, Fellowes v Lord Gwydyr (1829), 1 Russ & M 83 ; as to the identity of a money-lender, Gordon v Street, [1899] 2 Q B 641, C A , as to the ownership of property sold (wines, pictures, horses, &c), Bexwell v. Christie (1776), Cowp 395, R v. Kenrick (1843), 5 Q. B. 49, Arkwright v Newbold (1881), 17 C D 301, C. A (per JAMES, L J , at p. 314), and Whurr v Devenish (1904), 20 T L R 385.

(kk) Per Lord BLACKBURN at pp 275, 276 of McPherson v Watt (1877), 3 App Cas 254, H L Lord BLACKBURN's citation is from Prov xx 14

(l) Ranger v Great Western Railway Co (1854), 5 H L. C 72, per Lord CRANWORTH, L C , at pp 86, 87 (no duty to disclose difficulties occasioned by the nature of the soil to be excavated) Cp Thorn v Corporation of the City of London (1876), 1 App. Cas 120, H. L , where it was held that there was no implied warranty against difficulties precluding the execution of the specified work at a profit, which assumes that the contractor would have had no right to complain of the non-disclosure of those difficulties

(m) Boyd & Forrest v Glasgow & S W Railway Co , [1911] Sc Ct. of Sess. Cas. 33, where the principles of law laid down by the Court of Session were not dissented from on appeal, sub nom , Glasgow & S. W Railway Co. v Boyd & Forrest, [1913] A C. 404, H. L., though the finding of fraud, as a fact, was reversed

the weapons with which, perhaps at a great cost of time, labour and money, he has equipped himself for the business of life. No doubt such reserve and secrecy would be repugnant to a man of high honour and delicacy, who might recognize that it is not always right to exercise a right, that knowledge, like wealth, is power, which may be abused, and that *minimum libere cui multum licet*. Into these considerations, however, it is obvious that the law cannot enter. The only concern of jurisprudence must always be to declare under what circumstances, and in whom, a right is vested without inquiring whether the enforcement of that right is conformable to the higher standards of refined ethics (*n*).

167. A few further illustrations, of a general and miscellaneous character, suggest themselves. It is quite clear that there is no obligation on one of two negotiating parties to reveal to the other any legal status which may incapacitate him or her from contracting, either at all or except under certain conditions and within certain limits, such as infancy, or coverture (*o*), though a positive and fraudulent misrepresentation by a minor that he is of full age, or by a married woman that she is a spinster or widow, may, unless the fraud is directly connected with the contract, and enters into it, and is part and parcel of the entire transaction, give ground for an action of deceit at common law, and, under certain special conditions, may be the subject of indirect equitable relief (*p*). Nor, in general, need one who is contemplating a contract with another, reveal his past misfortunes, or misconduct (*q*), or his present impecuniosity (*r*), or, conversely, where it is a

(*n*) As to this, see App B, Sect. 2, § 667, *post*

(*o*) As to infancy, see *Stikeman* v *Dawson* (1847), 1 De G & Sm 90 (*per* KNIGHT-BRUCE, V.-C., at pp 113–116), *Re Jones, Ex p Jones* (1881), 18 C D 109, C A (*per* JESSEL, M R, at p. 120, and BAGGALLAY, L.J, at 123) *Evroy* v. *Nicholas* (1731), 2 Eq Cas Abr 488, is of no authority whatever if, and in so far as, it decided that the non-revelation by a minor of his own infancy, without any misrepresentation, is actionable. See the observations of KNIGHT-BRUCE, V.-C., on this case at p 115 of *Stikeman* v. *Dawson*, *sup*. As to coverture, see *Fletcher* v *Krell*, cited in note (*q*), *inf*

(*p*) This question is discussed in § 130 of the author's *Law of Actionable Misrepresentation*.

(*q*) See *Fletcher* v *Krell* (1873), 42 L. J (Q B.) 55, where it was held that a lady, on being engaged as a governess, is under no duty to reveal to her intending employer the fact that she has previously been married and divorced. At pp 449, 450 of *Andrewes* v. *Garstin* (1861), 10 C B (N S) 444 (where it was held that there is no duty on a person negotiating for partnership with another to divulge his dishonesty in a previous partnership with another person), Mellish, Q C., in argument for the plaintiff, observed—and his observations were obviously acceptable to the Court—"Take the case of a returned convict, ticket of leave man, or a drunken servant   . It would be monstrous to hold that every man who enters into a contract is bound to disclose against himself some circumstance of his former life which has no affinity to the contract, and as to which no inquiry is made." And to this passage the reporter, in a note, appends a reference to a case which had then recently been decided in France, where one of the parties had concealed from the other the fact that he was a "forçat," and the Cour de Cassation, reversing the Cour de Premier Instance, held that this non-disclosure was not actionable. As to the matters of the past which need not be disclosed, even when marriage is contemplated, such as previous insanity, or a former engagement, see § 147, *ante*. As to past misconduct of the person to be guaranteed in suretyship cases, see § 125, note (*yy*), *ante*

(*r*) COCKBURN, C J, at p 802 of *Beachey* v *Brown* (1860), E B & E 796, mentions such a fact as that the party "is in debt or subject to other liabilities" as one of the circumstances the non-disclosure of which, in the case of proposals of marriage, would not entitle the other party to be relieved of his engagement. Even when a contract of suretyship is in contemplation, there is no obligation on the creditor to disclose to the

question of obtaining favourable terms from the compassion of the other party, his wealth and prosperity (s) : though he must not, whether of his own accord or in answer to inquiry, make any false statement with regard to any of such matters (t). Nor is the creator of a security, on receiving notice of its assignment to a third person, bound to volunteer information to such assignee of any collateral equities affecting it, unless the notice discloses, on the face of it, that which induces the belief that the assignee has been deceived in accepting the assignment (u)

168. It must not be assumed that in every case where no legal duty of disclosure either existed originally, or arose from supervening circumstances, and where nothing amounting to actual fraud or misrepresentation has been proved, the party charged necessarily escapes scot free, or that, where obliquity of conduct, though not sufficient to ground a cause of action or affirmative plea, is established against him, the Court is altogether powerless to mark its sense of that conduct in a practical and effectual manner In the first place, though the Court may be compelled to withhold from the party complaining any form of relief which presupposes his absolute right to have the impeached contract avoided, or treated as void (v), it by no means follows

proposed surety the existing or past financial embarrassments of the debtor   see notes (v) and (w) to § 125, *ante*

(s) Instances will readily occur to any one, from ordinary life and social history, of professional men or tradesmen rashly drawing inferences from external indications of penury in the case of wealthy customers, clients, or patients, who, by display of such outward and visible signs, and by withholding the real state of their finances, whilst not making any positive misstatements, obtain reductions in fees or charges, prolongation of credit, or favourable settlements of disputed claims   Despicably mean as such conduct may be, no cause of action could be founded upon it

(t) As, for instance, was made by one of the *par nobile fratrum* who were the litigants in *Montefiori* v *Montefiori* (1762), 1 W Bl 362, with the connivance of the other, in order to enable the former to contract a favourable marriage, and as was alleged to have been made by the plaintiff in *Wharton* v *Lewis* (1824), 1 C & P 529, and *Foote* v *Hayne* (1824), 1 C & P 545 (two actions for damages for breach of promise of marriage, though on various grounds the party charged succeeded in each case, falsity not being proved in the one, and the defendant's knowledge of the truth being established in the other)   But there must have been a positive misrepresentation addressed to the party complaining   A mere general simulation of wealth by "keeping up appearances" will not do, any more than the general pretence of straitened circumstances alluded to in the last note   When Bassanio, not without an eye to the fair Portia, and before he had entered the lists, was "showing a more swelling port Than his faint means would give continuance," he was making no representation to the lady   When the moment came for declaring his suit, he stated the truth (" Gentle lady, When I did first impart my love to you, I freely told you, all the wealth I had Ran in my veins, I was a gentleman , And then I told you true "), but not quite the whole truth (" when I told you My state was nothing, I should then have told you That I was worse than nothing , for, indeed, I have engaged myself to a dear friend, Engaged my friend to his mere enemy, To feed my means ")   that is to say, he had stated his want of means, but not his contingent liability as a surety for Antonio   but, never having come under any legal duty to divulge either the one or the other fact, his conduct was irreproachable in point of law   So Lord BROUGHAM, at pp. 532, 533 of *Burnes* v *Pennell* (1849), 2 H L C. 497, puts the case of an owner of an estate making a pretence of its general prosperity by frequent remission of rent to his tenants, and ridicules the notion of any purchaser on the faith of these "appearances" claiming that this could have constituted a misrepresentation to himself

(u) *Per* Lord ST LEONARDS, L.C, at pp 782, 783 of *Marquis* v *Dixon* (1852), 3 H L C 762

(v) That is to say, rescission or analogous relief on the one hand, or a defence to an action to enforce the contract otherwise than *in specie*, on the other   See, as to these respective remedies, Sect. 5, Sub-ss (1) and (2), *post*

that it will not give effect to a defence raised by him to any action for the specific performance of such contract which may be brought against him by the party charged , for this is not to assert the legal right of the former party, but to decline the exercise of a discretionary jurisdiction in favour of the latter, and to deny him, not all remedy, but the particular and special remedy which he is soliciting (w). Secondly, a judge when sitting without a jury, can give fiscal expression to his view of the general behaviour of the party charged, as shown by the whole circumstances of the case, in judiciously moulded orders as to costs (x), and, "for good cause" he can do so, even when assisted by a jury (y) And, lastly, where the alleged non-disclosure is raised by way of defence to an action for unliquidated damages, the tribunal (whether a judge, or a jury under the direction of a judge) is entitled and bound to take such circumstances and conduct into consideration in estimating the sum to be awarded (z)

Sub-s. (9)   *The Effect of Warranties and Conditions as to Disclosure*

169. Before concluding this Section, it seems desirable to consider a topic which from time to time emerges prominently in the law relating to disclosure, and is not without considerable importance. It frequently happens, particularly where the contract is one of life insurance, that the

(w) Thus in *Walters* v *Morgan* (1861), 3 De G. F. & J. 718, a case which was very near the border line, it was evidently considered by Lord CAMPBELL, L C., that the party complaining, whom he held entitled to succeed in his defence to the action for specific performance, might not necessarily have been entitled to judgment if he had been suing for rescission, or defending himself against an action to enforce the contract otherwise than specifically   Conversely, in *Thompson* v *Lambert* (1868), 17 W. R 111, where the party complaining failed to obtain rescission, WALSH, M R (Ir.), at p 112, is careful to point out that it was not a case of a defence to a suit for specific performance, implying that, if it had been, he might have succeeded   And see, generally, § 245, *post*

(x) Thus, one of the parties charged (the undoubtedly dishonest infant), though the judgment was in his favour, was deprived of his costs in *Stikeman* v *Dawson* (1847), 1 De G & Sm 90 (*per* KNIGHT-BRUCE, V -C , at p 117)   And a similar order was made in *Walters* v *Morgan, sup* (in this case, both as to the costs of the hearing, and of the appeal also), and in *Thompson* v *Lambert, sup*   See, generally, on costs, Ch VIII, Sect 2, Sub-s. (4), § 619, *post*.

(y) See O 65, r 1, of the R S C , and the cases on "good cause" cited in the notes thereto in the practice books, and particularly *Roberts* v. *Jones* , *Willey* v *G N Ry Co* , [1891] 2 Q B 194

(z) In *Baddeley* v. *Mortlock* (1816), Holt N. P. 151, GIBBS, C J , directed the jury that, though the defendant (who had set up the plaintiff's non-disclosure of previous dishonesty and crime as a defence to his action against her for damages for breach of promise of marriage) had not proved enough to absolve her from the contract, added significantly " but it affects the damages," on which hint the jury gave the plaintiff a shilling   *Bench* v *Merrick* (1844) 1 C & K. 463, was a similar action where a similar direction was given (pp 407, 408), which, however, it was unnecessary for the jury to act upon, as they returned a verdict for the defendant.   In *Beachey* v *Brown* (1860), E B & E 796, where a demurrer was allowed to a plea of non-disclosure of a previous engagement in an action of the like nature, HILL, J , at p 805, observed .   "such circumstances may have a very material effect with the jury as to the amount of damages"   So, in *Andrewes* v *Garstin* (1861), 10 C. B. (N.S.) 444, an action for damages for breach of an agreement to take the plaintiff into partnership, to which the plaintiff's concealment of previous misconduct in another partnership was pleaded as a defence, which plea was successfully demurred to, WILLES, J , at p 452, whilst pronouncing that the case set up afforded no answer to the action, also observed that " if the allegations in the plea be true, the consequence may be that the plaintiff will recover but small damages."

parties expressly warrant, or make it an express condition of the contract, not only that certain questions specifically put have ' een, or shall be, truthfully answered, but also that nothing has been, or shall be, withheld by the one party, either relating to some specified subject-matter, or, generally, which it is important or material for the other party to know (a); the former may be called "contracts for the truth" (b) : the latter, "contracts for disclosure." There are other transactions, of which a policy of marine insurance is the typical example, in which there are expressed, or from which there are implied, warranties, not of the truth of any statement, or of the fact that full disclosure has been made, but of the existence of a certain fact or thing. In either case, it makes no difference for the present purpose what expression is used,—whether "warranty," "condition," "term," or "stipulation,"—provided that the thing warranted or promised or undertaken is made the basis of the contract, in the sense that unless the thing is, or (in the case of a promissory warranty) is made or procured to be, as warranted, the party warranting shall have no rights whatever under the contract of which the warranty or condition is a part or term (b) The question which now arises for consideration is as to the effect of these warranties and conditions on the principles of the law of disclosure, and on the rights and duties which would otherwise belong to, and lie upon, the negotiating parties respectively.

170. In the first place, the effect of an express or implied warranty of the existence of a specified thing, or state of things, is, on the one hand, to release the party complaining of the burden of establishing that any duty of disclosure was owed to him in respect of circumstances material to the thing warranted, or that such duty has been violated (c), and, on the other hand, to render it superfluous on the part of the party charged to make disclosure of any matter covered by the warranty (d). As to matters not so covered,

(a) See the cases cited in notes (c) and (d) to § 101, *ante*

(b) See *Hambrough* v *Mutual Life Insurance Co of New York*, cited in the next note.

(c) For it is the very object and office of a warranty or condition to make it impossible for either party to raise any such question thereafter See the citation from *Seymour* v. *London & Provincial Marine Insurance Co* in note (h), *post* Similarly, and on the same principle, neither falsity, nor fraud, nor inducement, nor materiality, all of which are vital elements in any proceedings founded on misrepresentation, has the slightest relevance to any issue in an action or defence founded on breach of warranty, or non-compliance with a condition, for the parties themselves have made that question of no importance : see *Pawson* v *Watson* (1778), Cowp 789 (*per* Lord MANSFIELD, C J, at pp 788–790); *Newcastle Fire Insurance Co.* v *Macmorran & Co* (1815), 3 Dow. H. L. 255 (*per* Lord ELDON, L C, at pp 262, 265); *Attwood* v *Small* (1838), 6 Cl. & F 232 (*per* Lord BROUGHAM at p 444), *Anderson* v *Fitzgerald* (1853), 4 H L C 484 (*per* Lord CRANWORTH, L C, at pp 503–505), *Towle* v *National Guardian Assurance Co* (1861), 30 L J (CH) 900; *Thomson* v *Weems* (1884), 9 App. Cas 671. H L (*per* Lord BLACKBURN at pp 683, 684, and Lord WATSON at p 689), *Hambrough* v *Mutual Life Insurance Co* (1895), 72 L T 140, C. A Cp., as to marine insurance, s 33 (3) of the Marine Insurance Act, 1906 Though called a warranty, the thing of which the non-fulfilment avoids the transaction must be, in substance and effect, a condition precedent see the observations of CHANNELL, B, at p 302 of *Wheelton* v *Hardisty* (1858), 8 E & B 232, Exch Ch

(d) The department of law which principally calls for the application of this rule, and supplies the most illustrations of it, is that of marine insurance See the observations of Lord MANSFIELD, C.J, in *Shoolbred* v *Nutt*, as cited in Park on Insurance, vol i, p. 493 · "there should be a representation of everything relating to the risk which the underwriter has to run, except it be covered by a warranty It is a condition or an implied warranty in every policy that the ship is seaworthy, and therefore there need be no

the duty of disclosure, though the specific warranty has been complied with (e), or discharged, or admitted to have been discharged (f), remains entirely unaffected. And, even as to the subject-matter of the warranty, it must not be supposed that the common law duty of disclosure is extinguished by, or even merged in, the contractual obligation which the warranty imposes. Both duties exist separately and independently, though the same facts are necessary to prove compliance with either of them. If and when, however, the party complaining insists on the performance of the contractual duty, as such, the other duty is in abeyance, because it is " superfluous " to discharge it, which presupposes that it still subsists ; just as, conversely, if and when the party complaining insists on his common law right, as such, the contractual duty is in abeyance. But it is open to the party complaining (and, being obviously to his advantage, this course is commonly adopted) to assert both rights simultaneously, but alternatively. If he fails to prove the express or implied warranty or condition, or the violation of it, he may fall back on his

representation as to that   If she sail without being so, there is no valid policy " To the same effect, Lord ELLENBOROUGH, C J , at p. 597 of *Haywood* v. *Rogers* (1804), 4 East 590 The rule is now declared and codified in s 18 (3) of the Marine Insurance Act, 1906 (6 Edw 7, c 41) —" In the absence of inquiry the following circumstances need not be disclosed, namely — . any circumstance which it is superfluous to disclose by reason of any express or implied warranty." In s 33 of the same statute a warranty is defined, s 35 relates to express warranties, s 36 to express warranties of neutrality, and ss 37, 39, 40, and 41 declare what matters are, and what are not, deemed to be impliedly warranted   All these marine insurance warranties are in the nature of conditions, such as are described in the text. As to the sale of goods, and what are express or implied warranties, giving a right to damages only, and what, on the other hand, operate as express or implied conditions, see the codifying provisions of the Sale of Goods Act, 1893 (56 & 57 Vict c 71), ss 10–15, and (for the definition of " warranty " therein) s 33 (1)

(e) See *Russell* v *Thornton* (1859), 4 H & N 788, where the defence to an action on a policy of marine insurance was the non disclosure by the plaintiff of information in a letter from the captain of the vessel that she had been aground, and had received very heavy blows, and was making her way in a sinking condition to a certain port, and, at p 797, BRAMWELL, B , points out that the above undisclosed letter " would have been all-important, even if there had been a warranty of seaworthiness,"—which there was not, it being a case of a time policy   " The underwriters might well say, ' You may patch her up, and render her seaworthy, but she will never be as good a ship as she was before this calamity '   It was therefore obviously a letter that ought to have been communicated to the defendants."   In other words, the implied warranty—if it had existed—would have rendered it superfluous for the party charged to communicate any fact tending to show that the vessel was unseaworthy, but not any fact tending to show that, though seaworthy, she was vitally damaged. So, in *Joel* v *Law Union & Crown Insurance Co* , [1908] 2 K. B 863, C A , a life insurance case, VAUGHAN WILLIAMS, L.J , at p. 878, and MOULTON, L J , at pp 892, 893, expressed a clear opinion that the mere fact that the party complaining fails—as the defendants in that case had failed—to establish that the alleged express condition precedent existed, or had been broken, does not deprive him of all his right to disclosure, though it may, in one sense, " partially relieve " the party charged.

(f) In *Cantiere Meccanico Brindisino* v *Janson*, [1912] 3 K B 452, C A , seaworthiness was admitted on the face of the policy, which discharged the assured from their implied warranty of seaworthiness of the floating dock insured   This, however, as was held by VAUGHAN WILLIAMS, L.J , at pp. 461, 463, MOULTON, L J , at p 467, and BUCKLEY, L J , at p 471, would still leave the assured under a duty to disclose any special circumstances (such as corroded plates, or a leak, or a surveyor's unfavourable report as to the unfitness of the floating dock to go to sea without some strengthening being added, &c) which would render the structure more unseaworthy than any floating dock must necessarily be   The only facts which the assured was relieved from divulging were facts connected with the nature of a floating dock which render all floating docks un seaworthy

right, independently of contract, to disclosure of any matter negativing or affecting the thing warranted   Conversely, if he fails to establish any common law duty of disclosure, he may still insist that in fact the party charged has expressly or impliedly contracted for the existence of the thing the absence of which would have been revealed by the disclosure of that which was not disclosed, and which, on the hypothesis, there was no duty to disclose (*g*)   Further, he may ask for and obtain judgment on both causes of action, or on both pleas, as the case may be, where it becomes of importance (by reason of the rules relating to costs of issues, or otherwise) to do so (*h*),—which establishes conclusively that the one right and duty is not merged in, or converted into, the other right and duty, or (if the right be regarded as one and the same right, and the correlative duty as one and the same duty, but springing from different sources), that the contractual character of the right and the duty may co-exist with their non-contractual character, and that the party to whom the duty is owed may rely on either, or both, of its two aspects, as may suit his convenience (*i*).

(*g*) See the extracts in note (*e*), *sup*, from the authorities there cited   Both rights were in this way asserted by way of alternative and independent pleas, which were separately and successively treated as such by the Court, in *Thames and Mersey Marine Insurance Co* v *Gunford Ship Co*, [1911] A C 529, H L (where the insurance company contended, first, that the master's record—he had not been to sea for 22 years, had lost his last ship, and his certificate had been suspended—was such as to render the vessel unseaworthy, and so constituted a breach of the assured's implied warranty, and, secondly, that, if there had been no such breach, there had been at all events a violation of the assured's duty to disclose the above facts, and the H L separately discussed the two pleas, and having first decided against the one, proceeded then to consider in detail, and reject, the other), and in *Joel* v *Law Union & Crown Insurance Co.*, [1908] 2 K B 863, C A (where, having first held that the truth in fact of the answers of the deceased to certain questions was not made a condition precedent to the validity of the policy, the Court of Appeal distinctly expressed their opinion, that it was still competent to the insurance company to resort to their second line of defence, viz breach by the deceased of her duty, independently of condition or contract, to disclose all material circumstances of the nature of those to which the questions were directed (*per* VAUGHAN WILLIAMS, L J , at p 878, intimating his entire dissent from the contention " that we ought to exclude from this contract the implied contract by an applicant for a policy to make full disclosure of all facts material to the risk," and *per* MOULTON, L J , who, at pp 892, 893, observes " *over and above the two documents signed by the applicant, and in my opinion unaffected by them, ther remained the common law obligation of disclosure of all knowledge possessed by the applicant material to the risk about to be undertaken by the company* ")

(*h*) In *Seymour* v *London & Provincial Marine Insurance Co* (1872), 41 L J (C P) 193, where the cargo insured was expressly warranted " no contraband of war," the Court of Common Pleas, whose judgment was delivered by WILLES, J , after coming to the conclusion that the cargo, part of which had been condemned by the U S Courts, was clearly contraband of war (pp 194–198), proceeded to refer to the separate plea which had been pleaded of non-disclosure, in the following terms —" We need not enter upon the other points of the case   It is enough to say that if there was contraband, it was concealed contraband from the underwriters, and though it is true that concealment of facts leading up to a breach of warranty is immaterial, *certainly it has never been held that a concealment of what actually falls within a warranty is not a concealment which would avoid the insurance apart from the warranty*   This may not be considered material with reference to the main question to be decided, but it is material for the purpose of *explaining why we give judgment for the defendants on the seventh plea, which deals with the concealment, as well as on the ninth plea, which is founded on the warranty* "

(*i*) Many obligations, such as that of a carrier, spring both from contract and from circumstances independent of contract   In all such cases, it is open to the injured party to assert the duty in either, or both, of its two characters.   Where a question of the right to High Court costs arises, under s 116 of the County Courts Act, 1888 (51 & 52 Vict c 43),

171. Where the warranty or condition which is made the basis of the contract is not of the foregoing type, but is expressed in a perfectly general form, as, for instance, that if the assured should (*inter alia*) " omit to communicate any matter material to be made known to the company in order to enable them to judge of the risk " (*j*), or that " if any information necessary to be made known to the company is withheld " (*k*), the policy is to be void, it is difficult to see what possible advantage is gained by the party who exacts such a covenant or proviso, since he is only stipulating for the performance of the precise duty, neither more nor less, which the law imposes on the opposite party One might as profitably insist on a general engagement to abstain from assault, defamation, or fraud (*kk*). And the attempt to fortify by contractual engagements the solid and impregnable fortresses of the common law, besides being " wasteful and ridiculous excess," is subject to special perils of its own In his anxiety to define and particularize that which the common law has left indefinite and general, and to substitute a rigid for a Lesbian and flexible canon (*l*), the party may find that, instead of defining and particularizing, he has limited and curtailed, his rights His confidence in the adequacy of contractual amplification to do for himself what the law has already done for him is wholly misplaced. Mistaking the universality or generality of a principle of jurisprudence for vagueness or obscurity, he foolishly attempts to improve upon it by language of his own which he puts into the mouth of the opposite party, the only result in many cases being to invite the Court to examine closely the precise contractual limits which the parties would appear to have assigned to an otherwise perfectly general obligation, and to encourage a severe application of the *expressio unius exclusio alterius* canon of construction, which otherwise would be entirely out of place (*m*). This attempt to " make assurance doubly sure "

---

this principle becomes of some practical importance It was successfully invoked in *Kelly* v. *Metropolitan Railway Co*, [1895] 1 Q B 944, C. A , *Turner* v *Stallibrass*, [1898] 1 Q B 56, C A, and *Edwards* v *Mallan*, [1908] 1 K B 1002, C. A , in all of which it was held that the plaintiff was entitled to have his action of negligence treated as one of tort, notwithstanding that the defendant's duty could also have been, and may in fact have been, pleaded by the plaintiff to have arisen out of contract Cp the case cited in the last note, where it was obviously of importance to the plaintiff, in accordance with the practice prevailing in 1872 with reference to the costs of separate pleas, to obtain judgment (as he did) on both the plea of concealment and the plea of breach of warranty

(*j*) *Pimm* v *Lewis* (1862), 2 F & F 778 (a fire insurance case)

(*k*) *Thomson* v *Weems* (1884), 9 App. Cas. 671, H L (a life insurance case), the condition is set out at p 680.

(*kk*) For this reason, an express condition in a contract for the observance of good faith was held nugatory in the Roman law see § 688, *post*.

(*l*) The Lesbian rule is cited, and the convenience and justice of its adoption in the law of disclosure (as, indeed, in most departments of our jurisprudence, to the genius of which it is entirely suitable) is discussed in § 649, *post*

(*m*) Thus, in *Jones* v *Provincial Insurance Co* (1857), 3 C B. (N s) 65, the " contract for the truth " entered into by the assured, and made the " basis " of the insurance, was that he " was not aware of any disorder or circumstance tending to shorten his Life, or to render an insurance on his life more than ordinarily hazardous," and, in reference to this condition, the Court (*per* CRESSWELL, J , at p 86), after referring to " the proposition, which as a general rule "—meaning, a rule of the common law of insurance, independently of contract—" is indisputable, that it is the duty of a party effecting an insurance on life or property to communicate to the underwriter or other insurer all material facts within his

in a literal sense, and to " take a bond of " the assured, is habitual in life insurance, but its utter inutility and absurdity, if not impropriety, in such cases, has been more than once judicially commented upon (n) : and for this, amongst other reasons, the party relying upon any such " contract for the truth," if the suggestion can plausibly be made that he has obtained something more by it than the ordinary principles of the law would give him (which is quite the exceptional case), is put to the severest and strictest proof that the warranty or condition is expressed in such clear and explicit terms as to entitle him to that " something more," and, further, that it has been made a condition precedent to the validity of the entire transaction (o).

SECT. 3. NATURE AND EXTENT OF THE BURDEN OF PROOF ON THE PARTY COMPLAINING.

172. In respect of alleged non-disclosure of any of the kinds which form the subject of this Chapter, the party complaining, in order to establish his

knowledge "—that is, facts within his knowledge which are material, whether the party believes them to be so or not—" touching the subject-matter of the insurance," proceeds to lay down that " it is, however, equally clear that the underwriters may in any particular case *limit* their rights in this respect to that of being informed of what is in the knowledge of the assured, not only as to its existence in point of fact, but also as to its materiality . and *in our opinion that is the effect of the limited declaration required in the present case.* . . Therefore, upon the construction of that clause which was alone relied upon at the trial, we are of opinion that the direction of the learned judge was right, and that the rule for a new trial ought to be discharged " Cp. the proviso contained in the life insurance policy which was the subject of *Armstrong* v *Turquand* (1857), 9 Ir C L Rep 32 Similarly, in *Watt* v *Assets Co*, [1905] A C 317, H L , a compromise case, in which a contributory in the liquidation of the City of Glasgow Bank was discharged from all liability as such, " on the basis of the truth, accuracy, and completeness of his answers to certain questions contained in a written statement, which answers he was required by the liquidators to verify in a statutory affidavit affirming that such answers were true and correct to *the best of his knowledge and belief*," and the result was that, in their blind confidence in the supposed saving virtues of a contract for the truth, and their insensibility to the advantages of the superior elasticity and comprehensiveness of the common law rule, the liquidators defeated their own object see the observations of Lord HALSBURY, L C , at pp 329, 330. The life insurance cases of *Wood* v. *Dwarris* (1856), 11 Exch 593, *Fowkes* v *Manchester & London Life Assurance & Loan Association*, No 2 (1863), 3 B & S 917, and *Hemmings* v *Sceptre Life Association*, [1905] 1 Ch 365, are illustrations of the application of precisely the same principle to misrepresentation. On the other hand, in the misrepresentation (life insurance) cases of *Duckett* v *Williams* (1834), 2 C & M. 348, 350, 351, and *Geach* v. *Ingall* (1845), 14 M & W. 95, 100, the insurers did succeed in enlarging materially the rights to the truth which they would have had independently of contract

(n) Notably by MOULTON, L J , at pp 885, 886, of *Joel* v *Law Union & Crown Insurance Co* , [1908] 2 K. B. 863, C A , who there points out, in some very weighty observations, the unwisdom, to put it at its lowest, and the possible trickery, to put it at its highest, of these " contracts for the truth " It is curious to find that, in marine insurance business, insurers are as habitually free from this particular form of unwisdom, as, in the case of other kinds of insurance, they are habitually guilty of it They know when they are well off, and are content with the general and unparticularized rules of the common law in relation to the assured's duty of disclosure, and in the equally general and unparticularized declarations of those rules in the codifying statute of 1906 (Marine Insurance Act, 1906).

(o) *Wheelton* v *Hardisty* (1858), 8 E & B 232, Exch. Ch (*per* MARTIN, B , at pp. 296, 297, CROWDER, J , at p 298, WILLES. J , at p 299, BRAMWELL, B , at pp 299–301, and CHANNELL, B , at p 302), *Fowkes* v *Manchester, &c, Association*, No 2, *sup.* (*per* COCKBURN, C J , at p 925, and BLACKBURN, J , at pp. 929, 930), *Hemmings* v *Sceptre Life Association*, *sup* (*per* KEKEWICH, J , at p 369); *Joel* v *Law Union & Crown Insurance Co* , *sup* (*per* MOULTON, L.J., at pp. 886, 887)

right to relief, must, whether he be plaintiff or defendant, and whatever be the form of proceeding in which the question is raised (p), allege and, having so alleged, prove each and every of the following matters, except in so far as any of them may be expressly or impliedly admitted before or at the trial by the party charged (q) :—

(A) That the party charged was under a duty to the party complaining to disclose to him the particular fact of which non-disclosure is alleged .

(B) That the alleged undisclosed fact was a fact at the material date :

(C) That the party charged did not disclose to the party complaining the alleged undisclosed fact at the time when he was under a duty to do so

(D) That the party charged had knowledge of the alleged undisclosed fact at the time when it was his duty to disclose it :

(E) That the party complaining had no such knowledge at the above-mentioned material date (r).

173. Proof of the above matters, though on the one hand essential to relief, is, on the other, sufficient. If the party complaining establishes all of them, he cannot be called upon to satisfy the tribunal as to any further or other issue, nor can judgment be given against him if he fails to do so (s).

(p) See Sect 5, post

(q) In most of the reported cases only some of the issues enumerated were contested There is scarcely one, unless it be *Elkin* v *Janson*, *inf*, in which all of them were As to the sense in which the abbreviated expressions " the party complaining," and " the party charged," are used in this book, and the reasons for selecting those expressions in preference to others which might be suggested, see § 12, *ante*

(r) For the reason given in the last note, it is almost impossible to find a judgment, or passage from a judgment, which comprises all the elements stated in the text, for judges do not profess to deliver exhaustive lectures on the whole branch of law which affects the particular case before them, but only to enunciate propositions sufficiently comprehensive to cover the matters which the parties have brought into debate The nearer approach to a complete judicial exposition of the main constituent elements of a title to relief for non disclosure in the course of negotiation for a contract of the character of those discussed in this Chapter is that contained in the judgment of ALDERSON, B , at p 664 of *Elkin* v *Janson* (1845), 13 M & W 655 (where to a declaration on a marine policy the defendants pleaded non disclosure of the facts that the captain of the insured ship had drawn a bill for her disbursements at Seville, and that she had sailed thence, long before the date of the execution of the policy, and was therefore a missing ship) " I take the plea to amount . to four propositions —first, that the facts relied on existed , secondly, that the knowledge of them was material to the underwriters . . , thirdly, that those facts were known to the plaintiff , and, fourthly, that they were not communicated to the defendant *The defendant must make out every one of those propositions* " It will be observed that the first of the above propositions corresponds to (B) in the text, the second to one of the constituents of (A)—see Sub s (1),—the third to (D), and the fourth to (C) There was no reference to (E), it not being disputed that the party complaining was ignorant of the undisclosed fact.

(s) Thus in *Stribley* v *Imperial Marine Insurance Co* (1876), 1 Q B D 507, where the defence to an action on a policy of marine insurance was non disclosure by the plaintiff of the receipt of a letter from the captain of the vessel, stating that he had arrived at the port several days previously, and had begun loading, but did not know when he would finish, and that there was very bad weather on the coast, and the jury (misled by the direction of GROVE, J , at the trial) found that the vessel was not " a missing ship " when the insurance was effected, the Court granted a new trial, on the ground that the defendants by their plea undertook no more than to prove that the plaintiffs received the letter, and the other facts alleged to have been withheld, and that those facts were known to the plaintiffs, were

Still less can he be required to sustain a burden of proof which would be only incumbent on him if he were relying upon a different, though somewhat similar, ground for relief, such as misrepresentation (*t*).

Sub-s. (1). *The Duty to Disclose (Materiality, &c).*

174. It may seem a somewhat self-evident and elementary proposition that the party complaining of a violation of duty, and who cannot succeed in obtaining relief without proving such violation, must begin by establishing that the duty existed (*u*)   But it must be remembered that this *probandum* which, when stated nakedly and generally, seems so obvious, comprehends and involves several subordinate and particular *probanda*   The party complaining, in order to prove the existence of the duty, must proceed by steps, and, if challenged, must, one by one, make good those steps   He must show, (i) that the relation between himself and the party charged was, or that the circumstances were, such as to give rise to a duty to divulge all facts material to be disclosed, (ii) that the party charged was the person, or a person, who owed that duty, (iii) that he (the party complaining) was the person, or a person, to whom the duty was owed, and (iv) that the particular fact alleged to have been undisclosed was a fact which, having regard to the particular class of contract which was the subject of the negotiation, or the special circumstances of the case, was material to be disclosed (*v*).

Sub-s. (2)   *The Existence or Occurrence of the Alleged Undisclosed Fact.*

175. Having established the duty to disclose, the next step, in logical order, is to show (unless admitted) that the alleged undisclosed fact *was* a fact at the material date   For it is obviously of no avail to prove that the party charged was bound at a certain time, or during a certain period, to

material, and were not communicated, and did not undertake to prove the fact that the ship was a missing ship, or non disclosure of *that* fact (*per* BLACKBURN, J, at p 511 " what the judge left to the jury was simply the question whether the ship was what is called ' a missing ship,' so that there was a presumption that she was lost when the insurance was effected.   I think that was not the real question   The real question was, whether the contents of the letter, the dates at which it was written and received, and the time which had elapsed since anything was heard of the vessel, were not facts which might properly have influenced the underwriter in accepting the risk."   To the same effect LUSH, J, at p. 514, and QUAIN, J, at pp 514, 515).

(*t*) An illustration of this is the case of *Morrison* v. *Muspratt* (1828), 4 Bing 60, where, the defence to a claim on a policy of life insurance being non disclosure of a grave pulmonary disease, ABBOTT, C J, at the trial, in directing the jury, treated the case as if the defendants had undertaken to prove misrepresentation, and the jury having negatived this, directed the verdict to be entered for the plaintiff; and the Court (see the judgment of BEST, C J., at p 62) held that this was quite wrong, and granted a new trial

(*u*) It has, however, been occasionally found necessary by judges to remind litigants of this obvious proposition   e g FRY, J, at p 474 of *Davies* v *London & Provincial Marine Insurance Co* (1878), 8 C D 469 (" it rests upon those who say that there was a duty to disclose to show that the duty existed ")

(*v*) See Sect 2 of this Chapter, *ante*, as to (i) and (iv), and Sect. 7, *post*, as to (ii) and (iii), of these several *probanda*   As to the meaning of materiality, see Ch II, Sect 2, Sub s (2), *ante*   From the cases cited in the notes to those parts of this work, it will be abundantly clear that the burden of establishing the several matters indicated is on the party complaining

reveal a fact of the particular character alleged, unless it be shown that there did exist at that time, or during that period, *in rerum naturâ*, a fact of the alleged character. Failure at this stage of the proof necessarily involves failure at the remaining stages: if the supposed fact never existed, or did not come into being until after the termination of the period during which the duty existed, there can be no question of the party charged having withheld it, or of his having wrongfully withheld it; nor can he possibly have been cognizant of it.

176. In order to make good the existence or occurrence of the alleged undisclosed matter, the party complaining must be prepared, if challenged, to establish two things (though the former of these is scarcely ever in dispute, and the latter not often), viz (i) that what is alleged to have been undisclosed is something which comes within the legal definition of a fact or circumstance, and (ii) that it existed, or (if a past event) had occurred, at the time when the party charged was subject to the duty of disclosure

177. The question of what " fact " or " circumstance " means and includes in law has been closely examined in a previous portion of this work (*w*), and it is unnecessary to repeat here what has already been said there.

178. Assuming that what is alleged to have been withheld is, in contemplation of law, a " fact " or " circumstance," the party complaining must next prove (if put to the proof by the pleadings) that the precise matter alleged to have been withheld existed, or (as the case may be) had happened, at the material date Thus, in a marine insurance case, if it is alleged that the assured omitted to communicate to the underwriters, for instance, the receipt of information from the captain of the vessel, or the putting on board of goods on which an excessive valuation had been effected, or a system of " treaties " for re-insurance with other underwriters similar to the treaty between the parties, on which loss had resulted to those underwriters pointing to the probability of a like loss on the treaty in question, the onus is on the party complaining to show, respectively, that the party charged had in fact received the alleged information from the ship (*x*); or that he had in fact put the goods on board, and had in fact effected the alleged insurances thereon, and that such insurances were excessive (*y*), or that there had in

(*w*) See Ch II, Sect. 2, Sub-s (1), *ante*

(*x*) *Elkin* v *Janson, sup.*—see note (*r*) to § 172, *ante*—where the jury found that the captain had in fact drawn the bill of disbursements, as alleged., *Morrison* v. *Universal Marine Insurance Co* (1873), L. R. 8 Exch 197, Exch. Ch, where, again, the first question put to the jury by BLACKBURN, J, at the trial was whether the plaintiff received the telegram alleged to have been sent to him by the master of the vessel, and to this the jury gave a negative answer, which, if no other fact had been alleged to have been undisclosed, would have entitled the plaintiff to a verdict, but there were other material facts admittedly undisclosed in respect of which the defendants were ultimately held entitled to judgment.

(*y*) See *Ionides* v *Pender* (1874), L R 3 Q B. 531 The alleged undisclosed fact there was a complex one, and involved the following (1) the putting of the goods on board, (2) the effecting of insurances thereon for certain amounts, and (3) the " excessiveness " of such insurances. At the trial, HANNEN, J, made (1) and (3) the subject of the first two of the seven questions which he put to the jury, (2) not being disputed, and the answer to both was in the affirmative, after the judge had directed the jury as to what, in law, constituted an " excessive valuation "

fact been " treaties " of the nature alleged with other underwriters, that such treaties had in fact resulted in loss to those underwriters, and that the " treaty " in dispute would probably result in a like loss to the party complaining (z) ; and similarly in cases of insurance generally (zz). Again, if it be alleged, in cases of vendor and purchaser, that the party charged has omitted to communicate the fact that the property is subject to incumbrances, such as a right of way, or if it be alleged, in such cases or in cases of marine insurance, that there has been no disclosure of some unusually restrictive covenants in a head lease or other instrument affecting the property, or of some unusual clause or condition in a maritime instrument which affects the underwriter's risk, it is for the party complaining to show, unless it be expressly or tacitly admitted by the party charged, that the right of way in fact existed (a), or that such covenant, clause, or condition not only in fact existed, but also was in fact an unusual covenant, clause, or condition (b). To take one further type of illustration, where one of the parties to a contract of marriage complains that the other has withheld his or her previous bad character or conduct from her or him during the negotiation, it must be proved that the party charged in fact had the bad character or was guilty of the evil conduct alleged (c).

(z) See *Glasgow Assurance Corporation* v *Symondson & Co* (1911), 104 L. T. 254. Here again the alleged undisclosed fact was a complex fact, subdivisible into the three facts stated in the text. SCRUTTON, J , who tried the case without a jury, found that none of the above alleged facts were facts, and on that ground, besides the ground that none of them were material, gave judgment for the defendant firm (the party charged, for the action was to set aside "the treaty" in question) There was another alleged undisclosed fact, which SCRUTTON, J , found to be a fact, but, as this too he held to be an immaterial one, the result was not affected.

(zz) See the "fidelity bond" case of *Allis Chalmers Co* v *Fidelity & Deposit Co. of Maryland* (1913), 29 T. L. R 506, where the defalcations of the manager, the non disclosure of which was complained of, occurred before what was held by the Court of Appeal, reversing PHILLIMORE, J , to be the date of the conclusion of the contract.

(a) See *Wilde* v *Gibson* (1848), 1 H L. C 605, where, at p 625, Lord COTTENHAM, L C , as one of his reasons for holding that the party complaining was not entitled to the relief prayed, stated that the plaintiff had failed to prove the fact that there was a public right of way over the property sold, which was the fact alleged to have been undisclosed On this much discussed case, see the detailed observations in Sect 8, Sub s (2), *post*

(b) Whether a restrictive covenant, in cases of the sale or demise of land, is, or is not, an unusual one at *the particular time in question* (for what is unusual at one period may be usual at another), is an issue of fact (see § 269, note (h), *post*), the burden of establishing which is clearly on the party complaining, if he is challenged , though, in almost all the reported cases on the subject of non disclosure of restrictive and unusual covenants in cases of vendor and purchaser,—see those cited in note (f) to § 115, *ante*,—the issue seems not to have been contested. In marine insurance cases, on the contrary, the question whether the alleged undisclosed clauses or conditions contained in maritime instruments, and affecting the underwriter's risk, were or were not in common use at the date of the alleged duty to disclose, has nearly always been the subject of contest and evidence, the onus being on the party complaining, as may be seen by a comparison of the cases cited in note (p) to § 96, *ante*, where the onus was sustained, with those cited in note (q) thereto, where it was not.

(c) See *Baddeley* v. *Mortlock* (1816), Holt N. P 151 (*per* GIBBS, C.J., at p 152 : "if a woman improvidently promises to marry a man who turns out upon inquiry to be of bad character, she is not bound to perform her promise. But she must show that the plaintiff is of bad character "); *Irving* v *Greenwood* (1824), 1 C & P 350 (where ABBOTT, C J , directed the jury, at pp. 350, 351, that the defendant was entitled to the verdict, if, after the contract, he discovered the plaintiff to be a loose or immoral woman, but that it was for the defendant to satisfy them that in fact she was of that character).

179. It is not sufficient to establish that the alleged undisclosed fact was in its literal sense a fact, if it was not so as regards that particular feature in it which made it material to be disclosed. Thus, where a purchaser complains of the non-disclosure of a restrictive covenant affecting the property sold, the feature in such alleged fact which makes it material to be disclosed is that he will be hampered in the enjoyment of the property; consequently, though he may establish the bare fact that the restrictive covenant exists, yet if in the course of the evidence facts are elicited which show clearly that the party who otherwise would be entitled to enforce the covenant has by his conduct or inaction long since forfeited his right to do so, the complaining purchaser fails to show the existence of the only element in the undisclosed matter which affects his interests, and, consequently, his title to relief (d). So, if it be a case of compromise, whereby a contributory in the liquidation of a company is to be released on disclosure of all the property of which he is possessed, and the liquidator sues to set aside the compromise on the ground of non-disclosure of (inter alia) certain shares in a shipping company, it is of no avail for the liquidator to establish that at the material date the contributory was the holder of the shares in question, for this is merely to show the existence of property in the literal and legal sense, but he must go on to prove that the shares constituted " property " in the only sense in which disclosure or non-disclosure of property can have the slightest importance, that is to say, that they had some value : and, if it is not pretended that they had any, he fails to sustain the burden of establishing that the alleged fact was a fact in its only substantial or material aspect (e).

180. On the other hand, whilst it is necessary, it is also sufficient, to prove the precise substantial fact alleged to have been withheld. For this purpose, the exact allegation made in each case must be critically examined (f). It has already been seen that the " fact " or " circumstance " may be, for instance, intelligence, information, or rumour, or a person's state of mind or will; his opinion, intentions, anticipations, or apprehensions; or an agreement between two persons; in all which cases, that which is to be proved is the possession of the information or the entertaining of the opinion, intention, hope, or fear, by the person to whom it is attributed, or the existence of the agreement,—but not the truth of the matters forming the subject of the information, or the correctness of the opinion, or the realization of the intention, expectation, or apprehension, or the validity of the agreement (g). A like caution is required in the analogous province of misrepresentation, where the representee can never be called upon to prove more than the existence of the precise fact which he avers to have been denied or falsely stated (h).

(d) This was the case in *Hepworth* v *Pickles*, [1900] 1 Ch 108, in which FARWELL, J., followed the similar decision of ROMER, J, against the party complaining, under similar circumstances, in *Re Summerson*, [1900] 1 Ch 112 n

(e) *Watt* v. *Assets Co*, [1905] A C 317, H L. (*per* Lord HALSBURY, L.C, at pp. 331, 332)

(f) See the case cited in note (s) to § 173, *ante*.

(g) See §§ 27, 28, 29, *ante*, and the cases cited in the notes thereto

(h) See *Duckett* v *Williams* (1834), 2 C & M. 348, the history of which case is rather peculiar One insurance company sued another (the parties named on the record being

181. It must not be forgotten that the duty of disclosure is strictly contemporaneous with the negotiation which gives rise to it. As there is no such duty before the parties are in treaty with one another, so there is none after the treaty has matured into agreement. The party charged is under no obligation to divulge any fact of which he acquires knowledge after the conclusion of the contract, and it is incumbent on the party complaining, therefore, as will be seen hereafter (i), to show that the party charged had such knowledge before that date. It follows, *a fortiori*, that, in proving the existence of the alleged undisclosed fact, he must prove that it existed before the conclusion of the contract, because if it did not then even exist, it is idle to attempt to show that the party charged then had knowledge of it (j). If it is sought to impose a duty on the party charged to reveal material facts supervening after the conclusion of the contract, but during its currency

their respective public officers) on a policy of insurance on the life of one Stephenson The defendant company pleaded misrepresentation by the plaintiffs that Stephenson was free from disease. The defendants proved the misrepresentation alleged, the jury found accordingly that "the life was not insurable," and the verdict was thereupon entered for the defendants, which, on appeal, the Courts of Exchequer refused to disturb, but, on the plaintiffs then contending (for the first time) that they were entitled to a return of the premiums paid by them, the parties (somewhat strangely) agreed that there should be a second trial to determine this particular subsidiary issue, and no other. On the second trial, the defendants (again very unaccountably) allowed the jury to consider the question which had already been decided on the first trial in a manner satisfactory to the Court, viz whether the life was insurable, and the second jury said that it was There was thereupon a deadlock, from which the parties extricated themselves by agreeing that the Court of Exchequer, on appeal, should be at liberty to look into the evidence, and form their own conclusions on all points This they did with the result (which might have been achieved at an earlier stage) that the real issue was discussed, and it was found that "at the time when the policy was effected, Mr Stephenson had upon him a disease which tended to shorten life," and held (in effect) that it was not incumbent on the defendants to prove more than, in the opinion of the Court, they had proved, viz the making of the representation, and its falsity and materiality (*per* Lord LYNDHURST, C B, delivering the judgment by the Court, at pp. 350, 351)

(i) See § 189, *post*

(j) An illustration of failure to establish that the alleged fact came into being before the conclusion of the contract is the case of *Pim & Rogers* v *Reid* (1843), 6 M & G 1, where to an action on a policy of fire insurance the defendants pleaded non disclosure of the fact that the plaintiffs had changed their business from that of paper-makers to that of dyers of cotton-wash, had accumulated large quantities of such cotton-wash on the insured premises, and had introduced a new furnace, but did not even allege that these admittedly undisclosed facts took place until after the execution of the policy, and the Court accordingly held that the insurance company's defence failed on the ground that the policy was not so clearly worded as to impose a contractual obligation to disclose supervening material facts, and also (and this is the only ground which concerns the present discussion) on the express ground that there was no such duty independently of contract (*per* TINDAL, C.J., at p. 19, COLTMAN, J, at p 21, MAULE, J, at p 22, and CRESSWELL, J, at p 24). On the other hand, where the party charged had begun to make alterations to his premises before the issuing of the fire insurance policy, it was held that the party complaining had established that the alleged undisclosed fact became a fact before the conclusion of the contract, and had sustained the onus which was upon him in this respect *Sillem* v. *Thornton* (1854), 3 E & B 868, at pp 881, 882 At least, this was one ground of the decision, which was enough to support it, but, at pp 882, *sqq*, the Court ventured on another, viz. that there was an implied warranty on the part of the plaintiff that no alterations would be made in the premises during the currency of the policy This was held to be a clearly bad ground in *Thompson* v *Hopper* (1858), E B & E 1038 (*per* WILLES, J, at p 1049) As regards marine insurance, the rule is stated in a codified form in s. 18 (1) of the Marine Insurance Act, 1906 (6 Edw 7, c 41) · "the assured must disclose to the insurer, *before the contract is concluded*, any material circumstance which is known to the assured "

or operation, or pending its completion, this must be done by the express agreement of the parties, as is usually the case in contracts of fire insurance (*k*), or else such a duty must be shown to arise out of some warranty or condition to be implied from the special character of the contract, as, for instance, in the case of guarantees (*l*), and, perhaps, contracts to marry (*m*).

182. The "conclusion of the contract," for the purpose of the rule now under discussion, and generally in relation to the duty of disclosure which exists during negotiation (*n*), in the act which, according to the principles regulating contracts in general or the species of contract which is in question in the particular case, effectually, finally, and unconditionally binds the parties to one another in law, or, as in the case of contracts of marine insurance (where the initialling of the slip is the contract, and not the policy subsequently issued), that which binds the parties according to rules of mercantile practice and good faith recognized by the law (*o*).

(*k*) See § 104, *ante* In *Pim & Rogers* v *Reid*, *sup*, the attempt to create the contractual obligation failed, because the language used was not, as in such cases it always should be, promise and unambiguous

(*l*) For the theory on which the duty is implied in the case of suretyship contracts, and the extent and nature of the duty, see § 129, *ante*

(*m*) Lord CAMPBELL, C.J, at p 759 of *Hall* v. *Wright* (1858), E B & E 746, expressed the view that "this contract of marriage likewise has peculiar incidents, by reason of which the performance of it may be excused If, *subsequently to the contract*, the woman has been guilty of incontinence, the man at his choice is excused from the performance of his promise which was given under the implied condition that the woman should continue chaste"

(*n*) See Sub ss (4) and (5), *post*, as to the knowledge of the party charged, and the ignorance of the party complaining. respectively, in relation to which the question of the "conclusion of the contract" is of considerable importance

(*o*) See *Morrison* v *Universal Marine Insurance Co.* (1873), L R 8 Exch 197, Exch. Ch, where the dissentient opinion of CLEASBY, B, on this question, in the Court of Exchequer (1872), L. R 8 Exch 40, at pp 59–61, was affirmed by the Exchequer Chamber See also the cases cited in the notes to § 189, and in those to § 195, *post* The mercantile rule of good faith was always supported to the fullest possible extent, short of defeating the claims of the revenue, and has now, to the same extent and within the same limits, received statutory recognition See ss. 21, 22 of the Marine Insurance Act, 1906, the former of which provides that "a contract of marine insurance is deemed to be concluded when the proposal of the assured is accepted by the insurer, whether the policy be then issued or not, and for the purpose of showing when the proposal was accepted, reference may be made to the slip or covering note or other customary memorandum of the contract, although it be unstamped", whilst the latter safeguards the fiscal requirements of the State by enacting that "subject to the provisions of any statute, a contract of marine insurance is inadmissible in evidence unless it is embodied in a marine policy in accordance with this Act The policy may be executed and issued either at the time when the contract is concluded, or afterwards." The same principle would doubtless be applied, wherever the same reason exists for its application, to any other mercantile document which binds the parties, though for revenue or other statutory purposes, the contract, concluded as between them, may have to be expressed in a more formal instrument. *A fortiori* is this the case where no requirement of the revenue stands in the way, as (*e g*) where a contract of fire insurance is constituted by a slip, as happens where a Lloyd's policy form is adopted, and where therefore there is no statutory reason why, for all purposes, the slip should not be deemed the concluded contract, just as much as a contract for the sale of land, though it requires to be completed by conveyance : see *Thompson* v *Adams* (1889), 23 Q B D 361 So, in *Yager* v. *Guardian Assurance Co* (1912), 29 T L R. 53 (another fire insurance case), the "document," which was a memorandum or note of much the same nature as the slip in the case last cited, would probably have been held to be the concluded contract between the parties, but for a clause or notice on the face of it that it should not have this effect until payment of the premium and the giving of a receipt therefor from the office, which clause, therefore, was in effect, by the express agreement of the parties, a postponement of the otherwise immediate binding operation of the document. For instances of

Sub-s (3) The Non-Disclosure.

183. Though absence of disclosure is a negative, and, ordinarily, *et incumbit probatio qui affirmat, non qui negat*, yet (as in the case of a similar *probandum* in actions of malicious prosecution, viz absence of reasonable and probable cause) it is for the party complaining to establish this negative element in the burden of proof, and he must accordingly tender some evidence that the party charged did not in fact disclose to him, or to all the parties complaining (if more than one), the particular matter which he alleges to have been withheld This means that while, on the one hand, it is enough to prove absence of full and clear disclosure (*p*), it is, on the other, necessary to prove that such disclosure was withheld on *all* the occasions (if more than one) at which it might reasonably have been made (*pp*) In most of the reported cases, the party charged appears not to have denied the alleged non-disclosure, so that the question of where the burden of proof ought to fall, became of no importance whatever, and was not discussed. But in one case (*q*), the question did become a vital one, and was carefully considered by the Court of Exchequer, with the result that the rule as above stated was solemnly laid down (*r*), though it was at the same time observed that the slightest possible evidence would always be sufficient to throw the burden on to the other side, if not to conclude the issue altogether, and that a very strong *primâ facie*, if not irrebuttable, inference of fact that the alleged undisclosed circumstance was not communicated arises from mere proof that the contract was entered into, where the undisclosed circumstance, and the contract, respectively, are of such a nature as to render it inconceivable that the latter would have been made if the former had first been divulged (*s*).

other insurance cases in which it became necessary to consider whether the express or implied intention of the parties was that the risk should commence only with the payment of the premium, or immediately on the issue of the policy, see *Canning* v *Farquhar* (1886), 16 Q B D 727, C A , *Roberts* v *Security Co* , [1897] 1 Q B 111, C. A , *Allis Chalmers Co* v *Fidelity & Deposit Co of Maryland* (1913), 30 T. L R. 445, C. A , *Harrington* v *Pearl Life Assurance Co* (1914), 30 T L R 613, C A

(*p*) As to what in law is meant by this, and particularly as to the essential requirements of completeness and freedom from ambiguity, see Ch II, Sect 1, *ante*, and the cases cited in the notes thereto

(*pp*) See note (*u*), *post*, and the case of *Watt* v *Assets Co* , cited in note (*w*), *post*

(*q*) This was *Elkin* v *Janson* (1845), 13 M & W 655, for the facts of which, and the rules as to burden of proof declared therein, see note (*r*) to § 172, *ante*

(*r*) *Ibid* , per ALDERSON, B , at p 664 (see the passage cited in note (*r*) to § 172, *ante*, in which the last of the four propositions, "every one of which" he holds must be made out by the party complaining, is that "they"—the facts relied on—"were not communicated to the defendant," who was there the party complaining), PARKE, B , at pp 662, 663, and PLATT, B , at pp 666, 667 POLLOCK, C B , at p 667, expressed some doubt, but did not dissent See also *Greenwood* v *Greenwood* (1863), 2 De G J & S 28 (at pp 38, 39, 41, 42), and *Joel* v *Law Union & Crown Insurance Co* , [1908] 2 K B 863, C A (*per* VAUGHAN WILLIAMS, L J , at p 880)

(*s*) *Elkin* v *Janson, sup* , per PARKE, B , at pp 662, 663 . "the burden of proof lay on the defendant, and he was bound to give some evidence of the non-communication, at the time he effected the policy, of the fact which the jury has found to be a material one for him to know , for although this allegation is negative in its terms, still, as it was the duty of the assured to make this communication, . . I think some evidence ought to have been given by the defendant, to show that that material communication was not made to him *Generally speaking, the mere fact of subscribing the policy would be sufficient evidence ;* in a case like the present, no prudent man with such information as the plaintiff was possessed of, namely, that the ship which it was proposed to insure had sailed from the

This decision has been adopted and acted upon in subsequent cases of marine, life, and other insurance (t), vendor and purchaser (u), com-

port for so long a period as to be a missing ship, would have executed a policy of Insurance on her In the present case, no doubt can exist that no such communication was made to the · underwriter, for the natural channel for it to come through would be the broker, who swore that he himself was ignorant of the date of this bill *That was enough to cast the burden on the other side*" So ALDERSON, B., at pp. 665, 666 · "in a case like the present, slender evidence of a material communication not having been made is all that can be required from a defendant "—the party complaining being here, as in nearly all the marine insurance cases, a defendant to an action on the policy—: "suppose the case to be that a ship about to be insured was burnt, and the plaintiff knew of it at the time he effected the insurance " . . &c. "So here, it is almost impossible to believe that the defendant would have insured this ship, had he known that she had sailed from [oville so long before. " &c Cp what is said as to this onus by KNIGHT-BRUCE, V C it pp 105, 106 of *Stikeman* v *Dawson* (1847), 1 De G & Sm 90 It should be remembered that these decisions were some years prior to the passing of the Evidence Act, 1851 (14 & 15 Vict. c 99), whereby (s 2) parties litigant and interested were for the first time allowed to give oral evidence, and it may have then seemed somewhat harsh, under such conditions, to require the party complaining to give any, even the slenderest, evidence of non disclosure but no such hardship can now be suggested as a ground for criticizing, or hesitating to enforce, the rule, when the party complaining has only to go into the witness box and give a simple denial on oath to any suggestion of disclosure which may be made by the party charged in his pleading, whether directly, or indirectly by a traverse of the allegation of non-disclosure in the pleading of the party complaining. In *Joel* v *Law Union & Crown Insurance Co*, *inf*, VAUGHAN WILLIAMS, L.J., at p 881, expressed the view that in the circumstances of that case the onus had not been shifted

(t) As in *Elkin* v *Janson, sup*, where it was held that the question was not put to the jury at the trial in such a form as to make it quite clear to them that the onus of proving non disclosure was on the party complaining—see note (a), *post, Ionides* v *Pender* (1874), L R 9 Q B 531, where the fifth of the seven questions left by HANNEN, J, to the jury was, whether the fact of the excessive valuation was concealed from the underwriters, which the jury answered in the affirmative (p 537), *Tate & Sons* v *Hyslop* (1885), 15 Q B D 368, C A, where (see pp 371, 372), MANISTY, J, left two questions to the jury on this point, (1) whether the fact there in question had been communicated to the underwriters, and (2) whether it had been concealed from them, and the jury having answered (1) by saying "not directly, but to the defendants' solicitors," and (2) in the negative, it was held on appeal (*per* BRETT, M.R., at p 374) that the disclosure to the solicitors mentioned in the answer to (1) was, in law, no disclosure at all,—see § 49, and note (z) thereto, *ante*,—and (*per* BRETT, M R, at p 378) that, therefore, there was no evidence to justify the answer to (2), which probably arose from the jury understanding the expression "concealed"—a most misleading one—to import fraud, *The Bedouin*, [1894] P 1, C A, where, affirming the decision of GORELL BARNES, J, the C A held that the burden was on the underwriters to prove non disclosure, and they had failed to sustain it (*per* Lord ESHER, M.R., at pp 12, 13), *Laing* v *Union Marine Insurance Co* (1895), 1 Comm Cas 11, where MATHEW, J, at pp 15, 16, found as a fact that the non disclosure alleged by the party complaining had been proved The above are all cases of marine insurance For life insurance cases, see *Joel* v *Law Union & Crown Insurance Co*, [1908] 2 K B 863, C A., where, besides other defences based on an alleged "contract for disclosure"—see Sect. 2, Sub-s (9), *ante*—which do not concern the present discussion, the defendants pleaded non disclosure, independently of contract, of a fact which the jury found to be material, viz that the assured had consulted a certain doctor, eight years previously, for a nervous breakdown, and it was held (*inter alia*) by the C. A that the insurance company had failed to discharge the onus, which was on them, of establishing non-disclosure of this fact, and that it was not enough to show, as they did, that the fact had not been divulged in a particular document, or on a particular occasion, when the disclosure might reasonably be expected to be made, but that evidence ought also to have been given, which it was not (though the persons who could have given it were in court at the trial), as to other documents, or other occasions, where the disclosure might, or might not, have been made · in short, that to establish non disclosure the evidence must deal with all reasonably possible occasions of disclosure, and exhaustively negative communication on any of them (*per* VAUGHAN WILLIAMS, L J, at p 874, and MOULTON, L J, at p 892) Cp *Thornton-Smith* v *Motor Union Insurance Co* (1913), 30 T L R 139

(u) See *Coaks* v *Boswell* (1886), 11 App Cas 232, H L, which is an excellent

promises (v), and others (w), whenever, as the result of the contentions of the parties, or in the opinion of the judge, it became necessary for the Court

Illustration of the distinction, in respect of the rules as to the burden of proof of disclosure, between cases of the class discussed in the present Chapter, and those of the types forming the subject of Chapters IV and V. The action was tried by FRY, J, sub nom., *Boswell* v *Coaks* (1881), 23 C. D. 302, who took the view that the relation between the parties was that of solicitor and client, and that there was therefore, in the first instance, a disability on the solicitor precluding him from purchasing *at all* from the client without having made full disclosure, or from sustaining the purchase, when impeached, without proving such full disclosure (see §§ 337, 338, *post*). The C. A. (1884), 27 C D 424, took the same view of the transaction, but differed from FRY, J, on the question whether this original disability had come to an end The H. L, whilst agreeing that if the relation between the parties had been what both the Courts below supposed it to have been, the onus would have been on the party charged to show the fullest disclosure in the clearest possible manner, held that the relation was not that of solicitor and client, but purely and simply that of purchaser and vendor, and that, this being so, it was not for the party charged to prove disclosure, but for the party complaining to establish the absence of it, and (in the special circumstances of that case) fraudulent suppression as well and, after a critical examination of the evidence, it was held that the party complaining, so far from having shown dishonest concealment, had failed to prove any non-disclosure in fact (*per* Lord SELBORNE, at p 239) And see also *Nottingham Patent Brick and Tile Co.* v. *Butler* (1886), 16 Q B D 778, C A

(v) See *Greenwood* v. *Greenwood* (1863), 2 De G J & S 28, 39, 38, 41, 42 In *Mostyn* (*Lord*) v *Brooke* (1866), L R 4 H L 304, a case of a family compromise, which had been sanctioned by the Master in the chambers of Lord ROMILLY, M R, a bill was filed by one of the parties to set aside the compromise, on the ground of non-disclosure by the other parties of certain material documents Lord ROMILLY, M R, dismissed the bill, *Brooke* v *Lord Mostyn* (1865), 33 Beav 457, on the ground that non-disclosure had not been shown with sufficient clearness to justify the upsetting of a family arrangement The Lords Justices, however, on the plaintiff adducing fresh evidence before them of the non-production of the documents referred to, considered the proof sufficient, (1865), 2 De G J & S 373 (*per* TURNER, L J, at pp 422–444, and KNIGHT BRUCE, L J, at pp 424, 425), and on this ground reversed the decision of Lord ROMILLY, M R But the H L, being of opinion that the complaining party's evidence, even as supplemented, was not sufficient to establish the non-disclosure, and on this ground alone, disagreed with the Lords Justices' decree, and restored the judgment of Lord ROMILLY, M R In *Watt* v *Assets Co*, [1905] A C. 317, H L, which was a case of an agreement of compromise between the liquidators of a bank and a contributory, whereby, on payment of certain moneys, and a declaration of all his property in a document referred to in the arguments and the judgments as "the statement," the contributory was released from all further liability to contribution The Assets Co, the successors in title (by purchase) of the liquidators, sued the trustees, executors, and beneficiaries of the deceased contributory for "reduction" of the compromise on the ground of non-disclosure of certain property by the contributory. The House of Lords reversed the Court of Session who had granted the relief prayed, and restored the interlocutor of the Lord Ordinary who had refused it, on the ground (amongst others) that the burden of proving that the deceased contributory had not divulged the existence of the assets alleged was on the Assets Co, and that this burden was not discharged by evidence that the assets were not included in the "statement," and that the only survivor of the liquidators, one Haldane, did not remember any communication (he could not swear that there had been none), which was all that the party complaining attempted to prove since, for aught that appeared, oral disclosure might have been made to any of the deceased liquidators, other than Haldane, if not to Haldane himself, and particularly might have been made to Cameron, who drew up the questions contained in the "statement," and the agreement which was based on it (*per* Lord HALSBURY, L C, at pp 329, 330) A stronger illustration of the rule stated in the text could not well arise for, if the burden had been on the representatives of the party charged to prove disclosure, the deaths of all the liquidators, except one (who remembered little or nothing of the facts), and of the party charged himself, must have been fatal to their case whereas it was the Assets Co whose case suffered from these circumstances. Cp. the case cited in note (u), *ante*, as to the duty on the party complaining of exhausting all possible means and sources of disclosure

(w) For instance, *Stikeman* v *Dawson* (1847), 1 De G & Sm 90, at pp 105–107 to give direction to the jury on the subject (x), or to lay down a rule for its own guidance (y)

184. It may be thought that the negative referred to is, like most negatives, capable of expression in some affirmative form, so as to render a rule which requires a man to prove that something did not happen more palatable to the normal intelligence of the jury box. for instance, that a jury may usefully be told that it is for the party complaining to prove that the party charged "neglected" to communicate, or "withheld," or "concealed," the fact in question. Attempts have been made in this direction, but they have usually led to trouble : because jurymen, not unnaturally, think (unless very carefully warned against so doing) that such positive terms must indicate some positive misconduct, and, in particular, that the expression "concealment" connotes a guilty and fraudulent hiding away, or covering up, or obscuring, of the thing undisclosed (z), and so their minds are diverted from the real issue, and concentrated on a false one. whilst they readily recognize the justice of the rule that he who alleges "concealment" or "keeping back" must prove it, they only do so in the persuasion that these terms necessarily involve deceit, or secretiveness, or other obliquity of conduct. On the other hand, if the question left to the jury is simply whether the fact was communicated, there is danger (unless the accompanying direction be very clear and precise) that the jury may infer that the burden is wholly on the party charged to prove the communication (a) The only safe rule, it would appear, for a judge to lay down for the guidance of the jury or for his own (as the case may be), where the matter becomes of serious importance, is

(x) The insurance cases of *Elkin* v *Janson, Ionides* v *Pender, Tate & Sons* v *Hyslop,* and *Joel* v *Law Union & Crown Insurance Co.*, cited in note (t), *ante*, were cases tried before a judge and jury

(y) *The Bedouin,* and *Laing* v *Union Marine Insurance Co*, cited in note (t), *ante*, and all the cases cited in notes (u), (v), and (w), *ante*, were heard before a judge alone

(z) HANNEN, J, left it to the jury to say whether there had been "concealment" in *Ionides* v *Pender*, cited in note (t), *ante*, and so did MANISTY, J, in *Tate & Sons* v *Hyslop,* cited in the same note No evil consequences resulted in the former case, because the jury answered the question in the affirmative · but, in the latter, where the jury negatived the "concealment," having previously answered another question in a manner which in law was equivalent to a finding of non-disclosure, it was held that the finding which negatived concealment could not stand, and that the jury had been misled by this inexact and inappropriate expression see, again, note (t), *ante* As to the ambiguity and inconvenience, generally, of the terms "concealment," and "withholding," see § 629, *post*, and note (nn) thereto

(a) This, it was held by the Court of Exchequer, might possibly have been the case in *Elkin* v *Janson* (1845), 13 M & W. 655, where the jury, having first found a general verdict for the defendant, and then having been asked specifically whether in their view the alleged undisclosed fact was communicated to the defendant, professed themselves unable to answer that question, whereupon POLLOCK, B, directed the verdict to be entered for the plaintiff But the question which the Court had to consider on appeal was whether the case was put to the jury in such a form as to make it quite clear on which party the burden lay in the first instance, and what amount of evidence would shift it from one to the other —see notes (r) and (s), *ante*—and, thinking that this had not been done, they granted a new trial without costs (*per* PARKE, B, at p 663, who, after stating that there was abundant, if not conclusive, evidence of non disclosure, and of the burden having been by this evidence thrown on to the plaintiff of showing the affirmative, concluded · "I however entertain some doubt whether my Lord Chief Baron, by the mode in which he left the case to the jury, did not cast the *onus probandi* on the wrong party ")

the rule propounded by the Court of Exchequer, with its qualification, as above stated.

Sub-s (4).   Knowledge of the Party charged.

185. Having established that the party charged did not disclose a certain fact which he was under a duty to disclose, if known to him, the party complaining must proceed to make good the next step in his proof, and show that the fact in question was known to the party charged at the time or during the period when it was his duty to disclose it : for, obviously, there can be no duty on any one, because it is an impossibility, to communicate or impart to another a knowledge which he does not possess himself (*b*).

186. The knowledge which must be proved is that which is deemed such in law It is, therefore, on the one hand necessary, but, on the other, it is sufficient, to establish either actual or presumptive knowledge, and, if the latter is relied upon, to point to such circumstances in evidence as will justify a legal inference therefrom of notice or knowledge on some one or more of the several principles which in a previous Chapter have been examined and dealt with once for all (*c*).

187. Where actual knowledge is ascribed to the party charged, the onus is satisfied by proof that the undisclosed fact was within his cognizance, though it may not have been present to his mind at the actual moment, or during the actual period, when the duty of disclosure existed.   Thus, in a suretyship case, where the surety complained of the non-disclosure by the creditor of a certain mortgage on the property which was the consideration for the guaranteed debt, it was held that the surety had established the fact of the creditor's knowledge as soon as the latter had admitted (which he did) that he had forgotten it (*d*).   On the same principle, in the law of misrepresentation, or statement from which, owing to pure forgetfulness, a qualifying circumstance is omitted, is thereby rendered false and, as such, amenable to proceedings for rescission, though not fraudulent or, as such, the subject of an action for damages (*dd*).

188. It must always be remembered that where the undisclosed fact is a complex one, as it not infrequently is, consisting of (1) circumstances capable of being apprehended by the senses or retained by the memory, and also (2) some thing, or state of things, to which those circumstances point, the

---

(*b*) This is the third of the four propositions mentioned by the Court of Exchequer in *Elkin* v *Janson*,—see note (*r*), § 172, *ante*,—as required to be established by the party complaining See also *Greenwood* v *Greenwood* (1863), 2 De G J & S 28, 38, 39, 41, 42 In both those cases it was established But it was not established in the marine insurance cases of *Bradford* v *Symondson* (1881), 7 Q B D 456, C A., and *Blackburn, Low & Co* v *Vigors* (1887), 12 App. Cas. 531, H L. (with which may be usefully contrasted the other case between the same assured and underwriters, but on another policy, *Blackburn, Low & Co. v. Haslam* (1888), 21 Q B D 184, where the knowledge of the fact by the assured's agents at the material date *was* shown), nor was it established in any of the life insurance cases cited in notes (*e*) and (*f*), *inf*, nor in the vendor and purchaser case of *Wilde* v *Gibson* (1848), 1 H L. C. 605.

(*c*) See Ch II, Sect. 3, *ante*.

(*d*) *Willis* v. *Willis* (1850), 17 Sim 218, 220. Cp. the observations of Lord CAMPBELL at p. 944 of *Railton* v *Mathews & Leonard* (1844), 10 Cl & Fin. 934

(*dd*) See § 112 of the author's *Law of Actionable Misrepresentation*

party complaining must prove not only that the party charged had knowledge
of those circumstances, but also that he fully appreciated their significance
as indicating the presence of that thing, or state of things Similarly, if the
undisclosed fact, in one of its aspects, is not necessarily of any importance
whatever, but, in another, is of vital materiality to the contract or transaction
which is the subject of the negotiation, it must be shown that the party charged
recognized not only the naked existence of the fact, but the existence of
that aspect of it which invests it with importance These observations,
which it is difficult to express in an abstract formula, are best illustrated by
cases of life insurance, where the person proposing to effect the insurance
of his own or another's life is under an obligation to disclose to the insurer
the existence of any present or past disease of a nature to affect the duration
of the life insured. In any such case where the insurer complains of the non-
disclosure of a disease, it is of no avail for him to prove that the assured
was, during the period of negotiation, aware of some incident or circumstance
in his physical history or condition indicative of a departure from normal
health, unless he is also in a position to prove that the assured realized, or
must, even with the normal intelligence of an inexpert mind, have realized,
that this incident or circumstance was symptomatic of existing, or premonitory
of approaching, mischief of a character to endanger or shorten life (e). An
assured may, for instance, be shown to have had occasional, or even constant,
headaches, and therefore to have been aware of them, and these may have
been of such a nature as to indicate to the trained professional intellect the
probable or certain existence or imminence of brain disease : but, unless the
insurer can satisfy the tribunal that the assured person inferred, or ought
to have inferred, from the phenomena what the physician would infer, or
(in other words) ought to have diagnosed his symptoms *secundum artem*,
he fails to establish the assured's knowledge of the undisclosed *disease*, which
means not only the actual phenomena, but all that is scientifically involved
in them (*f*). If it is desired to obviate this difficulty, the insurance company should frame specific questions directed not to particular diseases, but
to particular physical occurrences which they may be advised to have significance from a medical point of view, such as the question which was put in
one case where the insurance company established non-disclosure,—" have
you ever had blood-spitting ? " (*g*) ; though, even here, it was pointed out
in the direction to the jury that it would not be sufficient to show merely
that the assured knew that he had on occasions spat blood, because this
might happen after the extraction of a tooth, or from a collision, or fall, or
assault, but it must be proved that he was aware of having spat blood otherwise than as the result of some immediate external cause, or in technical
language, that the blood-spitting was idiopathic, and amounted to what a
doctor would designate hæmatoptysis. The same principle, as will be seen

(e) *Swete* v. *Fairlie* (1833), 6 C & P. 1 (at p. 8) ; *Fowkes* v. *Manchester and London Life
Assurance Co*, No 1 (1862), 3 F & F 440 (at pp 443, 444)
    (*f*) *Joel* v *Law Union & Crown Insurance Co.*, [1908] 2 K B 863, C. A. (*per* MOULTON,
L J , at pp 884, 885)
    (*g*) *Geach* v. *Ingall* (1845), 14 M. & W 95

presently, applies to the burden which is also on the party complaining of proving his own ignorance of the undisclosed fact (*h*).

189. It is on the one hand necessary, but, on the other, it is sufficient, to fix the party charged with knowledge   It is not necessary to prove knowledge on the part of a person for whose benefit the party charged is suing, for instance, as trustee for that person (*hh*).   Further, the knowledge which must be brought home to the party charged is a knowledge which existed during the negotiation.   It is of no avail to prove his acquisition of the knowledge after the conclusion of the contract   What the conclusion of the contract for this purpose means has already been explained, in relation to both contracts in general (*ι*), and contracts of marine insurance in particular, where the initialling of the slip, or other like note or memorandum, and not the policy, is, for all purposes which concern the parties, the act which operates as the "conclusion" (*ȷ*)   It has also been made clear that the party complaining must show that the alleged undisclosed fact existed or came into being before the conclusion of the contract (*k*).   But, if challenged, he must do more than this : he must establish that, whether it existed or came into being before that date or not, the party charged acquired knowledge of it before that date.   Thus, in cases of marine insurance, it has been held that, where underwriters pleaded non-disclosure of an accident to the insured vessel, and knowledge of that fact by the assured, as well as ignorance thereof on their own part, a replication by the assured was good which (without denying the accident or the happening of it before the conclusion of the contract) averred that "the plaintiff had no knowledge of the said fact before the initialling of the slip which the defendants were bound in honour, conscience, and good faith to embody in a policy," and that "the plaintiff relying upon the defendants' said obligation did in good faith abstain from communicating the said fact before the issue of the policy" (*l*)   Similarly, where a person made a proposal for an insurance on freight, which the underwriters accepted on a certain date, the assured was held entitled to demand (as he did) the issue of a stamped policy to him at a later date, though between the two dates he had ascertained the fact that the ship had been lost (*m*).   On the other hand, where by the agreement of the parties a later date is substituted for the date at which the contract would otherwise be deemed to have been concluded, the duty of the party charged continues, or is revived, as the case may be, and it is enough for the party complaining to prove that the party charged had knowledge of the undisclosed fact at any time before the termination of such extended, or renewed, period of duty   Thus, where a policy of marine insurance was

(*h*) See § 194, *post.*
(*hh*) See *Evans* v *Edmonds* (1853), 13 C. B. 777.
(*ι*) In § 182, *ante*
(*ȷ*) See note (*o*) to § 182, *ante*
(*k*) In § 181, and note (*ȷ*) thereto, *ante*
(*l*) *Cory* v *Patton* (1872), L R 7 Q. B 304, per BLACKBURN, J , delivering the judgment of the Court, at pp 308–310
(*m*) *Lishman* v. *Northern Maritime Insurance Co.* (1875) L R 10 C. P. 179, Exch Ch.

by mistake effected on the ship, instead of on the cargo, as intended, and, on the error being pointed out, it was put right by a corrective memorandum on the margin of the policy, it was held that it was enough for the underwriters to prove that the assured had knowledge of the undisclosed fact between the date of the issue of the original policy and the date at which the correction was made (*n*); and where, in a fire insurance case, the insurance company had, in a document which for that purpose was assumed to be analogous to the ship in a policy of marine insurance, inserted a note to the effect that no insurance was to be in force till the premium should have been paid, and a printed receipt issued from the office, it was held that the insurance company sustained the onus of establishing the knowledge of the assured during the existence of the duty by proof that after the delivery of the above document, but before the issue of the printed receipt, the assured had been apprised of the undisclosed fact (*o*).

190. Where the non-disclosure assumes the form of an omission to qualify facts stated absolutely, with the result of rendering the unqualified statement a misrepresentation, and the party complaining elects to rely upon this misrepresentation as his cause of action, and not on non-disclosure *simpliciter*, then, provided that he is only asking the Court to set aside the contract, or to treat it as a nullity, and is not seeking damages in an action of deceit, there is of course no obligation on him to prove any knowledge or belief whatsoever on the part of the person alleged to have (in the manner supposed) made the implied misrepresentation (*p*).

Sub-s. (5).   *Ignorance of the Party complaining.*

191. This, like non-disclosure, is a negative, but nevertheless, like it, is an essential element in the proof of the party complaining, who must aver, and, if denied, adduce at least some *primâ facie* evidence of, the fact that he had no knowledge of the particular matter in question either by means of a communication from the party charged, or from any other source   And this is a quite reasonable requirement, when the nature of the breach of duty which must be alleged by him is considered.   No duty is violated by the party charged *merely* because he observes silence as to something which he knows, or *merely* because he keeps to himself something which the party complaining does not know   The duty is only broken when he fails to disclose a material fact which is within his *special or exclusive* knowledge (*q*), that is

(*n*) *Sawtell* v *Loudon* (1814), 5 Taunt. 359
(*o*) *Yager* v *Guardian Assurance Co.* (1912), 108 L. T. 38, Div Ct.
(*p*) See most of the cases cited in notes (*t*), (*u*), and *v*), to § 118, *ante.*
(*q*) The duty is " not to conceal what he *alone* knows," as was said by the C A in their joint judgment, delivered by COZENS-HARDY, L J, at p 157 of *Law* v. *Law*, [1905] 1 Ch 140, C. A   That it is only matters within the presumed special or exclusive knowledge of the party charged which are required to be disclosed, has been insisted upon in several places in Sect. 2, *ante* · see §§ 84, 85 (generally), §§ 92, 93, 95, 96, 99 (illustrations from marine insurance cases), § 117 (vendor and purchaser cases), §§ 120, 122, 123 (suretyship), § 137 (compromises), § 141 (agreements for partnership), § 147, note (*p*), and § 148 (contracts to marry), and § 150 (deeds of separation), *ante*

to say, which is *both* known (actually or presumptively) to himself, *and is not known* (actually or presumptively) to the party complaining, who, therefore, unless he alleges, and (if challenged) proves, both the one and the other, alleges, or (as the case may be) establishes, no breach of duty whatsoever (r). At any rate, whatever its justification may be, and whether it is abstractedly justifiable or not (s), the rule has been definitely and unmistakably laid down (t), and, if it ever could have been, certainly

(r) The rules as to burden of proof in the law of misrepresentation, with regard to the knowledge or ignorance of the representee, may usefully be contrasted here When the representee has alleged and proved the misrepresentation (innocent, or fraudulent, as the case may be), and also materiality, inducement, and, where fraud is charged, damages, he has, though not saying a word about his ignorance of the truth, alleged and proved a good cause of action . the representor is from that point a convicted wrong doer, and the burden then lies heavily upon him to show affirmatively some reason why the representee should not obtain the appropriate relief, and one of such possible reasons is that, though the intention was to deceive him, yet in fact the representee was not deceived, because he actually and personally knew the whole truth at every material date: see *Mackintosh and Dreyer* v *Marshall* (1843), 11 M & W 116 (*per* Lord ABINGER, C B , and ALDERSON, B , at p. 127), and the other cases cited in the notes to §§ 206–209 of the author's *Law of Actionable Misrepresentation* In a case of non disclosure, on the contrary, if the statement of claim, or the evidence, of the party complaining, terminates without any averment, in the one case, or proof, in the other, of his own ignorance of the undisclosed fact, he has not alleged, or established, a complete cause of action, and the party charged is not an alleged, or (as the case may be) a proved, wrong-doer.

(s) Lord MANSFIELD, C.J , though he does not expressly say anything as to the burden of proof, leaves no room for doubt as to what he would consider to be the correct rule, in his observations on the foundation of the entire doctrine, and as to the fraudulent character of a claim to relief on the ground of non disclosure put forward by a person who has (even presumptive) knowledge of the undisclosed fact, at pp 1918, 1919 of *Carter* v *Boehm* (1766), 3 Burr 1905 " The reason of the rule against concealment is to prevent fraud, and encourage good faith If the defendant's objection"—which was non-disclosure set up by an underwriter who had not established, even if he had alleged, that he had no *presumed* notice of the undisclosed fact—" were to prevail in the present case, the rule would be turned into an instrument of fraud . If the objection ' that he was not told ' is sufficient to vacate it, he took the premium, knowing it to be void, in order to gain, if the alternative turned out in one way, and to make no satisfaction, if it turned out the other . If he thought that omission an objection at the time, he ought not to have signed the policy with a secret reserve in his own mind to make it void , if he dispensed with the information, and did not think that silence was an objection, then he cannot take it up now, after the event What has often been said of the Statute of Frauds may, with more propriety, be applied to every rule of law drawn from the principle of natural equity, that it should never be so turned, construed, or used as to protect or be a means of fraud " With this exposition should be compared that of COCKBURN, C J., who, at p. 605 of *Bates* v *Hewitt* (1867), L R 2 Q B. 595, takes up precisely the same ground " it will not lie in the mouth of the underwriter to say that a material fact was not communicated to him which he had present to his mind at the time he accepted the insurance , the law will not lend itself to a defence based upon fraud , it will not allow the underwriter to say, ' I have taken the premium with knowledge of the particular fact, but because the assured has not communicated it to me, I will not make good the loss.' " Cp. *Farrant* v *Blachford* (1863), 32 L. J. (CH) 237 (*per* Lord WESTBURY, L.C , at p. 240)

(t) For instance, KNIGHT-BRUCE, V -C., in his famous judgment in *Stikeman* v *Dawson* (1847), 1 De G & Sm 90, at pp 105–108, said that not only non-disclosure, but also his own ignorance from any other source, must be proved by the party complaining, and that, of the two, the latter should be established first, for, not until this is done, does the question of disclosure become of any importance , ERLE, C J , directed the jury, at p 672 of *Foley* v *Tabor* (1861), 2 F & F 663, a marine insurance case, in these terms—" did the assured neglect to communicate to the insurer any fact known to the assured, *and not known to the insurer*, material for his guidance, in respect of the premium to be demanded ? *Both parts of the question must be answered.* The material fact must have been known to the assured, *and unknown to the insurer*," and at p 673, after intimating to the jury that it was obvious that the assured had knowledge of the fact, he told them to consider whether

cannot now be, controverted. No doubt, there are one or two judicial pronouncements which, at the first blush, may appear to point in the opposite direction, and to throw on the party charged the onus of proving the knowledge *aliunde* of the party complaining, as soon as the latter has established non-disclosure : but on closer examination of such cases it will be seen that, in all of them, either the alleged ignorance of the party complaining was not disputed, or the burden of proving his knowledge was only thrown on the party charged at a stage in the trial of the case when the party complaining had already given some *primâ facie* evidence of his own ignorance, and the onus had so become shifted (*u*). For, as in the case of proof of non-disclosure (*v*), the allegation of ignorance in the pleading of the party complaining, which must certainly in any event be made (*w*), may be admitted. or at all events not disputed, in which case no proof is necessary . and, even where the averment is denied, very slight *primâ facie* evidence indeed, if non-disclosure has already been either admitted or proved, is sufficient to cast on the party charged from that point onwards the burden of establishing that the party complaining had acquired knowledge of the undisclosed fact through other channels than a direct communication from the party charged himself (*x*)

192. In accordance with the rule so established, it will be found, on reference to the authorities, that, wherever the party complaining has either (i) failed to give satisfactory *primâ facie* evidence of his own ignorance of the undisclosed fact, or (ii), having given such evidence, has been met by counter-evidence adduced by the party charged sufficient to sustain the

the other " part of the question " should be answered in favour of the underwriter At p. 383 of *Caxton and Accrington Union* v *Dew* (1899), 68 L J (Q B) 380, BRUCE, J, applied the same rule to the case of a fidelity guarantee , and Lord HALSBURY, L.C , at p 332 of *Watt* v *Assets Co.*, [1903] A C 317, H L , to the case of a compromise

(*u*) Thus, in *Elkin* v *Janson* (1845), 13 M & W 655, the ignorance of the party complaining was not stated to be one of the facts which, in the opinion of the Court of Exchequer, are required to be established by him but in that case it was not disputed that the underwriter had no knowledge of the material fact, if he did not acquire it from the assured; it was not necessary, therefore, to debate the question In *Bates* v. *Hewitt* (1867), L. R 2 Q B 595, COCKBURN, C J , undoubtedly put a question to the jury at the trial (viz whether the underwriters had a then present knowledge of the identity of the insured vessel with a late Confederate cruiser of the same name, which was the undisclosed fact) in such a form as to indicate that he considered the onus of proving the knowledge of the party complaining to be on the party charged, and, on the jury intimating that they were not satisfied as to this point, he directed the verdict to be entered for the underwriters (pp 598, 599), which again presupposed the same view, and his ruling was affirmed by the Court (pp 605 and 608), but this course was adopted at a stage of the proceedings when, *primâ facie* evidence of ignorance having been given by the underwriters (see p. 598), the burden had been shifted on to the shoulders of the assured of proving affirmatively the underwriters' knowledge, and (in the circumstances of that case) their actual then present knowledge.

(*v*) In Sub-s (3), *ante*.

(*w*) See, generally, the various pleas, answers, and defences (where relief was sought by way of defence), and the declarations, bills, statements of claim and counterclaims (where rescission was the relief claimed), set out in the reports of the cases cited in the notes to Sect. 2, *ante*.

(*x*) See the observations of KNIGHT-BRUCE, V.-C., at pp 105–107 of *Stikeman* v *Dawson* (1847), 1 De G & Sm 90, where he points out that, though slight evidence might be sufficient, the party complaining was not justified in his refusal or omission to give any at all

onus, which would then be on his shoulders, of affirmatively proving the knowledge (actual or presumptive) of the party complaining, all relief has been denied (y) . and that whenever, on the contrary, the party complaining has given evidence of his own ignorance which the party charged has either not attempted to refute, or has not succeeded in refuting, by countervailing evidence of knowledge (presumptive or actual), relief has been granted, or, where withheld, has been withheld on some other ground (z).

193. It must always be remembered that the complete burden of proof, in relation to this topic, is not sustained by merely showing that the party complaining had no actual or personal cognizance of the undisclosed fact. It must also be established, if disputed, that he had no presumptive knowledge (a). On the other hand, whilst it is necessary, it is at the same time sufficient, to prove the absence of either of these forms of knowledge: the party complaining is not required to go further, or to allege and establish that no means of knowledge were available to him, not being such means of which the mere presence and availability is tantamount to presumptive knowledge ; nor does the most conclusive proof, on the other side, of the existence of such means of knowledge in the least degree affect the claim of the party complaining to relief if otherwise well founded (b)

(y) One of the two things mentioned in the text happened, with the consequence that the party complaining failed to obtain relief, in the marine insurance cases of *Carter* v *Boehm* (1766), 3 Burr 1905, *Court* v *Martineau* (1782), 3 Dougl. (K B) 161, *Foley* v *Tabor* (1861), 2 F. & F 663, and (as regards some of the underwriters) *Cantimere Meccanico Brindisino* v *Janson*, [1912] 3 K. B 452, C A, amongst others, in the fire insurance case of *Pimm* v *Lewis* (1862), 2 F & F 778 ; in the vendor and purchaser case of *Bowles* v *Round* (1800), 5 Ves 508 , in the compromise cases of *Wason* v. *Wareing* (1852), 15 Beav 151, *Law* v. *Law*, [1905] 1 Ch. 140, C. A., and *Watt* v *Assets Co* , [1905] A C 317, H L , and in the promise of marriage case of *Irving* v *Greenwood* (1824), 1 C. & P 350

(z) This was what happened at the trial of the marine insurance cases of *Bates* v. *Hewitt* (1867), L R 2 Q B 595, *Harrower* v *Hutchinson* (1870), L R 5 Q B 584, Exch Ch , *Tate & Sons* v *Hyslop* (1885), 15 Q B D 368, C A, and (as regards some of the underwriters who, however, were deprived of relief on other grounds) *Cantimere Meccanico Brindisino* v *Janson*, *sup* , the horse insurance case of *Taylor* v *Yorkshire Insurance Co.*, [1913] 2 Ir R 1 , the vendor and purchaser cases of *Brandling* v *Plummer* (1854), 2 Drewry 427, *Phillips* v. *Homfray* (1871), 6 Ch App. 770, *Caballero* v *Henty* (1874), 9 Ch App. 447, *Ellis* v *Rogers* (1885), 29 C D 661, C A , *Re Hoedicke and Lipski's Contract*, [1901] 2 Ch 666, and *Re Puckett and Smith's Contract*, [1902] 2 Ch 258, C A ; the compromise cases of *Gordon* v *Gordon* (1821), 3 Swanst 400, and *Greenwood* v *Greenwood* (1863), 2 De G J & S 28 , and the promise of marriage case of *Bench* v. *Merrick* (1844), 1 C. & K 463

(a) The party complaining in the following cases failed to establish absence of presumptive knowledge, and it was accordingly held that on this ground alone, apart from others, he was disentitled to relief *Carter* v *Boehm* (1766), 3 Burr 1905 (see note (s) to § 191, *ante*), *Stikeman* v *Dawson* (1847), 1 De G & Sm 90 (per KNIGHT BRUCE, V-C, at pp 105–108), *Foley* v *Tabor* (1861), 2 F & F 663 (where the underwriters failed to show that they had no constructive notice through Lloyd's Shipping Lists) As to what is "presumptive knowledge," and the various species and forms of it, see Ch II, Sect 3, Sub ss. (2)–(6), *ante*.

(b) See *Bates* v *Hewitt*, *sup* , where, in answer to a question put for the express purpose of raising the point for the Court, the jury, though not satisfied as to the defendant's actual knowledge of the identity of the vessel, found that he "had abundant means of identifying the ships" (p. 599), and the Court held this finding to be irrelevant (per COCKBURN, C.J., at pp 606–608); *Brandling* v *Plummer*, *sup* (per KINDERSLEY, V-C., at p. 432), *Caballero* v *Henty*, *sup* , *Re Puckett and Smith's Contract*, *sup* (per COLLINS,

194. It has already been pointed out that, in order to establish that the party charged had knowledge of the undisclosed fact, the party complaining must show that he had cognizance of all those elements and features of the "fact" which made it material to be disclosed (c). Conversely, and on the same principle, in order to establish his own ignorance, it is sufficient for the party complaining to show that he was unaware of some one particular circumstance in the assemblage of undisclosed circumstances which gave significance to the others, though he may have been cognizant of those others ; or, where the fact is a complex one, that he had no knowledge or suspicion of the connection between two circumstances, or of the identity of two things, which rendered the non-disclosure of the entire "fact" of importance to him, notwithstanding that he was aware of the two circumstances, or of the two things, in their supposed disconnection. For this reason, it is in every case essential to inquire closely what element it is in the totality of the withheld matter which is the substantial ground of the complaint   Thus, in an action on a valued policy of marine insurance on goods on board a ship or ships at and from all or any of the Canary Islands to London, one of the ships on which the goods were laden having been wrecked, the underwriters pleaded non-disclosure of intelligence that such ship was in difficulties.   Now the undisclosed fact here obviously involved two facts: (1) the receipt of the news that a certain vessel was in distress, and (2) the identity of that vessel with a "ship" or one of "the ships" on which the goods were in fact laden which were the subject of the insurance. They did not pretend that they were ignorant of the intelligence as to a ship called "The President," for this had been posted up at Lloyd's before the conclusion of the contract, but they proved that they had no knowledge or suspicion that "The President" was a "ship," or one of the "ships," protected by the policy, and their defence accordingly succeeded (d).   So, where underwriters had issued a policy on the S.S. "Georgia," and one of these underwriters, being sued on the policy in respect of the capture of that vessel by a frigate of the United States, set up non-disclosure, he did not attempt to establish that he was ignorant of the fact that a steamship of that name had been a notorious Confederate cruiser, and that she had been sold at Liverpool, but he did allege, and prove,—and this was held to be sufficient,—that the identity of the insured vessel with this cruiser was not present to his mind when the insurance was effected, and that he did not know that he was asked to insure, and was insuring, the Confederate "Georgia" (e)   Again, in another marine insurance case, where the assured sued on a policy on the

M R , at pp 263, 264); *Nocton* v. *Lord Ashburton*, [1914] A. C. 932, H L (*per* Lord DUNEDIN, at p 962)   Cp. the misrepresentation cases cited in the notes to § 209 of the author's *Law of Actionable Misrepresentation*, where *a fortiori* (since—see note (r) to § 191, *ante*—there is no duty on the representee to prove ignorance of the truth) mere proof of means of knowledge available to the representee affords the representor no defence

   (c) See § 188, *ante*.
   (d) *Lynch* v *Dunsford* (1811), 14 East 494, Exch. Ch. (*per* Lord ELLENBOROUGH, C J , at p 497)
   (e) *Bates* v *Hewitt, sup* , at p 598 (see the judgment of COCKBURN, C J , at p 605)

freight of the "Pedro Ferrar" from St Iago in Cuba to the United Kingdom, the underwriters were, for the purposes of the judgment of the Exchequer Chamber, assumed to have had presumptive knowledge of the fact that at a material date "a British barque with copper ore was aground" at a certain place, this information having been published at Lloyd's: but they alleged, and proved, that they had not, and could not be expected to have, any knowledge or belief that this British barque was the "Pedro Ferrar" from any source other than information supplied by the assured, which information had been studiously withheld by him, though he had in his possession a letter from the captain stating that he was loading the ship *with copper*, that *there was no other vessel in the place*, and that he expected to sail on the 20th of a certain month; if, therefore, the assured had disclosed the contents of this letter, the underwriters, having regard to the fact that on *the 25th of that month* it was known at Lloyd's that a British barque *with copper ore* was aground at Iraqua, would have been able to put two and two together, and would not then have been in a position, as they were held to be in the absence of this information, to prove that they were presumptively ignorant of the only fact which gave the announcement at Lloyd's any significance to them (*f*). Similarly, where the plaintiff in an action on a policy of marine insurance, whose practice it was to insure at Lloyd's quantities of cochineal shipped by him from the Canaries on floating policies, knew, at the time of effecting the floating policy sued upon, and failed to disclose, two facts, (1) the publication of an anonymous letter stating that the owners of a vessel called the "Candida" intended to lose her on her next voyage, (2) that a cargo was to be shipped for him on board a vessel called the "Candida," the underwriters, without suggesting that they were ignorant of (1), because the letter was posted up at Lloyd's, alleged and proved their entire ignorance of (2), and it was held that this was enough, since obviously neither (1) nor (2) were of the slightest importance in themselves, and it was only the conjunction of the two facts, and their application to one another, which it was material for them to know (*g*).

195. Here too, as in the case of other elements in the burden of proof incumbent on the party complaining, the date of the conclusion of the contract may be of importance (*h*); for though, on the one hand, it is necessary, on the other, it is sufficient, to prove ignorance of the undisclosed fact before that date. Thus, in a case already referred to for another point, it was one of the contentions of the assured that the underwriters had elected to affirm the contract by issuing the policy with presumptive knowledge of the vessel being aground, but, the underwriters having proved that they had no knowledge (actual or presumptive) of this fact before the initialling of the ship (which, as between the parties, is the date of the conclusion of the contract),

(*f*) *Nicholson* v. *Power* (1869), 20 L T 580, Exch Ch (*per* COCKBURN, C J, at p. 580)
(*g*) *Leigh* v *Adams* (1871), 25 L. T. 566 (*per* COCKBURN, C J, at p 569)
(*h*) As to what "conclusion of the contract" means, see § 182, *ante*, and, in relation to marine insurance in particular, note (*o*) thereto As to the necessity of establishing that the alleged undisclosed fact was a fact, and that the party charged had knowledge of it, before the conclusion of the contract, see § 181, note (*j*), and § 189, *ante*, respectively

it was held that they had established all that they were bound to establish on this head, and that the fact that they acquired knowledge afterwards, though before the actual issue of the policy, was wholly immaterial (*i*).

Sub-s. (6). *Matters which it is not incumbent on the Party Complaining to establish.*

196. Except as above stated, there is no onus on the party complaining. In particular, he is not bound to prove either that the party charged was actuated by fraud, or that he (the party complaining) was induced by the non-disclosure, or rather by his belief in the non-existence of that which was not disclosed, to enter into the contract sought to be avoided or treated as void And not only is he not bound to prove either of these facts in the first instance, but he is not required to prove either of them at all, or at any stage of the proceedings In other words, the question is in each case wholly immaterial, and, if non-disclosure be established, no amount of proof of the innocence of the party charged, or of the party complaining having been induced to contract by other considerations, will render the contract valid It is true that it so happens that non-disclosure is usually *in fact* nothing less than fraudulent suppression, and that *in fact* the party complaining is generally deceived and induced thereby, but this, for the purposes of the present proposition, is a mere accident.

197. First, as to fraud It is now firmly established that, except in that artificial sense in which some equity lawyers, and also some writers on marine insurance, have spoken of the non-disclosure itself as " fraud " (*j*), it is quite useless and irrelevant to allege or prove fraud on the one side, or innocence on the other If the party complaining discharges the whole of his burden of proof, as above set forth, it is quite immaterial whether the breach of duty so established arose from a fraudulent or other guilty intention, or was the result of mere indifference, inadvertence, or mistake, or whether the party charged was consciously violating a known rule of law, or principle of honour, or, on the other hand, was ignorant of the very existence of any such rule or principle, and so was, in a sense, an unwitting trespasser upon the rights of others (*k*) The above proposition must of course be

(*i*) *Nicholson* v *Power*, cited in note (*f*), *ante* (*per* COCKBURN, C.J , at p. 581)
(*j*) This misuse, or misleading use, of the term " fraud " is discussed and criticized in App A, Sect 2, Sub-s (1), *post*
(*k*) The proposition stated in the text has been stated, and reiterated, in a large number of authorities The principal marine insurance cases are *Carter* v *Boehm* (1766), 3 Burr 1905 (*per* Lord MANSFIELD, C J , at p 1909 · " although the suppression should happen through mistake, *without any fraudulent intention*, yet still the underwriter is deceived, and the policy is void " and, again, at p 1912 " a concealment , fraudulent, if designed , or, *though not designed*, varying materially the object of the policy, and changing the risk understood to be run "), *Bridges* v *Hunter* (1815), 1 M & S 15 (*per* Lord ELLENBOROUGH, C.J , at p 18 ; " although no fraud is imputed to the plaintiffs, still that will not help them, provided they were bound to make the disclosure," and GROSE, J , at p 19 " it is not the less a concealment because made without any view to fraud "), *Gladstone* v *King* (1813), 1 M & S 35 (*per* Lord ELLENBOROUGH, C J , at p 38) , *Anderson* v *Thornton* (1853), 8 Exch 425 (*per* PARKE, B , at p 427) , *Bates* v *Hewitt* (1867), L R 2 Q B 595 (*per* COCKBURN, C J , at p 607 : " it is immaterial whether an omission to communicate a

understood as applying only to cases where a duty of disclosure arises from the mere relation of the parties as negotiators for a contract or transaction of one of the recognized types already indicated : it has no application to those cases where, there being no original duty to disclose anything, an obligation is created by, and solely by, special circumstances existing at the commencement, or supervening during the course, of the negotiation (*l*) ; for the " special circumstances " in question are nearly always such as indicate fraud, or such as, from the moment of their occurrence, or of their coming within the knowledge of the party charged, render the suppression by him of material facts dishonest In such cases it is obvious that, in being required (as he is) to prove these special circumstances, the party complaining is in effect required to prove fraud Moreover, it may be necessary for the party complaining to establish fraud in order to destroy certain affirmative answers which the party charged may set up, as will be seen hereafter, such as a plea of an agreement to waive the right of disclosure (*m*), or to dispense with

material fact arose from intention, or from indifference, or from a mistake, or from its not being present to the mind of the assured that the fact was one which it was material to make known'), *Ionides* v *Pender* (1874), L R 9 Q B 531 (*per* BLACKBURN, J , at p 537), and the American case there cited which is abstracted in note (*w*) to § 104, *ante* , *Tate & Sons* v *Hyslop* (1885), 15 Q B D 368, C A (*per* BRETT, M R , at p 378), *Scottish Shire Line, Ltd.* v *London & Provincial Marine & General Insurance Co* , [1912] 3 K B 51 (*per* HAMILTON, J , at p 70), *Gooding* v *White* (1913), 29 T L R 312 For statements of the same proposition in life insurance cases, see *Lindenau* v *Desborough* (1828), 8 B & C. 586 (*per* BAYLEY, J , at p 592) , *Everett* v *Desborough* (1829), 5 Bing 503 (*per* BEST, C J , at pp 515, 516) , *Traill* v *Baring* (1864), 4 De G J & S 318 (*per* KNIGHT-BRUCE, L J at p 327, and TURNER, L J , at p 328) , *Joel* v *Law Union & Crown Insurance Co* , [1908] 2 K B 863, C. A (*per* MOULTON, L J , at pp 883, 884) See also the fire insurance case of *Bufe* v *Turner* (1815), 6 Taunt 338 The vendor and purchaser cases to be referred to on this point are *Flight* v *Booth* (1834), 1 Bing N C 370 (*per* TINDAL, C J , delivering the judgment of the Court of C P , at p 376), *Dimmock* v *Hallett* (1866), 2 Ch App 21 (*per* TURNER, L J , at p 29, and CAIRNS, L J , at p 30), *Mostyn* (*Lord*) v *West Mostyn Coke & Iron Co* (1876), 1 C P D 145 (*per* BRETT, J , at p 151) , *Heywood* v *Mallalieu* (1883), 25 C D 357 (*per* BACON, V -C , at p 365) , *Carlish* v *Salt*, [1906] 1 Ch 335 (*per* JOYCE, J , at p 351) And, lastly, see the following suretyship cases *Railton* v *Mathews and Leonard* (1844), 10 Cl. & Fin 934 (*per* Lord CAMPBELL, who, at p 944, explains that it was quite irrelevant that the party charged did not know of his legal duty to disclose) , *Willis* v *Willis* (1850), 17 Sim 218 (*per* SHADWELL, V -C , at p 220) , *London General Omnibus Co* v *Holloway*, [1912] 2 K B 72, C A (*per* VAUGHAN WILLIAMS, L J , at pp 79, 80, FARWELL, L J , at pp 81, 82, and KENNEDY, L J , at pp 84, 85) The two solitary instances of any statement interrupting this steady current of authority are, first, an expression of personal opinion on the part of LOPES, L J , which is to be found at p 141 of *Hambrough* v *Mutual Life Insurance Co of New York* (1895), 72 L T 140, C A   " in policies of insurance on life," he there says (limiting the proposition apparently to this particular species of a particular class of contract), " mere silence respecting a material fact, in the absence of any fraudulent intention, does not avoid the policy," an amazing heresy, which was disposed of by the judgment of Lord ALVERSTONE, C.J , at p 439 of *Joel* v. *Law Union & Crown Insurance Co* , [1908] 2 K B 431 (trial of the action) , and, secondly, a like dictum at the end of the judgment of POLLOCK, C.B , at p 535 of *North British Insurance Co* v *Lloyd* (1854), 10 Exch 523 (" the non-disclosure   would not have vitiated the guarantee unless it had been fraudulently kept back "), which observation VAUGHAN WILLIAMS, L.J , at p 80 of *London General Omnibus Co* v *Holloway, sup*, found it impossible to understand, and quite inconsistent with the authorities The proposition is often expressed in another form, viz that disclosure is an implied condition of the validity of the contract , see § 83, and the cases cited in note (*t*) thereto

(*l*) See Sect 2, Sub s (8), *ante*

(*m*) See § 202, *post*

a particular form of relief (n); and, in some cases, it may be essential to show fraud in order to obtain the annulment of a contract after completion (o), or to get rid of the liability (to which otherwise the party complaining would be subject) of restoring to the party charged moneys which he has paid under the contract rescinded (such as, e g, premiums under a policy of insurance) as a condition of the rescission (p) The same rules, and for the same reason, apply to those cases of misrepresentation where the representee is not suing for damages in an action of deceit, but is merely claiming rescission of a contract induced by the misrepresentation, or is setting up the misrepresentation as a defence to an action on the contract (q), and both in the one class of case, and in the other, the irrelevancy of fraud is illustrated in a very striking manner by reference to the practical consequences, as regards costs and otherwise, with which the Courts have visited those litigants who, though establishing everything necessary for the purpose of the relief claimed, have unnecessarily, and therefore (having regard to the gravity of the charge) improperly, introduced accusations of dishonesty against their opponents which they have failed to prove (r).

198. Next as to inducement In cases of misrepresentation, the representee must not only establish the materiality of the falsehood, that is to say, its tendency to induce, but also the fact (which is a quite separate and distinct one) that he was in the particular case induced by his belief in its truth to alter his position to his detriment in the manner alleged.   However likely the misrepresentation may have been to influence a normal person to act upon it, however inconceivable even it may appear that such a person could have remained insensible to the allurement held out, yet if the particular representee is not in a position to allege, or, having alleged, to establish, that he was in fact so induced, he has no cause of action (s) It is otherwise in cases of non-disclosure When the party complaining has once proved that the undisclosed fact was material to be disclosed in the sense that, if it had been communicated to him, it *might* have influenced a person situated as he was, or belonging to the profession or business class to which he belonged, to enter into the contract in question on the agreed terms, it is quite unnecessary to institute the further inquiry (which is essential in a case of misrepresentation) as to whether he was actually so influenced in point of fact (t).   Any evidence on this head would be unnecessary and irrelevant It is quite true that evidence is always admissible, and often is essential, to prove the fact of materiality: but, as will be seen hereafter (u), such evidence must be

(n) See §§ 207, 208, *post*
(o) This question is discussed in § 230, *post*
(p) See § 232, *post*
(q) See § 250, and § 341, note (l), of the author's *Law of Actionable Misrepresentation*
(r) For a statement of these consequences, see Ch VIII, Sect 2, Sub-s (4), *post*
(s) Ch VI, Sect. 1, of the author's *Law of Actionable Misrepresentation* deals with this topic
(t) See Ch II, Sect 2, Sub-s (2), *ante*, as to what is meant by materiality for the purposes of the law of non-disclosure : and, as to the sufficiency of establishing no more than that a communication of the undisclosed fact *might* have had a deterrent influence, see §§ 31, 32, *ante*, and the cases cited in the notes thereto
(u) In Sect 6, Sub s (1), *post*

confined to the testimony of persons engaged in the business in question as
to the effect which would be produced upon their minds, as a class, by a
communication of the undisclosed circumstance, and must not include the
personal and individual impressions of the party complaining in relation to
the particular contract. On the other hand, if the party complaining fails
to establish materiality, it is of no avail whatever to allege, or to prove,
that, if the fact in question had been divulged to him, he would never have
entered into the contract at all (*v*).

199. Where the non-disclosure amounts to, or forms part of, or is preceded
or followed by, a misrepresentation, then, in so far as the party complaining
either elects, or is compelled, to treat it as misrepresentation, and to found
his title to relief upon it in that character, and not as non-disclosure *simpliciter*,
he is subject to the same burden of proof in all respects as a representee in
proceedings for misrepresentation, whether fraudulent or innocent, and must
therefore prove inducement as well as materiality (*w*).

SECT. 4 AFFIRMATIVE ANSWERS AVAILABLE TO THE PARTY CHARGED

200. Assuming the party complaining to have established, or to be in a
position to establish, each and every of the constituents of his burden of
proof, as stated in the last Section, and assuming the party charged to be
unable to resist, by way of direct negative, the case so made against him,
there are yet certain affirmative answers open to him whereby that case may
be displaced. These—apart from the answers and bars, whether statutory
or non-statutory, which are available to a party litigant in proceedings
relating to the enforcement or avoidance of contracts in general (*x*)—are
substantially two : first, waiver by the party complaining, whether express
or implied, of his right to disclosure, or of his right to insist on some particular
remedy in respect of non-disclosure ; and, secondly, affirmation by him of the
contract or transaction which he is seeking to have rescinded, or treated as

(*v*) See *Hamilton* v *Watson* (1845), 12 Cl & Fin 109, a suretyship case, in which Lord
BROUGHAM, at p 120, observes that "it is quite immaterial" whether "the cautioner
would have acted differently if he had known of the matter said to be concealed ", *North
British Insurance Co* v *Lloyd* (1854), 10 Exch 523, another suretyship case, where the
surety complained of the concealment from him of the fact that he was a substitute for a
former surety who had been released, and the Court of Exchequer upheld the finding of
the jury that this fact was not material, and (*per* POLLOCK, C B , at pp 532, 533) expressed
the opinion that it made no difference that the surety " swore that he would not have given
his guarantee had he been informed of the substitution "

(*w*) *Re Roberts*, [1905] 1 Ch 704, C A , was such a case   There the defendant resisted
an action to enforce a family compromise on the ground of conduct which was described
(at p 708) by Lord HALSBURY, L C , as non disclosure, or incomplete explanation, of a
certain opinion of counsel, but which VAUGHAN WILLIAMS, L J , delivering the judgment
of the Court of Appeal in favour of the defendant, treated as an " inaccurate statement, '
and positive " misrepresentation " (p 710), and, from that point of view, was careful to
point out the necessity of proving inducement in fact   No reference, of course, is made in
the text to cases of statutory non disclosure, which are regulated by the special terms of
the enactments themselves, and in many of which it is essential to prove inducement
These cases receive separate treatment in Ch VI, Sect. 1, *post*

(*x*) Such as the various Statutes of Limitation, on the one hand, or estoppel, accord
and satisfaction, and the like, on the other   With these the present treatise is not
immediately concerned

a nullity (y). The burden of allegation and proof, in the case of each of these, is of course on the party charged , though that burden may be satisfied, in whole or in part, by admissions expressly or impliedly made by the party complaining at or before the trial, or may in the course of the proceedings be shifted backwards and forwards (z)

Sub-s (1).   Waiver

201. *Modus et conventio vincunt legem.* If the party charged is in a position to prove either an express or an implied agreement, term, or condition, whereby the party complaining undertook to waive such right to disclosure as he otherwise would have had in respect of a class of facts to which the undisclosed fact belongs, the claim or defence, as the case may be, of the party complaining is defeated (a), just as, in cases of misrepresentation, the representee's right to the truth is defeated by a proved agreement on his part to waive that right (b)

202. First, as to express agreements to waive disclosure   There is no objection, on the ground of public policy, or otherwise to such an agree ment (c), any more than there is to an agreement not to take advantage of any misrepresentation (d), provided that no statutory prohibition stands in

(y) The former of these two affirmative answers is the subject of Sub s (1), the latter, of Sub s (2)   It may be asked why proof that the party complaining had knowledge *aliunde* of the undisclosed fact is not mentioned as one of the affirmative answers available to the party charged   The reason is, as pointed out in Sect. 3, Sub-s (5), *ante*, that there is no burden on the party charged to prove his opponent's knowledge unless and until some *primâ facie* evidence of the ignorance of the party complaining has been adduced on the other side   if and when this is done, the party charged may be said to assume the onus of establishing an affirmative case , but it is a transferred, not an initial, onus   The same may be said of the fact of disclosure which, at a very early stage of the proceedings, the party charged may be called upon to prove   but in strictness, he is, in so doing, negativing, by affirmative evidence, the negative which it is incumbent on the party complaining to make out   see Sect. 3, Sub s. (3), *ante*

(z) Illustrations of this tossing to and fro of the burden of proof will be found in several of the cases cited in the notes to Sub ss (1) and (2), *post.*

(a) A plea of waiver is thus the antithesis of a plea of knowledge   In the latter case no wrong is done to the party complaining, because he was aware (though not from the party charged) of the undisclosed fact   in the former, no wrong is done to him, because he was not, and did not want to be, aware of it, but was so eager to bind the party charged to a contract which promised profit and advantage to himself that he was content to run all risks, and dispense with all information   Obviously a plea of waiver is the more meritorious of the two   for the party setting up that plea is only insisting on effect being given to the contractual protection which he had stipulated for   whereas the other plea starts with the assumption that the party charged has not done his duty

(b) See § 213 of the author's *Law of Actionable Misrepresentation,* and the cases cited in notes (y), (z), (a), (b), and (c) thereto   Here also there is the same antithesis between a plea of the representee's knowledge of the truth, and a plea of his agreement to waive such knowledge   The mutually exclusive character of the two defences in misrepresentation cases is touched upon by JESSEL, M R , at p. 21 of *Redgrave v. Hurd* (1881), 20 C. D 1, C. A , and by Lord HALSBURY, L C , at p 369 of *Arnison v Smith* (1888), 41 C D 348, C. A.

(c) For a good illustration of an express waiver, see the marine insurance case of *Property Insurance Co v National Protector Insurance Co* (1913), 108 L T. 104 (*per* SCRUTTON, J , at p 106)   There are abundant illustrations of such terms or conditions, and of their being held valid and enforceable, in cases of life insurance · see several of the cases cited in note (m) to § 171, *ante*

(d) See, for examples of conditions, again in life insurance cases, which have been

tho way (*dd*), and that there is no stipulation that the contract shall not be impeached even for fraud (*e*) · and, if the language used is aptly framed so as to apply to or include the particular undisclosed matter, it is a *primâ facie* answer to the case of the party complaining, but not otherwise (*f*).

held to contain or imply an undertaking by the insurance company to waive or abnegate, either absolutely, or after the lapse of a specified period, the right to rely upon any mis representation other than fraudulent, *Wood* v *Dwarris* (1856), 11 Exch 593 (*per* ALDERSON, B, at p 503 " before the policy was entered into, the defendants issued a prospectus, by which they represented that all policies effected by them would be indis putable, except in cases of fraud That was holding out to all the world that they would require no proof of the truth of the matters stated in the proposal, but would only dispute the claim on the ground of fraud So that the defendants cannot now set up as a defence that the statement in this proposal was untrue, unless they add that it was fraudu lently untrue, for they have, in fact, said that they will never make any other defence "); *Wheelton* v *Hardisty* (1857), 8 E & B 232, Exch Ch. (a similar case, where, however, the representee failed to prove that the company's public announcement had come to his notice, and therefore failed to prove that he was a party to the alleged contract), *Hemmings* v *Sceptre Life Association*, [1905] 1 Ch 365 (where the condition was that the policy should not be avoided except for wilful misrepresentation), *Anstey* v *British Natural Premium Life Association* (1908), 99 L T 765 (policy to be indisputable after a certain time, except for fraud) So, where one of the articles of association of a company pro vided that no director should be liable for any loss or damage which might happen in the execution of the duties of his office, or in relation thereto, unless the same should happen through his own dishonesty, it was held that it is " not illegal for a company to engage its directors upon such terms ' *Re Brazilian Rubber Plantations and Estates, Ltd* , [1911] 1 Ch 425 (*per* NEVILLE, J , at p 440) For similar conditions in contracts for the sale of land, see several of the cases cited in note (*f*), *inf*

(*dd*) As in the case of " waiver clauses " in prospectuses of companies see § 562, *post*

(*e*) For such a stipulation is probably void It was a principle of Roman jurisprudence that any promise that a contract should not be impeached for fraud was wholly inefficacious, —see § 688, in App C, *post*,—and there is weighty authority in favour of the existence of such a principle in English law see *S Pearson & Son, Ltd* v *Dublin Corporation* [1907] A C 351, H L, *per* Lord JAMES at p 362 (" as a general principle, I incline to the view that an express term that fraud shall not vitiate the contract would be bad in law "), and Lord ATKINSON at p 365. The foundation of this rule is that the interests of the com munity, and of mercantile morality, imperatively demand it Consequently where no such reasons of public policy exist, as for instance, in the case of an agreement not to attempt to set aside the award of an arbitrator even for fraud or collusion, it has been held that the agreement is enforceable *Tullis* v *Jacson*, [1892] 3 Ch 440

(*f*) The general rule as to the absolute necessity of plain and clear language has been judicially stated over and over again notably by Lord ELDON, L C , at p 655 of *Jenkins* v *Hales* (1802), 6 Ves 646, by ROMILLY, M R , at p 94 of *Bousfield* v *Hodges* (1863), 33 Beav. 90, by FRY, J , at p 136 of *Re Banister* (1879), 12 C. D 131, C A. (" the vendor who means to exclude the purchaser from his common law right to have a good title shown, must do so by explicit and clear words "), by FRY, J , BAGGALLAY, L.J , and COTTON, L J , in *Re Marsh and Earl Granville*, as cited *inf* , in this note, and by BYRNE, J , at pp 669, 670 of *Re Hoedicke and Lipski's Contract*, [1901] 2 Ch 666 Accordingly, whenever the expressions used were not such as (expressly, or by necessary implication) to indicate, or to cover, the fact or class of fact in respect of which the waiver of disclosure was alleged, the party charged has always failed in making good his answer Thus, in cases of contracts between vendor and purchaser, a mere statement that " the title " is, or shall be in certain events, " accepted," or " deemed to be accepted," is not, *per se*, a waiver of the right to disclosure of material facts, known to the party charged (such as incumbrances, unusual restrictions, and the like), of a nature to affect or qualify such title · *Bousfield* v *Hodges*, *sup* (at p. 94 " a purchaser is only bound by his acceptance of the title so far as he is made cognizant of it, and if anything is kept back by the vendor, he is not, as to that, bound by his acceptance "); *Nottingham Patent Brick & Tile Co* v *Butler* (1886), 16 Q B D 778, C A , as to which, see note (*r*) to § 132, *ante* , *Re Cox and Neve's Contract*, [1891] 2 Ch. 109 (*per* NORTH, J , at pp 118, 119,—a case in which there was a condition of sale that the purchaser was to send in his objections and requisitions within 14 days of the delivery of the abstract, and, subject thereto, the title was to be deemed accepted, and all objections and requisitions not sent in within the time limited were to be deemed to have been waived Held that this condition operated as a waiver only in respect of

The party charged must show that he notified in clear and unambiguous terms to the party complaining, not indeed the specific fact which is the

what was revealed in the abstract, when delivered, and was not, as the vendor contended, so expressed as to relieve him of his ordinary duty of disclosure in that abstract, or otherwise, of deeds and covenants restrictive of the user of the premises), *Re Hædicke and Lipski's Contract, sup* (where, in reference to a clause in the contract, stating nakedly that "the vendor's title is accepted by the purchasers," BYRNE, J, held, at p 669, that this was no waiver of the right to disclosure of onerous and unusual covenants in a lease, for "it requires more than a condition couched in such general terms to bind the purchaser to take the title") On the other hand, a covenant, clause, condition, or stipulation, binding the purchaser to accept a conveyance of such right or title as the purchaser may have (*Early v. Garrett* (1829), 9 B & C 928), or to take land "with all risks as to errors" (*Brownlie v Campbell* (1880), 5 App Cas 925, H L), or to take a chattel "with all faults" (*Baglehole v Walters* (1811), 3 Campb 154, *Pickering v Dowson* (1813), 4 Taunt 779, *Schneider v. Heath* (1813), 3 Campb. 506, and *Ward v Hobbs* (1878), 4 App Cas 13, H L), operates as a clear waiver of disclosure of any fault, defect, or circumstance affecting title And it makes no difference, unless some fraudulent device be used, whether the fact of which disclosure is waived is known to the vendor or not see the observations of Lord ELLENBOROUGH, C J., at pp 156, 157 of *Baglehole v Walters, sup.* ("where an article is sold with all faults I think it is quite immaterial how many belonged to it within the knowledge of the seller The very object of introducing such a stipulation is to put the purchaser on his guard, and throw upon him the burden of examining all faults, both secret and apparent," which passage is cited and approved by Lord O'HAGAN, at p 27 of *Ward v Hobbs, sup*), and those of PARKER, J, at pp 530, 531 of *Shepherd v Croft,* [1911] 1 Ch 521 Accordingly, in all the cases last cited, the condition was held a good answer to the complaint of non-disclosure, except in *Schneider v. Heath, sup,* and there the ground of the vendor's failure was, not that the condition was not expressed in terms apt for the purpose, but that he was proved to have been guilty of a fraudulent device of the nature above indicated: see note (s), *inf* The vital distinction between the two types of condition referred to is insisted upon with lucidity and force by LINDLEY, L J, in the passage from his judgment in *Nottingham Patent Brick & Tile Co v. Butler, sup,* which is cited in note (r) to § 132, *ante,* and by BYRNE, J., at p 669 of *Re Hædicke and Lipski's Contract, sup* The double decision in *Re Marsh and Earl Granville* (1882), 24 C D 11, C. A, is an excellent illustration of what an obscurely expressed condition does, and what it does not cover There a clause in the contract provided that the title to the freehold portion of the estate sold should commence with a certain indenture of the year 1845, and that "the earlier title, whether appearing by recital, covenant for production, or otherwise, or not appearing at all, shall not be investigated or objected to" From the abstract of title it appeared that the deed in question, *quoad* the freehold parcels, was without consideration, and that there was power in the grantor to revoke the trusts (including a trust for sale) thereby declared Thereupon the purchaser made two objections, (1) that the deed in question was not a good root of title at all, and (2) that, for aught that appeared, the deed might have been avoided by a subsequent conveyance for value, or might have been revoked pursuant to the above power The vendor relied on the clause referred to as disentitling the purchaser to raise either of these objections It was held that the clause was expressed in terms adequate to show a contract to waive disclosure of such matters as those to which objection (2) related, but not of such as formed the subject of objection (1) · for, so far as regards the suggested waiver of information as to facts affecting the question whether a good root of title had been shown, the condition was not "expressed in clear and explicit terms" (*per* BAGGALLAY, L.J, at p 23), and "the Court will not compel a purchaser to take an estate with less than the ordinary title which the law gives him, unless the stipulation on which the vendor relies is fair and explicit" (*per* COTTON, L.J, at p 24, repeating, in effect, what FRY, J, had said in the Court below— see p 17—"a vendor who desires to limit the rights of a purchaser must do so by explicit and plain conditions") So, in a marine insurance case, *Cantiere Meccanico Brindisino v Janson,* [1912] 3 K. B 452, C A, where the policy, which was on a floating dock in tow of two tugs from Avonmouth to Brindisi, contained the clause "seaworthiness admitted," a nice discrimination was made between the kind of fact which this clause did, and the kind of fact which it did not, waive the disclosure of ; it being held that it operated to relieve the assured from divulging anything in the nature or condition of the dock which would render all floating docks unseaworthy, but not any "peculiar defect not usual in docks of this construction," such as corroded plates, a leak, or an unfavourable report from a surveyor as to its unfitness to go to sea without additional strengthening, and the like

subject of the dispute, for this would be a suicidal absurdity (q), but the class or type of fact of which the party complaining is required to assume the existence, and of which he is to dispense with further evidence (h)   But, though conforming to all requirements of the above nature, any condition purporting to waive disclosure is wholly defeated by proof (the burden of which, however, is in that event transferred to the party complaining) that it was characterized by fraud or dishonesty, or was otherwise misleading, "tricky," "catching," or unfair (i), or, where the party complaining is required to assume, without evidence or information, the existence of a specified fact, by proof that the party charged was aware of the non-existence of that fact, for stipulations of this nature can only have effect where the party charged believes, or at least does not disbelieve, the truth or reality of that which the other party is to take for granted, and is merely seeking to protect himself from difficult and expensive researches in procuring the necessary legal proof (j)   Where, however, the party complaining has not

(per VAUGHAN WILLIAMS, L J , at pp 461–463, MOULTON L.J , at p 467, and BUCKLEY, L.J , at pp 470, 471)   Cp *Hewitt Bros* v. *Wilson* (1914), 30 T L R 619, another marine insurance case, where BAILHACHE, J , was of opinion that the "held covered" clause in a policy (" in the event of any incorrect definition of the interest insured it is agreed to hold the assured covered at a premium, if any, to be arranged ") protects innocently mistaken non disclosure of material elements in the description, but not intentional concealments.

(g) *Re Sandbach and Edmondson's Contract*, [1891] 1 Ch 99, C A , per Lord HALSBURY, L.C., at p. 104, who there points out that if a waiver condition " could only be supported when the specific objection to the title was pointed out," the result would be that " no dealings with the estate would be possible in the future,"—to which it may be added that, as soon as the " specific objection," that is, the fact giving rise to the objection, is pointed out, disclosure is made, and it becomes ludicrous to ask the purchaser to waive information as to that of which, in making the request, the vendor informs him

(h) See § 132, and all the cases and judicial observations cited in notes (q), (r), and (s) thereto, *ante*, where this topic is fully discussed, and it is explained that contracts to waive disclosure are themselves subject to a duty of disclosure to the extent stated in the text.

(i) For illustrations of a waiver condition being defeated by proof of fraud on the part of the party charged, see *Schneider* v *Heath* (1813), 3 Campb 506 (where the plaintiff succeeded, on proof that the defendant had removed the vessel, which was to be taken "with all faults," from the ways in which she lay, and had kept her continuously afloat, so that her keel and bottom were always concealed, until the moment when the plaintiff was given possession of her)   In the following cases, though the fraud alleged was not proved, it was distinctly held that, if it had been proved, the waiver condition which was clearly expressed, and otherwise valid, would have been defeated   *Baglehole* v *Walters* (1811), 3 Campb 154 (per Lord ELLENBOROUGH, C J , in the case of a sale of a vessel " with all faults," at p 157   " unless the seller by positive means renders it impossible for the purchaser to detect secret faults "), *Early* v *Garrett* (1829), 9 B & C 928 (sale of land " with all faults " per PARKE, J , at p 952, " the purchaser cannot recover unless he prove fraud on the part of the seller "), *Ward* v *Hoobs* (1878), 4 App Cas 13, H L , a case of the sale of diseased pigs (where, at p 27, Lord O'HAGAN cites and approves Lord ELLENBOROUGH'S above statement, and concedes that if the defendant had been proved, as he was not—in fact it had not even been so alleged,—" guilty of any contrivance " to conceal or disguise the disease from which the pigs were suffering, the condition as to taking them " with all faults " would have gone for nothing)   The above cases all show that the burden of establishing the fraud which is to defeat an otherwise good waiver condition is shifted on to the shoulders of the party complaining, as soon as the condition itself, and its applicability to the particular undisclosed fact, is proved   As to the misleading, " catching," " tricky," and unfair waiver conditions referred to in the text, see again the citations contained in notes (q), (r), and (s) to § 132, *ante*.

(j) See *Re Banister* (1879), 12 C D 131, C A , where there was a condition that the purchaser was to assume that a certain person was, in the year 1835, entitled in fee simple to the property which was the subject of the sale, and this condition was held to be defeated

been made to assume the existence of any particular fact, or class of facts, but the agreement is to take property "with all faults," or "at all risks," the case is wholly different, and the validity of the condition is in no way affected by the fact that the party charged is aware of a fault or defect the disclosure of which is dispensed with. The reason is plain. In the former type of case, the party charged, in exacting the condition, makes an implied representation that he knows of nothing which negatives the fact required to be assumed, though, since it would be very troublesome to prove it by strict evidence, *and for no other reason*, he must ask the party complaining to relieve him of this obligation, and except on those terms he is not disposed to contract. Accordingly, if he does know of anything negativing the fact required to be assumed, he is guilty of a fraudulent misrepresentation (k). In the other class of case, the implied representation which the party charged makes is of an exactly opposite character. The seller of land or a

by proof that the vendor know that the fact was not what he had required the purchaser to assume that it was, *per* JESSEL, M R , at pp 142, 143 . "it is said, as regards this assumption, that the vendor know well that Esther Bannster was not, in the year 1835, entitled to the entire property in fee simple, and that, knowing that well, he ought not to have put in a condition asking a purchaser to assume that it was true , because it inferentially amounts to a statement that so far as he know anything to the contrary, she was so seised and entitled in fee simple   It appears to me this objection is well founded   I do not think a vendor is entitled to say that the purchaser shall assume that which he knows not to be true   The utmost that can be asked of a purchaser is to assume something of which the vendor knows nothing" To the same effect BRETT, L J , at pp 116–118, who also expressed the view that the condition was an implied representation, which the evidence showed to be inaccurate, though not, in his opinion, designedly so , and COTTON, L J , who, at pp 149, 150, describes the condition as "unfair," and as "misleading " Cp the misrepresentation case of *S Pearson & Son, Ltd v Dublin Corporation*, [1907] A C 351, H L , where it was a term of the contract, which was for the execution of works, that the contractors were to satisfy themselves of the accuracy of the information, drawings, and specifications supplied by the corporation's engineer, and where, on proof that the corporation knew of the inaccuracies complained of, the condition was held no bar to the contractors' claim for damages in an action of deceit (*per* Lord LOREBURN, L.C , at pp 353, 354, Lord HALSBURY, at p 356, Lord ASHBOURNE at pp 359, 360, Lord JAMES at p 362, and Lord ATKINSON at pp 364–366) On the other hand, where the party complaining fails to establish this guilty knowledge on the part of the party charged,—and it is for him to do so, as much as in the cases of fraud cited in the last note,—the condition has always been enforced, as, for instance, in the vendor and purchaser cases of *Nicoll v Chambers* (1852), 11 C B 996, *Cordingley v Cheeseborough* (1862), 3 Giff 496 , 4 De G F & J 379 , *Re Sandbach and Edmondson's Contract*, [1891] 1 Ch 99, C A , where the purchaser was required to assume that a certain person died intestate and without an heir before the year 1870, and where Lord HALSBURY, L C , at p 103, notices that no proof had been given that "the vendor knew that the assumption required to be made was false," which proof was necessary to defeat the condition, and, this being so, the condition was held to be enforceable, since it "was aptly and properly framed to prevent the purchaser insisting on proof of what was then and is now believed to be the fact, but which the vendor is not in a position to establish by legal proof" , *Blaiberg v Keeves*, [1906] 2 Ch 175, where a similar condition was supported, it being stated that the property had been assigned free from rent in 1828, and that the vendor had never paid rent, and that the purchaser was "required to assume that the said rent has been released," and the vendor having, in the particulars of sale, described the property as of freehold tenure (*per* WARRINGTON, J , at p 183   "all that the vendor has done is to describe the property as being held on a particular tenure, which he believed, and reasonably believed, on sufficient grounds, might be the true tenure on which it was held   Then, knowing that he might have a difficulty in proving the fact of freehold tenure, in the proper part of the document, i e the conditions, which show how he is going to establish his title, he throws upon the purchaser the burden of assuming the facts the proof of which might have been difficult ")

(k) See the observations of JESSEL, M R , in *Re Bannster, sup* , cited in the last note

chattel " with all faults " does not ask the purchaser to assume anything in favour of the title or quality of the thing sold : on the contrary, he inferentially declares to him that there are faults, and that he (the seller) may know of them, but will not sell except upon the terms that he is to be free of any duty to disclose any of them, and that the buyer must find them out for himself (*l*). Such a declaration is not rendered even false, much less fraudulent, by the mere fact that he is cognizant of any number of faults or defects in the quality, or blots on the title, of that which he is selling, or by anything short of the use of dishonest manœuvres to cover up, or hide away, any fault or blot of which he has knowledge (*m*) ; and it would be manifestly unjust, on this ground alone, to deprive him of the benefit of a condition, plainly expressed and honestly relied upon, which, to the knowledge of the purchaser, may probably have been the sole consideration for a reduction in the price otherwise obtainable for the property

203. An agreement or undertaking to waive disclosure may, like other agreements, be implied from acts and conduct, or from inaction, as well as expressed in words spoken or written. But, whilst it is by no means easy to establish even an express condition to this effect, the difficulties in the way of inferring such a condition from mere conduct, and still more from mere inaction (*mm*), are well-nigh insuperable, and it may be doubted whether there is any genuine example to be found in the authorities of a successful attempt in this direction Many of the decisions which are cited for this purpose are really cases where presumptive knowledge, judicially misdescribed as waiver of information, has been implied from neglect to inquire as to the matters which ought to have been divulged (*n*). Others are cases of affirmation, which, as will be seen (*o*), stand on a totally different footing from waiver. A third class consists of those decisions in which it has been held that the

(*l*) See the cases and judicial observations cited in the latter part of note (*f*) to this paragraph, *ante*

(*m*) See the cases cited in note (*i*), *ante*

(*mm*) At p 284 of *Selwyn* v *Garfit* (1888), 38 C. D 273, C A , BOWEN, L J , says "delay is not waiver Inaction is not waiver, though it may be evidence of waiver "

(*n*) If the party charged is under a duty of voluntary disclosure, it is obvious that the party complaining cannot be supposed to waive the performance of that duty merely because he asks no questions about the matters to be so communicated, any more than in a case of misrepresentation the representee can be said to have " waived the truth," merely because he abstained from the use of means of knowledge see § 209 of the author's *Law of Actionable Misrepresentation* It is neither incumbent on him, nor for his interest, to do so Indeed, exaggerated activity in such inquiries would, if anything, be more suggestive of, or consistent with, waiver than total abstention from them see note (*s*) to § 204, *post* When it is said, therefore, as it was by Lord MANSFIELD, C J , in *Carter* v *Boehm* (1766), 3 Burr 1905, at pp 1918, 1919—see the passage cited in note (*s*) to § 191, *ante*—that the party complaining " dispenses with the information," in virtue of his omission to put questions, all that is really meant by this somewhat loose expression is that he has presumptive knowledge, and that therefore the party charged has no private or exclusive knowledge, of the fact, and so need not disclose it, but *not* that, on the assumption of a duty to disclose (and this assumption must be made, for otherwise there is no occasion for this, or any, affirmative answer), abstention from inquiry would constitute or indicate an absolution from that duty It was vainly urged in *Laing* v *Union Marine Insurance Co* (1895), 1 Comm Cas 11, that conduct of this kind amounted to an implied waiver (*per* MATHEW, J , at p 16) and so also in *Thames & Mersey Marine Insurance Co* v. *Gunford Ship Co* , [1911] A C 529, H L (*per* Lord ALVERSTONE, at p 538)

(*o*) See Sub s (2), *post*

neglect to ask a question as to the alleged undisclosed fact, there being no duty to disclose, is fatal to the case of the party complaining ; but these are not cases of an implied waiver of the right to disclosure, because *ex hypothesi* no such right exists, but of an omission to do that which alone would create such a right, or rather a right to a truthful answer (*p*).

204. The kind of conduct from which in these cases waiver is vainly sought to be implied is negative   It is suggested, first, that inaction means indifference, and, secondly, that indifference amounts to waiver ; neither suggestion, as above pointed out, having any substance or foundation   There is, however, another type of case in which from an exactly contrary state of things the same inference is attempted to be deduced   It is sometimes contended that by active inquiries as to particular matters the party complaining has assumed the burden and responsibility of finding out for himself all that he desires to know, and has in this manner relieved the party charged of his common law duty of disclosure, either entirely, or at all events as to all facts outside the range of the specific investigation (*q*).   Such a contention, raised in this extreme form, is of course grotesque, and has never prevailed (*r*)   But, confined within more moderate limits, the argument may, in certain cases, present a more attractive and plausible appearance: for instance, if its application is restricted to the precise matters which form the subject of the express inquiries, where the answers to those inquiries are made the basis of the contract, as in most of the life insurance cases : for, under such conditions, it has been said that " the insurance office may, by requisitions of a specific sort which it makes of the proposer, relieve him partially from the obligation to disclose by an election to make inquiries as to certain facts

(*p*) This class of case is examined closely in §§ 159–162, *ante*   See also *Carter* v *Boehm*, *sup*

(*q*) The suggestion in the one case is that the party's inordinate and unsolicited diligence points to a total indifference to the acquisition of information from the other side, and a fixed intention to distrust it, if tendered, whatever it may be   In the other case, the argument is that, on the *expressio unius exclusio alterius* principle, his active investigation in certain directions implies absolute indifference to disclosure in all others

(*r*) As in *Maynard* v *Rhodes* (1824), 5 Dowl & Ry 266 , 27 R R 526 (where, in an action on a policy of life insurance, one of the points raised by the plaintiff who was charged with the non disclosure was that the defendant insurers had made such inquiries as they thought necessary, and " took upon themselves the burden " of investigating and ascertaining the facts, and both ABBOTT, C J , at the trial, and the Court of K B , on appeal, thought the contention a hopeless one), and again in *Everett* v *Desborough* (1829), 5 Bing 503 (another life policy case, in which the plaintiff before the Court of C P —see Serj WILDE's argument at p 510—raised the same point, and with the same result . *per* PARK, J , at p 519, and GASELEE, J , at pp 520, 521, who there point out that it should have been alleged and proved that the insurance company had dispensed with some specified condition of the policy, but that, so far from this being proved, it had not even been so averred in the declaration, which is set out at p 506)   The above were cases in which it was urged that a *total* waiver was to be implied from the conduct of the party complaining   In this form the contention does not seem to have been raised since 1829, but it has been from time to time suggested that a dispensation from disclosure as to the matters not specifically inquired into might be inferred,—a suggestion which, though not quite so ludicrous as the other, is equally vain   Indeed, even in the case of an express waiver, the corresponding contention has been held to be untenable   see the citation from *Cantiere Meccanico Brindisino* v *Janson*, [1912] 3 K B 452, C A , at the end of note (*f*) to § 202, *ante*

material to the risk to be incurred, against itself" (s). This, however, is only put as a possibility : that is to say, the whole circumstances of the case may be such as to show that the specific requisitions were intended by the parties to operate as a waiver or dispensation : and, even if such an intention be proved, the relief is only " partial," i.e confined to the particular matters which form the subject of the express inquiries

205. It is to be observed that, as in the case of any other contract or condition, it must be shown that the alleged contract or condition to waive disclosure was assented to by both parties It is not enough for the party charged to show that the party complaining proposed the waiver : he must establish that he himself accepted and relied upon that proposal In ordinary cases no difficulty arises on this score, because the condition which is suggested to constitute the waiver is contained in the contract which is sought to be set aside or treated as void, and the parties to the contract are therefore also parties to the condition : but, where the alleged proposal to waive is said to be contained in some instrument or document other than that which is sought to be avoided, the party charged must show that the proposal was addressed to himself, or to the public or a class of which he was a member, and that he acted upon it otherwise he proves no concluded agreement to waive, and his plea or answer accordingly fails(t) In this connexion, it is worth while to notice that, where an express waiver condition is relied upon, it is more likely to be established if it appears in the kind of instrument, or in that part of the instrument, in which such a condition would naturally be found, than if it is shown to have been inserted in some document, or part of a document, which is not the usual or normal place for it (u)

206. There may be on the part of the party complaining a waiver, not of his right to disclosure (which is the class of waiver hitherto discussed), but of his right to some specified form of relief in respect of non-disclosure. If the party charged can, for instance, show that the party complaining has undertaken not to exercise his right to avoid the contract by rescission or analogous proceedings, with or without the reservation of a substituted

(s) Per VAUGHAN WILLIAMS, L J , at p. 878 of *Joel v. Law Union & Crown Insurance Co*, [1908] 2 K B 863, C A

(t) In *Wheelton v Hardisty* (1857), 8 E & B 232, Exch Ch , a life insurance case, the plaintiff in his replication relied upon a public announcement by the company that no policy would be disputed except for fraud , but, though he proved the announcement, he failed to prove that it had come to his notice before the execution of the policy, and his attempted answer to the defendant's plea was accordingly held bad The replication here was in the same form as that in *Wood v Dwarris* (1856), 11 Exch 593 (which averred the issue by the insurance company of a prospectus containing a similar undertaking, and that the plaintiff had notice of it, and relied upon it) and was held good on demurrer, but, here again, the facts were not proved.

(u) See *Blaiberg v Keeves*, [1906] 2 Ch 165, where WARRINGTON, J , in a vendor and purchaser case, points out at p 184 that " it is not the function of the particulars to deal with title at all , that has to be dealt with on evidence, and it is the function of the conditions to say what evidence of title the purchaser is to have," or, in other words, what disclosure of facts relating to title the purchaser is to waive Conversely, descriptive matter should be in the particulars, and not in the conditions *per* MALINS, V C , at pp 131, 132, of *Torrance v. Bolton* (1872), L. R. 14 Eq. 124, who also strongly reprobated a suggested custom to the contrary.

right to pecuniary compensation, it is obvious that he has a *primâ facie* affirmative answer to any case of non-disclosure which may be made against him, whether in proceedings to obtain an annulment of the contract, or by way of defence to an action upon it (v). Here, in contrast with an agreement to waive disclosure, which may, in theory at all events, be implied from acts and conduct, as well as expressed in terms (w), the undertaking relied upon must be found, if at all, in the contract itself. The party charged must be in a position to point to some clause or condition in which the renunciation of the particular form of relief is expressly declared The question usually arises in contracts for the sale of land, a common condition of which is that the sale shall not be vitiated or annulled for any omission or error in the particulars of sale, but shall be the subject of compensation, abatement, or allowance, as the case may be, in money, and of that alone, or, in some cases, shall neither be avoided nor be the subject of compensation Where such a condition forms part of the bargain between the parties, the party charged is entitled to succeed (x), unless the party complaining, on whom the burden of proof thereupon rests, can bring the case within one or other of the two recognized exceptions to the rule.

207. These two exceptions are the outcome of the principles of interpretation applied by the Courts to clauses and conditions of the character in question. It has been found necessary to put some reasonable limitation upon the generality of the expressions, " error," " mistake," " omissions," " defects," and the like. In the first place, a deliberate and fraudulent concealment or misdescription has been held not to come within the protection of such a term or condition in the contract, the " errors " and " omissions " therein referred to being confined to such non-disclosure and misdescription as is purely innocent and accidental : secondly, all non-disclosure or misdescription which produces *error in substantialibus* is equally deemed to be outside the limits of what is covered by the expressions mentioned (y) In accordance with these rules, the waiver condition has

---

(v) There may be a similar waiver of the right to rescind the contract, or to treat it as void, on the ground of misrepresentation, or, indeed, upon any ground which would render a contract voidable For the purposes of this type of waiver, it is immaterial what is the invalidating cause The misrepresentation cases are, therefore, as much in point here as the non disclosure cases, and are accordingly cited in the ensuing notes.

(w) See §§ 203, 204, *sup*

(x) The waiver was established, and the party charged succeeded in resisting on this ground proceedings for rescission or analogous relief, and in limiting his liability to pecuniary compensation, in *Leslie* v *Thompson* (1851), 9 Hare 268 , *Nicoll* v *Chambers* (1852), 11 C B 996 (*per* JERVIS, C J , at p 1010), *Whittemore* v *Whittemore* (1869), L R 8 Eq 603, 605, 606 , *Debenham* v *Sawbridge*, [1901] 2 Ch 98 In the following cases the waiver, being proved, operated as a good answer to an affirmative objection or defence *White* v *Cudden* (1842), 8 Cl. & Fin. 766 , *Ayles* v *Cox* (1852), 16 Beav. 23 , *Price* v *Macaulay* (1852), 2 De G M & G 339 (where the condition relied upon by the plaintiff was held sufficient to defeat the defence as to one of the two lots therein question, but not as to the other) , *Re Fawcett and Holmes* (1889), 42 C D 150, C A , *Re Brewer and Hankin's Contract* (1899), 80 L. T 127, C A. It should be noted that, if the case is not brought within either of the two exceptions, the mere fact that the party charged had knowledge of the undisclosed fact does not render the condition inoperative . see note (*f*) to § 202, *ante*

(y) See, for a statement of both these exceptions, the judgment of the Court of C P

always been inefficacious as an answer to a proved case of non-disclosure or misrepresentation, and the contract has been rescinded or treated as void notwithstanding the condition, whenever fraud, or a wilful and calculated, as distinguished from an accidental and mistaken, omission has been established (z) Also, where the thing tendered in discharge of the contract materially differs in quality, character, substance, or title, from that which it was impliedly by non-disclosure, represented to be (a), or, if it is a case of express misrepresentation, " where the misdescription . . . is in a material or substantial point, so far affecting the subject-matter of the contract that it may reasonably be supposed that, but for such misdescription, the purchaser might never have entered into the contract at all, in such case the contract is avoided altogether, and the purchaser is not bound to resort to the clause of compensation " (b) This does not mean that the " material and substantial point " referred to must necessarily be a question of figures (c)

in *Flight* v *Booth* (1834), 1 Bing N C 370 (at pp 366, 367), *Re Terry and White's Contract* (1886), 32 C D 14, C. A (*per* Lord Esher, M R , at p 22, and Lindley, L J , at pp. 28–30), *Debenham* v *Sawbridge*, [1901] 2 Ch 98 (*per* Byrne, J , at p 109)

(z) As it was in *Dimmock* v *Hallett* (1866), 2 Ch App. 21, where the vendor had wilfully, and against good faith, though without express fraudulent intent, suppressed the fact that each of the tenants of certain farms forming part of the property had given notice to quit, and was therefore not allowed to take advantage of the condition, as against the purchaser who was seeking—it being a case of sale by direction of the Court—to be discharged from his contract (*per* Turner, L.J , at pp 26–29, and Cairns, L.J , at pp 30, 31) , *Nottingham Patent Brick & Tile Co* v *Butler* (1886), 16 Q B D 778, C A , where the purchaser sued for the return of his deposit on the ground of non-disclosure of certain restrictive covenants, and the vendor relied upon a very stringent waiver condition, which, however, was held wholly inoperative, on proof that the non disclosure amounted to a grossly fraudulent suppression (*per* Lord Esher, M R , at pp 787, 788, Lindley, L.J , at p. 790, and Lopes, L.J , at p 791), apart from the additional ground that the condition was not framed in sufficiently clear and explicit terms to bind the purchaser, as to which see note (r) to § 132, *ante*

(a) As in *Flight* v *Booth, sup* (*per Cur* , at pp. 377, 378), where the purchaser, on this ground, was held entitled to a return of the deposit, notwithstanding the condition pleaded by the vendor ; *Dobell* v *Hutchinson* (1835), 3 A & E 355 (a similar case) , *Madeley* v *Booth* (1849), 2 De G & Sm 718, a very strong case, but which, though depreciated by Jessel, M R , at pp 760, 761 of *Camberwell and South London Building Society* v *Holloway* (1879), 13 C D 754, met afterwards with the approval of Bowen, L J , who, at p 115 of *Re Beyfus and Masters's Contract* (1888), 39 C D 110, C A , expressed disagreement with the adverse criticism of Jessel, M R , *Stanton* v *Tattersall* (1853), 1 Sm & G 529 , *Re Davis and Cavey* (1888), 40 C D 601 (*per* Stirling, L J , at pp 608, 609), *Re Cox and Neve's Contract*, [1891] 2 Ch 109 (*per* North, J , at pp 119, 120) , *Jacobs* v *Revell*, [1900] 2 Ch 858 In all the above, the purchaser was the *actor*, either in a suit for rescission, or in an action for the return of the deposit, or in an application under the Vendor and Purchaser Act, 1874 In *Shackleton* v *Sutcliffe* (1847), 1 De G & Sm 609 (*per* Knight-Bruce, V -C., at pp 619–623), and *Re Puckett and Smith's Contract*, [1902] 2 Ch 258, C A , the purchaser was resisting the vendor's proceedings on the ground of non disclosure or misrepresentation, to which the vendor set up the condition, and the purchaser thereupon made good his right to have the condition ignored on the ground of discrepancy in quality and substance So also in *Price* v *Macaulay* (1852), 2 De G M & G 339 (*per* Knight-Bruce, L J , at pp 345–347, as to one of the lots therein question, but not as to the other, where the essential discrepancy was not made out, nor any fraud *per* Knight-Bruce, L.J , at p. 344) Cp *Portman* v *Mill* (1826), 2 Russ. 570, *per* Lord Eldon, L.C , at pp 574, 575

(b) *Flight* v *Booth, sup* , at p. 377
(c) *Re Terry and White's Contract* (1886), 32 C D 14, C A (*per* Lindley, L.J , at p 28), *Re Fawcett and Holmes* (1889), 42 C D 150, C A (*per* Lord Esher, M R , at p 156), *Jacobs* v *Revell, sup* , *per* Buckley, J , at p 865

The party complaining, if able to establish that he would not have entered into the contract at all but for the suppression or misdescription, is entitled to insist that the condition be ignored, though the difference in mere pecuniary value may be problematical, or even demonstrably insignificant (d). Conversely, where it is a question of compensation only, the question of difference in character is immaterial (e).

208. A much more stringent form of waiver of relief, as has already been hinted, is occasionally to be found in conditions of sale whereby it is stipulated that any error or omission shall neither vitiate the sale, nor be a ground for compensation. This type of condition is almost, but not quite, an agreement not to set up non-disclosure for the purpose of disputing or impeaching the sale in any form of proceeding whatever (f), which is much the same thing, or at least has much the same effect, as a total waiver of the right to disclosure (g). To any such case the same rule, with the same two exceptions, applies *mutatis mutandis*. That is to say, where the case is within the rule, and not within either of the exceptions, the condition is a bar to any form of relief which necessarily involves the annulment of the contract, or the treatment of it as a nullity, or the payment or allowance of pecuniary compensation (h). Where, however, the party complaining can establish either fraud, or *error in substantialibus*, he is entitled to rescission or analogous relief, no

(d) See *Flight* v *Booth*, *sup*, at pp 378, 379, *Madeley* v *Booth*, *sup*, where the difference in value between the residue of the term, as described, and an underlease for such residue, less three days, had actually been assessed by the arbitrator at the nominal figure of five shillings, and yet the difference in character between the two interests was held by KNIGHT BRUCE, V C, to be sufficiently vital to justify a disregard of the condition, and a decision that the purchaser was entitled to a return of the deposit, as well as to maintain his defence to the vendor's action for specific performance

(e) See *White* v *Cuddon* (1842), 8 Cl & Fin 766 (*per* Lord BROUGHAM, at pp 785, 786, and Lord COTTENHAM, at p 792), *Cordingley* v *Cheeseborough* (1852), 3 Giff 496, 4 De G J & F 379, *Re Leyland and Taylor's Contract*, [1900] 2 Ch 625 (at pp 630–632), *Shepherd* v *Croft*, [1911] 1 Ch 521 (*per* PARKER, J, at p 529)

(f) It is not quite a waiver of all remedies for instance, it would not debar the party complaining from setting up the non-disclosure as an answer to a claim for specific performance which, being a peculiar and discretionary form of relief,—see § 245, *post*,—may be refused notwithstanding the validity of the agreement. This was pointed out by PARKER, J, at p 531 of *Shepherd* v *Croft*, *sup*

(g) As to the class of case (mainly life insurance) in which the party complaining agrees not to dispute or question a policy on any ground other than fraud, see § 202, and notes (c) and (d) thereto, *ante*

(h) In the following cases, a double-barrelled condition of the nature in question was successfully set up by the party charged, and the party complaining failed in his attempt to bring the case within either of the two exceptions *Re Terry and White's Contract* (1886), 32 C D 14, C A, *Re Simpson and Thomas Moy, Ltd* (1909), 53 Sol J 376, *Shepherd* v *Croft*, *sup* In *Whittemore* v *Whittemore* (1869), L R 8 Eq 603, there were two conditions, one of the ordinary type, and the other in the more stringent form as to the former, MALINS, V -C—see note (x) to § 206, *ante*—held that it was a bar to rescission, and that, *under this condition*, the purchaser was entitled only to the alternative remedy of compensation It was then objected that, *having regard to the other condition*, he was not entitled to compensation either but the Vice Chancellor held that this latter was not enforceable against the purchaser, because of the vendor's " reckless and careless statements,"—a hopelessly illogical decision, for if the " recklessness " amounted to fraud, the first condition was as much invalidated as the second, if it did not, the second was as little invalidated as the first. This seems to have been the opinion of Lord ESHER, M R, judging from his observations on this case at pp 26, 27 of *Re Terry and White's Contract*, *sup*

less than if the condition had been in the more usual form (*t*). It should also be remembered that "it is obviously easier to arrive at the conclusion that the purchaser shall be compellable to take the land, and have money for the deficiency, than that he is to take less than he bargained for, and have no compensation" (*j*).

Sub-s. (2) *Affirmation of the Contract*

209. The second answer to a case of non-disclosure which is available to the party charged is of a totally different nature to that just discussed, which depends on some stipulation prior to, or forming part of, the contract itself ; whereas "affirmation" is concerned solely with the conduct of the party complaining after the contract, and after it has become voidable   In either case it must be assumed that non-disclosure has been established, but in the one case the party charged undertakes to show that the party complaining has agreed beforehand to surrender all or some of the rights which he would otherwise have had in respect of the non-disclosure . in the other, he sets out to prove that, though there was no such condition of waiver in the first instance, and though, therefore, the party complaining, on discovery of the undisclosed facts, became entitled to avoid the contract or to adhere to it, he has, since he became so entitled, deliberately chosen to adhere to it.

210. As will be shown hereafter, in discussing the nature and conditions of relief in respect of non-disclosure (*k*), the right of the party complaining is the right to choose whether he will affirm or disaffirm the contract during the negotiation for which the fact in question was withheld from him, and this option, when once exercised, is exhausted, so that he can never afterwards resile from it   It follows that if, with full and exact knowledge of all the facts which gave him a title to avoid the contract (*l*), the party complaining can be shown to have definitely and unequivocally elected to affirm it, the party charged has a valid answer to any case of non-disclosure set up against him, whether in proceedings for rescission or analogous relief, or by way of defence to an action on the contract.

211. It is incumbent on the party charged to make out two things ·
first, language, or acts and conduct, amounting to a clear and unequivocal election to affirm   secondly, that the party complaining had precise cognizance

<hr>

(*t*) See *Nottingham Patent Brick & Tile Co* v *Butler*, cited in note (z) to § 207, *ante*, where fraud was proved , and the following, in which substantial discrepancy was established   *Portman* v. *Mill* (1826), 2 Russ 570 , *Re Davis and Cavey* (1888), 40 C D 601 , *Jacobs* v. *Revell*, [1900] 2 Ch 858 ; *Re Puckett and Smith's Contract*, [1902] 2 Ch 258, C A (*per* STIRLING, L.J , at p 265)   In all the above, the "double condition" was disregarded, and the purchaser was held entitled to rescission, or to a return of his deposit, or to a declaration in his favour on an application under the Vendor and Purchaser Act, 1874
(*j*) *Per* BUCKLEY, J , at p 864 of *Jacobs* v *Revell*, *sup*
(*k*) See §§ 225, 226, *post*
(*l*) Whether the contract is sought to be avoided on the ground of non disclosure, or misrepresentation, or for any other cause   Obviously questions as to the affirmance or repudiation of a voidable contract are entirely independent of the particular ground on which that contract has become voidable   Accordingly, the rules stated in this Subsection will be illustrated by references to misrepresentation cases as well as strictly non-disclosure decisions

of the full extent of the non-disclosure in respect of which his alleged election was exercised.

212. The election may be indicated not only by express and direct language, but also by acts and conduct (*m*). In either case, however, it must be shown that the words used, or the acts and conduct, as the case may be, were inconsistent with any attitude of mind except that of a deliberate intention to adhere to the contract, or at all events were more consistent with such an intention than with an intention to repudiate it (*n*). Where this is not established, the party charged fails (*o*). It is idle to point to indecisive or equivocal acts or language which may evince no more than a state of doubt, suspicion, or suspended judgment; in that case the party charged proves, not an election, but an abstention from election, which not only does not support his plea, but negatives it (*p*).

213. Further, the party charged, though proving conduct on the part of the party complaining which *primâ facie* would amount to affirmation, must be prepared to show, if challenged on this point, that the party complaining had complete knowledge of all the material undisclosed facts, and not merely such a partial knowledge of some of them as might, perhaps, be sufficient to engender a suspicion as to the whole. This is only an application of the general principle of jurisprudence—a principle by no means confined to the present, or to any particular, subject-matter—that there can be no election where there is no precise cognizance of the facts, including the rights arising out of those facts, upon which the election is supposed to have operated, and from which alone it could have derived vitality and significance. This principle has been applied to cases of release and surrender

(*m*) Com Dig Election, C 1, *Clough* v *London & Northwestern Railway Co* (1871), L R 7 Exch 26, Exch Ch, *per Cur*, at p 34

(*n*) In the case of contracts for the sale of goods, this is the rule expressed in s 35 of the Sale of Goods Act, 1893

(*o*) Thus, where an agreement to affirm the contract is set up, a proposal and acceptance must be shown, and it is not enough to prove the proposal, followed by the silence of the other party *Russell* v *Thornton* (1859), 4 H & N 788 (a marine insurance case, where the assured contended in vain that a mere unaccepted and unanswered proposal by the underwriters to insure the vessel again after she had been surveyed and repaired was an affirmation *per* BRAMWELL, B, at pp 797-800, WATSON, B, at pp 801, 802, CHANNELL, B, at pp 803, 804) So in *Morrison* v *Universal Marine Insurance Co* (1873), L R 8 Exch 197, Exch Ch, also a marine insurance case, the Exchequer Chamber, reversing the Court of Exchequer, held that the issuing by the underwriters of the policy after knowledge of the undisclosed fact was not an unequivocal election to treat the contract as subsisting, the knowledge not having come to the underwriters before the initialling of the slip, since this was the usual course for underwriters to take in order to enable the assured to sue, and the act in question was at least as consistent with their intention to adopt that usual course as with an intention to affirm the insurance there was no conclusive election in law, and the verdict of the jury that there had been no such election in fact was one which it was competent for them to return, and could not be disturbed (*per Cur*, at pp 203-207) For illustrations of acts and conduct held or found not to amount to a positive and clear exercise of an election to affirm, or to have amounted, on the contrary, to clear exercise of an election to disaffirm, see the following misrepresentation cases *Wontner* v. *Shairp* (1847), 4 C B 404, *Clough* v. *London & Northwestern Railway Co*, *sup* (at pp 33-35), *Torrance* v *Bolton* (1872) 8 Ch App 118 (*per* JAMES, L J, at p 124), *Re Metropolitan Coal Consumers Association, Ex p. Edwards* (1891), 64 L T 651, *Re Same, Karberg's Case*, [1892] 3 Ch 1.

(*p*) See §§ 216-218, *post*.

of property and rights (q), and to cases of affirmation of contracts voidable for misrepresentation (r), or of impeachable transactions generally (s), as well as to cases of affirmation of contracts voidable on the ground of non-disclosure (t).

214. Where, however, the acts and conduct relied upon indicate with reasonable clearness a definite and unequivocal election on the part of the party complaining to affirm the contract, founded on an adequate knowledge of the material undisclosed facts, the party charged establishes a valid answer to any case of non-disclosure made against him (u).

215. It follows from what has been already said that the affirmation of a contract after discovery of one of two separate and distinct undisclosed

(q) *Leeds (Duke)* v. *Amherst (Earl)* (1846), 2 Ph 117 (per Lord COTTENHAM, L.C., at p 123 "for that purpose"—ι e to establish a case of release—"it is not only necessary to show that the plaintiff knew of the acts of waste having been committed, but that he knew of the rights which they gave him . and that, having such knowledge, he did some act amounting to a release of that right"), *Wilson* v *Thornbury* (1875), 10 Ch App. 239 (per JAMES, L J, at p 248, 'election by conduct must be by a person who has positive information as to his rights to the property, and, with that knowledge, rea'y means to give that property up," and MELLISH, L J, at p 249 "we have to see whether the plaintiff knew what his rights were, and what the material facts on which they depended were, and whether, knowing them, he determined to elect" . . . &c.) And see § 132, ante

(r) For illustrations of cases where the representor failed to make out his plea, because he failed to establish complete knowledge on the part of the representee, see *Jarrett* v *Kennedy* (1848), 6 C. B 319, 326, *Lachlan* v. *Reynolds* (1853), Kay 52, 101 R R. 523; *Clough* v *London & Northwestern Railway Co* (1871), L R 7 Exch 26, Ex Ch (per Cur., at pp 29, 30, 31), *Wakefield* v *Normanton Local Board* (1881), 44 L T 697, C A On the other hand, the representor proved the complete knowledge of the representee, and accordingly established his plea of affirmation, in *Ogilvie* v *Currie* (1868), 37 L. J (ch) 541, and in *Sharpley* v *Louth & East Coast Railway Co* (1876), 2 C D 663 C A (per JAMES, L J, at p. 685 "the plaintiff, after he knew what the company had done, what it was doing, and what it was able to do for months continued to act as a shareholder, with full knowledge of every circumstance which entitled him, if he ever was so entitled, to be relieved from his shares")

(s) *Murray* v *Palmer* (1805), 2 Sch & Lefr 472, per Lord REDESDALE, L.C (Ir), at p 485

(t) See *Maddeford* v *Austwick* (1826), 1 Sim 89 (per LEACH, V C, at p 96), *Clements* v *Hall* (1858), 2 De G & J 173 (per Lord CRANWORTH, L C, at pp 187, 188)

(u) As in *Armstrong* v *Turquand* (1857), 9 Ir C L R 32 (a life insurance case, where to a plea of fraudulent concealment the plaintiff pleaded a replication that the company, after knowledge of the concealed fact accepted a further premium, and thereby affirmed the contract of insurance, and, on demurrer, the replication was held good) The question, however, arises most frequently in cases of contracts voidable for misrepresentation, particularly contracts to take shares in companies, in the following of which the representor proved a clear affirmation, in virtue of acts and conduct, by the representee, with full knowledge of the truth —*Campbell* v *Fleming* (1834), 1 A & E 40, *Pulsford* v. *Richards* (1853), 17 Beav 87, *Re Royal British Bank, Mixer's Case* (1859), 4 De G & J 575, 586, 587, *Re Hop and Malt Exchange Warehouse Co, Briggs' Case* (1866), L R 1 Eq 483, 487, *Re Cachar Co, Lawrence's Case* (1867), 2 Ch App 412, 423, 424, *Re Russian (Vyksounsky) Ironworks Co, Kincaids Case* (1867), 2 Ch App 420, 426, 427, *Re Same, Whitehouse's Case* (1867), L R 3 Eq 790, *Re Same, Taite's Case* (1867), L R 3 Eq 795, *Scholey* v *Central Railway Co of Venezuela* (1868), L. R 8 Eq 266 n, 267 n, *Ogilvie* v *Currie, sup*, *Re Bank of Hindustan, China, and Japan, Campbell's and Hippisley's Cases* (1872), 9 Ch App 7, *Sharpley* v *Louth & East Coast Railway Co, sup*, *Cargill* v *Bower* (1878), 10 C D 502, 508, 509, *Re Wheal Unity Wood Mining Co, Chynoweth's Case* (1880), 15 C D 13, C A., *Reid* v *London and Staffordshire Fire Insurance Co* (1883), 63 L J (ch) 351, *Re Dunlop Truffault Cycle and Tube Manufacturing Co, Ex p Shearman* (1896), 66 L J (ch) 25, *Re Metal Constituents, Ltd, Lord Lurgan's Case*, [1902] 1 Ch 707; *Seddon* v. *North Eastern Salt Co*, [1905] 1 Ch 326, *Hemmings* v *Sceptre Life Association*, [1905] 1 Ch 365, 369, 370, *United Shoe Machinery Co of Canada* v *Brunet*, [1909] A C 330, 339, P C., *Re Christineville Rubber Estates, Ltd* (1911), 81 L J (ch) 63.

facts, is no bar to the right of the party complaining to avoid the contract on discovery of the other (v).

Sub-s (3). *Matters which, per se, constitute no Answer to the Case of the Party Complaining.*

216. Delay, laches, and acquiescence are constantly referred to in connection with contracts which have become voidable, whether by reason of non-disclosure, misrepresentation, or other cause (w), in such terms as to imply that, of themselves, they constitute a bar to the right to avoid any such contract This is quite a mistake. And it is a still graver mistake to use these expressions (as the term " laches " in particular is frequently used) with an underlying suggestion that the party entitled to avoid the contract owes a duty to the party whose conduct has rendered it voidable, the failure to discharge which renders him " guilty " of a wrong, and creates a personal equity against him, apart from anything else. The truth is that, in this, as in every case where a contract is rendered, not void, but voidable by the acts or omissions of one of the parties (x), the only legal result which can flow from the inaction or delay of the party complaining in availing himself of the remedies open to him is either to furnish evidence, with other facts, tending to negative some element in his burden of proof, such as the fact of non-disclosure, or the fact of his own ignorance (if either of these is in serious dispute), or to support a plea of waiver or affirmation raised by the party charged , or else to give scope and opportunity for the intervention of the *jus tertii*, or for the alteration of the character of the subject-matter of the contract in such a way as to enable the party charged to insist that on this ground one of the essential conditions of avoidance has disappeared But where the inaction, for however long a period, is not sufficient to constitute such evidence, or where, notwithstanding the lapse of time, no innocent person has in fact acquired rights or interests under the contract, and the property (if it is a case of sale) to be restored as the condition of rescission can be so restored in the same plight as that in which it was received, the delay, laches, or

---

(v) There is no direct authority for this proposition as applied to non disclosure, but, in relation to a contract voidable for misrepresentation, it has been held that, where the representee has affirmed the contract on discovering the falsity of one of two separate and distinct representations, though made in one and the same document, or at one and the same time, he may still sue for rescission on discovery of the falsity of the other representation *Re London and Provincial Electric Lighting and Power Co , Ex p. Hale* (1887), 55 L T. 670 But where only one misrepresentation is complained of, which is false in two or more particulars, the representee who has affirmed the contract with knowledge of one of such discrepancies is precluded from afterwards obtaining rescission on discovery of a fresh point of falsity in the same representation *Campbell v Fleming* (1834), 1 A & E 40 , *Re Russian (Vyksounsky) Ironworks Co , Whitehouse's Case* (1867), L. R. 3 Eq 790. The same principles would, without doubt, be applied, *mutatis mutandis*, to cases of non-disclosure

(w) Here again, for the purposes of this, as well as the two preceding Sub sections, the ground of the voidability of the contract being quite immaterial, misrepresentation cases are in point, and will be cited in the following notes

(x) Which is the position in cases of non disclosure . see §§ 225, 226, *post.*

so called acquiescence, go for nothing,—which is tantamount to saying that, per se, these matters constitute no answer (xx).

217. To take first the expressions "delay" and "laches," which in substance mean the same thing "Delay" indicates, either (like the French délai) the mere lapse of time, in which sense it is obviously ridiculous to impute it to any one as a fault, or an omission or neglect to avoid the contract within a reasonable time (and this is what the expression "laches" also means), which again cannot properly be described as a default on the part of him who so omits or neglects unless it can be shown (which it cannot) that he was under any duty to the other party in that respect The party complaining is neither punished for, nor prejudiced by, delay in itself ; though he may be seriously prejudiced by the rights which, during his inertia and supineness, he has allowed third parties to acquire against him "I take it to be a settled doctrine of equity," said JESSEL, M R (y), "not only as regards specific performance, but also as regards rescission, that this"—i e delay— "is not an answer, unless there is such delay as constitutes a defence under the Statute of Limitations That, of course, is quite a different thing" And the period during which the lapse of time counts against the party complaining does not even begin to run until the right of election accrues, that is, until he has knowledge of all the facts giving him that right (z) , and then only in the sense, and to the extent already indicated Indeed, if he asserts himself before he has acquired such complete knowledge, he may be exposed to the opposite objection that he is striking too soon (a) There may be cases, however, where, after full consciousness of all such rights as he ever had, the party's passivity was so pronounced and prolonged as to lend colour to the suggestion that from the first he never had any such rights as he pretends to have had, and that he was not ignorant of the facts which he alleges were suppressed or misrepresented (b), or that

(xx) See the observations of KNIGHT-BRUCE, V C, at p 579 of *Gibson* v *D'Este,* inf.

(y) At p 13 of *Redgrave* v *Hurd* (1881), 20 C D 1, C A This is what Lord DAVEY meant when he said that delay or *mora* is not a plea in law see the passage cited in note (m) to § 218, *post*

(z) *Clements* v *Hall* (1858), 2 De G & J 173 (*per* Lord CRANWORTH, L C, at pp 187, 188) , *Rawlins* v. *Wickham* (1858), 3 De G & J 304 (*per* KNIGHT BRUCE, L J , at p 314, and TURNER, L J , at pp 318–321) , *Lindsay Petroleum Co* v *Hurd* (1874), L R 5 P C 221, at p 241 ("in order that the remedy should be lost by laches or delay, . . . it is necessary that there should be sufficient knowledge of the facts constituting the title to relief") Cp the observation of TURNER, L J , as to acquiescence, at p 74 of *Life Association of Scotland* v *Siddall* (1861), 3 De G F & J 58, which is cited in note (q) to § 219, *post*.

(a) An objection of this sort was raised, though unsuccessfully (see the judgment of GRANT, M R , at p 318) in *Edwards* v *M'Leay* (1815), G Cooper 318, it being suggested that the plaintiff's action was premature, since he brought it before he knew that he would ever be evicted from the premises which were the subject of the contract sought to be rescinded on the ground of non disclosure of the fact that such eviction was legally possible. This case, and the danger of premature, no less than of belated action, is alluded to by KNIGHT BRUCE, V -C., at p 578 of *Gibson* v *D'Este* (1843), 2 Y & C (CH.) 542, as to which authority see Sect. 8, Sub s. (2), *post*, for a detailed discussion In that case the V.-C , held that the plaintiff had neither come too early (p 578), nor too late (p. 579)

(b) See Sect 3, Sub s (5), of this Chapter, *ante*

he agreed to waive disclosure (c), or that, without having so agreed in the
first instance, he afterwards deliberately elected to affirm the contract which,
if so minded, he might have avoided (d) . or again, the delay, without furnish-
ing, or contributing to, evidence of anything, may give "room and verge"
for the intervention of the *jus tertii*, or an alteration of the subject-matter of
the contract, or, in company cases, the winding-up of the company (e) ; and,
whether any of these events supervene or not in any particular case, it is
manifest that, the longer the delay, the greater must be the peril and probability of their so doing. "We think," said the Exchequer Chamber in a
famous judgment which is always appealed to as the *locus classicus* on this
topic, "that so long as he"—the person entitled to avoid the contract—
" makes no election, he retains the right to determine it either way, subject
to this, that, if in the interval while he is still deliberating, an innocent third
party has acquired an interest in the property, or if, in consequence of his
delay, the position even of the wrongdoer is affected, it will preclude him from
exercising his right to rescind" (f)   To the same effect, dealing with the
second of the above contingencies, the Privy Council has held that " the doctrine
of laches in courts of equity is not an arbitrary or technical doctrine   Where
it would be *practically unjust* to give a remedy, either because the party has,
by his conduct, done that which might fairly be regarded as equivalent to a
waiver of it, or where, by his conduct and neglect, he has, though perhaps not
waiving that remedy, yet put the other party in a situation in which it would
not be reasonable to place him, if the remedy was afterwards to be asserted,
in either of these cases, lapse of time and delay are most material.   But in
every case, if an argument against relief, which would otherwise be just, is
founded upon mere delay, that delay, of course, not amounting to a bar to

(c) See Sub s (1) of this Section, *ante*
(d) See Sub s (2) of this Section, *ante*, and §§ 374, 484, *post*, and the cases cited in the
notes thereto, with which cp the following, where the contract was voidable on the ground
of misrepresentation   *Clough* v *L & N W Railway Co* (1871), L R 7 Exch 26, Exch
Ch (*per Cur* , at p 34— " we think the party defrauded may keep the question open so long
as he does nothing to affirm the contract "—and, at p 35   " lapse of time without rescinding will furnish evidence that he had determined to affirm the contract, and when the lapse
of time is great, it probably would in practice be treated as conclusive evidence that he
had so determined ") , *Aaron's Reefs, Ltd* v *Twiss*, [1896] A C.273, H L. (*per* Lord DAVEY
at p 294 "lapse of time, without rescinding, may furnish evidence of an intention to affirm
the contract   But the cogency of this evidence depends upon the particular circumstances
of the case, and the nature of the contract in question) , *Mutual Reserve Life Insurance Co*
v *Foster* (1904), 20 T L R 715, H L ; *Cross* v *Mutual Reserve Life Insurance Co* (1904),
21 T L R 15 (BUCKLEY, J), *Merino* v *Same* (1904), 21 T L R 167; *Molloy* v *Same*
(1905), 22 T L R 59 (SWINFEN EADY, J), in which last four cases it was held that the
delay, though great, did not show affirmation , *Re Christineville Rubber Estates, Ltd* (1911),
81 L J (CH) 63 (*per* EVE, J , at pp 64–66, who held that, with the other circumstances of
that case, the delay was fatal to the applicant)
(e) As to these bars to relief, see § 231, 233, *post*.
(f) *Clough* v *London & Northwestern Railway Co* , *sup* , *per Cur* , at p 35   This
was a misrepresentation case , but the principles there enunciated by the Exchequer
Chamber have always been held to govern every branch of law which is concerned with a
voidable contract, on whatever ground it is voidable   and, in particular, they were afterwards expressly applied to a case of non disclosure by the Exchequer Chamber in *Morrison*
v *Universal Marine Insurance Co* (1873), L R 8 Exch 197, Exch Ch (*per Cur* , at
pp 203–205)   Cp the judgment of CHITTY, J (as to the intervention of the *jus tertii*) in
Re Murray, Dickson, and Murray (1887), 57 L. T 223, and, generally, §§ 374, 484, *post*

any statute of limitations, the validity of that defence must be tried upon principles substantially equitable " (g).

218. It would appear, therefore, that where the party complaining is said to have been "guilty" of delay and laches, what is meant is that his delay and laches have amounted to waiver or affirmation, or have given occasion for the supervening of facts constituting a bar to relief. Unless this is meant, the expressions in question, since they point to nothing which constitutes an answer at all to his right to have the contract rescinded or treated as a nullity, are wholly meaningless, except in the highly metaphorical sense in which a man may be said to have been guilty of a breach of duty to himself, or of a neglect of that regard for his own interests which is dictated by worldly wisdom and ordinary business sagacity (h). Very frequently, indeed, as may be seen on reference to the language used *arguendo* in the authorities, "laches" and "delay," like many other terms of equally convenient ambiguity in meaning and laxity in use (i), are mere disguises to veil a jejune contention. They would seem to indicate a consciousness on the part of the advocate that he cannot support a case of confirmation or waiver, or whatever may be the affirmative answer suggested, and must escape from rescission, if at all, like Venus in a mist, under cover of some such large and generous terminology, for the application of which to the case in question he may find specious warrant in not a few incautious deliverances of equity judges. Nor will he be without assistance from that unfailing resource of unsound reasoning, the "maxims of the law" (j) *Vigilantibus, non dormientibus, jus subvenit*, is extensively relied upon in this connection by those who fail to see that this, like other maxims, is only true with the proper restrictions and qualifications, and, when extended beyond these limits, is demonstrably false. It is true when limited to acquiescence in the proper sense of the word, or to those cases of "equitable estoppel," as it is sometimes called, in which inaction and standing by is deemed equivalent either to a representation which induces another to alter his position for the worse, or to a licence or encouragement to another to adopt or to persevere in

(g) *Lindsay Petroleum Co v Hurd* (1874), L R 5 C P 221, at pp 239, 240 The test of " practical injustice " was applied by KNIGHT BRUCE, V C, to the circumstances of *Gibson v D'Este* (1843), 2 Y & C (CH.) 542, at p 578, with the result that, no injury having in his opinion been caused to the vendor by the purchaser's delay, he held that such delay did not affect the latter's right to relief

(h) Embodied in such proverbial philosophy as " strike while the iron is hot," or Iago's "dull not device by coldness and delay." Of course these " γνῶμαι," like the maxims of the law—see note (j), *inf*—only represent one side of the question, and may be set off by some equally absolute aphorism bringing out the other side, in this case " more haste, less speed" is the antitheton, and Friar Lawrence's "too swift arrives as tardy as too slow" (*Romeo and Juliet*, Act 2, Sc 6) see the cases cited in note (a) to § 217, *ante*, for illustrations of this possibility The cautious Bacon steers a middle course between these extremes when he counsels that " generally it is good to commit the beginnings of all great actions to Argus with his hundred eyes, and the ends to Briareus with his hundred hands, first to watch, and then to speed "

(i) Such as " arrangement," a term always resorted to when it becomes necessary to dress up in the guise of a contract something which is not so in law

(j) Of such " maxims " an anthology might easily be settled, exhibiting a series of direct antinomies in parallel columns, on any question For further illustrations of these misleading and one sided *regulæ juris*, see App A, § 646, *post*

a certain course of conduct, such inducement, licence, or encouragement being implied from the party's abstention from exercising a right which he knows is his, and knows is being violated by a person who is expending money in the honest belief either that there is no such right, or that it is being waived. The maxim, however, has no application to cases where there has been no such inducement, licence, or encouragement. The law does not, and cannot, refuse its aid and countenance to the *dormiens*, if he wakes up and demands it before either the other party, or any third person, has acquired the right to insist that it shall be refused. He may have slept as long as Rip Van Winkle, but, if nothing has happened during his slumber which affects his title to relief, that relief is not to be granted or withheld accordingly as he has slept for a short or a long time. On the other hand, if something has happened which affects his title, it does not signify how brief his nap may have been. If Achilles wakes up in time to beat the tortoise at the winning post, neither the tortoise nor the law has any business to enquire how long it was before he woke up. No doubt, lapse of time, without any attempt to assert known rights, besides being a peril to the party complaining to the extent and in the manner above indicated, is also calculated to inspire a judicial leaning in favour of the party charged, at all events in the absence of any proof of fraud on his part, and a correspondingly critical attitude towards the slackness and laxity (which is the etymological meaning of "laches") exhibited by the party complaining in nursing a claim till it is stale. "It has beautifully been remarked," said Lord CAMPBELL, L C (k), " with respect to the emblem of Time, who is depicted as carrying a scythe and an hour-glass, that while with the one hand he cuts down the evidence which protects innocence, with the other he metes out the period when innocence can no longer be assailed." There is a strong and most justifiable disposition *in gremio judicis* to uphold, if possible, the position of one who, after many years, is charged, even on *primâ facie* plausible grounds, with non-disclosure or misrepresentation, where, in the course of that period, the persons and documents by which, if the accusation had been made *dum fervebat opus*, he could have established his defence, may have perished or been lost or destroyed, and in such cases the idea of an ethical period of limitation presents great attractions to the sternest and most unbending judicial mind, in this sense that, though mere delay is still no answer in itself, the fact of delay will invite, and indeed constrain, the Court to make every intendment in favour of the legality and validity of all the proceedings of the party charged, and to lay the burden of proving the contrary more heavily on the party complaining than if there had been no such delay (l), and,

---

(k) At p 617 of *Bright* v. *Legerton* (1860), 2 De G F & J 606

(l) Thus, in *Watt* v *Assets Co*, [1905] A C 317, H L, Lord HALSBURY, L C, at the outset of his speech, declared that the questions in debate rested " especially upon these two principles—that at this distance of time every intendment should be made in favour of what has been done as being lawfully and properly done, and that the persons who are now insisting on these rights have lain asleep upon their rights so long that as a matter of fact we know that witnesses have perished, and the opportunities which might have been had if the question had been earlier raised have passed away We are asked at a distance,

finally, it will make a serious difference in the way the whole case of the party complaining is regarded and investigated, and may damage and shake that case, even if otherwise strong, whilst, if otherwise doubtful or weak, it may serve to give it the *coup de grâce* (m) and it may always affect the question of costs (n) But the effect of delay not amounting to, or affording evidence of, or scope for, any of the answers or objections referred to cannot be put higher than this, even where the non-disclosure or misrepresentation is not proved to have been dishonest (o): and in any case where, on the contrary, such dishonesty is established, and where, therefore, the party charged is

in the one case of 20 years, and in the other case of 22 years, to rip up a transaction which has apparently been completely disposed of " And, at p. 333, he concludes his judgment by insisting again, and in equally emphatic terms, on the application of the above " two principles " See also the citation in note (p), *inf.*, from *Coaks* v. *Boswell* (1886), 11 App. Cas 232, H L

(m) In *Lawrance* v *Lord Norreys* (1880), 15 App Cas 210, H L , where the action was dismissed on the ground that it was an abuse of the process of the Court, delay was a prominent feature in the considerations which moved the decision that the plaintiff had no case which was even fit to be tried, Lord HERSCHELL observing, on this aspect of the case, at p. 213 " where an action is thus brought, on a title which accrued more than 70 years ago, to dispossess those who, or whose predecessors have been, in possession during that length of years, it is obvious that the allegations by which it is sought to prevent the statute being a bar '—these were allegations of concealed fraud—" need to be closely scrutinised ", and, again, at p 219 " this is not the first but the third edition of a statement of claim delivered with the object of recovering the Towneley estate , and when we review the history of the litigation there is much to lead to the belief that important allegations now made were an afterthought, the result of criticisms of the earlier form in which the charges of fraud were presented, and that the charges thus raised against persons long dead are wholly incapable of proof " So Lord WATSON, at p 221 " when a plaintiff, in order to escape from the Statute of Limitations, brings charges of concealed fraud, for the first time, at a distance of 70 years, it appears to me that the duty of making a full and candid statement is specially incumbent on him " Cp the observations of Lord DAVEY at p 334 of *Watt* v *Assets Co* , *sup* " in coming to this conclusion, I am not treating *mora* or delay as a plea in law I do not think it is a plea in law , but I think the lapse of time is a circumstance which ought to be taken into account and ought largely to influence our estimate of and the conclusion we come to upon the facts of the case " On the same principle, as is pointed out in § 247, *post*, the party complaining who waits to be sued on the voidable contract is generally in a worse position than he who, without so waiting, takes active proceedings for rescission. Cp. §§ 374, 484, *post*

(n) In either of two ways on the one hand, a party complaining who succeeds in obtaining relief may be deprived of his costs on the ground of delay, and, on the other hand, when he fails, but the conduct of the party charged has been so dubious and equivocal as to justify an order upon him to pay his own costs, the delay of the party complaining may be sufficient to prevent the Court from exercising this discretion in his favour, as it otherwise would have done An instance of this latter effect of delay is *Coaks* v *Boswell* (1886), 11 App. Cas. 232, H L (*per* Lord SELBORNE, at p 242 " as to costs, there are some things in this case which might have made me hesitate, if the action had been brought when the purchase was recent, and before what was then an uncertain, had turned out a profitable, speculation. But, as it was not brought until after a delay of more than eight years, and after the risk had been decided in the purchaser's favour, I think the costs ought to follow the event , The substitution of creditors who know nothing about the facts for those creditors by whom the sale had been conducted, and who, knowing all the facts, did not complain, is certainly no reason why the respondents should be exonerated from costs ")

(o) In *Gordon* v *Gordon* (1821), 3 Swanst. 400, a family compromise case, in which the party charged had probably been guilty of wilful, and not very honest, suppression, it was held that, even on the assumption of innocent non-disclosure, a delay of 19 years was not, of itself, a ground for refusing relief (*per* Lord ELDON, L C , at pp 474, 475 " in that view, taking the case, as I wish to take it, as a case of mere non-disclosure, the Court, even at this late hour, will give relief ")

B N D   O

shown to have enjoyed for the period of delay a wholly unmerited spell of good fortune, perhaps as the fruit of continued dishonesty, then, so far from being an object of legitimate commiseration, he comes before the Court in the character of one against whom, and not in whose favour, every presumption will be created by the delay. "No time will assure" such persons "in the enjoyment of their plunder, but their children's children will be compelled in this Court to restore it" (p).

219. "Acquiescence," in the sense of "laches" or "delay," for which expressions it is often loosely used as a mere synonym, is equally inefficacious as an affirmative answer to the right, if it otherwise exists, to avoid the contract. The true meaning of this term, however, has been well stated by Lord COTTENHAM, L C, thus : "if a party, having a right, stands by and sees another dealing with the property in a manner inconsistent with this right, and makes no objection while the act is in progress, he cannot afterwards complain. This is the proper sense of the word "acquiescence" (q). Acquiescence, in fact, is much more than "quiescence," which is all that is connoted by "laches" or "delay", it is a quiescence under such circumstances as indicate an assent to, and an encouragement of, a course of conduct on the part of the party charged. In any other circumstances, quiescence "amounts" to no more than "mere lapse of time" (r), and *mere* lapse of time amounts to nothing. Manifestly "acquiescence" has no possible meaning in relation to the right to avoid a contract, except where the term is used as the equivalent for affirmation, as it sometimes is (s).

220. It is no affirmative answer to a case of non-disclosure to allege or prove that the party charged honestly believed the undisclosed fact to be immaterial, for (as has already been pointed out) his belief on this question

---

(p) *Per* Lord LYNDHURST, L C, at p 741 of *Charter* v *Trevelyan* (1844), 11 Cl & Fin 714. The lapse of time here was no less than 37 years. At p 235 of *Coaks* v *Boswell*, *sup*, Lord SELBORNE prefaces his speech by observing that "the time which had elapsed between the purchase sought to be set aside and the commencement of this suit might have been a serious obstacle to the relief sought, if rested on any other ground than that of fraud, but, if fraud were proved"—which in that case it was not—"that difficulty would be overcome"

(q) At p 123 of *Leeds* (*Duke*) v *Amherst* (*Earl*) (1846), 2 Ph 117. Cp the observations of TURNER, L J, at p 74, and Lord CAMPBELL, L C, at p 77, of *Life Association of Scotland* v *Siddall* (1861), 3 De G. F & J. 58, and the exhaustive and luminous analysis of the doctrine by the Court of Appeal at pp. 314, 315 of *De Bussche* v *Alt* (1877), 8 C D 286, C A. Of course it must be shown that the party said to have acquiesced had full knowledge of his rights · *per* TURNER, L.J, *ubi supracit* ("acquiescence, as I conceive, imports knowledge, for I do not know how a man can be said to have acquiesced in what he did not know, and in cases of this sort I think that acquiescence imports full knowledge")

(r) *Murray* v *Palmer* (1805), 2 Sch & Lefr 472, *per* Lord REDESDALE, L C (Ir), at pp 486, 487

(s) In *Sharpley* v *Louth and East Coast Railway Co* (1876), 2 C D 663, C A, MALINS, V C, in the Court appealed from, though the C A studiously refrained from doing so, used the term "acquiescence" to describe conduct which was evidence of an election on the part of the representee to affirm the contract, and of nothing else. It should be noted that it is possible for *the party complaining* to rely upon the doctrine of acquiescence, *in its proper sense*, as a means of defeating the objection that by his acts and conduct he has altered the character of that which is the subject of the contract, and so cannot restore it *in specie* to the party charged. As to this, see § 231, and the case cited in note (i) thereto, *post*

has no relevance whatever (*t*). Noi is it of any avail to set up that the party charged had no intention to deceive oi mislead the party complaining, or acted in ignoiance of the equitable piinciples of disclosure, for neither (as has been seen) is it any pait of the *onus probandi* incumbent on the party complaining to show what motive actuated the party charged, or how far (if at all) he was conscious of his legal obligations in the matter (*u*).

221. Lastly, since the relative advantages oi disadvantages of adheiing to, oi of repudiating, the voidable contiact aie the exclusive concern of the party complaining, it follows that his right, if otherwise good, to adopt the lattei course, is in no way defeated or affected by the most irrefragable evidence or argument that the contract, if abided by, would have worked out rather to his benefit than to that of the paity charged, oi to the common advantage of both The party complaining is to be the sole judge of the expediency or piopriety of getting rid of the contractual relation between himself and the party charged It may be a mattei of honoui, and not of interest, with him. Having seen cause to regret his association with an undesiiable individual, company, or enterprise, and finding subsequently that the circumstances are such as to provide him with a means of escape, he may be anxious to avail himself of his iights irrespective of any immediate or tangible gain or loss Oi it may be a case of mere caprice The rationality of his motives foi insisting on avoidance is wholly immaterial He is always entitled to say, with Shylock, "it is my humoui" If the iight to avoid cannot be established, *cadit quœstio :* but, if it is established, the law no moie concerns itself with the ieasons which move the party complaining to exercise that right than it concerns itself with the motives influencing a litigant to insist on any other right of property or action to which he may be entitled When once his wrongdoing has been proved, the wrongdoei can neither be heard to speculate, noi invite the Court to speculate, on the supposed inadequacy or insagacity of such reasons oi motives (*v*)

(*t*) See § 33, *ante*
(*u*) See § 197, *ante.*
(*v*) See *Aberaman Ironworks, Ltd* v *Wickens* (1868), 4 Ch App 101, a misrepresentation case (*per* Lord CAIRNS, L C , at p 108 "the argument that the company would have bought with equal readiness had they known it to consist of less than 1100 acres, and that the real reason for rescinding was want of money to complete, appears to me hardly to require an answer If the deficiency is one that entitles them to rescind (and no one disputes that it is) they are entitled to rescind even though they might have been willing to pay an equal sum for the smaller quantity, and even although rescission may, in a financial point of view, have been convement to them") Cp the following misrepresentation cases where the party complaining was the defendant, and not the plaintiff, and where it was held that there is no more right to criticize or investigate his motives for resisting an attempt to enforce the contract than his motives for taking active measures to avoid it : *Knatchbull* v *Krueger* (1815), 1 Madd 153 (*per* PLUMER, V -C., at p 167), and, on appeal (1817), 3 Mer 121 (*per* Lord ELDON, L C , at p 146), *Flight* v *Booth* (1834), 1 Bing N C 370 (at pp 378, 379) ; *Brooke (Lord)* v *Rounthwaite* (1846), 5 Hare 298 (*per* WIGRAM, V C , at pp 302, 303), *Madeley* v *Booth* (1849), 2 De G & Sm 718 (*per* KNIGHT BRUCE, V C , at p. 722), *Ayles* v *Cox* (1852), 16 Beav 23 (*per* ROMILLY, M R , at pp 24, 25), *Denny* v *Hancock* (1870), 6 Ch App 1 (*per* JAMES, L J , at p 10) So, generally, in actions of contract, the party who has contracted foi one thing is not bound to accept another, and a different, thing, merely because most people might think the latter more valuable, or merely because it may have involved greater expense to the other party *Forman & Co Proprietary, Ltd* v *S S Lidderdale,* [1900] A C 190, P C (at pp 197, 201)

SECT. 5 RELIEF AND REMEDIES.

222. Where the party complaining has discharged the burden of proof which lies upon him (w), and the case so *primâ facie* established has not been displaced by any affirmative plea or answer on the other side (x), he is entitled to be relieved of his obligations under the contract in the negotiation for which the non-disclosure is proved to have occurred   It now becomes important to examine the nature of the remedies by which this relief is effected, and the principles upon which it is judicially granted or withheld

223. In substance, the right of any party complaining who elects to avoid a contract in the negotiation for which material facts have been withheld from him is to have the contract judicially annulled, or judicially treated as a nullity   And this is his only right   He is not entitled to recover damages against the party charged (y), unless the non-disclosure assumes the character of fraudulent concealment (z), or amounts to fraudulent misrepresentation (a), or is otherwise founded on, or characterized and accompanied by, fraud (b), and his case is so put (whether alternatively or not), and proved   in any of which events, however, the damages are recoverable for the fraud, and not for the non-disclosure as such (c)

224. For the above purpose, the law puts into the hands of the party complaining both a sword and a shield   The non-disclosure is regarded both as a dissolvent, and an absolvent   On the one hand, it constitutes a ground for rescission or analogous relief at the instance of the party complaining · on the other, it absolves him from liability under the contract, if it is put in suit against him   Both offensive and defensive proceedings

(w) See Sect 3, *ante*

(x) See Sect 4, *ante*

(y) Per SCRUTTON, J , at p 258 of *Glasgow Assurance Corporation* v. *Symondson & Co.* (1911), 104 L T 254, to take one of the most recent statements of a very familiar and well-established rule, as applied to contracts of insurance   There is no exception to the rule, for the cases of fraud mentioned in the text are only exceptions which prove it   And the " compensation " provided for in most contracts for the sale of land is not damages, but an agreed pecuniary substitute for avoidance (see § 206, *ante*), whilst the " compensation ' sometimes exacted by the Court in cases of specific performance is only imposed as a condition of this particular form of discretionary relief (see § 245, *post*)   The indemnity, again, which the party charged must give to the party complaining against liabilities under the contract set aside is not an indemnity against " losses arising out of the contract generally," and, therefore, not damages, as is explained in § 239, note (y), *post*   Statutory damages of course stand on a footing of their own   These are discussed in Ch VI, § 567, *post*

(z) As in *Wilson* v *Fuller* (1842), 3 Q. B 1009, Exch Ch , where the declaration charged both fraudulent misrepresentation and fraudulent concealment, the object of the action being to recover damages , and the Exchequer Chamber, whose judgment was delivered by TINDAL, C J , examined each head of complaint separately and successively, without expressing or implying the slightest doubt that proof of either would entitle the plaintiff to damages   The first is discussed at pp 1009, 1010, and thereupon consideration of the second (which occupies pp 1010–1012) is entered upon, prefaced by—" As to the statement in the declaration of *the second gravamen, the fraudulent concealment* .   " &c.

(a) This class of case forms the subject of Ch IV, Sect 4, Sub-s (2), of the author's *Law of Actionable Misrepresentation*

(b) As in most of the cases cited in Sect 2, Sub s (8), *ante*

(c) The same rule as that stated in the text applies to cases of innocent misrepresentation, where damages are equally not recoverable

aro open to him. It is proposed to consider separately the remedies thus placed at his disposal under these two main heads (d)

Sub-s. (1) Offensive Proceedings for the Avoidance of the Contract. Rescission and Analogous Relief.

225. It is now well established that any contract in the negotiation for which the party charged has broken his duty of disclosure is valid unless and until disaffirmed by the party complaining. in other words, it is not, *by reason only of the non-disclosure*, void (for, of course, it may happen to be in any particular case void for some other reason, such as statutory or common law illegality, or immorality, or injury to the public weal), but only voidable at the sole option of the party complaining (e). To hold otherwise would lead to the ridiculous and shocking result that the party charged, or (in cases of contracts induced by misrepresentation) the misrepresentor, or (in the case of any other invalidating cause) the wrongdoer, would be in the position, if he should find that the contract is profiting the party he has wronged rather than himself, to take advantage of his own wrong, and to insist that the other party shall not enjoy the benefit which he has involuntarily, by that wrong, conferred upon him (f). The Courts have been so

(d) In the remainder of this Section, there will be frequent references to cases of misrepresentation inducing contracts which the representee elected to avoid, for these are obviously in point, it being quite immaterial to the question of the procedure by, and form in which, relief against a contract may be obtained, whether the title to that relief arose from non-disclosure, or misrepresentation. or any other invalidating cause, and, if from non-disclosure, whether the breach was of duties forming the subject of this Chapter, or of duties dealt with in either of the next two Chapters. Consequently the present discussion of the general nature and conditions of rescission and analogous relief, and of the relief available by way of defence, is entered upon once for all, and will not be repeated in Ch IV, Sect 5, or in Ch V, Sect 5, *post*

(e) See, as to marine insurance cases, *Morrison v Universal Marine Insurance Co* (1873), L R 8 Exch 197, Exch Ch (at pp 203–205), as to life insurance, *Armstrong v Turquand* (1857), 9 Ir C L R 32, as to contracts to marry, *Hall v Wright* (1858), E B & E 746 (per Lord CAMPBELL, C J, at p 759) It is, however, in misrepresentation cases that it has been found most necessary to insist upon, and reiterate, the principle all these authorities are cited in note (u) to § 253 of the author's *Law of Actionable Misrepresentation* The most important of them are *Stevenson v Newnham* (1853), 13 C B 285, Exch Ch (per Cur, at pp 302, 303 "the effect of this, as of ordinary frauds, is not absolutely to avoid the contract or transfer which has been caused by that fraud, but to render it voidable at the option of the party defrauded It must be considered, therefore as established, that fraud only gives a right to rescind the contract or purchase, that the property rests until avoided, and that all mesne dispositions to persons not party to, or at least not cognizant of, the fraud are valid "), *Clough v L & N W Railway Co* (1871), L R 7 Exch Ch 26, Exch Ch (per Cur, at p 34—a passage, with others on the subject of election, cited and applied by the Exch Ch to cases of non disclosure in *Morrison v Universal Marine Insurance Co, sup* —"the fact that the contract was induced by fraud did not render the contract void, or prevent the property from passing, but merely gave the party defrauded a right, on discovering the fraud, to elect whether he would continue to treat the contract as binding, or would disaffirm the contract, and we further agree that the contract continued valid until the party defrauded had determined his election by avoiding it "), *United Shoe Machinery Co of Canada v Brunet*, [1909] A C 330, P C (at p 339 "a contract into which a person may have been induced to enter by false and fraudulent representation is not void, but merely voidable at the election of the party defrauded, after he has notice of the fraud Unless and until he makes his election, and by word or act repudiates the contract , the contract remains as valid and binding as if it had not been tainted with fraud at all ")

(f) See the cases cited in note (t), *inf* And cp. the estoppel case of *Goode & Bennion*

deeply impressed with the absurdity and injustice of such a result, that, even in cases where, not without encouragement from frequent examples of the misuse of the term in question by judges (g), and by the legislature (h), it has been expressly stipulated that in the event of non-disclosure, or fraud, or other breach of duty, the contract is to be " void," they have always held that, in using this expression, the parties must be taken to have meant no more than " void when the party wronged elects so to treat it," or, in other words, " voidable " at his option (i) There are other manifest absurdities which would flow from any doctrine that such contracts are void : for, on the one hand, the party complaining would be for ever precluded from taking active proceedings for relief, since the Courts will not ordinarily avoid what is void already (j), on the other hand,

\ *Harrison* (1821), 5 B & Ald 147, as to the contracts of an infant (*per* BEST, C J, at p. 150 . "the fallacy of Mr Littledale's argument, I think, arises from this circumstance—he considers the contract of an infant as absolutely void   But it is not void, for, if void, the infant himself could take no advantage of it ")

(g) In the earlier stages of our jurisprudence, the enormous importance of the distinction between voidability and *ipso facto* invalidity was either not fully appreciated, or not adequately expressed   Thus Lord ELLENBOROUGH, C J , in *Duffel* v. *Wilson* (1808), 1 Campb 401, distinctly described a contract induced by misrepresentation as " void," by which he may—as suggested by Sir GORELL BARNES at p. 548 of *Kettlewell* v *Refuge Assurance Co* , [1908] 1 K B 545, C. A —have meant " voidable " : but he could not have so meant, and the same excuse cannot be made for his actual decision (a hopelessly bad one) in *Hill* v *Gray* (1816), 1 Stark 434   In *Noble* v *Adams* (1816), 7 Taunt 59, the same terminological (if not substantial) error is traceable , and the verbal slip appears twice in the otherwise admirable judgment of the C P. in *Flight* v *Booth* (1834), 1 Bing. (N.C. 370 (" fraud avoids the contract altogether," p 376 . " in such cases the contract is avoided altogether," p 377)

(h) For instance, in the Infants Relief Act, 1874 (37 & 38 Vict c 62), s 1, as to which see Lord Halsbury's *Laws of England*, title *Infants and Children*, vol xvii, p 67, note (l), the unfortunate use of the term " void " might, if literally construed, deprive the infant of his remedy against the adult, and thus encourage and revive the fallacy put forward in *Goode & Bennion* v *Harrison*, *sup*

(i) As in the life insurance case of *Armstrong* v *Turquand* (1857), 9 Ir C L. R 32, and the lease cases (containing conditions that the lease should be void on failure to perform covenants therein) of *Rede* v. *Farr* (1817), 6 M & S 121 (*per Cur* , at pp 124, 125) , *Doe d Bryan* v *Bancks* (1821), 4 B & Ald 401 (*per* ABBOTT, C J , at pp 405, 406) , *Doe d Nash* v. *Birch* (1836), 1 M & W 402 (*per* Lord ABINGER, C B , at p 408)   In *Hyde* v *Watt* (1843), 12 M. & W. 254, a covenant in a composition deed that, if the debtor neglected to keep alive an insurance on his life, the deed should be void, was construed to mean that the indenture was only to be " void against the plaintiff if he chooses to treat it as such " (p 270), and PARKE, B , delivering the judgment of the Court of Exchequer, pointed (at pp 268, 269) to " the absurd consequences which would follow if the defendant, against the consent of the other parties who had all an interest in the continuance of the indenture and to whom it gave benefit as well as to the defendant, could avail himself of his own wrong, and absolve himself and his trustees from liability on their respective covenants " In *Sparenborg* v. *Edinburgh Life Insurance Co* , [1912] 1 K B 195, a life policy case, where there was a condition that, if the assured travelled outside certain geographical limits, the policy was to be void, it was strenuously contended by the plaintiff that " void " meant what it said, and that he having broken the condition, and the company having asserted that, strictly speaking, the policy was void on that account, he was entitled to a return of the premiums paid · but, inasmuch as it was expressly provided that, in that event, the premiums should not be recoverable, BRAY, J , decided in favour of the defendants without finding it necessary to express any opinion on the meaning of " void " as used in the policy (p 204), or on the company's argument that to construe the word otherwise than as " voidable " would enable the assured to take advantage of his own wrong   In *Taylor* v *Yorkshire Insurance Co* , [1913] 2 Ir R 1 (insurance of a stallion), " void " was treated as meaning " voidable " (*per* PALLES, C.B , at p 19)

(j) See §§ 232, 238, *post*   The Courts will not make unnecessary orders, or slay the slain.

even the party charged would be subjected to grave injustice, since he could never set up waiver, or affirmation, or (in the proper sense) acquiescence (k), as an affirmative answer to any case made against him, nor could he insist on the impossibility of mutual restoration *in specie* as a ground for with-holding relief from the party complaining (l).

226. It follows from the proposition above stated that, at the outset, the right of the party complaining is simply and solely a right of option, whether to affirm or disaffirm the contract (m). He is not bound to make any election at all, or he may postpone the exercise of his right for any period he pleases, though such omission or delay exposes him to serious perils of a nature already indicated (n). But the right, when exercised, is exhausted. *Quod in electionibus semel placuit amplius displicere non potest* He may keep the sword of Damocles suspended over the contract as long as he pleases, but if he takes the sword from its place, he can never put it back again, and, if he cuts the thread and lets it fall, whether he destroys the contract or not, he loses the sword If he once affirms, he can never after-wards avoid and, if he once avoids he can never afterwards affirm for his own purposes, nor, at the suggestion of the party charged, be held to have so affirmed (o). There is no *locus pœnitentiæ* in either case

227. If the party complaining elects to avoid the contract, and the refusal of the party charged to submit to the avoidance compels him to resort to the Court to have it judicially adjudged to be void, or treated as void, it must be remembered that, even though a case of actionable non-disclosure has been fully established, there are still certain conditions subject to which alone the relief can be granted

228. In the first place, it must appear, if the question is raised by the Court (for obviously, except in very special cases, the party charged is not interested in raising it), that there is something on which a judgment or order can operate, and for the undoing of which judicial intervention is requisite That is to say, there must be a subsisting contract which, unless and until set aside by the Court, is, and will continue to be, valid and binding on the parties. In strictness the Court, which is reluctant to make un-necessary orders (p), may decline to interfere when its aid is invoked to rescind that which in fact, or in contemplation of law, does not exist, as, for

(k) See Sect 4, *ante* Obviously no one can affirm, waive, or acquiesce in, what was void *ab initio*, or resuscitate that which was stillborn.

(l) See § 239, *post,* as to such mutual *restitutio ad integrum* being a condition of rescission But there can be no restoration of a *status quo* which never existed in law

(m) Com Dig Election, C 2, *Clough* v *L & N W. Railway Co* (1871), L R 7 Exch 26, Exch Ch , a misrepresentation case, *per Cur* , at p 34 , *Law* v *Law,* [1905] 1 Ch 140, C A , a non disclosure case, *per* COZENS-HARDY, L J , delivering the judgment of the Court, at p 159 (" he deliberately made his election, and by that he is bound See *Clough* v *London & North Western Railway Co* ")

(n) See §§ 216, 217, 218, *ante*

(o) *Clough* v *L & N W Railway Co* , *sup* , *per Cur* , at pp 34, 36 , *Re Thomas Edward Brinsmead & Sons, Ltd* , *Tomline's Case,* [1908] 1 Ch 104, a misrepresentation case, *per* WRIGHT J , at p 109 (" election once made is made for ever, and cannot be revoked even if the party wishes ')

(p) *Reeve* v *Gibson,* [1891] 1 Q B 652, *per* VAUGHAN WILLIAMS, J , at p 657, and WILLS, J , at p 659

instance, an alleged contract which was never " concluded " (q), or was not made by a person having the requisite authority in that behalf (r) ; or a contract which, having been made, was determined by the parties before the application for relief (s) ; or a contract which was a nullity *ab initio*, by reason of its object or consideration having been illegal, or immoral, or against public policy (t) , or a contract which, though not indictable or illegal, is rendered absolutely void, and not merely voidable, by statute (u). In many of such cases, however, relief is granted *ex abundanti cautelâ*, if the matter is not perfectly clear, or is not forced upon the attention of the Court (v) : and it will always be granted *ex debito justitiæ* where any entry in a statutory register, or other public document over which the Court has statutory jurisdiction, stands on record as *primâ facie* evidence against the party complaining, and where, therefore, it is just as necessary to get the entry expunged or rectified in the case of a void or non-existent contract as in the case of one which is voidable only, the relief being given not against the contract, which does not exist in fact, or in contemplation of law, as the case may be, but against the statutory register or other public document which declares that it does (w).

229. Not only where it is less, but also where it is more, than a contract in law, *e g* when it confers a permanent status upon the parties, besides establishing a contractual relation between them, the impeached transaction is incapable of being set aside, or treated as a nullity, except upon the grounds

(q) As in *Re Etna Insurance Co , Slattery's Case* (1873), Ir R 7 Eq 245   On the other hand, a concluded contract was proved in *Re Scottish Petroleum Co , Wallace's Case* (1883), 23 C D 413, C A , but it was recognized by the Court of Appeal (see pp 431, 432, 438) that, had it been otherwise, the applicant's right to have his name removed from the register would have rested on the voidness, or rather non existence, of the contract, and not on its voidability for misrepresentation

(r) See *Scottish Petroleum Co , Wallace's Case, sup* , where it was also recognized that, if it had appeared (which it did not) that the allotment had not been made by the requisite number of directors, it would have been a case of no contract at all, and not a case of a subsisting, but voidable, contract.

(s) As, for instance, by forfeiture of shares, pursuant to articles of association · *Re Home Counties and General Life Insurance Co , Ex p Woollaston* (1859), 7 W R 645 , *Re London & Mediterranean Bank, Wright's Case*, No 1 (1871), L R 12 Eq 334 n . *Re Same, Wright's Case*, No 2 (1871), 7 Ch App 55 , *Aaron's Reefs, Ltd v Twiss*, [1896] A C 273, H L. (at p 293)   The rule of course assumes that the forfeiture was *bonâ fide*   Where it was a fraudulent device of the shareholder, in collusion with the company's secretary, the contract was held not to have been put an end to   *Re London and Provincial Starch Co , Gowers' Case* (1868), L R 7 Eq 77, 81   As to the means of checkmating a similar manœuvre on the part of a company, see § 240, and note (d) thereto, *post*

(t) See Lord Halsbury's *Laws of England*, title *Contract*, vol vii, pp 391–403

(u) *Ibid* , pp 403–405   Further, any contract or transaction embodied in an instrument of which the class, quality, character, or nature has been wholly misdescribed, and any contract induced by *error personæ*, is void   This topic is fully discussed in §§ 256–259 of the author's *Law of Actionable Misrepresentation*

(v) Thus a contract which was clearly void, by reason of misrepresentation of the nature of the instrument, was nevertheless set aside in *Kennedy v Green* (1834), 3 My & K 699 , *Lewellin v Cobbold* (1853), 1 Sm & G 376 , *Vorley v Cooke* (1857), 1 Giff 230 , *Lee v Angas* (1866), 7 Ch App 79 n

(w) See, as to rectification of the register of members of a company, Lord Halsbury's *Laws of England*, vol v, pp 153–156, and as to variation of the list of contributories, *ibid* , pp 496–500, 502 , from some of the cases there cited it will appear that such rectification, or variation, has been ordered where the contract to take shares was not voidable, but void

on which such status can be dissolved   Marriage, and marriage settlements, as distinct from agreements to marry, furnish illustrations of this principle, as has already been explained (*x*)

230. Another condition of relief is that the contract must be executory on one side or the other   If it has been completed by conveyance, or otherwise fully executed and exhausted on both sides, the Court will peremptorily refuse to interfere (*y*), unless the non-disclosure, or (if it be a case of misrepresentation) the misrepresentation, was characterized by fraud, or unless it led to *error in substantialibus*, that is, a state of things in which, if the relief were refused, the party complaining would be compelled to keep something totally different in substance and nature from that which the contract purported to give him.   The first of these two exceptions, since fraud not only vacates and vitiates every transaction known to the law, but denies even to conveyance, completion, and long fruition the immunity which would otherwise attach to them, has never been in doubt.   Recognized in cases where the facts were not sufficient to establish the fraud alleged (*z*), the rule has always been rigorously applied wherever they were (*a*)   The second exception has been, from the earliest times, recognized in all the Scottish institutional treatises, such as Bell's *Principles*, the relevant passage from which has been cited and adopted in the House of Lords as representing not merely the law of Scotland, but that of England and Ireland as well (*b*), and it is now firmly established, though it was not perhaps always so, in our jurisprudence (*c*)   It should, however, be remembered that where, by a

(*x*) In § 149, *ante*
(*y*) On this ground rescission was refused in the following cases (in which it so happened that misrepresentation was the ground on which the contract was sought to be set aside, but the ground of voidability, as already stated, is immaterial)   *Attwood* v *Small* (1838), 6 Cl & Fin 232, *Wilde* v *Gibson* (1848), 1 H L C 605, *Brownlie* v *Campbell* (1880), 5 App Cas 925, H L., *Soper* v *Arnold* (1887), 37 C D 96, C A , affirmed (1889), 14 App. Cas 429, H L., *May* v *Platt*, [1900] 1 Ch 616 , *Debenham* v *Sawbridge*, [1901] 2 Ch 98   *Re Metal Constituents, Ltd , Lord Lurgan's Case*, [1902] 1 Ch 707, 709 , *Seddon* v *North Eastern Salt Co* , [1905] 1 Ch 326 , *Milch* v *Coburn* (1910), 27 T L R 170 , *Angel* v. *Jay*, [1911] 1 K B 666 (where it was vainly sought to distinguish a lease from a conveyance)   It should be noted that the mere fact that one of the parties, during the currency of the contract, has become entitled to benefits in certain events which have not happened, whilst the other has been at a corresponding risk, does not make the contract an executed one   *Kettlewell* v *Refuge Assurance Co* , [1908] 1 K B 545, C A (at pp 549–551)
(*z*) For instance, by Lord COTTENHAM, L C , at pp 349–352 of *Attwood* v *Small*, *sup* . and at pp 616, 617 of *Wilde* v *Gibson*, *sup* , by Lord CAMPBELL, at pp 632, 633 of the last case , by Lord SELBORNE, L C , at p 937 of *Brownlie* v *Campbell*, *sup* , by COTTON, L J , at pp 101, 102 of *Soper* v *Arnold*, *sup* , in the C. A , by FARWELL, J., at p 623 of *May* v *Platt*, *sup*
(*a*) Instances are   *Edwards* v *M'Leay* (1815), G Cooper 308, affirmed by Lord ELDON, L C (1818), 2 Swanst. 287 , *Charter* v *Trevelyan* (1844), 11 Cl & Fin 714   These were non disclosure cases.   Illustrations from misrepresentation cases are plentiful   see *Sturge* v *Sturge* (1849), 12 Beav 229 , *Reynell* v *Sprye* (1852), 1 De G M & G 660 ; *Garraud* v *Frankel* (1862), 30 Beav 445 , *Harris* v *Pepperel* (1867), L R 5 Eq 1 , *Lindsay Petroleum Co* v *Hurd* (1874), L R 5 P C. 221 , *Hart* v *Swaine* (1877), 7 C D 42 , *Paget* v *Marshall* (1884), 28 C. D 255
(*b*) See *Brownlie* v *Campbell*, *sup* , where, at p 937, Lord SELBORNE, L C , after citing the proposition in Bell's *Principles* as to *both* the exceptions mentioned, observes   "it appears to me that the cases which have been decided in this country and in Ireland are to the same effect."
(*c*) See *Bingham* v *Bingham* (1748), 1 Ves Sr 126 ; *Cooper* v *Phibbs* (1867), L R 2

term or condition of the contract, it has been agreed that compensation is
to take the place of rescission, and the period within which such compensation
is payable is not expressly limited, the exception last mentioned is not
admissible, it being deemed immaterial to the question of monetary relief
whether the contract has been completed or not. In any such case, accordingly, compensation cannot be denied to the party complaining, if his right
to it is established in all other respects, even after conveyance or full execution
on both sides, and at any time thereafter which is not beyond some period of
statutory limitation This doctrine was for some time doubted, on the
ground that the same rule ought to be applied to the substituted form of
relief as to the form for which it is substituted, and that the pecuniary equivalent of rescission ought to be payable within the same limits of time as those
within which the party complaining could have avoided the contract if he
had not agreed to take such equivalent instead : but it has now been definitely
declared to be law (d).

231. A third condition of rescission or analogous relief is complete *restitutio
in integrum* on both sides, and (where the property is specific) *in specie*.
It follows that where the party complaining, having received under the
contract something other than money, or securities, or goods incapable of
an individual character, has disabled himself from giving it back to the
party charged in the same plight as that in which he received it, he is unable
to satisfy this condition, in which case it would plainly be inequitable, as
between the parties, to deprive the party charged, however grievous a wrongdoer, of all rights and benefits, past and future, accruing to him under the
contract on the terms of receiving back, not the specific thing which he
delivered under the contract, but something of a different nature, quality,
or substance (e) Thus where, through the acts or omissions of the party
complaining, the property acquired by him under the contract, such as a
mine, a colliery, or a business, has been worked out or exhausted, or so dealt
with as to result in an entire destruction or alteration of its physical or commercial character (f), or where shares or securities so acquired have, owing

H. L 149 (*per* Lord CRANWORTH, at p 164, expressly approving the decision in the last-
cited case), *Jones* v. *Clifford* (1876), 3 C D 779 (*per* HALL, V.-C, at pp. 791, 792),
Debenham v *Sawbridge*, [1901] 2 Ch 98 (*per* BRYNE, J , who, at p 109, after referring to
the previous authorities, draws the unhesitating conclusion that " this "—i e. rescission—
" is relief which may undoubtedly be granted in a proper case, even after conveyance,
although there has been nothing in the nature of fraud ")

(*d*) *Bos* v *Helsham* (1866), L. R 2 Exch 72 , *Palmer* v *Johnson* (1884), 13 Q B D
351, C A , in which *Bos* v *Helsham* was distinctly approved and followed, whilst three
intervening decisions of MALINS, V -C , were overruled, and the opinion of WATKIN
WILLIAMS, J , in *Joliffe* v *Baker* (1883), 11 Q B D 255, Div Ct., if intended in any way
to contravene the principle of *Bos* v *Helsham*, was dissented from

(*e*) *Clough* v *London and Northwestern Railway Co* (1871), L. R 7 Exch. 26, Exch
Ch , *per Cur* , at p 35 (" if, in consequence of his delay, the position even of the wrongdoer
is affected, it will preclude him from exercising his right to rescind ")

(*f*) As in *Attwood* v *Small* (1838), 6 Cl & Fin 232 (collieries, and ironworks and mines,
described by Lord COTTENHAM, L.C, at p 537, as " a property . . varying from day
to day," and, therefore, as peculiarly the subject of the rule in its most stringent application) ; *Vigers* v *Pike* (1842), 8 Cl & Fin 562 (*per* Lord COTTENHAM, L C , at p 651, a case
of mines worked out and exhausted) , *Clarke* v *Dickson* (1858), E B & E 148 (the like,
where, at p 153, ERLE, J , likens the case to that of a man offering to return a lottery ticket

to the like conduct or default of the party complaining, become shares or securities of a different legal quality, and with different legal incidents (g), rescission will be refused. But mere depreciation or deterioration of the property which arises in the ordinary course of events, or from natural decay or inherent defects, and is in nowise attributable to the party complaining, is no bar to the grant of relief (h). Nor, even where the party complaining is responsible for the impossibility of restoring the property *in specie*, will the remedy be withheld if he can prove that the party charged has deliberately stood by and silently encouraged the acts which are alleged to have caused the alteration or extinction of the property, with full consciousness of his own wrongdoing, and for the sole purpose of providing himself with materials for raising the objection if and when proceedings should be taken against him (i). Where there is a doubt whether the party complaining will, or will not, eventually be able to make, or procure to be made, effective restoration *in specie*, the judgment may be framed in an alternative form, ordering rescission if the restoration be effected within a stated time, and, if not, dismissal of the action (j)

232. Where the party complaining has received nothing under the contract but money, *e g* premiums under a policy of insurance, or deposits on a contract of sale, or dividends on shares, no difficulty of the nature just referred to arises · the money, with or without interest (k), must be repaid, or brought into Court, or offered to be repaid, as a condition of rescission (l) ,

which had turned up a blank, and, at p 155, CROMPTON, J , to that of a butcher who had bought a beast from a glazier offering to return the carcase) ; *Sheffield Nickel and Silver Plating Co* v *Unwin* (1877), 2 Q B D 215, 223, 224 , *Ladywell Mining Co* v. *Brookes* (1887), 35 C D 400, C A (*per* LINDLEY, L J , at p 414 " rescission is not possible because the property acquired by the company does not belong to the company any longer The landlord has taken possession, and rescission is out of the question) , *Lagunas Nitrate Co* v *Lagunas Syndicate*, [1899] 2 Ch 392, C A (where, at p 433, LINDLEY, M R , says that " the real difficulty in the way of rescission lies in the impossibility of restoring the parties to their original position," and, at pp. 433, 434, enumerates the circumstances which resulted in this impossibility)

(g) *Clarke* v *Dickson, sup* (*per* ERLE, J , at pp 153, 154, and CROMPTON J , at p 155, where, besides the working out of the mines, the additional fact is relied on that the plaintiff, having been instrumental in getting the cost book mining com. converted into a joint stock company, had disabled himself from returning the shares in the same plight as that in which he had received them) , *Western Bank of Scotland* v *Addie* (1867), L R 1 H L (Sc) 145 (where a similar state of things was held a fatal objection to rescission, apart from the liquidation of the company before repudiation, which was a bar in itself ; see the observations of Lord CHELMSFORD, L C , at p 160, and Lord CRANWORTH, at pp 165, 166) On the other hand, in *Oelkers* v *Ellis*, [1914] 2 K B 139, where the party complaining had never in fact become a shareholder in the company which had gone into liquidation, there was no force in the plea raised against him, because he had never been put into possession at all of the shares which, it was urged, he could not restore (*per* HORRIDGE, J , at p 152)

(h) *Western Bank of Scotland* v *Addie, sup* (*per* Lord CRANWORTH, at p 166) *Adam* v *Newbigging* (1888), 13 App Cas 309, H L (*per* Lord WATSON, at p 323, and Lord HERSCHELL, at pp 330, 331)

(i) *Maturin* v *Tredennick* (1864), 12 W. R. 740

(j) See the form of the decree set out at p 245 of *Lindsay Petroleum Co* v. *Hurd* (1874), L R 5 P C 221, where there was a possibility that the company, though dissolved, might eventually, through other parties, procure the property to be reconveyed to the defendants

(k) See § 241, note (o), *post*

(l) Thus, in *Fitzherbert* v *Mather* (1785), 1 Term Rep 12 (marine insurance), the

and, if the party charged has concurred in the avoidance of the contract by the party complaining, so that there has been no necessity for judicial annulment, then the party complaining, if he fails to refund the money, is liable to the party charged in an action for money had and received (m) This general rule, however, is subject to two exceptions. first, where the non-disclosure or other breach of duty has been characterized or accompanied by fraud (n), and, secondly, where the parties have agreed to the contrary, which is almost universally the case as to premiums in contracts of insurance, other than marine (o), and is very commonly the case as to deposits on

underwriters paid the premium into court; in *Stainbank* v *Fernley* (1839), 9 Sim 556 (a case of a share transaction), the plaintiff by his bill offered to repay the dividends which he had received in respect of the shares t in *Anderson* v *Thornton* (1853), 8 Exch 425 (*per* PARKE, B , at p 428), and in *Russell* v. *Thornton* (1859), 4 H & N 788 (*per* BRAMWELL, B , at p 797), which were both cases of marine insurance, it was held that the underwriters were bound to return the premium, there being no fraud on the part of the assured So, in the life insurance case of *London Assurance Co* v *Mansel* (1879), 11 C D 363, the insurance company before action, and when repudiating the policy, had tendered the amount of the one premium which they had received from the assured ; and in *Joel* v. *Law Union & Crown Insurance Co* , [1908] 2 K B. 431, another life insurance case, the judgment in which was set aside by the Court of Appeal, [1908] 2 K B 863, C A , but not on any ground which affected the soundness of the observations now cited, Lord ALVERSTONE, C J , held in a considered judgment, after the jury had returned certain answers to specific questions, that " in order to entitle the defendants to revocation of the policy-- this not being a case of fraud—they ought to have tendered, or expressed their willingness to repay the premium . , in my judgment, fraud having been negatived, they were bound to repay the premium " (p 440), and he thereupon directed the judgment to be prefaced (as the judgment in *London Assurance Co* v *Mansel, sup* - ee p 372 of the report of that case—had been) by a recital of the fact that the insurance company were " willing and thereby offered to return the premium "

(m) *Everett* v *Desborough*, cited in note (o), *inf* , *British Workman's and General Assurance Co* v. *Cunliffe* (1902), 18 T L R 502, C A

(n) See the observations of PARKE, B , at p 427 of *Anderson* v *Thornton sup* (" in cases of insurance concealment vitiates the policy, and whether it be fraudulently made or not is a matter which is wholly immaterial, *except with reference to the return of the premium* "), and again, at p 428 (" with reference to the return of the premium, there is no doubt in my mind that the plaintiff would be entitled to recover it, *as there was no fraud in the representation* , if there had been, the case would have been different "), and those of BRAMWELL, B , at p 797 of *Russell* v *Thornton, sup* , and of Lord ALVERSTONE, C J , at p 440 of *Joel* v *Law Union & Crown Insurance Co* , as cited in note (l), *sup* The rules as to the return of premiums in cases of marine insurance are codified in ss 82, 83, 84 of the Marine Insurance Act, 1906 (6 Edw 7, c 41)

(o) In *Everett* v *Desborough* (1829), 5 Bing 503, there was an express condition that, if the assured's answers to the company's questions were untrue, the premiums should be forfeited, as well as the policy rendered void The assured had an alternative claim for the return of the premiums, in case his principal claim to the policy moneys should fail, as it did There can be no doubt that, according to the later decisions, this alternative claim would equally have failed, but it did not become necessary to decide the point in that case, because the insurers had paid the amount of the premiums into court Five years afterwards, however, in *Duckett* v *Williams* (1834), 2 C & M 348, where there was a similar condition, the point was distinctly raised, and decided in favour of the insurers and in *Thomson* v *Weems* (1884), 9 App Cas 671, H L , Lord BLACKBURN, at p 682, said that " it became usual, I do not know when, but at least for the last fifty years, to insert a term in the contract "—he is speaking of life insurance contracts only—" that, if the statements were untrue, the premiums should be forfeited That, no doubt, is a hard bargain for the assured, if he has innocently warranted what is not accurate, but if he has warranted it, ' untruth,' without any moral guilt, avoids the insurance, and in *Duckett* v *Williams*, in 1834, it was held, on reasoning to my mind irresistible, that in a declaration substantially as far as regards this point the same as this, what was untrue so as to have the effect of avoiding the insurance, was also untrue so as to cause the forfeiture of the premium."

contracts for the sale of land (*p*). Where, on the other hand, the contract is not one which, being voidable only in the first instance, the party complaining elects to avoid, but is one which either the parties have agreed in certain events shall be, or the law deems to be, void *ab initio*, the general rule is directly contrary. In such cases, the money is *primâ facie* not returnable. Of the former species of void contracts, it may be doubted whether there is a single illustration to be found in the authorities; for, as has already been shown, in every reported case where the parties have provided that the contract shall be void in the event of non-disclosure, misrepresentation, or breach of covenant, the term "void" has, for obvious reasons, been construed as "voidable" (*q*). It has been held, however, that if, in agreeing that the contract shall be void (even on the assumption that voidness, and not mere voidability, was really intended), the parties have also agreed that the money (*e.g.* a premium) shall not be returned, they have, whilst contracting for voidness, contracted themselves out of its normal consequences (*r*). As to the other species of void contract, the kind of contract which is void for illegality, the money is never returnable except in the event of the contract having been induced by a fraudulent misrepresentation on the one side, and an innocent belief on the other, that the contract was legal (*s*). Where both parties were honestly ignorant of the illegality, the general rule prevails (*t*), and so also, where both parties were guiltily conscious of the illegality (*u*).

233. Nor will rescission be granted even when complete restitution is practicable as between the immediate parties, if the undoing of the contract would prejudicially affect the rights or interests which any third party has acquired under it, in good faith and for value, whilst it was still unavoided: for this would constitute an obvious injustice to the third party who would thus be punished for no fault of his own, and for the benefit of the person by whose conduct and inaction he was encouraged to acquire those rights and interests (*v*). The refusal of relief in such a case, whilst operating as an act

(*p*) The stipulation may be express, or, in the case of deposits, implied from the mere use of the term "deposit," which has now, from long usage, acquired a definite business connotation, as a sum paid on the understanding that it is not to be returned if the purchaser makes default, but is to be absolutely forfeited · see *Howe* v *Smith* (1884), 27 C D. 89, C A (at pp 89, 95, 100-102)

(*q*) See § 225, and note (ı) thereto, *ante*

(*r*) *Sparenborg* v *Edinburgh Life Insurance Co*, [1912] 1 K B 195, *per* BRAY, J, at p 204 This was not a case of non disclosure, or even of misrepresentation, but of breach of a condition not to travel beyond specified limits, but the question discussed in the text is independent of the particular event agreed to be a ground of forfeiture

(*s*) As in *British Workman's and General Assurance Co* v *Cunliffe* (1902), 18 T L R. 502, C A. (*per* VAUGHAN WILLIAMS, L J, at p 503), *Tofts* v *Pearl Life Assurance Co.* (1913), 30 T L R 212, Div Ct (*per* BRAY, J, at p 213), affd (1914), 31 T. L. R 29, C A.

(*t*) This was the case in *Harse* v *Pearl Life Assurance Co*, [1904] 1 K B 558, C A, *Phillips* v *Royal London Mutual Insurance Co* (1911), 105 L. T. 136, Div Ct., *Evanson* v *Crookes* (1912), 106 L. T 264 (HAMILTON, J)

(*u*) As in *Elson* v *Crookes* (1912), 106 L T 462, Div. Ct, *Howarth* v *Pioneer Life Association* (1912), 107 L T 155, Div Ct

(*v*) *Clough* v *L & N W Railway Co* (1871), L R 7 Exch 26, Exch Ch, *per Cur*, at p 35 "if, in the interval while he is deliberating, an innocent third party has acquired an interest in the property , it will preclude him from exercising his right to rescind."

of bare justice to the third party, cannot be deemed unjust to the party complaining who, though he has actively done no injury to such third party, has at least enabled, if not induced, him to enter into transactions, make payments, incur liabilities, give credit, or otherwise alter his position to his detriment, on the faith of the continued subsistence and validity of the contract which it is sought to annul The party complaining is, as has been pointed out (*w*), under no obligation to make his election whether to affirm or avoid the contract within any specified time, or at all . he may sit on the fence and adopt a waiting policy for as long as he pleases, but he does so at his own risk, and cannot complain if in the meantime rights have been acquired by others which must be respected, and which cannot be respected without depriving him of remedies which otherwise he would have been entitled to enforce against the party charged (*x*)

234. Lastly, the rescission must be *in toto*, or not at all (*y*), where the contract is one entire and homogeneous thing In such cases the Court cannot permit itself the generous delicacy of the curate in the story, or affect to distinguish between the good and bad parts of the egg Where, however, there are separate and severable covenants or stipulations to be considered, or there are several parties or interests to be dealt with, or the instrument sought to be avoided has more than one object, and may be put in suit in more than one character, the Court may, if the other circumstances of the case justify such an order, rescind one of such covenants or stipulations, without interfering with any other (*z*), or set aside the contract against one of such parties in respect of some partial or severable interest of the party complaining, without affecting the position of the others or requiring them to be joined (*a*), or allow the instrument to stand in one of its characters, whilst rescinding it in the character in which it is put forward (*b*)

(*w*) In §§ 216, 217, 218, *ante*.

(*x*) The question is most frequently raised where the contract sought to be rescinded is a contract to take shares in a company which has been induced by misrepresentation. This class of case is fully discussed, with reference to the authorities (which are numerous), in § 310 of the author's *Law of Actionable Misrepresentation*

(*y*) *Myddleton* v *Lord Kenyon* (1794), 2 Ves 391 (*per* Lord ELDON, L C, at p 408), *Beaumont* v *Dukes* (1822), Jac 422, 23 R R. 110, a case of defence to specific performance (*per* PLUMER, M.R, at p 426 "it must stand or fall to the full extent"), *Clarke* v *Dickson* (1858), E B & E 148 (*per* CROMPTON, J, at p 155 . "the plaintiff must rescind *in toto* or not at all"), *Mostyn* (*Lord*) v. *West Mostyn Coke & Iron Co* (1876), 1 C. P D 145, another defence case (*per* LINDLEY, J, at p 154), *United Shoe Machinery Co of Canada* v *Brunet*, [1900] A C 330, P C (at p 310)

(*z*) As to a deed containing several covenants, which for that purpose may be regarded as two deeds written on one parchment, see Com Dig Fait, B 2, on the authority of which passage SWINFEN EADY, J, in *Bagot* v *Chapman*, [1907] 2 Ch 222, held that the mortgage deed there in question might be regarded as good *quoad* one of the covenants, and "*ab initio* void for the residue" (pp. 227, 228) In *Howatson* v *Webb*, [1908] 1 Ch 1, C A, though it was doubted whether the application of the principle to the facts of *Bagot* v *Chapman* was justified, no doubt was thrown on the correctness of the principle itself

(*a*) See the opinion to this effect of Lord LANGDALE, M R, at pp 356, 357 of *Harley* v *Stone* (1840), 3 Beav 355

(*b*) Thus in *Haygarth* v *Wearing* (1871), L R 12 Eq 320, WICKENS, V -C, made a declaration that the deed there in question was void as a conveyance, but good as a security. So also, in *Re Gomersall* (1875), 1 C D 137, C A, affirmed *sub nom Jones* v *Gordon* (1877), 2 App Cas. 616, H L, the bills of exchange which were the subject of the proceedings were held to be good as securities for certain portions of their face value, but void as to the residue

235. The above are the fundamental principles on which relief by way of avoidance is granted, or refused, in whichever of the various forms of active proceeding that relief may be sought   It remains to consider these several forms in order   They comprise, (1) the ordinary action (including counter-claim) for rescission, (2) the action (or counterclaim) for money had and received, (3) in cases of vendor and purchaser, proceedings under the Vendor and Purchaser Act, 1874, (4) in the like cases, where the sale is by the direction of the Court, applications to be discharged from the contract by way of motion to the Court directing the sale.

236. The object of the action (or counterclaim) for rescission being to avoid both the contract itself and also the consequences which have flowed and, but for its avoidance, may flow from it, it follows that the relief granted will comprise or involve, first, a decision, if not a declaration, that the contract is void, and must be deemed to have been so *ab initio* (c) , secondly, an order for the setting aside or cancellation of the contract, and, in certain cases, the physical surrender of the instrument of contract to the party complaining (d) , thirdly, provisions for repayment or retransfer to the party complaining of all moneys, property, or benefits, if any, which the party charged has received under the contract, on the terms of the like restitution to the party charged of all moneys, property, or benefits if any, which the party complaining has received thereunder (e) , and, lastly, such terms, if any, as may reasonably be required in order to protect the parties from future enforcement by either of them against the other of any rights derived therefrom (f).

237. Though not strictly necessary, it is not unusual to prefix to the order for rescission a formal or express declaration that the contract is void (g), the meaning and effect of which is that the contract, though voidable only till that date (h), is, when once declared or adjudged void by the Court, treated as having been void from the commencement, so as to nullify all mesne dispositions of property and acts consequential upon the contract which have taken place since it was concluded (i)   This intervening period may be likened to the " period of relation back " on adjudication of insolvency (j), and, on the other hand, contrasted with the period which elapses between the making of a contract and the date at which, without default of either party, the performance of it in the manner intended becomes impossible by reason of some event which destroys that which was contemplated as its

(c) See § 237, *inf.*
(d) See § 238, *inf*
(e) See § 239, *inf*
(f) See § 240, *inf*
(g) This was done in most of the rescission cases cited in this Chapter.
(h) See §§ 225, 226, *ante*
(i) *Reese River Mining Co* v *Smith* (1869), L R 4 H L. 64, *per* Lord HATHERLEY, L C , at pp 73, 74, Lord WESTBURY at pp 77, 78, and Lord CAIRNS at p 81   The same rule applies to the restitution which the party complaining has to make as a condition of relief *e.g* if he has received from the party charged both principal moneys and interest under the contract, he must restore the whole of both, which are treated as making one principal sum, and must pay interest to the party charged on the principal sum so constituted : see *Murray* v *Palmer* (1805), 2 Sch & Lefr 472 (at p 488)
(j) See the various treatises on bankruptcy, and the liquidation of companies

foundation, where the law regards what is past as irrevocably past, and gives neither party any right of recovery or otherwise against the other in respect of any payment, act, or liability, made, done, or incurred during such period (*k*)   Such declarations are convenient prefaces to, and the logical justifications of, the judicial orders and directions which follow   Like the preamble to a statute which in strictness *incipit a jussione* (*l*), a preface of this kind may be dispensed with, since the order for rescission presupposes a judicial determination to the same effect as that which is expressed in a declaration   but, for the prevention of subsequent disputes as to the meaning and grounds of the judgment (if, for instance, *res judicata* should be set up), it may serve a useful purpose (*m*), just as a preamble may, in cases of doubtful construction, be used as a key to the interpretation of the enactive provisions of the statute   And there may even be cases where a declaration is substantially the sole remedy which for the moment is required (*n*)

238. Where the contract consists of, or is contained in, more than one document, every one of such documents is the subject of the order for rescission ; and in certain cases, as has already been pointed out, conveyances or other instruments executed for the purpose of completing, or otherwise consequential upon, the contract may be set aside, as well as the contract itself (*o*)   The " tearing up," which is the literal meaning of rescission, is ordinarily understood only in a symbolical sense.   But, where the instrument is in the physical possession or control of the party charged, he will be directed by the Court to physically deliver it up to be destroyed or cancelled (*p*), unless its defect or invalidity appears on the face of it, and even

(*k*) As in *Taylor* v *Caldwell* (1863), 3 B & S 826, and the cases arising out of the postponed Coronation of King Edward VII , particularly *Krell* v *Henry*, [1903] 2 K B. 740, C. A , and *Chandler* v *Webster*, [1904] 1 K B 493, C A

(*l*) Jurists and political philosophers are not at one on the question of the utility of " prologues " or " proems " in legislation   see Plato, *Legg* iv, 722, 723 Seneca, *Ep* 93, Bacon *De Augm Sc* , Bk viii, Aphorisms 65, 69, 70, 71   Modern jurisprudence is (many think, unwisely) hostile to preambles, even to the extent of periodically massacring these innocents in successive Statute Law Revision Acts

(*m*) At p 478 of *Gordon* v *Gordon* (1821), 3 Swanst 400 (a family compromise case), Lord ELDON, L C , said   " I think the defendant is entitled to have a declaration inserted in the decree of the ground on which I proceed in holding the deeds void   Such declarations on the record are always useful, enabling the parties to deal with them as they think right."   It took 22 months to settle the decree, which is set out verbatim from the Register Book at pp 478–482 of the report   Of these five pages, two and a half are occupied with the declarations   It will be observed that Lord ELDON was in this case insisting on the right of *the party charged* (who was the defendant) to have the declaration, quite irrespectively of the right of the party complaining

(*n*) An example of such a case is *Brooke* v *Lord Mostyn* (1865), 3 De G J & S 373, where TURNER and KNIGHT BRUCE, LL JJ , reversing ROMILLY, M R , made a declaration that the compromise of a suit for the recovery of a legacy, and the order of the Court approving it, were not binding on the plaintiff, to whom they gave liberty to prosecute such further proceedings as he might be advised   And see *Clements* v *Hall* (1858), 2 De G & J 173 (where it was a question only of a chief clerk's certificate)   Cp also the case which is cited in note (*r*) to § 138, *inf*.

(*o*) See the cases cited in the notes to § 230, *ante*, and also *Reynell* v *Sprye* (1852), 1 De G M. & G 660 (*per* KNIGHT BRUCE, L.J , at pp 682, 683, and Lord CRANWORTH, L.J , at pp 710, 711), where a contract which would not have been made but for the deed immediately impeached was set aside, as well as the deed itself

(*p*) See, for instance, *Rivaz* v *Gerussi Bros & Co* (1880), 6 Q B D 222, C A , one of the few cases of marine insurance in which the party complaining was the *actor*   *Traill* v

then he will be required to do so if his conduct is proved to have been of such a character as to render it probable that he may in the future make an unconscionable use of the instrument by harassing and vexatious (even though hopeless) litigation, or if in any way it may, in his hands, or in the hands of third parties to whom he may transfer it, constitute a " cloud upon the title " of the party complaining, or otherwise hamper him in the enjoyment of his rights (q) And there may even be cases where, though the instrument has been delivered up to, or is in the possession of, the party complaining, such party will still be deemed entitled to an order of the Court for its cancellation (r)

239. Having decreed rescission, the next step in the remedial procedure of the Court is to provide for the undoing of the past on both sides by directions for mutual restoration *in specie* of all benefits received under the rescinded contract (s) The party charged must repay all moneys (t), and (unless the circumstances are exceptional) with interest (u), and reconvey or retransfer

Baring (1864), 4 De G J & S 318, and *London Assurance Co* v *Mansel* (1879), 11 C D 363 (at p 372), two of the equally rare instances in life assurance cases of the party complaining suing for rescission, and the vendor and purchaser cases of *Gibson* v *D'Este* (1843), 2 Y & C (CH) 542, and *Smith* v *Harrison* (1857), 26 L J (CH) 412.

(q) The principal cases in which this topic is debated are *Bromley* v. *Holland* (1802), 7 Ves. 3 (per Lord ELDON, L C, at p 21), *Ryan* v *Macmath* (1819), 3 Brown C C 15 (per Lord THURLOW, L C, at p 16), *Duncan* v. *Worrall* (1822), 10 Price 31 (at p 42), *Simpson* v *Lord Howden* (1837), 3 My & Cr 97 (per Lord COTTENHAM, L C, at p 102); *Cooper* v *Joel* (1859), 1 De G F & J 240 (per Lord CAMPBELL, L C, at pp 245, 246, differing from ROMILLY, M R, in the court below, reported 27 Beav 313, on this point, though affirming the decision itself), *Onions* v *Cohen* (1865), 2 H & M 354 (per PAGE WOOD, V C, at p 360), *Hoare* v *Bembridge* (1872), 8 Ch App 22 (per Lord SELBORNE, L C, at p 26), *Brooking* v *Maudslay* (1888), 38 C D 636 (per STIRLING, J, at pp 643, 644 646) The rules stated in the text are now well settled, though in early times equity judges seem to have been somewhat chary of exercising their jurisdiction in this matter, hesitating, as Portia did in a memorable suretyship case (*Shylock* v *Antonio*, reported *sub nom* The *Merchant of Venice* by William Shakespeare, Act IV, Sc 1), to lay profane hands on a solemnly executed instrument, or to "tear the bond," except with the consent of the parties Indeed in that case, even after the declaration of the court that the bond was void for illegality, it does not appear from the narrative of the gifted reporter that it was ordered to be delivered up to the defendant, or that it was in fact destroyed by the learned Nerissa, the acting associate, or any other officer of the Venetian Court

(r) As in *London & Provincial Marine Insurance Co* v *Seymour* (1873), L R 17 Eq 85, where the insurance company sued for rescission of two marine policies obtained from them by fraudulent concealment and misrepresentation, and, notwithstanding that they had by the date of the hearing succeeded in two actions brought against them at law on the policies, which decisions had been affirmed by the Exchequer Chamber, and not withstanding, further, that the policies had been given up to them, and were then in their possession, so that no *physical* cancellation was required, BACON, V C, decided cancellation, observing at pp 90, 91 "I cannot hesitate for a moment in making the only decree I am asked for now, viz that the policies which have been delivered up shall now be cancelled The plaintiffs to whom the policies have been delivered are entitled not only to retain possession of them, but to a decree of the Court that they be now cancelled "

(s) If the party charged has received nothing, this element in the relief is not required On the other hand, if the party complaining has received nothing, the remedy by way of money had and received, or analogous form of action—see § 241, *inf*—is open to him, and is often the more appropriate procedure

(t) No difficulty ever arises as to this See, generally, the rescission cases cited in this Section.

(u) Such interest is regarded as restitution, not damages *Re Metropolitan Coal Consumers Association, Karberg's Case,* [1892] 3 Ch. 1, C A, at p 17 As to the rate of interest, the practice has not been uniform Where fraud or misconduct is shown, the rate now usually allowed is 5 per cent see *Capel & Co* v *Sim's Ships Composition Co*

or redeliver (by appropriate instruments, where necessary) all property and rights, whether in possession or in action, which he has received (v), on the terms that the party complaining do on his part make a corresponding restoration or allowance in account (w). For this purpose, all necessary accounts and inquiries will be directed (x). The party charged must indemnify the party complaining against all payments made or liabilities incurred under the contract, but he is under no obligation to make good to him any loss or liability not strictly incurred under, though arising " out of," the contract, for the latter expression, if construed literally, would be wide enough to include damages in the ordinary sense, which are clearly not recoverable in rescission proceedings (y) In certain vendor and

(1888), 58 L. T. 807 (*per* KEKEWICH, J , at p 811) . *Greenwood* v *Leather Shod Wheel Co.,* [1900] 1 Ch 421, C. A On the other hand, in *Rawlins* v. *Wickham* (1853), 3 De G & J 304, *Aberaman Ironworks, Ltd* v. *Wickens* (1868), 4 Ch. App 101, and *Newbigging* v *Adam* (1886), 34 C D 582, C A , 4 per cent only was given. And this is the usual rate where the deposit is ordered to be returned on the rescission of a contract for the sale of land *Jacobs* v. *Revell,* [1900] 2 Ch 858 In *Henderson* v. *Lacon* (1868), L. R. 5 Eq 249, PAGE WOOD, V.-C , for some reason (not stated) disallowed interest altogether (pp 263, 264)

(v) This also is ordinary practice. See generally the rescission cases cited in this Section.

(w) To take the most common examples where the contract set aside is a contract to buy or take shares, the party complaining, if a purchaser, must retransfer the shares, and repay, or allow in account, any dividends he has received in respect of them, and indemnify the party charged against future liability thereunder, as in *Stainbank* v *Fernley* (1839), 9 Sim. 556 Where the contract is one of insurance, the insurer is required, in the absence of fraud or illegality, or express agreement to the contrary (see § 232, *ante*), to return the premiums Where the contract is one of sale, the party complaining, if he is the vendor, must return the purchase-money, or any instalment thereof which he has received (see the cases cited in the notes to § 259, *post*), but not, as a rule, the deposit (for the reasons given in § 232, note (p), *ante*), and must allow the costs of repairs or work done by the party charged to or on the property, if a chattel, or of permanent improvements thereto, if land see *Chesterfield (Earl)* v. *Harding* (1911), "Times," 2nd March (*per* WARRINGTON, J) as to chattels, and *Addis* v *Campbell* (1841), 4 Beav 101, and *Haygarth* v. *Wearing* (1871), L. R. 12 Eq 320, as to land. If a purchaser, the party complaining must retransfer all property of which he is in possession under the rescinded contract. Where the party complaining has to restore money received under the contract, he must do so with interest, even where the party charged has been guilty of fraud see *Chesterfield (Earl)* v *Harding, sup* (where WARRINGTON, J , fixed the rate of interest at 5 per cent., even in the case of a grossly defrauded vendor) : and, where he has received principal and interest under the contract, the two are massed together as one new principal sum, on which, and not merely on the original principal, he is required to pay interest to the party charged, as the condition of rescission : *Murray* v *Palmer* (1805), 2 Sch. & Lefr 472 (at p 488) Where the property received under the contract is not money, and the party complaining finds himself unable to restore it *in specie*, he is without remedy altogether, as has already been explained · see § 231, *ante*

(x) See *Addis* v *Campbell, sup* , *Haygarth* v *Wearing, sup* , and generally, the rescission cases cited in this Section

(y) In *Newbigging* v *Adam* (1886), 34 C D 582, C. A , this question was elaborately discussed The qualified proposition stated in the text represents the view of BOWEN, L.J Some of the expressions used by COTTON, L J (at pp 588–590), possibly, and the observations of FRY, L J (at p 596), are of a wider and more unqualified character In the House of Lords, this case, *sub nom Adam* v *Newbigging* (1888), 13 App. Cas. 309, H L. was so dealt with that it became unnecessary to decide the point in question, and Lord WATSON (p 324), and Lord HERSCHELL (p 341), expressly declined to deliver any opinion upon it. In *Whittington* v *Seale Hayne* (1900), 82 L T 49, FARWELL, J , after calling attention to the divergent language of the judgments delivered in the C A in *Newbigging* v *Adam, sup* , expressed his preference for that of BOWEN, L J , and held accordingly that the plaintiffs, who had been induced to take a lease of premises by misrepresentation, and on that ground were entitled to rescission and consequential relief, had a right, as

purchaser cases, the purchaser may be allowed the costs of investigating the title, and, where the purchase has been completed, the costs, charges and expenses to which he has been put in consequence of, or incidental to, the purchase and the conveyance (z).

240. Where the party complaining requires protection from possible attempts in the future on the part of the party charged to enforce against him any term of the rescinded contract, or to deal with property acquired by him thereunder as if there had been no rescission, a perpetual injunction may be granted at the trial in terms adequate to meet the particular mischief apprehended; as, for instance, to restrain the party charged from trans ferring shares (a), or making calls (b), in cases of purchase of, or subscription for, shares in companies, or from parting with furniture of which possession has been obtained under a lease which has been set aside (c). Further the party complaining is entitled, on proper terms, to an interlocutory injunction restraining the party charged until the trial of the action from forfeiting property of the party complaining under powers conferred by the contract sought to be rescinded, which contract the party complaining has repudiated and therefore cannot consistently with the attitude he has taken up recognize By such an order an ingenious manœuvre of companies, when sued by a shareholder for rescission of a contract to take shares on the ground of fraud, may now be frustrated The device is of this nature As soon as the share-holder repudiates his contract, which involves the necessity of refusing to pay calls, since such payment would be evidence of affirmation, the company, pursuant to the contract contained in its articles of association, purports to forfeit the shares with the view of doubly entrenching itself, the idea being that, even if the party complaining succeeds, it will be no worse off by reason of the forfeiture, whilst, if he should fail, and then claim to retain the benefits and exercise the rights secured to him under the contract which in that event would be held to be valid, it will be in a position to retort upon him that the contract has been determined pursuant to its terms. To meet this stratagem, it has now been held that an inter-locutory injunction may be granted to a plaintiff in such circumstances, on his paying the amount of the calls into court, and undertaking in damages, so that, if he be unable to establish a case for rescission at the trial, neither

part of such consequential relief, to an indemnity against the costs incurred by them in connection with the requirements of the local authority that the premises should be put into a sanitary state of repair, and against rent, rates, and taxes, and expenses of repairs generally, but not to payment of the value of stock lost during their occupation of the premises (which they had taken for breeding prize poultry), or of their loss of profit on the sale of such stock, loss of breeding season, &c, the latter being " losses arising out of the contract " generally, in other words damages, rather than a mere indemnity against payments and liabilities " so far as regards the rights and obligations which had been created by the contract." That damages, as distinct from indemnity and restitution, are not recoverable in any proceedings for rescission, which means that they are not recoverable at all where the ground of rescission is non disclosure, has never been doubted see § 223, note (y), ante

(z) See § 250, and note (b) thereto, post
(a) *Walsham* v *Stainton* (1863), 1 De G J. & S 678
(b) *Henderson* v *Lacon* (1868), L R. 5 Eq 249
(c) *Lempriere* v *Lange* (1879), 12 C. D 675

party is prejudiced : the shareholder still holds his unforfeited shares, and the company has, ready to be paid out to it, the amount of the calls, and also an undertaking to satisfy any damage it may have sustained (d).

241. The second form of active proceedings which may be instituted by the party complaining is the action (or counterclaim) for money had and received, or for the delivery of property, without asking for rescission of the contract This form of proceeding is properly resorted to where the party complaining has received nothing under the contract, and has nothing therefore to restore to the party charged as the condition of relief, but has paid money or transferred property thereunder, and where the only concern of the party complaining is to get back his money or property, and no judicial rescission is necessary (e), or where the party charged is not attempting or intending to enforce the contract (f), or has abandoned it (g), in which circumstances again a formal order to set aside the contract is not needed. In any such proceeding, whether by way of action or counterclaim, or, where authorized by statute (as in certain cases of life insurance), in the form of a claim before a court of summary jurisdiction (h), relief is given

(d) This was the decision of NEVILLE, J, in *Lamb* v *Sambas Rubber and Gutta Percha Co*, [1908] 1 Ch 845, and of the C A in *Jones* v. *Pacaya Rubber & Produce Co*, [1911] 1 K B 455, C A (see the observations of BUCKLEY, L J, at pp 457, 458), overruling *Ripley* v *Paper Bottle Co* (1887), 57 L J (ch) 327

(e) See *Re Ruby Consolidated Mining Co*, *Askew's Case* (1874), 9 Ch App 664, where relief in the nature of rescission, under s 32 of the Companies Consolidation Act, 1908 (6 Edw. 7, c 69), was refused on the ground that, the shares having been fully paid, rectification of the register was out of the question, the proper remedy being an action for money had and received In *London and Provincial Marine Insurance Co* v *Seymour* (1873), L R 17 Eq 85—as to which see note (r) to § 238, *ante*—cancellation was decreed, though the plaintiff had succeeded when sued at law, and the policies had been delivered up to them But the circumstances of this case were somewhat exceptional In *Oelkers* v *Ellis*, [1914] 2 K B 139, though rescission was formally claimed, it was quite unnecessary to ask for it at the trial, the contract not having been performed, and return of the money being sufficient relief

(f) As in *Flight* v *Booth* (1834), 1 Bing (N C) 370, where before the arbitrator the defendant had put forward no claim under the contract (see p 373)

(g) As in *Carlish* v *Salt*, [1906] 1 Ch. 335, where the defendants had themselves treated the contract as abandoned, and had pulled down the premises the subject of the sale

(h) By s 7 of the Collecting Societies and Industrial Assurance Companies Act, 1896 (59 & 60 Vict c 26), it is provided that "in all disputes between   an industrial assurance company and any member or person insured, or any person claiming through a member or person insured, or under the rules, that member or person may, notwithstanding any provisions of the rules of the society to the contrary, apply to   the court of summary jurisdiction for the place where that member or other person resides, and the court may settle that dispute," &c An "industrial assurance company" is defined by s 1 (b) as including "every such . . person or body of persons, whether corporate or unincorporate, granting insurances on any one life for a less sum than twenty pounds . as receives contributions or premiums by means of collectors at a greater distance than ten miles from the   principal place of business of the   . company, and   at less periodical intervals than two months" This has been construed to mean, though the section does not say so in terms, that a company, though answering to the statutory description, is only subject to the jurisdiction of the magistrates where the policy in respect of which the jurisdiction is invoked is for less than £20 *Cowling* v. *Topping*, [1906] 1 K B 466, Div Ct. "Disputes" under this provision would obviously include a claim for return of premiums, as well as a claim for the policy moneys, and such claims were the subject of applications to a court of summary jurisdiction in *British Workman's and General Assurance Co* v *Cunliffe* (1902), 18 T. L R 502, C. A., and in *Phillips* v *Royal London Mutual Insurance Co* (1911), 105 L. T 136, Div Ct. It will be observed that the assured obtains at least two advantages by resorting to the statutory procedure :

or withheld on precisely the same principles as in an ordinary action (or counterclaim) for rescission (i), for obviously the question of the title to relief can in no way be affected by the mere circumstance that in the one class of case the judicial treatment of the contract as vitiated and vacated by the non-disclosure, or misrepresentation, or whatever the invalidating cause may be, results in bilateral restitution, and, in the other, results in unilateral rescission only. Where it is sought to recover money only, as, for instance, sums paid by way of deposit, or on account of purchase-money, in contracts of sale and purchase (j), or premiums under insurance policies (k), or application and allotment moneys in respect of shares in companies (l), or other moneys (m), the claim, or counterclaim (n), is for money had and received, which is recoverable with interest if the money was both "obtained by fraud, and retained by fraud," but otherwise without interest (o) Where it is sought to recover property other than money, e g goods, which the party complaining has parted with under the contract, without having received anything in exchange, and therefore without having anything to restore, the remedy is trover or detinue (p), or other like form of proceeding (q)

242. The third and fourth kinds of active proceeding which, as above-mentioned, are available to the party complaining, viz an application under the Vendor and Purchaser Act, 1874, and an application by a purchaser of property sold by direction of a court in any cause or matter to the court directing the sale for an order discharging him from the purchase, are special

in the first place, he can apply to the court nearest to his, and not the company's, residence or place of business, and secondly, he cannot be excluded by the rules from his right to apply to this tribunal

(i) See *Flight* v *Booth*, *sup* (per TINDAL, C J , delivering the judgment of the Court, at pp 375, 376) , *Stone* v *City & County Bank* (1877), 3 C P D 282, C A (per BRETT, LJ , at pp 309, 310, and COTTON, L J , at p 312, affirming the views of LINDLEY, J , in the court below , at p 294) , *Manners* v *Whitehead* (1898), 1 F 171

(j) See §§ 250, 251, *post*

(k) There is no reported case of an assured suing for a return of premium on the ground of non disclosure by the insurer, because, ordinarily, no duty of disclosure lies upon the latter but, as Lord MANSFIELD, C.J , pointed out—see § 89, and note (f) thereto, *ante*,—there might very well be special circumstances which would cast such a duty upon him, in which case the remedy of the assured would be an action for money had and received, as it is where the assured claims a return of the premiums on the ground of the insurer's fraudulent misrepresentation of the validity of the policy, or of the right of the assured to a free policy at the expiration of a certain period see *British Workman's and General Assurance Co* v *Cunliffe*, *sup* , and *Kettlewell* v *Refuge Assurance Co* , [1908] 1 K B 545, C. A., "silently affirmed" in *Dom Proc.*, sub nom , *Refuge Assurance Co* v *Kettlewell*, [1909] A. C. 243, H L

(l) *Stone* v *City & County Bank*, *sup* , *Re Ruby Consolidated Mining Co* , *Askew's Case*, *sup*

(m) See the following miscellaneous cases, where the ground on which the money was returnable was misrepresentation *Duffel* v *Wilson* (1808), 1 Campb 401 (money paid to insure the plaintiff against being drawn for the militia), *Blair* v *Bromley* (1847), 2 Ph 354 (a sum paid for investment in a mortgage), *Moss & Co* v *Swansea Corporation* (1910), 74 J P 367 (a deposit paid to secure the performance of a contract), *Burdett* v *Horne et ux* (1911), 28 T L R 83, C A (subscriptions to various schemes)

(n) *Heywood* v. *Mallalieu* (1883), 25 C D 357, was a case of counterclaim

(o) *Johnson* v. *Regem*, [1904] A C 817, P C., at pp 821, 822

(p) *Jones* v *Keene* (1841), 2 M & Rob 348 , 62 R R 804 (trover for a life policy)

(q) *Moorhouse* v *Woolfe* (1882), 46 L T 374 (where the plaintiff sued a moneylender for delivery up of a bill of sale obtained by misrepresentation, he having repaid the whole of the money due with interest at the rate represented to be the rate charged) to contracts of sale and purchase, and will be dealt with hereafter when the nature of the remedies for non-disclosure in relation to this particular species of contract is separately considered (r).

Sub-s (2). Defensive Proceedings available to the Party Complaining.

243. Subject to the qualifications mentioned below (s), it may be stated broadly that, whenever the party complaining is in a position to obtain rescission of any contract on the ground of non-disclosure, he is equally in a position to establish a valid defence or answer on the same ground to any proceeding instituted against him by the party charged under or in respect of such contract, whether the proceeding be for specific performance (t), or for the direct, though not the specific, enforcement of the contract by recovery of a debt due thereunder (u), or for the indirect enforcement of it by recovery of damages for breach (v)   The non-disclosure in such cases may be set up not only as a defence to any action brought, but also as a reply or answer to any counterclaim pleaded, or affirmative case set up, by the party charged (w).   It may be insisted on as an answer to applications as well as actions (x)   It is immaterial whether the party complaining does, or does not, add to his defence or answer a counterclaim for rescission or analogous relief.   He may, if he pleases (y), but he is not in the least bound to do so (z)

(r) See §§ 251, 252, *post*

(s) See §§ 245, 246, *inf*

(t) For examples of successful defences on the ground of non disclosure to actions for specific performance, see the compromise case of *Re Roberts*, [1905] 1 Ch 704, C. A , and the vendor and purchaser cases cited in the notes to § 245, *post*

(u) Where the party complaining has succeeded in insurance or suretyship cases, he has almost invariably done so by way of defence to an action for the policy moneys, or to an action on the guarantee   see §§ 249, 254, *post   Mostyn (Lord) v West Mostyn Coke & Iron Co* (1876), 1 C. P. D 145, is an instance of a successful defence to an action for rent   In *Evans v Edmonds* (1853), 13 C B 777, the party complaining set up and made good a defence to a claim for arrears of annuity under a separation deed   In *Allis Chalmers Co v Fidelity and Deposit Co of Maryland* (1913), 30 T L R 445, C A , and in *Thornton-Smith v Motor Union Insurance Co* (1913), 30 T L R 139, the defence was to an action claiming a declaration that the policy was valid and subsisting

(v) Instances of defences to actions for damages are the vendor and purchaser cases of *Ellis v Rogers* (1885), 29 C D 661, C. A , and *Molyneux v Hautrey*, [1903] 2 K B. 487, C A , and the breach of contract to marry cases cited in note (f) to § 257, *post*

(w) As in the vendor and purchaser cases of *Fothergill v Phillips* (1871), 6 Ch App 770, and *Nottingham Patent Brick & Tile Co v Butler* (1886), 16 Q B D 778, C A   also in the release or compromise cases of *M'Carthy v Decaix* (1831), 2 Russ & M 614, and *Gilbert v Endean* (1878), 9 C D 259, C A

(x) As, for example, to applications under the Vendor and Purchaser Act, 1874 (see § 251, *post*), or to proceedings under O XIV   see *Re General Railway Syndicate, Whiteley's Case*, [1900] 1 Ch 365.

(y) A counterclaim for the return of the deposit, with interest, was added to the defence to an action of specific performance in *Heywood v Mallalieu* (1883), 25 C. D. 357, and *Re Roberts*, [1905] 1 Ch 704, C A , and in each case the party complaining succeeded both in defence and counterclaim   So also in *Shepherd v Croft*, [1911] 1 Ch 521, though there both defence and counterclaim failed   Cp the misrepresentation cases of *Redgrave v Hurd* (1881), 20 C D 1, C A , *Smith v Land and House Property Corporation* (1884), 27 C D 7, C A ; *Components Tube Co v Naylor*, [1900] 2 Ir R 1, where both defence and counterclaim were made good

(z) In marine insurance actions, for example, it is not the practice to do so, for obviously it would serve no useful purpose in such cases.

244. With the two exceptions mentioned below (a), the party complaining who relies upon non-disclosure as a defence or answer must allege and establish precisely the same facts and matters as those which the party complaining who relies upon non-disclosure as a ground for rescission is required to allege and establish (b), and the evidence which is necessary and sufficient for the latter purpose is necessary and sufficient for the former (c). Further, all such evidence as is essential and adequate to sustain any of the recognized affirmative pleas to active proceedings for relief (d), is equally essential and adequate to support an affirmative reply or answer to any case of non-disclosure raised by way of defence to an action on the contract (e).

245. The first of the above-mentioned exceptions arises where non-disclosure is set up by the party complaining as an answer to a claim for specific performance. In such cases it is not always necessary to prove as much as would be required if the party complaining were suing for rescission (f). The reason for this divergence in practice will be apparent from a consideration of the essential distinction between proceedings for the specific performance of a contract and proceedings for its enforcement otherwise than *in specie*. In the latter case, the party is entitled, if his cause of action is established, to the relief he claims *ex debito justitiæ*, and the other party can only invalidate this absolute title by strict proof of all facts required to negative the validity of the contract itself,—in other words, by proof of everything which it would be incumbent on him to establish in an action to rescind the contract; whereas, specific performance being a particular form of equitable remedy which it is within the discretion of the Court to grant or to refuse, either wholly or upon such terms and conditions as may appear in the circumstances of the particular case just and convenient, less evidence of questionable or unfair dealing will induce the Court to decline the exercise of the discretionary jurisdiction thus invoked, and to withhold from the party charged a form of remedy which is, in a sense, almost an indulgence, than will induce it to adjudge and declare, at the instance of the party

(a) Which are dealt with in §§ 245, 246, *inf*

(b) These are the subject of Sect. 3, *ante*.

(c) The cases cited in the notes to Sect. 3, *ante*, as authorities for the rules there stated as to the burden of proof which rests on the party complaining, include cases of defence, as well as cases of active proceedings

(d) See Sect. 4, *ante*

(e) See the cases, generally, cited in the notes to Sect. 4, *ante*, which are quite as often cases of affirmative answers to defences setting up non-disclosure, as defences to actions claiming rescission on that ground. In note (x) to § 206, and note (a) to § 207, *ante*, the two species of case are separately classified. Illustrations of the same identity of rules in cases of misrepresentation are given in note (n) to § 341 of the author's *Law of Actionable Misrepresentation*

(f) *Re Banister* (1879), 12 C. D. 131, C. A. (*per* JESSEL, M R., at p 142 "the considerations which induce a court to rescind any contract, and the considerations which induce a court of equity to decline to enforce specific performance, are by no means the same"), *Re Terry and White's Contract* (1886), 32 C. D 14, C. A (*per* LINDLEY, L.J., at p. 27 "in all applications to the court involving the exercise of that discretion which the court invariably does exercise in ordering or refusing specific performance, it is necessary not to confound the principles or rules by which contracts are interpreted with the principles or rules which guide the court in enforcing or declining to enforce specific performance ") complaining, that the contract is wholly and for all purposes unenforceable Or, inverting the proposition, more evidence of fair dealing on the part of the party charged is required to entitle him to this special relief, where unfair dealing or want of candour is suggested by the party complaining, than where the ordinary remedies only are in question (g). It cannot be said that this rule is in the slightest degree unjust to the party charged, since he is not being deprived of all possible relief for ever, as he is when rescission is decreed against him · he is still at liberty to proceed against the party complaining by way of alternative claim for damages (h), from which claim the party complaining cannot escape by proving less than what is essential to prove in proceedings for rescission ; and thus the party complaining, though his burden of proof may be less when resisting specific performance than when resisting any other mode of enforcing the contract, obtains a correspondingly less complete and final measure of relief when he has discharged that burden. Moreover, it is always open to the Court, in a proper case, instead of absolutely refusing specific performance, to refuse it only in the event of the party charged declining to make pecuniary compensation or allowance to the party complaining, or to submit to any other terms which in the circumstances may be deemed equitable (i) The party charged in such cases is given an option of obtaining equity on doing equity, which is the fundamental condition of all discretionary relief (j).

(g) *Cadman* v *Horner* (1810), 18 Ves. 10, *per* GRANT, M.R , at pp. 11, 12 . " if upon the evidence the plaintiff "—in a suit for specific performance—" has been guilty of a degree of misrepresentation, operating to a certain, though a small, extent, that misrepresentation disqualifies him from calling for the aid of a court of equity . . He must, to entitle him to relief, be liable to *no imputation in the transaction* "; *and such a case is to be sharply distinguished from* " a case where the court is called upon to rescind an agreement . . which would admit of a different consideration ") In accordance with these views, the House of Lords in *Wilde* v *Gibson* (1848), 1 H L C 605, whilst refusing rescission, conceded that the party complaining might have succeeded if he had been merely resisting specific performance (*per* Lord COTTENHAM, L C , at pp 616, 617 " the contract of purchase is perfected by a conveyance To be relieved against that, fraudulent concealment must be shown *This is different from a bill by the vendor for specific performance of the contract*") The relief given to the party complaining in *Ellard* v *Lord Llandaff* (1810), 1 Ball & B 241, and in *Walters* v *Morgan* (1861), 3 De G F & J 718, was put upon the ground that he was a defendant to a suit for specific performance, and, in the former case at any rate, can only be justified on that ground see Sect 8, Sub s (4), *post*

(h) The Court has now power to give damages not only in lieu of, or in addition to, specific performance, where there is a case for such latter form of relief, but also as an alternative thereto, where there is no such case See *Fry's Specific Performance*, § 1306 In earlier times, the party was remitted to his remedy at law

(i) Thus specific performance was only granted on such terms in *Scott* v. *Hanson* (1829), 1 Russ & M 128 (Lord ELDON, L C), *King* v *Wilson* (1843), 6 Beav 124 (*per* Lord LANGDALE, M R , at pp 128, 129), *Hughes* v *Jones* (1861), 3 De G F & J 307 (*per* KNIGHT-BRUCE and TURNER, LL JJ) Of course no reference is intended to be made in the text to the class of case dealt with in §§ 206, 207, *ante*, where compensation is a term of the contract, to which wholly different considerations apply

(j) It must not be supposed, however, that the party charged has an *absolute right* to specific performance with an abatement or an allowance in the absence of an express condition in the contract to that effect, nor on the other hand, that the party complaining, in the absence of such a condition, or if there is a condition excluding him from compensation, can claim as *his* right an order for specific performance with an abatement of price, though he may be in a position to resist an application for specific performance without abatement, or to obtain rescission, if he asks for it see *Cordingley* v *Cheeseborough* (1862), 3 Giff 496 , 4 De G F & J 379 , *Re Terry and White's Contract* (1886), 32 C. D 14, C. A

246. The second of the exceptions referred to concerns pleading, rather than substance. It has been held that, where the party complaining is the *actor* in proceedings for rescission, it is not, but, where he is on the defensive, it is, incumbent on him to allege in his pleading that from the time when he first acquired knowledge of the undisclosed fact, he has taken no benefit, exercised no right, made no claim, and recognized no interest or liability, under or in respect of the contract on which he is being sued (*k*)

247. It should be noted that though, if not sued at once on the contract (*l*), it may be justifiable and prudent to remain on the defensive where there is a doubt whether the evidence in the possession of the party complaining is sufficient to obtain rescission, it is by no means wise to do so where there is no such doubt, for, generally speaking, the party complaining who comes promptly to the Court to annul the contract before the actual accrual of any liability thereunder has a better equity to relief than he who waits to be sued on such accrual (*m*)

(*per* LINDLEY, L.J., at pp 30, 31), *Re Hare and O'More's Contract*, [1901] 1 Ch. 93, Fry's *Specific Performance*, §§ 1213-1238. And, where it appears to the court that it is impossible to estimate the compensation or allowance, or that for any other reason the case is not one for a qualified refusal or a conditional grant, specific performance is refused absolutely, or granted absolutely, as the case may be, and the decree of the court is that of Portia in *Shylock v. Antonio* · "Thou shalt have nothing but the forfeiture, To be so taken at thy peril, Jew." See *Knatchbull v Krueger* (1815), 1 Madd 153, *Beaumont v Dukes* (1822), Jac 422, 23 R. R 110 (*per* PLUMER, M R, at p 426); *White v Cuddon* (1842), 8 Cl & Fin 766 (at pp 786, 792-794); *Brooke (Lord) v Rounthwaite* (1846), 5 Hare 298 (*per* WIGRAM, V C, at pp 303-305)

(*k*) The mere allegation in the plea that the party complaining is then and thereby electing to avoid the contract is a sufficient act of repudiation *Clough v L & N W. Railway Co* (1871), L R. 7 Exch 26, 36, Exch Ch But it appears to have been held that this allegation is not enough without going on to make the additional averments referred to in the text. A plea containing these additional averments was held good in *Bwlch y-Plwm Lead Mining Co v Baynes* (1867), L R 2 Exch 324 Pleas omitting them were held bad in *Deposit Life Assurance Co v Ayscough* (1856), 6 E & B 761 (*per* Lord CAMPBELL, C.J, at p 763, COLERIDGE, J, at pp 763, 764, and CROMPTON, J, at p 764), *Meldon v Lawless* (1870), 18 W R 261, *Anderson v Costello* (1871), 19 W R 628 In *Dawes v Harness* (1875), L R 10 C P 166, it was held that, after verdict, the plea must be taken to have included these averments, *because otherwise it would have been bad* So in the non-disclosure case (the preceding being all misrepresentation cases) of *Mostyn (Lord) v West Mostyn Coke & Iron Co* (1876), 1 C. P D 145, LINDLEY, J, at p 154, though doubting whether the plea was not defective, expressed the opinion that it was to be taken as if the necessary averments had been made In *Aaron's Reefs, Ltd v Twiss*, [1896] A C 273, H L, where the allegations in question had been omitted from the defence, which did not, moreover, even allege repudiation, the contract had been put an end to by forfeiture of the shares, so that from that time, there being nothing to repudiate, repudiation would have been an idle and illogical proceeding, and "there was no evidence, or contention, that the defendant had adhered to the contract" no valid objection, therefore, could be raised to the plea under these special circumstances, though otherwise there might have been (*per* Lord HALSBURY, L.C, at pp 277-279, who refers to the decision in *Deposit Life Assurance Co v Ayscough, sup*, without any disapproval)

(*l*) As from the nature of the case he invariably is, in certain classes of contract, *e.g*, marine insurance

(*m*) *Fenn v Craig* (1838), 3 Y & C (Eq Exch) 216 (*per* ALDERSON, B, at p 222. "it seems to me that, if the allegations in the bill are taken to be true, the contract ought to be rescinded, and that, with reference to that relief, the plaintiffs stand in a better position now than they would have done after the death of the party had occurred"). The observations in the text are, of course, inapplicable to a case where the contract has been put an end to by the party charged *Aaron's Reefs, Ltd v Twiss, sup* (*per* Lord MACNAGHTEN at p 293) In any such case, indeed, it would seem illogical to ask for rescission of that which *ex hypothesi* does not exist see § 228, *ante*

Sub-s. (3)   *What Remedies are Respectively Appropriate to the Several Classes of Case mentioned in this Chapter.*

248. The general nature of the proceedings available to the party complaining, whether by way of offence or defence, having been described, it remains to discuss the suitability of these various remedies to the seven classes of transaction with which the present Chapter is concerned (*n*).

249. For obvious reasons of mercantile convenience, in cases of insurance, whether marine (*o*), or life (*p*), the party complaining almost invariably asserts his rights by way of defence to an action on the policy. It is nevertheless in theory open to the insurer to sue for rescission, or (if the loss has been paid) for recovery of the sums so paid as money had and received, and in a very few exceptional cases this procedure has been adopted both by underwriters (*q*) and by life insurance companies (*r*), whilst, in the rare, but conceivable, event of the assured being in a position to set up non-disclosure against the insurer, it is obvious that his remedy must be by way of active proceedings (*s*). A very curious form of halting or partial relief in cases of marine insurance, devised by Lord ELLENBOROUGH, C J, in the year 1813, which failed to survive the deadly criticism passed upon it in judicial observations of a later date, may be mentioned here, as having at least some historical interest The theory referred to was that an injury to a vessel may be a fact not so material as that the non-communication of it to the underwriter will render the policy void, but yet sufficiently material to justify a decision that such injury may be deemed "excepted out of the policy," that is to say, something which in contemplation of law the underwriters must be supposed not to have insured against (*t*). The result of this amazing decision would be that the assured would be worse off in the case of a partially or doubtfully material concealment, than in the case of one which is proved

---

(*n*) Which form the subject of Sub s. (2)–(8), respectively, of Sect 2, *ante*

(*o*) All the marine insurance cases cited in the notes to §§ 99–101, *ante*, are cases of defence, except those mentioned in note (*q*), *inf*

(*p*) The life and fire and other insurance cases cited in the notes to §§ 102–104, *ante*, are all cases of defence, except those mentioned in note (*r*), *inf*

(*q*) As in *Court* v *Martineau* (1782), 3 Dougl (K B) 161 (action for return of money paid as loss under the policy), *London and Provincial Marine Insurance Co* v *Seymour* (1873), L. R 17 Eq 85 (action for rescission), *Rivaz* v *Gerussi Bros & Co* (1880), 6 Q B D 222, C A (the like), *Glasgow Assurance Corporation* v *William Symondson & Co* (1911), 104 L T 254 (the like)

(*r*) As in *Fenn* v *Craig, sup* *Traill* v *Baring* (1864), 4 De G J & S. 318 (reinsurance), *Hoare* v *Bembridge* (1872), 8 Ch App 22, *London Assurance Co* v *Mansel* (1879), 11 C D 363

(*s*) *Carter* v *Boehm* (1766), 3 Burr 1905, *per* Lord MANSFIELD, C J, at p 1909   "the policy would be equally void against the underwriter, if *he* concealed, as if he insured a ship on her voyage, which he privately knew to be arrived, and *an action would lie to recover the premium*"

(*t*) *Gladstone* v *King* (1813), 1 M & S 35, where the underwriters complained of the non-disclosure of damage to the keel of the insured vessel to the extent of 15 per cent At the trial Lord ELLENBOROUGH, C.J, and afterwards the Court of King's Bench, presided over by him, distinctly held, on the one hand, that the policy was not rendered void by the non-disclosure, but that, on the other, "no mischief will ensue from holding in this case that the antecedent damage was an implied exception out of the policy," and that "if the principle be new, it is consistent with justice and convenience" (*per* Lord ELLENBOROUGH, C J, at p 38, to the same effect LE BLANC, J, at pp 38, 39)

to have been wholly and plainly so : for, in the former case, the policy not being avoided, he would not be entitled to a return of the premium (u), whereas, in the latter, unless fraud were proved against him, he would be so entitled (v). It is not surprising that this decision does not seem to have been relied upon or referred to in any judgment for upwards of half a century, or that, when it was first exhumed from its long and merited sepulture, it was doubted " whether this case will hereafter be maintained " (w) ; or that, at a still later date, it was ridiculed and discountenanced, if not expressly overruled, in the House of Lords (x).

250. In the second of the groups of transactions which form the subject of this Chapter, that relating to sales and purchases, the remedies resorted to by the party complaining are of a more diversified character than in any other group. They consist of actions for rescission (y), with the preliminary declarations and consequential accounts, inquiries, orders, and directions already described as incidental to the relief in question (z) ; actions (where the party complaining is a purchaser, not where he is a vendor) for specific performance with an abatement or allowance (zz) ; actions or counterclaims for the return of deposits or instalments of purchase-money paid under the contract (a), together with, in some cases, the costs of investigating

(u) And this in fact was part of the decision in *Gladstone* v *King, sup* It was argued for the plaintiff (see p 36) with unanswerable logic, but without effect, that the policy was either void, or not if it was not void, the assured was entitled to be paid the amount of the loss or damage ; if it was, no fraud being suggested, he was entitled to have back his premium to which Lord ELLENBOROUGH, C J , (at p 38) observed " I do not remember that the point respecting the return of the premium was made at the trial , and if it was, the answer to it must have been that this is not a case of a void insurance, but an exception out of the policy," and LE BLANC, J (at p 39) " the opinion which my Lord expressed at the trial must have precluded the plaintiff from demanding the premium "

(v) See § 232, *ante*

(w) *Stribley* v *Imperial Marine Insurance Co* (1876), 1 Q B D 507, *per* LUSH, J , at pp. 513, 514 There is an odd mistake on the part of some one at p 513, where LUSH, J , is reported as having said that " they "—i e the Court in *Gladstone* v *King*—" did not hold the policy to be void, for they recognized the right of the assured to recover back his premium ", whereas what the learned judge must have said, or meant, was " they did not hold the policy to be void, for they did not allow the assured to recover back his premium, which they recognized to be his right if, and only if, the policy was void "

(x) *Blackburn, Low & Co* v *Vigors* (1887), 12 App Cas. 531, H L , where Lord HALSBURY, L C , at p 536, after making a slightly contemptuous allusion in a parenthesis to *Gladstone* v *King, sup* (" whatever may be thought of the logic of that case "), cites (pp 536, 537) the extract from the judgment of Lord ELLENBOROUGH, C.J , which is given in note (t), *sup* , to which he appends the caustic comment " unfortunately his Lordship does not state what is the principle which he apparently admits to be new "

(y) As in *Edwards* v *M'Leay* (1815), G Cooper 308 , *Turner* v *Harvey* (1821), Jac 160 , 23 R R 15 , *Gibson* v *D'Este* (1843), 2 Y & C (CH) 542 , *Smith* v *Harrison* (1857), 26 L J (CH) 412 , *Torrance* v *Bolton* (1872), 8 Ch App 118 , *Re Banister* (1879), 12 C D 131, C A , *Baker* v *Moss* (1902), 66 J P 360 , *Mahomed Kala Mea* v *Harperink* (1908), 25 T L R 180, P C See the terms of the judgment in the several cases, for the consequential orders and directions deemed appropriate in the respective circumstances, and particularly *Gibson* v *D'Este, sup* , where the form of decree was specially minute and elaborate

(z) See §§ 237, 238, *ante*

(zz) See Fry's *Specific Performance*, §§ 1257–1286, and *James* v *Litchfield* (1869), L R. 9 Eq 51 (where, however, the claim failed on the ground of the purchaser's presumptive knowledge of the undisclosed fact)

(a) As in *Arnot* v *Biscoe* (1748), 1 Ves Sr. 94 , *Stevens* v *Adamson* (1818), 2 Stark 422 , *Coverley* v *Burrell* (1821), 5 B & Ald. 257 , *Flight* v *Booth* (1834), 1 Bing (N C)

title (*b*) ; defences to actions or counterclaims for specific performance (*c*), or answers to affirmative pleas relying upon the contract as subsisting and valid (*d*), or defences to actions for a debt alleged to be due under the contract (*e*), or to actions for damages for breach thereof (*f*) ; and certain special remedies

251. The first of these special remedies is the creation of the Vendor and Purchaser Act, 1874 (37 & 38 Vict., c. 78), s. 9 of which provides that " a vendor or purchaser of rent or leasehold estates in England, or their representatives respectively, may at any time or times and from time to time apply in a summary way to a Judge of the Court of Chancery in England in chambers, in respect of any requisitions or objections, or any claim to compensation, or any other question arising out of or connected with the contract (not being a question affecting the existence or validity of the contract), and the Judge shall make such order upon the application as to him shall appear just, and shall order how and by whom all or any of the costs of and incident to the application shall be borne and paid " (*g*) The words in parenthesis would seem, at first sight, to exclude from the benefits of the statutory procedure any vendor or purchaser who bases his application on the alleged invalidity of the contract by reason of non-disclosure and it has been held that it is not possible to obtain relief by way of rescission, or a return of the deposit, where a question of the validity of the contract on that or any other ground is raised expressly and *eo nomine* (*h*) . but, inasmuch as nearly all cases of non-disclosure may be asserted by the party, and dealt with by the Court, as cases of failure to show title under a condition impliedly inherent in the contract itself (*i*), it follows that the Court has generally seen its way to grant the party complaining all such relief

---

370 , *Heywood* v *Mallalieu* (1883), 25 C D 357 (here the return of the deposit was the subject of a counterclaim) , *Nottingham Patent Brick & Tile Co* v *Butler* (1886), 16 Q B D 778, C A ; *Carlish* v *Salt*, [1906] 1 Ch 335

(*b*) See *Edwards* v *M'Leay*, *sup* , *Re Hare and O'More's Contract*, [1901] 1 Ch 93 , *Carlish* v *Salt*, *sup*

(*c*) As in *Ellard* v *Lord Llandaff* (1810), 1 Ball & B 241 , 12 R R 22 , *Shackleton* v *Sutcliffe* (1847), 1 De G & Sm 609 , *Wilbraham* v *Livesey* (1854), 18 Beav 206 , *Walters* v *Morgan* (1861), 3 De G F. & J 718 , *Phillips* v *Homfray* (1871), 6 Ch App 770; *Caballero* v *Henty* (1874), 9 Ch App 447 , *Hyde* v *Warden* (1877), 3 Ex D 72, C A , *Jones* v *Rimmer* (1880), 14 C D 588, C A. , *Heywood* v *Mallalieu*, *sup*. , *Nottingham Patent Brick & Tile Co* v *Butler*, *sup* (where the defence was to a counterclaim for specific performance)

(*d*) See *Fothergill* v *Phillips* (1871), 6 Ch App 770, which was a cross action to, and was tried together with, *Phillips* v *Homfray*, *sup* , and where the party charged set up as a defence the contract of which he claimed specific performance in *Phillips* v *Homfray* This affirmative defence the party complaining successfully defeated on the same grounds as those on which his defence in *Phillips* v *Homfray* succeeded

(*e*) As in *Mostyn* (*Lord*) v *West Mostyn Coke & Iron Co* (1876), 1 C. P D 145

(*f*) As in *Ellis* v *Rogers* (1885), 29 C D 661, C. A , *Molyneux* v *Hawtrey*, [1903] 2 K B 487, C. A.

(*g*) In the remainder of the section, similar provisions follow as to real and leasehold estates in Ireland

(*h*) By STIRLING, J , at p 609 of *Re Davis and Cavey* (1888), 40 C D 601 It is curious, however, to note that in a later case, *Re White and Smith's Contract*, *inf* , the same judge, on a similar statutory application, made no difficulty about ordering rescission

(*i*) See § 111, and notes (*y*) and (*z*) thereto, *ante*

by way of the summary procedure in respect of non-disclosure as it would have granted him if he had been plaintiff or defendant in an ordinary action, and, even in the case in which jurisdiction was declined to the extent abovementioned, a declaration was made in favour of the party complaining, with liberty to him to sue for the return of the deposit, and for consequential relief, which was sufficient for all practical purposes (*j*) It must be remembered, however, that as in all cases where jurisdiction is conferred upon the Court to proceed *brevi manu*, the jurisdiction will not be exercised if in the discretion of the Court the case appears too complicated or serious to be disposed of summarily, and the party will be remitted to his common law remedies, or the summons may be set down and heard as an action (*h*) The relief under the summary jurisdiction has, in some cases, assumed the form of a declaration, rescission, return of the deposit, costs of investigating title, and the like (*l*) , whilst, in other cases, the relief has been obtained in the form of a successful resistance to the application of the party charged for a declaration that he has made a good title, or that the party complaining is not entitled to insist on certain objections or requisitions, or is precluded by the contract from refusing to accept the title made, or other like declaration (*m*)

252. Another form of relief which may be called special, in the sense that the purchaser who avails himself of it is not asserting his right to complain of non-disclosure in an action to which he is a party, is the following.   Where property is sold under the direction of the Court, in the course of administering a trust, partnership, or insolvent estate, or in any other cause or matter, a purchaser of such property who alleges non-disclosure on the part of the vendor, instead of suing or waiting to be sued in an ordinary action, may come to that Court, and apply, in that cause or matter, to be discharged from his purchase ; and an order will be made for that purpose, or for such other like relief as the nature of the case may admit of, on proof of the facts which

(*j*) See *Re Davis and Cavey, sup.*

(*h*) The latter course was adopted by JOYCE, J , in *Re Hare and O'More's Contract*, [1901] 1 Ch 93

(*l*) As in *Re Davis and Cavey, sup.* (where, as above stated, the purchaser obtained a declaration, with costs, but no other relief), *Re White and Smith's Contract*, [1896] 1 Ch 637 (where the purchaser obtained an order for rescission), *Re Hædicke and Lipski's Contract*, [1901] 2 Ch 666 (the like), *Re Ward and Jordan's Contract*, [1902] 1 Ir R 73 (where the purchaser applied for a declaration that the vendor had not made out a good title, but unsuccessfully in this case, the undisclosed fact being held immaterial)

(*m*) As in *Re Marsh and Earl Granville* (1882), 24 C D 11, C A (where the purchaser successfully resisted, on the ground of non disclosure, the vendor's summons for a declaration that he, the purchaser, was precluded by the contract from insisting on certain objections and requisitions), *Re Brewer and Hankins's Contract* (1899), 80 L T 127, C A , where the purchaser resisted (but unsuccessfully, owing to an express condition in the contract) the vendor's summons for a declaration that he had made out a good title; *Re Leyland and Taylor's Contract*, [1900] 2 Ch 625, C A (resistance, though again unsuccessful, to the vendor's summons for a declaration that the purchaser was not entitled to compensation under a certain condition in the contract), *Re Puckett and Smith's Contract*, [1902] 2 Ch 258, C A (where the purchaser successfully resisted the vendor's summons for a declaration that he had made a good title, and that the purchaser was not entitled to insist on certain requisitions, and where the purchaser further obtained a declaration in his favour negativing the above) it would be necessary to establish in an action for rescission (n). But, though this summary procedure is open to him under the conditions stated, and (being far less expensive and more convenient) is almost invariably resorted to in preference to the ordinary procedure, the purchaser is apparently not compelled to adopt it (o). And, in cases of gravity or intricacy, the Court will not permit him to do so (p). The fact that the sale is, in a sense, by the Court, and that the officers of the Court are responsible, in a sense, for the non-disclosure, does not in the slightest degree weaken the purchaser's title to relief It is the clear duty of the Court to see that its ministers are at least as honest as other people, and the no less clear right of the purchaser to rely with absolute confidence on the discharge of this judicial duty (q). Indeed, the fact in question ought, if anything, to render the contract more readily impeachable than if the sale had no judicial sanction or authority (r).

253. It happens occasionally that the vendor and purchaser provide in the contract itself for the relief which is to be available to either party, in

(n) Such orders were made in *Martin* v *Cooper* (1846), 3 Jo & Lat 496 , 72 R R 100 *Brandling* v. *Plummer* (1854), 2 Drew 427 , 100 R R 209 (here the relief asked for by the petition, and given by the Court, was compensation) , *Dimmock* v *Hallett* (1866), 2 Ch App. 21 ; *Re Banister* (1879), 12 C D 131, C A In the case of *Re Summerson*, [1900] 1 Ch 112 n., the purchaser's summons failed, but only because of his failure to establish one of the necessary elements in the burden of proof incumbent on the party complaining, whatever the nature of the proceedings may be The above are all non disclosure cases Cases in which the purchaser was discharged on the ground of misrepresentation are , *Lachlan* v *Reynolds* (1853), Kay 52 , *Whittemore* v. *Whittemore* (1869), L R 8 Eq 603 , *Re Arnold* (1880), 14 C D 270, C A

(o) Thus, in *Jones* v *Rimmer* (1880), 14 C D 588, C A , the purchaser waited until he was sued in an ordinary action for specific performance, and successfully set up the non disclosure as a defence to the action

(p) As happened in *Mahomed Kala Mea* v *Harperink* (1908), 25 T L R 180, P C , where the purchaser, on applying to the Court, was, after the proceedings had gone far enough to reveal the serious nature of the charges made against judicial officers, directed to bring his action

(q) "In my view," said Lord CAIRNS, L J , at p 29 of *Dimmock* v *Hallett, sup* , Court ought not to be less strict as to sales under its own order than as to sales out of Court " Indeed, it would be monstrous if the Court which, according to Lord SELBORNE's view, expressed at p 236 of *Coaks* v *Boswell* (1886), 11 App Cas 232, H L , ought to be "strict even to jealousy " in enacting the fullest disclosure and the utmost good faith from the purchaser, were to be content with less from its own officers as vendors In Roman law, the rules were different sales made by the authority of the State were not impeachable for anything except fraud, and then only if the purchaser would not have purchased at any price, had he known the truth D 21 1 1 3 In French law (Code Civil, Art. 1649), no action for rescission will lie, "dans les ventes faites par autorité de justice."

(r) "The Court," said Lord ST LEONARDS, when Sir EDW SUGDEN and L.C. (Ir), at p 505 of *Martin* v. *Cooper, sup* , "expects from vendors, and *particularly from officers of the Court,* a clear and express statement." So PAGE WOOD, V C , at p 55 of *Lachlan* v. *Reynolds, sup* · "it would be strange indeed if in sales made by the direction of the Court this rule "—i e. the rule of good faith—"should be less stringent " There should be, in such cases, as JESSEL, M R , insisted, at p 141 of *Re Banister, sup.,* "at least as much good faith towards the purchaser as, *and perhaps a little more than,* is required by ordinary vendors out of court," for "the conveyancing counsel, though in one sense the officer of the Court, is the conveyancing counsel of the vendor," and "if there has been a mistake,   as between vendor and purchaser, the vendor is no better off than if the mistake had been made by a conveyancing counsel not appointed by the Court ", with which cp his similar observations at pp 273, 274, 277 of *Re Arnold, sup* , and those of BYRNE, J , at p 107 of *Debenham* v *Sawbridge,* [1901] 2 Ch 98, and the strong animadversion by the Privy Council on the conduct of the officials of the Indian court in *Mahomed Kala Mea* v *Harperink, sup.*

the shape of fixed and liquidated payments, in which case this conventional relief, to the exclusion *pro tanto* of the ordinary remedies, is granted, if the party complaining establishes such facts as would entitle him to those remedies in an ordinary case (s).

254. Where non-disclosure is established in the course of negotiations for a contract of suretyship (t), the remedy usually resorted to, as in cases of insurance, and for the same reason, is defence (u), or (what, before the Judicature Acts, was equivalent thereto) an action to restrain or stay proceedings at law instituted by the party charged (v). In one or two cases only has the party complaining sought his remedy in rescission (w)

255. Where the contract impeached is a contract of release or compromise or waiver (x), both rescission (y), with its accompanying accounts, inquiries, directions, and other incidental and consequential relief (z), and also defence (a),

(s) See *Reeve* v. *Berridge* (1888), 20 Q B D 523, C A, where, in an agreement for the sale of leasehold premises, one of the terms was that either party making default should pay to the other £100. The purchaser paid a deposit of £20, and also £50 on account of the purchase money, but refused to pay more, or to complete, on the ground of the vendor's non disclosure of onerous and unusual covenants in the head lease The vendor, alleging that the purchaser had made default, sued to recover the agreed penalty of £100, less the £50 paid on account The purchaser, alleging that the default was the vendor's, by reason of the above non disclosure and his inability to make a good title, besides defending the action, counterclaimed for recovery of the £100 penalty from ⸺ ⸺d also for the return of the £20 deposit, and the £50 paid on account of purchase STEPHEN, J , whose decision was affirmed by the C A , gave judgment for the defe ⸺ r both on the claim, and on the counterclaim for the £170

(t) These are the subject of Sect. 2, Sub s (1), *ante*

(u) All the cases cited in the notes to Sect 2, Sub s (1), *ante*, were cases of defence, or its equivalent, except those cited in note (w), *inf*

(v) In such cases " what the one claims as his right in equity would constitute his defence in law," as Lord SELBORNE, L C , said, at p 27 of *Hoare* v *Bembridge* (1872), 8 Ch App 22 This was the procedure adopted in *Hamilton* v. *Watson* (1845), 12 Cl & Fin 109 , *Willis* v *Willis* (1850), 17 Sim 218 , *Stiff* v *Eastbourne Local Board* (1868), 19 L T. 408

(w) As in *Railton* v *Mathews & Leonard* (1844), 10 Cl & Fin 934 (in which the surety sued for "reduction" of the suretyship bond, besides defending an action *e contra* for its enforcement) , *Wythes* v. *Labouchere* (1859), 3 De G & J 593 (where, however, the action failed)

(x) This class of case is the subject of Sect 2, Sub s (5), *ante*

(y) As in *Bowles* v *Stewart* (1803), 1 Sch & Lefr 209 , *Leonard* v *Leonard* (1812), 2 Ball & B 171 , *Gordon* v *Gordon* (1821), 3 Swanst 400 , *Maddeford* v *Austwick* (1826), 1 Sim 89, affirmed (1833), 2 My & K 279 , *Smith* v *Pincombe* (1852), 2 Macn & G 653 , *Wason* v *Wareing* (1852), 15 Beav 151 (where, however, the action failed, on the ground of the presumptive knowledge of the party complaining) , *Greenwood* v *Greenwood* (1863), 3 De G J & S 28 , *Brooke* v *Lord Mostyn* (1865), 33 Beav 457 (where a declaration was the only relief necessary) , *Law* v *Law*, [1905] 1 Ch 140, C A (where the party com plaining failed, having by his acts and conduct affirmed the contract) ; *Re Roberts*, [1905] 1 Ch 704, C. A (by counterclaim) ; *Watt* v *Assets Co* , [1905] A C 317, H L (where, again, on various grounds, the party complaining failed)

(z) Such as are described in §§ 237, 238, *ante* For examples of these incidental and consequential orders and directions, worked out in considerable detail, see the form of decree in *Maddeford* v: *Austwick*, *sup* , *Gordon* v *Gordon*, *sup* , *Smith* v *Pincombe*, *sup*

(a) Under the general term " defence " is included any answer or reply to an affirmative case of release compromise or waiver set up by the party charged by way of defence to an action brought by the party complaining , see § 243, and note (x) thereto, *ante* The following are examples *M'Carthy* v *Decaix* (1831), 2 Russ & M 614 (reply to defence of renunciation or release) , *Moxon* v *Payne* (1873), 8 Ch App 881 (answer to case of compromise set up by party charged as defence to action to set aside certain deeds) , *Gilbert* v *Endean* (1878), 9 C D 259, C A (reply to a case of compromise set up by the party charged in answer to a motion to enforce a decree) , *Re Roberts*, [1905] 1 Ch 704 C A. (defence to action for specific performance, with counterclaim for rescission added) are resorted to by the party complaining, but more commonly the former. The question of the remedies available in cases of compositions with creditors and the question of the parties to and against whom they are respectively available in such cases, are discussed in another Chapter (b).

256. In the few reported cases of contracts to enter into partnership, or to alter existing partnership arrangements (c), the procedure adopted by the party complaining was a suit for rescission or analogous relief (d), except in one case, where non-disclosure was set up as a defence to an action by the party charged for damages for breach of the contract (e).

257. Where the contract sought to be avoided, or treated as void, has been a contract to marry, the party complaining, whether from considerations of prudence, or from motives of delicacy, has always awaited the onset of the *rejecta Lydia*, or (it may be) the jilted Corydon. Though, in theory, there is nothing to debar him or her from asking the Court to break off the engagement on the ground of concealment of any such fact as is deemed material, if the other party will not consent to do so, there is no recorded instance of such heroic remedy having been adopted, or of the non-disclosure having ever been set up otherwise than as a defence to an action for damages (f), whether with or without success—generally without (g) Of the two cases of separation deeds mentioned in this connection (h), in both of which the party complaining succeeded, one was a case of defence to an action for arrears of annuity under the deed (i), and the other a case of rescission (j)

258. In the last of the seven classes of case which form the subject of this Chapter (that, namely, in which, there being no duty of disclosure arising from the mere nature of the contract negotiated for, such a duty is nevertheless created by special circumstances antecedent to, or occurring in the course of, the negotiation) the question of the remedies available to the party complaining obviously depends upon the nature of the circumstances, and the conduct of the party charged, giving rise to the duty (k) Where, as is usual in this group of case, the circumstances and conduct in question are such as to render the non-disclosure tantamount to fraudulent misrepresentation or concealment, or fraud of any kind, the party complaining is entitled

---

(b) See Ch VII, Sect 3, Sub-s (2), *post*

(c) Sect. 2, Sub s (6), *ante* deals with this class of case

(d) As in *Maddeford* v *Austwick* (1826), 1 Sim 89 , *Clements* v *Hall* (1858), 2 De G & J 173 (where the relief was given indirectly in the form of a variation of a certificate made in chambers in the administration of an estate)

(e) *Andrewes* v *Garstin* (1861), 10 C B (N s) 444

(f) See *Aitchison* v *Baker* (1797), 1 Peake 103 , *Foulkes* v *Sellway* (1800), 3 Esp 235 , *Baddeley* v *Mortlock* (1816), Holt N P 151 , *Herbert* v *Edgington* (1844), 1 C & K 464n , *Beachey* v *Brown* (1860), E B & E 796 , *Baker* v *Cartwright* (1861), 10 C. B (N s) 124

(g) In the two earliest of the cases cited in the last note, the plea of the party complaining succeeded , in all the others, it failed

(h) These, together with cases of contracts to marry, are dealt with, as one class, in Sect 2, Sub s (7), *ante*

(i) *Evans* v *Edmonds* (1853), 13 C B 777

(j) *Evans* v *Carrington* (1860), 2 De G F & J 481

(k) This class of case, and its various species, form the subject of Sect 2, Sub-s (8), *ante* For the remedies applicable to the respective circumstances, see the cases cited in the notes thereto

not only to the relief granted in ordinary cases of non-disclosure, but also to the remedy in damages available to a plaintiff in an action of deceit (l).

SECT. 6. QUESTIONS OF LAW AND FACT.

259. The facts and matters required to be established by the party complaining in order to make out a case of actionable non-disclosure (m), and those which it is incumbent on the party charged to establish in order to make good any of the recognized affirmative answers to such a case (n), have already been considered. It now becomes necessary to inquire which of the questions arising on the judicial examination of these facts and matters, and the evidence and arguments in relation to them, in the course of the proceedings, are questions of law, and which are questions of fact. for every matter which is not a question of law must be a question of fact, and vice versa. When a question is loosely described as "a mixed question of law and fact," what is meant is that the question is a complex one, divisible into two or more contributory questions, but each of these contributory questions, taken singly, must be either wholly of fact, or wholly of law. It is proposed to deal with this subject in relation to the following topics separately and seriatim (o) (1) materiality, (2) existence of the alleged undisclosed fact, (3) non-disclosure, (4) knowledge of either party as to the alleged undisclosed fact, (5) waiver, (6) affirmation and election This detailed inquiry, however, should be prefaced by a statement of the two elementary rules of evidence which are of general applicability to all the above subject-matters, and indeed to every department of our jurisprudence, viz, first, that it is always a question of law whether a suggested legal inference should or should not be drawn from a proved or admitted state of facts, and, secondly, that it is always a question of law whether there is any evidence to support, or any evidence to negative, an averment of fact

Sub-s (1) As to Materiality.

260. It has been explained (p) that the first thing to be established by one who complains of the violation of a duty of disclosure by another is that such a duty was at the material dates owed to himself by the party charged, which involves proof not only that the relation between the parties, or the circumstances existing or occurring, at that time were such as to give rise to the duty (q), but also that the alleged undisclosed fact was material to be disclosed, for there is no duty to reveal any other The exact meaning

(l) This remedy, as has been pointed out, is not available in cases of pure non disclosure see § 223, ante
(m) See Sect 3, ante
(n) See Sect. 4, ante
(o) The subject is considered in relation to these topics in the six Sub sections respectively of this Section
(p) See § 174, ante
(q) It is a question of fact what the circumstances alleged to have created the relation or duty were, but it is a question of law whether the relation was constituted by, or the

of " material to be disclosed " has been fully examined (r). That, in the sense indicated, materiality is a question of fact whenever the question is raised at all (for in a large proportion of the cases it is not in issue), has been judicially declared in a series of decisions dating from the earliest times (s), relating to contracts of insurance, whether marine (t), life (u) or fire (v), sales and

duty arose out of, the proved or admitted circumstances · e g. in *Keates* v. *Cadogan* (1851), 10 B & C. 591, it was held, *on demurrer*, that the facts alleged gave rise to no duty of disclosure

(r) See §§ 30–33, *ante*

(s) Particularly those relating to marine insurance—see the next note—in which department of mercantile law, of all others, the subject has been most frequently debated

(t) See, for decisions and rulings before the passing of the Marine Insurance Act, 1906 (6 Edw. 7, c 41), the following *Littledale* v *Kenyon* (1805), 1 B & P. (N R.) 151 (*per* ROOKE, J , at p 153), *Bridges* v *Hunter* (1813), 1 M & S 15 (*per* Lord ELLENBOROUGH, C J., at p 1 it was a question certainly for the jury, and left to them as such ")—see, however do (r) to § 206, *post*, as to how the Court dealt with the verdict in this case; *Durrell* v *Bederley* (1816), Holt N. P. 283 (*per* GIBBS, C J., at p 285 · " the materiality of the facts known and suppressed is for the jury "). *Rickards* v *Murdock* (1830), 10 B. & C 27, *Elton* v. *Larkins* (1832), 8 Bing 198 (left to jury); *Westbury* v *Aberdein* (1837), M & W. 267 (left to jury), *Elkin* v *Janson* (1845), 3 M & W 655 (left to jury, as a specific question) ; *Foley* v *Tabor* (1861), 2 F & F 663 (left to the jury by ERLE, C.J. : see p 673), *Gandy* v *Adelaide Marine Insurance Co* (1871), L R 6 Q B 746 (*per* MELLOR, J , delivering the judgment of himself and HANNEN and LUSH, JJ., at pp 754, 755) , *Ionides* v *Pender* (1874), L R 9 Q B 531 (question specifically left to the jury, see p 535, and the judgment of the Court, *per* BLACKBURN, J , at p 537) , *Tate & Sons* v *Hyslop* (1885), 15 Q B D 368, C A , *Herring* v *Jackson* (1895), 1 Comm Cas 177 (left specifically by MATHEW, J , to the jury); *Fracis, Times & Co* v *Sea Insurance Co* (1898), 79 L T 28 (where BIGHAM, J , sitting without a jury, treated the issue as one of fact) The cases subsequent to the passing of the statute above mentioned are *Thames & Mersey Marine Insurance Co* v *Gunford Ship Co*, [1911] A C 529, H L (*per* Lord ALVERSTONE, at p 533, and Lord ROBSON, at p 550) , *Glasgow Assurance Corporation* v *William Symondson & Co* (1911), 104 L T. 254 (where SCRUTTON, J., treated and decided the issue as one of fact) , *Scottish Shire Line, Ltd* v *London & Provincial Marine & General Insurance Co*, [1912] 3 K B 51 (where HAMILTON, J , at pp 70, 71, found the materiality to be established as a fact on the evidence)

(u) See *Huguenin* v *Rayley* (1815), 6 Taunt 186 (*per* Cur , at p 189 " it ought to have been submitted to the jury, whether the omission of the fact relied upon was or was not a material omission "); *Morrison* v *Muspratt* (1827), 4 Bing 60 (*per* BEST, C J , at p 62 " whether or not it was material for the defendants to have been made acquainted with the fact which has been withheld from their knowledge is a question for the jury "), *Lindenau* v *Desborough* (1828), 8 B & C 586 (*per* LITTLEDALL, J , at p 593) , *Swete* v *Fairlie* (1833), 6 C. & P 1 (*per* DENMAN, C.J , at p. 7, in summing up " you will have to say whether the communication was or was not material "); *Wainwright* v *Bland* (1836), 1 M & W 32 (specifically left to the jury), *Rawlins* v *Desborough* (1840), 2 M & Rob 328 (Lord DENMAN, C.J , left the question to the jury see p 333) , *Jones* v *Provincial Insurance Co* (1857), 3 C B (N S) 65 (*per* CRESSWELL, J , delivering the judgment of the Court, at p 86 · " it is a question for the jury whether the particular fact was or was not material to be communicated "), *London Assurance Co* v *Mansel* (1879), 11 C. D 363 (where JESSEL, M R , in deciding that the undisclosed fact was material, evidently intended to find this as a fact, for he fortifies himself by the reflection that " any decent special juryman " would so find see p 369), *Joel* v *Law Union & Crown Insurance Co*, [1908] 2 K B 863, C A (*per* MOULTON, L.J , at p 893 " such materiality being a matter to be judged of by the jury, and not by the Court ")

(v) *Bufe* v *Turner* (1818), 6 Taunt 338 (where, though it does not appear that the question was left to them specifically, we are told that " the jury acquitted the plaintiff of any fraud, but thought that the circumstance of the fire on the 11th ought to have been communicated to the defendants, who without this communication did not engage on fair grounds with the plaintiff for whom under those circumstances they find their verdict," which finding the Court refused to disturb) , *Yager* v *Guardian Assurance Co* (1912), 29 T L R. 53, Div Ct (where, an arbitrator having found materiality as a fact, the Court held that this finding was conclusive) purchases (*w*), and guarantees (*x*), which are the more important of the contracts discussed in the present Chapter (*y*) In the case of marine insurance, the rule is now part of the statutory law of the land (*z*)

261. At one time it seems to have been doubted whether evidence of materiality is admissible in the form of declared opinions of those conversant with the class of business or transaction to which the matter giving rise to the dispute belongs (*a*). It is strange that such doubts should ever have existed, since, in determining that materiality is a question of fact, the Courts by necessary implication, and, as it were, in the same breath, determined that evidence may be given to establish, or negative, the fact, no fact being capable of proof except by evidence of some sort, though the character of the evidence will in each case depend upon, and have relation to, the class of fact alleged on the one side and denied on the other. A reluctance to recognize materiality as a question of fact at all would be intelligible . but no such hesitation can be traced in the deliverances of any of the masters of mercantile law since the time of Lord MANSFIELD   What is not intelligible is that, having accepted the rule, the Courts rebelled for a time against its inevitable corollary and consequence   One cannot but suspect that those who opposed the reception of evidence as to materiality were, in so doing, unconsciously expressing their regret that they had ever assented to the question being treated as one of fact at all, and had failed to foresee the formidable consequences which would logically flow from that assent   Be this as it may, the undoubted fact is that, for a century or more past, evidence of materiality has been, and still is, particularly in cases of marine insurance (*b*), and life

(*w*) See *Gibson* v *D Este* (1843), 2 Y & C (CH) 542 (where KNIGHT BRUCE, V.-C , at pp 550, 551, found the materiality of the existence of the public footpath, as a fact)

(*x*) See *Smith* v *Bank of Scotland* (1813), 1 Dow App Cas 272 , 14 R. R 67 (where the House of Lords, reversing an interlocutor of the Court below, allowed a proof of the alleged undisclosed circumstances, as "relevant" · in other words, held that their materiality was a question of fact, and not a question of law) , *North British Insurance Co* v *Lloyd* (1854), 10 Exch 523 (*per* POLLOCK, C B , delivering the judgment of the Court, at pp 532, 533)

(*y*) There are no cases relating to the other classes of contract discussed in which the point as to whether materiality is a question of fact has definitely and precisely arisen

(*z*) See s 18 (4) of the Marine Insurance Act, 1906, (6 Edw 7, c 41) "whether any particular circumstance, which is not disclosed, be material or not is, in each case, a question of fact "

(*a*) See the observations of Lord MANSFIELD, C J , cited in note (*f*) to § 263, *inf* which, however, as there explained, may admit of a construction consistent with a recognition of the admissibility of *proper* evidence under certain conditions   In *Campbell* v *Rickards* (1833), 5 B & Ad 840, however, the judges of the King's Bench, disagreeing with the observations of the same court three years previously—see the next note,—which they said were not necessary to the decision in that case, were uncompromisingly against the admissibility

(*b*) In *Rickards* v *Murdo* (1830), 10 B & C 527, the question, whether necessary to the decision or not, was carefully considered, and the Court of K B (*per* Lord TENTERDEN, C J) was distinctly of opinion that evidence must be received, if tendered, as to materiality ("I know not how the materiality of any matter is to be ascertained but by the evidence of persons concerned with the subject matter of the inquiry "· pp 540, 541)   This view, it is true, was dissented from in *Campbell* v *Rickards, sup* (an action brought by the principal of the unsuccessful plaintiff in the former case for negligence) but it ultimately prevailed, and evidence as to materiality has been received without objection in a series of cases both before and after the year 1830, and down to the present time   see, for

insurance (c) received as a matter of course, wherever it is tendered ; and it generally is so tendered when a question first arises as to the materiality of some novel class of fact which, from time to time, the growing volume and intricacy of mercantile practice and usages bring into prominence.

262. It must be remembered, however, that the now firmly established rule that evidence of materiality may be received does not mean that this evidence is always required or expected, or that, without it, the issues of materiality can never be established   There are some cases where evidence certainly is not required, as where the alleged materiality of the undisclosed fact is so obvious on the face of it, or has so repeatedly been found by a succession of mercantile verdicts or judgments, that to adduce evidence in support of it would be like calling a witness to testify to an axiom in Euclid, or to the operation of an elementary law of nature (cc)   On the other hand, there is an opposite class of case where the suggested materiality is so little apparent to the normal mind by the light of nature that (since *de non apparentibus et de non existentibus eadem est ratio*) expert evidence is not only useful but essential, if the party complaining is to have this issue found in his favour (d)   Intermediate between these two extreme types, is the far larger group of cases where the evidence, if tendered, must be received, and, when received,

examples   *Haywood* v. *Rogers* (1804), 4 East 590 , *Durrell* v. *Bederley* (1816), Holt N P 283 , *Berthon* v *Loughman* (1817), 2 Stark 258 (*per* HOLROYD, J , at p 259   " whether particular facts if disclosed to an underwriter would, in the opinion of a witness, or as a matter of judgment, make a   rence as to the amount of the premium is, I think, admissible evidence"), *Ionul*   *Pender* (1874), L R 9 Q B 531 (see pp 535, 539), *Stribley* v *Imperial Marine Insurance Co* (1876), 1 Q B D 507 (at p 508   " evidence was called to show that it would have induced an underwriter to suspect that some casualty had happened to the vessel ") , *Fracis, Times & Co* v *Sea Insurance Co* (1898), 79 L T 28 (where BIGHAM, J admitted the evidence, but was not convinced by it that the fact there in question was material), *Thames & Mersey Marine Insurance Co* v *Gunford Ship Co* , [1911] A C 529, H L (where " a great many witnesses were called   who stated that in their opinion it was material to the underwriters that they should be informed of the circumstances connected with the captain's experience "   *per* Lord ALVERSTONE, at p 533   This evidence, however, was ultimately held insufficient to establish the alleged materiality   Further evidence was tendered on both sides, and received, as to the materiality of another undisclosed fact, viz the over valuation   *per* Lord ALVERSTONE, at pp 538, 539, and Lord ROBSON at p 550) ; *Scottish Shire Line, Ltd* v *London & Provincial Marine & General Insurance Co* , [1912] 3 K B 51 (*per* HAMILTON, J , at pp 70, 71)

(c) See *Lindenau* v *Desborough* (1828), 8 B & C 586 (where physicians were called, without objection, to prove that certain symptoms and disorders were of such importance that they ought to have been communicated to the insurers), *Swete* v *Fairlie* (1833), 6 C & P 1 (*per* DENMAN, C J , who, at p 7, directed the particular attention of the jury to the medical evidence for, and against, the alleged materiality of the pathological facts there in question)

(cc) Thus, at p 550 of *Thames & Mersey Marine Insurance Co* v *Gunford Ship Co* , *sup* , Lord ROBSON says   " this is a question of fact, and there was evidence about it both ways in the form of underwriters' opinions on the point   Without depreciating the value of those opinions, I think a jury, or a Court of law acting as a jury, when once made acquainted with the general conditions of marine insurance, can easily decide for themselves how far any particular circumstance would influence the judgment of a prudent insurer "

(d) Thus, in *Glasgow Assurance Corporation* v *William Symondson & Co* (1911), 104 L T 254, SCRUTTON, J , at p 257, made a pointed reference to the fact that the defendants had not adduced any evidence whatever in support of their suggestion that the undisclosed circumstance in that case was material, and this absence of evidence clearly fortified him in the conclusion at which he arrived that it had no materiality whatever.

may or may not have weight, but where, if no evidence is tendered, the tribunal must determine the issue of fact, as best it can, without the assistance of witnesses, and the party charged has no right to say that no case of materiality has been made against him (e).

263. When it is said that evidence of materiality is receivable, it must be remembered that by "evidence" is meant the particular kind of evidence which is proper to the circumstances of the individual case. The rule does not mean that any sort of evidence will do, or that any person from anywhere, or of any trade or calling, can be allowed to testify with authority as to the materiality of the fact in question. Indeed, there are cases where, the individual fact being of such a nature as not to involve any consideration of precedent or current u or practices of any business or locality, it has been considered by high authority that *any* declaration of opinion by a witness is inadmissible altogether as evidence (*f*), or, if technically admissible, is a mere display of "wisdom after the event," and, as such, entitled to no weight whatever (*g*). If the undisclosed fact be, on the contrary, of such a character as to depend for its materiality upon the proved effect of its non-disclosure upon the judgment and conduct of men in a particular business, the only appropriate and admissible evidence is that of witnesses who can speak as to the effect of the non-disclosure upon such men as a class, and not that of a witness who only purports to testify to its effect upon his own mind (*h*)

(e) *Rickards* v. *Murdock* (1830), 10 B & C 527 (*per Cur*, at p 541 " if such evidence is rejected "—equally, of course, if not tendered—" the Court and jury must decide the point according to their own judgment unassisted by that of others ").

(*f*) This was the view expressed by Lord MANSFIELD, C J, at p 1918 of *Carter* v. *Boehm* (1766), 3 Burr 1905 " great stress was laid upon the opinion of the broker. But we all think the jury ought not to pay the least regard to it It is mere opinion which is not evidence. *It is opinion after an event It is opinion without the least foundation from any previous precedent or usage* It is an opinion which, if rightly formed, *could only be drawn from the same premises from whic* *the Court and jury were to determine the cause* · and therefore it is improper and irrelevant in the mouth of a witness " This is the passage which is usually cited as establishing Lord MANSFIELD'S objection to any evidence whatever on the question—see note (a) to § 261, *ante*—and certainly some of the expressions used point in this direction In so far as they do, they are not now law But, taking the passage as a whole, he seems to limit his objection (and, so far as thus limited, his observations are valid and sound) to the class of case mentioned in the text, where there is no established course of conduct or business on which the witness can express any opinion which will in the least assist the jury, or be of any more value than that which they are to form, or (for the mat of that) of any independent value at all The fact alleged not to have been disclosed in that case was the fact that designs had been formed by the French upon the insured fort a year previously, and abandoned, together with the supposed probability of their renewal,—a fact of such an isolated and unclassifiable a character that no marine insurance broker could speak with the slightest authority as to its effect on underwriters as a class

(*g*) See *Traill* v *Baring* (1864), 4 De G J & S 318 (*per* TURNER, L.J, at p 330, on the inutility of calling witnesses as to what in their opinion would have affected the plaintiff's mind, the undisclosed fact being the abandonment of an intention to take part of a certain life insurance risk), *Fracis, Times & Co* v *Sea Insurance Co* (1898), 79 L T 28 (where BIGHAM, J, though he admitted evidence of underwriters in support of the alleged materiality of an obsolete edict of the Persian Government, prohibiting the importation of arms into Persia, disregarded it altogether in arriving at his decision, thinking, as Lord MANSFIELD, C.J., thought in *Carter* v *Boehm*, *sup*, that it was merely a case of being wise after the event).

(*h*) *Berthon* v *Loughman* (1817), 2 Stark 258 (*per* HOLROYD, J, at p 259 "the question

264. It is, to say the least, extremely doubtful whether any evidence is admissible to establish, or to negative, the materiality of undisclosed facts which indicate a course of illegal conduct (i).

265. The rule that materiality is a question of fact is of course subject to the overriding and fundamental rule that there must be some evidence, or some capability (whether evidence is tendered or not), of the suggested materiality, which is a question of law   No Court can be deprived of its right, or rather can abnegate its duty, to pronounce that in law the undisclosed fact is wholly incapable of being deemed material, any more than it can renounce its function of declaring, in a case of defamation, whether the published matter is capable of the suggested, or of any, defamatory meaning. Even where evidence has been adduced as to the materiality of an undisclosed fact, it is still open to the judge to hold, as matter of law, that it cannot be material, as is impliedly recognized, even in those judgments where the fact has been held to be material, by prefatory judicial declarations that the particular case is not one in which this authority and duty of the Court can be exercised (j)   And there are several instances of an alleged undisclosed fact being held on demurrer (k), and of a proved undisclosed fact being held on appeal (l), incapable of materiality

266. Theoretically, one would suppose that it must also be a question of law whether the undisclosed fact is capable of being deemed otherwise than material, just as (invoking, again, the analogy of the law of defamation) it is open to the Court to rule that the published matter is incapable of a non-defamatory meaning, no less than it is to rule that it is incapable of a defamatory one   But, in cases of non-disclosure (as, indeed, also in cases of defamation), the Court has always been extremely reluctant to make such declarations, though by no means averse to ruling in the contrary sense. The cases in which juries have been directed, or advised by judges in such terms as to amount almost to a direction, that the fact in question is material, and ought to be so found, are mainly cases where no objection was taken to

---

is not what the private opinion of the individual may be as to the probable course of his conduct in a particular case, but what in his judgment the general opinion would be amongst those conversant with such matters ")   In cases of marine insurance, it is the opinion of " the prudent insurer " referred to in s 18 (2) of the Marine Insurance Act, 1906 (6 Edw 7, c 41), which is of importance, and of which evidence is admissible, and not the opinion of particular insurers, or even a large body of them, willing to take an " excessive or speculative risk," for " that opinion cannot bind others of more prudent temperament " (*Thames, &c , Co* v *Gunford Ship Co.* inf , per Lord ROBSON at p 550), not the opinion of the general public (*Glasgow Assurance Corporation* v *William Symondson & Co* (1911), 104 L T 254, per SCRUTTON, J , at p 257)

(i) *Thames & Mersey Marine Insurance Co* v *Gunford Ship Co*, [1911] A C 529, H. L. (per Lord ALVERSTONE at p 538)

(j) *Gandy* v *Adelaide Marine Insurance Co* (1871), L R 6 Q B 746 (at p 754); *Ionides* v *Pender* (1874), L R 9 Q B 531 (per Cur , at p 537), *Scottish Shire Line, Ltd* v *Provincial Marine Insurance Co* , [1912] 3 K B 51 (per HAMILTON, J , at p 70)

(k) As in *Beachey* v *Brown* 1860), E B & E 796 (successful demurrer to plea in a case of a contract to marry), *Andrewes* v *Garstin* (1861), 10 C B (N S) 444 (the like, in a case of a contract to enter into partnership)

(l) *Seaton* v *Burnand*, [1900] A C 135, H L (per Lord HALSBURY, L C., at p 139, and Lord BRAMPTON, at p 148)

the summing up, or to the verdict (*m*), or where the materiality had previously been admitted (*n*). But, though a judicial ruling in a particular case that the suppressed matter *cannot* be immaterial may be incorrect, and not justified by the circumstances, in which event a new trial will be granted (*o*), and though there is no right in any case to so rule unless there is " enough in the facts to enable the judge " to adopt this course (*p*), it has never been decided that, in a proper case, the Court has no power to hold, as matter of law, that the undisclosed fact must be material; and in one case, after a finding in the Court below of immateriality, based, moreover, on strong evidence, it was so held on appeal (*q*). Further, the Court has always retained its control (though much relaxed in modern times) over the verdicts of juries on this, as on any other, question of fact, to the extent of ordering a new trial in the event of a thoroughly irrational or perverse verdict, and this cautious mode of dealing with the strange verdicts, negativing materiality, which juries from quite intelligible motives have from time immemorial been very prone to return against insurers seeking to nullify their policies, has been freely resorted to in preference to the bolder and more summary course of entering judgment for the party complaining, even in cases where it is obvious that the Court entertained the strongest possible belief in the materiality alleged (*r*) Where, however, the case has been tried without a jury, the appellate Court is less reluctant to act upon its own opinion (*rr*).

(*m*) As in *Boyd* v *Dubois* (1811), 3 Campb. 132.

(*n*) As in *Bates* v *Hewitt* (1867), L R 2 Q B 595 (where—see p 598—COCKBURN, C J, directed the jury that the fact was material, but from his judgment *in banco* it appears that the materiality had previously been admitted   see p. 603)

(*o*) As in *Huguenin* v *Rayley* (1815), 6 Taunt. 186 (where DAMPIER, J, having held that the withheld fact must be material, and having therefore non suited the plaintiff, the Court of Common Pleas, at p 189, though evidently thinking that the fact probably was material to be disclosed, said that " it ought to have been submitted to the jury, whether the omission of the fact relied upon was or was not a material omission," and, therefore, they ordered a new trial

(*p*) *Gandy* v *Adelaide Marine Insurance Co* (1871), L R 6 Q B 746 (*per* MELLOR, J, delivering the judgment of himself and HANNEN and LUSH JJ, at p 753 " without putting it to the jury to draw the proper inference from the facts proved, there was not in the facts themselves enough to enable the judge to say ' aye" or " no " that there had been the concealment of a material fact ")

(*q*) See *Thames & Mersey Marine Insurance Co* v *Gunford Ship Co*, sup, where the H. L. held that the secret double insurance which was one of the two undisclosed facts in that case was material not only in fact, but *in law*, reversing the finding of the Court below, after hearing evidence, that it was not (*per* Lord ALVERSTONE at pp 538, 539, Lord SHAW at pp 542-545, and Lord ROBSON at p 550).

(*r*) See the following marine insurance cases, where, the jury having found that the undisclosed fact was not material, the Court ordered a new trial   *Willes* v *Glover* (180 , 1 B & P (N R) 14 (*per* Sir JAMES MANSFIELD, C J, at p 16), *Bridges* v *Hunter* (1815), 1 M & S 15 (*per* Lord ELLENBOROUGH, C J, at p 19, " it was a question certainly for the jury,   but still if this Court has reason to think that they come to a wrong conclusion upon it, we may set it right, as was done in *Willes* v *Glover*, by sending the case down to another inquiry "), *Sawtell* v *Loudon* (1814), 5 Taunt 359 (*per* HEATH, J, at p 364), *Kirby* v *Smith* (1818), 1 B & Ald 672, *Stribley* v *Imperial Marine Insurance Co* (1876), 1 Q B D 507 (*per* BLACKBURN, J, at p 511)

(*rr*) See *Thames & Mersey Marine Insurance Co* v *Gunford Ship Co*, sup, where one of the two findings of immateriality by the Lord Ordinary and the Court of Session was unhesitatingly reversed (*per* Lord ALVERSTONE at pp 538, 539, Lord SHAW at pp 544, 545, and Lord ROBSON at p 550)

Sub-s. (2)   *As to the Occurrence or Existence of the Alleged Undisclosed Fac*

267. It has been already explained that it is for the party complaining to establish, if either question should be in controversy, both that the fact alleged to have been undisclosed belongs to the class of matters which the law regards as "facts," and not to some other class, and that the alleged fact existed or occurred during the period in which the party charged was under an obligation to divulge it (s). It is manifest that, *ex vi terminorum*, the former of these is a question of law (t), and the latter (subject to the "previous question" whether there is any evidence in support of the allegation, which is for the Court) is a question of fact (u)

Sub-s (3)   *As to the Non-Disclosure.*

268. It has been seen that the burden is on the party complaining of establishing the fact (though a negative) of non-disclosure (v), but that very slight evidence indeed, and, in some cases, the dumb testimony of the *res ipsa*, that is to say, the mere fact that the contract was entered into in circumstances utterly inconsistent with any rational hypothesis of disclosure, will shift the burden on to the shoulders of the party charged of proving affirmatively that such disclosure was in fact made (u) Here again it is obvious that any issue as to whether the communication was or was not made must necessarily be one of fact (x), subject of course to the above-mentioned "previous question," and subject also to other questions of law which may incidentally arise, as, for instance, whether disclosure to any

(s) Sect 3, Sub s (2), *ante*
(t) See Ch II, Sect 2, Sub s (1), *ante*, and all the cases cited in the notes thereto.
(u) See all the cases cited in the notes to §§ 178–182, *ante*
(v) Sect 3, Sub s (3), *ante*
(w) See § 183, and note (s) thereto, *ante* As to what "disclosure" means, see Ch II, Sect 1, *ante*

(x) See, generally, the cases cited in the notes to Sect 3, Sub s (3), *ante*, in all of which the question of disclosure or no disclosure was left to the jury, or (where there was no jury) treated by the judge as a question of fact To these may be added the following (which are not cited in the notes referred to because they contain nothing which bears upon the question there discussed, viz the burden of proof) *Arnot* v *Biscoe* (1748), 1 Ves Sr. 94 (a vendor and purchaser case, in which Lord HARDWICKE, L C., directed three issues of fact to be tried at law, the first of them being whether the party charged had given notice to the party complaining of the incumbrance on the estate sold), *Rawlins* v *Desborough* (1840), 2 M & Rob 328 (a life insurance case, in which DENMAN, C J , in his summing up—see p 333—told the jury that it was for them to say whether the disclosure had, or had not been made), *Ionides* v *Pender* (1874), L R 9 Q B 531, a marine insurance case (*per* BLACKBURN, J , delivering the judgment of the Court, at p 537 "the jury must be taken to have found that it was no disclosure, and we cannot say that they were wrong") And note that in *Joel* v *Law Union and Crown Insurance Co* , [1908] 2 K B 863, C A , a life insurance case, the Court of Appeal, whilst holding that the facts supposed in the Court below to be evidence of non disclosure constituted in law no evidence at all, were of opinion that there were, or might be, other materials on which a jury could properly, and might possibly, find that there had been no disclosure, and on this ground they ordered a new trial, instead of entering judgment for the plaintiff, as they otherwise would have done, and as BUCKLEY, L J , was strongly disposed to think ought to have been done, even as it was (*per* VAUGHAN WILLIAMS, L J , at p. 883, MOULTON, L J , at p 893, and BUCKLEY, L J , at pp 897, 898).

person not being the party complaining can be deemed equivalent in law to a disclosure to that party himself (y).

Sub-s. (4) *As to Knowledge of the Undisclosed Fact possessed by, or imputed to, Either Party.*

269. It being incumbent on the party complaining to show that, during the material period, the party charged had (z), and he himself had not (a), cognizance of the undisclosed fact, the state of mind of both parties is obviously a vital issue, whenever it is a subject of controversy Knowledge, as has been fully explained, may be either actual or presumptive (b), and there are various classes and sub-classes of the latter (c) Ignorance is the absence of both actual knowledge, and of any of these classes or species of presumptive knowledge Obviously, any question as to whether either of the parties to whom it is being attributed had, or had not, actual knowledge of the undisclosed fact, if there is any evidence of the affirmative (which is a question of law), must be a question of fact (d) But, in the case of presumptive knowledge, it is a matter of more difficulty and nicety to determine which of the controverted matters are issues or inferences of fact, and which are questions or presumptions of law. That is to say, it often requires very careful discrimination to decide which of the general rules of evidence should govern, and how it, or they, should be applied to, the circumstances of any individual case : the principles themselves, however, are well established and clear. They are these . first, the rules as to the presumption of knowledge from certain classes of fact are rules of law secondly, any question as to whether given circumstances (that is, admitted, or undisputed, or proved) come within any of the specified classes is a question of law , but, thirdly, any question as to whether the facts are or are not as alleged is, *ex vi termini*, an issue of fact, subject to the question of law whether there is any evidence in support, or (as the case may be) to the contrary, of the allegation Thus, to take a

---

(y) See *Tate & Sons* v *Hyslop* (1885), 15 Q B D 368, C. A , a marine insurance case in which, the jury having found, in answer to a specific question, that the fact alleged not to have been disclosed had been communicated to the underwriters, " not directly, but to their solicitors," it was held on appeal that the disclosure to the solicitors was *in law* no disclosure at all (*per* BRETT, M R , at p 374), and, therefore, that there was no evidence to support a further finding of the jury that there had been no concealment of the fact in question (*per* BRETT, M R , at p. 378) This case is a good example of the application of the two primary conditions, subject o which alone any question can be treated as one of fact, as pointed out in the general observations prefixed to this Section in § 259, *ante*

(z) See Sect 3, Sub s (4), *ante*
(a) See Sect. 3, Sub s (5), *ante*
(b) See Ch II, Sect. 3, Sub s (1), *ante*
(c) The five main classes of presumptive knowledge, and their various species, are fully discussed in Sub ss (2), (3), (4), (5), and (6), respectively, of Ch II, Sect 3, *ante*.
(d) No authority is needed for this self-evident proposition but reference may be made to *Arnot* v. *Biscoe* (1748), 1 Ves Sr 94 (where Lord HARDWICKE, L C —see p 96— directed, amongst others, an issue to be tried at law whether the purchaser was cognizant of the undisclosed incumbrance or not), *Bates* v *Hewitt* (1867), L R 2 Q B 595 (*per* COCKBURN, C J , at pp 606-608) , *Cockburn* v. *Edwards* (1881), 18 C D 449, C A (*per* JESSEL, M R , at p 455), *Re White and Smith's Contract*, [1896] 1 Ch 637, 642

few examples out of many which present themselves (e), an underwriter of a marine insurance policy (as has been already indicated) is deemed, *as matter of law*, to be acquainted, whether he is so *in fact* or not, with all the usual and established customs, of the trade which he insures, or of particular ports, and all the usual and established forms and clauses in commercial instruments used for the purpose of marine adventures, and the rules and practices of underwriters generally, together with all such information as is derivable from the books and registers in ordinary use in an underwriter's business (f); *as matter of law*, he is not deemed to be cognizant of any unusual, or recent, or doubtful, practice, usage, custom, form, or clause (g). Now, in case of dispute, all questions as to whether the particular custom, practice, or clause which is the subject of the dispute is usual or unusual, established or recent, clear or ambiguous, are questions of fact, to be determined as such on the evidence (h). But if the allegation of fact is not in dispute or, having been disputed, is proved, it then becomes a question for the Court whether knowledge of the facts so established ought in law to be imputed to the party said to have been cognizant of them (i)

270. To take another species of presumptive knowledge, the actual knowledge of an agent, if he is "an agent to know," is imputed to his principal, with certain exceptions (j). This is a presumption of law (k). It is also a question of law whether, given the position occupied by the supposed agent in fact, such position amounted to an agency "to know," or to an agency at all (l). But all questions as to the position actually occupied by the alleged agent are questions of fact (m), if there is any evidence for, or against,

(e) See, generally, the cases cited in the notes to Ch. II, Sect 3, Sub-ss. (2)–(6), *ante*.

(f) § 42, *ante*.

(g, § 43, *ante*.

(h) Accordingly such questions were the subject of evidence, and were left to the jury in *Ougier* v. *Vallance* (1800), 1 Campb 504 n. (custom of Newfoundland fishing trade); *Vallance* v *Dewar* (1808), 1 Campb. 503 (the like), *Kingston* v. *Knibbs* (1809), 1 Campb 508 n. (custom of port), *Da Costa* v *Edwards* (1815), 4 Campb 142 (practice as to loading). In the following, a judge sitting without a jury received evidence, and otherwise treated the question as one of fact: *Mercantile Steamship Co.* v *Tyser* (1881), 7 Q B. D. 73 (*per* COLERIDGE, C.J , at p. 77 "the evidence showed that this provision as to a cancelling option was of comparatively recent introduction into charterparties"); *The Bedouin*, [1894] P. 1, C. A (clause in a time charter), *Charlesuc th* v. *Faber* (1900), 5 Comm. Cas 408 (clause in original policy, *per* BIGHAM, J , at pp 411, 412).

(i) See *Tate & Sons* v *Hyslop* (1885), 15 Q B D. 368, C. A (*per* BRETT, M R , at p. 378); *Laing* v. *Union Marine Insurance Co* (1895), 1 Comm Cas 11 (*per* MATHEW, J , at p. 18), *Wilson & Others* v. *Salamandra Assurance Co.* (1903), 8 Comm Cas 129 (*per* BRUCE, J , at p. 132); and, generally, the cases cited in the notes to §§ 42, 43, *ante*, except those referred to in note (h), *sup*

(j) See C 11, Sect. 3, Sub s. (4), *ante*.

(k) Which, however, may be rebutted on proof of facts bringing the case within any of the exceptions, but not otherwise : see § 57, *ante*

(l) And was so treated by the Court of Appeal in *Tate & Sons* v. *Hyslop*, *sup* (*per* BRETT, M.R., at p. 374 : "a solicitor is not the standing agent for one who has been, or may be, his client, to receive a mercantile notice in respect of mercantile business." This being held as a matter of law, the finding of the jury that in fact the underwriters had knowledge by this means was disregarded), by the House of Lords in *Blackburn, Lou & Co.* v. *Vigors* (1887), 12 App. Cas. 531, H L , and by the Court of King's Bench in Ireland, in *Taylor* v *Yorkshire Insurance Co* , [1913] 2 Ir. R. 1.

(m) See, generally, the cases cited in the notes to Ch. II, Sect 3, Sub-s. (4), *ante*.

the allegations made as to such position, which is a question of law (n) It is also a question of law, whether any proved, or admitted, or assumed circumstances are such as to bring the case within any of the recognized exceptions (o) ; but it is a question of fact what those circumstances actually were in the particular case (p), subject, again, to the preliminary question of law whether there is any evidence of their existence as alleged (q).

271. A third presumption of knowledge, also fully discussed in an earlier part of this work (r), is that by which, on proof of a party's actual knowledge of some fact or document, a knowledge of other facts or documents which would have inevitably followed from this actual knowledge, if reasonable inquiry had been made, is imputed to such party This is a presumption of law, when once the facts are ascertained or admitted (s) One of the subrules subordinate to the main rule, or one of the applications of the main rule, is this A party who, in any transaction for the sale or demise of land, has actual notice of the existence of a deed or document which may probably affect the property, has constructive notice of its *normal* contents, but not of any unusual restriction, condition, covenant, or clause which would not naturally be expected to find a place in the particular deed or document, unless, having been given a " fair opportunity " of inspection, he has neglected to avail himself of it, from which date the legal presumption, till then suspended, comes again into operation (t). This, again, given the facts, is a question of law (u) : but, if disputed, it is a question of fact whether the restriction, condition, covenant, or clause in question is usual, or unusual, unless there is no evidence in support of the allegation of normality or abnormality, as the case may be, which is a question of law (v). And

(n) See the same cases, generally, and especially those cited in the notes to §§ 50, 51, *ante.*

(o) These exceptions are discussed in §§ 54, 55, 56, *ante* See the cases cited in the notes thereto

(p) See § 57, and note (h) thereto, *ante.*

(q) See, generally, the cases cited in the notes to §§ 54–57, *ante*

(r) Ch. II, Sect. 3, Sub-s (5), *ante*

(s) See, generally, the cases cited in the notes to Ch. II, Sect. 3, Sub s. (5), *ante.*

(t) § 59, *ante.*

(u) It was so treated in *Hyde* v *Warden* (1877), 3 Ex. D 72, C. A., and in many of the other cases cited in the notes to § 59, *ante.*

(v) See *Wilbraham* v. *Livesey* (1854), 18 Beav. 206 (*per* ROMILLY, M R , at pp 209, 210); *Cockburn* v *Edwards* (1881), 18 C D 449, C A. (*per* JESSEL, M.R., at p 455, and COTTON, L.J., at p 462) In *Hampshire* v. *Wickens* (1878), 7 C D. 555, JESSEL, M R , at pp. 559-562, went into the matter closely. He clearly intended to deal with the question as one of fact, for he observes (p 560) that " usual covenants may vary in different generations. The law declares what are usual covenants *according to the knowledge of mankind.*" That is to say, the law declares to be " unusual" that which is found as a fact by evidence to be " unusual " at the time when the question arises. The proper kind of evidence of the contemporaneous " knowledge of mankind " would, in strictness, be the testimony of conveyancers, land agents, or other persons familiar with transactions in real property, just as foreign law is strictly proved as a fact by the evidence of those who practise it. But, just as in the latter class of case the Court will often receive as evidence of the fact references to statutes, or to works of authority, if the law to be ascertained is American or colonial, so it would seem to be justifiable to refer to the latest edition of some accepted treatise on conveyancing, at all events if neither side proposes to call evidence of experts, to determine the issue whether a particular covenant is "usual" or "unusual" And this was the course adopted by JESSEL, M R., in the case last cited But he was not thereby intending to treat the question as one of law, but was referring to the books merely as records of

as to the question of whether a "fair opportunity" was, or was not, given (w), and all the other questions which, as has been pointed out, may arise in cases belonging to this extensive branch of presumptive knowledge, the same general rules apply (x).

272. Instead of directing the jury (where there is one) to find the facts, and then ruling what inference in law ought to be drawn from them, it is open to the Court (and this course has been occasionally adopted) to leave the whole matter to the jury, with a proper and full direction as to what knowledge must in law be presumed from what facts, trusting to them to discriminate between their right to pronounce on the facts, and their duty, having so pronounced, to return a verdict which shall not contradict or disregard the direction given to them as to the legal consequences of the facts so found (y)

Sub-s. (5).   As to Waiver.

273. It has been pointed out that one of the affirmative answers to a case of non-disclosure is waiver (z); which is established by proof that the party complaining agreed, either in express terms or by acts and conduct, to waive his right to disclosure, or his right to some specified remedy for non-disclosure (a). Where such agreement is alleged to have been express, it is a question of fact, in case of dispute (which, however, is an extreme rarity),

"the then knowledge of mankind," or as, in the earlier part of the last century, the Annual Register was not infrequently cited without objection, by and to the courts, as evidence of modern or contemporary events   There is some danger, however, in allowing a departure from the strict rule, for the tendency of successive editions of text-books is to alter nothing except under the strong compulsion of a definite decision, to take an example, if the question should ever be seriously put in controversy, as it never has been yet, whether the covenant prohibiting assignment of a lease without the consent of the lessor, which is still stated in the treatises to be "unusual," is or is not so in fact according to the existing "knowledge of mankind," and the Court were to insist on that fact being proved in the proper way by the evidence of experts, it seems very difficult to suppose that such evidence would establish it to be "unusual"

(w) See *Re White and Smith's Contract*, [1896] 1 Ch 637 (*per* STIRLING, J., at p 642), and *Molyneux v. Hawtrey*, [1903] 2 K B. 487, C A (*per* COLLINS, M R., at p 492, and MATHEW, L J, at p. 496), as to ' fair opportunity " being an issue of fact.

(x) See the notes, generally, to Ch. II, Sect 3, Sub s (5), *ante*

(y) This seems to have been the course adopted in *Friere v. Woodhouse* (1816), Holt N P. 572 , 17 R R 679 , *Gandy v Adelaide Marine Insurance Co.* (1871), L R 6 Q B. 746 (see the second of the two questions left to the jury by BRETT, J , as set out at p 752, and the decision of the Court, at pp 755, and 759, that this question had been properly so left) ; *Morrison v Universal Marine Insurance Co.* (1872), L R 8 Exch 40 (where it appears—see p. 48—that one of the questions which BLACKBURN, J , put to the jury was "had the broker a right to suppose that the underwriters were acquainted with Lloyd's lists ?"   The Court of Exchequer thought that this question had been rightly left as one of fact, with the proper direction, to the jury, *per* MARTIN, B , at pp 52, 53.   The Exchequer Chamber did not deal with this point at all : it was on other grounds that they reversed the decision of the Court of Exchequer).   The same procedure is not uncommon in cases of defamation, where the judge, after advising the jury as to what facts in law give rise to immunity in respect of a defamatory publication, leaves to them the question, as a whole, whether the occasion was privileged or not, instead of getting a finding of the facts from them, and then declaring, as law, the consequences of the facts so found   See Article 36, note (g), of the author's *Code of the Law of Actionable Defamation*

(z) This topic is fully discussed in Sect 4, Sub s (1), *ante*

(a) The former species of waiver is the subject of §§ 202-205, *ante*, and the latter of §§ 206-208, *ante*.

whether it was made or not; but when, as is usually the case, the alleged agreement is in writing, whether in the form of a condition of the written contract itself which is impeached, or as the subject of an independent document, it is a question of construction for the Court (assuming that the document is entirely self-contained and self-luminous, and does not require or admit of interpretation by the light of surrounding circumstances) whether or not the language used amounts in law to a contract to waive (b). When the alleged agreement is sought to be implied from acts and conduct, then, assuming that there is any evidence at all, or any admissible evidence (c), which is a question of law, it is for the jury, or the Court acting as a jury, to determine, as a fact, what the acts and conduct were, and whether, in virtue of the acts and conduct so found, the party complaining did or did not intend to waive all, or any, and (if so) which, of his rights against the party charged (d)

Sub s (6) As to Affirmation and Election

274. Another ground of affirmative answer which is open to the party charged is established by proof that the party complaining, being in a position either to repudiate or to adhere to the contract at his option, has unequivocally elected to affirm it, and has signified such election, either by express language, or by acts and omissions inconsistent with any other view than that he meant thereby to exercise his option, and to exercise it in favour of adherence, and not avoidance This plea or answer has already been dealt with (e), and it has also been shown that any such election must have been exercised with full and precise knowledge of the undisclosed facts, otherwise it is no election at all (f), and that mere delay, laches, inaction, or quiescence do not, *of themselves*, amount to, or indicate, either affirmation, election, waiver, or acquiescence (g) The questions here involved are as to states of the mind and will, and the existence of any of those states, if controverted, is a question of fact (h), subject to the qualifications above referred to in the case

---

(b) See § 205, *ante*, and the cases cited in note (*t*) thereto, where it was decided, as matter of law, whether the alleged contract to waive was a *concluded* contract, or not ; and also those cited in the notes to §§ 206-208, *ante*, where questions as to whether a condition in the contract amounted to a waiver of rescission, or came within either of the two exceptions therein referred to, were dealt with as questions of law

(c) Thus, at p 538 of *Thames & Mersey Marine Insurance Co v Gunford Ship Co*, [1911] A C 529, H L, Lord ALVERSTONE observed, with reference to the evidence adduced before the Lord Ordinary as to disclosure of the double insurances being impliedly waived · "the practice of underwriters as to accepting risks or not making inquiries on particular points cannot, in my opinion, affect the duty as defined by statute, *and cannot properly be received as evidence of waiver in any particular case*"

(d) Thus, in *Laing v Union Marine Insurance Co* (1895), 1 Comm Cas 11, MATHEW, J, found as a fact that there had been no waiver of further information, and that such waiver was not to be implied from what the underwriters had said, done, or omitted

(e, In Sect 4, Sub s (2), *ante*.

(f) In § 213, *ante*

(g) See Sect 4, Sub-s (3), *ante*.

(h) See, generally, the cases cited in the notes to Sect. 4, Sub s (2), *ante*, for examples. As to belief, intention, and other states of the mind, being "facts" for the purposes of the rule as to the duty of disclosing material facts, see § 25, *ante*

of waiver. How far knowledge is a question of fact, and how far a question of law, has been discussed in an earlier part of this Section (i). Election, or choice, is a matter of intention, and presupposes a state of the will, as knowledge presupposes a state of the mind in its receptive or purely intellectual character: but the former no less than the latter is a fact, in the sense that it is for a jury, or judge acting as a jury, to find whether the alleged intention to elect in favour of affirmance did or did not exist, and whether such an intention ought in the particular case to be inferred from the language or acts and omissions proved (j), and, if disputed, what the alleged language acts or omissions, if any, were, subject, again, to the " previous question " of law, so often adverted to in the preceding Sub-sections, whether there is any evidence at all of such language acts or omissions, or whether the proved and admitted facts amount in law to an unequivocal election, or are such

(i) See Sub-s (4) of this Section, ante

(j) See particularly (besides other cases cited in the notes to §§ 212–215, ante) the marine insurance case of Morrison v. Universal Marine Insurance Co (1873), L R 8 Exch. 40 (trial, and decision of Court of Q. B), and 197 (decision of the Exchequer Chamber). Here it was contended by the assured that the underwriters by issuing the policy after discovery of the undisclosed fact, though they were ignorant of it when initialling the slip, had elected to adhere to the contract. BLACKBURN, J., (see p 43) left a specific question to the jury on this point, which was " did the defendant company, after knowledge that the broker had not disclosed this fact, elect to treat the policy as subsisting ? " The judge's direction to the jury in his summing up (see pp. 47, 48) was very explicit and complete. He told the jury that it was open to the defendants either to return the premium and make the contract a nullity, or to say that, having a right to get rid of the contract, they would nevertheless keep the premium, and go on. They could not do both. Then, after closely reviewing the evidence (somewhat too favourably to the plaintiff, in so far as he laid down that the election must be made within a reasonable time—which is not the law see §§ 217, 218, ante), he concluded " do you think that the defendants, having the opportunity (taking into account that they should make the election within a reasonable time), had elected to go on with the contract ? On this I express no opinion at all. I leave this entirely to you " It was obviously impossible for the plaintiff to escape from the consequences of the adverse finding of the jury on this point, except by establishing that the question was not one of fact at all, and that it was the duty of the judge to have ruled that the acts and omissions relied upon (viz issuing the policy, debiting the plaintiff in their books with the premium, and not protesting till afterwards) constituted, of themselves, a conclusive election in law to affirm the contract This contention prevailed with the majority of the Court of Exchequer, MARTIN, B , at p 53, expressing the view that it was a case of estoppel, and BRAMWELL, B , at pp 54–58, that it was for the defendants to explain away their conduct which, unexplained as it was, amounted to an election in law, and should have been so held by the judge. CLEASBY, B , in his dissentient judgment (see pp. 59–61) pointed out that the real contract was the slip, and that the issue of the policy was the merest formality (this has now for a long time been established as to law— see § 182, and note (o) thereto, ante), and of itself constituted no evidence, or no necessary evidence, of any election at all, whether with or without protest, or of anything except an intention to conform to the honourable practice of giving the assured that on which alone he could (by reason of the revenue legislation) legally sue, and so putting the dispute in train for decision. The Exchequer Chamber agreed with the dissentient judgment of CLEASBY, B , reversed the decision of the majority of the Court of Exchequer, and restored the judgment for the defendants which BLACKBURN, J., had entered on the findings of the jury. They entirely approved the summing up of BLACKBURN, J , except that they considered it too favourable to the plaintiff (p 205) they totally dissented from the idea of estoppel (p 206), and from the view that the facts constituted any conclusive election in law (pp 206, 207) Indeed, it would rather seem from the general tone of their exposition of the principles of election that, if they had considered the question to be one of law at all they would have held that, n the circumstances before them, it ought to have been decided in favour of the plaintiff, on the ground that those circumstances constituted no evidence in law of the alleged election, as CLEASBY, B., had evidently thought that an inference of an intention to affirm *can* possibly be drawn from them (*k*)

SECT. 7. PARTIES

275. It remains to consider what persons may assert a title to relief by reason of non-disclosure, and against what persons such title may be asserted, in any of the various forms of proceeding which are available for this purpose (*l*).

Sub-s (1). *Who are entitled to assert the Right to Relief.*

276. First, as to the persons entitled to assert the right to relief These comprise the person with whom the party charged made the contract in the negotiation for which he is alleged to have neglected the duty of disclosure, and the principal, or partner, of such person, or, if the party charged made the contract with two or more persons acting jointly, all such persons, and, if he made it with two or more persons acting severally, any of such persons (*m*). A second class consists of all such persons as by operation of law, or by voluntary assignment, are, or become, entitled to stand in the place of the person with whom the contract was so made (*n*).

277. The first of the above classes represents those to whom the duty of disclosure is due in the first instance That the principal or partner of a negotiating party to whom disclosure is due can assert the same rights in respect of non-disclosure as that party himself could, if he had no principal, or none who chooses to intervene, is a consequence of the elementary rules of the law of agency (*o*) That all or any of a number of joint contractors can claim in respect of non-disclosure to any of them, but that, where the party charged contracts severally with a number of persons, each of such persons can only assert his separate and individual rights in respect of the particular contract negotiated and made with himself, is a well-established principle of the general law of contracts (*p*), and needs no special observations in this place, beyond a reference to certain questions which have arisen in the application of this rule to contracts of marine insurance It is now undoubtedly the law, and declared to be so by a codifying statute, that where a policy of marine insurance is (as is nearly always the case) " subscribed by or on behalf of two or more insurers, each subscription, unless the contrary be expressed, constitutes a distinct contract with the assured " (*q*),

(*k*) See the concluding observations of the last note, and most of the cases cited in the notes to §§ 212, 213, *ante*.

(*l*) As described in Sect 5, *ante*

(*m*) See § 277, *inf*

(*n*) See §§ 278, 279, *inf*.

(*o*) See the various treatises on agency and partnership. Partnership is of course mutual agency, amongst other things. For examples of a principal complaining of the withholding of a fact from the solicitor who had negotiated the contract on his behalf, see the two compromise cases of *Gilbert* v. *Endean* (1878), 9 C D 259, C A , and *Turner* v. *Green*, [1895] 2 Ch 205.

(*p*) See any of the text-books on contracts.

(*q*) Marine Insurance Act, 1906 (6 Edw. 7, c. 41), s 24 (2)

that is to say, that each underwriter so subscribing, though his name appears with others at the foot of one and the same document, enters into a several contract with the assured to indemnify him in the event of loss to the extent of the amount set opposite his name, and does not contract jointly with the others to pay, in such event, the aggregate sum for which the policy is under-written *in solido* On one or two occasions, where special stipulations or expressions in the policy have seemed to lend plausibility to the contention, attempts have been made to fix the underwriters with a joint liability on the ground that, in the particular case, "the contrary" was "expressed", as, for instance, where a number of underwriters, each subscribing the policy for a fixed fraction of the whole, had described themselves as a syndicate, and, further, had contracted to reinsure the risk, and give the assured a charge upon such reinsurance . but it was held that conditions of this character did not even raise an implication of joint liability (*r*) , and, therefore, still less could they constitute, in the statutory phrase, an "expression" of it (*s*) The consequences of such a policy of marine insurance being regarded as so many separate and distinct contracts, no less than if they had been recorded in separate and distinct instruments, are that one of the underwriters so subscrib-ing does not, by mere proof of all the elements necessary to constitute a case of non-disclosure to himself, thereby relieve the others from the necessity of establishing the like elements as regards themselves nor, on the other hand, does the failure of any one of them to prove non-disclosure, or the success of any affirmative answer set up against any one of them, prejudice in the slightest degree the case of any of the others.   It is true that, in cases of misrepresen-tation, it was at one time thought that, though a false statement made to a subscriber of a policy cannot be deemed to have been made to one who underwrites at a later date, yet a misrepresentation made to the underwriter whose name appears first among the names of the subscribers to one and the same policy is deemed to have been made to all the underwriters whose names appear beneath his . but this absurdly illogical distinction cannot be maintained, consistently with the clear and plain rule now established (*t*).

(*r*) *Tyser* v. *Shipowners Syndicate* (*Reassured*), [1896] 1 Q B 135 (*per* MATHEW, J , at pp. 138, 139) , *General Insurance Co of Trieste* v. *Miller*, and *Leo Steamship Co* v *Corderoy* (1896), 1 Comm Cas 379, C A. (*per* Lord ESHER, M R., and A. L. SMITH and RIGBY, LL.JJ , affirming the decision of MATHEW, J., reported at p. 300 of the same volume)   In these cases, the policy, though otherwise in the ordinary form, was headed by the names of the syndicate and its manager, which names were repeated in the margin under the named aggregate amount of the insurance , but it was held that these merely descriptive expres sions were quite nugatory and meaningless, *quoad* the rights and liabilities of the parties, and could not control the operative part of the policy.   It was then contended that the covenant to reinsure and give a charge on the reinsurance to the assured made a difference, because this must have been the joint contract of the syndicate, as such but the obvious answer was that this stipulation carried the matter no further if the primary pro-mises were several, the accessory promises, whereby the assured obtained protection against the bankruptcy of each promisor, must be regarded as several also

(*s*) This term is noticeable . the section cited does not say—"unless a contrary intention is expressed *or implied*," but—"unless the contrary is *expressed*," which words may have been intended to confine the exception within closer limits than, previously to 1906, the common law of marine insurance might have permitted

(*t*) It seems to have always been recognized that one who comes in *after the date of the subscription of the policy* cannot take advantage of any misrepresentation made to such

It is also true that, in practice, the principles above stated are seldom invoked, because there is scarcely ever a suggestion of any distinction between the cases of the different underwriters (u) : but, on the rare occasions when such a distinction is shown, these principles become of importance, and they are both invoked and applied (v)

278. The second class of persons who are entitled to set up a case of non-disclosure, whether by way of offensive or defensive proceedings, consists of those to whom personally no duty of disclosure was owed, but who are, or become, whether by operation of law or by voluntary assignment, entitled to stand in the place of, or to represent, the persons to whom the duty was so owed. As regards the former kind of transmission which ensues upon the death, or disability (from insolvency, infancy, lunacy, or otherwise), of the party complaining, no special observations are required in this place. In all such cases, the right of the party complaining to claim in respect of, or to set up by way of defence, the failure of the party charged to fulfil his duty of disclosure devolves, upon the same persons, in the same events, and subject to the same conditions, as in the case of any other proceedings for the enforcement or avoidance of contracts (w)

279. As regards cases of transmission otherwise than by mere operation of law, that is to say, cases of assignment *inter vivos*, or of devise or bequest, there are two rules which require to be examined   In the first place, it is well settled that, where specific property is devised or conveyed or assigned from one to another, there pass with it all such equities to rescission, or

---

subscriber, or any of such subscribers , but as regards the list of subscribers themselves, it cannot be denied that no less an authority than Lord MANSFIELD, C J , at p 306 of *Barber* v. *Fletcher* (1779), 1 Dougl 305, committed himself to the statement that " a representation to the first underwriter extends to the others," which was followed in *Marsden* v *Reid* (1803), 3 East 571, where, at p 573, we are told that " the Court intimated upon the general question that if it had appeared that a material fact had been represented to the first underwriter to induce him to subscribe the policy, it should be taken to have been made to all the rest without the necessity of repeating it to each " But then dicta plainly contradict the theory of distinct contracts, which, if a sound theory (as it undoubtedly is), cannot depend for its validity upon the question whether the several contractors underwrote at the same time, or at different times   At a very early date Lord ELLENBOROUGH, C J , at pp 13, 14, of *Forrester* v *Pigou* (1813), 1 M. & S 9, expressed the gravest doubts on this question, which is now finally disposed of by the enactment cited

(u) And for that reason the procedure in marine insurance cases which is described in § 614, *post*, is habitually resorted to without objection

(v) Thus, in *Cantiniere Meccanico Brindisino* v *Janson*, [1912] 3 K. B 452, C A , there was clear evidence that some of the underwriters had, through a report addressed to them, complete cognizance of the fact alleged to have been undisclosed, and therefore were not in a position to establish one of the necessary ingredients in the burden of proof incumbent on them—see Sect. 3, Sub s (5), *ante*,—but it was pointed out by MOULTON, L J , at p. 468, that this circumstance in no way affected the case of the other subscribers to whom the report was not communicated, and who were in a position to establish the ingredient in question.

(w) See, generally, the treatises on contracts, parties, bankruptcy, companies (liquidation), infancy, and lunacy. For examples of transmission, on death, of the right to complain of non disclosure, see the release and compromise cases of *M'Carthy* v *Decaix* (1831), 2 Russ & M. 614 (where both parties to the litigation were representatives of the deceased parties to the negotiation) , *Law* v *Law*, [1905] 1 Ch 140, C A (the like). For an illustration of transmission on insolvency, see the life insurance case of *Re General Provincial Life Assurance Co , Ltd , Ex p Daintree* (1870), 18 W R 396 (where the liquidator of the company resisted the claim of an assured in the liquidation)

whatever ground, as the person devising, conveying, or assigning was previously entitled to (x) Secondly, it is no less firmly established, on grounds of public policy, that a bare right or equity to rescind, divorced from any specific property or fund, is not saleable or assignable ; for all such sales and assignments of litigated titles and claims savour of, if not actually constituting, champerty in the one case, and maintenance in the other (y). But the assignment of a claim, based on non-disclosure (or on any matter justifying avoidance of the contract), to recover a specific fund which is earmarked and can be traced, and which may properly be described as in equity the money of the claimant, or as an equitable debt, is not exceptionable on this ground (z), the fund in question being regarded as specific property within the meaning of the first rule. Hence it is that misfeasance claims against the delinquent directors and officers of a company have been held the proper subject of assignment and sale, whether by private treaty (a), or public auction (b), and this is so even where the purchaser is the agent of the very persons whose conduct is impeached (c)

(x) For, so long as the right is coupled with possession, physical or constructive (as by receipt of rents), the mere initiation or maintenance of an action *in relation to the property,* though proceedings for rescission may be involved in such litigation, is in no way obnoxious to the objections of champerty or maintenance see *Prosser* v *Edmonds* (1835), 1 Y & C (Eq Exch.) 481 (*per* Lord ABINGER, C.B , at pp 486, 487), *Cockell* v *Taylor* (1852), 15 Beav. 103 (at pp. 116, 117), *Dickinson* v *Burrell* (1866), L. R 1 Eq. 337 (*per* Lord ROMILLY, M R , who, in a passage which has repeatedly been cited and approved, at p 342, laid down that " the right of suit is a right incidental to the property conveyed," and " to each interest carved out of it," and, applying this doctrine to the facts with which he was dealing, " any interest which, but for the previous deeds, would have been sufficient to enable a person interested to ask this court to secure this property for the benefit of the persons interested therein, would, in my opinion, enable that person to ask this court to set aside the deed obtained by fraud, which, if valid would have prejudiced or destroyed his interest in the property purporting to be conveyed ") , *Dawson* v. *Great Northern and City Railway Co* , [1905] 1 K B 260, C A (*per* COLLINS, M R , at p 271 · " an assignment of property is valid, even although that property may be incapable of being recovered without litigation ") Accordingly, in *Clements* v. *Hall* (1858), 2 De G. & J 173, the suit was brought by the purchasers of the interest of a person under a will, to which person alone in the first instance the duty of disclosure was owed, and in *Watt* v *Assets Co.,* [1905] A C 317, H L , the pursuers in an action for " reduction " were a company who had bought the assets of the insolvent City of Glasgow Bank from the liquidator, and, with them, the right of the liquidator to sue in respect of the alleged withholding of certain material facts from him by a contributory with whom a compromise had been effected

(y) *Wood* v. *Downes* (1811), 18 Ves 120 (*per* Lord ELDON, L C , at p 125), *Prosser* v. *Edmonds, sup* (*per* Lord ABINGER, C B , at pp 496, 500), *Dawson* v *Great Northern and City Railway Co* , *sup* (*per* COLLINS, M R , at pp 270, 271 " a court of equity is as much bound as a court of common law by the rules relating to champerty and maintenance, and if an assignment of a chose in action is obnoxious to those rules, it is bad in equity no less than in law. An assignment of a mere right of litigation is bad ") , *Fitzroy* v *Cave,* [1905] 2 K. B 364, C. A. (*per* COZENS HARDY, L J , at p 371)

(z) See *Cockell* v *Taylor, sup* , where the distinction is drawn between an assignment of a mere right to sue, or of a bare litigated claim, which would be bad, and (as was the case there) the assignment of a claim to an interest in a specific fund which was actually lodged in court

(a) As in *Re Park Gate Waggon Works Co* (1881), 17 C. D 234, C A , *Re Anglo Austrian Printing and Publishing Union,* [1895] 2 Ch 891 n

(b) As in *Wood* v *Woodhouse & Rawson, United,* [1896] W N. 4.

(c) This was the case in *Re Park Gate Waggons Works Co* , *sup.,* where the liquidator of the company who sold all the company's property to the agent of the delinquents was held to have, in so doing, sold the misfeasance claim to those delinquents, who accordingly

Sub-s (2). *Against whom the Right to Relief may be asserted*

280. The persons against whom the right to relief in respect of non-disclosure may be asserted, whether by way of active proceedings or defence, may be classified under two heads, corresponding to those under which the persons entitled to relief have been classified   That is to say, the person called upon to answer for, or take the consequences of, non-disclosure may be, either (1) the person who in negotiating for the contract failed to comply with the duty of disclosure incumbent on him, or whose agent to effect the contract so failed, or (2) any person who, whether by operation of law in certain events, or by voluntary assignment, is required to stand in his place. Of these in their order.

281. If one of two persons contemplating a contract of any of the kinds described in this Chapter, being under a duty of disclosure to the other, chooses to delegate the negotiation for, and the making of the contract, to an agent, he cannot rely upon this fact as an excuse for the breach of the duty   If he has not himself performed that duty, he cannot be heard to say that he was personally ignorant of the fact required to be divulged, and that it was his deputy who was alone cognizant of it, and, therefore, alone responsible for not revealing it (*d*)   The fact remains that there has been no disclosure to the party entitled to it, and that this element in the burden of proof which lies on such party is accordingly established (*e*).   It makes no difference that the agent of the party charged was also the agent of the party complaining (*f*), or that he was also an officer of the Court in cases of sales pursuant to judicial order (*g*)   The agent who omits to divulge material matters known to him, being an agent employed to make the contract, is

---

obtained an injunction restraining the liquidator from attempting to enforce the claim, the order, however, was expressed to be without prejudice to any application which the liquidator might make to set aside the sale   So a man may under the conditions stated in the text devise, so as to defeat his heir, an equity to set aside a conveyance on the ground even of fraud to the very person guilty of it, just as he can devise away from his heir any other equitable and devisable interest attaching to specific property   *Stump* v *Gabey* (1852), 2 De G. M. & G. 632 (*per* Lord ST. LEONARDS, L C , at pp 630, 631)

(*d*) See § 49, and notes (*b*) and (*c*) thereto, *ante*, where also the distinction between "an agent to effect the contract," and "an agent to know" (the two characters being, however, usually united in the same person) is explained

(*e*) Brokers are commonly employed to negotiate or make the contract in cases of marine insurance see the authorities cited in the notes to §§ 91–99, *ante*, for illustrations of such brokers having failed in their duty   Land agents and solicitors are similarly employed in most vendor and purchaser cases, and their neglect to communicate material facts within their knowledge to the party complaining rendered their principals liable in many of the cases cited in Sect. 2, Sub-s (3) of this Chapter, *ante*   Solicitors are usually employed in negotiating a family arrangement, or a compromise of litigation, and it has never been disputed that suppression by them of facts within their knowledge which it is material to disclose affects the client   see *Bowles* v. *Stewart*, cited in note (*t*), *inf* , *Gilbert* v *Endean* (1878), 9 C D 259, C A , *Turner* v *Green*, [1895] 2 Ch 205 (though, whether rightly or wrongly, it was held in that case that there was no duty of disclosure on any one) , *Re Roberts*, [1905] 1 Ch 704, C A

(*f*) *Stewart* v *Stewart* (1839), 6 Cl & Fin 911 (*per* Lord COTTENHAM, L C , at p 970) , *Re Roberts*, *sup*   Both these were cases of a family arrangement ; a Scotch law agent in the former, and a solicitor in the latter, acted for all parties

(*g*) See § 252, and notes (*q*) and (*r*) thereto, *ante*

not only liable to his principal for the violation of his duty to him (*h*), but is also responsible to the party complaining to whom he equally owes a duty (*i*).

282. The first species of the second of the two classes above-mentioned demands no special observations. It is sufficient to say that, in case of the death or disability (whether by reason of insolvency, infancy, lunacy, or otherwise) of the party owing the duty of disclosure, the liability to proceedings for the breach of that duty devolves upon, or is transmissible to, the same persons, in accordance with the same rules, and subject to the same conditions, as in the case of any other proceedings to enforce or avoid contracts (*j*).

283. As regards the other species of the class of persons required to stand in the place of the party originally responsible, viz. that which comprises assignees from any such party otherwise than by mere operation of law, a distinction must in the first instance be drawn between an assignee of a chose in action, whether negotiable or non-negotiable, and an assignee of property in possession. The general principle applicable to assignments of these several kinds of property is that the assignor transfers what he has acquired, and no more: if he has only a limited or defeasible interest, he can only transfer an interest subject to the same limitations, or liable to be defeated by the same events: if he has no title at all, he can confer none. *Nemo dat quod non habet.*

284. Where any person has assigned a mere chose in action under a contract (not being a negotiable instrument) voidable at the instance of the other party to it, whether for non-disclosure or any other invalidating cause, his assignee, though taking in good faith, for value, and without notice,

---

(*h*) Thus, in *Campbell* v. *Rickards* (1833), 5 B. & Ad. 840, the plaintiff was suing for negligence his marine insurance broker who, by reason of proved non-disclosure, had failed in his action against the underwriters of the policy in *Rickards* v *Murdock* (1830), 10 B. & C. 527.

(*i*) Thus, in relation to a case of marine insurance, at p 543 of *Blackburn, Low & Co* v *Vigors* (1887), 12 App Cas 531, H L., Lord MACNAGHTEN observes that "the agent of the assured is bound, as the principal is bound, to communicate to the underwriters all material facts within his knowledge. Concealment of those facts is a breach of duty on his part to those with whom his principal has placed him in communication." On this theory, the solicitor of the other party to the contract was made a defendant, as well as that party himself, in the vendor and purchaser case of *Arnot* v. *Biscoe* (1748), 1 Ves. Sr. 94, and Lord HARDWICKE, L C, having first expressed his view that the second defendant, the vendor, was clearly liable (p 95), proceeded (p 96) to hold that the agent or attorney of the vendor had the same duty of disclosure to the purchaser as the vendor himself had, and "this, therefore," he added, "is a good equity for the plaintiff against Biscoe"—the attorney—"in default of the other defendant, if it comes out so." The same course was adopted in the release case of *Bowles* v *Stewart* (1803), 1 Sch & Lefr 209, where Lord REDESDALE, L.C. (Ir.), after holding that his client was liable, though he had no personal knowledge of the concealed deeds (p. 222), said, at p 227, with reference to the solicitor defendant, "his duty as a solicitor did not bind him to assist his client in an act of injustice . . . he has properly been made a party . . . and ought to be chargeable with the costs so far as they relate to the release, in case they cannot be recovered from Richard Bowles," his client, of whom the defendants Stewart and another were devisees.

(*j*) See the various text books on contracts, parties, bankruptcy, companies (liquidation), infancy, lunacy, &c. In *M'Carthy* v *Decaix* (1831), 2 Russ. & M 614, and *Law* v. *Law*, [1905] 1 Ch 140, C. A , the persons against whom relief was sought were the representatives of a deceased party to the negotiation and making of the contract impeached for non-disclosure. In *Bowles* v *Stewart, sup*, two of the defendants were devisees, as stated in the last note, of the vendor who had in his lifetime failed to make the necessary disclosure.

stands in no better position after the assignment than the assignor did before it No rule is better established, or more inflexibly applied, than the ancient equitable rule, now made part of the statutory law of the land (k), that the assignee of a chose in action takes subject to all equities which before the assignment were, and but for the assignment would continue to be, enforceable against his assignor ; and amongst such recognized equities is the equity to avoid (l). Desperate attempts have been made from time to time, on the appearance of any enactment which merely declares, or codifies, or recognizes this rule, to infer from some slight difference between the statutory language and that used in the authorities and text-books an intention on the part of the legislature to alter the existing law in favour of the assignee. Such attempts have always failed Thus, immediately after the passing of the Policies of Assurance Act, 1867 (m), and, again, shortly after the Marine Insurance Act, 1906 (n), it was vainly urged that s. 1 of the former statute, and s. 50 of the latter, conferred immunities upon the assignees of life and marine policies respectively to which the assignees of other choses in action are not entitled (o). There is, however, one well-established exception to the rule just stated. In the case of negotiable instruments, whether made so or

(k) Judicature Act, 1873 (36 & 37 Vict c. 66), s 25, sub s (6)
(l) As to what " chose in action " means, see Lord Halsbury's *Laws of England*, vol iv, pp 360–365 See, for examples of the application of the rule stated in the text, *Cory* v. *Gertcken* (1816), 2 Madd 40 (*per* PLUMER, V.-C, at p 51), a misrepresentation case , *Davis* v *Chester* (1855), 3 W R 321, where a compromise between five children, A , B., C., D , and E , was set aside not only as against B., by whose fraud it had been brought about, but also as against the innocent C , and D , and a purchaser without notice from E , *British Equitable Insurance Co* v *Great Western Railway Co.* (1868), 38 L J (CH) 132, affirmed, *ibid* , 314, where a policy of life insurance was avoided for non-disclosure against the assignees , *William Pickersgill & Sons, Ltd* v *London and Provincial Marine and General Insurance Co* , [1912] 3 K B 614, where a policy of marine insurance was treated as void against the assignees who were suing thereon It should be noted, however, that the party complaining may so conduct himself in relation to the assignee *after the assignment* as to give him an independent affirmative answer to the claim for relief · see what is said by LUSH, L J , at p 700 of *Wakefield & Burnley Banking Co* v *Normanton Local Board* (1881), 44 L T. 697, C A
(m) 30 & 31 Vict c 144
(n) 6 Edw. 7, c 41
(o) In *British Equitable Insurance Co* v *Great Western Railway Co* , *sup* , the contention was raised before MALINS, V.-C , (who rejected it, and was affirmed in so doing on appeal), that s. 1 of the Act of 1867 exempts assignees of life policies from equities to which they would otherwise be subject but it was pointed out that this section merely enables an assignee to sue in his own name, and in no way affects the equities to which such assignee is subject, whilst s 2 expressly preserves those equities In *William Pickersgill & Sons, Ltd.* v *London & Provincial Marine & General Insurance Co* , *sup.*, a similar suggestion was made with reference to s 50, sub-s (2) of the Act of 1906, which provides that " where a marine policy has been assigned so as to pass the beneficial interest in such policy, the assignee of the policy is entitled to sue thereon in his own name , and the defendant is entitled to make any defence arising out of the contract which he would have been entitled to make if the action had been brought in the name of the person by or on behalf of whom the policy is effected " It was urged that, by the words " arising out of the contract," the legislature (notwithstanding that the statute is expressed " to codify the law relating to marine insurance ") intended to limit the equitable rights of the underwriter against the assignee, and in particular to deprive him of his equity to avoid the policy against him for non disclosure But it was held by HAMILTON, J , at p 621, that this phrase was intended to describe, or was at least wide enough to include, " an implied condition, contained in the contract itself, precedent to the liability of the underwriter to pay," and the duty of disclosure is such a condition see § 83, and note (t) thereto, *ante*.

recognized as such by statute (p),—for instance, the Bills of Exchange Act, 1882 (q), and the Bills of Lading Act, 1855 (r),—or by the custom of merchants (s), the assignee is *primâ facie* free from all personal equities existing as between his assignor and the party complaining, and is presumed, until the contrary be shown, to have acquired and to hold the instrument " in due course," that is to say, for value and without notice and in good faith, and the onus is on the party complaining to show, not only the facts which would have entitled him to relief against the assignor, but also the fact that the assignee acquired his alleged title to the instrument otherwise than in due course (t), subject to the statutory proviso, with reference to bills of exchange, that " if in an action on a bill it is admitted or proved that the acceptance, issue, or subsequent negotiation of the bill is affected with duress, or force, and fear, or illegality, the burden is shifted unless and until the holder proves that, subsequent to the alleged fraud or illegality, value has in good faith been given for the bill " (u), which means that both value and good faith must be established, so that value without *bona fides* is as inefficacious to discharge the full burden imposed on the holder as *bona fides* without value (v)

285. On the other hand, where property in possession, physical or constructive (as by receipt of rents of profits), passes under the assignment to one who acquires it for value, without notice, and in good faith, no election to avoid the transaction which would have been available against the assignor will be in the slightest degree effectual to take the property out of the hands of the assignee. Such election to avoid must have been in fact exercised by the party complaining before the assignment, either in the form of a notice of repudiation, and that " resumption of the property " (in a legal sense) which is implied therefrom, or by the institution of proceedings for rescission, in either of which events the assignee is simply put in the possession of something which is nothing, since it was not in the power of the assignor to bestow it (w) But where there has been no such avoidance before the

(p) See Lord Halsbury's *Laws of England*, vol iv, pp 393 397.
(q) 45 & 46 Vict c. 61. See Chalmers on *Bills of Exchange*
(r) 18 & 19 Vict c. 111. See Carver's *Carriage of Goods by Sea*
(s) There are two marks of an instrument recognized as negotiable by the law merchant (1) it must pass from hand to hand by delivery, (2) with the intention and effect of conferring a right to sue thereon see *Crouch* v *Credit Foncier of England* (1873), L R 8 Q. B 374 (at pp 381, 382) As to what documents are comprised within the class of instruments negotiable by mercantile custom, see Lord Halsbury's *Laws of England*, vol ii, pp 564-570, *Sheffield (Earl)* v *London Joint Stock Bank* (1888), 13 App. Cas. 333, H L , *London Joint Stock Bank* v *Simmons*, [1892] A C 201, H L
(t) See, as regards bills of exchange, &c , ss 29, 30, and 38 (2) of the Bills of Exchange Act, 1882
(u) See s 30 (2) of the last cited Act
(v) *Tatam* v. *Haslar* (1889), 23 Q B. D. 345, Div Ct. The above provisions are applied by ss 73 and 89 of the Act to cheques and promissory notes respectively (with the necessary modifications) If the instrument comes to the hands of the holder when overdue, or after dishonour, or in a form which shows irregularity on its face, the rules stated in the text have no application, and the holder is in the position of any other assignee of a chose in action see s 36 of the Act.
(w) Thus in *White* v. *Garden* (1851), 10 C B 919, and *Pease* v *Gloahec* (1866), L. R 1 P. C. 219, which were both cases of misrepresentation, there had been no such avoidance before assignment, and the representee's defence accordingly failed

assignment, the assignee cannot be deprived of the property unless his acquisition of it was wanting in some one or more of the elements necessary to constitute that which (borrowing a phrase from the Bills of Exchange Act, 1882) may be termed " due course," that is to say, unless (1) he gave no value, and was a mere donee or volunteer, or (2) took with notice, or (3) in bad faith.

286. That the property may be taken out of the hands of an assignee who is a mere volunteer or the recipient of bounty, whether he acted in good faith, or without notice, or not, has been established from the earliest times (x). It is to be observed that for this purpose any person on whom property devolves by mere operation of law, such as an execution creditor, or a trustee in bankruptcy, is not a purchaser for value, and a party complaining may exercise against him any right of avoidance (thereby recovering property otherwise deliverable to the execution creditor, or distributable amongst the creditors) which he might have exercised against the execution debtor or the bankrupt (y) Secondly, if the assignee had notice of the fact which gave the party complaining his equity to avoid the contract and resume the property, he cannot retain such property, though he gave value, and though he was not guilty of any personal dishonesty or bad faith (z) Lastly, though the assignee gave value and in fact had no express notice of the circumstances which rendered the contract voidable, yet, if he acted in bad faith, that is to say, if with fraudulent deliberation he escaped notice of that which he had abundant reason to suspect, again he is not permitted to retain the property (a). In the first of the above three cases, the assignee has purchased no right to consideration, and therefore will suffer no *damnum* which the law can recognize in handing over that which came to him as a mere gift or windfall: in the other two of them, he will suffer a *damnum* but no *injuria*, because he will thereby be most righteously punished for direct or constructive complicity in the very breach of duty which is the subject of relief

287. The burden of establishing that the assignee was not an assignee " in due course " is on the party complaining. there is no onus on the assignee to prove that he was It has never. indeed, been doubted that, in the class of case now under consideration, it is incumbent on the party complaining to show that the assignee gave no value for the property, or had notice of

(x) See the cases cited in the notes to § 506, in Ch V, Sect 7, Sub s. (2), *post*, where the application of the rule becomes of more practical importance than in the class of case which is the subject of the present Chapter, and cp the misrepresentation cases of *Vaughan v Vanderstegen, Gates's Case* (1854), 2 Drew 363, *Same v Same, Othwaite's Case* (1854), 2 Drew 408, *Haygarth v. Wearing* (1871), L R 12 Eq 320, *Babcock v Lawson* (1880), 5 Q B. D 284, C A Contrast *Lloyd v. Passingham* (1815), G Cooper, 152, 14 R R 228 (per Lord ELDON, L C, at p 155)

(y) *Kennedy v Green* (1834), 3 My & K 699, *Load v Green* (1846), 15 M. & W 216, *Madell v Thomas*, [1891] 1 Q B 230, C A (per KAY, L J, at p 238), *Re Eastgate, Ex p. Ward*, [1905] 1 K B 645; *Tilley v Bowman*, [1910] 1 K B 745, 750

(z) See *Sheffield (Earl of) v London Joint Stock Bank* (1888), 13 App Cas. 333, H L , *London Joint Stock Bank v Simmons*, [1892] A C 201, H L In the former it was, and in the latter it was not, proved that the assignee had notice

(a) *Clough v L & N W Railway Co* (1871), L R 7 Exch 26, Exch Ch , where, though value had been given, the alleged bad faith was proved; *Whitehorn Bros.* v. *Davison*, [1911] 1 K B 463, C A , where the alleged *mala fides* was not made out.

the facts in virtue of which the contract had become voidable : but until recently there seems to have been some conflict of judicial opinion as to whether the onus of establishing good faith is not on the assignee   It has now, however, been decided by the Court of Appeal that this is not so, and that the party complaining must prove the assignee's absence of good faith, if he intends to rely on it, just as much as he must prove the absence of each of the two other elements which are required to constitute " due course " (b). Whenever the party complaining has either not alleged, or, having alleged, has failed to prove, the absence of some one of these three elements, his claim against the assignee has been dismissed (c), unless he has been in a position to rely upon some estoppel against the assignee (d), or has been able to show that there had never been any contract at all under which any property could have passed to him (e).

(b) *Whitehorn Bros* v *Davison, sup.*, where the rule, and the reason for it, are stated in the lucid judgment of VAUGHAN-WILLIAMS, L.J , at pp. 476, 477 : " where you have a contract of sale which is voidable on the ground of fraud, or for any other reason, and before it is avoided by the seller, the buyer, as against whom it could have been avoided, has transferred the subject-matter of the contract to an innocent third person who has given value and has accepted the transfer without either knowledge of anything wrong, or any knowledge of such circumstances as might lead him to wish not to make further inquiry lest he should find that there was something wrong, the contract cannot be avoided as against that person , and I am of opinion that the onus of proving that there are such circumstances as prevent the third person so purchasing from being such an innocent purchaser rests on the plaintiff who seeks to recover the subject-matter of the contract from him, and not on the defendant   . . The very statement which occurs again and again that in such cases the contract is a voidable and not a void contract, i e that it is valid till avoided, seems to me to indicate that the onus for the purpose of avoiding it against the third person must lie upon the person who is seeking to impeach that which up to that time is a valid contract.   Common sense appears to me to point to the same con clusion."   See also the observations of BUCKLEY, L J., in the same case, who, at pp. 481, 482, insists that a man in possession of property must be presumed to be in lawful and innocent possession of it until the contrary is shown, and that the form in which the proviso to s. 23 of the Sale of Goods Act, 1893 (56 & 57 Vict. c. 71) is expressed, though at first sight lending some countenance to the opposite contention, could not have been intended to evolutionize plain principles of evidence applicable to such cases   So also KENNEDY, L.J , at p. 487.
(c) As in *London Joint Stock Bank* v *Simmons, sup.* (where the plaintiff failed to prove notice) , *Truman* v. *Attenborough* (1910), 103 L T. 218 (where neither absence of value, nor notice, nor bad faith was even alleged, estoppel alone being relied upon) , *White horn Bros.* v *Davison, sup* (where, again, no allegation of, or attempt to prove, any of the above facts was made, it being insisted, wrongly as the C. A held—see the last note— that it was for the assignee to prove his good faith
(d) See *Mangles* v *Dixon* (1852), 3 H. L C 762 (per Lord ST LEONARDS, L C , at pp 732, 733) , *Truman* v *Attenborough, sup* (where, however, the estoppel was not made out).
(e) That is to say, where the contract must be deemed never to have existed at all, by reason of having been induced by misdescription of its character or class, or by *error personæ*, which type of case is discussed minutely in §§ 256–259, and in § 349, of the author's *Law of Actionable Misrepresentation* , or where the contract is void *ab initio*, and not merely voidable, by reason of statutory or common law illegality   It may be mentioned here, before leaving the subject, that one who acquires the subject matter of the contract without notice of the circumstances which would render it voidable can (except in the class of case mentioned by JESSEL, M R , in his observations cited below) confer a good title on another, even though that other had such notice   see *Lowther* v *Carlton* (1741), 2 Atk 242 ; *Sweet* v *Southcote* (1786), 2 Brown C C 26 , *Re Stapleford Colliery Co* , *Barrow's Case* (1880), 14 C D 432 (*per* JESSEL, M R , at p 445   "the only exception, and the well known exception, to the rule which protects a purchaser with notice taking from a purchaser without notice, is that which prevents a trustee from buying back property which he has sold, or a fraudulent man who has acquired property by fraud saying he sold it to a *bona*

SECT. 8. CRITICAL OBSERVATIONS ON CERTAIN DEBATEABLE DECISIONS RELATING TO MATTERS DEALT WITH IN THIS CHAPTER

288. There are certain decisions from time to time referred to in foregoing portions of this Chapter which would seem to invite a closer and more detailed examination than it was then possible or convenient to embody either in the text or in the appended notes. These decisions consist of : (1) the two " geometrical progression " cases (as they may be called) of *James* v. *Morgan,* and *Thornborow* v. *Whitacre,* (2) the vendor and purchaser case of *Wilde* v. *Gibson,* (3) the compromise case of *Turner* v. *Green,* and (4) the anomalous case of *Ellard* v *Lord Llandaff.* It is proposed now to examine these cases in the above order, and to consider how far, if at all, the propositions of law enunciated in them are sound

Sub-s. (1)   *The Cases of* James v. Morgan, *and* Thornborow v Whitacre.

289. These two cases, decided (if there can be said to have been in strictness any decision at all of either of them) in 1674, and in 1705, respectively, are really almost *lusus jurisprudentiæ* They can hardly be regarded as serious authorities   Each of them ended in, if not " a lame and impotent conclusion," at all events a *solvuntur risu tabulæ.* They were actions brought to recover damages for breach of contracts to deliver huge quantities of barley or rye calculated according to a stipulated scale of " geometrical progression," of the nature and consequences of which mathematical law the plaintiff in each case was presumably cognizant (though ὀψιμαθής), and the defendant presumably ignorant   We are not told in the report of either case what station in life the parties occupied, but we may suppose that they were farmers, and that, except *ad hoc,* they were not on intimate terms with any but the most elementary rules of arithmetic   In neither case does the Court seem to have been conscious of the serious nature of the questions of non-disclosure which were involved, and consequently there was no ruling which is of the slightest juridical value   Nevertheless these two " geometrical progression " cases raise problems which may conceivably have to be solved hereafter, and invite consideration of the principles on which any such question ought to be determined.   From that point of view, apart from the interest attaching to them as curiosities in the annals of our jurisprudence, they are perhaps not undeserving of examination

290. There are two reports of *James* v. *Morgan* (*f*).   One of them is as follows (*g*)   " Assumpsit to pay for a horse a barleycorn a nail, doubling it every nail, and avers that there were 32 nails in the shoes of the horse, which being doubled every nail, came to 500 quarters of barley   And on

fide purchaser without notice, and has got it back again ") ; *Nottingham Patent Brick & Tile Co* v. *Butler* (1886), 16 Q. B D 778, C A. (*per* LINDLEY, L J , at p 780) , *Wilkes* v. *Spooner,* [1911] 2 K B. 473, C A (*per* VAUGHAN WILLIAMS, L J , at p 483, and FARWELL, L.J , at pp 487, 488).   An illustration of the exception pointed out, *ubi sup.,* by JESSEL, M R., is the partnership case of *Gordon* v. *Holland* (1913), 82 L. J. (P C) 81.

(*f*) (1674), 1 Lev 111 , 1 Keb. 569
(*g*) That in 1 Lev. 111, the whole of which is transcribed *verbatim* in the text

non assumpsit pleaded, the cause being tried before HYDE at Hereford, he directed the jury to give the value of the horse in damages, being £8, and so they did. And it was afterwards moved in arrest of judgment for a small fault in the declaration, which was overruled, and judgment given for the plaintiff " (h).

291. It appears, therefore, that "HYDE at Hereford" took a short way with the jury and the situation, and that by his blunt direction, worthy of the summary and sub-ficulnal administration of a Cadi, brushed aside, or forestalled, the actual or potential suggestion of subtleties In those days, and in such cases, juries found as they were told to find The measure of damages was hopelessly unsound but no one seems to have been shocked or surprised by the judge's direction on that score, for the simple reason that damages were then awarded in an entirely haphazard fashion, and without any application or appreciation of the systematized body of rules which now govern the assessment of pecuniary compensation for breaches of contract (i) When moving to arrest the judgment, the defendant's counsel could think of nothing better than "the small fault in the declaration" above mentioned : any notion of fraud, or mistake, or non-disclosure was obviously not dreamed of in his philosophy (k)

292. *Thornborow* v. *Whitacre* was a similar case, except that the plaintiff was not, as in the former case, a vendor of a chattel for the stipulated number of grains, or rather an exchanger of goods for other goods to the stipulated amount, but the purchaser of the stipulated quantity of grains for a fixed price in money. The treatment, however, of the later case, both in argument and judgment, was entirely different. There are two reports of it (l) Putting

(h) The nature of the "small fault in the declaration," which was not allowed to have any effect "after verdict," appears from the report in 1 Keb 569, the whole of which runs thus "In action upon the Case on colloquium, on the sale of a Gelding, the defendant promised that the said horse should have four shoes, and in each eight nails and so for the first, the defendant was to give a barleycorn, for the second two, and four for the third, and so double to every nail, proximo, whereas it should have been proximo præcedenti Sed non allocatur after Verdict "

(i) Of course the proper measure was not £8, the value of the horse, but the value of the stipulated number of barleycorns, less £8, the (apparently agreed) value of the horse, if the horse had not been delivered, and without any deduction, if it had See the observations of VAUGHAN WILLIAMS, L J , at p 792 of *Chaplin* v *Hicks*, [1911] 2 K B 786, C A , as to the haphazard way in which damages were left to the jury in former days, without any rules or principles being laid down by judges for their guidance

(k) In neither report is the sum in geometrical progression exactly worked out, though Levinz estimates the result roughly at "500 quarters of barley," and, in the margin, cites a then well-known mathematical treatise "vide Mathesin Wallisn, cap 31 " The allusion is to the *Mathesis Universalis* (Oxford, 1657) of John Wallis, a very celebrated mathematician, man of science, and scholar, who was in 1649 appointed by Cromwell Savilian Professor of Geometry in the University of Oxford, and was one of the founders of the Royal Society The work in question " embodied the substance of his professional lectures " (*Dict of Nat Biogr* , sub nom , where we are also told that " in *Dunton's Life and Errors* (Nichols), ii 658, is a copy of verses on Wallis's funeral, beginning 'I'll have the solemn pomp and stately show *In geometrical progression go.*' " The precise figures are as follows the last doubling of the barleycorn gives 2, 147, 483, 648 barleycorns and the addition of the 32 sums, successively doubled, beginning with 1, and ending with the above figure, results in 4,294,966,395 barleycorns, a huge amount, but not nearly approaching the colossal result of the 52 doublings in *Thornborow* v *Whitacre*

(l) (1705), 6 Mod 305 , 2 Ld Raym 1164

aside the shorter and far less satisfactory of the two (m), we learn from Lord Raymond (n) that it was an "action upon the case, in which the plaintiff declares upon an agreement between the plaintiff and the defendant, that the defendant in consideration of 2s. 6d. in hand paid, and of 4l. 17s. 6d. to be paid upon the defendant performing the agreement of his part, *deliberaret* to the plaintiff two grains of rye corn on Monday, the 29th of March, and four grains of rye corn on Monday then next following, and eight grains of rye corn on Monday next after the Monday last mentioned, and sixteen grains of rye corn on Monday next after the said third Monday, and double the number of grains of rye corn, viz thirty-two grains of rye corn on Monday next after, being the fifth Monday, *et progressu sic deliberaret quolibet alio die Lunæ successivè infra unum annum ab eodem 29 Martii bis tot grana fecalis quot die Lunæ proximo præcedente (o) respectivè deliberanda forent.*" To this declaration the defendant demurred (p) It was felt that on some ground or other the Court ought to intervene at the earliest stage to prevent even the possibility of an outrageous result. but still it did not occur to the defendant's counsel to suggest any ground for the demurrer except impossibility (q), which, for obvious reasons, the Court (consisting of HOLT, C J., POWELL, J , and others) held to be an invalid ground (r). Thereupon

(m) Viz the report in 6 Mod. 305, the whole of which (*verbatim*) is as follows "Assumpsit, that in consideration of half a crown by the plaintiff in hand paid to the defendant, he promised to pay two grains of rye upon Monday the 29th March in such a year, four grains the next Monday after, and so on by progressional arithmetic every Monday for a year and non assumpsit pleaded Per Curiam, upon motion Let them go to trial, and though this may amount to a vast quantity, yet the jury will consider of the folly of the defendant, and give but reasonable damages against him" The "progressional arithmetic" mentioned is what is now called "geometrical progression" (1, 2, 4, 8, 16, &c), as distinct from "arithmetical progression" (1, 3, 5, 7, 9, &c) The "motion" referred to was, as we are told by Lord Raymond, a demurrer The statement that the consideration was half a crown is inaccurate it was, as again we find in Lord Raymond's fuller report, £5, whereof 2s 6d was paid down, and the remaining £4 17s 6d was payable on the completion of the defendant's 52 weekly deliveries of the successively doubled amounts of grain The observation of the Court as to what a jury would probably do with the case, which is not to be found in Lord Raymond's report, seems to indicate an intelligent anticipation of a repetition at the trial of the summary methods of HYDE, J , in *James* v *Morgan, sup* , which case (as we are told by Lord Raymond) was cited to, and discussed by, the Court see note (s), *inf*

(n) (1705), 2 Ld Raym 1164

(o) Observe that the cautious pleader, by using the phrase *proximo præcedente*, steered clear of " the small fault in the declaration " which imperilled the plaintiff's success on the trial of *James* v. *Morgan, sup* , and, but for the fact that the objection was taken after verdict, might have vitiated it

(p) His counsel was the eminent Salkeld, who was not willing to take the chance of a judge at the trial following HYDE, J 's direction in *James* v *Morgan, sup* , and telling the jury to give the plaintiff £5 as damages He evidently thought it quite possible that the jury might be directed or at all courts left free, to award as damages the value of the stipulated number of grains

(q) At pp 1164, 1165 of the report in 2 Ld Raym 1164, Salkeld's contention to this effect is stated He said that there were three kinds of impossibility, (i) *impossibilitas legis*, (ii) *impossibilitas rei*, and (iii) impossibility in fact. He admitted that the case did not fall within (i), but urged that it came within (iii), if not within (ii), " as all the rye in the world did not come to so much," and that the contract was therefore void

(r) *Ibid* , p 1165 " HOLT, C.J Suppose A for money paid him by B. will undertake to do an impossible thing, shall not an action lie against him for not performing it • . . though it cannot be performed, yet he shall answer damages *Per Curiam* And as to the impossibility, the Court said it was only impossible with respect to the defendant's ability,

" the counsel for the defendant, perceiving the opinion of the Court to be against his client, offered the plaintiff his half-crown and his costs ; which was accepted of, and so no judgment was given in the case " (s).

293. The result, therefore, of this action was as inconclusive as that of *James* v *Morgan*, and is, moreover, far less comprehensible On the one hand, HOLT, C J , seems to have been much troubled by the extraordinary and unforeseen consequences which would result from upholding the validity of the contract (t), and, with this in his mind, put an unnatural and impossible construction upon it which would at all events mitigate its absurdity (u) Yet POWELL, J , undoubtedly stated in plain terms the the contract " would hold in law " (v), and the rest of the Court must have agreed with him, since they were unanimous in considering the only ground assigned for the demurrer to be bad, and must therefore have been prepared, but for the compromise arrived at between the parties, to hold the declaration good, and the claim to its full extent enforceable. But then the very judge who expressed his view that the contract would hold in law observed in the same breath that " the defendant ought to pay," not the full stipulated sum, but " *something for his folly* " (w), and the Court, according to the shorter report, thought it probable that " the jury would give but reasonable damages against him " (x), which observations are totally inconsistent with the theory that

which was not such an impossibility as would make the contract void And the Chief Justice said, the words, *quolibet alio die Lunæ*, must be construed what we say in English, every other Monday, that is, every next Monday but one, and that would bring the contract nearer to the defendant's ability of performance. Powell said, that though the contract was a foolish one, yet it would hold in law, and that the defendant ought to pay something for his folly "

(s) *Ibid*, p 1166 We are told, at p 1165, that " upon this occasion .   *James* v. *Morgan* was remembered," and, at p 1166, that this case " was admitted of all hands to be good law, and did, as the plaintiff urged, rule this And Mr. Salkeld said that differed from this because that was possible to be performed, though an ill bargain, but this impossible " What was meant by its being " admitted of all hands " that *James* v *Morgan* was good law, it is impossible to imagine, because, if one thing is more clear than another about that case, it is that no question of law whatsoever was decided in it

(t) Here, as in *James* v. *Morgan*, the sum is not worked out We merely get a hint of its enormous magnitude by Salkeld's statement that " all the rye in the world would not come to so much " The amount is of course hugely in excess of that arrived at in the earlier case, since there are 52 doublings here, as against 32 there, and each additional doubling *vires acquirit eundo* The last duplication of the 2 grains, with which the series of 52 commences, results in the figure 2,251,799,813,663,248, or nearly 2252 billions of grains What the defendant, therefore, contracted to deliver (being the aggregate of the 52 sums, beginning with 2, and ending with the above) was no less than 4,503,599,627,326,494, or about 4503½ billions, of grains

(u) See note (r), *sup* The suggestion thrown out by HOLT, C J., that *quolibet alio die Lunæ* might,—indeed, as he said, must,— be construed as meaning every alternate Monday, is quite grotesque It sins against both decent Latinity and good sense In the first place, " alio," though perhaps not very good Latin for " every remaining Monday in the year (" cætero " being more appropriate), could by no possibility be taken to indicate alternate weeks Secondly, from the declaration, which carefully sets out the successive weekly duplications—2, 4, 8, 16, 32—for the first five Mondays, and proceeds, " et progressu *sic* deliberaret quolibet aliodie Lunæ successivè infrà unum annum," it is manifest that weekly doublings throughout the year, like the first five specified weekly doublings, were intended . for, otherwise, the word " sic " would have no meaning at all.

(v) See note (r), *sup*

(w) See, again, note (r), *sup*

(x) See note (m), *sup*.

the agreement was enforceable, and the stipulated sum recoverable according to its tenor. And, more than anything else, the defendant's offer, and the plaintiff's acceptance of it, absolutely contradict every pronouncement which is stated to have emanated from HOLT, C J , and POWELL, J For, if " the counsel for the defendant perceived the opinion of the Court to be against his client " to the extent of holding the declaration good (which was the only subject of the motion), it is inconceivable that this perception should have moved him to make, and still more inconceivable that the plaintiff (who presumably perceived the Court to be with him to the above extent) should have accepted, so ridiculously inadequate an offer as the return of the half-crown in hand paid ; indeed, a settlement on these terms is not only inconsistent with the hypothesis that the contract was valid and enforceable, but consistent with no other theory than that it was voidable and unenforceable (y).

294. The real problem in these cases was ignored or shirked : and it is no doubt for that reason that they have scarcely ever been cited as authorities, or regarded in any other light than as " flies in amber " But none the less they *donnent furieusement à penser*, and, like some of the apparently trivial discussions in the case books of the Jesuits, they raise questions of principle Let it be granted that a contract of the nature in question be made at the present day between two persons each of whom is of normal intelligence and education. On what principle, if any, could the party who promised to pay the sum calculable according to the law of geometrical progression be relieved of his promise ? Whether the party seeking to enforce the contract be a vendor, as in *James* v. *Morgan*, or a purchaser, as in *Thornborow* v *Whitacre*, there is ordinarily no obligation on him to instruct the other party in the simple rules of arithmetic (z)   And, generally, whatever be the nature of the contract in course of negotiation, each of the negotiating parties is presumed to be acquainted with, and neither of them need expound to the other, such rudimentary principles of science as form the subject of an ordinary education (a), unless there is independent evidence of fraud (b), or of oppression (c), when it may become incumbent on the party

(y) For, except as to the costs, this is just what would have happened if the defendant had insisted, and the Court had determined, that the contract was voidable at his option, or, if the defendant had been suing for rescission, and such rescission had been granted, in either of which cases he would have had to return the half crown as the condition of relief

(z) There is ordinarily no duty on a vendor to disclose matters not affecting title (see § 117, 118, *ante*), and there is no duty, except in very special circumstances, on a purchaser to disclose anything at all (see note (v) to § 111, and the latter part of § 165, *ante*)

(a) See § 40, *ante*

(b) As in many of the cases cited in the notes to Sect 2, Sub s (8), *ante*

(c) Thus, in *Howley* v *Cook* (1873), Ir R 8 Eq 370, one of the elements in the unconscionability of the bargain was that the money lender had introduced into the mortgage deeds unprecedented and oppressive clauses without any attempt to explain their effect to the borrower Another case, still more in point, is *Harris* v *Clarson* (1910), 27 T L R 30, an action by a moneylender, where, the defence being that the contract was " harsh and unconscionable " within the meaning of s 1 of the Moneylenders Act, 1900, by reason of a clause that on failure to pay any one instalment the whole amount was to become due at once, it was held by CHANNELL, J , that such a clause is harsh and unconscionable *primâ*

guilty of such conduct to explain the practical effect of even the simplest mathematical formula on the interests of the other negotiating party. The hypothesis, however, on which this discussion is based, excludes any such special circumstances : and the question is,—as between two persons of normal education and intelligence, or assumed to be so (for either party has the right to make this assumption with respect to the other), could the Court refuse to enforce a contract of the nature in question ? And, if so, on what theory ? Certainly not on the theory of impossibility (d), nor on that of common mistake, because in the case supposed there would have been no bilateral mistake, if, indeed, there can be said in strictness to have been any mistake of fact at all on the part even of the party complaining. If it could be shown that one of the parties, A., realized the serious practical consequences of the application of the law of geometrical progression in calculating the sum to be paid, and knew that B. did not realize them, and was contracting with himself in the belief, and on the basis, that no such serious consequences existed, it could plausibly be argued that the coexistence of these facts might of itself suffice to establish fraud on the part of A , that is, a fraudulent intention to trade on the known ignorance of B. for his own advantage, and to the damage of B. But reasons have already been given for concluding that such an argument, however attractive, is fundamentally unsound (e) And it would at any rate have no application to a case in which, instead of A contracting to sell property of fixed value, or pay a fixed sum, in consideration of the delivery to him by B. of a commodity to an amount to be calculated in accordance with the mathematical rule, A and B. are each contracting with the other for payment of sums so calculable in accordance with a law of which neither of them realizes the importance It may be said that such a case is never likely to arise. But

facie, or, in other words, that the insertion of it in the agreement casts upon the moneylender the duty of making its effect clear to the borrower · "what was harsh and unconscionable was the way moneylenders took advantage of such clauses They knew, if they inserted a clause to the effect that the whole amount for which the note was given became due if one instalment was unpaid, that the result might be, as in the present case, to increase the rate of interest from 140 to 600 per cent Not only did they know that, but they put in words which they thought a borrower would agree to, because he would think that he was asked to pay so much interest upon a loan which was to be for a certain period They knew equally well that the borrower would not see that the putting in of such a default clause made the interest payable, for example, in the case before him, not £35 for 12 months, but possibly £35 for one month " (p 30), accordingly, "he should decide that the case was one in which the defendant ought to have relief on the ground that this default clause, which was an unfair one unless it was very carefully explained, was put in for the purpose of being acted upon " (p 31)

(d) This was disposed of in *Thornborow* v *Whitacre, sup.*, being the only point of law which was decided, or raised, in that case

(e) See § 164, *ante* Lord HARDWICKE, L C , however, makes a passing reference to *James* v *Morgan*, at pp 155, 156 of *Chesterfield (Earl)* v. *Jannsen* (1751), 2 Ves Sr 125, in such terms as to indicate that in his view fraud was, or ought to have been, inferred in that case from the very nature of the transaction, without more Fraud, he there says, "may be apparent from the intrinsic nature and subject of the bargain itself; such as no man in his senses and not under delusion would make on the one hand, and as no honest and fair man would accept on the other . which are inequitable and unconscientious bargains , and of such even the common law has taken notice , for which, if it would not look a little ludicrous, might be cited 1 Lev. 111, *James* v *Morgan* " To this observation ROMILLY, M.R , draws attention, at p 115 of *Cockell* v. *Taylor* (1852), 15 Beav 103

it is conceivable (*f*). And, if a contract of this character should hereafter be made under the conditions stated, it is difficult to see on what principle any Court to whom either of the parties should apply to enforce it could refuse its aid

Sub-s (2). *The Case of* Wilde v. Gibson.

295. This much-discussed case occupied the attention of the Courts for nearly a decade in the middle of the last century. The party complaining was one Magnus Gibson, who had purchased by auction from Mdlle Augusta Emma D'Este (a daughter of Augustus Frederick, Duke of Sussex, by a morganatic marriage) an estate in Ramsgate. He filed his bill against the lady for rescission of the contract, and consequential relief, on the ground of non-disclosure of a serious incumbrance, viz. a public footpath or right of way, known as "the Liberty Way," over the property. The contract had been completed by conveyance before the plaintiff was apprised of the undisclosed fact. The suit came on for hearing before KNIGHT-BRUCE, V.-C, who granted the relief prayed (*g*). Five years later, the defendant, who had in the meantime (August, 1845) intermarried with Sir Thomas Wilde (afterwards Lord TRURO, L C), joined with her husband in seeking, and eventually obtaining, from the House of Lords a reversal of this decree (*h*)

(*f*) If contracts of gaming and wagering were, as they used to be in the time of Lord MANSFIELD, enforceable, a case of this description might well arise at any moment, under such circumstances, for instance, as those described in the newspapers of the 4th April, 1912 "A curious incident" (the report is taken from the issue of the *Daily Mail* of that date) "occurred in a bridge game on board the *Olympia* on her last voyage from New York to Plymouth. The players—two Americans, an Australian, and an Englishman—were friends. They were playing five cent (2½d.) points, or a little more than a sovereign a hundred, and they were all fairly matched. They played freely—i e they were calling on light hands and doubling the declaration with the smallest justification. The Australian had one of the Americans for his partner, the Englishman the other. The last-named made a heart call (for which each trick counts eight). This was promptly doubled by his Australian opponent. A redouble was again doubled by the Australian, and then the English partner of the American who had made the original call, raised the game still higher. This redoubling did not finish until, according to an onlooker keeping tally, the value had multiplied eighteen times. The game was played, and resulted in the loss of the odd trick by the man who had called hearts. When, however, the players calculated what the points were, they found that they had multiplied to 2,097,152, and that each trick was worth over £20,000" (in fact the value was £21,846 11s 8d) "The losers said this was absurd, that no one realized what he was doing, and eventually it was agreed that the losers should each pay £100 for the odd trick" Now, assume that no gaming statutes were now in force, and assume the absence of any rule of the game itself prohibiting doubling beyond a certain point, or an agreement of the parties not to be bound by such rule · if either of the winners, instead of arranging the matter in a sportsmanlike fashion, had chosen to sue either of the losers for £21,846 11s 8d, what answer could there have been in principle to the action? Each was equally ignorant of the magnitude of the figure resulting from eighteen doublings of eight points : each was equally ignorant of the other's ignorance. neither knew in whose favour the unexpected result of the application of the mathematical rule would operate. There could be no suggestion, therefore, of either player scheming to overreach the other. Equally there could be no breach of a duty to disclose, because there is never any duty to disclose anything except that of which the party under the supposed obligation has, or is presumed to have, *exclusive* knowledge. and here, *ex hypothesi*, each party knew what the other knew, no more and no less

(*g*) *Gibson* v *D'Este* (1843), 2 Y & C (CH) 542

(*h*) *Sub nom*, *Wilde* v *Gibson* (1848), 1 H L C. 605

296. The difficulties in dealing with the judgments delivered in the House of Lords, which have deservedly met with so much severe criticism, are in painful contrast with the ease and facility with which one is enabled to appreciate and accept the singularly lucid exposition of the law given by KNIGHT-BRUCE, V.-C., in the judgment appealed from. There were three members of the appellate tribunal. Lord COTTENHAM, L.C., Lord BROUGHAM, and Lord CAMPBELL. The speeches of the two latter were extremely hazy just where precision was most needed, and that of Lord COTTENHAM, L.C., certainly did not exhibit his usual clearness of expression. All of them present at times a confused medley of findings of fact with questions of law, of propositions necessary to the decision with propositions not so necessary, and of principles with pleadings. In the ensuing observations an attempt is made to disentangle this confusion, and to ascertain how far the decision of the House of Lords was based upon their view of the facts, and, therefore, is of no juridical importance, and how far it was founded upon propositions of law, and which of these latter were absolutely required to justify the reversal of the Vice-Chancellor's decree and which were not ; the former of course being, and the latter not being, authoritative.

297. All the facts which it was incumbent on the plaintiff as the party complaining to establish (*i*) were proved to the satisfaction of KNIGHT-BRUCE, V.-C. That is to say, he found (i) that the alleged undisclosed fact, viz the public right of way, existed (*j*) ; (ii) that this fact was material to be disclosed (*k*), (iii) that there had been non-disclosure of this fact, as alleged (*l*) ; (iv) that the plaintiff had no knowledge of the undisclosed fact, either actual or presumptive (*m*) ; (v) that the defendant had presumptive, if not actual, knowledge thereof (*n*) ; (vi) that the position of the defendant was in no way prejudiced by such delay on the part of the plaintiff as there had been after discovery of the undisclosed fact (*o*). The House of Lords did not dissent from any of these findings of fact, except the finding that the defendant had knowledge of the incumbrance (*p*), though Lord COTTENHAM, L.C., did also undoubtedly express his personal opinion that the alleged public right of way, and therefore the existence of the alleged undisclosed fact, was not proved (*q*). In so far as these views of the facts differed from those of the Vice-Chancellor, they were probably wrong (*r*) :

(*i*) See Sect. 3, *ante*
(*j*) 2 Y & C. (CH) 542, at pp 549, 550
(*k*) *Ibid*, at pp 550, 551
(*l*) *Ibid*, at p. 558
(*m*) *Ibid.*, at pp 558–560
(*n*) *Ibid*, at pp 560–570
(*o*) *Ibid*, at p 579.
(*p*) 1 H L C 605, *per* Lord CAMPBELL at pp 634, 635 (" there is no evidence to which we are at liberty to pay attention that . Wightwick was the agent of Lady Wilde, and if he was the agent, there is no evidence whatever that he in the course of his agency acquired any knowledge, or at any time had any knowledge, of the direction of the road, and on that the whole turns ")
(*q*) *Ibid*, at p. 625 (" if, therefore, the right of way complained of by the plaintiff had been proved—*which it was not* " &c)
(*r*) Lord ST LEONARD's detailed criticism of these views is summarily stated in § 301, *post*

and the above-mentioned personal conclusion of Lord COTTENHAM, L.C., was most certainly so (s). But it is of no interest to discuss these findings, which are not binding on any one, and they are only mentioned to be put aside and disentangled from the propositions of law which it is now proposed to consider.

298. The propositions of law enunciated in, or which lay at the root of, the Vice-Chancellor's judgment, were these :—(A) given the facts found by him as above stated (t), there was a proved case of a breach by the defendant of her duty of disclosure, in respect of which the plaintiff was entitled to relief : (B) it was immaterial that the defendant had no actual or personal knowledge of the undisclosed fact, if her solicitor and agent for that purpose was cognizant of it, for his knowledge must be imputed to her (u)   (C) the mere fact that the plaintiff had means of knowledge was not evidence that he had such knowledge, either actual or constructive (v) · (D) it was immaterial that neither the defendant, nor her agent, had any intention to deceive or injure the plaintiff, or to benefit themselves, or either of them, and that her solicitor honestly thought that silence was permissible under the circumstances, and was a duty which he owed to his client (w) . (E) where, as the Vice-Chancellor found to be the fact in this case, the position of the party charged is not altered for the worse by the delay (if any) of the party complaining, such delay is wholly inefficacious as a bar to relief (x)   All the above propositions or conclusions of law were undoubtedly sound in principle, and supported by a steady volume of authority, as has already been seen (y).   Nor did the House of Lords express the slightest disagreement with any of them : indeed, Lord CAMPBELL made a point of re-stating in his own language, and confirming, one of them (z)   But new ground was broken on the appeal, and great

(s) The observation of Lord COTTENHAM, L C , was parenthetical, but exp.ess He gives no reasons, and refers to no evidence, in support of his view. Both Lord BROUGHAM and Lord CAMPBELL abstain from expressing any concurrence

(t) See § 297, sup

(u) 2 Y & C (CH) 542, at pp 570, 571

(v) Ibid , at p 571 ("that he might have inquired, and learnt the truth by inquiry, is nothing, if there was not, as I think that there was not, any circumstance which, considering what he was told by the party contracting with him, was sufficient to apprize or warn him of the propriety of any such inquiry ")

(w) Ibid , at pp 571–577

(x) Ibid , at p 579 ("it is not suggested, at least it is not proved, that the defendant, by reason of that delay, has in respect of the property in question   . sustained any damage, or that the property in question has been treated or dealt with by the plaintiff at any time since April, 1839 "—the date when he first discovered the existence of the public right of way—"in a manner, relatively or otherwise, improper or unreasonable, or that the defendant has done, or omitted to do, anything   which, had she known earlier that the plaintiff would complain, or meant to make a claim against her, she would not have done, or would not have omitted to do ; nor   is it proved that the plaintiff ever intended to submit to the wrong done him, to acquiesce in it, or to waive his right to redress, or to accept compensation ")

(y) As to (A), see Sect 3, ante   as to (B), see Ch II, Sect 3, Sub-s (4), ante   as to (C), see § 193, ante   as to (D), see §§ 33, 197, 220, ante · as to (E), see §§ 216–219, ante.

(z) 1 H L C 605, at pp 633, 634   The proposition of KNIGHT-BRUCE, V -C , so restated was proposition (D) referred to in the te.t, as to the immateriality of absence of intention in the party charged to deceive the party complaining, or to injure him, or to benefit himself

importance was then for the first time attached to certain principles of law, as governing the case, which, it was said, the Vice-Chancellor should not have ignored, as he had.

299. The first of the principles so enunciated by the House of Lords was that, where the contract impeached has been completed by conveyance, it cannot be rescinded except for fraud, and that innocent non-disclosure, as distinguished from fraudulent concealment, is a ground for compensation (which in this case had been offered and refused) at most, and for no other relief (a) Now there is no doubt that this aspect of the matter was not present to the mind of KNIGHT-BRUCE, V.-C., who treated the case as one in which the most that could be said against the plaintiff was that there had been some delay (b), entirely overlooking the highly important facts that (1) the contract had been completed, and (2) the party complaining was asserting his right to rescission, and not to pecuniary compensation, and was not merely defending himself against a claim to enforce an executory contract There is also no doubt that, as a general rule, a contract completely executed on both sides cannot, in the absence of fraud, be annulled (c). But it is not true to say that fraud is the only exception, for there is a second, which consists in proof of a total or substantial difference in character between that which was transferred and that which was contracted to be transferred, so that, unless the contract be undone, the party complaining will be forced to retain that for which compensation will be no remedy at all (d). To this extent the main proposition on which the House of Lords based its reversal of the Vice-Chancellor's decision is incomplete, and, therefore, inaccurate (e) It would, however, in all probability, have made no difference to the result, if the proposition had been correctly and completely stated, because it is evident from numerous observations in the course of the judgments that the learned Lords considered the case as one that could be adequately met by compensation, and therefore no more came within the second exception than within the first (f). The case of *Wilde* v. *Gibson* is an authority,

(a) 1 H L C 605, *per* Lord COTTENHAM, L C., at pp 616, 617 (" the contract of purchase is perfected by a conveyance To be relieved against that, fraudulent concealment must be shown. This is different from a bill by the vendor for specific performance ")

(b) Which delay, not having affected the position of the defendant in any way, was in his opinion no bar to relief see note (x), *sup.* And, so far, the House of Lords did not disagree that is to say, they did not suggest that, if it had been a mere question of delay, without circumstances indicating affirmation or waiver, the plaintiff would on this account alone have been disentitled to relief

(c) See § 230, and notes (z) and (a) thereto, *ante*

(d) See § 230, and notes (b) and (c) thereto, *ante*

(e) It is quite open to the critic to suggest that a proposition formulated even by the tribunal of ultimate resort is unsound and devoid of authority, if (as in this case) it can be shown that in later decisions the House itself has laid down the law " en sons contraire " See, for instance, *Cooper* v. *Phibbs* (1867), L. R 2 H L 149 (*per* Lord CRANWORTH, L C, at p. 164), *Brownlie* v *Campbell* (1880), 5 App Cas 925, H. L (*per* Lord SELBORNE, L C, at p. 537)

(f) As to the first, they expressly found that no fraudulent concealment, or fraud of any kind, had been proved. And, if invited to do so by the course of the argument, they would doubtless have also found that there was no difference *in substantialibus*, i e no difference which could not be compensated for in money, between the property encumbered by the " Liberty Way," and the property free of such incumbrance.

therefore, for at least one branch or part of the rule which prohibits rescission of completed contracts, and the application by the House of Lords of that branch or part of the rule to the facts *as they found them* (whether correctly or not, is immaterial) properly and necessarily resulted in the refusal of relief to the plaintiff, and the setting aside of the Vice-Chancellor's decree. The question now arises whether the case is an authority for all or any of the other propositions or dicta contained in it (g).

300. These other propositions and dicta, which have occasioned so many difficulties, doubts, and debates, and to which either the House, or individual members of it, undoubtedly committed themselves, are the following · that the fraudulent concealment required to constitute an exception to the rule against rescinding a completed contract must be an actually or personally fraudulent concealment, as distinguished from a mere non-disclosure of facts of which the party charged has only constructive or presumptive knowledge through an agent (h) . that the mere constructive knowledge of an agent for sale, or for some purposes connected with the sale, or the knowledge acquired by such an agent otherwise than as agent, or before his agency commenced, can never be imputed to the principal (i) that when personal fraud is alleged, and not proved, the party complaining is debarred from relief on any other ground, such as constructive fraud or knowledge (j) and (this was the individual suggestion, during the argument, of Lord CAMPBELL only) that, in an action of deceit, a principal is not responsible for the misrepresentation or concealment of his agent (k) Of these four propositions, the first two require considerable qualification to render them completely accurate (l)

(g) Having found a principle on which the decision can properly be based, that is to say, a principle which is not at variance with the current of authority or with sound reasoning, one is at liberty to reject other propositions, enunciated as contributory to the result, which are so at variance Where a decision of the House of Lords is arrived at by one process of reasoning, and one only, in accepting the destination, as we must, we necessarily accept the only road by which it can be reached but where we are given a map on which the destination is marked as approachable by several routes, we are not, in accepting the destination, compelled to accept more than one of those routes we may accept a direct and good road, and reject those which are devious or foundrous

(h) 1 H L. C 605, *per* Lord CAMPBELL, at pp 632, 633 "if there be in any way whatsoever, misrepresentation or concealment, which is material to the purchaser, a Court of Equity will not compel him to complete the purchase , but where the conveyance has been executed, I apprehend, my Lords, that a Court of Equity will set aside the conveyance only on the ground of actual fraud And there will be no safety for the transactions of mankind if, upon a discovery being made at any distance of time of a material fact not disclosed to the purchaser, of which the vendor had merely constructive notice, a conveyance which had been executed could be set aside "

(i) *Ibid.*, *per* Lord COTTENHAM, L C , at pp 624, 625, and Lord CAMPBELL, at pp 634, 635

(j) *Ibid* , *per* Lord COTTENHAM, L.C , at pp 620–622, and p 627, Lord BROUGHAM, at p 628, and Lord CAMPBELL, at p 634

(k) It is not fair to impute this egregious dictum, even as a dictum, to the House of Lords. It was merely the personal observation of Lord CAMPBELL, interjected during the argument (see p 615 of the report): "in an action upon contract," he there says, "the representation of the agent is the representation of the principal , but in an action on the case for deceit, the misrepresentation *or concealment* must be proved against the principal "

(l) If by "actual fraud" Lord CAMPBELL meant the concealment of a fact personally known to the party charged, as distinguished from the non-disclosure of a fact known to the third, as stated, is now universally regarded as untenable (*m*) · whilst the fourth is ludicrously and hopelessly unsound (*n*).

301. Lord St. Leonards, in one of his treatises (*o*), has criticized adversely, and with some severity, the decision of the House of Lords in the case under discussion : but the criticism is not quite as valuable as one would have

his agent, the first of the four propositions stated in the text is not in accordance with the authorities   Even in an action of deceit, the principal is liable in damages for the fraud of his agent . see note (*u*), *inf*.   A *fortiori*, he is responsible for the like fraud of his agent, when sued for rescission   Lord Campbell himself admits (see p 633 of the report) that fraudulent intention need not be proved, it being enough to establish the *scienter* and it is now beyond question that principal and agent are one, and therefore to establish the *scienter* against the agent is to establish it against the principal   The second proposition, viz that constructive knowledge of the agent, or knowledge acquired by him otherwise than as agent in the particular matter, can *never* be imputed to the principal, is also somewhat too absolutely expressed   see § 56, and note (*z*) thereto, *ante*, and the observations of Lord St Leonards referred to in note (*t*), *inf*

(*m*) Lord Cottenham, L C , himself afterwards protested that he had never meant what he certainly is reported to have said in *Wilde* v *Gibson* on this topic   See his observations at pp 459, 460 of *Archbold* v *Commissioners of Charitable Requests in Ireland* (1849), 2 H L C 440 (" if fraud be imputed, and other matters alleged which would give the Court jurisdiction as the foundation of a decree, then the proper course is to dismiss so much of the bill as is not proved, and to give so much relief as under the circumstances the plaintiff is entitled to ")   And it is quite clear that there no longer exists any rule that a bill or statement of claim containing averments of fraud necessarily involves an undertaking to prove them, though not required for the purpose of making good a title to relief, and that, failing compliance with such implied undertaking, the whole action must be dismissed, or that the party complaining is affected otherwise than in the matter of costs   see the observations of Turner, V -C , at pp 264, 265 of *Espey* v *Lake* (1852), 10 Hare 260 , of Parke, B , at p 428 of *Anderson* v *Thornton* (1853), 8 Exch 425 , of Knight-Bruce, L J , at p 750 of *Small* v *Currie* (1854), 23 L J (cr) 746 , of Page-Wood, V -C , at pp 673, 674 of *Parr* v *Jewell* (1855), 1 Kay & J 671 , of the Court of Exchequer at pp 920, 921 of *Swinfen* v *Lord Chelmsford* (1860), 5 H & N 890 , of Turner, L J , at pp 323, 331, of *Traill* v *Baring* (1864), 4 De G J & S 318 , of Lord Chelmsford, L C , at p 331 of *Hickson* v *Lombard* (1866), L R 1 H L 324 , of the Privy Council at p 597 of *London Chartered Bank of Australia* v *Lempriere* (1873), L R 4 P C 572; of Lord Shaw, at pp 967, 968 of *Nocton* v *Lord Ashburton*, [1914] A. C 932, H L Where, however, the case pleaded is so bound up with fraud that, if the averments relating to it be struck out of the pleading, no intelligible cause of action remains, it is still the rule that, on failing to prove the fraud, the party complaining is not allowed to fall back on some other cause of action, such as negligence, which is independent of the question of good or bad faith (see *Thom* v *Bigland* (1853), 8 Exch 725, at pp 730–732, and *Connecticut Fire Insurance Co* v *Kavanagh*, [1892] A C 473, P C , at p 479), or, in an appellate court, rely upon admissions extracted from the party charged and his witnesses in the Court below which might establish such cause of action, because, if the claim had been so framed in the first instance, it might have been met by evidence of a very different character to that which was adduced on the supposition that fraud, and fraud only, was what the party charged was called upon to rebut : see *Hickson* v *Lombard, sup (per* Lord Cranworth, at p 336) , *Connecticut Fire Insurance Co* v *Kavanagh, sup* (at p 480)

(*n*) In *Udell* v *Atherton* (1861), 7 H & N 172, at pp 181, 182, Wilde, B (afterwards Lord Penzance and, it so happened, the nephew of the successful appellant in the case under discussion), in delivering the judgment of Pollock, C B , and himself, said " the only dictum in favour of it "—i e the notion that vicarious fraud will not support an action of deceit—" is, I believe, that of Lord Campbell, in the course of the argument in *Wilde* v *Gibson*. It may be doubted if it is correctly reported , at any rate it is to be taken, in my opinion, in reference only to the point then under argument " That the dictum was merely a suggestion thrown out during the argument, and not forming part of the judgment, and was personal to Lord Campbell, and in any case is utterly erroneous, is shown by reference to a long course of authority, before and since 1848, in § 162 of the author's *Law of Actionable Misrepresentation*

(*o*) " A Treatise on the Law of Real Property as administered by the House of Lords," by Sir Edward Sugden

expected in the case of so eminent an authority, inasmuch as it is largely occupied with an exhaustive analysis of the allegations and evidence in the case, and with an exposition of his reasons for dissenting from the Lords' inferences *of fact* therefrom,—an exposition which, though most convincing, is of no assistance in an investigation of the principles of law involved (p). The main difference between his views and those of the House of Lords relates to the question of the defendant's knowledge of the public right of way. The House considered that there was no evidence that Lady Wilde had actual knowledge of this fact further, that though the solicitor, Mr Wightwick, had at one time personal knowledge that there was some right of way in respect of which an annual payment was made, this knowledge was acquired long before he became Lady Wilde's agent for the sale of the property, and that he did not at any time become her agent for all purposes of the sale, and that, therefore, his knowledge was at most of a merely constructive, or presumptive, nature, and that any such knowledge cannot be, even if an agent's actual knowledge can ever be, imputed to a principal charged with personal knowledge and personal fraud in an action which Lord BROUGHAM and Lord CAMPBELL persisted in treating, and even describing, as an action *ex delicto*, founded upon deceit or fraudulent conceal-ment, rather than an action *ex contractu*, founded upon non-disclosure of a material fact within the knowledge of the party charged Lord ST LEONARDS shows in the most conclusive manner, by copious references to the evidence, that all these views and inferences were utterly erroneous In the first place, he points to the uncontradicted evidence of Mr. Wightwick himself, a witness for the defendant, as establishing beyond all reasonable doubt not only that he had actual knowledge of the undisclosed fact (q), but that his client also had such actual knowledge (r) Secondly, he shows quite clearly and con-vincingly that Mr Wightwick was the solicitor and agent for all purposes of the sale under such circumstances that the knowledge possessed by him during, and for the purpose of, such agency, however long previously it may have been acquired, was in law the knowledge of his client and principal (s), and that, even if such knowledge had been obtained altogether *in alid re*, it would still be a question whether or not it had passed from his mind at the time (t), but in this case it clearly had been obtained *in hâc re*, he having been employed to know matters affecting the title, that is to say, to acquire the knowledge, if he did not already possess it, and, if he did, to give his client the full benefit of it, which he could not do without at the same time charging her with

(p) The case is dealt with in Ch VI ("Of Purchases") The learned author commences with a summary of the facts (pp 614–618), followed by an abstract of the allegations in the bill (pp 618–621) He then deals closely with the evidence (pp 621–626), after which he summarizes, first, the judgment of KNIGHT-BRUCE, V -C (at pp 626–628), and then those delivered in the House of Lords (pp 628–634) His criticisms, on fact and law (but mostly on fact), occupy the rest of the space (pp 634–660) devoted to the discussion of this case.

(q) See pp 645–648 of the "Treatise."

(r) *Ibid*, at pp 636–640

(s) *Ibid*, at pp 640–643

(t) *Ibid*, at p 641, and see § 56, and note (z) thereto, *ante*

the full burden of it (u). Thirdly, even on the view (which he obviously disagrees with) that the bill was so framed as to put upon the plaintiff the onus of establishing the defendant's personal deceit and dishonesty, and that such onus had not been discharged, a case of non-disclosure only having been made, he expresses the opinion that this circumstance ought not to have influenced anything but the costs (v). Lastly, he demonstrates with the utmost clearness that the authority (w) relied upon by KNIGHT-BRUCE, V.-C. as governing the case, which the House of Lords thought inapplicable, was absolutely in point and undistinguishable (x); whilst that which the House of Lords regarded as undistinguishable, and as an authority for the decision at which they arrived (y), was, in all essentials, not only a different, but an opposite, type of case (z). It is noticeable, however, that Lord ST. LEONARDS does not combat, or deal with, the rule of law which alone of those propounded by the House of Lords may be thought to justify their decision, in connection with the facts as found by them (whether rightly or wrongly),—the rule, namely, that *primâ facie* a contract completed by conveyance cannot be rescinded, but that, where fraud is alleged, this form of relief may be granted if, but not unless, such fraud is strictly proved by the party complaining

302. On the whole, it is submitted that *Wilde* v *Gibson* is an authority for the proposition last stated, but is not an authority which can safely be accepted for anything else.

Sub-s. (3). *The Case of* Turner v Green.

303. It is proposed to submit reasons for questioning the correctness of the decision of CHITTY, J , in this case (a). It is not suggested that *on the*

(u) See p 641 of the "Treatise" "it was the duty of Wightwick, as the family solicitor, to make himself master of the real nature of the rights claimed, and his knowledge must in dealings between his client and third persons be deemed the knowledge of his client"

(v) *Ibid.*, at pp. 648, 649.

(w) *Edwards* v *M'Leay* (1815), G Cooper 308 (GRANT, M R), affirmed (1818), 2 Swanst 287 (Lord ELDON, L C)

(x) See pp 649–656 of the "Treatise"

(y) *Legge* v *Croker* (1811), 1 Ball & B 506 , 12 R R 49

(z) See pp 656–660 of the "Treatise" In *Legge* v *Croker*, the party charged had made disclosure of the fact that at one time certain public rights had existed, or had been claimed, over the property in question, and had stated (erroneously, but quite innocently) that those rights could no longer be effectually asserted for certain reasons which he gave, and which there was no proof that he did not believe to be reasons justifying his representation In *Wilde* v *Gibson*, there had been no disclosure at all It is impossible to conceive two cases more dissimilar in the essential point To establish any sort of parallel between the two, one would have to suppose that in the latter case, Lady Wilde, or her solicitor, had revealed to the purchaser all that they knew as to the past history of " Liberty Way," the recognition of the right of the public by payment of an annual sum, and the legal possibility of these dormant rights being actively revived in the future, together with a statement that there seemed little probability of such a revival In that case, the only cause of complaint which the purchaser would have had would have been that which the purchaser had in *Legge* v *Croker*, viz fraudulent misrepresentation, and the decision of the House of Lords against him on that state of facts would have been as correct as the similar decision in the earlier case As it was, there was nothing to justify any reliance upon, or reference to, the authority in question, except the delusion under which the House of Lords were labouring at the very onset, and throughout the hearing, viz that the case before them was practically an action of deceit

(a) [1895] 2 Ch 205 There are references to this case (with an intimation that it is

assumption made by all concerned in the case the result was other than what was properly to be expected, or that the judgment did not flow from a sound and logical application of well-established principles of law to the state of things so assumed What is contended is, that this assumption which underlay the decision was utterly erroneous, and thereby rendered the decision itself of no effect as an authority.

304. The party complaining was the defendant in an action for an account, which, after proceeding for a time, and passing through several of the preliminary stages in chambers, was compromised. The defendant, however, for the reason stated below, refused to perform his part, whereupon the plaintiff applied to the Court by summons for a stay of proceedings on the agreed terms. This application was treated, for the purposes of the argument and judgment, as though it were the trial of an action for specific performance of the agreement of compromise (b). The claim was resisted by the defendant on the ground of non-disclosure by the plaintiff's solicitor to the defendant's country solicitor, when negotiating the compromise with him at Portsmouth, of the fact (which the former had just learnt by a telegram from London) that an important interlocutory application on behalf of the plaintiff had been dismissed by the judge's chief clerk, or rather had been met with an adverse expression of opinion on his part which, unless the judge to whom the summons had been adjourned should take a different view, would operate as an adverse order (c). The non-disclosure, the knowledge of the undisclosed fact by the party charged, and the ignorance thereof by the party complaining, were clearly proved, and, indeed, hardly disputed, but the decision was against the party complaining, who, in the view of CHITTY, J., had shown no ground on which he could even resist the specific performance claimed by the party charged.

305. Now, the above being a case of compromise, it is quite clear on the authorities, which have been already discussed in the proper place (d), that there was a duty on each of the parties, in the course of the negotiation, to disclose to the other any material fact of which he may have acquired private and exclusive cognizance : and it is equally clear that any incident in the course of the litigation being compromised which would alter or affect the pre-existing relation to one another of the parties, and the chances of success or failure on the one side or the other, such as the fact above mentioned, would be a material one to be disclosed Nor can it be doubted that if this (somewhat obvious) aspect of the case had been pressed upon CHITTY, J , his judgment would have been in favour of the party complaining Yet, incredible as it may seem, this view was not only not urged upon the Court, but it was not even presented or mentioned in argument · and (what is still more strange)

to receive separate and detailed treatment later) in notes (n) and (r) to § 137, notes (y) and (g) to § 163, and note (o) to § 164, *ante*

(b) *Ibid* , at p 206

(c) *Ibid.*, at p 208 Though, as there pointed out by CHITTY, J , the chief clerk's opinion is not absolutely the same thing as the order of the judge in person, it becomes his order unless adjourned into Court, and, on the adjourned hearing, dissented from by him.

(d) See §§ 133, 137, *ante.*

it did not occur to the very learned and accomplished judge, to whom one might suppose that, independently of all argument, it would have inevitably suggested itself at some stage or other of the hearing Everybody concerned ignored, from first to last, the nature of the contract which was the subject of the negotiation , and the case was treated throughout as one in which neither party was under any initial duty of disclosure whatsoever by reason of the relation in which they stood to one another. This tacit assumption is made the foundation of the judgment "it *cannot be contended*," says CHITTY, J (e), " that Fowler "—the plaintiff's solicitor—" was under any obligation to disclose the result of the telegram " Obviously the judge was here merely inferring that this contention could not be raised because, if it could, it would have been, whereas it was not   Yet this was just the argument, and the only argument, which could have been presented, and to which, if it had been, there would have been no valid answer   Not relying upon or mentioning the only doctrine on which it was possible to claim relief, the party complaining was in a hopeless position   The broken reeds to which he was forced to resort, having left behind him the only sound and effectual weapon in his armoury, came to pieces, one after the other First, the case was boldly put as one of fraud, that is to say, since it was not pretended that there had been any positive representation, " fraudulent silence," or a dishonest trading on his known ignorance of a material fact within the other party's private and exclusive cognizance (*f*)   Then, it was suggested (but faintly) that the conduct of the party charged amounted to a breach of duty arising in the course of the negotiation out of something said or done by him which made it from that point dishonest in him not to exhibit the candour which—this being assumed throughout, as already stated (*g*)—was not incumbent on him in the first instance (*h*)   Lastly, abandoning the theory of " fraud " altogether (which was to abandon everything), it was contended that it was enough to establish " sharp practice," or a " shabby trick " (*i*), or that the case invited the application of such terms as " hardship," " unfairness," " inequality," " oppression," or any other of the misty and meaningless phrases coined in the cloisters of equity for the purpose of extending a paternal jurisdiction beyond the limits of sound and scientific principle (*j*)   All these arguments were of course unavailing   the first, because the principle invoked, though it has from time to time proved attractive, and has received some apparent judicial countenance,

(e) [1895] 2 Ch 205, at p 208
(*f*) *Ibid* , at p 206, in the argument for the defendant
(*g*) See note (*e*), *sup*
(*h*) [1895] 2 Ch. 205, at p. 207
(*i*) *Ibid* , at p 207, in the argument for the defendant, and at p 208, in the judgment, where CHITTY, J , observes that the defendant's counsel was driven to contend that it was " a shabby trick " on the part of the plaintiff's solicitor to keep the information to himself, and not such conduct as one would expect from a high-minded practitioner, and adds— " the question thus raised is *not one of fraud* " (the original theory of " fraudulent silence " having been by that time definitely jettisoned)

(*j*) *Ibid* , at p 207, where, in support of this contention, the case discussed in Sub s (4), *post*, and that alone, was relied upon.

is, as has already been explained, radically unsound (k). the second, because there was no evidence of any circumstance to bring the case within the proposition relied upon (l): the third, which was really an argument of despair, because conduct which *ex hypothesi* is not a subject of legal liability on the ground of fraud, or otherwise, cannot be made so by proof that it is not conformable to ethical standards, or is morally censurable (m). The criticism, therefore, pronounced by CHITTY, J , *on all the contentions presented to him* on behalf of the party complaining, was perfectly correct

306. If, however, instead of admitting that there was no duty of disclosure in the first instance, and only relying upon " fraudulent silence," and " unfair " conduct (n), the defendant had pointed out, or it had independently occurred, to the Court that the case belonged to a class where there *is* an initial duty of disclosure, and if the appropriate line of cases had been referred to and relied upon, the result must have been the opposite of what it was   The slightest allusion to either of the two cases now to be discussed (o) would have sufficed   But none was made, either by the defendant who failed to appreciate the strength of his position, or by the plaintiff who was obviously not concerned in correcting his opponent's omission

307. *Gordon* v *Gordon* (p) was the earlier of the two cases referred to. It is an authority of the utmost importance from several points of view, and it was handled by Lord ELDON, L.C , with even more than his usual patient care and discrimination (q)   The elder of two brothers (Harry) sued the

---

(k) See §§ 138, 163, 164, 165, 166, *ante*
(l) The principle itself is quite sound   see §§ 155–158, *ante*, and the cases cited in the notes thereto, particularly the observations of Lord ELDON, L.C , and Lord CAMPBELL, L C , cited in notes (h) and (ı), respectively, to § 155, *ante*   But CHITTY, J , at p 208 of the report, points out that there was no evidence before him of any " misleading conversation " as to what had taken place before the chief clerk, or of any " single word," or even " nod, wink, or smile," to bring the case within the exceptions mentioned, or the expressions used, by the two Lords Chancellors, or to create a supervening duty to break a silence which till then was assumed to be justifiable.
(m) See § 163, *ante*
(n) The argument for the defendant rested, for authority, on *Ellard* v *Lord Llandaff*, discussed in Sub s (4), *inf* , a very shaky reed, and gave the go-by to all the " compromise " authorities   Of course the plaintiff was not concerned to invite attention to these latter authorities, which were in point, but to rely (as he did) solely on certain vendor and purchaser cases, which were not   Accordingly CHITTY, J , founded his judgment (see pp 208–211) upon such authorities, on one side and the other, as (though wholly irrelevant) the parties had apparently agreed in considering to be alone relevant, and upon no others.
(o) See §§ 307, and 309, *post*, respectively
(p) (1821), 3 Swanst 400 , 19 R R 230   In notes (l) and (s) to § 137, and in note (z) to § 138, *ante*, reference is made to the present place for a fuller discussion of this decision than was there convenient
(q) As will be gathered from the following account of the proceedings   On the 17th December, 1816, the cause came before GRANT, M R , for trial, when an issue at law was directed to try the question of the elder brother's legitimacy   On the 27th February, 1818, the issue was tried and the jury found in favour of the legitimacy, and a motion to GRANT, M R , for a new trial was refused   On the 18th January, 1819, the case was before Lord ELDON, L C , on a motion for further directions, when he made several preliminary observations, suggested the lines on which further investigation should be conducted, and required the case to be reargued before him at a later date (see the report in 3 Swanst 400, at pp 457–465)   It appears, however, that the case had already been under his examination for a considerable time, for he prefaces his observations by a reference to

younger (James) for rescission of an agreement made between them 19 years previously for a division of family estates on the basis that Harry's legitimacy was doubtful. The ground on which it was sought to set aside the agreement was the non-disclosure by James of information which he had received, and rumours which had reached him, that a private ceremony of marriage had taken place which, if valid, would establish Harry's legitimacy (r). This fact was only discovered by Harry shortly before the commencement of the proceedings. Lord ELDON, L C., set aside the agreement. The grounds on which he proceeded were expressed somewhat differently at the various successive stages and rehearings of the case. At the outset, he draws particular attention to the circumstance that the compromise was of that special character known as a " family arrangement," and that such arrangements are less liable to be disturbed than ordinary compromises (s): indeed, he makes use of expressions which would seem to indicate that in his view nothing short of " imposition," " concealment," " suppression," or other unfair or fraudulent conduct, will avail to vitiate a family arrangement (t), which, if the matter were left there, would be tantamount to saying that there is no duty of disclosure in such cases. but his observations do not end there, for he immediately goes on to say that the fact of " imposition " would be clearly made out by proof of James's knowledge that there had been a marriage de facto, Harry's ignorance of that fact, and James's knowledge of Harry's ignorance (u), or in other words, that James was under

his " long indisposition," during which he had " considered this case with much attention " (p 457) On the 29th June, 1819, the case was reargued, the argument being both preceded and followed by some further observations from Lord ELDON, L C, which were, however, not intended to represent his final opinion and decision (pp 466–475) His ultimate judgment was delivered on the 16th August, 1819 (pp 475–478), and the decree, dated the 26th June, 1821, is set out at pp 478–482 And not only did the case, as is apparent from the above dates, receive the prolonged and patient attention of Lord ELDON, but it also occasioned him great anxiety, as may be judged from his striking remark on one of the above mentioned occasions :—" I have never known a case in which it was more the duty of the Judge to make a covenant with himself not to suffer his feelings to influence his judgment " (p 468) A decision arrived at after such protracted deliberation, and with such a keen vigilance against the distracting allurements of emotion, obviously commands a special degree of respect

(r) And in fact, as stated in the last note, the legitimacy was established eventually by the verdict of a jury

(s) (1821), 3 Swanst 400, at p 463,—a distinction which is drawn by him again in the later stages of the hearing, at pp 470, 477 See § 135, and the notes thereto, ante, for the other authorities in which this leaning of the courts in favour of family arrangements is declared and illustrated

(t) Ibid, at p 463 " where family agreements have been fairly entered into without concealment or imposition on either side, with no suppression of what is true, or suggestion of what is false, then, although the parties may have greatly misunderstood their situation and mistaken their rights, a court of equity will not disturb the quiet which is the consequence of that agreement, but where the transaction has been unfair, and founded upon falsehood and misrepresentation, a court of equity would have very great difficulty in permitting such a contract to bind the parties " Again, at p 464 " before the Court declares a contract like this void, it ought to be fully satisfied that the contract was entered into under circumstances of wilful concealment "

(u) Ibid, at pp 463, 464 " I suppose the most prominent mode of putting the fact of imposition is this that James Gordon knew that there had been a marriage de facto ; not that he knew the marriage was a legal marriage, but that a ceremony of marriage, whether valid or not, had been performed previous to the public marriage, and previous to the birth of Harry, that James Gordon was aware of this fact, and knew that Harry

a duty of disclosure, the breach of which would render him liable to Harry (v) On the next occasion, when the matter was before him for re-argument, he no longer insists on " misrepresentation," " suppression," or " imposition," but states roundly and plainly that if one of the parties to a compromise, even when it is a family arrangement, is " accessory to the mistake " of the other, though acting in perfect good faith, the arrangement will be set aside at the instance of that other (w). No clearer declaration could be made of the absolute duty of disclosure, independently of all question of honesty or fraud, than the perfectly general proposition enunciated by him in the course of his observations on this occasion that " in contracts of this sort, *full and complete communication of all material circumstances is what the Court must insist on* " (x) When the stage of final judgment is reached (to which alone, when all is said and done, we must look for *authority*), Lord ELDON reiterates, in even clearer and more emphatic language than he had used on any previous occasion, the inflexible principle that any non-disclosure of a material fact *of itself* vitiates not only any compromise of an ordinary nature, but even a family arrangement, and that it is no answer whatever

was not aware of it, and kept from him the knowledge of that fact It was his duty to communicate the fact of the private marriage "

(v) Though this result is arrived at with unnecessary circuity, and by taking two bites at the cherry The reasoning appears to be —" imposition " is necessary to vitiate the agreement, but this " imposition " is to be inferred from the mere fact of non disclosure It is obviously simpler to say, without introducing any such needless middle term as " imposition," that non-disclosure, without imposition, or without other imposition, is sufficient to vitiate the agreement A similar circuity is observable in the law of misrepresentation, when it is said that it is necessary to prove an intention to deceive, but that such intention is at once and peremptorily inferred from the making of a representation known to be false, or not believed to be true see § 102, and note (p) thereto, of the author's *Law of Actionable Misrepresentation* So, in the law of defamation, when it is stated that malice is necessary to constitute defamation, and in the same breath that malice is irrebuttably presumed from the mere act of publication, this is tantamount to saying that malice is not an essential constituent of defamation The topic is discussed in App II of the author's *Law of Actionable Defamation*

(w) (1821), 3 Swanst 400, at p 467 " my opinion is that if James Gordon, prior to the agreement, knew that there had been a private ceremony of marriage, and *conscientiously believing* that it was not a legal marriage, omitted to communicate the fact to his brother, the plaintiff would be entitled to relief , on the principle that, though family agreements are to be supported, where there is no fraud or mistake on either side, or none to which the other party is accessory, yet *where there is mistake, though innocent, and the other party is accessory to it*, this Court will interfere " Again, at p 470 " in every case it has been said, and it would be monstrous to hold otherwise, that if what one knows has been concealed from the other, who has been misled by that concealment, the Court will not sanction the agreement " At p 472 the principle is applied to the facts of the case " if he knew the fact of the ceremony and took on himself to determine its validity, and dealt with the elder legitimate brother without disclosing that fact, knowing that he was not otherwise apprised of it, he was wrong , it was his duty, as an honest man, to state the fact of that ceremony, and his opinion that it was not valid " At p 474, Lord ELDON, in summing up the position, makes a very definite pronouncement " the probability is that James Gordon knew, or had reason to believe, that there had been a private marriage, and that the plaintiff possessed no such knowledge , and then the parties did not meet on equal terms. In that view, taking the case, as I wish to take it, *as a case of mere non disclosure*, the Court even at this late hour will grant relief " So, at p. 475 " if in this case, therefore, the Court refuses relief, the refusal will be grounded on the fact that all parties acted in knowledge, if it grants relief, its interposition will support proof that some material circumstance known to one party was not communicated to the other "

(x) *Ibid* , at p 475.

to prove that the party charged acted with good faith and honest intention (*y*). Lastly, when the decree (as to the form of which Lord ELDON was very solicitous, specially directing that it should be prefaced by a proper declaration of the grounds on which it was made) saw the light after an incubation of no less than 22 months, it was so worded as to put it beyond all doubt that the ground, and the sole ground, of the rescission of the arrangement was the breach by the defendant of his duty to disclose to the plaintiff a material fact within his exclusive cognizance during the negotiation for such arrangement (*z*)

308. It will readily be understood from the above analysis that every principle and proposition of law which entitled the party complaining to relief in *Gordon* v *Gordon* must have equally entitled the party complaining to relief in *Turner* v. *Green* . or, rather, must have *a fortiori* so entitled him, because, putting aside the difference between the admitted good faith of the party charged in the one case and the at least indelicate conduct of the solicitor of the party charged in the other (which distinction is, on strict principle, an immaterial one), it must be remembered that in the former case the compromise was, whereas in the latter it was not, of a kind specially favoured by the law , in the former, the party complaining was suing for rescission, whilst, in the latter, he was merely resisting specific performance . and, lastly, in the former, the agreement impeached had been not only concluded but completed and fully executed for no less than 19 years, whereas, in the latter, it was executory and only a few weeks old

309. The second of the two cases referred to, as cases the citation of which, or of either of them, must have resulted in a judgment for the party complaining in *Turner* v *Green,* is *Gilbert* v *Endean* (*a*). As will be seen on reference to the abstract of this decision given in the part of this work which is concerned with compromises (*b*), the circumstances of the two cases were almost exactly parallel There, as here, the party complaining was resisting specific performance of an agreement for compromise of litigation between the parties there, as here, the agreement was negotiated at an interview between the respective solicitors : there, as here, the solicitor of the party charged, shortly before the conclusion of the agreement, had been

(*y*) (1821), 3 Swanst 400, at pp 476, 477   At p 477, Lord ELDON, L C , lays down in plain terms that "there must not only be good faith and honest intention, but full disclosure , and without full disclosure honest intention is not sufficient "

(*z*) *Ibid* , at pp 480, 481 (in the decree as transcribed from the Register Book at pp 478–482)   "inasmuch   as it is established by the evidence in the cause that, prior to the entering into the said agreement, the defendant James Gordon had been informed and knew that a ceremony of marriage had previously taken place between his father and mother before the birth of the plaintiff,   and *the said agreement having been entered into with such previous information on his part, and without such information being imparted to the plaintiff,*"   &c   It appears from p 478 of the report that, at the end of his judgment, Lord ELDON, L C , had expressly required "a declaration " to be "inserted in the decree of the ground on which I proceed in holding the deeds void," regarding this as a matter of justice to *the party charged* (" I think *the defendant* is entitled to have a declaration,"   . &c)

(*a*) (1878), 9 C D 259, C A

(*b*) In note (*r*) to § 137, *ante*

apprised of a material fact which, to his knowledge, was unknown to the solicitor of the party complaining. The Court of Appeal (affirming MALINS, V.-C.) in *Gilbert* v. *Endean* held that the contract was not enforceable, JESSEL, M.R. (*o*), expressing the grounds of his judgment in language of which every word, with the necessary substitution of names, was applicable to the facts of *Turner* v. *Green.* If, therefore, this case had been brought to the notice of CHITTY, J., it would have been impossible for him, without disregarding the authority of the Court of Appeal, to have decided otherwise than in favour of the defendant, the party complaining (*d*)

310. It is conceived, therefore, that the case of *Turner* v. *Green* is not an authority for the proposition that there is no duty of disclosure incumbent on parties negotiating for a compromise, because that proposition was assumed, and not debated, and the assumption was wholly contrary to all principle and authority   It is, however, undoubtedly an authority for the proposition (which is a perfectly sound one) that, given an absence of any duty of disclosure arising from the relation between the parties, such a duty is not created by the mere circumstance that one of the parties has exclusive knowledge of some material and undisclosed fact, of which the other, to his knowledge, is ignorant.

Sub-s. (4).   The Case of Ellard v Lord Llandaff

311. This case (*e*), in so far as the decision was based on the non-disclosure of a fact which the party charged was under no initial obligation to divulge, has created considerable difficulty   The facts were as follows   James Ellard was entitled to a leasehold interest in land for three lives, of which his uncle Thomas Ellard (then of the age of 70) was the sole survivor   The plaintiff proposed to his lessor, the defendant, to treat for a new lease for three lives in consideration of a surrender to the plaintiff of the existing lease. The defendant consulted his agent, one Lanigan, who advised him that Thomas Ellard's expectation of life was about six or seven years   During the negotiation, the plaintiff received private information that Thomas Ellard had just been seized with a strangury, and thereupon, after seeing the surgeon and ascertaining from him that no recovery was possible, he wrote an urgent letter to the defendant and Lanigan to meet him the next day to execute the agreement for the new lease and receive a surrender of the old, which they did, without any disclosure to them, or knowledge by them *aliundè*, of the above-mentioned fact. The terms of the agreement were settled entirely on the basis of Lanigan's estimate   It appeared in evidence that Thomas Ellard had died in the afternoon of the day on which the agreement was signed, and that the defendant had immediately afterwards

---

(*c*) (1878), 9 C D 259, C A, at p 267

(*d*) It might no doubt have been argued that the undisclosed fact in *Turner* v *Green* was not, as it undoubtedly was in the other cases, material   but no such question was raised by the parties, or considered by the Court

(*e*) (1810), 1 Ball & B 241, 12 R R 22   The case is mentioned, as one to be examined more closely at a later stage, in note (*h*) to § 163, and in note (*j*) to § 164, *ante.*

boasted to the surgeon that he had succeeded in getting the new lease, and " had made a pretty thing of it " The defendant, on discovering the facts, refused to abide by the agreement, and brought ejectment. The plaintiff filed his bill to restrain the proceedings in ejectment, and for specific performance of the agreement, to which the defendant pleaded two distinct defences. first, fraudulent concealment of the above material fact (*f*), secondly, that the agreement was void, as being a fraud on " the power which had to be exercised for its performance " Lord MANNERS, L C, on both grounds, which he considered separately and successively (*g*), gave judgment for the defendant.

312. It is quite clear that the second ground of itself justified the refusal of a decree for specific performance (*h*), and, therefore, that the actual decision was correct. The question is whether the other principle, on which also the judgment of Lord MANNERS was undoubtedly founded, is good law, viz the principle that non-disclosure by A. of a material fact known to him of which B, to his knowledge, is ignorant, gives B. a right to relief, there being no duty of disclosure on A arising from the nature of the contract contemplated It is submitted that, in accordance with reasons and authorities already stated (*i*), the supposed principle is without solid foundation, that non-disclosure under such circumstances does not amount to fraud (*j*), and cannot be made actionable on the theory that, though not constituting actual fraud, it may be properly described as " sharp practice " (*k*), or " suppression " (*l*), or even on the theory of " unfairness " or " hard-

---

(*f*) This is how it was put by PLUNKET in his argument for the defendant (see p 246 of the report) · " the performance is resisted on the ground of a *gross fraud* on Lord Llandaff "

(*g*) (1810), 1 Ball & B 241, at pp. 248–250, as to the first ground, and at p 251, as to the second

(*h*) See the observations of CHITTY, J, when dealing with this case, at pp. 209, 210 of *Turner* v. *Green*, [1895] 2 Ch 205 · " but there was another ground fatal to the plaintiff's case, which was, that the contract for a lease was void under the power which had to be exercised for its performance I may say, with regard to that latter ground, that it could not be questioned at the present day that it was quite sufficient for the decision of the case, but, as I have said, Lord MANNERS makes the non-disclosure of the life being *in extremis* the ground for refusing specific performance "

(*i*) See §§ 138, 163, 164, *ante*

(*j*) Lord MANNERS, though he does not actually use the word " fraud," seems in many parts of his judgment to have so regarded the plaintiff's conduct (see pp 248–250 of the report)

(*k*) (1810), 1 Ball & B 241, where, at p 250, Lord MANNERS so puts the case " the principles on which dealings of this description are to be carried on are now well understood, *this is too sharp a practice to be countenanced here.* The plaintiff must not be allowed to deal on a lease, as a good and subsisting one, when at the time he was conscious that it was worth nothing, and that the other party was ignorant of that fact "

(*l*) *Ibid*, at p 251, where Lord MANNERS uses the expression referred to " all the material facts must be known to both parties, and is it not against all principles of equity that a party, knowing a material ingredient in an agreement, should be permitted to suppress it, and still call for a specific performance ? " It is quite uncertain whether by the use of the word " suppression " here, and of the term " sharp practice " in the passage cited in the last note, Lord MANNERS did, or did not, intend to impute fraud to the plaintiff Indeed nothing could be vaguer than his language in these two deliverances It is clear that, as CHITTY, J, observed—see note (*o*) *inf*—his feelings were deeply enlisted, and that he had not, as Lord ELDON, L.C, did in *Gordon* v *Gordon*,—see note (*q*) to § 307. *ante*—" made a covenant with himself " to resist them, the result being that he was

ship" (m); and that, in so far as *Ellard* v. *Lord Llandaff* is grounded on any such theory, it has not survived either the mild scepticism of Sir EDWARD FRY (n), or the more searching criticism of CHITTY, J. (o).

forced to cast about for some liberal phraseology under cover of which he hoped to bring a case of purely ethical misconduct within a juridical principle large enough to render it amenable to a court of law as well as to the *forum conscientiæ*

(m) This is the only ground on which, according to Sir EDWARD FRY, and CHITTY, J (see the next two notes), the opinion of Lord MANNERS can be made to assume a plausible aspect. But, if the views expressed in §§ 138, and 163, *ante*, are sound, the proposition in question can no more be supported on the theory of "unfairness," or "hardship," than on that of "fraud," or "sharp practice," or "suppression"

(n) In his treatise on *Specific Performance*, where *Ellard* v. *Lord Llandaff* is referred to in two places, first, in Ch. V (" Of the Want of Fairness in the Contract "), and again in Ch XIV (" Fraud ") The passage in the former chapter (§ 402) is as follows "Unfairness arising from misstatements is considered under the head of Misrepresentation: and cases relating to the silence or suppression of a fact by one party are considered in the chapter on Fraud But it seems *possible* that there may be cases where silence is not fraudulent, and yet creates such a case of *hardship* as prevents the interference of the Court in specific performance On this ground was put a case where a lessee obtained the renewal of a lease on the surrender of an old one, knowing and suppressing the fact, which was unknown to the lessor, that the person on whose life the old lease depended was *in extremis*, and the Court declined to aid the lessee." The other passage is from § 717 in the Chapter on Fraud (Ch XIV). The learned author (§ 713) states that " it has never (it is believed) been held by our Courts that there is a *general* obligation of disclosure " —by which he means an obligation extending beyond the limited duty of disclosing matters affecting title—" on the part of a vendor or purchaser of chattels or realty, though the person maintaining silence may know that the other party is acting under an erroneous impression " then, after citing authorities in support of the above (§§ 713, 714), and after referring to the exceptional cases where fraud is established (§§ 715, 716), he alludes to the case under discussion (§ 717) in these terms " It is *possible* that silence which would not constitute fraud may yet constitute such *unfairness* in a contract as to stay the hand of the Court The case of *Ellard* v *Lord Llandaff*, *if it is to be supported on the ground of the silence of the lessee* as to the fact that one of the lives in the surrendered lease was, at the time of signing the contract, *in extremis*, rests upon this principle " It would seem from this latter passage, though not, perhaps, from the first, that Sir Edward Fry doubted very much whether innocent silence can be deemed actionable on the principle of "unfairness," any more than on any other principle

(o) At pp 209–211 of *Turner* v *Green*, [1895] 2 Ch 205, where, after a short statement of the cause of action in *Ellard* v *Lord Llandaff* (pp 209, 210), and an observation that it " was a trying case for any judge, and a case in which possibly a temptation might arise to strain the law " (p 210), he goes on (at pp 210, 211) to say " I have not been able to discover . any special mention of *Ellard* v *Lord Llandaff*, either approving or disapproving it as it stands reported But the learned editor of Fry on Specific Performance apparently questions the authority of the case," and he then cites the passage from § 717 of that work (inverting the order of the sentences), without, however, making any reference to the passage in § 402 He concludes (p 211) that " if the case is looked upon as one of *great hardship* upon the defendant in *very special circumstances*, and as one which presented a contract which ought not, on that ground, to be enforced, then the case will stand well upon the ground suggested by Sir Edward Fry " This concluding observation seems much too generous It is submitted that the case will not " stand " better " upon the ground suggested by Sir Edward Fry " than upon any other ground

CHAPTER IV.

THE DUTY OF DISCLOSURE INCIDENTAL TO RELATIONS OF CONFIDENCE

313. THE duty of disclosure which it is now proposed to examine arises under conditions of a wholly different character from those which give rise to the duty of disclosure discussed in the preceding Chapter There, the subject of consideration was the disclosure which *uberrima fides* requires to be made before the conclusion of a contemplated contract belonging to one or other of certain classes, in order that the parties may be on equal terms during the negotiation Here, there is no question of a contractual relation being in treaty between the parties : a fiduciary relation (whether contractual, or implied, or "resulting") is assumed to be already established, which relation involves an obligation, during its existence, of complete candour and good faith on the part of him in whom confidence is placed towards him who has placed it (*p*)   In the one case, the duty begins and ends with the negotiation (*q*) : in the other, it begins and ends with the relation (*r*)

314. Further, the class of case now to be discussed is distinguishable from, though it has many features in common with, that which is to form the subject of the next Chapter, where the relation to which the duty of disclosure is incidental is the relation existing between two parties of whom one is presumed or proved to exercise a dominating influence over the other, and who is, for that reason, placed by the law under a severe obligation to provide the party in subjection, not only with complete information, but

---

(*p*) The distinction between the two classes is emphasized by FRY, J, at pp 474, 475 of *Davies v London & Provincial Marine Insurance Co* (1878), 8 C D 469   He there mentions three kinds of case in which a duty of disclosure exists or may arise, first, where the relation already exists, whatever that relation be, whether fiduciary, or of the type described in Chapter V, *post*, secondly, where the parties are contemplating and nego tiating for a contract *uberrimæ fidei* (the subject of Chapter III, Sect. 2, Sub ss (2)–(7), *ante*), and, lastly, where a duty of disclosure is created by circumstances, though neither the nature of the contract in contemplation, nor that of the existing relation, is such as to impose any such duty in the first instance   The first type of case is described by him at p 474   "in the first place, if there be a pre-existing relationship between the parties, such as that of agent and principal, solicitor and client, guardian and ward, trustee and *cestui que trust*, then, if the parties can contract at all, they can only contract after the most ample disclosure of everything by the agent, by the solicitor, by the guardian, or by the trustee   *The pre-existing relationship involves the duty of entire disclosure*" He then proceeds to describe and distinguish the wholly different characteristics and conditions of the other two classes
(*q*) See § 181, note (*j*), § 189, and § 195, *ante*
(*r*) See § 353, *post*

with the means of exercising absolute freedom of will and action. It often so happens that the two relations, and the two duties arising out of them, coexist and coalesce (s), but this is accidental, and, even in such cases, it is very necessary to bear in mind the essential distinction, in thought and theory, between the two. In the cases of fiduciary relations discussed in this Chapter, *as such*, there is no question of "influence," and in the cases of "influence," *as such*, there is no question of a fiduciary relation (t); though usually, no doubt, the fiduciary relation gives scope and occasion for the "influence," whilst the "influence" leads to the establishment, or is exercised and expressed in the form, of a fiduciary relationship

Sect. 1. General Statement and Theory.

315. The general rule or principle (stated summarily) is that, where a fiduciary relation exists between two persons, the person in whom confidence is reposed in virtue of that relation owes to the person who has reposed it a duty (which begins with the creation of the relationship and continues until its dissolution) to place at his disposal all the knowledge, acquired or possessed by himself in the course and by virtue of such relationship, which has a bearing on any transaction, either between the parties themselves, or between either of them and a third person, with reference to any matter which is the subject of the confidence

316. The "knowledge" referred to means not merely knowledge of facts and circumstances (u), as in the class of case considered in the last Chapter, but also knowledge in the sense of experience, skill, and judgment, either in affairs generally, where the fiduciary office is of a general character, or as to professional or business transactions of a particular type, where the party in whom confidence is placed is employed in a special character as a person practising, or carrying on, or conversant with, a particular profession, trade, or vocation. It is often said that the party confided in has two other duties besides that of disclosure; for instance, that an agent or trustee,

(s) Particularly in the case of such relations as that of solicitor and client

(t) The observations of Lord Cranworth, at pp 770, 771 of *Smith v Kay* (1859), 7 H L C 750, are very pertinent here "there is, I take it, no branch of the jurisdiction of the Court of Chancery which it is more ready to exercise than that which protects persons in a situation of dependence, as it were, upon others, from being imposed upon by those upon whom they are so dependent The familiar cases of the influence of a parent over his child, of a guardian over his ward, of an attorney over his client, are but instances The principle is not confined to those cases . It is contended that it applies only to persons who stand in what is called a fiduciary relation I believe, if the principle is examined, it will be found most frequently applied in such cases, for this simple reason, that the fiduciary relation gives a power of influence but I could suggest fifty cases of fiduciary relation where the principle does not apply at all If a man makes me trustee of his estate, to pay certain securities, and then ultimately to stand possessed of it for him, . I have no influence upon him because I am his trustee It is only a particular sort of trusteeship which gives influence " It is suggested that the last sentence involves a slight inaccuracy, since no "sort of trusteeship," *as such*, "gives influence " That is to say, no trustee is presumed, from the mere fact of his trusteeship, to have a dominating influence over his *cestui que trust*, any more than one who has dominion and "influence " over another is, from that fact alone, presumed to be his trustee

(u) As to what are "facts" and "circumstances" for this purpose, see Ch II, Sect 2, Sub s (1), *ante*

when dealing with his principal or *cestui que trust*, must give him, or see that he has, independent and honest advice (*v*), or, if purchasing property from him, must pay full value (*w*), as a condition of the validity of the transaction. But, if "knowledge" be understood in the full, and (it is submitted) therefore correct, sense of the word above indicated, the so-called additional duty of honest advice is perhaps rather to be regarded as a case, or application, or corollary of the one primary obligation which requires the party trusted to inform and instruct the other party's mind with all the materials which are in his own,—that is, to transfer to him the whole of his own intellectual equipment so as to put that other in as good a position to exercise his judgment on the matter in hand as he himself would be. For this purpose, and in this sense, it is immaterial whether the equipment consists of known facts, or known methods or instruments of using those facts,—of intellectual material, or intellectual appliances and instruments. Thus, to take the most prominent of the fiduciary relations as typical of the rest, when it is said that a trustee who proposes to contract with his *cestui que trust* for the purchase of, or other dealing with, the trust property must advise him against himself, as if he were advising him against a stranger, it is not so much the actual advice which is essential, as the placing before the *cestui que trust* of both (1) all the material facts, and also (2) all arguments and considerations which the trustee's experience and skill (whether general or special) may suggest for the purpose of enabling the *cestui que trust* to view those facts in their true significance and bearing, whether they tell for or against the proposed dealing. The *cestui que trust* is then put in possession of all that his trustee knows, and there is (so far) no objection to the transaction, whether he has been actually and formally advised or not. So also, as to the necessity of proving full value in cases of purchases or other contracts, the duty of a trustee under the circumstances described is to impart to the *cestui que trust* all the facts of which he is cognizant which bear on the question, and also the full benefit of his honest opinion and judgment on those facts. If he fails in this duty, the transaction is voidable. If, however, he punctually discharges it, there is, it is conceived, nothing to prevent him from buying the property at an undervalue, that is, at a value less than that which results from his honest estimate on a full disclosure. The violation of duty (if any) consists, not so much in the mere fact of purchase at an undervalue as in the suppression and concealment of some matter, whether fact or opinion, which is essential to enable the *cestui que trust* to exercise a fully instructed judgment, just as, when it is said that a trustee, promoter, or agent must not make a profit out of his trust, promotership, or agency, when dealing with third persons, the meaning of this elliptical expression is, not that the mere act of making the profit, but that the non-disclosure of it, renders the recipient liable to disgorge (*x*).

(*v*) See § 324, *post*, and note (*r*) thereto.
(*w*) See § 323, and notes (*o*) and (*p*) thereto, *post*.
(*x*) See the promotership case of *Omnium Electric Palaces, Ltd* v *Barnes*, [1914] 1 Ch. 332, C. A (*per* SARGANT, J, at pp 344, 347 : promoter not a trustee of *disclosed* profit

317. There are two main theories upon which the above rule of disclosure has been based : public policy, and private right of ownership   The first of these theories has been stated, with more or less elaboration (more in the time of Lord ELDON, L.C , and less in later times, when the doctrine came to be accepted without question) in a long series of judicial deliverances It has been insisted over and over again that public policy, in the sense of public advantage, utility, and convenience, imperatively demands the establishment, and the strenuous and unflinching enforcement, of an absolute and general rule of disclosure in the class of case now under consideration For, were there no such absolute and general rule, every person who places trust in another by virtue of the relation would be insufficiently protected against him, because the latter would always be exposed to the temptation of preferring his interest to his duty whenever an occasion arises on which the two come into conflict   It is not a question of the particular individual, against whom there may be no proof, or even suggestion, of his having yielded to the temptation, or having either sought or gained any actual advantage to himself, in the particular case   It is the recognition and appreciation of the general tendency and probable influence of a right of concealment in such cases which justifies the doctrine,—a tendency and influence which on many occasions it might be difficult to resist, and the actual operation of which in any individual case it would be almost impossible to detect   From this onerous and odious task the courts can only exempt themselves by the declaration of a rule in absolute terms that the necessary disclosure shall be made, and that, if it be withheld, the transaction cannot stand, whatever the personal motives of the party withholding it may be, or whatever may be the actual pecuniary result of his so doing   By this means alone the protection of a large class of the community whose confidence requires protection is assured, and a public danger is averted (y).   Incidentally, no doubt, public

for the company)   Cp *Maxwell* v *Port Tennant Patent Steam Fuel & Coal Co* (1857), 24 Beav 495 (*per* ROMILLY, M R , at p 497 . "*as this was not communicated to the shareholders*, they cannot be bound by the contract," and, later,—"if, in their dealings on behalf of the company   . the directors gain a private advantage for themselves, it ought to be communicated to the body of shareholders"); *Cassels* v *Stewart* (1881), 6 App Cas 64, H L (*per* Lord BLACKBURN, at p. 69 . "if he, as an agent, makes a profit out of the concerns of his principal, and as acting for him, *he must communicate it to his principal*) , *Williamson* v *Hine*, [1891] 1 Ch. 390 (*per* KEKEWICH, J , at p 394   "there must be no *secret* arrangement and no *secret* profit," but there is no breach of duty " if it is fair and above board "), *Shipway* v *Broadwood*, [1899] 1 Q B. 369, C A (*per* CHITTY, L.J , at p 373   "the real evil is not the payment of the money, but *the secrecy* attending it "), *Swale* v *Ipswich Tannery, Ltd* (1906), 11 Comm Cas 88 (*per* KENNEDY, J , at p 96 "I agree that the gist of the wrong lies in *the secrecy* ")
(y) In the following authorities, the various aspects of public policy referred to in the text, are declared to be the foundation of the rule   *Ex p Lacey* (1802), 6 Ves 625 (*per* Lord ELDON, L.C , at pp 626A, 627, as to the difficulty of detection, and at p 629, as to the conflict between interest and duty) , *Lister* v *Lister* (1802), 6 Ves 641A (*per* GRANT, M R , at p 632   "the rule is a rule of general policy, *to prevent the possibility* of fraud and abuse") , *Ex p James* (1803), 8 Ves. 337 (*per* Lord ELDON, L.C , at pp 344–353, and particularly at pp 344, 345, where it is pointed out that " this doctrine   stands much more *upon general principle* than upon the circumstances of any individual case   It rests upon this that the purchase "—it was a case of an assignee of a bankrupt's estate purchasing part of the estate when put up for sale under the commission—" *is not permitted in any case, however honest the circumstances , the general interests of justice requiring it to*

morality is also advanced, because it is always for the moral well-being of society that its members should be freed from the temptation to do wrong . but the primary object and justification of the rule is public policy, in the

be destroyed in every instance , as no Court is equal to the examination and ascertainment of the truth in much the greater number of cases "), *Ex p Bennett* (1805), 10 Ves 381 (*per* Lord ELDON, L C , at pp 385, 386, as to the "rule being necessitated by the tendency and temptation" of the conflict between interest and duty, apart altogether from the effect in the individual case, and by the difficulty in ascertaining motives); *Ormond (Lady)* v *Hutchinson* (1806), 13 Ves 47 (where, at p 51, Lord ERSKINE, L.C , taking rather high ground, says that " the jurisdiction is most beneficial," because " confidential relations in life " are matters " in respect of which this Court assumes *a guardianship over mankind* "); *Harris* v *Tremenheere* (1808), 15 Ves. 34 (*per* Lord ELDON, L C , at p 39 " upon reasons of public policy," and, again, at p 42 " upon principles of public utility "), *Cook* v. *Collingridge* (1823), Jac 607 , 23 R R 155 (*per* Lord ELDON, L C., at p 621 : temptation, necessitating prohibitory rule), *Rothschild* v *Brookman* (1831), 5 Bligh (N.S) 165 (*per* Lord WYNFORD, L C , at pp 189, 190, 192, 196, 197, as to the temptation to evil doing which arises from the attempt to serve two masters, whether evil is done or contemplated in the particular case, or not) ; *Gillett* v *Peppercorne* (1840), 3 Beav. 78 (*per* Lord LANGDALE, M R , at pp. 83, 84, as to the conflict between interest and duty , at p 84 · " against the policy of the law "), *Greenlaw* v *King* (1841), 9 L J (CH) 377 (*per* Lord LANGDALE, M R , at p 383 difficulty of detection, requiring *absolute* rule "for the protection of mankind"), *Hamilton* v *Wright* (1842), 9 Cl & Fin. 111 (*per* Lord BROUGHAM, at pp. 121–124 tendency and temptation conflict between interest and duty), *Benson* v *Heathorn* (1842), 1 Y. & C. 326 (*per* STUART, V.-C , at pp 342, 343 . tendency and temptation—difficulty of detection—protection of the public), *Salmon* v *Cutts* (1850), 4 De G. & Sm 125 (*per* KNIGHT-BRUCE, V. C , at p 129 " in cases of this kind, there is a public as well as a private interest to be considered ") ; *Bentley* v *Craven* (1853), 18 Beav 75 (*per* ROMILLY, M R , at pp 76, 77), *Aberdeen Railway Co* v. *Blakie Bros* (1854), 1 Macq. H. L. 461 (*per* Lord CRANWORTH, L.C., at p 471) ; *Salomons* v. *Pender* (1863), 3 H & C. 639 (*per* MARTIN, B , at pp 643, 644, citing from Story on *Agency*, § 210, the following passage " if then the seller were permitted, as the agent of another, to become the purchaser, his duty to the purchaser and his own interest would stand in direct opposition to each other , and thus a *temptation*, perhaps in many cases too strong for resistance by men of flexible morals, or hackneyed in the common devices of worldly business, would be held out, which would betray them into misconduct, and even into crime ") ; *Turnbull* v *Garden* (1869), 20 L T 218 (*per* JAMES, V -C , at p 220) , *Panama & South Pacific Telegraph Co.* v *India Rubber, Gutta Percha, & Telegraph Co.* (1875), 10 Ch App 515 (*per* JAMES, L.J , at p 527 " *you must act on general principles, without regard to the particular facts or the particular conduct or misconduct of the parties in a particular case,*" because of " the impossibility which the Court finds itself in of ever ascertaining the real truth of the circumstances ") , *Robinson* v *Mollett* (1875), L R 7 H. L. 802 (*per* Lord CHELMSFORD, L.C , at p 838, adopting the opinions of the judges summoned, e g those of MELLOR, J , at pp 815, 816, BRETT, J , at p. 824, CLEASBY, B , at pp 828, 829, GROVE, J , at pp 831, 832, with which cp the judgment of WILLES, J , at pp 655, 656 of the report of the case in the Court below (1870), L R. 5 C P 646, as to the danger to the community which would result from the absence of the rule) , *Pearce* v. *Foster* (1886), 17 Q B D 536, C A (*per* Lord ESHER, M R , at p 540, and LINDLEY, L J , at pp 541, 542) , *Boston Deep Sea Fisheries & Ice Co* v *Ansell* (1889), 39 C D 339, C A (*per* COTTON, L J , at p 357) ; *Bray* v *Ford*, [1896] A. C 44, H L (*per* Lord HERSCHELL, at p 51—conflict between interest and duty) , *Shipway* v *Broadwood*, [1899] 1 Q B 369, C A (*per* CHITTY, L.J , at p. 373 : " a contrary doctrine would be most dangerous, for it would be almost impossible to ascertain what had been the effect of the bribe ") , *Costa Rica Railway Co* v *Forwood*, [1901] 1 Ch 746, C A (*per* RIGBY, L.J , who, at p 753, refers to the principle as " a most salutary one," the object and justification of which is " to make sure that people will do their duty when they are acting under circumstances of unusual difficulty," and *per* VAUGHAN WILLIAMS, L J , at p 761, describing the " doctrine " as a " wholesome " one, its object being " to protect directors trustees, and others against the fallibility of human nature ") ; *Re Haslam and Hier Evans*, [1902] 1 Ch 765, C A (*per* VAUGHAN WILLIAMS, L.J , at p 769, as to the conflict between interest and duty, when the attempt is made " to serve two masters ") , *King, Viall, & Benson* v *Howell* (1910), 27 T L R 114, C A (*per* COZENS HARDY, M R , at p 115, as to the " conflict of duties ") ; *Transvaal Lands Co.* v *New Belgium (Transvaal) Land and Development Co* , [1914] 2 Ch 488, C A (*per* Swinfen Eady, L J , at p. 503 · conflict of duties, again).

sense of public utility, security, and convenience, as is shown by the fact that, according to principles which are now thoroughly established (z), it is no answer to a case of non-disclosure to allege or prove that the party charged was not guilty of fraud on the party complaining, either in intention or result, which allegation and proof would be of the most vital materiality if the doctrine rested on a purely ethical foundation

318. The other theoretical basis of the duty of disclosure in fiduciary relations is the proprietary right of the person reposing confidence   Every such person is regarded as having, in virtue of the relation (whether founded on express contract, or arising from circumstances), acquired a title, whether paid for (as in the case of most agencies), or not (as in the case of most trustee-ships), to all the knowledge and information in the possession of the trustee or agent, or other person in whom the confidence is placed, as to all material facts   On this view, the latter's knowledge and information is not his own to communicate or withhold as he pleases · if he keeps it to himself, he is purloining, or converting to his own use, that which belongs to another (a)   To take two simple illustrations which are constantly used in the authorities, an agent's or trustee's private knowledge of the existence of a mine under an estate (b), or of the unsuspected value and history of a picture (c),

(z) See § 358, *post*   Cp *Bray* v *Ford*, [1896] A C 44 H L
(a) *Fox* v *Mackreth* (1788), 2 Cox 320 (*per* Lord THURLOW, L C, at p 326, "upon this arises a question which I think material, whether a trustee gaining a knowledge of the subject in the execution of the trust, and at the expense of the *cestui que trust*, . . *and that knowledge consequently belonging to the cestui que trust*, whether a trustee may not in this respect have the hand of justice laid upon him if this knowledge is made use of by him to circumvent his *cestui que trust*"), *Ex p Lacey* (1802), 6 Ves 625 (*per* Lord ELDON, L C, at p. 626), *Ex p James* (1803), 8 Ves 337 (*per* Lord ELDON, L C, at p 343 . "the principle is that, as the trustee is bound to acquire all the knowledge possible to enable him to sell to the utmost advantage of the *cestui que trust*, the question, what knowledge he has obtained, and whether he has fairly given the benefit of that knowledge to the *cestui que trust*, . . . no Court can discuss with competent sufficiency or safety to the parties"); *Coles* v. *Trecothick* (1804), 9 Ves. 234 (where Lord ELDON, L C, at p 247, adverts to "the danger that the trustee may buy with knowledge acquired at the expense of the *cestui que trust*"), *Hamilton* v *Wright* (1842), 9 Cl & Fin 111 (*per* Lord BROUGHAM, at p 124), *Luddy's Trustee* v *Peard* (1886), 33 C D 500 (*per* KAY, J, at pp 515, 519, 520)   See also the observations of Lord ELDON, L C, at pp 295, 296 of *Cane* v *Lord Allen* (1814), 2 Dow H L 289, an "undue influence" case
(b) *Ex p Lacey, sup* (*per* Lord ELDON, L.C, at p 627   "suppose a trustee buys an estate, and by the knowledge acquired in that character discovers a valuable coal mine under it, and locking that up in his own heart, enters into a contract with the *cestui que trust*," &c, which class of case he then contrasts with that of a purchaser who stands in no such fiduciary relation to the vendor, and whose knowledge therefore is his own to use as he pleases, and keep as he pleases), *Ex p James, sup* (*per* Lord ELDON, L.C., at p 343 . "a person"— he means a trustee—"knowing not only the surface value, but that there are minerals, buys upon the rent, and gains all that advantage   How can that be found out, if he chooses to deny it ?   Therefore the Courts have said," &c), *Coles* v *Trecothick, sup* (*per* Lord ELDON, L.C, at p 247, where he again illustrates the rule by "the case of mines" of which a trustee acquires secret knowledge), *Luddy's Trustee* v *Peard, sup* (*per* KAY, J, at p. 520   "taking the familiar illustration, if the agent becomes from his employment aware of the existence of a coal mine under his employer's land, of which the employer is ignorant, . . he could not purchase from the employer without disclosing that").
(c) *Lowther* v *Lord Lowther* (1806), 13 Ves 95, where an agent with whom a picture had been deposited discovered, after cleaning it, that it was (in his opinion at least) a Titian, worth £5000, and, without disclosing this discovery or opinion to his principal, claimed to have bought it of him for 300 guineas, and Lord ERSKINE, L C, at pp 102, 103,

which is the subject of his trusteeship or agency belongs to his principal or
cestui que trust, and cannot be kept from him, though, if there were no fiduciary
relation, that knowledge would be the party's own property, and, as has
already been explained (d), he would be legally entitled to make free use of it
for his own purposes and advantage, as he would of anything else belonging to
him   The same theory applies to "knowledge" in its other sense of "power"
This too belongs not to the agent or trustee, but to the principal or *cestui
que trust*, who is entitled to the exclusive benefit of the unbiassed and disinterested skill, judgment, discretion, and experience, of the person in whom
he has confided (e) , and, if the agent or trustee secretly uses his intellectual
armoury, no less than if he secretly uses his intellectual magazines, to undermine, instead of advancing, the service to which they have been devoted, or
if he surreptitiously alters the character with which the relation has invested
him, and turns himself from an agent into a merchant, from a protector
into a competitor, or from a watch-dog into a wolf, he is infringing and con-
spiring against proprietary rights which, whether contractually or otherwise,
he has bound himself to respect and promote (f)

said that "the principle upon which a court of equity acts in these cases " is, that "an
agent to sell shall not convert himself into a principal, unless he can make it perfectly
clear that he furnished his employer with all the knowledge that he himself possessed ")
See also the illustration given by Lord HATHERLEY, L C, at p 780 of *Phillips* v *Homfray*
(1871), 6 Ch App 770, as cited in § 165, *ante*, note (c)
(d) Numerous examples of the right to keep to one's self information, knowledge, or
opinions which no other person can claim as his property, are given in § 165, *ante*   as
to mines, in particular, see notes (w), (x), and (y) to that paragraph , and, as to pictures,
note (b) thereto
(e) *Whichcote* v *Lawrence* (1798), 3 Ves 739 (*per* Lord LOUGHBOROUGH, L C, at p 719 :
"knowledge *and abilities*") , *Sanderson* v *Walker* (1807), 13 Ves 601 (*per* Lord ELDON,
L C, at p 602 . "*bound to exert all his skill*, and apply all his knowledge, with strict
integrity, for their benefit ") , *Clarke* v *Tipping* (1846), 9 Beav 284 (*per* Lord LANGDALE,
M.R , at p 292   " among the most important duties of a factor are those which require
him *to give to his principal the free and unbiassed use of his own discretion and judgment* ") ,
Salomons v *Pender* (1865), 3 H & C 639 (*per* MARTIN, B , at p 643, citing Story on Agency,
§ 210   " this rule is founded upon the plain and obvious consideration that the principal
bargains, in the employment, *for the exercise of the disinterested skill, diligence, and zeal of
the agent, for his own exclusive benefit* ") ; *Pearce* v. *Foster* (1886), 17 Q B D 536, C A
(*per* LOPES, L.J , at p 543)
(f) *Crowe* v *Ballard* (1790), 1 Ves Jr. 215, 1 R R. 122, *Whichcote* v *Lawrence,
sup* (*per* Lord LOUGHBOROUGH, L C, at pp 749, 750), *Rothschild* v *Brookman* (1831),
5 Bligh (N S) 165 (*per* Lord WYNFORD, L C, at p 202   "if one of the parties is in
a situation which is not fairly disclosed to the other,"—he is dealing with the case of
an agent to buy or sell secretly converting himself into a vendor or purchaser
respectively—"which, if the other had known, he would not have relied on his
judgment and advice, nor have acted upon or adopted any act of his, such a transaction ought not to be allowed ") , *Gillett* v *Peppercorne* (1840), 3 Beav 78 (*per* Lord
LANGDALE, M R , at pp 83, 84, who there points out that the principal is betrayed by the
agent's secret change of character, since all the time he expects, and has a right to expect,
that "the agent will act in the matter purely and disinterestedly for the benefit of his
employer ") , *Robinson* v *Mollett* (1875), L R 7 H L 802 (*per* CLEASBY, B , at pp 828,
829, in delivering his opinion, as one of the judges consulted by the House, and Lord
CHELMSFORD, L C , at p 838) , *Panama and South Pacific Telegraph Co* v *India Rubber,
Gutta Percha, and Telegraph Co* (1875), 10 Ch App 515 (*per* JAMES, L J , at p 526, and
MELLISH, L J , at pp 528, 529 ; JAMES, L J , says that the case of a "surreptitious"
transformation of *persona*, such as is described in the text, is just as "if a man hired a
vetturino to take him from one place to another, and   the vetturino, after he had
accepted the hiring, had conspired with his servant to rob him on the way ") , *Re North
Australian Territory Co , Archer's Case*, [1892] 1 Ch. 322, C A (*per* BOWEN, L J , at p 341)

SECT. 2 THE SEVERAL RELATIONS TO WHICH THE PRINCIPLE IS APPLIED, AND THE NATURE OF THE DUTIES OF DISCLOSURE ARISING OUT OF SUCH RELATIONS RESPECTIVELY.

319. The fiduciary relations which give rise to the duty of disclosure may be classified as follows :—the relation between trustee and *cestui que trust ;* that between a promoter and the company promoted by him, and that between principal and agent (*g*)   There are, as will be seen (*h*), several species of the first and of the third class, whereas the second may be said to be *sui generis ;* but the above represent the main divisions or types of what it is convenient to term, and may with strict accuracy be described as, " relations of confidence," to distinguish them from those relations of " influence " of which " confidence," though often in fact a concomitant or result, is not a necessary characteristic (*i*).   These three classes it is now proposed to examine in the order above stated

Sub-s. (1)   *Trustee and Cestui que Trust*

320. There are many species of trusts, and, therefore, of trustees   A trustee may be declared such by the express terms of a deed, will, or other instrument · or he may be a trustee by implication, or construction, or as the " result " of certain circumstances and the legal situation which they create ; for instance, in the discharge of certain offices, such as that of an executor or administrator, or assignee of an insolvent estate, he may be deemed in law subject to many of the obligations of trusteeship, though not expressly declared to be a trustee by any instrument   Again, he may be a complete trustee of property for all purposes, as its legal owner, or he may be a trustee for certain specific or limited purposes, such as for sale, or for purchase (which type of trusteeship is hardly distinguishable from agency to sell, or to purchase, as the case may be), or for the mere execution of some term in a contract, or otherwise " a trustee by metaphor," in Lord WESTBURY'S phrase   But, however essential it may be to bear in mind these distinctions when applying the law of trusts in other directions (*j*), they have little significance for the purposes of the present subject   In all cases alike where one person is entrusted by another with the management, conduct, discharge, execution, or performance, of any property, business, office, service, duty, act, or matter respectively,

(*g*) These three form the subject of Sub ss (1), (2), and (3) respectively, *post*   Sub s (4) deals with a class of relation in which there is ordinarily no absolute duty of disclosure, but where, in the conduct of matters with which the relation is concerned, such a duty may arise
(*h*) As to the various forms of trusteeship, see § 320, *inf* , as to the peculiar nature of promotership, see §§ 327, 328, *post* , as to the different species of agency, see § 335, *post*
(*i*) See § 314, *ante*
(*j*) At p 566 of *Naylor* v *Winch* (1824), 1 Sim & St 555, SHADWELL, V C , says that an executor is " *in an artificial sense* a trustee for every legatee until the legacy is paid or invested "), and at pp 675, 676 of *Knox* v *Gye* (1872), L R 5 H L 656, Lord WESTBURY is at great pains to explain the vital distinction, for the purposes then under consideration, between a trustee by express declaration, or a complete trustee of property for all purposes, and " a trustee by metaphor," that is, a trustee by implication of law, and merely for the execution of some particular purpose or contractual obligation

by whatever name that person is called, and whatever may be the nature or limits of that which is confided to him, and whether he is placed in that position by express appointment under a deed, will, or contract, or by the necessity of the circumstances, he owes the same duty of disclosure, because there is in all these cases the same "confidence," or (in the largest sense of the word) "trust" (k); though, no doubt, the exact nature and limits of the matters to be disclosed may vary according to the particular species of trusteeship in which the duty of disclosure arises.

321. What, then, using the terms "trustee" and "*cestui que trust*" in the above large and general sense, are the matters which, being (actually or presumptively) within his knowledge, a trustee is bound to impart, and give the benefit of, to his *cestui que trust*, in the case of any dealing with him during the continuance of the relationship? They come under two heads In the first place, he is of course prohibited from suppressing his identity in any such transaction He cannot secretly procure an agent or nominee or trustee for himself to purchase the trust property from the *cestui que trust*, or otherwise contract with him in relation to the subject-matter of the trust, or mask his personality under an alias or *prête-nom* He must make a clear communication to the *cestui que trust* of the nature of the connection between himself and the person so procured or nominated, and reveal the transaction in its true light as a vicarious one, in which he is the real contracting party. otherwise, on discovery, the *cestui que trust* is entitled to the appropriate relief (l), without the necessity of considering any other breach of the trustee's duty of disclosure.

(k) *Gordon* v *Holland* (1913), 82 L J (P C) 81, 87 As to executors, and administrators, and assignees or trustees of an insolvent estate, who are in a fiduciary position to the beneficiaries, the creditors, and the bankrupt, respectively, see some of the cases cited in notes (l)—(r), inf

(l) See *Randall* v *Errington* (1805), 10 Ves 423, which was a case of two trustees, the defendant Errington and one Liddell, having purchased at auction the trust property by one Hodgson in trust for themselves The *cestui que trust* was one Wilkinson, whose next of kin sued Errington, the executors of Liddell (who had died in the meantime), and an assignee from them, for rescission of the sale, on the ground that these trustees were under a duty to inform their *cestui que trust* that H was not bidding for himself as a stranger, but as the agent and trustee for (in the case of certain cottages) E , and (in the case of certain shares) L GRANT, M R , granted the relief prayed, holding that the defendants had entirely failed to prove that the trustees had ever disclosed to either W or the plaintiffs, or that any of these latter knew at any material date, the above fact " as to W and these plaintiffs, it does not appear that they knew that E had become the purchaser " of the cottages (p 426), and, as to the shares, " there is no evidence that W knew that L had become the purchaser " (p 427), and, again (at p 429), " he did not know that it was a sale to L " So, in *Downes* v *Grazebrook* (1817), 3 Mer 200, Lord ELDON, L C , held that a trustee cannot purchase from his *cestui que trust* by an agent bidding and buying on his behalf, without bringing the fact of the agency to the actual and personal notice of the *cestui que trust*, and, further, obtaining his assent (pp 208, 209) See also *Baker* v *Read* (1854), 18 Beav 398 (ROMILLY, M R), 3 W R 118 (KNIGHT BRUCE and TURNER, LL.JJ), which was a case of an executor purchasing the estate from the beneficiaries by a trustee or agent, without disclosing the fact that he was the real purchaser, and in which it was held that, for the purposes of the rule of disclosure, executors are in precisely the same position as trustees the executor, however, in this case escaped, on proving that the beneficiaries were perfectly well aware from other sources that the purchase was made on his behalf , *Dyson* v *Lum* (1866), 14 L T 588 (a case of a person concealing the fact that in buying the property she was agent for her brother, one of the trustees under a will) On the other hand, in *Re Postlethwaite* (1888), 60 L T 514, C A , the alleged secret agency

322. The other, and the more common, type of case is where the trustee deals openly and professedly with his *cestui que trust*. It is now well established (though in very early times it was much doubted) that such a dealing is not absolutely prohibited (*ll*), but it is only permissible under the most stringent conditions that is to say, the transaction will be invalidated at the instance of the *cestui que trust*, unless the trustee can establish—and the burden of doing so lies heavily upon him, and is very seldom discharged—the propriety of his conduct in all respects, or, in other words, that he has taken no advantage of his exclusive or superior knowledge of the circumstances, that he has made a bargain as secure and advantageous for the *cestui que trust* with himself as could be made for the *cestui que trust* with any stranger, and that, generally, he has made a proper and fair use of the confidence placed in him (*m*); or, unless he can prove a clear assent by the

was not proved by the mere fact that the trustee bought the property from the purchaser shortly afterwards at a slightly increased price. It is of course in auction sales that the opportunity for suppression of identity most frequently arises see *Sanderson* v *Walker* (1807), 13 Ves 601 (*per* Lord ELDON, L C , at p 602 "there is no medium of sale that can be made a wider inlet to fraud than sales by auction "—he is referring to the ridiculous suggestion of a trustee that he was buying not from himself, but from the auctioneer, who, of course, as Lord ELDON points out, is not an interposed third person, but the mere agent of the trustee), *Knight* v *Marjoribanks* (1849), 2 Macn & G 10 (*per* Lord COTTENHAM, L C , at p. 12 " he must not, surreptitiously and without the knowledge of the *cestui que trust*, bid at an auction either in his own name, or by anybody for him , . This is the rule in the case of a trustee "), *Re Moore* (1881), 51 L J (CH) 72, with which contrast *Re Gallard*, [1897] 2 Q B 8

(*ll*) See *Coles* v *Trecothick*, and *Luff* v *Lord*, cited in the next note also *Whichcote* v. *Lawrence* (1798), 3 Ves 739 (*per* Lord ELDON, L C , at pp 749, 750 " it is stated as a proposition, that a trustee can never buy of the *cestui que trust* Certainly that proposition is not correctly true " He then goes on to say the same of " an emanation " from that proposition, viz "that the sale, where the trustee to sell is the purchaser, is *ipso jure* null; that there is no sale, no contracting party That is not the real sense of the proposition , but it is this , which is very plain in point of equity, and a principle of clear reasoning ; that he who undertakes to act for another in any matter shall not in the same matter act for himself "), *Sanderson* v *Walker*, *sup* (*per* Lord ELDON, L C , at p 601), as cited in note (*mm*), *inf* , *Downes* v *Grazebrook* (1817), 3 Mer 200 (*per* Lord ELDON, L C , at p 208), *Dover* v *Buck* (1865), 12 L T 136 (*per* STUART, V C , at p 137) Such transactions, however, though not *ipso jure* null, like a sale by a mortgagee to himself, which is regarded as not being an exercise of the power of sale at all,—see § 347, *post*,—are, if recorded in a formal instrument by a perfectly candid trustee, scarcely capable of expression in any terms which will not make the whole thing appear, on the face of it, an utter absurdity, as, for instance, in a case where the recitals of the deed made it clear that the trustee purported to sell to a person who was actually declared to be his agent *Franks* v *Bollans* (1867), 17 L T 309 (*per* STUART, V C , at pp 311, 312) See also *Thomson* v *Eastwood* (1877), 2 App Cas 215, H L (*per* Lord CAIRNS, L C , at p 236

(*m*) *Gibson* v *Jeyes* (1801), 6 Ves 266 (*per* Lord ELDON, L.C , at p 278 " that great rule of the Court that he who bargains in matters of advantage with a person placing confidence in him is bound to show that a reasonable use has been made of that confidence "), *Coles* v *Trecothick* (1804), 9 Ves 234 (*per* Lord ELDON, L C , at pp 246, 247 " a trustee may buy from the *cestui que trust*, provided that there is a distinct and clear contract, ascertained to be such after a jealous and scrupulous examination of all the circumstances, and there is no fraud, no concealment, no advantage taken by the trustee of information acquired by him in his character of trustee I own it is a difficult case to make out "), *Denton* v *Donner* (1856), 23 Beav 285 (*per* ROMILLY , M R , at p 290 " the burden of proof lies on the trustee to show that every possible security and advantage was given to the *cestui que trust*, and that as much as possible was gained for him in the transaction, and as could have been gained under any other circumstances "), *Smedley* v *Varley* (1857), 23 Beav 358 (*per* ROMILLY, M R , at p 359) , *Luff* v *Lord* (1864), 34 Beav 220 (*per* ROMILLY, M R , at p 227 " a trustee may purchase from his *cestui que trust*, when the *cestui que trust* chooses to sell him the property, though the burden of proof lies

cestui que trust to the termination of the trusteeship, and to the assumption by the trustee of the character of independent purchaser or contractor (*mm*), though this latter will not be an answer if the trustee has divested himself of his trusteeship within such a recent date that he cannot be supposed to have also divested himself of the exclusive or superior knowledge acquired by him in that character, in which case he is under the same duty of communicating his knowledge as if the relation had not been put an end to (*n*)

323. The knowledge which must be imparted to the *cestui que trust* is, in the first place, all the knowledge and information as to material facts which the trustee has acquired, or of which he has been in possession, in the course of his trusteeship, and, secondly, all the knowledge of how to use and appreciate those facts which he possessed before he entered upon his duties, and the possession of which, if he be an expert or skilled person who *spondet peritiam*

on the trustee to establish the propriety of the transaction ") The "difficulty" of " making out the case," which Lord ELDON acknowledges, was overcome by the trustee, who accordingly succeeded, in *Coles* v. *Trecothick*, *sup* , *Morse* v *Royal* (1806), 12 Ves. 355 (*per* Lord ELDON, L C , at pp 374, 375) , *Luff* v *Lord*, *sup* , *Hickley* v *Hickley* (1876), 2 C D 190   On the other hand, in the vast majority of cases the trustee was unable to " establish the propriety of the transaction," such as *Att.-Gen* v *Lord Dudley* (1815), G Cooper, 146 , 14 R R 226 (trustees of property for Anabaptists, under an enrolled deed, purchasing from the society) , *Cook* v *Collingridge* (1823), Jac 607 , 23 R. R. 155 (purchase by executors from co-executors of testator's share in partnership business) , *Williamson* v *Seaber* (1839), 3 Y & C (Eq Exch) 717 , *Hamilton* v *Wright* (1842), 9 Cl & Fin 111 (purchase by trustees in insolvency of annuity from debtor) , *Denton* v *Donner, sup* , *Smedley* v *Varley, sup* , *Lloyd* v *Attwood* (1859), 3 De G & J 614 (release of trustees), *Franks* v *Bollans*, cited in the note (*ll*), *sup* , *Gray* v *Warner* (1873), 42 L J 556 (purchase of a legacy by an executor); *Re Pepperell* (1879), 27 W R 410 (where an administratrix, by her husband, purchased part of the estate from another administratrix) , *De Cordova* v *De Cordova* (1879), 4 App Cas. 692, P C (at pp 702, 703 executors compromising a debt due from one of themselves) , *Plowright* v. *Lambert* (1885), 52 L T 646 (purchase of beneficiary's interest under a will by trustee of the will)

(*mm*) *Coles* v *Trecothick, sup* (see the earlier part of the passage from Lord ELDON's judgment which is cited in the last note) , *Sanderson* v *Walker* (1807), 13 Ves 601 (*per* Lord ELDON, L.C , at p 601 · " a trustee for sale may be the purchaser in this sense, that he may contract with his *cestui que trust* that, with reference to the contract of purchase, they shall no longer stand in the relative situation of trustee and *cestui que trust*, and the trustee, having through the medium of that sort of bargain evidently, distinctly, and honestly proved that he had removed himself from the character of trustee, his purchase may be sustained ")   Where the *cestui que trustent* are infants, there is no means of establishing such a contract, or consent to the termination of the relationship , for infants cannot so contract or consent, and it is only the Court who can do so on their behalf, and therefore it is only by obtaining judicial sanction that any dealing by the trustee with the beneficiaries can in such a case be sustained   *Mulvany* v *Dillon* (1810), 1 Ball & B 409 , 12 R R 43 (where an executor *de son tort* induced the executors named in the will to surrender a leasehold interest bequeathed to infants, and give him a new lease at a lower rent) , *Re New Haw Estate Trusts* (1912), 107 L T 191, where PARKER, J , held that, in this respect, the Public Trustee under the Public Trustee Act, 1906 (6 Edw 7, c 55), is in no different position than that of any other trustee

(*n*) *Robinson* v *Pett* (1734), 3 P Wms 249 (*per* TALBOT, L.C., at p 251 " the defendant's renouncing the executorship is not material . . if this were to make any difference, it would be an art practised by executors to get themselves out of this rule ") , *Ex p James* (1803), 8 Ves 337 (a case of the solicitor to the commission buying part of the bankrupt's estate, in which, at p 352, Lord ELDON, L C., said " if the principle is right that the solicitor cannot buy, it would lead to all the mischief of acting up to the point of sale, getting all the information that may be useful to him, then discharging himself from the character of solicitor, and buying the property ") , *Spring* v *Pride* (1864), 12 W R 892 (a case of a trustee retiring from the trusteeship "formally or colourably . for the purpose of . . . a better appearance to be made " *per* KNIGHT-BRUCE, L.J , at p. 893)

artis, may have been the reason for his appointment. As regards the first species of knowledge, the principal matters required to be disclosed are those facts and circumstances which have a bearing on the value of the trust property, and of which the trustee has special or private cognizance (o). The non-disclosure of such facts may obviously result in the trustee purchasing at a price which, if he had been put in full possession of the truth, the *cestui que trust* might not have been willing to accept. It has, indeed, been sometimes said, and still more often assumed, that the mere fact of undervalue is enough to vitiate a transaction between trustee and *cestui que trust* Unless this statement be taken to mean that any inadequate disclosure of facts bearing on value which results in the acceptance by the *cestui que trust* of inadequate value is such as to render the transaction voidable, or, unless it is confined to cases where undue influence, as well as abuse of confidence, is shown, it may be doubted whether it is strictly correct To test whether, in its literal sense, it is accurate, it must be assumed that the trustee has put at the disposal of the *cestui que trust* every single piece of knowledge or information which would tend to enhance the value, that he has placed him in communication with independent experts of the greatest skill and repute, that he has honestly given him the full benefit of his own experience and judgment, and that the bargain was in all other respects fair and proper and that the *cestui que trust* thereupon chooses, from motives of unsolicited and uninfluenced bounty, to sell the property at a price less than that which the knowledge so communicated, and the advice so given, would show to be the true value Would the mere fact of " undervalue " in such a case vitiate the purchase ? It is submitted that it would not , any more than, *e converso*, the mere fact

(o) Illustrations are —*Forbes* v *Ross* (1788), 2 Cox 113 (trustee lends money at less interest than, as he must have known, could have been obtained elsewhere), *Fox* v *Mackreth* (1788), 2 Cox 320 (trustee withholds information as to the real value of the estate which he had acquired by secretly sending down a surveyor to report), *Whichcote* v *Lawrence* (1798), 3 Ves 739 (*per* Lord Loughborough, L.C , at p 750 "Lawrence, being a banker, entered into the trust probably from the advantage he might derive that the money might he long with him , and it might draw custom to his shop From his situation he was not likely to be unacquainted with the real value," and, again, at p 751, "having a farm in the neighbourhood, he must have been well acquainted with the circumstances ") , *Ex p Lacey* (1802), 6 Ves 625 (*per* Lord ELDON, L C., at pp 626, 627) , *Ex p James* (1803), 8 Ves 337 (*per* Lord ELDON, L C , at p 350 · " Billingley's valuation stating it to be worth £12,000 at least was known to the assignee and some of the creditors Was not that material for the others to know ? " The case was that of an assignee of a bankrupt, and the solicitor to the commission, concealing this valuation, when purchasing part of the bankrupt's estate) , *Gregory* v *Gregory* (1815), G Cooper, 201 ; 14 R R 244 (where a trustee purchased at a sum which he was peculiarly qualified to know was grossly inadequate, having for 15 years been the acting trustee, during which period he "must have acquired a complete knowledge of the situation and value of the estates " *per* GRANT, M R , at p 204) , *Barton* v *Hassard* (1843), 3 Dr & War 461 (where an executor had purchased legacies from legatees at less than their face value, suppressing the fact, of which he had secret and exclusive knowledge, that the assets would be sufficient to discharge the legacies in full after satisfying the creditors) , *Plowright* v *Lambert* (1885), 52 L T 646 (where a trustee under a will bought a beneficiary's share for £900, with secret knowledge that it was worth about £4000 · *per* FIELD, J , at p 652) , *Dougan* v *Macpherson*, [1902] A C 197, H L (where a trustee of a marriage settlement purchased a beneficiary's interest without disclosing a valuation in his possession which estimated the value at a much higher figure *per* Lord HALSBURY, L.C , at pp 202, 203, Lord MACNAGHTEN, at pp 204, 205, and Lord LINDLEY, at p 206) of full value having been given and taken would validate a contract otherwise voidable on the ground of non-disclosure. There is no case in which, all the facts being as assumed in the above hypothesis, it has been so decided ; and any absolute rule to the contrary would seem to be hardly in accordance with sound theory or good sense (p)   No doubt, there may be a proved case of the offer and acceptance of undervalue so gross as to invite the suggestion, or even compel the inference, that weighty matters must have been suppressed in order to produce such a result, or that the whole transaction must have been fraudulent.   But this is a different proposition to that which is now being criticized (q)

324. Not only must the trustee put the *cestui que trust* in as good a position as himself in regard to the facts   he must put him in as good a position as himself as regards capacity to deal with the facts. He must transfer to him, for the purpose of the contemplated purchase or other dealing, all the judgment, discretion and skill (whether expert, or otherwise) which he would himself bring to bear upon the situation if he were not an interested

(p) It is quite clear, of course, that, in the absence of any relation between the parties which casts upon one of them the burden of establishing the righteousness of the transaction, the mere fact of inadequacy of price or consideration is wholly irrelevant and inofficacious as a ground of rescission, or even as a defence to specific performance see *Coles* v *Trecothick* (1804), 9 Ves 234 (*per* Lord El don, L C , at p 246) , *Abbott* v *Sworder* (1852), 4 De G & Sm. 448 (*per* Lord St Leonards, at p 461)   It is equally unquestionable that, where the relation of trustee and *cestui que trust* exists, and where, therefore, the burden is on the former of proving, generally, the fairness and honesty of the transaction,— see § 322, and note (m) thereto, *ante*,—one of the most effectual steps in sustaining that burden is to show that full value has been given   But is this a separate *probandum*, independent of and additional to all other evidence by which good faith may be established, such as disclosure, and, particularly, disclosure of all facts relating to the question of value ?   It is not to be denied that Lord Cairns, L C , at p 236 of *Thomson* v *Eastwood* (1877), 2 App Cas 215, H L , also Lord Halsbury, L C , at p 202, and Lord Macnaghten at p 204, of *Dougan* v *Macpherson*, [1902] A C. 197, H L , distinctly state the two things, full disclosure of knowledge as to value, and full value, as necessary to be shown by a trustee purchasing from his *cestui que trust* , but, in the latter case, the acceptance of an inadequate price was brought about by, and was inextricably mixed up with, grossly inadequate disclosure   And, though there are cases in which relief has been granted to the *cestui que trust* on no other ground, so far as appears from the report, than undervalue, in none of these had the trustee established—in some of them he had not even attempted to establish—the propriety of the transaction, and of his conduct, in all other respects. The correctness of the proposition canvassed in the text can only be made out by reference to some decision against a trustee under the above conditions (viz proof of entire discharge of every duty of good faith and honesty and candour on his part) on the mere ground of inadequacy of price   It is believed that there is no such decision.   It is true that in *Baker* v *Read* (1854), 18 Beav 398, Romilly, M R , intimated that, but for the *cestui que trust's* confirmation, he would have given relief against the trustee on the mere ground of undervalue   No decision, however, was called for, either from him or from the Lords Justices who affirmed him (1854), 3 W. R 118. On the other hand, there are expressions of high judicial authority which tend in the contrary direction, such as those of Lord Eldon, L C , at pp 273, 274, of *Gibson* v *Jeyes* (1801), 6 Ves 266 (who there distinctly said, when dealing with the question of undervalue, that if the case of the plaintiff " stood upon that ground merely, it would be very hazardous to rescind this transaction "), and of Lord Westbury, at p 9 of *Tennent* v *Tennent* (1870), L R 2 H L (Sc) 6 (" there is an equity which may be founded on gross inadequacy of consideration.   But it can only be where the inadequacy is such as to involve the conclusion that the party either did not understand what he was about or was the victim of some imposition ")

(q) As to the question of undervalue in cases of undue influence, see Ch V, Sect 4, Sub s (2), *post*, and, in relation to bargains and dealings with reversioners, which are governed by somewhat special rules in this respect, Ch V, Sect 2, Sub s (6), *post*

party. In other words, he is bound to use all his natural and trained faculties in advising the *cestui que trust* against himself, as if he were a stranger (r).

325. The discussion of the burden of proof which lies upon the *cestui que trust* in any proceeding is reserved for its proper place hereafter (s) ; and so also is the consideration of other topics, such as the affirmative defences available to the trustee, the relief and remedy available to the *cestui que trust*, questions of law and issues of fact, and the necessary parties to the proceedings (t).

Sub-s (2). *Promoter and Company.*

326. It is now well established that any person who "projects," "promotes," or "floats," a company—to use the three phrases in popular acceptation at successive stages in the history of joint stock enterprise (u)—stands in some sort of fiduciary relation to that company, and owes some duties to it, of disclosure and otherwise, which would not be incumbent on him but for the existence of that relation. But, as to the elements necessary to constitute promotership (v), the exact nature and extent of the promoter's

---

(r) *Whichcote* v. *Lawrence* (1798), 3 Ves 739 (*per* Lord LOUGHBOROUGH, L.C , at p 749 : "it is obvious that this estate has not been sold to that advantage which the knowledge *and abilities* of Mr L , the trustee, exerted towards this estate, *when his own*, obtained for himself , and, if that knowledge *and ability* had been applied at the original sale, when the estate was sold for the benefit of the creditors, it is obvious," &c   again, at p 751, he speaks of having before him " absolute demonstration that, if he had acted with regard to the trust with the same degree of *vigilance and attention* that he applied to his own affairs, when he came to act for his own benefit with some part of the trust estate   more, somewhat considerably more, would have been got than was obtained upon the former sale ") , *Gibson* v *Jeyes* (1801), 6 Ves 266, where the attorney and agent of an old lady in feeble health, in selling to her an annuity at an excessive price, withheld from her the benefit of the disinterested advice which he could and ought to have given her   The purchase was set aside, on the ground that the defendant, not having either given his client his own, or procured for her another's, impartial advice, had failed to comply with the duty which rested upon him, and with the rule of the Court which is that an agent or *trustee* (for afterwards Lord ELDON expressly applies the rule to the case of a trustee, amongst others, which is the reason for citing the case in the present connection) " shall, if the propriety of the contract comes in question, manifest that he has given [the *cestui que trust*, principal, or client] all that reasonable advice against himself that he would have given [him] against a third person " (*per* Lord ELDON, L C , at p 278)

(s) Sect 3, *post.*

(t) Sects 4, 5, 6, 7, respectively, *post*

(u) During the earliest period, a period covering such cases as *Hichens* v *Congreve* (1831), 4 Sim 420, *Society of Practical Knowledge* v *Abbott* (1840), 2 Beav 559, and *Maxwell* v *Port Tennant, &c , Co* (1857), 24 Beav 495, the phrase in common use was " projector "   Afterwards " promoter " came to be the accepted term, and it is used (and defined) in the Joint Stock Companies Act, 1844 (7 & 8 Vict c 110)   It finds no place in the Companies Act, 1862, but reappears in the Companies Act, 1867, and in subsequent company legislation, but without any attempt being made to define the expression, even in the Companies (Consolidation) Act, 1908, for, obviously, s 84 (5) of that statute, which says that " promoter " for the purposes of the section shall mean one particular species of the class, leaves the class itself undefined   The term " float " was almost contemporaneous in origin with " promoter," but has not been advanced to the dignity of statutory recognition.   The horribly malformed and grotesque word " flotation " is of comparatively recent growth.

(v) See § 327, *inf*

obligations to the company (w), and the theory on which those obligations rest (x), the law has not always spoken with so clear and certain a voice

327. First, as to the characteristics of promotership. This is not a relation which is ordinarily, as in the case of trusteeship or agency, established by instruments or express declarations The promoter, in the majority of instances which have come before the courts, has been restrained by a certain prudential modesty from assuming or acknowledging the name and style, and has preferred to be known, if he must be known at all, by his works. It is a question of fact, therefore, in each of such cases, whether a particular person was, or was not, a promoter of the company at the material date (y), and it lies on the party complaining, that is, the company, to prove that he was (z). As to what acts and proceedings are to be deemed indicia of promotership, the courts, like the legislature (a), and for the same wise reason, have steadily refused to lay down any universal rule. Any judicial catalogue of such acts and proceedings would be effusively welcomed by the astute and versatile fraternity concerned in the genesis of the baser sort of public undertakings, who would make haste to limit their activity to the uncatalogued operations, and thus keep on the windy side of all cast-iron definitions. It is not only the *dolosus*, in the ordinary sense of the word, whose interest it is *versari in generalibus.* There is a *dolus bonus* which, in the form of judicial astuteness, is equally concerned in refusing to condescend to particulars It is probably for this reason of policy, quite as much as from the intellectual difficulty inherent in the subject-matter, that all the descriptive references in the authorities to the constitutive elements of promotership are couched in language no less general, and in some cases even wider, than the term itself Indeed, not a few of them are as obviously, and (were it not for our consciousness of the excellent object in view) as ludicrously, of the *idem per idem*, or *obscurum per obscurius*, order as the famous definition of a poet which Lyly, in his *Endymion*, puts in the mouth of Sir Tophas (b).

(w) Thus, at p 1269 of *Erlanger* v. *New Sombrero Phosphate Co.* (1878), 3 App Cas 1218, H. L , Lord BLACKBURN limits himself to the proposition that promoters " stand with regard to the corporation, when formed, in what is called a fiduciary relation *to some extent*," and must " pay *some* regard to its interests," and, again, " are in a situation of confidence *to some extent* towards the company they form " With a like cautious indefinite ness, LINDLEY, J , at p 407 of *Emma Silver Mining Co* v *Lewis* (1879), 4 C P D 396, says that the word involves, amongst other things, " the idea of *some* duty towards the company imposed by or arising out of the position which the so-called promoter assumes towards it " Cp the observations of COTTON, L.J , at p 407 of *Bagnall & Sons, Ltd* v *Carlton* (1877), 6 C. D 371, C A , where he describes the relation as a fiduciary one, but adds that the description " is open to this observation that they "—*i e* promoters—" are not trustees as regards all matters nor at all times "

(x) See § 328, *post*
(y) This is discussed in § 389, note (y), *post*
(z) See § 352, *post*.
(a) See note (u), *sup*
(b) Act I , Sc 3 "Dost thou not know what a poet is ? Why, fool, a poet is as much as one should say—a poet ! " Of a piece with this is the bishop's description of an archdeacon as " a person who goes about performing archidiaconal functions," or Bardolph's heroic essay in lexicography in H 4, Part II, Act 3, Sc 2 " Accommodated ,

Thus, COCKBURN, C J., described a promoter as "one who undertakes to orm a company with reference to a given project and to set it going, and who takes the necessary steps to accomplish that purpose" (c). Lord BLACKBURN considered the expression "a short and convenient way of designating those who set in motion the machinery by which the Act enables them to create an incorporated company" (d) In the view of Lord BOWEN (e), "the term 'promoter' is a term not of law, but of business, usefully summing up in a single word a number of business operations familiar to the commercial world by which a company is generally brought into existence." Lord LINDLEY has characterized the expression as one that has "no very definite meaning" (f), and, again, as "an ambiguous term" (g) BACON, V -C, after citing the above observations, expresses his opinion that "not much assistance is to be derived" from them, and that they are "not satisfactory" (h), which is true in one sense, but not in another (i) Finally, in a still later case, COTTON, L J, boldly avowed his "dislike" of the term, and, after this pronouncement, succeeded in delivering the rest of his judgment without using it at all (j) Nothing could well be vaguer than the above descriptions . but nothing could be more deliberate or desirable than this vagueness *Quo teneam nodo mutantem Protea vultus?* The *nodus* which is to accomplish this feat must be as supple and transformable as the Proteus it is designed to imprison

328. The next question is as to the principle on which a person proved, as a fact, to have promoted a company is chargeable with duties of disclosure to that company during his promotership The inquiry admits of no very precise answer The relationship in question does not clearly and unmistakably belong either to the species of confidential relationship already discussed (k), or to that which remains to be considered (l) For, on the one hand, a promoter is not a trustee for the company he is forming, or

that is, when a man is, as they say, accommodated, or when a man is, being, whereby a' may be thought to be accommodated, which is an excellent thing "

(c) At p 541 of *Twycross* v *Grant* (1877), 2 C P D 469, C A

(d) At p 1268 of *Erlanger* v. *New Sombrero Phosphate Co* (1878), 3 App. Cas. 1218, H. L

(e) When BOWEN, J, at p 111 of *Whaley Bridge Calico Printing Co* v *Green* (1879), 5 Q B D 109

(f) This expression was used by him, when LINDLEY, J, at p 407 of *Emma Silver Mining Co* v *Lewis* (1879), 4 C P D 396, in the passage in which he also says that the term involves the idea of "some duty towards the company "—see the citation in note (w), *sup.*—as well as "the idea of exertion for the purpose of getting up and starting a company (or what is called floating it) "

(g) See *Lydney and Wigpool Iron Ore Co* v *Bird* (1886), 33 C D 85, C A, at p 93 He was then LINDLEY, L J

(h) At p. 46 of *Re Great Wheal Polgooth Co* (1883), 53 L J (CH) 42

(i) If meant as synthetical definitions, they are certainly "not satisfactory," for they are purely verbal and analytical but if (as they were) intended as mere explications of the concept, and designed for the express purpose of withholding such a synthetical description as would convey information, and teach the promoter what to avoid, they are eminently "satisfactory."

(j) See *Ladywell Mining Co* v *Brookes* (1887), 35 C D 400, C A, at p 411

(k) In Sub-s. (1), *ante*

(l) In Sub s (3), *post*

proposing to form, in the complete and strict sense of the term . he can, at most, be regarded as a " constructive trustee " for it (*m*), or what Lord WESTBURY called " a trustee by metaphor " (*n*) , and the courts have, on the whole, studiously refrained from calling him a trustee (*o*), though freely assigning to him a " fiduciary position " of a somewhat indefinite character (*p*)   Nor can he be deemed for all purposes an agent of the company, though the term "fiduciary agent " has occasionally been applied to him (*q*)   for, until the actual incorporation of the company,—and it is in the period which ends with that date that his duties of disclosure assume the greatest importance,—he certainly cannot be described with accuracy as its agent, for no man can have as his principal a person which, whether natural or artificial, is unborn or non-existent   And yet, as LINDLEY, L J., has observed (*r*), " although not an agent of the company, nor a trustee for it before its formation, the old familiar principles of the law of agency and trusteeship have been extended, and very properly extended, to meet such cases , and . . . it is perfectly well settled that a promoter of a company is accountable to it for all moneys secretly obtained by him from it, just as if the relationship of principal and agent, or of trustee and *cestui que trust*, had really existed between him and the company."   We are not here, or elsewhere, told on what precise reasoning or analogy the propriety of this extension is based   But some such theory as this may be suggested   There are certain characteristics of the promoter's position in reference to the company which would almost appear to justify the inclusion of this relation in the class of those from which " influence," rather than " confidence " merely, is presumed, and which form the subject of the next Chapter.   He is the creator of the company , he dictates the terms upon which it is to come into being as a legal entity , he is thus in a position of dominance and ascendancy towards his creature , and it is not, perhaps, too fanciful to suggest that the true theoretical justification and basis of the body of rules which prescribe duties of disclosure to promoters is the fact that promotership is a commercial parentage, involving the same judicial presumption of influence as is involved in cases of natural parentage, and the same burden on the parent of establishing that he has not abused that influence   This doctrine has never been expressed in precisely the above form · but there are abundant judicial expositions of the rules governing promotership cases which necessarily presuppose such a theory as their

(*m*) This was the view expressed by KAY, J , at p 147 of *Re Fitzroy Bessemer Steel Co.* (1884), 50 L T 144, and it was solely on this ground that he did not think it right that " vindictive damages," on a misfeasance summons, should be awarded against the promoter in that case   Cp the observations of SARGANT, J , at p 347 of *Omnium Electric Palaces, Ltd* v *Baines*, [1914] 1 Ch 332

(*n*) See § 320, *ante*, and note (*j*) thereto.

(*o*) Occasionally, however, one finds the relation referred to unqualifiedly as one of trusteeship   Thus, at p 823 of *Re Leeds and Hanley Theatre of Varieties, Ltd* , [1902] 2 Ch 809, C A , VAUGHAN WILLIAMS, L.J , refers to the company, and the " future allottees of shares " therein, as the "*cestuis que trustent*" of the promoters

(*p*) See note (*w*) to § 326, *sup*

(*q*) As, *e.g* , by Lord BLACKBURN, at p 1277 of *Erlanger* v *New Sombrero Phosphate Co* (1878), 3 App Cas 1218, H L

(*r*) At p 94 of *Lydney & Wigpool Iron Ore Co* v *Bird* (1886), 33 C D 85, C A

substructure, and which, indeed, would otherwise be meaningless (s). The result, therefore, is this A promoter is a " constructive trustee," but not a trustee in the strict sense of the word, for the company he promotes : he is an agent for it, when formed, but not before its formation · he is in any case the mercantile author of its being, and, as such, is presumed to have, and to exercise, an " influence " over it, which it is for him to show has been duly and properly exercised. It is by reason of this composite character of promotership that it has been thought proper and convenient to deal with it as a relation *sui generis*, rather than as a case of either trusteeship or agency, or as a species of the class of " influence " relations

329. There being, then, a relation between a promoter and the company he promotes which, whatever be its proper name or nature, undoubtedly involves a duty on the promoter's part of good faith and candid disclosure of all facts within his (actual or presumed) exclusive cognizance which are material to be communicated to the company (t), it remains to consider what classes of facts are the proper subject of the prescribed disclosure

330. It must be remembered that the promoter is only called upon to divulge during his promotership such matters. *if any*, as in the circumstances of the particular case are material for the company to know It may so

(s) Thus, to select a few examples out of many, at p 1236 of *Erlanger* v *New Sombrero Phosphate Co* , *sup* , Lord Cairns, L C , says " it is now necessary that I should state in what position I understand the promoters to be placed with reference to the company which they proposed to form They stand, in my opinion, undoubtedly in a fiduciary position *They have, in their hands, the creation and moulding of the company , they have the power of defining how, and when, and in what shape, and under what supervision, it shall start into existence, and begin to act as a trading corporation.*" It is clear from this passage that the doctrine of " the fiduciary position " of the promoter is based by Lord CAIRNS on the fact that he is the author and designer of the company's being, and the only person to whom, on its birth, it can look for information, guidance, and advice, just as the parent or guardian is the only person to whom the infant individual can look for the same purposes Lord BLACKBURN, at p 1269, expresses a similar view, though in somewhat different, and perhaps less forcible and convincing, language " the promoters," he observes, " can *create* such a corporation that the corporation, *as soon as it comes into being*, may be bound by anyth ng, not in itself illegal, which the promoters have chosen And I think that those who accept and use such extensive powers, which so greatly affect the interests of the corporation *when it comes into being*, are not entitled to disregard the interests of that corporation altogether They must make a *reasonable use of the powers* which they accept from the legislature with regard to the formation of the corporation, and *that requires them* to pay some regard to its interests " In other words, the privileges of mercantile parentage involve correlative duties which the parent is no more at liberty to disregard than the natural parent is to leave his offspring on the doorstep of a foundling hospital , and the statutory " influence " and ascendancy which flows from the position which the law enables promoters to assume involves an obligation not to make an unreasonable or undue use of that influence and ascendancy Cp the observations of COLLINS, L.J , at p. 181 of *Re Olympia, Ltd* , [1898] 2 Ch 153, C A , who says of the persons there found to have promoted the company that " *they did every act necessary to give it existence,   and generally dictated the conditions of the company's existence* "

(t) It is to the company that the duty is owed Whether the company be a public or a " private " one, as defined in s 121 of the Companies (Consolidation) Act, 1908, makes no difference see *Omnium Electric Palaces, Ltd* v *Barnes*, [1914] 1 Ch 332, C A (*per* SARGANT, J , at pp 347, 348) But the company, to whom alone the duty is owed, may mean more than the then existing shareholders Future allottees may be included. For a detailed examination of this question, see § 393, *post* The duty of disclosure in the prospectus which the promoter owes to individual applicants for shares is entirely the creature of statute This topic is dealt with in Ch VI, *post*

happen that there are no such matters. For instance, if the promoter is nothing but a promoter at an agreed remuneration for his services, and enters into no direct dealings, as vendor of property or otherwise, with the company, he is under no obligation of disclosure at all, at least in his character of promoter (*u*), any more than, conversely, a vendor to the company who is not its promoter is subject to any duty of communication other than that which lies upon him in his character of vendor (*v*). It is only where he assumes the position of vendor or lessor to, or contractor with, the company, concurrently with his position as its promoter, that the duty arises, for in any such case he is uniting in his own person two inconsistent characters, in one of which it is his interest to make the best bargain he can *for himself out of the company*, whilst in the other it is his duty to make the best bargain he can *for the company out of somebody else*. The following observations therefore are directed solely to cases of what, for brevity and convenience, we may call vendor-promotership

331. In the first place, as in the case of trustees (*w*), the vendor-promoter is not allowed to keep from the company the fact that he is a vendor-promoter He must not mask his identity under an alias, or by means of secret agents or nominees or associates, or by manipulation of names conceal from the company the fact that he is uniting in his own person two functions in which his interest must necessarily conflict with his duty If known to the company only as a vendor, or as a person otherwise dealing directly with it, he must reveal his promotership, or connection with the promoter or promoters, and, conversely, if known to the company only as a promoter, he must disclose his vendorship, or his association, however indirect, with those who, as vendors or otherwise, are contracting or treating direct with the company Whenever this duty has been violated, the company has succeeded in establishing its title to relief (*x*)

(*u*) He may of course, be liable to the duty in his character of agent for the company after its formation, or as trustee of property for the company when formed, if he should in fact be so declared or constituted

(*v*) As to the duties of disclosure which rest upon a vendor in an ordinary contract of sale and purchase, see Ch III, Sect. 2, Sub s (3), *ante* As to the duties which are not so incumbent on him in his mere character of ordinary vendor, though they would be upon him as a vendor-promoter, see the cases referred to in § 165, notes (*p*)-(*u*), *ante*, and contrast them with those cited in note (*x*), *inf*

(*w*) See § 321, *ante*

(*x*) For illustrations, see *Hichens* v *Congreve* (1831), 4 Sim 420 (where the promoters concealed the fact of their association with the vendor, who was willing to sell the property to any one for £10,000, but was induced to pose as a vendor to the company who would not take less than £25,000, which sum the company eventually paid in entire ignorance of arrangements between the vendor and the promoters, whereby the latter were to, and did, receive £15,000 from the vendor out of the £25,000), *Atwool* v *Merryweather* (1867), L. R. 5 Eq 464 n (where two promoters, one of whom was ready to sell the property for £4000, entered into a secret scheme, whereby the other was to pose as the sole vendor to the company for £7000, of which £3000 was to go to the first mentioned promoter), *Lindsay Petroleum Co* v *Hurd* (1874), L R 5 P C 221 (a similar clandestine arrangement); *Erlanger* v *New Sombrero Phosphate Co* (1878), 3 App Cas. 1218, H L (*per* Lord PENZANCE at p 1229 "there is no proof that they"—i e. the two directors who could alone be considered independent—"ever knew that the real vendors were all the promoters of the company," and Lord CAIRNS, L C, at p 1236, "if they"—the promoters—"are

332. In the next place, where the vendor-promoter deals with the company openly and avowedly in that double character, which course there is no rule of law to prohibit him from adopting, if he chooses (y), he is bound to make to the company (z) complete, precise, and unambiguous disclosure (a) of every matter within his own exclusive knowledge, whether actually or presumptively so, which it is material for the company to know Such matters comprise everything which bears upon the real value of the property or business which the vendor-promoter is selling to the company , the price at which he acquired such property or business, and the profit which he is making out of the company on the re-sale ; the commission or other advantages which have been, or are to be, paid or secured to him by or through the original owner or any intermediate vendor , all facts tending to show that the property or business might have been acquired from the owner or original vendor for a less sum than the company is agreeing to pay , and, generally, all circumstances which, if communicated, would affect the company's judgment in determining whether or not to purchase on the terms proposed, and which any person honestly advising the company in a contemplated transaction with a third person would bring before it   Whenever the vendor-promoter has failed to establish disclosure of facts of the above character, the appropriate relief has been obtained against him (b) . in the rare cases when he has succeeded in so doing, such relief has been refused (c).

doing all this "—r c. the various acts referred to in the citation from this judgment which is contained at the head of note (s), *ante*,—" in order that the company may, as soon as it starts into life, become the purchaser of the property of themselves, the promoters, it is, in my opinion, incumbent upon the promoters to take care that in forming the company they provide it with an executive, that is to say, with a board of directors who shall   be aware that the property which they are asked to buy is the property of the promoters,   . and who are not left under the belief that the property belongs, not to the promoter, but to some other person ") , *Re Leeds & Hanley Theatre of Varieties, Ltd* , [1902] 2 Ch. 809, C A (where the promoters concealed the fact that they, and not the ostensible vendors, were really selling to the company) , *Re Darby, Ex p Brougham*, [1911] 1 K B 95 (where the promoters of the company disguised their identity under the mask or alias of a corporation, and concealed the fact that this corporation, which sold to the company, was not independent of themselves, but was in fact either themselves in another name, or a mere piece of machinery devised and erected by themselves for the purposes of the above concealment   *per* PHILLIMORE, J , at pp. 101-103)

(y) As Lord CAIRNS, L C , is careful to concede, at p 1236 of *Erlanger* v *New Sombrero Phosphate Co* , *sup*   " I do not say that the owner of property may not promote and form a joint stock company, and then sell his property to it, but I do say that if he does he is bound, ' &c [he then lays down the conditions under which alone this kind of transaction can be supported]   Exactly the same principles obtain in the case of trustee and *cestui que trust*, as has been explained in § 322, *ante*

(z) As to the meaning of " the company " for this purpose, see § 393, *post*

(a) As to what this means, see Ch II, Sect 1, *ante*

(b) As in *Hichens* v *Congreve* (1831), 4 Sim 420 (secret profit or commission out of the vendor, who was made to sell at an enhanced price in order to provide for this payment to the promoters) , *Society of Practical Knowledge* v *Abbott* (1840), 2 Beav 559 (subscription

(c) *Re Sale Hotel & Botanical Gardens, Ltd* , *Ex p Hesketh* (1898), 78 L T 368, C A (where the alleged secret profit was fully disclosed, as part of the promotion expenses, both in the agreement of purchase and in the prospectus) , *Attorney General for the Dominion of Canada* v *Standard Trust Co of New York*, [1911] A C 498, P C. (alleged secret profits disclosed to a board which, though dependent on the promoter, was known to the company to be so) , *Omnium Electric Palaces, Ltd* v *Baines*, [1914] 1 Ch 332, C A (no secrecy even alleged)

333. It has sometimes been said, or assumed, that there is a further duty on the vendor-promoter, viz to provide the company with an executive, or board of directors, which shall be wholly independent of himself (d). By this, however, is meant no more than that he is under an obligation to disclose to the company the fact, if it be so, that the directors are his nominees and creatures, or are under obligations to him for favours, received or promised, in the shape of money or shares for qualification or otherwise, or are in any way interested with him in either of his two characters of vendor and promoter, and so are placed in a position of temptation and difficulty as long as any matters remain open between him and the company on which they may be called upon to represent the latter as against the former In short, such a fact as this is one of those which are material to be divulged, with the utmost candour and precision, by the vendor-promoter to the promoted and purchasing company The duty, therefore, is not independent of, or additional to, the duty of disclosure, but a branch of it For, in every case in which it has been shown that the company was made fully aware of the subjection of its executive to the will and interests of the promoter before entering into

for the whole share capital of the company among the promoters on payment of much less than the nominal value, and secret retention of the balance for themselves), *Lindsay Petroleum Co* v *Hurd* (1874), L R 5 P C 221 (secret arrangements with vendors and secret profit) ; *Re Hereford and South Wales Waggon & Engineering Co* (1876), 2 C D 621, C A (suppression of agreement whereby the promoters were to receive part of the purchase money from the vendors), *Phosphate Sewage Co* v *Hartmont* (1877), 5 C D 394, C A (non-disclosure of the fact that the concession sold to the company was forfeitable by the promoters' own default, of the names of the persons really interested, and of the profits made by such persons), *Erlanger* v *New Sombrero Phosphate Co* (1878), 3 App Cas 1218, H L (clandestine arrangements with owner, profits, and dependence of the directors upon the promoter) ; *Emma Silver Mining Co* v. *Grant* (1879), 11 C D 919 (a secret sub-agreement whereby the promoter was entitled to 20 per cent of the issued capital of the company), *Emma Silver Mining Co* v *Lewis & Son* (1879), 4 C P D 396 (secret receipt of shares from the vendor, afterwards converted into cash, and suppression of facts detrimental to the prospects of the mine, &c), *Whaley Bridge Calico Printing Co* v *Green* (1879), 5 Q B D 109 (secret arrangements with original and intermediate vendor, and profits secured thereby), *Re Fitzroy Bessemer Steel Co* (1884), 50 L T 144 (secret agreement with the vendors for shares), *Lydney and Wigpool Iron Ore Co* v *Bird* (1886), 33 C D 85, C A (sub agreement with vendors for payment of part of the purchase money), *Lagunas Nitrate Co* v *Lagunas Syndicate*, [1899] 2 Ch 392, C A (as to "secret profits," but the promoting syndicate escaped here, on the ground of the promoted company's affirmation by conduct As to the other matter alleged to have been concealed, see note (e), *inf*), *Gluckstein* v *Barnes*, [1900] A C 240, H L (clandestine purchase of debenture bonds of the vendor company at a discount, and of a mortgage for £10,000 at the price of £500), *Re Leeds & Hanley Theatre of Varieties, Ltd* , [1902] 2 Ch 809, C A (concealment of the fact that the ostensible vendor was trustee for the promoting company, who were the real vendors, and of the fact that this person had previously acquired the property, as trustee for such promoting company, at a much less price than that which the promoting company agreed to pay), *Re Darby, Ex p Brougham*, [1911] 1 K B 95 (concealment of profits made by promoters on re sale to the company, and of identity of promoters)

(d) "It is in my opinion," says Lord CAIRNS, L C, at p 1236 of *Erlanger* v *New Sombrero Phosphate Co* (1878), 3 App Cas 1218, H L , "incumbent upon the promoters to take care that in forming the company they provide it with an executive, that is to say, with a board of directors, who   shall be competent and impartial judges as to whether the purchase ought or ought not to be made I do not say that the owner of property may not promote and form a joint stock company, and then sell his own property to it, but I do say that, if he does, he is bound to take care that he sells it to the company through the medium of a board of directors who can and do exercise an independent and intelligent judgment on the transaction "

the transaction impeached, it has been held to its bargain (e), which shows that the vice is not in the thing itself, but in its secrecy (f). It is only when the promoter has failed to establish disclosure of this class of fact that the purchase is invalidated (g). No doubt, it is the interest of the promoter, and (in the highly metaphorical sense that every man owes a duty to himself to take care of his own interest) his duty also, to provide against any opportunity or suspicion of corruption in the relations between the directors and himself (h). He is deeply concerned in so doing, for the following, if for no other, reason: unless the board is impartial and independent, it will be extremely difficult for him to establish either disclosure by himself to the company, or the company's knowledge aliundė, of other material facts which he is bound to communicate; since disclosure to, or the knowledge of, an executive whom he has seduced beforehand, is not in law disclosure to, or the knowledge of, the company (i), as it is where the executive is independent; and to prove that the general body of shareholders, as distinct from the directors, was cognizant of the facts alleged to have been undisclosed, is

(e) This happened in *Lagunas Nitrate Co* v *Lagunas Syndicate*, [1899] 2 Ch 392, C A (*per* LINDLEY, M.R , at pp. 425, 426, who, in this point, distinguishes *Erlanger* v *New Sombrero Phosphate Co* , sup , where the company was told nothing of the dependence of the board) , also in *Att -Gen for the Dominion of Canada* v *Standard Trust Company of New York*, *sup* (where the disclosure was made to the four persons who alone constituted the company at the time pp 504, 505).

(f) Cp the cases cited in note (x) to § 316, *ante*

(g) In *Lagunas Nitrate Co* v *Lagunas Syndicate, sup* , though the company was informed that the board was not independent, and, so far, the promoter was held not liable—see note (e), *sup.*—it was not told of other facts material to be disclosed, and, as to these, the promoting syndicate vainly relied upon disclosure to the seven directors of the company who, so far from representing the company for this purpose, had, in the interests of the promoters, studiously concealed these facts from it on this ground, but for the subsequent dealing with the property by the company which precluded it from obtaining relief, the syndicate would have been held liable Other instances of the promoter's accountability for concealment of the dependence of the directors upon himself are *Hichens* v *Congreve* (1831), 4 Sim 420, where the vendor promoters actually appointed themselves to be the directors , *York and North Midland Railway Co* v *Hudson* (1853), 16 Beav 485, where the defendant, the notorious "railway king," suppressed the fact that he, being chairman of the board of directors, as well as vendor promoter, had used a large proportion of his shares in corrupting his fellow-directors , *Maxwell* v *Port Tennant Patent Steam Fuel and Coal Co* (1857), 24 Beav. 495 (where "the projectors" had made a clandestine arrangement for the corruption of the directors, the solicitor, and the secretary of the company by gifts of fully paid shares, and—*per* ROMILLY, M R , at p 497—"as this was not communicated to the shareholders, they cannot be bound by the contract," i e the contract of sale for the specific performance of which the "projector" was suing the company At p. 498, ROMILLY, M R , points out the natural result of these secret proceedings, viz that the directors took no "pains to examine into the value of the mine before they agreed to pay this sum for its purchase") , *Re Madrid Bank, Ex p Williams* (1866), L R 2 Eq 216, where the promoters had similarly seduced the board of directors , *Erlanger* v *New Sombrero Phosphate Co* (1878), 3 App Cas 1218, H L , where the vendor promoter had concealed from those directors who were independent of him the fact that the others were in his pay and power As to the position of the directors who are so "qualified" or otherwise bribed by the promoter, see § 340, *post*

(h) It was put somewhat in this way by Lord O'HAGAN, at p 1256 of *Erlanger* v *New Sombrero Phosphate Co* , *sup* "the promoters who so forgot their duty to the company they formed as to give it a directorate without independence *must take the consequences*" And so Lord PENZANCE, at p 1229 "they were . . bound .. , *if they wished to make a valid contract of sale to the company,* to nominate independent directors "

(i) Per LINDLEY, M R , at p 431 of *Lagunas Nitrate Co* v *Lagunas Syndicate, sup* , and *per* SARGANT, J , at p 342 of *Omnium Electric Palaces, Ltd* v *Baines*, [1914] 1 Ch 332, C A

by no means easy, and, when there is a possibility of future allotments and allottees, well-nigh impossible (*j*).

334. Such topics as the burden of proof incumbent on the respective parties, the forms of relief and remedy available to the company, questions of law and fact, and the persons who are respectively entitled, and liable, in any proceedings for the purpose of asserting the invalidity of transactions between promoter and company, are reserved for future discussion in the severally appropriate places (*k*).

Sub-s (3)   *Principal and Agent.*

335. The relation of principal and agent is undoubtedly a fiduciary one, and as such involves a duty on the part of the agent to impart to his principal, on the occasion of any transaction during the existence of the agency, all such matters within his actual or presumptive knowledge as are material to be disclosed, whether the transaction be between the agent and his principal, or between the agent and a third person. The species of this relation are manifold, varying in range from what is called "universal agency," which though conceivable in theory is almost unheard of in practice (*l*), to a mere mandate to perform a single act, such as to sign a document, or deliver a message. Thus, in some cases, the agent is a general business agent, or "homme d'affaires", in others, he is agent in a particular kind of business, or in a particular market, in others, again, he is appointed agent in relation to a particular property of the principal, whether for sale or purchase (*m*); or he may be a professional agent (*n*)   But, however differing from one another in the nature and extent of the functions which they respectively involve, these types of agency, including the various forms of sub-agency (*o*), of partnership, which is mutual agency (*p*), and of company-directorship, which, whatever else it may be, imports at least mercantile

(*j*) See § 393, *post*, on this important question of subsequent shareholders
(*k*) See Sub ss (3)–(7), respectively, *post*
(*l*) Probably no power of attorney ever known has made the attorney the *alter ego* of the grantor of the power for *all* purposes whatever, without limit as to space, time, subject-matter, or otherwise
(*m*) Such an agent is frequently called, though perhaps inexactly, "a trustee for sale," or "a trustee for purchase"   Having regard to this double designation, some of the cases included in this Sub section as examples of agency for sale, or for purchase, are, together with other cases of trusteeship "by metaphor," cited in Sub s (1), *ante*, though, on strict principle, it may be doubted whether they ought to have been referred to anywhere but in the present place
(*n*) Such as a solicitor, in so far as he exercises the functions of a confidential agent But a solicitor has other and further duties of disclosure and good faith, arising from his position of "influence" and ascendancy over the client   These are the subject of Ch V, Sect 2, Sub-s (2), *post*, where the cases which illustrate the solicitor's duty arising from "influence" are collected, though, inasmuch as the relief given to the client is based in some of these authorities on both aspects of the relation, a double citation of them in both places is inevitable.
(*o*) See *De Bussche* v *Alt* (1878), 8 C D 286, C A , *Powell & Thomas* v. *Evans, Jones & Co*, [1905] 1 K B 11, C. A
(*p*) *Erlanger* v *New Sombrero Phosphate Co* , *sup* (per Lord HATHERLEY, at p 1244 " as regards partners, there is no doubt that every partner is bound to exercise *uberrima fides* with regard to any transactions in which the partners may be engaged in common "); *Dean* v *MacDowell* (1878), 8 C D 369, C A (*per* JAMES, L J , at p 350 "it is quite

agency (q), possess the one common feature and foundation of " confidence," and, as such, are all alike subject to the general duties of disclosure which attach to this kind of relationship, and which it is now proposed to examine.

336. In the first place, as in the case of the relation of trustee and *cestui que trust* (r), an agent who is minded to buy from, or sell to, or otherwise deal with, his principal must do so openly and directly : he must not disguise his identity, or the character in which he is acting, under cover of a trustee, nominee, or associate, or conceal the true nature of the transaction by any device amounting to the assumption of an alias Such non-disclosure is of itself sufficient to vitiate the transaction, however fair it may have been in all other respects ; as has been invariably held in cases of both private

---

clear that in partnership matters there must be the utmost good faith, and there is to that extent a fiduciary relation between the partners "), *Cassels v. Stewart* (1881), 6 App Cas 64, H L. (per Lord BLACKBURN, at p 79   " a partner being an agent, *for I think it is because he is an agent that the fiduciary character arises*, if he, as an agent, makes a profit out of the concerns of his principal, and as acting for him, he must communicate it to his principal ,   *a partner is an agent, and the principle applying to him is a branch of that general rule which applies to agents* "), *Helmore v. Smith* (1887), 35 C. D 436 (per BACON, V. C , at p 414. "if fiduciary relation means anything, I cannot conceive a stronger case of fiduciary relation than that which exists between partners. Their mutual confidence is the life blood of the concern   *It is because they trust one another that they are partners in the first instance , it is because they continue to trust one a. other that the business goes on* ") A large number of the cases cited in the notes to this Sub section are, as will be seen, partnership cases   The duty of partners to one another during the subsistence of the partnership is of course a different duty of disclosure (though both are based on confidence, as is forcibly pointed out by BACON, V C , in the last of the above citations) to that which lies upon one who, being the owner of a business, is in treaty with another for the purpose of admitting him to partnership therein, or who, being the active partner in a firm, proposes to sell his share to his dormant partner, or to buy such dormant partner's share This latter duty belongs to another class altogether, and is discussed in Ch III, Sect 2, Sub s. (6), *ante*

(q) ROMILLY, M R , at p 491 of *York & North Midland Railway Co v Hudson* (1853), 16 Beav 485, expresses the opinion that directorship is " an office of trust," but the reason which he gives for so thinking, viz that " the directors are persons selected to manage the affairs of the company for the benefit of the shareholders," shows that he did not consider directors to be solely or for all purposes trustees   Cp the language used by him at p 497 of *Maxwell v Port Tennant Steam Fuel and Coal Co* (1857), 24 Beav. 495 (" the directors are persons who are entrusted to manage the affairs, and carry into effect the contracts, of a company for the shareholders who place implicit reliance upon them ")   The correct description of their dual character as, on the one hand, " trustees of the company's money and property," and, on the other, " agents in the transactions which they enter into on behalf of the company," is given by Lord SELBORNE, L C , at p 152 of *Great Eastern Railway Co v Turner* (1872), 8 Ch App 149   So JESSEL, M R , at pp 451, 452 of *Re Forest of Dean Coal Mining Co* (1878), 10 C D 450, observes that " directors have sometimes been called trustees, or commercial trustees, and sometimes they have been called managing partners, it does not matter much what you call them so long as you understand what their true position is, which is that they are really commercial men managing a trading concern for the benefit of themselves and all the other shareholders in it," adding (at p 453), " they are no doubt trustees of assets which have come into their hands, or which are under their control, but they are not trustees of a debt due to the company,   they are only the managing partners "   To the same effect, LINDLEY, L J , at p 631 of *Re Lands Allotment Co* , [1894] 1 Ch 616, C A (" directors are not, properly speaking, trustees," but, though this is so, " they have always been considered trustees of money which comes to their hands or is actually under their control "), and SWINFEN EADY, J , at p 425 of *Percival v Wright*, [1902] 2 Ch 421   It is only in their character as " agents," or " managing partners," that directors are considered in the present Sub section   Many illustrations of their duty of disclosure to the company, as such agents, are contained in the notes following   As to their statutory obligations of disclosure, see Ch VI, *post*

(r) See § 321, *ante*

bargains (s), and (where the facilities for concealment are of course much greater) market dealings (t). Further, where the agent or partner, though not within the class just mentioned, is connected in any way with any person, firm, or company doing business generally, or engaged in any particular transaction, with his principal or partner, and has a pecuniary interest of any sort, directly or indirectly, in that business, or transaction, he must divulge the fact that he is so connected or interested (u) ; but this is not

(s) As in *Crowe* v. *Ballard* (1790), 1 Ves Jr. 215 (agent to sell legacy secretly buys); *Benson* v. *Heathorn* (1842), 1 Y. & C. 326 (sale of a vessel "as from a stranger"); *Charter* v *Trevelyan* (1844), 11 Cl & Fin 714 (where a steward and agent to sell leasehold property concealed the fact that the ostensible purchaser was his trustee); *Murphy* v. *O'Shea* (1845), 2 Jo. & Lat. 422 , 69 R. R. 337 (agent clandestinely purchases through a nominee *per* SUGDEN, L C. (Ir.), at p. 429 "the moment it appears, in a transaction between principal and agent, that there has been any underhand dealing by the agent— *that he has made use of another person's name as a purchaser, instead of his own—however fair the transaction may be in other respects*, from that moment it has no validity in this Court "), *Lewis* v. *Hillman* (1852), 3 H. L C 607 (*per* Lord ST. LEONARDS, L.C., at p 630, where solicitors and agents for sale of reversionary interests sold them to a person who was a mere trustee for themselves), *Great Luxembourg Railway Co.* v. *Magnay* (1858), 25 Beav 586 (agent for company to purchase a concession conceals the fact that he, through a nominee, is the real owner and vendor), *Kimber* v *Barber* (1872), 8 Ch App 56 (agent to buy shares clandestinely sells his own), *Williams* v. *Scott*, [1900] A C. 499, P C (agent or trustee for sale of land becomes the real purchaser, disguising the truth of the transaction by a pretended sale to, and subsequent purchase from, an interposed third party)

(t) As in *Rothschild* v. *Brookman* (1831), 5 Bligh (N s) 165 (bankers employed to sell French rentes, and buy Prussian bonds, become the clandestine purchasers from, and vendors to, their principal of such rentes and bonds respectively), *Gillett* v *Peppercorne* (1840), 3 Beav 78 (stockbroker employed to purchase shares in the market buys of one who is merely a trustee for himself), *Wilson* v *Short* (1847), 6 Hare 366 (brokers pretend to make speculative purchases of iron in the market for their principal from a third person, suppressing the fact that there was no such third person, or principal vendor, and that they were therefore the real vendors), *Robinson* v. *Mollett* (1875), L. R 7 H L 802 (a similar dealing by brokers in the tallow market), *Oelkers* v *Ellis*, [1914] 2 K B 139 (stockbroker selling his own shares to his principal)

(u) The following are illustrations *Barker* v. *Harrison* (1846), 2 Coll 546 (concealment by agent, buying from his principal, of a bargain for resale at a profit to a third person), *Bentley* v *Craven* (1853), 18 Beav 75, where a partner in a sugar refining firm concealed the fact, not that he carried on a sugar dealer's business of his own (for this the other partners had expressly contracted to sanction), but that he had sold in that business his own sugar to the firm in which he was a partner, and by whom he was deputed to make the necessary purchases of sugar on their account, *Aberdeen Railway Co* v *Blakie Bros* (1854), 1 Macq H L 461 (where a director of the railway company concealed his interest, as managing partner, in a firm of ironfounders who sold iron chairs to the company), *Hesse* v. *Briant* (1856), 6 De G M & G 623 (where a solicitor and agent to sell property failed to disclose to his client and principal that the person to whom he sold it was another client of his), *Tyrrell* v *Bank of London* (1862), 10 H L C 26, as to which case see note (h) to § 339, *post*, *Salomons* v *Pender* (1865), 3 H & C. 639 (where a surveyor, employed to sell land, concealed from his principals the fact that the persons to whom he sold it were the promoters of a company in which he was interested as a shareholder, and afterwards as a director also), *McPherson* v *Watt* (1877), 3 App Cas 254, H L. (where an advocate in Scotland, though not the law agent of the party complaining, was employed by him as agent to sell four houses, and before selling them, as he did, to his brother, had made a clandestine bargain with him to take two of the houses off his hands at the price given, which two houses he resold at a profit to himself), *King, Hall, & Benson* v *Howell* (1910), 27 T L R 114, C A (which was a case of stockbrokers concealing from their principal the fact that the authorized clerk of the jobbers with whom they did their principal's business was, to their knowledge, the person employed by that principal as his agent to speculate for him on the Stock Exchange), *Re Republic of Bolivia Exploration Syndicate*, [1914] 1 Ch 139 (non disclosure to company that a solicitor-director was receiving profit costs), *Transvaal Lands Co* v. *New Belgium* (*Transvaal*) *Land and Development Co*, [1914] 2 Ch 489, C. A (a similar case to *Aberdeen Railway Co.* v. *Blakie Bros*, *sup.*)

all that is required of him . it is not enough merely to reveal the bare fact of his interest, unless he at the same time declares fully and plainly the precise nature and extent of that interest. Failure to perform the latter obligation, though he may have discharged the former, entitles his principal or partner to relief (v).

337. Secondly, on the assumption that the agent, without resorting to any manœuvre of the above-mentioned description, and without, therefore, having failed in any duty of disclosure up to that point, enters openly into a transaction with his principal—which in itself is not prohibited by the law (w),—he thereupon takes upon himself the whole burden of establishing, if and when called in question, the complete propriety, fairness, and righteousness of that transaction, and of his own conduct in bringing it about, and otherwise in relation to it ; and, as in the case of a trustee dealing openly with his *cestui que trust* (x), unless he sustains this burden, he cannot sustain the transaction either (y).

338. Frank and full communication of all knowledge which the principal is entitled to have, and which he legitimately relies upon his agent to impart,

(v) See *Dunne* v. *English* (1872), L R 18 Eq 524 (a partnership case, where one of the partners instructed to sell the firm's mine in England, revealed to the other partners the fact that he was interested in the purchase, but not " all the material facts " as to the nature and extent of that interest per JESSEL, M R , at pp 533, 535, 536), *Imperial Mercantile Credit Association* v *Coleman* (1873), L R. 6 H L. 189 (a like imperfect disclosure by a director of a company the observations of Lord CAIRNS at p. 205, cited in note (p) to § 21, *ante*, are of great weight on this question) ; *Costa Rica Railway Co* v. *Forwood*, [1901] 1 Ch 746, C A (another director's case see the views expressed by VAUGHAN WILLIAMS, L.J , at p 761, and STIRLING, L.J., at p 766 In this case, however, the director was protected by an express term in the articles of association)

(w) *Murphy* v *O'Shea* (1845), 2 Jo & Lat. 422 , 69 R R. 337, *per* Lord ST LEONARDS, then SUGDEN, L C (Ir), at p 425 (" the rule of the Court does not prevent an agent from purchasing from his principal, but only requires that he shall deal with him at arm's length, and after a full disclosure of all that he knows with respect to the property ") ; *Dunne* v *English* (1872), L R 18 Eq 524, where, at p 534, JESSEL, M R , cites the above proposition, and applies it to a case of partnership, adding that Lord ST LEONARDS' phrase, " all that he knows " &c , " of course means everything material which he knows " So, as to solicitor and client, Lord ELDON, L C , at p 276 *Gibson* v. *Jeyes, inf* · " it has been truly said, an attorney is not incapable of contracting with his client "

(x) See § 322, *ante*

(y) For statements of the general rule, and illustrations of failure on the part of the agent to satisfy its requirements, see *Gibson* v *Jeyes* (1801), 6 Ves 266 (*per* Lord ELDON, L C , who, at pp 278–280, expresses his conclusion that the attorney and agent in that case, purchasing an annuity from his client and principal, I ad failed to discharge the burden of showing that he had made " a reasonable use of the confidence " reposed in him (p 278) see the citations from the judgment in note (m) to § 322, and note (r) to § 324, *ante*), *Watt* v. *Grove* (1805), 2 Sch & Lefr 491 , *Harris* v *Tremenheere* (1808), 15 Ves 34 (where a steward, attorney, and agent failed to establish all that was required to sustain a purchase by him from his client, master, and employer, as to one of the leases there in question *per* Lord ELDON, L C., at pp. 42–44, the general nature of the burden incumbent on such an agent being stated at p 42 in a passage cited in note (b), *inf*), *Dunbar* v *Tredennick* (1813), 2 Ball & B 304 (*per* Lord MANNERS, L C (Ir), at pp 314–316 land and law agent fails to sustain the propriety of the purchase) , *Perens* v *Johnson* (1857), 3 Sm & G 419 (a case of solvent partners purchasing the interest of their insolvent partner, in which STUART, V -C , said, at p 425, that " the purchase cannot stand if there appear the slightest speck of unfairness in their "—the purchasing partners'—" conduct in regard to the sale," and he found many such " specks ") , *Barnard* v. *Hunter* (1856), 2 Jur (N s) 1213 , 106 R R 1014 (where a solicitor, employed to sell property for his client, omitted to advise and protect him sufficiently or properly, and, therefore, could not sustain the transaction *per* Lord CRANWORTH, L.C., at p. 1215, affirming STUART, V -C see note (b), *inf*) is the first, and most obvious, element in the requisite proof that the agent has not abused, but has made a fair use of, the confidence reposed in him. Indeed, it may be said to comprehend all the particular obligations which he assumes when dealing with his principal, if knowledge be understood in the double sense already indicated during the discussion of the relation of trustee and *cestui que trust* For the agent is bound to inform and instruct the mind of his principal, no less than the trustee is bound to inform and instruct the mind of his *cestui que trust*, in two respects On the one hand, he must put his principal in possession of all the facts, which means all the material facts (*z*), within his own knowledge, that is to say, all circumstances relating to the value of the property which is the subject of the transaction (*a*); and, secondly, he must impart to him all such knowledge, in the sense of power, capacity, skill, and judgment, as he himself possesses, and as he would bring to bear on the negotiation if he were the principal dealing with a stranger. he must fully and freely advise against himself (*b*). The latter is, no doubt, a task of peculiar difficulty in the accomplishment, and it is even more difficult to prove that accomplishment when the party is called upon to do so, perhaps long after the event. But this is no hardship whatever on the agent, being merely a condition of obtaining from the law what is, after all, in the nature of an indulgence

339. Lastly, in the course of his agency, the agent must not receive or

(*z*) See note (*w*), *sup*)
(*a*) See *Fox* v. *Mackreth*, and *Ex p James*, as cited in note (*o*) to § 323, *ante*, in both of which, as will be seen on reference to those citations, the non disclosure of valuations and reports as to, or facts bearing upon, the value of the property was held fatal to the purchasing agent and trustee) And see further *Lowther* v *Lord Lowther* (1806), 13 Ves 95, as abstracted in note (*c*) to § 318, *ante*, *Selsey* (*Lord*) v. *Rhoades* (1827), 1 Bligh (N S) 1 (*per* Lord ELDON, L C, at p 8, differing on this point from LEACH, V C. a case where a steward and solicitor did not divulge fully all facts which would tend to demonstrate the value of the property, though he escaped on the ground of affirmation by the client and principal), *Molony* v *Kernan* (1842) 2 Dr & Warr 37, 59 R R 635 (*per* SUGDEN, L C (Ir), at p. 40), *Carter* v *Palmer* (1842), 8 Cl. & Fin 657 (suppression of valuable information acquired in character of general manager *per* Lord COTTENHAM, L C, at pp 703–705), *Charter* v *Trevelyan* (1844), 11 Cl. & Fin. 714 (non disclosure of a valuation of the property in two parts which had been procured by the purchasing steward and agent, besides the concealment of his identity, as to which see note (*s*) to § 336, *ante* *per* Lord LYNDHURST, L C., at p 732, and Lord CAMPBELL at p 740), *Barker* v *Harrison* (1846), 2 Coll 546 (offers to purchase property, and arrangements for resale, not disclosed), *Patten* v *Hamilton*, [1911] 1 Ir R 40 (non-disclosure by agent of the mode in which he had been dealing with certain moneys see pp 57, 60)
(*b*) *Gibson* v *Jeyes* (1801), 6 Ves 266 (*per* Lord ELDON, L C, at pp 271, 278–280 see the citation in note (*r*) to § 324, *ante*), *Harris* v *Tremenheere* (1808), 15 Ves 34 (*per* Lord ELDON, L C, at p 42 "the defendant must be prepared to show that he made as good a bargain for his employer, as against himself as a provident, well-managing, honourable steward, acting most adversely, in a fair sense, would"), *Hesse* v *Briant* (1856), 6 De G M. & G 623 (*per* Lord CRANWORTH, L C, at p 628, adopting Lord ELDON's rule), *Barnard* v *Hunter* (1856), 2 Jur N S 1213 (*per* Lord CRANWORTH, L C, again, at p 1215 "when persons stand in confidential relations to one another, if the person whose duty it is to protect takes upon himself to deal with the person whose interest he has to protect, the onus is upon him to show that every sort of due caution was given to that person, and that he had the means, independently of his natural protection, of dealing at arm's length") In all the above cases, the agent failed to show that he had given to his principal the full benefit of all the skilled knowledge and advice which he was in a position to impart, or that his principal had obtained the equivalent elsewhere, *Lloyd* v *Attwood* (1859), 3 De G & J 614 (*per* TURNER, L.J, at p 649).

stipulate for any private advantage or profit out of any business which on behalf of his principal he may transact with a third person, without first disclosing to that principal the exact nature and particulars of the advantage or profit which it is intended or proposed that he shall receive. Here, again, the breach of duty consists not in the mere fact of accepting the benefit, or the promise of it, but in hiding the fact from the principal (c). The distinction is between a revealed and permitted gift, and a clandestine bribe · what in the one case is an increment to his remuneration honestly earned with the approbation, and, perhaps, for the benefit, or in relief, of the principal, is, in the other, the wages of betrayal, or at least an act calculated, if not intended, to seduce the agent from his allegiance, to the detriment of the principal, and to the secret advantage both of the agent and the contractor. Accordingly, in all cases where an agent, having received, or contracted to receive, from a third person with whom he is dealing on behalf of his principal any advantage or profit, whether money or money's worth, fails to sustain the burden which lies upon him of proving that, before the receipt, he had divulged all the circumstances, or that the principal had actual or presumptive knowledge of them, that agent is liable to account to his principal for the amount or value of what he has so received, and further the third person is liable to the principal in damages or otherwise for the corruption of the agent, besides being disabled from enforcing his contract (d). This has been invariably so held, in whatever form the clandestine advantage was received or promised,—whether in the more gross and obvious form of lump-sum bribes, or bonuses, in money (e), commissions, brokerages,

(c) See the cases cited in note (x) to § 316, ante, the partnership cases cited in the notes to § 341, post, and the following *Benson* v *Heathorn* (1842), 1 Y. & C. 326 (*per* SHADWELL, V C, at p 343 · "if in the present case, Mr Heathorn had openly and directly brought forward the matter before the body of shareholders generally, I consider it possible, if not probable, that he ... would now have been entitled to retain all the sums in question paid for commission. He has not elected to take that open and straightforward course; he has chosen that the matter should be undisclosed, and he must abide the inevitable result "), *Atwool* v *Merryweather* (1867), L R 5 Eq 464 n (*per* WOOD, V C, at p 467 n. "I do not in the least say that where persons with their eyes open know that the agent who secures them the bargain is going to take money for it, that would not be all right enough ")

(d) See Sect, 5, Sub ss (1), (2), *post*

(e) See *Fawcett* v *Whitehouse* (1829), 1 Russ & M 132 (where a partner, instructed to negotiate the terms of a lease, secretly stipulated for, and secretly received, "a conditional gift," as Lord LYNDHURST, L C, called it, of £12,000 from the parties with whom he treated), *Beck* v *Kantorowicz* (1857), 3 K & J 230 (where one of five partners or associates, employed to purchase a concession, stipulated for a bonus or bribe from the vendors to himself in the event of the five persons purchasing at a certain figure *per* WOOD, V -C, at pp 250, 251), *Morison* v *Thompson* (1874), L R 9 Q B 480 (where an agent to purchase a certain vessel, having ascertained that the owner had instructed his broker to sell it for not less than £8500, with liberty to him to keep any excess for himself, secretly arranged with this broker that he (the broker) should offer the vessel for £9250, and out of the £750 which he would thus become entitled to should pay him (the agent) £225), *Metropolitan Bank* v *Heiron* (1880), 5 Ex. D 319, C A (where a director received a bribe of £250 from a debtor to the bank to use his influence with the bank to obtain favourable terms for such debtor, but, by reason of the statute of limitations, and that alone, he escaped), *Andrews* v *Ramsay & Co*, [1903] 2 K B 635 (clandestine receipt by estate agents of a sum or bribe, under the name of "commission," from the purchaser whom they were instructed to procure), *Bartram & Sons* v *Lloyd* (1904), 90 L T 357, C A (the like, in the case of an agent to purchase a steamer) and like percentages on the value of business done between the third person and the principal (f), rebates and discounts (g), participation in the third person's profits on his contract with the principal (h); or in other less direct and more subtle shapes, as, for instance, where a member of a firm in course of dissolution secretly obtained for his own benefit, a renewal of the lease of the partnership premises (i); or where two of three partners in the business of common carriers entered into a contract on their own behalf, to the exclusion of the third, to carry bullion for the Mint on certain roads other than that which was the subject of the existing agreement between the three partners and the Mint, the second agreement being regarded as connected with, and a continuation of, the first (j); or where a chairman of the board of directors of a railway company made clandestine sales for his own profit of a large

(f) As in *Benson* v *Heathorn* (1842), 1 Y & C. 326, *Smith* v *Sorby* (1875), 3 Q B. D. 552 n , *Harrington* v *Victoria Graving Dock Co.* (1878), 3 Q B D 549, *Boston Deep Sea Fishing & Ice Co* v *Ansell* (1888), 39 C D 339, C. A., *Lister & Co* v *Stubbs* (1890), 45 C D 1, C. A , *Williamson* v. *Hine Bros* , [1891] 1 Ch 390; *Salford Cor. poration* v *Lever*, [1891] 1 Q B 168, C A , *Grant* v *Gold Exploration & Development Syndicate*, [1900] 1 Q B 233, C A , *Hovenden & Sons* v *Millhoff* (1900), 83 L T 41, C A , *Powell & Thomas* v *Evans, Jones & Co* , [1905] 1 K B. 11, C. A.; *Swale* v *Ipswich Tannery, Ltd* (1906), 11 Comm Cas 88.

(g) As in *Benson* v *Heathorn*, *sup* (where SHADWELL, V.-C , at p 344, observes that the secret receipt of discounts from tradesmen is morally worse than the receipt of secret commissions), *Turnbull* v *Garden* (1869), 20 L T 218 (discounts allowed to the agent by tradesmen), *Spain (Queen of)* v. *Parr* (1870), 39 L J (CH) 73 (discounts allowed by insurance companies to the agent, on punctual payment of premiums, for introducing the business), *Hippisley* v *Knee Bros* , [1905] 1 K B 1, Div Ct (rebates allowed to auctioneers by printers off printing charges, and by newspaper proprietors off advertising charges); *Green (E)* & *Son, Ltd* v *Tugham & Co* (1913), 30 T L R. 64 (rebates, &c , to insurance brokers)

(h) As in *Tyrrell* v *Bank of London* (1862), 10 H L C 26, where a solicitor for the bank, instructed by them to purchase certain premises in the City of London from one Read, the bank's secretary, suppressed the fact that, before the purchase was effected, he had entered into an agreement with Read to share with him the profits he was to make on his sale to the bank, and had, in fact, become joint owner with him of (amongst other properties) the premises in question, *Williams* v *Stevens* (1866), L R 1 P C 352, where the appellant, a creditor of a bankrupt in the Island of Jersey, was desirous of exercising her right (according to the law of Jersey) of taking over the estate, but, being herself insolvent, could only do so by appointing a surrogate to take it over She appointed one Snell. The respondent was her " procureur generale et spécial," and, as such, acted for her in the transaction He made a secret bargain with Snell to divide with him the estate so to be acquired, and afterwards sold his own moiety to him for £578, for which sum he was accordingly held accountable to the appellant, *Gordon* v *Holland* (1913), 82 L J (P C) 81 (secret profit on sale of property of partnership)

(i) *Featherstonehaugh* v *Fenwick* (1810), 17 Ves 298 (per Lord ELDON, L C , at p 310 " it is clear that one partner cannot treat *privately, and behind the backs of his copartners* for a lease of the premises where the joint trade is carried on, for his own individual benefit," and at p 312 " this *clandestine conduct* was very unfair towards the plaintiff *The defendant ought first to have given him notice* ")

(j) *Russell* v *Austwick* (1826), 1 Sim 52 Here the excluded partner, from whom the second agreement was concealed, sued the two non disclosing partners, Austwick and Maddeford, who immediately afterwards had a dispute between themselves, involving another point in the law of disclosure see *Maddeford* v *Austwick*, cited in note (d) to § 112, *ante* The original contract between the firm and the Mint was to carry coin from London to Falmouth it was contended for Austwick and Maddeford that they were under no obligation to divulge to the plaintiff the second agreement, because it was only for the carriage of silver on " provincial roads," with which the first contract had nothing to do, but, at p 62, LEACH, V -C , expresses the view that " the second agreement was entered into by the officers of the Mint as connected with, and in continuation of *the first* agreement, and in confidence of the responsibility of the parties to the first agreement "

number of shares which he ostensibly held for the purpose of buying off the opposition of landowners, and for " secret service " (k) ; or where directors of a company, having entered into a contract, pursuant to a resolution of the company, to sell to a certain person at a specified price all such shares as should not be taken up by the existing shareholders, and having been afterwards requested by the person in question to release him from his bargain, instead of either accepting or declining this proposal, secretly bought the shares back from him at the same price, and re-sold them at a profit, which they put into their own pockets (l) ; or where, there being an agreement between two telegraph companies that company B should construct and lay various submarine cables for company A at a price payable, as to part, on the receipt of the order, and, as to the residue, on the progress and final certificates of company A's engineer, company B, without the knowledge of company A., immediately afterwards entered into a sub-contract with this engineer to construct one of the cables which was the subject of their contract with company A at a price payable by instalments at the very dates on which company A was to pay instalments to them under the main contract, and on the certificate of the same engineer (m) ; or where, a shipowner having placed a vessel in the hands of certain agents for sale in Japan, and these agents having employed a sub-agent for that purpose, the sub-agent bought the vessel from the agents at the price named, and then re-sold it at a profit to a third person, pursuant to a secret agreement made by him with that third person *before* he bought from the agents (n) , or where a merchant's clerk, employed in handling the funds, securities, and investments of his employers, secretly gambled in differences on the Stock Exchange on an enormous scale (o) , or where a

(k) *York & North Midland Railway Co* v *Hudson* (1853), 6 Beav, 485

(l) *Parker* v *McKenna* (1874), 10 Ch App 96 This was an ingenious, but wholly unsuccessful, attempt to accomplish indirectly what the directors knew they could not do directly "If Stock"—who was the person who made the bargain with the directors of which, *before the time for performance had arrived*, he was anxious to be relieved—'had bought these shares and paid for them, and become the absolute owner of them, the directors were as free as any person in the market to go to Stock, and become the purchasers from him of these shares. The agency in that case would have been over, and there would no longer have been any conflict between interest and duty Here the agency had not been terminated" (Lord CAIRNS, L C , at p 118) If the directors had assented to Stock's request, the shares would still have been the company's to dispose of to another purchaser if they had declined to do so, the company would still have had Stock's liability In either case, there would have been no cause for complaint on the company's part But the course adopted was neither more nor less than "a profit made by an agent, *without the knowledge of his principal, in the course and execution of his agency*" (Lord CAIRNS, L C., ibid)

(m) *Panama and South Pacific Telegraph Co* v *India Rubber, Gutta Percha, and Telegraph Co* (1875), 10 Ch App 515

(n) *De Bussche* v *Alt* (1878), 8 C D 286, C A Here the sub agent had told his principal (through the agents) that he was to be the purchaser of the vessel at the price named, $90,000, but he had not told him, or his agents, of the secret agreement to resell it to a Japanese prince for $160,000 Having disclosed the former fact, he was quite free to buy from the agents, and then contract to sell at a profit, but he was not at liberty, *whilst he was still "in the course and execution of his agency,"* as Lord CAIRNS, L C , said in *Parker* v *McKenna, sup* , to enter into such an arrangement without the knowledge of the principal

(o) *Pearce* v *Foster* (1886), 17 Q B D 536, C A

person who held the fiduciary position of vice-chairman of a college, and was also its solicitor, made "secret profits" in the latter character (p), or where stockbrokers, being entitled to close their client's account, and to sell on the market shares of a like amount to those previously open with him, clandestinely arranged with the jobber to whom they sold the shares, *as part of the same transaction*, that they would buy them back, the result of which, according to the custom of the Stock Exchange, was that they would obtain an abatement from the price payable if it were an original purchase (q), or where one of two co-adventurers (who had made an improvident bargain for the supply of coal to the Austrian navy, and were afterwards permitted to reduce their loss by supplying cheaper coal), secretly provided the cheaper coal out of stocks supplied to his own coal depôt (qq), or where directors, without the knowledge of the company, received "qualification" shares or money, or other material favours, from the promoter.

340. The last-mentioned class of case is one which, since the introduction of the Companies Acts, has constantly occupied the attention of the courts As has already been stated (r), the promoter who has by such devices corrupted the executive of the company promoted by him is beyond doubt liable to the company, if he suppresses the fact that the directors are thus rendered dependent upon himself It is no less clearly established that the directors, as agents and officers of the company, are also liable for the concealment of this fact (s). It is quite immaterial what form the transaction assumes, or by what particular device "the watch-dog" is tempted "to take a sop from a possible wolf" (t): the bribe may be given for the express purpose of enabling the promoter's impecunious nominee to qualify as a director, where the articles of association require, as such qualification, the holding by him of so many shares in his own right, and in that case the gift may be of the shares themselves (u), or of the money necessary to acquire them (v). Or it may be a case of a naked present of shares (w) or debentures (x), without

(p) *Bray* v *Ford*, [1896] A C 44, H L

(q) *Erskine, Oxenford & Co* v *Sachs*, [1901] 2 K B 504, C A. If the two transactions had been independent of one another, there would have been no liability for non disclosure: but, since they were not so, the abatement represented a profit made in the course and execution of the agency, and therefore should have been disclosed (per A L SMITH, M R, at pp 511, 512, VAUGHAN WILLIAMS, L J, at pp 512, 513, STIRLING, L.J, at pp 516–518)

(qq) *Kuhlicz* v *Lambert Bros*, *Ltd* (1913), 108 L T 565

(r) See § 333, *ante*

(s) As to the form and measure of their liability, see §§ 379, 380, *post* As to their statutory liability, see §§ 566–572, *post*

(t) Per BOWEN, L.J, at p 341 of *Re North Australian Territory Co*, *Archer's Case*, [1892] 1 Ch 322, C A

(u) As in *Re Canadian Oil Works Corporation*, *Hay's Case* (1875), 10 Ch App 593, *Re Carriage Co operative Supply Association* (1884), 27 C D 322, *Re North Australian Terri ry Co*, *Archer's Case, sup* , *Re London & South Western Canal, Ltd* , [1911] 1 Ch 346

(v) As in *Re Englefield Colliery Co* (1878), 8 C D 388, C A

(w) As in *Maxwell* v *Port Tennant Patent Steam Fuel and Coal Co* (1857), 24 Beav 495 , *Re Disderi & Co* (1870), L R 11 Eq 242 , *Re Morvah Consols Tin Mining Co.*, *McKay's Case* (1875), 2 C D 1, C A , *Re British Provident Life and Guarantee Association*,

(x) As in *Re Anglo-French Co operative Society*, *Exp Pelly* (1882), 21 C D 492, C A.

any reference to qualification, or any other specific purpose. In all cases alike, if the transaction is not disclosed with the utmost candour and particularity to the company, the director is accountable. It is no answer to establish that the corrupt agreement with the promoter was made before the party charged became a director, if he received the fruits of it during his tenure of the office (y), nor that, in point of form, the director paid for the shares with his own cheque, if the cheque was paid against a cheque for the same amount handed back to him by the promoter out of several making up the purchase-money (z), nor (if there was a secret arrangement that, on demand at any time, the promoter would purchase them from the director at par) that, afterwards, when the shares had become valueless, the promoter did in fact, pursuant to this " private arrangement," as he had himself described it, pay their face value to the director (a). It does not improve the director's case, but on the contrary (for obvious reasons) make it much worse, to allege and prove that he received his qualification shares from the promoter, not as an absolute gift, but in trust for him (b). " it is not only improper, but it is misfeasance, to qualify by taking shares in trust for the promoter, and to execute blank transfers for the promoter to fill up at his pleasure   Directors so qualified hold office at the will of the promoter, and as long as they fulfil his wishes   But as soon as they act contrary to the promoter's wishes, he can fill up and lodge the transfers, and disqualify them " (c).   Nor can a director justify or excuse the bribe as a payment to him in the assumed character of vendor to the company, if in reality he had nothing to sell (d). And it is equally immaterial that it was made a condition of the bribe that the director should take, and pay for, other shares in the company (e)   On

De Ruvigne's Case (1877), 5 C D 306, C A , *Re Caerphilly Colliery Co* (1877), 5 C D 306, C A (here no qualification was required by the articles), *Nant y Glo and Blaina Ironworks Co* v *Grave* (1878), 12 C D 378 , *Re West Jewell Tin Mining Co* , *Weston's Case* (1879), 10 C D 579, C A (where, though some consideration passed, it was less than the then value of the shares, and, to the extent of the difference, the transaction was held to be a gift) , *Re Diamond Fuel Co* , *Milcalfe's Case* (1879), 13 C D 169, C A , *Eden* v *Ridsdale's Railway Lamp and Lighting Co* (1889), 23 Q B D 368, C A , *Re Postage Stamp Automatic Delivery Co* , [1892] 3 Ch 566 , *Re Westmoreland Green and Blue Slate Co* , *Bland's Case*, [1893] 2 Ch 612, C A

(y) *Re Morvah Consols Tin Mining Co* , *McKay's Case, sup* , per BRETT, J , at pp 7, 8

(z) This was the childish manœuvre resorted to in *Re Canadian Oil Works Corporation*, *Hay's Case* (1875), 10 Ch App 593 (see the observations on it of JAMES, L J , at p 600, and MELLISH, L J , at p 605)

(a) *Re North Australian Territory Co* , *Archer's Case*, [1892] 1 Ch 322, C A , where it was vainly contended that the director had genuinely paid for his shares, and, in the events which happened, had got nothing out of the company, and that the company had suffered no loss (per LINDLEY, L J , at pp 336-338)

(b) This was the device employed in *Re London & South Western Canal, Ltd* , [1911] 1 Ch 346

(c) *Ibid* , per SWINFEN EADY, J , at p 350   In the one case the director is swayed merely by a sense of gratitude for the past, in the other, he is subject to the continuous bondage of apprehension as to the future

(d) *Re Westmoreland Green and Blue Slate Co* , *Bland's Case*, [1893] 2 Ch 612, C A (per LINDLEY, L J , at p 617)

(e) *Re Postage Stamp Automatic Delivery Co* , [1892] 3 Ch 566 (per VAUGHAN WILLIAMS, J , at p 577)   Here each of the directors received (*inter alia*) 250 shares from the promoter, on the terms of his subscribing for 100 other shares   For further illustrations, see § 532, note (b), *post*, where the question of the statutory liability of directors and others to

the other hand, one who before becoming a director, or even a shareholder, acquired knowledge, in the course of certain transactions with the company, that the then directors had been corrupted by the promoter, but himself derived no benefit therefrom, was held free from any duty to impart this knowledge to the company on his subsequently joining the board (*f*)

341. Partnership, as has already been indicated (*g*), is a species of agency : but it has this peculiar feature, that all the partners are mutually agents and principals of one another : each member of the firm is acting not merely for, but with, the other member or members, in a common business or adventure It follows that, to this extent, a partner is subject to certain special duties of disclosure over and above those which are incumbent on other agents An ordinary agent, unless he has expressly or impliedly contracted with his principal for exclusive service, is at liberty to act as agent for, or to hold an interest in the business of, other persons, though they may be trading in competition with his principal, without revealing such agency or interest, provided that he is not deriving any private advantage from a transaction between any of those persons and his principal This is not so in the case of partnership No partner is allowed to conceal from the firm any interest which he may have in any trade, adventure, or concern which is akin to, in the sense that it is of a nature to compete with, the business of the partnership " One partner must not directly or indirectly use the partnership assets for his own private benefit He must not in anything connected with the partnership take any profit *clandestinely* for himself, nor must he carry on the business of the partnership, *or any business similar to the business of the partnership*, in his own or another name, separate from it, otherwise than for the benefit of the partnership " (*h*). In these, as in all the other cases which form the subject of this Chapter, the liability arises, not from the mere fact, but from its being kept secret (*i*). The burden is on the partner who is interested in the " similar " or rival undertaking, and whose conduct is impeached, to establish that he made due and candid disclosure to the firm, or that the firm was apprised *aliundè*, of both the existence and the exact nature and extent of his interest (*j*) ; but this burden does not rest upon him until the partners complaining have shown not only that he had the

disclose all material contracts in the prospectus is discussed , and where it will be seen that a common type of such contracts is the kind of arrangement for the corruption of the company's executive which is referred to in the text.

(*f*) *Re Forest of Dean Coal Mining Co* (1878), 10 C D 450 (*per* JESSEL, M R , at pp 456, 457)

(*g*) § 335, note (*p*), *ante*

(*h*) *Per* JAMES, L.J , at pp 350, 351 of *Dean v MacDowell* (1878), 8 C D 345, C A. At p 350, THESIGER, L J , lays down, as the second of the three principles which he considers applicable to this subject, that "a partner is not to derive any exclusive advantage by engaging in transactions in rivalry with the firm "

(*i*) See note (*x*) to § 316, *ante*, and the cases there cited And, for a further illustration from the agency or partnership class of case, see *Re Dover Coalfield Extension, Ltd* , [1908] 1 Ch 65, C A , where it was held that there was nothing wrong in a director of company A , who at the request of that company has become a director of company B , receiving director's fees from company B , for, in the first place he is not receiving any property of company A , to whom alone he is under a duty, and, secondly, there is no secrecy

(*j*) See Sect 4, Sub-s (2), *post*

interest alleged (k), but also that the business was of a "similar," in the sense of a competitive, nature : and this means not merely that the two businesses relate to the same commodity, or article of commerce, or subject-matter, but that their profits are earned in the same mercantile character, and by the same class of dealing For instance, a partner in a firm of salt brokers and merchants is under no duty to disclose the fact that he is also engaged in the business of a salt manufacturer (l) : nor is a member of a firm of ship-brokers bound to reveal to his partners the fact that he is assisting in the formation of a shipbuilding company (m) Another special obligation of a partner is to divulge to the firm of which he is a member any private or exclusive profit which he is making by the use of information acquired by him as a partner if, but only if, that information is " information *to which the partnership is entitled* " (n) The limitation conveyed by the last words must not be lost sight of , for " it is not the source of the information but the use to which it is applied, which is important in such matters To hold that a partner can never derive any private benefit from information which he obtains as a partner would be manifestly absurd. Suppose a partner to become, in the course of carrying on his business, well acquainted with a particular branch of science or trade, and suppose him to write and publish a book on the subject, could the firm claim the profits thereby obtained ? Obviously not, unless, by publishing the book, he in fact competed with the firm in their own line of business " (o). So, where three persons, under a partnership arrangement, bought from an individual, with a view to re-sale, certain plots of land or stands laid off for building, and also from a company owning other plots of land in the locality a certain number of shares in their undertaking, and one of the three partners, separately from, and without the knowledge of, the other two, bought certain other stands belonging to the company, and re-sold them at a profit to himself, it was held that he was not accountable in respect of this transaction, or bound to disclose it to his partners , for, though it was the knowledge which he obtained as partner which put him in a position to make the purchase, this knowledge was not used by him for the purpose of any business in competition with, or analogous

(k) See Sect 3, Sub-s (2), *post*
(l) *Dean* v *MacDowell* (1878), 8 C. D 345, C. A (*per* JAMES, L.J , at p 351, COTTON, L.J , at pp 353, 354, and THESIGER, L J , at pp 356, 357)
(m) *Aas* v *Benham*, [1891] 2 Ch 244, C A (*per* LINDLEY, L J , at pp 255, 256, BOWEN, L.J , at p 258, and KAY, L J , at pp 260, 261) And cp *Trimble* v *Goldberg*, [1906] A. C 494, P C , at p 499   see the citation in note (p), *inf*
(n) *Per* COTTON, L J , at p 354 of *Dean* v *MacDowell*, *sup*
(o) *Per* LINDLEY, L J , at p 256 of *Aas* v *Benham*, *sup* In this case, reliance was placed by the plaintiff on the third of the three principles enunciated by THESIGER, L.J , at p 356 of *Dean* v *MacDowell*, *sup* (viz " that a partner is not allowed, in transacting the partnership affairs, to carry on for his sole benefit any separate trade or business which, were it not for his connection with the partnership, he would not have been in a position to carry on "), but, for the reasons given by LINDLEY, L J , in the passage cited in the text, this statement of the proposition was thought much too broad, and the Court of Appeal preferred, and adopted, the more guarded language of COTTON, L J , in the earlier case, BOWEN, L J , observing, at pp 277, 278, that, when read carefully, that language is " perfectly precise and neat '

to, that of the firm (p).   The rules above stated have now received legislative recognition (q)

342. The topics of the burden of proof incumbent on the principal or partner complaining, and on the agent or partner charged, respectively, the forms of remedy and relief available, questions of law and fact, and parties, are reserved for separate treatment hereafter (r).

Sub-s. (4).   *Examination of Certain Relations not deemed* primâ facie *of a Fiduciary Character*

343. In any case where it is a matter of doubt and debate whether the relation between the parties is such as to cast the burden of sustaining the transaction upon the party charged, the courts will always put substance before form, and will consider the principle of the rule rather than the rule itself, the *ratio legis* rather than the *lex*.   It is not a question of names.   Many relations have been treated and described as relations of trusteeship, for the purposes of the doctrine discussed in this Chapter, which are not so in the full acceptation of the word, or otherwise than " in an artificial sense," or "by way of metaphor " (s)   On the other hand, there are cases where the party against whom relief is sought may be properly and strictly denominated a trustee or agent, and yet the circumstances may be such that, as regards the particular transaction impeached, it is impossible that any trust can have been reposed in him, or impossible that he can have derived any private and personal benefit, in either of which events he is not within the principle of the rule   *Cessante ratione cessat lex* (t).   The sole question in every case is whether the parties were so situated towards one another as to raise a presumption of confidence   If they were so situated, then, whatever be the correct definition of the relationship which in fact existed between them, or, whether such relationship admits of any definition or classification at all, the case is within what Lord ELDON, L C , describes as " that great rule of the Court, that he who bargains in matters of advantage with a person placing confidence

(p) *Trimble* v *Goldberg*, [1906] A. C **494,** P. C , at p 499 (" the subject of the purchase was not part of the business of the partnership, or an undertaking in rivalry with the partnership, or indeed connected with it in any proper sense   Nor was the information on which it seems Trimble acted acquired by reason of his position as partner ")   At p 500, with reference to the " secrecy of the transaction " which had impressed the court below, the Judicial Committee observed that " there was no legal obligation on Trimble or Bennett to tell Goldberg what they were doing, unless he had a right to take part in the speculation if he chose to do so "

(q) In the Partnership Act, 1890 (53 & 54 Vict c 39), which is mainly a declaratory and codifying statute   See s 29 (1)   " every partner must account to the firm for any benefit derived by him *without the consent of the other partners* from any transaction concerning the partnership, and from any use by him of the partnership property or business connection "   This is followed by s 30   "if a partner, *without the consent of the other partners*, carries on any business of the same nature as, and competing with that of the firm, he must account for and pay over to the firm all profits made by him in that business."

(r) See Sects 3, 4, 5, 6, 7, *post*.

(s) See § 320, *ante*.

(t) For illustrations, see § 344, *post*.

in him is bound to show that a reasonable use has been made of that confidence " (u) To this rule, as the fountain-head, or rather to its principle and reason, all subordinate and derivative rules, and all particular questions, must be referred for interpretation and solution (v).

344. There are several illustrations of transactions between parties who stand towards one another in a relation falling strictly within some one or more of the class denominations successively considered in the foregoing portions of this Section, where, nevertheless, the circumstances are not sufficient to bring the case within, or are sufficient to take it out of, the " principle of the rule " For instance, where an executor, described as a trustee " in an artificial sense," was also a residuary legatee, and, there being no question of assets, entered into a compromise with the other legatees solely in the latter character, it was held that there was no " confidence " on the one side, or " advantage " on the other, and that the compromise was unimpeachable (w) Similarly, a trustee of the estate of an insolvent, who is under a fiduciary duty, as such, to the creditors, is under no duty to the insolvent, where there is, and in the most favourable event can be, no surplus, or rather there is nothing upon which the trust can operate (ww) The like view was taken in the case of a trustee purchasing part of the trust property, not for his own benefit, but solely for that of certain of the *cestuis que trustent*, as between whom and the other *cestuis que trustent* there is no fiduciary relation or privity whatsoever (x) ; and in a case where an attorney and agent was

(u) *Gibson* v *Jeyes* (1801), 6 Ves 266, *per* Lord ELDON, L C, at p 278

(v) Lord COTTENHAM, L C, at p 130 of *Greenlaw* v *King* (1841), 10 L J (CH) 129, protests in forcible language against a narrow and literal view of the extent and applicability of the doctrine " some of the authorities referred to in the course of the arguments might lead persons to suspect that there was an absolute rule of the Court applicable only to particular classes of persons, such as solicitors, guardians, and trustees in the ordinary sense of that word, whereas the principle of the rule lies much deeper, and the rule has reference to, and *affects all persons coming within its principle*, which is, that no persons can be allowed to purchase interests where they have duties to discharge which are inconsistent with their character of purchasers. It is not sufficient to say, a particular person or class of persons is not within the rule . the question not being, whether a case is to be found in the books exactly similar to the present, but whether the transaction before me *comes within the principle* " Similarly, at p 342 of *Benson* v *Heathorn* (1842), 1 Y & C 326, SHADWELL, V -C, when applying the doctrine to the case of trustees, is careful to add—" and all parties whose character and responsibilities are similar, for there is no magic in the word " Cp the observations of Lord CAIRNS, L C, at pp 362, 363 of *McPherson* v *Watt* (1877), 3 App Cas 254, H L, and those of Lord HATHERLEY at p 1243 of *Erlanger* v. *New Sombrero Phosphate Co* (1878), 3 App Cas 1218, H L (" it is notorious that every mode which can well be conceived of dealing with contracts which ought not to be maintained . has from time to time come before the Courts of Equity, and there is scarcely any one which can be set on foot that is not struck at by the general doctrines of the Courts of Equity, though the precise circumstances of that case may never have yet come before the Court ")

(w) *Naylor* v *Winch* (1824), 1 Sim & St 555, *per* LEACH, V -C, at p 567 " where the policy of this Court prevents a trustee from dealing with his *cestui que trust*, it is upon the principle that his situation as trustee gives him an advantage in such dealing If this executor could in any sense be called a trustee, yet, inasmuch as there was no question of assets, and as the dealing proceeded entirely upon his character of residuary legatee, it is impossible that he could derive any advantage in dealing with the plaintiff and her trustees from his character of executor "

(ww) *Dover* v *Buck* (1865), 12 L. T 136 (*per* STUART, V -C., at p 137)

(x) *Barwell* v. *Barwell* (1865), 34 Beav. 371 (*per* ROMILLY, M R, at pp 374, 375)

also one of the judgment creditors of his client and principal, and attended a sale by the sheriff of the client's effects, and purchased part of them, solely in his character of judgment creditor (y).

345. From the above it will be seen that there is no privity of a fiduciary, any more than there is of a contractual, character between *cestuis que trustent*, legatees, or beneficiaries *inter se*, merely because there is such a relation between the trustee or executor, on the one hand, and each of such *cestuis que trustent*, legatees, or beneficiaries, on the other. A similar confusion of thought is responsible for the arguments from time to time "fondly invented," and vainly advanced, as to the supposed general fiduciary duties *urbi et orbi* of a director of a company. One would have thought it impossible to contend with any appearance even of plausibility that, merely because the word "fiduciary" is applied to the duties of this agency, anybody and everybody is entitled to claim the discharge of such duties, regardless of the question whether there is any privity or relation whatsoever between him and the directors, or the particular director attacked. But it has been so contended, and in each case the contention was treated seriously, and elicited solemn pronouncements of the law that there is no fiduciary relation between a director and an individual shareholder (z), or between a director and a third person to whom the company owes a fiduciary duty (a), or between a director and stockbrokers and other members of the outside public (b). There is, on the one hand, a relation of confidence between the director and the company, and, on the other hand, there is a contractual, or, it may be, a fiduciary, privity between the company and the shareholder or third person. It would, however, be a most perverse logic, comparable only to the syllogism whereby it was attempted to prove that the infant child of Themistocles ruled the

(y) *Austin* v *Chambers* (1837), 6 Cl & Fin 1, *per* Lord BROUGHAM, L C , who at pp 37, 38, points out that the respondent denies "that upon this transaction, with reference to this sale, he was acting as Mr Austin's attorney; he says he was acting for himself, that he was a judgment creditor; that he had a right to attend the sale, and had a right to purchase, and that he was acting in the character of judgment creditor. If he was not acting with a view to the interests of his client, who had been his client before, and was his client afterwards, he had a right undoubtedly, to throw off his character of solicitor at that particular time, and to exercise the right which belonged to him in another character'. The House of Lords considered that it was a question of fact whether this was the true aspect of the transaction, and offered the parties the opportunity of having this issue tried, which offer we are informed (at p 40) was accepted

(z) *Percival* v *Wright*, [1902] 2 Ch 421, *per* SWINFEN EADY, J , at pp 425, 426. Contrast *Allen* v *Hyatt* (1914), 30 T L R 444, P. C , where the circumstances were very special

(a) *Bath* v *Standard Land Co* , [1911] 1 Ch 618, C A , *per* COZENS HARDY, M R , at p 625. "the directors stand in a fiduciary relation to the company, but not to a stranger with whom the company is dealing," and to whom that company might be, and in the circumstances of this case was held to be—(see the judgment of COZENS-HARDY, M R , at pp 625, 626, and of BUCKLEY, L.J , at pp 642–647)—under a fiduciary obligation. The "confidence" is placed by the third person in the company, and by the company in the directors, but not by the third person in the directors

(b) *Tackey* v *McBain*, [1912] A C 186, P C , where it was held that a director and general agent of a company was under no duty to communicate to shareholders, much less to brokers soliciting the latest information, or to the general public, the receipt of favourable news by cable from the seat of the company's undertaking. Such a duty was alleged in the first instance as one of the causes of action, but little more was heard of it, and it was not even seriously relied upon in the arguments on the appeal, which were directed to the question of misrepresentation.

world (c), which could infer from these two separate relations the existence of a like relation between the director and the shareholder or the third person. A similarly illogical, but much more plausible, *saltus* has been attempted, in the case of the relation of partnership. It is undoubted law, as has been already stated (d), that partnership, being mutual agency, involves a fiduciary duty on the part of each member of the firm to the others to make no secret use of the partnership property to his own private advantage. From this duty another has been sought to be inferred, viz. a duty on any partner who is buying the share of another partner, and on that other partner who is selling it, to communicate this fact, and the circumstances attending the purchase, to the rest of the firm. It has been held, however, that this view (ignoring, as it does, the question of the matters which are the proper subject of, the purpose for which, and the persons by and in whom, the confidence is reposed) is fundamentally unsound (e)

346. Further illustrations of relations which do not, as such, involve any "confidence," or, therefore, any duty of disclosure, are the following A tenant for life at whose request a trustee is empowered to sell settled property is in no fiduciary relation to that trustee (f), nor is a purchaser of property in any such relation to the vendor merely because he has an option to become the trustee of the property when purchased (g). A solicitor or banker to a company, or to its promoters, is not, as such, a promoter, or subject to any duty of disclosure to the company (h), and an insurance broker employed to effect an insurance for, and who, as such, is under a fiduciary duty to, his principal, does not thereby bring himself into any fiduciary relation with the insurer (i)

(c) The pseudo syllogism was this Themistocles's baby rules his mother his mother rules Themistocles Themistocles rules Athens Athens rules Greece Greece rules the world. Therefore, Themistocles's baby rules the world

(d) In § 335, note (p), and § 341, *ante*

(e) *Cassels* v *Stewart* (1881), 6 App Cas. 64, H L , where it is pointed out that the share of an individual partner is his own property, and not that of the partnership *per* Lord SELBORNE, L C., at pp 73, 74, Lord PENZANCE, at p 77, and Lord BLACKBURN, at pp 79, 80 The kind of purchase now under consideration, where it is a question of the duty of the purchasing and the selling partner to the other partners must not be confounded with the totally different class of case which is the subject of § 142, *ante*, where it is a question of the duty of disclosure of the purchasing and selling partners to one another, when one of them has exclusive or superior knowledge of the concerns and dealings of the partnership

(f) *Dicconson* v *Talbot* (1870), 6 Ch App 32, *per* JAMES, L J , at p 37 " when a power of sale is given to trustees, to be exercised at the request or with the consent of the tenant for life, the trustees may sell to him as they might to any one else The ground of the rule is, that the power of consenting to or requesting an exercise of the power of sale is given to the tenant for life for his own benefit, and that he is not in a fiduciary position as to it He has, therefore, the same right to buy from the trustees that any one else has "

(g) *Clark* v *Clark* (1884), 9 App Cas 733, P C , at p 737 " their Lordships cannot agree that a sale is to be avoided, merely because when entered upon the purchaser may, at his option, become the trustee of the property purchased, though in point of fact he never does become such A man so placed might possibly use his power in such a way as to raise a case for setting aside the transaction . But that is a different thing altogether from the absolute disability attaching to one who would at the same time be a vendor in trust for others and a purchaser on his own account "

(h) *Re Great Wheal Polgooth Co* (1883), 53 L J (CH) 42, *per* BACON, V -C , at pp 46-48

(i) *Empress Assurance Corporation* v *Bowring* (1905), 11 Comm Cas 107 (*per* KENNEDY,

347. A debtor can never, merely as such, be deemed a trustee for his creditor, or liable to any of the duties which are incumbent on a trustee towards his *cestui que trust* (*j*), whether he be secured or unsecured. Desperate endeavours have from time to time been made to fix a mortgagee with some sort of fiduciary duty to the mortgagor, at all events in relation to his power of sale, but none of such attempts has succeeded. That is to say, it has never been held that a mortgagee, merely as such, stands in any other position than that of a secured creditor, with the rights, and (in the case of a sale of the property) subject to the duties, of such a creditor when dealing with his debtor's property in the manner contracted for, but not subject to any duty arising from confidence. He is not "trusted" to act *for* the debtor. he is entitled to act *against* him He certainly has in the first instance no fiduciary duties to the mortgagor in virtue of the contract (*k*) Nor is he a trustee of the power of sale, even if the mortgage is in the form of a trust for sale (*l*). It is true that if he sells openly to himself, the sale is a nullity, but this is not because he is violating any fiduciary obligation in so doing, but because a sale to himself is no exercise of the power at all (*m*), and, further, is an absurdity and a farce, because no man can contract with himself (*n*) It is also true that, if and when paid off, without any sale being

J , at p 112   " I know of no case or legal authority which can be cited to shew that the broker who is instructed to effect a marine insurance . . . becomes, for any part of the business of effecting the insurance, the agent also of the underwriter "), *Glasgow Assurance Corporation* v. *William Symondson & Co* (1911), 104 L T 254 (*per* SCRUTTON, J , at pp 254, 258)

(*j*) *Waters* v. *Groom* (1844), 11 Cl. & Fin 684 , *Re Diamond Fuel Co.* (1880), 13 C. D 815 (*per* MALINS, V -C , at pp. 819, 820) Moreover, where a party to whom a fiduciary duty is owed by another, by his own action converts that other's equitable liability into a debt, he loses his fiduciary rights, and substitutes for them those of a creditor only See *Re Thomas*, [1912] 2 Ch 348, C A , where, in an administration suit, a certain firm who were the only creditors of the estate, and between whom and the executor there undoubtedly existed a fiduciary relation in the first instance, chose to commence an action by originating summons against the executor for *personal* payment of the debt certified by the Master to be due to them, and obtained an order for such personal payment, and it was held that they had thereby made themselves judgment creditors only, and had entirely put an end to the pre-existing fiduciary relation, and disabled themselves from relying upon the third exception in s 4 of the Debtors Act, 1869, or from invoking the punitive jurisdiction of the Court against the defendant as " a trustee or person acting in a fiduciary capacity " (*per* COZENS-HARDY, M R , at pp 353, 354, FARWELL, L.J., at p. 354, and KENNEDY, L.J , at p 355)

(*k*) *Cholmondeley* v *Clinton* (1820), 2 J & W. 1 (*per* PLUMER, M.R , at pp 183, 184) , *Jones* v *Matthie* (1847), 11 Jur 504 (*per* Lord COTTENHAM, L C , at p 505) , *Knight* v. *Marjoribanks* (1849), 2 Macn & G 10 (*per* Lord COTTENHAM, L C , who at pp 12, 13, says that it would be " monstrous " to hold that a mortgagee cannot purchase from his mortgagor, which is equivalent to saying that he is not a trustee for him, since, if he were, he could not do so except on compliance with the fiduciary duties attaching to that position) , *Davey* v *Durrant* (1857), 1 De G & J 535 (*per* TURNER, L.J , at p 558) , *Robertson* v *Morris* (1859), 1 Giff 421 (*per* STUART, V -C , at pp. 424, 425) , *Adams* v *Scott* (1859), 7 W R 213 (*per* WOOD, V -C., at p 214) , *Farrar* v *Farrars, Ltd* , *inf* (*per* LINDLEY, L.J , at pp 410, 411) , *Nutt* v *Easton*, [1899] 1 Ch 873, at pp 877, 888

(*l*) *Kirkwood* v *Thompson* (1865), 2 H. & M 392 ; *Locking* v. *Parker* (1872), 8 Ch App. 30 ; *Re Alison* (1879), 11 C. D 284, C A , *Warner* v *Jacob* (1882), 20 C D 220 , *Haddington Island Quarry Co* v *Huson*, [1911] A C 722, P C

(*m*) *Martinson* v *Clowes* (1885), 52 L T 706, C A , *Farrar* v *Farrars, Ltd* (1880), 40 C D 395, C A (*per* LINDLEY, L J , at p 409)

(*n*) *Henderson* v *Astwood*, [1894] A C 150, P C , at p. 158   " the so called sale was of course inoperative A man cannot contract with himself A man cannot sell

necessary, he is from that moment, by implication, or, as Lord WESTBURY would say, "by metaphor," a trustee of the estate for the mortgagor (o), or, if the power of sale is resorted to, and a sum is realized which is more than enough to satisfy what is due to him, he is again, in the same sense, a trustee for the mortgagor of the balance (p) But, unless and until either of these events happens, he is "a mere indifferent stakeholder" (q), and is not, in any proper sense of the word, a trustee for the mortgagor of the power of sale, or of any other right given to him by the contract (r). Of course, in relation to his contractual obligation he owes the same duty of good faith, and in the same sense of the word, that every contractor owes to his contractee (s) That is to say, he must not only exercise his power of sale and other powers, in the manner, and at the time, and for the purposes expressed in the contract, but he must also perform all obligations which, though not expressed in the contract, *tacitè insunt.* When a man, by agreement of any kind, undertakes a duty, or stipulates for a right, he impliedly engages to perform that duty, and to exercise that right, where such exercise affects the interests of the other party, with absolute honesty, and with reasonable care and skill A mortgagee, therefore, in the exercise of his power to sell, and in his conduct of the sale, not only must refrain from contravening the express covenants of the mortgage deed, as by openly selling to himself, which would simply be a nugatory proceeding, but he must not secretly sell to an agent or trustee for, or to a person otherwise connected or interested with,

to himself either in his own person or in the person of another" The same fatuity was noted by STUART, V -C, in the case of a sale of trust property by a trustee to a person declared on the face of the instrument to be his agent see *Franks* v *Bollans* (1867), 17 L T 309 (at pp 311, 312)

(o) *Cholmondeley* v *Clinton, sup*, per PLUMER, M R, at p 184

(p) Per JAMES, L.J, at p 10 of *Locking* v *Parker, sup* In the same purely artificial sense, an ordinary vendor is, after the conclusion of the contract, described as a trustee of the property for the purchaser, and the purchaser as a trustee of the purchase money for the vendor

(q) The expression of PLUMER, M R, at p 184 of *Cholmondeley* v *Clinton, sup*

(r) At pp 424, 425, of *Robertson* v *Morris* (1859), 1 Giff 421, STUART, V -C, observes that Lord ELDON had undoubtedly committed himself—he is referring to *Downes* v *Grazebrook* (1817), 3 Mer. 200—to the expression "that the mortgagee is a trustee for the benefit of the mortgagor in the exercise of the power" But, the Vice Chancellor adds, "that expression is to be understood in this sense, that the power being given him to enable him to recover the mortgage money, this Court requires that he shall exercise the power in a provident way with a due regard to the rights and interests of the mortgagor in the surplus money to be produced by the sale" In other words, the contractor is to exercise his contractual rights against the contractee with due regard to the rights which the contractee reciprocally has against him under the same contract, which is no more than may be said of any contract in the world So PLUMER, M R, at p 183 of *Cholmondeley* v *Clinton, sup*. "it is only in a secondary point of view and under certain circumstances, and for a particular purpose, that the character of a trustee *constructively* belongs to a mortgagee No trust is expressed *in the contract*, it is only raised *by implication,* in subordination to the main purpose of it, and after that is fully satisfied . *its primary character is not fiduciary"* Again at p 293 of *Re Alison, sup*, JESSEL, M R, during the argument, observes with emphasis "a mortgagee *cannot* be a trustee for the mortgagor," that is, *as such,* and in the proper sense of the word, and "no duty is imposed on him"

(s) This is laid down distinctly by Lord HERSCHELL, at p 185, and Lord MACNAGHTEN, at p, 192, of *Kennedy* v *De Trafford*, [1897] A C 180, H L, who add that, in order to determine whether this general obligation of good faith has been discharged, the entire circumstances of the individual case must be regarded

himself , for in such a case that which, if done openly, would be a mere nullity, becomes at once a badge of *mala fides :* he puts himself, by thus masking his identity, in the position of one who has a clandestine design to acquire the property at an undervalue under pretence of effecting the sale to an ostensibly independent person (*t*)   This is fraud, and collusion.   And the use of the power given to the mortgagee by the contract to perpetrate this, or any other species of fraud (*u*), or for purposes of oppression (*v*), or, generally, for any evil purpose of his own which is " foreign to that for which " the exercise of the power " was intended " (*w*), will vitiate the sale (*x*)   Even the fact that the property was sold at a gross undervalue may be *primâ facie* evidence of, not merely a negligent and " improvident " exercise of the power in total disregard of the mortgagor's contractual rights and interests, but positive fraud : that is to say, this fact alone may be such as to indicate conduct not explicable on the theory of simple negligence, and pointing unmistakably to the alternative hypothesis of moral obliquity (*y*).   But it is for the mortgagor to establish facts of the above nature , nothing short of them will

(*t*) *Farrar* v *Farrars, Ltd* (1880), 40 C D 395, C A (*per* LINDLEY, L J , delivering the judgment of the Court, at pp 410, 411, 415), *Nutt* v *Easton*, [1899] 1 Ch. 873 (*per* COZENS-HARDY, J , at pp 877, 878), *Hodson* v *Deans*, [1903] 2 Ch 647 (*per* JOYCE, J , at pp 652, 653)   But " such a transaction is not necessarily a fraud, or evidence of fraud   The thing may be done with or without a dishonest intent   It may be a cloak for fraud, or it may be a mere blunder "   *Henderson* v *Astwood*, [1894] A C. 150, P C. at p 158

(*u*) *Jones* v *Matthie* (1847), 11 Jur. 504 (*per* Lord COTTENHAM, L C , at p 505   " if the power is exercised for fraudulent purposes, this Court will interfere "), *Davey* v *Durrant* (1857), 1 De G & J 535 (*per* TURNER, L J , at p 558   " fraud and collusion "), *Adams v. Scott* (1859), 7 W R 213 (*per* WOOD, V.-C , at p 214   " the plaintiff was bound to have shown that the power   had been exercised improperly, . . that there had been some fraud attending the sale ")

(*v*) *Jones* v *Matthie, sup* , *per* Lord COTTENHAM, L C , at p 505   " such a power as this may no doubt be used for the purposes of oppression, but, when conferred, it must be remembered that it is so by a bargain,   and it is for the party who borrows to consider whether he is not giving too large a power to him with whom he is dealing "   That is to say, the power itself raises no presumption of oppression, or of undue influence, as Lord REDESDALE erroneously thought in a case which is criticized in § 448, note (*r*), *post*   The facts indicating such an abuse of the power as to raise that presumption must be independently established

(*w*) *Robertson* v *Morris* (1858), 1 Giff, 421, *per* STUART, V -C., at pp 424, 425   " the legitimate purpose being to secure repayment of his mortgage money, if he uses the power for another purpose—from any ill motive to effect other purposes of his own, or to serve the purposes of other individuals—the Court considers that to be a fraud in the exercise of the power, because it is using the power for purposes foreign to that for which it was intended "

(*x*) As was the case in *Hodson* v *Deans, sup* , where the mortgagees, the trustees of a certain society, sold the property to a person who was a member of the investment committee of the society, and who had, through a nominee, instructed the auctioneer to sell   These proceedings, by means of which the society was in effect secretly selling to itself, were sufficient, in the opinion of JOYCE, J , to establish a *primâ facie* case of collusion between the trustees of the society and the member of its committee who purchased, and to throw the burden on to their shoulders of sustaining the transaction, which they totally failed to do

(*y*) *Davey* v *Durrant* (1857), 1 De G & J 535, *per* TURNER, L.J , at p 558   " the case made by the bill . . is this, that   . the price was grossly inadequate, *so much so indeed as to amount to evidence of fraud*   Of course he could not maintain a purchase made at a *fraudulent* undervalue "   In *Haddington Island Quarry Co* v *Huson*, cited in the next note, undervalue was proved, but, not having been alleged to constitute or indicate fraud, it was held quite unavailing as a ground for relief

suffice (z). It is not for the mortgagee to establish his good faith, until on the other side some proof has been offered of his bad faith : which is tantamount to saying that a mortgagee is not, *by virtue of the relation itself*, under any fiduciary duty to the mortgagor.

348. Two general observations should be made here. On the one hand, there may be cases where, though the fiduciary relation is proved, and also the transaction which is sought to be set aside, the connection between the relation and the transaction is not established, either because the relation did not operate *in hâc re*, or because the dealing was with some property or matter which was not the subject of the trust, agency, or other "confidence " (a). On the other hand, a relation which is not proved to be fiduciary may yet be such as to raise a presumption of " undue influence," which may subject the party to duties and liabilities of another character, to be discussed hereafter (b) ; and a transaction between parties not bound to one another at the outset by any relation of " confidence " may be accompanied by such acts and conduct as to give rise to independent and supervening duties of disclosure, on the one side, and rights to it, on the other (c).

Sect. 3. The Burden of Allegation and Proof on the Party Complaining.

349. The *cestui que trust*, company, agent, or other party complaining (like any other person who, coming to the Court for civil relief, is required to state and make out his cause of action) must establish against the trustee, promoter, principal, or other party charged, first, a duty of disclosure, and, secondly, its breach, or rather, a state of things sufficient to call upon the party charged to establish that the duty has been observed For this purpose he must allege, and, having alleged, prove, or be prepared to prove, both (1) that a fiduciary relationship existed between himself and the party charged at the material date, and (2) that the impeached transaction in fact took place, or that the alleged undisclosed fact was a fact Having established so much, and no more, he is entitled to call upon the party charged " to sustain the transaction," by means of some one or more of the affirmative

---

(z) The mortgagor failed to obtain relief, because he did not discharge this burden in (amongst others) the following cases *Davey v Durrant, sup* , *Warner v Jacob* (1882), 20 C D 220 (*per* KAY, L , at p 224 " no case of undervalue was made out there was no evidence of *mala fides* or collusion The sale could not be set aside, nor was there any case for damages in respect of the sale ") , *Nutt v Easton,* [1899] 1 Ch 873 (*per* COZENS HARDY, J , who, at p 878, points out that the mortgagor had not established that the ostensible purchaser was a mere trustee for the mortgagee, or that any other fraudulent device had been resorted to, or even that the price was inadequate This decision was affirmed, [1900] 1 Ch 21, C A , on the ground of delay, without considering any other question at all) , *Haddington Island Quarry Co* v. *Huson,* [1911] A C 722, P C , where no fraud, or collusion, or bad faith of any sort, was alleged in the pleadings, the mortgagors relying solely on the mere fact of undervalue On appeal, they sought to rely on this undervalue (of which they had given some evidence, not substantially contradicted at the trial) *as evidence of fraud,* but were not allowed to do so at that stage

(a) See §§ 361-365, *post*
(b) In Ch. V, *post*
(c) Cp the classes of case referred to in Ch III, Sect 2, Sub s (8), *ante*, where a duty of disclosure may be raised by supervening circumstances and conduct in the course of negotiation for contracts which do not, *per se*, involve any such duty in the first instance.

defences available to him, as hereafter stated (d). It is proposed to discuss these *alleganda et probanda* in the order above given.

Sub-s. (1) *The Existence of the Relation.*

350. The party complaining must allege, and prove, at the outset that a relation of "confidence" existed between himself and the party charged at the date of the transaction sought to be set aside. That is to say, he must prove, as facts (e), the contract or instrument whereby the relation is alleged to have been declared, or defined, or the circumstances from which it is said to be implied, and must further establish, if controverted, that, in law (f), the relation is constituted by the contract, instrument, or circumstances proved or admitted (as the case may be).

351. Thus, where the relation alleged is one of trusteeship, the *cestui que trust* must, if challenged (which, however, is rarely the case), prove, as a fact, the trust deed, will, or other instrument in which the party charged is declared or appointed a trustee for himself, or a class which includes himself, or, if the trusteeship is alleged to result, or to be implied, from circumstances, he must prove those circumstances (g) A question of law may then arise, as to the character and extent of the trusteeship created by the proved or admitted instrument, or as to whether a trusteeship in any sense (strict or metaphorical) is constituted by the proved or admitted circumstances, in which event it is for the *cestui que trust* to establish, as matter of law, that this question ought to be answered in the affirmative (h) And, further, in case of dispute he must show that the trustee entered into the transaction impeached for his own private benefit, and in his character of trustee, and in relation to some property or matter which was the subject of the trust (i)

352. Similarly, in cases of promotership, the company must prove, as an issue of fact (j), if it is disputed, all such acts and proceedings as are alleged to constitute the party charged a promoter (k), or the contract or other

(d) See Sect. 4, *post*
(e) See § 389, *post*
(f) *Ibid*
(g) Thus in *Mulvany v Dillon* (1810), 1 Ball & B 409; 12 R R. 43, Lord Manners, L C. (Ir), stated the question before him to be " whether Sir William Dillon has so far interfered with the management of the assets as to charge him with a fiduciary character, and to preclude him from taking a benefit to himself in the trust property " (p. 417) He thereupon proceeds to treat this question of fact as one which it was for the party complaining to prove, and, in the result, finds that it had been so proved " he principally interfered in the management of this part of the property, and made himself a sort of agent to the executors, and indeed acted as an executor " and, " by managing the testator's estate in the manner he has done, has so far acted as to have disabled himself   from retaining his purchase" (pp 417, 418) Cp , generally, the cases cited in the notes to Sect 2, Sub-s (1), *ante*, from an examination of which it will be seen that, in scarcely any of them, except the above, was there any question as to the existence of the instrument or facts alleged to constitute the relation.
(h) See the cases cited in notes (f), and (g), to § 346, *ante*, and in the notes to § 347, *ante* The propositions of law arising in all these cases were treated as propositions for the alleged *cestui que trust* to establish, and, on his failing to do so, he failed altogether
(i) See § 344, notes (w), and (x), *ante*
(j) Promotership is ordinarily a question of fact see § 389, note (y), *post*.
(k) The company must shew that the party charged was engaged in all those " business operations familiar to the commercial world by which a company is generally brought

document in which he is declared or expressed to be so (*l*) ; and, in the rare cases in which, the facts being agreed, the question becomes one of law, he must be prepared to satisfy the Court that promotership is a proper inference of law from those facts (*m*)   Further, it must be made clear that the party charged was at the precise material date the promoter of the particular company seeking relief, and it is not enough to prove that he had been previously, or that he afterwards became, a promoter, though such proof may (or may not) be sufficient to establish the company's title to some other form of remedy (*n*).   And, in this connection, it should be remembered that a man does not necessarily, or even usually, cease to be a promoter after formal incorporation of the company (*o*).

into existence," which is the definition given by BOWEN, J , of promotership at p. 111 of *Whaley Bridge Calico Printing Co* v. *Green* (1879), 5 Q. B. D 109   It is rarely disputed in modern times that the alleged promoter was in fact a promoter, because he has generally declared himself to be so in the prospectus or in the contracts of sale, or otherwise ; in addition to which, a long series of decisions has shewn the people engaged in this class of business the futility of contesting the point in the vast majority of cases   but in the early history of the Companies Acts, before the frame of mind in which judges and juries approach the subject had become fixed, and had assumed its present critical severity, the issue was frequently and fiercely debated   The burden of proving it was always held to be on the party complaining   The following are cases in which such acts and conduct and " operations " on the part of the party charged were proved as were considered by the tribunal to be sufficient to constitute the fact of promotership . *Nant y Glo and Blaina Ironworks Co* v. *Grave* (1878), 12 C D 738 (*per* BACON, V.-C , at p 744); *Emma Silver Mining Co* v *Grant* (1879), 11 C D 919 (*per* JESSEL, M R , at p 936) , *Gluckstein* v *Barnes*, [1900] A C 240, H. L (*per* Lord ROBERTSON, at p 256) , *Re Leeds and Hanley Theatre of Varieties, Ltd* , [1902] 2 Ch 809, C. A (*per* VAUGHAN WILLIAMS, L J , at p 823) , *Re Darby, Ex p Brougham*, [1911] 1 K. B 95 (*per* PHILLIMORE, J , at pp 101–103)   Cp the cases in which promotership was proved by a shareholder suing under the statutory provisions as to prospectuses, such as *Twycross* v. *Grant* (1877), 2 C P D 469, C A (*per* COCKBURN, C.J , at p 541), *Glasier* v. *Rolls* (1889), 42 C D 436, C A (*per* KEKEWICH, J , at p 443).   For a case in which the company failed to prove that the party charged was a promoter *at any time*, see *Re Great Wheal Polgooth Co* (1883), 53 L J. (CH) 42 (*per* BACON, V -C , at pp 47–50)   As to the cases in which the burden of proving that the party charged was a promoter *at the material date* was insisted on, see note (*n*), *inf*

(*l*) Which is now not infrequently the case   see the last note

(*m*) There appears to be no illustration of such a case, for the simple reason that, when the party charged is prepared to admit the " operations," he is not often inclined to controvert their legal complexion.

(*n*) Thus, in *Erlanger* v *New Sombrero Phosphate Co* (1878), 3 App Cas 1218, H L , so much of the company's claim as prayed an account of the profits made by the appellant on the resale of the island to the company was rejected, because the company had not sustained the burden which was upon them of shewing that, at the time when he purchased the property, he was intending to promote, or had in contemplation, *the* company suing, though he undoubtedly contemplated *a* company to be formed as the future purchaser (*per* Lord CAIRNS, L C , at p 1235, Lord BLACKBURN, at pp 1267, 1268, and Lord GORDON, at pp. 1283, 1284)   Afterwards, however, the appellant did promote the company suing, and from that moment his fiduciary duties commenced, for breach of which he was held liable to the appropriate relief, which was rescission   but the first-named head of relief which was alternatively claimed could only be given by erroneously antedating the period of his promotership   The same result, on the same ground, attended the company's claim to an account of profits in *Ladywell Mining Co* v *Brookes* (1887), 35 C. D. 400, C. A (COTTON, LJ , observing, at p 423, that the onus was on the company of proving facts sufficient to enable them to say with truth to the promoter—" when you bought this mine, you were acting for us   this purchase, although made by you, is one that must be considered as having been made by you for the company which was afterwards formed at your invitation ") ; also in *Re Lady Forrest (Murchison) Gold Mine, Ltd* , [1901] 1 Ch 582 (*per* WRIGHT, J , at pp 588, 589) , and in *Burland* v *Earle*, [1902] A C 83, P C (at pp 98, 99)

(*o*) See *Twycross* v *Grant* (1877), 2 C P D 469, C A (*per* COCKBURN, C J., at p 541) ,

353. Lastly, and similarly, in cases of agency and partnership, it is incumbent on the principal or firm complaining of the agent's or partner's fiduciary delinquency to establish the fact of the agency or partnership, either by proof of a deed or contract constituting it, or by evidence of the circumstances from which it is alleged to be implied (*p*). It is enough, however, to prove that for the purposes of the particular transaction in question the party charged was acting as agent for the party complaining, notwithstanding that such agent may not have been his general agent for matters of the class to which that transaction belongs (*q*). Next, the party complaining must show an agency or partnership of the precise character and type alleged, where such a question becomes material, and that its duties and functions (whether customary, or expressly agreed) are such that the transaction complained of must fall within them, and thus become material to be disclosed (*r*). Further, the agency must be shown to have existed at the time of, and not to have commenced after (*s*), or to have terminated before (*t*), the trans-

Emma Silver Mining Co v. *Lewis* (1879), 4 C P D 396 (*per* LINDLEY, J, at p 407), *Lydney and Wigpool Iron Ore Co* v *Bird* (1886), 33 C. D 85, C A (*per* LINDLEY, L.J, at pp 93, 94); *Ladywell Mining Co* v *Brookes, sup* (*per* LINDLEY, L J, at p 514, and LOPES, L J, at p 515); *Eden* v *Ridsdale's Railway Lamp and Lighting Co* (1889), 23 Q B D 368, C A (*per* LINDLEY, and LOPES, LL.JJ, at p 372, as to the receipt by directors of a bribe from the promoter, after the incorporation of the company, but before the contract between it and the promoter, on which their unbiassed advice was required, had been completed)

(*p*) In *Morgan* v *Elford* (1876), 4 C D 352, C A, the plaintiff wholly failed to prove the alleged agency, or any fiduciary relationship whatsoever between himself and the defendant, and on that ground judgment was given against him (*per* J   s, L J, at pp 384, 385) In *Oelkers* v *Ellis*, [1914] 2 K B 139, the plaintiff failed   prove, as to one of the several transactions there in question, that the defendant ha   ted as his agent (p 140)

(*q*) See *McPherson* v. *Watt* (1877), 3 App Cas 254, H L, where the party complaining failed to establish by evidence that the party charged was either his general agent, or his law agent in trust matters, and, so far as his case depended on sustaining that allegation, it would have failed (*per* Lord CAIRNS, L C, at pp 258, 259, Lord O'HAGAN, at p 267, and Lord BLACKBURN, at p 277) but he nevertheless succeeded on proof that in the particular transaction complained of the defendant did act, and was trusted in so acting, as his agent and adviser (*per* Lord CAIRNS, L.C., at pp 362, 363)

(*r*) Thus, in *Carter* v *Palmer* (1842), 8 Cl & Fin. 657, the onus was on the principal to shew that the agent acted not merely as his counsel, as was contended on the other side, but also, and principally, as his agent in the management of his affairs. This onus he discharged   "the *evidence proves*," said Lord COTTENHAM, L C (p 703), "that the employment was of a very different character," and (p 705), "*from the evidence* it is clear that the appellant is not to be considered as having acted merely as counsel for the respondent, but that he was so far his agent as to be affected with all the disabilities which attach to that character   See also *Williamson* v *Hine Bros*, [1891] 1 Ch 390, where KEKE WICH, J, directed an inquiry as to the duties and functions attaching to the particular type of agency there alleged, thinking it necessary for the party complaining to give evidence as to this issue, and, on the certificate of the chief clerk that the duties of the agency were of the character alleged, gave judgment for him (p 394)

(*s*) In *Re Forest of Dean Coal Mining Co* (1878), 10 C D 450, the transaction complained of took place long before the party charged became a director of the company, and the liquidator's summons accordingly failed (*per* JESSEL, M R, at pp 456, 457) The same result, and for the same reason (amongst others), attended the liquidator's misfeasance summons in *Bentinck* v *Fenn* (1887), 12 App Cas 562, H L (*per* Lord HERSCHELL, at p 658, after stating that the burden was on the principal to prove the agency at the time of the transaction in question "here it is beyond question that, *at the time when the purchase was made*, Mr Fenn and his co adventurers were none of them in any sort of fiduciary relation to the company, the existence of which at that time was not even contemplated ")

(*t*) See *Erskine, Oxenford & Co* v *Sachs*, [1901] 2 K. B 504, C A, where it was made

action impeached was entered into, or at least that the confidence was operative, though the agency may not have been literally or formally in existence, at the material date: for so long as the reasons upon which the fiduciary obligation is founded endure, the obligation continues, though the relation itself may be at an end (u). If, for instance, the principal is claiming relief against the agent in respect of a bribe, it is enough to establish the receipt of the money during the agency, though the corrupt agreement pursuant to which it was so received may have been made previously thereto, or (conversely) that the illicit commission or rebate became payable by reason of something done by the agent during his agency, though the actual payment was made after its termination and, generally, it is enough to prove that the act complained of, though done before or after the period of the actual subsistence of the relation, was so interwoven with some act done within that period as to form with it one entire transaction (v) Subject to these observations, the onus is undoubtedly on the party complaining to establish not only the fact of the agency, and (where this ⸱ ⸱ n issue) its character and extent, but also, if challenged on this head   transaction impeached was entered into, or the knowledge alleged to   ⸱ been withheld was acquired, by the agent " in the course and execution o⸱ ⸱⸱⸱ agency " (w), and by reason thereof. When this onus is not sustained, the party complaining fails at the threshold(x).

quite clear that it was for the client to prove that his brokers, when effecting the stock exchange transaction complained of on closing his account, were still his agents This onus was sustained   see note (v). *inf*

(u) *Carter v Palmer, sup*, per Lord COTTENHAM, L C, at p 705 "it is also proved that he did not actually act as counsel, or agent, for the respondent after August, 1831, but   . if his *previous* employment disqualified him from becoming the purchaser for his own benefit of those charges upon his employer's estates, such disqualification must continue *so long as the reasons upon which it is founded continue to operate* " He then (pp 705–707) proceeds to examine into the nature of these reasons (the special and exclusive information acquired, etc)

(v) Thus, in *Re Morvah Consols Tin Mining Co*, *McKay's Case* (1875), 2 C D I, C A, it was held sufficient for the liquidator to prove that the director received the bribe from the promoter during his directorate, though the arrangement pursuant to which he received it was made before he became a director So also, in *Erskine, Oxenford & Co v. Sachs, sup*, the client succeeded, because he was able to show that the brokers, in closing his account, and thereby terminating the agency, repurchased the very shares which they had sold for him when the agency existed, and from the same jobber, and as part of the same transaction, and it was only in virtue of the previous sale during the agency that they were entitled by the custom of the Stock Exchange to the rebate in the price in respect of which the plaintiff claimed relief (*per* A L SMITH, M R, at pp 511, 512, VAUGHAN WILLIAMS, L.J, at pp 512, 513, and STIRLING, L J, at pp 516–518) It was recognized by JESSEL, M R, at p 457 of *Re Forest of Dean Coal Mining Co* (1878), 10 C D 450, that in any case where the two transactions, that before, and that during, the agency are so connected as to form part of one entire scheme or "juggle," the whole will be deemed to have taken place in the course and execution of the agency, though the first of them was prior to its commencement.

(w) *Per* Lord CAIRNS, L.C, at p 118 of *Parker v McKenna* (1874), 10 Ch App 96 ("all that the Court can do is to examine whether a profit has been made by an agent, without the knowledge of the principal, in the course and execution of his agency ")

(x) As in *Austin v Chambers* (1837), 6 Cl & Fin 1 (where the party charged, though the attorney of the party complaining, was not proved to have acted in that character for the purposes of the transaction impeached, or in any other capacity than that of judgment creditor), *Great Western Insurance Co v Cunliffe* (1874), 9 Ch App 525 (where the plaintiffs, in proving no more than that their agents to effect reinsurances had received a customary commission from underwriters, not on any particular transaction, but on the

Sub s (2).   *The Existence or Occurrence of the Undisclosed Fact or Transaction.*

354. The next step in the proof necessary to make out a title to relief is to establish by evidence the existence of the fact, or the happening of the event, the concealment of which is complained of. Obviously, it is of no more use to prove the trusteeship, promotership, agency, or partnership, without also proving the existence or occurrence of the fact or transaction which, in virtue of such relation, the party charged was bound to disclose, than it is to prove the fact or transaction, without also proving the fiduciary relation   In the majority of cases, the party complaining is relieved of the burden of establishing this particular issue by the express or implied admission of the party charged   But this is by no means always so · and in every case, until so relieved, the party complaining must be prepared to sustain the onus

355. There are, as has been explained (*y*), two main classes of case in which the withholding of knowledge from the *cestui que trust*, company, or principal, constitutes a violation of fiduciary duty,—the one, where the related parties are dealing directly with one another   the other, where the trustee, promoter, or agent is dealing with third persons in the course and execution of his trusteeship, promotership, or agency   In the former type of case, relief is granted, whenever there has been either if the dealing was clandestine, non-disclosure by the trustee, promoter, or agent   the fact that he was the real purchaser or dealer in the matter, and that the ostensible dealer was merely the person under cover of whom he masked his identity, or, if the dealing was open, non-disclosure by him of any material fact as to the value of the property, or as to his previous transactions with reference to it, and the profit he was making on the re-sale, and the like   accordingly, it is for the party complaining to allege, and, having alleged, to establish by evidence, if secret dealing is alleged, that the party charged did in fact so deal, and that the ostensible dealer was in fact his mere nominee or agent for that purpose, in virtue of a corrupt pre-arrangement (*z*) , or, if the dealing is acknowledged to have been open, that the alleged undisclosed circumstance, transaction, or occurrence

net annual profits made by the underwriter out of all business introduced by the agents during the year, were held to have failed in proving that the transaction complained of occurred in the course and execution of the agency . *per* JAMES, L J , at pp 535–537)

(*y*) In Sect. 2, *ante*

(*z*) *Delves v Delves* (1875), L R 20 Eq 77, a case in which the *cestui que trust* failed to prove that the trustee for sale had made any bid at the auction, or taken any part in the purchase. *Re Postlethwaite* (1888), 60 L T. 514, C. A., was a case in which the beneficiaries under a will failed to establish (though the circumstances were a little suspicious) that one of the executors and trustees of the will, who had purchased part of the estate at a slight advance of price from the purchaser at the auction, was the real purchaser by arrangement with the first purchaser (*per* COTTON, L J , at pp 516–519, LINDLEY, L J , at pp. 519, 520, and BOWEN, L J , at p 520)   In *Re Gallard*, [1897] 2 Q B 8, the creditor of a bankrupt was unable to show that the ostensible purchaser of part of the estate was purchasing on behalf of a member of the committee of inspection who was alleged to have been the real purchaser, notwithstanding that these two persons were partners in a firm of solicitors (*per* VAUGHAN WILLIAMS, J , at pp 12, 13)   Accordingly in all these cases, the party complaining was refused relief, except in the last, where he was held entitled to damages on a different ground altogether, viz actual fraud

in fact existed or happened (a)   In the latter type of case, it must be proved by the party complaining, if it is not admitted, that the alleged secret bribe was in fact received, or that the alleged profits were in fact made (b), or that the trustee, promoter, or agent in fact entered into the exact transaction, or class of transaction, the secrecy of which is alleged as the foundation of the proceedings instituted (c) ; for it is obviously idle to complain of a party having concealed an alleged fact which never was a fact, or an alleged act of his own which he never committed.

Sub-s. (3).   *Matters which it is not incumbent on the Party Complaining to allege or prove*

356. There are no matters which the party complaining is required to allege or prove *in the first instance* beyond those stated   There are certain matters which, though he is not so required, he may yet find it necessary or desirable, to substantiate at a later stage of the proceedings, if and when a *primâ facie* affirmative case has been made against him of full disclosure or otherwise, and accordingly the onus is shifted back on to his shoulders of suggesting some particular material circumstance which the party charged has failed to communicate   But, unless and until such a case is made, he

---

(a) In all the cases, cited in the notes to §§ 323, 338, *ante*, of concealment of a report, valuation, or other fact relating to the value of the property, the existence of the fact appears to have been admitted   But, if denied, it is manifest that the party complaining would be called upon to prove it   To take a simple illustration from the hypothetical case of a concealed mine which is put by Lord ELDON, L C, at p 626A of *Ex p Lacey* (1802), 6 Ves 625 ("suppose a trustee buys an estate, and by the knowledge acquired in that character discovers a valuable coal mine under it, and, locking that up in his own breast, enters into a contract with the *cestui que trust*"),—if in such a case the trustee does not admit that there is or ever was in fact a mine for him to "lock up in his own breast," and the *cestui que trust* adduces no evidence of the existence of such a mine, or of its having any value, it is obvious that he would make out no title to relief   Again, in the cases where an agent is said to have made secret profits on the resale of the property to his principal, the burden would clearly be on the principal of establishing, if the allegation be denied, that the agent did in fact acquire the property by purchase before selling it to the principal, and acquired it at a less price than that at which he sold

(b) In the following cases, the party complaining failed to obtain relief because he did not sustain the burden on him of showing that the party charged had in fact received, or contracted to receive, any profit, as alleged, *Re Ambrose Lake Tin & Copper Mining Co.* (1880), 14 C D 390, C A (*per* JAMES, L.J, at p 395, BRETT, L J, at pp 396, 397, and COTTON, L J, at pp 398, 399), *Bentinck v Fenn* (1887), 12 App Cas 652, H L (where the contributory's misfeasance proceedings failed because, the alleged delinquent being the agent of the company to purchase *in the market*, it was never shown that the *market value* was less than the price paid by the company   *per* Lord HERSCHELL, at pp 659, 660), *Bath v Standard Land Co* , [1911] 1 Ch 618, C A (where the plaintiff could not prove that the *defendant company* had received the alleged secret profits, but only that certain of the directors had received them for their own individual benefit, *per* COZENS-HARDY, M R, at p 625   "it"—the company—"cannot be charged with profits which *in fact* the company did not receive, and which were received by the directors"), *Omnium Electric Palaces, Ltd v Baines*, [1914] 1 Ch 332, C A

(c) When once the relation is proved, and a transaction during the period of the subsistence of the relation, the burden is then on the party charged to allege, if he is minded to do so, and, having alleged, to prove that the relation was not operative upon the transaction, i e that some character other than, and in addition to that which would be inferred from such relation, and one not involving any fiduciary duty, belonged to him at the time, and that he entered into the transaction solely in that character   see Sect. 4, Sub s (1), *post*

need allege and prove no more than the relation, and the transaction, and he is thereupon entitled to call upon his opponent to justify the transaction, and demonstrate its propriety by some one or more of the means available to him (d). To take a simple illustration. A. alleges and proves that B. was his agent, and during his agency received a sum of money from C. with whom A. had entered into a contract which B. had negotiated for him. This alone entitles A. to judgment, if B. offers no evidence. It is not for A. to establish, in the first instance, that B. did not disclose the fact to him, or that it was material to be disclosed: it is for B. to show full and precise disclosure, or that the present was so trifling as to be immaterial, or that it was made pursuant to a custom of trade of which A. knew, or must be presumed to have known, or that it had been waived, or confirmed, by A. It may then be necessary for A. to go into evidence as to the want of completeness or candour in the disclosure, or as to the real importance of the bribe however trivial it may on the first blush appear to be, or as to his actual or presumptive ignorance of the custom, or its dishonesty, or as to circumstances attending the supposed waiver or confirmation which go to show that he was not told the whole truth of the matter at the time when he is alleged to have so waived and affirmed. Or A. may be a *cestui que trust* who alleges and proves that B., whilst his trustee, purchased from him part of the trust estate. It is then for B. to "sustain the transaction." A. need establish no more than the above at the outset (e), but, if B. makes out a *primâ facie* case of full disclosure of all material facts known to him, and honest advice either by himself or an independent third person, it may then be incumbent on A. to allege and prove some particular fact, not adverted to in B.'s general evidence, which was concealed (a report or valuation, for instance or the existence of a mine under the property, or the mark of a celebrated artist on a picture), or to point to some particular in which the advice was dishonest, or some reason for supposing that the third person was interested or biassed. But, unlike the party complaining of non-disclosure in negotiation for a contract *uberrimæ fidei* (f), the party complaining of non-disclosure in the course of a fiduciary relation need not, *in the first instance*, allege the withholding of any specific fact, known to the party charged, and material to be communicated (g).

(d) Described in Sect. 4, *post*.

(e) See *Dougan v. Macpherson*, [1902] A. C. 197, H. L., which was a case of trustee and *cestui que trust*, per Lord HALSBURY, L. C., who, at p. 202, lays down the clear duty of the trustee " to show that he has given full information—that he has kept back nothing .. and when I say that, it is not for those impeaching the transaction to prove negatively it is for the trustee to prove affirmatively that the information was given."

(f) See Ch. III, Sect. 3, Sub-ss (3), (4), and (5), where it is pointed out that, in that class of case, the party complaining must give some evidence, however slight, of the non disclosure of knowledge of the undisclosed fact possessed by the party charged, and the ignorance of the party complaining.

(g) The reason for the difference in the rules governing the two types of case is presumably that, in the former, there is nothing wrongful in negotiating for the contract with exclusive knowledge of a material fact, and the proceeding only becomes wrongful when non-disclosure is shown; whereas, in the latter, the law regards the transaction as wrongful in itself, unless and until it is justified by evidence of its propriety.

357. In addition to, and distinguishable from, the above is a class of matters as to which not only does no onus rest at the outset on the party complaining, but no onus rests on him at all, or at any stage of the proceedings, because the matters in question are wholly irrelevant, and it is, therefore, as idle for the one party to assert, as it is for the other to contradict, their existence. The first species of this class has reference to the motive, purpose, or intention by which the party charged was actuated: the second, to the material results, actual or anticipated, of the impeached transaction.

358. It has long since been established, in the present, as in the two other classes of case giving rise to a duty of disclosure (h),—though, for reasons given in another place (i), it has been found necessary to reiterate the statement for more than a century past with the regularity of a recurring decimal,—that it is wholly unnecessary, except for the purpose of defeating by anticipation some statutory or non-statutory affirmative plea which can only be displaced by proof of fraud (n), to allege that the breach of equitable duty complained of was animated or accompanied by actual and personal dishonesty, and wholly useless for the party charged to prove that his motives were honourable, that he intended no wrong or injury to the party complaining, and that he acted throughout in perfect good faith. The Court declines to enter into any such question. For the good of the community, it has established a general rule that non-disclosure shall entitle the party to whom the duty is owed to relief, and it will not go behind the fact, or investigate the state of mind and conscience which produced the violation of the rule, but will lend its assistance to the party voking it, on proof of such non-disclosure or breach of duty, though no fraud or moral obliquity of any kind be imputed to, or proved against, the party held liable, or even though, in the declared opinion of the tribunal, there has been positive demonstration of the complete candour and *bona fides* of such party's conduct throughout (j) ; or the case was obviously one of honest inadvertence

(h) See § 197, note (k), *ante,* and § 461, *post*

(i) In App A, §§ 629-631, *post*

(n) As, for instance, a plea that the contract has been completed by conveyance, or that disclosure has been waived, or a statutory plea, such as the Limitation Act, 1623 (21 Jac 1, c 16), on which, see *Oelkers* v *Ellis,* [1914] 2 K B 139, and the cases there reviewed. It was held that the above statute, which equity "applies by analogy," was a bar to a case of mere non disclosure, but as regards any case which could also be put as a case of implied fraudulent misrepresentation, the period of limitation only commences on discovery of the truth (per HORRIDGE, J , at pp 147-151)

(j) *Ex p James* (1803), 8 Ves 337 (per Lord ELDON, L C , at p 345 "the purchase is not permitted in any case, however honest the circumstances the general interests of justice requiring it to be destroyed in every instance "), *Ex p Bennett* (1805), 10 Ves 381 (per Lord ELDON, L C , at pp 385, 386) , *Cook* v *Collingridge* (1823), Jac 607 , 23 R R 155 (per Lord ELDON, L C , at p 169 "I should be sorry to be understood to impute any wrong motive to any one, for *I believe they all meant well* ") , *Rothschild* v *Brookman* (1831), 5 Bligh (N S) 165 (per Lord WYNFORD, L C , at p 619 "I do not mean to say that Mr Rothschild gave him that advice with any dishonest view whatever, *I have no doubt he acted fairly and properly* . God forbid that I should say that these gentlemen, or any of them, have taken advantage of the confidence that was reposed in them But the law which your lordships have to administer is a law of jealousy, it will not allow any n to be trusted with power that will give him an opportunity of taking advantage of

or mistake, or ignorance of, and inattention to, the equitable doctrine (k),—
a doctrine which, it seems to have been judicially conceded from time to
time, may appear to the laity artificial, rigid, and somewhat " too good for
human nature's daily food " (l). On the other hand, acts and conduct
showing a consciousness of the duty, and an attempt to evade it by disguising
the nature of the transaction, will operate against the party charged in case

employer ") ; *Gillett* v. *Peppercorne* (1840), 3 Beav. 78 (*per* Lord LANGDALE, M.R., at p 84) ;
Hamilton v. *Wright* (1842), 9 Cl. & Fin. 111 (*per* Lord BROUGHAM, at p. 124 · " the conduct
of the trustee not being blamable in the purchase is nothing to the purpose, for the Court
must act upon the general principle ; . . . it will be impossible for the Court to see in what
cases the transaction is morally unjust, and in what cases it is not ") ; *Bentley* v. *Craven*
(1853), 18 Beav 75 (*per* ROMILLY, M.R., at p. 76) ; *Imperial Mercantile Credit Association*
v. *Coleman* (1873), L. R. 6 H. L. 189 (*per* Lord CAIRNS, L C, at pp 209, 210) ; *Parker* v.
McKenna (1874), 10 Ch. App. 96 (*per* Lord CAIRNS, L C., at pp 119, 120) ; *McPherson*
v *Watt* (1877), 3 App. Cas. 254, H. L (*per* Lord O'HAGAN, at p. 269) ; *De Bussche* v. *Alt*
(1878), 8 C D. 286, C. A (*per* Cur., at p 317), *Erlanger* v. *New Sombrero Phosphate Co*
(1878), 3 App Cas. 1218, H L (*per* Lord O'HAGAN, at pp 1256, 1257 · not necessary to
show " evil purpose or conscious fraud," or " intention to do injustice," or " indirect and
improper motives ") ; *Re Carriage Co operative Supply Association* (1884), 27 C D 322
(*per* PEARSON, J , at pp 329, 331, in a case where the director's conduct was expressly
found to have been absolutely beyond reproach from first to last in its moral aspect) ;
Plowright v *Lambert* (1885), 52 L. T. 646 (*per* FIELD, J , at p 652) ; *Eden* v *Ridsdale's
Railway Lamp & Lighting Co* (1889), 23 Q B D 368, C A (*per* Lord ESHER, M.R , at pp
370, 371, and LINDLEY and LOPES, LL.JJ., at p 372), *Bray* v. *Ford*, [1896] A C 44,
H L (*per* Lord HERSCHELL, at p 51) ; *Re Sale Hotel & Botani d Gardens, Ltd , Ex p
Hesketh* (   ), 78 L T. 368, C. A. (*per* LINDLEY, M R , at p 370, this was a misfeasance
case), *Gray* v *Gold Exploration & Development Syndicate,* [1900] 1 Q B 233, C. A (*per*
COLLINS, L J , at pp 248–250), *Hovenden & Sons* v. *Millhoff* (1900), 83 L T 41, C A
(*per* ROMER, L J , at p 45), *Costa Rica Railway Co* v *Forwood*, [1901] 1 Ch 746, C A
(*per* RIGBY, L J , at p 753 " it does not depend on fraud," and—" it does not in the
least follow that, with perfect honesty of purpose, he may have done something which,
without his being aware of it, was contrary to principle "), *Kubliez* v *Lambert Bros ,
Ltd* (1913), 108 L T 565 (*per* SCRUTTON, J , at p 567)

(k) See the citations in the last note from *Imperial Mercantile Credit Association* v
Coleman, McPherson v. *Watt, Grant* v *Gold Exploration Syndicate,* and *Costa Rica Railway
Co* v *Forwood, sup* , also *Hippisley* v *Knee Bros* , [1905] 1 K B 1, Div Ct. (*per* Lord
ALVERSTONE, C J , at p 7, and KENNEDY, J , at p 9), *Patten* v *Hamilton,* [1911] 1 Ir R
40 (at pp 53, 58)

(l) *Greenlaw* v *King* (1841), 10 L J (CH) 129 (*per* Lord COTTENHAM, L C , at p 120
" the bishop was not, at the time of the transaction, aware, nor had he his attention drawn
to, the rule of this Court relative to purchases made by persons holding confidential
situations "), *Dougan* v *Macpherson,* [1902] A C 197, H L , where, as may be seen from
the report of his cross-examination, at p 199,—a human document of singular interest,
which is set out and discussed from the ethical point of view in § 656, note (d), *post,*—the
Scotch trustee was not only unconscious of the equitable rule, but could not conceive the
possibility of its existence, or that " fairness had anything to do with " his purchase from
the *cestui que trust* It is difficult, however, to understand why in the former case the
episcopal trustee, whose moral standard was presumably more refined than that of the
mercantile trustee in the latter, should have required the " equitable rule " to have been
brought to his notice, or why his conduct, in view of the facts stated in the narrative,
should have been palliated, if not approved, by Lord COTTENHAM, L C , or, for that matter,
why Lord WYNFORD, L C , should, in *Rothschild* v *Brookman* (1831), 5 Bligh (N S) 165,
have taken such a generous view of the conduct of " the many bankers and many
stockbrokers in London " who, he was convinced, had been with the most honourable
motives engaged in the pernicious practices which he invited the House to condemn,
unless the passage is to be read in the same sense as Mark Antony's appreciation of
Brutus and all " the honourable men whose daggers did slay Cæsar " One is disposed to
prefer the vigorous language of FRY, L.J , at p 369 of *Boston Deep Sea Fishing & Ice
Co* v *Ansell* (1888), 39 C D 339, C. A. " we were invited to consider the state of mind
of Mr Ansell ; whether he thought it wrong , in other words, we are invited to take as
the standard for our decision the alleged conscience of a fraudulent servant "

of doubt (*ll*)   From the rule which lays down that it is irrelevant to allege and prove actual fraud, it follows, as a necessary corollary, that to allege it without proving it is worse than futile, and entails a heavy visitation in the matter of costs, though such conduct is not a ground for denying relief altogether, if enough has been established otherwise to constitute a foundation for it (*m*)   In such cases the honest infringer of a fiduciary duty may derive to that extent some practical consolation from his honesty ; and, occasionally, some slight tribute may be paid to his personal merits in the form of a reduction in the rate of interest otherwise payable by him on money to be refunded (*n*), or even a total remission of such interest, together with a lenient application of the rules as to the measure of value in the case of property to be handed over (*o*) ; but, otherwise, on proof that in fact he has not complied with the fixed rules of equity, his honourable intentions will avail him nothing · *probitas laudatur et alget.*

359. Equally irrelevant is any question of material loss or gain resulting, or to be anticipated, from the transaction impeached   Thus it is quite unnecessary for the party complaining to prove that he has suffered tangible loss by reason of the contract or other transaction against which he seeks to be relieved, and quite useless for the party charged to establish that no such loss has been sustained (*p*)   Again, it is no answer to any claim for relief to establish, and it is therefore not only unnecessary, but irrelevant and improper, for the party complaining to offer anticipatory evidence to the contrary of, any of the following allegations . that the contract was in

(*ll*) As in *Watt* v *Grove* (1805), 2 Sch & Lefr 491 (at p 503)

(*m*) This question, with others relating to costs, is discussed in Ch VIII, Sect 2, Sub s (4), *post*

(*n*) As in *Imperial Mercantile Credit Association* v *Coleman* (1873), L R 6 H L 189 (*per* Lord CAIRNS, at pp 209, 210, reducing the rate of interest decreed in the Court below from 5 per cent. to 4 per cent on the ground that the director had acted on a mere error " honestly entertained ")

(*o*) As in *Re Fitzroy Bessemer Steel Co.* 1884), 50 L T 144 (*per* KAY, J , at p 147) In this case it was decided that the value of the shares which the director had received from the promoter should be taken at less than a third of their nominal value (though, according to the general run of the authorities—see § 380, *post*—they would have been valued at par), it " not being a case for vindictive damages,' in the opinion of the judge, nor a case for interest at all   This is the largest concession which has ever been made to a 'inquent director

(*p*) *Hamilton* v *Wright* (1842), 9 Cl & Fin 111 (*per* Lord BROUGHAM, at p 123), *Clarke* v *Tipping* (1846), 9 Beav 284 (where Lord LANGDALE, M R , at pp 287, 288, points out the irrelevance of the defendant's contention that his secret transactions were beneficial to the plaintiff) , *Parker* v *McKenna* (1874), 10 Ch App 96 (*per* Lord CAIRNS, L C , at p 118   " the Court will not inquire and is not in a position to ascertain whether the bank has lost or not lost by the acts of the directors "   and JAMES, L J , who, at pp. 124, 125, expresses the emphatic view that the Court is " not entitled, in my judgment, to receive evidence, or suggestion, or argument as to whether the principal did or did not suffer any injury in fact by reason of the dealing of the agent , for the safety of mankind requires that no agent shall be able to put his principal to the danger of such an inquiry as that") , *Harrington* v *Victoria Graving Dock Co.*, (1878) 3 Q B D 549 (*per* COCKBURN, C.J , at p 550, and FIELD, J , at p 552) , *Pearce* v *Foster* (1886), 17 Q B D 536, C A (*per* LINDLEY, L J , at p 542) , *Eden* v *Ridsdale's Railway Lamp & Lighting Co* (1889), 23 Q B D. 368, C A (at pp 370, 371, 372), *Bray* v *Ford,* [1896] A C 44, H L , *Kuhlicz* v *Lambert Bros , Ltd* (1913), 108 L T 565 (*per* SCRUTTON, J , at p 567)   The rule is otherwise in the case of certain kinds of statutory non disclosure, e g in relation to companies. as to which see § 559, *post*

a general sense, and abstracted from all considerations of the duties arising from the relation between the parties, a fair mercantile bargain (q); or that there is no reason, apart from such considerations, why the commission or profit (if it is a case of a bribe) should not have been taken (r), or that the party complaining was in such a position that he could not have earned the commission or profit himself (s); or that the party complaining has received the benefit of the agent's services (t); or, in a case of sale and purchase between the related parties where full disclosure has not been made, that the price was fair and adequate (u); or that the party charged made no profit, and

(q) *Aberdeen Railway Co.* v *Blaikie Bros* (1854), 1 Macq. H. L 461 (*per* Lord CRAN-WORTH, L C, at p. 472); *Imperial Mercantile Credit Association* v *Coleman* (1873), L R. 6 H L 189 (*per* Lord CAIRNS, L.C, at p 201 · "it is not the practice of a court of equity to inquire into the merits of a particular contract   The court does not permit such a contract to be made "); *McPherson* v. *Watt* (1877), 3 App Cas 254, H L (*per* Lord CAIRNS, L.C., at p 261); *Transvaal Lands Co.* v. *New Belgium, &c , Co*, [1914] 2 Ch 488, 502, C. A

(r) *Hichens* v *Congreve* (1831), 4 Sim. 420 (*per* SHADWELL, V -C, at pp 426, 127), *Costa Rica Railway Co* v *Forwood*, [1901] 1 Ch 746, C. A. (*per* VAUGHAN WILLIAMS, L.J, who, at p 761, points out that the rule is one which must be universally applied, though, in the particular case, "there may seem to be no reason of fairness why the profits should not go into the pockets of the trustees, and although the profits may be such that their *cestui que trust* could not have earned them all ")

(s) *Boston Deep Sea Fishing & Ice Co* v *Ansell* (1888), 39 C. D 339, C A , where it was held that it was no answer to contend, as the agent there did, that the company, his principal, not being a shareholder in the fish carrying or ice companies who contracted to give bonuses to such shareholders on their orders, was not qualified to obtain the bonuses the corrupt receipt of which by the agent was complained of (*per* COTTON, L J , at pp. 354, 355)   See also the passage from the judgment of VAUGHAN WILLIAMS, L.J , in *Costa Rica Railway Co* v *Forwood*, *sup*, which is cited in the last note

(t) *Salomons* v *Pender* (1865), 3 H & C 639 (*per* BRAMWELL, B , at p 642)

(u) *Randall* v *Errington* (1805), 10 Ves 423 (*per* Lord ELDON, L.C , at pp 427, 428), *Hichens* v *Congreve* (1831), 4 Sim 420 (*per* SHADWELL, V C , at p 427), *Rothschild* v *Brookman* (1831), 5 Bligh (N S) 165 (*per* Lord WYNFORD, L C , at pp 194–196), *Gillett* v *Peppercorne* (1840), 3 Beav 78 (*per* Lord LANGDALE, M R at p. 84), *Murphy* v *O'Shea* (1845), 2 Jo & Lat 422 , 69 R R 337, *per* SUGDEN, L C ( ) at pp. 424, 429), *Clarke* v *Tipping* (1846), 9 Beav 284 (*per* Lord LANGDALE, M R , at 288, 290), *Lewis* v *Hillman* (1852), 3 H L C 607 (*per* Lord ST LEONARDS, L C , at p 630), *Bentley* v *Craven* (1853), 18 Beav 75 (*per* ROMILLY, M.R , at p 78), *Beck* v *Kantorowicz* (1857), 3 K & J 230 (*per* WOOD, V -C , at pp 250, 251), *Dyson* v *Lum* (1866), 14 L T 588 (*per* STUART, V C), *McPherson* v *Watt, sup* (*per* Lord CAIRNS, L C , at p 264   "assume, if you please, that in every respect, as to price, and as to all other things connected with the sale, this was a sale which might have been supported had the McPherson family been told that Watt was the purchaser, in my opinion, it cannot be supported from the circumstance that that fact was not disclosed to them"   so Lord O'HAGAN, at p 266), *De Bussche* v *Alt* (1878), 8 C D 286, C A (*per Cur* , at p 316); *Whaley Bridge Calico Printing Co* v *Green* (1879), 5 Q B D 109 (*per* BOWEN, J , at p 111), *Hovenden & Sons* v. *Millhoff* (1900), 83 L T. 41, C A (*per* ROMER, L.J., at p 45)   In *Fox* v *Mackreth* (1788), 2 Cox 320, Lord THURLOW, L C , at pp 321, 322, committed himself to the proposition that "unless there be great inadequacy of value the case comes to nothing , the fraud or imposition of one party affords no ground of relief, unless damage be sustained by the other '   As applied to that form of equitable fraud which consists of non-disclosure by a trustee or agent, this statement is hopelessly incorrect, as Lord THURLOW tacitly acknowledged by his subsequent treatment of the case itself, for, though stating at an early stage that he should direct an inquiry as to value, we are told (at p 330) that "his Lordship, however, did not direct any such inquiries, but after the lapse of a considerable time, affirmed the decree, saying only that he had considered the case very much, and that he could not see that his Honour's decree was wrong"   Moreover, Lord ELDON, L C , in several cases took the opportunity of stating that Lord THURLOW afterwards acknowledged that the view in question had been expressed by him *per incuriam*, and ' went upon a clear mistake"   see the former's observations at p 277 of *Gibson* v *Jeyes* (1801), that the bargain was a bad one for him (v), or that he took risks, and stood to lose by it (w). Nor is it either requisite or relevant, in support of a principal's claim for relief against the party who has made a corrupt agreement with the agent, or as a ground for dismissal of such agent (x), to allege or prove that the agent was in fact thereby influenced or biassed in the advice which he gave to such principal (y), or even that the bribe was actually received at all, if it be proved to have been promised (z) ; or that the party charged was remunerated for his services by the party complaining (a).

6 Ves 266, p. 627 of *Ex p Lacey* (1802), 6 Ves 625, and p. 353 of *Ex p James* (1803), 8 Ves. 337, and cp the observation of GRANT, M R., as to Lord ELDON's correction of his predecessor's error, at p 148 of *Att -Gen. v Lord Dudley* (1815), G Cooper, 146, 1 R 226.

(v) *Ex p Bennett* (1805), 10 Ves. 381 (*per* Lord ELDON, L C, at pp 385, a case in which the trustee derived no advantage from, and was not personally interested in, the purchase) ; *Hamilton* v. *Wright* (1842), 9 Cl & Fin. 111 (*per* Lord BROUGHAM, at p 124) ; *Re Diamond Fuel Co*, *Metcalfe's Case* (1879), 13 C D 169, C A, (*per* JESSEL, M.R, at pp. 172, 173), *Re North Australian Territory Co*, *Archer's Case*, [1892] 1 Ch 322, C. A. (*per* LINDLEY, L J., at p. 336) ; *Dougan* v. *Macpherson*, [1902] A. C. 197, H. L. (*per* Lord HALSBURY, L.C, at p 201, during the argument "what has the fact that the trustee may have made a bad bargain to do with the question of unfair advantage on the part of the trustee ?")

(w) *Williams* v *Stevens* (1866), L R 1 P. C 352 (at p 359 "it is no answer to say that in the course of acquiring the bene it which has been derived by the trustee or agent, he incurred a possibility of loss. That may well be, but if the transaction has resulted in gain the consequence results that the whole benefit of the transaction belongs to the person whom he must be considered to have represented throughout")

(x) As to the principles on which the granting of relief against the contractee, as well as against the agent, is justified, and the nature of such relief, see Sect 5, Sub s. (2), §§ 383–385, *post*

(y) *Harrington* v *Victoria Graving Dock Co* (1878), 3 Q B D 549 (*per* COCKBURN, C.J, at p 550, and MELLOR, J , at p 552), the first definite decision on the point in question, which had been left open in *Smith* v *Sorby* (1875), *ibid*, 552 n , where it was only necessary to declare the immateriality of an issue as to whether there was an intention to influence or bias the agent , *Hovenden & Sons* v *Millhoff* (1900), 83 L T 41, C A (*per* ROMER, L J , at p. 45) The above are cases of claims for damages against the contractee for corrupting the agent The following are cases where the right to dismiss, or refuse payment to, the agent was in question —*Pearce* v *Foster* (1886), 17 Q B D 536, C A (*per* LINDLEY, L.J , at p 541), *Swale* v *Ipswich Tannery, Ltd* (1906), 11 Comm Cas 88 (*per* KENNEDY, J , at p 98, who, whilst expressly finding that the agent had not in fact been biassed in the slightest degree, held that in law this was wholly immaterial) As to this species of relief, see §§ 381, 382, *post*

(z) *Grant* v *Gold Exploration & Development Syndicate*, [1900] 1 Q B 233, C A (*per* A L SMITH, L J , at pp 242–244, COLLINS, L J , at pp 247, 248, and VAUGHAN WILLIAMS, L J , at pp. 253, 254), *King, Viall, & Benson* v *Howell* (1910), 27 T L. R 114, C A (*per* COZENS HARDY, M R , at p 115)

(a) *Gillett* v *Peppercorne* (1840), 3 Beav 78 (*per* Lord LANGDALE, M R , at p. 82 "the acting gratuitously makes no difference"), *York and North Midland Railway Co* v *Hudson* (1853), 16 Beav 485 (*per* ROMILLY, M R , at pp 499, 500), *McPherson* v *Watt* (1877), 3 App Cas 254, H L (*per* Lord CAIRNS, L C, at p 262, 263 "I care not whether this was done as a piece of business for which Mr Watt might have charged as a law agent, and sent in a bill of costs, or not " and, again, " whether Watt was a gratuitous adviser, or a paid adviser, of McPherson, he was not only an adviser, but the only adviser, of McPherson with regard to the sale of these houses"), *Luddy's Trustee* v *Peard* (1886), 33 C. D 500 (where KAY, J , at p 515, points out that the fact that the solicitor in that case was acting for a bankrupt, and probably, therefore, would not be paid, in no way negatived the fact that the bankrupt reposed confidence in him, and, therefore, was quite irrelevant), *Re Telescriptor Syndicate, Ltd* , [1903] 2 Ch 174 (*per* BUCKLEY, J , at p. 197 " an argument was suggested before me, but dropped, that, because the directors received no fees, it was not reasonable to suppose that they would be active It is, I think, of the first importance that it should be remembered that a director, whether paid or electing to serve without payment, owes duties which he cannot, in honour and honesty and legal

Still less relevant is any question as to the comparative advantages of adhering to, or avoiding, the transaction impeached. That is a matter of which the party complaining is to be the sole judge. The only function of judicature is to determine whether the right to relief is made out. The practical wisdom or unwisdom of asserting that right is no concern of the court, or of the party charged (b)

SECT. 4. AFFIRMATIVE ANSWERS TO THE CASE OF THE PARTY COMPLAINING.

360. When once the party complaining has proved the matters as to which the onus rests on him (c), it is incumbent on the party charged, unless he can repel the case made against him by direct contradiction, to establish some one or more of the affirmative answers available to him. Unless he succeeds in so doing, he must submit to judgment. Apart from those answers and bars, whether statutory or non-statutory, which are applicable to all proceedings for the avoidance of contracts in general (d), the only affirmative means by which the party charged can escape liability are these. He must establish,—the burden of course being on any party who avers that his opponent has in some way forfeited a *prima facie* right to relief to show how and why he has so forfeited it (e),—either that the relation had terminated before, or was in suspense at, the time of the particular transaction impeached, or that he fully discharged his duties of disclosure, and such other duties of good faith as flow from, or are ancillary to, this main and predominant duty, or that the party complaining had complete and exact knowledge *aliundè* of the undisclosed transaction or fact, or agreed to waive the performance of the duty by consenting in advance to any transaction or fact of the nature

liability, disregard"), *King, Viall, & Benson* v *Howell* (1910), 27 T. L R 114, C A (per COZENS-HARDY, M R, at p 115 "an agent to buy could not sell, whether he was remunerated for the sale or not")

(b) *Dyson* v *Lum* (1886), 11 L T 588, where it was in vain contended that the litigation would result in no benefit to the *cestui que trust*. And see § 221, *ante*, on this topic

(c) As stated in Sect 3, Sub-ss (1) and (2), *ante*

(d) Such as the non statutory pleas of accord and satisfaction, raised in *Salford Corporation* v *Lever*, [1891] 1 Q B 168, C A (at pp. 178–181), payment, raised in *Re Carriage Co operative Association* (1884), 27 C D 322, 330, set off, raised in *Re Anglo French Co operative Society, Ex p Pelly* (1882), 21 C D 492, C A (per JESSEL, M R, at pp 500–502, BRETT, L J, at pp 505, 506, and COTTON, L J, at pp 508, 509), and in *Re Carriage Co operative Association, sup* (where PEARSON, J, followed *Pelly's Case*), champerty, raised against an assignee in *Wilson* v *Short* (1847), 6 Hare 366 (per WIGRAM, V C, at p 384) In all these cases it so happened that, for reasons stated at the pages respectively indicated, the plea failed For instances of a statutory plea, see *Metropolitan Bank* v *Heiron* (1880), 5 Ex D 319, C A (per JAMES, L J, at p 323, BRETT, L J, at p 324, and COTTON, L.J, at pp 325, 326), and *Re Fitzroy Bessemer Steel Co* (1884), 50 L T 144 (per KAY, J, at p 147), in which the Statute of Limitations was relied upon,—in the former successfully, in the latter unsuccessfully, for the reasons stated in the references respectively given See also the very instructive case cited in § 358, note (u), *ante* As to the Trustee Act, 1888 (51 & 52 Vict. c 59), s 8, see *Re Lands Allotment Co*, [1894] 1 Ch 616, C A (per LINDLEY, L J, at pp 631, 632, and KAY, L.J, at pp 638, 639)

(e) See *Erlanger* v *New Sombrero Phosphate Co* (1878), 3 App Cas 1218, H L (per Lord PENZANCE, at p 1230 "it is for the vendors to show affirmatively that the company have forfeited that right", so Lord BLACKBURN, at p 1283, points out that the burden was on the promoters of showing "that the company have precluded themselves from the relief to which they have a right")

in question without the necessity for divulging it, or subsequently, with full knowledge of the facts and of his right of avoidance and otherwise in relation thereto, confirmed the transaction. These five affirmative pleas or answers, any one of which is sufficient, but some one of which is absolutely necessary, to entitle the party charged to succeed where he is unable to deny, or if denying, to disprove, the *primâ facie* case of the party complaining, require separate consideration (*f*).

Sub-s (1). *The Termination, or Suspense, of the Relation at the time of the Transaction.*

361. In the case of a direct dealing between the parties, it is a good answer to establish that the relation was not operative on the transaction, either because it had come to an end in fact before the transaction was entered into, or because there had been an agreement that it should be suspended for the occasion. Lord ELDON was accustomed to use the latter form of expression in enunciating this exception to the general rule. An attorney or trustee, he said, is not absolutely incapacitated from dealing with his client or *cestui que trust*, " but the relation must in some way be dissolved, or, if not, the parties must be put so much at arm's length that they agree to take the character of purchaser and vendor " (*g*) , and, again, " a trustee may buy from the *cestui que trust*, provided there is a distinct and clear contract, ascertained to be such after a jealous and scrupulous examination of all the circumstances " (*h*), and the *cestui que trust* has " clearly renounced the right of objecting," so that the parties may be said to have thus " bargained that the rule should be relaxed " (*i*) It is for the agent or trustee, he observes in another case, to show that he has " shaken off " his character as such, not only with the consent of the principal or *cestui que trust*, but as the result of " a new contract " between the parties to that effect (*j*). And, in still more precise language, he lays down elsewhere that " a trustee for sale may be the purchaser in this sense, that he may contract with his *cestui que trust* that, with reference to the contract of purchase, they shall no longer stand in the relative situation of trustee and *cestui que trust*; and the trustee, having through the medium of that sort of bargain evidently, distinctly, and honestly proved that he had removed himself from the character of trustee, his purchase may be sustained " (*k*). This (again using Lord ELDON's language) " is a difficult case to make out " (*l*), but it is not an impossible one, and, in the very authority in which the observation was made, it was so made out, it being there apparent from the evidence, and

(*f*) See the first five Sub sections of this Section, respectively
(*g*) At p 277 of *Gibson* v *Jeyes* (1801), 6 Ves 266
(*h*) *Coles* v *Trecothick* (1804), 9 Ves. 234, at p 246
(*i*) *Ibid*, at pp 247, 248
(*j*) *Ex p James* (1803), 8 Ves 337, at pp 348, 352, 353 Lord LANGDALE, M R , followed Lord ELDON's mode of putting the proposition see *Randall* v *Errington* (1805), 10 Ves. 423, at p 426
(*k*) *Sanderson* v *Walker* (1807), 13 Ves 601 And to the same effect, at p 208 of *Downes* v *Grazebrook* (1817), 3 Mer 200
(*l*) *Coles* v *Trecothick, sup*, at p 247.

from the instrument itself, that "the whole execution of the trust devolved upon the *cestui que trust* and he takes all upon himself, with the auctioneers if not chosen, at least approved by him, makes surveys, settles the plans, mode of sale and price, and therefore has all knowledge what is the proper price," so that, Lord ELDON concludes, "if any case can exist for relaxing the rule by consent of the parties, this is that case" (m) By the "contract," and "bargain" referred to, it must be supposed that Lord ELDON meant merely such a contract or bargain as must be inferred from the conduct of the parties . he cannot have meant an express and formal contract, because if the circumstances be sufficient to show that the relation was inoperative at the material date, it is not necessary for the party charged to prove a contract in words to that effect ; if on the contrary, it cannot be shown that it was inoperative at that date, an express bargain that the parties shall pretend, contrary to the fact, to be free from the relation, would be wholly ineffectual (n)

362. It follows from the above rule, as stated by Lord ELDON, that where, as in the case of infants, it is impossible to obtain a "consent," or a "new contract" or "bargain" to be implied from the circumstances, which will be effectual in law, it is impossible to sustain the transaction at all on this ground, except through the medium of the Court, who alone can sanction a contract on the infant's behalf (o)

363. It should also be remembered that where, as may often be the case, the reasons for the disability endure after the relation giving rise to it is at an end, the party charged must prove that those reasons, as well as the relation itself, have ceased to exist (p).

364. It is open to the party charged to allege that, though the relation existed at the time, he entered into the transaction in another, not being a fiduciary, relation which also happened to belong to him at that time and, if this allegation is established, the transaction is sustained (q)

(m) *Coles* v. *Trecothick* (1804), 9 Ves 234, at pp 247, 248 It will be noticed that the circumstances here were very special. In none of the other cases cited in the last five notes was the termination or suspension of the relation established.

(n) See § 322, and note (n) thereto, *ante*, as to the futility of a formal renunciation of the character of trustee, or agent, for the mere colourable purpose of escaping the rule The proposition is not now usually stated in the form adopted by Lord ELDON and the judges of his day The modern way of expressing it is to insist on the necessity of the parties having been in fact freed from the relation, and of their dealing with one another at arm's length see *Murphy* v. *O'Shea* (1845), 2 Jo & Lat. 422, *per* SUGDEN, L.C. (Ir), who, at p 425, says that "the rule of the Court does not prevent an agent from purchasing from his principal, but only requires that he shall deal with him at arm's length" The same high authority, when Lord ST LEONARDS, L.C., afterwards used the same language in *Cutts* v *Selmon* (1852), 21 L J. (CH) 750 (at p. 750) And see the citation from *Williams* v *Scott*, in note (z) to § 366, *post.*

(o) *Sanderson* v. *Walker* (1807), 13 Ves 601 (*per* Lord ELDON, L.C , at pp 601, 602) The Public Trustee, under the Public Trustee Act, 1906 (6 Edw 7, c. 55), is in no different position from any other trustee in this respect · *Re New Haw Estate Trusts* (1912), 107 L T 191.

(p) *Carter* v. *Palmer* (1842), 8 Cl & Fin. 657 (*per* Lord COTTENHAM, L C , at p 705 "it is also proved that he did not actually act as counsel or agent for the respondent after August, 1831, but . . . if his previous employment disqualified him from becoming the purchaser for his own benefit . ., such disqualification must continue so long as the reasons upon which it is founded continue to operate")

(q) See the cases cited in notes (w), (x), and (y), to § 344, *ante*

365. Where the trustee or agent is charged with having taken a present from a third party, it is a good answer to any claim for relief that his trusteeship or agency had come to an end before the date of the impeached transaction (*r*).

Sub-s. (2). *The Complete Discharge of the Duty of Disclosure and consequential Duties*

366. If not in a position to make good the kind of case just discussed, the party charged must be prepared with evidence sufficient to justify the transaction The conditions of disclosure, and otherwise, subject to which alone the trustee, promoter, or agent can deal with the *cestui que trust*, company, or principal, or can acquire personal profit in the course and execution of his trusteeship, promotership, or agency, have already been stated It has been seen that it is the duty of the party charged, when dealing direct with the other related party, to impart to him all the knowledge which he possesses, in both senses of the word (*s*), as to the nature of the transaction, and his own share and part in it, if it is being done in other names (*t*), and as to all material facts within his knowledge affecting the value of, and otherwise relating to, the subject-matter of the contract, together with impartial and disinterested advice against himself, as to the expediency of entering into it (*u*) : and that if, being an agent, he accepts in the course and execution of his agency any personal profit or advantage from the opposite principal, he is under an obligation to make full and precise disclosure of this fact to his own principal (*v*) By these means, and, further, by insisting on the intervention of an indifferent person to advise the party complaining, in the case of a direct dealing with him (*w*), and, where the transaction assumes the form of a contract, by giving full and fair value (*x*),—whether either of these

(*r*) *Parker* v *McKenna* (1874), 10 Ch App 96 (*per* Lord CAIRNS, L C., at p 118) ; *De Bussche* v *Alt* (1878), 8 C D 286, C A (*per Cur*, at pp 311, 312) , *Eden* v *Ridsdale's Railway Lamp & Lighting Co* (1889), 23 Q B D 368, C. A (*per* LINDLEY and LOPES, LL.JJ., at p 372) In none of these cases was the termination of the confidential relation established

(*s*) As to these, see § 316, *ante* See Ch II. Sect 1, *ante*, as to what disclosure means. *Oelkers* v *Ellis*, [1914] 2 K B 139, a principal and agent case, is a good instance of a pretended and partial disclosure which in law is none at all.

(*t*) See §§ 321, 331, 336, *ante*

(*u*) See §§ 323, 324, 332, 333, 337, 338, *ante*

(*v*) See §§ 339, 340, 341, *ante*.

(*w*) See § 316, and note (*b*) to § 318, *ante*, as to the duty to give impartial advice. As to the other duty, see *Gibson* v *Jeyes* (1801), 6 Ves. 266, where Lord ELDON, L.C, at p 278, says that the attorney's obligation in that case to the lady who was his client was *either* to have told her to get the advice of some other person, *or* to have " given her all that reasonable advice against himself that he would have given her against a third person." In *Harris* v. *Tremenheere* (1808), 15 Ves. 34, there was no advice by a third person in respect of such of the leases as were upheld · from which the inference is that Lord ELDON, L.C., who decided this case also, did not consider it a necessity in all cases.

(*x*) See § 323, and note (*p*) thereto, *ante*, as to the absence of any case of a *mere fiduciary* relation in which, the propriety of the transaction being proved in every other respect, the party charged has failed on the ground of undervalue alone Conversely, where the propriety is not established in other respects, full value will not entitle the party charged to succeed see § 359, note (*u*), *ante*. But proof of adequate value having been paid is undoubtedly of the greatest assistance in establishing the general fairness of the transaction, and the failure to prove it is correspondingly detrimental indeed, undervalue, with

is absolutely necessary as a separate and independent *probandum*, or not,—
he puts himself in a position to establish that righteousness and propriety
of the transaction which is the primary and predominant condition of its
being "sustained," if and when it should be called in question   From the
fact that these duties are imposed upon the party charged at the time of
the transaction, it follows, as a necessary consequence, that, when the transaction is impeached, a corresponding burden rests upon him of proving that
he has punctually and fully complied with them.   Indeed, the duties themselves
are only duties in the sense that the party owes it to himself, in his own
ultimate interest, to conduct the transaction under the conditions prescribed,
for there is nothing *ipso jure* void, illegal, or criminal in his doing otherwise (*y*) :   it is simply a case of his taking the risk of not being able to prove
what is incumbent on him to prove in order to justify the transaction, if
a time comes when it is challenged   The rule as to the burden of allegation
and proof which lies in this respect on the trustee, promoter, or agent,
has been expressly stated in numerous cases (*z*) , but, apart from any formal
enunciation, it underlies, and is presupposed by, the actual decisions arrived
at in all the authorities on the subject (*a*)

other circumstances, may be sufficient to show positive fraud, where the party complaining
is driven to allege and rely upon that as a ground for relief, as in *Re Collard*, [1897] 2 Q B
8   Even without other circumstances, it has been said that it may indicate fraud, if such
as "to shock the conscience", though it may be doubted whether the proposition,
stated in this extreme form, is not more calculated to shock the conscience than any undervalue which could be the subject of it.

    (*y*) See note (*ll*) to § 322, *ante*
    (*z*) To take an early, and a late, illustration, two clear statements as to the general onus on
the party charged are to be found in *Gibson* v *Jeyes* (1801), 6 Ves 266 (*per* Lord ELDON,
L C., at p 276), and in *Williams* v *Scott*, [1900] A C 499, P C (at p 508 "it ought not to
be assumed, in the absence of evidence to the contrary, that the transaction was a proper
one, and that the *cestuis que trustent* were informed of all necessary matters   The burden
of proof that the transaction was a righteous one rests upon the trustee, who is bound to
produce clear affirmative proof that the parties were at arm's length , that the *cestuis que
trustent* had the fullest information upon all material facts , and that, having this information, they agreed to and adopted what was done ")   For statements as to the onus of
proving disclosure of material facts with reference to the property, or its value, see *Selsey*
(*Lord*) v. *Rhoades* (1824), 2 Sim. & St 41 (*per* LEACH, V -C , at pp. 49, 50 . "the steward
is bound to make out that the employer was fully informed of every circumstance respecting
the property which was either within the knowledge of the steward, or ought to have been
within his knowledge, which could tend to demonstrate the value of the property ");
Charter v *Trevelyan* (1844), 11 Cl & Fin 714 (*per* Lord LYNDHURST, L C , at p. 732);
Thomson v. *Eastwood* (1877), 2 App Cas 215, H L (*per* Lord CAIRNS, L C , at p 236);
Dougan v *Macpherson*, [1902] A C. 197, H L (*per* Lord HALSBURY, L C., at p. 202, and
Lord MACNAGHTON, at p. 204).   As to the onus of proving disclosure of the receipt of a
personal profit by the agent, see the statement of JAMES, L J , at p 476 of *Re British Seamless Box Co.* (1881), 17 C D 467, C A   "the burden of proof is thrown on those who have
received it to satisfy the Court that it was intended to be, and was in fact, honestly
received "
    (*a*) See, generally, the cases cited in the notes to Sect 2, *ante*, of which those decided
against the trustee, promoter, or agent, were, for the most part, so decided because he failed,
or did not even attempt, to discharge the onus in question.   The following are cases in
which he discharged such onus, and judgment was accordingly given in his favour —
Coles v. *Trecothick* (1804), 9 Ves 234 (*per* Lord ELDON, L C , at pp 247, 248); *Harris*
v *Tremenheere* (1808), 15 Ves 34 (as to such of the leases as were held to be pure gifts,
per Lord ELDON, L C , at pp 39, 40) , *Morse* v *Royal* (1806), 12 Ves. 355 (*per* Lord ELDON,
L C , at pp 374, 375) , *Selsey* (*Lord*) v *Rhoades* (1824), 2 Sim & St 41 (*per* LEACH, V. C ,
at pp. 49, 50) , *Farrant* v. *Blanchford* (1863), 32 L J. (CH) 237 ; *Re British Seamless*

367. In strictness, perhaps, where it is a case of an agent receiving a personal profit from the opposite principal, the onus is on the party charged to establish not only disclosure of the fact on his own part, but the assent of the party complaining to his acceptance or retention of the profit (b). But, in substance, proof of the disclosure is enough. One can hardly imagine a case in which, after such proof, the principal would be heard to say that his agent is accountable merely because he has not formally expressed his consent. His silence, under such circumstances, would be taken to imply consent: otherwise, the Court would be lending countenance to the employment of discreditable strategy, and to the dishonest laying of traps, on the one side, and would be discouraging candour on the other.

368. It should be observed that the above rules are not necessarily applicable in their integrity to the statutory procedure by misfeasance summons in the case of promoters and directors of a company. For instance, in such cases, as will be noted in the proper place (c), the burden being on the liquidator, or other applicant, to prove misfeasance, and the non-disclosure being an element in such misfeasance, he must give some evidence of the non-disclosure, however slight, before he can call on the party charged for an answer.

Sub-s. (3). *Knowledge of the Party Complaining.*

369. Though not in a position to show that he has made the full disclosure required of him, the party charged is still entitled to set up that the party complaining had in fact, though from other sources, complete and precise knowledge of all the material circumstances, and, if he establishes this allegation by evidence, the burden being on him of so doing, he has a valid answer to the case for relief which is made against him, though otherwise unassailable (d). But, for this purpose, it is necessary to prove actual and

---

Box Co. (1881), 17 C D 467, C A (*per* JESSEL, M R , at pp 473, 474, JAMES, L J., at pp. 476, 477, and BRETT, L J , at p 478); *Re Sale Hotel and Botanical Gardens, Ltd , Ex p Hesketh* (1898), 78 L T. 368, C A , *Re Haslam and Hier-Evans*, [1902] 1 Ch. 765, C A , *Stubbs v Slater*, [1910] 1 Ch 632, C. A , at pp 641-644, 648), *Aston v. Kelsey*, [1913] 3 K. B. 314, C. A , *Blaker v Hawes & Brown* (1913), 109 L T. 320 , *Omnium Electric Palaces, Ltd v Baines*, [1914] 1 Ch 332, C A (*per* COZENS HARDY, M R , at pp. 360, 361, SWINFEN EADY, L J , at pp 354, 355, and PHILLIMORE, L J., at p 356).

(b) See *Charter v Trevelyan* (1844), 11 Cl. & Fin 714 (*per* Lord LYNDHURST, L C , at p. 732) , *Aas v. Benham*, [1891] 2 Ch 244, C A (*per* LINDLEY, L J , at p 255) , *Williams v Scott*, [1900] A. C 499, P C (at pp 503-505) In the case of a direct dealing between the related parties, of course the assent of the party complaining is essential . see *Downes v. Grazebrook* (1817), 3 Mer 200.

(c) See § 616, note (t), *post*

(d) In the following, this onus was sustained *Coles v Trecothick, sup.* , *Farrant v. Blanchford* (1863), 32 L J (CH) 237 (*per* Lord WESTBURY, L.C , at p 239); *Luff v Lord* (1864), 34 Beav. 220 (*per* ROMILLY, M R , at pp. 229-232) In the following the burden was not discharged *Rothschild v. Brookman* (1831), 5 Bligh (N S) 161 (*per* Lord WYNFORD, L C., at p 201) ; *Lindsay Petroleum Company v Hurd* (1874), L R. 5 P. C 221 (at p 241) Illustrations of cases in which the party charged proved the knowledge of the party complaining as to some of the transactions impeached, but not as to the others, are · *Williamson v Hine Bros* , [1891] 1 Ch 390 (*per* KEKEWICH, J , at pp 391, 394, 395) , *Hippisley v Knee Bros* , [1905] 1 K B 1, Div Ct (*per* Lord ALVERSTONE, C J , at p 7, and KENNEDY, J , at p 9) In all the above cases alike, it was either expressly held, or assumed, that the onus was on the party charged

personal knowledge on the part of the *cestui que trust*, company, or principal, as the case may be. The kind of knowledge which has been already discussed under the designation of " presumptive knowledge " (*e*) will not be imputed to the party complaining, so as to defeat his claim (*f*), however freely it may be imputed to the party charged, when it is a question of whether he has performed his duty of divulging all matters within his cognizance (*g*), or however material such knowledge would be in a case where no fiduciary relation exists between the parties (*h*). It is of no use, therefore, merely to prove that the party complaining had the means of knowledge (*i*), for instance, in a case of promoter and company, that the company was " put upon inquiry " by the general state of its books or documents (*j*), or by vague and dubious entries therein, such as an item under the heading " secret service," which it was contended in one case was enough to fix the company with notice of corrupt expenditure (*k*). Nor, in cases between principal and agent, is it to the purpose to establish the existence of customs and practices, however widely prevailing, as to the receipt of commissions, discounts, rebates, and other bribes by the agent, which defeat and undermine the very nature and essence of the relation, and are therefore dishonest, unless actual and personal cognizance of the custom is established against the principal; for no knowledge of it will be presumed against him from its mere prevalence and notoriety (*l*). Precisely the same strict rules as to the burden of proof

(*e*) In Ch. II, Sect. 3, Sub s (5), *ante*

(*f*) *Downes* v *Grazebrook* (1817), 3 Mer 200 (*per* Lord ELDON, L C, at pp 208, 209)

(*g*) *Watts* v *Bucknall*, [1903] 1 Ch 766, C A, a company prospectus case, is a good illustration of the court refusing to impute to the party complaining the kind of knowledge which it will always readily, and in this same case did, presume against the non disclosing party. " It will not suffice," says COLLINS, M R, at p 775, when dealing with the knowledge sought to be imputed to the party complaining, " to say merely that the party had such constructive notice that he might have been put upon inquiry, and might have searched the records which are not very easily accessible, and thus have arrived at a conclusion." With these observations contrast those as to position of the directors alleged to have " knowingly issued the prospectus " (pp 771, 772) Cp. *Nocton* v *Lord Ashburton*, [1914] A. C 932, 962, H. L A shareholder, however, is fixed with knowledge of the constitution of the company of which he is a member (see § 63, *ante*), and of the powers of its directors *Percival* v *Wright*, [1902] 2 Ch 421 (*per* SWINFEN EADY, J., at p 426)

(*h*) *Dunne* v *English* (1872), L R 18 Eq. 524 (*per* JESSEL, M R, at p 536 " even a statement which would in other cases be constructive notice .. will not be sufficient in cases of principal and agent ")

(*i*) *Swale* v. *Ipswich Tannery*, *Ltd* (1906), 11 Comm Cas 88 (*per* KENNEDY, J, at p 96)

(*j*) *York & North Midland Railway Co* v *Hudson* (1853), 16 Beav. 485 (*per* ROMILLY, M R, at pp 500–502), *Watts* v *Bucknall*, *sup*

(*k*) *York* v. *North Midland Railway Co.* v *Hudson*, *sup.* (*per* ROMILLY, M R, at pp 498, 499)

(*l*) *Gillett* v. *Peppercorne* (1840), 3 Beav 78 (*per* Lord LANGDALE, M R., at p. 85 " the knowledge "—i e of the alleged practice of brokers to sell their own shares—" in my opinion ought to have been brought home to the plaintiff," and merely to prove that it is " every day practice in the city "—p 83—is not to bring it home to any one not engaged in it) ; *Turnbull* v *Garden* (1869), 20 L T 218 (a similar case, *per* JAMES, V.-C, at p. 220 . " in answer to this the defendant depended upon what he alleged to be the custom of the trade It was not the first time the Court had heard of, and disapproved, the custom of ' salting invoices ' ") , *Robinson* v *Mollett* (1875), L. R 7 H L 802 (the same point, in regards tallow-brokers · *per* Lord CHELMSFORD, L C., at pp 837, 838, and see the opinion of BRETT, J, advising the House, at pp 816–819, 824, 825), *De Bussche* v. *Alt* (1878), 8 C D 286, C. A (*per Cur*, at p. 317, as to " an alleged custom or

where the wrongdoer sets up the knowledge of the injured party, and for the same reasons, are applied to cases of misrepresentation (*m*).

370. It is of course essential that the knowledge (as, indeed, the disclosure, where the party is attempting to make out compliance with his duty in this respect) should be brought home to the very person, or to all the persons, existing or to come into being (such as possible future allottees in a company case), to whom the fiduciary duty is owed, and where the person is an artificial one, the knowledge must be brought home to those officers and agents by whom alone the corporation can in law be said to acquire or possess knowledge This topic (a not unimportant one) is dealt with fully in the discussion of the question of parties (*n*)

Sub-s (4)   Contract to Waive Disclosure

371. As in the class of non-disclosure which forms the subject of Chapter III (*o*), waiver is a complete answer to the case of the party complaining. If it can be shown that it was an express term of any contract between the parties that the trustee, promoter, or agent should be free to enter into any transaction of the nature of that which is impeached without making the disclosure, or without making the full and exact disclosure, which the law would otherwise require of him, the claim to relief is gone, or rather is shown never to have existed, having been renounced in advance For instance, if a director of a company, charged with the receipt of secret profits, can point to a provision in the articles of association which expressly or impliedly excepts a certain class of matters from those of which disclosure is ordinarily required, and can show that the matter in question comes within the excepted class, he escapes liability (*p*) So also, a trustee under a will is entitled to rely on a clause in the will which contemplates and expressly sanctions the making of profits by him in his own business out of the business of the testator which he is to carry on as trustee (*q*) But such articles, terms, and clauses are subject to close scrutiny and criticism, and it must clearly appear that, in plain and perspicuous language, and not merely by

practice in the ports in which the defendant trades for an agent for sale, with a minimum limit, himself to take at that limit, and at his own option the thing he is employed to sell ") ; *Hippisley* v *Knee Bros* , [1905] 1 K B 1, Div Ct (*per* Lord ALVERSTONE, C J , at p 7, and KENNEDY, J , at p 9, as to an alleged custom of auctioneers to receive rebates or discounts from newspaper proprietors on orders for advertisements). As to all these cases in their ethical aspect, see §§ 656, 657, *post* In *Great Western Insurance Co* v *Cunliffe* (1874), 9 Ch App 525, which is sometimes cited in support of the view that the party complaining may be fixed with presumptive knowledge of a custom to take illicit commissions, the plaintiffs had impliedly, if not expressly, waived all objection,—see note (*s*), *inf* ,—and further, at a later stage, had acquired actual knowledge of the custom , apart from which, the commissions were not paid in respect of, or calculated upon, the particular transaction between the two principals And *Baring* v *Stanton* (1876), 3 C D 502, C A , was a case of the same class
(*m*) See § 209 of the author's *Law of Actionable Misrepresentation*
(*n*) It forms the subject of §§ 392, 393, *post* See also § 50, note (*f*), *ante*
(*o*) See Ch III, Sect 4, Sub s (1), *ante*
(*p*) As in *Costa Rica Co* v *Forwood*, [1901] 1 Ch 746, C A The conditions of the exemption must be observed *Transvaal Lands Co* v *New Belgium, &c , Co* , [1914] 2 Ch 488, 504, 505, C A.
(*q*) *Re Sykes*, [1909] 2 Ch 241, C A

what under other circumstances might be a reasonable implication, the trustee, promoter, or agent was distinctly absolved from the duty of disclosure by the very person, or by all the persons, if more than one, to whom the duty was owed (r). It is possible, however, to infer an intention to waive disclosure from an instruction by a principal to an agent to conduct the agency business in accordance with the usual customs and practices of that business, whatever they may be (s); just as a party may be bound by an agreement which he has not even read, on clear proof that he deliberately elected to execute it, whatever its contents might be, and without desiring or caring to know what in fact they were. So also, an intention to waive may be inferred from acts and conduct, but, to justify such an inference, the evidence adduced by the party charged must be of an extremely " clear and cogent " character (t) And, difficult as it is to establish an express absolution *ab ante* from a breach of fiduciary duty, it would seem all but impossible to establish an implied one. In certain classes of case, to be discussed hereafter (u), the legislature has thought fit to invalidate waivers altogether

Sub-s (5) *Confirmation of the Transaction.*

372. Another means of resisting the claim to relief is, as in the case of both the other two types of relation giving rise to a duty of disclosure (v), proof that the party complaining, though not having beforehand dispensed with the duty of disclosure, nevertheless elected to confirm the undisclosed transaction afterwards, either in the view that it would be more in his interests to adhere to it than to have it undone, or, where it is a case of an agent having taken a bribe or secret profit, from motives of pure generosity This plea admits the breach of fiduciary duty, and the right originally acquired by the party complaining to relief in respect of such breach, but asserts the subsequent loss of that right by the deliberate affirmance of that which he was free to disaffirm It is obvious that a case of this sort which depends on no merits whatever on the part of him who sets it up, but on the contrary begins by acknowledging his demerits, must always be a difficult one to make out, and especially so when the alleged confirmation amounts to a gratuitous remission of the consequences of the breach of duty, as in the case of the corruption of an agent (w). It can only, therefore, be made out by the clearest proof, not merely

(r) *Re Sykes,* [1909] 2 Ch. 241, C. A. (*per* COZENS-HARDY, M R , at p 247, and FARWELL, L J , at p. 250, recognizing the strictness of proof required, though there it was held sufficient) In the following, the proof was held insufficient —*Re Westmoreland Green & Blue Slate Co , Bland's Case,* [1893] 2 Ch 612, C A (*per* LINDLEY, L.J , at p 617); *Gluckstein* v. *Barnes,* [1900] A C 240, H L. (*per* Lord MACNAGHTEN, at p. 249), *Omnium Electric Palaces, Ltd* v *Barnes,* [1914] 1 Ch 332, C A (*per* SARGANT, J , at p 347, though there the party complaining failed on other grounds).

(s) *Great Western Insurance Co* v *Cunliffe* (1874), 9 Ch App 525 (*per* JAMES, L J , at p 537, referring to the evidence of the plaintiffs having said—" we meant it to be according to the usual practice ")

(t) *De Bussche* v *Alt* (1878), 8 C D. 286, C A. (*per Cur* , at p 313)

(u) In § 562, *post*

(v) See Ch III, Sect 4, Sub s (2), *ante,* and Ch V, Sect 4, Sub-s (3), *post.*

(w) See the observations of ROMER, L J., referred to in note (a), *inf*

of the act itself, and the intention to affirm supposed to be indicated thereby, but also of the fact that the party complaining, when so purporting to affirm, had the fullest and most detailed knowledge of all the material circumstances, and of all his rights in connection therewith, including the right to disaffirm, for he may have confirmed the transaction simply because he thought he could not help himself. There is very seldom much difficulty in proving the former and far less important of these two *probanda :* it is the latter,—the knowledge, in the absence of which there is nothing but the appearance, without the reality, of affirmation,—which creates the difficulty in the way of the party on whom the burden of proof lies. In the numerous cases in which the party charged has not sustained the onus of proving this knowledge, both of facts and of rights, on the part of the opposite party, the plea has failed (*x*)   in the comparatively few instances in which he has so sustained it, the plea has succeeded (*y*)

373. Difficult as it is to establish a case even of the most express affirmation,—for the courts are often astute to detect, instead of the suggested affirmation, a cunning design on the part of the trustee, promoter, or agent to entrench and fortify himself against future attack, and a continuance thereby of the very fraud or *mala fides* which is supposed to have been absolved (*z*),—it is yet more difficult to imply a confirmation from mere acts and conduct (*a*), and probably impossible to infer it from inactivity and delay alone (*b*)   And in any case where by reason of infancy or otherwise

(*x*) As in *Dunbar* v *Tredennick* (1813), 2 Ball & B 304, *Walker* v *Symonds* (1818), 3 Swanst. 1, *Rothschild* v *Brookman* (1831), 5 Bligh (N S) 165 (*per* Lord WYNFORD, L C, at p 201). *Perens* v *Johnson* (1857), 3 Sm. & G 419 (*per* STUART, V.-C, at pp 425, 426), *Lloyd* v *Attwood* (1859), 3 De G. & J 614; *Franks* v *Bollans* (1867), 17 L T 309 (*per* STUART, V -C, at p. 311), *De Bussche* v *Alt, sup* (*per Cur*, at pp 312-314), *Swale* v *Ipswich Tannery, Ltd* (1906), 11 Comm Cas 88 (*per* KENNEDY, J, at p 97).

(*y*) As in *Morse* v *Royal* (1806), 12 Ves 355 (*per* Lord ELDON, L C, at pp 373, 374, 376-378), *Selsey (Lord)* v *Rhoades* (1827), 1 Bligh (N S) 1 (*per* Lord ELDON, L C, at p. 8), *Salmon* v. *Cutts* (1850), 4 De G & Sm 125 (*per* KNIGHT BRUCE, V -C, at pp 129, 130), *Baker* v *Read* (1854), 3 W. R 118, *Dover* v *Buck* (1865), 12 L T 136 (*per* STUART, V. C, at p. 137), *Nutt* v *Easton,* [1899] 1 Ch 873 (*per* COZENS HARDY, J, at pp 878, 879), *Omnium Electric Palaces, Ltd* v *Baines,* [1914] 1 Ch. 332, C A (*per* SARGANT, J, at p 343, and COZENS-HARDY, M R, at p 350)

(*z*) This was the view of the evidence taken by Lord MANNERS, L C (Ir), at pp 316-318 of *Dunbar* v *Tredennick, sup*, where a trustee and agent, having failed to prove the propriety of the transaction (a purchase from his *cestui que trust* and employer), urged that the agreement had been confirmed by completion, but it was held that the conveyance having been obtained from the *cestui que trust* whilst the relation, and the confidence resulting from it, still existed, and without his being any more aware at the later date than at the earlier of his rights in the matter, and particularly his right to impeach the transaction, it was simply a case of the so called confirmation having been procured by the same dishonest means as the agreement which it purported to confirm

(*a*) See *Bartram & Sons* v *Lloyd* (1904), 90 L T 357, C A, where the Court of Appeal disagreeing with the view of BRUCE, L J, in the Court below (1903), 88 L. T 286, held that the agent's receipt of secret commission had not been confirmed by his principal's subsequent conduct, and where ROMER, J, at p 360, enlarged on the utter improbability of any employer, in his own interests, and as a matter of business, deliberately intending to abandon his rights in respect of a proceeding by which he has been robbed, after knowledge that he has been so robbed, without manifesting his intention by an express instrument or declaration

(*b*) See § 374, *post.* In *Farrant* v *Blanchford* (1863), 32 L J (CH.) 237, confirmation was inferred from long inactivity, *with other circumstances* (*per* Lord WESTBURY, L.C, at p 240)

it is impossible in law, or impracticable in fact, to procure evidence of the intention or the knowledge of the person, or all the persons or members of the class, to whom the duty is owed, a plea of confirmation is out of the question altogether (c).

Sub-s (6)   Matters which do not per se constitute Affirmative Answers.

374. It remains to consider certain matters which are not in themselves affirmative answers to the case of the party complaining. Foremost amongst these is delay This question has already been fully discussed in relation to the duty of disclosure which is incidental to the negotiation for contracts of a certain kind (d). It has been seen, in the course of that discussion, that lapse of time, unless it exceeds some statutory period of limitation, is of no legal significance in itself, though, with other circumstances, it may furnish evidence of a plea of affirmation, or acquiescence in the sense of affirmation, or of waiver, and may give an opportunity for circumstances to arise which may render it impossible to avoid the transaction complained of (such as a change in the substance of the property which is the subject of the transaction, or the intervention of the *jus tertii*), and though, where evidence is lost, it may raise a presumption against the party to whose delay and inaction such loss is to be attributed, and in any case may affect the exercise of judicial discretion in the matter of costs. All these principles, applicable to every case alike in which a party is seeking to be relieved of a voidable transaction (whether on the ground of non-disclosure, or misrepresentation, or any other ground), having been stated once, need not be re-stated now It is sufficient to say that there are many illustrations of their application to the particular class of non-disclosure which is the subject of the present Chapter (e).

(c) See §§ 392, 393, *post*.

(d) In §§ 216–219, *ante*

(e) The best statements as to the significance of delay as evidence, *with other circumstances*, in support of certain affirmative answers, or as a ground for making presumptions against the case of the party whose inaction has caused the loss of testimony, and as to its insignificance *per se*, in cases of fiduciary relationship, are to be found in the following·— *Morse v Royal* (1806), 12 Ves 355 (*per* Lord ELDON, L.C , at p 374   " as to the effect of length of time, when there is no bar by the statute of limitations, a court of equity will never lay down as a general proposition that .. the party is too late , . . . *The true operation of length of time is by way of evidence ,* . Considered in this way, length of time may have some operation   in what degree *depends upon the circumstances of the case* ") , *Erlanger v New Sombrero Phosphate Co* (1878), 3 App Cas 1218, H. L (*per* Lord PENZANCE, at p 1231 " delay, as it seems to me, has two aspects Lapse of time may so change the condition of the thing sold, or bring about such a state of things that justice cannot be done by rescinding the contract subject to any amount of allowances and compensation This is one aspect of delay, and it is in many cases particularly applicable to property of a mining character   But delay may also imply acquiescence, and in this aspect it equally bars the plaintiff's right, for such a contract as is now under consideration is only voidable and not void It conduces, I think, to clearness and to the exclusion of a certain vagueness which is apt to hang about the doctrine of delay as a bar to relief, to keep these two different aspects of it separate and distinct, when the consequences of delay come to be considered in connection with the circumstances of the individual case ") , *Re Postlethwaite* (1888), 60 L T 514, C A (*per* BOWEN, L J , at p 520   " we are asked to displace a transaction as impeachable which took place 34 years ago, and when all the parties who could give an explanation are dead.   . It seems to me that we ought to bring to the consideration of such a case this feeling, that if the correspondence and facts are capable of a reasonable

375. Other matters which are entirely irrelevant to any question between the parties, and which it is as idle for the party charged to affirm, as it is for the party complaining to contradict, have been incidentally dealt with in the examination of the matters which it is not incumbent on the party complaining to allege or prove (*f*) To these may be added the following miscellaneous illustrations. When a case has been established against the party complaining of failure to communicate knowledge which he in fact possessed during the subsistence of the relation, it is of no avail for him to set up that he acquired such knowledge before the relation commenced, or otherwise than in the execution of the duties appertaining to it (*g*)   It is equally ineffectual for the purpose of an affirmative defence, or even for the purpose of influencing costs, to rely upon an offer made before action, unless such offer comprises all the relief claimed to which the party complaining is by the judgment of the court declared to be entitled   Thus, where an administratrix, by her husband, purchased part of the estate of the deceased under conditions which rendered the transaction liable to be rescinded, it was held that an offer to reconvey the property at the price at which it was purchased, and the refusal of such offer, were irrelevant facts, inasmuch as, on such a re-purchase, the position of the party complaining would be different from what it would be on obtaining the relief to which he was entitled, though the immediate pecuniary result might appear to be much the same : in the one case, he would only hold the property under the title which the party charged could give him, which was a bad one *ex hypothesi*, whereas, in the other, the original sale being undone, he would continue to hold it under the same good title as he formerly had (*h*).

explanation consistent with the validity of the transaction, one ought not to draw inferences, which would really be guesses,   in favour of the invalidity of the transaction. The general presumption which the law makes is in favour of the good faith and validity of transactions, and not against them, and that presumption ought to acquire, and does acquire, weight from the length of time during which a transaction has subsisted ")
For further illustrations, see the following, in all of which the delay of the party complaining was held to constitute no answer to his claim for relief, either because it did not amount to confirmation, or acquiescence in the sense of confirmation, or because it had not resulted in any change in the condition of the property, or in the acquisition of rights and interests by innocent third persons for value, or in loss of evidence, or because it was otherwise natural or excusable   *Randall* v *Errington* (1805), 10 Ves 423 (*per* GRANT, M.R , at pp 426, 429) , *Greenlaw* v. *King* (1841), 10 L J (CH) 129 (*per* Lord COTTENHAM, L.C , at p 130) , *Charter* v *Trevelyan* (1844), 11 Cl & Fin 714 (*per* Lord CAMPBELL, at p 741) , *Barker* v. *Harrison* (1846), 2 Coll 546 (*per* KNIGHT-BRUCE, V -C , at p 555); *Lindsay Petroleum Co* v. *Hurd* (1874), L R 5 P C 221 (at pp 239, 240) , *De Bussche* v *Alt* (1878), 8 C. D 286, C A (*per Cur* , at pp 312-314, as to delay, and pp 314, 315, as to acquiescence) , *Re Pepperell* (1879), 27 W R 410 (*per* FRY, J , at p 411, who held that the facts did not amount to acquiescence, as defined by the C A in *De Bussche* v *Alt*, *sup*) , *Re Gallard*, [1897] 2 Q B 8 (*per* VAUGHAN WILLIAMS, J , at pp 13-15) , *Patten* v. *Hamilton*, [1911] 1 Ir R 40 (where, at pp 58, 60, 61, it was pointed out that delay, resulting in loss of evidence, operates against the party on whom the onus rests of producing the evidence, who was in that case not the principal seeking relief, but the agent against whom it was sought)
    (*f*) See Sect. 3, Sub-s (3), *ante*.
    (*g*) *Dougan* v *Macpherson*, [1902] A C 197, H L (*per* Lord MACNAGHTEN, at pp 204, 205, and Lord SHAND, at p 205)
    (*h*) *Re Pepperell*, *sup* (*per* FRY, J , at p 411 " as to the offer by Chamberlain to resell the brewery to the plaintiff on the terms on which he bought, I cannot see that there was any obligation on the plaintiff to accept the offer, and take Chamberlain's infirm title ")

SECT. 5   THE RELIEF AVAILABLE TO THE PARTY COMPLAINING.

376. The remedies to which the *cestui que trust*, company, or principal is entitled, on establishing a case for relief which is not displaced by any affirmative answer on the other side, are remedies, of an offensive and defensive character, against, on the one hand, the trustee, promoter, or agent, and, on the other, the opposite principal or contractee (if any) who has entered into a clandestine agreement or transaction with, and has thereby corrupted, the agent of, or other person owing a fiduciary duty to, the party complaining. These are two distinct classes of remedies which require separate examination

Sub-s (1)   *Remedies against the Party Charged.*

377. As against the party charged, the party complaining is, in the first place, entitled to rescission of the transaction complained of, together with consequential and analogous relief (*i*), subject to the conditions on which alone this particular form of remedy is available   The nature of these conditions has already been stated, once for all. It has been seen that transactions in respect of which there has been actionable non-disclosure are not void, but voidable at the option of the party complaining, and that important consequences follow from this leading principle (*j*)   that, with two exceptions —exceptions, however, which in cases of breach of fiduciary duty, go far to eat up the rule—rescission is only granted in the case of executory contracts (*k*)   that the possibility of mutual restoration *in specie* is a condition of the relief, and that, if the party complaining has by his own conduct disabled himself from making such restitution, he is precluded from obtaining

---

(*i*) The following are illustrations of rescission, with consequential relief (see the various forms of decree which, in some cases, are extremely elaborate)   *Fox v Mackreth* (1788), 2 Cox 320 , 2 R R. 55 , *Ex p James* (1803), 8 Ves. 337 ; *Ex p Bennett* (1805), 10 Ves 381 ; *Randall v. Errington* (1805), 10 Ves 423 , *Downes v. Grazebrook* (1817), 3 Mer 200 , *Rothschild v Brookman* (1831), 5 Bligh (N.S) 165 , *Gillett v. Peppercorne* (1840), 3 Beav 78 ; *Greenlaw v. King* (1841), 10 L. J (CH) 129 ; *Hamilton v. Wright* (1842), 9 Cl. & Fin. 111 (by cross-claim) ; *Molony v. Kernan* (1842), 2 Dr & War 37 ; 59 R R. 635 , *Carter v Palmer* (1842), 8 Cl & Fin 657 ; *Charter v Trevelyan* (1844), 11 Cl & Fin. 714 , *Murphy v O'Shea* (1845), 2 Jo. & Lat 422 , 69 R R 337 , *Wilson v Short* (1847), 6 Hare 366 , *Barnard v. Hunter* (1856), 2 Jur (N S) 1213 , 106 R. R. 1014 ; *Denton v Donner* (1856), 23 Beav. 285 , *Perens v Johnson* (1857), 3 Sm & G 419 , *Smedley v Varley* (1857), 23 Beav 358 ; *Spring v Pride* (1864), 12 W R 892 , *Dyson v Lum* (1866), 14 L T 588 ; *Franks v Bollans* (1867), 17 L T 309 ; *Atwool v Merryweather* (1867), L R 5 Eq 464 n., *Lindsay Petroleum Co v Hurd* (1874), L R. 5 P C. 221 ; *Bagnall (John) & Sons, Ltd v. Carlton* (1877), 6 C D. 371, C A , *McPherson v Watt* (1877), 3 App Cas 254, H. L , *Erlanger v. New Sombrero Phosphate Co.* (1878), 3 App Cas 1218, H L ; *Re Pepperell* (1879), 27 W R 410 , *Plowright v. Lambert* (1885), 52 L T. 646 , *Dougan v Macpherson*, [1902] A. C 197, H L ; *Transvaal Lands Co. v. New Belgium, etc., Co* , [1914] 2 Ch 488, C A

(*j*) See §§ 225, 226, *ante.* The cases cited in note (*p*), *inf* , are striking illustrations of the consequences of the transaction being voidable at the option of the party complaining   So also are the cases cited in note (*t*) to § 378, *post*

(*k*) See § 230, *ante*   In *Dunbar v Tredennick* (1813), 2 Ball & B. 304, no regard was paid to the completion, it being merely a "continuation of the fraud" (*per* Lord MANNERS, L C (Ir), at p. 318)   So, also, in *Lindsay Petroleum Co v Hurd, sup* , and *Transvaal Lands Co. v. New Belgium (Transvaal) Land and Development Co., sup.* (see p 505)

rescission, whatever other forms of relief may still be open to him (*l*) . that no contract or transaction can be set aside in which innocent third parties have acquired rights and interests for value (*m*) : that, ordinarily a transaction will be rescinded *in toto*, or not at all, but that, where covenants and stipulations, or parties, are separate and severable, relief may be given in respect of one part of, or against one party to, the transaction without interfering with any other part, or with the rights of any other party, and that an instrument possessing two characters may be set aside in one of those characters, and left to stand in the other (*n*) : and, lastly, that, where rescission is granted, the order is moulded in such a form as to comprise all prefatory declarations, and consequential or ancillary directions, as to cancellation (where necessary), repayment with interest, reconveyance or retransfer by the party charged (subject to the like restitution on the part of the party complaining), accounts, inquiries, injunctions, and otherwise, which may be appropriate to the circumstances of the individual case, and required to effect a complete *restitutio ad integrum* (*o*)   One of such incidental directions, in cases of purchases by trustees or agents in breach of fiduciary duty at auction sales, is of a somewhat anomalous character, since it neither annuls,

(*l*) See § 231, *ante ;* and, for applications of the doctrine there stated to cases of nondisclosure by persons in a position of confidence, see most of the authorities cited in note (*i*), *sup*, where adequate provision was made for mutual restoration *in specie* as a condition of the relief granted   For illustrations of cases where, the party complaining having so dealt with the property that it could not be restored in substantially the same plight and condition, rescission was refused, either absolutely, or unless certain conditions could be complied with, see *Great Luxembourg Railway Co.* v *Magnay* (1858), 25 Beav. 586 , *Lindsay Petroleum Co* v *Hurd* (1874), L R 5 P C 221 (at p 245, where the form of decree is set out) , *Re Worssam* (1882), 51 L J (CH) 008 (where the daughter of an intestate, being otherwise entitled to rescission of the sale of her interest to the administrator, had settled the purchase money on her marriage, and therefore could not restore it, and where, at p 671, Fry, J , laid down the rule, in general terms, that "those who come to set aside a voidable transaction must show two things—first, that the transaction was voidable , and, secondly, that they are in a position to avoid it "), *Ladywell Mining Co.* v *Brookes* (1887), 35 C. D 400, C A (*per* Lindley, L J., at p 414) ; *Lagunas Nitrate Co* v. *Lagunas Syndicate,* [1899] 2 Ch 392, C. A (*per* Lindley, M R , at pp 432–434, and Collins, L.J , at p 463) , *Re Leeds & Hanley Theatre of Varieties, Ltd.,* [1902] 2 Ch 809, C. A. (*per* Vaughan Williams, L. J , at pp 825, 826, pointing out that rescission was there impossible, because the property was in the hands of mortgagees, though this did not preclude relief of another kind, viz by way of damages, which was granted)   An illustration of the rule that, where the inability to make specific restoration is not the fault of the party complaining, he is not disabled from obtaining relief, is *Phosphate Sewage Co* v *Hartmont* (1877), 5 C D. 394, C. A (*per Cur* , at pp 454, 455)   Cp *Transvaal Lands Co* v *New Belgium, etc , Co* , *sup*

(*m*) See § 233, *ante,* and the following cases of fiduciary relationship in illustration thereof : *Featherstonehaugh* v *Fenwick* (1801), 17 Ves. 298 (where, at pp 312, 313, Lord Eldon, L.C , said that he would not have made the decree if it had been proved to his satisfaction, which it had not, that it would work injustice to the owner of the partnership premises, a renewal of the lease of which for the personal benefit of one of the partners was the transaction impeached) ; *Re Leeds & Hanley Theatre of Varieties, Ltd., sup* (the passage referred to in the last note)

(*n*) See § 239, *ante,* and, for further illustrations thereof taken from the class of case now under consideration, *Denton* v. *Donner* (1856), 23 Beav 285 (where an instrument was set aside so far as it purported to be an absolute conveyance, but allowed to stand as a security only, which the plaintiff was to be at liberty to redeem).   On the other hand, in *McPherson* v *Watt* (1877), 3 App Cas 254, H. L., two contracts were held to form part of one entire transaction, though distinct from one another in point of form, and between different parties (*per* Lord Cairns, L C , at p. 265, and Lord Blackburn, at p 276)

(*o*) See §§ 237–240, *ante,* and, for further illustrations, see the forms of decree or judgment in the cases cited in note (*i*), *sup*.

nor affirms, the purchase, but leaves it to stand or fall according to a future
event   The procedure is this   The property is ordered to be put up for
sale by auction again at the price at which it was knocked down to the purchaser, with the addition of such sum as may represent the increase in value
due to permanent improvements and repairs executed by the purchaser
since he acquired the property, if there were any such , and it is directed that,
if any higher bid is made on the second sale, the property is to go to the person
so bidding, and the original purchase is to be set aside, but, if no higher bid
is made, the original purchase is to stand.   In other words, if the original
purchaser is shown by the event to have made a good bargain, he is to be
deprived of it ; if a bad one, he is to be fixed with it (p)   This certainly seems a
somewhat unjust provision, and one which is hardly in accordance with the
fundamental principle on which a party is given his election to avoid or adhere
to a contract.   Though it may be perfectly fair and reasonable that the
wrongdoer should be at the mercy of the injured party's option, it cannot
be right that he should still be at his mercy when that option has been exercised   The party complaining comes to the Court to be relieved of the
contract, and must be supposed to have exercised, and therefore exhausted,
his right of election in favour of avoidance before doing so   The Court
thereupon, by the form of order in question, neither annuls nor affirms the
purchase, but permits the party complaining to keep the matter in suspense,
and encourages him in, and indeed itself practises, the vice of simultaneous
approbation and reprobation   "You have made your choice," it says to
him, " between two alternative and inconsistent courses , but, nevertheless,
if it appears *ex post facto* that your choice was an injudicious one, you shall
be at liberty to recall it, and resort to the alternative course which the event
will show to be that which you should have originally adopted, and you shall
be deemed to have so adopted it from the beginning "   It is not surprising
to find that GRANT, M R., was reluctant to follow the rule, and only did so in
deference to the high authority of Lord ELDON (q) , or that Lord ELDON himself,
its inventor, in a later case expressed some misgivings as to its fairness (r) ,

(p) This practice was instituted by Lord ELDON, L.C., and formed part of his decree
in many cases decided by him against the purchaser at an auction sale, as in *Ex p Lacey*
(1802), 6 Ves. 625 (see p. 630) , *Ex p. James* (1803), 8 Ves. 337, where, also, the solicitor was
prohibited from bidding on the resale by auction which had been ordered, for, though Lord
ELDON conceded that this might be unobjectionable if the consent of all the persons interested were first obtained, it would not be safe for the Court to give the solicitor even a con
ditional permission *ab ante* to do so . see pp 351, 352) , *Ex p Bennett* (1805), 10 Ves 381
In *Ex p. Hughes, Re Dumbell* (1802), 6 Ves 616, the order made by Lord ELDON, L C., was
that the property should be put up for sale again at a sum made up of the price at which
it was knocked down to the purchaser at the first sale, and the total value of the substantial
improvements and repairs effected by him whilst in possession of the property, which
value the Master was to ascertain.   The original purchase money was £2000, and the value
of the improvements was found to be no less than £6000.   The property was accordingly
put up again at £8000, and no higher bid being made, the purchaser was held to his
purchase (see pp 624, 625).
(q) In *Lister* v *Lister* (1802), 6 Ves. 631A, at p 632.
(r) ARDEN, M.R , directed the Master to inquire whether a resale would be for the
benefit of the infant *cestuis que trustent* in *Campbell* v *Walker* (1800), 5 Ves 677, and the
Master having reported that, in the case of one of the purchases complained of, the real
value was nearly double what had been given, a resale was ordered, and the property

though, half a century afterwards, it appears to have been still in force as a rule of convenience (s)

378. The principle that the transaction is voidable at the option of the party complaining involves the existence of the alternative right to adhere to it by adoption, or ratification, or simply by taking no steps to avoid it. In the latter event, the party complaining is not left without remedy against the party charged; but his remedy is of a different nature. It is a claim for an order on the party charged to account for the amount or value of the money or money's worth which he has received under the agreement or transaction impeached It is the right of the party complaining to elect between the two forms of relief: the party charged cannot compel him to resort to either in preference to the other If called upon to account, the party charged cannot set up that the party complaining might have, but has not, rescinded (t), any more than, if the party complaining chooses to insist that the transaction is a nullity, it is any answer to say that he might have adopted it and sued for an account and payment or delivery of the money or property improperly received thereunder (u) From time to time contentions to the contrary, founded on a total misreading and misapprehension of certain authorities (v), have been advanced · but it is now finally settled,

in question did in fact fetch nearly double the sum paid on the original sale by the trustee, who was accordingly not allowed to hold his bargain. Seven years later, this case, sub nom (Sanderson v. Walker (1807), 13 Ves 601, came before Lord ELDON, L.C, who, at p. 603, refers to "the principle laid down by me, that if it is for the benefit of the infants that the purchase shall not be disturbed, the Court will not disturb it, and will disturb it, if that will be for their benefit," and "that principle, open to considerable objection, must be admitted, if a better principle cannot be found"

(s) Dyson v. Lum (1866), 14 L. T 588 (per STUART, V -C, at p 589 · "the property must be put up for sale at the price at which it was purchased by the trustees, and if no more is then offered, they must be held to their bargain")

(t) See Hichens v Congreve (1831), 4 Sim. 420 (per SHADWELL, V.-C., at p. 428); Bentley v. Craven (1853), 18 Beav 75 (per ROMILLY, M.R., at p 76); Kimber v Barber (1872), 8 Ch. App 56 (per Lord SELBORNE, L.C., at p. 59); Bagnall (John) & Sons, Ltd v. Carlton (1877), 6 C. D. 371, C. A. (per JAMES, L.J, at p 399, and BAGGALLAY, L.J., at p. 404), where the separate and alternative nature of the two remedies was illustrated in a rather striking manner; the company having sued the representatives of the deceased vendor for rescission of the purchase, and the promoters for repayment of secret profits, it was held that they were entitled to elect either remedy in each of the two cases, and that, therefore, the promoters who were held liable to pay over these secret profits could not be heard to say that the sum for which the company had compromised its claim to rescind against the vendor's representatives should be credited to them as against the amount of the profits which they were ordered to disgorge; Emma Silver Mining Co v. Grant (1879), 11 C. D. 919 (per JESSEL, M.R , at pp. 957, 958, where he points out by a couple of forcible illustrations how independent of one another the two rights are); Emma Silver Mining Co. v. Lewis & Son (1879), 4 C P D. 396 (per Cur , at p. 409); Lydney and Wigpool Iron Ore Co v. Bird (1886), 33 C D 85, C A. (per Cur , at p. 94 · "nor is it necessary for the company to rescind the whole transaction of which the payment by the company of the money in question is found to be a part"), Re Leeds & Hanley Theatre of Varieties, Ltd., [1902] 2 Ch. 809, C A. (per VAUGHAN WILLIAMS, L.J., at p. 826 "although the Theatres company cannot give back the property, and ask that their money should be returned in toto, they are entitled to damages for this breach of duty")

(u) Re Hereford & South Wales Waggon & Engineering Co (1876), 2 C. D 621, C. A. (per Cur., at pp. 625, 626 : it was recognized here that it was open to the company to have adopted the contract with the agents, instead of repudiating it as they did, and that, in the former event, they would have been liable to pay for the agents' services, a claim for which remuneration, having adopted the latter alternative, they were successfully resisting)

(v) Such as Ladywell Mining Co. v. Brookes (1887), 37 C. D. 400, C. A. (per COTTON, L.J.,

and, indeed, has been so since 1831, that, as in the analogous case of fraudulent misrepresentation, both remedies are alternatively, but not cumulatively, available to the party complaining against the party charged; provided that, where there is more than one party charged, there is a choice of remedies against each, and rescission may be simultaneously claimed against one of them, and an account against the other or others, without any objection on the score of inconsistency (*w*).

379. Where the second of the above alternative remedies is pursued against the trustee, promoter, or agent, the right (whether it be called a claim for an account, or for money had and received, or for the recovery of damages) is a right to compel the delinquent to disgorge the amount or value of the secret profit or advantage which he has received under the transaction impeached. This profit or advantage may have been taken in the form of money, or of property other than money. In the former case, the *cestui que trust*, company, or principal, is entitled to an order for an account of the sums received, and payment over of such sums when so ascertained, or, in case of a single specific sum or an agreed total, a simple order for the payment thereof (*x*), with interest, which is usually fixed at 5 per cent (*y*), but in a

---

at pp. 407–409, LINDLEY, L.J., at pp 414, 415, and LOPES, L.J , at p. 415) It was not held here that the two claims were dependent on one another, so that if rescission failed, the right to recover the profit also failed   Quite the contrary . each claim was independently examined on its merits, and on the evidence, and each failed

(*w*) See the cases cited in note (*t*), *sup.*, and *Gluckstein* v. *Barnes*, [1900] A C. 240, H. L. (*per* Lord MACNAGHTEN, at p 249: " a third ground of defence was that the only remedy was rescission. This defence, in the circumstances of the present case, seems to me as contrary to common sense as it is to authority. The point was settled more than sixty years ago in *Hichens* v. *Congreve*, and, so far as I know, that case has never been questioned ").

(*x*) As in *Russell* v. *Austwick* (1826), 1 Sim. 52 (account of profits of secret agreement), *Fawcett* v. *Whitehouse* (1829), 1 Russ. & M. 132 (declaration of trusteeship, and account), *Rothschild* v. *Brookman* (1831), 5 Bligh (N S) 165 (account of dealings in securities); *Hichens* v. *Congreve* (1831), 4 Sim. 420 (payment of a certain sum already brought into court); *Barker* v. *Harrison* (1846), 2 Coll 546 (declaration of trusteeship); *Clarke* v. *Tipping* (1846), 9 Beav 284 (account of dealings), *York & North Midland Railway Co.* v. *Hudson* (1853), 16 Beav 485 (account of profits derived from sale and disposal of shares); *Bentley* v. *Craven* (1853), 18 Beav. 75 (account of profits); *Tyrrell* v. *Bank of London* (1862), 10 H L. C 26 (declaration, account, and payment); *Williams* v *Stevens* (1866), L. R. 1 P. C. 352 (payment of a specific sum), *Turnbull* v. *Garden* (1869), 20 L. T 218 (account of secret discounts); *Spain (Queen of)* v *Parr* (1870), 39 L J. (CH.) 73 (account of secret commissions), *Dunne* v. *English* (1872), L. R. 18 Eq 524 (account against partner of a moiety of the profits made on a secret transaction); *Kimber* v. *Barber* (1872), 8 Ch. App. 56 (payment of a specific sum), *Imperial Mercantile Credit Association* v *Coleman* (1873), L R 6 H. L 189 (the like), *Morison* v. *Thompson* (1874), L. R 9 Q B 480 (the like), *Parker* v. *McKenna* (1874), 10 Ch App. 96 (declaration of accountability, inquiry, and account); *Panama & South Pacific Telegraph Co.* v. *India Rubber, Gutta Percha, & Telegraph Co* (1875), 10 Ch App 515 (as against one of the defendants, payment of the amount of the bribe); *Phosphate Sewage Co* v *Hartmont* (1877), 5 C D 394, C A (payment of secret profit, as against some of the defendants); *Bagnall (John) & Sons, Ltd* v. *Carlton* (1877), 6 C D. 371, C A (the like); *De Bussche* v *Alt* (1878), 8 C. D. 286, C. A. (account and payment); *Re Englefield Colliery Co.* (1878), 8 C. D. 388, C. A. (payment, jointly and severally, against directors, of amount of bribe received from promoters), *Emma Silver Mining Co.* v. *Grant* (1879), 11 C. D. 919 (payment over of secret profits made by

---

(*y*) This rate of interest was ordered to be paid in several of the cases cited in the last note, being regarded as a punitive one, or, at all events, as a proper rate to charge against a trustee who had failed in his duty, which was the reason given by ROMILLY, M R , in *York & North Midland Railway Co.* v. *Hudson, sup.*

proper case, that is, where the party charged is shown to have been actuated by personal good faith, may be reduced to a less penal rate (z) A declaration is sometimes prefixed to the order (a) Only the net profits are recoverable : that is to say, the party charged is to be credited with the amount of all proper and legitimate expenditure incurred by him, and with remuneration for all proper and legitimate services rendered by him, for the purpose of entitling himself to the money which the party complaining is seeking to recover from him under and by virtue of a transaction which, though complained of, is not being repudiated, but adopted (b) It should be observed here that, where the transaction impeached is the secret receipt of a pecuniary bribe from the opposite principal or other third person, the money recoverable,

promoter), *Emma Silver Mining Co* v *Lewis & Son* (1879), 4 C P. D 396 (the like); *Whaley Bridge Calico Printing Co.* v *Green* (1879), 5 Q B D 109 (the like), *Metropolitan Bank* v. *Heiron* (1880), 5 Ex D 319, C. A. (recovery of bribe, but here the claim was held barred by the statute of limitations), *Lydney & Wigpool Iron Ore Co* v *Bird* (1886), 33 C. D 85, C. A. (payment of specific sum); *Boston Deep Sea Fishing & Ice Co* v *Ansell* (1888), 39 C. D 339, C A (account and payment of secret commissions, &c); *Lister & Co.* v. *Stubbs* (1890), 45 C D 1, C. A. (recovery of a specific amount), *Williamson* v *Hine Bros.*, [1891] 1 Ch. 390 (account), *Gluckstein* v. *Barnes*, [1900] A. C 240, H L (payment of specific sum); *Erskine, Oxenford & Co* v. *Sachs*, [1901] 2 K. B. 504, C. A. (account of secret profits, on counterclaim); *Re Leeds & Hanley Theatre of Varieties, Ltd* , [1902] 2 Ch 809, C A (payment of sum received by promoter as secret profit), *Hippisley* v *Knee Bros* , [1905] 1 K B 1, Div Ct. (payment of specific sums), *Powell & Thomas* v *Evans, Jones & Co* (the like, by counterclaim), *Nitedals Taendstickfabrik* v *Bruster*, [1906] 2 Ch 671 (account and payment of secret commissions), *Bath* v *Standard Land Co* , [1911] 1 Ch. 618, C A. (declarations and accounts), *Re Darby, Ex p Brougham*, [1911] 1 K B. 95 (proof in bankruptcy allowed for specific amount representing promoter-vendor's secret profit); *Green (E.) & Son, Ltd* v *Tugham & Co* (1913), 30 T. L R 64 (account and payment of rebates, discounts, and commissions); *Kuhlier* v. *Lambert Bros* , *Ltd.* (1913), 108 L T. 565 (account of profit)

(z) In *Imperial Mercantile & Credit Association* v *Coleman*, *sup* , Lord CAIRNS, at pp. 209, 210, advised the House to reduce the rate of interest from the more or less penal 5 per cent to 4 per cent , on the ground that the directors in that case had acted under an honest mistake, and were not ordinary delinquents The lower rate was ordered also in *Fawcett* v *Whitehouse*, *Emma Silver Mining Co* v *Grant*, *Lydney & Wigpool Iron Ore Co* v. *Bird*, and *Re Leeds & Hanley Theatre of Varieties, Ltd* , *sup*

(a) From note (x), *sup* , it will be seen that in some of the cases there cited declarations of trusteeship and accountability were prefaced to the mandatory part of the decree or judgment In *Powell & Thomas* v *Evans, Jones & Co* , *sup* , a somewhat special form of declaration was made on the counterclaim see note (d), *inf*

(b) In *York & North Midland Railway Co* v *Hudson*, *Dunne* v *English*, *Bagnall & Sons, Ltd* v *Carlton*, *De Bussche* v *Alt*, *Emma Silver Mining Co* v *Grant*, *Lydney and Wigpool Iron Ore Co* v *Bird*, and *Re Darby*, *sup* , the defaulting director, partner, agent, or promoter was held entitled to deduct from the sums to be handed over his expenses, and generally all just allowances, but not illegitimate expenditure, such as a payment incurred by a promoter in guaranteeing the subscription of shares in the company, for this would be " to make the company pay for the issue of its own shares," and so commit an illegal act (*per Cur* , at p 95 of *Lydney & Wigpool Iron Ore Co* v *Bird*, *sup*), though, in *Emma Silver Mining Co* v *Grant*, *sup* , JESSEL, M R , allowed the promoter his expenses of procuring the directors, engaging brokers "to sustain the market," and getting the concern written up in the papers (in other words, bribing the directors, rigging the market and corrupting the press), because the promoters would not have incurred these expenses, any more than he would have received the profits, but for the clandestine agreement complained of (pp 939-941) This generous view of the "just allowances " of corrupt promotership has not been adopted in any other case In *Bagnall (John) & Sons, Ltd* v *Carlton*, *sup* , the company made an offer to allow the promoters a reasonable commission for their services, and "by reason of this offer " (*per* JAMES, L J , at p 403, and COTTON, L.J , at pp 408, 409, adding, ' *this is the only ground on which we do it* ") a sum fixed by the Court was allowed Otherwise it would not have been

whether regarded as money had and received, or an equitable debt, or, as
some judges have preferred to call it, damages (c), is not trust money, or to
be treated as such   It is merely the subject of an ordinary debt or pecuniary
liability, and at no stage in the history of the transaction can the party complaining affirm that in equity it was his.   In the majority of cases, this distinction is of no practical importance · but, where there is a question of a
statute of limitations, or of a declaration as to the rights and liabilities of
the parties in respect of future receipts by the agent under the agreement
complained of, or where the agent is made bankrupt, it obviously becomes of
the utmost moment and materiality (d).

380. Where the property sought to be recovered is other than money,
and the party complaining is in a position to say that it was in equity his
property when received by the trustee, promoter, or agent, but not otherwise (e), he has the right either to have the thing itself delivered or trans-

(c) In *Re Fitzroy Bessemer Steel Co* (1884), 50 L T. 144, KAY, J , described a claim to
make the promoter of a company accountable as a claim for " damages " (p 147) , and,
at p 825 of *Re Leeds & Hanley Theatre of Varieties, Ltd* , [1902] 2 Ch. 809, C A , VAUGHAN
WILLIAMS, L J., said   " I am not sure that the Theatres Co can, in reference to this
breach of fiduciary duty by the promoters, maintain an action for money had and received.
I think that the safer way of putting it is to say that the remedy is in damages." This
particular terminological question, however, is never of any practical importance, because
the measure of damage always works out in precisely the same way as if the claim were for
an account, or for money had and received, the sum ordered to be paid in either case
being the amount received, less " just allowances " And, in the very case last cited, the
Court announced, at the end of the judgments, " we are all of opinion that the true measure
of damages is the amount of the profit which was made by the promoting company "
(p. 833).
(d) See *Metropolitan Bank* v *Heiron* (1880), 5 Ex. D 319, C A. (*per* JAMES, L.J , at
p 323, BRETT, L J , at p 324, and COTTON, L.J , at pp. 325, 326 : here the claim of the
bank to recover the amount of the bribe received by a director was held to be barred by the
Statute of Limitations, on the express ground that it was a debt, and, though dishonestly
received, was never in contemplation of law the principal's money, in which case, of course,
the statute would have been no bar) , *Lister & Co* v *Stubbs* (1890), 45 C D 1, C A.
(where the principal, in an action against the agent, to recover the amount of secret
commissions received by him, unsuccessfully moved the Court for an interlocutory
injunction to restrain the agent from dealing with real estate which he had purchased with
this money, it being held that the money was not a trust fund which could be followed
into investments, and identified as the principal's money, but only an ordinary debt ·
per STIRLING, J , at pp 9–11, COTTON, L J , at pp. 13, 14, and LINDLEY, L J , at p 15),
Re North Australian Territory Co , Archer's Case, [1892] 1 Ch 322, C A (*per* LINDLEY, L.J ,
at p 338 " to say that " the illicit profit is the money of the company " is to use
an ambiguous expression. In one sense it may be said to be the company's money—
that is to say, in the sense that the company are entitled to get it In another sense it is
not the company's money—that is to say, the company cannot follow it into investments
of it, nor, in the event of Mr. Archer's bankruptcy, could they withdraw the money from
his assets, instead of ranking as creditors against his estate ") ; *Powell & Thomas* v
Evans, Jones & Co , [1905] 1 K B 11, C A (*per* COLLINS, M.R , at pp 19, 20, STIRLING,
L J , at p. 22, and MATHEW, L J , at pp 23, 24, who, as regards any future sums to be
received by the agent under the secret agreement with the opposite principal, declared
that, when so received, they would constitute a debt to the principals, but refused the
more extended declaration pressed for, viz that the agent was the trustee of the agree
ment for them) With these cases contrast those in which the illicit profit was made
on a transaction between the related parties themselves, and where, as was pointed out by
Lord WYNFORD, L C., at pp 194–196 of *Rothschild* v. *Brookman* (1831), 5 Bligh (N S)
165, the party complaining *can* say that the money is earmarked
(e) *Erlanger* v *New Sombrero Phosphate Co* (1878), 3 App. Cas. 1218, H. L (*per* Lord
CAIRNS, L C , at p 1235, Lord HATHERLEY at pp 1242, 1243, and Lord BLACKBURN at
pp 1267, 1268)

ferred to him (unless it has disappeared, or has been parted with to a *bonâ fide*
purchaser for value), together with any proceeds or profits which may have
accrued in the meantime, or to be paid its value · the option is his to determine in what form he will take satisfaction, not that of the other party to
choose in what form he will give it (*f*) The former remedy is usually resorted
to where the property consists of land, or where there are difficulties in estimating the value (*g*) ; the latter, in other cases, and, particularly, where the
property consists of shares in a company which a director or other agent of the
company has taken under a clandestine agreement with the promoter (*h*) In
the last-mentioned class of case, there are certain established rules as to the
measure of value, or of damages, which, on the principle of *omnia præsumuntur
contra spoliatorem*, are applied against the delinquent with greater severity
than in cases where the party liable is not connected with the other party by
any relation of "confidence," and has not been guilty of fiduciary misconduct (*i*). The slightest *primâ facie* evidence on behalf of the company, or
its liquidator, that the shares were treated by persons dealing with them at
the material date as being worth their face value, is enough to throw the
burden on the delinquent of showing cause why he should not pay that
full value (*j*). Such *primâ facie* evidence may consist of no more than
proof of the fact that, at the date when the director or other officer of
the company received the shares, there were applications from the public

(*f*) *Re Caerphilly Colliery Co*, *Pearson's Case* (1877), 5 C D. 336, C A. (*per* JESSEL,
M.R , at p 341 "liable at the option of the *cestui que trust* to account either for the value
at the time of the present he was receiving, or to account for the thing itself, and its proceeds if it has increased in value"); *Naut y-Glo & Blaina Ironworks Co* v *Grave* (1878),
12 C. D. 738 (*per* BACON, V.-C , at pp 747, 748), *Eden* v *Ridsdale's Railway Lamp &
Lighting Co* (1889), 23 Q. B. D 368, C A (*per* Lord ESHER, M R , at p 371 · "if that which
the agent has received is money, he must hand it over to his principal , if it is not money,
but something else, the principal may insist on having it, or, if he chooses, the value of
it ") When the property has been parted with to a *bonâ fide* purchaser for value, the
party complaining must resort to his pecuniary claim, which he may elect to have measured
by the profit made by the party charged on the resale, as in *Whichcote* v *Lawrence* (1798),
3 Ves 739 ; *York & North Midland Railway Co* v *Hudson* (1853), 16 Beav 485 (as to
some of the shares there in question); *Barker* v *Harrison* (1846), 2 Coll 546
  (*g*) As in *Featherstonehaugh* v *Fenwick* (1810), 17 Ves 298 (a lease). *Att -Gen.* v.
Lord Dudley (1815), G. Cooper 146 , 14 R R 226 (land) , *Carter* v *Palmer* (1842), 8
Cl & Fin. 657 , *Tyrrell* v. *Bank of London* (1862), 10 H L. C. 26 (houses); *Luddy's
Trustee* v *Peard* (1886), 33 C D 500 (advantages under a will) In *Lowther* v *Lord
Lowther* (1806), 13 Ves 95, the relief sought was delivery of a valuable picture
  (*h*) As in *Society of Practical Knowledge* v *Abbott* (1840), 2 Beav. 559 , *Re Morvah
Consols Tin Mining Co* , *McKay's Case* (1875), 2 C D 1, C.A , *Re British Provident Life &
Guarantee Association*, *De Ruvigne's Case* (1877), 5 C D 306, C A , *Re Caerphilly Colliery
Co* , *Pearson's Case*, *sup* , *Naut-y-Glo & Blaina Ironworks Co* v. *Grave*, *sup*. , *Re West
Jewell Tin Mining Co* , *Weston's Case* (1879), 10 C. D 579, C A , *Re Diamond Fuel Co* ,
Mitcalfe's Case (1879), 13 C D 169, C A , *Re Fitzroy Bessemer Steel Co.* (1884), 50 L T.
144 , *Re Carriage Co-operative Supply Association* (1884), 27 C D 322 , *Re Postage Stamp
Automatic Delivery Co* , [1892] 3 Ch 566 ; *Re North Australian Territory Co* , *Archer's Case*,
[1892] 1 Ch. 322, C A.; *Re Westmoreland Green & Blue Slate Co* , *Bland's Case*, [1893]
2 Ch. 612, C. A , *Re London & South Western Canal Co* , *Ltd* , [1911] 1 Ch 346
  (*i*) *Shaw* v. *Holland*, [1900] 2 Ch 305 (*per* WEBSTER, M R , at p 310)
  (*j*) See *Weston's Case*, *sup*. (*per* JESSEL, M R , at p. 584), *Mitcalfe's Case*, *sup* (*per*
FRY, J , at p 173 "the obligation was on him to show that by reason of special circumstances he was not chargeable with the full value of any of the shares), *Eden* v *Ridsdale's
Railway Lamps & Lighting Co* , *sup*. (*per* Lord ESHER, M R., at p. 371)

which the company might have satisfied by allotting the shares in question
(which allotment of course could only be at par), or that shares of the description in question had been actually transferred at par, or had been treated
in the books of the company as worth their nominal value, or that the director
had himself purchased other shares than the shares in question, but of a
similar description, at par · and it is no answer to such evidence to prove
that the shares are at the date of the proceedings, or have been since they
were received, of less than their nominal value, or of no value at all (which,
indeed, is nearly always the case), or that the delinquent has sold them at a
sacrifice, the question not being whether he has gained by the transaction, but
whether and how much, the company has lost (k). It has been held in some
cases that, as against the wrongdoer, the shares may be presumed to have been
worth the highest price given for them at any date between the discovery
of the true facts relating to the bribe and the date of the institution of the
proceedings (l) To apply such a measure as this, however, can hardly be
equitable except under very special circumstances On the other hand, the
Court is not bound to give the face value, even when proved to have been
the real value at the material date : it exercises its discretion with reference
to all the circumstances, and these may be such as to induce it, in a
particular case, to apply the rules as to the measure of damage less rigorously
than in the ordinary type of case (m) It happens sometimes that the value,
so to speak, liquidates itself, as when the party charged has himself received
a sum of money in exchange for, or as representing, the shares, which sum
the party complaining is willing to take as their value (n) Interest on the
ascertained value is usually charged against the party held liable at the penal
rate of 5 per cent, on the ground that the concealment of the transaction in
the majority of cases amounts to actual misconduct (o), but in some instances
interest at 4 per cent. only is charged (p), and, in others, none at all (q)

(k) See, generally, the cases cited in note (h), sup
(l) As in *Re Morvah Consols Tin Mining Co*, *McKay's Case*, sup (per MELLISH, L J,
at pp 6, 7, and BRETT, J, at p 8), *Naut y Glo & Blaina Ironworks Co v Grave* (1878),
12 C. D 378 (per BACON, V C, at pp 749, 750) The rule was also so stated by Lord
ESHER, M R, at p 371 of *Eden v Ridsdale's Railway Lamp & Lighting Co*, sup Contrast
the observations of JESSEL, M R, at pp 584, 585 of *Weston's Case*, sup. "when a
director or any person in a fiduciary position accepts a present of this kind, he is to be
charged with and compelled to make good *the full possible value of the present or bribe at
the time* The full possible value—the Court is not to endeavour to reduce the value"
Here, it is conceived, the proposition receives its proper limitation. The "time" referred to is of course the time when the delinquent took the bribe
(m) As in *Re Fitzroy Bessemer Steel Co*, sup (per KAY, J, at p 147, who said that
vindictive damages ought not to be given against a merely "constructive trustee," and
fixed the value of the £10 shares at £3 only ; further, he refused to order the promoter
to pay any interest at all on the curious ground that he had received no dividends, and the
company had lost none) This treatment seems as unduly lenient to the party charged
as that adopted by the Court in the cases cited in the last note was unduly severe
(n) As in *Re North Australian Territory Co*, *Archer's Case*, [1892] 1 Ch 322, C A (per
BOWEN, L J, at p 340) Cp the cases cited at the end of note (f), sup, where the party
complaining was content to take the profit which in fact the party charged made on his
own dealings with the property
(o) As in *De Ruvigne's Case* (1877), 5 C D 306, C A, and *Archer's Case*, sup
(p) As in *Naut y Glo & Blaina Ironworks Co. v Grave*, sup.
(q) See note (m), sup.

381. In addition to the active proceedings above described, the party complaining has the right to defend himself on the ground of non-disclosure against any proceedings instituted against him by the trustee, promoter, or agent for the direct or indirect enforcement of the impeachable contract or transaction ; for the breach of the fiduciary duty is as much an invalidating cause, when raised by way of defence or answer, as it is when made the foundation of offensive proceedings The substantial identity, with certain exceptions, of the conditions under which a voidable transaction generally, whatever the ground of its voidability, may be annulled, and the conditions under which it may be treated as a nullity when sued upon, has already been considered , and, in the course of this examination, it has, in particular, been pointed out that, for reasons there stated, the party complaining is in a stronger position when resisting the claim of the party charged to the discretionary assistance of the Court in the form of a judgment for specific performance, than when resisting his claim to the enforcement of the contract as of right ; though, on the other hand, he incurs some peril in neglecting or delaying to exercise his right to take active measures for the judicial undoing of the impeached transaction (r)

382. Subject to these observations, it is well established that every fact which entitles the party complaining to rescission, or to other active relief, equally entitles him to be absolved from any action or counterclaim instituted against him by the party charged, whether for specific performance (s), or for the direct performance otherwise than specifically (t), or for the indirect performance in the shape of compensation in damages (u), of the contract invalidated by the non-disclosure, or, in the case of an agent, the contract of

(r) In Chapter III, Sect 5, Sub s (2), *ante*

(s) See *Watt* v. *Grove* (1805), 2 Sch & Lefr 491 (coupled here with cross bill for rescission), *Cutts* v *Salmon* (1850), 4 De G & Sm 130, affirmed (1852), 21 L J Ch 750, *Maxwell* v *Port Tennant Patent Steam Fuel & Coal Co* (1857), 24 Beav 495   *Cutts* v. *Salmon, sup* , is a good illustration of the stronger position of the party complaining, when resisting specific performance, than when taking active proceedings for in *Salmon* v *Cutts* (1850), 4 De G & Sm. 125, rescission was refused by KNIGHT-BRUCE, V C , who, however, at p. 130, gave a very significant hint to the defendant as to what would happen, if he should proceed with his cross-suit, which *Cutts* v *Salmon* was, for specific performance   Nothing daunted, the defendant did proceed with the cross-suit, with the result foretold by the Vice-Chancellor, viz dismissal with costs

(t) As in *Hamilton* v. *Wright* (1842), 9 Cl. & Fin 111 (defence to action for money due under annuity bond, together with cross claim to "reduce" the bond) , *Aberdeen Railway Co* v *Blakie Bros.* (1854), 1 Macq H L 467 (to action for price of goods sold, or alternatively damages) , *Salomons* v *Pender* (1865), 3 H & C 639 (to surveyor's action for agreed commission for services) , *Re Madrid Bank, Ex p Williams* (1866), L R 2 Eq 216 (to promoter's claim for balance of agreed remuneration) , *Robinson* v *Mollett* (1875), L R 7 H. L. 802 (to tallow broker's claim for indemnity against differences) , *Re Hereford & S. Wales Waggon & Engineering Co* (1876), 2 C D. 621, C A (to claim for services) , *Harrington* v *Victoria Graving Dock Co* (1878), 3 Q B D 549 , *Boston Deep Sea Fishing & Ice Co.* v. *Ansell* (1888), 39 C D 339, C A (defence to agent's counterclaim for salary and commissions) ; *Andrews* v. *Ramsay & Co* , [1903] 2 K B. 635, Div Ct (which was a case of a principal recovering from his agent the commission which he had allowed him to retain for his services whilst in ignorance of the corrupt agreement impeached, on the ground that, if the agent were making the claim, the principal would be entitled to resist it , so that this is really a "defence" case . *per* WILLS, J., at p. 638)

(u) As in *Aberdeen Railway Co* v. *Blakie Bros* , *sup* (*quoad* the alternative claim for damages) , *Swale* v *Ipswich Tannery, Ltd* (1906), 11 Comm Cas 88 (defence to action for damages for wrongful dismissal).

agency; and this, whether he chooses, or not, to counterclaim in the proceeding either for rescission of the contract, or for an account, or damages, or money had and received; for all these last-named species of relief are cumulative to the remedy by way of defence, and may be pursued simultaneously with it (v).

Sub-s. (2). Remedies against the Contractee who has corrupted the Agent of the Party Complaining.

363. In the case of an agent who has secretly taken or stipulated for a bribe, commission, or other private advantage or profit, from the person with whom he has negotiated a contract on behalf of his principal, the remedies available to that principal are not limited to his above-mentioned rights against the agent. He can also obtain relief against the contractee who has secretly given or promised the bribe, and has thereby conspired with the agent in the concealment and in the breach of fiduciary duty. And this relief is of the same threefold character as the relief to which he is entitled against the agent: that is to say, first, the conspiracy in the non-disclosure of the corrupt bargain is a valid answer to any action which the contractee may institute against him to enforce the contract (w), secondly, he is entitled to rescission of such contract against the contractee (x); thirdly, he has a valid claim against the contractee for the recovery of the damages he has sustained by reason of the contractee's procurement of, and complicity in, the agent's fiduciary misconduct (y).

364. Where the principal recovers money from the contractee, he so

---

(v) *Andrews* v. *Ramsay & Co., sup.* (per Lord ALVERSTONE, C J , at pp 636–638)

(w) As in *Maxwell* v. *Po t Tennant Patent Steam Fuel & Coal Co* (1857), 24 Beav 495 (per ROMILLY, M R., at p 497 . "there was a private arrangement between them"—i e. the plaintiff, who was suing the company for specific performance of a contract of sale, and the company's directors—"that the directors should obtain a personal benefit by the transaction, and, as this was not communicated to the shareholders, they cannot be bound by the contract "); *Smith* v *Sorby* (1875), 3 Q. B D. 552 n (defence to action for damages for breach of agreement to supply coal, on ground of secret bargain between plaintiff and defendant's agent for commission); *Harrington* v *Victoria Graving Dock Co* (1878), 3 Q. B D 549 (defence, on a similar ground, to a claim for agreed remuneration for services in this case the party prejudiced directly was not the defendant company, but another company for whom the defendants were executing certain work); *Shipway* v. *Broadwood*, [1899] 1 Q B 369, C A (defence to an action on a cheque for the price of a pair of horses, on the ground that the plaintiff had secretly promised money to the defendant's veterinary surgeon on his giving a certificate of soundness, subject to which the price was to be payable; per A L. SMITH, L.J , at p. 372 "it was the plaintiff's duty to inform the defendant of the promise made to P."—the veterinary surgeon—"if he wished to escape the consequences of having made it "); *Bartram & Sons* v. *Lloyd* (1904), 90 L. T 357, C A. (the same kind of case : per COLLINS, M.R , at p. 359), *King, Viall, & Benson* v. *Howell* (1910), 27 T L R. 114, C A. (defence to stockbroker's action for money paid and commission, on the ground that the plaintiff had, without any disclosure having been made of the fact, executed the transactions with a firm of jobbers whose authorized clerk was the defendant's agent to speculate for him on the Stock Exchange)

(x) As in *Panama & S Pacific Telegraph Co.* v *India Rubber, etc , Co* (1875), 10 Ch. App 515; *Transvaal Lands Co* v. *New Belgium, etc., Co.*, [1914] 2 Ch. 488, C. A.

(y) As in *Whaley Bridge Calico Printing Co* v *Green* (1879), 5 Q B D 109 , *Salford Corporation* v. *Lever*, [1891] 1 Q. B. 168, C. A.; *Grant* v. *Gold Exploration & Development Syndicate*, [1900] 1 Q. B. 233, C A. ; *Hovenden & Sons* v *Millhoff* (1900), 83 L. T. 41, C A.

recovers it as damages, and not as money had and received (z), though, inasmuch as the measure of damages is *primâ facie*, if not irrebuttably, presumed to be at least the amount of the bribe, the result is practically the same   This measure is adopted on the theory that the contract price or consideration must have been augmented by at least that amount in order to enable the contractee to pay it to the agent without any sacrifice of his normal mercantile profit (a)   It follows that, for this purpose, the question of whether the stipulated bribe was actually received by the agent, though of vital importance to any claim against such agent, is wholly immaterial to the question of the principal's right to damages against the contractee, or to the question of the *quantum* of such damages (b)

385. The above remedies against the contractee on the one hand, and the agent on the other, are cumulative remedies (c) : they may be pursued successively, and in any order the principal pleases, or simultaneously in one and the same proceeding ; and the money to which the principal is entitled as against the agent is entirely distinct from, and therefore recoverable independently of, the money to which he is entitled on compensation from the contractee, though it so happens that the two sums are ordinarily equal to one another , and it is no answer to the principal's claim against the contractee to prove that the former has agreed not to press, or has in fact omitted to press, his claim against the agent, though, in estimating the damages recoverable against the contractee, any sum which the principal has actually received from the agent goes in reduction of damages (d).

(z) *Grant* v. *Gold Exploration & Development Syndicate, sup* , where the money recoverable was regarded as damages, though quantified and liquidated by the application of the measure stated in the text.

(a) *Salford Corporation* v *Lever, sup* (per Lord ESHER, M R , at pp. 174, 175) , *Grant* v. *Gold Exploration & Development Syndicate, sup* (per A L SMITH, L J , at pp. 242-245, VAUGHAN WILLIAMS, L.J., at pp. 253, 254, 256, and COLLINS, L J., at pp 247, 248, 250, who also held that it was quite immaterial to the question of damage whether the bribe was actually paid, or not, if it was promised to be paid) , *Hovenden & Sons* v *Millhoff, sup* (per ROMER, L.J , at p. 45, expressing the view that the presumption—probably an irrebuttable one—against the contractee is that the contract price was enhanced by *at least* the amount of the sum given or promised as a bribe to the agent   The jury in this case had awarded nominal damages only, which the C. A. said was against all principle, and gave judgment for the plaintiff for the amount of the secret commissions, as the *minimum* damage recoverable)   .

(b) *Grant* v *Gold Exploration & Development Syndicate, sup* (passages cited in the last note)   And see *Whaley Bridge Calico Printing Co* v. *Green, inf*

(c) *Lister & Co* v *Stubbs* (1890), 45 C D 1, C A , per COTTON L J , at p. 12

(d) The following cases, in which relief was obtained, or was held to be obtainable, against both the contractee and the agent, illustrate the principles stated in the text · *Panama & S. Pacific Telegraph Co* v *India Rubber, Gutta Percha & Telegraph Co* (1875), 10 Ch App. 515, where the principal was held entitled to rescission and repayment against the contractee, and also to payment over of the amount of the bribe against the agent (per JAMES, L J , at p 526   " any surreptitious dealing between one principal and the agent of the other principal is a fraud on such other principal . . . ; if a man hired a vetturino to take him from one place to another, and found that the vetturino, after accepting the hiring, had conspired with his servant to rob him on the way, he would be entitled to get rid both of the vetturino and the servant ") , *Whaley Bridge Calico Printing Co* v. *Green* (1879), 5 Q B D 109 (where the principal recovered from the agent the money actually received by him, and from the opposite principal, as damages, certain other moneys promised, but unpaid, by him to the agent under the corrupt agreement, and an injunction restraining the negotiation of bills given to the agent in pursuance thereof) ;

Sub-s. (3). Miscellaneous Forms of Relief.

386. Apart from statutory remedies, whether for statutory or common law non-disclosure, which are dealt with separately elsewhere (e), there are certain miscellaneous forms of relief which have been granted under special circumstances, and to which some reference ought to be made before leaving the topic. In one case, besides granting relief as to the past, a prospective declaration was made on a principal's counterclaim against his agents and the person employed by them as sub-agent, that any moneys which might thereafter be received by such sub-agent in pursuance of the secret bargain complained of would be payable over as a debt to the principal (f) In another case, where an executor *de son tort* had obtained from the beneficiaries a surrender of a leasehold interest and a grant to himself of a new lease at a lower rent than had been paid by the testator, it was held that the beneficiaries were entitled to have this new lease declared a trust for them, as a graft on the surrendered lease (g).

387. Relief on the ground of non-disclosure in breach of a fiduciary duty has often been given indirectly and incidentally in the course of proceedings instituted with other objects, such, for instance, as the following proceedings under one of the Trustee Acts (h), a vendor and purchaser action, where it has been held that a vendor who can show no better title than that of a trustee who has purchased part of the trust estate shows none at all which

---

Salford Corporation v *Lever*, [1891] 1 Q B 168, C A (where the corporation recovered damages against a coal merchant who had clandestinely promised the manager of the corporation's gasworks a commission of a shilling per ton on all orders for coal given by the plaintiffs to the defendant, and it was held that the defendant's liability was in no way reduced or affected by the fact that the plaintiffs, having the right to make their manager disgorge the commissions received by him, had agreed not to sue him on his giving them certain information as to the persons who had corrupted him, and guaranteeing that the sums to be recovered from such persons should amount to a specified aggregate sum the two rights being wholly distinct rights, and the moneys recoverable not being the same moneys, though exactly equivalent, the principal was entitled to pursue the two remedies successively, or in one and the same action, and, for this and other reasons, the defendant's plea of accord and satisfaction was held wholly inadmissible   *per* Lord ESHER, M R , at pp 176–178, and LINDLEY, L J , at pp. 179, 180) , *Grant* v *Gold Explora tion & Development Syndicate*, [1900] 1 Q B 233, C A. (where the company recovered by counterclaim against the vendor, as damages, a sum equal to the amount of the bribe which he had given to one of their directors for procuring the company to purchase, less what they had previously, without the necessity of suing for it, extracted from the agent , it was here recognized that the two rights were distinct and cumulative, but that in calculating the damages it was impossible to ignore the money and shares actually received from the agent, the amount of which must go in reduction · *per* A L. SMITH, L.J , at pp. 245, 246, VAUGHAN WILLIAMS, L J , at p 255, and COLLINS, L J , at p 251)

(e) See Ch VI, Sect 7, and Ch VIII, Sect. 2, Sub-s (3), *post*

(f) *Powell & Thomas* v *Evans, Jones & Co* , [1905] 1 K. B. 11, C A. As to the reason for this declaration, and for its limited form, see § 379, note (d), *ante*.

(g) *Mulvany* v *Dillon* (1810), 1 Ball & B. 409 , 12 R. R 43

(h) *Re Bloye's Trusts* (1849), 1 Macn. & G. 488 (*per* Lord COTTENHAM, L C , at p 498 " I am bound to make such an order as I should have made if there had been a bill filed to set aside the deed "), affirmed, *sub nom Lewis* v *Hillman* (1852), 3 H L C 607 (*per* Lord ST. LEONARDS, L C., at pp 631, 632, to the same effect) This was a case in which a petition, and cross petition, had been presented under the Trustee Relief Act then in force, and where it became necessary to decide whether a certain sale was valid or, by reason of non-disclosure of identity by the solicitors and agents purchasing from their client and principal, invalid

can be forced on a purchaser (*i*), an action for sale in lieu of partition, where a question arising as to whether a certain charge on the property had been paid off or not depended upon whether a fiduciary duty of disclosure had or had not been complied with (*j*), an action for libel, where justification was pleaded of a defamatory charge against the plaintiff of having taken "secret profit" when in a fiduciary position (*k*); and an administration suit (*l*).

388. Relief by way of rescission may be obtained in bankruptcy proceedings against a trustee in bankruptcy who has failed in his fiduciary duty of disclosure to the creditors and to the bankrupt, on the motion of the bankrupt himself (*m*), or of a creditor (*n*). Where it is sought to recover from an insolvent promoter or agent the amount of secret profit made by him, the non-disclosure is regarded, not as a tort, but as a breach of an implied contract to perform the trust, and as giving rise to an equitable debt, and the company or principal is accordingly entitled to a proof (*o*), but, for reasons already given (*p*), is not entitled to relief on the footing that the money can be segregated from the assets divisible among the creditors, and set apart, as an earmarked trust fund, to answer the claim in full, unless it can be truly said that the money or property was, when received or held by the promoter or agent, the property or money of the company or principal Where a company in liquidation is entitled to relief in respect of non-disclosure against any of its directors or officers, the relief may be given in any one of three possible forms : in the first place, the liquidator, in the name of the company, may sue the delinquent, or prove against him, if insolvent (*q*), secondly, he may claim that the shares, if it be a case of a present of shares from the promoter to the director, have not been paid for, and settle the

---

(*i*) *Spencer* v *Topham* (1856), 22 Beav. 573 (where, however, the discharge of the fiduciary duty was proved, and the title accordingly held good) , *Williams* v *Scott*, [1900] A C 499, P C. (at p 508   " it would be inequitable to force such a title as this "—the title of one who, when trustee for sale, had purchased from himself—" upon the appellant. It is not merely that the purchaser would be running the risk of proceedings being taken by the *cestuis que trustent* to reopen the transaction The purchaser would be saddled with a property which he would be unable for many years to put upon the market, unless recourse was had to some special restrictive condition which might seriously reduce the price a purchaser would be willing to pay for it ")

(*j*) *Patten* v. *Hamilton*, [1911] 1 Ir R. 40

(*k*) *Bray* v *Ford*, [1896] A. C 44, H L

(*l*) As in *Gray* v *Warner* (1873), 42 L J (CH) 556, where a question arose whether the defendant could properly exercise his right of retainer, as executor, in respect of a legacy which he had purchased from a legatee, that is, whether he could sustain the propriety of the transaction

(*m*) As in *Re Moore* (1881), 51 L J (CH) 72   Cp *Re Spink* (1913), 108 L T 572, 811

(*n*) As in *Re Gallard*, [1897] 2 Q B 8.

(*o*) *Emma Silver Mining Co* v *Grant* (1879), 17 C D 122 (per JESSEL, M R , at pp 130, 131) , *Re Darby, Ex p Brougham*, [1911] 1 K B 95 (per PHILLIMORE, J , at p 100)   Where, however, after paying money into court, the party charged becomes bankrupt, the party complaining is entitled to have that money paid out to him in full, and is not remitted to a mere right of proof.   *Hichens* v *Congreve* (1831), 4 Sim 420 (per SHADWELL, V.-C , at p 429)

(*p*) See § 379, and note (*d*), thereto, *ante*.

(*q*) As in *Imperial Mercantile Credit Association* v. *Coleman* (1873), L. R 6 H L 189 , *Metropolitan Bank* v *Heiron* (1880), 5 Ex D. 319, C. A , *Re Darby, Ex p. Brougham*, *sup* (proof in bankruptcy)

director's name on the list of contributories (r) ; and, lastly, he may resort to the statutory misfeasance procedure (s).   The choice between these modes of asserting his claim to relief is the right of the liquidator (t).   It should be mentioned here that fiduciary misconduct on the part of the company's officers is not only a ground for the compulsory winding up of an insolvent company (u), but also a ground for refusing a stay of proceedings in a pending winding up, though the creditors are desirous that it should be granted (v).

SECT. 6.   QUESTIONS OF LAW AND FACT

389. It is always a question of law whether any, and, if so, what, legal rights or obligations result from a proved or admitted state of facts, and it is equally a question of law whether any admissible evidence has been adduced in support, or (as the case may be) in contradiction, of any material allegation of fact.   Subject, however, to these two cardinal rules, every matter in dispute between the parties in any proceeding based upon alleged breach of fiduciary duty, by non-disclosure or otherwise, is an issue of fact.   Thus to take *seriatim* the principal matters to be established in any such proceeding, on one side or the other (w) :—where the existence of the relationship is challenged, it is a question of law whether a relation of the precise character alleged can properly be inferred from the instrument purporting to create it, or from the proved facts, but it is a question of fact whether the alleged circumstances existed or not ; that is to say, whether the course of dealing between the parties, and the various acts said to constitute the party a trustee (x), a promoter (y), or an agent (z), of the particular kind alleged,

(r) As in *Re Diaders & Co.* (1870), L R 11 Eq. 242 ; *Re Canadian Oil Works Corporation, Hay's Case* (1875), 10 Ch. App 593.

(s) As to this procedure, see § 616, *post*

(t) See *Hay's Case, sup.* (per MELLISH, L J, at p 605, who points out that the company has the option of asserting that the director has never paid for the shares at all, or of treating him as if he had paid, and saying—" in that case you have paid with our money, and we will have it back now "), *Re Carriage Co operative Association* (1884), 27 C D. 322 (per PEARSON, J, at p 332).

(u) See Lord Halsbury's *Laws of England*, title *Companies*, vol v, pp. 397, 398

(v) *Re Telescriptor Syndicate, Ltd*, [1903] 2 Ch 174

(w) See Sects 3, 4, *ante*

(x) *Mulvany* v. *Dillon* (1810), 1 Ball & B 409 ; 12 R. R 43, where Lord MANNERS, L C (Ir) treated the question of whether the defendant had interfered with the assets and management of the estate so far as to constitute himself an executor and trustee, as one of fact (pp. 418, 419)   And see, generally, the cases cited in the notes to Sect 2, Sub-s (1), Sect. 3, Sub s (1), and Sect 4, Sub s (1), *ante*

(y) *Lydney & Wigpool Iron Ore Co* v *Bird* (1883), 33 C. D 85, C A (per LINDLEY, L J, at p 93 · " it is necessary in each case to see what the so-called promoter really did before his legal liability can be accurately ascertained   In any case, it is better to look at the facts and ascertain and describe them as they are ").   Cp., generally, the cases cited in the notes to Sect 2, Sub s (2), Sect 3, Sub s (1), and Sect. 4, Sub s (1), *ante*

(z) *Carter* v. *Palmer* (1842), 8 Cl & Fin. 657 (where, as to the contention of the party charged that he acted as counsel only, and not as general agent and manager, which was the allegation on the other side, Lord COTTENHAM, L C, said, at p. 703   " *the evidence proves* that the employment was of a very different character ") ; *Barker* v *Harrison* (1846), 2 Coll 546 (where KNIGHT BRUCE, V -C, at p 553, refers to the evidence as to the nature of the employment alleged, which he finds to have been established thereby as a fact), *Harrington* v *Victoria Graving Dock Co* (1878), 3 Q B D 549 (where the question was left as an issue of fact to the jury), *Williamson* v *Hine Bros*, [1891] 1 Ch 390 (where KEKEWICH,

did or did not exist or take place at the material date. So it is a question of fact, if there is evidence both ways, whether disclosure was made or not (a), and whether the party complaining had knowledge *aliundè* or not (b), of the transaction or fact which is said to have been unrevealed to, and unknown by, the party complaining; whether the party complaining by his acts and conduct affirmed the transaction impeached (c) ; and whether the transaction or matter alleged to have been undisclosed was entered into, or existed, as alleged (d). And any question of fair value which may arise is a question of fact (e).

SECT. 7. PARTIES.

390. It remains to consider what persons may assert a right to relief of any of the kinds already indicated (f), and against what persons, on the ground of non-disclosure of material facts during the existence of a fiduciary relation.

Sub-s (1) Who are entitled to assert the Right to Relief

391. The persons entitled to assert the right to relief comprise, (1) those to whom the fiduciary duty was owed in the first instance, and (2) those who by operation of law, or voluntary assignment, are, or have become, entitled to stand in their place.

392. The fiduciary duty is owed to the person, whether natural or artificial, or, in the case of a partnership (g) or class (h), to all the members of the firm

J , directed an inquiry as to the duties recognized in the mercantile world as attaching to the agency, though the C A thought the inquiry unnecessary, as it could only be answered in one way). And see, generally, the cases cited in the notes to Sect. 2, Sub s (3), Sect 3, Sub s (1), and Sect 4, Sub s (1), *ante*

(a) As to what "disclosure" means, see Ch II, Sect 1, *ante*. In *Harrington* v. *Victoria Graving Dock Co*, *sup*, this question also was left as one of fact to the jury So, in *Re Postage Stamp Automatic Delivery Co*, [1892] 3 Ch 566, VAUGHAN WILLIAMS, J , found, "as a fact" (p 576), that disclosure had been made with respect to certain of the shares there in question, but, with respect to the others, had not been made to future allottees, whom he also found "as a fact" that it was intended to deceive As to questions of disclosure to the precise person, and to all the persons, entitled to it, see § 392, 393, *inf* And, generally, cp the cases cited in the notes to Sect 4, Sub s (2), *ante* Where the disclosure is alleged to have been solely documentary, the question is for the Court *Oelkers* v *Ellis*, [1914] 2 K B 139 (per HORRIDGE, J , at p 147)

(b) As to what "knowledge" means, see Ch II, Sect 3, *ante* In *Whaley Bridge Calico Printing Co* v *Green* (1879), 5 Q B. D. 109, BOWEN, J , left this question, amongst others, to the jury (p 110) See, generally, the cases cited in the notes to Sect 4, Sub-s (3), *ante*

(c) In *Lowther* v *Lord Lowther* (1806), 13 Ves 95, Lord ERSKINE, L C , at pp 103, 104, offered to direct an issue as to what the exact nature of the transaction between the parties was, if the agent desired it, which he did. See, generally, the cases cited in the notes to Sect 4, Sub s (3), *ante*.

(d) See the cases cited in the notes to Sect 3, Sub s (2), *ante*

(e) In *Gibson* v. *Jeyes* (1801), 6 Ves 266, Lord ELDON, L C , treated this question as one of fact, depending on the evidence, and discussed the kind of evidence proper to be adduced for the purpose of determining it (p 274)

(f) See Sect 5, *ante*

(g) In *Fawcett* v *Whitehouse* (1829), 1 Russ & M 132, the circumstances were such as to render it proper to join *an intending partner* as a plaintiff entitled to the relief prayed

(h) Such as creditors—see note (n), *inf*—or a class of beneficiaries or class, between whom and the party charged the relation of confidence is proved to exist (*i*). The party charged may be a trustee for, though he cannot be an agent of, a person not yet in existence, or not yet having a full legal status, and in that event the person in question, when brought into being, or on becoming *sui juris*, is a person to whom the duty is deemed to have been owed in the first instance   Thus, if a person acquires property with the intention of selling it to a particular company to be promoted by him for the purpose of purchasing it, he may be deemed to have acquired the property as trustee (in a limited sense, not in the sense of " out-and-out trusteeship ") for the unborn, but intended, company, which, therefore, when incorporated has a right to relief against him in the event of any breach of such fiduciary duty arising out of the quasi-trusteeship (*j*) . but if, when acquiring the property, he did not contemplate any future sale at all, or any future sale to a company, or, though intending a sale to *a* company to be formed by him, did not contemplate *the* particular company in question, the company complaining has no right to say that he owed any duty to it when so acquiring the property, though it may have a right to relief against him on other grounds in respect of his subsequent acts (*k*).   So, in the case of infants, the duty is owed to those who are not yet *sui juris* ; for that reason, it is extremely difficult to prove that the duty has been discharged, and, indeed, it can only be so discharged by making the necessary disclosure to, and obtaining the sanction of, the Court (*l*).   Again, where a person is appointed to discharge certain fiduciary duties in relation to the re-building of a rectory, and fails to perform them, he is liable not only to the existing rector, but to his successors, any one of whom may come to the Court for relief (*m*)

393. In the case of a class of persons, such as a general body of creditors, the duty is owed to them all, and, for that reason, it is difficult to establish a case of disclosure to, or knowledge or assent or acquiescence on the part of, the entire body entitled to relief (*n*).   Where the person to whom the duty

(*i*) For illustrations of cases in which the relation does not exist, or is not operative on the transaction impeached, see Sect. 2, Sub s. (4), and Sect 3, Sub-s (1), *ante*

(*j*) *Beck* v. *Kantorowicz* (1857), 3 K & J 230 , *Gluckstein* v *Barnes*, [1900] A C 240, H L (*per* Lord HALSBURY, L C , at p 247).   As to the distinction between a promoter's limited trusteeship and the out-and-out trusteeship which gives rise to the obligation of restoring property and profits to the *cestui que trust*, irrespectively of disclosure or non disclosure, see the valuable observations of SARGANT, J , at p 347 of *Omnium Electric Palaces, Ltd* v *Barnes*, [1914] 1 Ch 332, C A

(*k*) *Erlanger* v. *New Sombrero Phosphate Co* (1878), 3 App Cas 1218, H L (*per* Lord CAIRNS, L C , at p 1235), *Bentinck* v *Fenn* (1887), 12 App Cas 652, H. L (*per* Lord HERSCHELL, at p 658), *Ladywell Mining Co* v *Brookes* (1887), 35 C D. 400, C A (*per* COTTON, L J , at p 413), *Re Lady Forrest (Murchison) Gold Mine, Ltd.*, [1901] 1 Ch 582 (*per* WRIGHT, J , at pp 588, 589)   *Burland* v *Earle*, [1902] A C 83, P. C (at pp 98, 99) See note (*n*) to § 352, *ante*, for the language used in some of these cases

(*l*) *Sanderson* v *Walker* (1807), 13 Ves 601 (*per* Lord ELDON, L C , at pp 601, 602). The statutory Public Trustee is, in this respect, in precisely the same position as any other trustee · *Re New Haw Estate Trusts* (1912), 107 L. T 191 (PARKER, J.).

(*m*) *Greenlaw* v. *King* (1841), 10 L J (CH) 129 (*per* Lord COTTENHAM, L C , at p 130 " the bishop was selected to take care of the interests of those who were not and could not be present in the transaction, viz of those who might thereafter be appointed rectors or the living "

(*n*) *Whichcote* v *Lawrence* (1798), 3 Ves. 739 (*per* Lord LOUGHBOROUGH, L C., at p 752 " you cannot argue upon the acquiescence, when there is a large body of creditors ')

is owed is a juridical, and not a natural, person, nice questions frequently arise as to whether the disclosure has been made to the particular persons on behalf of the corporation, or to all the persons constituting or representing it, who are entitled to the disclosure. The question of the proper agents or officers of a company, through whom alone under any circumstances it can be deemed to have received the necessary information as to the material facts, has been already discussed (o). But where the directors, or other agents, through whom under ordinary circumstances knowledge would be imputed to the company, are parties charged, or are implicated in the misconduct of the party charged, disclosure to them, or to their confederates, is of course no disclosure at all to the company, that is, to the party entitled to relief (p). And, independently of all questions of the complicity of the directors, the circumstances may be such that the fiduciary duty can only be discharged by disclosure to the general body of shareholders, or to the public: for instance, if it be proved in evidence that the shares are being offered to the public, or that a further issue is expressly or impliedly contemplated, these probable or possible future allottees are deemed to be constituents of the company which is entitled to the performance of the duty (q). It is only when there is no such intention, or contemplation, that disclosure to the directors, or to the actually existing members of the company, is deemed disclosure to the company (r) On the other hand, the company being a

---

This was the case of one who, being trustee for sale of a debtor's property for the benefit of the creditors, purchased part of the trust property

(o) See § 50, and the cases cited in note '*f*' thereto, *ante*

(p) *Benson* v *Heathorn* (1842), 1 Y & C 326 (*per* SHADWELL, V.-C, at p 343), *Re Fitzroy Bessemer Steel Co.* (1884), 50 L T 144 (*per* KAY, J, at p 147), *Costa Rica Railway Co* v. *Forwood*, [1901] 1 Ch 746, C A (*per* VAUGHAN WILLIAMS, L J., at p 761), *Omnium Electric Palaces, Ltd* v *Baines*, [1914] 1 Ch 332, C A (*per* SARGANT, J, at p 342)

(q) *Hichens* v *Congreve* (1831), 4 Sim 420 (*per* SHADWELL, V-C, at pp 427, 428); *Society of Practical Knowledge* v *Abbott* (1840), 2 Beav. 559, *Re Postage Stamp Automatic Delivery Co*, [1892] 3 Ch 566 (*per* VAUGHAN WILLIAMS, J, at p 576 "I find as a fact that the intention was to get the public to subscribe . . The fact of the knowledge of the actual members of the company will not in such a case avail the directors"), *Gluckstein* v *Barnes*, [1900] A C 240, H L. (*per* Lord MACNAGHTEN, at p 249 "disclosure is not the most appropriate word to use when a person who plays many parts announces to himself in one character what he has done and is doing in another To talk of disclosure to the thing called a company, when as yet there were no shareholders, is a mere farce To the intended shareholders there was no disclosure at all." So Lord HALSBURY, L.C., at p 247), *Re Leeds and Hanley Theatre of Varieties, Ltd*, [1902] 2 Ch 809, C A. (*per* VAUGHAN WILLIAMS, L J, at p 823, explaining that the fiduciary relation of promoters to the company "does not mean that they stood in such a relation to these directors, and these seven signatories. It means that they stood in a fiduciary position to the future allottees of shares—to the persons who were invited to come and take up the shares of the company . . among their *cestuis que trustent* are included the future allottees of shares"), *Re Darby, Ex p Brougham*, [1911] 1 K B 95 (*per* PHILLIMORE, J, at p 103), *Omnium Electric Palaces, Ltd* v *Baines, sup.* (*per* SARGANT, J, at pp 347, 348 . this was a case of a "private company")

(r) As was the case in *Re Ambrose Lake Tin & Copper Mining Co*, *Ex p Taylor, Ex p Moss* (1880), 14 C D 390, C A (*per* JAMES, L J, at p 395 "there was no fraud on any future allottees of shares, because there could be, at the time the arrangements were made and contemplated, no future allottees of shares," all the capital having been subscribed), *Re British Seamless Box Co* (1881), 17 C D 467, C A (*per* JESSEL, M R, who distinguishes between the two types of case, the one, where future shareholders are expressed to be contemplated, or where it is clear from the facts, *e g* a further issue shortly afterwards, that they must have been contemplated, and where therefore "it is intended

person in law, independently of its members, no shareholder can claim a right to relief on the ground of non-disclosure to himself, as if he were the company the duty to the company, as a juridical entity, involves no personal duty to any individual member of it (s)

394. The second class of persons entitled to set up a case of non-disclosure against the party charged comprises those to whom personally no duty was owed in the first instance, but who are, or become, entitled to stand in the place of, or to represent, the persons to whom such duty was owed, whether by operation of law (t),—as, for instance, on the death (u), insolvency (v), infancy, lunacy, or other disability, of the party complaining,—or by voluntary assignment. The conditions under, and the equities subject to, which an assignment of a chose in possession, and of a chose in action, respectively, may be made, and the application of the law on this subject to the case of a voidable contract, have been fully considered in an earlier Chapter (w).

395. There is a class of case in which, though there has been no transmission of the right to relief by operation of law or by voluntary assignment, persons other than the party to whom the duty is owed are entitled to sue in respect of a breach of fiduciary duty ; and that is, where the party charged is under a duty of disclosure or otherwise to a corporation, which he has failed to discharge, and the corporation, which alone (as has been seen) is *primâ facie* entitled to assert rights in respect of such breach of duty, refuses to take proceedings, being under the control of a majority of share-

to cheat the future shareholders "—pp 471, 172—and the other, where no future allottees are either expressly or impliedly contemplated, which was the case then before the Court " the company consisted of eight men, and it was not intended to consist of any more There was power of course to issue the remainder of the shares, but the intention of these eight men was to carry on the company with these shares,"—p 473,—and though there was in fact " a subsequent allotment of a portion of the shares," this was " not part of the original scheme"—p 475 And see the observations of JAMES, L.J , at pp 476, 477, BRETT, L J , at p 477, and COTTON, L J , at p 480, affirming the views of JESSEL, M R)

(s) *Percival* v *Wright*, [1902] 2 Ch 421 (*per* SWINFEN EADY, J , at p 426 " it was strenuously urged that, though incorporation affected the relations of the shareholders to the external world, the company thereby becoming a distinct entity, the position of the shareholders *inter se* was not affected, and was the same as that of partners or shareholders in an unincorporated company I am unable to adopt that view ") In *Allen* v *Hyatt* (1914), 30 T. L. R 444, P. C., the duty to the shareholders arose from special circumstances

(t) In all such cases the right to relief for breach of the fiduciary duty is conferred, or devolves, upon other persons in accordance with the same principles as in the case of any other proceedings for the enforcement or avoidance of contracts.

(u) As in *Randall* v *Errington* (1805), 10 Ves. 423 (next of kin of *cestui que trust*), *Lowther* v *Lord Lowther* (1806), 13 Ves 95 (beneficiaries under a will), *Ormond (Lady)* v. *Hutchinson* (1806), 13 Ves 47 (heiress at law of principal), *Charter* v *Treiclyan* (1844), 11 Cl. & Fin 714 (devisee of principal), *Barnard* v *Hunter* (1856), 2 Jur (N S) 1213 (executors of principal), *Turnbull* v *Garden* (1869), 20 L T 218 (widow of principal), *Plowright* v. *Lambert* (1885), 52 L T 646 (widow of *cestui que trust*)

(v) Assignees or trustees of the estate of an insolvent individual asserted the rights which the insolvent would otherwise have been entitled to assert, in *Pitt* v *Mackreth* (1788), 2 Cox 320 ; 2 R R 55 , *Luddy's Trustee* v. *Peard* (1886), 33 C D 500 As to the liquidator of an insolvent company, see § 388, note (t), *ante*, and, as to misfeasance proceedings, § 616, *post*

(w) See § 279, *ante*, as to what claims are, and what are not, obnoxious to the objections of champerty or maintenance For an illustration of an assignment of a contract which, though it so happened that litigation became necessary to enforce it, was held not champertous, see *Wilson* v. *Short* (1847), 6 Hare 366 (*per* WIGRAM, V.-C , at p 384)

holders who are themselves the persons against whom 't is desired to proceed, and who abuse their voting power to coerce and oppress the minority, and prevent justice being done. In such a case the minority may obtain leave from the Court, on establishing the facts, to use the name of the corporation in an action against the delinquents, or (which is the modern practice, in order to avoid circuity of proceedings) may sue on behalf of themselves and all other shareholders adopting their view (x). In the latter form of proceeding, although, as representing the company in a sense, the minority have no less rights than the company would have had if the action were in its name, on the other hand they have no greater rights, and if unable to make a case for the company, are unable to make one for themselves (y).

Sub-s (2)   Against whom the Right to Relief may be Asserted.

396. The persons against whom the right to relief may be asserted are classified under two heads corresponding to those under which the persons entitled to relief have been classified. That is to say, the persons liable are, (1) all those who have come under the fiduciary obligation in the first instance, and (2) those who, either by operation of law, or in virtue of a voluntary assignment, are called upon to stand in the place of the persons originally liable, or to take the consequences of their breaches of duty.

397. As regards the first class, *qui facit per alium facit per se* is a general principle which applies to breaches of the fiduciary duty of disclosure as much as to other breaches of duty. If a man chooses to delegate the duty of disclosure to another, he is responsible to the *cestui que trust*, company, or principal, if the duty is not discharged by the person so delegated (z). Conversely, an agent who is acting for a person liable to the duty, still more if he is also his professional adviser, cannot do what his principal is not allowed to do. If the latter is under an obligation to disclose to the other related party any personal advantage which he is acquiring in the course of the relation, so also is the former bound to disclose to such related party any private profit which in the course and execution of his delegated functions he may be so acquiring; and, generally, the agent is in no better position than his principal (a)   Further, a person who employs as his agent one whom

(x) *Hichens* v *Congreve* (1828), 4 Russ 562 (*per* Lord LYNDHURST, L C , at pp 575-577) *Atwool* v. *Merryweather* (1867), L R 5 Eq. 464 n. (*per* WOOD, V -C , at p 468 n), *Shaw* v. *Holland*, [1900] 2 Ch 305, C. A.   And, for judicial explanation of the principles of the law on this subject, see the citations in the next note

(y) *Burland* v. *Earle*, [1902] A C 83, P C , at p 93 , *Dominion Cotton Mills Co* v. *Amyot*, [1912] A. C. 546, P C. (at pp 551-553).   In both these cases the shareholders failed, because the company itself would have failed, if they had been plaintiffs

(z) As to when the knowledge of the agent is imputed to the principal, see Ch II, Sect 3, Sub-s (4), *ante.*

(a) See *Ex p James* (1803), 8 Ves. 337, which was a case of an assignee in bankruptcy purchasing part of the estate from the creditors, and the solicitor to the commission entering into a like transaction, where Lord ELDON, L C , after dealing with the assignee's purchase, which was clearly invalid, proceeds to consider the case of the solicitor: " as to the solicitor," he says at pp 346, 347, "if there is any utility in applying the principle against the assignee, the application as against the solicitor is more loudly called for.   He is to do his duty to the assignees, enabling them to do their duty to the creditors, always

he knows to stand in a fiduciary relation to a third party takes upon himself the same duties of good faith towards the third party as the person so employed is under towards him (b). The same consequences result when he accepts employment from one whom he knows to stand in such a position: for instance, one who becomes the sub-agent of a person known by him to be the agent of X., or known to be the agent of someone who afterwards turns out to be X , places himself in direct privity with X , as regards all fiduciary duties of disclosure, and otherwise, and so also, if he purchases from an agent of X , known to him to be such, he comes under the same liability to X as the agent (c). On the other hand, one who is bound by a relation of confidence to another does not escape from his obligations by making himself the agent of a person who is not so bound, and who actually effects the transaction complained of . his duties are neither diminished, nor increased, by such a proceeding (d), nor is he excused by the mere fact that, as trustee for another, he had no beneficial interest in the transaction (dd). It is, however, open to him to shew, if he can, that he was dealing directly independently, and adversely, with some third person in respect of property which the latter had validly, not being under any fiduciary duty to him, acquired from the party complaining, in that case the interposition of the independent third person would result in each transaction having been entered into by a pair of persons of whom neither was under any fiduciary duty to the other (e)

remembering also their duty to the bankrupt . . Upon the same principle that requires the assignees to make no benefit, the solicitor who is to direct and inform them in the very act by which they are to make no benefit, cannot possibly make any benefit "), *Ex p Bennett* (1805), 10 Ves 381 (*per* Lord ELDON, L C , at p 383), *Downes* v *Grazebrook* (1817), 3 Mer. 200 (*per* Lord ELDON, L C., at pp 208, 209); *Re Bloye's Trusts* (1849), 1 Macn & G 488 (*per* Lord COTTENHAM, L C , at p 494 " if the principal is incapacitated, can the agent do what the principal could not ? "), *McPherson* v *Watt* (1877), 3 App Cas 254, H L. (*per* Lord CAIRNS, L C , at p 265, and Lord BLACKBURN, at p 276), *Lydney & Wigpool Iron Ore Co.* v *Bird* (1886), 33 C D 85, C A (*per Cur* , at pp 94, 95), *Hodson* v. *Deans* [1903] 2 Ch 647 (*per* JOYCE, J , at pp 652, 653)

(b) *Watt* v *Grove* (1805), 2 Sch & Lefr 491, *per* Lord REDESDALE, L C. (Ir), at p 502. It is partly on this theory that relief is given against the contractee who has secretly employed the agent of the party complaining for commission and reward, as stated in Sect. 5, Sub-s (2), *ante.*

(c) *Molony* v *Kernan* (1842), 2 Dr & W 37 , 59 R R 635 (*per* SUGDEN, L C (Ir), at pp 41, 42 . " a party who buys from an agent with distinct notice that the party with whom he is dealing is an agent, has cast upon him the burden of sustaining the lease, just as much as the agent himself, and, if the lease could not be upheld by the agent, neither could it be supported by a purchaser from that agent, if he deals with him in his character as agent "), *De Bussche* v. *Alt* (1878), 8 C D 286, C A (*per Cur* , at pp 310, 311), *Powell & Thomas* v. *Evans, Jones & Co* , [1905] 1 K B. 11, C A (*per* COLLINS, M R , at pp 18, 19, STIRLING, L J , at pp 21, 22, and MATHEW, L J., at p. 23), *King, Viall & Benson* v *Howell* (1910), 27 T L R 114, C A

(d) See *Coles* v *Trecothick* (1804), 9 Ves 234 (*per* Lord ELDON, L C , at p 248 " if the trustee is to be the agent of the buyer, there is as much hazard that the sale may turn out to be that which may be fraudulent But the same circumstances that would authorize the trustee to contract would authorize him to be the agent of the buyer, and cannot be carried higher against the agent ") In that case the purchase, if made by the trustee himself, would have been quite unimpeachable, and it was held that his having acted as agent for the actual purchaser was equally so

(dd) *Transvaal Lands Co* v *New Belgium, etc* , *Co* , [1914] 2 Ch 488, 501, C A

(e) *Williams* v *Scott*, [1900] A C. 499, P C (at pp 505–508) Here the party charged failed to sustain the burden, held to be incumbent on him, of proving the interposition of

398. Where the duty of disclosure is owed by more than one person, and these persons are associated as partners (*f*), or as co-agents each of whom with the knowledge of the others enters into an illicit transaction with the same person at the same time, and all the transactions, though for a separate consideration in the case of each co-agent, are part of one entire scheme of corruption (*g*), the liability is joint and several . that is to say, each is liable *in solido* for the entire aggregate of the separate bribes (where it is a question of bribes) given to the persons in question, and not merely for the amount of his own separate bribe. But in any case where it appears on the evidence that none of the parties charged had any knowledge of the corruption of his associates, though each was conscious of his own, the liability is several, and not joint (*h*)

399. The person subject to the fiduciary obligations may be an artificial, as well as a natural person (*i*) , and, in that event, it may become of great importance to remember that the corporation which owes the duty is a distinct entity in contemplation of law from the individuals composing it, who, as such, owe no duty to the party complaining (*j*)

400. The second of the two above-mentioned classes of persons against whom the right to relief may be asserted consists of those to whom, whether by operation of law or by voluntary assignment, the liability for the consequences of any breach of that duty is transmitted

401. As regards the former species of the class, no special observations

the third party, his independence of himself, and the fact that the transaction with him was completed, or intended to be completed, or was anything more than a device to conceal identity by substitution and manipulation of names

(*f*) *Imperial Mercantile Credit Association* v. *Coleman and Knight* (1873), L R H L 189 (*per* Lord CHELMSFORD, at pp 202, 203, and Lord CAIRNS, at p 208)

(*g*) *Re Englefield Colliery Co* (1878), 8 C D 388, C A , *Re Carriage Co operative Supply Association* (1884), 27 C D 322 (a case of five directors, each of whom had accepted a present of 20 shares from the promoter one of them, General Roberts, strenuously contended that he was liable, if at all, for no more than the value of his 20 shares, viz. £100, but it was held otherwise, *per* PEARSON, J , at p 331 "there were four other directors, who accepted in the same way, and at the same time, and all in the presence of each other and of General Roberts, a transfer to each of them of 20 shares in the same way as General Roberts did " , and, accordingly, he was held accountable for £500, the value of the whole 100 shares), *Gluckstein* v *Barnes*, [1900] A C 240, H L (a case of four co-promoters of a company, who were held jointly and severally accountable for the whole of a sum of £20,000 received by them as secret profit, with penal interest, though inasmuch as, for some inconceivable reason, the liquidator had claimed relief against Gluckstein alone, and had limited the amount of such claim to £6341, with 3 per cent interest only, it was impossible for the House of Lords, in dismissing the appeal, to give him more than he had asked for and was content to accept in the court below *per* Lord HALSBURY, L C , at p 247, and Lord MACNAGHTEN, at pp 248, 255) , *Re Kent County Gas Light & Coke Co* , [1913] 1 Ch 92 (co promoters *per* NEVILLE, J , at p 96)

(*h*) *Re London & South Western Canal, Ltd* , [1911] 1 Ch 346 (*per* SWINFEN EADY, J., at pp 350, 351 . "then comes the question of what each director ought to pay It is only a several liability, as it is not established that the several directors knew the terms on which their co-directors were qualified Each director therefore is liable for £100 ")

(*i*) Thus, in *Lagunas Nitrate Co* v *Lagunas Syndicate*, [1899] 2 Ch 392, C A , and *Re Leeds & Hanley Theatre of Varieties, Ltd* , [1902] 2 Ch 809, C A , the party charged, or one of the parties charged, as promoter, and in *Bath* v *Standard Land Co* , [1911] 1 Ch 618, C A , the party charged as agent, was a limited company

(*j*) See *Bath* v *Standard Land Co.*, *sup* (*per* COZENS HARDY, M R , at pp 625, 626, and BUCKLEY, L J , at pp 642-647) are necessary. It is sufficient to say that, in case of the death (k), or disability, whether by reason of insolvency (l), infancy, lunacy, or otherwise, of the party owing the duty of disclosure, the liability to proceedings for rescission or analogous relief devolves upon, or is transmitted to, the same persons, in accordance with the same rules, and subject to the same conditions, as in cases of contract generally; and that the liability to damages, where damages are sought as for a wrong, is transmissible, if at all, under the same conditions as in any action of tort (m).

402. Where relief is sought against an assignee from a person who has entered into a transaction with the *cestui que trust*, company, or principal, which is impeachable on the ground of non-disclosure, the position of such assignee is determined with reference to a well-settled code of principles, equally applicable to any kind of contract which, on whatever ground, is voidable at the option of one of the parties. These principles accordingly are applied to the kind of non-disclosure which is the subject of the present Chapter, as well as to those which are the subjects of Chapter III, and of Chapter V, respectively. In connection with the former, they have already been fully discussed (n), and, without discussing them again, they may be summarily recapitulated as follows. Where the thing assigned is a chose in

(k) In the following cases, the proceedings were instituted, or, where the death occurred *pendente lite*, were continued or revived, against persons in law required to stand in the place of the party originally owing the duty. *Randall* v *Errington* (1805), 10 Ves 423 (executor of one of the trustees), *Morse* v *Royal* (1806), 12 Ves 355 (executors of the trustee), *Greenlaw* v *King* (1841), 10 L. J. (CH) 129 (personal representatives of one of the persons originally subject to the duty), *Hamilton* v. *Wright* (1842), 9 Cl & Fin. 111 (trustees of will of trustee for sale), *Charter* v *Trevelyan* (1844), 11 Cl & Fin 714 (executor and heir at law of the agent, and, on his death during the proceedings, the personal representatives of the executor), *Bagnall (John) & Sons, Ltd* v *Carlton* (1877), 6 C D 371, C. A. (personal representatives of one of the promoters who died during the proceedings, and trustees of the estate of another, who died before action brought), *Erlanger* v *New Sombrero Phosphate Co* (1878), 3 App Cas. 1218, H L (executors of some of the members of the promoting partnership per Lord BLACKBURN, at pp 1265, 1266), *Plowright* v. *Lambert* (1885), 52 L T 446 (widow of one trustee, and executors of the other), *Lydney* v. *Wigpool Iron Ore Co* v. *Bird* (1886), 33 C D 85, C. A (executors of one of the promoters who died during action), *Ladywell Mining Co* v *Brookes, Same* v *Huggins* (1887), 35 C. D. 400, C A (where the first action was against two living promoters, and the second against the respective executors of the three others), *Lagunas Nitrate Co.* v. *Lagunas Syndicate,* [1899] 2 Ch 392, C. A (respective executors of two of the directors of the promoting syndicate, which was in liquidation. It was pointed out here by LINDLEY, L.J, at p 438, that these executors might have been held liable for the secret profits obtained by their respective testators, if the action had been brought for that purpose, but were not liable for damages), *Costa Rica Railway Co* v. *Forwood,* [1901] 1 Ch 746, C. A (executors of the agent who died during the proceedings)

(l) Where the act or omission of the party charged can properly be described as a breach of trust, the insolvency of such party is not a discharge from the liability, being a case expressly excepted by the Bankruptcy Acts see *Emma Silver Mining Co* v *Grant* (1880), 17 C D 122 (per JESSEL, M R , at pp 128–130) For an instance of a claim in an action against the trustee of the estate of an insolvent individual, see *Erlanger* v *New Sombrero Phosphate Co , sup* (as regards some of the defendants), *Re Kent County Gas Light & Coke Co ,* [1913] 1 Ch 92 As to the right to prove in bankruptcy, see § 388, *ante* In the following cases, the relief was sought against the liquidator of an insolvent promoting company ; *Lagunas Nitrate Co* v *Lagunas Syndicate, sup , Re Leeds & Hanley Theatre of Varieties, Ltd ,* [1902] 2 Ch 809, C A

(m) These conditions are stated in the cases cited in note (l) to § 246 of the author's *Law of Actionable Misrepresentation*

(n) See §§ 283–287, *ante.*

action, the assignee takes it subject to all equities which before the assignment were, and but for the assignment would continue to be, enforceable against the assignor by the other party to the contract, including the equity to avoid it (o) : but where the subject of assignment is property in possession which the assignee takes for value, without notice, and in good faith, no right to avoid the original contract which would have been available against the assignor, at the suit of the other party to it, will be effectual to take the property out of the hands of the assignee, unless that right has been actually exercised before the date of the assignment (p) ; if, however, the assignee takes without valuable consideration, though without notice (q), or with notice, though for value (r), or both for value and without notice, but in bad faith (s), he stands in no better position than his assignor , the onus being on the party asserting his right to relief against the assignee to establish such absence of value, notice, or bad faith, as the case may be (t).

403. Questions as to the effect on costs of any unnecessary or improper joinder of parties not liable with those who are, and on the other hand of joining persons properly added as formal parties, and for conformity, or from whom, though eventually exculpated, it was reasonable to seek relief in the first instance, are considered hereafter in their proper place (u)

(o) *Greenlaw* v *King*, *sup* , where the assignee of an annuity was held responsible in respect of his assignor's breach of fiduciary duty , *Barnard* v *Hunter* (1856), 2 Jur (N S) 1213) where STUART, V -C , held that those defendants to whom a claim to a fund in Court had been assigned, though they took for value and without notice, yet, since they were "claiming under an assignment of an equity, must take as he"—the mortgagor—"took," which was in that case nothing   Cp the cases cited in note (l) to § 284, *ante*

(p) See § 285, *ante*, and, for an application of the rule there stated to cases of the description dealt with in this Chapter, see *Randall* v *Errington* (1805), 10 Ves 423, where it was recognized that, if the assignee of the property from the trustees whose purchase from the *cestui que trust* was impugned should turn out to have taken for value, without notice, and in good faith, no relief could be obtained against him, and the relief would in that event assume the form of an account against the trustees, and not of rescission   As to a purchase with notice from one who has acquired property for value and without notice, and as to when such a transaction confers a good title, and when not, see § 287, *ante*, and the cases cited in note (e) thereto

(q) See § 286, and notes (x) and (y) thereto, *ante*, and cp , for an instance of the application of the rule to cases of the present description, *McPherson* v *Watt* (1877), 3 App Cas. 254, H. L (per Lord CAIRNS, L C , at p 265, and Lord BLACKBURN, at p 276)

(r) See § 286, and note (z) thereto, *ante* , and cp , as illustrations of the application of the principle there stated to cases of the present class, *Molony* v *Kernan* (1842), 2 Dr & Warr 37 , 59 R R 635 (per SUGDEN, L C (Ir), at pp. 40-42) ; *Spencer* v *Topham* (1856), 22 Beav 573

(s) See § 286, and note (a) thereto, *ante*

(t) See § 287, *ante*

(u) In Ch VIII Sect 2, Sub s (4), *post.*

CHAPTER V.

THE DUTY OF DISCLOSURE AND OTHER DUTIES INCIDENTAL TO RELATIONS OF INFLUENCE.

404. THERE are certain relations which are deemed to give rise to what the law calls "influence", that is to say, from the mere existence of which the law presumes that one of the related parties, whom it may be convenient to call "the dominant party" (*v*), is in a position of ascendancy or predominance over the other, who may be called "the servient party," such that the former is placed under a duty of complete candour and good faith towards the latter, as regards disclosure and otherwise, in respect of any transaction which he may be minded to enter into with him while the relation, and the influence springing therefrom, continues   These relations may exist by nature, independently of human will, such as the parental or quasi-parental relationship, or may be constituted by the voluntary action of the parties, such as the professional relations of solicitor and client, spiritual director and penitent, or medical man and patient, or may be created by circumstances and conduct generally.   All these forms of relation will be classified and examined *seriatim*, and in detail, presently (*w*)   It is sufficient to note here that their common feature, or *differentia*, is clearly distinguishable from that of the class of relations considered in the last Chapter (*x*).   Subjection to the dominating influence of another is not the same thing as confidence in that other · indeed, the two states of mind may be mutually destructive, though it may frequently happen that, on the other hand, they co-exist in the same person, and engender one another.   An agent or trustee, for instance, exerts, as such, no influence.   On the other hand, a person in mental servitude places no trust in his owner or oppressor   Antonio reposes no confidence in Shylock, or the captive in his gaoler, if he does, it is only that spurious sort of confidence which is artificially induced by

---

(*v*) On the analogy of the expressions "dominant tenement," and "servient tene ment," in the law of easements   The terms "party complaining," and "party charged," which have been used hitherto (see § 7, *ante*), will be abandoned for the purpose of this Chapter, except where referring to the class of case in which the party sought to be made liable is not himself the party exerting the influence, but is utilizing and trading on it, and where it therefore becomes necessary to make a distinction between the former, who is the party charged, and the latter, who is the "dominant party"

(*w*) See Sect 2, *post*

(*x*) See *Torrance* v *Bolton* (1872), 8 Ch. App 118 (*per* JAMES, L J , who, at pp 124, 125, mentions, as two separate classes, "contracts obtained by persons from others over whom they have dominion," and "contracts obtained by persons in a fiduciary position" Cp § 314, *ante*, and note (*t*) thereto, where also the distinction is emphasized.

the hypnotism of the influence, and not that which, as in the case of a *cestui que trust* or principal, is voluntarily bestowed. The two types of relation are, it is true, often loosely classed together as "fiduciary relations"; but, except in the sense that fiduciary duties are incidental to each class, the expression is not strictly accurate, for in the one case it is the abuse of confidence which the law forbids, in the other, the abuse of influence. From this point of view, it is only the former kind of relation which is properly termed "fiduciary" The essential difference between "confidence" and "influence" is forcibly illustrated by the fact that gifts which are regarded with "almost invincible jealousy" when the result of influence, are quite unobjectionable as between parties related to one another merely by a tie of confidence, whilst, on the other hand, a present from a third person which, when made to an agent, for instance, is the subject of relief, when made to a dominant party is quite free from objection Nor is the distinction a purely academical one; for, though the same general considerations of public policy (y) which move the Courts to throw their protection round those who confide, whether they are influenced or not, move them also to protect those who are in subjection and servitude of will, whether they confide or not,—in the one case providing that the party shall not be cheated of his legitimate expectations, in the other, that he shall not be coerced or cajoled,—the duty cast upon a "dominant party" is, as will be seen (z), in some respects of a different nature to, and of a larger scope and measure than, that which is cast upon a trustee, promoter, agent, or other person in whom only confidence is reposed

SECT 1 GENERAL PRINCIPLES AND THEORY

405. The general proposition and cardinal rule as to the rights of the servient party on the one hand, and the duties of the dominant party on the other, is as follows Where a relation of the character indicated subsists between two persons, and, during its subsistence, a transaction of any kind takes place between them, the law presumes in favour of the servient party, against the dominant party, (1) that the relation placed the dominant party in a position to exercise influence and dominion over the servient party, (2) that such influence and dominion operated upon, and procured, the transaction, and (3), that the influence was an improper and unfair, or (to use the accepted phrase) an "undue influence" (a) Accordingly any such transaction,

(y) Cp § 407, *post*, with Ch IV, Sect 1, *ante*
(z) For instance, in the case of transactions other than gifts, it must be shown, as a separate and independent *probandum*, that full value was given, if the transaction is to be maintained see § 475, *post* In the case of relations of "confidence," this is at least doubtful: see § 323, note (p), *ante* Again, in the case of gifts at any rate, when the relation is one of influence, the independent advice of a third person must be shown, in addition to and apart from all other matters, by the dominant party—see § 478, *post* · but, in the case of "confidence" relations, this does not appear to be essential, if in all other respects the transaction was proper and conscientious see § 324, note (r), *ante* Lastly, the question of the receipt of bribes from a third party, which plays such an important part in the law relating to "confidential" relations, has no place at all in the case of any relation in which influence alone is concerned
(a) *Per* Lord LANGDALE, M R , at pp 558–560 of *Archer v Hudson* (1844), 7 Beav 551,

whether it be a contract for valuable consideration (b), or a gift (c), will be undone, or otherwise relieved against, unless the dominant party is able to show affirmatively—and the onus is on him to do so—either that, by reason of the termination or suspension of the relation itself, or otherwise, the influence *in fact* had no effect upon the transaction,—proof of which, if satisfactory, rebuts the first two of the above presumptions (d),—or that the influence was not "undue", in other words, that it was not abused, but conscientiously used, and that the transaction resulting from such use was in every respect fair, just, righteous, and reasonable (c),—proof of which will rebut the last of the above presumptions. It will thus be seen that none of the presumptions in question are irrebuttable, and that the view which appears to have been in early times frequently contended for, if not judicially countenanced, that even transactions for value between the related parties are absolutely prohibited by the law is a complete mistake (f). A more widely prevalent and persistent, and a much more excusable, heresy—but a heresy nevertheless—is the doctrine or suggestion that no gift made by the servient to the dominant party can ever stand under any circumstances. This is not so. the Courts have never held in modern times that it is absolutely impossible to sustain such a gift, indeed, the most they have ever said at any time is that, particularly in the case of attorney and client, it is "*almost impossible*" to do so, and that any such transaction will be scrutinized "with a jealousy that is *almost* invincible" (g)   Gifts and contracts are now, how-

and *per* Lord LYNDHURST, L C, at pp 211-213 of the report of this case when affirmed (1846), 15 L J (CH) 211   See also *Liles* v *Terry*, [1895] 2 Q B 679, C A. (*per* Lord ESHER, M R., at p. 683, LOPES, L J, at p. 684, and KAY, L.J, at pp 685, 686), *Powell* v *Powell*, [1900] 1 Ch 243 (*per* FARWELL, J, at p 245), *Wright* v *Carter*, [1903] 1 Ch 27, C A. (*per* VAUGHAN WILLIAMS, L J, at p 50, and STIRLING, L J, at p 57)   For applications of the rule to the various types of relation, see, generally, the cases cited in the notes to Sects 3 and 4, *post*

(b) Such as a purchase, sale, lease, mortgage, or any other transaction which a con veyancer would include under the term "purchase", a loan, security, &c, &c   See, generally, the cases cited in the notes to Sect 2, *post*.

(c) These include, besides donations or settlements of money, land, chattels, securities, and the like, all transactions which, as between the servient and the dominant party, are without valuable consideration, though not so as between either of such parties and the creditor of the dominant party, such as, for instance, a guarantee of the dominant party's debt, given by the servient party to such creditor, whether by express instrument of suretyship, or by becoming joint acceptor or maker of a negotiable instrument, or by joining as a party in any other contract between the dominant party and a third person   Several examples of this latter class of case are to be found in the notes to Sect 2, *post*

(d) See Sect. 4, Sub-s (1), *post*

(e) See Sect. 4, Sub-s (2), *post*

(f) In *Cane* v *Lord Allen* (1814), 2 Dow. H L 289, it appeared not improbable that the Court below had granted relief on the sole ground that a purchase by an attorney from his client was in any circumstances unsustainable   The House of Lords, however, in reversing the decree, held that there is "no such doctrine in our law" (*per* Lord ELDON, L C, at p. 294, and again at p. 299, and Lord REDESDALE, at p. 296)   See also *Tomson* v. *Judge* (1855), 3 Drew 306 (*per* KINDERSLEY, V C., at p 313: "a solicitor can purchase his client's property even w hile the relation subsists, but the onus lies on the solicitor to show that the transaction was perfectly fair"); *Allison* v *Clayhills* (1907), 97 L. T. 109 (*per* PARKER, J., at p 711: "a solicitor is not wholly incapacitated from purchasing or taking a lease from his client, but the onus is on him of upholding the transaction")

(g) In *Welles* v *Middleton* (1784), 1 Cox 112, it was undoubtedly said by Lord THURLOW, L.C., at p 125, that a gift from client to attorney cannot stand, though "once ever, in the best and most carefully considered of the various judicial exposi-tions of the doctrine, classed together as alike subject to the general and fundamental rule that the *primâ facie* presumption of impropriety may be repelled by affirmative evidence of propriety in fact (*h*), though the means by which the propriety of the transaction is to be established are not quite the same when the transaction was without, as when it was for, valuable consideration (*i*)

406. When the dominant party is called upon " to sustain the transac-tion," which is always the case unless he can show that the presumed influence was in fact non-existent or inoperative at the material date, he must, in order to do so, establish by evidence, in the case of both gifts and contracts, that, before the transaction took place, he (1) made full disclosure to the servient party of all material facts relating to the subject-matter of the transaction, its legal and business character and complexion, and the servient party's rights in respect of it, including his right to refuse to enter into it, and his right, having entered into it, to revoke or avoid it ; and (2) gave the servient party as honest and disinterested action against himself as he would have given him against a stranger, and placed at his disposal for that purpose the whole of his natural or acquired skill, judgment, and discretion   In the case of gifts, probably, but not in the case of contracts, he must further prove that the servient party, before making the gift, had the honest and competent advice of a third person, entirely independent of himself   In the case of contracts, but not of course in that of gifts, he must also show that he gave full and fair value for that which was conveyed or transferred to him under the contract   Under these conditions alone can the dominant

extricate him, and it may be otherwise."   To the same effect Lord ERSKINE, L C , at p 137 of *Wright* v. *Proud* (1806), 13 Ves 136 , Lord ELDON, L C , at pp 312, 313 of *Montesquieu* v. *Sandys* (1811), 18 Ves 301, distinguishing for this purpose a gift from a purchase , KINDERSLEY, V C , at pp 313–317 of *Tomson* v *Judge*, *sup* , BACON, V C , at p 645 of *Morgan* v *Minett* (1877), 6 C D 638, though, after stating the rule as without qualifica-tion, he proceeds to mention two himself.   On the other hand, with respect to gifts in the case of other relations of " influence," Lord ELDON, L C , at pp 297, 298 of *Hatch* v *Hatch* (1804), 9 Ves 292, limits himself to the statement that is " *almost* impossible " that a gift can stand, and that such a case is watched by the Court with " a jealousy which is *almost* invincible ", whilst, with reference to gifts in general, Lord BROUGHAM, L.C , at p 138 of *Hunter* v *Atkins* (1834), 3 My & K 113, remarks that " the cases supposed to decide that a gift can never stand, do not really decide this, but only that such cases should be approached with great suspicion ", and, even with reference to a gift from client to attorney, STUART, V -C , at p 345 of *Re Holmes's Estate, Bevan's Case* (1861), 3 Giff 337, said that it is " almost impossible that the gift can prevail   The principle of influence vitiates the gift , but the presumption of influence may be rebutted by circumstances short of the total dissolution of the relation of solicitor and client "   See also *Wright* v *Carter*, [1903] 1 Ch 27, C A (at pp 49–53, 56–58, and 61)

(*h*) Thus, in *Grosvenor* v *Sherratt* (1860), 28 Beav 659, ROMILLY, M R , at p 665, expresses the view that both alike, without making the slightest distinction between them, are " almost impossible " to sustain " in these cases," he says, " the persons who take the grant, *whether it be by a gift or a sale*, or a lease of the property, put themselves in a position which, in a Court of Equity, makes it almost impossible for them to succeed   They must show "   &c)   So, after mentioning various relations of " influence," Lord PENZANCE, at p 1230 of *Erlanger* v. *New Sombrero Phosphate Co.* (1878), 3 App Cas 1218, H L observes that they " all furnish instances in which the Courts of Equity have given pro tection and relief against the pressure of unfair advantage resulting from the relation and mutual position of the parties, *whether in matters of contract or gift* "

(*i*) See § 406, *inf*.

party accept a gift from, or enter into a contract with, the servient party: or rather, since the transaction is neither illegal nor void in itself, it is more correct to say that he can only have any dealings with the servient party at the risk of their being afterwards, if challenged, invalidated, unless he is then in a position to prove a strict compliance with these conditions, which (from lapse of time and consequent loss of evidence) he may find himself unable to do, though in fact he did comply with them It is a question, therefore, not of what he did at the time, but what, after perhaps a long interval, he can satisfy the Court by evidence that he then did,—which is a very different thing   Accordingly the proper occasion for a detailed discussion of the obligations of the dominant party is when the question of the affirmative answers available to him against a *primâ facie* case of breach of duty comes to be examined (*j*)

407. The theory upon which these rules are founded, and by which they are justified, is much the same as in the case of relations of " confidence " (*k*), that is to say, " public policy " in its proper sense of public utility, convenience, and security (*l*)   It may be—indeed, it has been, and by no less an authority than Lord ESHER (*m*)—objected that the code of presumptions and principles applied to relations of " influence " is an artificial and arbitrary code, inimical to freedom of individual action, and not called for or necessitated by the imperative requirements of the common weal   The objectors freely admit that the principle of public policy justifies the framing of strict rules in the case of any relation of " trust," and that there is no injustice in calling upon a trustee, promoter, or agent, to account—in the intellectual, and, if he cannot, in the fiscal, sense—for a bribe which he is discovered to have taken, or in presuming its impropriety until the contrary is shown, any more than there is in calling upon one whose hand is in another's pocket, or who is found on another's premises at dead of night, for an explanation of conduct which is at least *primâ facie* dubious   But they insist that, whereas the receipt of personal profit by a trustee, promoter, or agent is *ipso facto* wrongful, until shown to be rightful, no such presumption ought to be made against acts which result merely from " influences," all of which are, in themselves, negatively innocent, and even, as in the case of parental or spiritual influence, positively praiseworthy (*mm*)   To presume that an influence which in its nature is " due " must have been " undue," unless

(*j*) This is the subject of Sect. 4, Sub-s (2), *post*
(*k*) See § 317, *ante*
(*l*) As defined by Lord HARDWICKE, L C , at p 156 of *Chesterfield (Earl of) v Jannsen* (1751), 2 Ves Sr 125 , 1 Atk 301   The passage is cited in note (*y*) to § 646, *post*
(*m*) At pp 683, 684 of *Liles v Terry*, [1895] 2 Q B 679, C A   But, in the same case, at pp 684, 685, 687, both his colleagues expressed dissent from Lord ESHER's adverse criticism, and so did LINDLEY, M R , at pp 131, 132 of *Barron v. Willis*, [1900] 2 Ch 121, C A
(*mm*) Thus Lord THURLOW, L C , at p 125 of *Welles v Middleton* (1784), 1 Cox 112, describes parental influence as " the true, honest, and just influence, as it is in itself," and at pp. 299, 300, at *Hoghton v Hoghton* (1852), 15 Beav 278, ROMILLY, M R , speaking of influence relations generally, says   " not that the influence itself, flowing from such relations, is either blamed or discountenanced by the Court , on the contrary, the due exercise of it is considered useful and advantageous to society "

and until the contrary be shown, is, in the view of these critics, a flat contravention of the fundamental principle of our jurisprudence that every man shall be deemed innocent of wrongdoing until his guilt be proved : *usum non tollit abusus*, and accordingly every abuse of anything that admits of being properly used should be established as a fact, and not inferred as a proposition of law   To these objections—by no means unworthy of consideration—the answer given by the great masters of equity, and given so frequently and consistently for two centuries back, that, whether sound or not, it is now too late in the day to disturb it, is that the presumptions and rules in question, however unfair they may appear, if regarded without reference to the interests of the community at large, have been found to be absolutely required by that *suprema lex*, the *salus reipublicæ*   Admitting that nothing less than " public utility " and the preservation and " safety of society " can justify them, it has been held, over and over again, that this indispensable condition of their validity, as shown by all past experience, undoubtedly exists (*n*). The Court of Chancery, from the earliest times, has professed to be " the guardian and protector of the weak and helpless of every denomination " (*o*), and it has found that this guardianship and protection must be wholly inefficacious unless supported by, and armed with, a set of presumptions and principles which shall be entirely independent of any consideration of personal

(*n*) *Hylton* v *Hylton* (1754), 2 Ves Sr 547 (*per* Lord HARDWICKE, L C, at p 549 " all depends upon public utility ; and therefore the Court will not suffer it, though perhaps in a particular instance there may not be an actual unfairness "), *Norton* v. *Relly* (1764), 2 Eden 286 (*per* Lord NORTHINGTON, L C, at p 291   " public concernment and utility "), *Welles* v *Middleton* (1784), 1 Cox 112 (*per* Lord THURLOW, L C, at p 125 · " general principles of policy "), *Hatch* v *Hatch* (1804), 9 Ves 292 (*per* Lord ELDON, L C, at pp 297, 298   " public policy "), *Huguenin* v *Baseley* (1807), 14 Ves 273 (*per* Lord ELDON, L C, at p 300   " principle of public utility "), *Griffiths* v. *Robins* (1818), 3 Madd 191 (*per* LEACH, V -C, at p 192   " the policy of this Court "), *Archer* v *Hudson* (1846), 15 L. J (CH) 211 (*per* Lord LYNDHURST, L C, at p 211   " the principle of general policy "), *Nottidge* v *Prince* (1860), 2 Giff 246 (*per* STUART, V -C, at p 270 · " public utility which requires this Court to guard against such influences "), *O'Brien* v. *Lewis* (1863), 32 L J (CH) 569 (*per* Lord WESTBURY, L C., at p 573   " I am not going to return him "—the client who had made his attorney a present—" this £300 on account of his own merits, but because I must uphold the general rule, founded upon considerations of public policy "), *Brown* v *Kennedy* (1864), 4 De G. J & S 217 (*per* KNIGHT-BRUCE, L J., at p 222—" public policy,"—and TURNER, L J , at p 223—" the best interests of society "), *Baker* v. *Monk* (1864), 4 De G J & S 388 (*per* KNIGHT BRUCE, L J , at p 389   " the general good of society,"— " society is as much interested as are individuals "), *Morgan* v *Minett* (1877), 6 C D. 638 (*per* BACON, V -C, at p 645   " required for the safety of society "), *Allcard* v. *Skinner* (1887), 36 C D 145, C A (*per* BOWEN, L J , at p 190 " public policy and fair play "), *Liles* v *Terry*, [1895] 2 Q B 679, C A (*per* LOPES, L J , at p 684   " founded on public policy,"—a " highly beneficial " rule   So KAY, L J , at p 685   " a rule of public policy of great importance," which for that reason, he adds at p 687, " commands my strongest respect and approval "   As to Lord Esher's repugnance to this view of " public policy," see note (*m*), *sup*)

(*o*) The phrase used by Lord NORTHINGTON, L.C , at p 288 of *Norton* v *Relly*, *sup* , in which case, however, he permits himself certain extravagances in expression which are not so acceptable, such as—" this Court can extend its hands of protection   it has a conscience to relieve, and the constitution itself would be in danger, if it did not " (p 288) The same somewhat pontifical ground is taken by Lord THURLOW, L C., when, at p 125 of *Welles* v. *Middleton*, *sup* , he speaks of " the preservation of mankind," and by Lord ERSKINE, L C , when, at p 51 of *Ormond* (*Lady*) v *Hutchinson* (1806), 13 Ves 47, he claims for the Court of Chancery ' a guardianship over mankind "   Not even the Pope, or an Œcumenical Council, pretends to quite so extensive a jurisdiction and authority as this

merits or motives in the individual case (p)   If the rules are to be of any value, the Court must be relieved of the necessity of searching particular consciences ; and must not be impeded by difficulties which would otherwise arise in tracing the property to, and getting it out of the hands of, the dominant party (q)   The whole doctrine is based upon a recognition, and a necessary distrust, of the infirmities of human nature (r).   It is a question of tendency and temptation, rather than of individual good or bad faith in the particular instance   *usum non tollit abusus*, however true a saying, is one that the law cannot afford to adopt or countenance : it must prohibit the *usus* except under prescribed conditions, for fear of the possible, or, rather, inevitable *abusus* which will result if it does not   It is forced, in the interests of the community, to presume as against every person standing to another in a relation of " influence," however unjustifiable and contrary to the fact the presumption may be in any individual case, the existence of those elements and possibilities in his character which Lady Macbeth foresaw in that of her lord .

> " What thou wouldst highly
> That wouldst thou holily . wouldst not play false,
> And yet wouldst wrongly win " (s)

Such a person cannot be allowed to call for proof that he has " played false," or " wrongly won."   The burden must be placed on his shoulders to establish that in fact he did act " holily," did not " play false," and did " rightly win."   It is true that *omnia præsumuntur rite esse acta :* but it is no less true that *omnia præsumuntur contra spoliatorem*, and in cases of " influence " the general good requires the further presumption that the dominant party, being a potential *spoliator*, is actually so, until it be proved otherwise   And, say the apologists for this system of presumptions, this is not an extravagant burden to impose on a dominant party.   In the first place, there is no compulsion on him to enter into any transaction at all with the servient party during

(p) See the passages cited in note (n), *sup*, from *Hylton* v *Hylton, sup* , *O'Brien* v. *Lewis, sup*   In *Welles* v *Middleton, sup* , where, at p 119, Lord THURLOW, L C , after observing that " this case was opened as a transaction of fraud," but that none had been proved, and that, in his belief, " they "—the defendants—" stand very fair in the world," proceeds to point out the utter irrelevance of these considerations   At pp 646, 647 of *Morgan* v *Minett* (1877), 6 C D 638, BACON, V C , observes that " these Courts have not those golden scales which are said to be used in the mythological heaven to regulate the destinies of mankind," and therefore will not attempt the delicate task of appraising the merits or demerits of the individuals concerned, but will lay down, and act upon, a general prohibitive rule   The possibility of abuse of the influence is enough to justify such a rule " Cp the cases cited in the notes to §§ 461 and 486, *post*
(q) *Hatch* v *Hatch* (1804), 9 Ves 292 (*per* Lord ELDON, L C , at pp 297, 298)
(r) *Morgan* v *Minett, sup* (*per* BACON, V -C , at p 647   " suspicion is the basis of that rule of influence "), *Barron* v *Willis*, [1900] 2 Ch 181, C. A (*per* LINDLEY, M R , at p 132 " I think the rule is based upon a knowledge of human nature ")   Cp the like opinion of Lord HERSCHELL, in reference to " confidence " relations, at p. 51 of *Bray* v *Ford*, [1896] A C 44, H. L , " it does not appear to me that this rule is, as has been said, founded upon principles of morality   I regard it rather as based upon the consideration that, human nature being what it is, there is danger, in such circumstances, that "   . &c , &c
(s) *Macbeth*, Act 1, Sc. 5, ll 21–23

the existence of the relation : in the next place, any such transaction is not illegal or void (t), any more than a wager is, and no Court can undo it, or prohibit it, or punish for it, except on the initiative of the servient party, if he is so minded, which in the vast majority of cases he is not and, lastly, even where it is impeached, the presumptions made against its validity are not irrebuttable, and it is not demanding too much of a party who need never have entered into the transaction at all to require that, if challenged, he shall establish its propriety, and must understand that, in entering into it, as he may, he can only do so at the risk of its being set aside if the servient party should afterwards seek to be relieved of it, which he may never do, and if in such event he (the dominant party) is not in a position, as, however, he may be, to sustain it by the proper evidence. From this point of view, as has been justly observed (u), the doctrine, so far from infringing freedom of alienation of property, "secures the full and ample and uninfluenced enjoyment of it "

SECT. 2. THE CLASSES OF RELATION FROM WHICH INFLUENCE IS PRESUMED

408. The relations which give rise to the presumption of undue influence are, —in the first place, the domestic relation of parentage, or quasi-parentage (v), secondly, what may be called the professional relations, such as those which exist between solicitor and client, between spiritual director and penitent or disciple, and between medical adviser and patient (w),—all the above being often classed together as the " recognized," or the " known " (x), or the " suspected " (y), relations ,—thirdly, such relations as, not being within either of the two above-mentioned classes, are constituted by the circumstances of the particular case (z), including the relation, to which somewhat special rules are applicable, between purchasers or lenders and expectant heirs or reversioners (a) All these it is proposed to examine seriatim and in detail . but, in the meantime, it is necessary to make the general prefatory observation that, just as in the case of fiduciary relations, in reference to which a similar warning has been given (b), it is not a question of names,

(t) See § 488, note (d), post
(u) By Sir S Romilly in his reply at p 287 of *Haguenin* v *Baseley* (1807), 14 Ves 273, as to the recognized quasi-judicial authority of which, see note (c) to § 408, inf The argument against the policy of restricting freedom of purchase has been urged with greater plausibility, and with not a little judicial countenance, in the case of dealings with "expectants " in reversions see § 435, note (l), post
(v) See Sub s (1), post
(w) These relations are dealt with in Sub ss (2), (3) and (4), post, respectively
(x) The expression of Lord BROUGHAM, L C , at p 135 of *Hunter* v *Atkins* (1834), 3 My & K 113
(y) So termed in the felicitous language of Sir Frederick Pollock, at p 601 of his treatise on *The Principles of Contract* (7th ed) See also, as justifying the expression, the observation of BACON, V -C , cited in note (r), sup , that ' suspicion is the basis " of the rule
(z) See Sub-s (5), post
(a) See Sub s (6), post.
(b) § 343, ante.

but of things ; for, as was said by Sir Samuel Romilly, " the relief stands upon a general principle applying to all the varieties of relations in which dominion may be exercised by one person over another " (c). It is enough that any such " variety " which may hereafter come before the Courts, though its name and title be unknown to the reports, should be within the principle of the rule, to justify its immediate admission to the circle of " suspected relations " The only question is whether it is proper, in the interests of the community, to presume the " influence ", as, in cases of " confidence," the only question is whether the relation necessarily involves the " confidence." Many cases may be imagined of influences which, though not yet " suspect," may at any moment become so : for instance, the influence of a teacher or instructor (d) , of a master in literature, science,

(c) In his reply in *Huguenin* v *Baseley* (1807), 14 Ves 273, at pp 285, 286 The passage in the text is cited, not as argument, but as authority, because it has been textually adopted as such in more than one subsequent judgment Indeed, the whole of this reply is, as Sir Frederick Pollock justly observes (p vi of his Preface to 9 R R.), " perhaps the only modern case in which a reported argument has acquired by later judicial approval an authority equal to that of the judgment itself,"—which, considering that the judgment was that of Lord ELDON, is a somewhat startling result On reading the cold printed page, it is difficult to see why this chorus of laudation should have followed the argument, or in what respects it surpassed, or even equalled, the judgment, or, indeed, why Sir Samuel Romilly's reply should be so favourably distinguished from his opening, as to which the chroniclers have observed a conspiracy of silence One can only suppose that the effect produced by the effort was largely rhetorical, and depended upon a personal ascendancy and authority which has evaporated in the record, and can no more be reproduced in a report, than the art of Betterton, Garrick, or Kean can be made to live again in memoirs and critiques Of the reality, however, of the impression made at the time, and for many years afterwards, there can be no possible doubt Twenty-seven years later, Lord BROUGHAM, L C , at pp 139, 140 of *Hunter* v *Atkins* (1834), 3 My & K. 113, refers to " the famous case of *Huguenin* v *Baseley*, remarkable, amongst other things, for the display of those transcendent talents, and that pure taste, by which among many other accomplishments, Sir Samuel Romilly elevated and adorned the bar " , and, five years later still, Lord COTTENHAM, L C , who had heard the argument delivered, when citing the passage which appears in the text, speaks of " Sir Samuel Romilly s celebrated reply in *Huguenin* v *Baseley*, from hearing which I received so much pleasure that the recollection of it has not been diminished by the lapse of more than 30 years " *Dent* v *Bennett* (1839), 4 My & Cr 269, at p 277 After this date, its merits of necessity became matter of tradition only But the tradition was faithfully preserved, and the argument has been cited again and again, and always with the same laudatory description as " the celebrated argument," or " the celebrated reply," by a long line of judges from STUART, V C , in *Nottidge* v *Prince* (1860), 2 Giff 246 (at p. 263), to BYRNE, J , in *Cavendish* v. *Strutt* (1903), 19 T L R 483 (at p 489) The only judicial reference to the case which is free from these somewhat uncritical raptures, and exhibits a saner and more measured appreciation of the respective merits and authority of the argument on the one hand, and the judgment on the other, is to be found in *Middleton* v *Sherburne* (1841), 4 Y. & C. (Exch in Eq) 358, where Lord ABINGER, C B , seems not to have been greatly impressed by the laudatory allusion during the argument (p 367) in the consecrated formula to " the celebrated reply," and, at p 391, points out, with merciless exactitude, that Lord ELDON's judgment (which he, at least, it would appear, regarded as the only *authority*) carefully avoided the adoption of the " spiritual influence " contention on which the greater part of the reply was founded, and which earned for it its celebrity, and proceeded upon other grounds, viz the existence of a relation created by the actual " circumstances and conditions," as described in Sub s (5), *post*. It is, however, the undoubted fact that certain passages from " the celebrated reply " have been judicially adopted *in ipsissimis verbis* as representing the law. These passages, therefore, and these only, will be cited in this Chapter as authorities

(d) Pothier, in his *Traité des Donations entre Vifs*, Sect 2, Art 11 (vol. vii, p 441 of his *Œuvres*, ed Dupin, 1825), mentions the case of the master of a school

theology, or any of the arts (e) ; or of a political leader (f) Any of these, in the course of time, may be proved capable of perverting to the baser uses of material and personal advantage that ascendancy which is justly due to him in the sphere of intellect only. If and when the occasion arises, the Courts will be no more debarred from adding a relation to the list of those marked " dangerous," merely because no opportunity of doing so may have previously presented itself, than, in 1764, Lord NORTHINGTON, L C., hesitated to proclaim as *ipso facto* suspect the theretofore unassailed relation of spiritual director and disciple, or than, in 1839, Lord COTTENHAM, L C., hesitated to adopt the like course in the case of the previously unsuspected relation of medical attendant and patient. It is, indeed, for the very reason that this possibility exists of relations coming up for judicial investigation which, though new in name, will of necessity involve and invite the application of principles which are old, and because of the vital importance of any such future investigation being wholly unfettered, that the law of this country has steadily refused to draw up—for the sole benefit (as it would be) of persons minded hereafter to abuse the influence springing from any unspecified " variety "—a list or catalogue of proscribed relations (g) For a like reason, the law makes no distinction between the degrees and limits of influence to which the several types of relation give rise (h) From the point of view of psychology, or ethics, or sociology, such distinctions are, no doubt, of interest , and certain judgments have enlarged upon the special features in some particular variety of influence—at one time, the parent's, at another the solicitor's, at another the priest s, at another, that of the dealer in " expectancies "—which, in the opinion of the particular judge, constitute

(e) From the letters of Charlotte Bronte which have lately been deposited in the British Museum, it appears that an almost unbounded dominion over her intellect and heart was possessed by Professor Heger,—a dominion which he never used for any bad purpose, or, indeed, for any purpose at all But it is not difficult to imagine the case of a great teacher similarly situated exercising an influence so acquired over an adoring pupil for the purpose of extracting from her, or him, benefits of a more material kind than the incense of mere intellectual idolatry A modern Abelard might conceivably exert pressure upon a modern Heloise in financial directions

(f) Here, again, one can see the possibility of abuse Suppose that Fox, instead of his gambling debts having been voluntarily paid by his political friends, had deliberately used his political influence with the party of which he was the leader to induce them to come to his relief, it might be that the Courts, if appealed to, would have considered political leadership as one of the relations which ought to be " recognized," and from which influence ought to be presumed

(g) See *Dent* v *Bennett* (1839), 4 My & Cr 269 (per Lord COTTENHAM, L C , at pp 276, 277 " I will not narrow the rule, or run the risk of in any degree fettering the exercise of the beneficial jurisdiction of this Court, by any enumeration of the description of persons against whom it ought to be most freely exercised ") , *Smith* v *Kay* (1859), 7 H L C 750 (per Lord CRANWORTH, L C , at p 770 " the familiar cases of the influence of a parent over his child, of a guardian over his ward, of an attorney over his client, are but instances The principle is not confined to those cases ") , *Tate* v. *Williamson* (1866), L R 1 Eq 528 (per WOOD, V C , at pp 536, 537).

(h) " The degree of influence need not be inquired into. The fact of the influence is enough if it be established," says BACON, V. C , at p 646 of *Morgan* v *Minett* (1877), 6 C D 638 , though, as STUART, V -C , says, at p. 270 of *Nottidge* v *Prince* (1860), 2 Giff. 246, it is true that " *the same ground of public utility* which requires the Court to guard against such influences, *has its most important application* to that influence which is the strongest."

its characteristic strength and danger, and render it peculiarly the subject of vigilance (*hh*)   Further, such considerations are by no means irrelevant to any contention which may be raised by a dominant party that, in the particular case, the influence was not operative on the transaction, or was not in fact unduly exercised   But, for the purpose of the three *primâ facie* presumptions above-mentioned, viz that the relation gave rise to the influence, that the influence was operative upon the transaction, and that it was unduly exercised, the law does not discriminate in any way—indeed to do so would be highly dangerous, and would destroy all the utility of the presumptions— between the nature and force of the influence arising from one class of relation, and the nature and force of that which arises from any other

Sub-s (1)   *The Relation between Parent and Child, and Analogous Relations.*

409. The domestic relation which exists between parent and child is the relation which most obviously invites a presumption of influence, since, long before jurisprudence had anything to say in the matter, human nature itself had already created it   It is true that human nature also encourages the presumption that the influence is likely to be exercised for the common good of both child and parent , and this latter presumption has had its effect upon the jurisprudence of the subject , but, subject to the affirmative defence of " family arrangement " which will be considered presently, the relation in question gives rise to the three presumptions in favour of the servient party which have already been mentioned (*i*), and casts upon the dominant party the onus of sustaining, if and when impeached, any transaction which was entered into during the existence of the relationship, or of the influence arising from it, by such proof as is requisite for that purpose (*j*) , that is to say. proof that in fact the influence was not operative upon the transaction impeached, or that in fact it was not abused, either because it was proper under the circumstances (as in the case of a family arrangement), or because it was righteously and conscientiously exercised, in that the dominant party made full disclosure to the servient party, or that the servient party was otherwise fully cognizant, of the exact nature and effect of the transaction, and of his rights and interests in respect thereof, including his right to reject or avoid it, and of all material facts as to its subject-matter, and in that the servient party, in the case of a gift, had the competent and honest advice of an independent third person, and, in the case of any other transaction, received full value   Or the dominant party, notwithstanding his inability to sustain the transaction in all or any of the above respects, may excuse himself by proof that the servient party, with full knowledge of all material facts, and of his right to avoid the transaction, and when entirely emancipated from the influence attending the relation, deliberately elected

(*hh*) See §§ 409, 415, 421, 425, 435, *post,* as to the special characteristics of the influence arising from the various relations respectively
(*i*) See § 405, *ante.*
(*j*) Stated summarily in § 405, *ante,* and examined in detail in Sect 4, *post*

to confirm it. A long series of decisions has firmly established the above principles in the case of parent and child (k) , it being understood, of course, that "child," for the purposes of the doctrine in question, does not mean an infant in the legal sense (for infancy is protected under other heads of jurisprudence, both statutory and non-statutory), nor, on the other hand, a son or daughter of mature age and no longer under the roof or protection or guardianship of the parent, but one who is just emerging from infancy at the time when the influence is brought to bear upon him (l), or who, though past his majority, is still living with, and entirely dependent upon the parent for protection and means of livelihood (m) , for the governing principle of the established rules exists in the one case as much as in the other And it is with strict regard to this governing principle that the law has refused to limit the application of the doctrine to the simple case of parent and child, but has extended it to all cases of what may be described as " domestic " (to distinguish it from " professional ") relationship where the dominant party, though not the parent of, is in loco parentis to, the servient party, and the conditions are such as to indicate subjection, dependence, and pupilage (in a popular sense) on the one side, and dominion, supremacy, or tutelage (again in a popular sense) on the other (n)   Where the same mischief exists, the same relief against it will always be available to the servient party.

(k) Wycherley v Wycherley (1763), 2 Eden 175 (son joins his father in a settlement which, however, was held to constitute a family arrangement   see note (p), to § 410, post) , Bellamy v. Sabine (1847), 2 Ph 425 (disentailing deed) , Thornber v Sheard (1850), 12 Beav. 589 (release and conveyance of property by daughter to pay father's debts), Hoghton v Hoghton (1852), 15 Beav 278 (son bars entail) , Baker v Bradley (1855), 7 De G M & G. 597 (mortgage by son as security for father) , Dimsdale v Dimsdale (1856), 3 Drew 556 (resettlement of estates, but held to amount to " family arrangement "— see note (p) to § 410, post—as to part, and as to the residue, confirmation and other answers established) , Savery v King (1856), 5 H L C 627 (mortgage and other transactions by son to pay off father's debt to solicitor) , Hartopp v Hartopp (1856), 25 L J (CH) 471 (resettlement of estates held, however, to be a " family arrangement " see note (p) to § 410, post) , Wright v Vanderplank (1856), 8 De G M & G 133 (deed of gift of life estate by daughter to father   but the father proved confirmation here) , Jenner v Jenner (1860), 2 De G F & J 359 (resettlement of family estates   held, however, to be a " family arrangement "—see note (p) to § 410, post—besides which, the father proved full knowledge by son of all material facts) , Berdoe v Dawson (1865), 34 Beav 603 (son gives securities for father's debts) , Potts v. Surr (1865), 34 Beav 543 (settlement of estates   held, however, a " family arrangement "—see note (p) to § 410, post—and proved also that the son had independent advice) , Turner v Collins (1871), 7 Ch App 329 (gifts of reversionary interest and power of appointment) , Bainbrigge v Browne (1881), 18 C D 188 (daughter gives charges to a creditor to secure payment of father's debts) , Hoblyn v. Hoblyn (1889), 41 C. D 200 (resettlement of family estates   held, however, a ' family arrangement " : see note (p) to § 410, post) , De Witte v Addison (1879), 80 L T 207, C A (a daughter gives mortgage to secure her father's debt) , London & Westminster Loan & Discount Co v. Bilton (1911), 27 T L R 184 (a daughter grants bill of sale to, and charges a legacy in favour of, her father's creditor, to secure his debts)

(l) Powell v Powell, [1900] 1 Ch. 243 (per FARWELL, J , at pp 245, 246)   In nearly all the cases cited in the last note, the servient party was just emerging from infancy, and this fact was emphasized in some of the judgments as a necessary or, at all events, an important feature

(m) London & Westminster Loan & Discount Co v Bilton, sup , per JOYCE, J , who, at p 185, points out that, though the lady had come of age for ten years, she had been living under the parental roof for all that time, without any means of her own

(n) Thus, in the following cases, proof of the following domestic relations, with the other conditions mentioned in the text, was considered sufficient to raise the presumption

410. On the other hand, where the reason for the presumption is not apparent, which happens when the presumption is met by a counter-presumption of equal strength, the doctrine has no application. *Cessante ratione, cessat lex ;* and the *ratio* ceases to have any force, as soon as it is shown by the dominant party—it is for him, probably, to do so—that he dealt with the servient party solely in the character of the head of a family making necessary or desirable provision for the benefit of all its members, or all those materially interested in the family property, and not for his own benefit, except as such member   This kind of dealing is known as " a family arrangement." Obviously, on proof of any such arrangement, not even a *primâ facie* inference ought not to be made of any undue influence. Influence there may have been, but not only is there no presumption that it was improper, but every presumption that it was proper and commendable   To all such transactions it is often said that the Court exhibits " favour " or " leniency," or " indulgence," but these expressions are not very happily chosen   It is not a question of " favour," " leniency," or " indulgence," but of bare right.   In any such case as supposed, it would be an act of monstrous injustice to impute an abuse of influence, and there is no generosity in refraining from doing so   Without, however, examining too nicely questions of mere terminology, it may be stated that the rule is clear that, wherever it is established to the satisfaction of the Court that the impeached transaction was, or formed part of, " a family arrangement," such transaction will be upheld, and the dominant party will be relieved from those duties of full disclosure and otherwise to which, but for the " family arrangement, ' he would have been subject , just as, under the like conditions, in the case of negotiations for releases and compromises discussed in an earlier Chapter,

---

of influence, and to cast the burden of " sustaining the transaction " on the dominant party   *Aylward* v *Kearney* (1814), 2 Ball & B 463 (grandfather obtains lease from grand son, just of age, of whom he had been the guardian during his minority) , *Sercombe* v *Sanders* (1865), 34 Beav 282, was a case of two brothers influencing a third to give a mortgage to their creditor to secure their indebtedness. In *Sharp* v *Leach* (1862), 31 Beav 491, the influence was by brother and sister (sale of reversionary interest, and voluntary settlement). In *Espey* v *Lake* (1852), 10 Hare 260, and *Kempson* v *Ashbee* (1874), 10 Ch App. 15, the influence was that of a stepfather over stepchildren (suretyship and bonds to secure debts of stepfather)   In *Powell* v *Powell*, [1900] 1 Ch. 243, the influence was by stepmother over stepdaughter (voluntary and irrevocable settlement)   In *Hylton* v *Hylton* (1754), 2 Ves Sr 547, *Dawson* v *Massey* (1809), 1 Ball & B 219, *Archer* v *Hudson* (1846), 15 L J (CH) 211, and *Lloyd* v *Attwood* (1859), 3 De G & J 614, the influence was that of an uncle over a nephew or niece under his care and protection (annuity, release, and charges given in the first case, leases in the second, guarantee to bank in the third, and release to trustees of breaches of trust in the fourth)   In *Toker* v *Toker* (1863), 3 De G J. & S 487, the influence was that of a nephew over his aunt (gift of real estate   the nephew, however, in this case, sustained the burden of proof cast upon him by the presumption)   In *Hatch* v *Hatch* (1804), 9 Ves 292, the influence was that of a brother in law and late guardian over a sister in law and late ward, just emerging from infancy (conveyance of advowson)   In *Wright* v *Pound* (1806), 13 Ves 136, the influence was that of a keeper of a private lunatic asylum, and so a guardian or quasi guardian, over an inmate (conveyance by the inmate of the whole of his property)   In India, a " pardanishin " woman is treated as constructively an infant in relation to any person having dealings with her, to the extent of requiring a donee from her to establish substantially the same " propriety " in the transaction as in any case of parental influence . see *Kali Baksh Singh* v. *Ram Gopal Singh* (1913), 30 T L R 138, P C

the party charged will be so relieved (o). The test is this. Was it the sole object and effect of the transaction to make a settlement or redistribution of family estates or interests in such a way as to confer benefits on the family as a whole, and to preserve its common property, peace, or honour ? If so, it will not be invalidated (p). Or, whether so intended or not, did the transaction result in the parent obtaining an exclusive advantage for himself out of the child's concession or bounty, for which no equivalent was given ? If it did, the presumptions against the parent are not in the slightest degree disturbed or shaken, and the transaction will be relieved against, unless the parent can establish some one or more of the only affirmative answers which are available to a dominant party in any ordinary case (q).

(o) See §§ 135, 136, ante.

(p) As in *Wycherley* v. *Wycherley* (1763), 2 Eden 175, where a son upon his marriage joined with his father in settling the estate, and by a memorandum executed at the same time agreed to secure a certain sum to each of his sisters, and this memorandum was held to be unimpeachable (*per* Lord NORTHINGTON, L C, at p. 178 · "the Court will . . attend to slight considerations for confirming family settlements and modifications of property They pay a regard to reasonable motives and honourable intentions In these cases they will not weigh the value of the consideration. They consider the ease and comfort and security of families as a sufficient consideration"), *Bellamy* v. *Sabine* (1847), 2 Ph 425 (*per* PEPYS, M R, at pp 439-441, as to one of the two transactions there impeached), *Dimsdale* v *Dimsdale* (1856), 3 Drew. 556 (where part of the transaction was upheld as a family arrangement, "which sort of arrangement," said KINDERSLEY, V C, at p 569, "whether it be entered into for the purpose of securing the peace of a family, or for preventing litigation, or for preserving the property in the family, the Court will look upon in a different light from ordinary transactions between father and son while the parental influence continues"), *Hartopp* v *Hartopp* (1856), 25 L J (CH) 471 (*per* ROMILLY, M R, at p 479,—a clear and careful statement of the criterion referred to in the text), *Jenner* v *Jenner* (1860), 2 De G F & J 359, *per* Lord CAMPBELL, L C, who on the evidence, which he examined at pp 369-374, found that the father was deriving no exclusive advantage (p 367), and that the transaction was a family arrangement (p 368) of a "laudable," and "natural" character (pp 368, 369), *Potts* v. *Surr* (1865), 34 Beav 543, where, though the father obtained an advantage, he gave valuable consideration for it, and the transaction was for the benefit of the family as a whole (*per* ROMILLY, M R, at pp 552-554), *Hoblyn* v *Hoblyn* (1889), 41 C D 200, where the transaction was, except as to a certain part of it which the father offered to abandon, held to be a family arrangement (*per* KEKEWICH, J, who, at pp 204-206, pointed out that some degree of influence is natural and proper in such a case, rendering independent advice not essential, though—pp 206, 207—when the father obtains a benefit to himself from the arrangement, the jealousy of the Court is easily aroused) And see note (b) to § 135, ante

(q) As in *Hoghton* v *Hoghton* (1852), 15 Beav 278 (*per* ROMILLY, M R, at pp 305, 306 · "if the settlement of the property be one in which the father acquires no benefit not already possessed by him, and if the settlement be a reasonable and proper one, the Court will support it, even though it may appear that some influence was exerted by him to induce the son to execute it . When, however, the son confers on the parent by the transaction some advantages which he did not formerly possess, the principle which prevails in the first class of cases interposes" The "first class of cases" is that discussed by him at pp 299, 300, where the influence is presumed, and there is no ground for the plea of "family arrangement" At pp 307, 308, he points to circumstances which satisfy him that the case before him belongs to this first class, and not to the second), *Baker* v *Bradley* (1855), 7 De G M & G 597 (*per* TURNER, L J, at pp 620, 621 "transactions between parent and child may proceed upon arrangements between them for the settlement of property In such cases, the Court regards the transaction with favour On the other hand, the transaction may be one of bounty from the child to the parent, soon after the child has attained twenty one In such cases this Court views the transaction with jealousy, and anxiously interposes its protection to guard the child from the exercise of parental influence" The case before the Court was, in the proved circumstances, held to belong to the latter class "mother and son," says KNIGHT-BRUCE, L J, at p 613, "seem merely to have been the father's instruments under the guidance of

411. It is not only the parent, or person *in loco parentis*, against whom the relief may be obtained   Any third person is equally liable who is proved to have had actual or presumptive knowledge of the relation existing between the servient and the dominant party, and to have utilized and traded on the influence arising from it for the purpose of obtaining from the servient party payment or a guarantee of, or a security for, a debt owed to him by the dominant party (r).

412. The transaction impeached may be a gift or equivalent transaction, or it may be a contract for valuable consideration   The presumptions against it are the same, though the means of displacing those presumptions somewhat differ, in the two cases   In nearly all the authorities on the parental relation, the transaction before the Court was, as between the parties to the relation, an actual donation, or a transaction tantamount the to (s).

413. Putting aside cases of " family arrangement " (t), there are extremely few recorded examples of the success of any affirmative plea to a *primâ facie* case of abuse of the parental relation, that is, where the parent, or person *in loco parentis*, was able to sustain the transaction by proof of disclosure and compliance with his other duties, or to make out a case of subsequent confirmation by the servient party with full knowledge of the facts, and appreciation of his rights, after the relation, and the influence arising for it, had entirely come to an end (u)

the lawyer of the father's creditors "), *Savery* v *King* (1856), 5 H L. C 627 (*per* Lord CRANWORTH, L C , at p 657   family arrangements supported only where all derive benefit, not when the son gives up everything, and gets nothing) , *Turner* v *Collins* (1871), 7 Ch App 329 (*per* Lord HATHERLEY, L C , at pp 338, 339), *De Witte* v *Addison* (1899), 80 L T 207, C A (*per* ROMER, J , at p 209, and LINDLEY, M R , at p 212)

(r) In the following cases relief was given against the creditor (usually a solicitor, banker, or moneylender) who had used the parental influence, or knowingly allowed it to be used, over the servient party, in his own interests   *Archer* v *Hudson* (1846), 15 L J (CH) 211 , *Thornber* v. *Sheard* (1850), 12 Beav 589 , *Espey* v *Lake* (1852), 10 Hare 260 (*per* TURNER, V -C , at pp 263, 264), *Bl doc* v. *Dawson* (1865), 34 Beav 603 (*per* ROMILLY, M.R , at p 608   " where there is pressure used by a third person who by means of threats against the father induces him to compel his sons to join in a security of which he derives the sole benefit, the Court holds that neither he nor the third person can retain the benefit of that security as against the sons "), *Sercombe* v *Sanders* (1865), 34 Beav 382 (*per* ROMILLY, M R , at p 385   " it is important that creditors should understand that they cannot improve their security, taken from persons to whom they have given credit, by inducing them, at the last moment, to compel near relations, or persons under their influence, and not in a situation to resist their importunity, to pay their debts ") , *Kempson* v *Ashbee* (1874), 10 Ch App 15 (*per* JAMES, L J , at p 21), *De Witte* v, *Addison, sup.* (*per* LINDLEY, M R , at p 211)   On the other hand, in *Bainbrigge* v *Browne* (1881), 18 C D 188, the creditors escaped, though the father did not, because it was not proved against them that they had either actual or constructive notice of the influence, or knew anything beyond the bare fact that the same solicitors acted for father and daughter, which by itself was insufficient (*per* FRY, J , at p 198)

(s) The only cases of contract, as between the servient and dominant party, amongst those cited in the notes to this Sub-section are *Dawson* v *Massey* (1809), 1 Ball & B 219, and *Sharp* v. *Leach* (1862), 31 Beav 491 (as to one of the two transactions there in question)

(t) See the cases cited in note (*p*) to § 410, *ante*

(u) In *Toker* v *Toker* (1863), 3 De G J & S 487, full explanation to, and knowledge by, the servient party of all her rights was proved (*per* KNIGHT BRUCE, L J , at pp 489, 490)   In *Potts* v *Surr* (1865), 34 Beav. 543, the servient party fully appreciated the effect of the settlement, and had independent advice (*per* ROMILLY, M R , at pp 551, 552)   In the following cases, the dominant party succeeded in showing that though he had failed

414. The consideration of certain domestic relations which are not, *per se*, deemed in law to raise any presumption of undue influence whatsoever is reserved for another place (*v*).

Sub-s. (2). *The Relation between Solicitor, or other Legal Adviser, and Client.*

415. This was the first of the "professional" relations to engage the attention of the Courts, for the natural reason that the attorney in law, or solicitor, exercises his functions *in facie curiæ*, and is at all times under the immediate control and disciplinary jurisdiction of the judges. Though the presumptions against the validity of any transaction between solicitor and client during the existence of the relationship are precisely the same as in the case of any other relation (*w*), it is, nevertheless, the fact that there are features in this relation which render it specially desirable that the equitable doctrine of "influence" should be applied to it with the utmost alacrity and rigour. In the first place, as was weightily observed of advisers in general by Bacon (*x*), "the greatest trust between man and man is the trust of giving counsel. For in other confidences men commit parts of their life · their lands, their goods, their child, their credit, some particular affair— but to such as they make their counsellors, they commit the whole, by how much more they are obliged to all faith and integrity." A solicitor is in a position to acquire the most intimate knowledge not only of his client's property and affairs, but of his character and disposition, he is frequently the custodian not merely of the money and securities, but of the secrets and honour, of the client and his family. If minded to enter into a transaction with him of any kind, he knows best "the seasons when to take occasion by the hand,"—the *mollia tempora fandi* when with most safety and advantage to himself he may suggest, or entertain the suggestion of, a purchase, a sale, or a gift. He approaches the matter with, in most cases, a far more accurate appreciation of the title to, and the value and circumstances of, the property, or other subject-matter of the proposed transaction, than the client has added to which, the client is not infrequently in his debt. In these various ways his personal ascendancy is of a remarkable, and may be of an overwhelming, character (*y*), and, where he is conducting

in his duty, the servient party had afterwards confirmed the transaction. *Dimsdale* v *Dimsdale* (1856), 3 Drew 576 (as to parts of the transactions, the residue being upheld on the ground of family arrangement · *per* KINDERSLEY, V -C., at pp. 575-578), *Wright* v. *Vanderplank* (1856), 8 De G M & G 133 (*per* KNIGHT-BRUCE, L J, at pp 137, 138, and TURNER, L J, at pp 147-151), *Turner* v *Collins* (1871), 7 Ch App 329 (*per* Lord HATHERLEY, L C, at pp 340-342, as to one of the two transactions there in question) And see Sect 4, Sub-s (3), *post*, as to confirmation generally.

(*v*) See § 446, *post*
(*w*) See § 408, *sub fin*, *ante*
(*x*) Essay **xx**, "Of Counsel" (vol vi, p 423, in the edition of his Works by Spedding, Ellis, and Heath)
(*y*) At p 316 of *Tomson* v *Judge* (1855), 3 Drew 306, KINDERSLEY, V -C, adopts the language of Lord THURLOW, L C., who, in *Welles* v *Middleton* (1784), 1 Cox 112, at p. 125, had spoken of "the crushing influence of the power of an attorney", whilst, at p 712 of *Allison* v *Clayhills* (1907), 97 L T 709, PARKER, J., points out the twofold force and durability of the influence, arising from the solicitor's special information as to his client's affairs, and the personal ascendancy involved in the position of trusted adviser

litigation for his client over valuable estates or property, the temptation on the one side to make, and on the other to accede to, proposals of a champertous nature is of considerable force. A second reason for enforcing the rules with special strictness against the solicitor is that, as an officer of the Court, he is allowed several important privileges (z), and owes correlative duties of disclosure and good faith to the Court by whom he is so trusted, apart from those which he owes to his client (a) A third consideration which moves the Court, not indeed to make any distinction between a solicitor and any other dominant party, but to enforce its rules against the former with less of that reluctance and consciousness of inflicting a hardship on the individual which it feels, and sometimes expresses, in the case of a layman, is that a lawyer, in contemplation of the law which he professes and serves, and which he is presumed to know, enters into any transaction with his client with full appreciation of its impeachability at any future time, and of the risks which he is consequently incurring, and so, unlike many others who err from mere ignorance, must always be sinning against the light (b)

416. In so far as a solicitor is acting merely as the agent for sale or purchase, or as the land agent or steward, of his client, or is representing him commercially in some particular transaction, his duties are of a purely fiduciary character in the strict sense of the word, and, as such, have already been considered in a previous portion of this work (c) It must also be remembered that in every case a solicitor belongs to the class of agents, and that he is accordingly under the obligation of not abusing the confidence reposed in him as an agent, as well as that of not abusing the influence which is imputed to him as a legal adviser · and it is in the character of agent, rather than in his special character as solicitor, that the grave impropriety of his making secret arrangements for sharing profit costs with a solicitor acting for one whose interest conflicts with that of his own client has been recognized by the Court in its disciplinary jurisdiction (d).

417. It has been found convenient to describe the relation now under discussion as the relation between solicitor and client , but of course the rule is applied whenever its principle is applicable, that is, to any species of

(z) See *Newman* v *Payne* (1793), 2 Ves 199 (*per* Lord LOUGHBOROUGH, L C , at p 201)

(a) *Goddard* v *Carlisle* (1821), 9 Price 169 (*per* RICHARDS, C B , at p. 662, and GARROW, B , at pp 665, 666) ; *Re Four Solicitors*, [1901] 1 Q B 187, Div Ct (*per Cur* , at pp 189, 190) And, as to a solicitor's duty of disclosure to the Court, apart from that which he owes to his client, see § 575, note (a), *post*

(b) *Ex p James* (1803), 8 Ves. 337 (where, at pp 347, 346, Lord ELDON, L C., points out that the application of the equitable doctrine to the case of a trustee or agent in relation to his *cestui que trust* or principal is " more loudly called for " in the case of that trustee's or agent's solicitor, because of the latter's special position and duties in relation to his own client, over whom he ought to exercise his restraining influence to prevent his making a secret profit) ; *Gresley* v *Mousley* (1859), 4 De G & J 78 (where, at p 90, KNIGHT-BRUCE, L J , and, at pp 94-99, TURNER, L J , point out that an attorney, who ought to know that the transaction may be impeached at any time, is the last person to complain of delay) ; *Liles* v *Terry*, [1895] 2 Q. B 679, C A (*per* KAY, L J , at p 686, observing that least of all on a solicitor is the rule a hardship)

(c) Accordingly, it will be found that some few of the cases cited in the notes to this Sub section find a place also in the notes to Ch IV, Sect 2, Sub s (3), *ante* As to the position of a solicitor who is also mortgagee, see § 449, note (w), *post*.

(d) This was the decision in *Re Four Solicitors, sup*

professional relation between parties whereby one of them undertakes to give legal advice to the other, whatever be the name or the precise functions attaching to the relationship. For instance, the doctrine has been applied to counsel (e), to a certificated conveyancer (f), to a Scottish law-agent (g), and to a colonial advocate (h).

418. Against any solicitor, or other person occupying a similar position, who enters into any transaction, whether gift or contract, with his client during the subsistence of the relation, the law makes the same presumptions and casts upon him the same duties of disclosure and otherwise, and the same burden of proving that he fully discharged those duties in the event of the transaction being impeached by the client, as in the case of any other relation of influence (i) That is to say, when once the client has proved the relation, and the transaction, alleged, and the fact that the transaction was entered into at a time when the relation was subsisting—for unless and until he does so, no onus rests upon the solicitor at all (j)—it is incumbent on the solicitor, if he cannot show that the influence which is presumed from the relation did not in fact operate on the particular transaction, to establish the propriety of his conduct in all respects ; and the transaction is invalidated, or otherwise relieved against, if he fails to sustain this onus, which is of a somewhat different character, accordingly as the transaction is a gift, or a contract for valuable consideration

419. Any gift, or transaction equivalent to a gift, will be the subject of relief at the instance of the client, if the solicitor is unable to establish that he fully explained to the client the exact nature and meaning of the transaction, and its legal effect upon his rights and interests, and also—for this alone is not enough—advised his client that he was at liberty to revoke or avoid it at any time (k), and otherwise gave him all such cautious counsel and

(e) As in *Kingsland (Viscount)* v *Barncwall* (1706), 4 Brown P C 154 ; *Carter* v. *Palmer* (1842), 8 Cl & Fin 657 (though it was there found that the defendant acted in many other characters than that of counsel) , *Brown* v. *Kennedy* (1864), 4 De G J & S 217

(f) As in *Rhodes* v *Bate* (1866), 1 Ch App 252 (though the decision proceeded on the relation proved to have been constituted by the circumstances, rather than on the relation of legal adviser and client)

(g) As in *McPherson* v *Watt* (1877), 3 App Cas 254, H L

(h) As in *Pisani* v *Att.-Gen. of Gibraltar* (1874), L R 5 P C 516

(i) See § 405, *ante*, and Sect. 4, *post*

(j) See Sect. 3, Sub-ss (1) and (2), *post*, and, particularly, such of the cases cited in the notes thereto as are solicitor and client cases

(k) As in *Bulkeley* v *Wilford* (1834), 2 Cl & Fin. 102 (where the jury found that the solicitor had fraudulently omitted to explain to the client that the effect of the instrument executed by him was to revoke the will he had previously made in favour of his wife, and to confer a benefit on the solicitor, who was the heir-presumptive at law) ; *Procter* v. *Robinson* (1867), 15 L T 431 (where the solicitor failed to explain to the client that he need never have executed the deed at all, and that, after execution, it was not binding on him per TURNER, L J , at pp 431, 432, and CAIRNS, L J , at p 433) , *Morgan* v *Minett* (1877), 6 C. D. 638 (a similar neglect of duty on the part of the solicitor per BACON, V.-C , at p 648) , *Willis* v *Barron*, [1902] A C 271, H. L (where it was held that the solicitor had not fully discharged his duty to his client by merely explaining to her—as he had—the exact nature and extent of what she was giving up by the transaction, and what she was receiving under it,—it was a case of the extinction of a power of appointment,—and that he ought to have advised her, or seen that an independent person advised her, that no one could compel her to consent to the abnegation of her rights, instead of leaving her to

protection as he would have given him if the proposed donee had been a
stranger (*l*) ; and, further, that the client, before making the gift, had been
protected by the competent and honest advice of an independent third
person (*m*) , and, generally, that the whole transaction was righteous and
conscientious, and characterized by absolute candour and good faith on the
part of the solicitor (*n*) It is doubtful whether a single case can be found
in which a solicitor has in fact been able to sustain the above onus in the case
of a gift, that is to say, the onus of showing that, during the existence of the
relation and the influence springing from it, he received the gift under the
conditions stated ; though there are one or two instances of a solicitor succeeding on proof that both the relation and influence had come to an end
before the gift was made (*o*), or that the gift was subsequently confirmed by

suppose that she was powerless in the matter, and that the sole object of the transaction
was to rectify a mistake or slip in a previous deed on which the deed in question was
consequential. *per* Lord HALSBURY, L C , at p 276, and Lord MACNAGHTEN, at pp 280,
281)

(*l*) See the cases cited in the last note, and the observations of BUCKLEY, L J , at p 378
of *Clare* v. *Joseph*, [1907] 2 K. B. 369, C A , as to the common law duty—which, however,
as there explained has been in some respects modified by statute—" of the solicitor to
advise his client that it was contrary to his interests to pay more " than his taxed costs,
before obtaining from him any agreement to do so And " further," he adds, "if there was
an agreement between them by which the client was to pay less, the solicitor   owed
the duty of advising him that he ought not to enter into such an agreement, if other
provisions in it were contrary to the client's interest "

(*m*) As in *Goddard* v *Carlisle* (1821), 9 Price 169 (where, though it was expressly found
that full disclosure and explanation had been made, the annuity deed executed by the
client in favour of the solicitor was held to be invalidated because the solicitor was unable
to discharge the burden of establishing that the client had been independently advised
by some third person) , *Bulkeley* v *Wilford* (1834), 2 Cl & Fin 102 (where Lord ELDON,
at pp. 177–182, and Lord WYNFORD, at p 183, supported the decision of the Court below
on the ground of want of independent advice, apart from the non disclosure which had
been found by the jury, as stated in note (*k*), *sup*) , *Rhodes* v *Bate* (1866), 1 Ch App
252 (an extremely strong case, because, though it was established to the satisfaction of
the Court that the defendant Bate had punctually and honourably complied with every
other duty towards his client, even to the extent of " cautioning her " as to the suretyship
which she undertook in order to secure the indebtedness to him of the defendant Codrington, and that he " meant to give, and did give her honest advice," he was nevertheless held
liable on the sole ground that he had not insisted on his client having, and she did not in
fact have, the advice of a third person independent of Bate   *per* TURNER, L J , at pp
257, 259, 261, 262). The above decision has never been overruled, however distasteful
it may appear to some minds, and apparently did appear even to the Lords Justices
who yielded only to what they conceived to be an inexorable rule of equity in arriving
at it (" so far as she succeeds," said TURNER, L J , at p 262, " she does so by force of
the law of the Court, and not by any merits of her own," and the assent of KNIGHT-BRUCE,
L.J , was given with obvious hesitation) After this, it may seem superfluous to
cite the later decisions which follow it under conditions much less favourable to the
solicitor, such as *Morgan* v *Minett* (1877), 6 C D 638, 648 , *Liles* v *Terry*, [1895] 2 Q B
679, C A. (*per* LOPES, L J , at pp 685, 686, and KAY, L J , at pp 686, 687 Lord ESHER,
M.R , expressing, at pp. 683, 684, his antipathy to the doctrine, which he only followed
" under compulsion ") , *Powell* v *Powell*, [1900] 1 Ch 243 (*per* FARWELL, J , at pp 246,
247) , *Willis* v. *Barron*, [1902] A C 271, H L (at pp 276, 280, 281) As to the meaning
of competent and honest independent advice, see § 477, *post*.

(*n*) As in *Welles* v. *Middleton* (1784), 1 Cox 112 , *Tomson* v *Judge* (1855), 3 Drew 306 ,
Walker v *Smith* (1861), 29 Beav 394 , *Re Holmes's Estate, Bevan's Case* (1861), 3 Giff.
337 ; *O'Brien* v *Lewis* (1864), 32 L J (CH) 569 , *Brown* v *Kennedy* (1864), 4 De G J &
S 217 ; *Wright* v *Carter*, [1903] 1 Ch 27, C A (as to those of the deeds there in question
which were held to be in the nature of gifts   *per* VAUGHAN WILLIAMS, L J , at pp 49–53,
STIRLING, L.J., at pp 56–58, and COZENS-HARDY, L J , at p 61)

(*o*) *Oldham* v *Hand* (1751), 2 Ves Sr. 259 (*per* Lord HARDWICKE, L C , at p 260.

the client with full knowledge of all material facts and rights, and when entirely emancipated from the influence (p).

420. In the case of a purchase, or other transaction for valuable consideration, the client is entitled to relief against the solicitor, if the latter fails to establish any of the following :—full disclosure of all material facts (q), including his own identity as the person actually purchasing, or otherwise dealing in the matter, where the ostensible purchaser or dealer is another person, acting as agent, nominee, or trustee for him (r) ; full explanation of the legal character, effect, and incidents of the transaction, and of its bearing upon the client's rights and interests (s), either all such advice against himself as he would properly have given his client, if acting for him against a third person (t), or the competent and honest advice of a person independent of himself (u), and, lastly, payment of full and fair value (v). Where, however,

---

"this is a very large gratuity indeed, but, though there had not been that subsequent ratification,"—for this too was established—" I do not see how I could come at it, for it is not obtained by the attorney during the course of the cause, or before it, but the whole was over "). And see, generally, Sect 4, Sub s (1), *post*

(p) *Lyddon* v. *Moss* (1859), 4 De G. & J 104 (*per* TURNER, L J, at pp 132-134, and KNIGHT BRUCE, L J, at pp 134, 135) And see, generally, Sect 4, Sub s. (3), *post*.

(q) *Wright* v *Carter*, [1903] 1 Ch 27, C. A (where, as to those of the transactions which were for value, there had been no complete disclosure of all the material facts, and particularly as to the degree of pressure which was being exercised by a certain bank on the client *per* VAUGHAN WILLIAMS, L.J., at pp 51, 52, 54, 55, and STIRLING, L J, at p 59)

(r) As in *Wood* v *Downes* (1811), 18 Ves 120, *McPherson* v. *Watt* (1877), 3 App Cas. 254, H. L (*per* Lord CAIRNS, L C, at p 264, and Lord O'HAGAN, at p 266)

(s) As in *Moore* v *Prance* (1851), 9 Hare 299 (where the solicitor had not even read over the deed to his client *per* TURNER, V.-C, at pp 303, 304), *Smith* v *Kay* (1859), 7 H L C 750 (where the whole object and effect of the securities executed by the client was concealed by the solicitor *per* Lord CHELMSFORD, L C, at pp 761, 762, and Lord CRANWORTH, at pp 770-773), *Cockburn* v *Edwards* (1881), 18 C D 449, 455, 460, 462, C. A (no explanation of unusual covenant in deed), *Lala Mahabir Prasad* v *Mussamat Taj Begum* (1914), "Times," 13th March (legal adviser procures mortgage without any explanation)

(t) *Gibson* v *Jeyes* (1801), 6 Ves 266 (*per* Lord ELDON, L C, at p 278, where he states the two duties as alternative to one another " he should have said, if he was to deal with her for this, she must get another attorney to advise her as to the value or, if she would not, then out of that state of circumstances this clear duty arises from the rule of this Court, and throws upon him the whole onus of the case, that, if he will mix with the character of attorney that of vendor, he shall, if the propriety of the contract comes in question, manifest that he has given her all that reasonable advice against himself that he would have given her against a third person "), *Champion* v *Rigby* (1840), 9 L J (CH) 211, *Moore* v *Prance*, *sup* (*per* TURNER, V C, at p 303), *Holman* v *Loynes* (1854), 4 De G M & G 270 (*per* Lord CRANWORTH, L C., who, at p. 272, describes the attorney's duty as being to show "that no industry he was bound to exert could have got a better bargain for" the client, and " that his diligence to do the best for his vendor had been as great as if he were only an attorney dealing for that vendor with a stranger " and this " he must show to demonstration " the matter "must not be left in doubt " In that case the attorney bought property from his client with an annuity, without having made the slightest inquiry as to the price which could have been obtained), *Savery* v *King* (1836), 5 H L C 627 (*per* Lord CRANWORTH, L C, at pp 665, 666), *Gresley* v *Mousley* (1859), 4 De G & J 78 (*per* KNIGHT BRUCE, L J, at pp 88, 89, and TURNER, L J, at pp 97, 98); *Nocton* v *Lord Ashburton*, [1914] A C 932, H L (*per* Lord SHAW, at p 962)

(u) As in *Gibson* v *Jeyes*, *sup* (*per* Lord ELDON, L C, at p 278), *Barnard* v *Hunter* (1856), 2 Jur N S 1213, 106 R R 1014 (*per* STUART, V C, at p 1215, " the onus is

---

(v) As in *Jones* v *Thomas* (1837), 2 Y & C (Exch in Eq) 498, *Champion* v. *Rigby*, *sup.*, *Holman* v *Loynes*, *sup* (*per* TURNER, L J, at p 284), *Wright* v *Carter*, *sup* (*per* STIRLING, L J, at p 60, and COZENS HARDY, L J, at p 61, in reference to such of the transactions there impeached as were contracts, and not gifts)

the solicitor has been in a position to prove all the above elements in the burden of proof incumbent on him, or rather all such of them as have been in question (for it is not always the case that every one of them is a matter of controversy), he has always been held entitled to succeed, and the client has been denied relief (w).

Sub-s (3). The Sacerdotal Relation.

421. The spiritual relation has been frequently described, not only by social philosophers and psychologists, but also by judges and jurists, as the most powerful, comprehensive, and persistent of all the relations to which "influence" is imputed   The priest or spiritual director, or the ecclesiastical corporation or conventual establishment, exercises, it is said, a dominion which endures from the cradle to the grave ; which is present, either in the foreground, or in the background, at each of the most solemn acts of life, to command, to forbid, or to advise ; which works upon the strongest feelings of human nature,—faith, hope, and fear as to this life, and as to the life to come The priest holds the double keys : to him are confided the *arcana* of both worlds   From the religious point of view, he must hold it to be not merely his right, but his duty, to intermeddle with the temporal affairs of each member of his flock so far as to render them subservient to spiritual interests.   He is entrusted by Divine authority with a vicarious supremacy over the soul, heart, mind, and worldly concerns, of the penitent or disciple   his jurisdiction, therefore, extends to regions which are not ordinarily invaded by even the legal, or the medical, adviser, or by the usurer, or trader " in the necessities of mankind," to each of whom in turn jurisprudence and ethics have, from different points of view, assigned the premiership amongst " influences " (x) Though it is true that all this knowledge and power purports to be held on trust

upon him to show that every sort of due caution was given to that person, and that he had the means, independently of his natural protection, of dealing at arm's length What is meant .   when it is said that parties are to have protection is, that they are to have some person to look into the facts, and explain the matter to the client, in order that the client, with that assistance, may exercise his judgment "), *Smith* v *Kay* (1859), 7 H L C 750 (*per* Lord CHELMSFORD, L C , at pp 761, 762, and Lord CRANWORTH, at pp 770-773) , *Wright* v *Carter,* [1903] 1 Ch 27, C A (as to the purchase transactions, *per* VAUGHAN WILLIAMS, L J , at pp 51-55, STIRLING, L J , at pp 58, 59, and COZENS HARDY, L J , at pp 61, 62)   As to what is meant by *competent* independent advice, see § 477, *post*

(w) Thus, the solicitor proved a fair bargain and full value, in *Kingsland (Viscount)* v *Barnewall* (1706), 4 Brown P C 154 , no abuse of influence or unfair advantage taken of his exclusive knowledge, in *Cane* v *Lord Allen* (1814), 2 Dow H L 289 (*per* Lord ELDON, L C , at pp 297, 298) , full disclosure, and utmost value, in *Edwards* v *Meyrick* (1842), 2 Hare 60 (*per* WIGRAM, V.-C , at pp 71, 72) , " that the sale was as advantageous to the client as it would have been if the solicitor had used his utmost endeavours to sell the property to a stranger," in *Spencer* v *Topham* (1856), 22 Beav 573 (*per* ROMILLY, M R , at pp 577-583) , " that he acted in perfect good faith," and that the bargain " was in fact a fair one, and that he had not lost, for want of due diligence, better terms for his client," in *Pisani* v. *Att -Gen of Gibraltar* (1874), L R 5 P C 516 (at pp 538, 539) , knowledge and assent of the client, in *Re Haslam and Hier Evans,* [1902] 1 Ch 765, C A (*per* VAUGHAN WILLIAMS, L J , at p. 769, and STIRLING, L.J , at pp 772, 773) , full disclosure and liberal value, in *Allison* v *Clayhills* (1907), 97 L T 709 (*per* PARKER, J , at p. 713)

(x) See § 409, *ante* (as to the special features in the parental relation) , § 415, *ante* (the

for pious uses, the temptation to pervert "the good deposit" to the baser uses of personal and temporal advantage is held by the law to justify a special degree of vigilance in applying its presumptions and rules to this class of relation, and, on the principle of *corruptio optimi pessima*, a special feeling of repugnance to any violation of those rules. But, as has been pointed out (*y*), the presumptions and rules are in every case precisely the same, and therefore, without paying an exaggerated deference even to "the celebrated reply" of Sir Samuel Romilly in *Huguenin* v *Baseley* (*z*), or any at all to the violent, and slightly vulgar, tirade of Lord NORTHINGTON, L.C., at an earlier date (*a*), with reference to the particular relation in question, it is enough to say that it has been judicially declared in plain terms to constitute one of the recognized or "suspected" relations (*b*)

422. There have been very few cases in which "spiritual" influence has been brought before the Courts: the obvious explanation of this fact being,

---

like, as to the solicitor and client relation), § 425, *post* (as to the medical profession), and § 435, *post* (as to usurers and expectant heirs or reversioners)

(*y*) See § 108, *sub fin*, *ante* And cp the latter part of the citation from the judgment of STUART, V C, in the next note

(*z*) (1807), 14 Ves 273 See note (*c*) to § 408, *ante*, as to the extent to which this argument is entitled to quasi judicial authority, and as to the fact that Lord ELDON's judgment gives the go-bye to so much of it as is directed specifically to the spiritual relations. In *Nottidge* v *Prince* (1860), 2 Giff 246, at p 270, STUART, V C, expresses his opinion, for which he gives reasons, that "the strength of religion is far beyond that of gratitude to a guardian, trustee, or attorney," but he adds—"*the same ground of public utility* which requires this Court to guard against such influences, has its most important *application* to that influence which is the strongest"

(*a*) In *Norton* v *Relly* (1764), 2 Eden 286, where a maiden lady having granted an annuity of £50, secured on certain estates, to a methodist or "independent" preacher, the deed was decreed to be delivered up, and the defendant ordered to execute a release, on the general ground of spiritual ascendancy and fraud though it would appear from the extremely racy and vehement tone of the judgment that Lord NORTHINGTON, L C., was moved quite as much by his intense antipathy (political and religious) to the particular sect as by a distrust of spiritual influence in general "Shall it be said," he asks, at p 288, "that it"—the Court—"cannot relieve against the *glaring impositions of these men?*", and he declares that "*the constitution itself would be in danger*, if it did not" He then denounces "these men" as "false pastors," who are working "to the destruction not only of the temporal concerns of many of the subjects, *but to the endangering their eternal welfare*" Again, at p 289, he characterizes the "independent" preacher as "a subtle *sectary* who preys upon his deluded hearers, and robs them under the mask of religion, *an itinerant who propagates his fanaticism* even in the cold northern countries, where one should scarcely suppose that it could enter," and concludes, at p 291, with a ferocious jocosity not unworthy of JEFFREYS, C.J, at the Bloody Assize "one of his counsel tried to shelter him under the denomination of an independent preacher I have tried, in the decree I have made, *to spoil his independency*" Notwithstanding that STUART, V C., at p. 263 of *Nottidge* v *Prince*, *sup*, says that *Norton* v. *Relly* "is of unquestionable authority," one cannot but be sensible how gravely that authority is impaired by expressions of animus such as those which are above cited, and which in the argument for the dominant party in the later case were not unjustly described as "violent"

(*b*) See *Allcard* v *Skinner* (1887), 36 C D 145, C. A (*per* COTTON, L J, at pp 171 *sqq*, LINDLEY, L.J, at pp 181 *sqq*, BOWEN, L J, at pp 189 *sqq*), *Morley* v *Loughnan*, [1893] 1 Ch. 736, C. A. (*per* WRIGHT, J, at p 752) At p. 183 of the former case expressions are to be found which show that LINDLEY, L J., could not resist the temptation to make unnecessary comparisons between this and other influences "of all influences religious influence is the most dangerous and the most powerful" He does, however, at the same time seem to recognize the harmlessness, and possible utility, of "enthusiasm" inspiring and working upon "the enthusiast," but even here he excepts any enthusiasm which is the outcome of "external influence" The meaning and scope of this qualification is obscure

not, as has been judicially suggested on two occasions (c), the rarity in this country of its abuse, but rather, on the contrary, its prevalence, power, and persistence. For it must be remembered that any transaction entered into under the influence is not illegal or void (d): no policeman stands by to forbid it, and no bureaucracy has as yet ordained a house to house inspection of accounts between priest and penitent. No person can invite the assistance of the Court to recall a gift once made, except the donor; and in the enormous majority of the cases, the donor does nothing, for the simple reason that the power which is strong enough to forge the fetters is strong enough to prevent their being broken or relaxed.

423. The first of the "spiritual influence" cases was decided in 1764 (e). In this, and the few which succeeded it (f), the doctrine was applied indifferently to individuals, such as a nonconformist preacher (g), a Roman Catholic

(c) By Lord NORTHINGTON, L.C, in *Norton* v *Relly, inf*, and by STUART, V.C. in *Nottidge* v *Prince, inf*, at p. 270 ("fortunately the excellent character of Christian ministers in this country renders the occurrence of such questions extremely rare").

(d) *Re Metcalfe's Trusts* (1864), 2 De G. J. & S. 122, is a striking illustration of the elementary principle stated in the text. In that case a professed nun, having executed a deed assigning all her property to the trustees of the Brompton Oratory, required her own trustees to assign such property accordingly. Her trustees, instead of doing so, brought the question, and paid the fund, into court. The lady petitioned to have the fund paid out to her, or rather, according to her direction, to the trustees of the Brompton Oratory. Her trustees raised the plea of "spiritual" influence: but the Lords Justices, reversing ROMILLY, M.R., held that, since the only person entitled to avoid the transaction was not seeking to avoid it, but, on the contrary, insisted on its being carried out, the order must be made as prayed (*per* KNIGHT BRUCE, L.J., at p. 126. "this lady may be about to deal with her property in a way which we should think inadvisable, but we have no jurisdiction to take that into consideration. She comes here asking for her own property, and we have no power to refuse the application." The lady's trustees were deprived of costs: but, considering that they never had any right to raise the question at all, or put their *cestui que trust* to expense in the matter, and, further, that, instead of adopting a neutral attitude, they argued in Court against the petition being granted, it seems strange that they were not ordered to pay the lady's costs, as well as bear their own.

(e) *Norton* v *Relly* (1764), 2 Eden 286, where, at p. 287, Lord NORTHINGTON, L.C., remarks: "this cause, as it has been very justly observed, is the first of the kind that ever came before this Court, and, I may add, before any court of judicature in this kingdom." Sir Samuel Romilly, in his opening argument, at p. 280 of *Huguenin* v *Baseley* (1807), 14 Ves. 273, states that "the English Courts of Justice do not afford an instance of influence exercised by such means,' from which it would appear that he was not aware of *Norton* v. *Relly, sup*, which, though mentioned in a then published compilation, the *Collectanea Juridica*, as we are told by STUART, V.C., at p. 263 of *Nottidge* v *Prince* (1860), 2 Giff. 246, did not appear in any volume of professed reports until 1818, when it was included in Eden's collection, in two volumes, "of cases argued and determined in the High Court of Chancery from 1757 to 1766 from the original MSS of Lord Chancellor NORTHINGTON, collected and arranged, with notes and references to former and subsequent determinations, and to the registrar's books." Eden was a near relative of Lord NORTHINGTON, and in that way, as he tells us in his Preface, came "to be in possession of his law MSS," which "consisted of six volumes of notebooks, and a large quantity of loose papers," the latter containing Lord NORTHINGTON'S judgments, which, in cases of difficulty,' had been written out at length," and had probably been read in Court in the same state in which they now appear." Presumably the report of the judgment in *Norton* v *Relly* was taken from one of these separate papers.

(f) Namely, those cited in notes (h)–(m), *inf*. From these it has been thought better to exclude *Huguenin* v *Baseley, sup*, where the dominant party, though he happened to be a clergyman, and though, in "the celebrated reply," he was sought to be made liable in that character principally, was not in fact held liable on that ground, but solely on the ground of a relation of "influence" created by his conduct. The case therefore is dealt with as one of the authorities relevant to the kind of relation discussed in Sub-s (5), *post*.

(g) *Norton* v *Relly, sup*.

priest and confessor (h), and a Plymouth brother (i); and to ecclesiastical or conventual establishments, such as a Roman Catholic convent (j), an Agapemone (k), the Brompton Oratory (l), and a Protestant sisterhood (m)

424. Against the dominant party in these cases the law makes the same presumptions, and casts upon him the same burden of proof, as in all other cases of a "suspected" relation (n), if any transaction entered into during the continuance of the relation be afterwards called in question by the servient party, but not if challenged by any other person, for nobody else has anything to say in the matter (o) If and when, but not unless or until, the servient party has established the existence of the relation, and the fact of a transaction having taken place between the parties during its continuance (p), he is entitled to relief on failure by the dominant party to prove,—where the transaction was a gift, or in the nature of a gift, as it ordinarily is in a case of sacerdotal influence (q),—either that the influence was not in fact operative in hâc re (r), or that it was in fact properly used (s), and, in particular, for the purpose of establishing such propriety, that the servient party was fully informed as to the nature and effect of what he was doing, and had the

(h) *Middleton* v *Sherburne* (1841), 4 Y & C (Exch in Eq) 358
(i) *Morley* v *Loughnan*, [1893] 1 Ch 736
(j) *White* v *Meade* (1840), 2 Ir. Eq R 420
(k) *Nottidge* v *Prince*, inf
(l) *Re Metcalfe's Trusts* (1864), 2 De G J. & S 122
(m) *Allcard* v *Skinner* (1887), 36 C. D 145, C A
(n) See § 405, ante, and Sect. 4, post.
(o) Which it was not in *Re Metcalfe's Trusts*, sup see note (d) to § 422, ante.
(p) See Sect 3, Sub ss (1) and (2), post
(q) For a statement of the somewhat different kind of proof required in the case of transactions for value, see, generally, §§ 456 and 478, post: as applied to parent and child, see § 409, ante · as applied to solicitor and client, see § 420, ante.
(r) See Sect 4, Sub-s (1), post In *Allcard* v *Skinner*—see note (t), inf—the dominant parties set up, but failed to establish, a case of cesser of relationship and influence
(s) As in *Norton* v. *Relly* (1764), 2 Eden 286, *Nottidge* v *Prince* (1860), 2 Giff 246 (per STUART, V -C., at pp 269, 270 no one "can accept a gift or benefit from the person who is under the dominion of that influence, without the danger of having the gift set aside," as it will be unless the donee prove "that a sufficient protection has been interposed," which in that case he wholly failed to do) In *Middleton* v *Sherburne* (1841), 4 Y. & C (Exch in Eq) 358, both gifts by will, and gifts inter vivos, were impeached after explaining the different principles applicable to the two cases—see § 447, post, as to this question—the Court directed an issue as to the former, and it was not thought necessary to deal with the latter immediately but it was intimated that it might afterwards become so (per Lord ABINGER, C B , at pp. 392, 393); for, if the jury should decide that the will had not been procured by that amount of undue influence which is necessary to upset a will, this would not conclude the question whether the other gifts had not been obtained by the much less degree of influence necessary to invalidate transactions inter vivos, and further inquiry "might be essential" as to those, but if the jury should find to the contrary, then "further interference by the Court would be vain and profitless," because if the will were invalidated, a fortiori the gifts inter vivos ought to be. At p 392, he points out some "very strong facts" for the consideration of the jury, and impliedly indicates that, unless countervailed by evidence of complete propriety, they would operate even more strongly against the dominant party in any investigation which might be required thereafter of the gifts inter vivos No such investigation took place because, as we are informed at p 293, on the issue coming on for trial, it was compromised, together (presumably) with all other questions in the litigation.

competent and honest advice of an independent third person (t), and made the gift with a perfectly unfettered and instructed mind. It is, however, open to the dominant party, even if he can prove none of these things, and cannot therefore displace any of the presumptions which the law makes against him in the first instance, to set up that, though he failed in his duty, yet afterwards the servient party, with full knowledge of his rights, and when emancipated from the influence, deliberately elected to confirm, instead of avoiding, the transaction (u).

Sub-s. (4). *The Relation between Physician and Patient*

425. The profession of medicine resembles the other two of the professions commonly called "learned," as regards the kind of influence to which it gives rise. It involves, on the part of the medical adviser, such an intimate and exclusive knowledge of his patient's physical, and sometimes his mental, life, habits, history, weaknesses, and perils, and, on the part of the patient, such a dependence upon the doctor or surgeon for health of body and mind, or, it may be, for life itself, that the law has found itself constrained to make the same *primâ facie* presumptions against those who exercise it, as it makes against the solicitor or priest. Though there are very few recorded instances of litigated questions of "influence" between doctor and patient, and in many even of these few instances the relation was not solely and entirely a professional one, but was partly created by special "circumstances and conditions," such as are dealt with at a later stage (v), it has been distinctly held that, of itself, and apart from any such special conditions, the medical is one of the "suspected" relations (w). To some minds, indeed, inclined to a more prosaic and practical view of the meaning of "influence" in life than would be accepted by the psychologist, it may seem that this influence is stronger than any other, even than the sacerdotal; though no such pre-eminence has been judicially imputed to the medical relation as has been assigned to some of the other relations (x)

(t) As in *White* v *Meade* (1840), 2 Ir Eq R. 420 ; *Allcard* v *Skinner* (1887), 36 C D 145, C. A. (*per* COTTON, L.J , at pp 171–173), LINDLEY, L J , at pp 181 *sqq*., and BOWEN, L.J., at pp. 189–191 . in that case, however, the dominant parties succeeded, solely on the ground of the servient party's subsequent confirmation · see the next note) , *Morley* v *Loughnan*, [1893] 1 Ch 736 (*per* WRIGHT, J., at pp. 752–757. Here the dominant party was not only quite unable to show that the servient party had any independent advice, but it was proved against him that he had taken active measures to remove or neutralize any disturbing influences, and so preclude the possibility of the servient party listening to any disinterested voice)

(u) *Allcard* v *Skinner*, *sup.* (*per* LINDLEY, L J , at pp. 186–189, and BOWEN, L.J , at pp 191–195), diss COTTON, L.J., on this point for reasons which will commend themselves to many minds). See, generally, as to confirmation, Sect 4, Sub-s (3), *post*

(v) In Sub-s. (5), *post*, where accordingly are to be found several of the cases here cited.

(w) *Dent* v *Bennett* (1839), 4 My. & Co. 269 (*per* Lord COTTENHAM, L C , at p. 276), *Ahearne* v *Hogan* (1844), Dru. 310 (*per* SUGDEN, L C. (Ir), at pp 322, 325) , *Billage (or Billing)* v. *Southee* (1852), 9 Hare 534 ; 21 L. J (CH) 472 (*per* TURNER, V -C., at p 540) , *Mitchell* v. *Homfray* (1881), 8 Q B D 587, C A. (*per* Lord SELBORNE, L.C., at p 591)

(x) See §§ 409, 415, 421, *ante*, and § 435, *post*.

Louis XI, it is remembered, feared his confessor, but feared his barber-surgeon more. Other views, however, may be put forward with just as much plausibility, and just as little utility (y) ; for it must always be a question of the individual temperament, which, in framing its general presumptions and principles in the interests of society at large, jurisprudence cannot take into account (z).

426. Accordingly, the same presumptions are made against, and the same burden of " sustaining the transaction,"—neither more nor less,—is cast upon, the dominant party in the case of the relation between medical adviser and patient, as in the case of any other of his recognized relations (a). That is to say, as soon as the servient party has established the relation and the transaction (b), it lies upon the dominant party to prove, and relief will be granted against him whenever he fails to prove, either that the influence in fact did not affect or operate upon the transaction (c), or that in fact it was not abused, and that the transaction was in all respects righteous and proper (d),—which means, in cases of both gifts and contracts, that he made full and candid disclosure to the patient, before entering into the transaction, of all material facts, and explained to him its exact nature and effect (e) ; further, in the case of a gift (f), and perhaps in the case of a contract

(y) See App. B, Sect. 2, Sub-s. (3), post.
(z) See § 408, sub fin , ante
(a) See § 405, ante, and Sect 4, post.
(b) See Sect 3, Sub ss. (1) and (2), post.
(c) See Sect. 4, Sub-s (1), post In Dent v Bennett, inf., this contention was set up, but not established (per Lord COTTENHAM, L C , at p 277) So, also, and with the same result, in Ahearne v Hogan, inf. (per SUGDEN, L C (Ir), at p 323) In both cases, however, it was recognized that the plea of non existence or cesser of the relation (not merely of acts proper to that relation, such as actual administration of remedies, or attendances), if established, is a valid one
(d) See Sect. 4, Sub-s (2), post
(e) As in Popham v Brooke (1828), 5 Russ. 8 (where a surgeon was the recipient from his patient of an annuity, for which there was no consideration suggested, except the surgeon's promise to attend to him for the rest of his life   the instrument securing the annuity was set aside on the ground that the surgeon had failed to disclose to the patient the nature and effect of the deed, or the fact that, as he knew, and the patient did not, the latter had only a few weeks to live   If the transaction could be regarded as other than a gift, then the surgeon, it was held, must equally fail, not having shown that he gave full, or any, value per LEACH, M.R , at pp 10, 11) , Ahearne v Hogan (1844), Dru 310 (where a medical man had not only failed to explain to his patient the nature and effect of the transaction, which was the assignment of various policies of insurance, but had in various ways, and on the face of the deed itself, grossly misrepresented it per SUGDEN, L.C (Ir), at pp. 323–326) , Billage v. Southee (1852), 9 Hare 534 (where a medical man obtained from a poor patient a promissory note for £325 in pretended consideration of services rendered, but which, as to so much of the £325 as was in excess of the amount of his fees calculated on a proper scale, was regarded as a gift.   The promissory note was ordered to be set aside as to this excess, and to stand as security for the residue, on the ground that the medical attendant had failed to establish that he had made full, or any, disclosure or explanation whatsoever as to the amount of his alleged charges, and as to how much of the £325 was supposed to be due for his services, and how much to represent his patient's bounty · per TURNER, V -C , at p 540).
(f) Dent v. Bennett (1839), 4 My & Cr 269, where an agreement by a patient, more than 85 years old, to pay his medical attendant £25,000 in supposed gratitude for saving his life, and in consideration of the continuance of his services, was set aside by Lord COTTENHAM, L C , on the ground that not only was there no independent advice, but the agreement had been " carefully concealed from his "—the patient's—" professional

also (g), that he procured for the patient the competent and honest advice of a third person, and, further, in the case of a purchase or sale, that he gave no less, or received no more, as the case may be, than a fair and just price or consideration (h)   It is only where he succeeds in sustaining this onus to its full extent (i), or where, though unable to do so, he is in a position to prove that the servient party, with full knowledge and in entire freedom from the influence, subsequently elected to affirm the transaction (j), that he is protected, and that the presumptions made against him in the first instance are rebutted

Sub-s (5)   Relations created by the particular Circumstances and Conditions of the Case

427. Notwithstanding that there is no proof of the existence of any of the recognized relations, domestic or professional, hitherto dealt with, the conduct of the parties, and the other "circumstances and conditions" of the individual case, may be such as to constitute a relation *ad hoc*, so to speak, from which the law will make the same three presumptions of influence in favour of the servient, and against the dominant, party, as it makes in the case of any of the specific relations (k), or, to put it more simply, the law will presume from the proved existence of certain "circumstances and con-

advisers, and all other persons" (p 277)   This was on the theory of the transaction being in substance a gift, as Lord COTTENHAM thought it was (p 273)   If, however, it was not, then it was open to the further objection that he had sold his services at a grossly excessive price (p 272)   Cp *Gibson* v *Russell* (1843), 2 Y & C 104 (where "the intimate friend and medical attendant" of the servient party failed to establish, in respect of a certain conveyance which he had obtained from his patient, and which was impeached, that the patient "well understood the whole matter, and needed no other advice or assistance respecting it than such as he had". *per* KNIGHT-BRUCE, V.-C, at pp 115, 117–119), *Mitchell* v *Homfray* (1881), 8 Q. B. D 587, C. A. (where—*per* Lord SELBORNE, L C, at p 591, and BRAMWELL, L J, at p 593—it was held that a gift by patient to medical adviser was originally voidable on the ground that the patient admittedly received no independent advice, or explanation of her rights, and it would have been avoided accordingly, had she not afterwards, when the influence was removed, confirmed it)

(g) *Ahearne* v *Hogan* (1844), Dru 310 (*per* SUGDEN, L C (Ir), at p 322   "while such a relation continues, the Court is called upon to look at *a contract* entered into, without the intervention of a third party, with considerable jealousy")

(h) *Popham* v *Brooke, sup* (see the view of LEACH, M R, stated in note (e), *sup*, on the transaction in that case, if regarded as not being a gift), *Dent* v *Bennett, sup.* (see the similar opinion of Lord COTTENHAM, L C, as to the transaction in that case, if regarded in the light of a sale, as stated in note (f), *sup*)

(i) As in *Pratt* v *Barker* (1826), 1 S m 1 (where the surgeon who had received a bounty from his patient proved that the patient had had the honest and sound advice of his own solicitors, and full explanation of the exact legal consequences of the voluntary settlement which he deliberately executed, instead of leaving the property to the surgeon by his will, for the purpose of saving legacy duty), *Blackie* v *Clark* (1852), 15 Beav 595 (where, in the case of a transaction for value, the confidential medical attendant proved that the patient had the separate advice of her own solicitor as to some of the deeds, and thoroughly understood the effect of the others, and received fair terms   *per* ROMILLY, M R., at pp 601–604)

(j) As in *Mitchell* v *Homfray, sup.* . see note (f), *sup.*, and, generally, as to confirmation, Sect 4, Sub s (3), *post*

(k) See § 405, *ante*

ditions " surrounding a transaction, that one of the parties exercised " an undue influence " over the other in bringing it about, unless and until the contrary be shown The proposition is sometimes framed in this way,— whereas, it is said, in the case of the " suspected " relations, undue influence is presumed, in all other cases it must be proved as a fact but this is not a strictly accurate statement, for, since in every case of a *præsumptio juris* from given facts there must first be evidence of those facts, so here there must be proof of the existence of the " known " relation, where it is a case of such a relation, just as much as there must be proof of the necessary " circumstances and conditions," where it is not and exactly the same *primâ facie* inferences in law are drawn from the foundation of fact so established, whatever be the nature of the foundation in the particular case Lord HARDWICKE, L.C., in a case of established authority on the subject now under consideration, distinctly states that undue influence is not a matter for proof, but is always presumed in equity from proved " circumstances and conditions of the kind which he describes " In enumerating various species of undue influence (which he calls " fraud ") he mentions, as a " third kind of fraud," that " which may be *presumed from the circumstances and conditions of the parties contracting ;* and this goes further than the rule of law, which is that it must be proved, and not presumed · but it is wisely established in this Court to prevent taking surreptitious advantage of the weakness and necessity of another: which knowingly to do is equally against conscience as to take advantage of his ignorance . a person is equally unable to judge for himself in one or the other " (*l*) . and, again, when dealing with his " last head of fraud," viz. " catching bargains with heirs, reversioners, or expectants," he insists that " that is always fraud *presumed or inferred* from the circumstances and conditions of the parties contracting . weakness on the one side, . on the other, . . . advantage taken of that weakness " (*m*) And, more than a century later, in another leading case on this topic, the passages cited from Lord HARDWICKE's judgment were adopted by Lord SELBORNE, L C , *in ipsissimis verbis* (*n*), and they have always been accepted as an accurate and sound statement of the rules applicable, and of their theoretical basis. So manifest, indeed, has it appeared to some judges that a relation of some sort must be deemed to be established by these " circumstances and conditions," from which relation alone the presumptions can be made, that they have described the position of the dominant party under such circumstances and conditions as being constructively or metaphorically tantamount or analogous to that of the dominant party in some one or

(*l*) *Chesterfield (Earl of)* v *Janssen* (1751), 2 Ves. Sr. 125, at pp 155, 156
(*m*) *Ibid* , at pp 156, 157
(*n*) *Aylesford (Earl of)* v. *Morris* (1873), 8 Ch App 484, at pp 489–491 At p 491 he observes that " *the element of personal influence is here wanting* But it is sufficient for the application of the principle, if the parties meet under such circumstances as, in the particular transaction, to give the stronger party dominion over the weaker " . which is as much as to say that it is unnecessary to prove undue influence in fact, but that a relation will be established by proof of the circumstances under which the parties meet, from which relation the " *primâ facie* presumption " to which he afterwards refers will arise

other of the "known" relations,—that of a parent (o), for instance, or an attorney (p), or a guardian (q).

428. There must, then, as an essential condition precedent to the applicability of the equitable doctrine, be an "inequality" between the parties in the sense above indicated, that is to say, in Lord HARDWICKE's language, there must be *both* "weakness on the one side," *and* "advantage taken of that weakness, on the other." Inequality in any other sense is absolutely irrelevant. A mere disparity in natural qualities, resources (r), or fortuitous advantages, comes to nothing. The "inequality" must have been a factitious one. a case must be shown of marked cards, loaded dice, or "a little shuffling" of the rapiers; it must appear that the dominant party either brought about the unevenness in the conditions, or, finding it ready to his hand, utilized and traded on it to extract from the servient party a gift or contract which he would not otherwise have made. Nor is it to the purpose to establish a case of "hardship," unless by "hardship" is understood a taking advantage, that is, an unfair or unconscientious advantage, of the subjection of the servient party (s). Wherever the servient party has been unable to establish "circumstances and conditions" of the kind contemplated by Lord HARDWICKE (t), he has been held disentitled to any relief (u); for he has not

---

(o) As in *Murray* v *Palmer* (1805), 2 Sch & Lefr 472 (per Lord REDESDALE, L C (Ir), at p 485 " this young woman, evidently in great distress, is persuaded that, unless she takes what Palmer chooses to give her, she shall get nothing , he was formidably armed against her, . Palmer had *put himself into the situation of the father, and made himself a trustee for the children, as the father was*"), *Harvey* v. *Mount* (1845), 8 Beav. 439 (per ROMILLY, M R, at p. 447)

(p) As in *Taylor* v *Obee* (1816), 3 Price 83, where, at p 93, RICHARDS, B, states his comprehensive view that " any one possessing the confidence of a party must be regarded as in the situation of attorney of that party, and should not be allowed to take advantage of that situation "

(q) See *Revett* v *Harvey* (1823), 1 Sim & St 502, the facts of which are stated in note (a) to § 429, *post*, where, at p 507, LEACH, V C, says " this case must be governed by the principles which apply to a guardian and his ward "

(r) *Osmond* v *Fitzroy* (1731), 3 P Wms 129 (per JEKYLL, M R, at pp. 129, 130 · the Court " will not measure the size of people's understandings and capacities," unless circumstances have first been shown making the question a relevant one That is to say, mere " inequality " of this description is not a fact from which, without more, a presumption of improper influence will be drawn

(s) See *Middleton* v *Brown* (1878), 47 L J (CH) 411, C A (per JESSEL, M R , at p 413 " what is the meaning of the term ' hard bargain ' ? If it has any distinct meaning at all, as distinguished from a mere term of abuse, it means in equity an unconscientious bargain, that is, a taking advantage of the position of one of the parties to the contract, and when I say ' taking advantage,' I mean of course taking an unfair advantage When you come to that point and you have brought your proof up to that, there is a case in which equity will relieve against such a bargain ") In that case the agreement impeached was held not to be the subject of relief. Sir GEORGE JESSEL's language is adopted by WALKER, L.C. (Ir), at p 510 of *Rae* v *Joyce* (1892), 29 L R (Ir) 500, having, at p 509, pointed out how " ambiguous " the expression is

(t) See the citation from his judgment which is given in § 427, *ante*

(u) Thus, no relation was held to have been constituted by the circumstances and conditions proved, and therefore no presumption of undue influence was made against the dominant party, in *Farmer* v *Farmer* (1848), 1 H L. C 724 , *Harrison* v *Guest* (1860), 8 H L C 481, *Haygarth* v *Wearing* (1871), L R 12 Eq 320 (per WICKENS, V.-C., at p. 327); *Armstrong* v *Armstrong* (1873), Ir R 8 Eq 1 , *Henry* v *Armstrong* (1881), 18 C D. 668 (per KAY, J , at p 669), *Howes* v *Bishop*, [1909] 2 K B 390, C A (per Lord ALVERSTONE, C.J , at p 398, and MOULTON, L.J , at p 399), *Re Coomber*, [1911] 1 Ch 723, C A In all the above cases relief was refused, except in *Haygarth* v. *Wearing, sup* , and

established any relation from which the Court can draw even a *primâ facie* inference against the servient party, or cast upon him any onus to displace such an inference. It is of no more use to prove the transaction without proving the relation, than it is to prove the relation without proving the transaction (v). If and when, however, satisfactory evidence has been given of facts of a nature to constitute the relation, the same presumption in favour of the servient party is made, and the same burden of repelling it is at once cast upon the dominant party, as in the case of any of the domestic or professional relations (w). The presumption is of " an unconscientious use of power arising out of the circumstances and conditions of the parties contracting "; and, in the admirably precise phraseology of Lord SELBORNE, L C , in the second of the *loci classici* on this subject, " when the relative position of the parties is such as *primâ facie* to raise this presumption, the transaction cannot stand unless the person claiming the benefit of it is able to repel the presumption by contrary evidence, proving it to have been in *point of fact fair, just, and reasonable* " (x). " Fairness " here connotes both moral propriety, and adequacy of value from a business point of view : " justice " involves principally the former element, and " reasonableness " the latter. The three qualities of the transaction which the dominant party is called upon to make out, if he is to escape liability, may be established, and can only be established, by proof of the same matters as in the case of any other of the " influence " relations (y),—namely, whether the transaction was a gift or a contract, full disclosure of all material facts, and a clear explanation of the exact nature of the transaction, and of the servient party's liabilities and rights in respect of it, including his right to refuse to enter into it, and, when entered into, his right to repudiate it further, if the transaction was a gift, the honest and competent advice of an independent third person (which fact is also of great importance in considering the general propriety of any transaction other than a gift, though it may not in all cases of the latter description be an absolutely indispensable *probandum*), and, in the case of transactions for valuable consideration, the fact that an adequate and just price was paid by the dominant party, if a purchaser, and no more than a just price paid to him, if a vendor It should be observed here that, though in the form in which the rule is stated it is assumed, as a the   ical possibility, that a dominant party may be in a position to repel by al   itive evidence the *primâ facie* presumption raised against him, the possibility is practically a very remote one because, in proving a case sufficient to raise the presumption,—and until he does so, no answer is called for,—the servient party must of necessity have already negatived that conscientiousness, righteousness, and propriety which is the necessary foundation of any affirmative

then it was given solely on the ground of misrepresentation. See generally, as to the onus of proving the " relation," Sect. 3, Sub s. (1), *post*

(v) See Sect. 3, Sub s (2), *post*
(w) See § 405, *ante*, and Sect. 4, *post*
(x) At p 491 of *Aylesford (Earl of)* v. *Morris* (1873), 8 Ch App 484.
(y) See Sect 4, Sub s (2), *post*

answer (z) ; or, putting it the other way, any evidence of such conscientious-ness adduced by the dominant party is, if believed, not so much an affirma-tive answer as an obstacle to the right of the servient party to require any answer at all : it silences the adversary's guns by spiking them, rather than by any answering fire of its own artillery

429. It is not very easy to classify the "circumstances and conditions of the parties contracting" which are deemed sufficient to constitute the relation now in question, or the various acts and omissions by which the one party has been held to have made an unconscientious use of the power arising out of those circumstances and conditions, and to have taken an unfair advantage of the other party's weakness, or the different forms of that which the law recognizes as "weakness": the reason being that, in nearly all the reported cases, there has been a combination of several modes of "taking advantage," and of several forms of "weakness." But a rough attempt may be made in this direction. In the first place, on consulting the authorities, it is noticeable at once that a common feature in many of them, and a very important one in establishing both the advantage and the unconscionable use of it, is that, the servient party being in financial distress, the dominant party constituted himself his manager, adviser, or agent, professed friendship for him and an anxiety to serve him, officiously intervened and intermeddled in his affairs, obtruded himself upon his notice, assumed the office of "guide, philosopher, and friend," and, in his self-appointed character, proffered his aid in extricating him from his difficulties and em-barrassments , and, then, having established and consolidated his dominion over the servient party's will, judgment, and concerns, proceeded to take unconscientious advantage of his distress by obtaining from him either gifts or profitable contracts, the unconscientiousness being shown by concealment of material facts as to the subject-matter of the transaction, the failure to explain the effect of such transaction upon the servient party's rights and interests, and, in the case of gifts, to see that the servient party obtained honest advice from a disinterested third person, or, in the case of contracts, to pay him full value on a purchase, or to exact no more from him than full value on a sale (a)   Another class of case is where a similarly self-constituted

---

(z) See *Aylesford (Earl of)* v *Morris, sup*, per Lord SELBORNE, L C , at p 496   " no attempt has been made to show by any independent evidence (*if such a thing could be conceived possible*) that the terms here imposed upon the plaintiff were fair and reasonable "

(a) As in *Twisleton* v *Griffith* (1716), 1 P. Wms. 309 (where the servient party was in distress and debt, and the dominant party who bought his remainder in tail " took upon himself to advise and direct the plaintiff in everything, and professed great friendship for him " : *per* Lord COWPER, L C , at p 310), *Proof* v *Hines (circ. 1740)*, Forr. Cas. temp Talbot, 111 ("the case of a tradesman who officially interfered " so described by Sir Samuel Romilly, at p 284 of *Huguenin* v. *Baseley, inf.*), *Murray* v *Palmer* (1805), 2 Sch. & Lefr 472 (see the citation in note (o) to § 427, *ante*), *Huguenin* v. *Baseley* (1807), 14 Ves 273 (where the dominant party, with the object and result of obtaining from a widow a voluntary settlement of her estates, procured an introduction to her, ingratiated himself with her, took upon himself to manage all her affairs, and to advise her, received her rents, induced her to get rid of her solicitors, and employ as her agents in their stead himself and his own solicitor and surveyor, concealed from her the real facts as to the value of her property, failed to explain the nature and effect of the instrument, and particularly a clause in it which made it irrevocable except in the presence of persons whom

manager or adviser by similar means takes an unrighteous advantage of other infirmities or disabilities of the servient party, such as mental or physical imbecility, ignorance or incapacity for business, or general helplessness, unaccompanied by pecuniary embarrassment, or even accompanied by great affluence; or where, though neither in actual distress, nor even labouring under any positive infirmity of body, the servient party has suddenly come into property quite disproportionate to his previous possessions, or an expectation of acquiring such a property whether by litigation or otherwise, and, being quite unfitted by his previous mode of life to cope with the situation, is anxiously looking round for some one to give him the necessary counsel and aid, and is entirely dependent on, and at the mercy of, the first person who offers it, and the dominant party constitutes himself such a person (b) In the two classes of case hitherto mentioned, by interfering

it might not be easy to get together, and not only failed to see that she had, but took active steps to prevent her having, the independent advice of a third person : *per* Lord ELDON, L.C., at pp 293–300), *Wood v. Abrey* (1818), 3 Madd 417 (*per* LEACH, V.-C., at p 424 "I consider . this plaintiff entitled to relief, . . . because the purchase was made at an inadequate price from vendors who were in great distress, and without the intervention of any other professional assistance than the purchaser's attorney, and because *these circumstances are evidence that in this purchase advantage was taken of the distress of the vendors*"), *Revell v. Harvey* (1823), 1 Sim & St 502 (where a solicitor, appealed to by the mother of an infant in financial difficulties, professed great sympathy and anxiety to render assistance, asked the mother to bring him to his chambers, and then, besides acting as solicitor, entered upon a series of money-lending transactions, in respect of which he obtained an acknowledgment from the infant, on his attaining his majority, of indebtedness in a lump sum, without giving any information whatever as to the figures or the state of the accounts, or how the lump sum was made up, and without the servient party having any independent advice *per* LEACH, V C, at p. 507: "the defendant thought fit to *place himself in a relation with* this infant which gave him great influence over his mind, and he cannot be permitted to conclude the infant by an acknowledgment signed by him, within a month after he came of age, and without the intervention of any friend or adviser on his part") *Davies v Cooper* (1840), 5 My & Cr 270 (where the dominant party bought certain reversionary interests and an equity of redemption at an inadequate price from a drunkard and an imbecile, having "assumed in a great degree the management of his affairs," and being a person who "from his connection with the vendor, and from his interference with his affairs must have had much influence over him" *per* Lord COTTENHAM, L.C, at p 277, who also points out, at pp 277–279, that there had been concealment of material facts as to the inadequacy of the consideration, which was an annuity, the defendant knowing, and the plaintiff to his knowledge being ignorant, that the life was an extremely bad one An attempt to show that an independent person had been called in as referee wholly failed,—p 278), *Middleton v Sherburne* (1841), 4 Y & C (Exch in Eq) 358 (*per* Lord ABINGER, C B, at p 392, as to the priest in that case who took advantage of his position as spiritual adviser to become the self-constituted manager of the servient party's temporal affairs, and, in both capacities, obtained unbounded influence over him, whereby he became the recipient of gifts by deed as well as by will), *Cockell v Taylor* (1852), 15 Beav 103 (where the dominant party took advantage of a poor person's distress and need of money in order to prosecute a claim against the Crown to a fund in Court, and obtained from him conveyances and mortgages at an undervalue), *Tate v Williamson* (1866), L. R 1 Eq 528 (where the dominant party took advantage of a young man's pecuniary embarrassments, intemperance, and weakness of character, in making a purchase from him at an inadequate price, and without any disclosure of a certain valuation of the property obtained by him, which clearly indicated such inadequacy, and without the servient party having any independent advice, it being especially noted by WOOD, V.-C, at p 540, that the dominant party "took upon *himself to advise* the young man in reference to the arrangement of his difficulties," and "professed to give him advice," &c, and express mention being made in the declaration which prefaced the decree, set out at p. 541, of "*the duties which the defendant . . . had undertaken* of advising him with respect to the arrangement of the claims of his creditors")

(b) As in *MacCabe v Hussey* (1831), 5 Bligh (N.S) 715 (where an Irish barrister

in the concerns of the servient party without being invited to do so, it may almost be said that the dominant party at once raises a *primâ facie* presumption against himself, based upon that fact alone, since he voluntarily invests himself with the position and duties attaching to any of the recognized relations, just as an executor *de son tort* by intermeddling with the assets puts himself in the same position as if he had been expressly appointed to the office which he tortiously assumes. A third class consists of cases where, though there is no such intrusion or voluntary assumption of protectorship in the first instance, the dominant party utilizes and trades on his knowledge of the servient party's infirmities of mind, character, will, judgment, or otherwise, or his extreme youth and senility,—a knowledge acquired by long personal attendance, in the case of a servant (c), or long personal intimacy,

quitted his profession for the express purpose of constituting himself the adviser and assistant of a lady in certain matters, and manager of her affairs which fact alone— p 728—was held to be "singular and suspicious" enough to raise a presumption against him He obtained from the lady gifts and champertous agreements), *Baker* v. *Louder* (1873), L R 16 Eq 49 (where the dominant party thrust himself upon an old lady who had suddenly come into a large property, and made himself manager of her affairs : no advice, &c.); *Morley* v *Loughnan*, [1893] 1 Ch. 736 (which was treated by WRIGHT, J , separately from both points of view, first, as a case of spiritual influence, at pp 751, 752, and, then, as a case of the class now under discussion, at pp 752-757. A "Plymouth brother" in this case had taken advantage of the religious monomania and epileptic morbidity of a wealthy man to despoil him of sums in the shape of gifts, which amounted ultimately to £140,000 He "took absolute possession of" the servient party's mind, will, and life, and constituted himself, to the careful exclusion of all others, his sole manager, secretary, banker, doctor, and adviser), *Rees* v *Bernardy*, [1896] 2 Ch 437 (where a next-of-kin agent, having ascertained that two women were the co-heiresses at law of a wealthy intestate, forced his attention upon them, and procured for them an agreement to make over to him a moiety of what might be recovered, and a charge on the property The women were, though not in actual distress, in humble circumstances, and illiterate, and generally helpless The defendant never disclosed to them certain most material facts as to the real value of the property. The women had no independent advice, though the defendant had made a show of offering to procure it,—a perfectly illusory offer, since they had not the means of paying for it, as the defendant well knew The transaction was hurried through All these were considered abundantly sufficient "circumstances and conditions" to raise the presumption *per* ROMER, J , at pp 443-445), *Curtis* v *Bottomley* (1911), "Times," 1 Aug , C A (which was an action for fraudulent misrepresentation, but which MOULTON and BUCKLEY, LL JJ ,in the Court of Appeal, treated as what it ought to have been, an action for abuse of influence or confidence created by the defendant's proffers of friendship and assistance to one who had lost money by his association with the former's past speculations and schemes Having obtruded himself upon the plaintiff's notice, in the guise and under the profession of a sincere friend and adviser anxious to recoup the losses of "one of my oldest and best supporters," the defendant proceeded to build up a dominating influence over him, and obtain his financial support to fresh schemes as disastrous as the former, without disclosing to him their real perils, or that his object in putting them before him was, not to get back his losses for him, but to enrich himself at his expense)

(c) As in *Osmond* v *Fitzroy* (1731), 3 P. Wms 129 (where a servant engaged by the parents of a lad of seventeen to attend the latter on his travels, and " to prevent his being imposed upon "—the youth was of weak capacity and character—obtained an ascendancy over him in the course of ten years which was strong enough to extract from him a bond for £1000, whereby, instead of "preventing his being imposed upon" by others, or concurrently with such prevention, which was in his own interests, the servant "himself imposed upon him". *per* Lord COWPER, L C , at p 130), *Bridgeman* v *Green* (1757), Wilmot's Opinions and Judgments, 58, *per* WILMOT, C J , and other Lords Commissioners of the Great Seal, affirming the decision of Lord HARDWICKE, L C , (1755) 2 Ves Sr 626 (where a footman and valet acquired sufficient ascendancy over his master to obtain from him, first, a conveyance of land, and then a gift of a large sum of money raised on a mortgage of it) in the case of a friend (d). Or the unconscientious advantage may be taken by a moneylender in his transactions with the borrower (e), or by a mortgagee in his dealings with the mortgagor (f), when there are other " conditions and circumstances " present ; for neither of these relations, apart from statute (g), of itself gives .ise to any presumption of influence. In another type of case, the parties stand to one another in a relation which, though not one of the " suspected " domestic relations, and, therefore, not *per se* capable of raising any presumption against the dominant party, is yet an important factor, amongst other " circumstances and conditions," in determining whether a presumption of influence should be made in the particular case : as, for instance, where a husband takes unfair advantage of his wife's conjugal devotion and submissiveness (h), or a wife, of her husband's weakness and

(d) As in *Bennett* v *Vade* (1742), 2 Atk. 324 (weakness, amounting almost to idiocy, on the one side, and, on the other, non disclosure of the effect of a deed of gift of land, and of the distinction between a deed and a will, as to revocability ; and omission even to read over to the servient party the instrument, either when in draft, or when engrossed *per* Lord HARDWICKE, L C., at pp. 325–327) ; *Purcell* v. *M'Namara* (1807), 14 Ves. 90A (a case of conveyances and assurances obtained from a foolish and illiterate woman by one on whom she absolutely depended for advice in the management of her affairs, having no other friend or relation in the world to whom she could look for protection *per* GRANT, M.R , at p 108. No disclosure was made, or advice given, as to the effect of the deeds, which contained false recitals, and terms and covenants of such an outrageous character,— see pp. 109–120,—as, of themselves, to raise the presumption of " undue influence exerted to obtain from these unprotected women that which the defendant had no right to demand, and they had no rational motive to give ". p 115), *Griffiths* v *Robins* (1818), 3 Madd 191 (*per* LEACH, V -C , at p. 192 . " it appears that Mary Morris "—the servient party—" was upwards of 84 years of age , and at the period in question blind, or nearly so, and altogether dependent on the kindness and assistance of others . She had entire trust and confidence in them,"—the dominant parties,—" and it may be stated that they were the persons upon whose kindness and assistance she depended. They stood therefore in a relation to her which so much exposed her to their influence that they can maintain no deed of gift from her unless they can establish that it was the result of her own free will, and effected by the intervention of some indifferent person " and, later, he concludes that " the defendants have not made out that case which the policy of this Court requires from persons standing in *that relation to the donor in which they had placed themselves* ") , *Cavendish* v *Strutt* (1903), 19 T. L R. 483 (the case of a voluntary settlement made by a young man of great expectations, prodigal, self indulgent, and easily led, though obstinate at times, in favour of a person with whom he lived as a sort of boarder, and between whom and himself a great intimacy had grown up, and who attended to all his business affairs, opened and suggested or wrote answers to his letters, and advised him as to his investments *per* BYRNE, J , at pp 484, 485. No independent advice,—pp 485, 487, 489,—and no explanation of the legal effect of the instrument,—pp 488, 489)

(e) As in *Crowe* v *Ballard* (1790), 1 Ves Jr 215, *Houley* v *Cook* (1873), Ir R 8 Eq 370 , *Nevill* v *Snelling* (1880), 15 C D 679 (oppressive and extortionate terms exacted from a youth transaction not explained, &c), *Raja Maneshar Bakhsh* v *Shadi Lal* (1909), 25 T L R 635 (oppressive terms and absence of independent advice, held to constitute circumstances in which the lender " was in a position to dominate the will " of the borrower, who was necessitous and improvident), *Harris* v *Clarson* (1910), 27 T. L R 30 (unexplained clauses as to interest in a contract with a moneylender who, being in a position of domination and superiority, was held by CHANNELL, J , bound to give such explanation to the borrower), *J King, Ltd* v *Hay Currie* (1911), 28 T L R 10 (where the rule was recognized, but the lender discharged the onus here), *Stirling* v *Rose* (1913), 30 T L R 67 (*per* AVORY, J) , *Lewis* v *Mills* (1914), 30 T L R 438

(f) See Sub s (7), § 448, *post*, as to the extent to which the relation of mortgagor and mortgagee may, with other circumstances, give rise to a presumption of undue influence

(g) See § 508, *post*

(h) The relation of husband and wife is not one of the parental or quasi-parental relations which of themselves raise the presumption of influence see § 446, *post*. But it is

docility, or where other family influences, not being either parental or quasi-parental, are unconscientiously used (*i*). It happens sometimes that there are two co-existing relations between the parties, one being of the nature now under discussion, and the other being one of the " professional influence " relations, such as the legal (*j*), spiritual (*k*), or medical (*l*), or one of the " confidence "

a circumstance which, *with others*, may constitute " circumstances and conditions " of the kind now being considered, as it did in *Turnbull & Co* v *Dural*, [1902] A C 429, P C (see p 234 " it "—*i e* the transaction impeached, which was a security given by a married woman to her husband's creditors—" is open to the double objection of having been obtained by a trustee from the *cestui que trust* by pressure through her husband, and without independent advice, and of having been obtained by a husband from his wife by pressure and concealment of material facts "), *Chaplin & Co* v *Brammall*, [1908] 1 K B 223, C. A. (a similar case · *per* VAUGHAN WILLIAMS, L J , at p 237), *Bank of Montreal* v *Stuart*, [1911] A. C 120, P C (the like see p 137 " overpowering influence,"—" the transaction immoderate and irrational,"—" unfair advantage of Mrs Stuart's confidence in her husband was taken by Mr Stuart, and also, it must be added, by Mr. Bruce," the solicitor to the bank, who were the husband's creditors, and to whom —p 138— " the bank left everything ")

(*i*) As to the influence of wife over husband, see *Groves* v. *Perkins* (1834), 6 Sim 576 (coupled with concealment of material facts as to value, distress and ignorance of the husband, and absence of independent advice), *Procter* v *Robinson* (1867), 15 L. T. 431 (coupled with pressure, and absence of independent advice, and no explanation of rights *per* TURNER, L J , at pp 431, 432, and CAIRNS, L J , at pp 432, 433) Examples of other such influences are ·—the influence of elder sister over younger, coupled with absence of proper protection and advice, as in *Harvey* v. *Mount* (1845), 8 Beav 439 (*per* ROMILLY, M R , at p 452 *quære*, however, whether the decision did not go too far, and whether it was not founded on the view always entertained by ROMILLY, M R , but now quite exploded—see § 451, *note* (*c*), *post*—that *all* gifts require to be " sustained "), the influence of younger brothers over the eldest, coupled with pecuniary pressure on the one side, and advantage taken on the other, no fair disclosure, no independent advice, and inadequate value, as in *Sturge* v *Sturge* (1849), 12 Beav 229 , and, lastly, the influence of a family generally over one of its members, coupled with undue advantage taken of his gross ignorance, dissolute habits and weakness of character, want of professional advice, and false recitals in the deed itself, as in *Dunnage* v. *White* (1818), 1 Swanst 137 (*per* PLUMER, M R , at pp 150, 151, who also, at pp 151, 152, disposes of the rather impudent suggestion that this was a family arrangement) As will hereafter be pointed out (see § 446, *post*), none of the above relations are *per se* quasi-parental relations, and it was so recognized in the cases themselves As to the protection given by British Indian law to a " parda nishin " woman under the influence of her " mukhtar " (or man of business and general manager of her affairs), particularly when illiterate, and estranged from her natural advisers, or living with the mukhtar, see *Tewarry* v *Nawab Syed Hossein Khan* (1874), L R 1 Ind App 192 ; *Sudisht Lal* v *Mussummat Sheobarat Kunwar* (1881), L. R. 8 Ind. App 39 , *Shambati Koeri* v *Jago Bibi* (1902), L R 29 Ind App 127 , *Sajjad Husain* v *Wazir Ali Khan* (1902), 39 Ind. App 156 ; *Kali Bakhsh Singh* v *Ram Gopal Singh* (1913), 30 T. L R. 138, P C

(*j*) Thus in *Revett* v *Harvey* (1823), 1 Sim. & St. 502, the dominant party, who was a solicitor, gave legal advice, as well as financial assistance, to the young man whom he professed to befriend . in *Rhodes* v *Bate* (1866), 1 Ch App 252, one of the defendants, Bate, was a certificated conveyancer, and the plaintiff's professional adviser , in *Procter* v *Robinson*, *sup* , one of the defendants was not only solicitor to the wife, who obtained from her husband the gratuitous settlement in question, but, as the Lords Justices held, though not apparently ROMILLY, M R , in the Court below, solicitor to the husband also *per* TURNER, L.J , at pp 431, 432, and CAIRNS, L.J , at pp 432, 433). All the above cases are accordingly cited in Sub-s (2), *ante*, as well as in this Sub section.

(*k*) As in *Morley* v. *Loughnan*, [1893] 1 Ch. 736, where, as stated in note (*b*), *ante*, WRIGHT, J , decided in favour of the plaintiff on both grounds separately This case accordingly find a place also in the notes to Sub s. (3), *ante*.

(*l*) As in *Gibson* v *Russell* (1843), 2 Y & C. 104 ; *Ahearne* v. *Hogan* (1844), Dru. 310 Both these cases are dealt with in the notes to Sub s (4), *ante* See also *Allen* v *Davis* (1850), 20 L J (CH) 44 (the case of a dentist)

relations, such as that of trusteeship (m), or agency (n), in which cases the two are often separately considered and adjudicated upon, and the decision against the dominant party is based upon each relation, independently of the other   Occasionally imbecility is the sole "weakness" of the servient party of which unconscientious advantage is shown to have been taken (o); or the "weakness" of the servient party may have been, not constitutional, but temporary, if it was created by the pressure, importunity, or imposition of the dominant party at the critical time, or consisted in the servient party being "rushed" or hurried into the transaction, without any opportunity for deliberation or for taking counsel of his friends (p)   But whichever of these various forms the "circumstances and conditions" may assume, they must go to show each of the three prerequisites to the establishment of the relation, viz. (1) weakness or disability of "mind, body, or estate" on the one side, (2) advantage taken of that weakness or disability on the other side in the transaction impeached, and (3) the use of unfair or unconscientious means to procure that advantage

430. There are certain extreme cases where *res ipsa loquitur*, and the necessary "circumstances and conditions" are established by a mere reference to the enormity of the transaction itself (q), the provisions and contents of

(m) As in *Grosvenor* v *Sherratt* (1860), 28 Beav. 659 (where the dominant party was also executor of the will under which the servient party derived an interest, and acted as trustee for her, besides being a person on whom in fact she was absolutely dependent for advice and protection. This was a case of a purchase at an undervalue, made with no advice, or disclosure)

(n) See *Dally* v *Wenham* (1863), 33 Beav 154 (where the dominant party was agent and receiver for the servient party, though ROMILLY, M R , did not put it as a principal and agent case   there was non communication of special knowledge as to the property purchased, and undervalue)

(o) See *Willan* v *Willan* (1814), 2 Dow H L 274 (advantage taken of an uncle's bodily and mental imbecility: no independent advice, pressure, &c), *Longmate* v *Ledger* (1860), 2 Giff 157 (purchase of cottages and land, at an undervalue, from an old farm labourer, a "strange and eccentric creature" who "though not absolutely incompetent or incapable, was in such need of protection that whoever entered into any contract with him would be bound to show that no unfair advantage had been taken of his weakness, and that a fair price was given to him", neither of which was held to have been proved   per STUART, V -C , at pp 164, 165)   We learn from p 402 of *Clarke* v *Malpas* (1862), 4 De G F & J 401, that *Longmate* v *Ledger* was affirmed in the H L.

(p) This was an important element in the "circumstances and conditions" which raised the presumption of undue influence in *Evans* v *Llewellin* (1787), 1 Cox 333 (*per* Lord KENYON, M R , at p 339 . "I lay great stress upon the situation of the parties to it" —an agreement for sale at an inadequate price—"and the persons who compose the drama   The plaintiff Thomas in mean circumstances, and totally ignorant of his rights until the moment of the transaction taking place"   not permitted to consult his friends, and "undue advantage taken of his situation"), *Willan* v *Willan, sup* , *Ahearne* v *Hogan*, cited in note (*l*), *sup* , *Addis* v *Campbell* (1841), 4 Beav 401 (where there was actual imposition and pressure, and no independent advice), *Clarke* v *Malpas, sup.* (where the transaction, a purchase of cottages from a poor, old, and illiterate man, was rushed through without giving him any time for deliberation, or obtaining advice, at an inadequate price · *per* KNIGHT-BRUCE, L J , at pp 403–405), *Procter* v *Robinson* (1866), 35 Beav 329 (*per* ROMILLY, M.R , at pp 332–335), affd (1867), 15 L T 431, *Lewis* v *Mills* (1914), 30 T L R 438 (moneylender's device to prevent discussion of terms and investigation of methods)

(q) Lord HARDWICKE, L.C , at p 155 of *Chesterfield (Earl of)* v *Janssen* (1751), 2 Ves Sr. 125, mentions, as his second head of fraud, that which is "apparent from the intrinsic nature and subject of the bargain itself, such as no man in his senses and not under delusion would make on the one hand, and as no honest and fair man would accept on the other; which are inequitable and unconscientious bargains"   Illustrations of such

which may be so extravagant and oppressive *ex facie* as to raise a presumption at once against the dominant party, without inquiring further. It is also a material element in the consideration of the question whether such a presumption should be made, that the instrument embodying the transaction contained, if such be the fact, false recitals or statements of its consideration, or its object and effect, inserted by the dominant party ; such misrepresentations being regarded as betraying a consciousness on the part of the dominant party that the transaction was unrighteous, and could not be justified, if challenged, unless made by these means to appear other than in fact it was, and so amounting to an attempt to mislead not only the servient party into making the gift or contract, but the Court into upholding it, if a judicial investigation should afterwards be demanded (r). Another important consideration in this class of case is the fact, if it be so shown, that the dominant party by misrepresentation, calumny, or other active measures, endeavoured (whether successfully or not) to detach the servient party from his natural protectors or advisers, or prevent his access to the relations, friends, or agents (professional or mercantile) to whom he had always previously resorted for guidance and counsel (s)

431. In certain cases it is shown that two persons, though in different ways, derived advantage from the transaction : in that event, if each used unconscientious means to obtain the advantage, or if one of them induced, or knowingly left, the other to exert his influence over the servient party, the presumption is made against each (t)

432. In all the instances—they are extremely few—in which the *primâ facie* case made by the servient party was repelled by proof on behalf of the

---

"bargains" are   *Purcell* v *McNamara*—see the citation from this case in note (d) to § 429, ante , *Dunnage* v *White* (1818), 1 Swanst 137 (per PLUMER, M R , at pp 150, 151), *MacCabe* v *Hussey* (1831), 5 Bligh (N S) 715 (at p 729) , *Ahearne* v *Hogan* (1840), Dru 310 (per SUGDEN, L C (Ir), at p 326 , "the deed itself shows that the transaction was an improper one")

(r) As in *Bridgeman* v *Green* (1757), Wilm Opns & Judgts , 58 (fictitious consideration stated in the deed) , *Purcell* v *McNamara*, cited in note (d) to § 429, ante (false recitals) , *Dunnage* v *White*, sup (per PLUMER, M R , at pp 150, 151 · false recitals and misleading statements) , *Ahearne* v *Hogan*, sup (where SUGDEN, L C (Ir), after noticing, at pp 323-326, the various false recitals in the deed which showed the dominant party's consciousness of his liability to the equitable doctrine unless he could put an appearance upon the transaction which would take it outside the rule, states emphatically, at p 326 . " in any case which may come before me   in which one party may exercise influence over the other, . .   whenever there is a dealing between two parties, one of whom is subject to the influence of the other, I shall expect to find a fair and correct statement of the transaction upon the face of the deed itself ").

(s) See *Twisleton* v *Griffiths* (1716), 1 P Wms. 309 (where the purchaser of the reversion dissuaded the vendor from selling it to his father), *Osmond* v *Fitzroy* (1731), 3 P Wms. 129 (where " the secreting of the bond from the parents " was held to be " a further evidence of fraud " · per JEKYLL, M R , at p 131) , *Bridgeman* v *Green*, sup (where the valet induced his master to separate from his wife) , *Huguenin* v *Baseley* (1807), 14 Ves. 273 (where the dominant party induced the lady to get rid of her solicitors, and employ his own, by false aspersions on their skill and competence) , *MacCabe* v *Hussey* (1831), 5 Bligh (N. S) 715 (where the dominant party misrepresented and aspersed the conduct of the servient party's son, see p 728); *Middleton* v *Sherburne* (1841), 4 Y & C (Exch in Eq) 358 (where the dominant party induced the servient party to expel his nieces from his house).

(t) As in the cases cited in note (h) to § 429, ante, and also in *Procter* v *Robinson* (1807), 15 L. T. 431 (where the solicitor, as well as the wife, influenced the husband)

dominant party that, " in point of fact," the transaction was " fair, just and reasonable," the latter has been held entitled to judgment (*u*).

433. Further, any other of the defences available to a dominant party in the case of the " suspected " relations, is of course equally open to a dominant party in the present type of relation, such as " confirmation," or " family arrangement " Of the raising of the latter plea there is one example, though the attempt—a rather ludicrous one under the circumstances of the case—wholly failed (*v*)

Sub s (6) *The Relation between an " Expectant " and a Person dealing with him in respect of his Expectancy.*

434. It has from the earliest times been established that any unconscionable dealing with an " expectant heir," or a reversioner, for the purchase of, or otherwise in relation to, his expectancy or reversionary interest, gives rise to a presumption against the person so dealing which, unless repelled by affirmative evidence of the propriety of the transaction in all respects, will entitle the expectant heir, or reversioner, to relief As so stated, the rule governing this type of case would seem to be the source as that which governs any other relation constituted by the particular " circumstances and conditions " , but, inasmuch as the rule has been applied in a special manner, as will be seen presently, to bargains with expectant heirs (*w*), and such application has been based on a special theory of its own (*x*), and has further been the subject of special statutory modification (*y*), it has been thought proper to consider this type of case separately, and to assign to it in this commentary the same exceptional position which has been assigned to it in successive judicial expositions for there can be no doubt that, whether the description be correct or not (*z*), and whether, assuming it to be correct, there is any rational justification for the doctrine or not (*a*), the Courts

(*u*) As it was in *Kingsland (Viscount)* v *Barnewall* (1706), 4 Brown P C. 154 , *Pratt* v *Barker* (1826), 1 Sim 1 , *Nicol* v *Vaughan* (1833), 1 Cl & Fin 495 , *Hunter* v *Atkins* (1834), 3 My & K 113 , *Re Coomber,* [1911] 1 Ch 723, C A. , *J King, Ltd* v *Hay Currie* (1911), 28 T L. R 10

(*v*) *Dunnage* v *White* (1818), 1 Swanst 137 See the citation in note (*i*), to § 429, *ante* For an instance of a successful plea of confirmation, see *Cole* v *Gibbons* (1734), 3 P. Wms 290 (*per* Lord TALBOT, L C , at p 293)

(*w*) So DENMAN, J , seems to have considered, judging from his observations at pp 702, 703 of *Nevill* v *Snelling* (1880), 15 C D 679 (" the real question in every case seems to me to be the same as that which arose in the case of expectant heirs and reversioners *before the special doctrine in their favour was established* ")

(*x*) See § 435, *post.*

(*y*) See § 437, *post.*

(*z*) In the same way, and, perhaps, with no more justification, the Courts have persistently described a surety as " a favoured debtor," and a prisoner as entitled to " the benefit of the doubt " All these are extremely unfortunate phrases jurisprudence does not distribute " favours " or " benefits " , it enforces and secures " rights " It is not of grace and favour that the surety is held not liable on a contract that he never made, or that the accused is held not guilty of that which has not been proved against him And so, it may be argued, an " expectant " is not, or at all events ought not to be, set apart from or placed above, any other servient party of whose weakness unconscientious advantage has been taken

(*a*) As to this, see § 435, *post*

have in fact expressly described expectant heirs, and reversioners, as the objects of their peculiar favour (b).

435. The doctrine as to "catching" or "unconscionable" bargains with "expectants" has, in the two leading cases on the subject, been stated by Lord HARDWICKE, L.C (c), and Lord SELBORNE, L C. (d), in language which (save for the necessary substitution of specific terms for general) is identical with that used in stating the general proposition applicable to all relations constituted by "the circumstances and conditions of the parties contracting" (e)   That is to say · given the "expectancy," the "expectant," the dealer, the "bargain" between the parties relative to the expectancy, and circumstances and conditions indicating an unfair and unconscientious advantage taken by the dealer of the expectant's distress, a *primâ facie* presumption is raised against the dealer which will entitle the expectant to relief, unless the dealer can rebut the presumption by establishing that in point of fact the bargain was, in Lord SELBORNE's phrase, "fair, just, and reasonable." The theoretical foundation of the proposition is, broadly speaking, the same "public policy," in the proper sense of the word (f), on which the whole doctrine of abuse of influence is based   But, conscious, perhaps, of the need for a more detailed justification of their somewhat special and severe treatment of bargains with expectants, the equity judges of the eighteenth century, and particularly Lord HARDWICKE, were at great pains to point out the precise particulars in which public interests are served and safeguarded by that treatment.   In the first place, it was said that, in the exercise of its duty to suppress and mitigate the most prominent evils of the day, the Court is bound to use its best endeavours to restrain the follies, extravagances, and moral imbecility of one of the two classes of persons who become parties to these bargains, the rapacity, extortion, and fraud of the other, and the gambling in human lives which is the vice of both   Then, from the point of view of the "expectant," it was stated to be for his good, and indirectly for the good of the community, that he should not be "devoured," and, particularly, should not be prevented from resorting to the aid and advice of his natural guardians, protectors, and advisers, and so deprived of all chance of either financial relief on reasonable terms, or moral reformation   Again, the country is deeply concerned,—and this is the point on which Lord HARDWICKE laid special emphasis,—in the preservation

(b) As, for instance, in *Chesterfield (Earl of)* v *Jannsen* (1751), 2 Ves Sr 125 (*per* Lord HARDWICKE, L C, at pp 156, 157, where he describes the class of case in question as his "last head of fraud," separating it from his third "head," which is that dealt with in Sub-s (5), *ante*, but in such terms as to show no real difference between them) , *Gowland* v *De Faria* (1810), 17 Ves 20 (*per* GRANT, M R , at pp 24, 25) , *Bromley* v *Smith* (1859), 26 Beav 644 (*per* ROMILLY, M R , at p 662) , *Rae* v *Joyce* (1892), 29 L R (Ir), 500 (*per* FITZGIBBON, L J , (Ir) at p 523)   And note that this last case was after 1867, the date of the statute referred to in § 437, *post*, which deprived the "expectant" of the only privilege which he could be said to have ever enjoyed over other servient parties

(c) See the reference to *Chesterfield (Earl of)* v *Jannsen, sup* , in the last note

(d) At p 491 of *Aylesford (Earl of)* v *Morris* (1873), 8 Ch App 484

(e) For this proposition, see § 427, and § 429, *ante*

(f) Viz that which is ascribed to it by Lord HARDWICKE, L C , at p 156 of *Chesterfield (Earl of)* v. *Jannsen, sup*   The passage is cited in note (y) to § 646, *post*

of ancient family estates, which cannot be secured if the ancestor is allowed to be deceived and defrauded by these clandestine transactions. This last consideration may strike modern minds as a little extravagant and sentimental: the real injury to the ancestor, or other person from whom the future benefit is "expected," is now described in more prosaic and practical terms as consisting, not in the bargain being kept secret from him when it is made, but rather in the probability of its being traded on by the usurer, after being made, to extort payment from him under fear of exposure. All these several views, or combinations of them, have been expressed in the various expositions which from time to time have been given of the theoretical basis of the doctrine (g). But the substance which underlies the different

(g) Thus, in *Chesterfield (Earl of)* v *Janssen* (1751), 2 Ves Sr 125, Lord HARDWICKE, L.C (at p. 154), bases the doctrine, first, on the ground that "such bargains proceed from excessive prodigality on the one hand, and extortation on the other, which are *vitia temporis*, and pernicious in their consequences; and then it is the duty of the Court, if it can, to restrain them," and (at p 157) on the further, and distinct, ground to which he, and other judges of his time, obviously attached the greatest importance, that "in most of these cases have concurred deceit and illusion on other persons not privy to the fraudulent agreement the father, ancestor, or relation from whom comes the expectation of the estate, has been kept in the dark the heir or expectant has been kept from disclosing his circumstances, and resorting to them for advice, which might have tended to his relief and also reformation This misleads the ancestor, who has been seduced to leave his estates not to his heir or family, but to a set of artful persons who have divided the spoil beforehand." It is here that "public utility" comes in (see the passage, at p 156, which is cited in note (y) to § 646, *post*) Lord SELBORNE, L C, in *Aylesford (Earl of)* v *Morris* (1873), 8 Ch App 484, follows Lord HARDWICKE, L C, closely in his exposition of the three purposes for which relief is given, viz suppression of the *vitia temporis* on both sides; protection of the expectant against being cut off from all chance of relief or reformation at the hands of his natural advisers, and protection of the ancestor from fraud, and the family from ruin At p. 491, he speaks of the presumption which is made against "those who trade upon the follies and vices of unprotected youth, inexperience, and moral imbecility," whilst, at pp 491, 492, he points out that "the victim comes to the snare , excluded, and known to be excluded, by the very motives and circumstances which attract him, from the help and advice of his natural guardians and protectors, and from that professional aid which would be accessible to him, if he did not feel compelled to secrecy," and, at p 492, he notices, without expressing any disagreement with it, the view entertained by "great judges" of an earlier time that "there is a principle of public policy in restraining this, that this system of undermining and blasting, as it were, in the bud the futures of families, is a public as well as a private mischief, that it is a sort of indirect fraud upon the heads of families from whom these transactions are concealed" Cp *Cole* v *Gibbons* (1734), 3 P Wms 290, where Lord TALBOT L C, at p. 292, enlarges upon "the policy of the nation to prevent what was a growing mischief to ancient families, that of seducing an heir apparent from a dependence on his ancestor, which would probably have supported him, . this tended to the manifest ruin of families" In *Twisleton* v *Griffith* (1716), 1 P. Wms 309, Lord COWPER, L C, rests the doctrine on the duty of the Court "to discourage a growing practice of devouring an heir," and to the objection that "at this rate an heir without difficulty would not sell a reversion," replies that his inability to do so is exactly what the policy of the Court requires, for "this might force an heir to go home, and submit to his father, or to bite on the bridle, and endure some hardships, and in the meantime he might grow wiser, and be reclaimed" (p 312) In dealing with the less objectionable form of bargain, where the dealer is not a purchaser on obviously extortionate terms or a mortgagee of a reversion, but is gambling on the event, and stands to lose heavily, if the event goes against him, Lord HARDWICKE, L.C., at p 135 of *Burnardiston* v *Lingood* (1740), 2 Atk 133, says that, even in these cases, the relief is given "with the greatest justice in the world, *for the sake of the public*, to prevent people's gaming, as it were, to the prejudice and damage of young improvident persons, and the heads of families" Lastly, in *Nevill* v *Snelling* (1880), 15 C. D 679, if (which, however, seems doubtful) this case is to be regarded as an "expectancy" case, the circumstances were such that Lord HARDWICKE'S theory

forms in which the theory has been stated is, that it is for the benefit of society at large that a class of persons who, in the picturesque phraseology of Lord Thurlow, L.C., are in a state of constructive infancy (h), and on whom the circumstances of the cases impose a sort of *diminutio capitis*, should be protected against the depredations of those whom the misanthrope stigmatized as "bawds between gold and want," and equity judges, as "a set of artful persons who have divided the spoil beforehand," "those who trade upon the follies and vices of unprotected youth," or "common and professed annuity-mongers who deal in the distresses of mankind" (i). No one has put forward, as one of the elements in the "public utility" involved, the possible peril to the life of the ancestor which is, in some cases, the event on which the wager is to be won or lost, though in Roman law this was expressed to be the basis of the famous Senatus-consultum Macedonianum (j), and, in our own jurisprudence, was the avowed foundation of the statutes rendering life insurances without any insurable interest illegal and void. It should be observed here that, with reference to dealings in reversions, as distinct from expectancies in the strict sense of the word, grave doubts, notwithstanding the contrary opinion of Lord Cowper (k), may well be entertained, and in fact have on more than one occasion been judicially expressed (l), as to whether there is any reason in public policy for the special doctrine, or for its specially rigorous application to the cases in question, and whether, on the contrary, both public policy and private justice do not tend in the opposite direction Nothing is more certain than that restrictive rules, whether judicial or legislative, which are directed against a particular class of the community, merely aggravate the oppression which they are intended to curb, for the extortioner is driven to add to the burden which he has

---

of the fraud practised on the ancestor could have no application, but DENMAN, J., rested his decision on a ground which may seem more sound, and less fanciful, to modern minds, viz the duty of the Court to protect the ancestor, not from concealment in the beginning, but from being forced to pay by fear, or under threats, of exposure afterwards (see pp 687, 694, 695, 704)

(h) At p 9 of *Gwynne* v *Heaton* (1778), 1 Brown C C 1 ("there is a policy in justice, protecting the person who has the expectancy, and *reducing him to the situation of an infant*, against the effects of his own conduct")

(i) The expressions used by Lord HARDWICKE, L C, and Lord SELBORNE, L C, in the citations from their judgments contained in note (g), sup, and by Lord THURLOW, L C., at p 324 of *Fox* v *Mackreth* (1788), 2 Cox 320, respectively.

(j) This S C is discussed, together with the various judicial references to it, in App C, §§ 685, 698, post!

(k) Cited in note (g), sup

(l) As in *Davis* v *Duke of Marlborough* (1818), 2 Swanst 108 (per Lord ELDON, L C, at p 139 "in many cases those who have obtained relief from their annuities have really taken as much advantage of the annuitants as those annuitants have taken of them "), *Shelly* v *Nash* (1818), 3 Madd 232 (per LEACH, V -C, at p 236 "the principle and the policy of the rule may be both equally questionable "), *Wood* v *Abrey* (1818), 3 Madd 417 (per LEACH, V -C, again, at p 422 "the policy of this rule, *as to reversions*, may be well doubted, and if the cases were looked into, it might be found that the rule was only originally referred to expectant heirs, and not to reversioners,"—which is a correct surmise as to the application, but not as to the expression, of the rule—see note (t) to § 438, post), *Aldborough (Earl of)* v *Trye* (1840), 7 Cl & Fin 436 (per Lord COTTENHAM, L C, at p 457), *Judd* v. *Green* (1875), 45 L J (CH.) 108 (per BACON, V C, at p 109).

already laid on his victim a further load sufficient to cover the extra risk (m). The tooth of usury, says BACON, must be "grinded, that it bite not too much": but the action of the legislative, if not of the judicial, grindstone has usually been to sharpen, and not to blunt, the tooth of usury.

436. The history of the doctrine dates from very early times. The jurisdiction was exercised as far back as the days of the Star Chamber (n), that great censorian court of criminal equity, as it has been styled, the special function of which was to deal with powerful offenders not easily reached, or not adequately punishable, by the ordinary process of the Courts. It has, from time to time, been contended (quite unsuccessfully in the one case, and with only partial success in the other) that this ancient jurisdiction has been twice invaded or curtailed by the legislature, first in 1854, and again in 1867. In the former year, the Usury Laws Repeal Act, 1854 (o), was passed; and it was thereupon argued, in a series of cases, that this statute set the dealer in expectancies free to make any bargains on any extortionate terms he pleased, without interference by the Courts. This argument could only succeed on the hypothesis that the sole rule of law which ever enabled the Court to lay its restraining hand on the dealer was the rule contained in the repealed statutes against usury. On the hypothesis being, as it was in all the cases referred to (p), condemned as a sheer fallacy, the argument necessarily fell with it. There had always existed the ancient doctrine of equity, large and general in scope and flexible in nature, which at a later stage was to a certain extent assisted by the more specific, defined, and rigid provisions of the usury statutes, giving an entirely independent and concurrent, and in some cases a more summary and effectual, remedy. The only effect of the abolition of this partial and ancillary remedy was to leave the more ancient and comprehensive jurisdiction exactly as it had originally stood. so far from diminishing the need for its exercise, the Act of 1854 imposed upon the Courts the duty of enforcing it with greater vigilance than ever.

437. The second of the statutes referred to is the Sales of Reversions

(m) This is acknowledged by ROMILLY, M R, at p 665 of *Bromley v Smith* (1859), 26 Beav 644, but he says that it cannot be helped. The same result has attended the attempts of the legislature to curb the usurer, such as the Bills of Sale Acts, and the Moneylenders Acts

(n) As we are reminded by Lord NOTTINGHAM, L C, in *Berney v Pitt* (1680), 2 Swanst. 143 n ("the Star Chamber used to punish it, and the Court did always relieve against it")

(o) 17 & 18 Vict c 90

(p) *Croft v Graham* (1863), 2 De G J & S 155 (*per* TURNER, L J, at p 161), *Tyler v Yates* (1871), 6 Ch App 665 (*per* Lord HATHERLY, L C, at pp 668, 669), *Aylesford (Earl of) v Morris* (1873), 8 Ch. App 484 (*per* Lord SELBORNE, L C, at p. 490); *Benyon v Cook* (1875), 10 Ch App 389 (*per* JESSEL, M R, at pp 391, 392), *Nevill v Snelling* (1880), 15 C. D 679 (*per* DENMAN, J, at pp 697, 698), *Rae v Joyce* (1892), 29 L R (Ir) 500 (*per* WALKER, L.C (Ir), at pp 514, 515, and FITZGIBBON, L.J, (Ir) at pp. 524, 525) In *Chesterfield (Earl of) v Jannsen* (1751), 2 Ves Sr 125, Lord HARDWICKL, L C, speaking of "the acts of parliament instanced," which were the Usury Acts then in force, says (at p 158) "that they will be found to be made (many of them) not for want of power in this Court to give relief in many of these contracts, but to make them void in law, to give the party a short remedy against them" Accordingly, when this short remedy was abolished, "from that moment," says STUART, V-C, at p 795 of *Barrett v Hartley* (1866), L. R 2 Eq 789, "the jurisdiction of the Court which prevailed independently of the usury laws was likely to be called into active operation," and "to a greater extent than formerly" And to the same effect, KAY, J, at pp. 459, 460 of *James v Kerr* (1888), 40 C. D 449

Act, 1867 (*q*), by s. 1 of which it is enacted that " no purchase, made *bonâ fide* and without fraud or unfair dealing, of any reversionary interest in real or personal estate, shall hereafter be opened or set aside merely on the ground of undervalue," and, by s. 2, that " the word purchase shall include every kind of contract, conveyance, or assignment, under or by which any beneficial interest in property may be acquired " These provisions undoubtedly effected a change in the law, to the extent of abolishing an extravagant sub-rule which had grown out of the doctrine, and so removing what was after all only an unhealthy excrescence, but they did not in the slightest degree repeal the doctrine itself, and all the arguments to this effect which have been persistently advanced since the passing of the Act have invariably failed (*r*)

438. It so happened that the first class of persons who invoked the juris-diction, and to whom the doctrine was therefore first applied, are heirs, apparent or presumptive (*s*) : whereupon, in a manner very characteristic of English terminological habits, the doctrine took its title from the earliest subject of the experiment, instead of from its governing principle, with the result that, for a time, it was thought inapplicable to any transactions except " bargains with expectant heirs," that is to say, bargains with those who, whatever the description of heirdom might be, were "heirs" in the strict legal sense of the word (*t*)   This limitation, however, was soon pronounced to be unwarranted by the principle and reason of the rule, which equally applies to remainderman or reversioner, whatever the exact nature and extent of the remainder or reversionary interest may be, and, indeed, to any person who has any sort of expectation of deriving benefit from the death of an ancestor or relative, whether that expectation is based on the express provisions of any instrument, or on the law of descent, or is merely an expectation in the popular, and not the legal, sense of the term   As soon as these successive applications of the doctrine were made, as they were

(*q*) 31 Vict c. 4.

(*r*) See *Tyler* v. *Yates, sup.* (*per* Lord HATHERLEY, L C , at pp 668, 669) , *Aylesford (Earl of)* v *Morris, sup* (*per* Lord SELBORNE, L C , at p 490) , *Fry* v *I ane* (1880), 40 C. D 312 (*per* KAY, J , at p 321) , *Rae* v *Joyce, sup.* (*per* WALKER, L.C. (Ir), at pp 515–517) As to the exact nature and extent of the alteration in the law which really was effected by the statute, see § 442, *post*

(*s*) As, for instance, in *Berney* v *Pitt* (1680), 2 Swanst. 143 n , where the expectant promised to pay the moneylenders " five to one," if he survived his father , *Wiseman* v *Beake* (1690), 2 Vern 121, where the expectant bargained to pay the dealer " ten for one" upon the death of his uncle, a tenant for life of real estate, in the event of the uncle dying without issue before the expectant , *Chesterfield (Earl of)* v *Janssen* (1751), 2 Ves Sr 125, where John Spencer, having an expectation of a great increase of fortune on the death of his grandmother, the Duchess of Marlborough—" she was a good old life, and he but a bad young one "—agreed, in consideration of a loan of £5000, to pay the dealer £10,000 on the death of the Duchess, but nothing if he predeceased her (p 124)

(*t*) Thus in *Cole* v *Gibbons* (1734), 3 P Wms. 290, Lord TALBOT, L C , at pp 292, 293, declined to apply the doctrine to the case of one who was not an heir, apparent or presumptive, but a reversioner only, and held that the case fell within the ordinary rules of the Court, as described in Sub s (5), *ante*   A few years later, Lord HARDWICKE, L.C , in *Freeman* v *Bishop* (1740), 2 Atk 39, pointed out that it is immaterial whether the expectancy comes to the expectant " as heir to his father, or by descent, or from any other relation," and, later still (see the next note), he expressly included reversioners in a variety of authorities (*u*), it became obvious how ridiculously incomplete is the title—which, however, still survives—"catching or unconscionable bargains with expectant heirs," inasmuch as reversioners and remaindermen, who are certainly not expectant heirs, and, indeed, are strictly the very antithesis of them, are undoubtedly within the doctrine, the feature which lies at the root of that doctrine, viz the fact that the subject of the bargain is not a possession, but a chance, a hope, or an expectation of possession in the future, being common to both classes of case. This discrepancy between the label and the thing supposed to be designated by it has been noticed by JESSEL, M R., in the course of an exhaustive definition of the persons to whom the special protection of the Court is extended, as (1) any one who has a remainder, vested or contingent, (2) any reversioner; (3) " every one who has the hope of succession to property of an ancestor, . . by reason of his being the heir apparent or presumptive ", and (4) every one who has the like hope " by reason merely of the expectation of a devise or legacy on account of the supposed or presumed affection of the ancestor or relative " (*v*). But the existence of this *spes successionis*, of whatever kind that *spes* may be, though sufficient, is at the same time necessary, to justify the application of the special doctrine   If the element of futurity and contingency is wanting, that is, if the property in question is in possession, the alleged " expectant " is no " expectant " at all, and his rights are regulated and determined by the same considerations as the rights of any other servient party claiming to be such in virtue of the " circumstances and conditions " of the case (*w*). It will be noticed that the terms " expectant " and " expectancy " have been, and they will continue to be, used in this discussion as generic terms to include all the species enumerated in the above classification, for which use there is some warrant in the language of Lord HARDWICKE (*x*), and others.

439. The doctrine is said to be applicable to any unconscionable bargain with an expectant "with respect to," or "relative to," his expectancy. The expressions " with respect to," and " relative to," which are used in several of the authorities, are of a designed generality   They are wide enough, as has been held, to include not only the common case of a purchase or mortgage of, or charge on, an expectancy, but also the following :—an advance which the dealer in fact makes to the expectant on the credit or faith of his expectancy, though there may be nothing which is, or perhaps can be,

---

(*u*) For instance, the expectant who obtained relief was a remainder-man in *Barnard-iston* v *Lingood* (1740), 2 Atk 133, and in *Aylesford* (*Earl of*) v *Morris* (1873), 8 Ch App 484   He was a reversioner in *Gwynne* v *Heaton* (1778), 1 Brown C C. 1, in *Nesbitt* v *Berridge* (1863), 32 Beav 282, in *Benyon* v *Cook* (1875), 10 Ch App 389 n., and, generally, in the great majority of the more modern cases   Even as early as the date of *Chesterfield* (*Earl of*) v *Jannsen* (1751), 2 Ves Sr. 125, though that was not a reversioner's case, Lord HARDWICKE, L.C, includes " reversioners " as subjects of the relief (at p 156 " catching bargains with heirs, reversioners, or expectants ").

(*v*) At p 391 n of *Benyon* v *Cook* (1875), 10 Ch App 389 n.

(*w*) See § 440, and notes (*d*) and (*e*) thereto, *post*.

(*x*) See the citation in note (*u*), *sup*   By the expression " heirs, reversioners, or expectants " it was obviously meant, first, to name the two most important, and mutually exclusive, species, and then to conclude with a reference to the genus " expectants," which comprehends these, and other, species "

the subject of an instrument of charge (y), and whether "it is said so, or not " (z) , a transaction which is nothing but a wager on survivorship (a) , and even a series of sales of goods (sufficient to indicate a practice) by the dealer to the expectant at exorbitant prices, on the (though unexpressed and unavowed) faith of the expectancy (b).

440. To bring himself within the principle and (if it be so) the privilege of the doctrine, the burden is on the servient party to establish that he was an " expectant," within the meaning of that term above stated (c), at the time of the bargain If the property in question was not in reversion, or " expected," but in possession, he must succeed, if at all, in some other character than that of an expectant . he is not within the special class of servient party now under consideration (d). It is enough, however, if a substantial part of the property consisted of reversionary interests, and in that case the " dealer " cannot escape on the mere ground that property in possession was thrown in, and the bargain related to mixed and composite interests (e).

441. Secondly, the expectant must prove that the alleged bargain was of the character above indicated (f), and was made with him by the dealer with respect to, or on the faith and credit (expressly or tacitly) of the expectancy If, or to the extent to which, he fails in establishing this, he fails to bring himself within the doctrine (g).

442. Lastly, the necessary " circumstances and conditions " must be

(y) As in *Croft* v *Graham* (1863), 2 De G J & S. 155 ; *Aylesford (Earl of)* v *Morris* (1873), 8 Ch App 484 (*per* Lord SELBORNE, L C , who, at p. 497, points out the utter immateriality of the fact that there was no direct dealing with the expectant's estate in remainder, it being established that in truth the plaintiff " was trusted on the credit of his expectations " Indeed, as he adds at pp 497, 498, the tacit, but real, trust thus given was far more dangerous, and a more fit subject for the application of the doctrine, than if there had been an express charge), *Nevill* v *Snelling* (1880), 15 C D 679

(z) The expression of Lord HARDWICKE, L C , cited and adopted by Lord SELBORNE, L.C , at p 497 of *Aylesford (Earl of)* v *Morris, sup.*

(a) See the cases cited in note (s) to § 438, *ante*

(b) These were the circumstances in *Freeman* v *Bishop* (1740), 2 Atk 39, decided by Lord HARDWICKE, L C   See also *Berney* v *Pitt* (1680), 2 Swanst. 113 n , which was a case of combined loans and sales . that is to say, the dealer, having agreed to make the advances, purported to implement his agreement by sales of wine, cambric, jewels, &c , at exorbitant prices (more than four times the value of the goods)

(c) See § 438, *ante*

(d) See *Webster* v *Cook* (1867), 2 Ch App 542 (*per* Lord CHELMSFORD, L C , at pp 546, 547), where only property in possession was proved In *Wood* v *Abrey* (1818), 3 Madd 417, the alleged " expectant " joined with his father, the tenant for life, in selling the property, and it was held that he was not an " expectant," within the meaning and mischief of the rule (*per* LEACH, V C., at pp 422, 423 " the rule has no application here It proceeds upon the notion that he who has only a future interest to sell does not meet a purchaser upon equal terms But here the father, tenant for life, and his son, tenant in tail by remainder, concurring together to sell the estates, *form a vendor with a present interest*, and meet a purchaser with the same advantages as if a single person had the whole power over the estate ")

(e) See *Davis* v *Duke of Marlborough* (1818), 2 Swanst 108 (*per* Lord ELDON, L.C , at p 154) ; *Portmore (Earl of)* v. *Taylor* (1831), 4 Sim 182 (*per* SHADWELL, V -C , at pp 208-210), *Nesbitt* v. *Berridge* (1863), 32 Beav 282 (*per* ROMILLY, M R , at pp 286, 287)

(f) In § 439, *ante*

(g) Thus, in *Tottenham* v *Green* (1863), 32 L. J (CH.) 201, the plaintiff, as to such of the securities there in question as were not post-obit bonds, was held not to be an " expectant " (*per* WOOD, V.-C , at p 201)

shown, as in the case of any other relation of influence which is not one of the "known" or "suspected" relations In the present class of case, these "circumstances and conditions" may be broadly described, in the language of Lord HARDWICKE, L C, as "weakness on one side, usury on the other, or extortion or advantage taken of that weakness" (h). The "weakness" always takes the form of financial difficulties and distress, coupled with, in nearly every case, youth, and the vices, follies, and extravagances of youth, or moral imbecility generally; and the "extortion" or "advantage" is ordinarily established by proof that the usurer or other dealer, being aware of the expectant's distress and other "weakness," and also his expectancy, traded on such knowledge to obtain a contract at an unjust or unfair price, or otherwise to extort exorbitant terms, without explaining to the expectant their effect, or permitting him to resort to his natural protectors and advisers for aid or guidance, and without making candid disclosure, either to him or to them, of all material circumstances Whenever such facts as these are proved in evidence, a *primâ facie* case is established of an "unconscionable bargain" within the meaning of the rule, which, unless rebutted, has always been held to entitle the expectant to relief (i)

(h) At p 157 of *Chesterfield (Earl of)* v. *Janssen* (1751), 2 Ves. Sr 125 So, at p. 135 of *Barnardiston* v. *Lingood* (1710), 2 Atk. 133, he had previously said that "what the Court is guided by in all these cases is the taking of an undue advantage of an heir's being in distressed and necessitous circumstances, and this is the principal ground of their decrees"

(i) As in *Berney* v. *Pitt* (1680), 2 Swanst. 143 n (where the expectant was "circumvented and beset," and the usurer forced upon him the dealings described in note (b) to § 439, *ante*), *Twisleton* v *Griffith* (1716), 1 P Wms 309 (where on the one side there was distress and debt, and, on the other, a person who "took upon himself to advise and direct the plaintiff in everything, and professed great friendship for him," and bought the expectant's remainder, after dissuading him from selling it to his father), *Barnardiston* v *Lingood*, *sup* (where the defendant "drew in the plaintiff," who was in "the utmost distress" *per* Lord HARDWICKE, L C, at pp 134, 135), *Gwynne* v *Heaton* (1778), 1 Brown C C 1 (where the terms were "very grossly unequal," and "the purchaser, knowing the actual state of the lives for which he was bargaining, the inequality which that introduced, and the indigence of the man with whom he was contracting," made an "enormous" bargain with him at an inadequate price *per* Lord THURLOW, L C, at pp 7, 10), *Peacock* v. *Evans* (1809), 16 Ves 512 ("advantage taken" of "a distressed man," and undervalue *per* GRANT, M R, at pp 515–517), *Gowland* v *De l arra* (1810), 17 Ves 20 (distress, inexperience, and undervalue), *Portmore (Earl of)* v *Taylor* (1831), 4 Sim 182 ("grinding distress," knowledge of that distress, and undervalue *per* SHADWELL, V -C., at pp 207, 212), *Edwards* v *Browne* (1845), 2 Coll 100 ("straitened circumstances," and undervalue *per* KNIGHT-BRUCE, V C, at p 106), *Talbot* v *Staniforth* (1861), 1 J. & H. 484 (purchase at an undervalue from an expectant who "was under such extreme pressure from his creditors as to be driven from the country, and to be in danger of arrest" *per* PAGE WOOD, V C, at p 503), *Croft* v *Graham* (1863), 2 De G J & S 155 (loans at exorbitant interest to an extravagant and embarrassed undergraduate), *Tyler* v *Yates* (1871), 6 Ch App 665 (on the one side, youth, ignorance, distress, and helplessness; on the other, usury on extortionate terms, and concealment and misrepresentation of material facts, and of the expectant's rights and liabilities *per* Lord HATHERLEY, L C., at pp 670, 671), *Aylesford (Earl of)* v *Morris* (1873), 8 Ch. App 484 (youth and distress on the one side, and, on the other, usury of the most oppressive and extortionate character, and a bargain unconscionable on the face of it *per* Lord SELBORNE, L C., at pp 492–495), *Benyon* v *Cook* (1875), 10 Ch App. 389 n (where the circumstances were similar to those in the last case), *Fry* v *Lane* (1888), 40 C D 312 (poverty and ignorance of the expectant, and undervalue, and absence of independent advice *per* KAY, J, at pp. 322–324), *Brenchley* v *Higgins* (1901), 70 L J (CH) 788, C A (want of independent advice, concealment from the plaintiff's trustees, gross undervalue, and want of good faith generally)

Very slight extrinsic evidence, if any, is required to throw the burden on the other side where, as is frequently the case, the intrinsic evidence is of overwhelming stress ; for example, where the very nature and terms of the bargain are so outrageous as, of themselves, to constitute unconscionableness, or where the instrument containing or recording it is so framed as to imply a consciousness, and a tacit avowal or confession, of its impropriety (j). And so strong and persistent is the jealousy, not to say prejudice, with which the dealer in expectancies has been regarded by the law that, in the earliest stages in the development of the doctrine, and continuously down to the year 1867, mere proof that the dealer paid, or received, as the case might be, a price or consideration which was shown afterwards to have been inadequate in the one case, or excessive in the other, was always held sufficient of itself to establish a *primâ facie* case of unconscionableness and undue advantage, and to cast upon the dealer the burden of sustaining the transaction,— a burden, moreover, which could only be discharged by clear and cogent counter-evidence that in point of fact the price or consideration was just, and was not in the least discharged by any amount of evidence as to the honesty, good faith, and candour, of the dealer, or as to his having given, or received, a sum which to the best of his belief, after the fullest inquiry, reasonably appeared to him to be righteous and proper, or as to his having tendered, or the expectant having received from a third person, sound and disinterested advice (k)   All this was of no avail to rebut the presumption

---

In *O'Rorke* v. *Bolingbroke* (1877), 2 App Cas 814, H L , though the dominant party succeeded in sustaining the onus cast upon him, it was held that the " circumstances and conditions" there proved (a purchase from " a penniless, and, except for his father, friendless lad," without any independent advice) were sufficient to cast this onus upon him per Lord BLACKBURN at p. 834

(j) *Chesterfield (Earl of)* v *Jannsen* (1751), 2 Ves Sr 125 (*per* Lord HARDWICKE, L C , at p 157   " there has been always an appearance of fraud from the nature of the bargain, the intrinsic unconscionableness of the bargain "), *Gwynne* v *Heaton* (1778), 1 Brown C C. 1 (where, at p 7, Lord THURLOW, L C , points to the manifest anxiety of the purchaser to insert such statements in the " preamble" of the deed as would bring the transaction outside the area of bargains with expectants, thereby showing a consciousness on his part of its impeachability) ; *Aylesford (Earl of)* v *Morris* (1873), 8 Ch App 484 (*per* Lord SELBORNE, L C., at p 495   " the nature and terms of the bargains themselves," which were "*primâ facie* oppressive and extortionate")   In *Barnardiston* v *Lingood* (1740), 2 Atk 133 (*per* Lord HARDWICKE, L C, at p 135), and *Portmore (Earl of)* v. *Taylor* (1831), 4 Sim 182 (*per* SHADWELL, V ·C , at p 212), one of the elements in the unconscionability of the transaction, viz the distress of the expectant, was inferred from the character of the dealings,—frequent loans of very small sum.   Cp § 430, and the cases cited in notes (q) and (r) thereto, *ante*, as to similar presumptions and inferences from the nature and terms of the transaction itself, in cases falling within the class dealt with in Sub s (5), *ante*

(k) This was distinctly held to be the law in *Gowland* v *De Faria* (1810), 17 Ves 20, by GRANT, M R (at pp 24, 25)   " the doctrine of the Court " is " perfectly established, that it is incumbent on those who have dealt with an expectant heir relative to his reversionary interest, to make good the bargain   that is, to be able to show that a full and adequate consideration was paid.   That is undoubtedly a heavy burden upon a purchaser : but in that particular case the burthen is imposed upon him, and *that case is an exception to the general rule that for mere inadequacy of value a contract is not to be set aside*"   So LEACH, V ·C., at pp 235, 236 of *Shelly* v. *Nash* (1818), 3 Madd 232, states the rule in equally clear terms, and recognizes that it is firmly established, much as he dislikes it   In accordance with these statements of the rule, than which nothing could be plainer, a series of decisions followed, between 1810 and 1867, in which relief was given to

against him arising from the mere fact of a difference between price and value, though that difference might be such as to turn the scale "but in the estimation of a hair." Judicial adhesion to this arbitrary and inexorable rule, when once established, though in many cases most reluctantly given, produced, as was inevitable, the most startling and outrageous results (l), which at last compelled the legislature to intervene. Accordingly a useful measure was placed upon the statute-book,—the Sales of Reversions Act, 1867,—which, whilst, as has already been pointed out (m), leaving intact all the sound (which was by far the larger) part of the doctrine, effectually excised that which was unsound That is to say, the law of unconscionable bargains with expectants, so far as regards purchases of reversions, and all that a conveyancer understands by that term (for, it is to be observed, the statute does not apply to any other kind of transaction with an expectant on the credit of his expectancy), was brought back to the condition in which it was before the introduction of the special rule in question, and in which it still is as regards other relations constituted by "the circumstances and conditions" of the particular case Inasmuch as the statute only applies to "a purchase made *bonâ fide* and without fraud or unfair dealing," and the purchaser is therefore not in a position to take the benefit of it unless his purchase answers that description, it follows that it is still open to the expectant to rely upon undervalue as one of the "circumstances and conditions" which raise a *primâ facie* presumption in his favour against the dealer, or even, if very gross, to rely upon it alone as constituting such "circumstances and conditions" but, whereas formerly he could in any case rely upon undervalue, however slight, as sufficient to call for an answer, he is now deprived of that right : and, whereas formerly no answer which, though establishing complete conscientiousness and good faith on the part of the purchaser, did not establish full value, was of the slightest avail, it is now open to the purchaser to defend himself by proof of the propriety of the transaction, even though he is not in a position to displace the evidence against

an expectant on the sole ground of undervalue, without any other "circumstance or condition" being proved, and, in some cases notwithstanding positive proof by the dominant party, to the admitted satisfaction of the Court, that in every other respect the transaction was perfectly conscientious It is unnecessary, now that the law in this respect has been altered, to cite these cases it is sufficient to say that the ruling of GRANT, M.R , was adhered to by such high authorities as Lord CRANWORTH and Lord COTTENHAM, though the latter, at p 457 of *Aldborough (Earl of) v Trye* (1840), 7 Cl & Fin 436, recognized that "that proposition had been the subject of much observation undoubtedly" It was to this line of decisions, wherein "all the fair dealing in the world was of no use," that reference was made, in *Brenchley v Higgins* (1901), 70 L J (CH) 788, C A, by RIGBY, L.J , at p 790 cp the like references by VAUGHAN WILLIAMS, L J , at p 792, and ROMER, L J , at p 793

(l) Such as *Edwards v Browne* (1845), 2 Coll 100 (price paid, £1700 value proved, £1900) , *Foster v Roberts* (1861), 29 Beav 467 (price £370, value £400) , *Jones v. Ricketts* (1862), 31 Beav 130 (purchase-money £200, value £238) It is evident that these cases were decided in obedience to what was understood to be an inexorable and arbitrary rule of equity, and with much doubt as to whether the expectant would derive any benefit from the exercise of his right. For instance, at p 107 of *Edwards v Browne, sup* , KNIGHT-BRUCE, V -C , significantly observes that "this dealing with a reversionary interest, *if the plaintiff considers it to be for his benefit to press the matter*, cannot stand "

(m) See § 437, *ante*

him of undervalue in fact (n).   It would appear, therefore, that the doctrine as to unconscionable bargains with expectants, though undoubtedly a "special" one before the introduction of the Act of 1867, can no longer be properly so regarded

443. It is incumbent on the expectant to prove not only the fact of his distress, but also that the dealer was aware of it (o) · and, where the expectancy is not expressed to be the subject of the purchase, or the security for the loan, he must establish both that he had the expectancy in fact, and that the dealer knew of it (p) . for otherwise he fails in the first step towards the necessary proof that the dealer took advantage of, and traded on, his distress, and trusted to his expectancy   And, though Lord BROUGHAM's view (q), that it is an indispensable element in the expectant's case that the bargain was kept secret from the ancestor, is certainly not correct (r), this fact is nevertheless a feature which is very commonly and properly relied upon, where it exists (as it nearly always does), as helping, with other circumstances, to raise the presumption of unconscientiousness (s)

444. Generally, it must always be remembered that it is not bargains with expectants that are struck at, but unconscionable bargains only.   "In each case," as Lord BLACKBURN found it necessary to point out (t), " it must depend upon the circumstances whether the presumption which Lord HARD-WICKE spoke of is raised.   Sometimes there may be a serious question whether it is or not "   Not till the presumption is raised is the opposite party called upon for an answer, because not till then does he even become, in contemplation of law, a dominant party at all   And the presumption is not raised (as has sometimes been assumed, if not expressed) by mere proof of the expectancy, the bargain with respect to it, and the inequality in the relative position of the parties ·   there must also be shown some probability at least that an advantage was taken of those circumstances in fact   .d that such advantage was unfair, undue, or unconscientious (u).

(n) *Brenchley* v *Higgins* (1901), 70 L J (ch) 788, C A (*per* RIGBY, L J , at p. 790, VAUGHAN WILLIAMS, L J., at p 792, and ROMER, L J , at p 793)   A good illustration of a purchase at an undervalue which, before 1867, must have been set aside, but which, on proof of propriety in other respects, was upheld, even though the expectant had no independent advice, is *O'Rorke* v *Bolingbroke* (1877), 2 App Cas 814, H L , as to the facts of which, see note (x) to § 445, *post*   Another hypothetical illustration is given by ROMER, L J , at p 793 of *Brenchley* v *Higgins, sup*

(o) See *Gwynne* v *Heaton* (1778), 1 Brown C C 1 (the passage cited in note (s), *ante*), *Portmore (Earl of)* v *Taylor* (1831), 4 Sim 182 (*per* SHADWELL, V -C , at p 207   'where a person who stands in the situation of an heir apparent is in distress, *and deals with a party who is aware of the distress*   " &c.)

(p) See the observations of JESSEL, M R , at p 392 n of *Benyon* v. *Cook* (1875), 10 Ch App 389 n

(q) In *King* v *Hamlet* (1834), 2 My & K 456 (at pp 473, 474)

(r) See Sugden, V & P (11th ed) p 316   At pp 491, 492 of *Aylesworth (Earl of)* v *Morris* (1873), 8 Ch App. 484, Lord SELBORNE, L C , observes that " Lord ST LEONARDS, with good reason, dissents from that opinion," viz that the presence of " the feature" in question is " an indispensable condition of equitable relief "

(s) This is emphasized in the two leading cases on the subject by Lord HARDWICKE, L.C., and Lord SELBORNE, L C , respectively   See the passages cited in note (g) to § 434, *ante*

(t) At p. 834 of *O'Rorke* v *Bolingbroke* (1877), 2 App Cas 814, H. L.

(u) Thus, in *Moth* v *Atwood* (1801), 5 Ves 845, the expectant proved the bargain made to purchase his expectancy, and also his indigence, but did not prove that any advantage

445. As has already been observed, the burden cast upon the dominant party, if and as soon as a *primâ facie* case is made against him, is not impossible, though extremely difficult, to sustain. The "contrary evidence" by which alone he can "repel the presumption" is evidence that the transaction was "in point of fact, fair, just, and reasonable" (v), or, in other words, that it was "fair" in both senses of the word, that is to say, that his conduct was morally "fair," and that the terms of the bargain were commercially "fair." In a very few cases, both before 1867 (w), when it was much heavier, and since that date when it was lightened (x), the burden was discharged. Of course the affirmative defences available to any dominant party, even if he is unable to sustain the transaction in the sense above indicated, are equally available to a dealer in expectancies. For instance, it may be shown, and in the very case which was the occasion of Lord HARDWICKE's exposition of the severe presumptions made against the dealer, and the difficulty of rebutting them, it was in fact shown, that the transaction, assuming it to

had been taken of it, and was therefore denied relief. The same result attended the expectant's claim, on a similarly defective proof, in *Judd* v. *Green* (1875), 45 L J (CH) 108 (*per* BACON, V C , at pp. 109, 110   "it has never yet been held that an expectant heir was incompetent to deal with his interest for substantial purposes, or that the parties dealing with him could have these transactions impeached unless there was something so morally wrong as to make it necessary to discou⁁   their dealings on the ground of public policy")

(v) *Per* Lord SELBORNE, L C., at p. 491 of *Aylesfor* ⁁ *rl of*) v *Morris* (1873), 8 Ch App. 484   The necessity of establishing *both* the f⁁   ⁁ and justice, *and* the reasonableness, is insisted on by FITZGIBBON, L J (Ir), at p 5⁁⁁ f *Mae* ⁁ *Joyce* (1892), 29 L R (Ir) 500 ("the burden is thrown upon the defendant of sustaining the transaction What has he to prove ?   Not merely absence of fraud and dishonesty on his own part, not merely understanding and volition on the plaintiff's part, not merely that a contract in the fullest sense was made, but affirmatively that the contract itself was not only fair and just, but was also reasonable ")   See also *Fry* v *Lane* (1888), 40 C. D 312 (*per* KAY, J , at p 322)

(w) In *Berney* v. *Pitt* (1680), 2 Swanst. 143 n , where there were seven defendants, Lord NOTTINGHAM, L C , gave judgment in favour of the defendant Pitt, whilst granting relief against the other six, on the ground apparently that the bargain was a fair gamble—(Pitt was to get "three to one," if the plaintiff survived his father , but, if he did not, "he was to lose his principal")—and there was no "circumvention or practice" whereas, in the case of the others, the terms were "five to one," and it did not appear that they were to lose all, if the expectant predeceased his father, and there was "circumvention" This decision, however, would not have been approved by Lord HARDWICKE, L C. see his observations at p 135 of *Barnardiston* v *Lingood* (1740), 2 Atk 133   In *Moth* v *Atwood* (1801), 5 Ves 845, it was proved that the expectant "was determined to sell the reversion"; that it was "offered over and over again to all the town, to twenty persons " , that the purchaser "was not going about, or lying by to avail himself of an opportunity to get a good bargain"; that "there was no fraud or circumvention" , and that the bargain, though "a very considerable one," was "done deliberately, and not in consequence of a plan laid to gain a good bargain"   In *Shelley* v *Nash* (1818), 3 Madd 232, *Fox* ⁁ *Wright* (1821), Madd & G 111, and *Aldborough* (*Earl of*) v. *Trye* (1840), 7 Cl & Fin 436, the purchaser of the expectancy proved full and fair value.

(x) See *O'Rorke* ⁁ *Bolingbroke* (1877), 2 App Cas 814, H L , where the expectant was expressly held to have established a case which shifted the onus on to the other side (*per* Lord BLACKBURN, at p. 834), but where it was also held that, though the expectant had no independent advice, and though the purchase was at an undervalue in fact, this onus was sustained by proof on the part of the purchaser that he had good reason to believe, and in fact believed, that the father's health was good, and that (as on that supposition it was) the price paid by him was not only adequate, but liberal   further, that everything was arranged with the father, and that the father and son, being penniless, could not afford to pay for the independent advice of a professional man, and, being friendless, had no one else to whom they could resort without payment (*per* Lord BLACKBURN, at pp 835-837)

have been unconscionable, was afterwards affirmed by the expectant (y)   So also acquiescence, amounting to an implied confirmation, is a good defence, but only if the distress of the expectant has then come to an end (z), and the distress is presumed not to have come to an end until the expectancy has fallen into possession (a).   Proof of the concurrence of the ancestor with the expectant in the impeached bargain is a valid answer, and may be put as a plea of " family arrangement " ; but, in the nature of things, it is seldom that such a case can be made out (b)

Sub-s. (7).   Examination of Certain Relations which, of themselves, give rise to no Presumption of Influence.

446. There are certain relations which have from time to time been claimed as properly belonging to the class of " influence " relations, but which are now definitely excluded from that category.   Foremost among these is the relation between husband and wife.   It has been in one case judicially stated (c), and, in another, expressly decided (d), that in transactions between spouses, it will be presumed that an undue influence was exercised by the husband over the wife, unless and until the contrary be shown   But the judicial statement, which was only a *dictum* in the strictest sense of the word, has long since been recognized as a slip, and was, indeed, afterwards silently corrected by the author of it himself (e), and the decision referred to

(y) *Chesterfield (Earl of)* v *Jannsen* (1751), 2 Ves Sr 215, where the dealer escaped on proof that the expectant, in 1714, after the death of the Duchess of Marlborough, from whom he had anticipated, and had received, large benefits, and when his distress had come to an end, gave a bond confirming an earlier one of 1738 (which was the transaction impeached) with full knowledge of all material facts and of his rights, and fully and deliberately (*per* Lord HARDWICKE, L C, at pp 158, 159)   As to the plea of confirmation, generally, see Sect, 4, Sub s (3), *post*

(z) *Gowland* v *Ferie* (1810), 17 Ves 20 (*per* GRANT, M R , at p 25   " there is no case in which, during the continuance of the same situation in which the party entered into the contract, acquiescence has ever gone for anything   it has always been presumed that the same distress which pressed him to enter into the contract prevented him from suing to set it aside ; thus it is only when he is relieved from that distress that he can be expected to resist the performance of the contract ")

(a) *Benyon* v *Cook* (1875), 10 Ch App 389 n (*per* JESSEL, M R , at p 393 n.), *Fry* v. *Lane* (1888), 40 C D 312 (*per* KAY, J , at p 324)   And see *Salter* v *Bradshaw* (1858), 26 Beav 161 (*per* ROMILLY, M.R , at p 165)

(b) *Wood* v *Abrey* (1818), 3 Madd 417, where father and son concurred in selling the son's remainder in tail, the father being the tenant for life, and where relief was refused, might be considered a case of this class   Where, however, the transaction was not " like a dealing between father and son for the purpose of relieving the necessities of the different members of the family," nor was the case that of father and son together resorting to a moneylender for the purpose of relieving the son, but simply a case of the father purchasing the reversion from the son, the plea of ' family arrangement " was held to be quite out of place   *Talbot* v *Staniforth* (1861), 1 J & H 484 (*per* WOOD, V C , at pp 500–503)   Cp *Dunnage* v *White* (1818), 1 Swanst 137—see note (g) to § 429, *ante*—for an instance of a similar failure of this plea in a case within Sub-s (5), *ante*   The plea, as an answer to a case of non disclosure in negotiations for a compromise, is discussed in §§ 135, 136, 137, *ante*

(c) By Lord PENZANCE at p 468 of *Parfitt* v *Lowless* (1872), L R 2 P & M 462

(d) By WRIGHT, J , in *Bischoff's Trustee* v *Frank* (1903), 89 L. T 188, reversed as stated in note (f), *inf*

(e) At p. 1230 of *Erlanger* v *New Sombrero Phosphate Co* (1878), 3 App Cas 1218, H L , where, in a passage of no less generality, and no more necessity to the actual decision, than that referred to in note (c), *sup* , Lord PENZANCE omits the relation of husband and

was, though there is no report of the appellate proceedings, reversed by the Court of Appeal (*f*) Both the one and the other are directly opposed to the entire current of authority from 1750 to the present time, wherein it is quite clearly laid down that such a relation is one from which, though influence may be presumed, undue influence certainly cannot be (*g*) ; for the latter presumption would contradict the whole course of human nature and experience, which has always recognized the influence in question as perfectly natural and proper (*h*) ; and, inasmuch as a presumption of undue exercise of the influence is the most important of the three which are made in favour of the servient party in the case of any of the recognized relations (*i*), this is tantamount to saying that the relation of husband and wife is altogether outside that class. It by no means follows, however, that, where it is sought to establish a relation from the circumstances of the particular case (*j*), or to prove actual undue influence, the fact that the alleged dominant party was the husband of the servient party is to be left out of account altogether On the contrary, in any case " where the act done by the woman is in some degree a transaction alone with the husband," it has been said by Lord HARDWICKE (*k*) that " a court of equity will have more jealousy over it . and if there is any proof that the husband had any *improper* influence in it by ill, or even extraordinary good, usage, to induce her to it, the Court might set it aside, *but not without that* " In other words, it is on the one hand sufficient, and on the other necessary, for the wife, when impeaching a transaction with her husband, to show that, in virtue of the actual facts, he stood in some other and further

wife from the " instances " which he there gives of " relations in which courts of equity have given protection and relief against the pressure of unfair advantage resulting from the relation," these instances being only " the relations of principal and agent, trustee and *cestui que trust*, guardian and ward, priest and penitent "

(*f*) This appears from *Howes* v. *Bishop*, [1909] 2 K B 390, C A (*per* Lord ALVERSTONE, C J , at pp. 397, 398. who referred to passages from the short hand note of the judgments of COLLINS, M R , and ROMER, L J , disapproving both the decision of WRIGHT, J , and the theory on which it was founded that the relation of husband and wife is one of the "suspected" class) In *Chaplin & Co* v *Brammall*, [1908] 1 K B 223, C A , VAUGHAN WILLIAMS, L J , relied to some extent on the decision of WRIGHT, J., not being aware that it had been reversed, but he also rested his judgment on the evidence of actual pressure and undue influence, " apart from that decision " (p 237) It appears from *Bank of Montreal v Stuart*, [1911] A C. 120, P C, that there had been a recent Canadian decision to the same effect, and on the same erroneous ground, as that of WRIGHT, J

(*g*) *Nedby* v *Nedby* (1852), 5 De G & Sm 377 (*per* PARKER, V C , at p 383) , *Boyse* v *Rossborough* (1857), 6 H L C 2 (*per* Lord CRANWORTH, L C , at p 18) , *Barron* v *Willis*, [1899] 2 Ch 578 (*per* COZENS-HARDY, J , at p 585, expressing an opinion on this point which was not affected in any way by the reversal of the decision itself, [1900] 2 Ch 121, C. A , and *sub nom Willis* v *Barron*, [1902] A C 271, H L) , *Howes* v *Bishop*, *sup* (*per* Lord ALVERSTONE, C J , at pp 395-398, MOULTON, L J , at p 399, and FARWELL, L J , at pp 399-403, where Lord PENZANCE's error is corrected, and the opinion of COZENS-HARDY, J , *sup* , was approved) , *Talbot* v *Von Boris*, [1911] 1 K B 854, C A (*per* FARWELL, L J , at pp 863, 864) , *Bank of Montreal* v *Stuart, sup* (at p 137)

(*h*) See the citations in the last note, and particularly the reference therein to the judgment of Lord CRANWORTH, L C., at p 48 of *Boyse* v *Rossborough*, *sup*, where he observes that " the relation constituted by marriage is of a nature which makes it difficult to inquire, as it would be impolitic to pursue inquiry, into all which may have passed in the intimate union of affection and interests which it is the paramount purpose of that connection to cherish "

(*i*) See § 405, *ante*

(*j*) As in the class of case dealt with in Sub § (5), *ante*

(*k*) At p 517 of *Grigsby* v *Cox* (1750), 1 Ves Sr 517

relation to her than that of husband (*l*) Similarly not only the relation of husband and wife, but every other domestic relation which is neither parental nor quasi-parental in the sense already indicated (*m*), stands outside the class of those from which, without further inquiry or evidence, undue influence is at once presumed (*n*)

447. The relation between a testator and a devisee or legatee is not a relation from which any undue influence is presumed to have been exercised by such devisee or legatee In the case of a gift *inter vivos*, where one of the recognized relations exists between the donor and donee, a *primâ facie* presumption of a very strong character is at once made against the donee which is not in the least rebutted by mere proof that the donor knew what he was doing, and had a real intention of doing it : a further question, as Lord ELDON said (*o*), has then to be considered—" how was that intention pro   d ? " , and, unless the dominant party can show affirmatively that the presumed influence was in fact duly, and not unduly, exercised, he is liable whereas, in the case of a will, there is no presumption at all against the validity of the gift On the contrary, the presumption is either that no influence was exercised at all, or that, if it was, it was a natural and proper influence. A will can, no doubt, be invalidated by affirmative proof on the part of the person disputing it that the so-called testament did not represent the testator's will at all, but another person's will superimposed upon his, and substituted for it, and was in this sense a forgery, just as if it had been physically forged : but if it was in truth and in fact his will, no amount of evidence that it was brought about by influence which, in the case of a gift *inter vivos*, would be called " undue," will be of the slightest relevance And, in any case, it is not for the devisee or legatee, as it is for any donee who is a dominant party, to sustain the gift, but for the party disputing the will to show why it should not be " established " (*p*)

(*l*) The sufficiency of such proof is shown by the cases in which, on adducing it, and only because she adduced it, the wife succeeded, such as *Turnbull & Co* v *Duval*, [1902] A C 419, P C ; *Bank of Montreal* v *Stuart*, *sup* the necessity of it is shown by the cases in which, not adducing it to the satisfaction of the Court, she failed, such as *Nedby* v *Nedby*, *sup* , *Bischoff's Trustee* v *Frank*, *sup* (in the C A), *Howes* v *Bishop*, *sup*.

(*m*) In Sub-s (1), *ante*

(*n*) Illustrations are *Beanland* v *Bradley* (1854), 2 Sm & G 339 (no presumption against a gift by an old man shortly before his death to his guardian and son in law *per* STUART, V -C , at p 343) , *Cobbett* v *Brock* (1855), 20 Beav 524 (no presumption of undue influence where the fianceé of a debtor gives a security to his creditor *per* ROMILLY, M R , at pp 530, 531) , *Taylor* v *Johnston* (1862), 19 C D 603 (no relationship of guardian and ward constituted by mere residence under the same roof for a few months *per* BACON, V C , at p 609) , *Re Coomber*, [1911] 1 Ch 723, C A (no domestic relationship shown by mere proof that the alleged dominant party was the alleged servient party's son, and manager of her business *per* COZENS-HARDY, M R , at pp 726, 727, MOULTON, L.J , at pp 728, 729, and BUCKLEY, L.J , at pp 730, 731)

(*o*) At p 300 of *Huguenin* v *Baseley* (1807), 14 Ves 273 And see the cases cited in note (*m*) to § 469, *post*

(*p*) See *Middleton* v *Sherburne* (1841), 4 Y & C (Exch in Eq) 358 (*per* Lord ABINGER, C B , at pp 389, 300) , *Hindson* v *Weatherill* (1854), 5 De G M & G 301 (*per* KNIGHT BRUCE, L.J , at p 311) , *Boyse* v *Rossborough* (1857), 6 H L C 2 (*per* Lord CRANWORTH, L C , at pp 17–19) , *l   v Lawless* (1872), L R 2 P & M 462 (*per* Lord PENZANCE, at pp 468–471) And, as to confirmations of voidable transactions, generally, by will, see *Stump* v *Gaby* (1852), 2 De G. M. & G 623 (*per* Lord St LEONARDS, L C , at p 631)

448. Another relation which in early times was considered, but erroneously, to carry with it some presumption, or suggestion, of undue influence, is the relation between mortgagee and mortgagor. It has already been shown that this relation is not, *per se*, of a fiduciary character (*q*), and the authorities upon which that statement has been based are *a fortiori* authorities for the proposition that no presumption whatever of influence is raised in favour of a mortgagor, as such, against a mortgagee, as such, though in earlier times, when land was of more importance as property than it is at present, and when mortgagees were regarded by equity judges with the same kind of distrust as usurers, or even extortioners, it was vaguely thought or assumed that the position of a mortgagee gave such scope to oppression and abuse of proprietary rights and power, and was so habitually assumed as a cloak to evade the usury laws then in force, that some sort of burden ought to be cast upon him of sustaining any transaction between him and the mortgagor relative to the property during the continuance of the relationship, if and when impeached; and, indeed, in one remarkable case which, however, cannot now be regarded as law, Lord REDESDALE went the full length of holding that any dealing with the mortgaged estate, not being a purchase of the equity of redemption (which he admitted to be unimpeachable), must be presumed in law, until the contrary be shown, to have been procured by " a silent threat "—in other words, the undue influence—of the mortgagee (*r*).

(*q*) See § 347, *ante*
(*r*) *Webb* v *Rorke* (1806), 2 Sch & Lefr 661; 9 R R 122   Here a mortgagor impeached the validity of a lease of part of the mortgaged land for a term of 999 years granted by him to the mortgagee when the mortgage debt was still unpaid, on the grounds (so far as material) that the transaction was brought about by a threat on the part of the mortgagee to foreclose unless the mortgagor, then of great age and of feeble health, assented to it, and that inadequate consideration was given   The latter ground need not be discussed, because no inadequacy of a sufficient character was established (p 674), and the jury expressly negatived it on an issue directed for this purpose (p 661)   Everything, therefore, depended on the "threat"   If the threat had been proved, there might have been some evidence of a case within the class which is the subject of Sub s (5), *ante* (undue advantage taken of the senility, feebleness, and distress of the mortgagor), except that the only threat alleged being a threat to do a legal act, it could not, according to *Allen* v *Flood*, [1898] A C 1, H L, of itself have been deemed improper. And it was in this spirit that Lord REDESDALE, L C (I), approached the question in the first instance, for the directed issues to be tried by a jury as to whether the lease had been obtained by influence and pressure, and also (as above stated) whether a full and fair rent had been given   A verdict was found by the jury in favour of the dominant party on both points   But, on reconsideration Lord REDESDALE repented of having sent any issue to a jury at all, and in most distinct and unmistakable terms held that the threat and pressure ought to be inferred in law from the relative situation of the parties, and that no evidence is required of the affirmative from the servient party, but that it was for the dominant party to prove the negative   Substantially, in fact, he rests his decision on the theory that a mortgagee is in the position both of a trustee, and of a person who is *prima facie* deemed to have taken undue advantage of the mortgagor , though it is true that, at pp 666, 668, 672, he also refers to "the statutes of usury," or rather ' the policy on which they are founded " "I did wrong," he says , at pp 668, 669, "in directing the issues , and in truth I sent to a jury to try a question properly triable only in a court of equity, viz whether the relation in which these parties stood, of mortgagor and mortgagee, did not put them in such a condition that, except under extraordinary circumstances, a transaction of this sort must be deemed *prima facie* an advantage taken by the mortgagee of the situation in which he stood, with respect to the subject matter of the contract   Now that the defendant did stand in such a situation cannot be doubted   He prevails without using a single word of threat . like the beggar in ' Gil Blas ' who, with his gun at his shoulder, extorted

Moreover, this ancient prejudice against the mortgagee still survives in the curious arbitrary rules relating to mortgages which prohibit absolutely any stipulation in the mortgage deed itself, or in any contemporaneous instrument forming part of the entire transaction, calculated to deprive the mortgagor of his right to get back the property, on payment of the debt, in the same condition as that in which it was assigned, and any contrivance or device which operates to prevent or impede redemption, or which assures to the mortgagee any future advantage by diminishing the property to be reconveyed, as distinct from a mere loading of the debt (s). These rules, when coming up for judicial discussion, have always been accounted for historically, for it is recognized that they have no rational justification or excuse, by reference to the "sentiment" of bygone times which was prone to impute fraud or oppression at sight to any mortgagee merely because he was a mortgagee (t) Scarcely any attempt has been made to defend them on principle and they have been enforced by the Courts with obvious reluctance (u), and like, for example, the rule against the validity of a contract to accept a smaller sum in satisfaction of a larger, or the rules in favour of an executor-creditor, from regard to the disturbance to general business which would result from suddenly abrogating long-established doctrines, however

money from the traveller without using a single word of threat . . The mortgagor is under the control of the mortgagee in the very subject-matter of the contract, and if the mortgagor had distinctly said to the mortgagee, ' You must let me have a lease for 900 years at the rent which I think fit to give, and if you will not, I will harass you by all the mean by which a mortgagee can harass his debtor ', it is plain a lease so obtained could not stand If the thing can be done without a word spoken, the same consequences ought to follow. Our evidence of such a conversation to be required ? Is it not better to hold, as in the case of a trustee, ' because this may be done, it shall be taken as done, and the act, if disputed, shall be invalid ' ? The policy of public justice seems to me to require that a dealing of this kind shall not stand, if disputed by the mortgagor, unless supported by such evidence on the part of the mortgagee as would put the relation between the parties out of the transaction " Nothing could be plainer than this and nothing could be more incorrect, or more directly opposed to the series of authorities cited in notes (k), and (l), to § 347, ante The case, however, has been discussed at such length for the reason that it is the ablest exposition of a view now determined to be unsound, and in order to guard against any hasty inference which might otherwise be drawn from the fact that it has never been expressly overruled, or, indeed, expressly disapproved, though it is generally referred to in terms of dubious courtesy as " a very strong case," and has never been followed or acted upon

(s) These rules are stated in *Gossip v Wright* (1863), 32 L J (CH) 648 (*per* KINDERSLEY, V -C, at p 653), *Biggs v Hoddinott*, [1898] 2 Ch 307, C A ; *Santley v Wilde*, [1899] 2 Ch 474, C A , *Noakes & Co, Ltd v Price*, [1902] A C. 24, H L ; *Bradley v Carritt*, [1903] A C 253, H L , *Samuel v Jarrah Timber & Wood Paving Corpn* , [1904] A C. 322, H L , *Fairclough v Swan Brewery Co*, [1912] A C 565, P C , *Kreglinger v New Patagonia Meat & Coal Storage Co* , [1914] A C 25, H L

(t) See *James v Kerr* (1888), 40 C D 449 (*per* KAY, J , at p 460), *Biggs v Hoddinott*, *sup* (*per* CHITTY, L J , at p 322, and COLLINS, L.J , at p 323), *Noakes & Co, Ltd v Price, sup* (*per* Lord DAVEY, at p 33), *Samuel v Jarrah Timber & Wood Paving Corpn* , *sup* (*per* Lord MACNAGHTEN who, at p 326, says that " the rule is founded on sentiment rather than on principle," and refers, in this connection, to the expression used by Lord HARDWICKE, L C, at p 495 of *Mellor v Lees* (1742), 2 Atk 494,—" a design to wrest the estate fraudulently out of the hands of the mortgagor "), *Kreglinger v New Patagonia Meat and Coal Storage Co* , *sup* (*per* Lord HALDANE, L C, at pp 35, 36)

(u) And not only has the slightest attempt to extend the doctrine one iota beyond the established limits been at once repelled, as in *De Beers Consolidated Mines, Ltd v British South Africa Co* , [1912] A C. 52, H L , but those limits themselves have been severely criticized, if not contracted, in *Kreglinger v New Patagonia Meat & Coal Storage Co* , *sup.*

irrational, and however repugnant to modern ideas, on the faith of which the community has acted in the various transactions of life.

449. Though no presumption of undue influence is raised by the mere fact that the transaction was one between mortgagee and mortgagor with reference to the mortgaged property, it is of course recognized that such presumption will be made if the dominant party can be shown to have united with his character of mortgagee some other character in virtue of which he stood to the servient party in one of the "suspected" relations, such as that of trustee (v), or solicitor (w) And, where a case is put forward of a relation in virtue of "the circumstances and conditions," and there is other and independent evidence of an unconscientious advantage having been taken of weakness, the fact that the dominant party was a mortgagee who had the servient party the mortgagor, completely in his power, will not be overlooked, or deemed without significance, in conjunction with the other circumstances of the case (x) It will have been noticed that, in a large number of the illustrations given of unconscionable bargains with expectants, the dominant party was a mortgagee of the reversion or other expectancy, but his liability in all such cases was not based on the fact of his being a mortgagee, but on the fact of the security being an expectancy (y).

SECT 3 BURDEN OF ALLEGATION AND PROOF ON THE SERVIENT PARTY

450. In order to establish a case entitling him to call upon the dominant party to show cause why a transaction entered into during the subsistence of the relation should not be set aside, or otherwise made the subject of relief, the servient party must allege and, having alleged, adduce some *primâ facie* evidence of, two things,—first, a relation between him and the dominant party of one or other of the kinds from which the law presumes undue influence, and, secondly, a gift, or contract, or other transaction made or entered into during the subsistence of that relation Not until he has discharged this

(v) As in *Barrett* v *Hartley* (1866), L R 2 Eq 789 (*per* STUART, V C, at p 795)

(w) As in *Eyre* v *Hughes* (1876), 2 C D 148, where BACON, V -C, after finding (p 158) that the relation of solicitor and client existed between the mortgagee and mortgagor "so as to influence the whole of the transactions," and also " a sort of relation something like that of a banker," granted relief against the solicitor mortgagee on the ground that it was his duty, *in his character as solicitor*, to have advised his client against the stipulation complained of The rule, now abolished by the Mortgagees Legal Costs Act, 1895 (58 & 59 Vict c 25), which prohibited a solicitor from charging costs in respect of a mortgage taken from his   t, though sometimes put as an application of the doctrine of " clogging the equity of redemption," as in *Eyre* v *Wynn-Mackenzie*, [1894] 2 Ch 218, must surely have been based on the fact of the mortgagee being a solicitor, as well as a mortgagee, and not on his mere character of mortgagee

(x) See *Ca ew* v *Johnston* (1805), 2 Sch & Lefr 280 (where the relief was given " on the ground of unconscientious advantage being   taken " by the mortgagee of the distress, and also " of the imbecility and absence of " the mortgagor *per* Lord REDESDALE, L C (Ir), at p 306, and cp the elaborate series of declarations with which the decree, set out at pp 306–313, was prefaced), *Ford* v *Olden* (1867), L R 3 Eq 461 (a similar case *per* STUART, V C, at pp 363, 364), *James* v *Kerr* (1888), 40 C D 449 (where the decision was based on advantage having been taken of the necessitous circumstances of a young man, quite independently of other grounds, such as champerty, and " clog on the equity of redemption " *per* KAY, J , at p 460)

(y) See, generally, the cases cited in the notes to Sub s (6), *ante*

BND   2 E

burden is the dominant party called upon for an answer · but if and when the servient party does discharge it, the three presumptions already referred to (z) are at once made in his favour, viz. that the dominant party had an influence over him in virtue of the relation; that the influence operated upon, and procured, the transaction, and that such influence was undue. The onus is then shifted on to the shoulders of the dominant party to justify or excuse the transaction by allegation and proof of some one or more of the various affirmative pleas available to him which are the subject of examination in their proper places (a).

Sub-s (1)   *Proof of the Relation.*

451. If the servient party is unable to establish the existence of the alleged relation, he fails at the threshold   for the old heresy that, in cases of gift, the burden is on the donee to support it, if the donor sues to avoid it, though no relation of any sort existed between the parties (b)   is now entirely exploded (c).   In cases of a " known " or " suspected " relation (d), there is seldom any dispute on this question, or, if there is, the proof is not difficult ·   but, where the relation is claimed to have been created solely by the particular circumstances of the case (e), the difficulty in proving the necessary conjunction and interaction of a number of such circumstances is obviously greater than in establishing the comparatively simple fact that the dominant party was at the material date the servient party's parent, or his legal, spiritual, or medical adviser   and in such cases the difficulty has not been always surmounted (f)   If neither a relation of influence, nor a relation of " confidence " (g) is made out, the party complaining can still succeed on other grounds, such as actual fraud, misrepresentation, duress (*dolus, vis metus*), or insanity, or other invalidating cause, but in that case he must assume the whole burden of proof: he has no presumptions to fall back upon (h)

(z) See § 105, note (a), *ante*

(a) In Sect 4, *post*

(b) This was the opinion persistently maintained by ROMILLY,   an opinion based not only on his own reasoning, but also on a wholly mistaken belief that it had the authority of Lord COTTENHAM, L C, if not also of Lord ELDON, L C   see his observations at pp 239-241 of *'ooke v Lamotte* (1851), 15 Beav 234, and at pp 298, 299 of *Hoghton v Hoghton* (1852), 15 Beav 278   MALINS, V -C, appears to have adopted this error, at p 567 of *Coutts v Ackworth* (1869), L R 8 Eq 558

(c) See *Phillips v Mullings* (1871), 7 Ch App 244 (*per* Lord HATHERLEY, L C., at p 247), *Henry v Armstrong* (1881), 18 C D. 668 (*per* KAY, J, at pp 668, 669)   It is quite true to say that, even where the relation is established, a gift is in some respects more difficult to justify than a contract,—see § 405, notes (g) and (h), *ante*, and §§ 475-479, *post*,—but the proposition put forward by ROMILLY, M R, is a very different one

(d) The subject of Sect 2, Sub ss (1)-(4)   See *Holman v Loynes* (1854), 4 De G M & G 270 (*per* Lord CRANWORTH, L C, at p 272)

(e) See Sect 2, Sub s (5), and (as to unconscionable bargains with expectants) Sub s (6), *ante*

(f) For instances of such failure, see § 128, note (u); § 140, note (d), § 441, and § 441, note (u), *ante*

(g) The subject of Ch IV, *ante*

(h) See the very clear exposition of Lord BROUGHAM, L C, at pp. 134, 135, 140, of *Hunter v Atkins* (1834), 3 My & K. 113, *Cur on v Belworthy* (1852), 3 H L C 742 (*per*

452. Besides proving the facts alleged to constitute the relation, the servient party must be prepared to establish, in case of dispute, that the facts so proved amount in law to such a relation (*i*). He must also show that the relation existed at the actual time of the transaction, if this is in controversy (*j*). And, if he is complaining of the conduct of a third person who has utilized the relation between the dominant party and himself in obtaining the gift or contract sought to be invalidated, he must further show that the third person was aware of such relation (*k*).

453. In considering whether it is made out that the relation subsisted or not at the material date, the Court will always regard its reality and substance, rather than its form, or technical designation. It is not a question of names (*l*). Thus, where it is disputed whether the relation of solicitor and client has been proved (that is, such a relation as involves influence), the Court will not hold in the negative merely because the dominant party had not been appointed or retained to act as the servient party's solicitor (*m*), or was not literally or technically acting as such in reference to the particular transaction (*n*). nor, conversely, will it answer the question in the affirmative, merely because the dominant party happened to be a solicitor. Thus, it has been held that, where a solicitor, at the request of a lady who was an entire stranger to him, endeavoured to raise money for her, and, being unable to do so, ultimately agreed to advance the money himself, and, in that sense, acted for her in this isolated instance, no relation of influence was established (*o*)

Lord ST LEONARDS, L C., at p 752), *Harrison* v *Guest* (1855), 6 De G M & G 124 (*per* Lord CRANWORTH, L C., at pp. 432–436) For an instance of failure to prove the alleged, or any, relation, followed by success in establishing misrepresentation entitling to relief, see *Hayyarth* v *Wearing* (1871), L R 12 Eq 320

(*i*) For illustrations of facts which are not deemed relations from which influence is presumed, see Sect 2, Sub s (7), *ante*

(*j*) See *Rhodes* v *Bate* (1866), 1 Ch App 252 (*per* TURNER, L J , who treats this as a matter to be established by the servient party, at p 259 "I am of opinion that the plaintiff has established that a confidential relation *for some time* subsisted between her and the appellant, and *it is then to be considered whether this relation subsisted at the time when the transactions took place* For this purpose it is necessary to examine each of these transactions separately " He then does so, and concludes as to one of them (p 260), " that *the plaintiff has failed to establish* the existence of any confidential relation between her and the appellant when this transaction took place,' but, as to the other (pp 260, 261), that the plaintiff had established the existence of the alleged relation at the material date, and that the defendant had not discharged the onus which thereupon rested on him to show that the influence was not operative *in hâc re*, or had then ceased)

(*k*) See § 504, note (*o*), *post*

(*l*) See § 408, *ante*

(*m*) *Willis* v *Barron*, [1902] A C 271, H L (*per* Lord HALSBURY, L C , at p 276, where he points out that the plaintiff came to the defendant Skinner as " the natural person to whom to apply for protection," and to say that he was not formally his solicitor is only "juggling with words" and see the observations of Lord DAVEY, at p 283) Cp *Allison* v *Clayhills* (1907), 97 L T 709 (*per* PARKER, J , at pp 711, 712)

(*n*) *Wright* v *Carter*, [1903] 1 Ch 27, C A (*per* VAUGHAN WILLIAMS L J , at p 53, STIRLING, L.J , at pp 58, 59, and COZENS HARDY, L J , at pp 61, 62)

(*o*) *Edwards* v *Williams* (1863), 32 L J (CH) 763 (*per* KNIGHT BRUCE, L J , at p 765 " it happens, it is true, that one of the parties was a solicitor, and the other of them had had no legal advice except from that solicitor , but there had existed no previous relation of solicitor and client between them, and therefore that confidence which was the basis of the rule of the Court in similar cases did not appear to have existed "). Cp *Pisani* v

Sub-s. (2). *Proof of the Transaction*

454. It is only the conjunction of the relation and the transaction which entitles the servient party to relief It is, therefore, of no more avail to prove the relation without the transaction, than it is to prove the transaction without the relation If the alleged transaction be a gift, the actual payment or delivery or transfer must be established : no relief is required against a mere promise or declaration of an intention to make a present, which is unenforceable from the first

455. In many cases, where the object of the proceedings is simply to annul the transaction whatever it was, it is not vital to establish the precise nature or terms of the transaction But there are other types of case in which it is essential, or at all events important, for the servient party to prove that the transaction belonged to the particular class alleged, or that its terms were the exact terms alleged, and no other.

456. In the first place, it may be a question of great materiality whether the transaction was a gift, or a purchase or other contract for valuable consideration · for, as has already been indicated (p), it is, generally speaking, far more difficult for the dominant party to sustain a gift than a contract, and consequently more in the interest of the servient party to allege, and in that event he must prove, that the transaction was in fact of this character, as against the dominant party who is concerned to establish that it was a purchase, and who, for that purpose, frequently relies upon the recitals or express terms of the instrument so describing it, which, however, the Court will wholly disregard, if by the servient party's evidence of what was really done and understood they are shown to be erroneous, and still more if they are shown to have been fraudulently inserted as a prophylactic against possible future invalidation (q) Again, there are cases where, the instrument having represented the transaction as a gift, the dominant party struggles against his own deed to show that for some reason or other this was a mis description, and that in fact some sort of pecuniary consideration was given (r) On the other hand, where the strength of the servient party's position lies in the fact that there was no real inquiry into the question of value, it is obviously in his interest to allege, and in that case, again, it is for him to prove, that the transaction was a purchase or other contract, and not a gift, because the evidence of such absence of inquiry which is calculated to defeat the dominant party's attempt to sustain the transaction, if it was a contract, is the very evidence which tends to support any contention on the other side that it was a gift, emanating from the pure bounty of the

---

Att Gen of Gibraltar (1874), L R 5 P C 516, where, though the Court would not go quite so far as the Lords Justices went in *Edwards v Williams, sup*, which was referred to in the judgment, they relied on the circumstances, which were very similar to those of the earlier case as (together with others) exculpating the dominant party (p. 537).

(p) See § 405, and notes (g) and (h) thereto, *ante* · and cp § 475, *post*.

(q) See the cases cited in note (h) to § 472, *post*

(r) As in *Huguenin v Baseley* (1807), 14 Ves 273 (where the dominant party vainly relied upon an illusory undertaking to repay the property, as evidence that it was not given to him *per* Lord ELDON, L C, at p 301)

alleged servient party, who on that view would be entirely unconcerned with, and indifferent to, any mercantile questions as to the property which he intended to give, whatever it was worth (s). Here the dominant party, if he finds it hopeless to support the transaction considered as a contract, by reason of the consideration having been palpably inadequate, may be forced to set up, even in the face of his own deed, that the transaction was in fact a voluntary one; in so doing he only substitutes one kind of difficulty in sustaining the transaction for another, but he may think that the Scylla to which he is steering cannot at all events be more fatal than the Charybdis he has avoided, and may be less so (t). It sometimes happens that the servient

(s) Thus, in *Harris v. Tremenheere* (1808), 15 Ves 34, which was, perhaps, rather a case of a "confidence," than an "influence" relation, but which laid down principles equally applicable to both classes, and, as such, is relied upon in the "influence" decisions next cited, Lord ELDON, L C, held that, as to three of the four leases there in question, the plaintiff had not sustained the onus of establishing that the grant of them was matter of contract, rather than "the spontaneous fruit of his own generosity, not weighing the value or amount of the consideration which should have been given, if it had been the subject of barter" (p 40). In *Nicol v Vaughan* (1833), 1 Cl. & Fin 495, the servient party alleged that the bond in question was given for services rendered, it being contended on the other side that it was a voluntary bond, and the Master reported in favour of the latter view the Court below thereupon, instead of either adopting or rejecting the Master's report, directed an issue to be tried. The House of Lords on appeal held that the Court below must decide the question of fact one way or the other, and the Court thereupon found that the bond was given partly as a counter security, and partly in consideration of past services, which, being no consideration at all, meant a gift. On a second appeal to the House of Lords, this finding was reversed, and the Master's report was confirmed Thereupon the representatives of the obligor desired to shift their ground, and to impeach the transaction, assuming it now to be a gift, and alleging that it was made during the subsistence of a relation between obligor and obligee of either confidence or influence, and leave was given to them to institute proceedings for this purpose On a third appeal to the House of Lords, the Court below was again reversed, on the ground that, having set up a case of contract from the first, and having failed to prove it, the representatives of the obligor ought not to be allowed to turn round at this late stage, and set up not only a new, but a contradictory, case which involved charges of misconduct against the obligee (*per* Lord BROUGHAM, L C., at pp 520-625) The opinion was expressed that the case was of precisely the same character as *Harris v Tremenheere, sup* The like inability to establish that the transaction was a bargain for value, and not a gift, resulted in a similar denial of relief to the representatives of the alleged servient party in *Re Coomber*, [1911] 1 Ch 723, C A, which again was held to be *Harris v Tremenheere, sup*, over again (*per* COZENS HARDY, M R, at p 727 "it was not made after weighing the value of the consideration, it was simply an out and out gift", MOULTON, L J, at p 729 'it is possible that there might have been a transaction between the son and the mother with regard to the purchase of this leasehold property, in which the son would have had to show that he had given her full information in every possible way as to the value But in this case the gift was not based on value in any way at all The mother knew the house She had lived in it for twenty years, and knew the son was managing it. She meant it to go to the son whatever its value was")

(t) There are some curious illustrations of this oscillation between the frying pan and the fire which is sometimes forced upon the dominant party In *MacCabe v Hussey* (1831), 5 Bligh (N S) 715, the servient party had promised the dominant party that, in consideration of his services in obtaining a commission of lunacy against her aunt, and her appointment as the aunt' committee, she would pay him one third of the proceeds of the aunt's estate, if the aunt should die intestate The aunt did die intestate, and the servient party succeeded to her estate, and conveyed the whole of it to the dominant party, and mutual releases were exchanged Afterwards she filed her bill for restoration of two-thirds of the property, recognizing the dominant party's right to the residue for his services pursuant to the contract The dominant party, however, instead of being content with the situation, which would have left him the stipulated third, foolishly set up a case of gift as to one half of the estate which, of course, at once stirred up the lady s

party seeks in the first instance, not to avoid the transaction in the character of a servient party, but to enforce it as a contracting party, and, on the contractee setting up that it was not a contract, but a gift, asserts by way of reply that, if so, it was made during the subsistence of a relation from which influence is presumed. Two alternative lines of attack are thus open to him; and it is a matter of comparative indifference to him which of the two characters is assigned to the transaction ; except that his case on the former hypothesis is generally a simpler one to establish, and less likely to be defeated by counter-evidence, than his case on the latter (*u*). As already stated, the question of gift or purchase is one of substance (*v*).

457. There are other considerations which may render the exact character of the transaction a matter of importance, and requiring therefore strict proof on the part of the servient party. For instance, in the case of an alleged unconscionable bargain with an "expectant," the expectant's burden of proof is in certain respects, which have been already stated (*w*), somewhat

---

advisers to take him at his word, and to claim, by supplemented and amended bills, restoration of *the whole* of the property as having been conveyed without consideration, which relief she obtained In *Tomson* v. *Judge* (1855), 3 Drew 306, the instrument was in the form of a purchase. If it was in truth a purchase, the value given was grossly in adequate. Alive to this difficulty, the dominant party alleged, *and established,* that the transaction was in reality a gift, only to find that he had brought himself within the absolute rule, as it was then conceived to be, prohibiting any gift under any circumstances from a client to his solicitor, which was the relation between the parties in that case per KINDERSLEY, V.-C., at p 316) In *Allen* v. *Davis* (1850), 20 L J. (CH) 44, the dominant party who had obtained a bill of exchange for £262 from the servient party alleged that £100 of this was for services rendered as a dentist, and, as to the residue, set up, first, that it was a gift, and, afterwards, that it was in consideration of his undertaking to attend to his patient's teeth for the rest of his life. *Billage* v. *Southee* (1852), 9 Hare 164, was a similar case

(*u*) The following are illustrations *Nicol* v *Vaughan* (1833), 1 Cl & Fin 495 ; *Walker* v. *Smith* (1861), 29 Beav. 394 (where a lady sued to recover, *inter alia,* £500 East India Stock, which she had transferred to her solicitor for certain purposes the solicitor alleged that the stock was a gift, whereupon he assumed a double burden, first, that of showing that it was a gift, and, secondly, that of sustaining its propriety : he established the second, that is to say, that in fact the influence was not abused, but not the first per ROMILLY, M R , at pp 398, 399) ; *Re Holmes' Estate, Bevan's Case* (1861), 3 Giff 337 (where the circumstances were similar, and the solicitor was under the same double burden : but in this case he failed to prove either that the transaction was a gift, or that, if it was, it could be sustained per STUART, V.-C., at pp. 345–352) ; *Mitchell* v *Homfray* (1881), 8 Q B D 587, C A (where the executors of a lady sued her medical adviser for the repayment of money advanced : the defendant alleged that the money was given to him, and the jury found, on a question left to them for this purpose, that the transaction was a gift, and not a loan the defendant, however, failed to prove explanation of the transaction to the lady, or independent advice, and would therefore have been held liable, but for a plea of confirmation, which he established · per Lord SELBORNE, L.C., at pp 591, 592, and BRAMWELL, L.J , at p. 593).

(*v*) The following were, on the evidence, treated as gifts —*Wright* v. *Proud* (1806), 13 Ves. 136 (where a conveyance purporting to be the completion of an agreement for purchase was held to be a gift) ; *Dent* v *Bennett* (1839), 4 My & Cr 269 (where a contract whereby a patient purported to promise his medical adviser £25,000 in consideration of past services, and also of future attendance for the rest of his life, was treated as substantially a gift, having regard to the fact that the past services had been duly paid for, when rendered, and the future services must necessarily have been a "negligible quantity" in the case of a patient 85 years of age per Lord COTTENHAM, L.C , at p. 273) ; *Wright* v *Carter,* [1903] 1 Ch. 27, C A (where, of the three deeds in dispute, two, which purported to have been executed with the intention to benefit the solicitor for unpaid services rendered in the past, were held to be gifts) And op , generally, the cases cited in the last three notes.

(*w*) See § 443, note (*p*), *ante.*

heavier when the bargain is not a purchase of, or charge upon, the expectancy itself, than when it is expressed to be so in any instrument Again, the question of whether the transaction was a purchase or a mortgage determines the particular form of relief which may be appropriate; and for a similar reason the exact terms and figures are often required to be proved at the trial, or made the subject of inquiries or accounts then directed, in order that the mutual restitution which is an essential element in the rescission of any contract may be effectively provided for (x). And in the case of a gift, apart from the above considerations, it may become material to show, by reference to the circumstances, that it was not, or to rebut the dominant party's suggestion that it was, of such a trifling amount or value as to raise no presumption of undue influence or impropriety (y).

Sub-s. (3) *Matters which the Servient Party is not required to allege or prove.*

458. There are two classes of matters as to which the servient party is under no burden either of allegation or proof These comprise, first, those matters which he is not bound to, but may (by way of anticipation), set up in the first instance secondly, those matters which he not only is not required to, but cannot with propriety, set up at any stage in the proceedings, and which are wholly immaterial.

459. It is a fundamental rule of pleading that nothing need be alleged (z), and it is a fundamental rule of evidence that nothing need be proved, by a party litigant, at the outset, which the law presumes in his favour, or the contrary of which it lies upon the opposite party to establish. Now, as has been indicated, on proof of a relation of the kind under consideration, and of a transaction between the parties during the subsistence of that relation, the law makes three presumptions in favour of the servient party, (1) that the relation gave rise to dominion and influence on the one side, and subjection and amenability to the influence on the other; (2) that the transaction resulted from the exercise of the influence by the dominant party, and (3) that the influence was unduly exercised (a). It follows that none of the three facts so presumed need in the first instance be alleged, or, if alleged, need in the first instance be established, by the servient party, though, where it is known that the dominant party is prepared with materials for an affirmative answer, it may be advisable, and in any case it is allowable, to allege such facts by way of anticipation at the outset, instead of exercising the undoubted right to adopt the alternative, and the more regular and logical, course of awaiting the answer, and then setting up these matters in reply. It may be said that this rule can have no application to the class

(x) See Sect. 5, *post*
(y) See § 479, *post*
(z) R S C, O 19, r. 25 "neither party need in any pleading allege any material fact which the law presumes in his favour, or as to which the burden of proof lies on the other side"
(a) See § 405, note (a), *ante.*

of case where the relation is alleged to have been constituted by " the circumstances and conditions," and still less to that peculiar species of the class
which is known as " an unconscionable bargain with an expectant " but,
as has been noted in the discussion of these relations, though the servient
party is bound to establish facts indicating that the dominant party took an
unconscientious advantage of his " weakness," and though the proof of such
facts necessarily has the additional effect of meeting in advance any case
that may be made, or intended to be made, on the other side, yet what he
technically achieves by so doing is proof of a relation,—neither more nor less,
—and a right thereupon to have the same presumptions made in his favour
as in the case of any of the " known " or " suspected relations " (b).

460. The second of the above-mentioned classes, consisting of matters
irrelevant to any question between the parties, is wholly distinguishable
from the first : for here it is not a case of a right to reserve evidence which
may, or may not, afterwards be required, but in the meantime is not : it is
a case of evidence which can never be material, or therefore admissible, at
any stage of the proceedings, and which, therefore, it is as improper for the
servient party to adduce, as it is needless for the dominant party to contest

461. The first species of this class embraces all facts serving to indicate
the motive, purpose, or intention by which the dominant party was actuated.
It has long since been established in the present, as in the two other classes
of case giving rise to a duty of disclosure which have already been examined (c),
and for the same reasons of public utility which lie at the root of the whole
doctrine (d), that it is not only unnecessary, but immaterial, to allege that
the dominant party's breach of duty was animated or accompanied by actual
and personal dishonesty, or other moral obliquity, or that he had the intention
of defrauding or injuring the servient party : and that it is equally futile
and unavailing, because equally irrelevant, for the dominant party to allege
or establish the personal innocence of purity of his intentions or motives (e),

---

(b) See Sect. 2, Sub ss. (5), (6), ante, and note (h), inf.
(c) See § 197, and § 358, ante, respectively, which, mutatis mutandis, may be taken as
repeated in this place.
(d) See § 407, ante, and the cases cited in the notes thereto.
(e) *Welles* v *Middleton* (1784), 1 Cox Eq Cas. 112 (per Lord THURLOW, L.C., at p 119),
Wright v *Proud* (1806), 13 Ves 136 (where, at p 138, Lord ERSKINE, L.C , points out that
the dominant party had been " clearly overreached himself ; and . . made the instrument
of overreaching another in the same transaction "), *Groves* v. *Perkins* (1834), 6 Sim 576
(per SHADWELL, V.-C., at p 583), *Gibson* v *Russell* (1834), 2 Y. & C. 104 (where the
personal fraud alleged against the dominant party was not only unproved, but affirmatively
disproved by evidence—irregularly admitted without objection—of his high character,
which, however, did not save him from being held liable : per KNIGHT-BRUCE, V.-C., at
pp 120, 121) ; *Harvey* v *Mount* (1845), 8 Beav 439 (per Lord LANGDALE, M.R., at p 452),
Thornber v. *Sheard* (1850), 12 Beav. 589 (per Lord LANGDALE, M.R., at pp. 602, 603),
Baker v *Bradley* (1855), 7 De G M. & G 597 (per KNIGHT-BRUCE, L.J., at pp 616, 617) ;
Longmate v *Ledger* (1860), 2 Giff 157 (per STUART, V -C., at p. 165) ; *Baker* v *Monk* (1864),
4 De G. J. & S 388 (per TURNER, L.J , at p 394) , *Tate* v *Williamson* (1866), L. R 1 Eq
528 (per PAGE WOOD, V -C, at pp. 536, 541) , *Morgan* v *Minett* (1877), 6 C D 638 (per
BACON, V -C., at p. 647), *James* v *Kerr* (1880), 40 C D. 449 (per KAY, J , at pp. 460, 461) ,
Rae v. *Joyce* (1892), 29 L R. (Ir) 500, 509 , *Willis* v *Barron*, [1902] A. C 271, H L (per
Lord MACNAGHTEN, at p 278), *Raja Maneshar Bakhsh* v. *Shadi Lal* (1909), 25 T. L R
635, P. C , *Nocton* v *Lord Ashburton*, [1914] A C 932, H L

or his ignorance or unconsciousness of the equitable rules or doctrine (f), or his honest belief that the terms of the transaction were not unfair (g). Even in the case of a relation constituted by "the circumstances and conditions," or an unconscionable bargain with an expectant, it is only necessary for the servient party to prove fraud in the sense of a "presumed or inferred" fraud, not in the sense of personal fraud (h), though it is true that in establishing the circumstances from which the one kind of fraud is presumed, he incidentally establishes, in the majority of cases, the other also   Conversely, the unmeritorious position of the servient party is no reason for depriving him of relief, if he is otherwise entitled to it (i).   So irrelevant, and therefore improper, are charges of personal fraud, that the making of them by the servient party without proof is always the ground of a special and punitive order as to costs (j), though it can have no effect on his substantive rights even in a case where the dominant party has affirmatively established his complete probity and honour in relation to the particular transaction, or has, by an extreme indulgence, been permitted to adduce evidence (not objected to) of his high personal character and reputation generally (k).

(f) *Welles* v. *Middleton, sup* (*per* Lord THURLOW, L C , at p 126   "they have taken the property, perhaps bluntly and inadvertently, but that is too far out of the sight of a court of justice"); *Huguenin* v *Baseley* (1807), 14 Ves 273 (*per* Lord ELDON, L C , at p 300); *Espey* v *Lake* (1852), 10 Hare 260 (*per* TURNER, V.-C , at pp 263, 264), *Rhodes* v *Bate* (1866), 1 Ch App 252 (*per* TURNER, L.J , at p 262   nothing " affecting the moral character of the appellant—I think that he meant to give, and did give, the plaintiff honest advice, and that his liability arises not from his having failed to do so, but from his not having sufficiently attended to the law of this Court with reference to persons standing in confidential relations") , *Nocton* v *Lord Ashburton*, [1914] A C. 932, H L (*per* Lord HALDANE, L C , at p 954)

(g) *James* v. *Kerr* (1880), 40 C D 449 (*per* KAY, J , at pp 460, 461)

(h) *Gwynne* v *Heaton* (1778), 1 Brown C. C. 1 (*per* Lord THURLOW, L C., at p. 177 . "fraud is not the ground of relief, it is the example and pernicious consequences "   This was a case of purchase of a reversion); *Rae* v. *Joyce* (1892), 29 L R (Ir) 500 (another case of an unconscionable bargain with an "expectant," *per* FITZGIBBON, L.J. (Ir), at p 523 · "the essential character of the inequality of the parties to the transaction is distinct from fraud ").   It is true that at p 156 of *Chesterfield* (*Earl of*) v. *Jannsen* (1751), 2 Ves. Sr 125, Lord HARDWICKE, L.C , describes "catching bargains with heirs, reversioners, or expectants " as a " head of fraud," but he makes it quite clear that the " fraud " he is referring to is " fraud presumed or inferred from the circumstances and conditions," and not actual or personal fraud, though, as he adds at p 157, it so happens that in such cases there is " sometimes proof of actual fraud.'   So, at p 887 of *Moxon* v *Payne* (1873), 8 Ch. App. 881, JAMES, L.J., points out that, though "gross and premeditated fraud " had not been proved in that case (which was one of a relation of influence created by the circumstances), the failure to do so was no ground for refusing relief, and that fraud had been proved in the only sense in which it is required to be established, viz. the sense in which " the undue and unconscientious abuse of influence by a person in whom trust and confidence are placed, has always been treated "—that is, by the Court, and inferentially—" as a fraud of the gravest character "   See also *Nocton* v *Lord Ashburton, sup*

(i) *Hatch* v *Hatch* (1804), 9 Ves 292 (where the brother of the dominant party, who had actually prepared the deed which was set aside, and had been party to the undue influence which had procured it, was not deprived of relief (though he was of costs), because he was suing *in jure uxoris*, and the wife, who had been unduly influenced by both brothers, was not to be prejudiced by her husband's misconduct · *per* Lord ELDON, L.C , at pp 298, 299)   With this contrast the case of *Wright* v. *Vanderplank* (1856), 8 De G M. & G· 133 (where the unmeritorious husband was suing in right of his equally unmeritorious wife, and on this ground TURNER, L.J , at pp 149, 150, distinguishes the case from *Hatch* v. *Hatch, sup*.)

(j) See Ch. VIII, Sect. 2, Sub s. (4), *post*.

(k) As was done in *Gibson* v *Russell*, cited in note (*e*), *sup.*, q v   One may assume

462. Not less immaterial is the question of the actual, or anticipated, result of the transaction from a financial or business point of view. Just as in the case of the equitable duties of disclosure and otherwise which arise out of negotiations for a contract *uberrimæ fidei* (*l*), or out of a relation of confidence (*m*), it is no answer to a claim for relief to allege or prove, and quite unnecessary therefore for the servient party to offer anticipatory evidence contradicting any allegation, that the dominant party incurred serious risk in the transaction, and stood to lose heavily by it (*n*).   Equally irrelevant is any suggestion on the part of the dominant party that the servient party is unwise in seeking to avoid the transaction, and would be better off by electing to adhere to it , this being a matter for the consideration of the servient party alone, whose right to relief is not to be in any way affected by the fact, if it be a fact, that he will be a loser by so doing (*o*), any more than, conversely, the right of the dominant party to judgment in his favour, on his establishing any of the affirmative defences available to him, or on the servient party's failing to prove a case against him, is to be affected by the fact, if it be a fact, that, in the event, the transaction has turned out greatly to his advantage (*p*).

SECT. 4   THE AFFIRMATIVE ANSWERS AVAILABLE TO THE DOMINANT PARTY.

463. As soon as the servient party has established the matters in respect of which the onus rests on him, with the result that the three presumptions

that, if any objection had been made to its reception, this evidence would have been rejected.   In *Moore* v. *Prance* (1851), 9 Hare 299, the dominant party, a solicitor, relied upon an offer which he had made before action to reconvey the property to the servient party if he would apologize for having made charges of personal fraud and imposition, but TURNER, V.-C , at pp 304, 305, held that he had no right to impose such a condition, or " to mix up matters of personal and private feeling " with his plain legal duties, and such an offer, therefore, could have no effect upon the result, or even upon the costs.

(*l*) See § 221, *ante*.

(*m*) See § 359, *ante*.

(*n*) *Barnardiston* v *Lingood* (1740), 2 Atk 133 (*per* Lord HARDWICKE, L C., at p 135 " as to the hazard the defendant ran of its being a losing bargain, it is a circumstance in common only with all people who are dealers in this way, and if this had been a reason for carrying such an agreement into execution, there never would have been any of them set aside "   The case was one of an unconscionable bargain of an aleatory description with an expectant)   On the other hand, in *Berney* v. *Pitt* (1680), 2 Swanst 143 n., as to which see note (*w*) to § 445, *ante*, Lord NOTTINGHAM, L.C., did undoubtedly excuse the principal defendant on no other ground than that his bargain with the expectant was in effect a fair gamble

(*o*) See *Edwards* v. *Browne* (1845), 2 Coll 100 (*per* KNIGHT-BRUCE, V.-C , at p 107 : " this dealing with a reversionary interest, if the plaintiff considers it to be for his benefit to press the matter, cannot stand."   In that case the actual value was only shown to be £38 more than the £200 paid, and the Vice-Chancellor was obviously surprised that the " expectant " did think it worth his while " to press the matter," but distinctly held t' it the wisdom or unwisdom of his doing so was absolutely immaterial to his rights) ; *Bake.* v *Monk* (1864), 4 De G J & S 388 (*per* KNIGHT-BRUCE, L.J , who again points out that the question whether the servient party would not have done better for herself by resting content with the sale, was not the question he had to determine, which was solely one of right · p 389)

(*p*) See *Moth* v. *Atwood* (1801), 5 Ves. 845 (where the bargain which was upheld was admitted to be " a very considerable one ") ; *Montesquieu* v *Sandys* (1811), 18 Ves 301 (where Lord ELDON, L C., in sustaining an attorney's purchase, characterized by entire good faith and propriety, and of a very speculative character, which he had been pressed by the client to make, pointed out the irrelevance of the fact that the bargain ultimately turned out to the attorney's advantage   p. 312)

above stated (q) are made in his favour, it lies upon the dominant party to show cause why there should not be judgment against him. He must displace the *primâ facie* case made against him by proof that, in some way or another, the servient party has forfeited his right to relief This, unless he is in a position to establish some one of the various affirmative answers or bars which are applicable to actions of contract in general (r), he can only do by proving actual facts which contradict the facts presumed against him in virtue of the three presumptions in question Of these, the first, viz. that influence in general results from the relation, is probably irrebuttable, but, on the other hand, the dominant party is not concerned to contest this harmless, because unparticularized, presumption : it is only the other two, for these connect the influence with the transaction impeached, which he is seriously interested in repelling, and one or other of which he must repel, in order to succeed The former he displaces by proof that in fact the influence was not operative upon the transaction : the latter, by proof that it was not in fact undue (s). Either of these answers is sufficient to exculpate him · if the influence had in fact no effect upon the transaction, it is immaterial that there is no proof that, if it had been operative, it would have been in fact a " due " influence , and, if the influence be shown to have been duly exercised in fact, it does not signify in the least that the dominant party has failed, or has not attempted to establish, that it was inoperative in point of fact It is only the conjunction of the presumptions which entitles the servient party to relief . and a displacement therefore of any one of them is enough to destroy this right It is necessary to examine these two main classes of affirmative answer separately, and in detail ; and then to consider a third plea available to the dominant party, if he is unable to rebut any of the presumptions against him, which depends for its success on proof that, after the transaction had been entered into, the servient party with full knowledge of all material facts, and of his rights, and in entire freedom from the presumed undue influence, elected to confirm the transaction.

Sub-s (1) *Proof that the Presumed Influence was not Operative upon the Transaction*

464. The servient party having proved that the transaction was entered into at a time when the relation was in existence—the burden of proof is so far on him, but no further (t)—it is open to the dominant party to repel the

---

(q) See § 459, *ante*, and the cases cited in note (a) to § 405, *ante*

(r) Such as accord and satisfaction, release, &c Statutes of limitation do not in terms apply · see *Allcard* v *Skinner* (1887), 36 C D 145, C. A (*per* LINDLEY, L J , at p 186) Nor are they applied by analogy, where the party "has got the property into possession " *Nocton* v *Lord Ashburton*, [1914] A C 932, 957, 958, H L In *Cockell* v. *Taylor* (1852), 15 Beav 103, a plea of champerty was raised, but unsuccessfully

(s) For clear and succinct statements of the general burden of proof on the dominant party, in the case of gifts, see *Bainbrigge* v *Browne* (1881), 18 C D 188 (*per* FRY, J , at p 196) : in the case of transactions for value, *Holman* v *Loynes* (1854), 4 De G M & G 720 (*per* TURNER, L.J , at pp 282-284).

(t) See § 452, and the citation in note (j) thereto, *ante*

presumption thereupon made against him that the relation was not only contemporaneous with, but also operative upon, the transaction, by establishing that in point of fact it was not so operative. This he may do in one of two ways, or (as often happens) by both combined. He may prove facts tending to show that the relation, or rather the influence presumed to arise from it, had no effect upon the particular transaction, by reason of its subject-matter, or that such presumed influence had ceased, or was suspended, at the material date.

465. The first of these possible answers is made good by evidence that, for instance, the dominant party was not employed, if the relation be a professional one, in the particular transaction, or that the transaction was of such a nature as to render it impossible or unreasonable to suppose that it could have been within the sphere of the influence alleged. If the dominant party can establish that in this way the influence was, as it has been termed, inoperative *in hâc re*, he is entitled to judgment, without the necessity of going any further (*u*), but, wherever his proof has been found insufficient in this respect, he has failed (*v*), unless in a position to make good some other of the affirmative answers available to him.

466. Alternatively, it is open to the dominant party to allege that the influence presumed to have resulted from the relation was entirely at an end when the transaction took place, and that the servient party was at that time in a state of complete freedom and emancipation, notwithstanding that formally and technically the relation itself might be deemed to be still subsisting. There are extremely few examples of such a case being made out; but, whenever it has been, the dominant party, on this ground alone, and whether he was in a position to establish the propriety of the transaction or not, has been held entitled to succeed (*w*), whenever it has not,

---

(*u*) As in *Montesquieu* v *Sandys* (1811), 18 Ves 301, a case of an attorney purchasing from his client (*per* Lord ELDON, L.C., at p 312 "there is no authority establishing, nor was it ever laid down that an attorney cannot purchase from his client what was not in any degree the object of his concern as an attorney, the client making the proposal, himself proposing the price, no confidence asked or received in that article, and both ignorant of the value. Under such circumstances he is not the attorney *in hâc re*, and therefore, not being under any duty as attorney to advise against the agreement, he may be the purchaser"); *Edwards* v. *Meyrick* (1842), 2 Hare 60 (*per* WIGRAM, V. C, stating the proposition at pp. 68, 69, and finding, at p. 71, that the solicitor had brought himself within it, and had established that he was not employed *in hâc re*); *Allison* v. *Clayhills* (1907), 97 L T 709 (*per* PARKER, J, at pp 712 *sqq*, where the solicitor—it was again a case of a solicitor purchasing from his client—was held to have purchased as a friend, and not in the exercise of any influence presumed to spring from the relationship)

(*v*) As in *Jones* v. *Thomas* (1837), 2 Y & C (Exch in Eq) 498 (*per* ADDERSON, B, at pp. 519, 520), *Holman* v. *Loynes* (1854), 4 De G M & G 270 (*per* TURNER, L.J., at pp 279-281).

(*w*) As in *Oldham* v *Hand* (1751), 2 Ves. Sr 259 (case of a gift from a grateful client to his attorney after the litigation was over, *per* Lord HARDWICKE, L.C., at p. 260 "though there had not been that subsequent ratification"—for the attorney had established this plea also—"I do not see how I could come at it, for it is not obtained by the attorney during the course of the cause, or before it, but the whole was over"); *Lyddon* v *Moss* (1859), 4 De G. & J 104 (another case of attorney and client, where the attorney, though he had failed to prove that he had advised his client that an agreement to allow interest on his bill of costs was unenforceable, succeeded in establishing that the relation had come to an end at the time of the transaction · *per* TURNER, L.J, at pp 132-134, and KNIGHT-BRUCE, L.J, at pp 134, 135)

the Court, whilst recognizing that the plea is a valid one if satisfactorily established, has always so far as this ground is concerned, pronounced judgment against the dominant party (x). And the same consequences ensue upon a failure to prove that the state of freedom in which the servient party may have been at the commencement of the relation continued down to the date of the transaction, as upon a failure to prove a cessation of an initial state of subjection and inferiority before that date (y) If the gaoler can prove that the prison gates were thrown open, and that there was no one in the background to recapture the liberated prisoner, at the time of the act impeached, it is immaterial how long the captive may have previously been in durance and, conversely, it does not signify how free and unconstrained he may have been when he entered the place in which he was afterwards forcibly detained, if the act complained of was done during such detention It will be afterwards shown that, when the dominant party relies upon a subsequent confirmation of the transaction, the same onus is on him to show that the transaction was affirmed, as here it is to show that it was entered into, after a complete cessation and extinction of the influence (z)

467. It must always be borne in mind that the vital thing to be established in support of the plea now under consideration is the non-existence or cessation of the influence deemed to spring from the relation, rather than of the relation itself, which latter is only of importance as presumptively conducing to the former (a). It is useless to show that the relation had come to an end, or

(x) See *Hatch* v *Hatch* (1804), 9 Ves 292 (*per* Lord ELDON, L.C., at p 296), *Archer* v *Hudson* (1846), 15 L J. (CH) 211 (*per* Lord LYNDHURST, L.C, at pp 212, 213), and, in the Court below (1844), 7 Beav 551 (*per* Lord LANGDALE, M R , at p 561), *Holman* v *Loynes* (1854), 4 De G M & G 270 (*per* TURNER, L.J , at pp 282, 283), *Wright* v *Vanderplank* (1856), 8 De G M & G 133 'ver KNIGHT BRUCE, L J , at pp 136, 137, and TURNER, L.J , at p 146), *Re Holmes's* ' e, *Bevan's Case* (1861), 3 Giff 337 (*per* STUART, V C , at pp. 346, 347), *O'Brien* v *Lew.* 863), 32 L J. (CH) 569 (*per* Lord WESTBURY, L.C , at p 572), *Morgan* v. *Minett* (1877), 6 C. D 638 (*per* BACON, V -C , at p 645); *Bainbrigge* v *Browne* (1881), 18 C D. 188 (*per* FRY, J , at p 196), *Liles* v *Terry*, [1895] 2 Q. B 679, C A (*per* LOPES, L.J , at p. 684), *Cavendish* v. *Strutt* (1903), 19 T L. R 483 (*per* BYRNE, J , at p 488) In *Gibson* v *Jeyes* (1801), 6 Ves 266, the dominant party failed to show that the partnership between himself and his son (who actually exerted the influence) was at an end before the date of the transaction see § 504, note (m), *post*

(y) *Allcard* v *Skinner* (1887), 36 C D 145, C. A (*per* COTTON, L J., at pp. 172, 173, and BOWEN, L J , at p 191, pointing out the irrelevance of the mere fact that the servient party's mind and will were entirely free and unfettered when she entered the sisterhood, if the gift impeached was made under the influence afterwards arising out of the relation which she had so entered into, or, in other words, when the initial freedom had come to an end)

(z) See Sub s. (3), *post*

(a) *Wood* v *Downes* (1811), 18 Ves. 120 (*per* Lord ELDON, L C., at p 127: "if the relation has completely ceased, *if the influence can be rationally supposed also to cease*, a client may be generous to his attorney or counsel, as to any other person : but it must go so far "), *Allison* v *Clayhills* (1907), 97 L T. 709 (*per* PARKER, J , at pp 711, 712 "there are cases in which it is laid down that this principle only applies when the solicitor is the solicitor of the client in the particular transaction the validity of which is in dispute , but, in my opinion, that only means that when the relationship is of such a nature that it does not impose any duty to his client in the particular transaction, then the principle has no application. It does not mean, in my opinion, that the principle has no application in any case in which the solicitor is not in the particular transaction actually retained by or actually acting for his client under such circumstances that, if he neglected his professional duty, he would be liable to an action at law for negligence " He then gives, at p. 712,

was not subsisting, at the date of the transaction, unless circumstances be shown sufficient to raise a presumption that the influence also had ceased, or was inoperative (b) : for the presumption of undue influence which is made against the dominant party in the first instance can only be displaced by this counter-presumption   Still more futile is it to prove merely the non-performance or cessation of acts or duties proper to the particular relation, as, for instance, that the solicitor was not actually retained to act for the client in the particular transaction, or that the physician was not in actual attendance on the patient ; for to prove so much only does not even establish the non-existence or cesser of the relation, much less that of the influence (c). The most that such evidence can indicate is that, at the time of the transaction, the relation was dormant or suspended because at the moment no occasion arose for calling it into activity   So important is the question of the influence, and so comparatively unimportant that of the relation, that, as has been distinctly held, proof of the termination of the former, even without proof of the termination of the latter, may be sufficient to support the plea (d) ; and proof of circumstances tending to show that,

illustrations of the two types of case, one that of a solicitor who, though at the moment actually representing the servient party in an action, buys a horse from him in the hunting-field , the other, that of one who having been employed in litigation respecting the servient party's estates, or in the management of them, after ceasing to so act, buys from him part of those estates   in the former case, there would be a technical relation at the time of the transaction, but no influence is deemed to have operated on it   in the latter, there would be no existing relation, but none the less the influence might be inferred)   And see the case cited in note (d), *inf*

 (b) As in *Hylton* v. *Hylton* (1754), 2 Ves Sr. 547 (*per* Lord HARDWICKE, L C., at p. 549 " undoubtedly, if after the ward or *cestui que trust* comes of age, and after being actually put into possession of the estate, he thinks fit, when *sui juris* and *at liberty*, to grant that or any other reasonable grant, by way of reward for care and trouble, when done with eyes open, the Court could never set that aside · but the Court guards against doing it at the very time of accounting and delivering up the estate,"—that is to say, at a time when the " influence " is still fresh, though the relation of guardian and ward is formally at an end) , *Wright* v *Proud* (1806), 13 Ves. 136 (*per* Lord ERSKINE, L.C., at p. 137)   Cp. the cases cited in the last note, and also those cited in the notes to § 409, *ante*, where the relief is given on the theory that though the infancy is at an end, it has come to an end so recently that the influence of parent over " the child " must be presumed still active

 (c) See *Dent* v. *Bennett* (1839), 4 My & Cr. 269 (*per* Lord COTTENHAM, L C., at p 277 " the relation does not cease because the patient has not medicine actually administered to him at the time, any more than the relation of attorney and client ceases because no suit may be actually in progress.   If it were otherwise, I do not know that it would have made any difference "   The last sentence apparently means that, even if the relation could be deemed at an end, the influence could not be) , *Ahearne* v *Hogan* (1844), Dru 310 (*per* SUGDEN, L C (Ir), at p 323 · " the relation of physician and patient does not properly cease because the physician may not happen to be in actual attendance at the time ") , *Holman* v *Loynes* (1854), 4 De G. M & G 270 (where, as to the contention that the relation had come to an end because the dominant party had not actually rendered any professional services to the servient party for 16 months before the transaction, TURNER, L.J , at p. 282, observes that during that period " there was not any cessation of the relation, but only a cessation of the circumstances that were necessary to call the relation into action ") ; *Rhodes* v *Bate* (1866), 1 Ch App. 252 (*per* TURNER, L.J , at p 260 · " the mere fact that the relation is not called into action is not, I think, sufficient of itself to determine it, for this may well have arisen from there having been no occasion to resort to it ") , *Wright* v *Carter*, [1903] 1 Ch 27, C. A (*per* VAUGHAN WILLIAMS, L J , at p 53, STIRLING, L J , at pp 58, 59, and COZENS-HARDY, L J., at pp 61, 62) ; *Allison* v *Clayhills* (1907), 97 L T. 709 (the passage cited in note (a), *sup*)

 (d) *Re Holmes's Estate*, *Bevan's Case* (1861), 3 Giff. 337 (*per* STUART, V -C, at p 345, though the relation existed, it was of such a character as presumably to give rise to an extremely slight degree of influence, though not sufficient of itself to make good the particular plea in question, will operate strongly in the dominant party's favour, and may, with other circumstances, be deemed sufficient to sustain the transaction on the ground of its general propriety (c).

Sub-s. (2) *The Propriety of the Transaction, and the Due Exercise of the Influence in Fact*

468. If the dominant party is not in a position to rebut the presumption that the influence arising from the relation brought about the transaction, a second line of affirmative defence is open to him. He may still escape if he can repel the other presumption made in the servient party's favour, viz that the influence was unduly exercised, by affirmative evidence that in point of fact it was not unduly, but duly, exercised,—not abused for his own advantage at the expense of the servient party, but properly used with due regard to the rights and interests of both, and that the transaction was absolutely righteous, just, conscientious, and, in every sense of the word, "fair" (f). By such exculpatory proof he defeats and displaces the

---

in a case of a gift from client to solicitor · "the principle of influence vitiates the gift, but the presumption of influence may be rebutted by circumstances short of the total dissolution of the relation. *That relation is only looked at as creating the influence*, and as soon as circumstances of evidence are introduced which remove all effect of the influence, *whether the relation subsists or not*, there is no incapacity on the part of the solicitor to become the object of the client's bounty") In the particular case, however, the solicitor failed to show the necessary "circumstances of evidence" (pp 346, 347)

(e) *Pisani* v *Att -Gen. of Gibraltar* (1874), L. R 5 P C 516, where the servient party called in the dominant party, a colonial lawyer practising at Gibraltar, who had never acted for her before, and, in fact, was a perfect stranger to her,—to advise as to the sufficiency of certain deeds in a proposed sale of her property to a third person at a certain price Everything being ready for completion, the lady refused to proceed further with the matter, on the ground of a personal objection to the proposed vendee The dominant party used his best efforts, but in vain, to induce her to complete with this person, and, on her still refusing, offered to purchase himself at the same price, and eventually did so In these circumstances, it was held that, though it would be going a little too far to say that there was no relation at all between the parties, as in *Edwards* v *Williams*, cited in note (o) to § 453, *ante*, or no influence arising out of such a relation, yet (p 537) "the circumstances of the employment may be considered, and the amount of influence estimated." The Court found, on such consideration and estimate, "no reason to suppose that in this case, a high degree of confidence existed, or that much influence had been acquired"; and this finding, coupled with findings of complete good faith, sufficed to exculpate the dominant party (pp 538, 539)

(f) See *Hunter* v. *Atkins* (1834), 3 My & K. 113 (*per* Lord BROUGHAM, L C, at pp 134, 135 "in order to support the deed, he ought to show that no single advantage was taken, that all was fair," and that he entered into the transaction "taking no advantage of his influence or knowledge, putting the other party on his guard, bringing everything to his knowledge which he himself knew" again, at p 136. "the proof is upon him . to show that he has placed himself in the position of a stranger, that he has cut off as it were the connection which bound him to the party giving or contracting, and that nothing has happened which might not have happened had no such connection subsisted"), *Tomson* v *Judge* (1855), 3 Drew. 306 (the passage cited in note (p) to § 470, *post*); *Spencer* v *Topham* (1856), 22 Beav. 573 (*per* ROMILLY, M.R., at p 577 "the validity and *bona fides* of the transaction"), *Erlanger* v *New Sombrero Phosphate Co* (1878), 3 App Cas 1218, H L. (*per* Lord PENZANCE, at p 1230 "the Courts have always cast upon him who holds that position"—i e a position of "unfair advantage resulting from the relation" presumptively—"the burden of showing that he has not used it to his own advantage") *Rae* v *Joyce* (1892), 29 L R (Ir), 500 (the passage cited in note (n) to § 469, *post*)

inculpatory presumption, and succeeds in (as it is usually termed) " sustaining the transaction." It has, indeed, been sometimes judicially stated that, in the case of gifts as distinguished from contracts, this second line of defence is not available, and that the dominant party can only succeed by proof of the non-existence or cessation of the influence but when these statements are examined, it will be found that they amount to no more than an emphatic insistence on the different kinds of proof which must be adduced by the dominant party in the respective cases, particularly in regard to independent advice (g), the necessity for establishing which in the case of a gift, as a separate and distinct *probandum*, as contrasted with the absence of such necessity in the case of a contract, has, as will be explained hereafter (h), been definitely and clearly laid down and it is this necessity which, in the statements referred to, is doubtless intended when it is said that the relation must be put an end to before the gift can be secured from avoidance at the option of the donor.

469. How, then, is the " fairness," or " righteousness," or " propriety," or " conscientiousness " of the transaction to be established ? To some extent the kind of evidence required will depend upon the circumstances of the individual case · an element which may be of the utmost importance in this case may be of little or none in that : that which is not a matter of serious dispute between one pair of litigants may be fiercely contested between another And, further, there are obvious reasons why, as Lord BROUGHAM remarked (i), it is not desirable to specify too closely, or draw up any authoritative catalogue of, particular facts which will be held by the law, in each and every case, sufficient to " sustain the transaction." This observation, however, is not intended to suggest that the law ought to abnegate, or has abnegated, its duty of formulating general principles The first of these general principles is that, as has been emphatically laid down, it is wholly insufficient, and, though indispensable as a preliminary to the evidence which

---

(g) Thus, in *Morgan* v. *Minett* (1877), 6 C. D 638, after stating (p 645) that " the rule is without qualification," i c. the rule against a solicitor accepting a gift from his client, BACON, V.-C , goes on to say that " there may be circumstances which would show that that relation had been put an end to, so that the parties are at liberty to deal," and (at pp 646–649) refers to " independent advice," apparently (for otherwise the whole of this part of his judgment would contradict his previous statement that the rule is unqualified) as one of the means by which the relation may be so put an end to Similarly, in *Liles* v *Terry*, [1895] 2 Q B 679, C A , statements that the rule is irrebuttable as to gifts, while the relation subsists, are followed by others which recognize that proof of the competent and independent advice of a third person may justify the transaction, because in that way the dominant party puts himself in a position to say that the relation did not operate upon the gift (*per* KAY, L J , at pp 685, 686). Again, at p 186 of *London & Westminster Loan & Discount Co* v *Bilton* (1911), 27 T. L. R 184, JOYCE, J , after a statement that the dominant party must show a cesser of the influence, adds that " practically this could hardly be done, except by seeing that " the servient party " had competent and independent advice." Cp Lord BROUGHAM's observations cited in the last note, as to the kind of evidence whereby the dominant party may establish that he " has cut off, as it were, the connection."

(h) See § 470, and § 475, *post.*

(i) At p 141 of *Hunter* v *Atkins* (1834), 3 My & K 113 · " if it were stated that certain things should be required in order to rebut the presumption of " undue influence, " how easy would it be for cunning men to protect themselves and to place their misdeeds beyond the denunciation of the law."

is to justify the transaction, is not even, strictly, an ingredient in such evidence, to prove that the servient party had a real and actual intention of doing or promising that which he is alleged to have done or promised This of course is the first thing that the dominant party must establish, if it is in dispute, as the foundation on which his plea of good faith and propriety is to be built (j); for, however clearly he may satisfy the Court that his conduct has been such as would have abundantly sustained the transaction if there had been any actual intention on the part of the servient party to enter into it, yet, if he fails to prove the existence of that intention, he fails altogether (k): he has built a house, indeed, but upon sand, like the defamer who proves a case of absolutely fair comment on certain facts, assuming them to have been true, but cannot establish that they were true. Having proved that the servient party had a real intention of making the gift or contract, which, if it were the case of a will, would be enough, without going further, as has already been explained (l), the dominant party is still only on the threshold. the next question, as Lord ELDON said (m), is, " how the intention was produced." And it is at this point that he takes up his burden; not, as has been vainly contended, that he lays it down. Accordingly whenever, having shown the existence of actual volition on the part of the servient party with full knowledge of what he was doing, the dominant party has either failed in establishing, or has not attempted to establish, the next step, namely, the freedom from influence and the spontaneity of that volition, contenting himself with the utterly fallacious argument that because proof of intention is an indispensable prerequisite to success it is therefore the only one, his plea has been held bad (n)

(j) As in *Gibson* v *Russell* (1843), 2 Y & C. 104 (where, at p. 115, KNIGHT-BRUCE, V.-C, states this as one of the three things which the dominant party was bound to establish, and at pp 115, 116, finds that he had failed to do so, the matter being left in doubt); *Moore* v *Prance* (1851), 9 Hare 299 (where the dominant party did not even attempt to prove that, as he had falsely stated in the recitals of the deed drawn up by himself, the servient party had any intention or desire in fact to restrict his power of dealing with his property, or to appoint the dominant party his trustee, or place his affairs in his hands *per* TURNER, V.-C., at p 303)
(k) *Walker* v *Smith* (1861), 29 Beav 394 (*per* ROMILLY, M R, at pp 398, 399)
(l) See § 447, ante.
(m) At p. 299 of *Huguenin* v *Baseley* (1807), 14 Ves 273 noted and applied by Lord HATHERLEY, L C, at pp 338, 339 of *Turner* v *Collins* (1871), 7 Ch. App 329
(n) As in *Billage* v. *Southee* (1852), 9 Hare 534 (*per* TURNER, V.-C., at p 540 : " it is said that he intended to be liberal . but intention imports knowledge, and liberality imports the absence of influence "), *Wright* v *Vanderplank* (1856), 8 De G M. & G 133 (where, though it was proved that the lady knew exactly what she was doing, it was not proved that she was " in mind, and in person, a free agent ". *per* KNIGHT-BRUCE, L J, at pp 136, 137, and TURNER, L.J, at p 146); *Rhodes* v *Bate* (1866), 1 Ch. App. 252 (*per* TURNER, L J, at p 257); *Turner* v *Collins, sup* , *Rae* v *Joyce* (1892), 29 L. R (Ir.) 500 (*per* FITZGIBBON, L.J. (Ir), at p 523 : " the burden is thrown on the defendant of sustaining the transaction What has he to prove ? Not merely absence of fraud and dishonesty on his own part, *not merely understanding and volition on the plaintiff's part, not merely that a contract in the fullest sense was made*, but affirmatively that the contract itself was not only fair and just, but was also reasonable " This was a case of a bargain with an " expectant "); *Bank of Montreal* v. *Stuart*, [1911] A C 120, P. C. at p 137 (wife's declarations of freedom of will " merely showed how deep-rooted and lasting the influence of her husband was ") It has been said that this spontaneity and freedom, where the transaction is a gift, is even more difficult to establish than it ordinarily is in such cases if the servient party makes the gift not in the form of a payment or transfer outright, but in the form of a security to the dominant party's creditor on terms which involve a

470. Assuming the foundation to have been laid, as just indicated, the elements essential to the success of the plea may be summarily stated, accordingly as the transaction is a gift or a contract, as follows. A gift is "sustained" by proof, (1) that the servient party had full disclosure, in the widest sense of the term, from the dominant party; and (2) that he had, not from the dominant party, but from a separate person entirely independent of him, and free from his influence, honest and competent advice (o) A contract is "sustained" by proof, (1) that the servient party had such full disclosure from the dominant party as is above-mentioned; (2) that he received honest advice either from an independent third person, or (for the third person's intervention is not an absolutely indispensable condition here) from the dominant party himself who, in that case, must show that he gave precisely the same advice against himself as he would have given if the transaction had been with a stranger; and (3) that he received not less, or parted with not more than, a fair and proper consideration (p). It is now proposed to consider each of these elements successively.

471. Whatever be the nature of the transaction, the dominant party can only justify it by proof that, before it took place, he had put the servient party in possession of all the knowledge, in both senses of the word (q), which he then, whether actually or presumptively (r), himself possessed. That is to say, he must be in a position to show, not only that he had communicated to the servient party all material facts within his exclusive cognizance, but also that he had placed at his disposal the whole of his knowledge in the sense of natural or acquired skill or judgment as to the wisest mode of dealing with those facts in the interests, not of himself, but of the servient party In a word, he must make all such disclosure, and give all such advice, to the servient party as would or might put him back in that position of equality of which the relation has, in contemplation of law, deprived him (s)

continued future liability . *Archer* v *Hudson* (1846), 15 L J (CH) 211 (*per* Lord LYND. HURST, L C , at pp 212, 213), *Kempson* v *Ashbee* (1874), 10 Ch App 15 (*per* Lord CAIRNS, L C., at p. 19).

(c) See *Archer* v *Hudson, sup* (*per* Lord LYNDHURST, L.C , at pp 212, 213), and, in the court below (1844), 7 Beav. 551 (*per* Lord LANGDALE, M R , at p. 561), *Grosvenor* v *Sherratt* (1860), 28 Beav. 659, 665; *Bainbrigge* v. *Browne* (1881), 18 C. D 188 (*per* FRY, J , at p. 196). The above are good general statements of all the necessary elements in the case of gifts · for illustrations of the elements in detail see the cases cited in the remaining notes to this Sub-section

(p) *Holman* v. *Loynes* (1854), 4 De G M & G 270 (*per* TURNER, L J , at p 284 : "these rules require no more than that the client"—the case was one of solicitor and client— "should be fully informed, and duly and honestly advised, and that the price should be just"), *Tomson* v *Judge* (1855), 3 Drew 305, another solicitor and client case (*per* KINDERSLEY, V.-C , at p 313 : "the onus lies on the solicitor to show that the transaction was perfectly fair , that the client knew what he was doing, and, in particular, that a fair price was given, and of course that no kind of advantage was taken by the solicitor"), *Wright* v *Carter*, [1903] 1 Ch 27, C A (*per* STIRLING, L.J , at p 60); *Allison* v *Clayhills* (1907), 97 L. T. 709 (*per* PARKER, J , at p 712) The above are clear statements of the main classes of prerequisites to the upholding of a contract For illustrations of the several elements, considered separately, see the cases cited in the remaining notes to this Sub-section, *passim*

(q) See § 316, *ante*.

(r) As to actual and presumptive knowledge, and the various kinds of the latter, see Ch. II, Sect 3, *ante*

(s) See *Grosvenor* v *Sherratt, sup* (*per* ROMILLY, M R , at p 665).

472. First, as to communication of knowledge in the former sense. The onus is on the dominant party to establish, and the plea fails at the outset unless he establishes, by evidence which must be "clear and decisive" (t), that he made complete and exact disclosure (u) to the servient party of all material facts (v) within his exclusive cognizance relating to or affecting the subject-matter of the transaction; such as, where property other than money is in question, all facts relating to the title to the property (w), or the extent and particulars thereof (x), or its value (y)—and such facts, it must be remembered, may be material even where the transaction is a gift, for, though no value is paid, the donor may be none the less concerned in knowing what he is giving (z); or, where the consideration for a contract is payable on a certain event, all facts which have a bearing on the probability, or probable time, of that event happening (a); or, where it is a question of a series of loans, or services rendered, or other matter of account, all items and details required in order to explain the account, and show clearly how it is

(t) *Toker* v *Toker* (1863), 3 De G J & S 487 (*per* TURNER, L.J, at p. 490). In this case, the evidence was "clear and decisive" . see note (s), *post.*
(u) As to what this means, see Ch. II, Sect. 1, *ante.*
(v) As to materiality, s e Ch. II, Sect. 2, *ante.*
(w) *Wright* v. *Proud* (1806), 13 Ves. 136 (non-disclosure of the fact that the party was purchasing property which was already his own).
(x) *Groves* v. *Perkins* (1834), 6 Sim. 576 (where the dominant party divulged the fact that an intestate's property, to a share of which the servient party was entitled, was "considerable," but gave no particulars of the property, or the amount or value of the share, and, accordingly, said SHADWELL, V.-C, at p 583, "there was that non-disclosure of a material fact which compels me to say that the deed cannot stand")
(y) *Hatch* v *Hatch* (1804), 9 Ves 292 (non-disclosure of the improving value of the property per Lord ELDON L.C., at p. 296); *Huguenin* v. *Baseley* (1807), 14 Ves. 273 (concealment of the real value of the property); *Grosvenor* v. *Sherratt* (1860), 28 Beav 659 (non disclosure of previous offers to take the lease, and the reversionary value of the minerals : per ROMILLY, M R , at pp. 665, 666) , *Tate* v. *Williamson* (1866), L. R 1 Eq 528 (concealment of a valuation which the dominant party had obtained from an experienced mining agent, and which put the value of the mines at a much higher figure than that at which he purchased per WOOD, V -C., at pp. 539, 540) , *Rees* v *De Bernardy*, [1896] 2 Ch 437 (non-disclosure of the value of the property to which the next-of-kin agent had informed the servient parties that they were entitled, and of the fact that he was stipulating for a larger share of the property on establishing the title to it than he had previously asked from another person whom at first he had thought to be the heir . per ROMER, J., at pp. 443–445).
(z) For instance, a man may make a present of what he believes to be grazing or prairie land, without the least intention of giving land with valuable minerals under the surface It is clearly material to him to know this. The two first of the cases cited in the last note were cases of gifts In *Harris* v *Tremenheere* (1808), 15 Ves 34, Lord ELDON, L.C , at pp 39, 40, with reference to the two leases which he there found to be pure acts of bounty, intimated that, if there had been any evidence of an account laid before the servient party, containing any inaccurate statement as to value, he would have set the leases aside, instead of upholding them as he did. Similarly, in a case where no relation was established, and where, therefore, it was necessary to make out a misrepresentation, it was held that such a misrepresentation as to the value of the property was material, whether the transaction were regarded as a gift, or as a purchase : per WICKENS, V. C , at p. 329 of *Haygarth* v. *Wearing* (1871), L. R 12 Eq 320. And in *Re Coomber*, [1911] 1 Ch 723, C. A , the observation of MOULTON, L.J , at p 729, that "*in this case* the gift was not based on value," implies that there may be cases in which a gift is based on value.
(a) *Davies* v. *Cooper* (1840), 5 My. & Cr. 270 (where the dominant party purchased a reversionary interest from the servient party without disclosing to him the fact, of which he was cognizant, and of which, to his knowledge, the servient party was ignorant— believing, indeed, the contrary,—that the life on which the reversion depended was a very bad one · per Lord COTTENHAM, L.C , at pp. 277-279)

made up (b). Further, the dominant party must be prepared to establish that he gave the fullest and most candid information as to the exact nature of the transaction, as well as of its subject-matter, accordingly, his plea falls to the ground whenever he is unable to prove that he clearly explained to the servient party the character of the instrument recording the transaction (c), or the purposes which it was designed to accomplish (d), or the servient party's rights, liabilities, and position at the moment immediately preceding it, with reference to the matters proposing to be dealt with thereby (e), or the effect which it was calculated to have on those pre-existing rights and liabilities (f), or the right of the servient party both to reject it

(b) *Revell* v *Harvey* (1823), 1 Sim & St. 502 (where the dominant party not only omitted, but failed to comply with an express request, to disclose to the servient party how his account for a series of advances was made up, or to give him any particulars or explanation of it); *Thornber* v. *Sheard* (1850), 12 Beav 589 (a similar non disclosure · *per* Lord LANGDALE, M R, at p 601), *Billage* v. *Southee* (1852), 9 Hare 534 (where the dominant party, a medical man, refused to give his patient any account or explanation of how a certain sum, for which he had obtained a promissory note, was made up, and how much of it consisted of professional charges, and what those charges were. *per* TURNER, V. C, at p. 540)

(c) *Chaplin & Co* v *Brammall*, [1908] 1 K B. 223, C A (where the nature and effect of a guarantee was not explained *per* VAUGHAN WILLIAMS, L J., at p. 237)

(d) *Willis* v *Barron*, [1902] A. C 271, H L (where the donor was left to suppose that the object of the deed in question was merely to put right a slip in a previous deed executed by her which had been so expressed as not to carry out the intention of the parties, though the real purpose of the deed was to deprive her of the general power of appointment conferred by the previous instrument. *per* Lord HALSBURY, L.C, at p 276, and Lord MACNAGHTEN, at pp. 280, 281)

(e) As in *Tyler* v. *Yates* (1871), 6 Ch. App 665 (where one of the two servient parties was not told that he was under no liability in respect of the bills of exchange given by the other, an infant, so that no situation had arisen which would make it necessary to enter into the transaction impeached, or what his position was generally *per* Lord HATHERLEY, L C, at p. 670), *Kempson* v. *Ashbee* (1874), 10 Ch App 15 (where the servient party was not informed of the invalidity of the bond which she was supposed to be confirming by the transaction in question *per* Lord CAIRNS, L C, at pp 20, 21, and JAMES, L.J, at p 21), *Bank of Montreal* v. *Stuart*, [1911] A C 120, P. C (where there was a total failure to explain the existing situation to the servient party, or the position of her husband, whose necessities she was asked to relieve) See also *Wright* v. *Carter*, [1903] 1 Ch. 27, C A (*per* VAUGHAN WILLIAMS, L.J, at pp 51–55)

(f) As in *Bennett* v *Vade* (1742), 2 Atk. 324 (*per* Lord HARDWICKE, L C., at pp 326, 327), *Huguenin* v. *Baseley* (1807), 14 Ves 273 (no explanation of the effect of a provision in the settlement making it revocable only in the presence of certain persons, or of the effect of the deed generally. *per* Lord ELDON, L.C, at pp 293–300), *Bayly* v *Wilkins* (1846), 3 Jo & Lat 630 (concealment from client that the effect of his purchase of an incumbrance on the estate of a debtor to the solicitor would be to benefit the solicitor as a prior incumbrancer, and not the client as heir at law · *per* SUGDEN, L.C. (Ir), at p 636); *Moore* v. *Prance* (1851), 9 Hare 299 (*per* TURNER, V.-C, at p 304), *Grosvenor* v. *Sherratt* (1860), 28 Beav 659 (no explanation of the effect of a reversionary lease on the servient party's interests *per* ROMILLY, M R, at p 666); *Sharp* v *Leach* (1862), 31 Beav 491 (not explained that the deed was irrevocable *per* ROMILLY, M.R, at pp 494–501), *Procter* v. *Robinson* (1867), 15 L. T 431 (servient party not made to understand that the effect of the deed was to benefit the solicitor: *per* TURNER, L.J, at p 432) · *Howley* v *Cook* (1873), Ir. R 8 Eq 370 (no explanation of effect of unprecedented clauses introduced into the mortgage deeds, such as a power of sale without notice), *Nevill* v *Snelling* (1880), 15 C D. 679 (no explanation by moneylender of the "penal clause" in the contract · *per* DENMAN, J, at pp 692, 693); *Re Haslam and Hier Evans*, [1902] 1 Ch. 765, C A. (*per* STIRLING, L J, at pp 769–772), *Cavendish* v *Strutt* (1903), 19 T. L. R. 483 (*per* BYRNE, J, at pp. 488, 489), *Cockburn* v *Edwards* (1881), 18 C D 449, 455, 460, 462, C A (a similar case to *Howley* v *Cook*, *sup*); *Harris* v. *Clarson* (1910), 27 T L R 30 (no explanation by moneylender of the operation of a clause as to interest); *London & Westminster Loan & Discount Co* v *Bilton* (1911), 27 T L R. 184 (a similar type

when *in fieri*, and to repudiate it after execution (g). Sometimes the dominant party seeks to fortify himself by false recitals, or other misrepresentations of the nature of the transaction or its subject-matter, which he introduces into the instrument in the belief that the servient party will not notice or appreciate their untruth. In such cases, of course, there is a double obligation of disclosure on the dominant party; and the very thing which he fondly hopes will be his salvation, turns out to be his undoing, and the fabricated recitals to be "scripta auctori perniciosa suo" (h) Where, however, the dominant party succeeds in satisfying the Court that he has made full disclosure in the above sense, his plea so far, but so far only, prevails (i).

473. The dominant party must next establish, in order to make good a case of disclosure in the fullest comprehension of the word, that, before the transaction took place, he put at the disposal of the servient party the whole of his knowledge, in the sense of capacity, skill, and judgment, which means that he gave him "all that reasonable advice against himself that he would have given him against a third person" (j). "He must show to demonstration, for this must not be left in doubt, that no industry he was bound to

of case to the last . *per* JOYCE, J. at p 185: "merely reading over the deed to the defendant or any one else would be of little or no use It could hardly be understood except after careful perusal and examination by a lawyer, and would require the skill of an actuary to calculate the exact rate of interest really charged"); *Stirling* v *Rose* (1913), 30 T L R 67 (the like), *Re Hoggart's Settlement* (1912), 56 Sol J 415 (no explanation of the effect of an agreement between solicitor and client for remuneration by a percentage of sums to be recovered in respect of non-contentious business. The solicitor in this case, however, escaped on proving an offer to have his costs taxed) Cp the Indian cases of " pardanishin " women, such as *Tewarry* v *Nawab Syed Ali Hossein Khan* (1874), L R 1 Ind App 192 (at pp 206, 207), *Sudisht Lal* v. *Mussummat Sheobarat Kunwar* (1881), L R. 8 Ind App 39 (at p 43) Here the onus was not discharged In *Kali Bakhsh Singh* v *Ram Gopal Singh* (1913), 30 T L R 138, it was

(g) As in *Procter* v *Robinson* (1867), 15 L T 431 (*per* TURNER, L J , at pp 431, 432, and CAIRNS, L J , at pp 432, 433 here the servient party was not told that he need never have executed the deed at all, and that, when he had executed it, it was of no validity); *Morgan* v *Minett* (1877), 6 C D 638 (*per* BACON, V-C, at p 648)

(h) See *Wright* v *Proud* (1806), 13 Ves 136 (the nature of the plaintiff's interest falsely recited in the deed *per* Lord ERSKINE, L.C., at p. 137); *Gibson* v *Russell* (1843), 2 Y & C 104 (a gift fraudulently recited to be a purchase *per* KNIGHT-BRUCE, V.-C., at p 106); *Moore* v *Prance* (1851), 9 Hare 299 (false recitals of the desire and intention of the servient party to place his affairs in the hands of the dominant party, and appoint him his trustee, which the dominant party did not even suggest to be true *per* TURNER, V-C, at p 303), *Broun* v *Kennedy* (1864), 4 De G J & S 217 (deed condemned on the face of it by its false recitals of the character and purport of the transaction: *per* KNIGHT-BRUCE, L.J, at p 221), *Moxon* v *Payne* (1873), 8 Ch App 881 (a false recital that the price paid to the dominant party in a previous transaction had been "ascertained upon an incorrect basis, and upon a mistake of facts," whereas in truth it was a fraudulent price deliberately obtained from the servient party, and not the result of any "mistake" whatsoever · *per* JAMES, L.J , at p 885) Cp the decisions as to false recitals and descriptions, in cases of relations constituted by the circumstances, which are cited in note (r) to § 430, *ante*

(i) As in *Edwards* v *Meyrick* (1842), 2 Hare 60 (*per* WIGRAM, V-C., at pp 71, 72), *Archer* v *Hudson* (1846), 15 L J (CH) 211 (*per* Lord LYNDHURST, L C , at pp 212, 213 but here the dominant party, though proving explanation of the meaning of the promissory note in question, and thus establishing one point in the requisite proof, completely failed to prove any of the others, and was accordingly held liable), *Hartopp* v *Hartopp* (1856), 25 L. J (CH) 471; *Toker* v *Toker* (1863), 3 De G. J & S 487 (*per* KNIGHT-BRUCE, L.J , at pp 489, 490, and TURNER, L.J , at p 490), *Allison* v *Clayhills* (1907), 97 L T 709 (*per* PARKER, J , at p 713)

(j) *Gibson* v. *Jeyes* (1801), 6 Ves. 266 (*per* Lord ELDON, L C , at p 278)

exert would have got a better bargain " for him (k). In all cases of failure to
satisfy the Court on this point, the plea has failed (l). It must obviously
be a matter of extreme difficulty for any man in any case to act up to a
" counsel of perfection " which requires him to use the whole of his natural
and acquired intellectual and moral powers, his sagacity, experience, and
skill, his zeal, energy, and industry, in direct opposition to his own interests :
and, assuming him to have surmounted this difficulty, a much heavier burden,
and the only one which concerns jurisprudence, awaits him when the transaction is challenged and subjected to judicial investigation,—the burden
of proving compliance with a duty so antagonistic to the ordinary impulses
and propensities of human nature. In a very few cases, however, the
dominant party has succeeded in discharging this burden (m)

474. There is a very simple and obvious means of escaping these difficulties,
and a means which affords an excellent test of the conscientiousness and
propriety of the transaction , and that is, to give no advice at all, but to
see that the servient party has the advice of a third person entirely independent
of the influence. This course so plainly suggests itself to an honest and
scrupulous man that, when proved to have been adopted by the dominant
party, it goes a very long way, and in most cases is sufficient of itself, to sustain
the validity and *bona fides* of the transaction (n) : whereas the omission to
resort to it raises an inevitable suspicion that the only reason for the omission
must have been a consciousness on the part of the dominant party that the
transaction was unrighteous and unfair, and that any impartial person would

(k) *Gibson* v *Jeyes* (1801), 6 Ves 266 (*per* Lord ELDON, L.C , at p 271), *Huguenin* v.
Baseley (1807), 14 Ves 273 (*per* Lord ELDON, L C , at p 299), *Holman* v. *Loynes* (1854),
4 De G. M & G 270 (*per* Lord CRANWORTH, L C , at p 272)   The principle is stated,
substantially in the same form of words, in all the cases cited in the next two notes, at the
pages of the several reports which are cited within brackets after the reference.

(l) As in *Gibson* v *Jeyes*, *sup.* , *Dawson* v *Massey* (1809), 1 Ball & B 219 (*per* Lord
MANNERS, L C (Ir), at p. 236), *Champion* v *Rigby* (1830), 1 Russ & M 539 (*per* LEACH,
M.R , at p 539 : the dominant party, however, escaped here on the ground of the servient
party's delay, amounting to implied confirmation, the decision being affirmed by Lord
COTTENHAM, L.C (1840), 9 L J. (CH) 211, on the further ground of additional delay in the
appellate proceedings) ; *Moore* v *Prance* (1851), 9 Hare 299 (*per* TURNER, V -C., at p. 303) ,
Holman v. *Loynes*, *sup.* , *Savery* v *King* (1856), 5 H L C 627 (*per* Lord CRANWORTH, L C ,
at pp 665, 666) . *Gresley* v. *Mousley* (1859), 4 De G & J 78 (*per* KNIGHT BRUCE, LJ , at
pp 88, 89, and TURNER, L J , at pp 97, 98) , *Clare* v *Joseph*, [1907] 2 K B 369, C A.
(*per* BUCKLEY, L J , at p. 378)

(m) As in *Edwards* v. *Meyrick* (1842), 2 Hare 60 (*per* WIGRAM, V.-C , stating the proposition, at pp 70, 71, and finding that in that case the onus was sustained, at pp 71,
72) ; *Spencer* v *Topham* (1856), 22 Beav. 573 (*per* ROMILLY, M R , at p 577, stating the
rule, and, at pp 577–583, finding that the burden was discharged) , *Pisani* v *Att -Gen of
Gibraltar* (1874), L. R 5 P. C 516 (at p 536, statement of the rule, and, at p 538, finding
that it had been complied with)

(n) In the following cases of gift, the dominant party succeeded, on proof of indepen
dent advice of a third person (with or without other facts showing the propriety of the
transaction) —*Pratt* v *Barker* (1826), 1 Sim 1 ; *Taylor* v *Johnston* (1882), 19 C D 603
(*per* BACON, V.-C., at p 610) , *Re Coomber*, [1911] 1 Ch. 723, C A (*per* COZENS-HARDY,
M.R , at p. 728)   The like result attended the like proof in the following cases where the
transaction impeached was a contract —*Blackie* v *Clark* (1852), 15 Beav 595 (*per*
Romilly, M R , at p 603, as to one of the transactions there in question) ; *Potts* v *Surr*
(1865), 34 Beav 543 (*per* ROMILLY, M R , at pp 551, 552   this was a case of a family
arrangement, in which the father was proved to have given valuable consideration, for
which reason the case may be regarded as one of contract, rather than gift)

so advise A party must ordinarily be in a very dubious position who asks a disinterested tribunal to approve, *ex post facto*, the propriety of a transaction which he carefully refrained from submitting to the judgment of an equally disinterested (though an unofficial) tribunal before the transaction was entered into By so acting he may be thought to have pronounced judgment against himself in advance It is one thing, however, to say that proof of the interposition of a non-conducting medium (so to speak), in the shape of an impartial third person's advice, between the influence and its object is of the utmost service in sustaining the transaction ; it is another to say that proof of this fact is *per se* an indispensable *probandum* in the sense that, however righteous the transaction may be demonstrated to have been in every particular, it still cannot stand in the absence of evidence that a third person intervened to protect the servient party The question now arises— and it is one of considerable importance—whether the latter proposition, which does not seem to have much principle or reason in its favour, is established by authority The correct answer, it is conceived, to this question is that, in the case of gifts, it probably is so established, but that, in the case of contracts, it is not

475. It has already been shown what a sharp division the law has from the first made between gifts, or transactions in the nature of gifts, on the one hand, and contracts, or transactions for valuable consideration, on the other ; how " invincible " is the jealousy with which the former have always been regarded by the courts ; and how " almost impossible " it has been thought to be for any gift between parties connected by a relation of influence to stand (*o*). Approaching the question in this spirit, it is not surprising to find that, in early times, equity only admitted a relaxation of its rigidity and severity towards gifts to the extent of allowing them to stand where the influence is shown to have come to an end ; to which it grudgingly added in modern times the further concession, already adverted to (*p*), that evidence of independent advice might be deemed evidence of the termination of the influence To hold these views is tantamount to laying down that proof of the servient party's having been advised by a separate and independent person is the only element in the propriety of the transaction which is of the least use or relevance in any attempt to sustain a gift, and that it is so relevant, not because it tends to establish that the influence was not abused, but because it proves that no influence was *in hâc re* exerted at all. And not only is this view to be implied from decisions in which the dominant party failed to sustain the propriety of the gift in other respects, and which, therefore, are not absolutely conclusive (*q*), but it has been expressed in plain and unmistakable terms in one most remarkable case, from which every

(*o*) See § 405, and note (*g*) thereto, *ante*.
(*p*) See § 468, and note (*g*) thereto, *ante*.
(*q*) Such as *Baker* v. *Bradley* (1855), 7 De G M & G 597 ; *Sharp* v *Leach* (1862), 31 Beav. 491 ; *Brown* v. *Kennedy* (1864), 4 De G J & S 217 ; *Willis* v *Barron*, [1902] A C. 271, H L. ; *Chaplin & Co* v. *Brammall*, [1908] 1 K B 223, C A , *Bank of Montreal* v. *Stuart*, [1911] A. C. 120, P. C ; *London & Westminster Loan & Discount Co* v *Bilton* (1911), 27 T. L. R 134.

other possible basis of the decision was eliminated with the utmost care and precision   It was there held by TURNER, L J., with the reluctant and tardy adhesion of KNIGHT-BRUCE, L.J., in favour of a servient party with no merits whatever against a dominant party whose conduct had been quite meritorious, that, though "the evidence on the part of the defendant"——who was the dominant party referred to—had established to the complete satisfaction of TURNER, L J, as stated in his judgment, "that the plaintiff signed the promissory notes and memoranda, and executed the bonds and deeds in question freely and voluntarily, and without pressure or solicitation on the part of the defendant, that their contents were fully explained to her, and that she perfectly understood them, and their nature, purport, and effect, and the consequences of her signing and executing them," and that the defendant had "cautioned her" as to the transactions, and "meant to give, and did give the plaintiff, honest advice,"—yet, because this full explanation of the transaction and of the plaintiff's rights in respect thereof, and this honest advice, did not proceed from a third person, the gift must be set aside (r).   One naturally inquires whether this startling decision has been observed upon, if not overruled, in any subsequent authority.   So far from it, it has received the express approbation of Lord SELBORNE (s) ; and the doctrine there laid down has been acted upon, though not always under such striking circumstances, in a series of decisions both before and after the date of that in question (t).   So that, however irrational and unjust

(r) *Rhodes* v. *Bate* (1866), 1 Ch App 252 (*per* TURNER, L J, at pp 257, 261, 262) The effective judgment of the Court is given by TURNER, L J, after which KNIGHT BRUCE, L J, at p 262, merely adds a few words, from which it appears that, at the last, he was won over to the opinion of his colleague   It will be observed that the plaintiff was deprived of costs (p. 257)

(s) At p 591 of *Mitchell* v *Homfray* (1881), 8 Q B D 587, C A ("in *Rhodes* v *Bate*, it was laid down in clear terms that in order to uphold a gift made to a person standing in a confidential relation, the donor must have had competent and independent advice in conferring it   This is undoubtedly the rule so long as the confidential relation exists ")

(t) See the following cases of gift, in which the dominant party was held liable on the *sole* ground of failure to prove that the servient party had the independent advice of a third person   *Griffiths* v *Robins* (1818), 3 Madd 191 (*per* LEACH, V -C, at p 192   "they can maintain no deed of gift from her unless they can establish that it was the result of her own free will, and *effected by the intervention of some indifferent person*"), *Goddard* v *Carlisle* (1821), 9 Price 169 (*per* RICHARDS, C B, at pp 661, 662, and GRAHAM, B, at pp 663, 664), *White* v *Meade* (1840), 2 Ir Eq R 420, *Harvey* v *Mount* (1845), 8 Beav 439 (*per* ROMILLY, M R, at p 452), *Archer* v *Hudson* (1846), 15 L J (CH) 211 (*per* Lord LYNDHURST, L C, at pp 212, 213), *Nottidge* v *Prince* (1860), 2 Giff 246 (*per* STUART, V -C., at p 269 . no proof that "a sufficient protection has been *interposed*"), *Sercombe* v. *Sanders* (1865), 34 Beav 382 (*per* ROMILLY, M R, at p 386), *Mitchell* v. *Homfray, sup* (but the dominant party escaped here on the proved plea of confirmation, and on that alone.   Otherwise he would have been held liable on the sole ground of absence of independent advice · *per* Lord SELBORNE, L.C, at p 591, and BRAMWELL, L J, at p 593), *Allcard* v *Skinner* (1887), 36 C D 145, C A (*per* COTTON, L J, at pp 171–173, LINDLEY, L J, at pp 181 *sqq*, and BOWEN, L.J, at pp 189–191   This also was a case in which the dominant party, who otherwise would have been held liable, succeeded on the ground of confirmation of the transaction by the servient party), *Liles* v *Terry*, [1895] 2 Q B 679, C A. (*per* LOPES, L J, at p 684, and KAY, L J, at pp. 685, 686), *Powell* v *Powell*, [1900] 1 Ch 243 (*per* FARWELL, J, at pp 245, 246), *Wright* v *Carter*, [1903] 1 Ch 27, C A (as to such of the deeds there in question as were voluntary   *per* VAUGHAN WILLIAMS, L.J at pp 49–53, STIRLING, L.J, at pp 56–58, and COZENS HARDY, L J, at p 61)   The few cases in which a dominant party has succeeded in establishing the interposition of the indifferent third person are cited in note (*n*) to § 474, *ante*

the doctrine may appear to some minds, and however distasteful it has in point of fact been to judges of no mean authority (u), and though the Privy Council has recently refused to accept it, in its absolute form, in the case of a gift by a "pardanishin" woman (uu), it is difficult to deny that it is now part of the law of England.

476. In the case, however, of any transaction for value, which, as has been pointed out (v), is not regarded by the law with that "almost invincible jealousy" which a gift arouses, the rule as to independent advice is not so stringent. Here, though proof of the interposition of a third person's protection and advice is of paramount value as a factor in the justification of the transaction (w), and though the absence of such proof is usually fatal (x), and, further, may contribute to establish that form of relation which is constituted by "the circumstances and conditions" of the case, as has already been shown (y); yet, as has been distinctly held, if the other facts of the particular case are such as to warrant an inference of complete fairness and conscientiousness in the conduct of transaction, and to indicate that the advice of an indifferent person was impracticable, or would have been of no use or importance, the dominant party's plea will not be defeated merely because he is unable to establish that such advice was given (z). In other

(u) The objections which have been, or may reasonably be, made to the rule in question are discussed in App B , § 665, *post*.

(uu) The passage referred to in this most important judgment (delivered by Lord SHAW) is as follows —"the Judicial Commissioners have laid it down that such a gift cannot stand unless it is proved that the lady had independent advice   In their Lordships' opinion, there was no rule of law of the absolute kind indicated   The possession of independent advice, or the absence of it, was a fact to be taken into consideration and well weighed on a review of the whole circumstances relevant to the issue whether the grantor thoroughly comprehended, and deliberately and of her own free will carried out the transaction   If she did, the issue was solved, and the transaction upheld , but if upon a review of the facts   the conclusion was reached that the obtaining of independent advice would not really have made any difference in the result, then the deed ought to stand "   *Kali Bakhsh Singh v Ram Gopal Singh* (1903), 30 T L R 138, P. C , at p. 139

(v) See § 405, and note (f) thereto, *ante*

(w) See the " contract " cases cited in note (n) to § 474, *ante*

(x) As in *Barnard v Hunter* (1856), 2 Jur (N S) 1213 , *Smith v Kay* (1859), 7 H L. C 750 (*per* Lord CHELMSFORD, L C , at pp 761, 762, and Lord CRANWORTH, at pp 770–773) , *Lloyd* v. *Attwood* (1859), 3 De G & J 614 (*per* TURNER, L J , at pp 649, 650) , *Wright v Carter*, [1903] 1 Ch 27, C A (as to such of the transactions there in question as were in the nature of contracts *per* VAUGHAN WILLIAMS, L J , at pp 54–56, and STIRLING, L J , at p 60) : *Re Hoggart's Settlement* (1912), 56 Sol J 415 (though in that case the servient party had put himself in the wrong by ignoring the offer of the dominant party—his solicitor—to submit his bill of costs to taxation)

(y) See, generally, the cases cited in the notes to Sect 2, Sub ss (5), and (6), *ante* , and, particularly, *Taylor v Obee* (1816), 3 Price 83 ; *Wood v Abrey* (1818), 3 Madd 417 ; *Revett v Harvey* (1823), 1 Sim & St 502 , *Davies v Cooper* (1840), 5 My & Cr 270 ; *Addis v Campbell* (1841), 4 Beav 401 ; *Sturge v Sturge* (1849), 12 Beav. 229 , *Baker v Loader* (1873), L R 16 Eq 49 ; *Fry v Lane* (1880), 40 C D 312 , *Rees v De Bernardy*, [1896] 2 Ch 437 , *De Witte v Addison* (1899), 80 L. T 207, C A , *Brenchley v Higgins* (1901), 70 L J. (CH) 788, C A , *Cavendish v. Strutt* (1903), 19 T L R 483

(z) *O'Rorke v Bolingbroke* (1877), 2 App Cas 814, H L (a case of a purchase of the servient party's reversion, where the dominant party proved that he had done everything in the matter which honesty and candour demanded, had made full disclosure both to the servient party, and to his father, and had paid a price which he had every reason to believe was not only fair, but liberal, though it turned out afterwards to have been inadequate no third person had advised the servient party, but since, to the knowledge of all parties, both father and son were unable to afford this expense, it was held that the conscientiousness of the bargain had been established in the whole circumstances of the case, which,

words, proof of this fact is not in every case, as it is where it is a question of a gift, an absolutely indispensable condition precedent to the success of the plea, and the "sustaining" of the transaction.

477. It must be shown that "the third person" introduced was both independent and competent. By independence is meant entire freedom of will and judgment from the influence of the dominant party, and from that of every other person whose interest may lie in the same direction. This freedom must be a freedom in substance, and not merely in form. A person who is merely called in by the servient party for the express purpose of approving, and putting into legal form, what has already been determined upon, and from whom any dissuasive counsel or attempted exercise of judgment would be immediately resented, or one who is employed by, or is in the confidence of, both parties, or one who is not likely to act in the sole interests of the servient party, though ordinarily his natural protector, by reason of some special circumstance, such as a quarrel or estrangement, is not an independent person in this sense (a) "Competence" (which, being manifestly a term *ancipitis sensus*, is an unfortunate one to have employed, as judges have constantly employed it, in this connection) imports the competence which arises from full instruction in the material facts on which the third person is to advise it does not of course mean the competence which arises from skill The plea therefore is not made out by proof that the servient party was advised by a person who, however independent and honest, was not completely acquainted with every detail of the situation (b), or at least as completely as the dominant party On the other hand, if the advice was in fact honest and independent it can hardly be supposed that the servient party can make the dominant party responsible for its want of skill, unless of course the latter had put the

said Lord BLACKBURN, at p 837, "made it impracticable for the lad to have that further advice which, I agree, if practicable, the purchaser should have insisted on his having"): *Cockburn* v *Edwards* (1881), 18 C D 449, C A (*per* BRETT, L J , at p 460 "if he can show that he has done nothing to which an independent solicitor would not   have assented, and that he fully explained the matter,   the law cannot interfere with the transaction"); *Readdy* v. *Pendergast* (1887), 55 L T 767 (*per* KEKEWICH, J , at p 768), *Allison* v *Clayhills* (1907), 97 L T 709 (*per* PARKER, J , at p. 712) Cp the observations of VAUGHAN WILLIAMS, L J , at pp 54, 55 of *Wright* v *Carter*, [1903] 1 Ch 27, C A

(a) As in *Clarke* v. *Malpas* (1862), 4 De G. F & J 401 (where the solicitor who was supposed to be advising the servient party was in fact more the solicitor of the dominant party than his . *per* KNIGHT-BRUCE, L.J , at p. 404), *Tate* v *Williamson* (1866), L R 1 Eq 528 (where the dominant party urged the servient party to consult his father with whom he had quarrelled,—a suggestion which under the circumstances was a mockery · *per* WOOD. V -C, at p 539), *Rae* v *Joyce* (1892), 29 L. R. (Ir) 500 (where the introduction of a solicitor whose function really was to approve and register, rather than to advise impartially, was held to have been quite illusory, and no protection at all to the servient party : *per* WALKER, L C (Ir), at p. 514, O'BRIEN, C J (Ir), at pp. 521, 522, and FITZGIBBON, L.J. (Ir), at pp. 525–527), *Powell* v *Powell*, [1900] 1 Ch. 243 (where "the third person" was the solicitor of both parties, which FARWELL, J , at pp 245–247, said was not enough ; what is required being "the intervention of an independent mind and will acting on behalf and in the interest of " the servient party "only "), *Willis* v *Barron*, [1902] A C 271, H. L (where a married lady was the servient party, and her husband's, or the family's, solicitor was the dominant party, and it was held that in telling the lady and her husband, *both together*, to get advice elsewhere, the dominant party was not discharging his full duty, which was to tell the lady *alone* to obtain the advice of some one independent both of himself *and of her husband* . *per* Lord MACNAGHTEN, at p. 282).

(b) *Wright* v *Carter*, [1903] 1 Ch. 27, C A. (*per* STIRLING, L J , at p 60)

former in communication with one whom he knew to be lacking in judgment, sagacity, and experience, and as likely to give bad counsel as good. It has, indeed, been said, in a case where the transaction impeached was a gift, that the dominant party must also be in a position to show that the competent and independent advice was followed by the servient party, and that " it is the action resulting from the advice, not action against the advice, which binds the donor " (c) ; but this view seems a highly extravagant and illogical one, and it is not surprising to find that it has since been expressly dissented from (d)

478. A further element in the necessary proof of the righteousness and fairness of any contract—it has no place or relevance, of course, in the case of a gift (e)—is the fairness of the value given, or received, by the dominant party, whose plea has always succeeded on his establishing, together with other facts showing his entire good faith and candour, the fact that he paid the servient party a full and just price, if a purchaser (which is the common case), or, if a vendor, received from him no more than a fair consideration (f) whenever, on the other hand, he has not succeeded in demonstrating by such evidence the mercantile propriety and justice of the transaction, any more than its moral propriety and justice, he has always failed to sustain the contract (g). " Full " or " fair " value, or " a just price," as it has been variously expressed, means for this purpose the utmost sum which the dominant party by the exercise of due diligence, inquiry, and skill, could have obtained under the conditions existing at the time, according to the best of the knowledge and information which he then possessed, or might and ought to have acquired (h) : it does not mean a price which, so far as he had any

(c) This was the view expressed by FARWELL, J , at p 246 of *Powell v Powell, sup.*
(d) By MOULTON, L J , at pp 729, 730 of *Re Coomber,* [1911] 1 Ch 723, C A . " all that is necessary is that some independent person, free from any taint of the relationship, and of the consideration of interest which would affect the act, should put clearly before the person what are the nature and the consequences of the act. It is for adult persons of competent mind to decide whether they will do an act, and I do not think that independent and competent advice means independent and competent approval "
(e) It has been seen—see § 456, and note (s) thereto, *ante*—that the ignoring, or the taking into consideration, of questions of value is a main test of whether the transaction belongs to the gift, or the contract, class, in cases where this is a matter of controversy.
(f) As in *Kingsland (Viscount) v. Barnewall* (1706), 4 Brown P C 154; *Allison v Clayhills* (1907), 97 L. T 709 , and the " unconscionable bargain with expectant " cases cited in note (w) to § 445, *ante*
(g) As in *Murray v Palmer* (1805), 2 Sch & Lefr 472 , *Dawson v Massey* (1809), 1 Ball & B 219; *Aylward v Kearney* (1814), 2 Ball & B 463 , *Taylor v. Obee* (1816), 3 Price 83 , *Wood v Abrey* (1818), 3 Madd. 417 , *Jones v. Thomas* (1837), 2 Y & C. (Exch in Eq) 498 , *Dent v Bennett* (1839), 4 My & Cr 269 , *Champion v. Rigby* (1840), 9 L. J. (CH) 211; *Davies v. Cooper* (1840), 5 My. & Cr 270 , *Sturge v. Sturge* (1849), 12 Beav 229 , *Cockell v Taylor* (1852), 15 Beav. 103 , *Holman v Loynes* (1854), 4 De G M & G 270 , *Grosvenor v Sherratt* (1860), 28 Beav 659 , *Longmate v Ledger* (1860), 2 Giff 157 ; *Sharp v Leach* (1862), 31 Beav 491; *Clarke v Malpas* (1862), 4 De G F & J. 401 , *Dally v Wonham* (1863), 33 Beav 154 , *Baker v Monk* (1864), 4 De G. J. & S. 388 , *Tate v Williamson* (1866), L. R 1 Eq 528; *Wright v Carter,* [1903] 1 Ch 27, C. A (as to such of the transactions there in question as were contracts) In the above are not included any of the cases of unconscionable bargains with expectants, which, as to undervalue, stand on a special basis of their own. As to these see § 442, and the authorities collected in notes (i), (k), and (l), thereto, *ante.*
(h) *Gibson v. Jeyes* (1801), 6 Ves 266 (*per* Lord ELDON, L C, at p. 271 . "that no industry he was bound to exert would have got a better bargain "), *Holman v. Loynes*

reason to believe, after all proper investigation and industry, he could not have then obtained, but which by evidence subsequently forthcoming is shown to have then been possibly procurable in some quarter or other (i) This question of value, as will be seen hereafter (j), is a question of fact, and of evidence. The same question now arises (though it is not of the same importance, because an affirmative answer to it would not involve the same injustice to the dominant party) as arises, and has been discussed, in reference to "independent advice". is this issue a wholly separate *probandum*, in the sense that failure to prove it, though the propriety of the contract be established in all other respects, is fatal to the case of the dominant party? To take a concrete example. assume the dominant party to have satisfied the Court that he made the fullest and frankest disclosure to the servient party of all material facts, and particularly those relating to value (k), that he gave him the same advice against himself that he would have given him against a stranger, that he recommended the servient party to obtain, and that the servient party did obtain, the independent report and advice of a disinterested third person as to value, and otherwise, that, in the result, the property was declared to be worth, say, £1000 (l) · assume that, in these circumstances, the servient party insisted on selling for no more than, say, £600. Could this contract be upset? If the issue is one which the dominant party must establish, or fail, whatever else be established, such a bargain could be upset; if not, not It is submitted that such a transaction would not be impeachable, though, no doubt, *quoad* the £400 difference, it would have to be sustained by all the evidence, and particularly evidence of independent advice, which is necessary to sustain a gift. but, in the case imagined, this evidence is assumed to have been forthcoming No actual case has yet been brought before the Courts for decision in which the circumstances were as above supposed : but a hypothetical case has been judicially suggested of much the same character (m), and it was said that, in such circumstances, the

---

(1854), 4 De G M & G 270 (*per* Lord CRANWORTH, L C, at p 272) In *Grosvenor* v. *Sherratt* (1860), 28 Beav 659, ROMILLY, M R, at p 661, said "the obligation falls on them to show that, *by no possibility*, could more have been obtained" The expression, "by no possibility," goes beyond Lord ELDON's rule, and, so far as it does so, is incorrect.

(i) *O'Rorke* v *Bolingbroke* (1877), 2 App Cas 814, H. L (*per* Lord BLACKBURN, at p 136) So in *Champion* v *Rigby* (1830), 1 Russ & M 539, LEACH, M R., at p 539, said that "a solicitor dealing with his client is bound to show that he has given his client the best price which he would have advised his client to accept from another person," that is, not necessarily the best that could be obtained by any one in the world, or the price which subsequent experience may show to have been in fact the best, but that which the solicitor, or other dominant party, to the best of his knowledge and skill, would be justified in considering, and therefore in advising, to be the best price. And see the first two of the cases cited in note (h), sup.

(j) See §§ 499, 500, *post*, where the proper kinds of evidence of value, and the principles on which it is estimated, are discussed

(k) See the cases cited in note (y) to § 472, ante.

(l) It will be observed that the case here put is not that of a price being paid which, though not in fact a fair price, is believed by both parties to be so, as in *O'Rorke* v *Bolingbroke*, sup, but that of a value which both parties know to be an undervalue

(m) By ROMER, L J, at p. 793 of *Brenchley* v *Higgins* (1901), 70 L. J (CH) 788, C A "you must of necessity consider some other circumstances of the purchase to some extent. For instance, it may well be that even gross inadequacy of price may not be sufficient in itself to upset the purchase of a reversionary interest under some special and peculiar

answer to the question now being propounded ought to be in the negative. And there are certainly to be found judicial statements and suggestions tending in the same direction (n). It is true that, as has been seen in the case of unconscionable bargains with expectants, undervalue alone, even of the most trifling character, was originally held sufficient *per se* to invalidate them : but this was the result of an avowedly special doctrine as applied to such cases, and the Sales of Reversions Act, 1867, may be regarded as having restored the law as to these bargains to the state in which it was before the special doctrine was introduced, and in which it always has been with respect to other " influence " relations (o).

479. It should be mentioned here that it has been judicially suggested that a gift may be sustained, that is, may be shown not to have been improper, or the result of influence which was improper, by proof of its trivial or trifling character (p). No case, however, has as yet arisen in which a dominant party has succeeded on this ground : nor is such a case very likely to arise , for, where the gift is really of this negligible description, it is not probable

circumstances that one could imagine   Suppose, for example, a father having a reversion, wishing to give his son an advantage, sells it to the son for, say, half its real value, the father well knowing the value of the reversion, and the son being perfectly innocent in the matter and not unduly persuading his father, of course, in such a case as that, you could not lay hold of the gross inadequacy of price, and say that in itself is sufficient to enable the father to upset the sale as against the son. To see whether gross inadequacy of price would be sufficient to set aside a sale, you must of course look at the general circumstances of the sale—between whom it was made, and how it was brought about "   These observations, it is true, were made in a case of the purchase of a reversion, where the Court had to consider what, if any, effect the Sales of Reversions Act, 1867,—see § 442, *ante*—had on the existing state of the law as to such purchases at an undervalue, but the Lord Justice's imaginary illustration admits of easy adaptation to any other relation of influence in such a way as to leave his reasoning and inferences equally applicable   for it is obvious that the same absurdity in pronouncing the transaction an unconscientious bargain on the ground of proved undervalue alone, in the one case, would equally characterize the view, in the other, that the dominant party's proof of the absolute righteousness of the bargain is to be of no avail merely because he fails to prove that full value was in fact given

(n) See, for instance, *Dawson v Massey* (1809), 1 Ball & B 219 (*per* Lord MANNERS, L.C. (Ir), at p 235   " I do not say that there might not be other considerations, besides the value of the land, to render a transaction of this nature between such parties fair and just , but they do not exist in this case ") , *Taylor v Obee* (1816), 3 Price 83 (*per* THOMPSON, C.B , at p 90, and WOOD, B., at p 92, where it is stated that the decision is not based on undervalue alone) , *Dally v Wonham* (1863), 33 Beav 154 (*per* ROMILLY, M R , at p 159. where he points out that if the dominant party, instead of keeping to himself all that he knew as to the value of the property, had imparted this knowledge to the servient party, and had said to him, " though I will not give it, the property is worth £900, or more," and the servient party had thereupon insisted on selling it for the less value which in fact was given, the transaction might have been supported on the ground of bounty, *quoad* the difference between the two sums). It is true that in *Wright v. Carter*, [1903] A C. 27, C A , STIRLING, L.J , at p 60, and COZENS-HARDY, L J , at p 61, do undoubtedly speak of full value as a fact which must be proved, in addition to others, in order to sustain a contract   but those observations were made in a case in which the dominant party failed to prove those other facts, and where, therefore, the precise point was not the subject of decision   See § 323, and note (p) thereto, *ante*, where the same views as those expressed in the text are stated with reference to relations of " confidence."

(o) See § 442, and the cases cited in notes (i), (k), and (l) thereto, *ante*

(p) *Rhodes v Bate* (1866), 1 Ch App 252 (*per* TURNER, L J , at p 258) , *Allcard v Skinner* (1887), 36 C D 145, C A (*per* LINDLEY, L.J , at p 185), *Barron v Willis,* (1900] 2 Ch 121, C A (*per* LINDLEY, M R , at p. 132) , *Wright v. Carter*, [1903] 1 Ch 27, C. A (*per* VAUGHAN WILLIAMS, L.J , at p 50) that the servient party will be sufficiently interested to litigate the question (q).

Sub s (3). Confirmation of the Transaction by the Servient Party.

48^. Though not in a position to repel any of the presumptions made against him, either by proof that the influence was not operative upon the transaction, or by proof that it was not unduly exercised (r), the dominant party may, as in the case of any other voidable transaction (s), whatever be the ground of its voidability, set up by way of answer to any claim for relief that the servient party elected to confirm that which, to his knowledge, he had the right to repudiate or not, as he pleased But this plea of confirmation can only be established by the same means as are essential to the validity of a plea justifying the transaction itself. For the latter purpose, as has been shown (t), the dominant party, after having proved (where this question is in dispute) that the servient party had a real intention of entering into the transaction, is required further to show that the intention proceeded from an uninfluenced or emancipated will, and from a fully instructed mind. So, in the case of confirmation the dominant party, as the groundwork of, and the preliminary to, his plea, must establish that there was an actual intention *in fact* on the part of the servient party to confirm, and, unless he can make this first step good, it is useless to proceed further, for he has no foundation on which to build, and he fails at the outset (u) The intention may be shown by acts and conduct (v), as well as by express agreement or declaration, though it is a much more difficult case to make out

(q) If and when the question comes up in a form, and under conditions, meriting serious discussion, it will have to be considered whether " triviality " means what the donor, or what the donee, would consider trivial Presumably it means the former Supposing " the widow's mite " had been given not to the poor, but to a Pharisee exercising undue sacerdotal influence, the latter could not be heard to defend himself by the plea that it was of trifling value to him. It was not so to the widow. In the citation from *Wright v Carter* in the last note, VAUGHAN WILLIAMS, L.J., speaks of " a gift made by a man with so ample a fortune that it must have been trifling to him "

(r) See Sub-ss (1), and (2), *ante*.

(s) See Ch. III, Sect 4, Sub s (2), *ante*, as to affirmation of contracts voidable for non-disclosure during the negotiation, and Ch IV, Sect 4, Sub-s (5), *ante*, as to affirmation of transactions voidable for breach of duties attaching to fiduciary relations.

(t) See § 469, *ante*.

(u) As in *Welles v Middleton* (1784), 1 Cox 112 (mere general expressions of satisfaction no proof of intention to confirm · per Lord THURLOW, L C, at p 126); *Murray v Palmer* (1805), 2 Sch & Lefr. 472 (where the servient party, "having received the interest " —of the purchase money—" whilst single, . . and she and her husband having received principal and interest after her marriage," was in the circumstances held not to have indicated an intention to confirm, because, to establish such an intention, it must be shown that the servient party "is aware that the act he is doing is to have the effect of confirming an impeachable transaction; otherwise the act amounts to nothing as a confirmation " · per Lord REDESDALE, L C (Ir), at pp 485, 486), *O'Brien v Lewis* (1863), 32 L J. (CH.) 569 (mere omission to debit in account held not to be an intentional recognition of the transaction, much less an intentional confirmation, per Lord WESTBURY, L.C., at p. 573).

(v) As it was in *King v Hamlet* (1834), 2 My. & K. 456 (per Lord BROUGHAM, L.C., at pp 480–484), *Wright v. Vanderplank* (1856), 8 De G M. & G 133 (per KNIGHT BRUCE, L J, at pp 137, 138, and TURNER, L.J, at pp 147–151), *Lyddon v. Moss* (1859), 4 De G & J. 104 (per TURNER, L J, at pp. 132–134, and KNIGHT-BRUCE, L J, at pp. 134, 135),

481. Assuming that the servient party's intention to confirm has been established, or is not in dispute, there then at once arises the same question which Lord ELDON considered to arise in respect of the transaction itself which is sought to be justified, as soon as the servient party's intention to enter into it is made out,—viz how was the intention produced? It is for the dominant party to show, in this case as much as in that,—and his plea fails whenever he cannot do so.—that the servient party, when intending and purporting to confirm or ratify the transaction, had received from himself full disclosure, or was otherwise fully cognizant, of all material facts (w), and of his rights in respect of those facts, and, particularly, his right to repudiate and avoid the transaction, and the absence of any obligation to adhere to it on the ground of its supposed validity (x); and, further, that the servient party was, at the time of the alleged confirmation, completely emancipated from the dominion and influence which operated upon the transaction purporting to be confirmed,—this last being a fact which, unless the disclosure or knowledge above-mentioned, or the independent advice of a third person, be first established, is almost unprovable, the inference under such circumstances being that the mere act of confirmation, so far from indicating the cessation of the influence, demonstrates its strength and persistence (y). As applied to unconscionable bargains with expectants, the rule, as has been

---

Turner v. Collins (1871), 7 Ch App. 329 (*per* MALINS, V -C, as to part of the transaction, at pp 340–342), *Mitchell v. Homfray* (1881), 8 Q. B. D 587, C A (*per* Lord SELBORNE, L C, at pp 591, 592, and BRAMWELL, L J, at p 593), *Allcard v Skinner* (1887), 36 C. D 145, C. A (*per* LINDLEY, L J, at pp 186–189, and BOWEN, L J, at pp 191–193)

(w) *Hylton v. Hylton* (1754), 2 Ves Sr. 547 (where a release given to the late guardian of the servient party was held to amount to nothing, as no proper account had been rendered *per* Lord HARDWICKE, L C, at p 549), *Thornber v Sheard* (1850), 12 Beav. 589 (*per* Lord LANGDALE, M R, at pp 601, 602), *Turner v Collins, sup* (as to part of the transaction *per* MALINS, V C., at p. 342, the plea being held good as to the other part, where knowledge was shown see the last note)

(x) *Crowe v Ballard* (1790), 1 Ves Jr 215 (*per* Lord THURLOW, L C, at pp 219, 220 new bond given "under the idea that the old one may be enforced against him"), *Murray v Palmer* (1805), 2 Sch & Lefr 472 (*per* Lord REDESDALE, L C (Ir), at p 486), *Purcell v M'Namara* (1807), 14 Ves 90A (*per* Lord ERSKINE, L.C., at p 122 "subject to the same influence and control, and with as little knowledge of their rights"), *Savery v King* (1856), 5 H L C 627 (*per* Lord CRANWORTH, L.C., at pp. 663, 664. ignorance of right to avoid), *Lloyd v Attwood* (1859), 3 De G & J 614 (*per* TURNER, L J, at p 650); *Berdoe v Dawson* (1865), 34 Beav. 603 (*per* ROMILLY, M R, at p. 610), *Kempson v Ashbee* (1874), 10 Ch. App 15 (*per* Lord CAIRNS, L C., at p. 20 "to constitute a confirmation there must be knowledge of the invalidity of the document")

(y) *Hylton v Hylton, sup* (*per* Lord THURLOW, L C, at p 549), *Crowe v Ballard, sup* (*per* Lord THURLOW, L C, at pp. 219, 220 new bond given under same distress and terror as the old), *Purcell v M'Namara, sup* (see the passage cited in the last note), *Wood v Downes* (1811), 18 Ves 120 (*per* Lord ELDON, L C, at p 128, where, at the time of the suggested confirmation, the servient party was still "labouring under all the pressure" which attended the original transaction), *Thornber v Sheard, sup* (*per* Lord LANGDALE, M R, at pp. 601, 602), *Savery v King, sup* (*per* Lord CRANWORTH, L C, at pp 663, 664), *Grosvenor v Sherratt* (1860), 28 Beav 659 (*per* ROMILLY, M.R, at pp 664, 665); *Moxon v Payne* (1873), 8 Ch App 881 (where the same influence which brought about the original deeds operated to bring about the alleged confirmatory deed, which was "of such a nature as to require the strongest evidence of knowledge, and freedom of will, and deliberate purpose, to sustain it"); *Barron v Willis*, [1900] 2 Ch 121, C A (where it was held that the confirmation deed relied upon demonstrated not a confirmed transaction, but a confirmed influence, and where also it was held that a delay of some years was to be accounted for by the same persistent influence *per* RIGBY, L J, at p 135, and COLLINS, L J, at p 137)

stated (z), results in the impossibility of establishing a case of confirmation until the distress of the expectant is at an end, which means, until the reversion, or other expected benefit, has fallen into possession. It follows also from the rule, as a necessary consequence, that if at the time of the suggested confirmation the servient party was mentally or otherwise incapable (a) of any act of the will, whether capable at the time of the transaction or not, the confirmation cannot have any effect, and this must be the dominant, not the servient, party's misfortune. But, difficult though it be to discharge the onus, yet, whenever the dominant party has been able to make good all the matters which have been laid down as necessary elements in his proof, he has always been held entitled to judgment (b). The rule, it should be observed, has no application to the confirmation of a voidable transaction by will (for the same reason which excludes gifts by testamentary disposition from the whole doctrine of undue influence in respect of gifts *inter vivos*), as was held in a case where a client by his will, after reciting the fact that he had made a conveyance to his solicitor which he, or those coming after him, might be in a position to dispute, proceeded to confirm the transaction, and it was said by Lord St. Leonards that, though in a case of contract the solicitor would have had " to show that the confirmation was made by the client with a full knowledge of his right to set aside the conveyance," yet " it is beyond dispute that . . if a client, dealing with his solicitor, executes a voidable instrument, and afterwards desires to confirm it by will, he clearly may ", and, in the case before him, " the party was disposing of his own property " —that is, a devisable equity to avoid the transaction as already explained— ' by will in favour of a person with whom he had previously been dealing, and it was equally competent to him to have disposed of the same property in favour of any other individual " (c)

Sub-s (4)   " Family Arrangement "

482. It is a good answer to the servient party's claim in respect of the alleged abuse of a parental or quasi-parental relation as has already been pointed out, to establish that the transaction sought to be rescinded was in the nature of a " family arrangement," in which the parent was deriving no exclusive or preponderating benefit at the expense of the child (d) : and,

---

(z) See the cases cited in note (z), and (a), to § 445, *ante*

(a) *De Witte* v *Addison* (1879), 80 L T 207, C A (*per* LINDLEY, M R , at p 212)

(b) As in the cases cited in note (v) to § 480, *ante* , and also in *Cole* v *Gibbons* (1734), 3 P Wms 290 (*per* Lord TALBOT, L C , at p 293, the servient party being " fully apprised of everything," and there being " not the least fraud or surprise "), *Chesterfield* (*Earl of*) v. *Jannsen* (1751), 2 Ves Sr 125 (where the expectant, after the state of expectancy had come to an end, and with it his embarrassments, deliberately and with full knowledge and in perfect freedom, and without any fraud, contrivance, or surprise, executed a bond confirming the bond impeached   *per* Lord HARDWICKE, L C , at pp 158, 159, STRANGE, M R , at pp 148–152, and BURNET, J , at pp 145, 146); *Oldham* v *Hand* (1751), 2 Ves Sr 259 (*per* Lord HARDWICKE, L C., at p 260)

(c) *Stump* v. *Gabey* (1852), 2 De G M & G. 623 (*per* Lord St LEONARDS, L C., at p 631) As to " undue influence " not applying to wills, see § 447, *ante*

(d) See the authorities cited in notes (p) and (q) to § 410, *ante*, which respectively illustrate the success, and the failure, of the plea in cases of parental influence

under the like conditions, a bargain between an " expectant " and a money-lender, where the father or other ancestor concurs with the " expectant " in resorting to the moneylender for financial assistance in their joint interests, may be supported (e).

Sub-s. (5). *Certain Matters which are not deemed valid Affirmative Answers*

483. It remains to consider certain matters which from time to time have been put forward in argument as affirmative answers to the servient party's case, but which have always been held ineffectual for that purpose.

483a. In the first place it is of course quite irrelevant to adduce evidence in contradiction of any of those facts, already discussed (f), which it is irrelevant for the servient party to establish.

484. Secondly, mere delay in instituting proceedings is not of itself an answer to the servient party's claim, unless that claim be obnoxious to the provisions of some statute of limitations This question has been fully discussed in the Chapter dealing with the duty of disclosure incidental to negotiations for contracts of a certain character (g). The principles there enunciated have also been applied to proceedings for breach of duty arising from relations of confidence (h). It is unnecessary to repeat these principles here *in extenso*, or to say more than that they are equally applicable to the subject of the present Chapter. Accordingly, to prove that for a period of time, however long, the servient party abstained from any repudiation of the transaction is to prove nothing, unless it be also affirmatively shown that at some stage in that period of time he was fully aware of his rights, and entirely emancipated from the influence which presumably brought about the transaction, and presumably also operated continuously against any attempt or desire to avoid it afterwards (i), that the inaction was accompanied by such acts and conduct during the period in question as to constitute evidence of implied confirmation (j), and that the dominant party was in some way injured

(e) See the cases cited in note (b) to § 445, *ante*. The "family arrangement" plea occupies a very important place in cases of compromise and release, as to which, see §§ 135, 136, *ante*
(f) See §§ 461, 462, *ante*
(g) In §§ 216-219, *ante* Statutes of Limitation do not in terms, nor, as a rule, " by analogy," apply to actions for the avoidance of transactions on the ground of undue influence : see note (r) to § 463, *ante*
(h) See § 374, *ante*, and the illustrations of such application which are given in note (e) thereto.
(i) *Aylward* v *Kearney* (1814), 2 Ball & B 463 (where, during the whole period of delay, the servient party was in a continuous state of " pupilage," and " the length of time under such circumstances can go for nothing " *per* Lord MANNERS, L C. (Ir), at pp 476-478) , *Sharp* v. *Leach* (1862), 31 Beav. 491 (*per* ROMILLY, M R , at p. 502   " it is obviously reasonable to conclude that the influence which vitiates the act of the person over whom that influence is exercised should also, as long as it lasts, excuse the omission of that person to complain of that act obtained by such influence ") ; *Rees* v *De Bernardy*, [1896] 2 Ch 437 (where the plaintiffs were ignorant of their equitable right to relief : *per* ROMER, J , at p 445)
(j) See several of the cases cited in note (u) to § 480, and in notes (w), (x), and (y) to § 481, *ante*, for illustrations of inaction and delay not amounting to confirmation, as

or prejudiced thereby (*k*). And, even in such a case, the plea will fail where the servient party is in a position to suggest any fair excuse for, or explanation of, his apparent inactivity, as, for instance, if the transaction was one of suretyship for the dominant party's debt, a reasonable belief, arising from the fact of his never having been pressed by the creditor during the whole of the period of alleged delay, that the primary liability had been duly discharged by the dominant party, in which case there would remain no liability on his own part for which it would be necessary to seek relief (*l*). Delay may, no doubt, affect judicial discretion as to costs (*m*) : but, though it is often urged on behalf of the dominant party that he has at least some moral claim to consideration arising from the loss of evidence (whether oral testimony of witnesses who have died or disappeared, or documents which have been destroyed or mislaid), this contention is usually met by the observation that lapse of time in such cases must count against the wrongdoer, who entered into what he knew, or ought to have known, was a transaction impeachable at any future time, and in so doing must be deemed to have taken all risks, amongst which is the risk in question (*n*).

485. Equally futile, as an affirmative answer, is proof by the dominant party of an offer made by him before action, or *pendente lite*, to surrender or renounce all or any of his rights under the transaction impeached, unless

contrasted with those cited in note (*v*) to § 480, *ante*, where the delay, coupled with other circumstances, was held to constitute confirmation, particularly *Allcard* v *Skinner* (1887), 36 C. D 145, C. A (*per* LINDLEY, L.J , at p. 186 : " this is far more than inactivity or delay on the part of the plaintiff. There is conduct on her part amounting to confirma tion of her gift ")

(*k*) *Murray* v. *Palmer* (1805), 2 Sch & Lefr 472 (where, at pp. 486, 487, Lord REDESDALE, L C. (Ir.), points out that the interests of the dominant party were not affected, nor was " his situation altered " in any way, " and therefore this acquiescence amounts to a mere lapse of time," though he also intimates at p. 488, that circumstances are conceivable in which the dominant party may have been lulled into a false security, and so tempted not to preserve his evidence, with which latter observation cp. those of BOWEN, L.J , at p 192 of *Allcard* v. *Skinner*, *sup.* , *Hatch* v. *Hatch* (1804), 9 Ves. 292 (where a delay of 24 years was held not fatal, no one having been injured by it · *per* Lord ELDON, L.C., at pp. 287, 288) ; *Baker* v. *Bradley* (1855), 7 De G M. & G. 597 (*per* KNIGHT-BRUCE, L J , at p. 618) , *Procter* v. *Robinson* (1867), 15 L. T 431 (where, again, nobody had been prejudiced by the delay : *per* CAIRNS, L.J , at pp. 433, 434) , *Rees* v. *De Bernardy*, *sup.* (*per* ROMER, J , at p 445 : defendant's position not affected)

(*l*) *Archer* v *Hudson* (1846), 15 L J (CH) 211 (*per* Lord LYNDHURST, L.C., at p 213) , *Kempson* v *Ashbee* (1874), 10 Ch. App 15 (*per* Lord CAIRNS, L.C , at p 21 · " so long as there was no claim asserted, the plaintiff might well be content to let matters remain as they were. She might expect that the creditor would enforce the debt against her step-father. There was, indeed, a threat of proceedings against her , but no real measures were taken till 1872, when the action was brought, and that immediately led to this bill ")

(*m*) See Ch. VIII, Sect. 2, Sub s (4), *post*.

(*n*) As in *Salter* v. *Bradshaw* (1858), 26 Beav. 161 (where the purchaser of a reversion who was sued for rescission of the transaction after 40 years found himself in difficulties on the question of " fair value," which, however, ROMILLY, M R , said were difficulties of his own creation, and for which he must suffer : pp. 164, 165) , *Gresley* v. *Mousley* (1859), 4 De G & J. 78 (where it was again held that the dominant party, who in that case was a solicitor, ought to have known that the transaction might be impeached at a distant date, and must suffer for not having preserved the evidence required to sustain it : *per* KNIGHT-BRUCE, L.J , at p 90, and TURNER, L.J , at pp. 94–99). And, as to the duty of the dominant party to have his proofs in order in any case, whether delay or not, and as to his responsibility for any difficulties which beset him at the trial in consequence of his having neglected this duty, see *Talbot* v *Staniforth* (1861), 1 J & H. 484 (*per* PAGE WOOD, V C , at p 503) ; *Cockburn* v *Edwards* (1881), 18 C. D. 449, C. A (*per* JESSEL, M R , at p 455)

the offer takes the form of a submission to the whole of the relief claimed by the servient party which by the judgment of the Court he is declared to have properly claimed (o). But where the dominant party has satisfied the Court as to the propriety of the transaction, with the exception of one particular and severable term or part of it, the abandonment of that term or part at the trial may have the effect of entitling him to a judgment in his favour which otherwise he might not have obtained at all, or not in a complete form (p). A proposal by a dominant party before action which in reality veils a threat, or is nothing but a device " to double hatch the cheat," is of course wholly inefficacious, and entitles him to no consideration, even in the matter of costs ; as where a usurer, having extorted an unconscionable bargain from an expectant in distress, offers to take repayment of the loan at ordinary interest, with the alternative of foreclosure, and to relinquish in that event his rights under the bargain, knowing full well that the distress of the servient party is such as to wholly disable him from accepting the offer, and probably to drive him in his desperation to submit to a new and a still harder bargain, in which whips will be exchanged for scorpions. In such a case the offer which the dominant party makes with the intention of using it, if unaccepted (as he knows it will be), as a testimonial to his reasonableness and good faith when he is called upon to sustain the transaction, naturally produces the exactly opposite effect (q) And no renunciation by the dominant party at or before the trial, or on appeal, of any rights derived from the transaction will in the slightest degree impede the Court in the exercise of its duty of investigating the circumstances under which those surrendered rights are alleged to have been acquired (r) Any offer, however,

(o) As was the case in *Re Hoggart's Settlement* (1912), 56 Sol J 415, where the solicitor whose agreement with a client as to costs was complained of had before action offered to renounce all rights and claims under the agreement, and to have the bill taxed in the ordinary way, which was the whole relief asked by, or available to, the servient party As to the general rule that a defendant is not entitled to judgment, or to any special order as to costs, if the offer which before action he has made, or in the proceedings he has placed upon the record, is an offer of something which falls short of the full measure of relief to which the Court ultimately declares him entitled, see the cases cited in the notes to O. 65, r. 1, in the Annual Practice (under the heading " Offer ") As to offers, in the case of relations of " confidence," see § 375, note (*h*), ante.

(p) As in *Hoblyn* v *Hoblyn* (1889), 41 C. D 200.

(q) *Wiseman* v. *Beale* (1690), 2 Vern 121, where an "expectant" sued to rescind a bargain with a moneylender as "unconscionable," and the representative of the deceased moneylender pleaded an offer made before action, and embodied in a bill (which was however not proceeded with, though exhibited) to take the actual money advanced, with interest, otherwise foreclosure, as a ground, if not for refusing relief altogether, at all events for ordering the expectant to pay the defendant's costs · but the Lords Commissioners of the Great Seal granted the relief prayed, and refused to make the plaintiff pay any costs (see pp. 121, 122 . " *when he had spent the money,* then a specious offer was made to relinquish the bargain on payment of the money lent with interest, *which at that time was impossible for him to do* · and though such bill was exhibited, it was not prosecuted, but was *a contrivance only to double hatch the cheat* ") Lord THURLOW, L C, at p 220 of *Crowe* v *Ballard* (1790), 1 Ves Jr 215, applies the above to a case of confirmation, quoting " the quaint expression " (as he calls it) with which the passage cited ends

(r) See *Dunnage* v *White* (1818), 1 Swanst. 137 (*per* PLUMER, M R , at p 152 " it is true that they are now willing to correct the error, but the instrument must be considered as it stood at the date ; and the question is, was it *then* a right disposition of the property ? "), *Moxon* v. *Payne* (1873), 8 Ch. App 881 (*per* JAMES, L J , for himself and

which is shown to have been not illusory and specious, but genuine and honest, will certainly be taken into consideration on the question of costs, particularly in the case of dealings with expectants, where the expectant is frequently regarded as occupying a position analogous to that of a mortgagor inviting the assistance of the Court to enable him to redeem his security (s).

486. Lastly, "the personal equation" is for the most part irrelevant It has already been shown that the personal motives of the dominant party are wholly immaterial (t). The personal situation or characteristics of the servient party are, generally, no less so Thus, it is no answer to the servient party's case for relief to allege or prove that he (or she) was of mature age (u), except in some of the cases of influence arising from the parental relation (v), and also in some of those where the influence arises out of "the circumstances and conditions," one of which may be the extreme youth of the servient party (w), or that he (or she) was a person of great business capacity, shrewdness, or experience, or of vigorous intellect (x), or that he (or she) was self-willed, or firm, or obstinate, on certain points or on certain occasions (y) As

MELLISH, L J , at p 886, as to an offer made by the defendant before action to give up all his rights under the two deeds impugned, and to let the earlier deed, which they purported to vary, stand unaffected, "the defendant Payne could not by such an offer . . purge himself of the additional fraud which these documents prove ") Cp the misrepresenta tion case (which, however, turned out to be quite as much a case of undue influence in a relation created by the circumstances, as one of misrepresentation) of *Curtis* v *Bottomley* (1011), "Times," 1 Aug , where the defendant, on appeal from a verdict against him for damages, abandoned so much of his notice of motion as prayed for judgment, and ex pressed his willingness to limit his argument to the residue which asked for a new trial, in the hope that the Court of Appeal would thereupon think it undesirable to deal closely with the merits, and would inquire solely into the question whether the former trial had been properly conducted The hope was vain, and the "astute" manoeuvre, so described by BUCKLEY, L J , was as abortive as that resorted to by the defendant in *Moxon* v *Payne, sup*

(s) See §§ 620 (generally), and § 624 (as to expectants), *post*

(t) See Sect 3, Sub s (3), *ante*

(u) *Wiseman* v *Beake, sup* (where the servient party was 40 years of age, and it was vainly argued that this made a difference), *Bromley* v. *Smith* (1859), 26 Beav. 644 (*per* ROMILLY, M R , at pp 663, 664), *Rhodes* v *Bate* (1866), 1 Ch App 252 (*per* TURNER, L.J., at p 257 "I do not think that either the age or the capacity of the person conferring the benefit . . . affects this principle Age and capacity are considerations which may be of great importance in cases in which the principle does not apply , but I think they are but of little, if any, importance in cases to which the principle is applicable "), *Rae* v *Joyce* (1892), 29 L. R (Ir) 500 (*per* FITZGIBBON, L J (Ir), at p 526, referring to the age of the servient party in *Wiseman* v *Beake, sup*)

(v) See § 409, and notes (l), and (m) thereto, *ante*

(w) See the cases cited in the notes to § 429, § 442, *ante.*

(x) *Welles* v *Middleton* (1784), 1 Cox 112 (*per* Lord THURLOW, L C , who at pp 124, 125, points out that the conflicting evidence as to the personal capacity of the deceased servient party was quite irrelevant), *Barnard* v *Hunter* (1856), 2 Jur (N s) 1213 (*per* Lord CRAN WORTH, L C , who, at p 1215, in reference to the argument that the servient party here was a shrewd man of business, expresses his view that the Court cannot regard "the particular competency of the particular man "), *Bromley* v *Smith, sup.* (*per* ROMILLY, M R , at p 661 immateriality of the fact that the servient party was a man of vigorous intellect), *Broun* v *Kennedy* (1864), 4 De G J & S 217 (*per* KNIGHT-BRUCE, L J , at p 222, describing the transaction there in question as "one from which the lady who executed it, *however clever she may be and probably is,* has a plain right to be delivered "), *Baker* v *Monk* (1864), 4 De G J & S 388 (where the servient party to whom relief was granted was "said to be a very shrewd old woman " *per* TURNER, L J , at p 393), *Rhodes* v *Bate, sup* (see the passage cited in note (u), *sup.*)

(y) *Cavendish* v *Strutt* (1903), 19 T L R 483 (where the servient party who obtained

regards this last feature, indeed, it is a commonplace of psychology that spasms of self-assertion are quite consistent with constitutional phancy; it was "the noble Othello" who, in the hands of one who knew how to work upon him, was "led by the nose as easily as asses are." Nor is it of any avail to rely on the fact that the servient party belonged to a profession of such a nature as to render those who exercise it peculiarly unamenable to influence in general, or to the kind of influence alleged in the particular case, or even that he belonged to the same profession as that of the dominant party, where the influence is alleged to have sprung from a professional relation (z) But where the influence is presumed from the particular circumstances of the case, and physical or mental incapacity is alleged as one of those circumstances, several of the last-mentioned considerations are strictly in issue, and cannot possibly be excluded (a).

SECT 5 THE RELIEF AVAILABLE TO THE SERVIENT PARTY.

487. The servient party may either assert his title to relief as an *actor*, claiming, whether by original action or cross-claim, that the transaction be judicially annulled, or he may wait till he is sued, and then stand on the defensive, asserting that, whether judicially annulled or not, the transaction ought to be judicially treated as a nullity There are also certain miscellaneous remedies open to him under special circumstances. These three classes of relief invite separate consideration

Sub-s (1). *Rescission and Consequential Relief*

488. The servient party is always entitled to rescission of any transaction, whether contract or gift, which he has successfully impeached, and which the dominant party has been unable to sustain by countervailing evidence,

relief was described by BIRNE, J, at pp 484, 485, as a clever man, and one who could be very obstinate at times, though on the whole easily led) At pp 339, 340, of *Turner* v *Collins* (1871), 7 Ch App 329, Lord HATHERLEY, L C, emphasizes the consistency of occasional firmness or fractiousness with normal docility and weakness in one and the same person ("some evidence is given to show that the young gentleman was not likely from his self-will to be subject to undue influence I should say that a young man like this was a person most requiring protection No doubt there are plenty of people in the world whom it is difficult to drive, but whom anybody can lead It is well known that people who are generally most difficult to drive are usually about the most easy to be led by others who understand them ") It is influence *of any kind* which the law presumes and guards against, irrespectively of the precise means by which it operates, whether by the domination of fear, or the close ties of affection and trust, whether by coercion or seduction, whether, as Lord HARDWICKE, L C, said, at p 517 of *Grigsby* v. *Cox* (1750), 1 Ves. Sr. 517, by "ill," or "extraordinarily good, usage "

(z) *Wiseman* v. *Beale* (1690), 2 Vern 121 (where the servient party was a proctor of Doctors' Commons, and it was held that this made no difference), *Rae* v *Joyce, sup* (per FITZGIBBON, L J (Ir), at p 526, referring to the above circumstance in the case last cited) In *Cooke* v *Fitzpayne* (coram WRIGHT, J , 14, 16 Nov 1901 *ex relatione auctoris*) the servient party was a solicitor who obtained relief against another solicitor

(a) See the cases cited in the notes to § 429, § 442, *ante*. In *Osmond* v *Fitzroy* (1731), 3 P Wms 129, JEKYLL, M R, at pp 129, 130, says that, though the Court "will not measure the size of people's understandings or capacities" in ordinary cases, it is bound to do so in any case such as that before him (which was one of undue influence by a confidential servant over a youth whom he was employed to protect) together with all such other remedies as are consequential upon the main relief (b), subject, however, to the conditions upon which alone any voidable transaction, on whatever ground it is voidable, can be set aside These conditions have already been stated in detail, and once for all (c) ; and it is unnecessary to restate them here It has been shown that important practical consequences flow from the leading principle that the transaction is not void, but voidable at the option of the party aggrieved (d) , that the possibility of mutual restoration *in specie* is a condition of the relief in cases of contracts (the rule has of course no application to cases of gift), so that, if the plaintiff has by his own conduct disabled himself from making such restitution, unless the defendant has by *his* conduct encouraged the plaintiff in so disabling himself, he is debarred from obtaining rescission, whether any other remedy be still available to him, or not (e) , that no transaction can be set aside under which any innocent third party has acquired rights for value, in the absence of such interested party (f) , that the transaction will be rescinded *in toto*, or not at all, and as against all the parties to it other than the servient party, unless (which frequently is the case) in the instrument containing or recording such transaction there are separate and severable covenants,

(b) This being the usual remedy resorted to by the servient party, and, in the case of gifts, his only remedy, it is idle to give a long list of illustrative cases Suffice it to say that all the authorities referred to in this Chapter, except those cited in the notes to Sub ss (2) and (3) of this Section, *post*, are cases of offensive proceedings (whether successful or not) instituted by the servient party. In the class of case which is the subject of Chapter III, the right to relief is nearly always asserted in the form of a defence, whilst in the class which is the subject of Chapter IV, the two forms of relief are more evenly matched (see Sect. 5 of these Chapters respectively) There are, in the case of each class, business reasons, easily intelligible, for the preference, or absence of preference, manifested by the party complaining for the one, over the other, kind of relief

(c) In Ch. III, Sect 5, Sub s (1), *ante*

(d) See §§ 225, 226, *ante* A striking application of this general rule to a case of a transaction voidable on the ground of undue influence is *Re Metcalfe's Trusts* (1864), 2 De G J & S 122, where the trustees of a lady refused to pay moneys forming part of the trust fund to a religious establishment, though directed to do so by their *cestui que trust*, and, when sued, set up the audacious, and of course unsuccessful, plea that the payment would be a gift resulting from spiritual influence,—a plea which could only prevail on the theory that such a transaction is void and illegal . *per* KNIGHT-BRUCE, L J , at p 126

(e) See § 231, *ante* , and, for applications of the doctrine there stated to cases of "influence," see, generally, such of the authorities cited in the notes to this Chapter as resulted in favour of a servient party claiming rescission of a contract, where adequate provision was always made for complete restoration *in specie* by the plaintiff as the condition of relief For an illustration of the servient party having so dealt with the property that he could not restore the benefits he had derived from the transaction, see *King* v *Hamlet* (1834), 2 My & K 456 (*per* Lord BROUGHAM, L.C , at pp 480–484) , *Dimsdale* v *Dimsdale* (1856), 3 Drew 556 (*per* KINDERSLEY, V -C , at p 577) On the other hand, where it was not the servient parties' fault that they were unable to give back what they had received (which was not tangible property, but information that they were entitled to such property), this inability was held not to be a bar to relief . *Rees* v *De Bernardy*, [1896] 2 Ch 437 (*per* ROMER, J , at pp 445, 446) So also, where the dominant party had led the servient party to suppose that he could do as he pleased with the property in question *Savery* v *King* (1856), 5 H L C 627 (*per* Lord CRANWORTH, L C , at pp 668, 669)

(f) See § 233, *ante,* and the following "undue influence" cases in illustration of the rule there stated *Farmer* v *Farmer* (1848), 1 H L C 724 (*per* Lord COTTENHAM, L C, at pp 748, 749, pointing out that the absence of any one to represent those interested in the personal estate comprised in the impeached conveyances was, of itself, fatal to the plaintiff's case) , *Dimsdale* v *Dimsdale, sup* (where the plaintiff had given to third persons interests under the instruments in question which he did not even offer to redeem . *per* KINDERSLEY V -C , at pp 575, 578)

terms, or stipulations, one or more of which is a proper subject of relief, whilst the residue is unimpeachable, in which case the court will set aside the former without interfering with the latter (g),—a course it will never adopt if they are all homogeneous parts of one entire transaction (h),—or unless some of the parties to the instrument, being innocent of any abuse of influence, can be detached from any other or others who may be liable, and their rights and liabilities deemed several, in which case the instrument may be set aside against the party or parties so held liable, and left to stand as a valid instrument in favour of, and enforceable by, the other or others (i) , and, lastly, that an instrument may be set aside in one character, and allowed to stand in another,—for instance, a conveyance may be declared void as such, whilst permitting it to remain in the dominant party's hands as a security (j), and, in the case of an unconscionable bargain, a security for

(g) See § 239, *ante* Illustrations of the application of the rules there stated to cases of the present class, are *Bellamy* v *Sabine* (1847), 2 Ph 425 (as to which see note (i), *inf*), *Turner* v. *Collins* (1871), 7 Ch App 329 (*per* Lord HATHERLEY, L.C , at p 342, where the servient party by deed of gift gave the whole of his reversionary interest in certain moneys to his father's second wife and daughter, and also conferred on his father a power of appointment over certain moneys coming to him from his mother, and the deed was sustained as to the former, but invalidated as to the latter) ; *Hoblyn* v *Hoblyn* (1889), 41 C D 200 (where part of the deed operated to confer an exclusive benefit on the father at the expense of the son, but the residue was held to be " a family arrangement," and the deed was upheld as to this residue only · *per* KEKEWICH, J., at p 207) , *Wright* v *Carter*, [1903] 1 Ch. 27. C A (a useful illustration, because it was there held as to two of the three deeds in question that it was possible to separate those parts of them whereby the servient party conferred a bounty on his children which was not the result of either presumed or proved undue influence from those parts whereby he benefited the dominant party, the solicitor, the latter being declared invalid, and the former left to stand whilst, on the other hand, in the case of the remaining deed, which was a contract, it was not possible to allocate the consideration, and the whole was set aside against both the solicitor and the children *per* VAUGHAN WILLIAMS, L J , at p 54, STIRLING, L.J , at pp 59, 60, and COZENS-HARDY, L J , at p 63)

(h) As in *Willan* v *Willan* (1814), 2 Dow H L 274 (*per* Lord ELDON, L C , at pp 280, 281, and Lord REDESDALE at pp 284, 285, where it was held that the Court " could not draw the line between " the objectionable and the unobjectionable parts of the instrument, and that it must be undone in its entirety) , *Wright* v. *Carter*, *sup* (as to one of the deeds there in question . see the last note)

(i) As in *Bellamy* v *Sabine* (1847), 2 Ph 425 (where there were two agreements following one another within the space of a fortnight, which were held, as against the solicitor who was one of the alleged dominant parties, to have constituted one entire scheme , but the earlier of the two which the servient party and his father, the other alleged dominant party, alone executed, was upheld as a " family arrangement," whilst the latter, which was executed by the servient party and the solicitor only, was set aside *per* PEPYS, M R , at pp 438, 439) , *Turner* v *Collins*, *sup* (where the deed was sustained in favour of the father's second wife and daughter, but invalidated as against the father see note (g), *sup*) , *Readdy* v *Pendergast* (1887), 55 L T 767 (*per* KEKEWICH, J , at p. 769) , *Wright* v *Carter*, *sup*. (see, again, note (g), *sup*) So, where the transaction consists in the servient party concurring in a security given by the dominant party to his creditor, the instrument is of course only set aside in favour of the servient party, leaving the dominant party liable to the creditor, as in *Archer* v *Hudson* (1846), 15 L. J (CH) 211 , *Savery* v *King* (1856), 5 H L C 625 (*per* Lord CRANWORTH, L C , at p 669 . "I do not think the son is precluded from setting aside the transaction as against him, merely because he concurred with another person who is bound by it ") On the other hand, where it is impossible to separate the responsible from the innocent parties, the transaction must be rescinded, if at all, against all of them, as in *Cooke* v *Lamotte* (1851), 15 Beav 234 (where, however, the innocent parties were relieved of having to pay costs : *per* ROMILLY, M R , at p 249) , *Wright* v *Carter*, *sup* (as to two of the deeds there in question · see note (g), *sup*)

(j) As in *Gwynne* v *Heaton* (1778), 1 Brown C C. 1 , *Newman* v *Payne* (1793), 2 Ves.

the repayment of an extortionate principal sum, or amount of interest, may be invalidated as a security for such amounts, without interfering with its enforceability in respect of the actual money advanced with reasonable interest (k), the servient party being in effect allowed to redeem on those terms in substitution for the agreed terms (l).   It has also been explained, in the course of the general discussion referred to, that whenever a voidable transaction, of whatever nature, or whatever may be the ground of its voidability, is set aside, the order of the Court is so moulded as to effect the first object of all rescission, namely, the undoing of the transaction on both sides, and the restoration of the parties to the position they respectively occupied immediately before entering into it (m)   This result is achieved, in cases of " undue influence," as in other cases, by providing in the form of the judgment for such declarations and directions of the following nature as may be deemed necessary or appropriate in the individual circumstances

489. In the first place, the order usually begins with a declaration, in the nature of a justificatory preface or preamble, that the transaction impeached is void (n); and, in special cases, it has been thought desirable or convenient to add a recital of the precise grounds for such declaration (o) Though it has occasionally been considered sufficient for all purposes to follow this with a further declaration that the dominant party is to be deemed a trustee for the servient party of the property which passed to him under the transaction declared void (p), in the normal type of case the order proceeds to direct the setting aside of the transaction   Where necessary or convenient, the dominant party may be required to deliver up to the servient party the instrument in which it is embodied, to be cancelled (q)   and, in

199; *Purcell* v. *M'Namara* (1807), 14 Ves 90A, *Thornber* v *Sheard* (1850), 12 Beav 589, *Billage* v *Southee* (1852), 9 Hare 534, *Longmate* v *Ledger* (1860), 2 Giff. 157, *Tate* v. *Williamson* (1866), L. R 1 Eq 528

(k) As in *Barnardiston* v *Lingood* (1740), 2 Atk 133, *Edwards* v *Browne* (1845), 2 Coll 100, *Croft* v *Graham* (1863), 2 De G J & S 155, *Tyler* v *Yates* (1871), 6 Ch App 665, *Howley* v *Cook* (1873), Ir R 8 Eq 370, *Nevill* v. *Snelling* (1880), 15 C D 679, *Rae* v. *Joyce* (1892), 29 L. R (Ir) 500.

(l) It is because the servient party is so regarded that the rules as to costs in cases of redemption of mortgages have been applied to relief against unconscionable bargains see § 624, *post*   Sometimes, as in *Benyon* v *Cook* (1875), 10 Ch App 389 n, the servient party, in express terms, asks for redemption   In *Carew* v *Johnston* (1805), 2 Sch & Lefr 280, there had actually been a decree of foreclosure, but Lord REDESDALE, L C (li), made a declaration that the servient party's equity of redemption should be deemed not to have been barred by this decree, which had been obtained by " a fraud practised on the Court " (p 306).   this case accordingly finds a place in Chapter VII, as to concealment from third persons (see note (c) to § 575, *post*)

(m) See §§ 237–240, *ante*

(n) See, generally, the cases cited in the notes to this Chapter.

(o) As in *Carew* v *Johnston*, *sup* (see the series of declarations set out at pp 306–313); *Tate* v *Williamson* (1866), L R 1 Eq 528   Cp the elaborate recitals of the grounds on which the decree proceeded, and the reasons of convenience given by Lord ELDON, L C, for such declarations, in the compromise case of *Gordon* v *Gordon* (1821), 3 Swanst 400, as to which see § 237, and note (m) thereto, *ante*

(p) As in *Wood* v *Downes* (1811), 18 Ves 120, *Tomson* v *Judge* (1855), 3 Drew 306. Where the servient party asks for, and is entitled to, rescission, the relief should not stop short at a declaration of right   *Tewarry* v. *Nawab Syed Ali Hossein Khan* (1874), L R. 1 Ind. App 192 (at p 207)

(q) As in *Norton* v *Relly* (1764), 2 Eden 286, *Willan* v *Willan* (1814), 2 Dow H L. 274, *Aylward* v *Kearney* (1814), 2 Ball & B 463, *Griffiths* v *Robins* (1818), 3 Madd 191;

any case, he is ordered to repay all sums with interest and redeliver all property which he has received, and restore all rights and benefits which he has acquired, under the transaction annulled, and to account for all rents, profits, dividends, and other fruits of the transaction enjoyed by him between the date thereof and the date of the judgment (r), and, where the transaction had been completed, to execute a reconveyance, release, re-assignment, or retransfer, of any property or rights which may have passed to him upon such completion (s); on the terms, however, in the case of a contract, that the servient party do, on his part, make the like repayment and redelivery or retransfer to the dominant party of all money, property, benefits, or rights which he has received or to which he has become entitled under the contract, together with just allowances for the value of any permanent improvements or repairs which the dominant party may have executed on or to the property, if consisting of land, whilst in his possession (t), or the value of any services he may have rendered to the servient party pursuant to, or as the consideration for, such contract (u). For this purpose, the order will direct all such accounts, inquiries, or issues (if any) as may be necessary or appropriate in the circumstances of the particular case (v)

490. Where a claim is made to rescind a voidable transaction, it is generally a matter of considerable importance whether the transaction has been completed or not. In a case, however, of " undue influence," the question scarcely ever arises, for the simple reason that the conveyance or other act by which the completion is effected is presumed to have been subject to the same influence as the transaction itself, unless and until the contrary is proved, or, in other words, unless and until the completion is shown to have amounted to a confirmation under the conditions, already stated (w), subject to which alone any confirmation is sustainable. Where, however, a contract

Revell v. *Harvey* (1823), 1 Sim & St 502, *Popham* v *Brooke* (1828), 5 Russ 8, *Dent* v *Bennett* (1839), 4 My. & Cr 269, *Baker* v *Bradley* (1855), 7 De G M. & G 597; *Sharp* v. *Leach* (1862), 31 Beav 491; *Dally* v *Wonham* (1863), 33 Beav 154, *Brenchley* v. *Higgins* (1901), 70 L J (CH) 788, C A ; *Turnbull & Co* v *Duval*, [1902] A C. 429, P C , *Wright* v *Carter*, [1903] 1 Ch 27, C A (as to the deed which was rescinded *in toto*) As to the theory and grounds upon which cancellation is ordered, when it is ordered, see § 238, and note (q) thereto, *ante*

(r) See, generally, the cases cited in the notes to this Chapter in which relief was granted

(s) See *Osmond* v. *Fitzroy* (1731), 3 P Wms. 129 (where release of the bond in question, it having been mislaid, was ordered), *Norton* v *Relly* (1764), 2 Eden 286 (release of annuity directed to be executed, as well as the deed delivered up to be cancelled); *White* v *Meade* (1840), 2 Ir Eq R 420 (reconveyance of land and retransfer of stock), *Addis* v. *Campbell* (1841), 4 Beav. 401 , *Nottidge* v. *Prince* (1860), 2 Giff 246 (retransfer of consols) , *Foster* v *Roberts* (1861), 29 Beav 467 (reassignment of reversionary interest) , *Clarke* v. *Malpas* (1862), 4 De G F. & J. 401 (reconveyance of land here it was said by KNIGHT-BRUCE, L J , at p 405, that, where a contract has been completed, the proper course is to set it aside, and order reconveyance, differing herein from the view taken by ROMILLY, M R , in the court below, and in *Hoghton* v. *Hoghton* (1852), 15 Beav 278, at p 321, that in such cases it is enough to declare the conveyance void) , *Dally* v *Wonham*, *sup* (reconveyance of land, as well as delivery up of conveyance to be cancelled)

(t) See the several forms of decree or order in the cases cited in the notes to this Chapter, generally

(u) As in *Rees* v *De Barnardy*, [1896] 2 Ch 437

(v) See, again, the authorities collected in this Chapter, generally

(w) In § 481, *ante*.

is sought to be invalidated by reference to "the circumstances and conditions" of the case, and, amongst those circumstances and conditions,
undervalue is wholly or principally relied upon, it has been said that the fact
of completion imposes a somewhat heavier burden on the servient party, in
his proof of the unconscionableness of the bargain, than would otherwise be
incumbent upon him (x).

Sub-s. (2). *Defensive Proceedings.*

491. As in the cases which form the subject of Ch. III (y), and of
Ch IV (z), respectively, it is always open to the party complaining, though
there are obvious perils in adopting this course, to await the enemy's attack
In that event, he has the same right to resist the attack, whether it be made
in the form of a claim, or cross-claim, or affirmative plea, and to have the
transaction judicially treated as invalid as he would have to its annulment
by the express order of the Court if he were taking active proceedings for
that purpose   All such matters as would justify an order for rescission in
the latter case will equally justify an answer to any claim or counter-claim
by the dominant party for specific performance of the contract (a), or to
enforce the security (b), or for payment of moneys alleged to be due thereunder (c); or to any claim in respect of the transaction in an administration
suit (d); or to any affirmative plea raised by the dominant party (e).   The
servient party may, and usually does, add to his defence a cross-claim for
rescission (f); or he may already be the plaintiff in an action for that
purpose, in which the dominant party is counter-claiming to enforce the
contract: in that event, his answer to such counter-claim is asserted by way
of reply (g)

(x) See *Longmate* v *Ledger* (1860), 2 Giff 157 (*per* STUART, V -C, at p. 164); *Clarke* v
Malpas, 4 De G F & J. 401 (*per* KNIGHT-BRUCE, L.J, at p 403)
(y) See Ch. III, Sect. 5, Sub-s (2), *ante*
(z) See §§ 381, 382, *ante*
(a) As in *Barnardiston* v. *Lingood* (1740), 1 Atk 133, *Peacock* v *Evans* (1809), 16
Ves 512; *Davies* v *Cooper* (1840), 5 My & Cr 270 (answer to cross-bill)
(b) As in *Bayly* v *Wilkins* (1846), 3 Jo. & Lat. 630; *Blackie* v. *Clark* (1852), 15
Beav 595 (the defence, however, failed here), *London & Westminster Loan & Discount
Co.* v. *Bilton* (1911), 27 T L. R 184.
(c) As in *Osmond* v *Fitzroy* (1731), 3 P Wms 129, *Chaplin & Co* v *Brammall*, [1908]
1 K B 223, C A, *Raja Maneshar Bakhsh* v *Shadi Lal* (1909), 25 L. T R. 635, P C   In
Ahearne v. *Hogan* (1844), Dru 310, the servient party successfully resisted the claim of the
dominant party to the policy moneys which the insurance company had paid into court
See also the cases in which, before the Judicature Acts, courts of equity restrained proceedings at law on an instrument impeached for undue influence, for these may be regarded as
illustrations of what would now be deemed a good defence to such proceedings, e g, *Goddard*
v *Carlisle* (1821), 9 Price 169; *Revett* v. *Harvey* (1823), 1 Sim & St 502, *Bulkeley* v.
Wilford (1834), 2 Cl & Fin. 102, *Espey* v *Lake* (1852), 10 Hare 260, *Smith* v. *Kay* (1859),
7 H L. C. 750.
(d) See note (h), *inf*
(e) See § 456, and the cases cited in note (u) thereto, *ante*.
(f) This happened in several of the cases cited in the notes to this Sub-section, such
as *Osmond* v. *Fitzroy, sup*, *Peacock* v. *Evans, sup*, *Blackie* v. *Clark, sup*, *Raja
Maneshar Bakhsh* v *Shadi Lal, sup*; *London & Westminster Loan & Discount Co* v
Bilton, sup, also in *Fry* v. *Lane* (1888), 40 C D. 312.
(g) As in *Davies* v *Cooper, sup*

Sub-s. (3)   Miscellaneous Forms of Relief

492. There are certain forms of proceeding, other than actions and counter-claims for the express purpose of obtaining rescission, in the course of which the servient party may be indirectly relieved against a transaction which he claims to be voidable on the ground of undue influence   Thus, he may resist a claim in an administration suit which is founded on such a transaction (*h*) ; or, if the question is between solicitor and client as to the validity of an agreement for costs, such question may be determined in proceedings for, or in relation to, taxation (*i*).

493. No relief by way of damages is possible, unless the servient party's case can be, and is, put in the form of a claim (whether alternatively, or not) for relief against a breach of duty of such a nature as to constitute a fraudulent misrepresentation or other tortious act (*j*), or unless the parties consent to the substitution of pecuniary compensation for rescission and mutual restitution *in specie* (*k*)   Of course neither this, nor any of the fore-going observations on the subject of remedy and relief, has any application to proceedings for statutory non-disclosure, which are the subject of separate and independent treatment hereafter (*l*)

SECT. 6.   QUESTIONS OF LAW AND FACT.

494. The three presumptions of the exercise of undue influence which arise as soon as the relation, and the transaction during the subsistence of that relation, are established as facts, are presumptions of law, as has been already explained (*m*)   Except the above, all matters in controversy between the parties in any proceedings founded on " undue influence " are issues of fact, subject to the two cardinal rules of evidence that it is always a question of law, (1) whether any, and, if so, what, legal rights or obligations result from a given state of facts ; and (2), whether there is, or is not, any admissible evidence in support, or (as the case may be) in con-tradiction, of any allegation of fact   It is proposed to illustrate this general statement by particular reference to three main classes of questions which

---

(*h*) The servient party successfully resisted the dominant party's claim in an administration suit, in *Re Holmes's Estate, Bevan's Case* (1861), 3 Giff 337 , *Fry v Lane ; Re Fry, Whittet v. Bush* (1888), 40 C D 312 (so far as regards *Re Fry, Whittet v Bush*).

(*i*) As in *Re Hoggart's Settlement* (1912), 56 Sol. J 415

(*j*) As in *Cockburn v Edwards* (1881), 18 C D 449, 459, 460, C A (claim based on a tortious sale); *Curtis v Bottomley* (1911), " Times," 1st Aug , C. A. (where the action was brought, and damages were recovered, for fraudulent misrepresentation, though, in the Court of Appeal, it was recognized, as appears clearly from the judgments of MOULTON, L.J , and BUCKLEY, L.J., that the case might have been put either as one of abuse of influence, or as one of fraud ; *Nocton v Lord Ashburton*, [1914] A C. 932, 956–958, H L

(*k*) Thus, in *Sturge v Sturge* (1849), 12 Beav 229, where the servient party established his right to rescission of a sale of land for £950, and, it appearing that the dominant party had sold it to a third person for more than this sum, Lord LANGDALE, M.R , instead of ordering a reconveyance (which would have been the regular relief), with the consent of the plaintiff—without this it could not have been done—directed the defendant to pay over to him the excess

(*l*) See Ch VI, *post*

(*m*) In § 405, note (*a*), *ante*

most commonly and prominently arise, viz. questions as to the relation, as to the transaction, and as to value, respectively (n)

Sub-s. (1). Questions as to the Relation

495. Subject to the two governing rules above-mentioned, all questions relating to the existence of the particular relation alleged, its commencement and termination, and its operation upon the transaction impeached, are questions of fact (o)   More particularly and obviously is this so, when the relation is said to have been created by the circumstances of the individual case , for here not only are facts to be considered, but they are wholly to be considered, inasmuch as they are avowed to be the very foundation of that which is sought to be established (p).   It is, however, always a question

(n) Being the subjects of the three Sub sections respectively which follow The citation of authorities in the notes to the first two of these is necessarily of a somewhat general character, for the reason that most of the judgments are given by equity judges who are not concerned to mark off, by any sharp dividing line, their findings of fact from their conclusions of law, so that it is a matter of some difficulty to point to any express judicial statement in these cases that this or that question is one of fact, or one of law, however clear it may be, as a matter of inference from the general character of the language used, and from references to the evidence adduced, that the particular question before the Court was treated as one of fact   There are however some cases, few but sufficient, where, the trial being before a judge and jury, questions were left to the jury, and which, therefore, are conclusive as to the questions so left being questions of fact   And, further, the frequent references by Chancery judges of certain matters to the Master for account, inquiry, or report, and the direction of issues to be tried at law, are tantamount to decisions that such matters are questions of fact

(o) See, generally, the cases cited in the notes to Sect 3, Sub s (1), and Sect 4, Sub s (1), *ante*, and, particularly, *Rhodes v Bate* (1866), 1 Ch. App 252 (*per* TURNER, LJ , at pp. 259–262).   As to its being a question of fact whether a party is so connected with a related person as to be himself also related to the servient party, see the cases cited in note (n) to § 504, *post*

(p) See, generally, the cases cited in the notes to Sect. 2 Sub ss. (5), and (6), *ante* , and in particular, *Gibson v. Jeyes* (1801), 6 Ves 266 (*per* Lord ELDON, L C , at pp 272, 273, as to the plaintiff's mental capacity, which, if necessary, he would have sent to a jury to determine) , *Willan v Willan* (1814), 2 Dow H L. 274 (where, at p 278, Lord ELDON, L.C., treated the question of the servient party's capacity as one of fact, and a matter for medical evidence, and said that, but for the strength of the other circumstances indicating the "weakness" of the servient party, he would have directed an issue) , *Wood v Abrey* (1818), 3 Madd 417 (*per* LEACH, V -C , at p 423, finding as a fact, on the evidence, that the servient party was in pecuniary distress at the date of the transaction) ; *Portmore (Earl of) v Taylor* (1831), 4 Sim. 182 (*per* SHADWELL, V -C., at p 212, finding the like "distress," and the dominant party's knowledge of that distress, as facts); *Howes v Bishop*, [1909] 2 K. B. 390, C A. (where the jury found, in answer to a question left to them by JELF, J , that influence had been exercised by the husband over the wife, but could not agree on another question left to them, whether the influence had been "unduly" exercised   The Court of Appeal, however, intimated that the second of these questions ought not to have been put, as there was no evidence in support of the affirmative   *per* Lord ALVERSTONE, C J , at p. 398, and MOULTON, L J , at p 399) , *Bank of Montreal v Stuart*, [1911] A. C. 120, P C (at p 137, where the existence of the circumstances and conditions necessary to raise the presumption of influence was treated as one of fact on the evidence)   As to undervalue, another and a very important element in the proof of the circumstances and conditions, being always a matter of fact and evidence, see § 499, *post*   The curious view expressed, and course taken, by Lord REDESDALE, L C (Ir), in *Webb v Rorke* (1806), 2 Sch & Lefr. 661, as stated in note (r) to § 448, *ante*, where the question of actual exertion of influence and threats, though at first thought to be one of fact, was ultimately pronounced to be one of law, is wholly at variance with the current of authority, and cannot be supported

of law whether a given state of facts constitutes a relation from which undue influence is to be presumed (*q*).

Sub-s. (2)   *Questions as to the Transaction*

496. Subject, again, to the primary rules above referred to, all disputed questions as to the nature and class of the transaction (and such disputes not infrequently arise, as, for instance, where the transaction is asserted to have been a gift on the one side, and to have been a contract on the other), and also as to its details (these being always necessary to enable the Court to frame the proper directions for mutual restitution in any case where rescission is granted), are questions of fact (*r*)

497. Further, inasmuch as only by establishing that, in point of fact, the transaction was proper, righteous, and fair, can the dominant party repel any presumption of law to the contrary which will otherwise be made against him, it is obvious that all controversies as to such propriety, righteousness, or fairness, must be controversies of fact, to be determined by the evidence (*s*) : for instance, it is always a question of fact whether the servient party had an actual and real intention of making the gift, or entering into the contract which is sought to be invalidated (*t*), whether the dominant party made full disclosure to the servient party of all material facts, and explained to him the nature of the transaction and his rights and liabilities in respect of it, and gave him such honest advice against himself as he would have given him against a stranger (*u*), and whether the servient party was protected by the intervention of an independent third person (*v*)

498. Lastly, all disputed questions which may arise as to whether or not the servient party intentionally and voluntarily confirmed the transaction,

---

(*q*) See Sect. 2, Sub s (7), *ante*

(*r*) See the cases cited in the notes to § 456, and § 457, *ante*, and particularly *Nicol* v. *Vaughan* (1833), 1 Cl. & Fin. 495 (where the question of whether the transaction was purely voluntary, with no consideration except past services, or was, on the contrary, in the nature of a counter security, was referred to the Master for report, as a question of fact   The case is abstracted in note (*s*) to § 456, *ante*), *Mitchell* v. *Homfray* (1881), 8 Q B D 537, C A (where the question was left specifically to the jury whether the transaction was a loan or a gift)

(*s*) Generally, see the cases cited in the notes to Sect 4, Sub-s (2), *ante*

(*t*) See the cases cited in the notes to § 469, *ante*, and, particularly, *Rhodes* v *Bate* (1866), 1 Ch App 252 (*per* TURNER, L.J, at p 257)

(*u*) See the cases cited in the notes to §§ 470–473, *ante*, and especially the following, in which such questions were specifically left to, and pronounced upon by, a jury · *Bulkeley* v *Wilford* (1834), 2 Cl & Fin 102 (where the jury found a fraudulent omission to disclose), *Howes* v *Bishop*, [1909] 2 K B 390, C A (where the jury found concealment, and neglect to explain the instrument), *Mitchell* v *Homfray, sup* (where the jury found, *inter alia*, that there had been no fraud, or undue influence, by which they meant presumably that there had been full disclosure of everything requiring to be disclosed)   For findings of judges, see *Rhodes* v *Bate, sup* (*per* TURNER, L J, at p 257), *Cockburn* v *Edwards* (1881), 18 C D 449, C A (*per* JESSEL, M R, at p 455, and COTTON, L J, at p 462)

(*v*) See §§ 471–477, and the cases cited in the notes thereto, *ante*, and, especially, *Wood* v *Abrey* (1818), 3 Madd 417 (*per* Leach, V -C, at p 423), *Rhodes* v *Bate* (1866), 1 Ch App 252 (*per* TURNER, L J, at pp 259, 260, referring to the evidence on the point) In *Mitchell* v *Homfray, sup*, the absence of independent advice was admitted by the dominant party, and therefore this issue was not left to the jury, with the others, as it would have been if any evidence of such advice had been adduced

and, if so, whether or not, at the time of the suggested confirmation, he was entirely emancipated from the influence which had operated on the transaction purporting to be confirmed, and whether or not he was then cognizant of every fact material for him to know and of his rights in respect of the transaction, are, if there is evidence on both sides, questions of fact to be resolved with reference to such evidence (*w*).

Sub-s. (3).   *Questions as to Value*

499. Whenever it is a question of the terms on which mutual restoration is to be effected, which is the primary object of rescission, disputes may arise not only as to the proper amount of the cash sums due or paid under the transaction, but also as to the value of allowances to be made, or credits to be given, by the servient party, as, for instance, for permanent improvements to the property made, or for services rendered, by the dominant party under or in pursuance of the transaction. All these are of course questions of fact, and, as such, are usually made the subject of inquiries or accounts directed by the judgment (*x*) It is, however, in cases where full value is relied upon by the dominant party as evidence of the propriety of the contract impeached, or where undervalue is set up by the servient party as one of the "circumstances and conditions" raising a presumption of undue influence, or of an unconscionable bargain in relation to an expectancy, that questions of value are most important. These, too, are of necessity matters to be decided, as facts, on a balance of conflicting evidence at the trial (*y*), or to be referred, as issues of fact, to others for inquiry, report, or assessment (*z*)

(*w*) See the cases cited in the notes to Sect 4, Sub-s (3), *ante*, and, particularly *Mitchell* v. *Homfray* (1881), 8 Q B D 537, C. A, where, amongst the questions left to the jury by STEPHEN, J., was the question whether after the cessation of the relationship, and of the effect produced by it, the servient party intentionally abode by what she had done, which the jury answered in the affirmative, and this fact so found by the jury, for whom alone it was to determine it, was held by the Court of Appeal to have justified the judgment for the dominant party which the judge had directed to be entered at the trial

(*x*) See § 489, *ante.*

(*y*) In the following cases, the question of value was dealt with by the Court itself, with reference to the evidence · *Moth* v *Atwood* (1801), 5 Ves 845 (*per* ARDEN, M R , at p 845), *Peacock* v *Evans* (1809), 16 Ves 512 (*per* GRANT, M R., at p. 517), *Gowland* v *De Faria* (1810), 17 Ves 20 (*per* GRANT, M R , at p 25), *Wood* v. *Abrey* (1818), 3 Madd. 417 (*per* LEACH, V.-C , at pp 423), *Portmore (Earl of)* v *Taylor* (1831), 4 Sim 182 (*per* SHADWELL, V -C , at p 210–212), *Edwards* v *Burt* (1852), 2 De G M & G 55 (*per* Lord CRANWORTH, L J , at pp. 57–62), *Salter* v *Bradshaw* (1858), 26 Beav 161 , *St Albyn* v *Harding* (1859), 27 Beav. 11 (*per* ROMILLY, M.R , at pp 13, 14); *Foster* v *Roberts* (1861), 29 Beav. 467 (*per* ROMILLY, M R , at pp 470, 471); *Talbot* v *Staniforth* (1861), 1 J & H 484 (*per* PAGE-WOOD, V -C., at pp 503–508); *Nesbitt* v *Berridge* (1863), 32 Beav 282 (*per* ROMILLY, M R , at pp 287, 288); *Baker* v *Monk* (1864), 4 De G J & S 388 (*per* KNIGHT-BRUCE, L J , at p. 391), *Tate* v *Williamson* (1866), L. R 1 Eq 528 (*per* PAGE WOOD, V -C., at p. 540); *Pisani* v *Att -Gen. of Gibraltar* (1874), L. R 5 P. C 516 (at pp 538, 539); *Fry* v. *Lane* (1888), 40 C D 312 (*per* KAY, J., at pp 322, 323) And see, generally, the cases cited in the notes to § 478, *ante*

(*z*) Thus, in *Webb* v. *Rorke* (1806), 2 Sch & Lefr 661, an issue was directed whilst the question was the subject of a master's report, or of an inquiry, in *Aldborough (Earl of)* v *Trye* (1840), 7 Cl & Fin 436 , *Boothby* v *Boothby* (1852), 15 Beav 212 , *Jones* v. *Ricketts* (1862), 31 Beav. 130.

500. So constantly has this question of value occupied the attention of the Courts in cases of bargains with "expectants" that, in the course of time, a set of working rules or principles for general use in determining the proper inferences of fact to be drawn from certain kinds of evidence has emerged and taken shape It has been held, in the first place, that the value to be ascertained in such cases is the value which the expectancy had at the time of the transaction, not that which it would have had if it had been then known how the event on which such value was contingent (for instance, the continuance or termination of the respective lives) would turn out (a) , further, it has been said that the expert evidence of actuaries as to market values, calculated according to the recognized tables, is of little or no use without proof of the particular circumstances of the individual reversion, such as the relative position, as regards health, of the "expectant" and of the person on whose death the expectancy falls into possession (b) . but that, if no other evidence is offered, the expert evidence must determine the issue (c) It has also been said that an auction sale, unless proved to have been a mere cloak for a fraudulent private bargain, is ordinarily the best test of value (d) None of these, however, are conclusive or infallible criteria Where, for instance, there is proof of an actual re-sale of the reversion at a profit immediately after the transaction, this may carry far greater weight than any other evidence (e) So also proof of the fact that the dominant party received on behalf of the servient party inquiries and applications with a view to purchase, all of which he ignored and concealed from the servient party, is, by itself, eloquent of inadequacy of value (f), just as, conversely, the fact of the servient party having offered the reversion in all directions without result is equally eloquent of adequacy (g) And the most decisive evidence of all is the opinion of an indifferent third person to whom both parties agreed to resort (h).

(a) *Gowland* v *De Faria* (1810), 7 Ves 20 (*per* GRANT, M.R., at pp. 25, 26) , *Nesbitt* v. *Berridge, sup* (*per* ROMILLY, M.R , at p. 287)

(b) *Gibson* v. *Jeyes* (1801), 6 Ves 266 (*per* Lord ELDON, L.C , at p. 274), *Aldborough* (*Earl of*) v. *Trye* (1840), 7 Cl & F 436 (*per* Lord COTTENHAM, L C , at pp 458–460); *Edwards* v. *Burt* (1852), 2 De G. M. & G 55 (*per* Lord CRANWORTH, L J., at pp 56, 57, 63, 64)

(c) *Portmore* (*Earl of*) v. *Taylor* (1831), 4 Sim. 182 (where, at pp 210, 211, SHADWELL, V.-C., says that he "cannot conceive" why the evidence of an actuary should not be accepted "when there is nothing to contradict it ")

(d) *Shelly* v *Nash* (1818), 3 Madd 232 (*per* LEACH, V.-C., at p 236, who, however, there excepts the case of "fraudulent sales by auction" . . . "to cover private bargains," which "will operate nothing"), *Fox* v *Wright* (1821), Madd. & G 111 , *Aldborough* (*Earl of*) v *Trye, sup.* (*per* Lord COTTENHAM, L.C , at p 460, and Lord BROUGHAM, at p. 465) , *Foster* v *Roberts* (1861), 29 Beav 467 (*per* ROMILLY, M R., at p. 471 " unless a person gives much more than the value, it is impossible to purchase a reversionary interest with safety, except under a sale by auction ")

(e) *Nesbitt* v *Berridge* (1863), 32 Beav 282 (*per* ROMILLY, M.R , at p 288)

(f) *Grosvenor* v *Sherratt* (1860), 28 Beav. 659 (*per* ROMILLY, M R , at pp 661, 662, 664)

(g) *Moth* v *Atwood* (1801), 5 Ves 845 (*per* ARDEN, M R , at p 845 "he was determined to sell this reversion . . It is clearly admitted, it was offered over and over again to all the town, to twenty persons That circumstance is decisive . . . The plaintiff offered it to the husband of the tenant for life, who refused it. . . The bill must be dismissed with costs ")

(h) *Foster* v. *Roberts, sup* (*per* ROMILLY, M R., at p. 471).

SECT 7. PARTIES.

501. It remains to consider by, and against whom, the right to relief may be asserted in respect of transactions impeachable on the ground of undue influence

Sub-s (1). *Who are entitled to assert the right to relief.*

502. The persons entitled to assert the right to relief comprise the servient party, and any person who by operation of law, as, for instance, on the death (*i*), or the disability of the servient party by reason of insolvency (*j*), insanity (*k*), or otherwise, or in virtue of a voluntary assignment from him (*l*), is or becomes entitled to stand in his place

Sub-s. (2) *Against whom the right to relief may be asserted.*

503. The persons against whom the right to relief may be asserted comprise, firstly, the person who is deemed to have exercised, or to be responsible for the exercise of, the undue influence ; and, secondly, any person who, whether by operation of law, or as assignee from the dominant party, is or becomes bound to stand in his place.

504. The first of these classes includes not only any person against whom individually the exercise of undue influence upon the servient party in respect of the transaction is presumed or proved, but also any person who, whether as partner, principal, or otherwise (*m*), was associated with

---

(*i*) A very large proportion of the cases cited in the notes to this Chapter are cases in which the plaintiff was the heir, devisee, executor, administrator, next of kin, or other representative of the estate of the deceased servient party, as will be seen on reference They are, indeed, so numerous that it would be a waste of space to give a catalogue of them in this note They range from *Bennett* v. *Vade* (1742), 2 Atk 324, to *Re Coomber,* [1911] 1 Ch. 723, C. A. The reason for this preponderance is plain. The servient party, having once come under the influence, usually remains under it until his death, when " another Pharaoh " comes upon the scene who, being unamenable to the influence, and having no interest except in the estate, at once takes active measures

(*j*) As in *Ford* v *Olden* (1867), L. R. 3 Eq 461 (where the plaintiff was the assignee of the estate of the bankrupt servient party for the benefit of his creditors), *Tyler* v *Yates* (1871), 6 Ch App 665 (the like)

(*k*) As in *De Witte* v *Addison* (1899), 80 L. T. 207, C A (where the plaintiff was the next friend of the servient party who was of unsound mind not so found by inquisition)

(*l*) The conditions under, and the equities subject to, which a chose in possession, and a chose in action, may be respectively assigned, without rendering any action by the assignee obnoxious to the doctrine of champerty or maintenance, and the application of the law on this subject to voidable contracts in general, have been fully considered, once for all, in § 279, *ante.* For an illustration of an assignment which was held not to be champertous, see *Cockell* v *Taylor* (1852), 15 Beav 103 (*per* ROMILLY, M R , at pp 116, 117). For a similar illustration, where the relation was one of confidence, see the case cited in note (*w*) to § 394, *ante*

(*m*) See *Gibson* v *Jeyes* (1801), 6 Ves 266, where a member of a firm of solicitors was held liable for the undue influence personally imputable to his partner and son (*per* Lord ELDON, L C , at p 279A " I am satisfied by this evidence, upon the question whether the defendant is affected by the conduct of Jeyes the younger, that there is no distinction between them ") In *Baker* v. *Bradley* (1855), 7 De G M & G. 597, the improper conduct of one of the mortgagees against whom relief was claimed, it being proved that he had acted as agent for all of them, was held sufficient to render all liable (*per* KNIGHT BRUCE, L.J., at pp. 614, 615). The liability of the parties in such cases is ordinarily joint, unless it appears on the face of the instrument, or otherwise, that an innocent party claims rights under covenants or parts of the instrument which are severable from those under

him in the transaction impeached, and must, therefore, take the consequences of its having been improperly brought about; and any person who, with knowledge of a relation of influence between two persons, procures or suffers the dominant party to exercise the influence belonging to that relation with the object and result of inducing the servient party, as surety or otherwise, to enter into or concur in a contract with himself, by which he, as well as the dominant party, will be benefited (n). The burden, in the last-mentioned case, is upon the servient party of showing, not only that the relation alleged existed between him and the dominant party, but also that the person in question was cognizant of, and whether by overt acts or tacitly utilized and traded on, such relation and the influence presumed by the law, and anticipated by him, as likely to result from it (o). A juridical or artificial person, it should be noted, is capable of undue influence (p), just as it is of fraud, or malice (q)

505. The second class consists of two species, the first of which includes any person to whom the liability is transmitted, or upon whom it devolves, by operation of law, in case of the death (r) or other legal disability of the dominant party (s).

which a guilty party derives title, in which case, as has been seen—see § 488, and note (*ı*) thereto, *ante*—the transaction will not be set aside as against such innocent party.

(n) See § 411, and the cases cited in note(r) thereto, *ante* (where a creditor made use of the parental influence); the cases cited in note (h) to § 129, *ante*, also § 431, and the cases cited in note (t) thereto, *ante* To these add *Rhodes* v *Bate* (1866), 1 Ch App 252 (where one of the dominant parties, Bate, besides exerting undue influence on his own account, took the benefit of that which the other dominant party, his co defendant Codrington, exercised, in order to obtain guarantees from the servient party of Codrington's indebtedness to himself It was on the latter aspect of the case that so much of the relief as ordered Bate to repay all that he had received under such guarantees was based *per* TURNER, L.J, at pp 260, 261)

(o) See *Cobbett* v *Brock* (1855), 20 Beav 521 (where it was vainly contended that mortgagees to whom a lady had mortgaged her reversion were deprived of all rights, merely because they knew that the lady was engaged to be married to the person whose debt the mortgage was intended to secure. *per* ROMILLY, M R , at p. 531 "the fact of Mr. Brock saying, 'I am about to marry a lady who will give you security,' does not amount to notice to them that this security could only be obtained by undue influence "), *Bainbrigge* v. *Browne* (1881), 18 C D 188 (where, a father having exercised undue parental influence over his children, which resulted in their giving a charge to certain creditors of his on their interest under a marriage settlement, it was held that the chargees could not be deprived of their security on the mere ground that they knew that the same solicitor was acting for both father and children (*per* FRY, J , at pp 198, 199, and see also the citation in note (t), *inf*)

(p) For instance, in *Bank of Montreal* v. *Stuart*, [1911] A C. 120, P C , the dominant party was a bank In *London & Westminster Loan & Discount Co , Ltd.* v *Bilton* (1911), 27 T L R 184, and in *J King, Ltd.* v *Hay Currie* (1911), 28 T L R 10, the dominant party was a limited company For cases of relations of "confidence" in which the party charged was a corporation, see the authorities cited in note (*ı*) to § 399, *ante.*

(q) The liability of corporations for fraud is discussed in § 165 of the author's *Law of Actionable Misrepresentation* , and their liability for malice in App IV, Sect 4 (*sub fin*) of his *Law of Actionable Defamation*

(r) As in *Wiseman* v *Beake* (1690), 2 Vern 121 ; *Kingsland (Viscount)* v *Barnewall* (1706), 4 Brown P C 154 (devisee and executors) , *Webb* v *Rorke* (1806), 2 Sch & Lefr. 661 ; 9 R R 122 (heir at law and personal representative) , *MacCabe* v. *Hussey* (1831), 5 Bligh (N s) 715 (administrator here the dominant party died pending suit) , *Addis* v. *Campbell* (1841), 4 Beav 401 (personal representatives); *Gresley* v *Mousley* (1859),

(s) As in other cases of actions of contract. Cp. § 401, *ante,* as to relations of " confidence "

506. The second of the above-mentioned species includes any one who has acquired property which was the subject of the impeached transaction by conveyance, assignment, or transfer, from the dominant party, if such property was a chose in action (t), or if, being a chose in possession, the servient party is in a position to establish (and in that case it is for him to do so) either that the assignee took as a volunteer, or sub-donee, or otherwise, without consideration, in which case it is wholly immaterial whether he had, or had not, notice of the circumstances rendering the transaction voidable (u), or that he took with notice of such circumstances, or in bad faith, in which case it is immaterial whether he gave valuable consideration, or not (v)

507. Questions as to the effect on costs, on the one hand, of adding "formal" parties, that is, parties whom, as trustees, holders of the legal estate, incumbrancers, stake-holders, or otherwise, it was necessary or proper to join "for conformity," or persons from whom, though eventually exculpated, it was reasonable to seek redress in the first instance, and, on the other hand, of any unnecessary or improper joinder of parties not liable with those who are, form the subject of separate examination in another place (w)

---

t De G. & J 78 (here the dominant party died during the appeal), *Baker* v. *Loader* (1873), L R 16 Eq 49 (executrix)

(t) See *Barnard* v *Taylor* (1856), 2 Jur (N S) 1213 (*per* STUART, V C., at p. 1215, as to so much of the mortgaged property as consisted of a fund in court)   The rules stated in the text as to choses in action, and choses in possession, respectively, acquired under voidable transactions in general, irrespective of the particular ground of voidability, have been enunciated and discussed, once for all, in §§ 283–287, *ante*, and need not now be re stated with the same detail   See, however, the statement by FRY, J , of the general rule, as applied to cases of undue influence, which is to be found at pp 196, 197 of *Bainbrigge* v. *Browne* (1881), 18 C D 188   "against whom does this inference of undue influence operate ?   Clearly .   against the person who is able to exercise the influence . .   and . . against every volunteer who claimed under him, and also against every person who claimed under him .   with notice of the circumstances from which the Court infers the equity   But .   it would operate against no others."   Cp for instances of the application of the rules to relations of "confidence," § 402, *ante*

(u) The *locus classicus* (perhaps, rather, the *purpureus pannus*) on the hopeless position of subdonees, however morally free from blame (which they rarely are, however), forms part of the constantly cited judgment of WILMOT, C J , as one of the Commissioners of the Great Seal, at p 64 of *Bridgeman* v *Green* (1757), Wilmot's Opns. & Judgts , 58, affirming the decision of Lord HARDWICKE, L.C (1755), 2 Ves Sr 626 ("there is no pretence that Green's brother, or his wife, was party to any imposition or had any due or undue influence over the plaintiff . but does it follow from thence that they must keep the money ?   No, whoever receives it must take it tainted and infected with the undue influence and im position of the person procuring the gift   His partitioning and cantoning it out amongst his relations and friends will not purify the gift, and protect it against the equity of the person imposed upon   Let the hand receiving it be ever so chaste, yet if it comes through a corrupt, polluted channel, the obligation of restitution will follow it ")   The principle so stated has been applied to all subsequent cases of volunteer assignees of property the subject of a transaction resulting from undue influence, such as *Carew* v *Johnston* (1805), 2 Sch & Lefr. 280 , *Huguenin* v *Baseley* (1807), 14 Ves 273 (*per* Lord ELDON, L C , at pp 288–290), *Goddard* v *Carlisle* (1821), 9 Price 169 (*per* RICHARDS, C B , at p 661, and GRAHAM, B , at p 664); *Morley* v. *Loughnan*, [1893] 1 Ch 736 (*per* WRIGHT, J , at pp. 757, 758), *Barron* v *Willis*, [1900] 2 Ch 121, C A (*per* LINDLEY, M.R , at p 133)

(v) As in *Tottenham* v *Green* (1863), 32 L J (CH) 201 (*per* WOOD, V C., at pp 205, 206, as to sub mortgagees who took with notice), *Nesbitt* v *Berridge* (1863), 37 Beav 282 (*per* ROMILLY, M.R , at pp 288, 289, as to sub purchasers with notice)   On the other hand, some of the defendants in *Rhodes* v *Bate* (1866), 1 Ch. App 252, succeeded in showing that they took for value in good faith, and no relief, therefore, was granted against them (*per* TURNER, L.J , at pp 261, 262).

(w) § 623, *post*

CHAPTER VI.

THE STATUTORY LAW AS TO NON-DISCLOSURE IN PROSPECTUSES OF COMPANIES.

508. HITHERTO this commentary has been concerned solely with the common (in the sense of non-statutory) law of disclosure, so far as it is the subject of civil jurisdiction and relief   It is now proposed to consider how far, and in respect of what matters, the legislature has modified that law   On a careful examination and analysis of the various statutes and enactments in which non-disclosure or concealment is dealt with, after excluding those which merely codify, declare, confirm, re-enact, recognize, or assume existing principles and rules of the common law, without purporting to alter them in any way (x), those which render either existing or newly created duties of disclosure amenable to criminal jurisdiction only (y), and with which this treatise is not concerned, those which merely provide a special and simpler or more summary procedure for the enforcement of common law rights already enforceable by action (z), and those which have already been dealt with in foregoing

---

(x) As, for instance, Marine Insurance Act, 1906 (6 Edw 7, c 41), the provisions of which as to disclosure have been frequently referred to in Ch II, Sect 3, and in Ch III, Sect. 2, Sub-s (2), *ante*, Conveyancing Act, 1882 (45 & 46 Vict c 39) s. 3 and other sections, as to presumptive knowledge, cited *passim* in notes to Ch II, Sect 3, Sub-ss (4), (5), (6), *ante*, Partnership Act, 1890 (53 & 54 Vict c 39), ss 16, 29, 30, cited in notes to §§ 44, 55, 56, 341, *ante*, Sale of Goods Act, 1893 (56 & 57 Vict. c 31), s 23 of which, as to disclosure of title, is cited in notes to §§ 110, 170, 287, *ante*   All these are either codifying or declaratory enactments   For an illustration of an enactment which needlessly prescribes, as a statutory remedy, a form of relief already existing at common law, see Law of Property Amendment Act, 1859 (22 & 23 Vict c 25), s 24, as extended by Law of Property Amendment Act, 1860 (23 & 24 Vict. c 38), s 8, which purports to render a vendor or mortgagor, or his solicitor or agent, liable in damages to the purchaser or mortgagee for the concealment of any incumbrance or document of title,—a liability which would clearly attach to such a concealment, being an implied fraudulent misrepresentation, independently of any statute, as explained in § 85 of the author's *Law of Actionable Misrepresentation*   For instances of statutes which, without altering existing civil rights and liabilities at common law in respect of non-disclosure, give new forms of civil relief, or confer additional rights and remedies in respect of other matters not being non disclosure, though akin to it, see Clandestine Mortgages Act, 1692 (4 & 5 W. & M, c. 16), ss 2, 3 (whereby any person who, having mortgaged his lands to one mortgagee, subsequently mortgages them to another is deprived of his equity of redemption altogether against that other); Moneylenders Act, 1900 (63 & 64 Vict c 51), the effect of which statute is considered in *Samuel v Newbold*, [1906] A C 461, H L , Moneylenders Act, 1911 (1 & 2 Geo. 5, c 38), s. 1 (3)

(y) See, for examples, Debtors Act, 1869 (32 & 33 Vict c 62), ss. 11, 14, now repealed, and re enacted, with extensions, by ss 154, 160, respectively, of the Bankruptcy Act, 1914 (4 & 5 Geo 5, c 59); Moneylenders Act, 1900 (63 & 64 Vict c 51), s 2 ; Prevention of Corruption Act, 1906 (6 Edw 7, c 34), s 1   As to the last, see *Re a Solicitor* (1909), 26 T L R 22, where the solicitor had been convicted of offences under this section).

(z) See § 616, *post*, for an example (misfeasance procedure).

Chapters, or which do not directly affect the substantive provisions of the general law (*a*), it will be found that in one class of case only, though that one is of the utmost importance, has the legislature thought fit to alter the existing law by making actionable certain kinds of non-disclosure which were not previously so. The class of case referred to is non-disclosure in prospectuses of companies, and the enactment which modifies the law, creates new duties, and renders them the subject of civil relief in respect of such non-disclosure is s. 81 of the Companies (Consolidation) Act, 1908 (*b*). To this enactment accordingly the residue of this Chapter is devoted

SECT. 1   ORIGIN AND OBJECT OF THE ENACTMENT.

509. In each of the three preceding Chapters, the discussion of the non-statutory duties of disclosure and good faith between persons standing to one another in the relations therein respectively described has been prefaced by some observations as to the theory on which the doctrine is based (*c*). Where statutory law is concerned, any such inquiry is of course entirely out of place. It is a case of " hoc volo, sic jubeo · sit pro ratione voluntas " No question of theory or principle arises But the occasion of any legislative modification of the common law is sometimes a guide to its construction, and in any case is not without historical interest. For this, and other reasons which will become apparent in the course of the discussion, it has been thought advisable to offer, as an introduction to the present inquiry, some historical observations as to the origin and object of the enactment which is the subject of this Chapter, before analysing in detail its somewhat multifarious and complicated provisions.

(*a*) The Sales of Reversions Act, 1867 (31 Vict., c 4) has been fully dealt with in Ch V, Sect 2, Sub-s. (*b*), *ante* so also have the statutes requiring registration of various documents of title, in so far as their provisions affect the doctrine of presumptive knowledge see Ch II, Sect. 3, Sub s (*b*), *ante* Disclosure to the world of various other matters is enforced by statutory requirements as to registration, *e g* persons and names, by the Moneylenders Acts, 1900 and 1911 (see s 1 (2) of the latter Act), associations, by the various Friendly Society, Building Society, and Trade Union Acts, and the Companies (Consolidation) Act, 1908; newspapers, by the Newspaper Libel and Registration Act, 1881 (44 & 45 Vict c 60), bills of sale, by the various Bills of Sale Acts But, except as affecting the rules relating to presumptive knowledge, they have no bearing on the law of actionable non disclosure, inasmuch as none of them gives any civil remedy, either expressly or impliedly, to any person injured by the non registration, though they may (or may not) have the effect of rendering contracts by the unregistered persons or societies, or the unregistered instruments, unenforceable, a question which in each case depends on the scope and language of the particular statute. see § 567, *post* The secret employment as to puffers at sales by auction, prohibited by the Sale of Land by Auction Act, 1867, being rather a form of implied misrepresentation than of pure non disclosure, is discussed in Ch XIII, Sect 2, of the author's *Law of Actionable Misrepresentation* And, generally, the legislation against fraudulent concealment, or fraud, is of course irrelevant, as such, to the law of non-disclosure, which, as such, does not depend upon fraud at all, as explained in §§ 197, 358, 461, *ante* So that, on the whole, it is not incorrect to say that substantially the only enactment directly imposing a duty of disclosure, pure and simple, unknown to the common law, and making that duty the subject of civil, and not of merely criminal, jurisdiction is the enactment which forms the subject of this Chapter,—a Chapter which therwise would have been headed generally, "Statutory Non Disclosure."

(*b*) 8 Edw 7, c 69 (hereinafter called the Act of 1908).

(*c*) See respectively, §§ 83, 317, 318, 407, *ante*

510. At common law there is no obligation of disclosure on any person who issues a prospectus inviting the public to subscribe for shares or debentures in a company, other than and beyond that which rests on everyone who negotiates, or offers to negotiate, for a contract which is not *uberrimæ fidei* with another person to whom he is not tied by any relation of confidence or influence,—the obligation, namely, to divulge every fact the withholding of which would render any statement which he chooses to make so fragmentary and defective as to amount to positive falsehood (*d*). He is in such a case under no duty, apart from statute, to disclose any fact which would not have this effect, however material it may be. It is established, though it has been said to be " well worth consideration " whether the law is not or ought not to be otherwise (*e*), that the issuer of a prospectus does not, by reason of the mere fact that the document in which he makes his offer is a prospectus, undertake for plenary disclosure, or any disclosure except to the extent above stated. Moreover, at common law there is no obligation on any company to issue a prospectus at all, or to take the public into its confidence in any way, or, if not issuing a prospectus, to file any statement containing particulars of the undertaking in any register or office accessible to the public.

511. This was considered to be an undesirable state of the law, and, accordingly, after the Overend and Gurney litigation had revealed its inadequacy in the matter of prospectuses, and had provided an object lesson sufficiently striking to excite public attention (*f*), the legislature intervened, and the Companies Act, 1867 (*g*), was passed, s. 38 of which was intended to cure the mischief. The section ran thus: " Every prospectus of a company, and every notice inviting persons to subscribe for shares in any joint stock company, shall specify the dates and names of the parties to any contract entered into by the company, or the promoters, directors, or trustees thereof, before the issue of such prospectus or notice, whether subject to adoption by the directors or otherwise, and any prospectus or notice not specifying the same shall be deemed fraudulent on the part of the promoters, directors, and officers of the company knowingly issuing the same, as regards any person taking shares in the company on the faith of such prospectus, unless he shall have had notice of such contract." This egregious piece of drafting was soon perceived to exhibit nearly every imperfection of which legislative expression is capable. The presumable object was to render nondisclosure of material contracts in a prospectus actionable: but instead of saying this in so many words,—than which nothing could have been easier,—

(*d*) Misrepresentation by omission of qualifying circumstances is dealt with in Ch. IV, Sect. 4, Sub-s. (2), of the author's *Law of Actionable Misrepresentation*, as to this type of misrepresentation in prospectuses particularly, see the cases cited in note (*c*) to § 85 in that Chapter.

(*e*) Per FRY, J., at p. 311 of *Arkwright* v. *Newbold* (1881), 17 C. D. 301, C. A.

(*f*) " The occasion of this Act must be remembered, viz. the omission from a prospectus of a company of a contract in the Overend and Gurney case which burdened the company " per BRAMWELL, L.J., at p. 499 of *Twycross* v. *Grant* (1877), 2 C. P. D. 469, C. A.

(*g*) 30 & 31 Vict., c. 131 (hereinafter referred to as the Act of 1867).

the legislature preferred to wrap up its meaning in a succession of *involucra verborum*, in comparison with which a Delphic oracle is simplicity itself. The consequence was that a series of decisions was required to reduce the loose and ill-defined language of the enactment to something like rationality and coherence. Ultimately, after much debate and conflict of opinion, in the course of which the judicial observations on the section were " painful, and frequent, and free," it was determined that the legislature must be taken to have meant, though they did not express their intention in apt terms, to impose a duty on the persons specified to disclose every contract material to be made known to anyone contemplating application for the shares offered in the prospectus for subscription (*h*).

512. After enduring 33 years of more or less derisive criticism, the section was repealed by s 33 (1), and the Schedule, of the Companies Act, 1900 (*i*), which statute at the same time prescribed the duty of disclosing in any prospectus of a company a long list of specific matters catalogued in s 10. This section, as varied and extended by s 2 of the Companies Act, 1907 (*j*), was reproduced in s 81 of the Companies (Consolidation) Act, 1908, which now contains the statutory code of the law of disclosure in prospectuses of companies (*k*), the general effect being to render actionable, at the suit of a subscriber for or purchaser of shares or debentures in a company, every omission from the prospectus of the kinds of facts which, at common law, a promoter would be under a fiduciary duty to disclose to the company promoted by him (*l*), or which a director or other officer of a company would be bound to divulge to such company as his principal (*m*), but which, at common law, such company promoter, director, officer, or agent, would be under no obligation to disclose to actual or possible shareholders, or to the public (*n*). Further, by s 1 (1), and Sched I, of the Act of 1907, now reproduced in s 82 and Sched II, of the Act of 1908, it was provided that every company which does not issue a prospectus, other than a " private company," and a company which has allotted shares or debentures before the 1st July, 1898, must file with the registrar of companies a " statement in lieu of prospectus" in the prescribed form, and containing the prescribed particulars (*nn*)

(*h*) See § 532, and note (*w*) thereto, *post*
(*i*) 63 & 64 Vict , c 48 (hereinafter referred to as the Act of 1900)
(*j*) 7 Edw 7, c 50 (hereinafter described as the Act of 1907)
(*k*) It follows that the authorities on so much of s 38 of the Act of 1867, s 10 of the Act of 1900, and s 2 of the Act of 1907, as is reproduced, or represented by equivalent provisions, in s 81 of the Act of 1908, are relevant to the present inquiry, and, as such, are cited in the following notes
(*l*) See Ch IV, Sect 2, Sub-s (2), *ante*
(*m*) See Ch IV, Sect 2, Sub-s (3), *ante*
(*n*) See § 345, and notes (*z*), (*a*) and (*b*) thereto, *ante*
(*nn*) The prescribed form is to be found in Sched II of the Act of 1908, which repeats Sched. I of the Act of 1907. The particulars required to be inserted in the " statement," pursuant to this Schedule, are substantially the same as those required to be inserted in a prospectus by s 81 of the Act of 1908 (with the omission of matters (a), (b) and (n) therein). A " private company " is defined in s 121 of the Act of 1908 (reproducing s 37 of the Act of 1907), as amended by the Companies Act, 1913 (3 & 4 Geo 5, c 25). This provision, however, is not of much practical importance. For, though an allottee of shares would have a theoretical right to damages in respect of non disclosure of any of the prescribed matters in the " statement," if in a position to prove that he subscribed for

513. It is thus seen that, so far as the duty of disclosure in prospectuses of companies exists, or has ever existed, it is, and always has been since 1867, purely the creature of the legislature (o), if " duty of disclosure " is understood in the strict sense above stated (p) : for non-disclosure which amounts to misrepresentation has always given, and still gives, a cause of action to the party aggrieved concurrently with, and independently of, any remedy which may be available for statutory non-disclosure (q)   And, though it was quite unnecessary to do so, the enactment itself which is now under consideration is careful by express words to safeguard these concurrent and independent rights (r).

514. Defective, however, as was the legislation of 1867, that of 1900, 1907, and 1908 may appear to some minds to have achieved a not much larger measure of success   A recognized master in this branch of the law, whilst characterizing s 38 of the Act of 1867 as " a notorious section," has also described s 81 of the Act of 1908 as a "monumental" one (s), probably not intending a compliment in the latter case any more than in the former   The enactment may not unfairly be criticized as combining two opposite vices in the art of legislative expression.   For it is specific, just where it ought to be general, and general or vague, just where it ought to be specific,   It was the ambiguity and obscurity of s 38 of the Act of 1867 which occasioned, or which at any rate was the justification for, its repeal, not its generality, for generality in such a case is a merit, and not a fault, and is quite consistent with lucidity and precision.   In laying down or developing any doctrine, our courts have always manifested a wise and healthy reluctance to tie their hands by enumerating the particular acts and omissions which are to be deemed within the doctrine, and have steadily limited their exposition to a statement of the rule, and the reason and principle of the rule (t) , whereas

his shares on the faith of it, it is obvious that such a case is not likely to arise, for the very object of a prospectus less company is to avoid giving the public any rights against it, and the requirements of the statute can be satisfied by filing the "statement" at such a short interval before the allotment—see s 1 (2), and Sched II of the Act of 1907, reproduced in s. 82 of the Act of 1908—that there will be no opportunity for any member of the public to inspect it before the allotment, which, it has been held, is not avoided by proved non-disclosure   *Re Blan Open Hearth Furnace Co* , [1914] 1 Ch 390, C A

(o) "The director is placed in a position which nothing short of a statute could have placed him   He is under an absolute obligation to disclose   &c   Therefore the conditions of his liability are fulfilled if he knows the dates and names of the parties to the contract, and does not state them   He is under an absolute obligation to state them "   *per* COLLINS, M R , at pp 774, 775 of *Watts* v *Bucknall*, [1903] 1 Ch 766, C A (a case under s 38 of the Act of 1867)

(p) See § 510, *ante*

(q) Thus it was held, in a case under s 38 of the Act of 1867, that mere formal compliance with the requirements of that section did not of itself negative or displace the shareholder's proof of fraudulent misrepresentation by omissions of material contracts and facts from the prospectus   *Aaron's Reefs, Ltd.* v *Twiss*, [1891] A C 273, H L (*per* Lord HALSBURY, L C , at p 279, Lord WATSON at p 287, and Lord DAVEY at pp 293, 294)

(r) Sub-s. (9) of s 81

(s) Buckley, *Companies Acts* (note to s 81 of the Act of 1908, at p 178 of the 9th edition)

(t) This judicial habit and disposition has manifested itself in the case of each of the main classes of relation dealt with in the three preceding Chapters, as pointed out in §§ 84, 343, 408, respectively, *ante,* where the preference of the courts for the flexible Lesbian rule (see § 649, *post*) is illustrated

lists and catalogues of *mala prohibita* have always presented irresistible attractions to the parliamentary draftsman, and the legislature, by its dangerous passion for particularity is constantly engaged in emasculating that which constitutes the essential merit of a judicial rule, its universal or general applicability to future cases (*u*). So here, erroneously supposing that only by the substitution of the specific for the general could the ambiguity of the former section be removed, and not appreciating the soundness and profundity of Bacon's observation—*ut exceptio firmat vim legis in casibus non exceptis, ita enumeratio infirmat eam in casibus non enumeratis* (*v*),—the legislature, instead of laying down a perfectly general, but none the less on that account a perfectly lucid and definite, rule prohibiting the omission from a prospectus of any fact (which would include a contract or document) material to be known to any person invited to subscribe for or purchase shares or debentures of a company, has preferred to set out a "monumental" specification of particular facts, and particular contracts, mixed up with general prohibitions against the withholding of "material" contracts, with the result of at least encouraging the argument that nothing is forbidden which is outside the four corners of the statutory catalogue or proscription list (*w*). On the other hand, in relation to the questions of remedy and relief, and of the persons respectively entitled and liable, where above all things specification is vital, and where even the despised provision of 1867 was clear and definite, to say nothing of other sections in the Act of 1908 itself (*x*), the enactment under discussion is utterly indefinite, or rather is absolutely silent (*y*).

SECT. 2. THE PROSPECTUS

515. Before examining the list of matters required to be stated in a prospectus by s 81 of the Act of 1908, it is obviously essential to ascertain

(*u*) Many instances of these cross currents, and conflicting tendencies, are to be found in other departments of our jurisprudence. The mischief is aggravated by the fact that a large proportion of modern statutes are of the "occasional" or "ad hoc" type, being designed to meet a sudden situation, or even provoked by some popular clamour of the moment, than which no conditions could be more unfavourable to well considered and enduring legislation. Thus, the Directors' Liability Act, 1890 (53 & 54 Vict., c 64), now reproduced by s 84 of the Act of 1908, was the outcome of *Derry* v *Peek* (1889), 14 App. Cas 337, H L, and the Moneylenders Act, 1900 (63 & 64 Vict., c 61) was largely stimulated by *Gordon* v *Street*, [1899] 2 Q B 641, C A. These measures may be referred to as illustrations of the hastily considered, and therefore ill-expressed, legislation resulting from the attempt to satisfy a momentary outcry by or against a particular section of the public without much regard to the requirements of the future, or the good of the community at large, which are what Bacon, in his "History of Henry VII" (vol vi, p 92 ed Spedding, Ellis, & Heath) contrasts unfavourably with the "laws" which "are deep, and not vulgar, not made upon the spur of a particular occasion for the present, but out of a providence for the future"

(*v*) *De Augm Scient*, Book VIII, App. 17
(*w*) See Sect 3, and particularly § 532, *post*
(*x*) As, for instance, ss 84, 85, and 86 of the Act of 1908
(*y*) See §§ 537, 540, 566, *post*. *In express terms* the enactment gives no remedy of any sort, and imposes no duty on any person whatever, but only on a thing "every prospectus must state," &c. The nature of the remedy, and the incidence of the liability, is left to be conjectured from the other provisions of the section, and from the application of general principles of statutory interpretation, as to which, see in § 567, *post*.

the statutory meaning of " prospectus " : for a document headed or described as a prospectus may not be a statutory prospectus ; whilst, conversely, that which is otherwise headed or described may nevertheless be a prospectus to which the section applies. By the conjoined effect of the definition of " prospectus " in the general interpretation clause of the Act of 1908, the opening words of s. 81, and the expressions used in sub-s. (7) of that section, the following result is arrived at. The prospectus in which the prescribed disclosure must be made means and includes " any prospectus, notice, circular, advertisement, or other invitation, offering to the public for subscription or purchase any shares or debentures of a company " (z), which is " issued by or on behalf of a company, or by or on behalf of any person who has been or is engaged or interested in the formation of the company (a), whether issued on or with reference to the formation of a company, or subsequently," not being a " circular or notice inviting existing members or debenture holders of a company to subscribe either for shares or debentures of the company, whether with or without the right to renounce in favour of other persons " (b). This definition involves a number of constituent elements which must be separately considered

516. In the first place, though the terms " notice " and " invitation " are in themselves neutral, it is quite clear from the context, and the collocation of such expressions as " circular," and " issue," as well as from other provisions of the statute requiring every prospectus to be dated and signed, and a copy filed for registration (c), that the prospectus contemplated by the enactment is a documentary, and not an oral, invitation or offer.

517. In the next place, no document can be a statutory " prospectus " which does not constitute, or contain, an " offer " or " invitation " to anyone to subscribe for, or purchase, shares or debentures (d). And the offer must be to the public, which expression, however, does not necessarily mean the entire community, but includes any class or section of the public, or any

---

(z) This is the definition of " prospectus," contained in s 285 of the Act of 1908

(a) The last cited words are from the commencement of s 81, from which it is clear that it is not every prospectus, as defined in s 285, that " must state " the matters prescribed, but only every prospectus answering to that definition which is issued by the company or persons specified See § 519, *post*

(b) The words last cited appear in sub-s (7) of s 81 Subject to the exception there stated, they constitute an extension or amplification of the introductory language of the section.

(c) See s 80 of the statute

(d) It is clear from the language of s 89, (1), (b), of the Act of 1908, that an offer *to the public* is essential to constitute the document a statutory prospectus, and that there may be " a circular or notice, *not being a prospectus,* inviting subscription for shares " , see § 571, *post* And, where a promoting syndicate which never intended to, and never did in fact, apply to the public, or carry on business, printed 1000 copies of a document headed " strictly private and confidential—not for publication," and relating to the prospects of the company of which they were contemplating the promotion, and handed 20 copies to one director, and 200 to the others, and one of these copies was, without any authority from the syndicate, sent to the plaintiff, it was held that the document was not a statutory prospectus, as it was not issued or intended as an offer or invitation at all, certainly not as " an offer of shares to any one who should choose to come in," which is one of the indicia of an " offer to the public " *Sherwell v Combined Incandescent Mantles Syndicate, Ltd.* (1907), 23 T. L R 482 (*per* WARRINGTON, J , at p 483)

selected number of persons, not being *exclusively* holders of shares or debentures in the company issuing the prospectus. In short, " the public " means the outside public, whom it is desired to bring into relation with the company, as contrasted with those who are already in relation with it, whether as members or secured creditors, and, if so, since *omne majus in se continet minus*, the expression covers any portion of that outside public (e), though existing members or shareholders may be included in that portion. If, however, such existing members or debenture-holders *only* are invited, the document is not a prospectus (f). And, generally, when it is clear that the thing alleged to be a prospectus was not " issued," or published at all in the business sense of the word, that is, *animo invitandi*, or with the intention of appealing to the public, but for some totally different purpose, the section has no application (g), and the document is not a statutory prospectus, even if it is capable of being termed a prospectus in any sense (h). The question whether the alleged prospectus does, or does not, constitute or contain an offer or invitation to the public to subscribe for, or purchase, shares or debentures, is a question of fact (i)

518. The securities offered for subscription or purchase must be either shares (j), or debentures (k)   Having regard to the extended statutory

(e) See *Re South of England Natural Gas and Petroleum Co*, [1911] 1 Ch 573, where the prospectus was issued only to shareholders in various gas companies likely to be interested in the projected company, and it was held that these persons were none the less " the public," *vis à vis* the company, because they were not the public at large, but a selected portion of it (per SWINFEN EADY, J, at p 576)   It so happened, however, that the claim in that case failed, because (and only because) the wrong remedy was pursued   see note (i) to § 568, *post*

(f) See sub s (7) of s 81, and the observations of FARWELL, J, at p 27 of *Burrows v Matabele Gold Reefs & Estates Co*, [1901] 2 Ch 23, C A

(g) *Sherwell v Combined Incandescent Mantles Syndicate* (1907), 23 T L R 482

(h) See *Baty v Keswick* (1901), 85 L T 18, a case under s 38 of the Act of 1867, which applies, *inter alia*, to " every notice inviting persons to subscribe for shares' (per FARWELL, J, at p 19. " the Act was not intended, and it is not expressed in such a manner as to impose the very serious consequences of disobedience to its provisions on persons engaged in settling prospectuses in respect of copies not authorized for publication, but shown to friends, or speculators, not as members of the public, but by way of anticipation of the public, and in order to induce them to co-operate with the promoters in placing the shares with the public ")   Here " the plaintiff signed his underwriting agreement and application for shares before any prospectus had been issued *to the public*, as he must have known, because the agreement mentions the prospectus as a document to be issued in the future " (*ibid*), and on this, amongst other grounds, he failed in his action

(i) *Sherwell v Combined Incandescent Mantles Syndicate, sup* (per WARRINGTON, J, at p 483)

(j) " Share " is defined in s 285 of the Act of 1908 as meaning " share in the share capital of the company," and as including " stock, except where a distinction between stock and shares is expressed or implied "

(k) *Drincqbier v Wood*, [1899] 1 Ch 393, is an instance of a prospectus offering debentures   In s 285 of the Act of 1908, it is enacted that " debenture includes debenture stock," but there is no statutory definition of either of these expressions   It has been held by CHITTY, J —see p 264 of *Levy v Abercorris Slate Co* (1887), 37 C. D 260—that "a debenture means a document which either creates a debt or acknowledges it, and any document which fulfils either of these conditions is a debenture"   " Debenture stock " combines the two opposite characteristics of " share " or " stock " on the one hand (a partnership interest), and of " debenture " on the other (a creditor's interest), but, in most cases, is far more in the nature of " stock " than of a " debenture "   JAMES, L J, delivering the judgment of the Court, at p 349 of *Attree v Hawe* (1878), 9 C D. 337, C A, described

meaning of these respective terms, it is difficult to imagine any type of security or instrument in relation to a company which would not come within either the one class, or the other, but, if there is such a form, no document inviting persons to subscribe for or purchase securities or instruments of that type is a statutory prospectus. Again, it is not easy to conceive any transaction in relation to such securities which would not be either a taking of them, in the sense of subscribing for them, or a purchase of them: but if there be any such dealing, any document inviting the public to so deal in respect of shares or debentures is not a document in which any disclosure is required to be made by the enactment.

519. Another essential feature in the statutory " prospectus " is its issue " by or on behalf of a company, or by or on behalf of a person who is or has been engaged or interested in the formation of a company " A document not so issued is not within the section (l). A " company " is defined by s 285 of the Act of 1908 as meaning a company formed and registered under that Act, or an " existing company "; and " existing company " means a company registered under " the Joint Stock Companies Act " (which expression is to include the Joint Stock Companies Acts, 1856, 1857, the Joint Stock Banking Companies Act, 1857, and the statute 21 & 22 Vict, c 91, but not the statute 8 Vict, c 110), or under the Companies Act, 1862 A company incorporated by act of parliament, or by a charter, is not a company to which the Act of 1908 applies It follows that there is no statutory duty of disclosure whatever in the case of a prospectus offering for subscription or purchase the shares or debentures of a parliamentary or chartered company (m) The company on whose behalf the offer is made of course means the company whose shares or debentures are offered (n) It will be observed that the

<hr/>

debenture stock issued under ss 22, 23, and 24 of the Companies Clauses Act, 1863 (26 & 27 Vict , c 118), as "nothing but preference stock with a special preference " It was one of the many defects of s 38 of the Act of 1867 that creditors' securities were entirely ignored, the enactment being limited to applications for shares, and the Courts finding it impossible to extend the remedy beyond the limits fixed by the express language of the legislature see *Cornell* v *Hay* (1873), L R 8 C P 328, where a bondholder was refused relief (*per* KEATING, J , at p 332, and HONYMAN, J , at p 334).

(l) See *Sleigh* v *Glasgow & Transvaal Options, Ltd* (1904), 6 F 420, where the so-called prospectus was not issued by the company, or on its behalf, and was never adopted or ratified by them, and, on this ground, was held not to be a prospectus within s 10 (1) of the Act of 1900, now s 81 (1) of the Act of 1908.

(m) This is an astonishing omission In his treatise on Companies, Bk I, Ch III, Sect 2 (6th ed), Lord Lindley points out that the very prospectus which was the subject of the decision giving rise to the Directors' Liability Act, 1890 (53 & 54 Vict , c 64), as to misrepresentations in prospectuses (now reproduced in s 84 of the Act of 1908), was a prospectus of a tramway company incorporated by Act of Parliament Whatever excuses may be made for the oversight in 1890, none can possibly be made for the deliberate perpetuation of the error, as regards misrepresentations, in 1908, and, as regards non-disclosure, in 1900, 1907, and 1908, when three opportunities of rectifying it successively presented themselves, and were successively neglected

(n) See *Booth* v. *New Afrikander Gold Mining Co* , [1903] 1 Ch 295, C A This was a case under s 89—as to which see § 571, *post*—where the company was concerned to prove that they had made " an offer to the public " of the shares in question, in order to bring themselves within the permissive and enabling portion, viz sub s. (1), of that section, and outside the prohibitive portion, sub-s (2), whereby the payment of commission under any other conditions was declared illegal With this object they gave evidence of an agreement by which they—being a " new " or reconstructed company—were to allot to the

reference to "purchase" contemplates the case of a promoter issuing a prospectus inviting the public to purchase shares or debentures which he has acquired as vendor or promoter or otherwise, and that by a later subsection of the enactment it is provided that any document which otherwise answers to the definition of a prospectus, and is not "a circular or notice inviting existing members or debenture-holders of a company to subscribe either for shares or for debentures of the company, whether with or without the right to renounce in favour of other persons," shall, "whether issued on or with reference to the formation of a company, or subsequently," be deemed a prospectus to which the section applies (o).

520. If, as often happens, there are several documents offering shares or debentures, or several editions of such a document, issued either successively,—first, as abridged, and then as complete (p), or first, as a "proof," or "advance" copy, or "subject to revision," and then as final, or finally approved (q),—or simultaneously in different forms, or in different places or newspapers (r), each of such documents is, or may be, a "prospectus". but only that one of them on the faith of which the aggrieved party subscribed for or purchased shares or debentures is *the* prospectus which entitles him to relief, so that, if *that* prospectus is not shown to have contravened the section, or to have been issued by the person sought to be made liable, the party fails, however obnoxious to its provisions the other or others of them may have been, and,

liquidator of the old company shares for distribution amongst as many shareholders of the old company, and, if not, as many members of the public, as would take them Held that this, if an offer to the public by any one, was certainly not an offer to the public by the company concerned (*per* VAUGHAN WILLIAMS, L J , at p 312, STIRLING, L J , at pp 314, 315, and COZENS-HARDY, L J , at p 316)

(o) Sub s (7) of s. 81 It is difficult to understand why, instead of being banished to an outlying subsection, this amplification, or qualification, was not inserted at the commencement of sub s (1), together with the expressions which it purports to amplify or qualify

(p) *White* v *Hayman* (1883), C & E 101, a case under s 38 of the Act of 1867, where the plaintiff complained of the omission of a material contract from an "abridged prospectus" advertised in a newspaper, and the defendant vainly urged that constructive "notice" was given to the plaintiff, within the meaning of that section, by the full prospectus afterwards issued, MATHEW, J , holding that, the plaintiff having established that he took his shares on the faith of the first prospectus, and had no actual notice of the second, there was no room for the application of the doctrine of constructive notice

(q) *Hoole* v *Speak*, [1904] 2 Ch 732 (*per* KEKEWICH, J , at p 735) This also was a case under s 38 of the Act of 1867 On the other hand, if it is made quite clear that the document was not intended to be, and was not in fact, a prospectus at all, and that the document really intended as a prospectus was to be issued at a subsequent date, the first document is not in law a prospectus see the case referred to in note (h) to § 517, *ante,* and the citations therein from the judgment of FARWELL, J

(r) In *Drincqbier* v *Wood*, [1899] 1 Ch 393, the plaintiff took his debentures on the faith of two documents, a prospectus (so headed and described), and a letter, under one cover. BYRNE, J , at p 403, expressed the view that each document rendered the defendants liable, the former as a prospectus, and the latter as a "notice," under s 3 of the Directors' Liability Act, 1890, which means that he would have held each of them to be a statutory "prospectus" within the more comprehensive definition contained in s. 285 of the Act of 1908 In *Roussell* v *Burnham*, [1909] 1 Ch 127, there was a prospectus issued in England, which stated the minimum subscription on which the company might proceed to allotment, as required by s 81, (1), (d) of the Act of 1908, and another advertised in a French newspaper, which did not The plaintiff claimed relief under ss 85, 86, in respect of the French prospectus, on the faith of which he established that he had subscribed for his shares, and PARKER, J , held that he was entitled thereto conversely, if *that* prospectus violates the statutory duty, it is no answer to point to another which complies with it (*s*).

521. Where a statutory prospectus is issued or published as a newspaper advertisement, or where it is issued after the lapse of a year from the date at which the company was entitled to commence business, the statutory duty of disclosure is relaxed to the extent specified in sub-ss. (5) and (8), respectively, of the section, and hereafter explained (*t*).

SECT. 3   THE MATTERS REQUIRED TO BE DISCLOSED IN THE PROSPECTUS

522. The meaning of the statutory prospectus having been ascertained, the next subject of inquiry is the nature and extent of the prescribed disclosure. The "monumental" section, in its first and most "monumental" subsection, sets out (in an order which is neither logical, nor chronological, nor based on any discoverable principle) a series of matters, or groups of matters, required to be stated in the prospectus, which, as is provided by another section of the Act of 1908, must not be issued until a copy, dated, and signed by every person named therein as a director or proposed director of the company, has been filed for registration, and must state on the face of it the fact that it has been so filed (*u*)

523. The first subject of the statutory disclosure is "the contents of the memorandum, with the names, descriptions, and addresses of the signatories, and the number of shares subscribed for by them respectively, and the number of founders' or management or deferred shares, if any, and the nature and extent of the interest of the holders in the property and profits of the company" (*v*). "Subscribed for," presumably means "subscribed for in the memorandum" None of these matters need be disclosed in any newspaper advertisement of the prospectus (*w*), nor "in any prospectus issued more than one year after the date at which the company is entitled to commence business" (*x*).

524. The next matters to be disclosed are "the number of shares, if any, fixed by the articles as the qualification of a director, and any provision in the articles as to the remuneration of the directors" (*y*)   These are exempt

(*s*) See *Roussell* v *Burnham*, *sup* (*per* PARKER, J, at pp. 130–132), with which compare the following under s 38 of the Act of 1867 · *White* v *Haymen* (1883), C & E 101, *Hoole* v *Speak*, [1914] 2 Ch 732 (where the defendants were not proved to have authorized the issue of the advance prospectus which contained the same defects as the further and final prospectus which was the subject of *Shepheard* v *Broome*, [1904] A C 342, H L, and which *was* shown to have had the authority of the directors for its issue   Accordingly, in the first case, the claim failed; in the second, it succeeded)

(*t*) See § 523, notes (*w*) and (*x*), § 524, note (*z*), § 525, note (*y*), and § 530, note (*p*), *post*

(*u*) S 80 of the Act of 1908   It will be noticed that this section applies to "every prospectus issued by or on behalf of a company or in relation to any intended company"; whereas s 81 is made to apply to "every prospectus issued by or on behalf of a company, or by or on behalf of any person who is or has been engaged or interested in the formation of a company"   Was this difference in language designed, and, if so, what was the design ?   Or was it merely inadvertent ?   It is impossible to say.

(*v*) S. 81, (1), (a).   "Memorandum" is the statutory shorthand for "memorandum of association": s 285

(*w*) S 81, (5).

(*x*) S 81, (8)   As to when the company is "entitled to commence business,' see s 87

(*y*) S 81, (1), (b)   "Articles" = "articles of association"   see s 285, where also

from disclosure in the case of a prospectus issued more than one year after the company is entitled to commence business (z).

525. Disclosure is next to be made of "the names, descriptions, and addresses of the directors, or proposed directors" (a), except in any prospectus issued more than one year after the date of the company's right to commence business (b)

526. Then follows a group of matters which, having regard to the other provisions of the Act of 1908, is (and has, indeed, been found in the course of actual litigation to be) of considerable importance   The prospectus is required to state "the minimum subscription on which the directors may proceed to allotment, and the amount payable on application and allotment on each share , and in the case of a second or subsequent offer of shares the amount offered for subscription on each previous allotment made within the two preceding years, and the amount actually allotted, and the amount, if any, paid on the shares so allotted" (c)   Any person responsible for the issue of the prospectus has a double interest in divulging the minimum subscription, since not only is he liable under the enactment for any omission to do so, but also, by a later section (d), allotment is prohibited unless the amount of such minimum subscription fixed by the memorandum or articles, *and named in the prospectus*, has been subscribed, and the sum payable on application for the amount so fixed *and named*, which is to be "not less than five per cent of the nominal amount of the shares," has been paid to and received by the company; and, if no amount is so fixed *and named*, then there can be no allotment unless the sum payable for the whole amount offered for subscription has been so paid and received   the consequence being that, if the amount of the minimum subscription fixed by the memorandum or articles is not also named in the prospectus, the company is prohibited from going to allotment except on receipt of the whole nominal value of the shares offered, and contravention of this provision entails very serious and special consequences (e) independently of, and in addition to, the liability in damages for the non-disclosure itself   Since *id certum est quod certum reddi potest*, the disclosure is sufficiently made if the prospectus states the proportion of the entire shares offered on subscription for which it is proposed to go to allotment (f).

"director" is defined as including "any person occupying the position of a director by whatever name called "

    (z) S. 81, (8) , and see s 87
    (a) S 81, (1), (c)
    (b) S 81, (8); and see s 87
    (c) S. 81, (1), (d)   There was held to have been a non compliance with this provision in *Re Wimbledon (Olympia), Ltd.*, [1910] 1 Ch 630, and *Re South of England Natural Gas & Petroleum Co*, [1911] 1 Ch 573 , but in each case the plaintiff pursued the wrong remedy · see § 568, and note (v) thereto, *post*.
    (d) S 85, on which see § 570, *post*.
    (e) Ss 85, 86 prescribe two forms of relief, one of which alone is available before any allotment has taken place, and the other only after an allotment : as to these, see § 570, *post*
    (f) As in *Re West Yorkshire Darracq Agency, Ltd* (1909), 25 T L R 77, where "ten per cent of the shares issued " was held to be a sufficient statement of "the minimum subscription "

527. The next class of facts to be disclosed consists of " the number and amount of shares and debentures which within the two preceding years have been issued, or agreed to be issued, as fully or partly paid up otherwise than in cash, and in the latter case the extent to which they are so paid up, and in either case the consideration for which those shares or debentures have been issued or are proposed or intended to be issued " (g)

528. Following the above are two groups of matters which, though separated in the section, can only be treated as one group, relating to the property which the company is formed to acquire. It is first provided that there must be disclosure of " the names and addresses of the vendors of any property purchased or acquired by the company, or proposed so to be purchased or acquired, which is to be paid for wholly or partly out of the proceeds of the issue offered for subscription by the prospectus, or the purchase or acquisition of which has not been completed at the date of the issue of the prospectus, and the amount payable in cash, shares, or debentures, to the vendor, and where there is more than one separate vendor, or the company is a sub-purchaser, the amount so payable to each vendor · provided that, where the vendors or any of them are a firm, the members of the firm shall not be treated as separate vendors " (h) Succeeding this, is a further requirement contained in a separate paragraph, though it is obviously a part of the first, and to some extent a mere repetition of it, that there shall be stated in the prospectus " the amount (if any) paid or payable as purchase money in cash, shares, or debentures, for any such property as aforesaid, specifying the amount (if any) payable for goodwill " (i) In other parts of the enactment the above expressions are elucidated and expanded by providing that " every person shall be deemed to be a vendor who has entered into any contract, absolute or conditional, for the sale or purchase, or for any option of purchase, of any property to be acquired by the company, in any case where the purchase money is not fully paid at the date of issue of the prospectus, or the purchase money is to be paid or satisfied wholly or in part out of the proceeds of the issue offered for subscription by the prospectus, or the contract depends for its validity or fulfilment on the result of that issue " (j); and that " where any of the property to be acquired by the company is to be taken on lease, this section shall apply as if the expression ' vendor ' included the lessor, and the expression ' purchase money ' included the consideration for the lease, and the expression ' sub-purchaser '

(g) S 81, (1), (e).
(h) S. 81, (1), (f)
(i) S 81, (1), (g). From the reference to " such property as aforesaid," it is obvious that this paragraph or item belongs to that which immediately precedes Moreover, so much of (g) as prescribes the disclosure of " the amount (if any)   payable as purchase money in cash, shares, or debentures, for any such property as aforesaid," is a mere repetition of, and adds nothing to, so much of (f) as requires disclosure of " the amount payable in cash, shares, or debentures to the vendor " The only new elements imported by (g) are the amount of any payment in fact made to the vendor, and the specification of the price paid for goodwill , and there is no apparent reason why both these should not have formed part of (f)
(j) S 81, (2), a reproduction of s. 10, (2), of the Act of 1900.

included a sub-lessee " (k). It has been held that "sub-purchaser" means "sub-purchaser" in the technical conveyancing sense, and not in its popular sense, so that where the company's vendor has paid the original vendor outright before selling to the company, the company is not a "sub-purchaser" within the enactment, and there is no obligation to state in the prospectus the amount so paid by the company's vendor to the ultimate vendor (l).

529. The next matter to be divulged in the prospectus is "the amount (if any) paid within the two preceding years, or payable, as commission for subscribing or agreeing to subscribe, or procuring or agreeing to procure subscriptions, for any shares in, or debentures of, the company, or the rate of any such commission provided that it shall not be necessary to state the commission payable to sub-underwriters " (m) An additional, though an indirect, means of enforcing disclosure of the amount of commission is provided by another section of the Act, which will be considered later (n).

530. There must be disclosure of "the amount or estimated amount of preliminary expenses " (o), except where the prospectus is "issued more than one year after the date at which the company is entitled to commence business " (p).

(k) S 81, (3), reproducing s 10, (3), of the Act of 1900 It is difficult to see why either this subsection, or s 81, (2), any more than s 81, (1), (g), was not incorporated with s 81 (1), (f)

(l) *Brookes* v *Hansen*, [1906] 2 Ch 129, where an action for damages against a director who had authorized the issue of the prospectus for non disclosure therein of the matters specified in ss 10, (1), (f), 10, (2), and 10, (3) of the Act of 1900, now represented by ss 81, (1), (f), 81, (2), and 81, (3), of the Act of 1908, was dismissed, on the failure of the plaintiff to prove anything beyond the circumstances stated in the text (*per* JOYCE, J , at pp 135-137, who observes, at p 136, that "there is no suggestion of any obligation to disclose the amount of the purchase money, however small, paid by the vendor upon his acquisition of the property, however recent,"—in that case the vendor had paid £15,000 for the property the day before he sold it to the company for £58,500,—but, he proceeds, "if what the company buys be merely the benefit of a contract for the purchase of a property, the consideration for which remains wholly or in part undischarged, and so, *pro tanto*, a burden on the company, the company which acquires the benefit of the contract would properly be termed a sub purchaser, and the amount payable by the company to the original vendor, as well as to their immediate vendor, would, under this subsection (f), have to be stated in the prospectus, and possibly also the name and address of that original vendor, as well as of the immediate vendor to the company "), *Re Christineville Rubber Estates, Ltd* (1911), 81 L J (CH) 63, where the plaintiff relied upon, amongst other causes of action, a non compliance with s 81, (1), (f), of the Act of 1908, and where it appeared that, though the company's immediate vendor had sold to the company for £51,250 a property which he had bought for £1000 only, he had paid the whole of the £1000 to the original vendor one day before the sale to the company, and it was accordingly held, or rather it was admitted, that in this state of the evidence the case could not be brought within the subsection (*per* EVE, J , at p 66) It is extraordinary, and only to be accounted for as suggested in note (u) to § 532, *post*, that it never occurred to the plaintiff in either of these cases to rest his claim on the omission of "a material contract " within s 81, (1), (k) Anything more "material" within *this* paragraph, whether it was specifically required to be disclosed by paragraph (f) or not, than the fact that the company had bought for £51,250 property which had the day before changed hands at £1000, can hardly be conceived It certainly would be held material as between the vendor promoter and the company see Ch IV, Sect 2, Sub-s (2), *ante*

(m) S 81, (1), (h)

(n) S 89, as to which see § 571, *post*

(o) S 81, (1), (i)

(p) S 81, (8) For "the date at which the company is entitled to commence business," see s 87 of the Act of 1908

531. The prospectus must also state " the amount paid within the two preceding years or intended to be paid to any promoter, and the consideration for such payment " (q).

532. Next follows, in a most unpretentious position, the highly important provision which was presumably intended to replace in an improved form the discarded s. 38 of the Act of 1867 This requires the prospectus to state " the dates of and parties to every material contract, and a reasonable time and place at which any material contract or a copy thereof may be inspected : provided that this requirement shall not apply to a contract entered into in the ordinary course of the business carried on or intended to be carried on by the company, or to any contract entered into more than two years before the date of issue of the prospectus " (r). It has already been shown how the wise generality of this requirement is weakened, rather than strengthened, by the number of specific requirements which accompany it (s). Disembarrassed of satellites which serve only to encumber freedom of movement, the provision would stand out as a good example of terse, lucid, adaptable, and useful legislation: but, surrounded as it is by these particular prescriptions as to particular contracts, some preceding, and others following it (t), the sphere of its operation and the extent of its applicability, is, or will naturally be thought to have been, deliberately curtailed (u) Moreover, the position which the requirement in question occupies in the statutory list or catalogue is most unfortunate It neither heads the list, nor closes it In the former case, adopting a form commonly used in statutory drafting, the enactment would have opened—" all material contracts shall be disclosed in the prospectus, and, in particular, the following   " In the latter, there would have been an enumeration of specific contracts ending with a final clause requiring the disclosure of all other material contracts of whatsoever kind Neither of these methods of legislative expression would be perfect, because each would invite the application of the *ejusdem generis* doctrine, and so tend to limit the generality, and with it the effectiveness, of the provision It may be said that a great many of the items in the list are facts, and not contracts. This is true, but the answer is that the criticism here offered applies, *mutatis mutandis*, to the facts as well as to the contracts. In this case,

(q) S. 81, (1), (j) As to what ' promoter " means and includes, see §§ 327, 328, *ante*
(r) S 81, (1), (k)
(s) In § 514, *ante.*
(t) For both (m), and (n), of s 81, (1), at least involve the existence of contracts
(u) And this view will derive great encouragement from the marginal heading of the section, which is—" *specific* requirements as to *particulars* of the prospectus " It must have been from some idea that, by the specification of particular contracts in (f) and (g) of s. 81, (1), the legislature intended to restrict the area and purview of the " material contracts " referred to in (k), that the plaintiffs, in *Brookes* v *Hansen*, [1906] 2 Ch 129, and *Re Christineville Rubber Estates, Ltd* (1911), 81 L J (Ch) 63, respectively, refrained from suggesting that the undisclosed contract was, if not within the special terms of (f), and (g), at any rate within the general language of (k), and with an exaggerated, but perfectly natural, deference to the *expressio unius* principle, contentedly assumed that failure to prove the former necessarily involved failure to prove the latter Definite provisions, it must have been thought, control and limit what is indefinite, whereas an indefinite generality cannot have the effect of expanding what is specifically stated, or indeed, any operation of any kind on any matters except such as are not the subject of the specific provisions preceding or following it

too, the desirable course would have been to prescribe the disclosure of all material facts, with or without, but preferably without, an enumeration of facts which " in particular " are to be stated. It seems reasonable to suppose that two short clauses, that now under consideration as to material contracts, and another in exactly the same form as to material facts, would have been sufficient to accomplish the intention of the legislature : or, best of all, one clause requiring the disclosure in the prospectus of all contracts and facts, or all facts—for a contract is a fact,—material to be made known to any person invited thereby to subscribe for or purchase shares or debentures of the company. Abandoning criticism, however, and dealing with the paragraph in question as it stands, without reference to the possible effect upon its construction of other paragraphs as to particular kinds of contract, it is necessary to consider the meaning, in this connexion, of the expression " material." What materiality connotes in general has already been the subject of a detailed examination (v), in the course of which it has been pointed out that in each case regard must be had to the class of persons to whom the duty of disclosure is owed in determining whether any particular fact is, or is not, material (w). Now the class of persons to whom the statutory duty is owed under the enactment consists of those who subscribe for, or purchase, shares or debentures on the faith of the prospectus in which they are offered   This (so far as regards subscribing for shares) was also the class entitled to be relieved against violation of the provisions of s 38 of the Act of 1867 , and, inasmuch as the " contracts " referred to in that section were judicially construed as limited to contracts " material to be made known to persons invited to take shares in order to enable them to form a judgment as to the policy of so doing " (x), which means neither more nor less than the " material contracts " of the present enactment, it follows that the authorities on the earlier section are also authorities on that which has replaced it, and that the kinds of contract which were in those authorities deemed material to be made known to persons invited to take shares would equally be deemed material to be made known to persons invited to take shares or debentures under the existing statutory conditions (y). From an examination of these decisions under the old section it

(v) See Ch II, Sect 2 Sub-s (2), *ante*

(w) See § 30, and the references in note (*ll*) thereto, *ante*

(x) This is from the definition given by THESIGER, L.J , at pp 460, 461 of *Sullivan* v *Mitcalfe* (1880), 5 C P. D 455, C. A , which was adopted and applied by SULLIVAN, M R (Ir), at pp 401–403 of *Jury* v *Stoker* (1881), 9 L R (Ir)̀ 385   Cp the similar language used by Lord COLERIDGE, C J , in the Common Pleas Division, and by COCKBURN, C J , in the Court of Appeal, at pp 485, 527, respectively, of *Twycross* v. *Grant* (1877), 2 C P D. 469, C A.

(y) It may be observed here that in *Shepheard* v *Broome*, [1904] A. C. 342, H L , it was held (*per* Lord LINDLEY, at p 346) that, in any case in which the right to relief accrued before the passing of the Act of 1900, the old section is alone applicable, however long after that date the trial of the action may be   The last reported cases of this description are *Macleay* v *Tait*, [1906] A C 24, H L , where the action was brought in 1902, and the cause of action arose in 1899, and *Shepheard* v *Bray*, [1906] 2 Ch 235, where the action was commenced in 1904, and the cause of action arose in 1898   It is almost impossible that there should be another

appears that, generally speaking, any contract or transaction which, at common law, a director or promoter would be required to disclose to the company to whom he stands in a fiduciary relation, though not to anyone else (z), was regarded as material to be disclosed by those who issue a prospectus to those who take shares on the faith of it in virtue of the new fiduciary duty created by the legislature. Accordingly, all, or nearly all, the cases in question range themselves under two main classes : first, the class in which the omission of contracts whereby promoters secured to themselves secret profits or advantages was held the subject of statutory relief (a), and, secondly, the class in which the non-disclosure of contracts whereby the promoter seduced the directorate or executive of the company in the form of qualification shares, cash, or other bribes, was held amenable to the section (b)

533. The next matter requiring disclosure is " the names and addresses of the auditors (if any) of the company " (c).

534. Then follows a very important group. The prospectus must give " full particulars of the nature and extent of the interest (if any) of every director in the promotion of, or in the property proposed to be acquired by, the company, or, where the interest of such a director consists in being a partner

---

(z) See Ch IV, Sect 2, Sub ss. (2) and (3), *ante*, as to the fiduciary relation between these parties, and, as to the non-existence of any such relation between the promoters and agents of a company, on the one hand, and shareholders or the public, on the other, see § 393, note (s), *ante*

(a) As in *Re Bagnall & Co*, *Exp Dick* (1875), 32 L T 536, *Re Coal Economizing Gas Co*, *Gover's Case* (1875), 1 C D 182, *Twycross* v *Grant* (1877), 2 C P D 469, C A, *Greenwood* v *Leather Shod Wheel Co*, [1900] 1 Ch 421, C A, *McConnell* v *Wright*, [1903] 1 Ch. 546, C. A ; *Watts* v *Bucknall*, [1903] 1 Ch 766, C A, *Shepheard* v *Broome*, [1904] A C 342, H L, *Stevens* v *Hoare* (1904), 20 T L R 407, *J & P Coats, Ltd* v *Crossland* (1904), 20 T L R 800, *Nash* v *Calthorpe*, [1905] 2 Ch 237, C A, *Macleay* v *Tait, sup*, *Shepheard* v *Bray*, [1906] 2 Ch 235 The plaintiff did not succeed in every one of the above cases, but in all of them the contract, being of the type stated in the text, was held or admitted to be material Many of them, it will be noticed, would now be within (f) and (g), as well as (k), of the present enactment

(b) Examples of this type of case are —*Cornell* v *Hay* (1873), L. R 8 C P 328, *Arkwright* v *Newbold* (1881), 17 C D 301, C A ; *Jury* v *Stoker* (1881), 9 L R (Ir) 385 ; *Capel & Co* v *Sim's Ships' Composition Co* (1888), 58 L T 807, *Cackett* v *Keswick*, [1902] 2 Ch 456, C. A In *Arkwright* v *Newbold, sup*, the alleged contract was held not to have been a contract at all, but only an "understanding" ; its materiality, however, was recognized In *Baty* v *Keswick* (1901), 85 L T 18, which was decided by FARWELL, J, on the same day as *Cackett* v *Keswick, sup* (affirmed by the C A, as above), and related to the same prospectus and the same omitted contract, the plaintiff failed because he did not satisfy the Court, as Cackett did, that he took his shares on the faith of the non existence of the undisclosed contract, but in both cases it was held that the contract was material, though not so obviously or certainly material to Baty, who took the shares for purposes of an underwriting speculation, as to Cackett who took his as an ordinary investor (*per* FARWELL, J, at p. 20) The above cases would now fall within s. 81, (1), (m), as well as within (k) There has as yet, probably for the reasons stated in note (u), *ante*, been no decision on the question of what is a "material contract" within paragraph (k) of s 81 (1) The only reported case in which that paragraph has even been relied upon is *Re Wimbledon (Olympia), Ltd*, [1910] 1 Ch. 630, where (amongst other things) it was suggested that the company had omitted a " material contract " from the prospectus, in that they had failed to state therein a mortgage of part of its property · but the action was dismissed on grounds not involving any necessity to consider the materiality of the contract, which, for the purposes of the judgment, was assumed The reluctance thus exhibited to base proceedings upon non compliance with this requirement seems to indicate how completely its vitality and utility has been squeezed out of it by the pressure of the particular and specific requirements in which it is imbedded

(c) S 81, (1), (l)

in a firm, the nature and extent of the interest of the firm, with a statement of all sums paid or agreed to be paid to him or to the firm in cash or shares or otherwise by any person either to induce him to become, or to qualify him as, a director, or otherwise for services rendered by him or by the firm in connexion with the promotion or formation of the company " (d). The term " director " is defined as including " any person occupying the position of a director by whatever name called " (e). The meaning of the terms " promotion " and " promoter " has already been considered (f).

535. The last item in the catalogue of particulars is, " where the company is a company having shares of more than one class, the right of voting at meetings of the company conferred by the several classes of shares respectively " (g).

536. It has already been explained that where there is a duty of disclosure at common law, that duty is not discharged except by a disclosure which is complete, precise, and plain ; and that any inadequate, partial, or un-particularized revelation, or any resort to " doubtful equivalents " for an express and perspicuous statement, is wholly inefficacious, or worse (h). The statutory " statement " in the prospectus (especially when regard is had to the terms of the marginal note to the section, " particulars of prospectus," and to the " full particulars " mentioned in another place), must certainly be not less candid, complete, exact, and unambiguous than the disclosure which is required at common law (i).

SECT. 4. THE PERSONS BY AND AGAINST WHOM THE STATUTORY RELIEF MAY BE CLAIMED

537. In s. 38 of the Act of 1867, and also in certain sections of the Act of 1908 (j), there is an express designation of the persons to and by whom the statutory duty of disclosure is owed   For some reason which it is impossible to divine, or for no reason at all, s 81 of the Act of 1908 omits to specify

---

(d) S 81, (1), (m)   This is the class of fact the withholding of which by promoters and directors from the company, in breach of their fiduciary duty, plays such a prominent part in the decisions on that subject   see §§ 333, 340, ante. Non compliance with this particular requirement, or rather with s. 10, (1), (m) of the Act of 1900, of which s 81, (1), (m) of the Act of 1908 is a repetition, was alleged by the plaintiff, and admitted by the defendants, in *Sleigh* v *Glasgow and Transvaal Options, Ltd* (1904), 6 F. 420, assuming the document relied upon as a statutory prospectus to answer to that description, which, however, was held not to have been made out

(e) S 285 of the Act of 1908

(f) See §§ 327, 328, *ante*

(g) S 81, (1), (n)

(h) See Ch II, Sect 1, *ante*

(i) See *Roussell* v *Burnham*, [1909] 1 Ch 127 (*per* PARKER, J , at p 133), a case in which there was no express statement of the amount of the minimum subscription, within s 81, (1), (d), in the prospectus on which the plaintiff took his shares, though there was such a statement in another prospectus which he never saw, and it was vainly argued that, by a process of reasoning and inference and " putting two and two together," the plaintiff ought to have gathered what the minimum amount probably was

(j) For instance, in s 84 (as to misstatements in the prospectus, where the designation is extremely precise and detailed), and ss 85, 86 (as to the minimum amount of subscription)

either class in terms. The intention, however, of the legislature, in this respect is a matter of clear and certain implication from various expressions used in the enactment itself, and in the interpretation clause of the statute (*k*).

Sub-s. (1) *By Whom the Statutory Relief may be Claimed.*

538. Where there is any right to civil relief in respect of the violation of a statutory obligation, that right can be asserted by any person who can prove that he has sustained loss or damage in consequence of such violation, and by no other person. Now the prospectus in which the disclosure must be made is defined by s. 285 of the Act of 1908 as "a prospectus, notice, circular, advertisement, or other invitation, offering to the public for subscription or purchase any shares or debentures of a company." It is obvious, therefore, that any member of the public who can, and no member of it who cannot, establish that he subscribed for or purchased shares or debentures of a company on the faith of a prospectus of that company in which the prescribed particulars were not stated, belongs to the class of persons entitled to protection. Such member may be either a natural or a juridical person (*l*). Where such person dies after his cause of action has accrued, his representatives may institute, or continue, the proceedings, as the case may be (*m*). So also, in the case of insolvency, the trustee of the insolvent individual, or the liquidator of the insolvent company, may, and, if the claim is to be pursued at all, must (for the cause of action passes to him by operation of law) claim relief in respect of the statutory, as he would in the case of any non-statutory, wrong done to the estate or property, as distinct from the person, of the insolvent (*n*). And, generally, whatever right any person, as representing a party aggrieved who is under disability of any kind or his estate, would have to sue for damages in respect of a tort at common law, he would equally have to sue for damages in respect of the statutory tort (*o*).

(*k*) See the introductory words of s. 81 (1), s. 81 (6), and s. 285 (definition of "prospectus")

(*l*) Thus, a limited company was the successful plaintiff in an action under 8 of the Act of 1867 (amongst other causes of action) in *J & R Coats, Ltd v Crosslan*)), 20 T L R 800

(*m*) See *Twycross* v *Grant* (1878), 4 C P D 40, C A, a case under s. 38 of the Act of 1867. In *Hoole* v *Speak*, [1904] 2 Ch 732, which was also a case under that section, the successful plaintiff was the executor of the person who took the shares on the faith of the prospectus and it was not suggested by anybody that on that account he was disentitled to relief. Nor was any objection on this score taken to the claim made by the executors of a person who had taken shares on the faith of the prospectus in *Re South of England Natural Gas & Petroleum Co*, [1911] 1 Ch 573, which was a case under s. 81 of the Act of 1908

(*n*) See, as to damages to the estate of a bankrupt, as distinguished from personal damage, *Hodgson* v *Sidney* (1866), L R 1 Exch 313, a case of misrepresentation, where it was held that the right to sue passed to the assignees, and a plea to the bankrupt's claim on this ground was held good. And see, generally, the treatises on bankruptcy. As to liquidation of a company, see Lord Halsbury's *Laws of England*, title *Companies*, vol v, pp 446–448

(*o*) For it can make no difference to the applicability of the principle in question whether the act in respect of which the claim to recover damages arises is prohibited by common law, or by statutory rules. As to the position of a married woman in relation

A bare right, however, to sue for damages is not the subject of assignment otherwise than by operation of law (p)

539. A number of persons may either sue separately, or join in suing, for damages for the breach of the statutory duty (q), as they can for the breach of any other duty. How far, and under what circumstances such proceedings may be the subject of a " representative order," or of an order to stay them pending the trial of a " test action," are questions to be examined at a later stage (r)

Sub-s (2). *Against whom the Statutory Relief may be Claimed*

540. The opening words of the enactment, which govern all the rest, are that " every prospectus issued by or on behalf of a company, or by or on behalf of any person who is or has been engaged or interested in the formation of the company, must state . . " &c. Now, as an obligation cannot be imposed upon a thing, the plain implication from this language (though it would have been far better to have said so expressly, instead of leaving it to inference, however clear) is that the prescribed duty of disclosure was intended by the legislature to be imposed upon any company by or on behalf of which, or any person engaged or interested in its formation by or on behalf of whom, a prospectus is issued   No person who was not " responsible for the prospectus " (s), which means of course, responsible for its issue, is liable to proceedings under the section, however engaged or interested he may have been, at or before the date of the issue, in the formation of the company   On the other hand, no person who was not acting on behalf of the company, or who was not engaged or interested in its formation, when issuing the prospectus, or had not previously been so, can be made liable, however clearly it may be proved that in point of fact he issued, or authorized the issue of, the prospectus

541. The words " issued by or on behalf of a company " are intended to strike at directors (t), and other agents of the company having its authority to issue the prospectus. They are also sufficient to render the company

to torts, see Lord Halsbury's *Laws of England*, title *Husband and Wife*, vol xvi, pp 445–462   As to the persons entitled to represent an infant, or a lunatic or person of unsound mind not so found by inquisition, in an action of tort, see R S C, O 16, rr 16, 17, 21, and the various treatises on Infancy, and Lunacy, respectively

(p) Because such an assignment would savour of champerty or maintenance   This question is discussed in § 279, *ante*.

(q) In *Arnison v. Smith* (1888), 41 C D. 348, C A , there were 52 plaintiffs in an action to recover damages for common law misrepresentation in a prospectus   In *Drincqbier v Wood*, [1899] 1 Ch. 393, several debenture holders joined in an action for damages for statutory misrepresentation under the Directors' Liability Act, 1890 (now s 84 of the Act of 1908), and it was held that they were entitled to do so, and were not bound to resort to separate actions (*per* Byrne, J , at pp 396, 397).

(r) See § 613, 615, *post*.

(s) This expression is to be found in sub s (6) of the enactment, where it is provided that " a director or other *person responsible for the prospectus* shall not incur " the liability " to which (it is implied) he would otherwise be subject, " if he proves ' the facts there specified

(t) A director " includes any person occupying the position of a director by whatever name called " : see s 285 of the Act of 1908

itself liable in damages, *quoad* subscriptions for debentures, and would be sufficient for that purpose as regards subscriptions for shares also, but for the fact that, as will be seen later (*u*), no remedy in the nature of avoidance is given by the enactment, expressly or impliedly, and there is a long and firmly established principle of law which, in the absence of such avoidance, debars a shareholder from recovery of damages in respect of his shares against the company of which he still remains a member (*v*).

542. The expression, "issued by or on behalf of any person who is . . . engaged or interested in the formation of the company," points to the class of promoters (*w*), and their agents, but is evidently not intended to be limited to them, because the word "promoter," which is used in other places in the Act (particularly in s 84, as to misrepresentations in prospectuses), is here carefully avoided, and the much wider terms "engaged," and "interested," are preferred, the latter, indeed, being of a comprehensiveness which would be almost dangerous, were it not for the fact that, in this as in the other cases, the "issue" must also be brought home to the "interested" person.

543. It will be observed that the enactment impliedly renders liable for any breach of its provisions, not only the class of those who, at the date of the issue of the prospectus by them, were engaged or interested in the formation of the company, but also the class of those who, when they issued the prospectus, had ceased to be, though they were originally, so engaged or interested This provision, bearing in mind the definition of "prospectus" in s 285, and the language used at the end of sub-s. (7) of s. 81 ("whether issued on, or with reference to the formation of, a company, or subsequently"), is doubtless designed to meet, amongst others, the possible case of a *quondam* promoter, after the incorporation of the company, issuing a prospectus "offering to the public for purchase" any of the shares or debentures of the company which he may have acquired as promoter, vendor, or otherwise.

544. Whoever be the person sought to be made liable, whether a director, promoter, or agent of the company, or other person engaged or interested in its formation, he must be shown either to have actually and personally issued the prospectus, or to have given authority in that behalf to the person

(*u*) See § 568, *post*.
(*v*) This principle, and the grounds for it, are very clearly and convincingly explained in *Houldsworth* v *City of Glasgow Bank* (1880), 5 App. Cas. 317, H. L, by Lord CAIRNS, L C, at pp 323–326, Lord SELBORNE, at pp 329, 330 ("here it is impossible to separate the nature of the pursuer's claim from his status as a shareholder, unless the status can be put an end to by rescinding the contract which brought him into it," and damages, in such a case, are "neither more nor less than the whole aliquot share due from him in contribution of the whole debts and liabilities of the company   But it is of the essence of the contract between the shareholders, as long as it remains unrescinded, that they should all contribute equally to the payment of all the company's debts and liabilities He is either suing all shareholders except himself, who are as innocent as himself, or if they are fraudulent, he is as fraudulent as they "), Lord HATHERLEY, at pp 332–335, and Lord BLACKBURN, at pp 338–341.   In the above passage from Lord SELBORNE's judgment, "guilty of statutory non-disclosure," in order to apply the principle to the present class of case, should be substituted for "fraudulent," which was the word there appropriate, the action being one of deceit   See also *Re Hull and County Bank, Burgess's Case* (1880), 15 C. D. 507 (at pp 511–514)   The rule has no application to the relation between a debenture holder and the company.
(*w*) As to what is involved in promotership, see §§ 327, 328, *ante*

who did so issue it, each of these being a question of fact (x). A promoter, or person " engaged or interested," may be an artificial person, as has been already observed (y), there being nothing to the contrary either in the enactment, or in the statute of which it forms part

545. The sole civil remedy for the statutory non-disclosure being, as will be explained hereafter, an action for damages (z), it follows that, where there are several defendants, the ordinary rules as to the joint and several liability of tortfeasors acting in concert, and as to the inadmissibility of contribution or indemnity between them, are applicable to such a case (a).

546. Where the person alleged to have been guilty of the statutory non-disclosure dies before judgment, the action cannot, any more than any other action for damages (b), be brought, or continued (as the case may be), unless the estate of the deceased was enriched at the expense of the plaintiff by the statutory tort (c)

547. In the case of the insolvency of a tortfeasor, the general rule is that the damages otherwise recoverable are not the subject of a proof in the

(x) In *Hoole* v *Speak*, [1904] 2 Ch 732, the plaintiff failed to sustain this onus, as to the " advance prospectus " on the faith of which alone he took his shares, and his action, therefore, was dismissed (*per* KEKEWICH, J , at p 735), whilst, on the other hand, a person who, having subscribed on the faith of the later or final prospectus of the same company, and who did establish that this final prospectus was issued with the authority of the directors, succeeded in *Shepheard* v *Broome*, [1904] A C 342, H L. In *Roussell* v *Burnham*, [1909] 1 Ch. 127, the plaintiff similarly proved that the person issuing the prospectus had the authority of the company for that purpose (*per* PARKER, J., at p 132, who there describes the question as one of fact).

(y) See the cases cited in note (i) to § 399, *ante*

(z) See Sect 7, *post*.

(a) For it can make no difference whether the wrongdoers are so by virtue of a breach of a common law, or of a statutory, duty. The rule that each of two or more wrongdoers acting together is liable *in solido*, and also severally, is an elementary one. For its application to statutory non-disclosure under s 38 of the Act of 1867, see many of the cases cited in notes (a) and (b) to § 532, *ante* It is still the law that a tortfeasor can recover neither indemnity nor contribution from his principal or associate in the wrong, except where one person employs another to do, or joins with another in doing, "acts not unlawful in themselves " (*per* Lord KENYON, C J , in *Merryweather* v *Nixan* (1799), 8 Term Rep 186). The doctrine, with the above qualification, has been followed, and noted upon, in *Adamson* v *Jervis* (1827), 4 Bing 66 , *Horwell* v *London General Omnibus Co.* (1877), 2 Ex D 365, C A , *The Englishman, and the Australia,* [1895] P 212 It has, however, been severely criticized in *Palmer* v *Wick*, [1894] A C. 318, H L , where the House of Lords declined to extend it, and where, also, it was stated not to be a part of Scots law   There is nothing, it will be observed, in s 81 corresponding to the exemption from the stringency of this rule which, in the case of persons jointly liable for untrue statements in a prospectus, is enacted by s 84, sub ss (3) and (4) of the Act of 1908.

(b) See *Peek* v *Gurney* (1873), L R 6 H L 377 (*per* Lord CHELMSFORD, at pp 392–395) , *Kirk* v *Todd* (1882), 21 C D 484 (*per* JESSEL, M R , at p 488) , *Phillips* v *Homfray* (1883), 24 C D 439, C A (*per* BOWEN, L J , at p 454) , *Re Duncan,* [1899] 1 Ch 387 (*per* ROMER, J , at p 392) ; *Davoren* v *Woolton,* [1900] 1 Ir R 273

(c) In *Shepheard* v *Bray,* [1906] 2 Ch 235, WARRINGTON, J , at p 253, decided that a claim under s 38 of the Act of 1867 is an *actio personalis* within the meaning of the rule · on appeal, [1907] 2 Ch 571, C A , the question was again discussed at considerable length, but ultimately the appeal and action were settled   In *Twycross* v *Grant* (1878), 4 C P D 40, C A , the rule was recognized, though it was not the subject of the decision itself   In *Frankenburg* v. *Great Horseless Carriage Co* , [1900] 1 Q B 504, C. A , an action for (*inter alia*) damages in respect of untrue statements in the prospectus under the Directors' Liability Act, 1890 (now s 84 of the Act of 1908), the point was debated (*per* LINDLEY, M R , at p 510, and ROMER, L J , at pp 511, 512), but it was not necessary to decide it.

bankruptcy, or a claim in the liquidation, unless the insolvent has gained what the claimant has lost, or the liability can be said to constitute an equitable debt, or to have arisen, however indirectly, out of some contractual obligation (d) There seems to be no reason why this general rule should not apply to the insolvency of a statutory tortfeasor under the Act of 1908, and it has been held that it does so apply (e)

SECT. 5. BURDEN OF PROOF ON THE PLAINTIFF IN AN ACTION FOR BREACH OF THE STATUTORY DUTY.

548. In considering the duty of disclosure which exists at common law between parties negotiating for a contract *uberrimæ fidei*, it was pointed out that the burden is always upon the party complaining (unless relieved of it, wholly or in part, by the express or implied admission of the party charged) to establish five matters, the first three of which are :—the existence of the duty as between himself and the party charged in reference to the particular fact the withholding of which is complained of (and this involves the onus of showing that the particular fact was material to be disclosed, having regard to the nature of the transaction); the existence of the alleged undisclosed fact; and (though this is generally not denied, and, even if it be, the slightest possible evidence is sufficient to shift the onus) the failure or omission to communicate it (f) The same three *probanda* exist, *mutatis mutandis*, in the case of the statutory obligation That is to say, the plaintiff (g) in any action to recover damages for non-compliance with any of the requirements of s 81 of the Act of 1908, must establish :—first, the existence of the statutory duty, as between himself and the defendant ; secondly, the existence or occurrence of the matter alleged to have been omitted from the prospectus , and, lastly, the fact that such matter is not stated at all, or is not stated with the requisite clearness and particularity, in the prospectus for the issue of which the defendant is responsible, and on the faith of which the plaintiff subscribed for or purchased his shares or debentures. There is no obligation, however, on the plaintiff to establish either that the defendant was cognizant of the undisclosed matter (with one

(d) See *Read* v *Bailey* (1877), 3 App Cas 94, H L (per Lord CAIRNS, at pp 99, 100, and Lord BLACKBURN, at pp 102-104) , *Ex p Adamson, Re Collie* (1878), 8 C D 807, C A (per JAMES, L J , at pp 818-821), *Jack* v *Kipping* (1882), 9 Q B. D 113 , *Re Giles, Ex p. Stone* (1889), 61 L. T. 82 , *Tilley* v *Bowman, Ltd* , [1910] 1 K B. 745 And cp , generally, Lord Halsbury's *Laws of England*, title *Bankruptcy*, vol ii, p 198 As to how far the bankruptcy rules as to provable debts or liabilities apply to the liquidation of companies, see Lord Halsbury's *Laws of England*, title *Companies*, vol v, pp 508-515 As to the conditions under which alone a party is entitled to segregate the amount of his claim from the assets distributable among the creditors, see § 379, note (d), *ante*.

(e) *Greenwood* v *Humber & Co (Portugal), Ltd* , [1908] W N 162.

(f) See Ch III, Sect 2, Sub ss (1), (2), (3), respectively, *ante*

(g) Throughout the remainder of this Chapter, instead of the expressions " party complaining," and " party charged " (which, for the reasons given in § 12, *ante*, have hitherto appeared appropriate), the terms " plaintiff " and " defendant " will be respectively used, for the reason that there can be no danger of their misleading any one when applied to a class of case in which, as here, the party complaining must of necessity always be a plaintiff : see § 568, *post*.

exception), or that he was himself ignorant of it, which are the fourth, and fifth, respectively, of the five above-mentioned *probanda* at common law in the case of a negotiation *uberrimæ fidei* (*h*). That this is so, is a clear inference, as will be seen later, from the language of the statute (*i*). On the other hand, his only remedy for the statutory wrong being the recovery of damages, it is incumbent on him to allege and prove that which is *ex vi termini* part of his cause of action, viz. the fact of damage, and also a causal connexion between that fact and the defendant's breach of the statutory requirement, as in the case of any other action for damages (*j*), though, in any case of common law non-disclosure, where rescission, avoidance, defence, and their equivalents, are the only remedies available, such matters are wholly irrelevant (*k*). It is now proposed to examine, separately and *seriatim*, each of the matters above stated in respect of which the onus rests at the outset (for it is often shifted at a very early stage) on any person seeking relief in respect of statutory non-disclosure in a prospectus.

Sub-s (1)   *The Existence of the Duty to Disclose in the Prospectus*

549. The plaintiff must in the first place establish that the statutory duty for the breach of which he claims damages was at the material date owed by the defendants to himself; which means that he must show that he, or (in case of death, or disability) the person whose estate he represents, belongs to the class of persons entitled to the statutory relief (*l*), and also that the defendant, or (in case of death, or disability) the person whose estate has devolved upon him, belongs to one or other of the classes of persons liable to the proceedings (*m*).

550. He must next show, if the matter is contre verted, that the document alleged to be a prospectus was a prospectus in the statutory sense already explained (*n*), and, in any case in which more than one prospectus was

---

(*h*) See Ch. III, Sect 2, Sub-ss. (4), and (5), respectively, *ante*.
(*i*) See §§ 557, 561, *post*
(*j*) See §§ 558, 559, *post*
(*k*) See § 359, *ante*
(*l*) That is to say, that he is a person who subscribed for, or purchased, shares or debentures offered by the prospectus, or a person who, by operation of law, is entitled to represent him, or his estate, within § 537, *ante*
(*m*) This means that the defendant must be shown to have issued or authorized the issue of the prospectus, being a promoter, director. or agent of the company, or a person who, at the date of the issue, was or had been, engaged or interested in its formation, as described in §§ 540-544, *ante*, or he must be shown to represent the estate of such a person, if deceased (see § 546, *ante*) or under disability, such as insolvency (see § 547, *ante*). The cases cited in the notes to §§ 540-544, *ante*, and in the notes to this Chapter, generally, show (though authority is hardly required for the proposition that he who asserts the breach of a duty to him by another must prove the existence of that duty) that the onus of establishing the matters in question is on the plaintiff All the above are questions of fact (see the above cases) As to promotership, and (when material) the date and duration of such promotership, being issues of fact, see (amongst other cases) *Twycross* v. *Grant* (1877), 2 C P. D 469, C A (where, from p 476, it appears that Lord COLERIDGE, C J , left it to the jury at the trial to find, as a fact, whether the defendant was a promoter, or not) As to the meaning of " promoter," see §§ 327, 328, *ante*.
(*n*) §§ 515-519, *ante* If the plaintiff is complaining of omission from the prospectus of any of the matters referred to in sub ss (5) or (8), of s. 81, he must show that the

issued, he must further show that the particular prospectus on the faith of which he took his shares or debentures was subject to the statutory duty of disclosure (o).

551. Lastly, in order to complete his proof of the existence of the statutory duty, it is incumbent on the plaintiff to establish that the undisclosed matter is one of those required by the enactment to be stated in the prospectus (p). With one important exception, the matters enumerated in s 81 are (as described in the marginal heading to the section) in the nature of " particulars," and the subject of " specific " requirements As to these it is not probable that any difficulty will often arise The requirement, however, as to " material contracts " (pp)—which constitutes the exception referred to—involves proof of a more general character, since the question whether the omitted contract is one of which disclosure is necessary, or not, depends entirely on whether it was, or was not, material ; and materiality depends on a variety of circumstances and considerations, and is not always self-evident or obvious The meaning of " materiality," for the purposes of disclosure in general, has been fully discussed in an earlier Chapter (q). It has also been already explained what this term, as applied to the particular statutory duty under consideration, has been held to mean in a succession of decisions under s. 38 of the Act of 1867, which, for the reasons given, are strictly relevant to this provision of the Act of 1908 (r). From these decisions it will be apparent that it is always incumbent on the plaintiff to establish the materiality of the omitted contract (s), which question, as in all other cases where materiality is an essential part of the burden of proof incumbent on a person complaining of non-disclosure (t), is a question of fact (u).

document on which he took his shares or debentures was not a copy of the prospectus " published as a newspaper advertisement," or (as the case may be) was not " published more than one year after the date at which the company was entitled to commence business " : see §§ 523, 524, 525, 530, *ante*.

(o) See § 520, and the cases cited in the notes thereto, *ante*, from which it is apparent that this onus rests on the plaintiff

(p) See Sect 3, in which all these " particulars " are discussed *seriatim*, and the notes thereto, *ante*.

(pp) This is s. 81, (1), (k)

(q) See Ch. II, Sect 2, *ante*

(r) In § 532, *ante*

(s) See the cases cited in the notes to § 532, *ante*. It is no answer, in any class of non-disclosure case where materiality is established, to allege or prove that the party charged believed the undisclosed fact not to be material : see § 33, *ante* So in the case of omission from a prospectus of a contract which is in fact material, it is quite useless for the defendant to set up that he believed, or was professionally or otherwise advised, that it was not of such materiality as to require disclosure : see the following cases under s 38 of the Act of 1867 —*Cackett* v *Keswick*, [1902] 2 Ch 456, C A (*per* FARWELL, J , at p 468) , *Watts* v *Bucknall*, [1903] 1 Ch 766, C A (*per* COLLINS, M R., at p 773) On the other hand, as in other cases (see § 33, note (s), *ante*), where the evidence is conflicting, and the issue is doubtful, the fact that the defendant by his conduct betrayed a consciousness or suspicion of the materiality may turn the scale against him : see, for instance, *Broome* v *Speak*, [1903] 1 Ch 586, C A , a case under s 38 of the Act of 1867, in which it was regarded as an important fact that the defendants had shown their belief in the materiality of the undisclosed contracts by referring to them in the first draft of the prospectus from which, as finally issued, they were omitted (*per* COLLINS, M.R , at p. 614)

(t) See Ch III, Sect 6, Sub s (1), *ante*.

(u) Thus, in *Charlton* v *Hay* (1874) 31 L T 437, where a demurrer to a count in the declaration was based on the contention that the omitted contract could not, as a matter

Sub-s (2). The Existence of the Matter omitted from the Prospectus.

552. As in cases where a non-statutory duty of disclosure is alleged to have been broken (v), it is obvious that any person who complains of the omission from the prospectus of any of the facts required by the statute to be inserted therein must prove, if challenged, that the alleged fact was a fact. Here, again, as regards most of the items enumerated in the enactment, the proof of the existence of the alleged fact is extremely simple but, whether easy or difficult to discharge, the onus in every case rests on the plaintiff of doing so, unless he is relieved of it by admission Thus, if he complains of the omission of a " material contract " from the prospectus, before any question of materiality arises, he must be prepared to prove that the alleged contract, or, if he relies on several contracts, that at least one of them, being a material one, was in fact made (w) For this purpose he must put in evidence the document or documents in which the contract in question is supposed to be contained or recorded, or from which it is to be implied (x), and must then show that it, or they, amount in law to a concluded and binding contract, as distinguished, for instance, from a mere "understanding," or an " engagement of honour " (y)

553. It is not necessary to prove a formal instrument of contract   If

of law, have been material, and the Court overruled the demurrer   In *Twycross v Grant* (1877), 2 C P D. 469, C A , it was left as a question of fact to the jury, whether the plaintiff would have taken his shares if he had known of the existence of the omitted contracts (p 476)   See also *Cackett v Keswick*, [1902] 2 Ch 456, C A (per FARWELL, J , who, at p. 464, expressed his opinion that the determination of the materiality, or otherwise, of the omitted contract depended upon "an inference of fact to be drawn by the Court, or a jury, from the circumstances of the case ")   All the above were cases under s 38 of the Act of 1867

(v) See Ch III, Sect 3, Sub-s (2), *ante.*

(w) See the following cases of omitted contracts under s 38 of the Act of 1867 : *Twycross v Grant* (1877), 2 C P D 469, C A (where the burden was discharged) , *Watts v Bucknall*, [1903] 1 Ch 766, C A. (where the plaintiff alleged ten omitted contracts, and proved six of them, all or some of which six were material)   On the other hand, in *Arkwright v Newbold* (1881), 17 C D. 301, C A , the plaintiff failed to prove the making of the alleged contract, and his action, so far as it was based on s 38 of the Act of 1867, failed though on other grounds it ultimately succeeded in the Court of Appeal   So, in *Stevens v Hoare* (1904), 20 T L R 107, out of six alleged contracts the plaintiff proved one only (per JOYCE, J , at p 410), and as to that one failed to prove either his own damage, or the defendant's knowledge, and his action was accordingly dismissed

(x) The contracts required to be stated in the prospectus are documentary contracts only   This is clear from the language of s 81, (1), (k), which requires a statement of " a reasonable time and place at which any material contract or a copy thereof may be inspected "   These words, it will be observed, are quite general and absolute, and are not prefaced by any qualification, such as—" where the contract was in writing " or the like   In the repealed s. 38 of the Act of 1867, there was no such reference to " inspection " or " copies," and it was accordingly held that oral contracts were within the statutory duty of disclosure   *Capel & Co. v Sim's Ships Composition Co* (1888), 58 L T 807 (per KEKEWICH, J , at p 810)

(y) In *Broome v. Speak*, [1903] 1 Ch 586, C. A , the plaintiff succeeded in establishing that a certain resolution of the company's board of directors was (in the sense that it related to previous contracts, and affected the mode of payment) a contract, or part of a contract, and not a mere " engagement of honour " (per BUCKLEY, J , at pp. 598-600, and, in the Court of Appeal, per COLLINS, M R , at p 617, and ROMER, L J , at pp 626, 627)   On the other hand, in *Arkwright v Newbold, sup*, the plaintiff failed to establish anything beyond an " understanding " (per FRY, J , at pp 308, 309), and, so far as his claim was based on s 38 of the Act of 1867, his action failed.

the particular contract alleged can be spelt out from the documents in evidence, however informal they may be, this is enough (z). It is necessary on the one hand, and sufficient on the other, to establish that the "real" or "true" contract, the non-disclosure of which is complained of, is to be found in undivulged documents construed by the light of all the other circumstances of the case, where it is suggested that the documents disclosed in the prospectus present a superficial appearance of something which is not the "real" or "true" contract (a) It may be enough, in certain circumstances, to prove the omission of a contract which had been completely executed, or had been cancelled, at the date of the issue of the prospectus, and, *a fortiori*, of one which at that date had merely been modified (b)

554. Whether the omitted contract was made or not (c), and whether, in cases of the kind above indicated, it was the "real" or "true" contract (d), are questions of fact. Whether the document or documents proved amount to a binding and enforceable contract, or not, is a question of law (e).

Sub-s (3) The Omission from the Prospectus

555. It has been shown that, where one of the two parties to a negotiation complains of a breach by the other of a common law duty of disclosure, it is incumbent on such complaining party to give some evidence if challenged,

(z) *Broome* v *Speak*, [1903] 1 Ch 586, C A

(a) *Cackett* v *Keswick*. [1902] 2 Ch 456, C A (*per* FARWELL, J , at p 465, ROMER, L J , at p 476, and STIRLING, L J , at p 477, *dubitante*, on this point, VAUGHAN WILLIAMS, L J , at pp. 472, 473) The Court, however, was unanimous in thinking that, in this case, it did not matter whether the "real" contract was the expressed contract, or not, for either would be within the section

(b) See *Broome* v *Speak*, *sup*, where the omitted contracts were (i) a contract, contained in a letter and minute of the board, whereby the promoter was to receive a bonus of £7500, (ii) a contract, contained in another letter and minute, whereby the promoter agreed to share this bonus with Speak, and (iii) a subsequent resolution of the company's board of directors, with the assent of the promoter, that, in lieu of the £7500, such sum should be paid as the board should think reasonable It was contended that (iii) had cancelled (i) and (ii), and that (i) and (ii) were accordingly extinct contracts when the prospectus was issued, and not required, therefore, to be disclosed under s 38 of the Act of 1867, whilst (iii), which had performed its sole function as the extinguisher, was equally outside the duty But it was held by BUCKLEY, J (pp 600-602), and, in the Court of Appeal, by COLLINS, M R (pp. 615-626), that (iii) had not the effect of putting an end to (i) and (ii), but only of substituting another method of payment, and, further, that, even if it had the former effect, so that (i) and (ii) at the date of the issue of the prospectus might be called non-existent contracts, still (iii) was a contract, viz a contract of rescission, and all three were contracts which at various dates had in fact been made, and the non-disclosure of any one of them, all being material, was a breach of the statutory duty

(c) See, generally, the cases cited in the notes to this Section, and, particularly, *Twycross* v *Grant* (1877), 2 C P D. 469, C. A, where it appears from p 476 that the first of the questions left to the jury by Lord COLERIDGE, C J , was, whether the alleged contracts had been made or not

(d) See *Cackett* v. *Keswick*, *sup* (*per* FARWELL, J , at p 465 . "I find *as a fact* that the consideration for the 10,000 shares was the agreement by Mathesons to take the company into their offices," the expressed consideration being something else, viz commission for underwriting these shares)

(e) In *Arkwright* v. *Newbold* (1881), 17 C D 301, C A , and in *Stevens* v *Hoare* (1904), 20 T L R 407, FRY, J , and JOYCE, J , respectively, in so far as they decided that the contents of the documents proved did not import a concluded or binding contract, seem to have treated the question as one of law

of the non-disclosure alleged, though the slightest possible proof of this negative will at once shift the onus on to the other side of establishing the affirmative (*f*)   So, in the case of the statutory non-disclosure under consideration, the burden is technically on the plaintiff to prove the omission from the prospectus of the particular matter which he alleges to have been omitted,— a burden, in the vast majority of cases, easily and instantly discharged by merely reading the prospectus, which at that stage will already have been produced and put in evidence, and pointing to the place where the omitted matter ought to be, and is not   It sometimes, however, happens that the proof is less simple, and more argumentative : for instance, where the prospectus contains some more or less distant and oblique references to the matter in question, it is incumbent on the plaintiff to establish in argument, and it may be by evidence, that these allusions conveyed no real knowledge to him, and fell short of that candid, complete, exact, and unambiguous statement which is demanded by the law from every person who is under a duty of disclosure to another, whether the duty arises at common law or is imposed by a statute (*g*)

Sub-s (4)   *The Defendant's Knowledge* (*in one class of case only*).

556. The party complaining of another's non-compliance with a common law duty of disclosure must, as has been explained in an earlier Chapter, establish that the party charged was cognizant of the undisclosed fact (*h*)   Where, however, a statute imposes the duty, there is no such onus on the plaintiff, unless the legislature, in describing the act which constitutes the offence, qualifies it by language importing that the defendant's knowledge is to be a necessary ingredient in it   In s 38 of the Act of 1867 such a qualification was introduced by virtue of the word " knowingly "   Only a person who " knowingly issued " a prospectus omitting a material contract was rendered liable by that section : and, in a series of decisions, " knowingly issuing " was construed to mean no more, and no less, than " issuing a prospectus with knowledge that the undisclosed contract at the date of such issue was, or at some material date had been, in fact entered into " (*i*)   In the case, however, of the enactment now under consideration there is no such qualification, except as to one particular class of matter to be mentioned presently.   The general duty is prescribed by the introductory words of the enactment in absolute, indeed in impersonal, terms : " every prospectus issued by   must state " . . &c , and no question of " knowledge " is made relevant, or referred to in any way, in s 81 (1), of the Act of 1908, though a later sub-section of the enactment in specific language creates one exception (*j*)

(*f*) See Ch III, Sect 3, Sub s (3), *ante*
(*g*) As to what " disclosure " means and involves, see Ch II, Sect 1, *ante*   The statutory obligation " to state " cannot possibly have a narrower connotation than the common law duty to " disclose " or " communicate "
(*h*) See Ch III, Sect 3, Sub s. (4), *ante*
(*i*) *Twycross* v *Grant* (1877), 2 C. P D 469, C A ; *Cackett* v *Keswick*, [1902] 2 Ch 456, C A , *Watts* v *Bucknall*, [1903] 1 Ch 546, C A , *Shepheard* v *Broome*, [1904] A C 342, H L , *Macleay* v *Tait*, [1906] A C 24, H L
(*j*) See § 557, *ante*.

Subject to this exception, it is clear, on ordinary principles of construction, that no knowledge or other state of mind of the defendant is a necessary factor in constituting the statutory tort, or, therefore, requires to be established by the plaintiff as part of his case : and this is made still clearer by the express provision that ignorance of the undisclosed matter shall be a good affirmative plea, the burden of proving which is placed on the defendant (*k*) , and by the fact that, in other parts of the Act of 1908, when it is intended to make "knowledge" of the essence of the prohibited act, it is so stated (*l*)

557. The exception above referred to is created by the proviso to sub-s (6) of s. 81, "that in the event of non-compliance with the requirements contained in" a certain paragraph "of sub-section (1) of this section, no director or other person shall incur any liability in respect of the non-compliance unless it be proved that he had knowledge of the matters not disclosed " The paragraph in question embraces the very important class of facts which relate to the interest of the directors of the company in the promotion, and to their qualification by, or other corrupt relations with, the promoter (*m*) Where omission of any matter of this class is complained of, the plaintiff must prove the defendant's (actual or presumptive) knowledge of such omitted matter at the date of " non-compliance " (that is, the date of the issue of the prospectus which fails to comply with the statutory requirement), and, as in cases under s. 38 of the Act of 1867 (*n*), unless he establishes this knowledge as a fact (*o*), his action falls to the ground The provision is for the protection of a director who, being himself free from blame, was ignorant of the illicit relations existing between his fellow-directors and the promoter . where the plaintiff sues a director solely in respect of the non-disclosure of his own delinquencies in this regard, it is of course unnecessary to prove the defendant's knowledge of his own acts.

(*k*) See s 81, (6), (a) of the Act of 1908, and § 563, *post*

(*l*) As in s 80 (5),—"every person who is knowingly a party to the issue, '—and s 86 (2),—"knowingly contravenes "

(*m*) The paragraph is (m) of s 81, (1), and runs as follows ' full particulars of the nature and extent of the interest (if any) of every director in the promotion of, or in the property proposed to be acquired by, the company, or, where the interest of such a director consists in being a partner in a firm, the nature and extent of the interest of the firm, with a statement of all sums paid or agreed to be paid to him or to the firm in cash or shares or otherwise by any person either to induce him to become, or to qualify him as, a director or otherwise for services rendered by him or by the firm in connexion with the promotion or formation of the company " As to this clause see § 534, *ante*

(*n*) This was the result in *Stevens* v *Hoare* (1904), 20 T L R 407, where the plaintiff failed to prove that the defendant knew of the existence of the only one of the six alleged contracts which was held to be a contract at all (*per* JOYCE, J , at p 410) The " knowledge " to be proved need not necessarily be an actual and personal knowledge It is enough to show circumstances from which it may fairly be imputed to, or presumed against, the defendant, as in *Watts* v *Bucknall*, [1903] 1 Ch 766, C A (*per* COLLINS, M R , at p 772, ROMER, L.J , at p 777, and COZENS HARDY, L J , at p 779) As to " presumptive knowledge," and its various forms and species, see Ch II, Sect 3, Sub-ss (2)–(6)

(*o*) See, generally, the cases cited in note (*n*), *sup* , and particularly *Twycross* v *Grant* (1877), 2 C P D 469, C A , where one of the questions left to the jury by Lord COLERIDGE, C J (see p 476), was, whether the defendants had "knowingly omitted mention of the contracts from the prospectus "

Sub-s (5) Inducement and Damage.

558. Where, as in the three classes of non-disclosure considered in previous Chapters (p), or as in cases of innocent misrepresentation (q), the only remedy available is rescission, or its equivalents, the questions of inducement and damage are wholly irrelevant. But where the case is one of fraudulent misrepresentation (r), or other fraud or tort, or where a breach of statutory duty is complained of for which no special civil remedy is provided by the statute,—this, as will be seen hereafter (s), is true of the enactment under consideration,—and where, therefore, recovery of damages is the appropriate form of relief, such damage is, ex vi termini, an essential ingredient in the cause of action, and the plaintiff must prove that he has sustained some tangible loss or damage in fact (t), to an amount which is either ascertainable at once, or of which sufficient general evidence is available to justify an inquiry or reference (u)

559. To prove, however, the mere fact of damage, without going on to establish a causal relation between the damage and the statutory wrong, is to prove nothing. To establish this relation of cause and effect, the plaintiff must show, first, that his subscription for or purchase of the shares or debentures resulted in loss to himself, and, secondly, that the non-compliance with the statutory duty of disclosure was the cause of that subscription or purchase, in the sense that he was induced by his belief that such duty had been observed to so subscribe or purchase. It is true that no express words to this effect are to be found in the enactment, such as are to be found in other statutory requirements as to prospectuses,—for instance, " by reason of any untrue statement," or " on the faith of the prospectus " (v) But this circumstance is of no significance whatever, in view of the obvious and universal rule that no man can obtain from another compensation for damage which is not shown to have resulted from the proved actionable wrong. The plaintiff, therefore, in an action for damages for the omission by the defendant from the prospectus of any of the matters required to be stated therein by s 81 of the Act of 1908, is bound to establish no less, though

(p) See §§ 221, 359, 462, respectively, ante
(q) See Ch XI, Sect 1, Sub s (2), of the author's *Law of Actionable Misrepresentation*
(r) *Ibid* , Ch X, Sect 1
(s) See § 568, post
(t) Thus, in *Stevens v. Hoare* (1904), 20 T L R 407, an action for damages for breach of s 38 of the Act of 1867, one of the reasons for dismissing the action was that the plaintiff proved no damage (per JOYCE, J , at p 409) So also in *Nash v Calthorpe*, [1905] 2 Ch 237, C A Of course the question of damage, or no damage, and also the amount of such damage (if any), are questions of fact, subject to certain rules of law as to what constitutes damage and the principles on which it should be measured, as to which see § 569, post
(u) As in *Cackett v Keswick*, [1902] 2 Ch 456, C A (per FARWELL, J , at p 468), *McConnell v Wright*, [1903] 1 Ch 546, C A (per ROMER, L J , at p 558), *Shepheard v Broome*, [1904] A. C 342, H L (per Lord LINDLEY, at pp 347, 348), *J & P Coats, Ltd v Crossland* (1904), 20 T L R 800 (per SWINFEN EADY, J , at p 807)
(v) The latter expression is to be found both in s 38 of the Act of 1867, and in s 84 of the Act of 1908 (reproducing the Directors' Liability Act, 1890), which latter also contains the words " by reason of any untrue statement " in the prospectus, a curiously elliptical phrase for " by reason of his having acted in the belief of the truth of any untrue statement therein " See the observations of FARWELL, J , at p. 463 of *Cackett v Keswick, sup*

he need establish no more, than that he took his shares or debentures, and so incurred the alleged loss, on the faith of the non-existence of the particular undisclosed matter (*w*) This, as was observed by Lord LINDLEY in one of the cases under s 38 of the Act of 1867 (which, *mutatis mutandis*, are strictly relevant to the present inquiry) means that the plaintiff must show not merely that, on reading a prospectus which turns out to have been in contravention of the enactment, he subscribed for or purchased the shares or debentures, but also that he was induced to do so by his persuasion that the identical fact or contract, the omission of which is the ground of his action, was non-existent " proof that he applied for the shares on the faith of " the " prospectus, and that he obtained them and paid for them and lost his money, is *primâ facie* evidence, but only *primâ facie* evidence of damage   But if the plaintiff is challenged on this point, he must go a step further and prove that he was misled by . the omission to disclose some document which ought to have been disclosed " (*x*)   For this purpose, the plaintiff must establish at least that, if the existence of the omitted fact had been revealed to him at the time, he *might* not have taken the shares or debentures , and, in one view (which, however, it is conceived, goes too far), it is incumbent on him to show that he *would* not have done so, and that due disclosure would have had a *certainly* prohibitive, and not merely a probably or possibly deterrent, effect (*y*)   The question of inducement is one of fact (*z*)

(*w*) Accordingly, in all the cases under s 38 of the Act of 1867, where the plaintiff failed to show that he was induced to take his shares by a belief (whether there were other inducements or not) that the omitted contract did not exist, he failed altogether, as in *Baty* v *Keswick* (1901), 85 L T 18 (*per* FARWELL, J , at p 20), *Stevens* v *Hoare* (1904), 20 T L R 407 (*per* JOYCE, J , at p 410), *Sleigh* v *Glasgow & Transvaal Options, Ltd* (1904), 6 F 420 , *Nash* v *Calthorpe*, [1905] 2 Ch 237, C A (*per* VAUGHAN WILLIAMS, L J , at pp 246, 247, and STIRLING, L J , at pp 254–256) , *Macleay* v *Tait*, [1906] A C 21, H L (*per* Lord HALSBURY, L C , at p 26, Lord ROBERTSON, at pp 27, 28, and Lord LINDLEY, at pp 33, 34)

(*x*) At p 31 of *Macleay* v *Tait, sup*

(*y*) Divergent views on this point (generally, however, unnecessary for the decision itself) have been expressed by high authorities in cases under s 38 of the Act of 1867 On the one hand, VAUGHAN WILLIAMS, L J , at pp 244–246 of *Nash* v. *Calthorpe, sup* , and Lord HALSBURY, L C , at p 26 of *Macleay* v *Tait, sup* (a case which related to the same company, and the same prospectus, as *Nash* v *Calthorpe*), expressed a clear opinion that it is incumbent on the plaintiff to establish that he *would* not have taken the shares if he had known of the omitted contract   The expressions to the same effect used by COCKBURN, C J , at p 543 of *Twycross* v *Grant*, 2 C P D 469, C A , and by THESIGER, L J , at p 460 of *Sullivan* v *Metcalfe* (1880), 5 C P D 455, C A , are by no means conclusive, because they occur in conjunction with, or in proximity to, other expressions tending distinctly in the opposite direction   The same observation may be made as to the fact (on which VAUGHAN WILLIAMS, L J , relies in *Nash* v *Calthorpe, sup*) that one of the questions left to the jury in *Twycross* v *Grant, sup* , was whether the plaintiff would have taken the shares if he had known of the contracts   for it appears from the report of that case (p 476) that it was also left to the jury, as a separate and independent question, whether the plaintiff subscribed for the shares " on the faith of the prospectus " , and, as the jury answered both questions in favour of the plaintiff, no decision was called for on the point under discussion   On the other hand, the opposite view is expressed in no less strong and unmistakable language, by COLLINS, M R , at pp 620–622 of *Broome* v *Speak*, [1903]

(*z*) See the cases, generally, under s 38 of the Act of 1867, where the question has always been so treated.   In *Twycross* v *Grant, sup* , as stated in the last note, two questions, based on the two above-mentioned views of inducement, were left to the jury by Lord COLERIDGE, C J

B.N D

2 K

SECT. 6.   AFFIRMATIVE DEFENCES TO THE ACTION FOR STATUTORY NON-DISCLOSURE

560. The remedy for the statutory non-disclosure being an action for damages, it follows that a defendant may avail himself of the affirmative pleas which would be available to a defendant in any other action for damages, except in so far as the enactment itself by express language curtails, increases, or varies them, as in three important respects it does (a).

Sub-s. (1)   *Non-statutory Affirmative Pleas unaffected by the Enactment*

561. There is nothing in the enactment which purports to deprive the defendant of such affirmative common law defences to any action for damages as accord and satisfaction, in activity and delay amounting to acquiescence or affirmation (b), and the like, or of a defence founded on some other statute, such as a statute of limitations (c). Again, a plea based on proof of the plaintiff's

1 Ch. 586, C A, by ROMER, L J, at pp. 251, 252, of *Nash* v *Calthorpe*, [1905] 2 Ch 237, C A, and by WARRINGTON, J, at pp. 250-253 of *Shepheard* v *Bray*, [1906] 2 Ch 235, and, it is submitted, is the more sound of the two. It may be, however, that the difference lies more in form and expression than in thought and substance, and that the apparent opposition is capable of reconciliation, if the proposition is put as FARWELL, J, expressed it, at p. 464 of *Cackett* v *Keswick*, [1902] 2 Ch 456, C A. "if the Court sees that the fact omitted is of such a nature that it might reasonably deter, or tend to deter, the ordinary investor from entering into the contract, this is sufficient . . If a material fact is omitted from a statement put forward to induce a person to enter into a contract on the faith of that statement, it is a fair inference that he would not have contracted if he had known of the fact." In other words, though technically it is necessary for the plaintiff to prove that he would not have subscribed for the shares if the omitted fact had been disclosed, he discharges that burden—*prima facie*, at least—by showing that the contract was of a nature to produce hesitation, and "give pause" to a normal person. This is only to say, as is abundantly established (see § 32, and note (p) thereto, *ante*, and, as applied to cases of misrepresentation, cp §§ 120, 131, of the author's *Law of Actionable Misrepresentation*), that inducement may be inferred as a fact, but not as a conclusion of law, from materiality, and that the question, ' would you have taken the shares if something had been left out, and something else put in ? ", may, in some cases, be properly and sufficiently met without destroying a case of inducement otherwise established, by the reply,—"I cannot say, I have never seen such a prospectus,"—as was observed by BYRNE, J, in a case under the Directors' Liability Act, 1890 (now s 84 of the Act of 1908), at p 404 of *Drincqbier* v *Wood*, [1899] 1 Ch 393

(a) See Sub-ss (2), (3), (4), *post*

(b) In *Re Christineville Rubber Estates, Ltd* (1911), 81 L J (CH) 63, the applicant's inaction and delay, after knowledge of his rights, was held fatal to his motion for rectification of the register, which was based on the ground of both misrepresentation in the prospectus (which was admitted), and also non disclosure of matters required to be stated therein by s. 81, (1), (f) of the Act of 1908 (*per* EVE, J, at p 66)

(c) The period of limitation is six years, as in the case of any non statutory action. It was decided in *Thomson* v *Lord Clanmorris*, [1900] 1 Ch 718, C A (*per* LINDLEY, M R, at pp 725, 726, and VAUGHAN WILLIAMS, L J, at pp 727, 728) that sect 3 of the Civil Procedure Act, 1833 (3 & 4 W 4, c 42), which enacts that "all actions for penalties, damages, or sums of money given to the party grieved by any statute . shall be commenced and sued within two years after the causes of such actions or suits," has no application to the cause of action "given" by the Directors' Liability Act, 1890 (now s 84 of the Act of 1908), and that "damages and sums of money" refers only to statutory imposition of pecuniary liability *in poenam*, and not to compensation by way of civil relief. If this be so, still less has the section referred to any application to the enactment now under consideration which "gives" no cause of action at all *nomination*, as the Act of 1890 did, and s 84 of the Act of 1908 does. The six years period runs from the date of the plaintiff's subscription for, or purchase of, the shares or debentures, for then first his cause of action accrues. *Thomson* v *Lord Clanmorris, sup* (*per* LINDLEY, M R, at pp. 726, 727, and VAUGHAN WILLIAMS, L.J, at pp 728, 729)

actual and personal (not presumptive) knowledge of the truth, which is always available in an action for damages for misrepresentation (d), is equally available in an action for damages for breach of the enactment, as it was held to be in the case of actions for damages for breach of s 38 of the Act of 1867 (e) The existence or non-existence of such actual and personal knowledge on the part of the plaintiff is a question of fact (f)

Sub-s (2) Waiver—how affected by the Enactment

562 To a common law action for damages for misrepresentation in a prospectus, or otherwise, it is a valid answer to allege and prove that, either expressly, in the form of a term or condition in the contract, or impliedly, by acts and conduct, the plaintiff agreed to waive, renounce, or surrender, any right to relief to which he might otherwise have been entitled (g) This defence was not abolished, or affected, by s 38 of the Act of 1867, and the " waiver clause," which became a common feature in prospectuses of the period, was accordingly recognized as valid if, but only if (which was rarely the case), it was so expressed as to satisfy all the conditions of complete candour and good faith which are required by the law in all cases of waiver, release, or compromise (h) By s 10 (5), however, of the Act of 1900, repeated in s 81, (4), of the Act of 1908, it was expressly enacted that " any condition requiring or binding any applicant for shares or debentures to waive compliance with any requirement of this section, or purporting to affect him with notice of any contract, document, or matter not specifically referred to in the prospectus, shall be void " (i) It will be observed that the latter part of this clause covers a much wider area than the first part, since it invalidates every attempt to fix the party beforehand with contractual knowledge of any undisclosed matter whatsoever, whether it is or is not a matter required by the enactment to be stated in the prospectus So far, therefore, as express contracts or conditions are concerned, the defence

---

(d) This topic is dealt with in Ch X, Sect. 2, Sub-s (1), of the author's *Law of Actionable Misrepresentation*

(e) See *Watts* v *Bucknall*, [1903] 1 Ch 766, C. A. (*per* COLLINS, M R , at p 775 At p 776, he explains why there is no logical inconsistency between the rule which requires actual knowledge to be brought home to the injured party, who is under no statutory liability in the matter, and the rule which denies to the wrongdoer, who is under an absolute statutory duty, a means of escape by pleading that the same facts which prove that the plaintiff had no knowledge, because he had no actual notice, ought to be sufficient to acquit the defendant of " knowingly issuing," because he too had no actual notice) As to " actual " and " presumptive " knowledge, see Ch II, Sect 3, *ante* As to the defendant's onus of proving the plaintiff's actual and personal knowledge, in an action of misrepresentation, see § 209 of the author's *Law of Actionable Misrepresentation*

(f) In *Twycross* v *Grant* (1877), 2 C P D 469, C A , one of the questions left to the jury (see p 476) was whether the plaintiff had " notice," within s 38 of the Act of 1867, of the omitted contracts

(g) See Ch X, Sect 2, Sub s (2) of the Author's *Law of Actionable Misrepresentation*

(h) See § 132, *ante*, and all the cases which are cited in note (s) thereto, in connexion with the principles regulating the duty of disclosure in negotiations for compromise

(i) It is remarkable that there is no corresponding prohibition of a waiver condition in s 84 of the Act of 1908 (relating to " untrue statements " in the prospectus). On the other hand, there is such a prohibition in s 85, as to allotment of shares on less than " the minimum subscription " · see sub s (5) of that section

of waiver is now, and since the 1st January, 1901 (the date of commencement of the Act of 1900) has been, totally extinct The defence of waiver by acts and conduct, for what it is worth, still remains

Sub-s. (3)   The Defendant's Ignorance of the Undisclosed Matter.

563 It has been already pointed out that, except in the case of one specified class, the enactment does not require the plaintiff to allege or prove that the defendant was cognisant of the matter alleged to have been omitted from the prospectus (*j*). It is expressly provided, however, that " in the event of non-compliance with any of the requirements of this section, a director or other person responsible for the prospectus shall not incur any liability by reason of the non-compliance, if he proves that, as regards any matter not disclosed, he was not cognisant thereof " (*k*) This means that the defendant is not to be deprived of the plea of ignorance, but it is for him to allege and prove it, and not, as in certain common law cases of non-disclosure (*l*) and in the class of case expressly excepted by the enactment itself, for the plaintiff to establish the defendant's knowledge

Sub-s (4)   The Defendant's " Honest Mistake of Fact."

564. The above cited provision of the enactment, after allowing the defendant a plea of ignorance as compensation for depriving him (except as above stated) of his common law right to insist on his knowledge being proved by the plaintiff, proceeds to create an entirely new affirmative defence, not subject to any exception in this case, constituted by proof on the part of the defendant that " the non-compliance (*i e* " with any of the requirements of the section ") arose from an honest mistake of fact on his part " (*m*)

565 This is an affirmative plea unknown to the non-statutory law relating to breaches of the duty of disclosure It is to be observed that there are two conditions subject to which alone the " mistake " is to operate as a valid defence. It must, in the first place, be " honest," by which curious expression (*n*) is meant no more than that the mistake must be purely and genuinely a mistake, arising from mere accident or inadvertence, and not a self-induced error into which the defendant has deliberately determined to fall, or for which he has fraudulently prepared the ground beforehand, in the hope of qualifying himself to take the benefit of the plea, in which case the pretended mistake is in truth and fact no mistake at all Secondly, the mistake must be one of fact this requirement being obviously designed to render impossible a repetition of the kind of contention to which the

(*j*) See § 557, *ante*   The excepted class is that comprised in s 81, (1), (m)
(*k*) 81, (6), (a) of the Act of 1908. As to what " cognizance " or " knowledge " means for this purpose, see § 556, *ante*
(*l*) See Ch III, Sect 3, Sub-s. (4), *ante*
(*m*) S 81, (6), (b), of the Act of 1908
(*n*) See, as to the lax terminology of such expressions as " honest belief," and " honest mistake," § 639, *post*.

indefiniteness of the phrase "knowingly issued" in s. 38 of the Act of 1867 lent some encouragement in proceedings under that section, viz. that a man does not "knowingly issue" a prospectus who is ignorant of the legal effect of the section, or who has been advised by counsel that the particular omitted contract does not in law belong to the class of contracts required thereby to be disclosed, and the like (o).

SECT 7. THE STATUTORY RELIEF.

566 The enactment undoubtedly in express terms imposes a new duty of disclosure upon certain persons in certain events; and, equally without doubt, it omits to provide any specific remedy for the breach of that duty, though expressions are used which clearly imply that the legislature assumed the existence of a civil liability of some sort in the case of any contravention of its provisions The question is whether, on the application of the principles which govern the interpretation of statutes to the above conditions, any civil relief is available to the party aggrieved and, if so, what is its nature.

567 A clear general statement of the doctrine in question, which has always been accepted and applied, though in some respects it has required and received supplementary amplification, is the following. "There are three classes of cases in which a liability may be established by statute There is that case where there is a liability existing at common law, and which is only re-enacted by the statute with a special form of remedy; there, unless the statute contains words necessarily excluding the common law remedy, the plaintiff has his election of proceeding either under the statute or at common law Then there is a second class, which consists of those cases in which a statute has created a liability, but has given no special remedy for it, there the party may adopt an action of debt or other remedy at common law to enforce it. The third class is where the statute creates a liability not existing at common law, and gives also a particular remedy for enforcing it, with respect to that class it has always been held that the party must adopt the form of remedy given by the statute" (p) The above

(o) As in *Twycross* v *Grant* (1877), 2 C P D 469, C A (per Lord COLERIDGE, C J, at p 489, and COCKBURN, C J, at pp 541, 542), *Cackett* v *Keswick*, [1902] 2 Ch 456, C A (per FARWELL, J, at p 463, and STIRLING, L J, at p 478), *Watts* v *Bucknall*, [1903] 1 Ch 766, C A (per COLLINS, M R, at p 773), *Broome* v *Speak*, [1903] 1 Ch 586, C A (per COLLINS, M R, at p 619, and ROMER, L J, at p 628), *Macleay* v *Tait*, [1906] A C 24, H L (per Lord LINDLEY, at p 29)

(p) This is from the judgment of WILLES, J, in *Wolverhampton New Waterworks Co* v *Hawkesford* (1859), 28 L J (C P) 242 (at p 246) The citation is made from the Law Journal report, in preference to that in 6 C B (N S) 336, which, in the description of the second class, is evidently somewhat inaccurate It was probably for this reason that FARWELL, J, cites the former, and not the latter, report at p 903 of *Stevens* v *Chown*, *inf* Illustrations of the application of the above principles to enactments of the first class are — *Lichfield Corpn* v *Simpson* (1845), 8 Q B 65 (per Lord DENMAN, C J, at p 74, WILLIAMS, J, at p 74, COLERIDGE, J, at pp 74, 75, and WIGHTMAN, J, at p 75), *Great Northern Steam ship Fishery Co* v *Edgehill* (1883), 11 Q B D 225 (but see the next note as to this case), *Stevens* v *Chown*, [1901] 1 Ch 894 (per FARWELL, J, at p 903) For examples of enact ments held to belong to the second class, see *Doe d Rochester (Bishop of)* v *Bridges* (1831),

statement should be enlarged by the observation that, in the case of all three classes, and not merely the first of them, a *primâ facie* presumption only is raised, which is subject to be rebutted by proof of a contrary intention expressed in, or necessarily to be implied from the tenor and purport of, the statute (*q*), and by the further observation that in every case, whether the statute recognizes an existing duty or creates a new one, the party injured, or the Attorney-General, as the case may be, is entitled to resort to the Court for the purpose of obtaining an injunction to restrain the violation of such duty, unless that resort is by express words taken away by the statute (*r*). The ordinary civil remedies at common law are (apart from injunction) an action for damages or debt. Relief by way of rescission of, or recovery of money paid under, a contract entered into in contravention of the statute, or by a person carrying on business under conditions prohibited thereby, is only available where

---

1 B & Ad 847 (*per* Lord TENTERDEN, C.J , at p 859), and, possibly, *Johnston* v. *Connecticut Gas Co of Toronto*, [1898] A. C 447, P C (but see the next note as to this case) The third class is illustrated by *Wolverhampton New Waterworks Co* v *Hawkesford, sup* , *Ross* v *Rugge Price* (1876), 1 Ex D 200; *Atkinson* v *Newcastle & Gateshead Waterworks Co* (1877), 2 Ex. D 441, C A , *Saunders* v *Holborn District Board of Works*, [1895] 1 Q B 64; *Johnston* v *Connecticut Gas Co of Toronto, sup* (perhaps, but see the next note); *Att -Gen* v. *Ashbourne Recreation Ground Co* , [1903] 1 Ch 101, C A

(*q*) This qualification has been applied, or recognized, in cases belonging to each of the three classes   Thus, in *Great Northern Steamship Fishery Co.* v *Edgehill, sup* , where a new remedy was provided by the statute for an existing common law wrong, and where, therefore, the case fell within the first class, it was recognized that, unless by express words or fair implication the legislature evinces an intention to take away the ordinary common law remedy, the party aggrieved has his choice between that, and the new statutory remedy (p 226), but it was held that, by clear implication, the legislature had there manifested such an intention (pp 227, 228)   So, in cases of the second class, where the statute creates a new liability without specifying any particular remedy, and where, therefore, *primâ facie* the party has a right to resort to the ordinary common law forms of relief for a breach of duty, it is still open to the party sued to show, if he can, a fair inference from the language of the statute that this *primâ facie* right was intended to be taken away   and the defendant succeeded in showing this in *Johnston* v *Connecticut Gas Co of Toronto, sup* , assuming the case to be within the second, and not, as the Court seemed rather to think it was, within the third class   Lastly, it was recognized in *Atkinson* v *Newcastle and Gateshead Waterworks Co* , *sup* , that, even where the enactment creates a new liability, and prescribes a new and special remedy (which is the third class of case), and where, therefore, *primâ facie* the aggrieved party can only pursue the statutory remedy, it is nevertheless, open to him to establish, if he can, for the burden is on him of doing so, that by express words, or necessary implication, the legislature has manifested its intention not to take away the common law remedy   In that case, however, the plaintiff wholly failed to sustain this onus   There is one other qualification on the general principles enunciated by WILLES, J , which must always be borne in mind, and that is, that no person is entitled to relief of any kind against a breach of statutory duty unless he belongs to the class of persons intended to be protected, and the injury in respect of which he claims, besides resulting from the breach of statutory duty, was that kind of injury which it was the object of the statute to guard against   see *Gorris* v *Scott* (1874), L R 9 Exch 125, where the plaintiff sued for damages for loss of cattle washed overboard by reason of the defendant's non observance of the provisions of a statute as to the disposing of cattle on board vessels in such a way as to prevent or minimize the danger of infection by cattle disease, and it was held that, not having sustained the precise sort of damage which the enactment contemplated, or was designed to prevent or relieve against, he had no remedy

(*r*) See *Ross* v *Rugge Price* (1876), 1 Ex D 200 (where the right to an injunction was assumed), *Stevens* v. *Chown*, [1901] 1 Ch 894 (where FARWELL, J , at p 903, expressed a clear opinion that nothing but express words can destroy the right of an interested party, or the Attorney General, as the case may be, to resort to the Court for the purpose of restraining the breach of a statute), *Att -Gen* v *Ashbourne Recreation Ground Co* , [1903] 1 Ch 101, C A

there is a clear indication in the statute itself that parliament intended all contracts so made to be void, or voidable (s).

568. Applying the above rules to s 81 of the Act of 1908, it is manifest that the section falls within the second of the three classes enumerated by WILLES, J , that the aggrieved party is, therefore, *primâ facie* entitled to enforce the statutory duty by a common law action, that this *primâ facie* presumption is in no way destroyed by anything contained in the statute, but, on the contrary, is recognized and assumed by the legislature in the very section itself (t), and that civil relief in the ordinary forms of damages, debt, or injunction (though the last two are obviously inappropriate or useless in the class of case under consideration) is available to any person who has subscribed for or purchased shares or debentures on the faith of a prospectus from which any of the specified matters has been omitted, but that, on the other hand, rescission or analogous relief is impossible, there being no indication in the enactment, any more than there was in s 38 of the Act of 1867 (u), of an intention on the part of the legislature to render the contract itself either void or voidable (v), and it being, further, made specially clear by other provisions of the statute that parliament was quite alive to the importance of this particular remedy, and that, whenever it was thought a suitable one in any particular case, it was so enacted in express terms (w).

569 The *quantum* of damage recoverable by a successful plaintiff in proceedings for breach of the statutory duty is determined in accordance with well-established rules which, in their application to contracts to take or purchase shares or debentures of a company, are as follows. On the one side of the account must be placed all sums which the plaintiff has paid,

(s) See *Whiteman* v *Sadler*, [1910] A C 514, H L. (*per* Lord DUNEDIN, at pp 525-527), and the cases there cited, and the observations of SWINFEN EADY, L J , at pp 408, 409 of *Re Blair Open Hearth Furnace Co* , [1914] 1 Ch 390, C A.

(t) See s. 81, (6), where a "liability in respect of the non-compliance" (i e "with any of the requirements of this section") is twice alluded to as a liability which, under certain conditions, is not to be incurred, thereby clearly implying (as SWINFEN EADY, J , observed, at p 577 of *Re South of England Natural Gas & Petroleum Co* , [1911] 1 Ch 573), that, in the absence of those conditions, such liability exists And, since no special remedy is prescribed by the enactment for the breach of the duty which it has created, that liability can only mean a liability to damages In none of the cases as yet decided under s 81 has it been suggested that damages is not the proper form of relief, if the liability of the defendant is established

(u) See, for instance, *Re Coal Economizing Gas Co* , *Gover's Case* (1875), 1 C D 182, C A (*per* JAMES, L J , at p 189, and BRAMWELL, B , at p 193)

(v) See *Re Wimbledon (Olympia), Ltd* , [1910] 1 Ch 630 (*per* NEVILLE, J , at p 632 "the section does not in terms so provide, and I cannot attribute to the legislature the intention that the mere fact of the omission of any of the facts required by this section to be stated should give the shareholders this right to get rid of their shares " The motion here was to rectify the register on the ground of the omission from the prospectus of matters required by s 81, (1), (d), and (k), to be stated therein), *Re South of England Natural Gas & Petroleum Co* , sup (per SWINFEN EADY, J , at p 576) In *Roussell* v *Burnham*, [1909] 1 Ch 127 (*per* PARKER, J , at p 133), it was not necessary to decide the point and in *Sleigh* v *Glasgow & Transvaal Options, Ltd* (1904), 6 F. 420, the company, who succeeded on other grounds, did not raise it

(w) As in s. 86, (1), of the Act, on which see § 570, note (c), *post* , also s 82 which prohibits allotment, and therefore avoids it, and any contract founded on it, unless a statement in lieu of prospectus has been filed in the prescribed manner and form see *Re Blair Open Hearth Furnace Co* , sup

and the estimated present value of all sums (if any) which he is liable to pay, under the contract, or in respect of the shares or debentures. On the other side is to be placed the real or actual value (if any) of the shares or debentures at the date of the allotment or transfer. The excess (if any) of the total of the sums so paid or payable over the real value (if any) of the shares or debentures at the date named is the measure of damage. Such "real value" means the price which the securities would have fetched in any reasonable dealing, if the whole truth of the undisclosed facts had been within the knowledge of those fixing the price it must, therefore, be ascertained in the light of the evidence adduced, and without regard to current or market prices, which may be the mere manufacture of the very persons whose misconduct has given the plaintiff his right to damages If the real value at the material date is found to be *nil*, as not infrequently is the case, the plaintiff is entitled to the whole of what he has paid On the other hand, if it is a complete equivalent, he has sustained no damage at all It is the duty of the plaintiff to minimize the damages in the interests of whom it may concern, if a real opportunity is afforded him of doing so Thus, he would not be justified in continuing to pay calls with his eyes open, and so heaping up the damages, after a sincere and *bonâ fide* offer by the company to avoid the contract, and restore everything received by them under it, but a mere half-hearted and obscure admission of a breach of duty, unaccompanied by any such offer, would clearly leave the plaintiff entitled, and bound, to go on meeting all liabilities under the contract, and adding the amount of his payments to the damages (x).

(x) For instances of the application of the measure of damage stated in the text to cases under s 38 of the Act of 1867, see *Twycross v Grant* (1877), 2 C P D 469, C A (per Lord COLERIDGE, C J, at pp 489-491, BRAMWELL, L J, at pp 503-505, and COCKBURN, C J, at pp 542-546), *Jury v Stoker* (1881), 9 L R (Ir) 385, C A , *Cackett v Keswick*, [1902] 2 Ch 456, C A (per FARWELL, J, at pp 468, 469), *McConnell v Wright* [1903] 1 Ch 546, C A (per COLLINS, M R, at pp 552-555, ROMER, L J, at pp 556-9 and COZENS HARDY, L J, at p 559), *Broome v Speak*, [1903] 1 Ch 586, C A (per BUCKLEY, J, at p 605, COLLINS, M R, at pp 622, 623, and COZENS HARDY, L J, at p 630); S C, sub nom *Shepheard v Broome*, [1904] A C 342, H L (per Lord LINDLEY, at pp 347, 348), *Stevens v Hoare* (1904), 20 T L R 407 (per JOYCE, J, at p 409), *J & P Coats, Ltd v Crossland* (1904), 20 T L R 800 For a statement of the rule in its application to the Directors' Liability Act, 1890 (now s 84 of the Act of 1908), as to "untrue statements" in the prospectus, see *Thomson v Lord Clanmorris*, [1899] 2 Ch 523 (per KEKEWICH, J, at p 529, whose decision was affirmed, [1900] 1 Ch 718, C A) For cases of common law misrepresentation in prospectuses where the principles on which the damage is to be calculated are enunciated and applied, see *Arkwright v Newbold* (1881), 17 C D 301, C A (per FRY, J, at pp 312, 313 the decision itself was reversed by the C A, who gave judgment for the defendant, and, therefore, found it unnecessary to consider the question of the measure of damages), *Peek v Derry* (1887), 37 C D 541, C A (per COTTON, L J, at pp 591-593, and Sir JAMES HANNEN, and LOPES, L J, at p 594 the principles there laid down being of course unaffected by the subsequent reversal of the decision itself in the H L), *Arnison v Smith* (1888), 41 C D 348, C A (per Lord HALSBURY, L C, at pp 369, 370), *Glasier v Rolls* (1889), 42 C D 436, C A (per KEKEWICH, J, at p 455 here, again, the statement of the rule as to measure of damages is unaffected by the fact that the C A reversed the decision of KEKEWICH, J, in favour of the plaintiff) In *Twycross v Grant, sup*, and *Jury v Stoker, sup*, the damages were assessed by a jury, under a proper direction from the judge In the remainder, which were tried before a judge alone, the Court first laid down the principles, and then either applied them to the circumstances of the case for the purposes of an immediate assessment,

570. It should be mentioned here that, as regards two of the matters required to be stated in the prospectus, there may be cases in which, indirectly but effectually, additional protection and security is provided for the public by other sections of the statute   The first of these matters is the " minimum subscription on which the directors may proceed to allotment," which is one of the most important of the items specified in the statutory catalogue (*y*). There are, in ss. 85, 86 of the Act of 1908 (*z*), further provisions in regard to this subject of a somewhat stringent character.   No allotment can legally be made unless " the amount (if any) fixed by the memorandum or articles *and named in the prospectus* as the minimum subscription . .   or, if no amount is so fixed *and named*, then the whole amount of the share capital so offered for subscription, has been subscribed, and the sum payable on application for the amount so fixed *and named*,"—which sum must not be less than five per cent of the nominal amount of the share—" or for the whole amount offered for subscription has been paid to and received by the company " (*a*) ; and, if these conditions are not complied with before the expiration of forty days after the first issue of the prospectus, all moneys received by the company must be repaid to the applicants without interest, failing which repayment within a period of eight further days, the directors are to be jointly and severally liable for the amount with five per cent interest, except as to any director who can prove that the loss of the money was not due to any misconduct or negligence on his part (*b*) ;   any allotment made without conforming to the stated requiremen   be voidable at the instance of any applicant within one month of t   utory meeting of the company, and not later, and may be so avoided notwithstanding that the company is in liquidation, and, as an alternative remedy, any director

or (where the evidence, though sufficient to sustain the plaintiff's burden of proving some damage, was not specific enough for the purpose of quantifying it at once) directed an inquiry, as in *Cackett* v *Keswick, sup* (*per* FARWELL, J , at p 468), *McConnell* v. *Wright, sup* , *Shepheard* v *Broome, sup* (*per* Lord LINDLLY, at pp 347, 348, who there points out the convenience of adopting this course), *J & P Coats, Ltd* v *Crossland, sup* (*per* SWINFEN EADY, J , at p 807)   In *Arkwright* v, *Newbold, sup* , though the evidence was inadequate,—indeed, there was none at all,—for the purpose of ascertaining the amount, FRY, J , in order to save expense, and without objection on the part of the defendant, made an extemporaneous and summary estimate of the damage, which he put at one half of what the plaintiff had paid (p 313)   In *Twycross* v *Grant, sup* , *Jury* v *Stoler, sup* , and *Thomson* v *Lord Clanmorris, sup* , the application of the rules to the evidence resulted in a finding that the shares were wholly valueless at the material date, and the amount of damage was, therefore, the whole sum paid for the shares, without any deduction   On the other hand, in *Stevens* v *Hoare, sup* , the opposite extreme resulted, it being there found by JOYCE, J (p 409), that the plaintiff had failed to prove that the real value of the shares at the material dates was not fully equal to the sum which he had paid for them   In the present class of case the remedy by injunction, which is theoretically available to the plaintiff, as stated in the text, is wholly out of place   contrast the classes of case referred to in note (*c*), *post*, and in § 571, note (*m*), *post*, where it is of distinct utility to the party aggrieved.

(*y*) S 81, (1), (d) of the Act of 1908, as to which see § 526, *ante*

(*z*) These are reproductions of ss 4 and 5, respectively, of the Act of 1900

(*a*) S 85, sub ss (1), (2), (3), which repeat s 4, sub ss (1), (2), (3), of the Act of 1900

(*b*) S 85, sub s (4), to which s 4, sub s (4) of the Act of 1900 corresponds   Relief under s 4, as well as under s 5, of the Act of 1900, was sought in *Burton* v *Bevan*, [1908] 2 Ch 240, but was refused for the reason given in note (*q*), *inf*   The plaintiff's case for relief under s 5 failed for the reason stated in note (*f*), *inf*

who knowingly contravenes this provision, or permits or authorizes the illicit allotment, is rendered liable to compensate either the company, or any allottee, for any loss, damages, or costs which it, or he, may have sustained or incurred thereby, provided that proceedings for the recovery of such compensation must be instituted within two years from the allotment (c), and any stipulations for the waiver of these requirements is to be void (d). An additional stimulus to the due observance of the provisions of s 81 (1) as to the disclosure of the minimum subscription is thus provided ; for, unless the minimum subscription fixed by the memorandum and articles is also "named in the prospectus," the company and directors will be liable to the various consequences indicated if they do not receive the whole of the amount of the capital offered for subscription, and not merely the "fixed" amount, or (as the case may be) if they proceed to allotment without having received such whole (e). To "knowingly contravene" the statutory provisions means to allot with a knowledge of the facts which render the allotment a contravention of such provisions (f). The return of the application moneys is the only remedy available before the directors have proceeded to allotment; the avoidance of the allotment and the compensation is the only remedy available after that date (g). None of the remedies provided by ss 85, 86, have any application to the latter part of the earlier enactment which, in the case of a second

(c) S 86 of the Act of 1908   For examples of relief under this section, or rather under s 5 of the Act of 1900 which it reproduces, see *Re National Motor Mail Coach Co., Anstis's and McLean's Claims*, [1908] 2 Ch 228 (rectification of register, which, since the company was in liquidation, would have been impossible but for the express words in the statute which are referred to in the text, *per* SWINFEN EADY, J., at p 234), *Roussell* v *Burnham*, [1909] 1 Ch. 127 (removal of name from register, and return of money paid. *per* PARKER, J) In *Burton* v *Bevan*, *inf*, the action failed, so far as it rested on s 5 of the Act of 1900, not, however, because the wrong relief was applied for, but for the reason given in note (f), *inf*   Interlocutory injunctions to restrain the company from allotment were applied for in *Means* v *Western Canada Pulp & Paper Co*, [1905] 2 Ch 353, C A, and a *Sherwell* v *Combined Incandescent Mantles Syndicate, Ltd* (1907), 23 T L R 482, successfully in the former case   but (there being no proof of an "offer to the public") unsuccessfully in the latter

(d) S 85, (5)

(e) See *Roussell* v *Burnham*, *sup*, which is an excellent illustration of the indirect enforcement of the requirements of s 81, (1), (d), by means of ss 85, 86   for in that one alone of the cases cited, the minimum subscription had been "fixed" by the articles, but had not been also "named" in the prospectus, or rather (which makes the case a still more striking illustration) had been named in one of the two prospectuses issued, but not in the other, on the faith of which latter the plaintiff took his shares , and it was held that the company was bound to cancel the plaintiff's application, remove his name from the register, and return his money, for, though they had not in fact proceeded to allotment on less than the amount of the minimum fixed by the articles, yet, as against the plaintiff, they could not lawfully allot unless the whole amount of the issue had been subscribed (*per* PARKER, J , at pp 130–132)

(f) *Burton* v. *Bevan*, [1908] 2 Ch 240 (*per* NEVILLE, J , at pp 247, 248)   In so far as this action was based on s 5 of the Act of 1900 (= s 86 of the Act of 1908), it was dismissed on the ground that the defendant was not shown to have been aware of the facts which made the allotment a contravention of the section   For the similar interpretation of "knowingly issued" in s 38 of the Act of 1867, see the cases cited in note (s) to § 556, *ante*

(g) *Burton* v *Bevan*, *sup* (*per* NEVILLE, J , at pp 245, 246)   The plaintiff here sued for relief under both s 4 and s 5 of the Act of 1900 (corresponding to s 85, and s 86, respectively, of the Act of 1908), and his claim under the former section for a return of the application moneys was defeated on the ground that the allotment had been already made when the plaintiff took proceedings.

or subsequent offer of shares, requires a statement in the prospectus of the amount offered for subscription on each such previous allotment, and the amounts actually allotted, and paid on allotment (h). The avoidance by the applicant of the allotment, which must be within the time above specified, means notice of repudiation and intention to avoid, not the institution of proceedings for that purpose, which need not be commenced within the "one month" (i) The payment to, and receipt by, the company which is required by s 85, (1), is a payment and receipt in cash, not by cheques which are subsequently dishonoured (j)

571. The second of the two matters above mentioned is "the amount (if any) paid within the two preceding years, or payable, as commission for subscribing, or agreeing to subscribe, or procuring or agreeing to procure subscript , for any shares in, or debentures of, the company, or the rate of any su commission " (k). Here, again, there is a later section of the statute which, in the same indirect manner as in the case of "the minimum subscri ion," may in some cases operate as an additional security for the performance of the duty to disclose This is s. 89, reproducing s 8 of the Act of 1900, which, as regards shares only, prohibits payment of commission for any of the purposes stated, unless the payment of such commission is authorized by the articles, *and the amount or rate per cent of the commission paid or agreed to be paid is disclosed in the prospectus* (l) Consequently, any company or director paying a commission to an amount, or at a rate, authorized by the articles of association, will nevertheless be committing an illegal act, unless such amount or rate is also disclosed in the prospectus the remedies being either an injunction at the instance of a shareholder to restrain the company from applying its shares or capital money, directly or indirectly, in payment of any such commission, or of any equivalent in the form of a discount, or allowance (m), or an action by the company itself against its directors for the restoration and replacement of moneys so misapplied (n)

572 There being nothing in the enactment, or in the residue of the Act

(h) See *Re South of England Natural Gas & Petroleum Co*, [1911] 1 Ch 573 (*per* SWINFEN EADY, J, at pp 576, 577)

(i) *Re National Motor Mail Coach Co, Instis s and Maclean's Claims*, [1908] 2 Ch 228 (*per* SWINFEN EADY, J, at pp 234, 235) As to the "statutory meeting," see s 65 of the Act of 1908

(j) *Mears v Western Canada Pulp & Paper Co*, [1905] 2 Ch 353, C A ; *Re National Motor Mail Coach Co*, *sup* (*per* SWINFEN EADY, J, at pp 233, 234), *Burton v Beran*, [1908] 2 Ch 240 (*per* NEVILLE, J, at p 245) In all the above cases, the cheques which the company treated as cash were not in fact honoured, and the defendants were accordingly held liable It may be otherwise, however, where the cheque is immediately afterwards duly met, as in *Glasgow Pavilion, Ltd v Motherwell* (1903), 6 F 116, which case, being distinguishable on this ground, may be good law . see, however, the powerful dissentient judgment of Lord MONCRIEFF

(k) S 81, (1), (h), of the Act of 1908, as to which see § 529, *ante*

(l) See *Re Worthington*, [1914] 2 K B 299, C A , for a case held not within the section

(m) As in *Burrows v. Matabele Gold Reefs & Estates Co*, [1901] 2 Ch 33, C A ; *Booth v New Afrikander Gold Mining Co*, [1903] 1 Ch 295, C A

(n) As in *Dominion of Canada Trading & Investment Syndicate v Brigstocke*, [1911] 2 K B 648, Div Ct Conversely a payment of commission which, though named in the prospectus, is not authorized by the articles would be equally illegal, as was recognized in *Re Republic of Bolivia Exploration Syndicate*, [1914] 1 Ch. 139

of 1908, which affects any right or liability under the existing law, whether statutory or non-statutory, and no special remedy being provided by s. 81, it follows that, on general principles, all such rights and liabilities remain undisturbed (o), but, for greater caution, sub-s. (9) of s. 81 expressly provides that "nothing in this section shall limit or diminish any liability which any person may incur under the general law or this Act apart from this section." And, as was the practice in the earlier cases (p), a combination of statutory and common law remedies may be enforced in one and the same proceeding against the same or different defendants, if the imperfections of the prospectus constitute the one common ground of complaint.

(o) See § 513, ante

(p) See (to take a few examples out of many) *Greenwood* v. *Leather Shod Wheel Co.,* [1900] 1 Ch 421, C. A , where the plaintiff sued for rescission, and rectification of the register, on the ground of common law misrepresentation, damages under the Directors' Liability Act, 1890 (now s. 84 of the Act of 1908), and damages for omission of contracts under s 38 of the Act of 1867 ; *J & P. Coats, Ltd.* v *Crossland* (1904), 20 T. L R. 800 (the like combination), *Hoole* v. *Speak,* [1904] 2 Ch 732 (where the plaintiff sued for relief under each of the two enactments above referred to).

CHAPTER VII.

CONCEALMENT FROM COURTS, PUBLIC AUTHORITIES, AND OTHER THIRD PERSONS

573. THERE are a variety of cases in which one of two parties may have a right to relief in respect of the other's failure to disclose material facts to a third person or to a public authority, if such failure injuriously affects his (the first party's) proprietary interests. These cases do not fall within the scope of any of the preceding Chapters, because the duty which is violated is not (primarily and directly, at least) a duty owed to the party aggrieved. They have accordingly been reserved for separate treatment in this place (q). The main types of such non-disclosure or concealment are three: first, where a judicial tribunal, English or foreign, is misled by non-disclosure or concealment to pronounce a judgment, or make an order, or execute any other judicial act, to the prejudice of one of the parties to the litigation; secondly, where the Crown or the State, or a public authority, is similarly misled to make a grant to, or confer a right or privilege upon, one subject to the prejudice of another or others; thirdly, where material facts are withheld from a third person, or class of persons, not being a judicial or executive officer, or a public authority.

SECT. 1. CONCEALMENT OF MATERIAL FACTS FROM A JUDICIAL TRIBUNAL.

Sub-s (1) English Judgments, &c., procured by Non-Disclosure

574 It has been undoubted law since at least the time of Coke, and probably from a much earlier date (r), that "acts of the highest judicial authority," though "not to be impeached from within," are yet "impeachable from without", for, "although it is not permitted to show that the court was mistaken, it may be shown that they were misled. Fraud is an extrinsic collateral act, which vitiates the most solemn proceedings of courts of justice. Lord COKE says, it avoids all judicial acts, ecclesiastical or

(q) A corresponding class, in cases of misrepresentation to persons other than those entitled to relief, is separately considered in Ch XIV of the author's *Law of Actionable Misrepresentation*

(r) For *deceptio curiæ* was punishable both as a contempt of the Crown, and as a wrong to the party, as early as the time of King John, and was indeed the principal, if not the only, subject of the writ of deceit in its earliest form, as explained in App A, Sect. 1, Sub s. (1), of the author's *Law of Actionable Misrepresentation*

temporal " (s)   Accordingly every " judicial act " procured by the fraud of
one of the parties to the litigation has always been held voidable at the instance
of the other party, but, unless and until so impeached, valid ; where, however, it is the result of the collusion of both parties, it is a *fabula, non judicium,*
and is void *ab initio* (t). The " fraud " referred to usually assumes the form
of fraudulent misrepresentation, with or without fraudulent suppression
of material facts   But, in the large sense of the term, " fraud " includes
any breach of the duty—where it exists—of full and candid disclosure to
the Court, and there are several cases, putting aside all those of pure misrepresentation (u), in which judgments and orders obtained by means of
non-disclosure have on that ground been set aside at the instance of the
party against whom, or to whose detriment, they were pronounced, though
it has often so happened that positive mendacity constituted a further
ground of avoidance   The duty of disclosure to the Court, apart from
the duty to abstain from falsehood, must of course be shown in order
to entitle the party to relief.   When does such a duty exist ?   In the first
place, whenever the Court, in its capacity of guardian and protector of
persons under disability, is concerned to inquire whether a particular compromise or other transaction would, or would not, be for the benefit of any such
person, and ought or ought not to be approved accordingly, every party has
the same obligation of candour and good faith to the Court for the purpose
of procuring its sanction as he has towards the other parties to the proposed
compromise in the course of his negotiations with them for the purpose of
procuring their assent (v)   Similarly, when the Court, in the course of

(s) *The Duchess of Kingston's Case* (1776), 2 Sm L C (11th edtn) 731
(t) *Boswell* v *Coaks* (1804), 6 R 167, H L (*per* Lord SELBORNE, L C , at pp 168, 169)
(u) Such as *Priestman* v *Thomas* (1884), 9 P D 210, C A ; *Cole* v *Langford*, [1898]
2 Q B 36, Div Ct , *Sharrock* v *Littlejohn* (1898), 68 L J. (Q B) 165, Div Ct , *White* v
Ivory (1900), *Times*, 27th April
(v) See *Brooke* v *Lord Mostyn* (1865), 2 De G J & S 373   This was a case of a compromise which required the sanction of the Court, infants being concerned   In the
proceedings before the Master with th view of obtaining this sanction, the defendant
failed to disclose a certain valuation of the property, which was of the utmost materiality
to the question of the terms on which the proposed compromise ought to be approved   On
this ground, KNIGHT BRUCE and TURNER, LL JJ , reversing the Court below, set aside
the decree sanctioning the compromise, as well as the compromise itself (*per* TURNER, L J ,
at pp 421–424, and KNIGHT-BRUCE, L J , at pp 424, 425)   The case was treated as one
of non disclosure, and not of misrepresentation, for, though misrepresentation was also
alleged it was not satisfactorily proved (*per* TURNER, L J , at pp 419–421), and the
concealment was dealt with as a breach of duty to the Court, and precisely the same
principles (substituting the Court for the party) were applied to the determination of this
question as would have been applied in a compromise case of non disclosure as between
the parties   " the orders of the Court cannot be set aside on grounds less strong than
those which would be required to set aside the transaction between competent parties "
(*per* TURNER, L J , at p 416)   " I think it plain," said KNIGHT-BRUCE, L J (at pp
424, 425), " that there were before the Master persons whose duty *to the Court*, and to
the infant, it was to bring under the attention of the Master every material fact within
their knowledge, but who omitted to lay before him material facts within their knowledge "   And, similarly (at p 424), TURNER, L J , concluded —" under all the circumstances of the case, but more especially having regard to the non production of Sisson's
valuation, my opinion is that this compromise cannot stand and that the decree, *therefore*, cannot be supported " (meaning that the same non disclosure which, in relation to
the party, was sufficient to invalidate the compromise was, when proved to have been

administering an estate, or otherwise, directs a sale of property, and so (in a sense) becomes the vendor, every purchaser is subject to such duty of disclosure—it is an extremely limited one—to the judicial vendor as he would owe to a non-judicial vendor in the case of a sale with which no Court had any concern (w). The like duty arises where a transaction requires the approval of the Court in bankruptcy proceedings (x), or where the Court orders an inquiry before an expert to inform its own mind on any particular subject (y), or where, there being at common law a duty of full disclosure to the Crown or the State, as in the case of patents for an invention, the legislature has substituted the Court for the Crown, or for the King in Council, as the authority to deal with applications for the grant or for the extension of any such patent, in which case the disclosure is owed no longer to the original, but to the substituted, authority (z).

practised on the Court, equally sufficient to invalidate the judicial sanction which had been given to that compromise

(w) Thus, in *Coaks* v *Boswell* (1886), 11 App Cas 232, H L, Lord SELBORNE, L C, was at great pains to explain that the duty of a purchaser of property sold by direction of the Court is to make such disclosure to the Court as is required to be made in other cases of sale by the purchaser to his vendor,—no more and no less and that this duty is an extremely restricted one, has been explained in § 165, *ante*. "At pp 153, 154 of 27 C D," he observes at p 240, "it is said that 'a person desirous of buying property which is sold under the direction of the Court must either abstain from laying any information before the Court in order to obtain its approval, or he must lay before it all the information that he possesses, and which it is material that the Court should have to enable it to form a judgment on the subject under consideration' As a general and abstract proposition, this seems to me to be too broadly stated I do not think that because information on some material point or points is offered, or given on request, by a purchaser from the Court, it must also be given on all others, as to which it is neither offered nor requested, and concerning which there is no implied representation, positive or negative, direct or indirect, in what is already stated The case of *Brooke* v *Lord Mostyn* was unlike the present" The concluding remark means that *Brooke* v *Lord Mostyn*, *sup*—see the last note—was a case of a compromise, which involves a duty of disclosure between the parties, and, consequently, a duty from each of them to the Court which is asked to sanction it; whereas *Coaks* v *Boswell* was a case of sale and purchase, in which a purchaser ordinarily owes no duty to the vendor except to tell the *whole* truth on any matter as to which he volunteers information, or is asked a question, and, therefore, owes no greater duty to the Court when he is (in a sense) purchasing from the Court

(x) *Motion* v *Moojen* (1872) L R 14 Eq 202, where, amongst other forms of deceit practised upon it, the party had concealed the existence of a certain supplemental agreement from the Bankruptcy Court, whose approval was sought to a proposed sale and purchase (*per* BACON, V -C, at pp 214, 215 "there is no suggestion that that"—i e the agreement—"was communicated to the Chief Clerk, so that when he approved the sale, he was aware of the terms contained in the supplemental agreement" It so happened that here the motion failed, because there was held to be no jurisdiction to entertain it Cp *Re Spink* (1913), 108 L T 572, a case in which the leave of the Court of Bankruptcy was required, and, on full disclosure made, was given, to a sale of the bankrupt's business to a company promoted ' trustee and committee of inspection, a transaction which otherwise would have been not only voidable at common law, but also void in virtue of the prohibition contained in Rule 316 of the Bankruptcy Rules, 1886 See another motion in the same case (1913), 108 L T 811, where PHILLIMORE, J, on application and disclosure to him of the facts, sanctioned the payment by the trustee (then carrying on the business) of cost prices out of the estate, but not profit-charges (this being contrary to Rule 317 of the above Bankruptcy Rules)

(y) As in *Flower* v *Lloyd* (1879), 10 C D 327, C A, where, an inquiry having been directed before an expert, it was alleged (see pp 329, 330) that part of a certain process which was the subject of the inquiry had not been disclosed to the expert In this case, however, the ' concealed part, ' even assuming concealment to have been established, was held immaterial See § 576, note (f), *post*

(z) See note (j) to § 581, *post*

575 More especially is complete disclosure and the utmost good faith required from a solicitor who is an officer of the Court (a). It is also essential in all cases of *ex parte* applications to any judicial tribunal (b). Thus, where a decree of foreclosure had been made against an absent mortgagor, under the provisions of 7 Geo. 2, c. 14, at the instance of a mortgagee who, though complying with the formal requirements of the statute, omitted to inform the Court that the mortgagor's absence was due to his imbecility, and also withheld documents and material information from the Master on taking the account, relief was given to the mortgagor by a declaration that his equity of redemption was not to be deemed barred by the decree, on the ground that the mortgagee had violated his duty of disclosure to the Court, as well as to the party (c). So an order made under 3 & 4 W. 4, c. 74, s. 91, and 20 & 21 Vict. c. 57, s. 1, on the *ex parte* application of a married woman, enabling her to charge her interest in personal property without the concurrence of her husband, was set aside on proof of suppression of material information from the Court making the order (d). And where the executor dative of a deceased owner of land in Natal had obtained from the Court *ex parte* orders for delivery of certified copies of the title deeds, without disclosing the fact that the occupier of the lands held under a possession alleged by him to be lawful, and which might possibly have been accompanied by possession of the title deeds, and such executor had then proceeded to effect and register the transfer, the orders, as well as the transfer, were set aside on the ground (as regards the former) of " material concealment " from the Court (e).

576 The burden of proof on the party seeking the annulment of a " judicial act " procured by non-disclosure to the Court is, *mutatis mutandis,*

(a) See *Harbin v. Masterman*, [1896] 1 Ch 351, C A, where it was established that a solicitor, purporting to have the conduct of an appeal on behalf of a client, and in her interests, was in truth doing so entirely in his own interests, and on the terms that the client should be indemnified, and should suffer no loss, and derive no benefit, in either event whereupon the Court of Appeal, taking the matter into their own hands, called upon the solicitor to show cause why he should not pay the costs of the unsuccessful appeal and, on his failure to give any satisfactory explanation made an order accordingly, on the ground that he had deceived the Court by withholding from them the above understanding with his client (*per* RIGBY, L.J , at pp 369–372) It will be observed that the concealment here was not from the client (who was, moreover, perfectly indifferent as to the solicitor's proceedings), but solely and entirely from the Court Cp *Re S, a Solicitor* (1910), 55 Sol J 127, where, on the ground that material facts had been withheld from the Court, an order to tax, obtained *ex parte* on a petition of course, was discharged

(b) *Dalglish v. Jarvie* (1850), 2 Macn & G 231 (*per* ROLFE B, one of the Commissioners of the Great Seal, at p 243, holding that an interlocutory injunction obtained *ex parte* by suppression of material facts ought to be dissolved immediately the undisclosed facts are brought to the notice of the Court), *London Assurance Co v Mansel* (1879), 11 C D 363, a case of insurance, in which JESSEL, M P (at p 368) used the last cited case as an illustration of the principles of good faith in the matter of disclosure which are applicable to all transactions *uberrimæ fidei*

(c) *Carew v. Johnston* (1805), 2 Sch & Lefr 280, *per* Lord REDESDALE, L C (Ir), at pp 298–301, and again, at p 306, where the decision is based " on the ground of unconscientious advantage being (*by means of a Court of Justice*) taken of the imbecility and absence of this man, by which gross injustice has been done, and *in fact a fraud practised on the Court* "

(d) *Ex p Cockerell* (1878), 4 C. P. D 39 (*per* Lord COLERIDGE, C J , at p 39, and LINDLEY, J , at p 40)

(e) *Crowly v. Bergtheil*, [1899] A. C. 374, P C (at pp 388, 389).

or rather, perhaps, *additis addendis*, substantially the same as that which rests on a party seeking rescission of a transaction voidable on the ground of non-disclosure to himself In the ordinary type of case, the first matters to be established by the party complaining are the existence of the duty of disclosure to himself by reason of some relation which gives rise to the duty, and the fact that the undisclosed circumstance was the subject of the particular duty, that is, was material to be communicated as between persons standing to one another in the relation proved So, in the present class of case, facts must be shown which indicate a duty of communication *to the Court*, and the materiality of the undisclosed fact *for the Court* to know (*f*) for, unless such a duty can be established, no party litigant is bound to divulge to the Court, any more than to his opponent, any evidence against himself Of course, if required to make an affidavit of documents, he must reveal every material document, and he must further answer truthfully all questions put to him in the witness-box, or by interrogatories but, if not so required, or if not called as a witness, or interrogated, he is under no legal obligation to throw his cards on the table, or allow his hand to be over-looked for his own protection, and in the defence of his rights and interests, he is entitled in any ordinary case to use all that legitimate reserve and secrecy which the Roman jurists denominated *dolus bonus*. Where there would be no duty of disclosure, or only a limited duty, as between two individuals, no duty, or only an equally limited duty, is owed by either of the litigants to the Court which is protecting the other, or which has assumed the conduct and direction of the transaction

(*f*) See Ch III, Sect 3, Sub s (1), *ante*, as to the onus on the party complaining of proving the relation between the parties which gives rise to the duty of disclosure, and as to he necessity of establishing the materiality of the undisclosed fact As to the meaning of materiality, see Ch II, Sect 2, *ante* For illustrations of the burden of showing that the withheld fact is one which it was material *for the Court* to know, in the class of case now under discussion, see *Charter v Trevelyan* (1844), 11 Cl & Fin 714 (where the correct copies of certain documents withheld from the Court would not have affected the result if disclosed, and relief on this ground was accordingly refused *per* Lord LYNDHURST, L C, at p 739), *Brooke v Lord Mostyn* (1864), 2 De G J & S 373, where the materiality of the suppressed valuation, together with the other ingredients in the necessary proof, having been duly established, relief was granted (*per* TURNER, L J, at pp 422, 423 ' the materials necessary to enable a fair judgment to be formed upon the question whether the compromise was for the benefit of the infant were not fairly and properly brought before the Master's consideration,'' and, again, at p 423 "I am satisfied that information was withheld which was material to have been given, and which, if given, might have altered the conclusion arrived at"), *Flower v Lloyd* (1879), 10 C D 327, C A (where the party endeavouring to upset the judgment failed for the reason, amongst others, that he had not shown that if every one of the lithographic stones alleged to have been concealed had been disclosed to the expert appointed by the Court, his report would have substantially differed *per* BAGGALLAY, L J, at p 333), *Boswell v Coaks* (1894), 6 R 167, H L (where the plaintiff wholly failed to satisfy the Court that the omitted passage from a certain letter would, if disclosed, have affected the result. *per* Lord SELBORNE, L.C, at pp 171–174), *Crowly v Bergtheil*, [1899] A C 374, P C (where the concealment was shown to be material p 388), *Re Johnson's Patent*, [1909] 1 Ch 114 (*per* PARKER, J, at p 126, who held that the undisclosed fact was "obviously material" for the Court to know) In *Birch v Birch*, [1902] P 130, C A, it was held that there must be a suggestion in the statement of claim, if it is to escape being struck out as frivolous and vexatious, of facts discovered since the trial, and not disclosed thereat, which, if proved, would constitute a reasonable ground for reversing the judgment, though they need not necessarily be such as would have been evidence at the trial (*per* VAUGHAN WILLIAMS, L.J, at pp 136, 137)

or is asked to sanction it (g).   Next, as in cases where there is no intervention of any judicial tribunal, the party seeking relief from the judgment, order, or other "judicial act" must establish the existence or occurrence of the alleged undisclosed matter, and the fact of its non-disclosure, though here it is the Court, and not the party, or not the party alone, who must be shown to have been kept in the dark (h)   Lastly (again as in the ordinary type of case) he must show that the party charged had knowledge of the uncommunicated fact (i), and that he was himself ignorant of it (j), at all material dates

577   It does not signify what is the precise nature of the "judicial act" which is sought to be invalidated   It may be a judgment, decree, or order, pronounced or made by a court of equity, or by a court of common law, in an ordinary action, or an adjudication or order in bankruptcy, or an order conferring a privilege or power or licence, or imposing duties, or making an appointment, whether in the exercise of inherent jurisdiction or pursuant to a statutory provision, or the sentence of an ecclesiastical or matrimonial tribunal, or a judgment of a court of probate establishing a will (k)   Questions of jurisdiction, however, sometimes arise, for the purpose of determining which the nature of the "judicial act" impugned may have to be considered. Thus, an application to set aside a bankruptcy order should be made to the judge exercising bankruptcy jurisdiction (l), and a claim to set aside a judgment establishing a will should be asserted in the Probate Division (m)

(g) See the observations of Lord SELBORNE, L C, cited in note (w) to § 571, ante   As to the classes of case where there is no duty of disclosure as between negotiating parties, see §§ 165, 166, 167, ante

(h) As to the necessity of proving the existence or occurrence of the alleged undisclosed fact, and also its non disclosure to the party complaining, in ordinary cases, see Ch III, Sect 3, Sub ss (2) and (3), ante, respectively   In most of the cases cited in the notes to the present Section, neither of these issues was disputed.

(i) The onus on the party complaining to prove that the party charged had knowledge of the undisclosed fact, in the ordinary type of case, is discussed in Ch III, Sect. 3, Sub s (4), ante   In the following cases of non disclosure to the Court it is stated, or assumed,—*Brooke* v *Lord Mostyn* (1864), 2 De G J & S 373 (per TURNER, L J, at p 423 this was a suppression of material facts which were within the knowledge of Lord Mostyn and his advisers, and were not within the knowledge of the plaintiff or of those who acted for him"), *Re Johnson's Patent*, [1909] 1 Ch 114 (per PARKER, J, at p 126 "neglect to state a fact which is within the petitioner's knowledge, and which it is obviously material that the Court should also know, is not consistent with the candour and good faith which is always required of a petitioner for extension of a patent")

(j) That, as between negotiating parties, the party complaining must, if challenged (which, however, is rarely the case), give some evidence of his own ignorance of the undisclosed fact, is shown in Ch III, Sect 3, Sub s (5), ante   The rule equally applies in cases of suppression of facts from the Court   for, if the party claiming to have the judgment set aside had cognizance of the fact in question, and did not inform the tribunal, he cannot with any justice complain of the result   See the cases cited in the last note, and also *Birch* v *Birch*, [1902] P 130, C A   In *Dunn* v *Cox* (1855), 11 Hare 61 (a case of misrepresentation to the Court), the plaintiff, though averring that he was ignorant of the true facts at the date of the consent order whereby the defendant was ordered to pay him a certain sum of money, abstained from suggesting that he did not know of them when he received the money   and on this ground, amongst others, PAGE-WOOD, V C, allowed the demurrer to the bill

(k) Illustrations of all these types of "judicial act" are to be found in the cases cited in the notes to this Section

(l) *Motion* v *Moojen* (1872), L R 14 Eq 202, *Bowler* v *Power*, [1910] 2 K B 229, 232, C A   And see, generally, on this question, Lord Halsbury's *Laws of England*, title "Bankruptcy and Insolvency," vol ii, p 56, 299, 300

(m) *Priestman* v *Thomas* (1884), 9 P D 70 (per HANNEN, P, at p 76)

Subject to such questions of exclusive jurisdiction there seems to be no reason why the judgment of any court should not be invalidated by proper proceedings instituted in either the King's Bench, or the Chancery Division (n).

578 The nature of the relief which, on proof of the requisite facts, may be granted to the party invoking the jurisdiction is twofold Either the "judicial act" impeached will be set aside, or declared inoperative, at the instance of the party aggrieved (o), or the non-disclosure will furnish the party with a good answer to any action brought, or to any plea or allegation made, against him which is founded upon the "judicial act" in question, or depends for success upon its validity (p). It should be noted here that the court of bankruptcy has peculiar powers in this respect It may inquire into the consideration of a judgment debt, and go behind and ignore a judgment proved to have been obtained by fraud (whether in the form of suppression and concealment or in that of positive misrepresentation), but it is by no means bound, and ought not, to do so except upon a very strong *primâ facie* case (q)

579 A claim for the setting aside of a judgment or order procured by suppression of material facts from the Court must be asserted by an action for that purpose, not by motion or application to the Court itself in which the judgment was pronounced or the order made (r), except in the case of an interlocutory order (s), or a judgment by default (t), in which latter event even a third person may invoke the jurisdiction on motion, if the judgment and the default were collusive (u) It should be remembered, however, that, even in the excepted classes of case, the jurisdiction to entertain an action still exists, though any resort to this procedure, where a cheaper and more convenient one is provided by the practice rules (O 27, r 15), may be penalized by a special order as to costs (v) The trial of the action is

(n) Thus, in *Dunn* v *Cox* (1853), 11 Hare 61, the bill in Chancery prayed the setting aside of an order made in the Court of Exchequer, and, though the plaintiff failed because his proof was insufficient, the jurisdiction was not disputed

(o) This was the nature of the relief prayed in most of the cases cited in the notes to this Section In *Carew* v *Johnston* (1805), 2 Sch & Lefr 280, cited in note (c) to § 575, *ante*, the decree of foreclosure was not formally set aside, but a declaration was made that the mortgagor was to be deemed to be still entitled to his equity of redemption *non obstante decreto*, which had much the same effect

(p) See the following misrepresentation cases (which are in point on this question) — *The Duchess of Kingston's Case* (1776), 2 Sm L C (11th edtn) 731 , *Perry* v *Meddowcroft* (1846), 10 Beav 122 , *Eyre* v *Smith* (1877), 2 C P D 435, C A

(q) See *Re Flatau* (1888), 22 Q B D 83, C A , *Bonler* v *Power*, [1910] 2 K. B. 229, C A

(r) *Flower* v *Lloyd* (1877), 6 C D 297, C A

(s) *Wyatt* v *Palmer*, [1899] 2 Q B 106, C A

(t) As in *Dalglish* v *Jarvie* (1850), 2 Macn & G 231.

(u) As in *Harrod* v *Benton* (1828), 8 B & C 217 (*per* Lord TENTERDEN, C J , at p 219) an execution creditor here successfully intervened on motion to set aside a collusive warrant of attorney, judgment, and execution), *Nixon* v *Loundes*, [1909] 2 Ir R 1 (*per* GIBSON, J , at p 7, KENNY, J , at pp 8, 9, and DODD, J , at p 11 here a judgment creditor, in the enforcement of a judgment honestly obtained and registered against his judgment debtor, was impeded by a judgment mortgage previously registered against such debtor by another judgment creditor whose judgment had been procured by fraudulent collusion, and on his moving to have the latter judgment set aside, the jurisdiction to grant relief on motion was asserted by the Court)

(v) *Wyatt* v *Palmer*, *sup* (*per* LINDLEY, M R , at pp 109, 110).

ordinarily by a judge, bu   nore is no reason why it should not take place
before a judge and jur\   the parties so desire, and if this mode of trial
is ordered on the summons for directions (*w*).   The old learning as to the
precise distinction between a suit by "original bill," and a suit by "supplemental bill of review," with or without leave, and, indeed, the whole procedure
by bill of review, is now obsolete (*x*).

Sub-s (2).   *Foreign Judgments procured by Non-Disclosure.*

580 A foreign judgment, that is to say, a judgment pronounced by any
court not within the English jurisdiction, whether a court of a foreign State,
or an Irish, Scottish, British-Indian, or Colonial Court, is, no less than an
English judgment, and on no other principle, treated as void by courts within
the jurisdiction, on proof that it was obtained by the fraud of one or both
of the parties (*y*), whether that fraud consisted in pure misrepresentation (*z*),
or in the suppression of material facts from the tribunal (*a*), accompanied
or not by other forms of deception practised upon it   An allegation of
such fraud, whether of a positive or negative character, is, if established,
a good plea to any action on the foreign judgment   It is not necessarily
an answer to the plea that the evidence to prove the fraudulent suppression
is the very same evidence which was used in support of the case set up by the
aggrieved party before the court which pronounced the judgment (*b*) , nor
that the foreign court was not ignorant of the truth, or was, in fact, itself
guilty of fraud (*c*).   For obvious reasons, the party can only put forward
his case by way of defence or answer, where any action is instituted within
the jurisdiction for the purpose of executing or enforcing the judgment against
him (*d*), or where, in the course of any proceedings in England, the foreign
judgment is sought to be made use of in any manner as an obstacle to the
success of his claim or defence, as the case may be, in which event he is entitled

(*w*) As was done in *White* v. *Ivory* (1910), "Times," 27th April (where CHANNELL, J ,
remarked that this was the first case in his experience, or reported, in which the issue had
been so tried, but that there was no objection in law or practice to the adoption of this
course.

(*x*) *Boswell* v. *Coaks* (1894), 6 R   167, H. L. (*per* Lord SELBORNE, at p 170)

(*y*) The principle is that the defendant has entered into an implied contract to pay
the amount of the debt declared by the judgment to be payable, and this principle is
applicable to English and foreign judgments indifferently   *Grant* v *Easton* (1883), 13
Q B. D. 302, C A (*per* Lord ESHER, M.R , at p. 303)   See, as to foreign judgments,
Abouloff v *Oppenheimer* (1882), 10 Q B. D 295, C. A. (*per* Lord COLERIDGE, C J , at p 303),
Vadala v. *Lawes* (1890), 25 Q B D 310, C. A (*per* LINDLEY, L.J , at p 316)   Anything,
therefore, which would invalidate any contract, such as breach of a duty to disclose, would
invalidate this particular type of implied contract

(*z* *Bank of Australasia* v *Nias* (1851), 16 Q B 717 (*per* Lord CAMPBELL, C J , at
p 735); *Cammell* v *Sewell* (1858), 3 H & N 617 (*per* MARTIN, B., at p 646) , *Gossain* v
Gossain (1860), 8 W. R. 196, P. C (an Indian judgment), *Ochsenbein* v. *Papelier* (1893),
8 Ch App 695 ; *Abouloff* v. *Oppenheimer, sup*

(*a*) *Vadala* v *Lawes, sup.* (see para. 7 of the statement of claim, set out at p 311),
Crowly v. *Bergtheil,* [1899] A. C 374, P. C (at p 388), cited in note (*f*) to § 576, *ante.*

(*b*) *Abouloff* v. *Oppenheimer, sup* (*per* BRETT, L.J , at p 307) , *Vadala* v. *Lawes, sup*
(*per* LINDLEY, L.J., at pp. 316–320).

(*c*) See the citations in note (*z*), *sup* , and *Price* v. *Dewhurst* (1837), 8 Sim. 270 (*per*
SHADWELL, V -C., at pp. 308, 309)

(*d*) See the cases cited in the notes to this Sub section, generally.

to ask the English Court to declare it to be. or to treat it as, an absolute nullity (e).

SECT 2.   CONCEALMENT OF MATERIAL FACTS FROM THE CROWN OR THE STATE

581. Whenever the Crown, or an officer or department of the State, is induced by suppression, or perversion, of material facts within the actual or presumptive knowledge of the grantee, to confer any privilege on a subject, whereby the rights and interests of any other subject, or of the King's other subjects in general, are proportionately curtailed, such grant, on the proper proceedings being taken by the proper parties, will be repealed, revoked, withdrawn, or avoided, or (without being formally avoided) treated as void. " The rule arises out of a duty which the law casts upon the subject of making known any previous inconsistent grant of which he may himself have notice If he neglect this duty, he is held to have deceived the King, when accepting the grant made to him, with the result that he takes nothing by his grant " (f). This rule, established from the earliest times, has been applied to grants by the Crown of estates (g), charters of incorporation (h), markets (i), monopolies in respect of inventions (j), and other exclusive rights and licences (k).

(e) As in *Price* v *Dewhurst* (1837), 8 Sim 279, *Gossain* v *Gossain* (1860), 8 W. R. 196, P C (where a party, for the purpose of establishing his claim, was forced to rely upon an Indian judgment procured by fraud, and in breach of a compromise of previous litigation, and, this judgment being treated as a nullity, his claim fell with it.

(f) *City of Vancouver* v. *Vancouver Lumber Co.*, [1911] A. C. 711, P C, at p 721. For other statements of the nature and theory of the duty, see the *Case of Alton Woods* (1600), 1 Coke Rep 40 b (*per* the Lord Keeper EGERTON, at p 51 b), Com Dig Grant, G. 8 At p. 894 of *Eastern Archipelago Co.* v. *R* (1853), 2 E & B 856, Exch. Ch (the number of the page is misprinted 568 in the report), PARKE, B, says that a charter obtained by "fraudulent concealment," as well as one procured by "false suggestion," is "void at common law " Similar rules obtained in Roman law with reference to the *fallax petitor* who obtained grants and privileges from the Emperor by fraud : see C. 1, 22, 2, 3, 4, 5.

(g) See the *Case of Alton Woods*, *sup*, *City of Vancouver* v. *Vancouver Lumber Co.*, *sup* In these, the subject was alleged to have failed to disclose to the Crown the existence of a previous inconsistent grant In the former, the case was made out · in the latter, it was not. For illustrations of cases where the King was deceived by misrepresentation, see *R et Reg.* v. *Kempe* (1694), 1 Ld Raym. 49, *Gledstanes* v. *Earl of Sandwich* (1842), 4 M & G. 995.

(h) See the misrepresentation cases of *R* v. *Boucher* (1842), 3 Q B. 641 ; *Eastern Arch·pelago Co* v *R*, *sup*, *La Banque D'Hochelaga* v *Murray* (1889), 15 App Cas. 414, P C

(i) As in *R.* v. *Butler* (1685), 3 Lev 220 ; *Great Eastern Railway Co* v *Goldsmid* (1884), 9 App Cas. 927, H. L In these cases concealment of a previous grant of a market was alleged In the former, it was proved in the latter, it was not. see note (x) to § 584, *post.*

(j) See *R* v *Wheeler* (1819), 2 B & Ald 345, *Hill* v *Thompson* (1818), 8 Taunt 375 ; *Brunton* v *Hawkes* (1821), 4 B & Ald. 541; *Morgan* v. *Seaward* (1837), 2 M & W 544; *Nickells* v *Rolls* (1849), 8 C B 679 Letters patent for inventions are now sealed with the seal of the Patent Office, pursuant to s 14, sub s (1), of the Patents and Designs Act, 1907 (7 Edw. 7, c 29), and no longer, as they were during the period of the cases above cited, with the Great Seal of the United Kingdom, and the procedure for obtaining revocation is altered, but the theory on which a patent is revoked, viz that the State is misled

(k) Such as a right to take wreck · *Alcock* v. *Cooke* (1829), 5 Bing 340. Also, an order of the Board of Trade for the release of a trustee in bankruptcy Bankruptcy Act, 1914 (4 & 5 Geo 5, c 59), s 93 (3)

582. The party entitled to raise the question of the invalidity of the grant by reason of the withholding of material information from Crown or State is, in the first place, the Attorney-General, as representing the Crown or State (*l*) ; and, secondly, every fellow-subject of the grantee who is directly or indirectly prejudiced by the grant (*m*), or even one who is not interested, provided that those who are interested would be entitled to relief if they chose to apply for it (*n*), since the prerogative of the Crown in this respect is the privilege of the subject, and the King cannot fetter the exercise and enjoyment of a privilege which is vested in him for the public good , so that, whether directly, or indirectly in virtue of his right to call upon the Crown to exercise its powers of revocation and repeal, the subject is entitled *ex debito justitiæ* to have a franchise procured by the suppression of material facts forfeited (*o*).

583. Relief against a grant which is void on the ground of non-disclosure may be given in either of two forms. The charter or patent may be repealed at the instance of the Attorney-General, whether moving *ex officio*, or on the relation of an aggrieved subject (*p*) ; in which case the repeal must ordinarily be *in toto* or not at all (*q*), but it has been held that, in cases where the undisclosed fact is a prior inconsistent grant, " the rule is qualified to this extent that, if the subject had no actual or constructive notice of the previous grant, the second grant will be good to the extent to which it may be consistent

into granting a privilege which it otherwise would not have granted, remains It is on this theory also that a petition for prolongation of the term of a patent, formerly made to the King in Council, but now to the Judge of the Chancery Division appointed to exercise this jurisdiction pursuant to s 18 of the above statute, may be dismissed on the ground of secrecy and reticence on the part of the petitioner, as it was in *Re Johnson's Patent*, [1909] 1 Ch 114, though there were many other grounds justifying the dismissal in that case See the observations of PARKER, J , at pp 125, 126 " again, it appears that in the present case the petitioner applied for a patent to protect his invention in Germany, but did not obtain one, partly, at any rate, because of a prior German patent, which was brought forward as an anticipation. It may well be that the prior patent did not in reality anticipate the petitioner's invention, but *it was, in my opinion, the duty of the petitioner to state this fact in his petition*, referring to the alleged anticipation, and giving such explanation as he might think possible or desirable. It ought not to be left to some opponent to bring out such facts as these *Neglect to state a fact which is within the petitioner's knowledge, and which it is obviously material that the Court should also know, is not consistent with the candour and good faith which is always required of a petitioner for extension of a patent.*"

(*l*) As in the *Case of Alton Woods* (1600), 1 Coke Rep 40 b ; *R.* v *Butler* (1685), 3 Lev 220 Cp. the misrepresentation cases of *R. et Reg.* v. *Kempe* (1694), 1 Ld Raym 49 , *R* v *Wheeler* (1819), 2 B & Ald. 345 , *Eastern Archipelago Co* v *R* (1853), 2 E & B 856, Exch. Ch , *La Banque d'Hochelaga* v *Murray* (1889), 15 App Cas 414, P. C (where the defendants, who were entitled to raise the question of the invalidity of a grant of a charter of incorporation to a certain company, as corporators of which they were being sued, thought it nevertheless wise to fortify their position by procuring the Attorney-General of the Colony to proceed, on their relation, by way of *scire facias* against the company for the repeal of the charter, such proceeding being consolidated with the action)

(*m*) *Alcock* v *Cooke* (1829), 5 Bing 340 , *Morgan* v *Seaward* (1837), 2 M & W 544 (*per* PARKE, B., at p 561 · "such a grant is void not against the Crown merely, but in a suit against a third person ") , *Eastern Archipelago Co* v *R* , *sup* , *La Banque d'Hochelaga* v. *Murray*, *sup*

(*n*) *Great Eastern Railway Co.* · *Goldsmid*, [1884] 9 App Cas 927, 940, H L

(*o*) *Eastern Archipelago Co.* v. *R* , *sup* , at pp 884, 886, 914

(*p*) See the cases cited in notes (*l*) and (*m*), *sup* , respectively

(*q*) *La Banque d'Hochelaga* v *Murray*, *sup* , at pp. 426–428

with the first grant, though void as to the rest " (r). Or the charter, patent, or other instrument may be treated by the Court as a nullity on the establishment by a party litigant of his right to have it so treated, when it is relied upon by the opposite party as the foundation of his case, or a link in his chain of proof (s). The procedure to obtain a repeal is information or action by way of *scire facias*, for which, however, the legislature has now substituted, in the case of patents for inventions, a petition to the Court for revocation at the instance of the Attorney-General, or of any person aggrieved (t), and, in the case of trade marks, an application to the Court by any person aggrieved, or, where the registration has been procured by fraud, the registrar himself, to make, expunge, or vary any entry in the register of trade marks (u). The right to defensive relief may be asserted by way of plea to an action for infringement of the patent (v), charter, or other instrument by which the grant is made (w)

584 The burden of proof on the party claiming relief is, *mutatis mutandis*, substantially the same as that which rests on a party complaining of the non-disclosure to him of material facts in the course of a negotiation with a view to a contract or transaction *uberrimæ fidei* That is to say, the Attorney-General, or the aggrieved subject, as the case may be, must allege and establish circumstances raising the duty of disclosure as between the grantee and the Crown, and must show that it was material for the Crown to be informed of the particular undisclosed fact (x) Secondly, he must show if challenged, the existence or occurrence, in point of fact, of that which he alleges to have been withheld from the King's notice, for instance, if it be a question of a previous inconsistent grant of land, it must be made quite clear that the grant relied upon was, in fact and in law, a grant of, or a grant which included, the very land or estate which purported to pass by the

(r) *City of Vancouver* v *Vancouver Lumber Co*, [1911] A C 711, P C, at pp 720, 721.

(s) As in the cases cited in note (m), *sup* In *R* v *Boucher* (1842), 3 Q B 641, the Court, though with great doubt and hesitation, thought it safer not to decide the question of the validity of the charter incorporating a borough, though it was involved in the question immediately before them of the validity of a rate made by that borough; the ground of the refusal being that the borough existed *de facto*, and none of the inhabitants had ever taken any steps to get the charter revoked

(t) This procedure was introduced, and the old *scire facias* procedure abolished, in the cases of patents for inventions, by s. 26 of the Patents, Designs, and Trade Marks Act, 1883 (46 & 47 Vict c 57), which is reproduced in s. 25 of the Patents and Designs Act, 1907 (7 Edw. 7, c. 29) The petition may be presented by the Attorney-General, or by any person authorized by him, or by a party aggrieved · s 25 (3) of the Act of 1907.

(u) See ss 12 and 35 of the Trade Marks Act, 1905 (5 Edw 7, c. 15)

(v) This ground of defence is expressly reserved by s 25 (2) of the Patents and Designs Act, 1907 (7 Edw. 7, c. 29) See several of the cases cited in note (j) to § 581, *ante*, for illustrations

(w) See the cases cited in note (m), *sup*

(x) As to the onus of establishing the circumstances and relation giving rise to the duty of disclosure in the course of negotiations with a view to a transaction between individuals, and of establishing that the undisclosed fact was the subject of the duty, i e was material, see Ch. III, Sect 3, Sub s (1), *ante*. As to what materiality means and includes, see Ch II, Sect. 2, *ante* The necessity of proving that the undisclosed fact was one which it was material for the Crown, or (in the case of inventions) the Court, to know is illustrated by *Johnson's Patent*, [1909] 1 Ch 114 (*per* PARKER, J, at p 126 . see the citation in note (j) to § 581, *ante*)

impeached grant (y)   Thirdly, he must establish the non-disclosure alleged (z).
but in the ordinary type of case, that is, where there is no recital in the charter
or other instrument of any inconsistent grant, or whatever the undisclosed
fact may happen to be, the onus is discharged by a mere reference to the non-
recital, from which alone, notwithstanding the usual prefatory expression, *ex certâ scientiâ*, there is an irrebuttable presumption of law that the
King could not have been informed of the withheld fact either by the grantee
or any other person, for the contrary inference would necessarily involve
an imputation upon the honour of the Crown (a).   Fourthly, it must be
shown that the subject to whom the impeached grant was made had either
actual or presumptive knowledge of the undisclosed fact, and he is presumed,
in the common case of a prior inconsistent grant, to have had knowledge of
such prior grant, if it was enrolled or otherwise recorded in some document
publici juris (b).   Lastly, it must be established that the King had no knowledge *aliunde* of the undisclosed fact.   This, however, will ordinarily be

(y) *City of Vancouver v Vancouver Lumber Co.*, [1911] A. C 711, P C   The same
obligation rests upon the party complaining in the ordinary type of case, as is explained in
Ch III, Sect 3, Sub s (2), *ante*
(z) This issue, though a negative, must be established by the party complaining in the
case of a transaction between individuals, though very slight evidence is sufficient to
throw the burden on the other side, and sometimes it may be inferred as a fact from the
nature of the transaction itself   see Ch III, Sect 3, Sub s (3), *ante*.   As to what "dis
closure" means, see Ch II, Sect 1, *ante*.
(a) *Case of Alton Woods* (1600), 1 Coke Rep 40 b (at p 51 b), *Alcock v. Cooke*
(1829), 5 Bing 340 (*per* BEST, C.J., delivering the judgment of the Court of Common Pleas,
at p 354)   Cp., as to cases of "misdescription or mistake," whereby the Crown is
deceived, *Gledstanes v Earl of Sandwich* (1842), 4 M & G 995 (*per* TINDAL, C J, at
pp 1028, 1029)   "But," says HOLT, C J, in *R et Reg. v Kempe* (1694), 1 Ld. Raym 49,
"where the words are the words of the King," that is, where the inconsistent grant,
or other alleged undisclosed fact, is recited in the charter or patent, "and it appears that
he has only mistaken the law, then he shall not be said to be deceived, to the avoidance
of the grant"   And see *Alcock v Cooke*, *sup*, at p 350   An actual and personal intention
to deceive the Crown is no more required to be proved in the present class of case, than
actual and personal intention to deceive the party complaining in the ordinary type of
case (as to which, see §§ 197, 358, 461, *ante*): truthful and complete disclosure to the
Crown being put as an implied condition of the validity of the grant, just as it is to the
validity of a contract or transaction between individuals (§ 83, *ante*), see *Eastern Archipelago v. R* (1853), 2 E & B 856 (the page is misnumbered 568 in the report), Exch Ch
(*per* MARTIN, B, at pp 871, 872)
(b) This must be proved by the party complaining in ordinary cases, as shown in
Ch. III, Sect 3, Sub s (4), *ante*.   As to "actual" and "presumptive knowledge," see
Ch. II, Sect 3, *ante*   For the rule as to the knowledge of the grantee being presumed from
the fact that the undisclosed inconsistent grant is enrolled, or otherwise of record, see the
Case of Alton Woods (1600), 1 Coke Rep 40 b (*per* Lord Keeper EGERTON, at p 51 b
"the King ought to be informed of his own estate, for if it be a lease   . of record,
whereof the subject may take notice, then   it is void"), *Alcock v Cooke*, *sup*. (*per*
BEST, C.J., at p 349: "if an individual grants a lease, and the estate of which that individual grants a lease afterwards comes to the King, if the King regrants that, as the
subject could not know with certainty that there was a previously existing lease, the
position I have been laying down would not apply.   The doctrine I am delivering is
applicable to a case where the subject cannot be deceived, and he must be deceiving the
King.   for if the King's prior lease be enrolled, the subject has the means of knowing the
existence of that lease, and it is his duty to inform the King of its existence") ; *City of
Vancouver v. Vancouver Lumber Co*, [1911] A C 711, P C (at pp 720, 721)   Here,
amongst other *probanda* which the party impeaching the grant failed to establish, was the
fact that the grantee had actual or constructive notice of the alleged previous grant of
the island in question, assuming such a grant to have been in fact made, which also was
not satisfactorily proved

presumed, just as the grantee's omission to give the required information will be presumed, and for the same reason (c) : but, where the impeached grant was made (as frequently happens in the case, for instance, of markets) after the holding of an inquiry under a writ of *ad quod damnum*, not only is no such presumption made, but a strong *primâ facie* presumption arises to the contrary, which can only be rebutted by the clearest possible evidence on the part of the subject who impeaches the grant that the inquiry was surreptitiously and dishonestly conducted (d).

SECT. 3 CONCEALMENT OF MATERIAL FACTS FROM PRIVATE THIRD PERSONS.

585. In the two classes of case hitherto considered, relief is given to a person who, though no duty of disclosure is owed to him in the first instance, is yet prejudicially affected by another's breach of duty to the Court or the State, and who, therefore, has a legitimate ground of complaint on his own merits, as an injured or aggrieved person But there is a third type of case, in which the law provides a party who has suffered no wrong, and has no merits whatever, with a way of escape from liability to an action brought against him by one who has practised a fraud, not upon him, but upon a third person. This course is adopted, not because jurisprudence desires to adopt it, but because it cannot achieve its paramount purpose of rendering such frauds unprofitable to those who resort to them without at the same time setting unmeritorious persons free In such cases the delinquent is deprived of the remedy to which he would otherwise be entitled on those considerations of public policy, morality, and decency—and on those alone—which imperatively demand the interposition of the Court (whether the party raises the point or not) whenever the assertion of a claim, or of an affirmative defence, depends for its success upon allegations or facts which disclose illegality, immorality, or other *turpis causa* The result, no doubt, is that the party who is devoid of merits, and has of course no rights of his own

(c) It has been explained that, in ordinary cases, some evidence of the ignorance *aliunde* of the party complaining must be adduced, if the matter is in dispute, as it rarely is see Ch III, Sect 3, Sub-s (5), *ante* In cases of the description now under consideration, where there is no recital of the undisclosed fact, the ignorance of the Crown will always be presumed in the first instance at all events, on the same principle that non-disclosure to the Crown will be see note (a), *sup*

(d) See *Great Eastern Railway Co.* v *Goldsmid* (1884), 9 App. Cas. 927, H. L. (*per* Lord SELBORNE, L C , at pp. 939, 940, 942) Here there had been an inquiry of the nature indicated, and the presumption therefore was that the Crown was not ignorant of the existence of the competing market, no suggestion being made that the inquiry had been improperly conducted On the other hand, in *R* v *Butler* (1685), 3 Lev. 220, where it was alleged that the defendant had obtained a grant of a market at Chatham, to the prejudice of an existing market at Rochester, by non-disclosure to the King of material circumstances, and that the King had no knowledge from other sources of the undisclosed facts, notwithstanding that a writ of *ad quod damnum* had been issued, followed by the usual inquiry, this latter allegation (supported by averments that the inquiry had been held at a place thirty miles distant from Rochester, whereas Chatham was only 1½ miles distant, and without notice to the Corporation of Rochester. and had been otherwise " mismanaged, ' and conducted " surreptitiously, fraudulently, and in deceit of them ") was held, on demurrer, to have been well pleaded.

which he can set up in any active proceedings, and who not infrequently is implicated in the very misconduct which defeats the claim made, or affirmative defence pleaded, against him, derives benefit and relief, but this is inevitable   Fraud, whether it assumes the form of conscious falsehood, or of a breach of any duty of good faith and candour, is a head of misconduct to which this principle of our law is perhaps in modern times most frequently and most inflexibly applied (e)   So familiar to us has this application now become that it is difficult to realize that there was a time when the doctrine appeared to some minds a little novel, if not dangerous.   That there was such a time, appears from the almost apologetic terms in which Lord HARDWICKE, in a memorable judgment, introduced the doctrine to the notice of his contemporaries : " a fourth head of fraud," he says, " may be collected or inferred in the consideration of this court from the nature and circumstances of the transaction, as being an imposition and deceit *on the other persons* not parties to the fraudulent agreement.   It may seem odd that an agreement may be infected by being a deceit on others not parties   but such there are, against such there has been relief " (f)

Sub-s. (1).   *Concealment from Private Third Persons in General*

586 The concealment of material facts from private third persons which provides an unmeritorious party with a defence or answer to the case of the opposite party, as above stated, may be a concealment either from a specific individual (g), or from one who fills a certain character, and in that character

---

(e) " A contract which is a fraud upon a third person may on that account be void as between the parties to it "   *per* BAYLEY, J , at pp 610, 611 of *Pidcock v Bishop* (1825), 3 B. & C. 605   For a discussion of this rule in its application to cases where the fraud on the third person consists purely of misrepresentation, see Ch XIV, Sect 2, of the author's *Law of Actionable Misrepresentation*

(f) In *Chesterfield (Earl of)* v *Jannsen* (1751), 2 Ves Sr 125, at p 156

(g) As in the following   *Neville* v *Wilkinson* (1782), 1 Brown C C 543 (as to which, see *Dalbiac* v *Dalbiac, inf*), *Jackson* v *Duchaire* (1790), 3 Term. Rep 551 (a very curious case, in which the defendant, having agreed to buy certain goods from the plaintiff at a valuation, procured one Welch to buy them for her of the plaintiff for £70, which was the consideration expressed in the bill of sale granted by the plaintiff to Welch   It appeared, however, that there was a contemporaneous agreement between the plaintiff and the defendant, *kept secret from Welch by both of them*, that the defendant should pay the plaintiff an additional £30 for the same goods, secured by two promissory notes for £15 each, on one of which the plaintiff was suing the defendant   Lord KENYON, C J , at the trial, without the defendant having raised the point, ruled that the action would not lie, on the ground that the transaction was a fraud, not upon the defendant (who had no merits of her own on which she could rely in answer to the claim), but upon Welch, and this ruling was supported by the Court of King's Bench   *per* ASHURST, J , at p 552   " it is clear both on the principles of law and equity, that when any friend advances money to relieve another person from the pressure of his necessities, and the parties interested enter into a private agreement over and above that with which the friend is acquainted, such agreement is void in law, as being a fraud on such friend "   To the same effect, BULLER, J , at p 553, who observes that, if Welch had been informed of the clandestine bargain, " he probably would not have advanced his money ") ; *Dalbiac v Dalbiac* (1809), 16 Ves 116 (*per* GRANT, M R., at p 125 " the defendant, procuring himself to be appointed trustee "—of the marriage settlement there in question—" by suppressing the fact that he was a creditor, cannot, upon principles clearly established, revert back to that character, and set up again the debt which he has suppressed   Many cases have been determined upon that principle   The case is much stronger than *Neville* v *Wilkinson*, where the creditor, having suppressed the fact of his

is deceived or wronged, such as, in the case of unconscionable bargains with expectants, the ancestor (h), or from a certain class, such as, in the case of invitations to subscribe to commercial undertakings, the investing or speculating public (i), or, as in the case of dealings by an insolvent debtor, from a particular creditor (j), or the general body of creditors The last named type of non-disclosure to third persons, in the course of negotiations for composition arrangements, is of special importance, and demands separate consideration.

Sub-s (2)   Concealment from Creditors in Negotiations for Composition Arrangements

587. In all cases in which an insolvent enters into a composition deed or arrangement with his creditors, the essence of the transaction is equal distribution of the insolvent's estate, and a rateable abatement of each creditor's claim. Good faith, therefore, and complete candour is required from each of the parties towards the others in the negotiation for, or in the carrying into effect of, the arrangement If any of the creditors stipulates with the debtor for a separate advantage to himself, without divulging the transaction to all the other creditors, he is obviously violating this duty of good faith

debt, was not permitted to set it up even against the person in whose favour and at whose instance he made the suppression "), *Sims* v *Tuffs* (1834), 6 C & P 207 (where the plaintiff, fearing an execution, entered into a secret and collusive agreement with his landlord, the defendant, whereby the latter agreed to, and did, destroy his receipts for rent, and make a nominal and sham distraint upon the plaintiff's goods for pretended arrears of rent ; whereupon the defendant, who was as ready to cheat the plaintiff, as the plaintiff was to cheat his execution creditor, proceeded to distrain upon the goods in real earnest, and, when the plaintiff sued him for conversion, justified as landlord, to which plea the plaintiff set up the clandestine agreement in reply It was held that this agree- ment, having been kept secret from the execution creditor, could not stand as an answer to the defendant's affirmative plea which, therefore, grossly iniquitous as it was, was allowed to prevail), *Harrington* v. *Victoria Graving Dock Co* (1878), 3 Q. B D 549 (a principal and agent case, where the agreement to pay the agent a commission or bribe was proved to have been concealed, not from the principal, the defendant company, but from third persons, and on this ground the agent's claim was defeated).

(h) *Chesterfield (Earl of)* v *Jannsen* (1751), 2 Ves. Sr 125, per Lord HARDWICKE, L C , at p. 157 "in most of these cases have concurred deceit or illusion on persons not privy to the fraudulent agreement the father, ancestor, or relation, from whom was the expectation of the estate has been kept in the dark " Cp. the observations of Lord SELBORNE, L.C , at p 492 of *Aylesford (Earl of)* v. *Morris* (1873), 8 Ch App 484 (" great judges have said that there is a principle of public policy in restraining this, that this system of under- mining   the fortunes of families is a public as well as a private mischief , that it is a sort of indirect fraud upon the heads of families from whom these transactions are con- cealed ")   See Ch V, Sect 2, Sub s (5), *ante*

(i) *Begbie* v *Phosphate Sewage Co* (1875), L R 10 Q B 491 (concealment from prospective shareholders of the fact that the plaintiffs had not, nor could ever acquire, a right to exercise the invention which they purported to sell), *Re Great Berlin Steamboat Co* (1884), 26 C D 616, C A. (concealment from subscribers to an undertaking of a private arrangement whereby certain moneys deposited with the company were not to be the moneys of the company, having been deposited for the sole purpose of enabling it to obtain a delusive credit with bankers and others per COTTON, L J , at p 619), *Scott v. Brown, Doering, McNab & Co* ,[1892] 2 Q B 724, C A (concealment from the investing public that certain contracts for sale and purchase of shares on the Stock Exchange had been entered into for the sole purpose of creating a fictitious market)

(j) See the cases cited in note (u) to § 579, *ante*

and candour, with the result that the clandestine agreement cannot be enforced even against the debtor, for, though the favoured creditor has done no wrong, and infringed no duty, to him, he has failed in his duty to third persons,—the class of creditors other than himself. The relation between the creditors *inter se* is sometimes described as based on an implied representation by each of them to the others that he is deriving no benefit from the debtor over and above the agreed composition in which view, any creditor who has derived, or bargained for, such a benefit is guilty of an implied fraudulent misrepresentation (*k*). But it may, with at least equal propriety, be described as a relation between members of a class which imposes on each member a duty to reveal to the rest of them any transaction between himself and the debtor which is calculated to destroy or alter the equality of treatment on which such relation is founded In whichever way it is put, the clandestine bargain entered into between the insolvent and the favoured creditor is a fraud upon the other creditors, though not upon the insolvent, and is accordingly invalidated on the same principle of public policy as any other kind of concealment from third persons (*l*)

588 There are various forms of transaction by which an advantage may be stipulated for between a creditor and the debtor It is quite immaterial, however, in what precise mode the creditor is favoured If he is in fact favoured, and if the arrangement for the conferring of the favour

---

(*k*) The subject is treated from this point of view in § 364, note (*b*), of the author's *Law of Actionable Misrepresentation.*

(*l*) See § 139, *ante,* where the type of case now under discussion is treated as belonging to the subject of compromises generally, so far as the duty of disclosure is concerned, but is reserved for more appropriate handling in this place, by reason of the duty being owed to third persons The favoured creditor's secret agreement is put as fraud in the following cases : *Fawcett* v *Gye* (1796), 3 Anstr 910 (*per* MACDONALD, C B , at pp 914, 915 "the principle is that in such cases each must conduct himself openly, and in the manner in which he appears to the world to act. If his conduct is such as has a natural tendency to induce the other creditors to believe that all are acting upon equal terms, and receiving equal shares, as they may be induced by that appearance, any private arrangement for greater benefit to one is a fraud upon the rest, and therefore void ") ; *Pidcock* v *Bishop* (1825), 3 B. & C. 605 (*per* BAYLEY, J , at pp 610, 611 "where by a composition deed the creditors agree to take a certain sum in full discharge of their respective debts, a secret agreement whereby the debtor stipulates with one of the creditors to pay him a larger sum is void upon the ground that that agreement is a fraud upon the rest of the creditors. So that a contract which is a fraud upon a third person may on that account be void as between the parties to it ") *Re Cross* (1848), 4 De G & Sm 364 n. , *Higgins* v *Pitt* (1849), 4 Exch. 312 (*per* PARKE, B , at p 324 "every secret bargain is a fraud on the creditors, and is void when it is made, and being executory, cannot be enforced even against a fraudulent party "), *Ex p Milner* (1885), 15 Q B D 605, C A (*per* BRETT, M.R , at pp. 613, 614, BAGGALLAY, L.J , at p 615, and BOWEN, L J , at p 616). As to "public policy " lying at the root of the doctrine, see *Chesterfield* (*Earl of*) v. *Jannsen* (1751), 2 Ves. Sr 125 (*per* Lord HARDWICKE, L.C , at p 156, who there mentions secret bargains for the private advantage of a particular creditor in cases of composition deeds as one of the examples of his "fourth head of fraud," referred to in note (*n*) to § 586, *ante* "In this," he says, "there can be no particular deceit on the debtor, who is party thereto , but it tends to deceit of the other creditors, who relied on an equal composition "), *Jackman* v *Mitchell* (1807), 13 Ves. 581 (*per* Lord ELDON, L C., at p 587 : "in these cases, which proceed upon grounds of public policy, the relief is given on account not of the individual, but of the public "), *Re Cross, sup* , *Atkinson* v *Denby* (1862), 7 H & N 934, Exch Ch. (*per* COCKBURN, C J , at p 936 "contrary to the policy of the law ") As to the inconvenience and slight ambiguity of the term "public policy," as explained by Lord HARDWICKE, see § 646, note (*y*), *post*

is kept secret from the other creditors, it will be relieved against, on the proper steps being taken by the proper parties

589 The most common and simple type of transaction is a promise by the debtor to pay the favoured creditor at some future date the difference between the composition debt and the full debt, whether the deficiency be or be not also secured by the debtor's bond, promissory note, or acceptance, or to pay him a larger dividend than the composition deed provides for, or to give him some other advantage over and above the other creditors, by cash payment, or otherwise (*m*).

590 A second, and more subtle, form of transaction is where the debtor, though not promising any extra payment to the favoured creditor from his own purse, or from the estate, promises a third person to enter into such an engagement, or to guarantee the discharge of the composition debt. Thus, clandestine agreements of the following nature have been treated as void . where the debtor, as a condition of the favoured creditor's signing the certificate under the old insolvency law, induced his sister to pay a certain sum in cash to the creditor, and to give him a promissory note for a further sum (*n*), where the debtor procured a third person to give the creditor security for the payment of certain instalments which were not secured by the composition deed, and where it was held to be no answer to say that the favoured creditor was to receive no greater amount than the other creditors, his advantage consisting in the fact that his debt was to be better secured than theirs (*o*), where the third person was to satisfy the deficiency by deliveries of goods to the favoured creditor (*p*), or by his acceptance (*q*), where the debtor arranged with the favoured creditors (his bankers) that they should be entitled to reserve their remedies against the third person who had guaranteed the debtor's account with them (*r*), where an advantage, not coming from the debtor's estate, was secured to the creditor (*s*), where the debtor's brother gave an undertaking to make additional payments to the creditor, and it was again held that the fact of the secret favour not being at the expense of the estate was quite immaterial (*t*), and where, the third person having given the favoured creditor his promissory note or acceptance for an amount beyond the composition instalments, the debtor afterwards guaranteed payment of such negotiable instrument in consideration of the creditor's forbearance,

(*m*) See, for illustrations, *Cockshott* v *Bennett* (1788), 2 Term Rep. 763; *Fawcett* v *Gye, sup.*, *Jackman* v. *Mitchell, sup*, *Smith* v. *Cuff* (1817), 6 M. & S 160, *Pendlebury* v *Walker* (1841), 4 Y & C (Exch. in Eq.) 424, *Horton* v *Reilly* (1843), 11 M & W 492; *Re Cross, sup*, *Higgins* v *Pitt, sup*, *Mallalieu* v *Hodgson* (1851), 16 Q B. 689, *Ex p. Oliver, re Hodgson* (1851), 4 De G & Sm. 354, *Atkinson* v *Denby, sup*, *Ex p Phillips, re Harvey* (1888), 36 W. R. 567, C. A, *Re Otway*, [1895] 1 Q B 812, C A, *Re Shaw, ex p Gill* (1901), 83 L T 754, C A.; *Re Goldberg* (1904), 21 T. L R 139, C A
(*n*) *Smith* v *Bromley* (1766), 2 Dougl. (κ в) 695 n
(*o*) *Leicester* v. *Rose* (1803), 4 East 371
(*p*) *Knight* v. *Hunt* (1829), 5 Bing. 432 (*per* BEST, C J, at p. 434)
(*q*) *Howden* v *Haigh* (1840), 11 A & E 1033 (*per* Lord DENMAN, C J, at p 1038)
(*r*) *Davidson* v *M'Gregor* (1841), 8 M & W 755 Here, however, no relief was given, because the ignorance of the other creditors was not proved see § 601, note (*q*), *post*
(*s*) *Dauglish* v *Tennent* (1866), L. R 2 Q B 49
(*t*) *Ex p. Milner* (1885), 15 Q. B D 605, C. A (*per* BRETT, M R, at pp. 613, 614)

and it was held that the third person's debt, and consequently also the debtor's guarantee, was illegal and void (u)

591 The following case was of a somewhat special character The debtor, who, by the composition deed, had covenanted to pay the creditors eight shillings in the pound, entered into a secret agreement with one of them that, in consideration of the creditors guaranteeing payment of this amount to all the creditors, he (the debtor) would pay to the creditor the residue of his debt It was held that this agreement was void, and, when it was urged that the stipulation was for the advantage of the creditors generally, it was answered that the creditors, as a body, may or may not have considered it in that light · but it was for them to judge, and they had not been asked their opinion it was a case, therefore, of the suppression of an agreement which, as it *might* have deterred them from executing the composition deed, was material to be disclosed to them (v).

592. In a subsequent case, of a similarly anomalous character, the circumstances were these The debtor, Lenzberg, owed various sums to one Kearns, as security for which he had deposited a policy for £5000 on the joint lives of himself and his wife He had for some time previously been making monthly payments of certain amounts to nominees of Kearns These payments were entirely voluntary As a condition of executing the composition deed, Kearns secretly stipulated that Lenzberg should, and he did in fact, continue to make these voluntary payments to Kearns's nominees On the death of Lenzberg's wife, the insurance company paid the policy moneys into Court to abide the result of the conflicting claims of Lenzberg and Kearns. It was held that Lenzberg was entitled to credit for the amount of the allowances which, though previously voluntary, he had bound himself by the clandestine bargain to pay to Kearns's nominees, on the ground that the agreement was void as a fraud on the other creditors The debtor, it is true, was obtaining an advantage out of a fraud to which he was a party, but this circumstance could not be allowed to interfere with the application of an absolute and inflexible rule, founded on considerations of public utility(w)

593 The secret arrangement between the debtor and the favoured creditor may be relieved against, or treated as a nullity, in a variety of forms The first, and simplest, class of case is that in which the favoured creditor sues the debtor to enforce the clandestine bargain, or otherwise asserts a claim against the debtor thereunder, and the debtor's plea or answer of non-disclosure to the other creditors is allowed to prevail (x).

(u) *Geere* v *Mare* (1863), 2 H & C 339 (where the debtor assigned to the creditor a policy on his life to secure a bill of exchange, covenanting to pay premiums . held that the assignment was bad)

(v) *Wood* v *Barker* (1865), L. R 1 Eq 139 (*per* STUART, V.-C, at p 144 · "the secrecy puts them to this disadvantage, that but for the secrecy they might be willing to forego the guarantee in consideration of receiving a higher rate of dividend. It is plain that the concealment prevented them from exercising this option ")

(w) *Re Lenzberg's Policy* (1877), 7 C D. 650 (*per* HALL, V -C , at p. 654)

(x) As in *Cockshott* v. *Bennett* (1788), 2 Term Rep 763 , *Howden* v *Haigh* (1840), 11 A & E. 1033 , *Re Lenzberg's Policy, sup* (where the favoured creditor and the debtor were claiming adversely to one another in respect of a fund in court, under the circumstances stated in § 592, sup.)

594. A record type of case is where the favoured creditor sues, or sets up a right against, a third person who, by procurement of the debtor, has entered into the impeached agreement with such creditor, and the third person successfully pleads the concealment of the agreement from the other creditors by the debtor, the favoured creditor, and himself (y)

595. In a third class of case, the debtor himself, if coerced, but not otherwise, is granted relief against his own iniquity, on the principle that though, where an action is brought under or in respect of an illegal transaction, the general rule is that *potior conditio est defendentis*, an exception exists where there is proof or presumption that the party suing was constrained by the pressure of circumstances " to bow to the rod which the other party held over him " Thus, on proof of the secret agreement, and of the pressure and coercion, a debtor has been held entitled, in proceedings instituted by him against the favoured creditor, or in a contest between himself and the creditor as rival claimants to a fund, to have the agreement set aside or delivered up to be cancelled, or to recover the moneys which he has paid to the favoured creditor or to *bonâ fide* holders for value of negotiable instruments given by him pursuant to the impeached agreement, or to have such payments credited to him in account   In other cases the debtor has been held entitled to a declaration that the favoured creditor has no claim to the extra payment stipulated for, or has obtained an order that the original composition deed be set aside (z)

(y) As in *Leicester* v. *Rose* (1803), 4 East 371 (where the successful defendant was a person whom, unknown to the other creditors, the favoured creditor and the debtor had procured to give collateral security for payment of two composition instalments which were unsecured by the deed of arrangement), *Knight* v *Hunt* (1829), 5 Bing 432 (secret agreement to satisfy balance of favoured creditor's debt by deliveries of coal to be made by the debtor's brother   *per* BEST, C J , at pp 433, 434), *Davidson* v *M'Gregor* (1841), 8 M. & W. 755 (where a bank, by its public officer, sued the defendant as guarantor of the debtor's account with the bank   plea, that the debtor had executed a composition deed with his creditors, of whom the bank was one, whereby the debtor was to be released on payment of 10s 6d. in the £, which had been done, and, there being no longer any principal debt, there was no secondary liability either   replication, express reservation of the bank's rights against the surety : rejoinder, that this express reservation was not disclosed to the other creditors, and was therefore void   It was held that the agreement would have been invalid on this ground if the defendant had proved—which he did not—that the other creditors were ignorant of it   see note (q) to § 601, *post*) , *Clay* v *Ray* (1864), 17 C B (N S) 188 (where a guarantee given by the debtor's son was held void); *Mayhew* v *Boyes* (1910), 103 L. T 1, C A (where the defendant was sued by the favoured creditor on a promissory note which he had joined with the debtor in making, and succeeded on proof of a secret bargain between him, the debtor, and the favoured creditor, whereby he had promised at some future date to discharge the whole of the debtor's liability to the favoured creditor with interest)

(z) Thus, at the debtor's suit, the bond given in pursuance of the secret agreement was ordered to be delivered up to be cancelled in *Fawcett* v *Gae* (1796), 3 Anstr 910 ; *Jackman* v *Mitchell* (1807), 13 Ves 581 (*per* Lord ELDON, L.C , at pp. 585–587)   The debtor successfully sued for the return of sums paid to the favoured creditor under the clandestine agreement, as money had and received, in *Atkinson* v *Denby* (1862), 7 H. & N 934, Exch Ch (*per Cur* , at p 936), and for the recoupment of moneys which he had been compelled to pay to a holder in due course of a negotiable instrument given by him to the favoured creditor pursuant to the impeached arrangement, in *Smith* v *Cuff* (1817), 6 M & S 160 (*per* Lord ELLENBOROUGH, C.J , at p 165, pointing out that the agreement had been obtained from the debtor " extorsively and by oppression," and that " when one holds the rod, and the other bows to it," the oppressed party, in this sense and to this extent, is not *in pari delicto* with the other), and in *Horton* v. *Reilly* (1843), 11 M. & W. 492 (*per*

596. A fourth species of case is where, on the same principle, similar relief is granted to a third person who, at the favoured creditor's and the debtor's instance, has contracted to confer an advantage on such creditor, without the knowledge of the other creditors. Such relief may be given in the form of an order for repayment of moneys paid under the agreement (a), or, if the transaction consisted in the third person guaranteeing a composition instalment, an order discharging him from his suretyship (b)

597. The next class of case in which the validity of a secret bargain with a particular creditor may be successfully impeached is where the favoured creditor institutes, or threatens to institute, bankruptcy proceedings against the debtor, founded on the non-payment of the composition debt, and such creditor is held disentitled to a receiving order on proof, either of a clandestine agreement made by him with the debtor for a special advantage over the other creditors, or of an attempt by him to extort such an advantage, whether the attempt succeeded or not, as a condition of forbearance from the threatened proceedings, or of withdrawing or suspending proceedings already instituted. Such last mentioned conduct constitutes, if concealed from the other creditors, a sufficient cause, within s. 7 (3) of the Bankruptcy Act, 1883 (now s. 5 (3) of the Bankruptcy Act, 1914), for refusing to make a receiving order (c). Further, it has been held that the favoured creditor in such a case deprives himself of the right to relief of any kind, and, in the attempt to overreach the other creditors, overreaches only himself . for, on

Lord ABINGER, C.B , at p 493, and PARKE, B , at pp 493, 494) The decision in *Wilson* v. *Ray* (1839), 10 A. & E 82, which is apparently in direct conflict with each of the two cases last cited, cannot be accepted as law, unless it is possible to distinguish it, which Lord ABINGER, C B , at p. 493 of *Horton* v *Reilly*, *sup*., and the Court of Exchequer, but not the Exchequer Chamber, in *Atkinson* v *Denby*, *sup* , attempted to do, on the ground that there the pressure was over when the debtor executed the agreement   In *Wood* v. *Barker* (1865), L R. 1 Eq. 139, the debtor sought, and obtained, relief in the form of an order for an account, and a declaration that, on the taking of the account, the favoured creditor was not to be allowed more than the percentage payable to each of the creditors under the composition deed (*per* STUART, V C, at pp 144, 145) In *Re Lenzburg's Policy* (1877), 7 C D 650, for an abstract of which see § 592, *ante*, the debtor established his claim to be credited in account with sums paid to the favoured creditor's nominees under the secret arrangement.

(a) *Smith* v. *Bromley* (1760), 2 Dougl. (K B) 695 n (*per* Lord MANSFIELD, C.J)

(b) *Pendlebury* v *Walker* (1841), 4 Y & C (Exch in Eq) 424 (*per* ALDERSON, B., at p 441) In this case a bank, one of the creditors of the insolvent, agreed with him and the other creditors that, upon obtaining guarantees from one person for £5000, and from twenty others for £1000 each, they would provide a sum sufficient to pay 10s. in the £ to the creditors, and, after such payment, to enable the debtor to carry on business. The plaintiff was one of the £1000 guarantors, and he filed a bill on the equity side of the Court of Exchequer alleging a secret agreement between the bank and the debtor for the payment by the debtor to the bank of the remaining moiety of his indebtedness to them, and claiming that the composition deed was thereby rendered no longer binding on any of the creditors, and that he, therefore, as a guarantor of a supposed indebtedness which no longer existed in law, was discharged from the obligations of his suretyship. It was held that these allegations disclosed a good cause of action, and a demurrer to the bill was overruled

(c) *Ex p Phillips, Re Harvey* (1888), 36 W R 567, C. A ; *Re Otway*, [1895] 1 Q B. 812, C. A. (*per* Lord ESHER, M.R., at pp. 813, 814 : this was a case of an attempted exaction by the creditor of an additional payment, as a condition of the creditor's consent to an adjournment of the hearing of a petition for a receiving order   The attempt failed, but the Court held that this made no difference); *Re Shaw, Ex p Gill* (1901) 83 L. T 754, C. A , *Re Goldberg* (1904), 21 T L R 139, C. A.

the one hand, he cannot enforce the secret agreement . nor, on the other hand, can he proceed in bankruptcy on the original debt, because the release contained in the composition deed stands in his way, which release, though expressed to become void on non-payment of the composition debt, is in law absolute, since the condition of avoidance is illegal and void (d)

598. Another variety of case presents itself where the debtor sues one of the creditors on a covenant for indemnity in the composition deed against claims in respect of liabilities from which he is thereby released, and the creditor repels such claim on proof of an agreement between himself and the debtor, undisclosed to the other creditors, whereby special terms were stipulated for in the creditor's favour (e)

599 The cases in which an unfavoured creditor invokes the assistance of the Court constitute another distinct and separate class. It has been held that any such unfavoured creditor, on discovering that a secret agreement was entered into between the debtor and a favoured creditor, has the right to insist that the composition arrangement is void, and should be judicially ignored, leaving him free to claim the full original debt by action (f), or to make it the subject of bankruptcy proceedings (g)

600 The following is an anomalous and unique case A creditor sued the debtor for the price of goods sold and for moneys paid The debtor pleaded his release by a composition deed to which the plaintiff was a party. In his replication to this plea the plaintiff, with comical impudence, set up

---

(d) *Re Cross* (1848), 4 De G & Sm. 364 (at p. 365), *Mallalieu v Hodgson* (1851), 16 Q B 689 (*per* ERLE, J, at p. 711), *Ex p Phillips, Re Harvey* (1888), 36 W. R 567, C. A ; *Mayhew v. Boyes* (1910), 103 L. T 1, C A (*per* COZENS-HARDY, M.R , at p. 3).

(e) *Higgins v Pitt* (1849), 4 Exch. 312 (*per* PARKE, B , at pp 324, 325) Here the debtor had executed a composition deed whereby he covenanted to give the creditors bills (to the extent of 5s in the £) in substitution for existing bills, and, in consideration thereof, each of the creditors covenanted to indemnify him against all claims in respect of any existing bills which he might have negotiated to holders in due course The debtor, having been compelled to pay to one of such holders the full amount of an old bill indorsed to him by a creditor, sued the creditor on the above covenant to indemnify The creditor pleaded his own and the debtor's fraud on the other creditors in virtue of a clandestine agreement between him and the debtor whereby he (the creditor) was to be paid 5s in the £ in cash beyond the amount of the composition bill, and, in respect of certain goods sold, was to be paid in full. The plea was held good on demurrer It will be observed that the decision in this case proceeded upon the ground that the debtor was not, as he was in the cases cited in note (z) to § 595, ante, proved to have been under pressure . if it had been so proved, he might, as in those cases, have been held entitled to relief It is on this distinguishing feature that *Wilson v Ray* (1839), 10 A & E 82, may be supported

(f) *Dauglish v. Tennent* (1866), L R 2 Q B 49 (*per* COCKBURN, C J , at p 54) Here the unfavoured creditor sued the debtor on the original debt, to which the defendant set up release by the composition agreement, whereupon the plaintiff pleaded a replication setting up a secret agreement between the defendant and certain creditors, other than himself, by which such creditors became entitled to special advantages, though not at the expense of the estate On demurrer, the replication was held good

(g) *Ex p Milner* (1885), 15 Q B D 605, C. A (*per* BRETT, M.R , at pp. 612–614, BAGGALLAY, L J , at p 615, and BOWEN, L J , at p 616) In this case the unfavoured creditor, on discovery of the secret bargain with the favoured creditor, issued a bankruptcy notice against the debtor in respect of a judgment for the full amount of the original debt, ignoring, and insisting that the Court should ignore, the composition deed as altogether a nullity, by reason of the non-disclosure to the creditors other than the favoured creditor The debtor moved to set aside the notice The Registrar refused to do so, and the C A held that this refusal was correct

that, when giving him a secret advantage over other creditors, the defendant fraudulently misrepresented to him that he was not conferring similar favours on any other creditor, whereas in fact he had entered into such agreement with another creditor. In other words, whilst avowing, and indeed pro claiming, his own complicity in a fraud on the other creditors, he complained of other similar frauds, not because they were frauds, but because he derived no benefit from them The replication was held bad (*h*).

601. The burden of allegation and proof on the party seeking relief is, *mutatis mutandis*, precisely the same as that which, in an ordinary case, rests on the party who complains of the non-disclosure of a material fact by the other party to a negotiation for a compromise or other contract *uberrimæ fidei*. That is to say, the party impeaching the alleged secret bargain with the favoured creditor must allege and prove each of the following matters : first, the existence of a relation between the parties giving rise to the duty of disclosure to the creditors of any material agreement of the nature in question (*i*),—which duty, it must be remembered, is to divulge to *all* the creditors, and continues until the last of them has executed the composition deed (*j*),—and the fact that the particular agreement impeached was the subject of such duty (*k*) by reason of its materiality, which means no more than that its disclosure *might* have influenced the general body of creditors, or some of them, to decline to accede to the proposed composition arrangement (*l*) , secondly, the execution in fact of the alleged secret agreement (*m*) , thirdly, its non-disclosure to *all* the creditors (*n*) ; fourthly, that the persons concerned had knowledge of it (*o*), which fact is of course established by mere proof of the making of the agreement between those persons ,

(*h*) *Mallalieu* v. *Hodgson* (1851), 16 Q B 689 (*per* ERLE, J , at pp 712, 713, and COLERIDGE, J., at pp 714-716). It is somewhat surprising to find that WIGHTMAN, J. (whose decision was reversed by the Court of Q. B), had at the trial directed a verdict for the plaintiff, and still more astonishing to find that as a member of the Court, after full argument, he adhered to his view at *nisi prius*, and dissented from the rest of the Court

(*i*) See Ch. III, Sect 3, Sub s (1), *ante*.

(*j*) *Ex p. Milner* (1885), 15 Q B D. 605, C A (where it was held that the duty of disclosure, being a duty to all the creditors, continues until all of them have executed the composition deed, and it is therefore immaterial that the secret bargain is made after the unfavoured creditor complaining of the non-disclosure has executed the composition deed, if it is still unexecuted by some of the creditors (*per* BRETT, M R , at p 613)

(*k*) *Ex p. Burrell, Re Robinson* (1875), 1 C D 537, C. A , is a good illustration of the sort of fact which a debtor is under no duty to disclose to the creditors

(*l*) As to the meaning of "materiality" in general, see Ch II, Sect. 2, *ante*. For illustrations of the application of the principles there enunciated to cases of the character now under discussion, see *Knight* v *Hunt* (1829), 5 Bing 432 (*per* BEST, C.J , at pp 433, 434, explaining that it is sufficient to establish that the other creditors *might* have been influenced by the disclosure of the suppressed agreement, in determining whether or not to accede to the composition deed) ; *Wood* v *Barker* (1865), L. R 1 Eq. 139 (*per* STUART, V.-C., at p 144,—the passage is cited in note (*v*) to § 591, *ante*) , *Dauglish* v *Tennent* (1866), L R. 2 Q B. 49 (*per* COCKBURN, C J , who, at p 54, points out that the disclosure of the secret stipulation might have resulted in the deed of arrangement not going through , for any particular creditor may distrust his own judgment, and may be induced to accede to the arrangement by his belief that the entire body of creditors, persuaded thereto by fair means and not bribed, have considered it to their advantage to concur).

(*m*) See Ch. III, Sect. 3, Sub-s (2), *ante*

(*n*) See Ch III, Sect 3, Sub-s. (3), *ante* Generally, as to what constitutes " dis closure," see Ch II, Sect 1, *ante*

(*o*) See Ch III, Sect. 3, Sub-s (4), *ante*.

and, lastly, that the persons to whom the duty was owed were ignorant from any other source of the undisclosed agreement (p), such persons being the entire body of creditors (q).

602. The affirmative defences of waiver, and affirmation, available to a party charged in an ordinary case of compromise (r), are equally available to a party against whom relief is sought in respect of a clandestine bargain with a particular creditor: but, inasmuch as the duty is to disclose to the general body of creditors, neither of these pleas can be established except on proof that *all* the creditors waived their right to disclosure, or acquiesced in the non-disclosure (s)

(p) See Ch III, Sect. 3, Sub s (5), *ante* Generally, as to the constitutive elements of "knowledge," actual and constructive, see Ch II, Sect. 3, *ante*

(q) See *Davidson* v. *M'Gregor* (1841), 8 M & W 755, the facts of which are abstracted in note (y) to § 594, *ante* (*per Cur.*, at p. 768. "it does not appear on the pleadings, nor was it proved at the trial, that this reservation of the plaintiff's rights against the defendant was not known to the other creditors. . . Inasmuch as the defendant is seeking to establish that this agreement, which he in fact entered into, was invalid in law, we think that the fact ought to have been proved by him. In the absence of this proof, we see nothing to show that the agreement was not binding on him ")

(r) Ch. III, Sect. 4, Sub-ss (1) and (2), *ante.*

(s) *Geere* v. *Mare* (1863), 2 H. & C. 339 (where it was argued for the plaintiff that " here the defendant chose to waive the illegality by not availing himself of it in the action on the note " on which ERLE, C J, at p. 192, observed that " the fraud is upon the general body of creditors, and there is no sign of waiver by them "). Cp. the case of *Whichcote* v. *Lawrence* (1798), 3 Ves 739, cited in note (n) to § 393, *ante*, as to the burden being on a trustee for the sale of a debtor's property for the creditors to establish, if he sets up acquiescence, that the entire body of creditors acquiesced,—an almost impossible onus to sustain where the creditors are, as they were in that case, very numerous

CHAPTER VIII.

JURISDICTION AND PROCEDURE.

603. To complete this commentary, it remains to examine the question of the jurisdiction of Courts in cases of non-disclosure, and to consider certain rules of pleading, practice, or procedure which are special to such cases, or which, though general, have a special character or importance in their application to the topic of non-disclosure.

SECT. 1   JURISDICTION

604. Where the right to relief in respect of non-disclosure is asserted by way of affirmative defence (*t*), no question as to the jurisdiction of the Court to entertain the plea arises   for, in such cases, the party complaining has not chosen the forum, but is cited to appear in it, *nolens volens*, and, as a general rule, if the jurisdiction is challenged at all, it must be the jurisdiction to entertain the action, not the defence, any Court which is competent and bound to try the one being, generally speaking, competent and bound to try the other   It is only necessary therefore to consider the cases in which the party complaining is the *actor* in the proceedings, whether those proceedings be instituted for the purpose of obtaining rescission, and consequential or analogous remedies, or for pecuniary relief in the form of an action for money had and received, or otherwise (*u*)   For any of these purposes, the Courts having jurisdiction are the Chancery Division (*v*), and (subject, where rescission is claimed, to transfer in a proper case) the King's Bench Division (*w*), or

(*t*) As it frequently is. see Ch III, Sect 5, Sub-s. (2), Ch IV, Sect 5, and Ch V, Sect 5, Sub-s (2), *ante*
(*u*) See Sect. 5 of Chapters III, IV, and V, *ante*, respectively   As to the action for money had and received against the bribed agent, and for damages against a party who has corrupted such agent, see Ch. IV, Sect. 5, Sub-s (2), *ante*
(*v*) By s 34 of the Judicature Act, 1873 (36 & 37 Vict. c 66), " the setting aside, or cancellation of deeds or other instruments " is assigned to the Chancery Division   This provision, however, is materially qualified by s. 24, sub ss (1), (2), (3), (4), and (7), of the same statute, which empowers and requires any Division of the High Court to give effect, not merely to any equitable claim so far as it is pleaded or operates as a defence,—see *Mostyn (Lord)* v *West Mostyn Coke & Iron Co* (1876), 1 C. P D 145 (*per* BRETT, J , at p 150, ARCHIBALD, J , at pp 153, 154, and LINDLEY, J , at p 154),—but also to any equitable claim to relief set up *by a plaintiff*, " against any deed, instrument, or contract or against any right, title, or claim whatsoever asserted by *any defendant* "
(*w*) It results from the combined effect of the two sections cited in the last note that actions for rescission may be instituted, and, if no application is made by the defendant to transfer to the Chancery Division, may be maintained, in the King's Bench Division   Such actions have been quite commonly brought in the latter Division, without objection, since 1873 see, for instance, *Rivaz* v *Gerussi* (1880), 6 Q B D 622, *Mitchell* v *Homfray* (1881), 8 Q B D. 587, C A , *Plowright* v *Lambert* (1885), 52 L T 646,

the High Court of Justice, the two Chancery Courts of the Counties Palatine of Lancaster, and of Durham, respectively (x), and (subject, in each case, to the local and pecuniary limits of the jurisdiction) the Mayor's Court (y), any County Court (z), and any borough or local court of civil jurisdiction having authority (by statute, charter, or custom) to entertain proceedings instituted for the objects mentioned (a) Where, on the liquidation of a company, which automatically stays all actions, leave is obtained to prosecute an action in the K B D, and for a trial by jury, there is nevertheless jurisdiction to transfer the action to the Winding-up Court, notwithstanding that fraud is charged, if the parties charged do not object (aa)

605. For the purpose of the various statutory proceedings by which, or in the course of which, questions of non-disclosure may be raised and determined, the Courts having jurisdiction are those (if any) specified in the respective enactments. Thus, misfeasance proceedings are, in England, subject to the jurisdiction of such judge or judges of the Chancery Division as the Lord Chancellor may assign to deal with the winding up of companies, or the judge who for the time being exercises the bankruptcy jurisdiction of the High Court, or, where the company is within the district of either of the two above-mentioned Palatine Courts, or of certain County Courts having bankruptcy jurisdiction, or is within the stannaries, to the jurisdiction of such Courts respectively (within certain pecuniary limits), in Ireland, to the jurisdiction of the Irish High Court of Justice (though, in a proper case, they may be transferred to the Court of Bankruptcy having jurisdiction in the place where the registered office of the company is situate); and, in Scotland, to the jurisdiction of the Court of Session, though that Court, in its discretion, may remit the winding up proceedings, in the case of any particular company, to one of the permanent Lords Ordinary (b) Applications under the Vendor and Purchaser Act, 1874, are

Liles v *Terry,* [1895] 2 Q B 679, C A , and the misrepresentation case of *Moore* v *Explosives Co* (1887), 56 L. J. (Q B) 235, C A. When an application is made to transfer, the Court has a discretion to make the order, or to retain the action, as in all the circumstances may be deemed just and convenient , see s 11 of the Judicature Act, 1875 (38 & 39 Vict , c 77), and Lord Halsbury's *Laws of England,* title "Courts," vol ix, pp. 60, 61. An order may be made in a proper case for the transfer of an action for rescission from the C D to the K B D , as in *Forrester* v *Jones,* [1899] W N 78.

(x) See Lord Halsbury's *Laws of England,* title "Courts," vol ix, pp 120–127.

(y) *Ibid ,* title "Mayor's Court," vol xx, p 286

(z) *Ibid ,* title "County Courts," vol viii, p 444 *Re Pepperell* (1879), 27 W R 410, is an instance of an action to set aside a sale, on the ground of abuse of a fiduciary relation, which was commenced in the County Court, but removed to the Chancery Division on its appearing to be outside the pecuniary limit of the equitable jurisdiction.

(a) See Lord Halsbury's *Laws of England,* title "Courts," vol ix, pp 129–213. As to when the judge appointed to exercise bankruptcy jurisdiction, or one of the judges appointed to deal with the winding up of companies, is empowered, or required, to entertain claims made by or against insolvent persons or companies in respect of non disclosure, see § 388, *ante ,* note (l) to § 401, *ante ,* and § 616, *post*

(aa) *Re Pacaya Rubber & Produce Co ,* [1913] 1 Ch 218, C A

(b) See ss. 132, 133 (as to England), 134 (as to Ireland), 135, 136 (as to Scotland), of the Companies (Consolidation) Act, 1908 (8 Edw. 7, c 69) The Court of the Vice-Warden of the Stannaries was abolished by the Stannaries Court (Abolition) Act, 1896 (59 & 60 Vict , c 45), and by order made thereunder the jurisdiction was transferred to the Cornwall County Courts, and is now vested in the Courts having bankruptcy jurisdiction in Cornwall.

(as has been already stated) within the exclusive jurisdiction of the Chancery Division (c). Questions of non-disclosure arising in a certain class of life insurance case may, as has also been indicated, be dealt with by a court of summary jurisdiction, pursuant to statutory authority (d). The Companies (Consolidation) Act, 1908 (e), and the Money-lenders Act, 1900 (f), the former of which expressly relates, and the latter may be applied, to cases of statutory and common law non-disclosure respectively, are statutes which do not limit the jurisdiction to any particular court, the consequence being that any of the courts above mentioned as having jurisdiction in relation to non-statutory breaches of the duty of disclosure has the like jurisdiction, and within the same limits, in respect of the non-disclosure to which those Acts relate, or are applicable. Questions as to the Courts having jurisdiction to deal with cases of concealment from judicial tribunals, the State, or private third persons, have been incidentally touched upon in the course of the general discussion of these topics (g)

SECT. 2   PROCEDURE.

606 Under the head of procedure, it may be convenient to notice such rules of pleading, discovery, and practice as are either peculiar to, or have a special interest and importance in connection with, cases of non-disclosure ; then, to deal separately, and in some detail, with the entire subject of the statutory procedure (in the widest sense of the word) relating to misfeasance (having regard to the large proportion of the authorities illustrating the duty of disclosure incidental to relations of confidence which consists of misfeasance cases) ; and, lastly, to examine the principles on which judicial discretion in the matter of costs has been exercised

Sub-s (1)   Certain Rules of Pleading and Discovery in Proceedings for Non-Disclosure

607. Every fact, the burden of establishing which is upon the party complaining of non-disclosure (h), must in the first instance be distinctly alleged

see s 280 of the Act of 1908, as to the winding up part of the jurisdiction, which, as was decided in *Dunbar* v *Harvey*, [1913] 2 Ch 530, C A. is exclusive, and not concurrent with that of the High Court   See also *Re Radium Ore Mines, Ltd.* (1913), 30 T L R 66, C A   As to the procedure in misfeasance, see § 616, *post*

(c) See § 251, *ante*

(d) 37 & 38 Vict, c 78   See the statute and cases referred to in § 241, and note (h) thereto, *ante*

(e) 8 Edw 7, c 69   See Ch VI, Sect. 7, *ante*

(f) 63 & 64 Vict. c 51   By s 1, (1), (2), " any court " may give the statutory relief both to a borrower who is defending himself, and to one who is taking active proceedings against, the moneylender   whilst, by s 1 (3), courts of bankruptcy are empowered to apply the remedial provisions of the Act to claims and proceedings in bankruptcy.   The question of "unconscionableness" appears to be one of law for such "court," and not one of fact · *Abrahams* v *Dimmock*, [1914] 2 K B 372, affd, [1914] W N 449, C A

(g) See, as to the Courts having jurisdiction to set aside or otherwise deal with judgments, Ch VII, Sect. 1, and particularly § 577, *ante*   as to setting aside, or treating as void, Crown grants or charters, see Ch VII, Sect. 2, *ante*   as the jurisdiction of bankruptcy courts in reference to undisclosed agreements made with a favoured creditor by an insolvent compounding with his creditors, see § 597, *ante*

(h) See Sect 3 of Chapters III, IV, and V, respectively

in that party's statement of claim (i), or defence (j), as the case may be. This means that the particular "suspected" relation (k), or the particular "circumstances and conditions" (l), relied upon as giving rise to the duty of disclosure or other fiduciary duty must be stated, as well as the facts showing the alleged non-observance of such duty. In a case where the cause of action, or ground of defence, is "undue influence," it is not essential to make use of the actual expression (m), provided that matters of fact are pleaded sufficient to raise the legal presumption of the existence and undue exertion of such influence (n). But these matters of fact, whether in a pleading, or in an affidavit, must be averred with precision and particularity, and nothing must be left to conjecture (o). The kind and degree of particularity required varies according to the nature and circumstances of the individual case (p). And it must be remembered that, though in proceedings based on the violation of a duty other than fiduciary the party alleging such violation must give all necessary particulars without first receiving any assistance by means of discovery from the other side (q), this is not so where

(i) See O 19, r 6, of the R. S C , where not only "fraud," but "undue influence," is expressly mentioned As regards "fraud," see *Myddleton* v. *Lord Kenyon* (1794), 2 Ves 391 (*per* Lord ELDON, L C , at p 412), and *Davy* v *Garrett* (1878), 7 C D 473, C. A (the passage cited in note (m), *inf*)

(j) R S C , O 19, r 15 *Wallingford* v *Mutual Society*, *inf* , was a case of fraud as a defence see note (o), *inf*.

(k) See Ch V, Sect 2, Sub ss (1), (2), (3), (4), *ante*

(l) *Ibid* , Sub ss (5), (6), *ante*

(m) See, as to the analogous case of fraud, *Davy* v *Garrett*, *sup* , *per* THESIGER, L J , at p. 489 . "there is another still stronger objection to the statement of claim The plaintiffs say that fraud is intended to be alleged, yet it contains no charge of fraud . It may not be necessary in all cases to use the word 'fraud'—indeed, in one of the most ordinary cases, it is not necessary" &c but "the plaintiff is bound to show distinctly "—i e by pleading facts amounting in law to fraud—"that he means to allege fraud."

(n) As to the presumptions made in favour of the servient party from a proved relation of influence, see § 405, and the cases cited in note (a), thereto, *ante* That a party need not aver anything which the law presumes in his favour, is expressly provided by O 19, r 25

(o) The observance of this rule has been always strictly insisted upon in cases of fraud *Redgrave* v. *Hurd* (1881), 20 C D. 1 (*per* JESSEL, M.R,, at p 12) ; *Lawrance* v. *Lord Norreys* (1890), 15 App Cas 210, H L (*per* Lord HERSCHELL, at p 219, and Lord WATSON, at pp 221, 222) , *Bentley* v *Black* (1893), 9 T L. R 580, C A , *Birch* v *Birch*, [1902] P 130, C. A (*per* COZENS-HARDY, L J , at p 138) The rule equally applies to an affidavit see *Wallingford* v *Mutual Society* (1880), 5 App -Cas 685, H L (*per* Lord SELBORNE, L C , at p 697, with reference to an affidavit of a defendant in proceedings under O XIV , setting up fraud as a ground for leave to defend "with regard to fraud, if there be any principle which is perfectly well settled, it is that general allegations, however strong may be the words in which they are stated, are insufficient even to amount to an averment of fraud of which any court ought to take notice ")

(p) "The amount and kind of explanatory statement required in order to impart relevancy to such charges will necessarily vary according to circumstances" *per* Lord WATSON, at p 222 of *Lawrance* v *Lord Norreys*, *sup* Similarly, where actual damage is a necessary element in the cause of action, "as much certainty and particularity must be insisted on as is reasonable, having regard to the circumstances, and to the nature of the acts themselves by which the damage is done "*per* BOWEN, L J , at p 532 of *Ratcliffe* v *Evans*, [1892] 2 Q B 524, C A

(q) For, where misrepresentation is alleged, it is obvious that the party who sets it up is in a position to give full particulars without discovery, or, if he is not, he should not have brought his action, or raised his affirmative plea. On precisely the same principle, the duty alleged to have been broken is one of good faith In all such cases, as will be seen hereafter, the party complaining has an absolute right to discovery, if he insists upon it, before delivering his particulars (r).

608. It is not ordinarily permissible to raise at the trial a case of non-disclosure which has not appeared in any pleading of the party seeking relief, and which is a new case, not merely in point of form and expression, but in substance (s). Where, however, on the cross-examination of a party at the trial, admissions are made by him which show that such a case might have been made by the other party in the first instance, if he had been then aware of the facts which he has succeeded in eliciting on such examination, leave will be given to amend, and judgment may be given for the latter party on such amended case, or, subject to penalization in the matter of costs, even where no such amendment has been made or asked for (t) In that event, if the former party is taken by surprise, but not otherwise, it is proper to offer him a reasonable adjournment (u).

609. Where non-disclosure is set up as a defence to an action to enforce a contract, it is incumbent on the defendant to allege in his pleading that, from the time when he discovered the existence or occurrence of the undisclosed fact, he never recognized any liability, or asserted any right, or derived any benefit, under the contract impeached, but did what in him lay to disaffirm it (v)

610. In all cases of non-disclosure, the party complaining is entitled to have an affidavit from the party charged containing such discovery of facts and documents as will enable him to deliver, if otherwise unable to do so,

---

the defamer who pleads justification to an action of defamation is not entitled to discovery to enable him to give particulars of his plea · *Zierenberg* v *Labouchere*, [1893] 2 Q B 183, C. A.

(r) See § 610, *post*, as to non disclosure cases, generally, and § 611, *post*, as to marine insurance cases in particular At p 187 of *Zierenberg* v *Labouchere, sup*, KAY, L.J, is careful to distinguish non disclosure cases, in this respect, from the class of case there under consideration

(s) *Nicol* v *Vaughan* (1833), 1 Cl & Fin 495 (where, after two trials and two appeals to the House of Lords, it was sought, on a third hearing, to raise an entirely new case for impeaching the bond there in question, viz that it was in the nature of an undisclosed gift by principal to agent, in breach of the latter's fiduciary duty On a third appeal to the House of Lords, it was held that this could not be done · *per* Lord BROUGHAM, L.C, at pp. 520–525) Cp *Lawrance* v *Lord Norreys* (1890), 15 App. Cas 210, H L., at p 213, where it appears that the plaintiff had been, in the Q B. D, refused leave to amend by setting up concealed fraud, or an expanded statement thereof In *Omnium Electric Palaces, Ltd* v. *Barnes*, [1914] 1 Ch 332, C A , SARGANT, J , at the trial, whilst allowing a very limited amendment, refused to permit the plaintiffs to transform their whole case by adding a new claim for account on the theory of secret profits, which (as he said, at p. 544), if raised at the proper time, would have altered the entire course of the defendant's interlocutory proceedings and evidence

(t) *Shipway* v. *Broadwood*, [1899] 1 Q B. 369, C A (a case of fraud).

(u) *Riding* v *Hawkins* (1889), 14 P. D 56, where, in a probate action, it appeared from admissions made by the defendant in cross examination at the trial that the plaintiff might have had a possible case of fraud, which he had not pleaded, and BUTT, J , thereupon gave the latter leave to amend by adding an allegation, with particulars, that the execution of the will had been obtained by fraud, at the same time offering the defendant a postponement of the trial to enable him to meet the new charges. This course (though a new trial was ordered on other grounds) met with the approval, on appeal, of Sir JAMES HANNEN, P., and A L SMITH, J   see the observations of the latter at p, 59.

(v) See § 246, and the cases cited in note (k) thereto, *ante*.

proper particulars of his claim, or (as the case may be) of his defence (w). In ordinary cases, the party alleging a breach of contract or tort would not be so entitled : but, where the wrong complained of is the withholding of information which, by reason of the relation between the parties, ought in good faith to have been divulged, the same considerations which give rise to the initial obligation of disclosure justify the imposition of a like duty of discovery at the earliest stage in the litigation.

611. In actions of marine insurance, a fuller measure of discovery is exacted from the assured even than that which is required in other proceedings for non-disclosure. "In cases of this nature, the underwriters are entitled not only to discovery of all the circumstances attending the original contract, but to the whole history of the adventure and loss," and "nothing" could be "more dangerous than to limit the rights of the underwriters to discovery "(x) The order is made without any affidavit on the part of the applicant, and it provides for a stay of the action until the assured, *and all persons interested*, do produce all the ship's papers and documents, such production being (in the case of the assured) verified and vouched on oath (y). This rule, as a rule special to marine insurance business, was adopted by the Courts at an early stage in the history of our commercial law, and (as has been held, in spite of vigorous contentions to the contrary) was neither impliedly abolished, nor affected in any way, by the Judicature Acts, and remains part of the established practice (z) It has further been distinctly laid down that, if any question arises as to the sufficiency of the affidavit of discovery, the assured must satisfy the Court that he has taken all possible steps, not only to produce the documents from his own or his agent's custody, but to procure their production by other interested parties over whom he has no absolute legal control, and he must further give all possible information as to the

(w) *Whyte* v *Ahrens* (1884), 26 C D 717, C A ; *Leitch* v *Abbott* (1886), 31 C. D 374, C A., *Sachs* v *Spielman* (1887), 37 C. D 295 , *Edelston* v *Russell* (1888), 57 L T 927

(x) Per Lord ABINGER, C B , at pp 136, 137 of *Janson* v *Solarte* (1836), 2 Y & C (Exch in Eq) 127 So also BRETT, L.J , at p 145 of *China S S Co* v *Commercial Assurance Co* (1881), 8 Q B. D 142, C. A , emphasizes the fact that "long before the Judicature Acts, *the peculiarity of insurance business* had given rise to a practice   of granting discovery *to a larger extent than in ordinary business*." The same explanation of the special rules as to discovery in marine insurance cases is given in *Boulton* v *Houlder Bros* , [1904] 1 K B 784, C A , by COLLINS, M.R , at p 790 ("the discovery allowed in an ordinary action would be ineffectual in such a case as the present "), and by MATHEW, L.J , at pp 791, 792 (" it is an essential condition of a policy of insurance that the underwriters should be treated with good faith, not merely with reference to the inception of the risk, but in the steps taken to carry out the contract *That being the meaning of the contract*, effect is given to it by means of the order of discovery of ship's papers, and the affidavit with relation to them In order that the underwriters should be on equal terms with the assured, *a stringent form of order for discovery* has been long in use ")

(y) See *Twizell* v. *Allen* (1839), 5 M & W 337 , *Rayner* v. *Ritsen* (1865), 6 B & S 888 , *West of England Bank* v *Canton Insurance Co.* (1877), 2 Ex D 472 (where, DENMAN, J , having struck out of the order the words " and all persons interested," the Court restored them) ; *China S S. Co* v. *Commercial Assurance Co* , sup , *China Trading Insurance Co* v *Royal Exchange Assurance Co* (1898), 3 Comm. Cas 189 , *Boulton* v *Houlder Bros* , sup

(z) Per CLEASBY, B., at p 474 of *West of England Bank* v *Canton Insurance Co* , sup "the old practice, *which is confined to actions on marine policies*, was not superseded by the Judicature Acts " This statement was followed by BRETT, L J., in *China S S Co* v *Commercial Assurance Co* , sup (see the passage cited in note (x), sup.).

contents of such documents as he cannot produce, or procure to be produced(a). The practice in question, as a matter of history, is supposed to have originated at the time when applications first began to be made by assured parties for orders consolidating separate actions brought against the several underwriters, and the Courts thereupon required the assured, as a condition of this indulgence, to make ample discovery (b)

Sub-s. (2). Certain Rules of Practice in Proceedings for Non-Disclosure.

612. There are certain rules of practice, as to joinder of parties and causes of action, which, in relation to proceedings for non-disclosure in prospectuses of companies and to marine insurance cases, require to be noticed

613. First, as to joinder of parties. It generally happens, where there has been statutory non-disclosure in the prospectus of a company, that relief is claimed by a number of allottees. In that case, each of them can sue separately, or all, or any two or more, of them can join in suing (c), but, in the latter event, each plaintiff must establish his separate right to relief as regards matters which are peculiar to his own case (d). No "representative" proceedings, therefore, can be instituted, that is to say, it is

(a) See *West of England Bank* v *Canton Insurance Co* (1877), 2 Ex. D 472, where the plaintiffs, mortgagees of the insured vessel, in vain protested that they had no control over the mortgagor in whose custody were the required documents (*per* CLEASBY, B., at p 175 : "they cannot say, 'We will do no more than make an affidavit that we have no papers ourselves, or none under our actual control'   No; they must go further, and endeavour to comply with the practice in substance , that is to say, they must endeavour to produce the ship's papers , they must satisfy us that they have made application to the mortgagor"); *London & Provincial Insurance Co* v *Chambers* (1900), 5 Comm Cas 241 , *Boulton* v *Houlder Bros* , [1904] 1 K B 784, C A, where the underwriters were not being sued, but were plaintiffs in an action to recover policy moneys already paid so far as they exceeded the sums properly payable, on the ground of the bad faith of the assured in ignorance of which the excessive payments had been made, and the plaintiffs were held entitled to the same measure of full discovery from the defendants, according to the established practice, as if they had not already paid the money, and were being sued for it on the policies (*per* COLLINS, M R , at pp 789, 790, and MATHEW, L J , at p. 792) , the order for discovery here made was to the same effect as, but more elaborate than, that which was made in *West of England Bank* v *Canton Insurance Co* , *sup.*, though, as in that case, it was again fruitlessly contended on behalf of the assured that they ought not to be compelled to produce documents which were not in their custody, or only in their custody as agents for other persons (*per* COLLINS, M.R , at p. 790, who said that the discovery " ought certainly to embrace a statement on oath by the defendants as to the steps they have taken to put themselves in a position to produce the documents, and failing to produce them, they should be directed to give such information as to them as they can obtain by reasonable exertions on their part ", to which MATHEW, L.J , at p 791, added that the defendants ought " to state what they know as to the contents of " the documents in question)

(b) *Twizell* v *Allen* (1839), 5 M. & W 337 (*per* MAULE, B , during the argument, at p 339); *Boulton* v *Houlder Bros* , *sup* (*per* COLLINS, M R , at p 790)

(c) See § 539, and the cases cited in note (*g*) thereto, *ante*

(d) *Arnison* v. *Smith* (1888), 41 C D 348, C A (a case, not of non disclosure, but of misrepresentations in the prospectus   for the present purpose, however, this circumstance is immaterial) furnishes a good practical illustration of what is stated in the text.   There 12 of the 52 plaintiffs did not appear at the trial, in the mistaken expectation that a judgment for the 40 who established their right to relief would enure for their benefit also KEKEWICH, J , who decided in favour of the forty who appeared, was compelled to give judgment against the twelve absentees, which latter judgment the C A were no more able to disturb than the former, though their order affirming it was expressed to be " without prejudice to a fresh action " (pp 374, 375)

not permissible for any one of the subscribers to sue on behalf of himself and all others constituting the class of persons claiming to have been injured, for, though questions as to the issue of the prospectus, and as to the omission therefrom, and the materiality (in some cases), of the undisclosed matter, are common to every member of the so-called "class," other important questions, and particularly those relating to inducement and damage, are special to the individual (e). If, however, where a "representative" suit is instituted, no application is made by any defendant before the trial to strike out so much of the title of the action as purports to give it a representative character, the plaintiff's case will not be dismissed, but will be heard as if he were suing on his own behalf alone (f) The usual practice in such cases is to resort to the "test action" form of order, the procedure being as follows The subscribers claiming relief issue separate writs in the first instance, whereupon an application is made at chambers for an order whereby one of the actions is selected as a test, and the others are stayed until the trial of the action so selected, upon proper terms for the protection of the defendants on the one hand, and, on the other hand, for the prevention of prejudice to any of the plaintiffs in the outstanding actions from collusive or incompetent conduct of the test action (g)

614 Similarly, in the case of a number of underwriters of a marine insurance policy, though (as has been explained) the contract of each underwriter with the assured is a separate and distinct one (h), yet in practice some one underwriter is habitually sued without objection, and, being so sued, sets up any defence he may have, including that of non-disclosure, on behalf of himself and all the others, who by express or tacit agreement consent to be bound by the result No doubt, the assured has the right, if so minded, to sue each underwriter separately, but in that case the defendants would immediately apply for, and, in the absence of special circumstances obtain, a consolidation order (i) To avoid this circuitous process, the more business-like course referred to is always adopted. It sometimes,

---

(e) Community of interest or of liability alone justifies a representative suit: *Jones* v. *Garcia del Rio* (1823), 1 T. & Russ. 297, *Long* v *Yonge* (1830), 2 Sim 369, *Markt & Co.* v *Knight S S. Co.*, [1910] 2 K B 1021, C A, *Allen* v *Hyatt* (1914), 30 T L R. 444, P. C There is no such community in the case of several allottees suing in respect of statutory non disclosure, any more than there is where several persons sue for misrepresentation (common law or statutory), in a prospectus. In both classes of case the "inducement," or the taking of the shares "on the faith of" the prospectus, is a separate issue in relation to each individual plaintiff see *Croskey* v *Bank of Wales* (1860), 4 Giff 314 (*per* STUART, V C., at p. 330), *Hallows* v. *Fernie* (1868), 3 Ch App. 467 (*per* Lord CHELMSFORD, L C, at p 471) The old rule as to representative actions is now embodied in the R S C, O 16, r 9. The case of *Beeching* v *Lloyd* (1855), 2 Drew 229, which was approved in the dissentient judgment of BUCKLEY, L J, at pp 1045, 1046 of *Markt & Co* v *Knight S S Co*, would seem to be in direct conflict with *Hallows* v *Fernie, sup*, which latter case was not noticed either by BUCKLEY, L J, or by the majority with whom he disagreed
(f) This course was adopted in *Hallows* v. *Fernie, sup* Cp. *Allen* v *Hyatt, sup*
(g) For an elaborate form of an order in a test action, see that made by FIELD, J., in *Bennett* v *Lord Bury* (1880), 5 C. P. D 339, as set out at p 346.
(h) See § 277, *ante* In *Janson* v. *Property Insurance Co.* (1913), 19 Comm Cas 36, this principle seems to have been entirely overlooked
(i) Both under the old practice in cases of marine insurance, and now under O 49, r. 8.

though very rarely, happens that the underwriters, without waiting to be sued on the policy, take the field themselves and institute proceedings against the assured for rescission of the policy or analogous relief. In that case, unless objection is made by the defendant, any one or more of them can sue in a representative character (j), and there are instances of the adoption of this procedure (k).

615 Secondly, as regards joinder of causes of action in one proceeding by, or against, several parties   The general rule, applicable to non-disclosure as to other cases, but specially illustrated by the decisions in proceedings against companies and their officers, is that several plaintiffs may sue, and several defendants may be sued, together in respect of several causes of action, if (in the case of plaintiffs) those causes " arise out of the same transaction, or series of transactions," or if (in the case of either plaintiffs or defendants) evidence in support of one cause of action would be evidence in support of the other or others (l), but not otherwise (m)

Sub-s (3)   Misfeasance Procedure in the Liquidation of Companies

616 It will have been noticed that a considerable proportion of the authorities cited in an earlier chapter to illustrate the fiduciary duty of disclosure which is owed to a company by its promoter (n), or by its agents (o), were cases in which the company was being wound up, and that in nearly all these cases the relief granted, or applied for, was of a statutory nature, pursuant to successive enactments framed with the object of providing a summary remedy for " misfeasance " (which includes cases of non-disclosure) in the liquidation of companies   The procedure referred to was introduced in 1862 (p), extended in 1890 (q), and re-enacted, with some further

(j) Under O 16, r 9   See *Janson* v *Property Insurance Co.* (1913), 19 Comm Cas 36, a case of a policy on a motor car according to the practice at Lloyds'

(k) As in *Rivaz* v *Gerussi* (1880), 6 Q B. D 222 (successful representative action for rescission), *Brooking* v *Maudslay* (1883), 38 C D 836 (representative action for declaration and injunction, which failed on the merits)

(l) As regards plaintiffs, see O 16, r 1, which should be read in conjunction with O 18, r 1. As regards defendants, see O 16, rr 4, 7, which, though not expressed in terms so wide as those of O 16, r 1 in its present extended form, have been liberally interpreted so as to bring the companion rules into harmony   see *Compania Sansinena de Carnes Congeladas* v *Houlder Bros & Co*, [1910] 2 K B 354, C. A , *Œsterreichische Export, &c* v *British Indemnity Assurance Co*, [1914] 2 K B 747, C A (per KENNEDY, L J , at pp 752, 754, and SWINFEN EADY, L J , at pp 756, 757)   Illustrations of actions against several defendants in respect of different causes of action, one of these causes of action being statutory non disclosure in a prospectus, which have been held unobjectionable, on the principles stated in the text, are —*Frankenburg* v *Great Horseless Carriage Co*, [1900] 1 Q B. 504, C A (per LINDLEY, M R , at pp 508, 509, and ROMER, L.J , at pp 510–512) *Greenwood* v *Leather Shod Wheel Co*, [1900] 1 Ch 421, C A , *J & P Coats, Ltd* v *Crossland* (1904), 20 T L. R 800.

(m) See *Gower* v *Couldridge*, [1898] 1 Q B. 348, C A , which was recognized as a sound decision, and distinguished, by LINDLEY, M R , at pp 508, 509 of *Frankenburg* v *Great Horseless Carriage Co*, sup., *Stroud* v *Lawson*, [1898] 2 Q B 44, C A (per A L SMITH, L J , at pp 50, 51, CHITTY, L J , at p. 52, and VAUGHAN WILLIAMS, L.J , at pp 54, 55)

(n) In Ch. IV, Sect. 2, Sub s. (2), *ante*

(o) See Ch IV, Sect. 2, Sub s. (3), *ante.*

(p) By s 165 of the Companies Act, 1862 (25 & 26 Vict , c 89)

(q) By s 10 of the Companies (Winding Up) Act, 1890 (53 & 54 Vict , c 63)

amplification, in the consolidating statute of 1908 (r). In its present form, the enactment runs as follows · " where in the course of winding up of a company it appears that any person who has taken part in the formation or promotion of a company, or any past or present director, manager, or liquidator, or any officer of the company, has misapplied or retained or become liable or accountable for any money or property of the company, or has been guilty of any misfeasance or breach of trust in relation to the company, the court may, on the application of the official receiver, or of the liquidator, or of any creditor or contributory, examine into the conduct of the promoter, director, manager, liquidator, or officer, and compel him to repay or restore the money or property or any part thereof respectively with interest at such rate as the court thinks just, or to contribute such sum to the assets of the company by way of compensation in respect of the misapplication, retainer, misfeasance, or breach of trust as the court thinks just." It is now proposed to analyze and interpret this provision in the light of the authorities The question of the courts having jurisdiction in misfeasance procedure has already been considered (s) The application for relief is by summons in the High Court, and by motion in any other court, supported by affidavit The liquidator is not bound to resort to the summary remedy : he can sue, if he pleases, in the name of the company, or (as in certain cases may be expedient) he can seek to attain his object by settling the name of the delinquent on the list of contributories in respect of shares which he has secretly received from the promoter as a gift or bribe (t). If he elects to pursue the statutory remedy, it is not a matter of course that he will be allowed to proceed : the court has a discretion, as in the case of summary applications to rectify the register, though it is very seldom that it refuses to exercise the jurisdiction, and the circumstances must be very special to justify such a refusal (u). The procedure is *primâ facie* applicable to a winding up by the court, or subject to its supervision, but on the application of the liquidator, or any contributory or creditor, it may in a proper case, and on such conditions as may appear just, be applied to a voluntary winding up (v). The burden of proof on the applicant is as

(r) Companies (Consolidation) Act, 1908, (8 Edw 7, c 69), s 215 Each of the cases cited below is a decision on the particular one of the three sections which was in force at the time

(s) See § 605, note (b), *ante* The authorities cited in the remaining notes to this Sub-section relate to " misfeasances " of all kinds, for the reason that illustrations of procedure in " misfeasance " are obviously independent of the particular delinquency in respect of which the procedure is resorted to In fact, it is only a few of the non disclosure cases dealt with in Ch IV, Sect 2, Sub s (2), *ante*, which are of importance in connection with the present topic of procedure

(t) See § 388, notes (q), (r), and (s), *ante*

(u) In the peculiar circumstances of *Re Sunlight Incandescent Co* (1900), 16 T L R 535, WRIGHT, J , declined to give statutory relief GIFFARD, L J , however, at p 494 of *Re Mercantile Trading Co., Stringer's Case* (1869), 4 Ch App 475, observed "I think the instances are rare in which the jurisdiction ought not to be exercised "

(v) See *Re County Marine Insurance Co* (1870), 6 Ch App 104, where (*per* JAMES, L J , at pp 114, 115, and MELLISH, L.J , at pp 120, 121) it was held that s 138 of the Act of 1862 (now s 193 of the Act of 1908) enabled the misfeasance procedure authorized by s. 165 of that Act (now s 215 of the Act of 1908) to be applied, under the prescribed conditions, to voluntary liquidations

follows   First, he must establish that the respondent's conduct was such as to constitute " misfeasance " within the section, which is not the same thing by any means as misfeasance at large   " It has been settled," said Lord MACNAGHTEN in a well-known judgment (w), " and I think rightly settled, that that section "—he was referring to s. 165 of the Act of 1862, which in this respect is the same as s 215 of the Act of 1908—" creates no new offence, and that it gives no new rights, but only provides a summary and efficient remedy in respect of rights which apart from that section might have been vindicated at law or in equity. It has also been settled that the misfeasance spoken of in that section is not misfeasance in the abstract, but misfeasance in the nature of a breach of trust resulting in a loss to the company." Besides proving that the non-disclosure or other wrongful act complained of was actionable at law or in equity, that it was, if not a breach of trust, a violation of some fiduciary duty to the company, and that it occasioned damage or loss to such company, the applicant must also, if challenged on any of these matters, establish that he belongs to one of the classes entitled to the benefit of the statutory procedure (that is, official receiver, liquidator, creditor, or contributory), and, if a creditor or contributory, that he has an interest in the result of the application (x), and that the respondent was at the date of the alleged misfeasance a member of some one or more of the classes of persons rendered by the section amenable to its provisions, that is to say, was a person " who took part in the formation or promotion of the

(w) At p 669 of *Bentinck* v *Fenn* (1889), 12 App Cas. 652, H L   Cp the observations of JAMES, L J , at p 670 of *Re Canadian & Land Reclaiming & Colonizing Co , Coventry and Dixon's Case* (1880), 14 C D 660, C. A   " misfeasance in that section means   something which the officer of the company has done wrongly by which   the company's property has been wasted, or the company's credit improperly pledged   It must be some act resulting in loss to the company "   " Misfeasance in the abstract " will not do (*per* BRAMWELL, L J , *ibid* , pp 672, 673).   The wrong must have been committed " in relation to the company," as is expressly provided by the section.   Though there may be a misfeasance which is not actually a breach of trust, as in the case of *Re Cardiff Savings Bank, Davies's Case* (1890), 45 C. D 537, the act complained of must at least constitute a violation of some fiduciary obligation to the company, in such a way as to diminish its assets, as distinguished from mere negligence, for instance, or other breach of non-fiduciary duty   *Re Forest of Dean Coal Mining Co* (1878) 10 C D 450 (*per* JESSEL, M R , at pp 458, 459), *Re Hill's Waterfall Estate & Gold Mining Co* , [1896] 1 Ch 947 (see note (b), *inf*), *Re Kingston Cotton Mill Co* , *No* 2, [1896] 2 Ch. 279, C. A (*per* LINDLEY, L J , at p 283, LOPES, L J , at p 288, and KAY, L J , at p 291)   In short, it is an entire mistake to suppose that because the section provides a summary means of getting what could be got by the ordinary procedure (*per* LINDLEY, L J , at p 334 of *Re North Australian Territory Co* , *Archer's Case*, [1892] 1 Ch 322, C A), and because every misfeasance must be actionable, therefore everything that is actionable is a misfeasance

(x) *Bentinck* v *Fenn* (1887), 12 App Cas 652, H. L (*per* Lord HERSCHELL, at pp 664, 665, Lord WATSON, at p. 667, and Lord MACNAGHTEN, at pp 669, 672)   In that case the applicant, being, though a contributory, the holder of fully paid shares, was held to have had no interest in the result of his application   Perhaps this was the reason why, in the case of *Re Westmoreland Green & Blue Slate Co* , *Bland's Case*, [1893] 2 Ch 612, C A , a contributory obtained the leave of the Court to institute the proceedings in the name of the liquidator   It was on precisely the same principle that, where one of three partners in an insolvent firm filed a bill for the rescission of a purchase of the estate at an undervalue by a person who was trustee for the sale thereof for the benefit of the creditors, the bill was dismissed, it appearing that, even if the estate could have been sold for what the plaintiff alleged to be its full value, there would have been no surplus for the partners, after satisfying the creditors' claims, and therefore the plaintiff had no substantial interest in the suit : *Dover* v. *Buck* (1865), 12 L T 136 (*per* STUART, V -C , at p 137)

company " (*y*), if the company is being wound up in England,—for, if it is being wound up in Ireland or Scotland, such a person is expressly exempted from liability under the section (*z*),—or that such respondent was a past or present director (*a*), manager, liquidator (*b*), or "officer" of the company This last expression means and includes any permanent official constituted as such either by statute, or by the memorandum or articles of the company (*c*), but not any person otherwise appointed or employed, such as (ordinarily) the company's banker (*d*), nor its solicitor (*e*), nor its liquidator, where (there being no case against him as such liquidator) he is sought to be made liable in his character of "officer," unless in connection with the alleged misfeasance he was executing duties imposed on him as a receiver or otherwise under the Companies Winding Up Rules (*f*), nor a trustee for the company's debenture-

(*y*) As to what constitutes "promotership," see §§ 327, 328, *ante* Presumably "formation" is not used as a mere synonym of "promotion," and the legislature must be supposed to have contemplated the case of a person who, without being a promoter, assisted in bringing the company into being The class of "promoters" are not mentioned in s. 165 of the Act of 1862

(*z*) See s 215, sub s (4), of the Act of 1908

(*a*) A *de facto*, as well as a *de jure*, director is within the section *Re Canadian Land Reclaiming & Colonizing Co*, *Coventry and Dixon's Case* (1880), 14 C D 660, C A (*per* JESSEL, M.R., in the Court below, at p 666, and, in the C A, *per* JAMES, L J, at p 670, and BRAMWELL, L J, at p 673, so far agreeing with him, though the actual decision was reversed), *Re Western Counties Steam Bakeries & Milling Co*, [1897] 1 Ch 617, C A (*per* LINDLEY, L J, at pp 626, 627, and A L SMITH, L J, at pp 629, 630) "Director" is defined in s 285 of the Act of 1908 as including "any person occupying the position of director by whatever name called"

(*b*) A liquidator can only be proceeded against in the character of one who, as such, has property of the company in his hands or under his control, in relation to which he is contravening, or omitting, some fiduciary obligation to such company A claim against a liquidator based on his alleged neglect to allot shares to the applicant in pursuance of a reconstruction scheme is in reality nothing more than a personal claim for damages, in respect of a breach of non-fiduciary duty, and so fails to satisfy either of the two conditions —see note (*w*), *sup*—required to bring the case within the section *Re Hill's Waterfall Estate & Gold Mining Co*, [1896] 1 Ch. 947 (*per* STIRLING, J., at p 953)

(*c*) Such as, for instance, a secretary, as in *Re Morvah Consols Tin Mining Co*, *McKay's Case* (1875), 2 C D 1, C A (*per* MELLISH, L.J., at p 6, and BRETT, J., at pp 7, 8): a trustee of a Savings Bank, as in *Re Cardiff Savings Bank*, *Davies's Case* (1890), 45 C. D 537, or an auditor, if so constituted as stated in the text, as in *Re London & General Bank*, [1895] 2 Ch 166, C A, and *Re Kingston Cotton Mill Co*, No 1, [1896] 1 Ch 6, C A, but not otherwise, *e.g*, an accountant called in to audit the company's accounts, who holds no "office" under the articles, or by statute, is not amenable to the section · *Re Western Counties Steam Bakeries & Milling Co*, *sup* (*per* LINDLEY, L J, at pp 627, 628, who points out that, where the section specifies a particular office by name, such as a "director," a directorship *de facto* is sufficient, but, where it is a question whether the misfeasant comes within the generic description of "officer," it is essential to establish the "office," and mere proof of the *de facto* performance of acts proper to the execution of such an office, if it had been created, does not establish this fact A solicitor may, perhaps, under very special circumstances, be deemed an "officer," but *primâ facie* he is not so see note (*e*), *inf*

(*d*) *Re Imperial Land Co of Marseilles* (1870), L R 10 Eq 298, *Re General Provident Assurance Co* (1872), 14 Eq 507

(*e*) *Re Great Wheal Polgooth Co* (1883), 53 L J (CH.) 42 (*per* BACON, V C, at p 47), *Re Great Western Forest of Dean Coal Consumers Co*, *Carter's Case* (1886), 31 C D 496 But a solicitor who undertakes all the company's business at a fixed salary has been held to come within the description of "officer" *Re Liberator Benefit Building Society* (1894), 71 L T 406 (*per* CAVE, J, at pp 407, 408, and COLLINS, J, at p 408)

(*f*) *Re Hill's Waterfall Estate & Gold Mining Co*, [1896] 1 Ch 947 (*per* STIRLING, J., at pp 954, 955) The rules there relied upon, though unsuccessfully, were Rules 89, 90 of the Companies (Winding Up) Rules, 1890, which correspond to Rule 75 of the present Companies (Winding Up) Rules.

holders (q) On the death of an alleged misfeasant, his representatives do not become amenable to the procedure (h). An ambassador, or other diplomatic representative of a foreign State, or his secretary, or a member of his suite, is no less exempt from liability as a misfeasant than he is from liability to any other civil process (hh) It should be noted that, though in ordinary cases of a fiduciary relation it is not incumbent on the party complaining to prove non-disclosure as a condition precedent to relief, this burden is placed upon the shoulders of one who resorts to the statutory remedy, for, the onus being on him to prove the statutory misfeasance, it follows that, where the misfeasance is alleged to have consisted in non-disclosure, such non-disclosure must be established (i) The grounds of the application should always be stated on the face of the summons, or in the affidavit filed in support (j). It is not necessary to aver, or prove, actual or personal fraud (k) The remedies provided by the enactment are:—repayment of money with interest, restoration of property (other than money), or compensation in the nature of damages, as the circumstances of the case may require (l) The questions which may arise as to the measure of value, or of damages, the rate of interest, and the like, have already been discussed (m). A misfeasance claim is the subject of assignment (n) In an earlier chapter, the question of the nature and extent of the liability of a deceased delinquent's estate has been considered (o) A right to the recovery of money or damages against a misfeasant under the statutory procedure is not the subject as set off (p), though, to the same extent and under the same conditions as any common law right, it may be the subject of release (pp).

(g) *Astley v New Tivoli, Ltd*, [1899] 1 Ch. 151 (*per* NORTH, J, at p 154)

(h) *Re East of England Bank, Felton's Executors' Case* (1865), L. R. 1 Eq 219, *Re British Guardian Life Association Co* (1880), 14 C D 335 (*per* HALL, V C, at pp 340, 341)

(hh) *Re Republic of Bolivia Exploration Syndicate*, [1914] 1 Ch. 139 (*per* ASTBURY, J, at pp. 148–157).

(i) *Bentinck v. Fenn* (1887), 12 App Cas. 652, H L. (*per* Lord WATSON, at p 666, and Lord MACNAGHTEN at pp 670, 671), *Re North Australian Territory Co*, *Archer's Case*, [1892] 1 Ch 322, C A (*per* LINDLEY, L J, at p. 335, and BOWEN, L J, at p 341)

(j) *Bentinck v Fenn*, *sup* (*per* Lord HERSCHELL at pp 662, 663), *Re New Mashonaland Exploration Co*, [1892] 3 Ch. 577 (*per* VAUGHAN WILLIAMS, J, at pp. 583, 584)

(k) *Re Sale Hotel & Botanical Gardens, Ltd*, *Ex p Hesketh* (1898), 78 L T 368, C A (*per* LINDLEY, M.R, at p 370 ' such application need not be based on fraud, except so far as secrecy involves fraud The word ' fraud ' is not to be found in the section, and fraud need not be either alleged or proved to bring a person within its operation ")

(l) See s. 215, sub s (1) of the Act of 1908 By sub s (2), the section is to apply though the misfeasance may be one for which the misfeasant is criminally responsible By sub-s (3), an order for payment of money made under the section is to be deemed a final judgment within the meaning of s 4, (1), (g), of the Bankruptcy Act, 1883 (46 & 47 Vict c 52), now s. 1, (1), (g), of the Bankruptcy Act, 1914 (4 & 5 Geo 5, c 59) By sub s, (4), " so much of the section as relates to " (*inter alia*) " property of the company other than money " is not to " apply to a winding up in Scotland or Ireland."

(m) In §§ 379, 380, *ante*

(n) See § 279, *ante.*

(o) See § 379, note (d), and § 388, note (o), *ante*

(p) *Re Anglo French Co operative Society*, *Ex p Pelly* (1882), 21 C. D 492, C A (*per* JESSEL, M R, at pp 502, 503, BRETT, L J, at p. 507, and COTTON, L J, at pp 599, 510), *Re Carriage Co operative Supply Association* (1884), 27 C D. 322 (*per* PEARSON, J, at pp 330, 331)

(pp) See *Re Joint Stock Trust and Finance Corporation* (1912), 56 Sol J 272. As to the conditions on which releases are valid at common law, see § 132, *ante*

Sub-s. (4). Costs in Proceedings for Non-Disclosure.

617. It is often said that, whereas in cases heard without a jury, the discretion of the judge as to costs is unfettered, in cases tried before a judge and jury the judge has very little discretion at all, since, in the absence of a special order, "the costs follow the event," that is, the verdict of the jury: but the difference between the two modes of trial, as regards the nature, limits, and conditions of the judicial control over costs, has been greatly exaggerated, such control being, in the former case, considerably less, and, in the latter, considerably more, than is generally supposed (*q*). In deference, however, to the supposed distinction, it is proposed to limit the succeeding observations to the consideration of rules as to costs in proceedings for non-disclosure heard before a judge alone

618. Any judge would strongly and justly resent the statement that there are, or the suggestion that there ought to be, any rules of law or practice dictating to him the lines on which he is to exercise his discretion in the matter of costs,—a discretion which must necessarily have regard to the individual circumstances of the particular case, the conduct and attitude of the parties, and a variety of matters which no cast-iron formula is capable of coping with, or foreseeing. At the same time it must not be forgotten that, firstly, it is a condition precedent to the exercise of any discretion at all that there be some materials on which to exercise it (*r*), and that, secondly, even in relation to the cases where such materials are present, great equity judges, without listening for a moment to any dictation or intrusion *ab extra*, have nevertheless from time to time enunciated certain leading principles or rules of conduct, for their own guidance and convenience, as to the disposition of costs in certain circumstances and conditions. The first, and the most firmly established, of these "rules of conduct" is that which visits a party who succeeds in his action or defence with the costs of any unproved charge of fraud which he may have unnecessarily made—and in every case of non-disclosure, as has already been explained in the proper places, such a charge is wholly gratuitous (*s*) In all such cases, though the party, if otherwise entitled to succeed, is not ordinarily deprived of his right to judgment (*t*), he is, in the absence of special circumstances, mulcted in costs, to a greater or less degree according to the view which the judge takes of the conduct of both parties throughout the litigation, by some one of the many

(*q*) For, by O 65, r 1, where there is a jury, the judge may make any "exceptional order" which may appear to him just as to costs, that is to say, any order which will prevent the costs "following the event" in the usual course Illustrations of the various forms of such "exceptional orders" are given in the notes appended to this Rule in the books of practice It is true that the discretion does not exist where there is no "good cause," that is, where there are *no* materials on which it can be exercised but equally, according to the modern authorities, a judge sitting without a jury has no jurisdiction to make an "exceptional order" as to costs in the absence of any materials at all . see the cases cited in the next note

(*r*) *New Brunswick and Canada Railway and Land Co* v *Conybeare* (1862), 9 H L. C. 711 (see note (*v*), *post*), *Civil Service Co operative Society* v *General Steam Navigation Co*, [1903] 2 K B 756, C A.; *King (F) & Co* v. *Gillard & Co*, [1905] 2 Ch 7, C A

(*s*) See § 197, and note (*k*) thereto, § 358, § 461, and note (*k*) to § 616, *ante*

(*t*) See note (*m*) to § 300, *ante*

varieties of order which have been framed for this purpose (u). On the other hand, a judge has no right to exercise his discretion in the opposite direction by dismissing without costs the action of a plaintiff who has based his case on fraud, and has failed to prove it, the defendant being entitled in such a case to have the action dismissed with costs in the ordinary way (v), unless, again, there are special circumstances, as, for instance, where the party unjustly charged with fraud has been guilty of dubious conduct in other respects (w), or has withheld explanations which he was in a position to give, and which, if given when required, would have prevented the continuance of the litigation (x)   In a proper case, the court may give the party unnecessarily and unsuccessfully accused of fraud his costs as between solicitor and client, so far as his general costs have been increased by such charge (y) : but there is no jurisdiction to give him costs " on the higher scale," merely because he has been so accused, whether the case is simple (z), or complicated (a)

619. Another such " rule of conduct," as to costs, is the following   A party who succeeds in resisting a claim for non-disclosure is nevertheless frequently deprived of his costs, if his conduct is shown to have been devoid of all merits (b), or characterized by obliquity in other respects (c), or if he

(u) The following are selected illustrations of various forms of order as to costs whereby the party complaining of non disclosure was punished for making unnecessary charges of fraud which were not proved   *Welles* v *Middleton* (1784), 1 Cox Eq Cas 112 (*per* Lord THURLOW, L C , at p 119, who deprived the successful plaintiff of his costs) , *Groves* v. *Perkins* (1834), 6 Sim 576 (the like per SHADWELL, V C , at p 583) , *Champion* v *Rigby* (1840), 9 L. J (N S). (CH) 211 (*per* Lord COTTENHAM, L C., at p 216, dismissing a bill with costs which otherwise would have, and in fact in the Court below had, been dismissed without costs) , *Gibson* v *Russell* (1843), 2 Y. & C 104 (successful plaintiff deprived of his costs up to the filing of the replication, when an offer was made which the defendant ought to have accepted   per KNIGHT-BRUCE, V -C , at pp 120, 121) , *Shackleton* v *Sutcliffe* (1847), 1 Dr & Sm 609 (successful defendant deprived of his costs " so far as increased by the defendant having imputed fraud or unfair intention to the plaintiffs or their solicitors "   per KNIGHT-BRUCE, V C , at p 623) , *Dimsdale* v *Dimsdale* (1856), 3 Drew 556 (a similar case to *Champion* v *Rigby*, *sup*   per KINDERSLEY, V C , at p 578) , *Parker* v. *McKenna* (1874), 10 Ch App. 96 (so much of the bill as alleged fraud dismissed with costs, and plaintiff to have no costs of the residue on which he had succeeded   per Lord CAIRNS, L C , at pp 122-124, and JAMES, L J , at p 125) , *Thomson* v *Eastwood* (1877), 2 App Cas 215, H L (the like form of order, except that the plaintiff was not deprived of his costs of the residue of his claim   per Lord CAIRNS, L C , at p 244) . *J P Coats, Ltd* v *Crossland* (1904), 20 T L R 800 (where, as against one of the defendants only, the plaintiff was deprived of the costs of unfounded charges of fraud, so far as the costs of the other issues on which he had succeeded had been increased thereby, but he was not ordered to pay any costs to that defendant   per SWINFEN EADY, J , at p 807)   See also the cases cited in note (z) to § 624, *post*

(v) *New Brunswick and Canada Railway and Land Co* v *Conybeare* (1862), 9 H L C 711 (*per* Lord WESTBURY, L C , at pp 735, 736)

(w) See the cases cited in notes (c), (d), (f), (g), and (h), to § 619, *post*

(x) See § 619, note (e), *post*.

(y) As in *Forester* v *Read* (1870), 6 Ch App 40 (*per* JAMES and MELLISH, LL JJ , at pp 42, 43)

(z) *Paine* v. *Chisholm*, [1891] 1 Q B 531, C. A

(a) *Assets Development Co* v *Close Bros & Co* , [1900] 2 Ch 717 (*per* BUCKLEY, L J , at pp 719-721)

(b) As in *Hatch* v. *Hatch* (1804), 9 Ves 292 (*per* Lord ELDON, L C , at pp 298, 299) , *Rhodes* v. *Bate* (1866), 1 Ch App 252 (*per* TURNER, L J , at p 257)

(c) As in *Montesquieu* v *Sandys* (1811), 18 Ves 301 (*per* Lord ELDON, L.C , at p 313, dismissing without costs a bill to set aside the purchase by an attorney of his client's

refused, or delayed, when requested, to make to the party complaining a communication (d), or explanatory statement (e), which, if made, might be expected to put a stop to the litigation, and the withholding of which reasonably invited suspicion ; or if his conduct has been "indiscreet," or "injudicious" (f), or "precipitate" (g), or if, the alleged non-disclosure having been established against him, he escapes from its consequences solely by reason of supervening or fortuitous circumstances (h), or, generally, if the proved concealment was deliberate and morally censurable, whilst the proved exculpatory facts involved no personal merit on the part of the wrongdoer (i).

620. A third principle which is sometimes applied in a certain type of case is that according to which a party is punished in the matter of costs who has unreasonably refused or ignored a reasonable offer from the other

reversionary interest, on the ground of the attorney's dubious conduct in mis stating the nature of the transaction in a receipt), *Harrison* v *Guest* (1860), 6 De G M & G. 424 (where a solicitor, who succeeded in his defence, had chosen, quite unnecessarily, to mis state the consideration for a certain contract, thinking it would look better when the title came to be examined, though no one was misled or damaged · *per* Lord CRANWORTH, L C, at p 438); *Armstrong* v *Armstrong* (1873), Ir R 8 Eq 1 (where the successful defendant in an undue influence case had concealed a certain deed), *Taylor* v *Johnston* (1882), 19 C D 603 (*per* BACON, V C, at pp. 610, 611 . "suspicious circumstances" in the conduct of the successful defendant)

(d) As in *Harris* v *Tremenheere* (1808), 15 Ves 34 (*per* Lord ELDON, L C, at p. 40, who, whilst dismissing the bill with costs as to some of the leases sought to be set aside, and granting relief with costs as to another of them, dismissed the bill as to the remaining leases without costs, because "a suspicion attaches to the transaction, and justified an examination"), *Hunter* v *Atkins* (1834), 3 My & K 113 (*per* Lord BROUGHAM, L C, at p 157 successful defendant deprived of costs because of his persistent refusal to give particulars, which was calculated to excite some suspicion)

(e) As in *Patch* v *Ward* (1867), 3 Ch App 203 (*per* Lord CAIRNS, L J, at pp 210, 211)

(f) *Harvey* v *Mount* (1845), 8 Beav 439 (where one of the defendants succeeded, but was deprived of his costs because of his injudicious conduct in attempting to serve two masters *per* Lord LANGDALE, M R, at pp 452, 453), *Baker* v *Loader* (1872), L R 1 Eq 49 (where a solicitor defendant had been guilty of "a great want of discretion and judgment" *per* MALINS, V -C, at p 56), *Bagnall (John) & Sons* v *Carlton* (1877), 6 C D 371 (where the solicitor defendants who were successful, and against whom "charges had been made considerably beyond what ought to have been made," had nevertheless been guilty of "impropriety and indiscretion," in "arming some person with that which might have been made the means of fraud," and were accordingly deprived of their costs down to a certain date *per* JAMES, L J, at pp 401, 402)

(g) As in *Pisani* v *Att -Gen of Gibraltar* (1874), L R 5 P C 516 (at p 540)

(h) As in *Re Summerson*, [1900] 1 Ch 112 n (*per* ROMER, J), *Hepworth* v *Pickles*, [1900] 1 Ch 108 (*per* FARWELL, J , at p 111), *Greenhalgh* v *Brindley*, [1901] 2 Ch 324 (*per* FARWELL, J , at pp 328, 329) In all these cases, the vendor was proved to have clearly failed in his duty of disclosure to the purchaser with respect to incumbrances and restrictive covenants, but he was nevertheless held entitled to succeed in his defence to a claim for rescission in the first two cases, and in his action for specific performance in the third, because of the accidental circumstance (accidental in the sense that it involved no merits, or rather no expunging of proved demerits, on the part of the vendor) that the alleged restrictive covenant had ceased to be enforceable, and that the alleged incumbrance was therefore in law no longer an incumbrance at all It does not appear from the report of *Re Summerson*, *sup* , that ROMER, J , dismissed the summons without costs, but it is so stated at p 329 of *Greenhalgh v. Brindley*, *sup* , by FARWELL, J , who had been counsel in the case

(i) See *Re Hoggart's Settlement* (1912), 56 Sol J 415 (where a solicitor who had made an agreement for costs with his client which was impeachable on the ground of absence of explanation or independent advice, and who only escaped because he had abandoned the agreement and offered taxation before the proceedings were instituted, was deprived of his costs) And see further, the cases cited in § 168, notes (x) and (y), *ante*

side (*j*), but not, where he has properly and justifiably declined to entertain an offer which was obviously unreasonable, illusory, or intended as a trap (*k*).

621. Where the party charged fails on the issue of disclosure, but succeeds on the ground of illegality, which he has not pleaded, or which he has concurred with his opponent in requesting the judge to ignore, but which the Court takes notice of, as it must, if it is apparent on the face of the transaction, or on the whole of the relevant facts, but not otherwise (*kk*), he may be ordered to bear his own costs, or even to pay the costs of the other party (*l*).

622. The delay of a successful party complaining may affect his costs (*m*). So also may that of a successful party charged (*n*).

623. Trustees, incumbrancers, stakeholders, and, generally, parties joined for conformity merely, who are in no way implicated in the non-disclosure or other breach of duty charged, or guilty of any other misconduct, and have not made common cause with any of the substantial parties held liable, are entitled to their costs (*o*), in which case the guilty parties are ordered

---

(*j*) As in *Gibson* v *Russell* (1843), 2 Y & C 104 (where, though, for the reason that he had been unnecessarily charged with fraud which was not proved, the defendant was excused from paying any costs down to the date of the replication, he was made to pay the plaintiff's costs after that date, because an offer was then made which he ought to have accepted. *per* KNIGHT BRUCE, V C, at pp 120, 121), *Howley* v *Cook* (1873), Ir R 8 Eq. 370 (where a borrower, though he succeeded in obtaining rescission of certain deeds executed by him at the instance of the moneylender under pressure, was ordered to pay the defendant's costs, having refused an offer of all that he was entitled to) And see the "unconscionable bargain" cases cited in notes (*d*) and (*e*) to § 624, *post*

(*k*) As in *Moore* v *Prance* (1851), 9 Hare 299 (where the trustee against whom judgment was given had offered to reconvey the premises which had passed to him under the impeached instrument, but only if the plaintiff would apologize for having charged him with imposition and fraud, and it was held that, since the trustee had no right to impose such a condition, or "to mix up matters of personal or private feeling with the discharge of his trust," the offer was not such as should affect the costs. *per* TURNER, V-C, at pp. 304, 305) Cp the cases cited in notes (*f*), and (*g*), to § 624, *post*

(*kk*) *North Western Salt Co* v. *Electrolytic Alkali Co*, [1914] A C 461, 469, 475, H L

(*l*) See *Gedge* v *Royal Exchange Assurance Corporation*, [1900] 2 Q B 214 (*per* KENNEDY, J, at p 224, depriving the successful party of his costs), *Charlesworth* v *Faber* (1900), 5 Comm Cas 408 (*per* BIGHAM, J, at p 413, who ordered the successful defendant to pay the plaintiff's costs)

(*m*) As in *Att. Gen* v *Lord Dudley* (1815), G Cooper 146, 14 R R 226 (*per* GRANT, M R, at p 148 "the length of time in this case ought to weigh, and therefore the decree must be without costs") For examples of converse cases in which the delay and confirmation to be inferred therefrom was fatal to relief, but the bill was dismissed without costs, see *Gregory* v *Gregory* (1815), G Cooper 201, 14 R R 244 (*per* GRANT, M R, at pp 204, 205), *Champion* v *Rigby* (1830), 1 Russ & M 539 (*per* LEACH, M.R, whose decision, however, was varied on appeal by making the plaintiff pay the costs, he having in the meantime introduced new and unfounded charges of fraud see note (*u*) to § 618, *ante*), *Salmon* v *Cutts* (1850), 4 De G & Sm 125 (*per* KNIGHT-BRUCE, V-C, at pp 129, 130) See also the case cited in note (*n*) to § 218, *ante*.

(*n*) As in *Cane* v *Lord Allen* (1814), 2 Dow H L. 289, where Lord REDESDALE, at p. 298, pointed out that the party charged, who succeeded in obtaining a decree for specific performance, and rebutting the case of undue influence made against him by the defendant, had allowed the cause to sleep after his replication in 1786, down to 1807, and on that account ought to be deprived of costs, though not of his right to specific performance, because, as Lord ELDON, L C, observed at p 300, the defendant had been equally supine in not moving to dismiss the bill during the above period of 21 years, as he ought to have done.

(*o*) See O 65, r 1 (as to trustees), and *Bentley* v *Craven* (1853), 18 Beav 75 (two of four partners made defendants for conformity in a suit in which the third partner sued the fourth to recover secret profits for the firm), *Beck* v *Kantorowicz* (1857), 3 K & J 230 (a similar case), *Tottenham* v *Green* (1863), 32 L J (CH) 201 (*per* WOOD, V.-C, at p 206 .

either to indemnify any successful party who has to pay the costs of a formal party (*p*), or to pay such costs to the formal party direct (*q*). But any party who has at any time claimed an interest (*r*), or has been guilty of improper conduct (*s*), is not only not entitled to costs, but may have to pay them. Sometimes, a party who is both a trustee of, and a beneficiary under, an instrument which is set aside, though he is disallowed all costs in his character of beneficiary, is granted leave to apply at a subsequent date, as he may be advised, for his costs as trustee out of the trust property (*t*) A not uncommon form of order against a solicitor who has aided his client in committing, or made it possible for him to commit, the breach of duty complained of, is an order whereby, though judgment goes against the client only, the solicitor is made a guarantor of the costs primarily payable by such client (*u*) On the other hand, the old and disreputable practice of adding agents, and particularly solicitors, as defendants in proceedings based on breaches of fiduciary duty, or undue influence, without sufficient grounds, in the hope that something will turn up at the trial which may justify an order against such an agent or solicitor for costs, or with the still more shameful motive of inducing him to put pressure upon his client and co-defendant to settle the action, has frequently been denounced by high judicial authority (*v*)

sub mortgagees to have their costs), *Kimber* v *Barber* (1872), 8 Ch App 56, *Turner* v *Collins* (1871), 7 Ch App 329, 349 (trustees), *Fry* v. *Lane* (1888), 40 C D 312 *per* KAY, J, at p 325 (trustee)

(*p*) As in *Smith* v *Pincombe* (1852), 2 Macn & G 653, *Cockell* v *Taylor* (1852), 15 Beav 103 (*per* ROMILLY, M R, at p 129), *Sharp* v *Leach* (1862), 31 Beav 491 (*per* ROMILLY, M.R., at p 503), *Rhodes* v *Bate* (1866), 1 Ch App 252 (*per* TURNER, L.J, at p 262)

(*q*) As in *Cavendish* v *Strutt* (1903), 19 T L R 483 (*per* BYRNE, J, at p. 489)

(*r*) As in *Tate* v *Williamson* (1866), L R 1 Eq 528 (where a defendant who, though claiming no interest at the trial, had originally done so was deprived of his costs *per* WOOD, V -C, at p 540)

(*s*) See *Bennett* v *Vade* (1742), 2 Atk. 324 (*per* Lord HARDWICKE, L.C, at p 327, as to a solicitor defendant who had been guilty of improper conduct, and had obtained a benefit under the impeached deed), *Beadles* v *Burch*, cited in note (*v*), *inf* (the like), *Phosphate Sewage Co* v *Hartmont* (1877), 5 C. D 394, C. A (*per* MALINS, V -C, at pp 443-447 here the guilty agents were ordered to pay costs), *Powell* v *Powell*, [1900] 1 Ch 243 (*per* FARWELL, J, at p 248, who disallowed costs to the solicitor who was one of the trustees of the settlement, though he did not order him to pay costs) And see, further, the cases cited in note (*f*) to § 619, *ante*

(*t*) This was the order made in *Wright* v *Carter*, [1903] 1 Ch 27, C A, as regards one of the defendants who, as trustee, had submitted to the direction of the Court (see the minutes of the order, at p 65)

(*u*) As in *Bowles* v *Stewart* (1803), 1 Sch & Lefr 209 (*per* Lord REDESDALE, L C (Ir), at p 227), *Baker* v *Loader* (1873), L R 16 Eq 49 (*per* MALINS, V -C, at p 59) In *Tyrrell* v *Bank of London* (1862), 10 H L. C. 26, it was considered in the House of Lords, *per* Lord WESTBURY, L C, at p 47, that ROMILLY, M R, might properly have made such an order against Read, one of the defendants, who was associated with Tyrrell, the other defendant, who unsuccessfully appealed, that is, an order that he should pay to the Bank whatever Tyrrell did not pay, and it was regretted that this course had not been adopted However, since the Bank were not cross-appealing from this part of the decision, whilst Read was (for obvious reasons) not joining with Tyrrell in his original appeal, the House had no jurisdiction to interfere

(*v*) Though, as SHADWELL, V -C, said in *Beadles* v *Burch* (1839), 10 Sim 332, at pp 337-339, a solicitor, to whom "purity of intentions" may fairly be attributed, may nevertheless be properly joined as a defendant, if there has been any actual impropriety of conduct, and even made to pay costs, the practice referred to in the text was vigorously denounced by Lord SELBORNE, L.C, at p 255 of *Barnes* v *Addy* (1874), 9 Ch App 244,

624. In the class of case in which relief is sought against an unconscionable bargain between an "expectant" and a person dealing with him in relation to, or on the faith of, his expectancy—a class of case to which special attention has been devoted in an earlier chapter (w)—something approaching to a code of "rules of conduct" as to costs has gradually emerged (x) It was, in the first instance, considered a sound general principle that the expectant, being in the position of a mortgagor coming for redemption against a mortgagee in possession, ought to pay the dealer's costs, assuming the latter to have been guilty of no actual or personal misconduct, as well as the debt, interest, and charges, just as in an ordinary case of redemption of a mortgage (y). It was then thought that, in some cases, the expectant should pay only the costs of the inquiry as to the value of the expectancy, and of the taking of the necessary account (z), but that in another type of case, as for instance where he had made unfounded charges of personal fraud, or where he succeeded on the ground of undervalue alone, the expectant ought, as a condition of relief, to pay all the dealer's costs except the costs of such inquiry or account (a). Subsequently, in that very common kind of case in which the merits, or the demerits, of the parties are very evenly balanced, or where the decision proceeded solely or mainly on undervalue, it became a not unusual practice to do a sort of rough justice, and save both parties the expense of taxation, by giving no costs to either side (b) Where, however, the dealer is shown to have been guilty of personal misconduct, and not merely to have infringed a doctrine of law, the general rule has always been that he is required to pay all the expectant's costs (c) Where an offer has been made by either party to the other, the nature of the offer, and the manner in which it was met or dealt with, are matters of considerable importance in deciding how the costs should be borne Generally speaking, the

and again at pp 40, 41 of *Burstall* v *Beyfus* (1884), 26 C D 35, C. A , and by JESSEL, M R , at p 502 of *Mathias* v. *Yeits* (1882), 46 L T 497, C A (a misrepresentation case)

(*w*) See Ch V, Sect 2, Sub-s (b), *ante*

(*x*) Both ROMILLY, M R , at pp 14, 15 of *St Albyn* v *Harding* (1859), 27 Beav 11, and KAY, J , at p 324 of *Fry* v *Lane* (1888), 40 C D 312, attempted a rough classification of the various forms of order made in this description of case, though each of them acknow ledges that there is "no imperative rule in these cases" (*per* ROMILLY, M R , ' no absolute rule," is the expression of KAY, J)

(*y*) See *Twisleton* v *Griffith* (1716), 1 P Wms 309 (*per* Lord COWPER, L C , at p 310) , *Peacock* v *Evans* (1809), 16 Ves 512 (*per* GRANT, M R , at p 518) , *Gowland* v *De Faria* (1810), 17 Ves 20 (*per* GRANT, M R , at p 26)

(*z*) As in *Gwynne* v *Heaton* (1778), 1 Brown C C. 1 (*per* Lord THURLOW, L C , at pp 10, 11) ; *Portmore* (*Earl of*) v. *Taylor* (1831), 4 Sim 182 (*per* SHADWELL, V C , at pp 213, 214)

(*a*) See *Edwards* v *Burt* (1852), 2 De G M & G 55 (*per* Lord CRANWORTH, L J , at p 65) , *Boothby* v *Boothby* (1852), 15 Beav 212 (*per* ROMILLY, M R , at p 214) , *Jones* v *Ricketts* (1862), 31 Beav 130 (*per* ROMILLY, M R , at p 132)

(*b*) As in *Salter* v *Bradshaw* (1858), 26 Beav 161 , *Foster* v *Roberts* (1861), 29 Beav 467 (*per* ROMILLY, M R , at pp 471 472), *Tottenham* v *Green* (1863), 32 L J (CH) 201 (*per* WOOD, V -C., at p 206, stating it to be a general rule that where the transaction is set aside on the ground of undervalue alone, there should be no costs on either side, but where there has been misconduct on the part of the dealer, the "expectant" should have his costs) , *Croft* v *Graham* (1863), 2 De G J & S 155 (*per* STUART, V -C , at p 159) , *Aylesford* (*Earl of*) v *Morris* (1873), 8 Ch App 484 (*per* Lord SELBORNE, L C , at p 499) , *Fry* v *Lane* (1888), 40 C D 312 (*per* KAY, J , at p 325) , *Rae* v *Joyce* (1892), 29 L R (Ir) 500 (*per* WALKER, L C (Ir), at p 517)

(*c*) See *Tottenham* v *Green, sup.*, as cited in the last note

expectant who has refused the dealer's reasonable offer of redemption, or the dealer who has refused, or met with an impossible counter-proposal, the expectant's reasonable offer of payment, will be ordered to pay all the costs of his opponent (d) ; and, in the absence of special circumstances, this rule has been often applied to the case of a dealer declining, or ignoring, an offer made by the expectant before trial to pay the debt, with interest at 5 per cent, and charges and costs (e). In the less common case of the dealer offering to accept payment, or to allow redemption, on certain terms before the trial, the Court narrowly examines the nature of the offer, and the time when it was made, and the conditions with which it was clogged, for the purpose of ascertaining whether it was a genuine and a reasonable offer, or, on the contrary, a specious and insincere " contrivance to double-hatch the cheat " (f), or an utterly unreasonable proposal (g) , in either of which events, the dealer will receive no indulgence in the matter of costs. As in the case of any other party complaining of non-disclosure (h), the expectant who makes unnecessary charges of personal misconduct, which he fails to prove, will be penalized in costs (i)

(d) Per ROMILLY, M R , at pp 14, 15 of St Albyn v Harding (1859), 27 Beav 11

(e) As in Nesbitt v Berridge (1863), 32 Beav 282 (per ROMILLY, M R , at p 289) ; Benyon v Cook (1875), 10 Ch App 389 n. , Nevill v. Snelling (1880), 15 C. D. 679 (per DENMAN, J , at p 705)

(f) Wiseman v Beake (1690), 2 Vern 121 (per Cur , at pp. 121, 122 " when he had spent the money, then a specious offer was made to relinquish the bargain on payment of the money lent with interest, which at that time was impossible for him to do and though such bill "—i e a bill by the moneylender in Chancery offering to allow redemption on payment of principal and interest only—" was exhibited, it was not prosecuted, but was only a contrivance to double hatch the cheat ")

(g) As in St Albyn v Harding, sup , where the dealer, on the offer being made, insisted on an immediate formal tender, which, in the case of the costs charges and expenses, was (as he well knew) an impossible condition to comply with (per ROMILLY, M R , at pp 14, 15)

(h) See § 617, and the cases cited in note (u) thereto, ante

(i) Thus, in Bromley v Smith (1859), 26 Beav 644, the "expectant," though he obtained relief, had to pay the defendant's costs of the charges of fraud, and was disallowed his costs of the residue of the claim (per ROMILLY, M.R , at pp 675, 676) , so, also, in St. Albyn v Harding, sup (per ROMILLY, M R , at p 15) For illustrations of cases in which the successful " expectant " was deprived of costs on the ground that he had pitched his case too high, see Talbot v Stanisforth (1861), 1 J & H 484 (per WOOD, V C , at p 508) , Tyler v. Yates (1871), 6 Ch App 665 (per Lord HATHERLEY, L.C., at p 671)

APPENDICES.

APPENDIX A.

TERMINOLOGICAL QUESTIONS.

625. EXTREMELY little criticism of an adverse nature can justly be made as to the substance of the English law of disclosure and kindred duties of good faith It may fairly be claimed for it that, in this department as in many others, our jurisprudence yields to none of the codes of other nations, ancient or modern, whilst, in the richness of its subordinate propositions and the variety of its illustrations, it surpasses them all (*j*). Not quite the same commendation, however, can be bestowed on the English terminology of the subject, which in some particulars invites observation Sir J. F. Stephen remarked (in the Preface to his *Digest of the Law of Evidence*) that, the longer he studied and practised the law, the more forcibly he was impressed with, on the one hand, the conspicuous merits of our jurisprudence in point of substance, and, on the other, its equally conspicuous defects in point of form, arrangement, and terminology. The same contrasted merits and defects were attributed by that remarkably acute jurist and moralist, Lord Kames, to the Roman system, when insisting on "the supreme importance" of analysis and arrangement in any scientific exposition of law (*k*). The particular province of our law which is the subject of this treatise, it must be admitted, has not altogether avoided the faults, whilst in no way falling short of the merits, ascribed by these high authorities to the entire system · it is undoubtedly, however, less characterized by vicious terminology than many other departments (*l*)

SECT 1. GENERAL OBSERVATIONS ON THE IMPORTANCE OF TERMINOLOGY.

626. "All human Spirit and Reason does yet what Father Adam began life by doing, strive to name the new Things it sees of Nature's producing,—often helplessly enough '(*m*). The importance of terminology, in any department of knowledge which pretends to rank as a science, one would suppose to be obvious. And yet, in nearly every branch of English law, precision and lucidity of nomenclature has been, if not openly disparaged, in practice treated as a thing of quite subsidiary

---

(*j*) In App B, *post*, occasional conflicts between popular ethics and legal doctrines, as to certain topics, are pointed out, but with no suggestion in any case, except that of gifts (§ 665, *post*), that the popular view is preferable to the juridical The "law" referred to in the text is of course the non statutory law built up by the judges, not the manufactures of the legislature As to these, and the points in which they are obnoxious to criticism, see Ch VI, *ante*

(*k*) At pp xiii, xiv, of the Preface to the third edition (1778) of his *Principles of Equity* "in an institute of law, or of any other science, the analysing it into its constituent parts, and the arranging every article properly, is of supreme importance One would not conceive, without experience, how greatly accurate description contributes to clear conception. . Witness, in particular, the famous body of Roman law compiled under the auspices of the Emperor Justinian, remarkable even among law books for defective arrangement

(*l*) Such as, for instance, misrepresentation, as to which see App A, Sect 5, Sub s (1), of the author's *Law of Actionable Misrepresentation*, and defamation, the loose terminology in which branch of the law is the subject of App xxi, Sect 2, of the author's *Code of the Law of Actionable Defamation*

(*m*) Carlyle's *French Revolution*, Book V, Ch I

interest It is an old fallacy, exposed again and again by accurate thinkers, but still flourishing like a green bay tree in the English mind, that things and thoughts are the realities, and that names do not matter. But the fact is that terminology reacts on thought. Loose definitions encourage loose conceptions. It is as true of scientific, as it is of artistic, expression that "φῶς ἴδιον τοῦ νοῦ τὰ καλὰ ὀνόματα" (n). Bacon describes "the Idols of the Market-place" as "the most troublesome of all; idols which have crept into the understanding through the alliance of words and names. For men believe that their reason governs words, but it is also true that words react upon the understanding " (o). And, in another place, he insists that "the juggleries and charming of words will in many ways seduce and forcibly disturb the judgment, and (after the manner of the Tartar bowmen) shoot back at the understanding from which they proceeded " (p). No doubt, there are circumstances and conditions in which this attitude of indifference to names is not merely excusable, but entirely proper and requisite Where, for instance, a discussion arises as to whether a particular state of things, or a particular relation between persons, is covered by a general proposition of law, it is quite sound, and in accordance with a healthy intellectual instinct, to enter upon the inquiry in a spirit of suspicion towards every contention of those who "for a tricksy word defy the matter" (q), or which is based on a pedantic servility to mere nomenclature, and to insist that the question is not one of names, or whether the state of things, or the relation, under discussion bears a label identical with that of any of the objects to which that proposition has hitherto been applied, but whether or not the case presented falls within, not the words of the rule, or even the rule itself, but its reason and principle. In several parts of this work, illustrations have already been given of this salutary and justifiable independence and distrust of names under the conditions stated (r) But, where the concepts to which the proposition itself relates, and the terms in which it is enunciated, are in question, it is quite another matter Here a judicious choice of distinct names to express distinct ideas in the first instance, followed by a loyal recognition afterwards of the authority of the names so selected, is essential to the stability of the science. "it is most necessary," said Lord WESTBURY, "to mark this again and again, for there is not a more fruitful source of error in law than the inaccurate use of language " (s).

627. The expressions in relation to which inexact, ambiguous, or misapplied terminology has characterized the branch of law dealt with in this treatise are "fraud;" "negligence;" "mistake;" "confidence;" "influence;" "actual," "constructive," and "imputed" knowledge; and others of minor importance

SECT. 2. CRITICISM OF THE USE OF THE TERMS "FRAUD," "NEGLIGENCE," AND "MISTAKE" IN RELATION TO NON-DISCLOSURE, &c.

628 These three terms have been considerably abused both by judges in their judicial deliverances and by writers in treatises even of the highest authority They

---

(n) Longinus, *De Subl* Or, descending from the "sublime" of Longinus to the "ridiculous" of Justice Shallow, "good phrases are surely, and ever were, very commendable" (Henr IV, Part II, Act 3, Sc 2).

(o) *Nov Org*, lix.

(p) *De Augm Scient.*, Book V, Ch IV Lord PARKER, at p 53 of *Kreglinger v New Patagonia Meat & Coal Storage Co*, [1914] A C 25, H L., doubtless had this passage in mind when he observed that maxims, such as "once a mortgage, always a mortgage," invariably " beg the question, and, like Bacon's idols of the market-place, lead to misconception and error "

(q)   " The fool hath planted in his memory
         An army of good words ; and I do know
         A many fools, that stand in better place,
         Garnish'd like him, that for a tricksy word
         Defy the matter "—*Merch. of Ven.*, Act 3, Sc 1.

(r) See, for instance, § 85, § 343, and note (v) thereto, and § 408, *ante.*

(s) At p 676 of *Knox v Gye* (1872), L. R 5 H L 576; and cp. the observations of Lord Kames cited in note (k), *sup*

have been applied, as will now be seen, sometimes ambiguously, sometimes incorrectly, and still more often, unnecessarily

Sub-s (1). *Double Use of the word " Fraud "*

629. At a very early stage in the growth of equitable principles, it was clearly laid down that proof of fraud is not necessary to render non-disclosure actionable, where a duty of disclosure exists (*t*) And yet, after having been so established, the proposition has been again and again solemnly re-asserted (*u*). "What needs this iteration ? " Why was it found necessary, at secular intervals, to remind the world of the existence of the ancient rule, and, with more or less elaboration, to justify and explain its continued vitality ? The answer is to be found in the unfortunate use of the one word "fraud " to describe two wholly distinct, and even opposite, things. Whilst constantly proclaiming that fraud in its proper, plain, and natural sense of "actual," "active," "positive," "personal," "moral," "intentional " or "conscious " fraud, or fraud "in the odious " or "offensive " sense (*v*), need never be alleged or proved in proceedings for non-disclosure, the courts have nevertheless alternated these definite declarations, in regularly recurring strophe and antistrophe, with equally frequent and definite declarations, that fraud in another sense—a totally unnatural and incorrect one (it is submitted)—must always be established in such proceedings : that is to say, that the duty, and its breach, must be shown, and that such breach thereupon is deemed to constitute "constructive," "legal," "technical," "artificial," "unconscious," "equitable," or "presumptive" fraud. Thus, in the law of marine insurance, expressions are used by Lord MANSFIELD (*u*), and in at least one accepted treatise on the subject (*x*), which clearly involve the terminological heresy in question, —a heresy which, in the course of his remarkable judgment in a very valuable case (*y*), Lord ESHER vigorously condemned (*z*), adopting the sound and philosophical language of an excellent text-book writer who had previously, and no less convincingly, condemned it (*a*). So also, in relation to transactions between vendor and purchaser,

(*t*) See § 197 (in Ch III), § 358 (in Ch IV), and § 461 (in Ch V), *ante*

(*u*) See the cases cited in note (*k*) to § 197, and in the notes to §§ 358, 461, *ante*

(*v*) All these expressions are to be found either in the authorities cited in the immediately succeeding notes, or else in the misrepresentation cases referred to in the notes to § 157 of the author's *Law of Actionable Misrepresentation*, where the use of the contrasted terms "legal," and "moral," as applied to fraud, is shown to have been necessitated by the same initial error as is the subject of the present criticism.

(*w*) At p 1909 of *Carter* v *Boehm* (1766), 3 Burr 1905 : "the keeping back such a circumstance *is a fraud*, and *therefore* the policy is void Although the suppression should happen *through mistake, without any fraudulent intention*, yet still the underwriter is deceived, and the policy is void."

(*x*) Arnould's *Marine Insurance* See note (*a*), *inf.*

(*y*) *Blackburn, Low & Co.* v *Vigors* (1886), 17 Q B D. 553, C A The dissentient judgment of Lord ESHER was supported, and the decision of the majority reversed, by the House of Lords, (1887), 12 App Cas 531, H. L

(*z*) At p 562 of *Blackburn, Low & Co* v *Vigors, sup*, in the C A As might be expected from his well known, and constantly avowed, antipathy to all legal or equitable "presumptions" of fraud, malice, intention, and the like, Lord ESHER vigorously condemned the view expressed in Arnould's work—see the next note—as one of those "figures of speech " and "oracular phrases " which were so exceedingly distasteful to him

(*a*) Phillips, in a passage which Lord ESHER cites at length at the page of his judgment referred to in the last note, and warmly approves (" this seems to me to be true doctrine "), stated and criticized Arnould's theory as follows "since a representation through mistake or inadvertence has the same effect, in reference to the underwriter, as an intentional or literally fraudulent concealment, he deems it to be excusable to apply the term 'fraud' But I cannot think that the anomalous use of the term is justifiable on this ground, since ambiguous phraseology is not to be tolerated in any science, and least of all in that of law, where it can possibly be avoided, as it may easily be in this case by stating the practical doctrine in direct terms." The "direct terms " in which, according to Phillips, Lord ESHER, and, in the House of Lords, (1887). 12 App Cas 531, H L., at p 539, Lord WATSON, the doctrine ought to be stated are, that full disclosure is "an implied condition of the contract of insurance " Phillips was an American writer

even Lord St Leonards (b) committed himself to a proposition similarly misleading without the necessary qualification and explanation which, omitted by himself, was afterwards added by Sir William James (c), and made use of expressions which at least encouraged, though they may not have justified, the ridiculous theory of a possibly actionable "fraudulent silence,"—a theory to which advocates in distress have resorted, as to a *tabula in naufragio*, in every case where no breach of any recognized duty of disclosure could be suggested (d). And Lord Hatherley mentions cases "between vendor and purchaser" as constituting the first of "the three particular classes of cases of *what the Court terms fraud*," the other two being cases of partnership, and cases "in which an agent for a purchaser receives a gratuity from the vendor" (e), which latter Lord St. Leonards also described as cases of "fraud," though not in the "odious" or "felonious" sense (f). Lastly, in respect of the "undue influence" type of case, we find Lord Hardwicke describing breaches of the equitable duties involved therein as "presumed fraud" (g); whilst Sir William James, in a case in which "preconceived design," and "premeditated fraud," had not been made out, observed that this made no difference, because "the obtaining of property, or any benefit, through the undue and unconscientious abuse of influence by a person in whom trust and confidence are placed, has always been regarded as fraud of the gravest character" (h),—a statement which is only correct if 'fraud' be understood in the artificial and comprehensive meaning previously assigned to that term by himself (i), and absolutely incorrect if the word is taken in its natural meaning,—the meaning which Lord Thurlow, and Sir George Jessel, put upon it, when they emphatically denied its relevance, even in that (morally speaking) gravest species

on marine insurance, whose treatise, published at Boston about the middle of the last century, has always been highly commended by the best authorities on the subject in this country, such as Sir John Willes and Sir James Mathew, as well as Lord Esher The first of these cited § 1183 of the 1853 edition of Phillips's book, describing it as "a very able work," in the "Memorandum on Over Insurance, Valued Policies, and Constructive Loss" which he prepared, in 1867, for the Commission on Unseaworthy Ships, whose report was published in 1874 The Memorandum of Sir John Willes, including the passage cited by him from Phillips, was adopted by Sir James Mathew in his judgment in *Herring v Jackson* (1895), 1 Comm Cas 177, at p 179 Lord Esher (then Brett, L.J), at p 463 of *Bradford v Symondson* (1881), 7 Q B D 456, C A, expressed his opinion that "of all the great text authorities on insurance law, Phillips is the one most to be considered," and at pp 561 and 563, respectively of *Blackburn, Low & Co v Vigors* (1887), 12 App Cas. 531, H L, described him as "always the more accurate guide," and his "propositions" as "always nicely accurate"

(b) In his *Vendor and Purchaser* (14th ed), p 244. And cp. the language used by him judicially in the case cited in note (f), inf , in relation to agency and partnership

(c) At pp 124, 125 of *Torrance v Bolton* (1872), 8 Ch App 118 · "it was very strongly impressed upon us that Lord St Leonards had said in his book that contracts for sale, though they might not be enforced in this Court, could only be set aside on the ground of fraud The word 'fraud' there is *nomen generalissimum*, and it must not be construed so as to mislead persons into the notion that contracts for the sale and purchase of lands are in any respect privileged, so as to be free from the ordinary jurisdiction of the Court to deal with them as it deals with any other instrument or transaction in which the Court is of opinion that it is unconscientious for a person to avail himself of the legal advantage which he has obtained. Indeed, the books are full of cases in which the Court has dealt with contracts of that kind—contracts obtained by persons from others over whom they have dominion, contracts obtained by persons in a fiduciary position. . A contract for sale, like every other contract, is subject to the ordinary rules and jurisdiction of this Court, and that passage of Lord St Leonards must be understood as meaning that the same kind of case must be made when a party comes here to set aside a contract for sale as must be made in setting aside any other contract or dealing between the parties"

(d) See, as to the futile contentions based on this meaningless or, rather, misleading phrase, § 305, *ante*, with which cp. §§ 153–158, and note (y) to § 163, *ante*

(e) At p 1243 of *Erlanger v New Sombrero Phosphate Co* (1878), 3 App Cas 1218, H L

(f) At pp 751, 752 of *Cutts v Salmon* (1852), 21 L. J (ch) 750

(g) At pp 155, 156 of *Chesterfield (Earl of) v Jannsen* (1751), 2 Ves Sr 125

(h) At p 887 of *Moxon v Payne* (1873), 8 Ch App. 881.

(i) See note (c), *sup*.

of "undue influence" which is constituted by unconscionable bargains with "expectants" (j). Again, Lord LINDLEY has spoken of "undue influence" as "including one of the many varieties" of "fraud" (k), and KAY, J., in a case in which he expressly found that "no moral fraud has been proved," said that, nevertheless, "such transactions" - the case was one of an unconscionable bargain with an expectant—"amount to unfair dealing, which equity considers a fraud," though, as he immediately added, he "would rather the word were used only for moral delinquencies" (l). The same unfortunate use of the term is noticeable in cases relating to composition arrangements with creditors (m), and in cases of innocent misrepresentation against which relief by way of rescission is given without the slightest necessity for proving "fraud" in its ordinary sense (n); and it is encouraged by digests and text-books, in which non-disclosure is habitually classed under the general head of "fraud," and by the constant use of the terms "concealment," and "withholding the facts," as exact synonyms of non-disclosure, which scientifically they may be, but certainly are not to the mind of the layman who, rightly or wrongly, infers a distinct moral imputation from these positive expressions which he does not attach to the negative term (nn).

630. As has been already hinted, all this seeming conflict and confusion can be traced back to the needless, and worse than needless, use of the word "fraud" in a secondary and enlarged sense, not only alternately, but concurrently, with its use in the natural and proper sense. Chancery judges have thus wantonly converted a name which, if ever a name did, always signified one thing, and one thing only, into a name *ancipitis sensus*. To the plain man "fraud" has never suggested anything short of actual deception practised by one man upon another with a wicked intent. In equity, on the other hand, it has from the earliest times connoted no more than a non-compliance with equitable rules, or a violation of equitable duty, and has denoted, therefore, no less than every act or omission which answers to that description (o).

631 In applying the term in question indifferently to cases falling within either, or both, of these two definitions, the Courts have disregarded that first law of scientific terminology which requires that every term used for the purpose of the science,

(j) At p 10 of *Gwynne v Heaton* (1778), 1 Brown C C 1, Lord THURLOW, L C, says that "fraud is not the ground of relief", and, at p 391 n. of *Benyon v. Cook* (1875), 10 Ch App 389, JESSEL, M.R., explains that "the doctrine has nothing to do with fraud" Both these were cases of unconscionable bargains with expectants

(k) When LINDLEY, L.J., at p 183 of *Allcard v Skinner* (1887), 36 C D 145, C. A

(l) At p 324 of *Fry v Lane* (1888), 40 C. D 312.

(m) *Mayhew v Boyes* (1910), 100 L T 1, C. A, per COZENS-HARDY, M.R., who there describes such a secret agreement as one "which the law declines to recognize, as being against public policy, and *in the eye of the law fraudulent, though not morally so.*"

(n) As to which, see §§ 456, 457 of the author's *Law of Actionable Misrepresentation*

(nn) As to this, cp § 184, note (z), *ante.* JESSEL, M R, at p 370 of *London Assurance Co v Mansel* (1879), 11 C D. 363, says that "concealment properly so called means non-disclosure of a fact which it is a man's duty to disclose" But describe non-disclosure to a jury as "concealment," and they will hesitate in the plainest case see *Taylor v Yorkshire Insurance Co*, [1913] 2 Ir R 1.

(o) See the observations of JAMES, L.J, cited in note (c), *sup*, and those of Lord HALDANE, L.C., at pp 629-632 of *Nocton v Lord Ashburton*, [1914] A C. 932, H L So, too, Dr. Story (Eq Jurispr vol. i, ch vii, § 258) includes within his description of "constructive fraud" all "such acts and contracts as, although not originating in any actual evil design . are yet, by their tendency to deceive or mislead other persons . deemed equally reprehensible with positive fraud, and therefore are prohibited by law, as within the same reason and mischief as acts and contracts done *malo animo.*" He admits that these doctrines "may seem to be of an artificial, if not of an arbitrary, character", yet, he contends, "on closer observation they will be perceived to be founded on an anxious desire of the law to apply the principle of preventive justice" The apology, however, should have been made, not for the doctrines, but for the nomenclature There is nothing "artificial" or "arbitrary" in applying the principles of public policy and "preventive justice" to acts of which the tendency is mischievous, whatever the intention may have been The arbitrariness is in describing these acts by a name in popular use to which they do not answer

whatever it be, should denominate one concept, and not more than one. No doubt the science of jurisprudence, since it is concerned with the application of logic and ethics to the common affairs and transactions of life, is forced to draw largely upon the popular vocabulary for purposes of expression. But this course should be adopted only when it is unavoidable, because, though not without certain advantages, it is commonly attended by inconveniences and perils which far outweigh them. Of these the most serious are, as Dr. Whewell (p) has pointed out, the danger that the laxity of vernacular usage may infect the terminological apparatus of the science, and the disturbing element due to the fact that, for the most part, expressions *sermoni propiora* are tinged with sentiment, emotion, imagination, and other subtly pervading personal associations. It is unwise, therefore, to father a term current in the *vulgare eloquium* for the purposes of any scientific proposition, if it is possible to state that proposition clearly and fully without resort to it. But, if it is impracticable, and would be pedantic, to avoid the use of the term altogether, it is at any rate essential that the position which it is to occupy in its adoptive home should be exactly defined at the outset, and afterwards strictly maintained. Both these principles have been flagrantly disregarded in the case of this unhappy term. In the first place, it was from the beginning wholly unnecessary to use the word at all for the purpose of stating the fundamental principles of the law of non-disclosure. In one of the two "opinions" between which equity has "halted," it is said that fraud is essential to liability, but that the omission to disclose material facts as between two persons standing to one another in certain relations amounts in law to fraud, and raises a conclusive presumption of it. But what is this but a confession that the essential thing is the non-disclosure? If so, there was no need for the introduction of this middle term at all (q). It is as true of *nomina* as of *entia*, that they are *non multiplicanda præter necessitatem*; and the application of this useless label would seem to sin gravely against the above philosophical canon. It would have been quite sufficient to have simply stated the existence of the duty of disclosure under certain conditions, and to have then laid down that any breach of the duty under those conditions is actionable; and when judges have gone out of their way to describe such omissions of duty as fraud "in the eye of the Court," whilst lamenting that the word has not been confined to its proper sense of "moral delinquency" (qq), it is strange that they have never perceived that it has always been in their own hands to remove the cause of their lament, or at all events give no further occasion for it, by the very simple expedient of eschewing, or abandoning, the use of the word altogether. Secondly, the employment of the word lacks the negative, as well as the positive, merit of Shylock's "harmless necessary cat." It has been as misleading and harmful in its life as it was unwanted at its birth. Being a term of all others "tinged with sentiment," in Whewell's phrase, and suffused with inevitable suggestions of moral reprobation and odium, it should at least have been rigidly confined to its popular signification. Yet, as has been pointed out, this is exactly what has not been done; the courts having been as guilty in general, as the legislature has been occasionally (r), of the terminological crime of branding with one common *nota*

(p) In his *Novum Organon Renovatum*, Book IV

(q) "Whenever," as is wisely observed by Dr. Wendell Holmes, "it is said that a certain thing is essential to liability, but it is conclusively presumed from something else, there is always ground for suspicion that the essential is to be found in that something, of what is said to be presumed" (*The Common Law*, Lect. IV, at p 134)

(qq) See, for instance, the language of KAY, J., in the citation given in note (l), *ante*

(r) It was said by Sir GEORGE MELLISH, as counsel, at pp 608, 609, of *Re Overend, Gurney & Co, Ex p Oakes and Peek* (1867), L R 3 Eq 576, that "there are certain statutes . which make things fraudulent which may be most innocent things in the eyes of the world. As, for instance, under the statute of Elizabeth against fraudulent conveyances, a man may have made a conveyance without consideration, and yet under that statute it would be held to be fraudulent against a subsequent conveyance for value. It is a misfortune that the word 'fraud' has ever been applied to transactions which do not involve any moral fraud at all." It is a curious fact that this was the very case which is supposed to have occasioned the introduction of s 38 of the Companies Act, 1867, (see Ch. VI, *ante*) a few months later in the same year,—the enactment (now happily

infamiæ actions and persons which the common conscience would, and those which they would not, designate as dishonest, notwithstanding that, in all other connexions, judges have never wearied in denouncing the enormity of making such a charge as fraud without adequate grounds (*s*).

632. The error in question has been encouraged, and the mischief resulting from it aggravated, by that persistent judicial tendency to trespass upon the provinces of the preacher, the priest, and the pedagogue, on occasions where no moral question is raised to justify the intrusion, which has of late aroused no little resentment when manifested in other departments of law (*t*).

633. A corresponding double use of the terms *bona fides,* "honesty," and the like, with the same results, may be noticed in some of the authorities (*u*). So also, in the law of misrepresentation (*v*), and in that of defamation (*w*), the like twofold application of the words "fraud" and "malice," respectively, has been responsible for the ridiculous division of the former into "moral" and "legal" fraud, and of the latter into "malice in law," and "malice in fact," to the confusion of all clear thought and exposition.

Sub s. (2)   *Misuse of the term "Fraud" in connection with the Doctrine of Presumptive Knowledge.*

634. In the discussion of the various species of presumptive knowledge, it was seen that one of them consists in the knowledge which a party is presumed in law to have acquired of some document or fact in virtue of his actual knowledge of some other and connected document or fact under such circumstances that reasonable investigation, if made, would have led him from the latter to the former knowledge (*x*), and it was explained that this presumption is made for the general convenience of the community, and that accordingly any characterization of the party's motives or morals in omitting to pursue the necessary inquiry is logically irrelevant and indefensible (*y*)   No doubt, in a large number of cases, it has so happened that the

repealed) which presents the most flagrant example of the "misfortune" referred to by Sir GEORGE MELLISH, and which, had it then been in force, would have added point and weight to his argument   The judicial attitude towards this and all other statute made frauds, which are even more repulsive than judge-made frauds, was forcibly expressed by VAUGHAN WILLIAMS, L J , at p 471 of *Cackett* v *Keswick,* [1902] 2 Ch 456, C A   "I think that the 38th section, which in effect provides that a man   shall although acting honestly be deemed fraudulent, is a section which no judge can give effect to, not only without a feeling of repugnance, but without a feeling that that which he is doing does not really tend to the maintenance of commercial honesty and commercial morality   To herd together, under a collective word like 'fraudulent,' people who are honest and people who are dishonest, to my mind, cannot possibly tend to the maintenance of commercial morality"   Cp , on "the painful duty" thrust upon the Court by this enactment, the observations of COZENS-HARDY, L J , at pp 628, 629 of *Broome* v *Speak,* [1903] 1 Ch. 586, C A , concurred in and adopted by Lord HALSBURY, L C , at p 315, and Lord LINDLEY at p 346, of the same case, on appeal to the House of Lords, *sub nom Shepheard* v *Broome,* [1904] A C 342, H L , and those of BRAMWELL, L J , at pp 19, 20 of *Re Wheal Unity Wood Mining Co , Chynoweth's Case* (1880), 15 C D 13, C A , on a similar enactment in the Stannaries Act, 1869 (32 & 33 Vict , c 19), s 35

(*s*) "A charge of fraud is a terrible thing to bring against a man," said Lord ESHER, M R , who always expressed himself very strongly on this subject, at p 498 of *Le Lievre* v *Gould,* [1891] 1 Q. B 491, C A   This is why gratuitous and unproved charges of fraud are visited with such heavy penalties in the matter of costs · see § 618, *ante*

(*t*) See § 670, *post*

(*u*) Thus, in *Foster* v *Roberts* (1861), 29 Beav 467, ROMILLY, M R , at p 470, after observing that "there is perfect *bona fides* on both sides," that is, in the moral sense, goes on to say that "the burden of proof lies on the defendant to prove that the transaction was a *bonâ fide* one in the sense that a full and sufficient price was given for the reversion"

(*v*) This is the subject of §§ 458, and 465, of the author's *Law of Actionable Misrepresentation*

(*w*) See App II of the author's *Code of the Law of Actionable Defamation*

(*x*) See Ch II, Sect 3, Sub s (5), *ante*

(*y*) See § 58, *ante,* where the terminological questions arising were expressly reserved for discussion in this Appendix

B N D   2 O

conduct of the party was dishonest in the sense that, whilst conscious of something in the background affecting the validity of his title or of the transaction in which he was engaged, he deliberately refrained from ascertaining what that something was, with the intention of putting himself in a position to assert with literal truth, when subsequently sought to be "fixed" with notice, that he was in fact ignorant of that which is alleged to have taken place with his cognizance. In every such case, judges have not been slow in ascribing to the party "fraudulent blindness" (z), "wilful blindness"(a), "diligence in ignorance" (b), and all manner of wickedness. And so frequent have been the cases in which the conduct of the party has been such as to call down this thunder from Olympus, that at least two great masters of equity, Lord ELDON (c), and in more recent times, JAMES, L.J. (d), have been tempted to lay down that fraud is not only a very usual concomitant of the abstention from inquiry which raises the presumption of knowledge, but is a condition precedent to that presumption being made at all, and this in face of the considerable number of reported decisions wherein omissions to take the necessary precautions have been held to be actionable which undoubtedly proceeded from nothing more than sheer laziness, stupidity, or unfamiliarity with the recondite principles on which equity imputes to a man a knowledge which he never had (e). The explanation of the uncompromising and unqualified language in which the above proposition came to be expressed is the same as that which accounts for so much that is unsatisfactory and perplexing in our jurisprudence, as will be noticed hereafter (f). The process is this. A judicial statement of a general rule is accompanied by ethical reflections on the conduct of the parties which may be justified by, but in any case are only relevant to, the circumstances of the particular case. Under the like circumstances the same thing happens again and again, until at last the accompanying reflections are thought to be an integral part of the proposition itself, and that which was never more than an accidental annex comes to be treated as a substantive and essential condition of the applicability of the rule.

635. That the proposition stated by Lord ELDON and JAMES, L J., is too absolute, and to that extent inaccurate, is now abundantly clear. It runs counter to the main current of authority, according to which not only a fraudulent, but a negligent, "blindness" or abstinence from inquiry is sufficient to raise the presumption of knowledge (g), and it is in still wider disaccord with the statutory expression of the

(z) The expression of WIGRAM, V C, at p 61 of *Jones* v. *Smith* (1841), 1 Hare 43, by which he meant (see p 56) "a suspicion of the truth, and a fraudulent determination not to learn it"

(a) *Per* COCKBURN, C J., at p 605 of *Bates* v *Hewitt* (1867), L. R 2 Q B 595 Cp. the "wilful ignorance" of Lord ST LEONARDS at p 1035 of *Owen* v *Homan* (1853), 4 H L. C 997

(b) A favourite locution of Sir JAMES KNIGHT BRUCE

(c) In *Evans* v *Bicknell* (1801), 6 Ves 174, at p 190 In *Northern Counties of England Fire Insurance Co* v *Whipp* (1884), 26 C D 482, C A, FRY, L J, delivering the judgment of the Court, at pp 488–490, elaborately analyses and explains Lord ELDON's judgment and phraseology in the above case, and, at p 490, concludes "all this language of Lord ELDON, though loose and difficult to construe, appears to us to point to fraud as the necessary conclusion before the Court can deprive the owner of the legal estate of his legal rights derived from that estate." Cp *Manners* v *Mew* (1885), 29 C D 725 (*per* NORTH, J, at p 727)

(d) At p 654 of *Ratcliffe* v *Barnard* (1871), 6 Ch App 652.

(e) For which unfamiliarity small blame can be imputed, in the case of doctrines and rules so complicated and refined that judge after judge has exclaimed against them, protested against their extension in the slightest degree, and rejoiced in their apparent restriction by statute. see Ch II, Sect 3, Sub s (7), *ante*

(f) See § 647, *post*.

(g) For examples, see *Jones* v *Smith* (1841), 1 Hare 43 (*per* WIGRAM, V C, at p 55, where he mentions, as two distinct and separate "classes" of constructive notice, first, the cases in which knowledge of a fact or instrument is imputed to a party who would have acquired actual knowledge thereof if he had pursued the inquiries it was reasonable for him to make, and negligent, therefore, not to make and, "*secondly*, cases in which the Court has been satisfied from the evidence before it that the party charged had designedly abstained from inquiry for the very purpose of avoiding notice"), *Jones* v *Williams* (1857), 24 Beav 47 (*per* ROMILLY, M.R., at pp 58, 59, distinctly stating that

rule introduced in 1882, which mentions neither fraud, nor negligence, as necessary to found the presumption (*h*).

636. The only cases in which fraud is a necessary condition of the presumption are cases in which it is sought to deprive a party of the special statutory advantages to which he is entitled as the holder of a negotiable instrument (*i*), or as having duly registered a title to land pursuant to any of the Registry Acts (*j*). Obviously these are nothing but exceptions which prove the rule.

Sub s. (3). Misuse of the term " Negligence," as the Equivalent of " Fraud," in Connection with the Doctrine of Presumptive Knowledge.

637. Those who were responsible for the view that, in the class of case just considered, a party to whom it is sought to impute knowledge of a fact must be proved to have been guilty of fraudulent ignorance before the imputation can be made (*k*), found themselves in a difficulty when confronted with the decisions of unquestionable authority in which it had been held that negligence, at all events if "gross" and "culpable," is equally adequate to raise the presumption (*l*). Recognizing that the proposition enunciated by them was unsustainable unless negligence could be in some way identified with fraud, they proceeded to evolve the amazing theory that negligence, if "gross" enough, *is* fraud, or at all events is evidence of it (*m*). Both Lord ELDON (*n*) and Sir GEORGE TURNER (*o*) committed themselves to the first,

fraud is not necessary) ; *Hunt* v. *Elmes* (1860), 2 De G. F. & J 578 (*per* TURNER, L.J., at p 588), *Bates* v *Hewitt* (1867), L R 2 Q B. 595 (*per* COCKBURN, C.J., at p 605 " if the insurer chooses to *neglect* the information which he receives,   it is his own fault "). Then came the disturbing judgment of JAMES, L.J , in 1871, cited in note (*d*), *sup* , which, however, after eleven years, was corrected or qualified by the statement of the rule which is contained in the enactment mentioned in the next note   Ultimately, though not until after the lapse of another seventeen years, a definite note of dissent to the extreme view of JAMES, L.J , was struck in the case of *Oliver* v. *Hinton*, [1899] 2 Ch 264, C A (*per* LINDLEY, M.R , at p. 274   " the actual decision in that case was, I think, perfectly right   But I think that JAMES, L J , went too far in the language which he used   To deprive a purchaser for value without notice of a prior incumbrance of the protection of the legal estate, it is not, in my opinion, essential that he should have been guilty of fraud ; it is sufficient that he has been guilty of such gross negligence as would render it unjust to deprive the prior incumbrancer of his priority ")   And see the subsequent cases of *Berwick & Co* v *Price*, [1905] 1 Ch 632 (*per* JOYCE, J , at p 640   " the omission by a purchaser to investigate the title, or to require delivery or production of the title deeds, is not to my mind either fraudulent or culpable, nor does it since the judgment of LINDLEY, M R , in *Oliver* v *Hinton*, seem necessary to characterize it by any such epithet "), *Walker* v *Lynom*, [1907] 2 Ch 104 (*per* PARKER, J , who, after referring to *Northern Counties of England Fire Insurance Co* v *Whipp*, cited in note (*c*), *ante*, which certainly supports the now discarded heresy, observes, at p 113   " there are, however subsequent cases that   fraud is not necessary "   He then cites and adopts the language of, and the qualifications introduced by, *Oliver* v *Hinton*, *sup* , and *Berwick & Co* v *Price*, *sup*

(*h*) See § 66, *ante*, in which the enactment referred to, s 3 (1) of the Conveyancing Act, 1882 (45 & 46 Vict c 39), is set out , § 67, *ante*, in which it is explained with reference to the authorities , and § 68, *ante*, in which it is shown that neither " fraud," nor " negligence," nor any other motive or state of the mind, is expressly or impliedly alluded to in the section as a condition precedent to presumption of notice   It is rather strange, therefore, that, in the cases after 1882 which are cited in the last note, greater reliance was not placed on the statutory rule

(*i*) See § 70, *ante*

(*j*) See § 73, *ante*

(*k*) For examples, see the cases cited in note (*c*) to § 634, *ante*

(*l*) See the cases cited in note (*g*) to § 635, *ante*

(*m*) Cp the similar process described in Sub s (1), *ante*, where it is shown that, having once said that non disclosure must be fraudulent to be actionable, the Courts were driven to buttress up the initial error of substance by another of terminology

(*n*) In *Evans* v *Bicknell* (1801), 6 Ves 174 (at p 191·   " negligence so gross as to amount to fraud ")

(*o*) In *Hewitt* v *Loosemore* (1851), 9 Hare 449 (at p 458·   " gross and wilful negligence which in the eye of this Court amounts to fraud ")

and bolder, of these propositions, which is now entirely exploded. Not only is negligence not the same thing as fraud, or (as it is otherwise expressed) "equivalent" or "tantamount" to it; it is its direct *antithcton* "It has been said," observes Sir Edward Fry, "that there may be negligence which amounts to fraud. That language has always seemed to me not strictly accurate. Fraud imports design and purpose Negligence imports that you are acting carelessly and without that design. But what is meant is this—that conduct which might be negligent, or might be attributable to negligence, is really attributable to a design not to know more" (*p*). One can only say, in reference to the attempted excuse so courteously made for the astounding heresy under criticism, that if that was the meaning, the very opposite was said ; and so Sir Edward Fry himself, two years later, seems to have thought. The milder, and more superficially plausible, of the two views above referred to, which was alternatively propounded by Lord ELDON (*q*), and others (*r*), viz. that negligence is evidence of fraud, even if it be not identical with it, is in reality not less inaccurate. Negligence no more indicates fraud than it constitutes it. White cannot be evidence of black, any more than it is black. It is true that the *alleged* white may be of so dubious and dingy a hue that any person called upon to decide whether it is black or white, there being no middle colour possible, may be justified in saying that what is described as white is in fact black   But this does not justify the proposition that white ever can be evidence of black   One might as reasonably say that because there are many cases in which a jury find that what is suggested to be justifiable homicide is murder, therefore the former is evidence of the latter.   Here, again, Sir Edward Fry delivers some sound criticism · "the expression 'gross negligence that amounts to evidence of a fraudulent intention' is certainly embarrassing, for negligence is the not doing something from carelessness or want of thought and attention ; whereas a fraudulent intention is a design to commit some fraud, and leads men to do or omit doing a thing not carelessly, but for a purpose. But Lord ELDON seems to have meant by his words the not doing of something so ordinarily done by honest men under the given circumstances as to be really attributable not to negligence or carelessness, but to a fraudulent intention. In short, it appears to us that, in the mouth of Lord ELDON, the word 'negligence' was used simply to express non-feasance." Then follows the criticism, above referred to, of Lord ELDON's bolder proposition . "in one place he speaks of negligence so gross as to amount to fraud, which seems like speaking of carelessness so great as to amount to design " (*s*), or, returning to the simple illustration above given, it may be said that it is like speaking of an object so white as to amount to black.

(*p*) At p 706 of *Kettlewell* v *Watson* (1882), 21 C D 685. The later case referred to in the text is *Northern Counties of England Fire Insurance Co* v *Whipp*, 26 C D 482, C A , at p 490 of which, in criticizing the language of Lord ELDON cited in note (*n*), *ante*, he uses somewhat more caustic language   Similar attempts have been vainly made to identify gross negligence with fraud in the law of misrepresentation (see § 110 of the author's *Law of Actionable Misrepresentation*), and with malice in the law of defamation (see *Pittard* v *Oliver*, [1891] 1 Q B 474, C A , at p 476)

(*q*) In *Evans* v *Bicknell* (1801), 6 Ves 174, at p 189 ("that gross negligence that amounts to *evidence of fraud*"), at p 190 ("that gross negligence that amounts to *evidence of a fraudulent intention*"), and at p 193 (" a circumstance of so gross negligence that it is *conclusive evidence of fraud* ")

(*r*) See *Jones* v *Smith* (1841), 1 Hare 43 (*per* WIGRAM, V -C , at p 71) ; *Ratcliffe* v *Barnard* (1871), 6 Ch App 652 (*per* JAMES, L J , at p 654   "that wilful negligence which leads the Court to conclude that he was an accomplice in the fraud "), *Manners* v *Mew* (1885), 29 C D 725 (*per* NORTH, J , at p 727   "the gross negligence may be such that, looking to the circumstances of the particular case, the Court will see that there was fraud , or it may be in itself, or coupled with other circumstances, sufficient to show fraud,"— than which a more confused or confusing statement it would be impossible to imagine) *Oliver* v *Hinton*, [1899] 2 Ch 264, C A (*per* JEUNE, P , at p 275   " negligence so gross as would justify the Court of Chancery in concluding that there had been fraud in an artificial sense of the word ")

(*s*) *Northern Counties of England Fire Insurance Co* v *Whipp*, *sup* , at pp 189, 490

Sub-s. (4). *Whether such terms as " Negligence" and " Duty " are applicable at all to cases of Presumptive Knowledge.*

638. For the purpose of demonstrating that fraud need not necessarily be established against a person whose knowledge of a fact is presumed from omission to make reasonable inquiry, certain authorities have been relied upon which support the above negative position in virtue of the affirmative statement that negligence of a certain character and degree is a good ground for the imputation of such knowledge ; and it has hitherto been assumed that this latter proposition is correct. But it may well be doubted whether, strictly speaking, it is so ; and whether, notwithstanding the reiterated use of such phrases as "gross," " wilful," " culpable," and the like (*t*), there is really any question of a duty at all, in the proper sense of a duty owed by one person to another, or of " negligence " in the proper sense of the breach or disregard of such a duty. The foundation of the presumption in question, as of all other legal presumptions, is public utility and convenience. The Courts declare, or properly declare, no more than that, under certain circumstances, a man will be deemed to have acquired all that knowledge to which he would have been led by reasonable inquiry : if he does not make such inquiry, his omission to do so is at his own risk and peril. And, in the codifying enactment on the subject in s. 3 of the Conveyancing Act, 1882 (*u*), as well as in several of the authorities (*v*), the proposition is stated in a form which negatives, or at least in no way suggests, the existence of any duty in the matter, except in the metaphorical sense of a duty to one's self, or any motive for pursuing the necessary investigation other than the protection of the party's own interests, or any " guilt," or " culpability," in not doing so. Lord SELBORNE, indeed, is very emphatic on the point. In a registry of title case he observes with his usual felicity and accuracy of expression: " it has been said in argument that investigation of title and inquiry after deeds is the ' duty ' of a purchaser or a mortgagee, and no doubt there are authorities (not involving any question of registry) which do use that language But this, if it can properly be called a duty, is not a duty owing to the possible holder of a latent title or security. It is merely the course which a man dealing *bonâ fide* in the proper and usual manner *for his own interest*, ought by himself or his solicitor to follow *with a view to his own title and his own security* " (*w*)

(*t*) See, generally, the cases cited in the notes to this Sub section It is, however, in *Ware* v *Lord Egmont* (1854), 4 De G M & G 460, a case which in other respects is a very valuable authority on presumptive knowledge, that the error in question is expressed in its most aggravated form Lord CRANWORTH, L C., commits himself distinctly to the full proposition which is canvassed in the text " The question," he says at p 473, " when it is sought to affect a purchaser with constructive notice, is not whether he had the means of obtaining and might with prudent caution have obtained, the knowledge in question, *but whether the not obtaining it was an act of gross and culpable negligence* " Here what is stated not to be the question is precisely what the enactment of 1882 declares to be the only question, whilst the enactment, on the other hand, contains not the remotest reference to those considerations of duty and guilt which Lord CRANWORTH describes as being the sole question.

(*u*) As to this section, see §§ 66, 67, 68, *ante*

(*v*) In the following cases, for example, the doctrine of presumptive knowledge or notice was stated without the slightest suggestion of any duty on the part of the person to whom the knowledge is imputed towards the person in whose favour the presumption is made, or of any culpability, or " guilt " attaching to the former, or of anything being in question except his own " protection " and " interest " *Eyre* v *Dolphin* (1813), 2 Ball & B 290 (*per* Lord MANNERS, L C (Ir), at p. 301), *Sadler* v *Lee* (1843), 6 Beav 324 (*per* Lord LANGDALE, M R , at p 351), *West* v *Reid* (1845), 2 Hare 249 (*per* WIGRAM, V -C., at pp 259, 260, 261), *London Joint Stock Bank* v *Simmons*, [1892] A. C 201, H L. (*per* Lord HERSCHELL, at p 220 " when it is said that a person is put on inquiry, the result in point of law is that he is deemed to know the facts which he would have ascertained if he had made inquiry He cannot better his position by abstaining from so doing "), *Berwick & Co* v *Price*, [1905] 1 Ch 632 (*per* JOYCE, J , at p 640 see the passage cited in note (*g*) to § 635, *ante*) , and see, also, the cases cited in the next two notes Cp the similarly erroneous phrase, " guilty of laches," which is criticized in § 217, *ante*

(*w*) At p. 157 of *Agra Bank, Ltd* v *Barry* (1874), L. R 7 H. L. 135

It would seem, therefore, that "negligence" in this connection means simply neglect of a man's own interests, and the word "ought," which is used both in the above citation and in the enactment of 1882, imports no idea of "duty" in the juridical sense, but bears the same meaning as it does when a person is told that, if he wishes to catch a certain train or vessel, or to obtain a certain appointment, he "ought" to be at a certain place not later than a certain hour , or that he "ought " to be armed, if he intends to travel in a dangerous district, or " ought " to take a guide in the ascent of a particular mountain, or that, if engaged in a business transaction, in order to prevent the possibility of disputes he "ought" to reduce the terms of his agreement into writing, and the like.   In reference to s. 3 of the Act of 1882, in which presumptive notice is made to depend on the probability of actual knowledge resulting from such inquiries as "ought reasonably to have been made," it has been distinctly held that the word " ought " there used "does not import a duty or obligation, for a purchaser need make no inquiry. The expression ' ought reasonably ' must mean ' ought as a matter of prudence,' having regard to what is usually done by men of business under similar circumstances " (x).

Sub s. (5)   Lax Use of the term " Mistake " in the Law of Non-Disclosure

639. In connection with certain types of case, particularly where there is great difficulty in establishing the existence of a relation between the parties of such a character as to give rise to a duty of disclosure, occasional tendency is manifested to indulge sympathy at the expense of justice, and grant relief on the general ground of " mistake,"—not " mistake " as known to the law, but " mistake " as a *nomen generalissimum*, with a large and generous meaning far transcending the definite and sober limits assigned to that concept by jurisprudence.   Some instances of this loose use of the word have been given in a previous chapter (y)   Another misuse of the word, not, however, by judges, but by the legislature, is its association with the adjective " honest."   As has already been pointed out (z), one of the affirmative pleas available to a person sought to be made liable for non-disclosure in a prospectus under s. 81 of the Companies (Consolidation) Act, 1908, is " honest mistake." This expression is meaningless.   If " honest " is to import any addition to the connotation of " mistake," it can only do so on the basis that there is such a thing as dishonest mistake   But there is no such thing   A man may dishonestly pretend to be mistaken, but he cannot be dishonestly mistaken.   Dishonesty and error are mutually exclusive.   To speak, therefore, of an honest mistake, is as tautological as to speak of a rectangular square ; whilst " dishonest mistake " is as self-contra-dictory an expression as " unrectangular square."   The similar phrases " honest satisfaction " (zz), and " honest belief," are subject to the same criticism   It has, it is true, been found possible to give a meaning, though a very strained one, to " dishonest belief " (a)   but, assuming the possibility of a real and actual belief

(x) *Per* STIRLING, L J , at p 135 of *Bailey* v *Barnes*, [1894] 1 Ch 25, C A   Cp *Gains-borough (Earl of)* v *Watcombe Terra Cotta Clay Co* (1885), 54 L. J. (CH) 991 (*per* NORTH, J , at p 994)   Cp *Scriven Bros & Co* v *Hindley & Co*, [1913] 3 K B 564 (*per* A T LAWRENCE, J , at p 569   "a buyer when he examines a sample does so for his own benefit, and not in the discharge of any duty to the seller, the use of the word " negligence " in such a connection is entirely misplaced , it should be reserved for cases . . . where some duty is owed by one person to another ")   Similarly, as to the term "fault," used by COCKBURN, C J , at p 605 of *Bates* v *Hewitt* (1867), L R 2 Q B. 595 (" if he shuts his eyes to the light, it is his own fault "), it is clear from the context that nothing was meant but that one who omits to take precautions for his own protection has only himself to blame
    (y) See § 138, and note (n) thereto, *ante*.
    (z) See Ch. VI, Sect 6, Sub s (4), *ante*
    (zz) See the observations of A L SMITH, L J , at p 307 of *Harward* v *Hackney Union* (1898), 14 T L R. 306, C A .   "a dishonest satisfaction would be no satisfaction at all "
    (a) Thus, in the celebrated misrepresentation case of *Derry* v *Peek* (1889), 14 App Cas 337, H L , Lord HERSCHELL, after saving, at p 374, that " to prevent a false statement being fraudulent, there must always be an honest belief in its truth," proceeds in a later passage of his judgment to explain precisely what he means by " honest belief "   " If

which may yet be regarded as dishonest, because dishonestly produced, how can fraudulent manufacture be ascribed to a mistake? If the thing is a mistake, it cannot be a fraud: if it is a fraud, it cannot be a mistake.

SECT. 3 CRITICISM OF TERMINOLOGY APPLIED TO RELATIONS OF CONFIDENCE AND INFLUENCE.

640. In connection with the duty of disclosure and other duties incidental to relations of confidence and influence, expressions have occasionally been used with some laxity. In the first place, the term *uberrima fides*, as applied to contracts in the negotiation for which full disclosure is required, has been referred to as possibly open to exception (b), though in this case the comment may be considered somewhat hypercritical.

641. Secondly, as regards relations of confidence, Lord MOULTON, in language remarkable for its force and lucidity, has drawn attention to the confusion arising from the lax and indiscriminate use and application of the general term " fiduciary relation " (c), and Lord WESTBURY has strongly condemned the like misuse of the word " trustee " in connection with one particular class of fiduciary relation (d)

642. Thirdly, with respect to relations of " influence," it has already been pointed out how frequently " influence " and " confidence " are confounded with one another, and the distinction between them hazily defined, or altogether disregarded (e), whilst the ambiguities and difficulties, in this case perhaps unavoidable, which surround the expression " undue,"—applied, as it is, to " influence " in at least three senses (the popular sense, the " testamentary " sense, and the sense in which it is used by lawyers in relation to transactions *inter vivos*),—have been observed upon by Lord CRANWORTH (f) and Lord ABINGER (g)

I thought," he observes, at p 376, "that a person making a false statement had shut his eyes to the facts, or purposely abstained from inquiring into them, I should hold that honest belief was absent, and that he was just as fraudulent as if he had knowingly stated that which was false " That is to say, in any action of deceit, where it is necessary to prove that the representor did not believe in the truth of his representation, a belief actually held, but dishonestly engendered, will be deemed as clear a badge of fraud as the absence of any belief at all But this principle has no application whatever to the case of non-disclosure which is actionable without fraud

(b) See §§ 1, 2, 85, 87, 106, *ante*

(c) At pp 728, 729 of *Re Coomber*, [1911] 1 Ch 723, C. A " it is said that the son was manager of the stores, and therefore was in a fiduciary relationship to his mother This illustrates in a most striking form the danger of trusting to verbal formulæ Fiduciary relations are of many different types , they extend from the relation of myself to an errand boy who is bound to bring me back my change up to the most intimate and confidential relations which can possibly exist between one party and another, where the one is wholly in the hands of the other All these are cases of fiduciary relations, and the Courts have again and again interfered to set aside acts which, between persons in a wholly independent position, would have been perfectly valid Thereupon in some minds there arises the idea that, if there is any fiduciary relation whatever, any of these types of interference is warranted by it They consider that every kind of fiduciary relation justifies every kind of interference Of course this is absurd The nature of the fiduciary relation must be such that it justifies the interference " Cp § 143, note (h), *ante*

(d) At pp 675, 676 of *Knox v Gye* (1872), L. R 5 H. L 656 See note (b) to § 646, *post* Cp *Omnium Electric Palaces, Ltd v Baines*, [1914] 1 Ch 332, C A (*per* SARGANT, J , at p 347), and the criticism of Lord WESTBURY'S views in the Privy Council, at pp 87, 88 of *Gordon v. Holland* (1913), 82 L J (P C) 81

(e) In § 314, note (t), and § 404, *ante*

(f) At pp 47, 48 of *Boyse v Rossborough* (1857), 6 H L C 2 " the difficulty of deciding such a question arises from the difficulty of defining with distinctness what is undue influence In a popular sense we often speak of a person exercising undue influence over another, which influence is certainly not of a nature which would invalidate a will A young man is often led into dissipation by following the example of a companion of riper years ; the companion is then correctly said to exercise an undue influence But if in these circumstances the young man, influenced by his regard for the person who had thus led him astray, were to make a will, and leave to him everything that he possessed, such a will certainly could not be impeached on the ground of undue influence "

(g) At p 367 (during the argument) of *Middleton v. Sherburne* (1841), 4 Y & C. (Exch

643. Lastly, the vague and misleading use of such mere figures of speech as "unfairness," "inequality," "mistake," and the like, in connection with the duties incidental to the negotiation of compromises and other contracts *uberrimœ fidei* (h), as also with those incidental to relations of influence (i), has already been criticized. The use of the terms "fair" and "unfair" in a variety of meanings has been particularly productive of pitfalls in the law of non-disclosure (j), as it has been in other departments of our jurisprudence (k). And the same is true, as has been emphatically noted by Sir GEORGE JESSEL, of the haphazard application of the terms "hardship" (l) and "oppression" (m).

SECT. 4   CRITICISM OF CONFLICTING TERMINOLOGY APPLIED TO THE DOCTRINE OF ACTUAL AND PRESUMPTIVE KNOWLEDGE.

644. An examination of the phraseology used in the authorities as to "actual," "constructive," and "imputed" knowledge will reveal an extremely inconvenient and perplexing want of consistency in the application, and unanimity in the interpretation, of those respective adjectives. Conflicting definitions have been given,

in Eq.) 358, where he also mentioned an unreported case in which "Mr Justice Chambre, who tried the case and who was the best lawyer of his day, told the jury he hardly knew what undue influence was." Cp. the cases cited in note (p) to § 447, *ante*, and *Wingrove v. Wingrove* (1885), 11 P. D. 81 (*per* HANNEN, P., at p. 82).

(h) See § 138, *ante*, and the cases cited in notes (e), (f), (g), (h) to § 163, *ante*.

(i) See § 128, *ante*.

(j) Thus, at p. 324 of *Fry v. Lane* (1888), 40 C. D. 312, KAY, J., speaks of "*unfair dealing*, which equity considers a fraud," though "no moral fraud has been proved"; at p. 662 of *Bromley v. Smith* (1859), 26 Beav. 644, ROMILLY, M.R., uses the expression "fairness of the transaction" as indicating adequacy of price only; whilst Lord SELBORNE, L.C., at p. 491 of *Aylesford (Earl of) v. Morris* (1873), 8 Ch. App. 484, and, following him, FITZGIBBON, L.J. (Ir.), at p. 523 of *Rae v. Joyce* (1892), 29 L. R. (Ir.), 500, seem to regard the term as negativing the taking of any unconscionable advantage of the distress and weakness of a servient party, as distinguished from the reasonableness, in a commercial aspect, of the bargain.

(k) The unfortunate ambiguities in the application of the term "fair" to "comment" are minutely discussed and criticized in App. XII, Sect. 4, of the author's *Code of the Law of Actionable Defamation*. Similar difficulties have arisen, in connection with the law relating to contracts in restraint of trade, whenever reliance has been placed on a supposed standard of "fair restraint," "fair competition," and the like. See *Mogul Steamship Co. v. McGregor, Gow & Co.* (1889), 23 Q. B. D. 598, C. A., *per* BOWEN, L.J., at p. 615 "we were told that competition ceases to be the lawful exercise of trade, . . . if carried to a length that is not fair or reasonable.   This seems to assume that, apart from fraud, intimidation, molestation, or obstruction, of some other personal right *in rem* or *in personam*, there is some natural standard of "fairness" or "reasonableness" (to be determined by the internal consciousness of judges and juries) beyond which competition ought not in law to go.   There seems to be no authority, and I think, with submission, that there is no sufficient reason for such a proposition.   The defendants, we are told by the plaintiffs' counsel, might lawfully lower rates provided they did not lower them beyond "a fair freight," whatever that may mean.   But where is it established that there is any such restriction on commerce?   And what is to be the definition of 'a fair freight'?" So, at p. 47 of the report of the same case on appeal to the House of Lords, [1892] A. C. 25, H. L., Lord BRAMWELL observes "it is admitted that there may be fair competition in trade, that two may offer to join and compete against a third.   If so, what is the definition of a 'fair competition'?   What is unfair that is neither forcible nor fraudulent?", and, to the same effect, Lord MORRIS, at p. 51 "I am not aware of any stage of competition called 'fair,' intermediate between 'lawful' and 'unlawful.'   The question of 'fairness' would be relegated to the idiosyncrasies of individual judges."

(l) At p. 413 of *Middleton v. Brown* (1878), 47 L. J. (CH.) 411, C. A., in a passage, cited in note (s) to § 428, *ante*, which was adopted in *Rae v. Joyce* (1892), 29 L. R. (Ir.) 500 (*per* WALKER, L.C. (Ir.), at p. 510).

(m) At p. 260 of *Wallis v. Smith* (1882), 21 C. D. 243, C. A.   "he"—Lord ELDON— "perfectly well knew that, whatever had been the doctrine of equity at one time, it was not then the doctrine of equity to give relief on the ground that agreements were oppressive, where the parties were of full age, and at arm's length."

not only of the expressions "constructive," and "imputed," but (which one would hardly expect) even of the word "actual" also (n). Thus Lord ERSKINE, after using "actual notice" in its ordinary meaning, proceeded to distinguish it from, on the one hand, "notice by construction of law, as where notice to the agent is notice to the principal," and, on the other hand, from "imputed" notice, which he understood as "that notice which from the nature of the transaction every person of ordinary prudence must have" (o). Lord CHELMSFORD, however, expressed his preference for a limitation of the phrase "constructive notice" to the notice which a person is deemed to have had of that which reasonable inquiry would have revealed, whilst that which Lord ERSKINE called "constructive," viz. the knowledge which a principal is deemed to have in virtue of his agent's knowledge, should in his view be denominated "actual," or, if not, then "imputed" knowledge (p). The former of the two adjectives thus suggested as proper to be applied to cases of knowledge through an agent was afterwards expressly adopted by Lord HATHERLEY (q) and Lord CAIRNS (r), and impliedly by the various judges who have insisted that, for purposes of knowledge as of all others, the principal is "identified" with his agent (s). the latter was preferred by Sir GEORGE TURNER and Sir EDWARD FRY (t). Lord ESHER strongly objected to the use of any such phrase as "constructive" or "imputed" notice, but his repugnance was not so much to the names, as names, but to the theories to which they were applied. "The doctrine of constructive notice," he observes, "is wholly equitable," and "is a dangerous one." He protests that "it is not known to the common law," and insists that the cases at common law of "wilful blindness," in order to avoid knowing the truth, are not really cases of constructive notice at all, but of actual notice "when a man has statements made to him, or has knowledge of facts, which do not expressly tell him of something which is against him, and he abstains from making further inquiry because he knows what the result would be—or, as the phrase is, he wilfully shuts his eyes—then judges are

(n) In Ch. II, Sect 3, *ante*, the various species of knowledge are discussed
(o) At p 120 of *Hiern* v *Mill* (1806), 13 Ves 114
(p) At p. 554 of *Espin* v *Pemberton* (1859), 3 De G & J 547 "I think it would tend very much to clearness in these cases if it"—*i e* knowledge through an agent—"were classed under the head of actual notice . . . Constructive notice, properly so called, is the knowledge which the Courts impute to a person upon a presumption so strong of the existence of the knowledge that it cannot be allowed to be rebutted, either from his knowing something which ought to have put him on further inquiry, or from his wilfully abstaining from inquiry to avoid notice I should therefore prefer calling the knowledge which a person has, either by himself, or through his agent, actual knowledge, or, if it is necessary to make a distinction between the knowledge which a person possesses himself, and that which is known to his agent, the latter might be called imputed knowledge ' The definition here given of "constructive notice," as distinct from "actual" and "imputed notice," is somewhat unfortunately expressed, because it describes constructive notice as something which the Courts "impute" It is taken almost *verbatim* from a passage in the judgment of TURNER, V C, in *Hewitt* v *Loosemoore* (1851), 9 Hare 449, at p 455, but it is plain from the context that the Vice-Chancellor meant by his "constructive," "imputed," and "presumed" knowledge—for in his view all three epithets are equally applicable—the knowledge which a principal is deemed to have in virtue of the actual knowledge of his agent, and no other kind of knowledge
(q) In *Rolland* v *Hart* (1871), 6 Ch App 678, at pp 681, 682 "it has been held over and over again that notice to a solicitor of a transaction, and about a matter as to which it is part of his duty to inform himself, is actual notice to the client"
(r) At p 148 of *Agra Bank, Ltd.* v *Barry* (1874), L R 7 H L 135 ("actual notice either to the principal, or to the agent, whose knowledge is that of the principal")
(s) See *Stribley* v *Imperial Marine Insurance Co* (1876), 1 Q B D 507 (*per* LUSH, J , at p 514 "when the master of a ship, or the agent or correspondent of the owner withholds any fact material to the risk, the owner, in making any insurance, is identified with his agent, and liable for his default" Cp the following misrepresentation cases S Pearson & Son, Ltd v Dublin Corporation, [1907] A C 351, H L (*per* Lord LOREBURN, L.C , at p 354, and Lord HALSBURY, at pp 357, 358) , *Lloyd* v *Grace, Smith & Co*, [1912] A C 716, H L
(t) *Hewitt* v *Loosemoore, sup* (*per* TURNER, V. C., at p 455); *Bradley* v *Riches* (1878), 9 C D 189 (*per* FRY, J , at p 196).

in the habit of telling juries that they may infer he did know what was against him.

. There is no question of 'constructive notice,' or 'constructive knowledge'; it is actual knowledge which is inferred " (u).

645 In this marked divergence of nomenclature, the course which suggests itself as the best adapted to avoid confusion, when dealing with this topic, is to employ the principle of dichotomy, and divide all knowledge into two main classes—knowledge which is acquired personally and directly, and is the subject of evidence, on the one hand ; and knowledge which is not so acquired, and not so proved, but is inferred in law, on the other. The former class it cannot be wrong to call " actual." For the latter a class name should be chosen which has not been appropriated to any particular variety, or applied by different judges to different varieties, of the class, and which at the same time expresses its full connotation No term answers these requirements so satisfactorily as " presumptive," which, moreover, has received the countenance of a strong body of authority (v). Accordingly, in the treatment of the subject of knowledge in an earlier chapter (w), and throughout this work generally, the terminology described has been adopted

SECT 5. OBSERVATIONS ON THE PROVERBIAL PHILOSOPHY OF THE SUBJECT, AND ON JUDICIAL EXPRESSION OF PROPOSITIONS

646 The branch of law which forms the subject of this work is, in common with others, overrun by elliptical formulæ, gnomic phrases, metaphors, and figures of speech These should always provoke a somewhat cautious and critical attitude. A principle or proposition of law can seldom be concentrated in terminological tabloids and quintessences A phrase can, as a rule, only present one facet of the truth the whole truth is more than these " broken lights " Proverbial wisdom, attractive though it be on the surface, is of necessity so imperfect and one sided that he who relies upon it for solid support in any question of science is leaning on a broken reed Even in common affairs, popular sayings are often untrue to life, as Charles Lamb has wittily demonstrated in matters of philosophy and science, they are still more unsafe guides. For, indeed, as against almost every accepted maxim, paradox, or even dilemma, it is possible to formulate a contradictory one, which shall be just as good, or just as bad Bacon was so impressed with this possibility,

(u) At pp 707, 708 of English & Scottish Mercantile Investment Co v Brunton, [1892] 2 Q B 700, C A   He had previously protested, in Allen v Seckham (1879), 11 C D. 790, at p 795, that " the doctrine of constructive notice ought to be narrowly watched   . Indeed, anything 'constructive' ought to be narrowly watched, because it depends on a fiction."

(v) As in Noble v Kennaway (1780), 2 Dougl (K B) 510 (per Lord MANSFIELD, C J, at p 512 " every underwriter is presumed to be acquainted with the practice of the trade he insures ") , Friere v Woodhouse (1817), Holt N P 572 (per BURROUGH, J, at p 573 " presumed within the knowledge of the underwriter ") , Stewart v Bell (1821), 5 B & Ald 238 (per Cur, at p 239 " the underwriter is presumed to be acquainted with the usual course of the voyage ") , West v Reid (1843), 2 Hare 249 (per WIGRAM, V C, at pp 260, 261 " a purchaser must be presumed to investigate, &c.,   and may therefore be presumed to have examined, &c   and that presumption I take to be the foundation of the whole doctrine But it is impossible to presume that a purchaser examines instruments not directly nor presumptively connected with the title ") , Smith v Capron (1849), 7 Hare 185 (per WIGRAM, V-C, at p 192 the presumption, therefore, would be that he had made himself acquainted with the whole of the instrument I do not think that I ought to allow this presumption to be rebutted by the averment that   &c) , Heuitt v Loosemoore (1851), 9 Hare 449 (per TURNER, V C, at p 455 " a presumption so strong that it cannot be allowed to be rebutted ") , Espin v Pemberton (1859), 3 De G & J 547 (per Lord CHELMSFORD, L C, using the like expression : see note (p), ante) , Harrower v Hutchinson (1870), L R 5 Q B 584, Exch Ch (per KELLY, C B, at pp 591–593, where the word " presumed " is repeatedly used, as also in the treatises of Phillips, and of Duer, there cited, and per CLEASBY, B, at p. 594) , Leigh v Adams (1871), 25 L T 566 (per COCKBURN, C J. at p 569 " the knowledge that every underwriter is presumed to possess ")

(w) See Ch. II, Sect 3, ante.

in regard to science in general, that he recommended (*De Augm. Scient.*, Book vii) special attention to be given to "Antitheses of Things," and with that object sketched out the beginnings of a suggested "Promptuary," or "Preparatory Storehouse," with examples of antithetical aphorisms arranged in parallel columns. In relation to jurisprudence in general, and the law of non-disclosure in particular, Lord ESHER expressed his strong distrust of, and distaste for, these "oracular phrases," and emphasized the "danger which always arises from the use in law of these figures of speech. Their terseness prevents them . . . from expressing accurately the proposition they are used to enunciate. They are generally larger than that proposition " (*x*). Of such are the meaningless *caveat emptor* (*xx*), in the law relating to sale and purchase, "estoppels are odious," *de minimis non curat lex*, and the like Similarly metaphorical and analogical modes of expression have found small favour with great judges. Even the phrase " public policy," which figures so largely in the law of non disclosure as the name applied to that general utility which is the theoretical foundation of nearly all its rules, was thought at one time of a sufficiently figurative complexion to demand judicial apology and explanation at the hands of Lord HARDWICKE (*y*). The word " justice " itself has not escaped the attention of the metaphor-mongers, and has been used as a figure of speech (*z*). Lord MANSFIELD, indeed, roundly declared that " nothing in law is so apt to mislead as a metaphor " (*a*), and, in particular relation to the case of a " trustee by metaphor," was heartily supported in this view by Lord WESTBURY (*b*) It may be doubted, however, whether such unqualified denunciation of the metaphor is just The use of this mode of conveying thought is quite proper in itself Its application may of course be incorrect, as may be that of analogy, which is only expanded metaphor, as metaphor is condensed or crystallized analogy. If so, it is not ἀνὰ λόγον. The alleged ratio does not exist. One does not, however, denounce the Rule of Three, because many schoolboys cannot apply it correctly Half our language is metaphorical The word " metaphor " is itself a metaphor

647. From time to time judges show an inclination to reproach advocates with the vice of misapplying, or accepting too broadly and literally, the language in which they have expounded or enunciated a rule or principle of law. Advocates, on the

(*x*) At p 557 of *Blackburn, Low & Co* v *Vigors* (1886), 17 Q B D 553, C A Cp the observations of Lord PARKER cited in note (*p*) to § 626, *anti*

(*xx*) See note (*c*) to § 91 of the author's *Law of Actionable Misrepresentation*

(*y*) At p 156 of *Chesterfield (Earl of)* v *Janssen* (1751), 2 Ves Sr 125, where, after describing the various classes of unconscionable transactions, he added " these cases show what courts of equity mean when they profess to go on reasons drawn from public utility To weaken the force of such reasons, they have been called political arguments, and introducing politics into the decision of courts of justice This was showing the thing in the light which best served the argument for the defendant, but far from the true one, if the word *politics* is taken in its common acceptation but if in its true original meaning, it comprehends everything that concerns the government of the country , of which the administration of justice forms a considerable part , and in this sense it is admitted always To apply this thus far, and in this sense, is relief in a court of equity founded on public utility as the rest of mankind besides the parties contracting are concerned it is properly said to be governed on public utility " It must have been the use of the word " policy," instead of " utility," and not the thing itself, which prompted, and gave an air of plausibility and wisdom to, the exceedingly inept description of it by BURROUGH, J , as the " unruly horse " See § 668, *post*, for a more detailed examination of the various shades of meaning assigned to this term

(*z*) See § 670, *post*

(*a*) See the next note

(*b*) In *Knox* v *Gye* (1872), L R, 5 H L 656, Lord WESTBURY, L C, after speaking of " the advantage of correcting an inaccurate use of a word although that use may be found in treatises of reputation," and giving an instance of it from his own experience (p 675), goes on, at p 676, to say that the case before the House—(the case of a man who was " improperly and by metaphor only called a trustee," but whom it was sought to fix with the same liabilities " as if he were a trustee by declaration—in other words, a complete trustee ")—" well illustrates the remark made by Lord MANSFIELD that nothing in law is so apt to mislead as a metaphor '

other hand, and *jurisperiti* retort that it is unfair in a judge who has not used suffi- ciently guarded language to blame his hearers for supposing that he had meant what he said, and for taking him at his word *Non nostrum est tantas componere lites.* It is sufficient to call attention to the prevalence (in the present, as well as in other departments of our law) of two opposite errors, or alleged errors, in the treatment of judicial deliverances. On the one hand, it has been made a subject of complaint (by no means justly, however, in many cases) that, in argument, a general proposition stated by a judge is cited without reference to the circumstances of the particular case to which that proposition was intended to be confined (c). The only observation proper to be made on this complaint is that its justice depends on the form in which the proposition was declared   If it purported to be a *summum axioma,* and the case itself was decided as it was because, and only because, it was a particular instance of the general rule, then the proposition ought to be cited without reference to the particular circumstances . if, on the other hand, it was *expressed* to be confined to those circumstances, it ought not to be relied upon apart from them   The converse error (for which again, however, it is submitted, judges are themselves partly re sponsible) arises when a pure general proposition is intended to be declared, but the expression of it is adulterated by the admixture of some of the particular facts of the case of which the proposition is really quite independent, and afterwards (not alto gether unnaturally) the advocate supposes this adventitious and alien element to be an integral part and an essential condition or qualification of the proposition itself, and to have been so intended (d)

(c) Thus, Sir JAMES MANSFIELD, C J , at p 162 of *Brisbane* v *Dacres* (1813), 5 Taunt 143, in a passage cited with approval by HAMILTON, L.J., at p 138 of *Baylis* v *Bishop of London,* [1913] 1 Ch. 127, C. A , said : "it is certainly very hard on a judge, if a rule which he generally lays down is to be taken up and carried to its full extent   This is sometimes done by counsel, who have nothing else to rely on , but great caution ought to be used by the Court in extending such maxims to cases which the judge who uttered them never had in contemplation " RIGBY, L J , at p 270 of *Oliver* v *Hinton,* [1899] 2 Ch 264, C A , expressed the view that "the Court is not bound to treat the mere language used by a learned judge in the particular case with which he was dealing as laying down a principle of law governing other cases ". Lord HALSBURY, L C., at p 506 of *Quinn* v *Leathem,* [1901] A C 495, H L , insisted that "every judgment must be read as applicable to the particular facts proved, since the generality of the expressions to be found there are not intended to be expositions of the whole law, but governed and qualified by the particular facts of the case in which such expressions are to be found " The soundness of these various *dicta* seems somewhat questionable   If taken literally, they would render vain all induction and deduction in the study of jurisprudence, and turn science into chaos. But the warning conveyed by Lord HALDANE, L C , at pp 38, 10, 42, 43, of *Kreglinger* v *New Patagonia Meat & Cold Storage Co ,* [1914] A C 25, H L., against the judicial—not the forensic—habit of paying too much attention to the rule, and too little to the principle of the rule, is heartily to be commended   See §§ 475, 478, *ante,* for examples of this error.

(d) Many of the cases cited in the notes to § 635, *ante,* are illustrations of this type of misapplied learning   Another, and a very striking example, is furnished by the mis- representation case of *Lloyd* v *Grace, Smith & Co ,* [1912] A C 716, H L.

APPENDIX B.

COMPARISON BETWEEN JURISPRUDENCE AND ETHICS IN RELATION
TO THE DUTY OF DISCLOSURE AND THE USE AND ABUSE OF
CONFIDENCE AND INFLUENCE

648. It is proposed in this Appendix to consider where, and why, ethical and juridical doctrines, as to the various subject-matters of this treatise, coincide, and where, and why, they diverge, and in what respects they have influenced one another (e)

Sect 1 As to the Substantial Correspondence between the Moral and Juridical Treatment of the Duty of Disclosure and Fiduciary Obligations generally.

649. Ethical philosophy, conventional or customary morality ("sittlichkeit"), and the juridical body of doctrine which is known as "equity," concur in their distaste for rigid and unprogressive formulæ, and in their preference for elastic and adaptable principles, in all matters concerned with the conceptions of Good Faith and Honour . " τοῦ γὰρ ἀορίστου ἀόριστος καὶ ὁ κανών ἐστιν, ὥσπερ καὶ τῆς Λεσβίας οἰκοδομῆς ὁ μολύβδινος κανών πρὸς γὰρ τὸ σχῆμα τοῦ λίθου μετακινεῖται καὶ οἱ μένει ὁ κανών " (f) The flexible Lesbian rule which appealed thus strongly to Aristotle, as the only fit instrument to be applied to all moral questions, has appealed with at least equal force to jurists in relation to the various topics dealt with in this work, and particularly (as has been already noticed) to the equitable duty of candour in negotiations with a view to transactions *uberrimæ fidei* (g), the principles affecting " contracts for disclosure (h), and the use and abuse of confidence (i), and influence (j), as it has also in relation to other provinces of our law, such as defamation (k), or the doctrine of restraint of trade (l) Philosophical equity, again citing from Aristotle, aims at τὸ ἐπιεικές, as a necessary expansion or correction of the absoluteness of moral formulæ which, if universally applied, would on occasions shock the conscience, " καὶ ἔστιν αὕτη ἡ φύσις ἡ τοῦ ἐπιεικοῦς, ἐπανόρθωμα νόμου, ᾗ ἐλλείπει διὰ τὸ καθόλου " (m) And this is precisely

(e) In App B of the author's *Law of Actionable Misrepresentation*, a similar comparative treatment is to be found

(f) *Eth* V 10. Bacon (*De Augm Scient* , lib 8, cap 3, aph 32) says that equitable principles also must proceed *ex arbitrio boni viri et discretione sanâ, ubi legis norma deficit, lex enim non sufficit casibus*, adding that Time is *sapientissima res, et novorum casuum quotidie auctor et inventor*, adopting Xen *Hellen* , III 3, 2 Cp Lord Kames in the Introduction to his *Principles of Equity* (vol 1, pp 24, 25)

(g) See § 85, *ante* (insurance) , § 109, *ante* (vendor and purchaser) , § 120, *ante* (suretyship)

(h) § 171, *ante*

(i) § 343, *ante.*

(j) § 453, *ante*

(k) In connection with the rules relating to protected or " privileged " communications, the praiseworthy elasticity of the law (miscalled by some " fluctuation ") is noted and illustrated in App XXI, Sect 1, of the author's *Code of the Law of Actionable Defamation*

(l) See *Nordenfeldt v Nordenfeldt Maxim Gun & Ammunition Co* , [1894] A C 535, H L (*per* Lord Watson, at pp 553, 554, and Lord Ashbourne, at p 558)

(m) *Eth* , V. 10

the function of juridical equity, as stated by Bacon (n), and Lord Kames (o), in almost identical language ; and so it always has been of " sittlichkeit," as reflected in the summary judgments of those organs of current sentiment, " the man in the street," the Homeric " τίς " (p), or the modern juryman. The represen tatives of those three points of view are at one in their keen appreciation of the danger of cantoning out the denotation of bad faith, or *dolus*, or fraud, and in their aversion to cast iron definitions, or itemized catalogues (q). This is the real meaning of the reiterated judicial statement that it is impossible to define fraud, and it is only in this sense that it is strictly accurate. Thus Lord REDESDALE observed · " *Crescit in orbe dolus.* Cases cannot always be found to serve as direct authority for subse-quent cases ; but if a case arises of fraud, or presumption of fraud, to which even no principle already established can be applied, a new principle must be established to meet the fraud . . ; for the possibility will always exist that human ingenuity in contriving fraud will go beyond any cases which have before occurred " (r). And Lord HATHERLEY : " the Courts of Equity have at all times abstained from attempt ing a nice definition of imposition. . . It is notorious that every mode that can well be conceived of dealing with contracts which ought not to be maintained . has from time to time come before the consideration of Courts of Equity, although the precise circumstances of the case may never yet have come before the Court " (s) In other words, it is not a case of intellectual impossibility of defining fraud, or bad faith, in the sense of declaring the connotation of those terms, but of the refusal of the Courts, on grounds of high policy, to map out their denotation, and provide the wrong-doer with an inventory or specification of particular acts to be avoided It is, therefore, inaccurate to say, as Lord LANGDALE did, that " nobody *has been able* to define fraud," because " it is so multiform " (t), for multiplicity of species is no obstacle to a definition of the genus , but it may be perm ss. 'le to say, with Lord LINDLEY (u), that " no Court *has attempted* to define frai d," or " to define undue influence," if " define " is understood in the above limited (and not very correct) sense

650. Further, there appears to be, and to have been from the earliest times, a general agreement between the attitude of the community, as expressed in the works of dramatists, poets (v), and other writers not professedly philosophic, on the one hand, and that of jurisprudence, on the other, towards the simpler problems, and the main and rudimentary principles, of the subject Popular sentiment, and public authority, whether ecclesiastical or civil, reflecting that sentiment, have at all times and in all civilized countries denounced abuses of power, and of knowledge, for the purpose of extorting p ivate advantage from the necessities of the helpless. " Cursed

---

(n) " Adjuvandi, vel supplendi, vel corrigendi juris civilis gratiâ." See, generally, as to the functions of prætorian courts, his *De Augm Scient* , lib 8, cap 3, aphh 32–46

(o) Lord Kames considered the doctrines of ethics and equitable jurisprudence so intimately allied that he prefixed to his *Equity Jurisprudence* (in the first two editions) a " preliminary discourse on the principles of morality "

(p) See Sir Richard Jebb's Essay on " Ancient Organs of Public Opinion " (*Collected Essays*, pp 130–132)

(q) It is true that theological casuistry revels in particular instances,—indeed it would not be true to its name if it did not,—but even here the Jesuits always insist that the minutiæ to which at first sight such disproportionate importance seems to be attached in their " case books " are chiefly used to illustrate great principles

(r) At p 666 of *Webb* v. *Rorke* (1806), 2 Sch & Lefr 661 , 9 R R 122

(s) At p 1243 of *Erlanger* v *New Sombrero Phosphate Co* (1878), 3 App Cas 1218, H L

(t) At p 303 of *Franks* v. *Weaver* (1847), 10 Beav. 297

(u) When LINDLEY, L J , at p 183 of *Allcard* v *Skinner* (1887), 36 C D 145, C A

(v) At p 50 of *Piggott* v *Stratton* (1859), 1 De G F & J 33, Lord CAMPBELL, L C , vouches " moralists and jurists " for a proposition in the law of misrepresentation So, at p 291 of *Cox* v *Lee* (1869), L R 4 Exch 284, PIGOTT, B , in considering the effect on a man's reputation of a charge of ingratitude, referred to the " light " in which " it is re garded by *poets and moralists,* who are the mirrors and exponents of the universal feelings and judgments of mankind " Homer is frequently cited in the Institutes and Digest. and, in one of the *epistolæ* prefixed to the latter, Justinian describes him as *patrem omnis virtutis.*

be he that maketh the blind to go out of his way," said the Mosaic law (w), and the commination was deemed, or expanded, to cover the negative offence of not putting the blind on his way. This may be regarded as the earliest recognition of a duty of disclosure arising out of a relation between the strong and the weak. A breach of the duty was visited with public execration in Athens (x), and was denounced both by the Roman poet, and the Roman moralist (y), as one of the gravest crimes against humanity. In all drama and fiction questions as to the duty of breaking silence, over and above the mere duty of veracity (z), and problems arising out of the conflict between interest and honour (a), have supplied the strongest, because the most human, situations, and have appealed the most powerfully to audiences and readers, —a fact which is only explicable on the hypothesis of a popular appreciation of the existence and sanctity of such a duty. Of the close correspondence in all essentials between professed moral philosophy and jurisprudence as to the doctrine of Good Faith, no less than as to other doctrines which form the common subject of the two sciences, no better proof can be suggested than an examination of the writings of Paley, and, the fact, which such an examination will abundantly reveal, that most of his ethical rules are reasoned out on precisely the same basis as those of jurisprudence, whilst jurisprudence has made many avowed references and appeals to his philosophy in support and elucidation of her own principles. This great moralist had qualifications and gifts which specially commended his views to jurists. "An Englishman," said Mr. F. D. Maurice (b), "can never allude to Paley without remembering how eminently English he was in all the habits of his mind, in his exquisitely transparent style, in a kind of quaint, homely humour . . and in his detestation of everything which appeared to him unpractical. These, with a most genial temperament and an acuteness developed by visits to our law courts, and the study of evidence, may assure us that he will give us much that his predecessor (c)—however he may have been excelled by him in the special refinement and richness of the Greek mind— could not give" (d) It is not a matter of surprise, therefore, that his works have

(w) This is the third Curse in the Commination Service. The duty in question is noticed by Juvenal as one imposed by the Jewish Code, but it is described by him, and made a subject of reproach on that account, as a duty of a strictly tribal character, and owed to no one who is not a co-religionist "non monstrare vias eadem nisi sacra colenti" (Sat xiv 103). The Mosaic prohibition of usury was similarly limited see § 664, note (t), post.

(x) See Cic, De Off, III 13 "quod Athenis exsecrationibus sanctum est"

(y) Cic, De Off, I 16, citing Ennius, where he contrasts the humanity of him "qui erranti comiter monstrat viam" with the meanness of refusing or omitting such an obvious service to a fellow creature,—a service which, like the act of permitting another to light his lamp or fire from one's own, can be rendered without any extinction or diminution of the light or heat from which the other borrows In this sort of view the duty of candour appeared not so much a dictate of justice as of humanity, just as the theologians of a later date, such as Augustine, spoke of honest disclosure, and even of veracity, as a branch of the specially Christian virtue of charity, rather than as a requirement of honour

(z) The double duty is recognized in Horace's "justitiæ soror, incorrupta fides, Nudaque veritas" (Carm I xxiv), and still more markedly in the pathetic exclamation of Neoptolemus in Soph Philoct, 908, 909, which appears on the title page of this work

> ὦ Ζεῦ, τί δράσω, δεύτερον ληφθῶ κακός,
> κρύπτων θ' ἃ μὴ δεῖ, καὶ λέγων αἴσχιστ' ἐπῶν,

(a) In Tro & Cress, Act 4, Sc 5, Agamemnon welcomes Hector in terms which admirably express the whole duty of disclosure and disinterested candour in relations of confidence and influence

> "faith and troth,
> Strained purely from all hollow bias drawing,
> Bids thee, with most divine integrity,
> From heart of very heart, great Hector, welcome"

(b) In his "Inaugural Lecture to a Course on Casuistry, Moral Philosophy, and Moral Theology, delivered in the Senate House, Cambridge, on the 4th December, 1866"

(c) The reference is to Aristotle

(d) That Paley had a more than bowing acquaintance with the practical side of law, we learn as a fact from the Memoirs of William Paley, by G W Headlam (2nd ed., 1810),

attracted the attention of practical lawyers as well as of philosophic jurists. ERSKINE, at a trial before Lord ELLENBOROUGH, C.J., in 1803, recommended the study of his writings to all members of his profession (e). In his reference to "moralists," in 1859, there can be no doubt that Lord CAMPBELL, L.C., had Paley especially in mind (f). In 1871, HANNEN, J., in dealing with the question of the conditions necessary to create a duty to remove the delusion of a negotiating party, said that the rule of law applicable to such a case is "a corollary from the rule of morality, which Mr Pollock cites from Paley " (g). In 1873, BRAMWELL, B , strongly advised certain judicial persons to "read and inwardly digest Paley's *Moral and Political Philosophy* . . in which the necessity for positive rules of general application, the doctrine of particular and general consequences, and the superior importance of, and regard due to, general consequences are clearly expounded " (h) : whilst Archbishop Whateley, as a training in the principles of evidence, recommended to students of the law a study of the philosopher's writings, and particularly his *Horæ Paulinæ* (i) It will be noticed that many occasions have already been taken (j), and will hereafter arise (k), in these pages, to illustrate and enforce the principles of non-disclosure and fiduciary duty by references to Paley. Writers on other departments of our jurisprudence are no less in the debt of this great casuist for suggestion and illumination in connection with, for instance, the law of representations and promises (l), or that of bailments, or defamation (m). It is true that COLERIDGE carped at Paley's principles, which he considered unworthy of the higher philosophy, and described as "time serving" (n) ; but, if this criticism be just, which it is not, the ground of it, viz. that his doctrines reflect current sentiment, is the very circumstance which makes his works so apt an illustration of the point now insisted upon, that there is a substantial sympathy, as regards moral questions, between jurisprudence on the

though no one reading the *Moral and Political Philosophy* with attention could fail to infer it As a boy, he attended the Lancaster Assizes (*Memoirs*, p 5) On the 3rd May, 1759, he heard the trial of Eugene Aram, whom he shrewdly described as "a man who got himself hanged by his own cleverness " (*ibid*, pp 7–9) He also paid regular visits to the Old Bailey, where he had a special place near the Bench, and took in the Old Bailey Session Papers from 1763 to 1765 (*ibid*, pp 142, 143) He was a local magistrate from 1795 (*ibid*, pp 100, 101)

(e) Headlam's *Memoirs*, p 208

(f) At p 50 of *Piggott v Stratton* (1859), 1 De G F & J 33　　See note (v), *ante*

(g) At p 610 of *Smith v Hughes* (1871), L R 6 Q B 597

(h) At p 59 of *R v Middleton* (1873), L R 2 C C R 38

(i) In his *Miscellaneous Lectures and Reviews*, Lect IV, where, after speaking of Paley s "remarkably clear and forcible style, very simple, with an air of earnestness generally devoid of ornament, and often homely, but occasionally rising into a manly and powerful eloquence," he proceeds to draw special attention to the *Horæ Paulinæ*, in which, he says, the task the author had set himself "is done so ably and satisfactorily that I have often recommended the study of this work to legal students , not merely on account of its intrinsic value, with a view to its own immediate object, but also as an admirable exercise in the art of sifting evidence "

(j) See § 20, note (d), § 83, note (u), and § 86, notes (w), (x), *ante*

(k) See § 654, note (v), § 659, note (z), and § 667, notes (g), (t) and (u), *post*

(l) Dr Story, for instance (*Equity Jurisprudence*, vol 1, § 205) cites Paley with approval, as to a vendor s duty of disclosure And in Austin's *Lectures on Jurisprudence*, vol 1, p 456, the philosopher's doctrine of deceptive promises is approved in the main, though corrected in one particular

(m) See Story on *Bailments*, § 182 " Dr. Paley, in his Treatise on Moral Philosophy, has, with his usual good sense, put the case of mandates on a reasonable ground " So in the law of defamation, the view insisted on by Paley (*Principles of Moral and Political Philosophy*, Book III, Part II, ch xii) that "truth may be made instrumental to the success of malicious designs as well as falsehood," is adopted in Bacon's Abridgment, title *Slander*

(n) William Hazlitt, in giving us his early impressions of Coleridge, alludes to an interview with him, in the course of which the latter " mentioned Paley, praised the naturalness and clearness of his style, but condemned his sentiments, thought him a mere timeserving casuist, and said that the fact of his work on *Moral and Political Philosophy* being made a text book in our universities was a disgrace to the national character " one ha d, and "Sittlichkeit" (of which, in Coleridge's view, Paley was merely an exponent) on the other.

651. Whilst, however, jurisprudence and ethics (popular and philosophical) undoubtedly concur in the recognition of trust as a necessary condition of human society, and are alike persuaded that confidence on the one side necessarily involves certain duties of candour and good faith on the other (o), it is no less true that, when it comes to the consideration of the exact nature and incidence of these duties under given conditions, occasional differences of attitude emerge, which it is now proposed to examine.

SECT. 2. COMPARISON BETWEEN JURISPRUDENCE AND POPULAR SENTIMENT OR MORAL PHILOSOPHY IN RELATION TO PARTICULAR DOCTRINES AND RULES OF DISCLOSURE AND GOOD FAITH.

652. The points at which the law finds itself not altogether in sympathy with some of the views of the general, or the mercantile, community, or with philosophical casuistry, may conveniently be discussed under the following heads :—negotiations for contracts *uberrimæ fidei* (particularly insurance), relations of confidence; relations of influence (particularly the parental and sacerdotal relations); oppression and usury; gifts, and "wilful ignorance" (p). It will be seen that, in all cases of divergence, the ideals of jurisprudence are not lower than those of ethics; whilst in most of them, whether designedly or (so to speak) accidentally, they are higher.

Sub s. (1) *In respect of the Duty of Disclosure in Negotiations for certain Contracts.*

653. In this class of case (q), whilst, on the one hand, jurisprudence and mercantile morality condemn with equal severity the resort to forms of law for the purpose of defeating expectations legitimately entertained on the faith of honest and laudable trade customs, as in the case of the "slip" in marine insurance (r), there are, on the other hand, numerous questions on which the practices, if not the avowed views, of the commercial community are in direct conflict with the more stern, stringent, and exalted requirements and principles of the law.

654. Custom being, for good or evil (s), "the principal Magistrate of Man's life "(t), or, as Pascal puts it, "une seconde nature " (u), it follows that jurisprudence must

(o) Lord Kames acutely observes that "veracity, and a disposition to believe what is affirmed for truth, are certainly principles which make one entire branch of the human nature Veracity would be of no use were men not disposed to believe , and, abstracting from veracity, a disposition to believe would be a dangerous quality ": *Essays on the Principles of Morality and Natural Religion*, Part I, Essay II, Ch vi (" Justice and Injustice ") Lord Kames was both a jurist and a moral philosopher, and thought and wrote excellently in both characters He occupied much the same position in Scotland as Paley held in England, the same lucidity of expression and style characterized the writings of both, and their ratiocinative methods and conclusions were very similar For instance, on the very point mentioned in the text, the passage from Paley which is cited in note (u) to § 83, *ante*, runs on parallel lines with Lord Kames's reflections Accordingly, as (in a sense) *doctus utriusque juris*, Lord Kames is an author to whose treatises references may usefully be made for the purposes of the subjects discussed in this Appendix.

(p) These are the subjects of the six Sub-sections respectively of this Section

(q) See Chapter III, *ante*

(r) See § 189, notes (l) and (m), *ante.*

(s) For good, on the whole, as most people believe ; for ill, in the view of those who think with J S Mill (*Liberty*, Ch III) that "the despotism of custom is everywhere the standing hindrance to human advancement "

(t) Bacon, *Essays and Counsels*, Essay xxxix (" Of Custom and Education ").

(u) "La coutume est une seconde nature qui detruit la première Pourquoi la coutume n'est elle pas naturelle ? J'ai bien peur que cette nature ne soit elle même qu'une première coutume, comme la coutume est une seconde nature " *Pensées*, Art III, § 13. So Greek philosophers, poets, and historians were never tired of extolling the paramountcy of custom in morals, and in social life Pindar's " νόμος ὁ πάντων βασιλεὺς, θνατῶν τε καὶ ἀθανάτων " (*Fragm*) is cited with approval by Herodotus (III 18, who again, in VII. 104, speaks of the " δεσπότης νόμος '), and by Plato (*Gorgias*, 484 B)

mould, and from time to time vary or expand, its rules so as to give effect and expression to the usages and requirements of contemporary society. Within certain limits, as "homo est minister et interpres naturæ," in the Baconian phrase, so "jus est minister et interpres consuetudinis"; and Justice, by waiting on Custom, wins faith and acceptance from those with whom that custom originated. To say this, however, is not to concede for one moment "that custom possesses any proper authority to alter or ascertain the nature of right and wrong" (v): for "sunt certi denique fines, Quos ultra citraque nequit consistere rectum." Where usage has transcended those *certi fines*, and rebelled against the primary rules of right and wrong, the law has always set its face sternly and unflinchingly against it, however violently the trading community may have resented the condemnation, and however closely and impenetrably the "damnèd custom" may have "brassed" the public conscience "so that it be proof and bulwark against sense." In such cases to apply the principle of "non nisi parendo vincitur," justly applied to innocuous practices, would be a base abnegation of the highest function of judicature; for Custom is here no longer the subject, whose lawful wishes, sentiments, and habits are to be respected, but the insurgent, with whose treason no terms can be made. The occasions on which the law is called upon to frustrate and suppress these persistent attempts upon its purity occur and recur with increasing frequency. It may be that, as Buckle thought (w), the main principles of morality have remained fairly constant in the history of civilization; but this proposition, if true, in no way conflicts with the equally true one that the science of casuistry, or the application of these simple principles to particular cases, has become more and more difficult, in proportion as the cases themselves have multiplied, together with those "divided duties" which are the inevitable outcome of a growing complexity in social conditions. In primitive days, the questions addressed to jurisprudence and ethics admitted of a prompt and plain answer—generally the same answer—from both, and there was little occasion for any conflict between juridical and popular sentiment. But when, in the course of time, the problems submitted for decision became less easy of solution, for the reason that the same simple principles had to be applied to a variety of much more complicated facts, and when the mercantile community, in this change of the "old order, yielding place to new," seized on the opportunity to introduce and encourage dubious practices, and, after a decent interval, clamoured for their recognition by the law as established customs. the courts of the land stood at the parting of the ways, and were faced with a clear duty which, unmoved by the *civium ardor prava jubentium*, they discharged with unbending constancy. Then commenced that warfare between the uncompromising inflexibility of jurisprudence, in reference to commercial customs opposed to plain principles of honesty, and the pliant casuistry of commerce which has been waged, in one form or another, ever since, and is not even now by any manner of means extinct. For the moral fibre, once relaxed, does not easily regain its tone, "nec vera virtus, quum semel excidit, Curat reponi deterioribus" so long as the convenient "justification by custom" remains an article of mercantile faith, and the individual trader's conscience is stupefied, and subjected to base transformations, by the Circean enchantments of "Commodity." As early as the time of Lord Mansfield, and probably much earlier, merchants began to solicit the courts to incorporate their knaveries into the common law on the sole ground that they had been consecrated by usage. The solicitations were vain. The law of England, which is founded on "the reason and custom of generations" (x),—not on custom alone, irrespective of whether it conforms, or not, to the requirements of reason and

---

(v) Paley, *Principles of Moral and Political Philosophy*, Book III, Part I, Ch. viii

(w) Lecky (see his *Rise and Influences of the Spirit of Rationalism in Europe*, vol I, ch 3, and his *History of European Morals, passim*) and J S Mill are entirely opposed to this view. The latter has recorded his opinion that "the human intellect has not improved in anything like the same ratio as the sentiments" (*Letters of J S Mill*, ed Hugh Elliot, vol II, p 374)

(x) Lord Acton, *Hist. of Freedom, &c*, p 72. The expression used in one of the old cases is "the common laws comply with the Genius of the Nation"

conscience,—"rejecit alto [jussa] nocentium Vultu, et per obstantes catervas Explicuit sua victor arma."

655. The duty of candid and complete disclosure in negotiations for contracts *uberrimæ fidei* has, amongst other duties of good faith, been the subject of persistent attempts to undermine or emasculate, by means of dishonest practices and dubious customs, the unqualified severity of the law's requirements. Particularly in cases of marine insurance efforts were made from the earliest times to win the countenance and connivance of the law in debasing the moral currency. In every case the failure was complete, and, in denouncing the particular immoral usage relied upon, the courts have always spoken with no uncertain voice, as witness (to take a few examples out of many) the powerful judgment of COCKBURN, C.J., in one memorable case (y), and those of Lord ALVERSTONE (z), and Lord SHAW (a), in another. This uncompromising stringency of jurisprudence not only conflicts with the views of the dishonest traders who justly suffer from it,—this is only to be expected,—but also, it must be admitted, finds little favour even with the average non-mercantile citizen, and is not altogether in harmony with current sentiment, as reflected in the jury-box, the journals, and the market-place. It seems impossible to persuade the man in the street to take up any but a *contra proferentem* attitude against the insurer (b), or to stir a step outside his simple creed that the man who receives the premiums ought to pay the insurance moneys, disclosure or no disclosure, unless the non-disclosure amounts to positive fraud, or to convince him that the man whose ship or life or health has been assured ought to be under any obligation to divulge anything that he is not asked about by the underwriter or insurance society. Roger North (c) bears witness to the enormous strength of this popular feeling in the middle of the seventeenth century (though he expresses his sense of its irrationality), and it is certainly no less strong at the present day.

(y) Who, at pp 606, 607 of *Bates* v *Hewitt* (1867), L R 2 Q B 595, after pointing out how dangerous it would be to allow an assured who has failed in his duty of disclosure "to speculate as to what may or may not have been in the minds of the underwriters," proceeds :—"if we were to sanction such a course, especially in these days, when parties frequently forget the old rules of mercantile faith and honour which used to distinguish this country from any other, we should be lending ourselves to innovations of a dangerous and monstrous character."

(z) At p 538 of *Thames & Mersey Marine Insurance Co* v *Gunford Ship Co*, [1911] A. C 529, H L, with reference to the contention that the duty of disclosing double insurances had been impliedly waived by "the practice" in the marine insurance world — "the practice of underwriters as to accepting risks, or not making inquiries on particular points, cannot in my opinion affect the duty."

(a) At p 543 of the case last cited. "the argument for the respondents is this, that the policies are gambling and wagering policies, but that the shipping and insuring world is aware that such things go on, and that every insurer of ship or hull takes his risk that the scales may be weighted in favour of the destruct of the vessel by that kind of underwriting." Again, at p 545. "the practice is co ned because underwriters pay upon such policies. They go by the much-abused name 'honour'", and the illegitimate "honour" policies constitute that incentive of self interest towards the destruction of the vessel which . &c

(b) The law is not altogether unsympathetic towards this attitude, if there is evidence that the underwriter had even presumptive knowledge of the undisclosed fact, but not otherwise. It took a very little evidence of this kind to satisfy Lord MANSFIELD, with his Guildhall merchants, that the underwriters had taken the premium with a suspicion of the truth, and with the fraudulent intention of repudiating their obligations, if necessary, on the ground of a supposed non-disclosure which never deceived them in the least. See the passage from his judgment in *Carter* v *Boehm* (1766), 3 Burr 1905, which is cited in note (s) to § 191, *ante*.

(c) "I have had occasion to wonder," he says in his *Autobiography*, "that insurers of ships have a sort of obloquy, which either chance or custom has given them, and they come not to the law without prejudice, such as extortioners, usurers, or pawnbrokers usually meet with, and the insured is favoured, and all presumptions taken on his part. Whereas the insurer cannot be a cheat,"—Lord MANSFIELD thought he could be, and often was,—"and is very often cheated by the insured, for the falsities come on their side who know their own motives, which are secret to the insurers."

Sub s. (2). In respect of the Duty of Disclosure in Relations of Confidence.

656 In two of the principal authorities on the fiduciary duty of a trustee towards his *cestui que trust,* there is a remarkable revelation of the astounding discrepancy between the juridical and the ethical conception of the obligations involved in a situation of trust. In one of these, we are permitted to explore the conscience of a Scottish merchant; in the other, that of an English bishop. In the former, the merchant, under cross-examination, laid bare his view on the question with engaging frankness, which was (shortly), that a trustee bargaining with his *cestui que trust* is under no duty of disclosure of any sort or kind; indeed, it was a matter of profound and obviously genuine astonishment to him to hear it suggested that there is such a duty, or that "fairness had anything to do with it" (*d*). In the other case, the bishop was not called upon to declare his moral attitude, but it must be assumed, in that spirit of charity and courtesy which, in their observations, the judicial, manifested towards the episcopal, bench, that in his clearly proved violation of his equitable duty the bishop was entirely unconscious of having broken any moral duty within the range of his cultivated ethical knowledge and experience; for otherwise a high ecclesiastical dignitary must be assumed (*nefandum dictu!*) to have been capable, and in fact guilty, of gross moral delinquency (*e*). Nothing could be more eloquent than are the reports of these two cases, of the gulf which separates the doctrines of jurisprudence in this particular relation, not merely from the views of conventional or commercial morality, but even from the presumably exalted and refined principles of expert casuistry. In the face of these two glaring examples, it need occasion no surprise to find that the mercantile community either cannot understand, or will not be reconciled to, the elementary proposition of law that an agent who receives a present, or bribe, or private advantage from a third person in the course or execution of his agency, without disclosing the fact to his principal, or a director of a company who is clandestinely qualified or otherwise bribed by its promoter, is guilty of any moral impropriety. Expressions of amazement that this wide discrepancy should continue in existence, and not only continue but grow wider with each succeeding year, and denunciations of the deplorable moral laxity— for so it seemed to them—of the mercantile community on this question of commissions, have proceeded from judge after judge, such as (in order of date) Lord

(*d*) *Dougan* v *Macpherson,* [1902] A C 197, H L   The highly instructive examination referred to in the text is set out *verbatim,* as it deserves to be, in the narrative, at p 199   It is as follows   "When I concluded the bargain," the trustee stated, "I estimated that I would make a few hundred pounds" (Q) "If you were told that the profit would be between £800 and £900, would that alter your opinion as to its fairness?" (A) "I simply would not believe it   *I do not see that fairness has anything to do with it, if a man sells at his own valuation, and another buys, it has nothing to do with fairness*   I did not personally at any time submit to him a statement of his interest under either deed   *I was not called upon to do so, because I was never asked*" (Q) "Did you think it was a duty upon you as trustee, and holding a fiduciary relation to your brother, to disclose to him the extent of his interest in the trust estate?" (A) "*Certainly not,* when he could get all information from the law agents of the trust"   The curious state of mind revealed in these ingenuous avowals is commented upon by Lord HALSBURY, L C, at pp 202, 203, Lord ASHBOURNE at p 204, and Lord LINDLEY, at p 206

(*e*) *Greenlaw* v. *King* (1840), 9 L J (CH) 377, before Lord LANGDALE, M R, affirmed (1841), 10 L J (CH) 129, by Lord COTTENHAM, L C   It certainly appears, on a perusal of these reports, that this was a plain, and a rather gross case   Yet both Lord LANGDALE and Lord COTTENHAM went out of their way to acquit the Bishop of any want of personal good faith   the latter observing, at p 129, that "the bishop was not, at the time of the transaction, aware, nor had he his attention drawn to the rules of this Court relative to purchases made by persons holding confidential situations"   One would have thought that episcopal erudition and conversance with ethical problems would not have required a reminder from the Courts as to the obligations of good faith, though Scottish commercialism might   and it must therefore be presumed that, in the exculpatory observations which Lord LANGDALE and Lord COTTENHAM made, they intended to express their recognition of the hiatus which separates the moral standards of jurisprudence, in the matter of fiduciary duty, from those of the rest of the community, even when represented by a specially cultured class

WYNFORD, L C (*f*), Lord LANGDALE, M R. (*g*), Lord ESHER (*h*), JAMES, L.J., in no less than four cases (*i*), MELLISH, L J. (*j*), THESIGER, L.J., on behalf of himself and the other members of the Court of Appeal (*k*), FIELD, J. (*l*), FRY, L.J. (*m*),

(*f*) At p 202 of *Rothschild* v *Brookman* (1831), 5 Bligh (N.S) 165 . "Mr. Rothschild has only followed a practice which I believe has been acted on in London. It is fit your Lordships say now that such practices cannot be endured. If they are common, it is fit your Lordships say, in language that cannot be misunderstood, that such practices must not continue to prevail."

(*g*) At p 83 of *Gillett* v. *Peppercorne* (1840), 3 Beav. 78 (" it is said that this is everyday practice in the city. I certainly should be very sorry to have it proved to me that such a sort of dealing is usual ").

(*h*) When BRETT, J , delivering his opinion as one of the judges summoned by the House of Lords, at pp. 816, 817 of *Robinson* v. *Mollett* (1875), L. R. 7 H. L 802 " it is when merchants dispute about their own rules that they invoke the law The Courts, therefore, being appealed to, have been obliged to apply some rule When merchants have disputed as to what the governing rule shall be, the Courts have applied to the mercantile business brought before them what have been called legal principles, which have almost always been the fundamental ethical rules of right and wrong They have decided in favour of that course of business which was in accordance with such principles or rules, and against that course which was inconsistent with them. Customs of trade are generally courses of business invented or relied upon in order to modify or evade some application which has been laid down by the Courts of some rule of law to business, and which application has seemed irksome to some merchants And when some such course of business is proved to exist in fact, and the binding effect of it is disputed, the question of law seems to be whether it is in accordance with fundamental principles of right and wrong."

(*i*) The four cases referred to (in the first of which he was Vice Chancellor, and in the others a Lord Justice) are the following —*Turnbull* v. *Garden* (1869), 20 L T 218 (at p 220 . "the defendant depended upon what he alleged to be the custom of the trade The defendant said, ' True it is I never paid the actual sums charged in my account to you, but I was authorized in charging you more than I actually paid by the custom of the trade of army agency ' It is not the first time the Court has heard of, and disapproved, the custom of ' salting invoices ' "); *Panama & South Pacific Telegraph Co* v *India Rubber, Gutta Percha, and Telegraph Co* (1875), 10 Ch App 515 (at pp. 527, 528 · " this is a contract as to which *res ipsa loquitur*, and at which I am bound to express my strongest disapprobation and reprehension "), *Re Canadian Oil Works Corporation, Hay's Case* (1875), 10 Ch App 593 (at p 599, expressing amazement "that a body of English gentlemen consented and condescended to become on these terms the hired retainers of unknown adventurers from the other side of the Atlantic "), *Re Caerphilly Colliery Co , Pearson's Case* (1877), 5 C D 336, C A (at p 342 " that a gentleman of Sir Edwin Pearson's position should have allowed this matter to be discussed in one Court is strange enough , that it should have been brought up by him for further discussion in a Court of Appeal passes my comprehension ")

(*j*) At p 529 of *Panama & South Pacific Telegraph Co* v *India Rubber, Gutta Percha, & Telegraph Co.*, sup " I cannot help expressing my astonishment that gentlemen like Sir Charles Bright, and the directors of the Telegraph Works Company, should actually think that this is a mere technical rule of a Court of Equity, and that there is nothing morally wrong in itself in the man who is engineer of a telegraph company, and who has to certify to them when the money becomes payable by them to a construction company, having behind their backs a sub contract with that construction company for part of what they had contracted to do for the purposes of the telegraph company "

(*k*) At p 317 of *De Bussche* v *Alt* (1878), 8 C D 286, C A " one matter, alleged by the defendant, and actually supported by evidence, although in argument admitted to be untenable, ought not to pass without notice or reprobation, namely, an alleged custom or practice in the ports in which the defendant trades for an agent for sale with a minimum limit himself to take at that limit, and at his own option, the thing he is employed to sell. We cannot but express a hope that the Court will never again hear of such a contention, or have before it such evidence "

(*l*) At p 552 of *Harrington* v *Victoria Graving Dock Co* (1878), 3 Q B D 549 "the present case affords an instance how sadly loose commercial practice has become in transactions of this nature "

(*m*) At p 369 of *Boston Deep Sea Fishing & Ice Co* v *Ansell* (1888), 39 C D 339, C A · " we were invited to consider the state of mind of Mr Ansell, whether he thought it wrong ,

ROMER, J. (n), Lord ALVERSTONE, C.J. (o), KENNEDY, J. (p), BUCKLEY, J (q), and Lord MACNAGHTEN (qq).

657. Though, in this long series of authorities, the decisions themselves have had valuable results in settling and enforcing sound legal doctrine, it may be doubted whether the hortatory and moralizing portions of the judgments have in the slightest degree succeeded in their presumed object of commending the ideals and principles of jurisprudence to the mercantile conscience. Indeed, it may be questioned whether these judicial exercises in homiletics have not been a little overdone, and whether they are in any case either necessary or advisable. The equitable rules of disclosure are entirely independent of personal motives or intentions (as has been pointed out many times already), and, this being so, these excursions are quite needless for all purposes of juridical exposition. If they are undertaken in the hope of reconciling the commercial community to the law, the hope is doomed to disappointment. If the object is to advise and warn the merchant, *pro salute animæ*, the answer is that this is foreign to the business of a judge (r), who is not the pastor of a spiritual flock, but an officer of State entrusted with the sole duty of administering justice according to law,—a sufficiently exalted and responsible office of itself, without adding to it alien functions, or intruding upon the domain of the preacher or pedagogue, and thereby provoking public uneasiness and irritation. The plain trader is much like the schoolboy who has no particular objection to a whipping without a lecture, or to a lecture without a whipping, but strongly protests against being made the subject of both at one and the same time. He understands, and accepts with resignation, the adverse operation of a rule of law, if it is put to him as a rule of law simply, and he is told that he is " within its danger " · but he chafes at a simultaneous philippic against his personal character. If, therefore, the judges were to content themselves with the mere proclamation to the laity of the rules which, for the general good, they have seen fit to make, and their determination to see that they are observed, without any running ethical commentary, there would be no occasion for resentment and antipathy on

in other words, we are invited to take as the standard for our decision the alleged conscience of a fraudulent servant   I decline to accept any such rule as one on which the Court is to decide such questions "

(n) At p 15 of *Hovenden & Sons* v *Millhoff* (1900), 83 L T 41, C A   " some persons undoubtedly hold laxer views   Not that these persons like the ugly word ' bribe,' *if that word be used*, but they differ from the courts in their view of what constitutes a bribe "

(o) At p 7 of *Hippisley* v *Knee Bros*, [1905] 1 K B 1, Div Ct   " unfortunately there appears to prevail in commercial circles, in which perfectly honourable men desire to play an honourable part, an extraordinary laxity in the view taken of secret profit by agents "

(p) At p 9 of *Hippisley* v *Knee Bros*, *sup* (" I should be sorry to say that the practice itself is an honest one ")   and again, at p 95 of *Swale* v *Ipswich Tannery, Ltd* (1906), 11 Comm. Cas 88 (" I believe, I am sorry to say from experience as well as from hearsay, that in business there are a good many people who profess, and apparently genuinely, to see no harm in doing things which they ought unquestionably to see there is the greatest harm in doing ")

(q) At pp 196, 197 of *Re Telescriptor Syndicate, Ltd*, [1903] 2 Ch 174   " I regret to say that transactions of this kind are so far from uncommon that many persons will condescend to them without the intent which is the matter relevant to a question of personal integrity   The giving and acceptance of commissions and presents have grown to such an extent that legislation is now pending to deal with that which is admitted to be a great evil "   Again, at p 197, he observes, " with great regret,' with respect to one of the respondents, that, " although he was a director of this company, he considered himself as having really no responsibility   This is a frame of mind strongly to be condemned '   The " pending legislation " referred to materialized, but not until after three more years' incubation, in the Prevention of Corruption Act, 1906 (6 Edw 7, c 34).

(qq) At p 192 of *Tackey* v *McBain*, [1912] A C 186, P C   " brokers examined on behalf of the plaintiff were shocked to think that the manager of a company could tell an untruth to a broker, but there was not one of them who seemed to have thought that there was any harm in a broker trying to worm out secrets from the confidential manager of a company "

(r) See § 670, *post*   And cp. § 632, *ante*

the one side, or for lamentations over mercantile perversity on the other, any more than there is when the legislature, without any moral reflections, nakedly commands or prohibits certain acts in a statute which *incipit a jussione*, and gets to business at once, after the fashion of the "plagosus Orbilius" who expounded the Beatitudes to the *animosa juventus* of Eton in a manner which none of his audience misunderstood or resented ("blessed are the pure in heart. Boys, take care to be pure in heart. Boys, if you are not pure in heart, you will be whipped"). As it is, the chasm between the two points of view remains, and the well-meant efforts to bridge it over by disquisitions on morals serve only to aggravate, and not to heal, the dissension. The Launcelot Gobbos of commerce, between the Fiend and Conscience, or what the law tells them is, or ought to be, their Conscience, will always conclude that the latter "is but a kind of hard conscience," and that "the Fiend gives the more friendly counsel" (s). This, indeed, is recognized by RIGBY, L.J., almost in the very words of "honest Launcelot," when, in discussing the rule against clandestine commissions, he takes occasion to observe that "many people think it a hard principle" (t). If judges will reiterate that the practice is dishonest, instead of simply saying "we forbid it," the trader will persevere in his protest that it is not dishonest; and how favourably this protest is received by juries will be manifest to any one conversant with the sort of verdicts which they return in commission cases, when injudicious references to "fraud" from the bench give them an opportunity of declaring their views on the moral aspect of the question. To take one instance out of many, there was a case in which the facts were so strong that the jury felt bound to record their opinion that "the practice" of receiving a commission "calculated to bias" the recipient was reprehensible, and yet insisted on finding that there had been "no fraud" (u). It is easy to characterize such an attitude in terms of reprobation and ridicule: "I am quite aware," said LINDLEY, L.J., in a case as to secret creation of fictitious prices by rigging the market, "that what the plaintiff has done is very commonly done; it is done every day. But this is immaterial. Picking pockets and various forms of cheating are common enough, and are nevertheless illegal" (t). But this sort of rather obvious criticism is wanting in a just appreciation of all that is involved in the public feeling on this matter, which rests upon the supposition that the practices in question are not merely usual, but that they are generally known to prevail, or are so common that everybody ought to know, if he does not, that everybody else is resorting to them daily. It is not suggested that this hypothesis corresponds with fact. But it is not right to ignore its importance altogether, as the foundation of the popular sentiment, and this is what judicial denunciations of the above type frequently do. The whole and sole vice, morally as well as juridically, of the condemned customs is their secrecy, as has already been noted (w) and if the receipt of commissions by agents in general business should ever become of such universal notoriety (like the receipt by domestic servants, or postmen of Christmas presents from tradesmen or the public, respectively) as to justify an imputation of knowledge of the practice to all concerned the only element which renders it objectionable, and with it the objection itself, would disappear. That time has not yet come, nor is it likely that it ever will: but, in the meantime, the belief that it is rapidly approaching explains in some degree the violent opposition of the mercantile community, not so much to the juridical code itself, as to that particular theoretical justification of it, occasionally put forward, which involves the imputation of personal dishonesty. The strength and persistency of this divergence, however it is to be explained, between the common law and the common conscience in these matters is responsible for the steady under-current of opposition which Sir EDWARD FRY and Lord RUSSELL encountered before they could obtain legislative recognition of the criminal character of clandestine commissions in the form of the Prevention of Corruption Act, 1906 (6 Edw. 7, c 34), and for the enormous difficulties which

---

(s) *Merchant of Venice*, Act II, Sc 2
(t) At p 753 of *Costa Rica Railway Co v Forwood*, [1901] 1 Ch 746, C. A
(u) *Smith v Sorby* (1878), 3 Q B D 552 n
(v) At p 729 of *Scott v Brown, Doering, McNab & Co*, [1892] 2 Q B 724, C. A.
(w) See the cases cited in note (x) to § 316, *ante*

notwithstanding the energetic efforts of societies and leagues, are still met with in enforcing the provisions of the statute, and, when a prosecution is instituted for that purpose, in obtaining verdicts against the accused. And so it will always be until harmony is somehow established between the views of the man in the street and those of the man of law. *quid leges sine moribus Vanæ proficiunt?*

658. The above observations as to the unwisdom of giving an ethical colour to such rules of disclosure as are in law independent of moral considerations for their efficacy have of course no application to cases where breaches of these rules are committed by persons over whom, as its officers, the Court has disciplinary jurisdiction Here it is obvious that judicial reflections on professional ethics (*x*) are not only not misplaced, but essential.

659. As to the fiduciary duties involved in the relation of partnership, as distinguished from other forms of agency, jurisprudence is at one with mercantile, ard (we may add) religious, sentiment. The baseness of concealment from a partner is recognized and condemned by commerce quite as heartily as it is by the law (*y*), or even by the Church, as illustrated in the story of Ananias, whose offence was simply and solely concealment of material facts from those associated with him in an informal κοινωνία of goods for pious uses (*z*),—an offence which, nevertheless, St. Peter expressly characterized as a lie, condemning the name of Ananias to eternal infamy as that of the typical liar, notwithstanding that he had in fact made no false, or indeed any, representation whatever (*a*), and associating him for all time with Sapphira who had undoubtedly made a false statement, and had lied in the ordinary sense of the word (*b*), as persons equal in guilt, and meriting the same swift and tragic fate.

Sub-s. (3). As to the "Suspected Relations" of Influence

660 The "man in the street," not without some support from a certain school of jurists is by no means in sympathy with the equitable presumptions of undue influence applied to certain of the relations which have been called, after Sir Frederick Pollock, "suspected" (*c*), and thinks it an unjust imputation upon humanity, and an unwarrantable interference with individual freedom, that these relations should be so "suspected" Influence he urges, is a fundamental condition of society. Man is not man except in relation to his fellows He is "φύσει πολιτικός" It is only the supreme spirits who can endure the loneliness of regulating each action of their lives by pure reference to principle, rather than by imitation of some living ideal or personal model The average man must necessarily exercise, and come under,

(*x*) Such as those of Lord ALVERSTONE, C J , at p 191 of *Re Four Solicitors*, [1901] 1 K B 187, Div Ct , and, again, in *Re a Solicitor* (1909), 26 T L R 22 Div Ct

(*y*) Indeed, it must be admitted that, in one case, no less an authority than Lord BLACKBURN appears to have entertained a somewhat less exalted conception of the fiduciary duties of partners to one another than the popular one, when he says "I generally think it is advisable. *as a matter of prudence* as well as on other grounds, to let everything be above board " *Cassels v Stewart* (1881), 6 App Cas 64, H L (at p 80) One is not surprised to find that, in a later case, Lord MACNAGHTEN, with gentle irony, characterized this as "a very proper sentiment, worthy perhaps of a more unhesitating acceptance " · *Trimble v Goldberg*, [1906] A C 494, P C (at p 500)

(*z*) *Acts*, iv 32–35 See, as to this κοινωνία, Paley's *Principles of Moral and Political Philosophy*, Book III, Pt II, Ch V

(*a*) *Acts*, v 1–6, from which it is quite clear that the crime of Ananias consisted, not in his mere retention of part of the price of the possessions which he sold for the supposed benefit of the common fund, but in the secrecy of his retention, and in his false pretence (by the mere act of delivery without express reservation) that what he was transferring was the whole price (" whiles it remained, was it not thine own ? and after it was sold, was it not in thine own power ? ") It was the breach of the fiduciary duty, and not any direct falsehood, which made the offence a lie " not unto men, but to God "

(*b*) *Acts*, v 8 " and Peter answered unto her, Tell me whether ye sold the land for so much ? And she said, Yea, for so much "

(*c*) As to the various ' uspected relations," see Ch V, Sect 2, Sub-ss. (1)–(5), *ante* As to the presumptions of law which arise on proof of any such relation, see § 105, *ante*

influences of all kinds from the cradle to the grave,—influences moral, religious, social, professional, artistic, scientific, or that which "bright eyes rain,"—as well as those which are immediately concerned with the direction of his temporal and business affairs. Why, it is often asked, should the law look kindly on the former, and askance at the latter? It is firmly established that even the latter class of influence is not presumed to have been undue or improper in the case of a testamentary disposition of property (d), and popular ethics finds it difficult to appreciate the reasons which move jurisprudence to draw a distinction between such a mode of disposition and a disposition *inter vivos*, and, whilst making no unfavourable presumption against the one, to cast grave suspicion on the other.

661. Of the four "suspected" relations, two (viz that between medical attendant and patient, and that between legal adviser and client) do not, perhaps, give rise to any very great difference of opinion. The two others, however, do. These are the parental and the spiritual relations.

662. The plain man can conceive nothing more natural and proper than the parental influence (e). And, to a certain extent, jurisprudence goes along with him in so thinking. For example, as has already been noted, not only in the discussion of this particular species of influence (f), but also in that of compromises, and bargains with expectants (g), the law makes no presumption of impropriety against, but distinctly favours, "family arrangements" Again, it refuses to "suspect" the influence of a husband over his wife when he appeals to her for succour in his financial distress, or to deem him a *spoliator* against whom *omnia præsumuntur* (h). Why, then, asks the layman, should a parent who has a natural, and, indeed, in certain circumstances a legal, right to look to his child for support in his pecuniary difficulties, be accounted a presumptive *spoliator* by reason of his parentage alone, and be at once put to the proof of the purity of his motives, and the good faith of the transaction? Why should not the child, as the wife is, be required to make out some *primâ facie* case of impropriety before the parent is called upon for an answer?

663 In the case of the sacerdotal relation, the ordinary man either agrees vehemently, or disagrees vehemently, with the doctrines of jurisprudence. The Laodicean attitude of the "spiacenti a Dio ed a nemici suoi" is not common. There is, no doubt, a strong body of popular opinion which supports the law in gravely suspecting this relation (i), as is shown by the history of the persistent, and ultimately successful, warfare waged by the Crown and its judges, with the hearty sympathy of the community, against the usurped jurisdiction of ecclesiastical tribunals (j). It is commonly felt that an influence which dominates every stage in man's pilgrimage,—now at his side with counsel, now at his back to support or spur forward, now in front of him to bar access to prohibited ground,—must necessarily hold such pervading and persistent sway over his temporal concerns as to provoke suspicion and invite vigilance. In modern times the seductive and coercive power of the priest and monk is not nearly so universal as it was in the middle ages, when, as we may read in the eloquent pages of the historian of European morals, "the more pious minds recoiled from the disposing of their property in a manner which would not redound to the advantage of their souls" (k), and in time "the evil attained such a point that a law was made under Valentinian depriving the Christian priests and monks of that power of receiving legacies which was possessed by every other class of the community, and St. Jerome mournfully acknowledged that the prohibition was necessary" (l). But the influence, though more sporadic and occasional at the

(d) See § 447, *ante.*
(e) See §§ 409, 410, *ante*
(f) In § 410, *ante*
(g) In § 135, and § 482, *ante,* respectively.
(h) See § 446, *ante*
(i) See § 421, *ante*
(j) This is traced historically in the author's *Code of the Law of Actionable Defamation,* App V, Sect 4
(k) Lecky's *History of European Morals from Augustus to Charlemagne* (9th ed.), vol ii, pp 133, 134
(l) *Ibid.,* vol ii, p 151 See also p 216 of the same vol

present day than formerly, exercises, when it exists at all, as powerful a dominion as ever, and excites as deep a distrust. Accordingly current English sentiment, no less than English law, is still in accord with the views of Pothier, and other French jurists, as regards the impropriety of gifts to confessors and spiritual directors (m), or to the conventional establishments or monastic orders of which they are members (n). The ecclesiastical point of view is of course violently antagonistic. The influence which the law presumes to be a breach of duty to man, the Church presumes to be an absolute duty to God. Spiritual persons strongly, and, in the opinion of many, justly, resent judicial interference with dispositions in favour of ecclesiastical bodies and institutions, though willing to concede that the individual priest who uses his sacerdotal authority for the purpose of extracting private gain for himself is a desecrator of his divine office, and a fraudulent trustee of the authority placed in his hands (o), and that, even in matters strictly within his province, it is not the function of a wise director to establish too great a personal dominion over the penitent, "le rôle d'un confesseur" being, according to Bossuet, "de mettre les âmes en état de se passer de lui." "You countenance and encourage," they say to jurists, "the exertion of influence for the preservation of family honour and estates (oo). Why should a presumption be made against the influence which we exert for the honour and peace and temporal welfare of the spiritual families committed to our charge?" To which jurisprudence replies· "we do not prohibit these gifts. Let Nicodemus give all his possessions to the Church, if he will· but if he should afterwards be minded to revoke his gift, we will call on the establishment which is in receipt of his bounty to sustain the transaction. The Church may censure the back-sliding of one who is no longer "a cheerful giver," but the law cannot allow her to retain, if and when challenged, anything which she has obtained by the abuse of her spiritual ascendancy" The Church on this protests that what she complains of is not the taking away of property acquired by proved abuse of influence, but the presumption of law, without proof in the first instance, that there must have been such an abuse. The conflict, therefore, ultimately turns on the fairness or unfairness of the presumption, and on this issue jurisprudence, supported by a large mass of popular opinion, is, and probably always will be, hopelessly and irreconcileably opposed to sacerdotalism

(m) See Pothier, *Traité des Donations entre Vifs*, Sect 2, Art 1 (*Œuvres*, ed Dupin, 1825, vol vii, p 441), and *Traité des Donations Testamentaires*, Ch III, Art 3, also Merlin, *Repertoire de Jurisprudence*, tit *Confesseur*, Art 3 The first of these references was in the mind of Sir SAMUEL ROMILLY, in his opening argument, at p 280, and in his reply, at p 286, of *Huguenin v Baseley* (1807), 14 Ves 273 As to the authority of the "celebrated reply," see note (c) to § 108, *ante* All three passages were cited (in argument) in *Middleton v Sherburne* (1841), 4 Y & C (Exch in Eq) 358

(n) See the citations from Pothier in the last note, and the observations of STUART, V-C, at p 270 of *Nottidge v Prince* (1860), 2 Giff 246 "the law of France, as stated by Pothier, absolutely prohibited not only all gifts by a penitent to his confessor, but all gifts to that religious community of which the confessor is a member"

(o) The view so forcibly expressed by Prince John of Lancaster, when denouncing the rebellious Archbishop of York (Scroop) for prostitution of his sacred office (*Henry IV*, Part II, Act 4, Sc 2) —

> " Who hath not heard it spoken
> How deep you were within the books of God ?
> To us the speaker in His parliament,
> To us the imagined voice of God himself,
> The very opener and intelligencer
> Between the grace, the sanctities of heaven
> And our dull workings O, who shall believe
> But you misuse the reverence of your place,
> Employ the countenance and grace of heaven,
> As a false favourite doth his prince's name,
> In deeds dishonourable ? "

(oo) See §§ 135, 410, 482, *ante.*

Sub-s. (4). As to Oppression and Usury.

664. In relations not of the "suspected" types, but such as are created by the particular "circumstances and conditions" of the case, where the weakness of the servient party is taken advantage of by unconscionable conduct on the part of the dominant party (*p*), and particularly in the relation between an "expectant" and a person dealing with him on the faith of his expectancy (*q*), it has been seen that oppression and usury play a prominent part. Here the moral sense of the community has always enthusiastically supported the judicial code in all its stringency. Indeed, it has at times shown an anxiety to go even further than the judges, and to force unwise measures upon the legislature. The general hatred of the oppressor was probably responsible for some of the more grotesque of the rules and presumptions made by Courts of equity against mortgagees (*r*). The abuse of power and riches to extort advantages from distress and helplessness by unconscientious means, and particularly by usury, has been the subject of execration in all civilized times and countries, whether we look to the ethical and theocratic code of Israel (*s*),—though, as in the case of misleading the blind (*t*), the prohibition was purely tribal, and directed against usury *domi*, and not *foris*,—or to the decrees of the Christian Councils, such as the Fifth Council of Lateran, 1515; or to Greek philosophy which insisted specially on the tendency of usury to propagate sedition and disorder (*u*), and on the unnatural character of fecundity in a naturally unproductive material (*v*); or to Athenian legislation (*w*), or to Roman law (*x*), and history (*y*);

(*p*) This is the subject of Ch V, Sect. 2, Sub s (5), *ante*

(*q*) Separa ely treated in Ch V, Sect. 2, Sub-s (6), *ante*

(*r*) Such as the rule that " a mortgagee is not allowed at the time of the loan to enter into a contract for the purchase of the mortgaged property,"—a rule which, at p. 326 of *Samuel* v *Jarrah Timber & Wood Paving Corporation*, [1904] A C 322, H. L., Lord MACNAGHTEN characterized as " founded on sentiment rather than on principle," and framed, in accordance with that sentiment (the sentiment of Lord HARDWICKE'S day), in order " to protect embarrassed landowners from imposition and oppression," and to checkmate a supposed " design " on the part of the extortionate mortgagee " to wrest the estate fraudulently out of the hands of the mortgagor "

(*s*) See *Deuteronomy*, xxiii 20 (prohibition of usury, except to the stranger) The Old Testament is full of denunciations of the oppressor and the usurer, and of him who " grindeth the face of the poor " The last of the nine Curses in the Commination Service is directed against (*inter alios*) " the unmerciful," and " the extortioner " " He that hath given his money upon usury " is excluded from the Lord's tabernacle, and an outcast from " His holy hill " Ps xv 6 The cruelty inflicted by the manufacture of " corners " in commodities of necessity is reprobated in Prov xi 26 " he that withholdeth corn, the people shall curse him , but blessings shall be upon the head of him that selleth it "

(*t*) See § 650, notes (*x*) and (*y*), *ante*

(*u*) Plato (*Rep* vii 555, 556) insists that the inevitable result of allowing χρηματισταί to ply their trade and force their attentions upon dissolute and ruined youths must be to engender a class of drones (κήφηνες) and of " νεατερισμοῦ ἐρῶντες who will bring disorder into the State

(*v*) See Plato, *Rep* vii 556 (" τοῦ πατρὸς ἐκγόνους τόκους πολλαπλασίους), and Legg 742 c also Aristotle, *Polit* I 10 4, 5 (' ὁ δὲ τόκος γίνεται νόμισμα νομίσματος ὥστε καὶ μάλιστα παρὰ φύσιν οὗτος τῶν χρηματισμῶν ἐστίν ') The same idea is expressed by Bacon in his Essay on Usury (*Essays or Counsels, Civil and Moral*, Essay XLI " it is against nature for money to beget money "), and by Shakespeare in the lines cited in note (*a*), *post*

(*w*) Solon legislated against usury see Plutarch, *Solon*, 15 , Lysias, *Contra Theom nestum*, I 18; Schol in Demosth , *Timocr* 766 (" μή λαμβάνειν πολλοὺς τόκους ')

(*x*) The XII Tables limited the rate of interest to an *unciarium foenus* The Lex Genucia (a plebiscitum of 340 B C) further restricted usury In Cicero s Time, 12 per cent was the maximum, and compound interest was not allowed Tacitus, in Ann vi ,

(*y*) See Livy, VII, 16, 27, 42 , Lucan, *Pharsalia*, I, 181, 182 —

" Hinc usura vorax, avidumque in tempore foenus, Et concussa fides, et multis utile bellum '

Cp the passages cited in the last note from Tacitus It was said that the revolt of Boadicea was precipitated, if not caused, by Seneca's sudden calling in of a huge loan

or to mediæval sentiment (z) ; or to the later views of renaissance poets (a), and sociologists (b) ; or to the laws for the suppression of usury in modern states, including our own (c). So overpowering has been the public detestation and distrust of this particular form of "influence" that the community, in this as in other countries, has always refused even to contemplate the other side of the question, though presented to them by the wisdom of a Bacon (d), and has been blind and deaf to every suggestion of compensating mercantile advantage. In their feverish hankering for repressive legislation, the multitude has never stayed to consider " how small of all the ills that men endure, The part which kings or laws can make or cure," or how easily statutes of this character are evaded, or (if not evaded) in what consequences they will inevitably involve the very classes which it is intended to benefit and protect,—consequences of the utmost gravity, not only financially, since, in order to repay him for his increased risk, the usurer must exchange whips for scorpions (e), but also morally, in that the borrower's conscience is debauched by the strong temptation held out to him to cheat his oppressor under forms of law (f).

Sub s (5) As to Gifts.

665 With reference to donations, as distinct from transactions for value, between living persons standing to one another in any of the "suspected" relations, the

16, 17, gives a short account of the legislation against moneylenders down to the time of which he is writing and, in Ann xiii, 42, reports Suilius as stating, in his spirited defence to Seneca's charges, against him under the Lex Cincia de Donis et Muneribus (as to which see § 680, note (u), post), that the provinces, as well as Italy, had been drained by usurers, and (lest there should be any mistake as to the person he was aiming at) asking by what sort of philosophy Seneca in four years of imperial favour had amassed 300,000,000 sesterces (£2,500,000) Justinian prescribed different scales of permissible interest, graduated according to the risk (12 per cent. being the maximum in maritime contracts, 8 per cent in other mercantile transactions, 6 per cent. in the case of private dealings with ordinary persons, and 4 per cent where the borrower was in an exalted station, or an agriculturist) Cp Bacon's suggestion referred to in note (b), inf As to the S C Macedonianum with reference to usurious bargains with "expectants," see § 685, in App C, post.

(z) The Nine Circles of Dante's *Inferno* are largely peopled by extortioners, oppressors, usurers, and other abusers of trust and power

(a) See the *Merchant of Venice*, *passim*, where Antonio represents the current feeling of Shakespeare s day against lending "upon advantage, ' and "the giving or the taking of excess," particularly in the case of a friend, "for when did friendship take A breed for barren metal of his friend ? " (Act I, Sc 3, ll 134, 135)

(b) See Cicero, *De Off* . I, 42, and II, 25, and Bacon's *History of Henry VII* in which he speaks of usury as "the bastard use of money," and his above cited Essay ("Of Usury "), where he sets forth its various "discommodities," as reflected in popular sayings,—for instance, that the Devil takes the tithe, instead of the Church, that it is unnatural for " barren metal ' to propagate its kind,—see note (r), *ante*,—that the usurer s plough goes every Sunday, which is a violation of Christian law, that it is contrary to the Divine decree, *in sudore vultus tui comedes panem* (not *in sudore vultus alieni*) ; that it is a breeder of drones, that it engenders disorder and sedition, that it concentrates wealth in a few hands, that it prevents money circulating, and money "is like muck, not good except it be spread ", and that its tendency is to "dull and damp all industries " (cp Polonius's borrowing dulls the edge of husbandry ") These popular views are repeated in other of his Essays, such as Essay XV (" Of Seditions and Troubles "), and Essay XXXIV (" Of Riches ") Bacon was, however, too wise a thinker to accept all this proverbial philosophy of the multitude without qualification He says that usury is and must be *concessum propter duritiem cordis* he sets out its " commodities," and concludes that "to speak of the abolishing of usury is idle,"—"that opinion must be sent to Utopia,"—but its "tooth must be grinded that it bite not too much," and he then suggests a graduated scale, like that of Justinian —see note (x), *ante.*

(c) See § 436, *ante*, as to the Usury Acts, and their abolition Cp Lecky's *Rise and Influence of Rationalism in Europe*, vol ii, ch 6

(d) See note (b), *sup*

(e) See § 435, note (m), *ante.*

(f) As was observed by Lord ELDON, L C , at p 139 of *Davis v Duke of Marlborough* (1818), 2 Swanst 108, and by FARWELL, L J , at p. 891 of *Sadler v Whiteman*, [1910] 1 K B 868, C A

equitable code of duties is of an almost Draconian severity. It has already been explained (g) that at one time it was deemed "impossible" to sustain a gift made under such conditions; then "almost impossible"; then impossible unless the relation, and the influence presumed from it, has been first absolutely terminated, or unless the donor is proved to have acted on the independent and competent advice of a third person. The common sense and conscience of the public vehemently, and not without reason, rebels against the stringency, and (it almost may be said) savagery, of these rules. The community at large cannot be reconciled to a doctrine which lays down that, however real was the intention of the donor to make the gift, and however honest, impartial, and candid the conduct and advice of the donee may have been, yet, if the relation, or the influence created by it, existed or lingered at the material date, the gift may be afterwards undone at any time most convenient to the donor, or most inconvenient or ruinous to the donee, merely because the disinterested and unbiassed advice given by the latter did not pass through the lips of the indispensable "third person," and a non-conducting medium was not thus interposed between the related parties. "Sittlichkeit" thinks that mankind should not be encouraged in practices which even the gods did not permit themselves (h) A man's gift by will cannot be upset unless his supposed will is proved not to have been in truth his will at all, but somebody else's will, superimposed upon his (hh). But if he chooses to give the devised or bequeathed property to the objects of his bounty before he dies, and becomes (as William of Wykeham is said to have done) the executor of his own will, the gift is revocable under the conditions, and subject to the exceptions, above stated. What good reason, it is asked, can there be for such a distinction? How can the mere fact that the donor is dead make the donation a matter of less suspicion than if he still lived? If anything, the law's distrust and suspicion ought to be less in the latter case than in the former, at any rate where the will is a death-bed one made by a testator in a state of bodily or mental weakness, and perhaps a prey to morbid apprehensions as to the future, or exaggerated remorse as to the past · but, certainly, it ought not to be greater The ordinary man appreciates the policy of the law in refusing to enforce a promise to make a gift, just as it refuses to enforce a wager · but in the case of a wager the law equally refuses to enforce restoration of the amount of the wager, when once paid Why, it is asked, is not the same equality of treatment meted out to donor and donee? What fairness is there in allowing the giver to suddenly recall his gift, perhaps long years afterwards, when the recipient has spent it, or has altered the style of his living on the faith of the honesty and validity of the transaction? It is this very circumstance which the law has allowed to operate even as an estoppel against the recovery of moneys paid or credited in error (i). To this the law answers "we only allow a completed gift to be undone when the suspected relation is proved, from this relation we presume undue influence, though even then not quite irrebuttably" Whereupon the plain man protests that it is just this "almost irrebuttable" presumption to which he objects Why should security and stability be denied to a gift honestly made and honestly accepted, and the donee's enjoyment of it, and his legitimate expectations of its continuance, be defeated by the belated caprice, or vanity, or senile imbecility of a donor who, perhaps, takes offence at what he (or, more commonly, she) may consider a falling off in the profuse servility expected as the life-long interest on the gift, or by the exchange of one particular form of influence for another (j)? Why should it

(g) See § 405, note (g), and § 475, *ante*

(h) "The gods themselves cannot recall their gifts" Tennyson's *Tithonus*

(hh) See § 447, *ante*

(i) See *Brisbane v Dacres* (1813), 5 Taunt 143 (*per* GIBBS, J, at pp 152, 153, and Sir JAMES MANSFIELD, C J at p 162), *Skyring v Greenwood* (1825), 4 B & C 281 (*per* ABBOT, C.J, at p 290, and BAYLEY, J, at pp 290, 291)

(j) For example, the decisions in *O'Brien v Lewis* (1863), 32 L J (CH) 569, *Broun v. Kennedy* (1864), 4 De G J & S 217, *Rhodes v Bate* (1866), 1 Ch App 252, and *Liles v Terry*, [1895] 2 Q B 679, C A, are decisions of judges, or appellate tribunals, which popular sentiment would in fact condemn (whether rightly or wrongly, is another question), and which no jury would have given, any more than they did in the similar cases of

be made impossible to take a bounty, except on the terms of giving the donor a promissory note to repay it on demand ? The donee is thus made, instead of " taking a bond of Fate," to give a bond to Fate, and, instead of " making assurance doubly sure," to shatter it to pieces. This feeling, indeed, has not only been recognized, but shared, by more than one eminent judge (k). As for the view of the law that the donor usually gives in haste, and repents at leisure, this is by no means in complete accordance with the facts of life. Quite as often as not, the gift is deliberate, and the revocation hasty and capricious. Further, the revocation is often, perhaps more often than not, the revocation not of the donor, but of those whom he leaves behind him, and in such a case the equitable rules operate with double cruelty, for they disappoint the life-long desire and intentions of the donor who has gone hence in the pathetic confidence that he has securely provided for the object of his affection, as well as the trust and faith of the donee in the permanence of his possession. For these reasons, or some of them, high authorities, such as Lord BROUGHAM (l), Lord CAMPBELL (m), Lord ESHER (n), and Lord SHAW, delivering the judgment of the Judicial Committee of the Privy Council (nn), have expressed opinions by no means in disaccord with popular sentiment as to the unfairness of the supposed absolute requirement of equity that a gift, made in perfect good faith in every other respect, can nevertheless be successfully impeached if the *consilium tertii* be not proved, whereby it results that, to use the felicitous phrase of Lord SHAW in the case last mentioned, " the legal protection " intended to be thrown round the donee is " transmuted into a legal disability."

Sub-s. (6). As to the Doctrine of " Wilful Ignorance."

666. In examining certain questions of terminology, it has been noticed that, under such phrases as " wilful ignorance," " intentional " or " fraudulent blindness," " diligence in ignorance," ' dishonest belief," and the like, English law has exhibited a distinct tendency to impute moral blame in certain circumstances to passive and

Kennedy v *Brown* (1803), 13 C B (N S) 677, and *Mitchell* v *Homfray* (1881), 8 Q. B D. 587, C A, which were tried by a judge and jury   Even in *Brown* v. *Kennedy*, *sup* (where current morality, if disagreeing with the decision, would clearly have been at fault), it would not seem otherwise than human in the normal person to recoil with disgust from the base ingratitude of the client towards her " able and effectual advocate " (*per* KNIGHT-BRUCE, L J, at p 218), to whom she was indebted for her success in the protracted litigation with reference to her step father's will   In *Allcard* v *Skinner* (1887), 36 C D 145, C A (where, as in *Mitchell* v *Homfray*, *sup*, the donor, though successful, succeeded only on the ground of confirmation), it was proved that the donor had come under religious influences opposed to, and deeply interested in obliterating, the particular kind of spiritual influence under which she had made the gift. In all the cases cited in this note, except *O'Brien* v *Lewis* (1863), 32 L J (Ch) 569, the donor was a woman

(k) Thus, in *O'Brien* v *Lewis, sup*, Lord WESTBURY, L C, at p 573, was careful to point out that his decision was not based on any merits on the part of the donor, in *Rhodes* v *Bate* (1866), 1 Ch App 252, KNIGHT-BRUCE, L.J, at p 257, expressed his extreme repugnance to a judgment against a donee who had abundant merits, in favour of a donor who had none, and in *Liles* v *Terry*, [1895] 2 Q B 679, C A, Lord ESHER, M.R, at pp 683, 684, protested against the hard and fast equitable doctrine, and said that he only followed it under compulsion " the learned judge has found, and I believe it to be the truth, that   she did precisely what she intended to do, and that no undue influence whatever was exercised upon her "   Then, after stating the equitable rule, he proceeds " I submit to that rule   I own that I think it unfortunate that such a rule should have been laid down, because in particular instances it may work great injustice, and I do not think that a hard and fast rule which may work such injustice ought to be the rule of law in the matter   But I feel bound by the authorities to hold that there is such a rule in equity   *On that ground only*   I think the female defendant must lose the benefit which the plaintiff, her aunt, intended to confer upon her "

(l) At p 526 of *Nicol* v *Vaughan* (1833), 1 Cl & Fin. 495, and, again, at p 137 of *Hunter* v *Atkins* (1834), 3 My & K 113

(m) At p 374 of *Jenner* v *Jenner* (1860), 2 De G F & J. 359

(n) In *Liles* v *Terry, sup*.   see note (k), *sup*

(nn) At p. 139 of *Kali Bakhsh Singh* v. *Ram Gopal Singh* (1913), 30 L T 138, P C.

negative states of mind (o). In so far as expressions have been judicially used which imply that fraud, as distinct from negligence, must always be established when it is sought to presume against a man a knowledge of that which in fact he does not know, some reasons have been given for concluding that these expressions go too far (p); but there can be no doubt that there is one species of the actual ignorance deemed in law equivalent to knowledge which is marked off from the rest by the circumstance that the party to whom the knowledge is imputed deliberately and dishonestly closed his eyes and ears to the truth which for purposes of his own he did not want to see or hear. With the attitude of jurisprudence in respect of this particular species ethics is in hearty accord. Theology reprobates " blindness " and " hardness of heart," from which, in two petitions of the Litany, the congregation prays to be delivered, whilst, in a third, it seeks forgiveness for " all our sins, negligences, *and ignorances*." Quite a common expression with divines is " sinful blindness " (q), and " false doctrine, heresy, and schism," and matters of faith and belief generally, are accounted by them questions of the will and the heart, quite as much as of the intellect. Similarly, popular sentiment appreciates the deep guilt of that ignorance of crime which it is vainly hoped will be evidence of innocence hereafter,—the ignorance in which Macbeth desired his wife to remain,—

> " *Macb.* . . . There will be done
> A deed of dreadful note.
> *Lady M* What's to be done ?
> *Macb.* Be innocent of the knowledge, dearest chuck,
> Till thou applaud the deed " (r),—

or the ignorance which Pompey rebuked Menas (proposing the murder of the other two " world-sharers," Lepidus and Octavius) for not leaving him in,

> . . . " Repent that e'er thy tongue
> Hath so betrayed thine act : being done, unknown,
> I should have found it afterwards well done,
> But must condemn it now " (s).

As to the remaining species of presumptive knowledge, the man in the street (Aristotle's " ὁ φρόνιμος ") would in some cases make the same imputations as the law, in others, he would not (t) . and with his views as to these latter (consisting principally of various kinds of " constructive notice " in mercantile transactions) jurisprudence is so far in sympathy that both judges (u), and the legislature (v), have indicated in the strongest possible manner their intention to restrict, rather than to extend, the operation of the doctrine.

SECT 3   WHEN, AND WHY, JURISPRUDENCE DISREGARDS ETHICS.

667. There are undoubtedly cases in which the law neglects the moral quality of the act which is the subject of its civil principles and process   It is true that Lord ESHER, in a famous judgment, has stoutly maintained that " *every* general proposition laid down by judges as a principle of law .   . is the statement of some ethical

---

(o) See App A, § 634, *ante*
(p) *Ibid* , §§ 635, 637, *ante*
(q) See *Archbishop Trench's Letters and Memorials* (Kegan Paul & Co , 1888), vol. ii, p 188 (a letter from Dr Pusey to the Archbishop, dated the 2nd April, 1875).
(r) *Macbeth*, Act III, Sc 2, ll. 43–46
(s) *Ant & Cleop* , Act III, Sc 7, ll 83–86
(t) The normal person, for instance, would not be disposed, as a rule, to presume knowledge to the same extent as the law does in the classes of case which are dealt with in Sub ss (4) and (5), but would probably agree with the rules which are the subject of Sub ss (2), and (3), of Ch II, Sect 3, *ante*
(u) See Ch II, Sect 3, Sub s. (7), *ante*.
(v) See §§ 66, 67, 68, *ante*

principle of right and wrong, applied to circumstances in real life, that is, in the life of social intercourse, or in the life of business. If the suggested principle is not obviously a rule of right and wrong, or if the suggested application cannot be supported by the suggested principle, the proposed application must be wrong, or must be supported *by some other principle of right and wrong, or cannot be supported at all* " (w). But this language is obviously much too wide (since it includes several propositions of law which are entirely devoid of all ethical content whatever, such as those to which relate to the passing of property, or are otherwise based on public convenience alone), and is recognized as being so in other judicial expositions for which the same high authority is responsible, and which introduce the proper qualifications. In one case, for instance, we find him justifiably protesting that "unless we are forced by paramount authority to hold that it is law, nothing which is *contrary to* natural justice can be part of the law of England " (x), and, in another, that "legal principles have *almost* always been the fundamental ethical rules of right and wrong " (y). The fact is that jurisprudence and ethics view their common subject, the field of human action, from opposite standpoints, and must necessarily do so, if they are to remain true to their respective functions. The law must refer its problems to the ultimate standard of public utility, convenience, and expediency, rather than that of morals (z), except in so far as public morality is a part of public policy, and except, of course, in cases where fraud or malice or other personal wickedness constitutes an essential ingredient in the cause of action, or the criminal offence. It is true that the resultant conclusion is in most cases practically identical, but this is (scientifically considered) an accident (a). It is also true that, as has been already pointed out, ethical considerations may affect the question of costs (b), or, in certain classes of case, may aggravate or reduce the damages, or, in another kind of case, where the form of remedy prayed is discretionary (e g. specific performance), may even be a ground for refusing relief (c). But subject to these qualifications and exceptions, the law can only enquire whether a legal duty has been violated. It can only regard the effect upon the temporal interests of the party injured, whereas ethical casuistry devotes itself to the examination of the motive and intention of the alleged wrongdoer Jurisprudence is the surgeon, whilst the moralist is the physician, of human conduct,—the one is concerned with visible and palpable results, the other with internal feelings, habits, causes, and diatheses The distinction between the

(w) In *Blackburn, Low & Co* v *Vigors* (1886), 17 Q B D 553, C. A., at p. 558.

(x) At p 531 of *Stumm* v *Dixon* (1889), 22 Q B D 529, C A

(y) See the passage from pp 816, 817 of *Robinson* v *Mollett* (1875), L R 7 H L 802, which is cited in note (h) to § 656, *ante*

(z) See §§ 197, 358, and 461, *ante*, and the cases cited in the notes thereto, and particularly *Hunter* v *Atkins* (1834), 3 My & K 113 (per Lord BROUGHAM, L C, at p 134 "the various departments of its"—the Court's—"jurisdiction are not in any portion accurately defined   but at least its outer boundary is sufficiently marked, and separates it plainly enough from the province of the moralist,—from the regions under the sway of what are not very accurately termed duties of imperfect obligation '), *Liles* v *Terry*, [1895] 2 Q B 679, C A (per LOPES, L J, at p 684, and KAY, L J, at p 685), *Barron* v *Willis*, [1900] 2 Ch 121, C A (per LINDLEY, M R, at pp 131, 132)

(a) In *Gillett* v. *Peppercorne* (1840), 3 Beav 78, Lord LANGDALE, M R, at p 84, said "these transactions cannot be supported, not only are they in themselves so extremely likely to lead to the commission of fraud, as to make them directly against the policy of the law, but in those cases which have occasionally come to the knowledge of the Court,   it has invariably been found that fraud has been the result of such transactions ' In *Cooke* v *Lamotte* (1851), 15 Beav 234, ROMILLY, M R, at p 241, refers to the coincidence of ethics and jurisprudence, but in such a way as to indicate that the coincidence is rather incidental than consciously aimed at ("if the doctrine there stated were carried to the extent here contended for,"—he is speaking of some of the expressions used by Lord BROUGHAM in *Hunter* v *Atkins*, *sup*,—"it might   prevent this Court from exercising a jurisdiction by which it has not only established a rule of equitable jurisprudence, but has, at the same time, enforced a principle of high morality ')

(b) See §§ 168, 618, 623, *ante*

(c) See, as to the damages, § 168, note (z), *ante* ; and, as to specific performance, § 245, *ante*.

two attitudes somewhat resembles that which exists between the judgments of history and the social verdicts of the moment: and not merely by the theologian, but even by the most utilitarian philosopher, many matters which are vital from the juridical point of view are deemed of comparatively slight account in forming ethical judgments (d). The *officia virtutis* which Lord KENYON, Lord ELDON, and (though not altogether approving the phrase) Lord BROUGHAM, described as duties of "imperfect" obligation (e), are precisely those which are deemed by such moralists as Kant (f) at one end of the scale, and Paley (g) at the other, duties of "perfect" obligation; whilst the *officia juris* which alone the law regards as of "perfect" obligation, are, in a strictly ethical aspect, since their sanction is not purely moral, considered of "imperfect" obligation. Nothing could more neatly illustrate the totally opposite standpoints in relation to all such questions of conduct as are the common subject of both systems Dr. Story, after an exposition of the equitable doctrine of good faith, adds: "the principles of natural justice and social morals do, indeed, go further; and require the most scrupulous good faith, candour, and truth in all dealings whatever. But courts of justice generally find themselves compelled to assign limits to the exercise of their jurisdiction, far short of the principles deducible *ex æquo et bono*, and with reference to the concerns of human life, they endeavour to aim at mere practical good and general convenience" (h). Or, as Cicero puts it, "aliter leges,

(d) "Contemporaries look at the agents, their motives, and characters, history looks rather at the acts and their consequences" (Hare, *Guesses at Truth*) J. S Mill, in his diary, under date 2nd March, 1854, wrote "it is a common saying that the only true test of a person's character is actions. There is much error in this. . . Actions, no doubt, are the fittest test for the world at large, because all they want to know is the actions they may expect from him But to his intimates who care about what he is, and not merely about what he does, the involuntary indications of feeling and disposition are a much surer criterion of them than voluntary acts" (*Letters of J. S. Mill*, ed Hugh Elliot, vol ii, p 376) So also Canon Mozley (*Bampton Lectures*, vol i, p 11), after saying that "a perfectly sinless character . . would be as great a miracle as any that could be conceived," proceeds "where is the proof of perfect sinlessness? No outward life or conduct, however just, benevolent, and irreproachable, could prove this, because goodness depends upon the inward motive, and the perfection of the inward motive is not proved by the outward act"

(e) "It is not every moral and social duty the neglect of which is the ground of an action For there are some which are called in the civil law duties of imperfect obligation, for the enforcing of which no action lies" *Pasley* v *Freeman* (1789), 3 Term Rep 51 (per Lord KENYON, CJ, at p 63) So Lord ELDON, LC, at p 273 of *Gibson* v *Jeyes* (1801), 6 Ves 266 "this Court cannot proceed upon those nice and delicate considerations in matters of propriety that would suggest that, as matter of moral, and *therefore imperfect*, obligation," &c Lord BROUGHAM L C, also used the expression in the same sense—see the citation in note (z), *ante*—but not without a suggestion of its inaccuracy

(f) In the Second Section of his *Metaphysic of Morals*

(g) *Principles of Moral and Political Philosophy*, Book II, Ch x "I call these obligations 'imperfect' in conformity to the established language of writers upon the subject The term, however, seems ill chosen upon this account, that it leads many to imagine that there is a less guilt in the violation of an imperfect obligation than of a perfect one, which is a groundless notion For an obligation being perfect or imperfect, determines only whether violence may or may not be employed to enforce it, and determines nothing else The degree of guilt incurred by violating the obligation is a different thing, and is determined by circumstances altogether independent of this distinction" In another passage (Book III, Part I, Ch vii), when speaking of contracts of sale, he draws a distinction between "what the parties ought to do, and what a judge or arbitrator would award to be done," that is to say, between the lawyer's "imperfect" obligation and the lawyer's "perfect" obligation It is in reality only a question of words From the point of view of jurisprudence, that only is a 'perfect" duty which is unadulterated (if the word may be permitted) with moral sanctions to the moralist, that only is a perfect duty which derives its authority from within, and is independent of any external monitor If for the term "perfect obligation," which suggests different ideas in the two connections, and in both of them inappropriate associations, there were substituted the term "purely legal," or "purely moral," obligation, as the case may be, there would be no difficulty

(h) *Equity Jurisprudence*, vol i, § 194

aliter philosophi, tollunt astutias : leges, quatenus manu tenere possunt, philosophi, quatenus ratione et intelligentiâ " (ı). Even "the Chancery" of earlier times, described by Bacon as "the Prætorian power for mitigating the rigour of law in case of extremity by the conscience of a good man," conceived itself to be under this disability. "With such a conscience," said Lord NOTTINGHAM, L.C., "as is only *naturalis et interna* this court has nothing to do ; the conscience by which I am to proceed is merely *civilis et politica*, and tied to certain measures " (ȷ) ; and, in the same spirit, JEKYLL, M.R., observed that "though proceedings in equity are said to be *secundum discretionem viri boni*, yet, when it is asked, *vir bonus est quis ?* the answer is, *Qui consulta patrum, qui leges juraque servat*" (k). "There is a well-known case in the books," said Lord CRANWORTH, L.C., "with which those who practice in the courts are very familiar (l), in which, upon a counsel saying to Lord THURLOW, ' Your lordship would think in point of honour, so and so,' Lord THURLOW said, ' upon that point you must apply to the party himself. I do not give any opinion on that subject ' " (m). Accordingly, in the matter of disclosure, juris-prudence, though requiring the utmost openness and candour in specific relations and transactions which are deemed to give rise to fiduciary duties, and though pro-hibiting such concealment as amounts to implied misrepresentation and fraud even in cases where there is no such specific relation or transaction (n), has found it impracticable and impolitic to enforce conformity to the high Stoical ideals of complete disclosure, in any and every kind of dealing, of everything which the other party to the transaction is interested in knowing (o) Thus Lord THURLOW, L C in reference to the common illustration of a man purchasing an estate without dis-closing to the vendor the existence of a valuable mine under the surface, says "the question is, not whether the transaction be such as a man of honour would disclaim and disdain, but it must fall within some settled definition of wrong recog-nized by this court ", otherwise the court would be "undoing all the common transactions of mankind," and "rendering all their dealings too insecure " (p) "Simple reticence," observes Lord CAMPBELL, L.C., "does not amount to legal fraud, however it may be viewed by moralists " (q). And, according to Dr Story, " Pothier has expounded this subject with his usual force and sterling sense. As a matter of conscience,' says he, ' any deviation from the most exact and scrupulous sincerity is repugnant to the good faith that ought to prevail in contracts Any dissimulation concerning the object of the contract and what the opposite party has an interest in knowing, is contrary to that good faith ; for, since we are commanded to love our neighbours as ourselves, we are not permitted to conceal from him anything which we should be unwilling to have concealed from ourselves. But in civil tribunals something plainly injurious to good faith ' (that is, to positive rules of jurisprudence) ' must be shown to justify their interference ' " (r) The same disclaimer of the pretensions of civil courts to invade the domain of pure ethics has

(ı) *De Off* III 17

(ȷ) At p 600 of *Cook v Fountain* (1676), 3 Swanst 585 He had previously observed that the "trust, security, or agreement " which was vainly sought to be proved in that case was " such 　　as is only between a man and his confessor "

(k) At p 753 of *Cowper v Earl Cowper* (1734), 2 P Wms 720 In this case JEKYLL, M.R , felt himself constrained to give judgment for the plaintiff, though " were I "—he says at p 734—"to consider the matter, not as sitting in judicature, but taking in all manner of considerations, such as honour, gratitude, private conscience, &c , I must think this claim should never have been made "

(l) *Fox v Mackreth,* cited in note (p), *inf*, may have been the case which was in Lord CRANWORTH'S mind A fortiori, all considerations of perverted "honour" (so called) will be contemptuously rejected by the law, as in the case of the "honour" policies referred to in note (a) to § 655, *ante*

(m) At p 773 of *Smith v Kay* (1859), 7 L C 750

(n) See Ch III, Sect 2, Sub-s (8), *ante*

(o) As to the Stoical and Ciceronian view of the question, see § 675, in App C, *post*

(p) At p 321 of *Fox v Mackreth* (1788), 2 Cox 320 , 2 R R 55

(q) At pp 723, 724 of *Walter v Morgan* (1861), 3 De G F & J 718

(r) *Equity Jurispr* , vol 1, § 194

been made by jurists of high authority from Lord ELDON, L.C., to Lord MAC-
NAGHTEN (s). The above, it will be observed, are illustrations of cases where juris
prudence deems it injudicious, and inconsistent with its main purpose and utility,
to regard ethical considerations, either because it is impracticable to secure the
"equality" of conditions in the full sense that casuistry might require, or (it may be)
because it is impossible to devise a suitable remedy, which are amongst the reasons
suggested by Paley, and by Lord Kames (t); though the former, in other passages,
treats the rules of law, in relation to particular kinds of transaction, as based on
identically the same considerations as the rules of morality, and insists that the one
and the other pay the like regard to both motive and effect (u).

668. There is another type of case in which the law peremptorily and deliberately

(s) See *Gibson* v *Jeyes* (1801), 6 Ves 266 (*per* Lord ELDON, L C., at p. 275. the passage
is cited in note (c), *ante*); *Harris* v *Tremenheere* (1808), 15 Ves 34 (*per* Lord ELDON,
L C, at p. 39 · " I am not entrusted with a jurisdiction to say what a delicate and prudent
consideration would have suggested"), *Blackburn, Low & Co.* v *Vigors* (1887), 12 App.
Cas. 531, H. L. (*per* Lord MACNAGHTEN at p. 543. "I apprehend that it is not the function
of a Court of Justice to enforce or give effect to moral obligations which do not carry with
them legal or equitable rights") For a variety of illustrations of the dividing line
between legal, and purely moral, obligations, see §§ 165, 166, 167, and the cases cited in
the notes thereto, *ante.*

(t) *Principles of Moral and Political Philosophy*, Book III, Part I, Ch viii " what
some say of this kind of contracts "—i e wagering and insurance contracts—" ' that one
side ought not to have any advantage over the other,' is neither practicable nor true.
It is *not practicable;* for that perfect equality of skill and judgment, which this rule
requires, is seldom to be met with I might not have it in my power to . . underwrite
a policy of insurance once in a twelvemonth, if I must wait till I meet with a person whose
art, skill, and judgment in these matters is neither greater nor less than my own Nor is
this equality requisite to the justice of the contract . The proper restriction is that neither
side have an advantage by means of which the other is not aware " The whole of the
above passage accords with jurisprudence, except the last sentence, which states a proposition wider than the law would now accept see § 164, *ante* For another sense in which
the enforcement of certain moral obligations is said to be "impracticable," see Lord
Kames, *Principles of Equity, Introduction,* vol 1, p 23 He there points out that the
nature of such obligations is entirely dependent upon the individual conscience and
circumstances, whilst those "founded on interest" admit of closer definition and limitation, and that "viewing the matter in this light, it will appear that such duties are left upon
conscience, not from neglect or insensibility, but from the difficulty of a proper remedy"

(u) *Principles of Moral and Political Philosophy,* Book III, Part I, Ch vii ("Contracts of Sale") "the rule of *Justice,* which wants with most anxiety to be inculcated in
the making of bargains, is, that the seller is bound *in conscience* to disclose the faults of
what he offers for sale Amongst other methods of proving this, one may be the following
I suppose it will be allowed that to advance a direct falsehood, in recommendation of
our wares, by ascribing to them some quality which we know that they have not, is
dishonest Now compare with this the *designed concealment* of some fault which we know
that they have The motives and the effects of actions are the only points of comparison
in which their moral quality can differ but the motive in these two cases is the same, viz
to procure a higher price than we expect otherwise to obtain the effect, that is, the
prejudice to the buyer is also the same If, therefore, actions be the same, *as to all
moral purposes,* which proceed from the same motives, and produce the same effects ,
it is making a distinction without a difference to esteem it a cheat to magnify beyond truth
the virtues of what we have to sell, but none to conceal its faults " It is not quite certain,
having regard to the several expressions italicized above, whether this passage is intended
as the statement of a rule of "justice," or a rule of "conscience" if the former, it is not
quite a correct statement, unless by "designed concealment" is meant the actual covering
up, or hiding away, or disguise of a fault by positive artifices, or unless the "fault" is
of a kind which, as affecting the title, the vendor is under a duty to disclose see Ch III,
Sect 2, Sub-s (8), *ante* If, however, it was intended to enunciate a purely moral principle,
the statement is quite sound, as ethics, and it serves in that case to indicate the precise
point at which law and morals diverge Theological casuists accentuate this point of
divergence more than other moral philosophers Thus, St Thomas Aquinas (*Summa
Theologicæ, Secunda Secundæ,* Quæst lxxvii, Art 3) holds that the seller should reveal all
except manifest faults, whilst the law lays down the exact opposite, viz that he need
disclose none unless actively concealed

refuses to give effect to the principles which would be applied by ethics as between individuals, on the ground of that higher justice, or *suprema lex*, usually termed "public policy" or (better, perhaps) "public utility," which is recognized as overriding the particular interests, and, sometimes, even the private rights, of the parties concerned. There are various conditions under which "public policy," or the higher kind of "justice," becomes the dominating factor in judicial determinations, and correspondingly various senses which those expressions bear. In the first place public utility demands that persons under disability, whether by reason of status or circumstances, and persons unable to help themselves, or not represented in the immediate inquiry, such as infants, creditors, "expectants," and the like, shall be protected, even where the protection results in persons who are morally guilty going free (v). Secondly, it is an element in this larger and controlling "justice" that its rules should peremptorily ignore the personal innocence of the party to whose prejudice they operate, on the ground that mankind at large must be preserved from the temptation and tendency to evil doing which would otherwise result ("how oft the sight of means to do ill deeds Makes deeds ill done"),—the disregard of moral considerations under such circumstances being dictated by what is sometimes described as "the policy of the law" (w). Lastly, in establishing and enforcing its presumptions (irrebuttable or rebuttable, as the case may be) of knowledge, confidence, or influence, the law defers to that general convenience which almost amounts to a public necessity, when it disregards the individual conscience of the actors, a close introspection of which, if required to be pursued on each occasion, instead of being dispensed with, as it is, by the presumptions in question, would result in a paralysis of business (x). The respective claims on jurisprudence of utility, justice, and interest, have been acutely and soundly analyzed by Lord Kames (xx),

(v) As to infants, see *Stikeman v Dawson* (1847), 1 De G & Sm 90, *per* KNIGHT-BRUCE, V-C, at p 111 "fraud is certainly odious, and to be repressed But neither is protection to be withheld from the imbecility of youth Is not allowance to be made for its exposure and obnoxiousness to influence, to temptation, and seduction, especially in a state of legal nonage?" And, again, at pp 116, 117 "there may be a want of delicacy, or indeed of morality, in the conduct of a young man of twenty buying a picture or a statue upon credit, without mentioning his age, but laws cannot vindicate every deflection from propriety, and it must be preferable surely that men of full age, in or out of trade, should sometimes suffer for acts of carelessness or imprudence, than that there should be given the obvious facility and plain encouragement to minors to be their own destroyers, and to others to make them a prey, which would be afforded by the rule that mutual silence, with an appearance of manhood, should expose a boy, upon the ground of fraud, to be fixed after his majority with the most rash and foolish contracts, or with the liability to restore money wasted in childish extravagance *Nulla lex satis commoda omnibus est, id modo quæritur, si majori parti et in summam prodest*" As to creditors, in the case of secret agreements whereby one of them is favoured, see § 587, and note (l) thereto, *ante* As to these, and "expectants," and third persons generally, see *Chesterfield (Earl of) v Janssen* (1751), 2 Ves Sr 125 (*per* Lord HARDWICKE, L C, at pp 156, 157)

(w) The expression used by Lord LANGDALE, M R,—see the citation in note (a) to § 667, *ante*—and by others For illustrations of this aspect of "public policy," and for the theory that the equitable rules of good faith, in disclosure and other matters, are founded on a recognition of the general tendency and temptation to wrong doing which would result in wrong being done, if there were no such rules, see § 317 (in Ch IV), and § 407 (in Ch V), *ante* Cp Lord Kames, *Principles of Equity*, Book II, Ch 1 (vol II, pp 84–88), where he points out that "acts in themselves lawful are reprobated in equity as having a *tendency* to corrupt morals," and that "wrong must be done before justice can interfere, but *utility* lays down measures to prevent wrong," and removes "*temptation* to fraudulent practices" He then gives instances from the rules relating to the fiduciary position of trustees, agents, and the like, observing with respect to the receipt of secret profit by a person in such a position · "an act of this nature may in itself be innocent, but is poisonous with respect to consequences"

(x) As to certain rules of presumptive knowledge being founded on public convenience of the kinds mentioned in the text, see §§ 41, 47, *ante* as to the like, in the case of relations of confidence, and of influence, see § 317, and § 407, *ante*, respectively

(xx) His *Principles of Equity* (as announced by him in his *Introduction*) is divided into two Books, the first of which is devoted to "The Powers of a Court of Equity derived

who says that though "in opposing *private* utility to justice, the latter ought always to prevail," yet public utility, in the proper sense, and within the proper limits, ought to prevail against not only private utility, but private justice too. "It is not, however," he adds, "every sort of public utility that can outweigh justice; it is that sort only which is preventive of mischief affecting the whole or bulk of society: public utility, as far as it concerns positive additional good to the society, is a subject which comes not within the sphere of a court of equity," but, with this exception, "wherever it is at variance with justice a court of equity ought not to enforce the latter." The principles of public utility, and of private justice, it is true, "for the most part are good friends," but there are "branches of utility which are not so strictly attached to justice," and cases sometimes arise where the two "are in declared opposition," to the extent of defeating the enforcement of just *moral* claims, but no further; for "the influence of public utility stops there, and never authorizes a court of equity to enforce any positive act of injustice." What is called "public policy," therefore, whether the word "policy" is happily chosen or not, is a real and sound principle in jurisprudence, and by no means deserves the disparaging reflections of BURROUGH, J., or his somewhat inept comparison of the doctrine to an "unruly horse." Public policy, said this judge in an oracular passage which has been cited *ad nauseam*, as if it had been drawn from the very fount of wisdom. "may lead you from the sound law. It is never argued at all but when other points fail. It is a very unruly horse, and when once you get astride it, you never know where it will carry you." A. L. SMITH, M.R., however, described it, in equally metaphorical, but more accurate, phraseology as "a high horse to mount, and difficult to ride when you have mounted it" (y). The fact is that this steed, which might very well have been allowed to rest during the many years since it was led out of the stables in 1824, is a horse of excellent race, mettle, and temper, and, whenever he has come to grief, it has been due not to himself, but to bad riding. The best horse in the world, if put to impossible fences, will bring himself and rider to the ground. No doubt, he is "a high horse," but is none the worse for that · and he may be "difficult to ride, when you have mounted him," but this does not necessarily involve unruliness. Of course the doctrine in question "*may* lead you from the sound law": so may any other, if misapplied: but to say that it is never argued at all but when other points fail" is simply contrary to the fact, and BURROUGH, J., when he made this observation, was singularly oblivious of "the celebrated reply" of Sir S. ROMILLY in the leading case on "influence" relations, and of judgment after judgment of Lord HARDWICKE, and of Lord ELDON, prior to 1824. No doubt, the circumstances to which, sometimes properly, and sometimes improperly, the rule of ' public policy" is applied, are infinite in variety, but the fluctuation, or (more properly speaking) the development, of the forms in which the rule is from time to time expressed in no way negatives, but rather emphasizes and illustrates, the essential unity of the doctrine itself ' the determination of what is contrary to the so-called policy of the law varies from time to time," but " the rule remains," notwithstanding that " its application necessarily varies with the principles which for the time being guide public opinion " (yy).

from the principles of Justice" (vol i, and vol ii, pp 1–83), and the second to "The Powers of a Court of Equity founded on the principle of Utility" (vol ii, pp 84 *ad fin*) The citations in the text are from the concluding chapter of Book II, entitled ' Justice and Utility Compared " (vol ii, pp 127–131)

(y) At p 605 of *Driefontein Consolidated Mines, Ltd* v *Janson* (1901), 17 T L R 604, C A The "unruly horse" originally came from the judgment of BURROUGH, J, at p 252 of *Richardson* v *Mellish* (1824), 2 Bing 229 Lord MERSEY, at p 46 of *Kreglinger* v *New Patagonia Meat and Cold Storage Co*, [1914] A C 25, H L, prefers "the unruly dog" as a simile

(yy) *Eventurel* v *Eventurel* (1874), L R P C 1, at p 29 Cp the like observations, as to the "public policy" rules against restraint of trade, in *Nordenfeldt* v *Nordenfeldt Maxim Gun & Ammunition Co*, [1894] A C 535, H L, and, with respect to the theory on which immunity is granted to certain classes of defamatory publication, in *Lewis* v *Levy* (1858), E B & E 537 (*per* Lord CAMPBELL, C J, at p 560), *Wason* v *Walter* (1868), L R 4 Q B 73 (*per* COCKBURN, C.J, at p 93), and *Usill* v *Hales* (1878), 3 C P. D 319 (*per* COLERIDGE,

669. Moral teachers and casuists, on the other hand, look at every problem from the other end of the telescope Personal character, and the springs that set conscience in motion, are more to them than the general effect of actions on society at large, or even than their individual effect on the material interests of the parties concerned. The utilitarian Mill, no less than the theologian Mozley, has expressed himself in language (z) which distinctly implies this attitude. Indeed, there are certain types of theological casuistry which insist that the confessor should, in his devotion to the *salus animæ*, occupy himself entirely with the task of "directing the intention," to the total, or almost total, exclusion of the effect. This is one of the doctrines which Pascal makes a subject of reproach to the Jesuits, a member of which Society, in an imaginary conversation with himself, he represents as justifying the system of "diriger l'intention, qui consiste à se proposer pour fin de ses actions un objet permis," by reference to the fact that "les juges, qui ne pénètrent pas dans les consciences, ne jugent que par déhors de l'action, au lieu que nous regardons principalement à l'intention ; et de là vient que nos maximes sont quelquefois un peu différentes des leurs." It is this same "diriger l'intention," without reference to results, which excited Boileau's scorn in the satire addressed to "L'Equivoque " · " tu sçus, dirigeant bien en eux l'intention, De tout crime laver la coupable action ' (a). The general spirit, however, of philosophical, and even of theological, ethics is not fairly obnoxious to this censure. The soundest moralists by no means entirely ignore the effect of acts, just as for certain purposes, such as costs, damages, or discretionary relief (b), the law does not entirely ignore motive and intention. Paley gives weight to both in determining the moral complexion of a certain class of transaction (c), and St Augustine plainly avows that it is no answer for a man who intended the act to say, " I did not intend to sin " (d). Pascal, indeed, in the Letter in which he ridicules the above-mentioned practice of the Jesuits, expresses his own views on the subject in such terms as to suggest that, so far from ignoring the effect, he is disposed rather to ignore the intention, and to think more juridically than jurisprudence itself · "l'intention de celui qui blesse ne soulage point celui qui est blessé . il ne s'aperçoit point de cette ' direction ' secrète, et il ne sent que celle du coup qu'on lui porte. Et je ne sais même si on n'aurait pas moins de dépit de se voir tuer brutalement par des gens emportés, que de sentir poignarder consciencieusement par des gens devots " (e). And it must be remembered that ecclesiastical authority has always so far regarded temporal consequences as to require restitution to the injured party, where possible, as a part of the penance inflicted *pro salute animæ*, and a condition of absolution. indeed, the King's Courts in early times found in this practice evidence of an intermeddling with temporal concerns sufficient to justify them in wresting back from the Church the exclusive jurisdiction over slander and certain other causes of action, which she had previously usurped (f)

670. The main purpose of jurisprudence being as above stated, and the ἀρετή of any art or science consisting, according to Plato, in accomplishing its own ἔργον, it follows that the law falls short of that excellence when it concerns itself with moral themes, and inquires into personal motives, which are not an element in, or germane

C J , at p 327)   As to the unsuitableness of the term " policy," by reason of its suggestion of other associations, see the remarks of Lord HARDWICKE, L C , cited in §646, note (y), *ante*. And it cannot be denied that " the policy of a statute " is not only an absurd expression, but stands for a preposterous method of reasoning

(z) Cited in note (d) to § 667, *ante*

(a) The passages cited are from Pascal's *Les Provinciales, ou les Lettres écrites par Louis de Montalte à un Provincial de ses Amis set aux révérends Pères Jesuites, Letter VII*, and Boileau's *Satires*, XII, 287, 288

(b) See §§ 168, 618, 623, *ante*

(c) See the citation in note (u) to § 667, *ante*

(d) *Liber Retract* , ch xv

(e) *Les Provinciales*, Letter VII   This is exactly the view of English jurisprudence, and also of the civilians   " neque enim interest emptoris cur fallatur, ignorantia venditoris, an calliditate " (in contracts of sale) D 21 1 1 1

(f) See App V, Sect 4, of the author's *Code of the Law of Actionable Defamation*

to, either some cause of action, or some ground of defence, or some form of relief. *Ne sutor ultra crepidam* This is the belief and the practice of the large majority of English jurists and judges It cannot be denied, however, that in recent times there has been manifested in this country a growing tendency to administer, or coquet with, eccentric forms of justice, and to stray beyond the bounds of "justice according to law." Amongst these spurious types are "natural justice" (g); "poetic" or "dramatic justice" (h), "substantial justice," when ear is given to the urgent entreaty,—"wrest once the law to thine authority, To do a great right, do a little wrong" (i); and what has been described by Lord SUMNER as "that vague jurisprudence which is sometimes attractively styled 'justice as between man and man'" (j), as if, except in the Platonic metaphor, there ever could be any justice except between two human beings ("ἀεὶ ἐν πλείοσιν ἀναγκὴ εἶναι τὸ ἄδικον"). Further, it cannot escape notice that a judicial propensity to intrude upon the domain of ethics where it is unnecessary, and therefore wrong, to do so, and to improve the occasion by parenthetical sermons or lectures, is on the increase, and that the community deeply resents this intrusion as an impertinence We are told in the Articles of Religion that "the other books, as Hierome saith, the Church doth read for example of life and instruction of manners, but yet doth not apply them to establish any doctrine" But these non-canonical digressions of judges not only do not establish any doctrine, but, unlike the non canonical books of Scripture, are not even read "for example of life and instruction of manners," or regarded at all except upon their merits as homilies, which are often not very conspicuous, inasmuch as the moral denunciations of the particular conduct passed under review represent merely the individual attitude of the particular judge to the particular delinquency or delinquent, exhibit the widest variations in the strength or mildness of the censure, and are often the outcome of the personal sentiment   price, or even prejudice of the moment (k). The wisest exponents of our law   erved upon the growth of this tendency, and its accompanying perils, with no int   prehension "I for one," said BOWEN, L J, "should deeply regret the day,   came, when courts of law or equity thought themselves justified in interfering more than is strictly necessary with the private affairs of the people of this country " (l). A generation or so later,

---

(g) Relied upon by Cicero, and the Stoics whom he followed, as the foundation of their ethico jural views on disclosure . see § 675, *post* Lord ESHER, too, considered that no rule of law should prevail which is contrary to " natural justice" see § 667, note (x), *ante* And, as was pointed out by HAMILTON, L J, at pp 199–201 of *R* v *Local Government Board*, [1914] 1 K B 160, C A, and by Lord SHAW in the H L (July 20, 1914—not yet reported), the expression either means no more than "justice" *simpliciter*, or, if intended to recall the old *jus naturale*, is totally misleading

(h) The justice which is illustrated by "the engineer hoist with his own petar," and the falling into the pit dug for another, and which forms the περιπέτεια of " The Merchant of Venice," " Measure for Measure," and the story of Phalaris

(i) *Merchant of Venice*, Act iv, Sc 1, ll 215, 216

(j) At p 140 of *Baylis* v *Bishop of London*, [1913] 1 Ch 127, C A

(k) See the cases cited in note (i) to § 656, *ante*, and particularly *Panama & South Pacific Telegraph Co* v *India Rubber, Gutta Percha, & Telegraph Co* (1875), 10 Ch App 575, where, before his moral lecture, JAMES, L J , observed, at p 527 : " I might have been content to have allowed this case   to have been based upon the application of a plain principle of equity which is to be enforced   without regard to the particular facts or the particular conduct or misconduct of the parties in a particular case " A just and wise remark, which it would have been better to have acted on But the craving for homiletic exercises and excursions was too much for him " But I cannot," he proceeds, " content myself with disposing of this case merely upon that general principle, and only saying that it is the general principle which has crushed this contract " It is submitted that the judgment would have gained, and not lost, in authority and power, if he had so contented himself After the moral reflections, he concludes by saying, at p 528, " res ipsa loquitur " He had begun by implying that *jus ipsum loquitur* Then, *cur judex loquitur ?*, it might be asked The mild handling of the Bishop's conduct in the case cited in note (e) to § 656, *ante*, is in sharp contrast with the severe strictures upon that of the mercantile Scot in the case cited in note (d) thereto, *ante* If any ethical discourse was necessary, why this distinction in its personal application ?

(l) At p 335 of *Re Agar Ellis* (1883), 24 C D 317, C. A.

when the time which BOWEN, L J., foresaw as a possibility had arrived, MOULTON, L.J., expressed his views on the subject in much more trenchant and spirited language : " I own," he said, " that not only as an individual but as a member of the Judicial Bench, I rebel against the suggestion that according to English law he "—the litigant—" may do this only so far as it may accord with the notions of some judge who, as such, has no more authority to act towards him as a moral director than has the man in the street. .   The Court has the right and duty to decree the proper relief against him, but it can do no more.   It cannot add to this relief directions or comments as to his future conduct   If they are not part of the relief itself, they are pronounced without authority.   The conception of the Court interfering with litigants otherwise than by granting the relief which it is empowered and bound to grant, is wholly vicious and strikes at the foundation of the status and duties of judges.   We claim and obtain obedience and respect for our office because we are nothing other than the appointed agents for the enforcing upon each individual the performance of his obligations. That obedience and that respect must cease if, disregarding the difference between legislative and judicial functions, we attempt ourselves to create obligations and impose them on any individual who refuses to accept them " (m).   Even when expressly invited by the parties to pronounce on the ethical aspects of the case, a judge, though not to be blamed overmuch if he accedes to the invitation, will yet act more correctly if he declines it, as TURNER, L.J., did in a celebrated case ·   " the defendant," he observed, " in the course of his argument, invited us to give an opinion on his conduct   I advisedly decline to do so further than by saying it has been wholly at variance with the principles of the Court " (n)   The unnecessary homilies of judges are, as has already been pointed out (o), responsible for various terminological errors, and have set public feeling against doctrines which, but for their faulty expression, would have been readily accepted by the laity   It has been the cause of not a few incorrect decisions ·   added to which, the authority of even a correct decision is weakened, and not strengthened, when it is needlessly based upon moral grounds, and great judges such as Lord ELDON (p), and JERVIS, C.J. (q), have even expressed distrust of their own decisions, and grave fears as to being unduly swayed by moral indignation, in cases where the personal merits of one party were in such sharp contrast with the utter demerits of the other as to be a source of temptation (r)

(m) At p 273 of *Scott* v. *Scott*, [1912] P 241, C A
(n) At p 223 of *Brown* v *Kennedy* (1864), 4 De G J & S 217   But, in *Re Telescriptor Syndicate, Ltd* , [1903] 2 Ch 174, BUCKLEY, J , did, more or less under protest, think fit to accede to a similar application   The directors, he said at pp 195, 196, " invite the judgment of the Court upon the matter from the point of view of their personal integrity This Court is not a court of conscience, and the question of legal liability is not at present ripe for decision   In the absence, therefore, of the invitation held out to me by their counsel to express an opinion on their case as affecting them in their personal character, and as apart from legal liability, I should have added nothing upon the case as regarded from that point of view   But upon that invitation I add that which follows "   That ' which followed " was not exactly what the directors hoped for when they proffered their exceedingly ill advised " invitation,' as will be seen by the extracts given in note (q) to § 656, *ante*
(o) See §§ 652 and 657, *ante*
(p) Who, at p 468 of *Gordon* v *Gordon* (1821), 3 Swanst 400, said that he " had never known a case in which it was more the duty of a judge to enter into a covenant with himself not to suffer his feelings to influence his judgment "
(q) Who, at pp 784 785 of *Evans* v *Edmonds* (1853), 13 C B 777, concluded his judgment in these words   " I cannot help saying that I somewhat distrust my judgment in this case   It was impossible to avoid having one's feelings enlisted in favour of the defendant   It is one of the most scandalous cases I ever met with "
(r) In *Fllard* v *Lord Llandaff* (1810), 1 Ball & B 241, Lord MANNERS, L.C (Ir), would seem to have yielded to this temptation, and, as regards some at least of the principles he there laid down, to have ' wrested the law to his authority "   See Ch III. Sect 8, Sub s (4), *ante*, where this case is the subject of special consideration and criticism

APPENDIX C.

THE ROMAN LAW OF NON DISCLOSURE AND ABUSES OF CONFIDENCE AND INFLUENCE.

1. Some of the English rules relating to disclosure and good faith in transactions and relations of confidence and influence are, if not founded on, at least fortified and illustrated by, the principles of the Roman jurists in reference to Dolus and actions *bonæ fidei*, whilst, as regards others, our courts have arrived at conclusions which are in substance identical with those transcribed in the Digest (s) from Ulpian and the other great Roman authorities, as supplemented by scattered legislation in the Codex (t) It may, therefore, be of interest to institute a comparison between the two systems in this department of jurisprudence (u)

Sect 1. General View of Dolus, as involving Non Disclosure, in Roman Jurisprudence.

672. In Roman law there were certain classes of transaction which were the subject of actions *bonæ fidei*, as opposed to others called *stricti juris*. In an action of the former description, it was the duty of the judex to inquire whether good faith had, or had not, been observed, by both or either of the parties, the formula being—*quicquid paret dare (facere) oportere ex fide bonâ, &c*, whereas, in the latter class of action, bad faith, whether by concealment or otherwise, was not relevant at all before the introduction of the Aquilian Formula, and, even after that date, could only become so if affirmatively raised as the ground of either an *actio*, or an *exceptio, doli mali*. Cicero, in this respect concurring with those equity judges of this country who (rightly or wrongly) have construed the term "fraud" as a *nomen generalissimum* applicable to any and every breach of fiduciary principles, constantly insists on the adaptability, and corresponding utility, of the *ex fide bonâ* clause, which, he says, ought to be applied alike to all transactions where confidence must be reposed on one side, and good faith therefore required on the other, if human society is to be kept together in any enduring bond He cites Q. Scævola as declaring ' summam vim esse in omnibus arbitriis, in quibus adderetur *ex fide bonâ*, fideique bonæ

(s) The title prefixed to the First Book of this collection of extracts from the treatises of the great Roman jurists is "Domini Nostri Sacratissimi Principis Justiniani juris enucleati ex omni vetere jure collecti *Digestorum* sive Pandectarum Liber Primus" We ought, therefore, strictly to speak of "the Digests," not "the Digest" It is curious that, whilst the Greek title "Pandects" is always correctly used in the plural, jurists have conspired to use the singular number in the case of the equally plural Latin equivalent

(t) The Codex referred to in this Appendix is Justinian's collection of Imperial Constitutions

(u) The mode of citing from the Corpus Juris in the following notes is that now generally used "D" stands for "Digest," and "C" for "Codex" The first figure after the "D" or the "C," as the case may be, indicates the number of the Book, the second, the number of the Title (or Chapter), the third, that of the section, and the fourth (where there is a fourth), the number of the clause (or paragraph, or "fragment") When the clause is an introductory one, and has no number, the abbreviation "pr" (for "principium") is used

nomen . . . *manare latissimè*, idque versari in tutelis, societatibus, fiduciis, mandatis, rebus emptis venditis, conductis locatis, *quibus vitæ societas contineretur*" (v). In other passages, he mentions *negotiorum gestio*, and *res uxoria*, as transactions which are the subject of a *bonæ fidei* action. It will be recognized that the classes of transaction and relation enumerated correspond closely with some, but by no means all, of the classes which are stated in Chapters III, IV, and V, of this treatise to give rise to duties of disclosure and good faith generally. It remains now to consider the circumstances and conditions under which, with reference to a transaction not *bonæ fidei* in the above sense, the Roman law allowed an action, or plea, of *dolus malus* to be raised, and what kind of non disclosure in such a case was deemed indicative of *dolus malus*.

673. It was C. Aquilius Gallus, an official colleague, personal friend, and relative of Cicero, who invented the *judicium de dolo malo*, enthusiastically extolled by the latter as the "everriculum malitiarum omnium" (w). The Aquilian Formula, as set out in the Digest, is in designedly general and simple terms · "quæ dolo malo facta esse dicentur, si de his rebus alia actio non erit, et justa causa esse videbitur, judicium dabo ' (x) The introduction of this new cause of action, and ground of affirmative defence can be traced to the Stoical teaching by which Aquilius, like Cicero, was deeply influenced. The Stoic philosopher Panætius taught Mutius Scævola, of whom both Aquilius and Lucius Balbus were disciples. The latter, who is made to represent the Stoical side of the discussion in Cicero's *De Naturâ Deorum*, instructed the renowned jurist, Servius Sulpicius. Cicero's *De Officiis*, whether it is to be regarded as a treatise on law or on ethics, on *officia juris* or on *officia virtutis* (y), was avowedly founded on Panætius (z), and is saturated with Stoical doctrine which, through him and others, sank deeply into the fabric of the Digest in relation to all departments of the *corpus juris* (a), but pre eminently in relation to Dolus.

674 Having in view its Stoical parentage, one is not surprised to find that the doctrine "manabat latissimè,' that Roman jurisprudence shrank from restricting the meaning or range of Dolus, and that not only bad faith or fraud, in the ordinary sense, of whatever kind, but also any other oppressive, unconscionable, extortionate, or malicious conduct, evincing a wicked and deliberate intention to overreach or injure another, as distinguished from mere negligence and unintentional wrong (*culpa*), was included within its purview, just as the term "fraud" has been extended by our equity judges to embrace a similarly miscellaneous assortment of trans-

(v) *De Off* III, 17 Cp *De Nat Deorum*, III, 30 (where substantially the same list is given, with others "inde tot judicia de fide malâ, tutelæ, mandati, pro socio, fiduciæ, reliqua, quæ ex empto aut vendito aut conducto aut locato contra fidem fiunt"), and *Top* xvii 66 (where *negotiorum gestio*, and *res uxoria*, are added) In *Pro Cæc* iii, 7–9, Cicero mentions *tutela, societas, res mandata*, and *fiducia ratio*, and adds that a decision against a party in a *bonæ fidei actio* was a *turpe judicium*, that is, involved *infamia*. In *Just Instit* 4 6 28, the complete list of *bonæ fidei* actions is given as follows . "ex empto vendito, locato conducto, negotiorum gestorum, mandati, depositi, pro socio, tutelæ, commodati, pigneraticia, familiæ erciscundæ, communi dividundo, præscriptis verbis quæ de æstimato proponitur, et ea quæ ex permutatione competit, et hereditatis petitio "

(w) *De Nat Deorum*, III, 30

(x) D 4 3 1 1

(y) It has generally been regarded as a juridical treatise both by Roman lawyers and by English judges (see Sect 6, *post*), as also by English, American, and French writers on jurisprudence, e g Sir Edward Fry (*Specific Performance*), Dr. Story (*Equity Juris prudence*), and Pothier In one or two passages, however, Cicero himself admits, with regret, that he is expounding some purely ethical principle ("lege naturæ sanctum ') which is not, though it ought to be, part of the positive law. For instance, speaking (*De Off* III 17) of certain customary breaches of good faith in transactions of purchase and sale, he laments that they incur no legal penalty, nor even moral or social censure *hoc* video, *propter depravationem consuetudinis* (Hamlet's "damnèd custom"), *neque more turpe haberi, neque aut lege sancici aut jure civili.*

(z) "Panætius qui sine controversiâ de officiis accuratissimè disputavit, quemque nos, correctione quâdam adhi ", potissimum secuti sumus " *De Off* III, 2

(a) In the very beginning the Digest, Chrysippus, described as "philosophus summæ stoicæ sapientiæ," is cited for his definition of νόμος (D 1 3 2)

gressions against *æquum et bonum* (b). Even *culpa*, the direct antithesis of *dolus*, was, in its more serious degrees (*latior*, or *latissima*, as distinguished from *levis*), frequently described, as it has been by our own lawyers,—erroneously in both cases,—as either equivalent to *dolus* (c), or next door to it (d). In the passage of the Digest which is usually cited for the definition of *dolus malus* in the more restricted sense of bad faith (e), the Aquilian rule is stated to have been aimed at all manner of *dolosi*, with the object of rendering their fraud, or want of candour, both unprofitable to them, and innocuous to their intended victims (f). The definitions of the rival schools of Servius and Labeo are then contrasted, with the result that the former is found too narrow in one respect, and too broad in another, and the latter is preferred. Labeo's definition is : "every kind of craft, deceit, or covin, used for the purpose of circumventing another" (g),—a definition which presents an almost ludicrous example of a *circulus in definiendo*, but which, from the higher standpoint of jurisprudence, commands approbation by reason of the very generality and vagueness which constitutes its defect in the eyes of the mere precisian in logic or language (h). It is now proposed to inquire what sort of non disclosure in transactions other than those which might be the subject of a *bona fide* action, which will be considered later (i), and other than reticence of a kind which amounts to misrepresentation (j), was deemed by Roman law to constitute, or indicate, *dolus malus*.

675. The *locus classicus* on the vexed question of the dividing line between guilty concealment and permissible reticence, as drawn by the Roman jurists, is the passage in the *De Officiis* in which Cicero puts, and debates, the famous case of the Alexandrian corn-merchant and the famished Rhodians (k). He supposes that the *frumentarius* carries corn from Alexandria to Rhodes, where there is a famine, and sells it to the Rhodians at famine prices, without disclosing the fact that on his voyage he had passed several vessels bound for the starving city with abundant supplies,—a fact which, if known, would have at once reduced the market price to normal proportions, and which was, therefore, in one sense of the word, an obviously material fact. The question is · was this fact material in the other sense of the term ? that is to say, was it material to be disclosed ? The *frumentarius* is assumed, in this "case of conscience," to be a man honestly anxious to do what is right, but "perplexed in the extreme" as to the course which duty enjoins. Cicero assigns the advocacy of the opposing views to Diogenes Apollonius, and his disciple, Antipater, respectively, both disputants being Stoical casuists. but, in this and like matters,

---

(b) See §§ 629, 630, 631, *ante*

(c) D 16 3 32. "quod Nerva diceret latiorem culpam dolum esse, Proculo displicebat, mihi verissimum videtur,"—Celsus, *Digesta*, lib xi is here being transcribed,—"nam . nisi ad suum modum curam in deposito præstat, fraud non caret nec enim salva fide minorem is quam suis rebus diligentiam præstabit " Th is is the same terminological error as that for which English judges are responsible in those incautious pronouncements in which they have treated negligence as either the equivalent of fraud, or as evidence of it the topic is discussed in § 637, *ante* Even for the purposes of an action of deceit, this was the view entertained by many equity lawyers before *Derry v Peel* (1889), 14 App Cas. 337, H L

(d) D 17 1 29 pr · "dissoluta negligentia prope dolum est " Again see § 637, *ante*

(e) Which is taken from Ulpian, *Ad Edictum*, lib xi.

(f) D 4 3 1 pr

(g) D 4 3 1 2 "Labeo sic definit dolum malum esse omnem calliditatem, fallaciam, machinationem ad circumveniendum, fallendum, decipiendum alterum adhibitam "

(h) Dr Hunter, in his valuable work on Roman law, characterizes the definition as "neither very precise nor very accurate " It certainly is not very precise, but for that reason it is not inaccurate, for the thing to be defined is not precise

(i) See § 676, *post*

(j) These forms of implied misrepresentation by silence, and by conduct, as the subject of Roman jurisprudence, are discussed in Appendix C (§§ 509, 510, 511, 513) of the author's *Law of Actionable Misrepresentation*

(k) *De Off* III, 12, 13

drawing different conclusions from their common principles (*l*). Antipater is represented as pressing the unconditional and inviolable claims of what in the language of modern ethical philosophy would be termed "the categorical imperative" (*m*). To this exalted view Cicero himself obviously inclines (*n*); but he states, fairly and forcibly, the counter arguments of Diogenes Babylonius, who, after further debate (*o*), is allowed to have the last word, and the credit of a first attempt to distinguish between silence and concealment (*p*). Then follows a series of further illustrations, mostly taken from the law of vendor and purchaser (*q*), after which, Cicero finally delivers his own judgment both in the matter of the *frumentarius*, and in the other cases put (*r*), and, in so doing, defines justifiable reticence, and unjustifiable concealment, respectively, in a formula which, though a little more scientific than that of Diogenes Babylonius, and though constantly cited in our courts (*s*), is open to grave exception. The

(*l*) "In hujusmodi causis aliud Diogeni Babylonio videri solet, magno et gravi Stoico, aliud Antipatro, discipulo ejus, homini acutissimo"; *De Off.* III, 12.

(*m*) *Ibid.*: "omnia patefacienda, ut ne quid omnino, quod venditor norit, emptor ignoret." The duty is thus stated as universal, and absolute, neither dependent on any condition, nor limited in any way as to the subject-matter of the disclosure.

(*n*) See note (*r*), *inf.*

(*o*) Diogenes Babylonius urges that no wrong can be done where there is no legal duty of disclosure, and there can be no such duty where the purchaser has no right to expect that the vendor will depreciate his chances of making the most of his own property: to which Antipater answers, in the spirit of modern theological casuistry, that the duty of disclosure springs from the general and primary obligation of benevolence to mankind, or to one's neighbour, and expresses surprise that a Stoic who accepts as amongst the "principia naturæ, quibus parere et quæ sequi debeas," the duty of so acting "ut utilitas tua communis sit utilitas" (our "public policy" in one of its senses), should yet reject one of its most obvious applications, the duty of imparting "hominibus, quid us adsit commoditatis et copiæ." Diogenes objects that silence is not concealment, that there can be no universal obligation to instruct mankind in useful knowledge, and that abstention from such instruction in matters of far greater moment than the price of corn, such as theological or moral philosophy, has never been called concealment ("*aliud est celare, aliud tacere* neque ego nunc te celo, si tibi non dico quæ natura deorum sit, qui sit finis bonorum, quæ tibi plus prodessent cognita, quam tritici vilitas. *Sed non quicquid tibi audire utile est, id mihi dicere necesse est*"). Thereupon Antipater, instead of recognizing that his proposition stood in need of at least some qualification, vehemently adheres to it in its absolute form, and bases it again on the paramount claims of the members of any human *societas* upon one another, which gives Diogenes the obvious retort that it would be a curious *societas* which denies to its members the right of private property, and that under such conditions any transaction between man and man, other than a gift, would be unrighteous ("num ista societas talis est, ut nihil suum cujusquam sit? Quod si ita est, non vendendum quidem quidquam est, sed donandum") *De Off.* III, 12.

(*p*) See the last note, and the "aliud est celare, aliud tacere" passage there cited, which is so frequently relied upon in English judgments (see § 694, *post*) The mere distinction, however, is in itself quite colourless, and does not advance matters in the least. It is only when Cicero's distinction between permissible and improper reticence is tacked on to it, that it has any real meaning or importance

(*q*) *De Off.* III, 13. These illustrations are referred to in note (*h*) to § 676, *post* Antipater and Diogenes express the same contrary opinions on the merits of these cases as on the conduct of the corn merchant, the former comparing the concealment in question to the refusal or neglect to put a wanderer on the right path,—see notes (*v*), (*x*), and (*y*) to § 650, *ante*,—or rather to the much graver offence of deliberately misleading him ("quid est enim aliud, erranti viam non monstrare, si hoc non est, emptorem pati ruere et per errorem in maximum fraudem incurrere? Plus etiam est quam viam non monstrare nam est scientem errorem alterum inducere"), and the latter insisting that the vendor, who is admittedly not bound by mere laudatory generalities on the merits of his own property, to which no one is supposed to attach any importance, is still less required "to cry stinking fish." In short, Antipater represents the extreme, not to say grotesque, attitude of ethics *in excelsis*, whilst Diogenes reflects the strictly juridical view, and, in so doing, perhaps goes to the other extreme

(*r*) "Non igitur videtur nec frumentarius ille Rhodios, nec hic ædium venditor celare emptores debuisse" *De Off.* III, 13

(*s*) See § 694, *post*

proposition runs thus: "neque enim id est celare, quicquid reticeas; sed quum quod tu scias, id ignorare emolumenti tui causâ velis eos quorum intersit id scire" (t). In its most literal sense, the statement is so inconformable to the principles even of sound ethics (u), not to speak of law, that one at first doubts whether Cicero intended it to be so understood. But, on examining the context, and the examples which he gives, and, above all, the theory which he enunciates as the groundwork of the whole doctrine, viz. that "it is contrary to natural justice for one man to take advantage of the ignorance of another" (u), it is evident that he did mean the proposition to be taken *au pied de la lettre*, and without any qualification other than as stated by himself. Regarded in the light of a jurisprudental maxim, as most writers (whether justly or not) have regarded it, it is certainly a proper subject of the criticism which has been applied to it by Pothier (v), Grotius (w), Pufendorf (x), Kent (y), Story (z), and Sir Edward Fry (a), some of whom suggest qualifications, subject to which the proposition, it is said, may be assented to by jurists. Thus Grotius is of opinion that the undisclosed fact must be material (b), which is true, so far as it goes, but more than this is required to make the rule consonant with English jurisprudence Sir Edward Fry inclines to the view that the only additional element necessary in order to make the proposition a sound juridical one may be obtained by expanding "velis" into "desire, *and take active steps to procure*" the ignorance of which the guilty party seeks to take advantage (c). But, surely, even this is not enough, unless "interest" be also enlarged so as to include not only the interest of the opposite party in knowing the uncommunicated matter, but also his right to have it communicated.

SECT 2 THE DUTY OF DISCLOSURE BETWEEN NEGOTIATING PARTIES IN ROMAN LAW.

676 It has already been explained that in English law there is a duty on parties negotiating for contracts of certain specified and defined types to disclose all matters respectively deemed material (d). Roman jurisprudence had no such detailed or scientific classification. It enjoined *bona fides* in general terms on a surety (e), and as between parties compromising litigation (f), and, in negotiations of whatever kind, dissimulation was accounted a form and badge of *dolus* (g) But no specific

(t) *De Off* III, 13 The passage follows, and is put as the ground of, the decision
(u) See Thomas Aquinas, *Summa Theol.*, II, ii, Quæst lxvii, Art 3, and Pothier, note (v), *inf*
(u) *De Off* III, 17 "ex quo intelligitur, quoniam juris natura fons est, hoc secundum naturam esse, neminem id agere, ut ex alterius prædetur inscitiâ"
(v) *Traité du Contrat de Vente*, pp 233–242, and pp 297, 298 At p 241 he remarks that most writers on the subject regard "la décision de Cicéron" as "outrée," and expresses his opinion that it "souffre beaucoup de difficulté, même dans le for de conscience"
(w) *De Jure Belli et Pacis*, lib II, ch. xii, s. 9 "non ergo generaliter sequendum illud ejusdem Ciceronis, celare esse, quum quod tu scias, id ig. orare emolumenti tui causâ velis eos quorum intersit id scire, sed tum demum id locum habet, *quum de iis agitur quæ rem subjectam per se contingunt*"
(x) *Law of Nature and Nations*, Book V, Ch 3, § 4
(y) *Commentaries*, vol ii, Lect 39, pp 485–491
(z) *Equity Jurisprudence*, vol i, § 205
(a) *Specific Performance*, §§ 705, 713 see the citations in note (c), *inf*
(b) See the citation in note (w), *sup* This was also the qualification upon which Diogenes Babylonius insisted see note (o), *sup*
(c) In note (1) to § 705 of his *Specific Performance*, he observes that the limitation suggested by the Dutch jurist would probably bring the Ciceronian proposition into conformity with English law; but in note (2) to § 713 of the same treatise he supplements this opinion by the further suggestion that "if the whole is to express the principles of our law, *velis* must, it is conceived, import not only will, but some act consequent thereon"
(d) In Ch III, Sect 2, *ante*
(e) Sponsio, Fidepromissio, Fidejussio
(f) Called "transactio" in Roman law
(g) D 18 1 43 2 ('qui insidiose et obscurè dissimulat") Cp Cic *De Off* III, 15 ('ex omni vitâ simulatio dissimulatioque tollenda est Ita nec, ut emat melius, nec ut vendat, quidquam simulabit aut dissimulabit vir bonus')

duties of disclosure were prescribed in respect of special classes of contract, except that between vendor and purchaser. Here the vendor was required in all cases to divulge to the purchaser facts of a material character, known only to himself (h), in substantial accordance with the rules of English law (i), and, in cases expressly provided for by legislation, certain named defects in the thing sold, whether he knew of them or not (j), as in the corresponding cases of statutory disclosure in our juris. prudence (k). The Ædilician Edict (l) prescribed the disclosure of the particular defects ("vitia") specified therein on every market sale, and made the failure in this duty the subject of both an *actio redhibitoria*, and an *exceptio*. The requirements, at first very limited, both as regards the subject matters of the sale, and the "redhi bitory" defects, were by degrees enlarged until they embraced nearly every kind of property, and most of the ordinary material defects (m). The *actio redhibitoria* was so called because the seller was thereby forced to take back what he had before, or, in other words, submit to an undoing or annulment of the sale: "redhibere est facere, ut rursus habeat venditor quod habuerit" (n).

SECT 3.   ROMAN LAW AS TO THE DUTY OF DISCLOSURE IN RELATIONS OF CONFIDENCE.

677. The obligations of disclosure and otherwise incidental to relations of "confidence" form the separate subject of one of the foregoing Chapters (o). The relations in question are those classified under three main heads (p). One of these, the relation between a promoter and the company promoted by him has no analogue in Roman law; but, under the name of *fiduciæ* (q) *mandata*, and *societas* (r), we find,

(h) Such facts, for instance, as that the vendor was selling a slave with vices, physical, mental, or moral, or diseased cattle, decayed timber, incumbered land, and the like   See D 19 1 1, D. 19 1. 4 pr , D 19. 1 6 9 ; D. 19 1 13 pr , 1, 2, 3, D. 19 1. 21 1, D 19 1 41, D 19 2 19 1.   The non disclosure of such defects, if known to the vendor and unknown to the purchaser, is *dolus*   See also Cic *De Off* III, 12, 13, 16, 23   The examples there given are, besides the case of the *frumentarius* (III, 12), which is discussed in § 675, *ante*, sales of houses which the vendor knows, but the purchaser does not know, to be insanitary, or infected with serpents (the English cases are concerned with a minuter pest), or dilapidated, or ruinous, or jerry built (III, 13), or to have been condemned by the augurs as an obstruction to the taking of the auspices, or to be subject to servitudes (III, 16), or sales, under the like conditions, of wine which is "going off" (*fugiens*) or of slaves addicted to lying, gambling, thieving, or drunkenness (III, 23)

(i) Some of them fall within the classes of case which are the subject of Ch III, Sect 2 Sub s (3), *ante*, dealing with facts material to be disclosed in the negotiation for a contract of sale   The residue are of the same character as those referred to in Ch III Sect 2 Sub s (8), dealing with cases of negotiation where there is no duty of disc   in the first instance, though supervening conduct or circumstances, or fraud, ma   de such a duty

(j) D. 21 1 1 2   "dummodo sciamus venditorem, etiamsi ignoravit ea quæ ædiles præstari jubent, tamen deberi tenetur"

(k) The subject of Ch VI, *ante*

(l) Set out in D 21 1 1 1

(m) For the history and development of the rules introduced by this Edict, see Cic *De Off* III, 16, 17, and see D 21 1 (De Ædilicio et Redhibitione et Quanti Minoris) generally, for illustrations of its application

(n) D 21 1 21 pr , (from Ulpian s Commentary on the Ædilician Edict)

(o) Ch IV, *ante*

(p) See Ch IV, Sect 2, *ante*

(q) Cicero mentions *fiduciæ* amongst the transactions or relations which are the subject of *bonæ fidei* actions, in *De Off* III, 17, *De Nat Deorum*, III, 30, *Pro Cæc* ii, 7, *Pro Roscio Com edo*, vi   The equitable rule against direct purchases from the *cestui que trust*, or principal, is stated, but in an absolute, not a qualified form, in D 18 1. 34 7   "tutor rem pupilli emere non potest   porrigendum est ad similia, id est ad curatores, pro curatores, et qui negotia aliena gerunt"   Cp D 18 1 46, D 26 8 5   The relation of trustee and *cestui que trust* is dealt with in Ch IV, Sect 2, Sub s (1), *ante*

(r) *Mandata* (res *mandatæ*) are included amongst *bonæ fidei* transactions in Cic *De Off* III, 17, *Top* x, xvii ; *De Nat. Deor*, III, 30, *Pro Cæc* ii, 7, and *societas*, and the

both in Cicero and in the Digest, frequent references to relations corresponding to the other two English types of confidential relation, those, namely, which exist between trustee and *cestui que trust*, and between agent and principal, including partnership As regards these, the Roman jurists always insist in the strongest terms on the general duty of *bona fides*, without, however, except in a very few instances, condescending to particulars, or working out the theory in any detail.

SECT. 4. THE ROMAN DOCTRINE OF GOOD FAITH IN RELATIONS OF INFLUENCE.

678. In the Chapter devoted to this class of relation (s), six species of influence have been separately considered, that of the parent or guardian (domestic), those of professional advisers or directors (legal, sacerdotal, and medical), and that which is created by the special circumstances and conditions of the individual case, and particularly, in this connection, the influence of the moneylender or dealer over the "expectant." It is proposed to compare the two systems of jurisprudence in relation to these several species.

Sub-s. (1). As to the Parental or Quasi-Parental Relation.

679. Roman law, from the very earliest times, numbered *tutela* among its "suspected" relations, in the sense that the *tutor* could not deal directly with his *pupillus*, and might always be required to establish his good faith   But the notion, so deeply implanted in our jurisprudence, that a parent, merely as such, and apart from actual guardianship, is properly the subject of vigilant scrutiny when entering into a transaction with a son just emerging from infancy, is foreign to the Roman system, in which the duty of good faith was strictly limited to the actual juridical relation of guardianship, and no presumption of improper influence was made, as it is with us, against those who were in a position of purely domestic and natural ascendancy (t)

Sub s (2).   As to the Relation between Legal Adviser and Client.

680. The influence of the advocate was from an early stage in Roman history the object of deep distrust.   The growing domination of the Senate (from whom came most of the advocates) over the subservient plebs, by means of this particular type of influence, stimulated the passing of the Lex Cincia de Donis et Muneribus, in the year 204 B C, which prohibited the acceptance of gifts by an advocate from his client " ob causam orandam,"—he could not stipulate for a fee (*merces*) by the existing

action *pro socio*, in the same passages, as well as in *Pro Roscio Amerino*, xl (where Cicero explains the theory on which good faith is especially required of partners in substantially the same language as an English Court of equity would use)   See also, as to the relation of partnership in Roman law, D 17 2 (on the action *pro socio*), C 4 37. 3 ("in societatis contractibus fides exuberet "), Just *Instit* 3 25 1 (si quis callidè in hoc renunciaverit societati, ut obveniens aliquod lucrum solus habeat,   cogitur hoc lucrum communicare ")   The English law as to the duty of disclosure and good faith in the relation of principal and agent, including partnership, is the subject of Ch IV, Sect 2, Sub-s (3), *ante*

(s) The subject of Ch V, *ante*

(t) As Cicero tells us in *De Off* III, 15, the duties incidental to *tutela* were the subject of express provisions in the XII Tables   See Lib 36 (De Tutelis) of the Digest, and all the passages from Cicero cited in note (r), *sup*, except *Pro Rosc Am* xl   The parental or quasi parental relation in English law is the subject of Ch V, Sect 2, Sub s (1), f m which it will be seen that our jurisprudence includes among the domestic relations which raise a presumption of influence on one side, and a corresponding duty of good faith on the other, many relations which would not come within the well defined limits of the Roman *tutela*   On the other hand, Roman law recognized transactions relating to *res uxoria* as giving rise to duties of good faith (see Cic *Top* xvii), whereas English law now draws no presumption of influence from the relation of husband and wife (see § 446, *ante*)   It is curious to find that in Athens there was a law of Solon which invalidated transactions due to the influence of the wife over the husband (" ἄκυρα ταῦτα πάντα, ὅταν τις γυναικὶ πειθόμενος πράττη " Demosth *In Olymp* 1183).

law,—and enabled the donor to recover any such gift at any time during the joint lives of himself and the donee (u). This *plebiscitum* is referred to, as an important measure, by Livy (v), Cicero, and Tacitus (w). It was re enacted as a *senatus con sultum* in the principate of Augustus (with a severer penalty, viz. repayment of the gift fourfold). The practice, however, went on, unchecked by either old *plebiscita* or new *senatus consulta*, till, in the principate of Nero, "nihil publico merois tam venale fuit quam advocatorum perfidia," and, in the case of one Publius Suilius, the scandal was so flagrant that even the corrupt Senate of that day was shamed into prosecuting him. It was recognized at last that these donations could not be stopped, and Claudius, adopting a middle course, limited the amount of my one gift to *dena sestertia* (about £80). At one time the Senate required an o ch from the litigant parties in every cause that they had not made, promised, or secur d, any donation to their respective advocates. Constantine relaxed these provisions considerably; but we still find references in the Digest to the liability of an advocate receiving more than the maximum to disgorge the overplus, though his right is recognized to take a present made to him after the litigation is terminated (x). Any champertous agree ment (called a *pactum de quotâ litis*) was prohibited by a constitution of Constantine.

Sub s. (3)   *As to Spiritual Influence.*

681. Sacerdotal dignity and supremacy, in the pagan times of Rome, was never the object of suspicion, but on the contrary claimed, and received, the deepest respect, recognition, and confidence. Still less did the law exhibit any of that hostility to the exercise of spiritual influence in worldly matters which is so deeply emb dded in both the jurisprudence and the popular sentiment of this country (y). During the later period when Christianity had become firmly established in the constitution of the Empire, so far from distrusting the temporal influence of the Church, and of its sacerdotal administrators and officers, both the executive and the judiciary encouraged it by every possible means. Justinian, in particular, took great pains to provide facilities for effectuating testamentary gifts in favour of ecclesiastical institutions, and precautions against their invalidation by the (then very common) omission of any human person or earthly place as the object of the bequest Thus, in one of his Constitutions, he notes the prevailing practice of instituting as heir to the whole or a portion of the testator's property either "our Lord Jesus Christ," or "one of the Archangels or Martyrs," without naming any priest or church, and he ordains that in all such cases the gift shall not be defeated on that account, but shall take effect cy près in various prescribed forms (z)

Sub-s. (4)   *As to Medical Influence*

682. As has been already pointed out, this type of influence is the object of suspicion in English law (a) It was also, apparently, distrusted, or subjected to vigilant scrutiny, in Roman jurisprudence Gifts to *archiatri* were legislated

---

(u) This *lex* was a *plebiscitum*, introduced by the tribune M Cincius For the English law as to the relation between legal adviser and client, see Ch V, Sect 2, Sub-s (2), *ante*

(v) *Hist* xxxiv, 4, where M Porcius Cato, speaking *pro Lege Oppiâ*, is represented as asking "quid legem Cinciam de donis et muneribus [excitavit], nisi quia vectigalis jam et stipendiaria plebs esse senatui cœperat?"

(w) Cic *De Senect* iv De Oratore, II, 71 Tacitus, in his report of the speech of Pætus Thrasea—see § 685, note (m), *post*—mentions this law

(x) The authorities for the account of the Lex Cincia in the text are Tacitus, *Ann* xi. 5, xiii 42, xv 20, Pliny, *Epist* V 20, D 50 13 10 12

(y) See § 421, *ante*

(z) See C 1 2 26, pr "quoniam in pler sque nuper testamentis invenimus hujusmodi institutiones, quibus ex asse quis scripserit Dominum nostrum Jesum Christum hæredem, non adjiciens oratorium aut templum ullum, aut ex semisse". &c Again, in C. 1 2 26, 1, 2 "si vero unius ex Archangelis meminerit, vel venerandorum Martyrum, nullâ sacræ ædis mentione" &c

(a) The subject of Ch V, Sect 2, Sub s (4), *ante*

against (b), on the same lines as gifts to advocates (c), in an imperial constitution which, besides prescribing certain counsels of perfection (such as that the physician should devote himself to the service of the poor and needy, rather than basely pander to the imaginary diseases of wealth and fashion), prohibited the acceptance of gifts promised by a patient when in the throes of a dangerous illness, but permitted the receipt of a present made after complete restoration to health.

Sub s. (5). As to Undue Influence in Fact.

683. The species of influence, viz. that which is presumed from a relation constituted by the particular "circumstances and conditions" of the case, and which plays such a prominent part in the English law of undue influence (d), is the subject of occasional denunciation in general terms by the Roman jurists, such as Cicero in the oft-cited passage where he characterizes as the vilest form of fraud and oppression that which is made possible by the dominant party's preliminary professions of friendship, and the assumption of the character of honest adviser, to the servient party in his distress (e). But, except as to bargains with expectants,—the topic next to be considered,—these general principles are not worked out in any detail.

Sub-s. (6). As to Unconscionable Bargains with Expectants.

684. Oppressive bargains with "expectants," which it has always been the special object of our jurisprudence to relieve against, as already explained (f), occupied in a no less degree the attention of the Roman legislature. As early as 200 B C. (circ), a statute was passed which prohibited the circumvention of *adolescentes*, that is, young men who, though of age (*puberes*), were less than 25 years old, by abuse of influence, or other unconscionable means (g) There were also various statutory attempts to repress, or curtail, usury in general (h) In course of time, however, the rapid growth of extravagance, luxury, and indebtedness on the part of these "adolescentes," bringing in its train the inevitable, and equally rapid, multiplication of extortioners, demanded much more stringent and specific measures to cope with this particular evil

685. Accordingly the famous Senatus-consultum Macedonianum, not infrequently referred to in judgments on bargains with expectants in our courts (i), was passed, either in the principate of Claudius (j), or in that of Vespasian (k) This enactment was a piece of occasional legislation in the sense that it was immediately provoked by the enormities of its eponymous hero, one Macedo, a peculiarly infamous usurer of the day (l), just as the like enormities of the Polish usurer known to our courts as Alexander Gordon were the immediate occasion of the passing of the Moneylenders

(b) C 10 52 9 "archiatri honestè obsequi tenuioribus malint quam turpiter servire divitiis Quos etiam ea patimur accipere, quæ sani offerunt pro obsequio, non ea quæ periclitantes pro salute promittunt "

(c) See § 680, note (x), ante

(d) Dealt with in Ch V, Sect 2, Sub s (5), ante

(e) "Totius injustitiæ nulla capitalior est quam eorum qui, cum maxime fallunt, id agunt ut viri boni esse videantur" (Cic *De Off* I 13), a passage cited by Sir S Romilly, in his "celebrated reply" in *Huguenin* v *Baseley* (1807), 14 Ves 273 (at p 285),—as to which see § 408, note (c), ante,—in support of his denunciation of "undue influence" in all its many varieties Plato (*Crito*, 52 E) speaks of contracts being invalidated in Athenian law on the ground of coercion, or pressure, with no time given to reflect or take counsel "τὰς ξυνθήκας καὶ μολογίας μὴ παραβαίνειν τὸν οὐχ ὑπ' ἀνάγκης ὁμολογήσαντα, οὐδὲ ἐν ὀλίγῳ χρόνῳ ἀναγκασθέντα βουλεύσασθαι "

(f) In Ch V, Sect 2, Sub s (6), ante

(g) The Lex Plætoria (or Lætoria), mentioned by Cicero in *De Off* III, 15, and *De Nat Deor* III, 30

(h) For a brief account of legislation against usury, see § 664, ante

(i) Particularly, in those of Lord HARDWICKE, L C see § 698, note (j), post

(j) As Tacitus says, *Ann* xi 13

(k) According to Suetonius, *Vesp* 11

(l) It has been sometimes said that Macedo was the name of a notorious spendthrift of the day, and the principal prey of the moneylenders, and not that of a moneylender at

§ 800 (m). The actual words are set out by Ulpian in a passage which is incorporated in the Digest (n). There is first a short preamble, reciting the misdeeds of Macedo, and the temptation to crime which was thereby placed in the way of the expectants to whom he lent money: "cum inter cæteras sceleris causas, quas illi natura administrabat, etiam æs alienum adhibuisset, et sæpe materiam peccandi malis moribus præstaret, qui pecuniam (ne quid amplius diceretur) mortis nominibus crederet." Then follow the operative words ("placere ne cui, qui filiofamilias mutuam pecuniam dedisset, etiam post mortem parentis ejus cujus in potestate fuisset, actio petitioque daretur"), with a statement that the intent of the enactment is that no usurer shall have a cause of action in respect of a loan on the faith of the expectation of the ancestor's decease ("ut scirent qui pessimo exemplo fœnerarent, nullius posse filiifamilias bonum nomen *expectatâ patris morte* fieri"). Ulpian does not in terms say that the object of the Senate was to prevent attempts upon the life of the ancestor, as well as upon his property, but it is so stated plainly by Justinian in the Institutes (o). It will be observed that in most respects this measure was less far-reaching than the flexible principles of our equitable doctrine on the subject. Thus, it only gave the expectant an *exceptio* to an *actio* or *petitio* by the usurer for the recovery of the loan "ne cui . . . actio petitioque daretur" (p). It gave no relief to the expectant, by way of rescission or otherwise, if he had once paid the money, which is quite contrary to English law (q), and must have gone far to emasculate the statute. Also the enactment gave no remedy to any one who was more than 25, or was otherwise "suæ potestatis" (r), whereas all that our law requires to be proved is that, whatever his age or exact legal status may have been, the servient party had an expectation of benefit from some ancestor or relative, on which the moneylender was trading (s). The *exceptio* was not available against a lender who was reasonably induced by the acts and conduct and "holding out" of the borrower to believe that he was a *paterfamilias* (t), or who could not have known that the borrower was under disability in point of age or status (u). The bar to relief only operated against one who either knew, or could have discovered, that the borrower was under

all. How this notion could ever have gained ground, it is difficult to understand. The preamble of the S. C., which recites the usurer's crimes (see the text, *sup*), entirely negatives the suggestion.

(m) 63 & 64 Vict., c. 51. The revelations made in *Gordon* v. *Street*, [1899] 2 Q. B. 641, C. A., as to the practices of this Macedo of the period, self-described as "the hottest and bitterest" of his tribe, "with a gross of aliases," stimulated and provoked this measure. For other instances of Roman legislation occasioned by scandals of the day, see the speech of Pætus Thrasea, when prosecuting Claudius Timarchus for corruption as an administrator of Crete in the principate of Nero, as given by Tacitus (*Ann.* xv. 20). The orator there insists that the notoriety and spread of some particular vice has always been the cause of repressive legislation, and mentions, as illustrations, the Lex Cincia De Donis et Muneribus (see § 680, notes (u), (v), (w), (x), *ante*), provoked by the growing licence and rapacity of advocates, the Leges Juliæ, occasioned by corrupt practices at elections, and the Leges Calpurniæ, by the extortions of magistrates.

(n) D. 14. 6. 1 pr. (taken from Ulpian, *Ad Edictum*, lib. xxix.)

(o) *Instit.* 4. 7. 7. "quæ ideo senatus prospexit, quia sæpe onerati ære alieno creditarum pecuniarum quas in luxuriam consumebant, *vitæ parentum insidiabantur.*"

(p) See also D. 14. 6. 1. 1. "deneganda est actio." On the other hand, the moneylender was debarred from recovering anything: he lost the whole of his principal, as well as the benefit of the special terms made. This is directly contrary to our law.

(q) See Ch. V, Sect. 5, *ante.*

(r) C. 4. 28. 1.

(s) As explained in § 438, *ante.*

(t) D. 14. 6. 3 pr.. "si quis patremfamilias esse credidit, non vanâ simplicitate deceptus, nec juris ignorantiâ, sed quia publicè paterfamilias plerisque videbatur, sic agebat, sic contrahebat, sic muneribus fungebatur, cessabit S. C." As to the exceptions of "vana simplicitas," and "juris ignorantia," and the conditions under which these states of mind affect legal presumptions of knowledge, see §§ 40, 41, *ante*, respectively. As to presumed knowledge or ignorance of infancy in English law, see the passages from the judgment of KNIGHT BRUCE, V.-C., in *Stikeman* v. *Dawson* (1847), 1 De G. & Sm. 90, which are cited in note (t) to § 164, *ante.*

(u) D. 14. 6. 3. 2.

the proscribed age, or was "in alienâ potestate" (v). If credit was really given to the parent, and not to the expectant, the statute had no application (w),—which corresponds with the like rule in English law (x). So also, if the *paterfamilias* was cognizant of the whole transaction (y), or if it was done at his instance (z), or with his authority and consent (a): and this again accords with our law (b). If the *filiusfamilias* was *fidejussor* for another, the *exceptio* was available to both (c). It was no answer to the *exceptio* that the transaction was not in form a loan, but a sale to the *filiusfamilias* (d), or a guarantee of his indebtedness (e).

SECT. 5 ROMAN LAW AS TO BURDEN OF PROOF, AFFIRMATIVE DEFENCES, AND RELIEF, IN CASES OF NON-DISCLOSURE.

Sub-s. (1) As to the Facts required to establish the Actio or Exceptio Doli.

686. Those nice and difficult questions of the burden of proof with which our law has been so busily concerned are not very minutely discussed in the Digest. But the general principle, *ei incumbit probatio qui dicit, non qui negat* (ee), pervades both systems, and, in regard to *dolus* in particular, there is an imperial constitution requiring, as English law requires, the utmost strictness of proof (f) In ordinary cases of non-disclosure the party complaining was, as he is in English law, bound to establish that the party charged had knowledge, actual or presumptive, of the undisclosed fact (g). Where it was a question of a statutory duty of disclosure, the precise terms of the enactment had to be considered in order to determine whether any, and what, knowledge on the part of the alleged delinquent was required to be proved before a breach of the duty could be said to have been established: thus, to take two illustrations, it has already been pointed out that the non-disclosure of certain redhibitory defects under the Ædilician Edict was actionable independently of the question whether the vendor knew of them, or not (h), whilst, on the other hand, actual or constructive knowledge on the part of the usurer as to the expectant's disability was apparently a necessary ingredient in the proof required to establish the statutory *exceptio* given by the S. C Macedonianum (i) Illustrations have been given of what the Roman jurists regarded as amounting to presumptive knowledge (j) in one of its various forms, as known to English law (k) With respect to another of these types of presumptive knowledge, it seems clear that Roman jurisprudence, agreeing with ours (l), as a general rule, imputed the knowledge of the agent to his principal (m).

(v) D 14 6 19 "exceptionem S. C. nulli obstare nisi qui sciret, aut scire potuisset, filiumfamilias esse eum cui credebat."
(w) D. 14 6. 3 4, D 14 6 6
(x) See § 482, note (e), *ante*.
(y) D. 14 6 12.
(z) C. 4. 28 2.
(a) C. 4 28. 4
(b) See note (e) to § 482, *ante*.
(c) D 14 6 7 pr. , D. 14. 6 7. 1.
(d) D 14.6 3 3; D 14 6.7 3
(e) D 44 1 7 1 ("etsi pro filiofamilias contra S. C. quis fidejusserit, aut pro minore vigintiquinque annis circumscripto")
(ee) D. 22 3 2
(f) C 2. 20 (or 21) 6 "dolum perspicuis insidiis probari convenit" Pothier cites the passage with "indiciis," instead of "insidiis." The former certainly makes better sense, and better Latin
(g) See § 676, note (h), *ante*, which accords with English law, as stated in Ch. III, Sect 3, Sub s (3), *ante*.
(h) See § 676, note (j), *ante*, and cp the like rules in cases of statutory disclosure in prospectuses (§ 556, *ante*)
(i) See notes (t), (u), (v), to § 685, *ante*
(j) In § 676, note (j), and § 685, notes (t), (u), (v), *ante*
(k) Viz. that which is the subject of Ch. II, Sect. 3, Sub-s (2), *ante*
(l) See Ch II, Sect 3, Sub s. (4), *ante*
(m) D 14. 4 5 pr (citing Ulpian, *Ad Edictum*, lib xxix) "procuratoris scientiam et dolum nocere debere domino neque Pomponius dubitat, nec nos dubitamus."

Sub s. (2) *As to the Affirmative Answers available to the Party Charged.*

687. Proof that the party complaining had actual knowledge of the undisclosed fact was a good answer in Roman law (*n*), as it is in our jurisprudence (*o*). So also was proof of a certain kind of presumptive knowledge, viz. that which is imputed to a vendor in the case of "objects of sense" (*p*); and herein the Roman rules substantially, though not exactly, corresponded with our own (*q*). Generally, also, the knowledge of the agent was imputed to the principal complaining of the non-disclosure (*r*), as with us (*s*) It has been said that Roman law presumed against the party complaining a knowledge of the *conditio* of the party charged (*t*) If this really was so, which does not seem quite certain, the Roman rule was certainly at variance with the English (*u*). The burden of establishing this, or any other affirmative plea was, as it is with us, on the party charged: "reus in exceptione actor est" (*uu*).

688. The rule that an express engagement to waive disclosure, inquiry, or investigation constitutes an answer to a case of concealment is a part of the Roman law on the subject (*v*), as it is of the English (*w*) And the countervailing rule of English law (*x*), that the answer is destroyed by proof of fraudulent devices for the purpose of covering up or hiding away any particular defects or risks or facts, prevailed in

(*n*) D 19 1. 1 : "non videtur esse celatus qui scit, neque certiorari debuit qui non ignoravit." This was the rule even in the case of statutory relief see § 685, note (*y*), *ante*

(*o*) See Ch IV, Sect. 4, Sub s. (3), *ante*, as to relations of confidence, and § 445, *ante*, as to bargains with "expectants." In negotiations for contracts *uberrimæ fidei*, it would seem that the burden is on the party complaining to establish his own ignorance, though very slight evidence is sufficient to shift the onus on to the shoulders of the party charged, and call upon him for affirmative evidence of the former's knowledge see Ch. III, Sect. 3, Sub-s. (5), *ante*

(*p*) D 18 1. 43 pr. (whether a slave is good-looking, or a house well-built, *palam apparet*, and must be known to the *emptor :* English law would certainly not agree as to the house, though it might as to the slave) ; D 18 1 43. 1 (sale of a slave *luminibus effossis* op. the insurance of the one eyed man in *Bawden v London, Edinburgh & Glasgow Assurance Co.*, [1892] 2 Q B 534, C A), D 21 1 1 (patent blemishes), D 21. 1. 14 (a visible scar, or blindness) On the other hand, no knowledge is imputed of the intellectual or artistic capacity of a slave to the party complaining D 18 1 43 pr., *sup.* Plato (*Legg* xi. 916, 917) draws a distinction between physical defects which would be patent and palpable to a layman, and morbid conditions or tendencies, such as epilepsy, which could only be detected by the expert eye and knowledge of a physician or trainer

(*q*) See § 39, note (ii), and § 193, *ante*

(*r*) D 21 1 51.

(*s*) See § 49, notes (*x*) and (*y*), *ante* , but the agent to whom the knowledge is sought to be imputed must be "an agent to know" · see *ibid* , note (*z*), *ante*.

(*t*) "Qui cum alio contrahit vel est, vel debet esse, non ignarus conditionis ejus." KNIGHT-BRUCE, V.-C, at p 107 of *Stikeman v Dawson* (1847), 1 De G. & Sm 90, cites this as a rule of the civilians, without giving any reference, and he appends, as a gloss on this rule appearing in the best commentaries, the following "conditio accipitur pro statu, servus sit an liber, paterfamilias an filiusfamilias Ita significat ætatem, mores, fortunam, valetudinem"

(*u*) At p 107 of *Stikeman* v. *Dawson, sup* , KNIGHT-BRUCE, V.-C., adds, after stating both the rule and the gloss cited in the last note "I am not satisfied that, as a general rule, the law of England dissents" The opinion is expressed in a halting, qualified, and negative form, it is true but it is amazing to find in the mouth of so sound and erudite a judge even the faintest suggestion or hint that the law of England imputes, or ever did impute, to a party alleging non-disclosure, knowledge of the opposite party's age, character, financial circumstances, and bodily health. The rule was not even, as stated, one of Roman law, see note (*u*) to § 685, *ante* , much less was the gloss. English law utterly repudiates it.

(*uu*) D 44. 1 1

(*v*) D 50 17 23 . "nisi si quid nominatim convenit, legem enim contractus dedit." See also the citations in note (*y*), *inf.* Such an express term was called a *pactum* Like estoppel in English law, it gave rise to no cause of action, and could only operate as a bar or *exceptio.*

(*w*) See § 202, *ante.*

(*x*) *Ibid* , notes (*k*) and (*m*), *ante.*

Roman jurisprudence also (y). Again, as in our system (z), an express contract to exclude liability for fraudulent concealment, or other fraud, was wholly inefficacious (a); and, for the same reason, an express stipulation for the general observance of good faith is declared in the Digest to be nugatory (b), just as an express contract for full disclosure in general terms is equally futile in English law (c).

Sub-s. (3). As to Relief

689. In so far as non-disclosure constituted an element in *dolus*, it was the subject of both offensive and defensive proceedings,—both an *actio* and an *exceptio* (d). The terms in which the Aquilian action was made part of the prætorian law have already been stated (e). The formula used for the purpose of raising the *exceptio doli mali* was. "Si paret Numerium Negidium Aulo Agerio . . . dare [facere] oportere, s. in eâ re nihil dolo malo Auli Agerii factum est, neque fiat, condemna. Si non paret, absolvito" (f). Redhibitory relief could be granted to a defendant setting up the *exceptio*, which means that every such plea involved a counterclaim for rescission. So, in English law, as has been pointed out (g), the party complaining has his choice between offensive and defensive proceedings, or he may add a counterclaim for rescission to his defence. Whatever was sufficient to support the action was, as in our law, sufficient to support the defence (h). In any case of statutory relief, the exact form of remedy prescribed by the express language of the *plebiscitum*, *senatus consultum*, or imperial constitution, as the case might be, was to be followed (if any remedy at all was provided, which was almost invariably the case in Roman legislation), and no other. which corresponds to one of our canons of statutory interpretation (i). To take one example, the benefit of the S. C. Macedonianum, as has been explained (j), could only be taken in the form of a defence, for the enactment, though giving the aggrieved party an *exceptio*, was silent as to any *actio*.

690. The active remedies for *dolus* consisted of rescission, the subject of an *actio redhibitoria*, and also compensation, recoverable in an *actio quanti minoris*, or *æstimatoria*, which latter form of relief is not ordinarily permissible in our law, where the case is one of mere non-disclosure (k).

691. The *actio redhibitoria* was the outcome of the Ædilician Edict (l). The rules laid down in the Digest as to redhibition, or specific restitution, in cases of sales are, first, that where it is the vendor's fault that the purchaser cannot give back what he has received the inability to restore constitutes no defence to the redhibitory action; secondly, that where neither party is in fault the like result follows; but, thirdly,

(y) D 19 1 1. 1 (where the case is put of a man who, on selling a house, declares that, so far as he knows, it is not subject to any servitude, but he wishes to protect himself by an express condition against the consequences of any servitude being afterwards discovered here, if he knows of no servitude, the condition protects him; if he does know of any, and is concealing it, the condition is no defence) See also D 19 1 6 9; D. 19 1 13 6, D. 21 1 14 9 (concealment is a good *replicatio doli mali* to an *exceptio pacti*).

(z) See § 202, note (e), *ante*

(a) D 2 14 27 3; D 13 6 17, pr.

(b) D 18 1. 68. 1; D 50. 17. 23 (where, after the sentence cited in note (v), *sup.*, the following exception to the rule is noted "excepto eo, quod Celsus putat, non valere si convenerit, ne dolus præstetur, hoc enim bonæ fidei judicio contrarium est"

(c) As to which, see Ch. III, Sect 2, Sub s. (9), *ante*.

(d) See § 672, *ante*.

(e) In § 673, *ante*.

(f) For illustrations, see D 44 4 (De Doli Mali et Metus Exceptione), *passim*

(g) See Ch. III, Sect 5, Ch IV, Sect 5, and Ch. V, Sect 5, *ante*

(h) D 44 4 2 pr "palam est autem hanc exceptionem ex eâdem causâ propositam, ex quâ causâ proposita est de dolo malo actio"

(i) See the last of the three rules mentioned in § 567, note (p), *ante*.

(j) See § 685, note (c), *ante*

(k) As stated in Sect. 5 of Chs III, IV, and V, *ante*, subject to the exceptions therein respectively mentioned.

(l) Cic *De Off* III, 16, 17, D 21. 1 See § 676, notes (l), (m), (n), *ante*, for an account of this Edict.

if it is the purchaser's fault entirely, as (for instance) if he has manumitted the slave who, or alienated the thing which, passed by the contract, there is a complete answer to proceedings of any kind. The first and third rules are the same as in English law The third rule points to what in our courts would be regarded as also a case of affirmation. The second rule is not in accordance with the English decisions (m)

692 In any action *bonæ fidei*, as distinguished from an action *stricti juris*, no *exceptio doli mali* was required, because the action itself imposed on the *judex* the duty of examining whether complete good faith had been observed on the one side, and on the other, the formula being: *quicquid dare [facere] oportere ex fide bonâ*, &c As in the case of the equitable action for money had and received, which Lord MANSFIELD is said to have introduced into our jurisprudence, the utmost latitude was permitted both to the *actor* in formulating his equitable claims, and to the *reus* in resisting them on equitable grounds The principles of *æquum et bonum* could be invoked on either side, without any special *exceptio*, or *replicatio*, and the *judex* was invested with ample authority to do what was right between the parties, entertain cross claims, order reduction of prices, strike a balance (*compensatio*, or *deductio*), and give effect to equities all round (n).

SECT 6   APPLICATIONS OF, AND REFERENCES TO, THE PRINCIPLES OF THE ROMAN LAW OF NON-DISCLOSURE AND DOLUS IN ENGLISH JUDGMENTS.

693. The references to Cicero and the Digest in the judicial deliverances of our courts on questions of non disclosure and good faith are not infrequent or unimportant. In most of these, the principles of Roman jurisprudence are appealed to in support of established rules of English law ; but, in one or two cases, they are prayed in aid of the individual judge's personal predilections in favour of an extension of those rules (o). The topics now to be considered are those in reference to which the most frequent judicial allusions are made to the views of Roman jurists

694. The definition and examples of *dolus malus* given in Cicero and the Digest, as already cited (p), are adopted, or referred to, by Lord HARDWICKE (q), Lord BROUGHAM (r), KNIGHT-BRUCE, V.-C. (s), WILLES, J (t), SHEE, J (u), and the Privy Council (v), in important judgments

(m) For the third rule, see D. 21. 1. 47 pr   For illustrations of the other two, see D 21 1, *passim*   As to these three rules in English law, see § 231, § 377, note (l), and § 488, note (e), *ante*

(n) See Just. *Instit* 4. 6. 28, with which cp the description given by Lord MANSFIELD, C.J., of the nature, fairness, and convenience of the action for money had and received, at p 1012 of *Moses* v *Macferlan* (1760), 2 Burr 1005

(o) As, for instance, those of Lord MANSFIELD, C J (observed upon by Lord ELDON, L C, in *Conolly* v *Parsons* (1797), 3 Ves 625 n.), and those of SHEE, J (see note (u), *inf*).

(p) In § 673, *ante*.

(q) In *Le Neve* v *Le Neve* (1747), Ambl. 436 (at p 445), 1 Ves 64 (at p 68), 3 Atk 646 (at p 654)   In Ambler, the spelling of the words cited is hopelessly inaccurate

(r) In *Attwood* v *Small* (1838), 6 Cl & Fin 232, 444, 445 ("dolus dans locum contractui")

(s) At p 109 of *Slikeman* v *Dawson* (1847), 1 De G & Sm 90, where the reference is given as D 4 3 12, instead of D 4 3 1 2, as it should be, and as it is in the reporter's note (4) to p 210 of the report in 16 L J (CH) 205

(t) At p 1047 of *Thompson* v *Hopper* (1858), E B & E. 1038   He there says that "it" (i e. the judgment below) "appears to me to be founded on a misapplication of the maxim, *Dolus circuitu non purgatur* 'Dolus' therein stands for *dolus malus*, and cannot mean simply anything which may lead to the damage of another indeed, some such acts constitute what has been called *dolus bonus*, and some are *danna absque injuriâ* Without entering into a discussion of the precise meaning of *dolus*, or *dolus malus*, in the civil law, I may say that if *dolus*, in the sense in which it is used in the maxim, can exist independently of evil intention, it cannot so exist without either the violation of some legal duty, independently of contract, or the breach of a contract, express or implied, between the parties "

(u) At p 496 of *Lee* v *Jones* (1864), 17 C B (N.S.) 482, Exch Ch , a suretyship case, wherein he gives a translation of D 18 1 43 2 (which the reporter incorrectly cites as D 43. 2), as to that form of *dolus* which consists in dissimulation   At p 502 he cites D 17. 1 29, as to extreme negligence being near akin to *dolus* · see note (l) to § 673, *ante*

(v) At p 382 of *Crowly* v *Bergtheil*, [1899] A C 374, P C , where it is pointed out that

695. The Ciceronian view of the distinction between innocent reticence and culpable concealment (*w*) is cited freely by both common law and equity judges, such as Lord MANSFIELD, C.J. (*x*), Lord ABINGER, C.B. (*y*), KNIGHT-BRUCE, V.-C. (*z*), SHEE, J. (*a*), CLEASBY, B. (*b*), and CHITTY, J. (*c*). It is to be noted that many of these eminent judges (*d*), and several jurists, including that extremely accurate writer, as well as judge, Sir EDWARD FRY (*e*), were content to adopt Lord MANSFIELD'S citation on trust, without checking it with the original. Had they taken this precaution, they would have discovered that the first half of the words cited by Lord MANSFIELD as forming one continuous sentence (" aliud est celare, aliud tacere ") occurs in the middle of the argument of Diogenes Babylonius, and the latter half expresses the ground of the opinion which Cicero himself delivers, much later, on the case of the *frumentarius*, in a passage which is separated by a considerable quantity of intervening disputation from the former,—" longo intervallo," and not even " proximus huic "

696. Lord CRANWORTH illustrates the English rules as to the impropriety of a trustee buying from his *cestui que trust*, or an agent from his principal (*f*), and KNIGHT BRUCE, V.-C , the like rules as to a legal adviser accepting gifts from his client (*g*), by references to the Roman law on these subjects.

697. As to the good faith which should exist between partners, TURNER, V.-C., cites the Roman doctrine (*h*).

698. The S. C Macedonianum (*i*) is referred to both by Lord HARDWICKE, L C (*j*), and by Lord THURLOW, L C (*k*), in illustration of the English law as to bargains with " expectants "

dolus malus in Roman Dutch law, which governed the case then before the Court, no less than fraud in English law, is sufficient to prevent a registered owner of land from relying on his registration

(*w*) See § 675, *ante*
(*x*) At p. 1910 of *Carter* v *Boehm* (1764), 3 Burr 1905.
(*y*) At pp 380, 381 of *Cornfoot* v *Fowke* (1840), 6 M. & W 358, where almost the entirety of *De Off* III, 12, 13—see notes to § 675, *ante*—is either cited or abstracted
(*z*) At p 571 of *Gibson* v *D'Este* (1843), 2 Y. & C 542, and again at p 221 of *Nellthorpe* v *Holgate* (1844), 1 Coll 203.
(*a*) At p 498 of *Lee* v. *Jones* (1864), 17 C B (N S) 482, Exch Ch
(*b*) At p 595 of *Harrower* v *Hutchinson* (1870), L R 5 Q B 584
(*c*) At pp 208, 209 of *Turner* v. *Green*, [1895] 2 Ch 205
(*d*) See § 675, *ante* Lord MANSFIELD, C J , in *Carter* v *Boehm*, *sup*.—see note (*x*), *sup*—was the beginner, and the error was copied, without examining the text, by SHEE, J , at p 498 of *Lee* v *Jones*, *sup*—see note (*a*) of the reporter on that page,—and by CHITTY, J , in *Turner* v *Green*, *sup*—(see the last note) In *Gibson* v *D'Este*, *sup*—see note (*z*), *sup*—KNIGHT-BRUCE, V C , makes "non quicquid . &c " follow immediately upon " aliud est celare, aliud tacere," omitting the intervening matter set out in note (*o*) to § 675, *ante*.
(*e*) In note (2) to § 713 of his *Specific Performance*
(*f*) At p 474 of *Aberdeen Railway Co* v *Blaikie Bros* (1854), 1 Macq. (H L.) 461 See Ch IV, Sect 2, Sub ss (1), (3), as to the English law The passage cited is D. 18 1. 34 7, set out in note (*g*) to § 677, *ante*
(*g*) At pp 733–736 of *Kennedy* v *Broun* (1863), 13 C B (N S) 677, where, in justice to the plaintiff's erudite and brilliant argument, he traces the whole history, with appropriate citations, of the position of the advocate in Roman jurisprudence as to remuneration and gifts . see § 680, *ante* As to the English law, see Ch V, Sect 2, Sub s (2)
(*h*) At p 523 of *Blisset* v *Daniel* (1853), 10 Hare 493 The passage cited is from *Just Instit* 3 25 4, and is set out in note (*r*) to § 677, *ante* The English rules are stated in Ch IV, Sect 2, Sub s (3)
(*i*) See § 685, *ante* For the English law on bargains with expectants, see Ch V, Sect 2, Sub s (6), *ante*.
(*j*) At pp 157, 158 of *Chesterfield* (Earl) v *Jannsen* (1751), 2 Ves Sr , 125 "the senate and law makers in Rome were not so weak as not to know that a law to restrain prodigality, to prevent a son's running in debt in the life of his father, would be vain in many cases · yet they made laws to this purpose, viz the Macedonian decree, happy, if they could in some degree prevent it est aliquod "—(sic it should be " aliquo ")—" prodire tenus "
(*k*) At p 9 of *Gwynne* v *Heaton* (1778), 1 Brown C C. 1

699. The doctrine of our law as to the knowledge which is imputable to the party complaining, so as to establish an affirmative answer to his complaint (*l*), is illustrated by references to the Digest in a judgment of KNIGHT-BRUCE, V.-C. (*m*); whilst the Roman rule according to which both the knowledge and the *dolus* of an agent is deemed to affect his principal (*n*) is cited by JERVIS, C.J. (*o*). And, in support of a personal suggestion that the English doctrine of presumptive knowledge may without undue violence be stretched so far as to impute to one of two contracting parties a knowledge of the other's *conditio* (including his status, age, character, financial position, and state of health),—a suggestion of amazing unsoundness,—KNIGHT-BRUCE, V.-C., prayed in aid the supposed opinions and dicta of certain civilians and glossators (*p*).

700. The rules, statutory and otherwise, of our jurisprudence as to the secret employment of puffers at auction sales have not been dealt with in this treatise, for the reason that they were considered to belong rather to the department of misrepresentation law (*q*). But they may also be regarded as part of the law of non-disclosure, and, in whichever light the practice in question be viewed, Cicero considered it indicative of *dolus*, and denounced it, as such, in a passage (*r*) which was the foundation of several of Lord MANSFIELD'S decisions on sales by auction (*s*), and at a later date was cited by BYLES, J., in dealing with the same question (*t*).

(*l*) See § 687, *ante*

(*m*) At p 687 of *Reynell* v. *Sprye* (1852), 1 De G M. & G 660, citing D 22 6 9 2—the passage is set out in § 40 (*sub fin*), *ante*, the phrase, however, which he also purports to quote, "qui vult decipi, decipiatur," and the similar expression, "haud decipitur qui scit se decipi," which is cited by Lord CRANWORTH, L.C, *ibid*, at p. 710, are not to be found in the part of the Digest to which the reference is given

(*n*) D 14 4 5, pr, set out in note (*m*) to § 686, *ante*

(*o*) At p. 108 of *Coleman* v *Riches* (1855), 16 C. B 104 The spelling and syntax are hopelessly inaccurate here, "procurationis" being substituted for "procuratoris," and "dominus" for "dominum"

(*p*) At p 107 of *Slakeman* v *Dawson* (1847), 1 De G & Sm. 90 See note (*t*) to § 687, *ante*.

(*q*) See § 508, note (*a*), *ante* In Ch XIII, Sect 2 of the author's *Law of Actionable Misrepresentation*, this topic is fully discussed

(*r*) *De Off* III. 15. "non illicitatorem venditor, nec qui contra se liceatur, emptor apponet"

(*s*) Lord ELDON, L.C, though agreeing with the decisions themselves, thought that some of Lord MANSFIELD's dicta, following too closely the exalted Stoical doctrines, went further than our jurisprudence would permit · see *Conolly* v. *Parsons* (1797), 3 Ves. 625 n

(*t*) At p 208 of *Green* v *Baverstock* (1863), 14 C B (N s) 204, where, however, instead of *qui contra se liceatur*, the citation is, *qui contra asse liceatur*,—which makes nonsense of the whole passage When Serj. Byles, he had previously cited the passage in his argument in *Thornett* v *Haines* (1846), 15 M. & W. 367, as "the rule of ethics laid down by Cicero," on which "this doctrine of our law is founded," and which, he adds, Lord MANSFIELD always followed

APPENDIX D.

THE SCOTTISH LAW OF NON-DISCLOSURE.

701. Scots law, in the department of non-disclosure, as in most others, follows, or at all events is in conformity with, the leading principles of Roman jurisprudence. The consequence is that, in substance (*u*), its rules as to the duty of disclosure and good faith differ very little from those of English law on such questions, for these latter also coincide in the main with, and in some instances even purport to be derived from, the doctrines of the Digest (*v*). Where any such difference exists, it will generally be found that the Scottish rule is the more logical and just (*w*). It is now proposed to compare very briefly the two systems in connection with the following topics :—(1) the duty of disclosure in negotiating for contracts *uberrimæ fidei*, (2) the duties of disclosure and good faith in relations of "confidence", (3) the like duties in relations of "influence", (4) questions of remedy and relief ; and (5) statutory duties and provisions (*x*).

SECT. 1. AS TO THE DUTY OF DISCLOSURE IN NEGOTIATIONS FOR CONTRACTS DEEMED UBERRIMÆ FIDEI.

702. The rules of English law as to the duty of disclosure in negotiations with a view to any contract or transaction falling within certain recognized classes are the

---

(*u*) See, generally, Lord Kames's *Principles of Equity*, and Bell's *Principles of the Law of Scotland*, §§ 13, 13A There are great differences, however, in terminology, since Scottish jurisprudence has always adopted a special and highly technical system of nomenclature which, though sometimes provoking the derision of unreflecting persons, presents this enormous advantage that it tends to accuracy in definition, which means precision in thought, whereas the English practice of drawing upon popular language serves only to promote confusion : see App. A, *ante*. There are also differences in the rules of pleading and practice, all of them to the advantage of the Scottish system, as to which see §§ 546, 547 in App D to the author's *Law of Actionable Misrepresentation*

(*v*) See App. C, Sect. 6, *ante*

(*w*) Lord Cockburn, not without warrant, boldly asserts, in his *Life of Lord Jeffrey*, that " with a little deduction on account of the feudality which naturally adheres to real property, it is perhaps the best and the simplest system in Europe It is deeply founded on practical reason, aided by that conjoined equity, which is equity to the world, as well as to lawyers There can be no more striking testimony to its excellence than the fact, that most of the modern improvements in English law, on matters already settled in the law of Scotland, have amounted, in substance, to unacknowledged introductions of the Scotch system." This " striking testimony " has been added to since Lord Cockburn's time For example, in the Sale of Goods Act, 1893, the legislature deliberately adopted the Scottish rules in preference to the English, where there was a discrepancy between the two, as the rules which were to govern the sale of goods in the United Kingdom. One reason of the greater logicality and simplicity of Scots jurisprudence is that, following (as it does) the Prætorian law of Rome, it has never had occasion to establish or recognize a pair of parallel and conflicting sets of rules, as in England, or to hamper themselves with such ridiculous distinctions as that, for instance, drawn so persistently in our courts at one time between " legal " and " equitable " fraud, or between " legal " and " equitable " estoppel, and the like. See the observations of Lord BROUGHAM (on certain points of difference which existed in his day) referred to in note (*g*) to § 703, *post*

(*x*) See the five Sections, respectively, of this Appendix.

subject of separate treatment in an earlier chapter of this work (y). The rules of Scottish jurisprudence are precisely the same, as has always been held by the House of Lords in every case in which the question has been argued, or in which for any other reason it was deemed necessary to express an opinion on it, whether in relation to contracts of marine or life insurance (z), contracts between vendor and purchaser (a), contracts of suretyship or, in Scottish phrase, "cautionary obligation" (b), compromises (c), or "family arrangements" (d).

Sect 2.　As to the Duties of Disclosure and Good Faith in Relations of Confidence

703. The two systems are completely at one in respect of these duties. The rules of our jurisprudence as to their nature and limits, and as to the relations which give rise to them, and the conditions under which they are deemed to continue, or to cease (e), are precisely the same rules as those which are applied in Scotland, whether examples be sought from cases of trustee and *cestui que trust* (f), of principal and agent (g), or of partnership (h).

Sect. 3.　As to the like Duties in Relations of Influence

704. Here, too, there is no difference whatever between English and Scottish jurisprudence. The same principles are applied in the same way, and to the same classes of case, and on the same theory; the duties being deemed to arise on a presumption of the existence, and the undue exercise, of influence by the dominant

(y) Ch III, *ante*

(z) As to the duty of disclosure in negotiating for marine insurance, dealt with in §§ 91–99, *ante*, see the Scotch case of *Thames and Mersey Marine Insurance Co* v. *Gunford Ship Co*, [1911] A C 529, H L   As to the like duty, in the case of life insurance (see §§ 100–102, *ante*), Lord WATSON, at p 687 of *Thomson* v *Weems* (1884), 9 App Cas 671, H L., says that the principles applicable are precisely the same in the two systems

(a) For an instance of the application of the English rules of disclosure in cases of vendor and purchaser (see Ch III, Sect 2, Sub s (3), *ante*) to a Scotch case, see *Brownlie* v *Campbell* (1880), 5 App Cas 925, H L.

(b) The English law of disclosure in negotiations for suretyship (see Ch III, Sect 2, Sub-s (4), *ante*) was applied to Scotch cases of "cautionary obligations" in *Smith* v *Bank of Scotland* (1813), 1 Dow. (App. Cas.) 272 ; 14 R R 67 , *Mactaggart* v. *Wilson* (1835), 3 Cl & Fin 525 , *Railton* v. *Mathews & Leonard* (1841), 10 Cl & Fin. 934 , *Hamilton* v *Watson* (1845), 12 Cl & Fin 109 ; *Bonar* v. *Macdonald* (1850), 3 H. L. C 226

(c) The English principles as to the duty of disclosure in negotiating compromises were applied, as laid down in Ch III, Sect 2, Sub s (5), *ante*, to the Scotch case of *Watt* v *Assets Co*, [1905] A. C 317, H L

(d) The rules of good faith in "family arrangements," discussed in §§ 135, 136, *ante*, were applied to Scotch cases in *Stewart* v *Stewart* (1839), 6 Cl & Fin. 911 (where Lord COTTENHAM, L C., after first reviewing the English cases, cites, at pp 970, 971, three Scotch cases, and passages from Lord Stair's *Institutes*, with the view of showing that Scotch law is the same as ours on this subject) , *Tennent* v *Tennent* (1870), L R. 2 H L (Sc) 6

(e) In Ch IV, *ante*

(f) See *Hamilton* v *Wright* (1842), 9 Cl & Fin 111 ; *Dougan* v *Macpherson*, [1902] A C. 197, H. L. (*per* Lord MACNAGHTEN, at p 204, and Lord SHAND, at p 205).

(g) See *Aberdeen Railway Co* v *Blaikie Bros* (1854), 1 Macq H. L. 461 (*per* Lord CRANWORTH, L C , at pp 473, 474, and Lord BROUGHAM, at pp 479, 482, 483, though the latter takes occasion in one of these passages to express his regret that English law had not up till then adopted the Scotch doctrine of *bonâ fide consumptio et receptio*, that is, that ' *fruges* bonâ fide perceptæ et consumptæ " remain the property of the actual possessor, until dispossessed, and, in the other, to lament the then divided, legal and equitable jurisdiction of the English Courts, as contrasted with their union in Scottish law,—an objection now partially removed) , *McPherson* v *Watt* (1877), 3 App Cas 254, H. L. (*per* Lord BLACKBURN, at p. 272)

(h) See *Cassels* v *Stewart* (1881), 6 App Cas 64, H L.

over the servient party, and the presumption being made in every case where, either by reason of a "suspected" relation existing between the parties, or by reason of the actual circumstances, the one party must be supposed to be in a state of subjection and inferiority, and the other in a position of predominance and ascendancy,—a relation which in Scottish terminology, reminiscent of the Roman *circumscriptio adolescentium*, is sometimes aptly termed a relation of "facility" on the one side, and "circumvention" on the other (i).

SECT. 4. AS TO RELIEF.

705. Speaking broadly, our law gives any party entitled to complain of non-disclosure two remedies, a right to rescission (and analogous or consequential relief), and a good answer to any proceedings instituted for the purpose of enforcing the impeached contract or transaction (j). And, though the terminology used is somewhat different, the like double set of remedies is placed by the law of Scotland at the disposal of the party complaining.

706. Thus, as regards offensive proceedings, a contract or transaction may be "reduced" (rescinded), and the parties "reponed" to their former position (mutual restoration *in specie*), where such contract is voidable, whether on the ground of non-disclosure (k), or misrepresentation (l), or for any other reason. Further, in a proper case, the aggrieved party may sue for "repetition" (m), which answers to our action for money had and received, and also to the Roman *conductio indebiti* (n), or he may obtain an order for an account (o)

707. Defensive relief against an impeachable contract is also available to an aggrieved party in Scots law under precisely the same conditions as it is in our courts, whether the ground on which the contract is impeached be non-disclosure (p), or misrepresentation (q), or otherwise, and whether the party complaining adds, or does not add, to his defence a cross claim for "reduction."

708. It not infrequently happens in Scots procedure that two cross actions are raised, or cross claims are made, by the opposing parties : the one seeking to enforce a contract, and the other claiming "reduction" of the contract so sought to be enforced, or "suspension" (stay) of the first action In such cases, whether the ground on which the "reduction," or the "suspension," is sought be non-disclosure (r),

(i) Bell's *Principles of the Law of Scotland*, vol i, § 13A The "influence" cases are the subject of Ch V, *ante*. The cases dealt with in Sect 2, Sub-ss (5) and (6), of that Chapter are termed in Scotch law, cases of "facility and circumvention"

(j) See Sect 5 of Chs. III, IV, and V, respectively

(k) In the following non-disclosure cases "reduction" was the subject of the action, or cross claim *Stewart v Stewart* (1839), 6 Cl. & Fin. 911 ; *Railton v Mathews & Leonard* (1841), 10 Cl. & Fin 934 , *Hamilton v Wright* (1842), 9 Cl & Fin. 111 (cross-claim) , *Tennent v Tennent* (1870), L R 2 H. L. (Sc) 6 , *Watt v Assets Co.*, [1905] A C. 307, H. L

(l) Such as *Burnes v. Pennell* (1849), 2 H L C 497 ; *Davidson v. Tulloch* (1860), 3 Macq H L. 783 ; *Tennent v City of Glasgow Bank* (1874), 4 App Cas 615, H. L ; *Stewart v Kennedy* (1890), 15 App Cas 108, H. L. , *Edinburgh United Breweries, Ltd v Molleson*, [1894] A. C. 96, H L ; *Life & Health Assurance Co v Yule* (1904), 6 F 437 ; *Ferguson v Wilson* (1904), 6 F 779 ; *Gamage (A. W.), Ltd. v Charlesworth*, [1910] S C 257

(m) As in *Brownlie v Campbell* (1880), 5 App Cas. 925, H L

(n) Bell's *Principles of the Law of Scotland*, §§ 531–535

(o) As in *Cassels v Stewart* (1881), 6 App Cas 64, H L

(p) For illustrations, see *Smith v. Bank of Scotland* (1813), 1 Dow (App. Cas.) 272 , *Hamilton v Wright* (1842), 9 Cl. & Fin. 111 (with a cross-claim for reduction) , *Aberdeen Railway Co v Blaikie Bros* (1854), 1 Macq H L. 460 , *Thomson v. Weems* (1884), 9 App Cas 671, H. L , *Thames & Mersey Marine Insurance Co v Gunford Ship Co* , [1911] A C 539, H L

(q) See the cases cited in note (s), *inf* , and *National Exchange Co. of Glasgow v Drew* (1855), 2 Macq H. L 103

(r) As in *Smith v Bank of Scotland*, *sup* (claim for "reduction" on one side, and for "suspension" on the other) , *Hamilton v. Watson* (1845), 12 Cl. & Fin 109 (the like) ; *McPherson v Watt* (1877), 3 App. Cas 254, H L (action for "reduction" heard together with action on the other side claiming the "implementing" of the contract) or misrepresentation (s), the actions or claims are "conjoined," and heard together as parts of one entire proceeding.

709. It has been shown that delay, unless amounting to affirmation, or some other recognized head of defence, is of itself no bar to relief in our courts (t). It is the same with the Scots "mora" (u).

SECT. 5. AS TO STATUTORY DUTIES AND PROVISIONS.

710. A special chapter has been devoted to the statutes and enactments affecting (whether by way of codification, or amendment) the English common law of disclosure (v). Most of these statutes, with such variations as may be prescribed, apply to Scotland. For example, the Companies (Consolidation) Act, 1908 (8 Edw. 7, c 69), subject to certain adaptative provisions (w), is part of the Scottish statutory law (x): and so also is the Marine Insurance Act, 1906 (6 Edw. 7, c 41), the effect of which is wholly declaratory and codifying (y). On the other hand, the Vendor and Purchaser Act, 1874 (37 & 38 Vict., c 78), does not apply to Scotland (z). The Sale of Land by Auction Act, 1867 (30 & 31 Vict c. 48), is expressed not to extend to Scotland (see s. 9), but this was because Scots law, following the Roman, was already in the condition in which the statute provided that it should thereafter be for England and Ireland (a). Scotland has its own statute law on such matters as the limitation of actions (b), registration of titles to land (c), and others of the like more or less domestic character

(s) As in *Sibbald* v. *Hill* (1814), 2 Dow. (App. Cas) 273 , *Burnes* v *Pennell* (1849), 2 H L. C 497.

(t) See §§ 217, 218, *ante.*

(u) See *Watt* v. *Assets Co* , [1905] A C. 317, H. L (*per* Lord DAVEY, at p 334).

(v) Ch. VI, *ante.*

(w) See § 616, notes (z) and (l), *ante.*

(x) Such as *Glasgow Pavilion, Ltd.* v *Motherwell* (1903), 6 F. 116, cited in note (j) to § 570, *ante , Sleigh* v. *Glasgow and Transvaal Options, Ltd.* (1904), 6 F. 420, cited in note (n) to § 545, *ante.*

(y) See *Thames & Mersey Marine Insurance Co.* v. *Gunford Ship Co* , [1911] A C 539, H. L.

(z) See s. 10 of the Act   And, generally, as to this statute, see § 251, *ante.*

(a) Bell's *Principles of the Law of Scotland*, §§ 130–132   See, as to this Act, Ch XIII, Sect. 2, of the author's *Law of Actionable Misrepresentation,* to which subject it more properly belongs than to the law of non-disclosure

(b) Bell's *Principles*, §§ 589–604

(c) *Gordon-Cumming* v *Houldsworth,* [1910] A C 537, H L., was concerned with the Scottish "Register of Sasines." In this case it was observed by Lord SHAW, at p. 555, that "the system of registration of title in Scotland   . was substantially perfected in the seventeenth century, beginning particularly with the Act of 1617, c. 16."

INDEX.

ABANDONMENT,

of supposed rights, good consideration for compromise, 108

of right to relief, when conduct of party amounts to, 194

of contract by one party, gives the other a right to sue for money had and received, without rescission, 212

offer of, when given effect to at the trial, 451, 452

of contract, when not affecting the duty to disclose the abandoned contract in a prospectus, 493

ABATEMENT,

of price, agreement to accept in lieu of rescission, 181—184

waiver of, as well as of right to rescission, 184, 185

specific performance with, 216

ABNORMAL. *See* UNUSUAL.

ABRIDGED, prospectus, when subject of statutory duty of disclosure, 476

ABSTENTION, from inquiry, when raising a presumption of knowledge, 41—47

ABUSE,

of confidence. *See* CONFIDENCE.

of influence. *See* INFLUENCE.

of voting power in a company, 356, 357

ACCEPTANCE,

of offer to waive, necessary to sustain plea of waiver, 181

of negotiable instrument, affected by fraud, rules as to, 246

ACCESS,

of light, deed acknowledging absence of right to, need not be disclosed, 83

of servient party to natural protectors, where dominant party prevents, 398, 400

ACCESSIBLE TO PUBLIC,

documents, registration or entries in *See* PUBLIC DOCUMENTS.

ACCIDENT,

personal, as subject of insurance, 74. *And see* LIFE AND HEALTH INSURANCE.

to property, as subject of insurance, and duty of disclosure in negotiation therefor, 74, 75

to ship, as subject of marine insurance, 64, 65

vendor's non-disclosure merely by, protected by waiver clause or condition, 177—179, 182, 183

omission in prospectus by honest, subject of statutory defence, 500, 501

ACCOUNTANT,

when not " officer " of company, for purposes of misfeasance, 543

[1]

Index.

ACCOUNT,
    guarantees of, what duty of disclosure in negotiations for, 90, 91
    disclosure, and explanation of, in partnership cases, 110, 111
                        in "influence" cases, 435, 436
    directions for taking, as incident to rescission, 210
                       as to value where undervalue alleged, 462
    right of party complaining to, in "confidence" cases, 341—346
         servient party to, in "influence" cases, 457
    rules as to costs of taking, in "expectant" cases, 550

ACCURATE,
    information in fact received is material to be disclosed, whether accurate, or not, 13, 14
    opinion in fact given, or entertained,—the like, 15
    in sense of exact. *See* EXACT.

ACQUIESCENCE,
    amounting to affirmation, a good plea, 194
                    of party charged in the other party's dealing with property, may destroy the validity of a plea of impossibility to restore *in specie*, 203
ACT,
    when knowledge of agent for purposes of single act in a transaction is, and when it is not, deemed the knowledge of the principal, 35
    of mind or will, servient party incapable of, cannot confirm a transaction, 448

ACTS AND CONDUCT. *See* CONDUCT.

ACT OF PARLIAMENT. *See* STATUTE.

ACTING UPON,
    independent advice, not necessary for dominant party to show that there was any, on part of servient party, in order to sustain the transaction, 443
    acceptance of offer of waiver by, 181

ACTION,
    when, and what form of, is the proper proceeding to obtain relief in cases of non-disclosure. *See* RELIEF.
    when will lie. *See* ACTIONABLE.
    causes of. *See* CAUSE OF ACTION.
    chose in. *See* CHOSE IN ACTION.

ACTIONABLE,
    when non-disclosure, and other breaches of fiduciary duty, are, in—
        negotiations for certain contracts, 60—119   *And see* NEGOTIATION.
        relations of confidence, 279—306.   *And see* CONFIDENCE.
        relations of influence, 369—412   *And see* INFLUENCE.
        prospectuses of companies, 468—489.   *And see* PROSPECTUS.
        cases of concealment from the Court, 509—517
                     the State, 517—521
                     third persons, 521—523
                     creditors, 523—531
        cases where, though no duty of disclosure in first instance, a duty is created by the special circumstances of the case, such as—
            pre-existing or incidental fraud, 120—123
            supervening circumstances, 123—130
            question asked, and answer given, 131—134
    when non-disclosure is not, in—
        negotiations for contracts of certain kinds, 134—144
        relations of confidence, 306—313

[2]

INDEX.

[3]

INDEX.

INDEX.

[7]

INDEX.

ASSIGNMENT,
  of lease, duty of disclosure on intending assignee in negotiation for, 81
  of specific property, carries with it equity to avoid for non-disclosure, but assignment of naked right to avoid is invalid, as maintenance, and may be champertous, 241, 242, 356
  of claims to money, right of parties in respect of, accordingly as the money is unspecific, or is an earmarked and traceable fraud, 242, 356
  misfeasance claims may be subject of, 242
  right of parties on assignment of securities, accordingly as they are non-negotiable, or negotiable, 245, 246
  of property in possession, effect of, is that assignee takes free from equity to avoid the contract for non-disclosure, not having been already avoided, 246, 247, 360, 361, 466,—
  unless party complaining can establish that party charged took as volunteer, or with notice, or in bad faith, or is estopped, 247, 248, 360, 361, 466
  no duty on creator of security of which there has been an, to disclose to assignee collateral equities, except under certain conditions, 143
  of property on insolvency *See* INSOLVENCY.

ASSOCIATION,
  articles of. *See* ARTICLES OF ASSOCIATION
  memorandum of. *See* MEMORANDUM OF ASSOCIATION

ASSURANCE, ASSURED *See* INSURANCE, MARINE INSURANCE, LIFE INSURANCE, FIRE INSURANCE

ATTENDANT,
  medical, name and attendance of, when material to be disclosed, in life insurance, 73
  relation between medical, and patient, is one of the recognized relations of "influence" *See* MEDICAL RELATION

ATTORNEY,
  in fact. *See* AGENCY.
  in law. *See* SOLICITOR

ATTORNEY-GENERAL,
  position of, in cases of concealment from Crown, 518, 519

AUCTION,
  sales by, subject to duty of disclosure, 79
  Lord Eldon's practice as to putting up property again for sale by, where first sale avoided, 339—341
  misfeasance claims may be sold by, 242

AUDITOR,
  of company, knowledge of, as such, does not affect company, 31, 32
  names of, to be disclosed in prospectus, 483
  when "officer" of company, for purposes of misfeasance, 543

AUTHORITY (IN SENSE OF MANDATE). *See* AGENCY.

AUTHORITY (IN SENSE OF PUBLIC OR LOCAL OFFICER OR BODY),
  concealment from, 517—521
  orders of, in respect of land, when to be disclosed, 82

AVOIDANCE,
  of contract or transaction by party. *See* ELECTION, and VOIDABLE
  court. *See* RESCISSION.
  of judgments, 509—517
  of grants by Crown or State, 517—521
  where right of, has not been exercised, assignee takes free from equity to rescind, 246, 247
  right of, dominant party must explain to servient, 437

[10]

INDEX.

BOARD,

of directors of company, knowledge of, sitting as board, is imputed to company, but not knowledge of individual director, &c., 32

duty of promoter to disclose dependency of board of directors of company on himself, 202, 203, 355, 356

BODY,

general, of shareholders, what disclosure promoter must make to, 293, 294

general, of creditors, what disclosure favoured creditor must make to, 523—531

BONA FIDES,

generally. *See* GOOD FAITH.

Roman law as to, 601—605

BONUS,

agent must disclose to principal the receipt or promise of, by third person, 299—302

BOOKS,

of partnership, when to be disclosed, 110, 111

accessible to public. *See* PUBLIC DOCUMENTS.

generally. *See* DOCUMENTS.

BORROWER *See* MONEYLENDER.

BREACH,

of duty of disclosure, when actionable. *See* ACTIONABLE.

of promise of marriage, when non-disclosure justifies, 113—116

of implied contract to perform trust, non-disclosure may be regarded as, and in that character is subject of proof or claim in insolvency, 351

of trust, act or omission must be in nature of, in order to constitute "misfeasance" in company cases, 542

BRIBE,

receipt of, from third person, must be disclosed by agent, &c , to principal, &c , 299—302

of directors of company by promoter, must not be kept secret from company, 291—294, 302—304

directors who receive, jointly and severally liable for the whole amount of, in ordinary cases, 359

BROKER,

in stocks and shares. *See* STOCKBROKER.

in insurance, ordinarily owes duty to his own principal, not to the other negotiating party, 309

in marine insurance *See* MARINE INSURANCE.

BROTHER,

may be in *loco parentis* to brother, and so within the parental relation of influence, 373 *And see* PARENTAL RELATION.

BURDEN OF ALLEGATION AND PROOF:

(A) *On Party Complaining of Non-Disclosure, &c —*

1. in negotiations for contracts *uberrimæ fidei*, to establish (i) duty and materiality, (ii) existence or occurrence of undisclosed fact, (iii) non-disclosure, (iv) knowledge of party charged, and (v) his own ignorance, 151—170,—

    but not to establish personal fraud, actual inducement, or loss, 170—183, 195

2 in relations of confidence, to establish (i) existence of relation at material date, (ii) the undisclosed transaction or fact, 314—319,—

    but not to establish personal fraud, or loss, 321—326

INDEX.

CONFIDENCE—*continued.*
relations of :—
     general description of, and statement as to duties in, 273—278
     distinguished from relations between negotiating parties for certain contracts, 272
     distinguished from relations of influence, 272, 273, 362, 363
     duties of disclosure, in two senses of the word, and of giving disinterested advice and fair value, and of not disguising identity, where dealing direct, in, 273, 274
     rules as to, applied to three species of. *See* TRUSTEE, PROMOTER, and AGENCY (B), respectively.
     what are not, 306—313
     burden of proof on party complaining in, 314—319
     affirmative answers available to party charged in, 326—336
     relief and remedy in proceedings for breaches of duty in, 338—352
     questions of law and fact in proceedings as to, 352, 353
     parties in such proceedings, 353—361
  laxity in use of the term, and, generally, of the language employed in discussing relations of, 111, 112, 557
  ethical views as to duties involved in, as compared with juridical, 580—584
  Roman law as to relations of, 606, 607
  Scots law as to relations of, 618

CONFIRMATION. *See* AFFIRMATION (CONFIRMATION).

CONSCIENTIOUS,
  use of confidence or influence must be proved, in order to sustain impeached transaction. *See* PROPRIETY OF TRANSACTION
  motives of party charged, when irrelevant, *See* MOTIVE.

CONSCIOUSNESS,
  of materiality, shown by conduct of parties, when relevant, 17—19
  of illegality of insurance by insurer, the assured being unconscious thereof, renders premium returnable . but where consciousness of illegality on both sides, or want of it on both sides, premium not returnable, 205
  of violation of duty, need not be proved by party complaining, but only the fact of non-disclosure or other breach, 170, 171, 321—323, 424, 425
  of impropriety of transaction shown by false recitals, statements, &c., 398, 420, 437
  absurdity of application of term, to " fraud," 557

CONSENT,
  of creditor required to vary contract between him and surety, 95, 96
  absence of real, must be proved to annul marriage, 117
  of party complaining to waiver must be shown, 181
  of infants, only to be obtained through the Court, 328
  of principal, to receipt of commission by agent, must strictly be shown, but usually inferred from disclosure or knowledge, 331
  of ancestor, in " expectant " cases, when a good answer to claim by expectant, 412, 449
  orders by, when set aside for non-disclosure, 510, 511
  when " silence gives," and when not, 121, 127, note (*t*), 331

CONSIDERATION,
  valuable. *See* VALUE.
  for compromise, abandonment of uncertain rights, 108
  false statement of, by party charged, important in considering the propriety of the transaction impeached, 398
  for shares paid otherwise than in cash, to be disclosed in prospectus of a company, 479

Index.

CONTRACT—*continued.*

voidable, not void, for non disclosure, 197—199, 204, 205, 338, 369, 454

sought to be rescinded, must be shewn to be subsisting, and not void, or illegal, or something more than contract, 199—201

difficulties in executing engineering, need not be disclosed, 141

by which relation of confidence created, must be proved, 314—317

now, "shaking off" relation, proof of, may be affirmative defence, 327, 328

but, in case of infants, such contract must be sanctioned by Court, 328

with agent of party complaining, relief against third person who has entered into, for commission or profit, 318, 340

by debtor with favoured creditor, must be disclosed to other creditors, 523—531

implied, to perform obligations of trust, in cases of non-disclosure, results in claim being subject of proof in insolvency, 351, 352, 489

election to adhere to, or avoid. *See* Election.

affirmation, or confirmation, of impeachable *See* Affirmation.

rescission of impeachable, conditions of, and rules as to *See* Rescission.

expenses under, but not those arising out of, may be subject of indemnity, in relief against non-disclosure, 210

non disclosure as defence to proceedings for enforcement of *See* Defensive Proceedings.

CONTRIBUTION, none between tortfeasors, whether statutory or not, 488

CONTRIBUTORIES IN LIQUIDATION OF COMPANY,

liquidator may settle a director who has received his qualification from promoter on list of, 351, 352, 541

rights of, against a "misfeasant," 541

CONVENT, gifts to, when invalidated, 385 *And see* Sacerdotal Relation.

CONVEYANCE,

contract completed by, when not subject of rescission, 201, 202

may be rescinded where fraud or substantial error, 201, 202

will be set aside in cases of influence as a rule, 457, 458

of specific property, carries with it equity to avoid, 241, 242

CONVEYANCER,

certificated, may be deemed within the relation of legal adviser and client, 379

of Court, is in same position as conveyancing counsel of vendor in ordinary case, for purpose of duties of disclosure, 222

CONVEYANCING LAW,

rules of presumptive knowledge in, 48

"sub-purchaser" according to, is a "sub-purchaser" for the purpose of certain matters required by statute to be disclosed in prospectuses, 479, 480

CONVICTION,

personal, of licence-holder, not a matter of title requiring disclosure by vendor to purchaser, 83

CORRECTION,

of opposite party's mistake, when required to be made, as part of the duty of disclosure, and when not, 125—130, 134—143

CORRUPTION,

of agent by third person. *See* Commission and Profit

relief in respect of, 348, 349. *And see* Relief (B).

legislation against, 467, 583

parties engaged in, jointly and severally liable, 359

[23]

COSTS,

of investigating title, when part of relief in vendor and purchaser cases, 211, 221

undue influence of solicitor may be relieved against in proceedings for taxation of, 459

special orders as to, jurisdiction to make, unless no materials on which discretion can be exercised, 545, 546, 551

unnecessary and unproved charges of fraud visited with punitive orders as to, of various kinds, 545, 546

where no legal duty of disclosure, conduct of successful party may justify order depriving him of, or otherwise affecting him in the matter of, 144, 323, 516, 547, 550

refusal or withholding of reasonable explanation may affect successful party's right to, 546, 547

where party guilty of non disclosure, and only succeeds by supervening, or accidental, circumstances, adverse order as to, may be made, 547

mode of dealing with offers before action, how affecting the, 547, 548, 550, 551

delay, as affecting, 548

of formal parties, how dealt with, 548, 549

when solicitor-defendant, though escaping judgment, made to guarantee his co defendant's, 549

special code of rules, and various forms of order, made as to, in cases of bargains with " expectants," 550, 551

effect of illegality on, when point raised by Court, and not by the parties, 548

may be affected, where party resorts to action instead of summary procedure authorized by statute or rules of Court, 515

of amendment, or adjournment, where new case of non-disclosure raised at the trial for the first time, 536

solicitor not entitled to receive profit costs, without disclosure to client to whom he stands in another fiduciary relation, 300, 302

COUNSEL,

within the relation of legal adviser and client, 379

opinion of, when material to be disclosed, 15

does not support the statutory plea of " mistake in fact," in cases of non-disclosure in prospectuses, 501

actual knowledge of, when presumptive knowledge of client, 48

conveyancing, of Court, regarded as counsel of the vendor, in sales under direction of the Court, for purposes of duty of disclosure, 222

COUNTERCLAIM,

for rescission, on the ground of non-disclosure, &c , 207

for money had and received, on like grounds, 212, 213

non-disclosure may be set-up as reply to, 214

COUNTY COURT, jurisdiction of, in proceedings for non-disclosure, &c , 533

COURSE,

and execution of agency. *See* AGENCY.

ordinary, of business, or events. *See* ORDINARY

holder in due. *See* NEGOTIABLE INSTRUMENT, CHOSE IN POSSESSION.

COURT,

sales by order of, subject to same rules of disclosure as other sales, though relief is given in a different form, 221, 222, 510, 511

can alone give consent for, or sanction contract with, infants, 328

relief against judgments obtained by concealment from *See* JUDGMENT.

jurisdiction of various kinds of, in non-disclosure cases, 532—534

COVENANT,

presumptive knowledge of usual, in head lease, or documents of title, and no duty therefore to disclose, 39, 40, 67

INDEX.

DILIGENCE,
"in ignorance," effect of, on presumptive knowledge, 38, 30, 502
want of. *See* NEGLIGENCE.

DIRECT,
notice, is "actual" knowledge. *See* KNOWLEDGE (A).
enforcement of contract, non disclosure is good defence to action for, 214
transactions between parties related to one another by a relation of confidence.
See CONFIDENCE.

DIRECTION,
of court, kinds of, ancillary to rescission, 210
in case of "influence" relations, 456, 457
rules by, of court, some rules of disclosure apply to, as to other cases of sale,
221—223, 510, 511

DIRECTOR OF A COMPANY,
presumptive knowledge of company through actual knowledge of, when acting
officially, but not otherwise, 32
stranger not presumed to be aware of absence of authority of board of directors
to do acts on behalf of company, when, 46
when disclosure to, or knowledge of, directors is not disclosure to, or knowledge
of, company, 293, 335
no duty of disclosure owed by an individual director to a stranger, or even to an
individual shareholder, when negotiating with him a sale or purchase of shares,
except that which lies on any other vendor or purchaser, 138, 139, 140, 308,
356
when pleas of payment, and set-off, are not available to a delinquent, 326
waiver of disclosure by, in articles of association, 333, 334
when liability of directors for non-disclosure is joint and several, and when
several only, 359
liability of, for statutory non-disclosure in prospectuses, 486—488   *And see*
PROSPECTUSES.
when liable in misfeasance proceedings, 541—544
described as "fiduciary agent," "commercial trustee," or "managing partner,"
295
duties of disclosure incumbent on, as to certain classes of material facts, 302—304
person exercising duties of, liable as a, whether so called or not, 484

DIRECTOR (SPIRITUAL). *See* SACERDOTAL RELATION.

DISABILITY,
transmission of rights on disability of party entitled, or charged. *See* TRANS-
MISSION
of parties related by relations of confidence and influence from dealing with one
another directly, except under certain conditions. *See* CONFIDENCE and
INFLUENCE
by reason of infancy, coverture, &c, need not be disclosed, but must not be
misrepresented, 142
persons under, can only consent to termination of relation, or to waiver, with
sanction of court, 328
the like, as to affirmation of an impeached transaction, 335, 447
unless termination of, be established, it is of no use for purposes of affirmative
plea, to prove mere termination of the relation, whether of confidence or of
influence, 328, 429—431

DISAFFIRM. *See* ELECTION and VOIDABLE.

DISCHARGE,
of surety, from contract, 95, 96.   *And see* SURETY.

[30]

INDEX.

DISCHARGE—*continued.*

    delay of guarantor who reasonably thinks that there has been a discharge of the suretyship he has assumed as a servient party, is excusable, and is not evidence of affirmation, 450

    of warranty, proved or admitted, does not necessarily negative or excuse the duty of disclosure, 146

    of purchaser from contract, in sales by order of court, where non disclosure proved, 221, 222

    of burden of proof. *See* BURDEN OF ALLEGATION AND PROOF.

    of duties of disclosure, &c. *See* DUTY.

DISCIPLE,

    relation between, and spiritual director, religious order, conventual establishment, &c. *See* SACERDOTAL RELATION.

DISCLOSURE,

    must be exact, complete, and unambiguous, 7—12

    duty of, as regards facts material to be disclosed (but no others) in—

        negotiations for certain contracts *uberrimæ fidei*, 61—119

        relations of confidence, 270—306

        relations of influence, 372—412

        prospectuses of companies (statutory duty), 408—489

        obtaining judgments, English or foreign, 509—517

        applying for grants from Crown or State, 517, 518

        in transactions involving rights of third persons, 521—523

        in composition arrangements with creditors, 523—531

        in circumstances creating duty of, though none originally owing, 120—134

        in transactions where full disclosure is expressly contracted for, 144—149

    facts which are respectively deemed the proper subject of, in the above relations and circumstances. *See* MATERIALITY (C).

    where no duty of, in—

        negotiations for certain classes of contract, 134—144

        relations of confidence, 306—313

        relations of influence, 412—417

    question of, whether or not, is question of fact, if any evidence, 232, 233, 353

    ethical views as to duty of, 573—600

    Roman law as to, 601—616

    Scots law as to, 617—620

DISCOUNT,

    receipt of, or stipulation for, to be disclosed by agent to principal, 300

    when principal deemed to have presumptive knowledge of custom to allow agent, in the particular class of business, 26

DISCOVERY (IN THE ORDINARY SENSE),

    of all facts and documents to which actually known facts and documents would have led, if reasonable inquiries, is deemed to have been in fact acquired, 38—47

    of falsity of representation when made, or of facts supervening which render it false, raises a duty of disclosure on the party, 120—130

    of undisclosed fact, no affirmation until, 185, 186, 334, 335, 417

DISCOVERY (IN THE PROFESSIONAL SENSE),

    same duty of, in an action, as of disclosure in the relation or circumstances which gave rise to it, 534, 535

    must be full and exact, and generally required to be given before the party complaining furnishes particulars, 534—537

    special practice as to, in cases of marine insurance, 537, 538

DISCREPANCY. *See* DIFFERENCE

[31]

DISCRETION,

of court, as to granting or refusing specific performance, with or without conditions, consequences of, 215, 216

exercise of judicial, as to whether action should be ordered instead of summary procedure authorized by statute or practice, in—

    cases under the Vendor and Purchaser Act, 221

    motions to discharge purchaser from purchase on sale ordered by Court, 222

    misfeasance cases, 541

    application to set aside judgments, 515

of court, as to costs, how exercised   *See* COSTS.

DISEASE,

bodily or mental, when to be disclosed in negotiating contract to marry, and when not, 115

when material to be disclosed in negotiation for contracts of life and health insurance, 72, 73   *And see* LIFE INSURANCE

relation between person affected with, and medical adviser or attendant. *See* MEDICAL RELATION.

taking advantage of servient party's, by dominant party, one of the " circumstances and conditions " creating a relation of influence, 393

mental, in sense of lunacy. *See* LUNACY.

DISGUISE,

of identity, is breach of duty in trustee, agent, or partner dealing directly with the *cestui que trust*, principal, or firm, under other names, or through nominee, &c , 280, 290, 295, 296

burden on party complaining to prove the above, 318

DISHONESTY,

no presumptive knowledge of customs and practices characterized by, 269, 332

of person whose fidelity is guaranteed, known to person to whom guarantee is given, or even suspicion thereof, must be disclosed to surety, 91—93

of one whose credit or overdraft merely is guaranteed, need not be disclosed to surety, 91

in conduct of inquiry pursuant to writ of *ad quod damnum*, negatives presumption otherwise made of Crown's knowledge of inconsistent grant, 521

in sense of " fraud," generally. *See* FRAUD.

DISINTERESTED,

advice, opinion, and judgment, when duty to give   *See* ADVICE, and INDEPENDENT AND COMPETENT ADVICE.

DISPUTE,

negotiations for settlement of. *See* COMPROMISE.

DISQUALIFICATION,

of directors, power of, reserved to promoter, a device for the corruption of the company's executive, 303.   *And see* DIRECTOR OF COMPANY.

DISTINCT. *See* SEPARATE.

DISTRESS,

financial, when party negotiating not bound to disclose his own, 142

    of grantor of annuity being sold, not material to be disclosed to the purchaser, 83

    not material to be disclosed in negotiations for marriage, 113

    need not be disclosed in negotiations for guarantees of cash credit, 90, 91

of servient party, and taking advantage thereof by dominant party, are circumstances creating a relation from which undue influence will be presumed, 392—397

of " expectant," taking advantage of, in cases of unconscionable bargains. *See* EXPECTANT.

INDEX.

DIVIDEND,
secret bargain of debtor to give or secure larger, to a favoured creditor than to the others, will be relieved against, 525

DOCTOR. *See* MEDICAL RELATION.

DOCTRINE,
ignorance of equitable, as to disclosure, is no answer to charge of having in fact contravened it, 170, 321, 322, 424, 425

DOCUMENT,
when presumptive knowledge of form and contents and clauses of a mercantile, and when not, 25—27
when knowledge of existence and contents of one, is presumed from proved knowledge of existence and contents of another, and when not, 38—47
fundamental, of company (memorandum and articles of association), statutory irrebuttable presumption that every member is acquainted with contents of, 45, 46
accessible to public, when every member of public presumed to know contents of, in case of—
    books and registers of a company, 46
    enrolments of grants, 520
    registers of title, and other public documents, 52—55
of title   *See* TITLE
ship's documents, rules as to production of, in marine insurance cases, 537, 538
entry in public, may justify rescission of contract which is not voidable, but already void, 200
condition in prospectus purporting to affect party with notice of any undisclosed, is made void by statute, 499, 500

DOLUS, in Roman law, 601—605

DOMESTIC RELATIONS,
raising a presumption of influence. *See* PARENTAL RELATION
from which no influence is presumed (husband and wife, &c), 412—414

DOMINANT, DOMINATION, DOMINION,
meaning of expression " dominant party," as used in this work, 362
relations raising a presumption of domination or dominion of one party over the other. *See* INFLUENCE.

DONATION, DONOR, DONEE. *See* GIFT.

DORMANT,
partner, duty of disclosure to, when, 110, 111
relation, no answer to case of servient party, if the influence springing from it was not, at the time of the transaction, 429—431

DOUBLE INSURANCE,
may be material to be disclosed in negotiations for marine insurance, 66

DUE,
course, holder in   *See* NEGOTIABLE INSTRUMENT, CHOSE IN ACTION, and CHOSE IN POSSESSION.
use of confidence, or influence   *See* PROPRIETY OF TRANSACTION.

DURATION,
of life, what facts affecting, must be disclosed in negotiations for life insurance, 72, 73
generally. *See* TIME

[33]

INDEX.

EFFECT—*continued.*

statutory non disclosure and damage must be proved to have been connected with one another as cause and, 496, 497

and intention, ethical and juridical views compared as to the relative importance of, 508

ELECTION,

to avoid transaction for non disclosure, or to affirm it, is the right of the party complaining, but, when once exercised, is exhausted, 185, 199

what is not an exercise, but a suspension of the right of, 186, 189, 190

delay in exercising right of, not *per se* a bar to rescission, 189—194

party complaining has right of, between rescission and account, as against agent, 341, 342

right of, either to take the thing itself which has been corruptly received by agent, or its value, 344—346

liquidator of company entitled to relief has right of, between three remedies, action, putting party charged on list of contributories, and misfeasance proceedings, 351, 352

duty on surviving partner to disclose facts to executor of deceased partner to enable him to exercise his right of, whether to be treated as a partner, or to take interest on his capital, 111

EMANCIPATION,

of servient party must be proved, to support the dominant party's plea of cesser of relation at time of transaction by agreement, 428, 429

the like, to support a plea of confirmation, 447, 448

whether or not, is a question of fact, 462

EMBARRASSMENT, financial. *See* DISTRESS.

EMPLOYMENT,

guarantee of fidelity of servant, clerk, or officer in, rules as to duty of disclosure by employer to surety, in negotiations for, 91—93

of a person standing in relation of confidence or influence to another, may result in the employer, if he knows of the relation, coming under the same duties to that other, 357, 358, 465

where there was no, of dominant party in the particular transaction, effect of, on affirmative plea that influence inoperative *in hâc re*, 428

mere absence of actual, at the moment of the impeached transaction, not necessarily evidence of cessation of the relation, much less of the influence, 430

of solicitor to carry out that which has been pre-determined, is not the procurement of independent advice, 442

ENACTMENT. *See* STATUTORY.

ENGAGEMENT,

of marriage, duties of disclosure in negotiation for, 112—116

previous, which was broken off, need not be disclosed in negotiations for marriage, 113

of honour, need not be disclosed in prospectus, 492

of interest in formation of company, renders any person so engaged or interested liable to statutory duty of disclosure in prospectus, 486, 487

ENTIRETY,

of material facts to be disclosed, 7—11

transaction impeached must be set aside in its, if set aside at all, subject to certain exceptions, 206, 339, 454, 455, 518

of bribes received by directors, when each is jointly and severally accountable to company for, and when not, 359

INDEX.

EQUIVOCAL,

disclosure, is no disclosure at all, and may be worse than none, 11, 12

language or conduct, may create duty of disclosure, though none originally, 124—126

not evidence of affirmation, 186

does not support plea of waiver, 333, 334

admission or offer, ineffectual in reduction of damages, 504

ERROR. *See* MISTAKE.

ESTATE,

no presumptive knowledge of law affecting title to particular, 23

duty of disclosure in negotiations for contracts of sale and purchase of, in land. *See* VENDOR (A).

arrangements for settling family. *See* FAMILY ARRANGEMENT.

preservation of family, said to be one of the objects of the equitable doctrine as to bargains with "expectants," 400, 401

grant of, by Crown, when impeachable for non disclosure, 517—521

rights and liabilities of persons representing the, of a party complaining, or party charged, respectively, who is deceased, or under disability. *See* DEATH, INFANCY, INSOLVENCY, LUNACY

immaterial that advantage secretly secured to a favoured creditor in negotiations for composition is not to come out of debtor's, 525

ESTOPPEL,

distinguished from non disclosure, 6

none against infant misrepresenting his age, 142

against party charged who has encouraged the party complaining to alter or destroy the subject matter of a contract voidable for non disclosure, whereby party charged is precluded from setting up impossibility of restoration *in statu quo*, as bar to rescission, 203

against assignee of property in possession, when party complaining is in a position to establish, 248

by silence, where duty to speak, but not otherwise, 126, 127, note (*t*)

ETHICS,

of non-disclosure, good faith, undue influence, &c., as compared with jurisprudence, 573—600

EVENT,

past, is a "fact," and, as such, if material, must be disclosed, in any negotiation or relation involving a duty of disclosure, 13

burden on party complaining of proving the occurrence in fact of any, which he alleges to have been undisclosed, 151—156, 318, 319

contract of insurance is wager on future, 61, 62, 70

some types of bargain with "expectant" are wagers on future, 406

everything is material to be disclosed (where there is a duty of disclosure) which has a bearing on the future, if any, on which liability under the contract is contingent, 435

supervening, may give rise to duty of disclosure though none existed originally, 120—134

subsequent, showing compromise to have been unwise, is no ground for relieving against it, 108

rules as to costs following the, 545

EVIDENCE,

when, under what conditions, and what kinds of, admissible on the question of materiality, 17, 18, 227—230

actual knowledge, whether or not, is matter of, 20, 234

what kinds of presumptive knowledge are, and what are not, rebuttable, by, 36—38

GENERAL,

notoriety, presumptive knowledge of facts of, 21

usages in trade, presumptive knowledge of, but not of recent or unestablished practices, 24—27

practices, what evidence as to, admissible on question of materiality, 18

principles of law, presumptive knowledge of, but not of particular titles or rights, 23

meeting of shareholders, when disclosure must be made to, by promoter or director, in order to discharge his duty of disclosure to the company, 203, 204, 355

body of creditors, burden on party charged of proving disclosure of special bargain with favoured creditor to, or waiver, or affirmation by, or knowledge of, 530, 531

releases, construction of, 97   And see RELEASE.

waiver conditions, construction of, 171—179.   And see WAIVER.

questions as to disclosure put by insurers in life insurance cases, inutility of, 148, 149

good of the community   See PUBLIC POLICY.

GENUINE,

offer by one party to the other, before trial, effect of, on relief, 450—452
　　　　　　　　　　　　　　　　　　　damages, 504
　　　　　　　　　　　　　　　　　　　costs, 547, 548, 551

GIFT,

receipt or promise of, by third person to agent or partner, must be disclosed to principal or firm, 298—302

by promoter to directors of company, must be disclosed, 302—304

from servient to dominant party during the existence of a relation of influence will be set aside unless the dominant party can sustain the gift, 363—365

by what affirmative proof sustainable, and wherein the dominant party s evidence differs from that which he is required to adduce in the case of a transaction for value, 432, 438—442   And see INFLUENCE

above distinction between, and contract, as to the mode of "sustaining" it, illustrated in the case of the parental, legal, sacerdotal, and medical relations, 376, 379—382, 385, 387, 388

importance in certain cases of showing that the transaction was a gift, and not a contract, or vice versâ ; burden of proof in such cases, 420—422

old doctrine that donee is called upon to support any sort of, though no relation proved, is erroneous, 418

triviality of, may rebut the presumption of undue influence, 423, 445, 446

whether transaction is, or a contract, is question of fact, 461

ethical views as to, 588—590

GOOD FAITH,

duties of, generally   See DUTY

"utmost."   See UBERRIMA FIDES.

proof of, in what sense, and in what respects, necessary to sustain a transaction in relations of confidence, and of influence.   See PROPRIETY OF TRANSACTION.

personal, proof of, is no answer to a case of non-disclosure, or other breach of fiduciary duty, 170—172, 321—323, 424, 425

compromises entered into in, favoured by the Court, 101—108

mercantile, customs and practices involving, are upheld and given effect to, 156, 577

assignee of non-negotiable chose in action is subject to personal equities, though taking in, 244, 245

transferee of negotiable instrument, when fraud in the inception or negotiation thereof is established, is required to prove his, 245, 246

contractual, only, to be observed by mortgagee to mortgagor, 311—313

[47]

INDEX.

IDENTITY,

of vessel subject of marine insurance with a vessel which has become liable to capture, must be disclosed, 65, 66

of party charged with person in whose name, or through whom, he is dealing with the party complaining, during the subsistence of a relation of confidence, must be disclosed to party complaining—

in cases of trustee and *cestui que trust,* 280

promoter and company, 290

agent or partner, and principal or firm, 295—297

the, above referred to, must be proved as a fact by the party complaining, 318

IGNORANCE,

actual, of certain classes of fact, does not negative presumed knowledge. *See* KNOWLEDGE (B)

of both parties, renders non-disclosure innocuous, 19

wilful, intentional, or fraudulent, when deemed to be knowledge in law, as illustrated in various kinds of transaction, 46, 47, 50, 53—55, 57, 247. *And see* WILFUL

of one party as to the undisclosed fact, to the knowledge of the other party, does not of itself create a duty of disclosure, if there is otherwise none, 136—138

party complaining must prove his own, of the undisclosed fact in—

negotiations for certain contracts, 164—170

cases of judgments obtained by concealment, 514

grants from Crown obtained by concealment, 520, 521

composition arrangements with creditors, 531

but no burden on party charged to prove his own, as to any undisclosed fact, in relation of confidence or influence, 320, 424, 425

means absence of presumptive, as well as of actual, knowledge, 167

is not negatived by proof that the party had means of acquiring knowledge, 167

of equitable rules or doctrines, is no answer to a case of non-disclosure, 170—172, 321—323, 424, 425

honest, of illegality of transaction, induced by misrepresentation of legality on the other side, renders premium, deposit, or other sum paid, recoverable, 203—205

of servient party, where dominant party takes unconscientious advantage of, the transaction is impeachable, 388—397

of any matter omitted from prospectus which is required by statute to be disclosed therein, is good statutory defence to action, 500

of law, or statutory rule, or wilful, is not a " mistake of fact," within the meaning of the statutory plea to actions for non-disclosure in prospectuses, 500, 501

" diligence in," 39, 562

ethical views as to wilful, 590, 591

ILLEGALITY,

in wagering or gaming, duty to disclose fact showing, in marine insurance cases, 66

of contract, renders it void, not voidable, 197—199

Court will not, as a rule, rescind a contract already void for, 200

in cases of contracts of insurance void for, premiums not returnable if both parties ignorant, or both cognizant, of the illegality, but if one party is induced to believe the contract to be legal by the fraud of the other, he is entitled to a return of such premium, 203—205

whether evidence is admissible as to the materiality of facts disclosing, 230

of condition on which release of debtor is to be cancelled, renders the release absolute, 528, 529

when duty of Court to take notice of, without either party raising the point, or desiring it to be decided, or even when both concur in inviting the Court to ignore it, 548

INDEX.

ILLUSORY. *See* DELUSIVE.

IMBECILITY,
physical, mental, or moral, of servient party, when taken advantage of by dominant party, creates a relation from which undue influence will be presumed, 392—397

IMMATERIAL. *See* MATERIAL.

IMPARTIAL advice. *See* ADVICE.

IMPEACHABLE,
when, and how, a transaction is, for non disclosure and other breaches of fiduciary duty. *See* ACTIONABLE, and RELIEF.

IMPLIED,
notice or knowledge. *See* KNOWLEDGE (B)
condition. *See* CONDITION
misrepresentation, when non disclosure is. *See* MISREPRESENTATION.
waiver, 179, 180. *And see* WAIVER.
affirmation, 186, 188, 194. *And see* AFFIRMATION.
trustee, subject to same duties as express trustee, 279, 280
mortgagee is not, except for one purpose, 310—312
from circumstances, a relation of confidence or influence may be, in which case the party complaining must prove those circumstances, 314—317, 418, 419
contract to perform trust obligations, when non-disclosure may be regarded as, and when on this theory, party entitled to proof or claim on insolvency, 351, 352, 489
consent to agent, &c , receiving a gift, from silence after disclosure, 331
contract, must be disclosed in prospectus, 492, 493

IMPUTED, knowledge or notice. *See* KNOWLEDGE (B)

IN HÂC RE,
knowledge acquired by agent, imputed to principal, but not as a rule knowledge acquired *in aliâ re* *See* AGENCY (A)
employment, when necessary in relations of confidence, 315—317
influence, 428

IN LOCO PARENTIS. *See* PARENTAL RELATION.

IN SPECIE,
performance *See* SPECIFIC PERFORMANCE
mutual restitution, a condition of rescission, 202, 203, 209, 210

IN TOTO,
when rescission, if at all, must be, and when it need not be, 206, 339, 404, 405
when repeal of Crown grant must be, 518, 519

INACTION,
waiver not to be inferred from mere, 179, 180, 188—194, 199
affirmation not to be inferred from mere, 188—194, 199, 449, 450

INADEQUATE,
disclosure, is no disclosure at all, 7—11
value or price *See* VALUE.
generally. *See* COMPLETE.

INADVERTENCE,
no answer to case of non-disclosure to show that such non-disclosure arose from, in—
negotiations for contracts *uberrimæ fidei*, 170—172
relations of confidence, 321—323
influence, 424, 425

INDIFFERENT,

third person, advice of. *See* INDEPENDENT AND COMPETENT ADVICE, &c.

opinion of, best evidence of value, 463

INDIVIDUAL,

opinion of witness as to effect of disclosure of undisclosed fact upon his own judgment as an, not evidence of materiality, 229

shareholder, no duty of disclosure on director of company towards, 138—140, 308, 356

member of company, is not, as such, under any duty to the public, merely because the company is, 359

temperament, capacity, &c., when disregarded in relations of influence, 386, 387, 452, 453

case, when circumstances of, create a relation of influence. *See* CIRCUMSTANCES AND CONDITIONS OF THE PARTICULAR CASE

circumstances, opinion of one who has no knowledge of, is of no importance in determining value of reversion, 463

motives and conduct of the, irrelevant to the absolute equitable rules of disclosure and good faith, in—

negotiations for contracts *uberrimæ fidei*, 170—172

relations of confidence, 321—323

influence, 424, 425

INDUCEMENT,

actual, of party complaining, not, as a rule, necessary to be proved, 172, 173

but must be proved, where no duty of disclosure, and non-disclosure is relied upon as an implied misrepresentation, 133, 173

must be established in statutory action for damages by reason of omissions from prospectus, 496, 497

in connection with materiality. *See* MATERIAL (B)

INEQUALITY. *See* EQUALITY.

INFANCY,

need not be disclosed, but must not be subject of misrepresentation, 142

position of representatives of parties under disability by reason of—

in asserting claim to relief for non-disclosure, &c., 241, 356, 464

in resisting claim to relief for non-disclosure, &c , 244, 360, 465

persons under disability by reason of, cannot consent to termination or suspension of relation, or confirm a voidable transaction, except through the Court, 328, 335, 336

duties of disclosure and good faith owed to parties during, 354

youth just emerging from, has right to full disclosure and good faith from his parent in any transaction, unless a family arrangement, 373. *And see* PARENTAL RELATION.

constructive, attributed by Lord Hardwicke to the servient party in certain relations of influence constituted by circumstances, 402

INFERENCE,

of law. *See* PRESUMPTION, and QUESTIONS OF LAW AND FACT.

of fact. *See* QUESTIONS OF LAW AND FACT.

INFERIORITY,

on the one side, and dominion or superiority on the other. *See* INFLUENCE.

of knowledge, duties of disclosure and of good faith to party who is necessarily labouring under, when. *See* EXCLUSIVE.

INFIRMITY. *See* WEAKNESS.

INDEX.

INFLUENCE,

 relations of, classified as follows :—

  (i) "suspected" : (a) domestic,   372—376.   *And see* PARENTAL RELATION.

    (b) professional : legal, 377—379. *And see* SOLICITOR.

      sacerdotal, 382—385 *And see* SACERDOTAL RELATION.

      medical, 386, 387. *And see* MEDICAL RELATION.

  (ii) created by the circumstances and conditions of the particular case, 388—398. *And see* CIRCUMSTANCES AND CONDITIONS, &c

  (iii) unconscionable bargains with expectants, 399—406. *And see* EXPECTANT

 what are not relations of, 412—417

 nature of, as distinguished from, "confidence," 272, 273, 276, 362, 363

 "dominant party," and "servient party," in relations of, 362

 law draws no distinction between kinds and degrees of, in the various relations, 369—372

 burden on servient party, in proceedings for breach of duty incidental to relation of, to establish the existence of the relation, and the fact and nature of the transaction which is said to have been influenced, 418—423

 on proof of relation of, and of the transaction, the law presumes, in favour of the servient party, (1) the existence of the influence, (2) its exercise and operation upon the transaction, and (3) its impropriety and abuse, 363—365, 426, 427

 the second and third of the above presumptions as to, are rebuttable respectively by proof on the part of the dominant party that in fact the influence did not operate on the transaction, or in fact was duly exercised, 427

 good answer to show that the, was inoperative *in hâc re*, by reason of the subject-matter, or otherwise, 427, 428

 termination or suspension of the, presumed from the relation is a good answer, but it is not enough to prove termination or suspension of the relation itself, still less the dormancy of the duties attaching to it, if the influence was not entirely extinguished, or inoperative, 428—431

 valid answer is constituted by proof of a due use of the, 431, 432

 proper use of the, is shown by proof of real intention on the part of the servient party, fairly produced, in complete freedom of will and judgment, and after full disclosure of all material facts, and explanation of effect of proposed transaction on servient party's interest, and his right to reject and revoke, &c , and after honest advice from dominant party against himself, or from disinterested third person, 434—438

 in cases of gifts, fair and conscientious use of the, must be shown by proof of the independent and competent advice of a third person, but in the case of contracts, such proof not indispensable, if impracticable to obtain such third person's advice, or unreasonable to seek it, 438—443, and, as to what constitutes such independent and competent advice, *see* INDEPENDENT AND COMPETENT ADVICE OF THIRD PERSON.

 in transactions for value, proof of fair value is of the utmost importance in proving the proper and due exercise of the, but doubtful whether indispensable, if full information and honest advice given as to value, 443—445

 triviality of gift may show absence of undue, 445, 446

 above presumptions and rules as to, illustrated in cases of—

  parental relation, 372—377

  relation between legal adviser and client, 379—382

  sacerdotal relation, 385, 386

  medical relation, 387, 388

  relation created by the particular circumstances, 388—399

  bargains with "expectants," 399—412

INDEX.

INDEX.

duty of disclosure ordinarily on the assured, but may in special circumstances be on the insurer, in negotiation for, 63

contract of, compared with contract of suretyship, in respect of duty of disclosure, 87, 88

express stipulation in contracts of, other than marine, for true and complete answers to questions put, how affecting duty of disclosure, 144—149

excessive, when duty to disclose, in negotiations for marine policies, 66

duty of disclosure in negotiations for marine *See* MARINE INSURANCE

life and health *See* LIFE AND HEALTH INSURANCE

fire *See* FIRE INSURANCE

miscellaneous, 74, 75

popular ethics as to disclosure in negotiations for, 577—579

INTENTION,

when a " fact," material to be disclosed, and when not, 14, 15, 91, 94, 154

expression of, by agent, not to communicate a certain fact to his principal, in collusion with opposite party, prevents knowledge of that fact being imputed to such principal, 37

existence of real, on the part of the servient party to enter into the contract, or make the gift, which is impeached, must be established, as the first step in the dominant party's plea of propriety in the exercise of the alleged influence, 432, 433

proof of such, not sufficient in itself to establish such plea, 433

whether such real, on the part of the servient party existed or not, is question of fact, 461, 462

proof of, sufficient to establish a will, 414

to waive, on part of party complaining, when waiver pleaded as affirmative defence, must be proved to have been expressed in clear language, and with full knowledge *See* WAIVER

of party complaining to affirm, when plea of affirmation set up, must be proved by party charged to have been evinced by unambiguous language or conduct, and with full knowledge of facts and rights, and in absolute freedom of will and judgment, 237, 238, 334, 335, 446—448, 461, 462

to infringe known equitable rules of disclosure, not necessary to establish, when the infringement in fact is proved, 170—172, 321—323, 424, 425

to avoid knowledge, when knowledge is presumed from proof of. *See* WILFUL

and effect, of acts, ethical views as to relative importance of, compared with those of jurisprudence, 591—598

INTEREST (IN THE ORDINARY SENSE),

of agent in not communicating a fact to his principal, proof of, does not of itself prevent imputation of knowledge of that fact to the principal, 38

duty to disclose facts showing absence of, in negotiation for contract of marine insurance, 68

the like, in negotiation for life insurance, 73

conflict between, and duty, is one of the grounds of the doctrine of disclosure and good faith in relations of confidence and influence, 275—277, 290, 292, 302—304, 368, 369, 377, 378, 382, 383

duty of agent to disclose the exact nature of his, or of any company or firm dealing with his principal, when, 295—297

duty of partner to disclose to firm his, in any similar or competing business, 304—306

where no surplus assets, beneficiary not having any, cannot obtain relief against executor or trustee of insolvent estate, 307

party charged under duty to party complaining to explain effect of proposed transaction on the latter's, 274, 329, 436, 437, 447

INDEX.

IRREBUTTABLE,
  presumptions of knowledge, what are, and what are not. *See* KNOWLEDGE (B).
  presumptions, generally. *See* PRESUMPTIONS.

IRREGULARITY,
  in acts of company, when no knowledge of, imputable to stranger, 46

IRRELEVANT. *See* MATERIAL.

ISOLATED,
  knowledge of agent employed solely for the purposes of one isolated act or
    step in the entire transaction is not imputed to the principal, nor is the
    ignorance of a person brought in for such a purpose credited to him, 35
  the fact that an alleged relation of influence is only proved in respect of one
    isolated transaction is a strong element in establishing a due use of the
    influence by the dominant party, even if it does not negative the existence
    of the relation, 419

ISSUE (IN THE ORDINARY SENSE),
  of prospectus, statutory duty of disclosure arising on. *See* PROSPECTUS
  of shares by company, as fully paid, and consideration, must be stated in
    prospectus, 470
  amounts received on previous, of shares, required by statute to be disclosed
    in the prospectus, 470
  of negotiable instruments affected with fraud, proof of, rebuts presumption that
    holder is a holder in due course, 245, 246

ISSUE (IN TECHNICAL SENSE),
  of fact, what is. *See* QUESTIONS OF LAW AND FACT.
  directions for trial of, or inquiry as to *See* RELIEF, PROCEDURE, COSTS.

JOINDER,
  of parties, generally, 538, 539
  of parties in statutory proceedings for non-disclosure in prospectus, 486
  of underwriters in marine insurance cases, 539, 540
  of causes of action, generally, 540
                              in prospectus cases, 508
  of remedies, generally, 540
                              in prospectus cases, 508

JOINT,
  contracts, rights in respect of, 239
  subscriptions of underwriters are not, 239—241
  and several liability of co-agents and co-directors, when, 359
  liability of statutory tortfeasors in prospectus cases, 488

JUDGE,
  when trial by, with, and when without, jury, 532—534
  rules as to costs on trial by, with, and without jury, respectively, 545

JUDGMENT (IN ORDINARY SENSE),
  fact disclosure of which is likely to affect the, of a normal person, is in one sense
    of the word material, 17, 482
  duty on party charged to give the party complaining the benefit of his honest
    and impartial, in—
      relations of confidence, 273, 274, 278, 282—285
      influence, 434, 437, 438
  freedom of *See* FREEDOM.
  infirmity of, in servient party, coupled with fact that dominant party takes
    unconscientious advantage of it, is one of the " circumstances and conditions "
    by which a relation of influence may be constituted, 394—397

Index.

KING. *See* Crown.

KING'S BENCH DIVISION,
>   jurisdiction of, in cases of non-disclosure, 532, 533

KNOWLEDGE,
>   (A) *Actual Knowledge,*
>>   means personal and direct knowledge, or express notice, only, 20
>>   when alleged, not sufficient to show vicarious knowledge, 20
>>   must be proved against party complaining, where a plea of knowledge is set up against him, and mere proof of means of knowledge not enough, 331, 332
>>   must be brought home to the very person who is alleged to have possessed it, 333, 498, 499
>>   is matter of proof and evidence, 20, 233
>>   necessary to defeat registered title, or statutory presumption of ignorance, 50—55

>   (B) *Presumptive Knowledge,*
>>   expression used in this treatise to denote every kind of knowledge other than actual, 20
>>   rules as to, are questions of law, 21, 233— 236
>>   of five classes of matters, as follows —
>>>   (i) Matters of public notoriety, objects of sense, topics of general information, elementary laws and facts of nature, general principles of law, &c , 21—24
>>>   (ii) Matters of common knowledge in business of parties, usages and practices of trade, and usual conditions, clauses, &c , 24—27
>>>   (iii) Matters known to the agent of the person to whom the knowledge is imputed, if he is the " agent to know," and if employed *in hâc re,* unless he is shown to have been perpetrating a fraud upon his principal at the material date, 27—30
>>>   (iv) Facts or documents to the discovery of which such inquiries and inspections as were reasonable under the circumstances, having regard to the party's actual knowledge of connected facts or documents, would have led, 38—47
>>>   (v) Matters of which knowledge is imputed by statutes (whether codifying, or modifying common law rules and presumptions), 48—55

>   (C) *Knowledge in General,*
>>   equal, of parties, negatives duty of disclosure, 19
>>   necessarily exclusive on one side, and corresponding trust on the other, is foundation of duty of disclosure in negotiation for contracts *uberrimæ fidei,* 58—60, 70—73, 78, 88, 89, 97, 104—106, 110—116, 118, 119
>>   in two senses (knowledge of facts, and capacity, skill, experience, &c), must be imparted in relations of confidence and influence, 273—278, 281—285, 434—438
>>   of undisclosed fact by party charged must be proved by party complaining, in—
>>>   negotiations for certain contracts, 161—164
>>>   proceedings for relief against a judgment, 514, 517
>>>   grant, 520
>>>   composition arrangements with creditors, 530
>>   condition in prospectus purporting to affect applicant for shares with, of any undisclosed fact, is rendered void by statute, 499
>>   no valid affirmation or confirmation of transaction impeached without full and exact, 185, 186, 334—336, 417
>>   possessed by party charged during relation of confidence, though acquired by him previously, must be communicated, 282, 283

INDEX.

MAINTENANCE,
assignment of naked right to avoid a transaction is, or savours of, 242

MAJORITY,
in sense of full age   *See* INFANCY.
oppression of minority of members of company by, may entitle the minority to use of name of company, or to institute a representative suit, 356, 357

MALA FIDES. *See* BAD FAITH.

MANAGEMENT,
internal or "indoor" of company, stranger has no presumptive knowledge of, 46

MANAGER,
self-constituted, of affairs of servient party, stands towards him in a relation of "influence," 392—394
of company, may be liable to misfeasance proceedings, 543

MANAGING PARTNERS, directors of company described as, 205 note (*q*)

MANŒUVRE. *See* DEVICE

MARINE INSURANCE,
in negotiations for, it is the duty of the assured to disclose to the underwriter all material facts within his (actually or presumptively) exclusive knowledge, such as—
  (i) facts relating to voyage, accidents, injuries, storms, dates of departure and arrival, so far as they bear on question of whether overdue or missing ship, disposal of goods on board, &c, 64, 65
  (ii) facts relating to war-risks, capture, re-capture, prize, regulations of foreign governments affecting ship's safety, articles contraband of war, &c, 65, 66
  (iii) places of loading and discharge, if not recognized ports, 66
  (iv) material facts as to over valuation, double insurance, illegal gaming, &c, 66
  (v) in cases of insurance of chartered freight, or of reinsurance, any unusual conditions in charterparty, or in original policy, respectively, 67
  (vi) detention of ship at places other than contemplated, or unusual methods of loading or stowing cargo, and other miscellaneous facts, 68, 69
illustrations of facts material either to the risk, or the amount of premium payable, in cases of, 68, 69
"material," in contracts of, means what a rational and prudent underwriter would consider as, 69
in negotiation for, the assured must communicate the particular element which gives significance to the undisclosed fact, 154
if two facts, each of which is meaningless except in conjunction with the other, the assured must disclose both in negotiation for, 67
what facts the assured, and the underwriter, respectively are, and what they are not, presumed to know in cases of, 22, 24, 25, 30, 31, 40
initialling of slip, not the issue of the policy, is the conclusion of contract of, 156
importance of the above rule to the party complaining illustrated in connection with the burden on him of establishing—
  the existence of the undisclosed fact, 155, 156
  the knowledge thereof on the part of the party charged, 163, 164
  his own ignorance thereof, 169, 170
subscription of each underwriter to a policy of, constitutes a separate and distinct contract, 239—241,—
but, in practice, one of the underwriters of policy of, usually defends, or sues, on behalf of the others, 539, 540

[63]

INDEX.

MARINE INSURANCE—*continued.*

specially stringent rules as to discovery by the assured in proceedings on a policy of, where non-disclosure is set up by the underwriter, 537, 538

relief on ground of non-disclosure in negotiation for, 218, 219

MARKET,

presumptive knowledge of usages of, 25, 26

agent's duty of disclosure of identity in dealing on, for his principal, 205, 206

prices, not conclusive as to value of reversion, 463

in assessing damages for statutory non-disclosure in prospectus, 504

grant of, when impeachable for non disclosure to Crown, 517—521

MARRIAGE,

(A) *Contract to marry (" pre-contract of marriage ") :—*

duty in negotiation for, to disclose—
   unchastity in the woman, 112
   permanent disease, bodily or mental, tending to show incapacity for marriage state, 114, 115
   loose behaviour, or reputation, in the woman, to what extent, 114, 115
   criminal conduct or character on the part of the man, 114

no duty to disclose—
   past and cured bodily or mental disease, 113
   past, and broken off, engagement to marry a third person, 113
   on part of the woman, the " adulteries of art," 113, 115, 116,
   on the part of the man, defects of temper, disposition, &c., or financial distress, &c., 113

(B) *Contract of Marriage —*

stands on a totally different footing from contract to marry confers status, and therefore not capable of annulment on the ground of non disclosure or fraud inducing the assent, but only on proof that the party never assented at all, 116, 117

above principle applies to a marriage settlement, or licence, as much as to a, but not to a deed of separation, which is not void, but voidable, for non disclosure, 117—119

is never voidable at option of party complaining, but, when subject of relief at all, can only be declared null and void by the proper tribunal, 200, 201

(C) *Relation constituted by Marriage —*

is not one of the recognized relations of " influence," but may be important, with other circumstances, in constituting a particular relation of influence, 395, 396

Roman and Attic law as to, 607 note (*t*)

MATERIAL, MATERIALITY,

(A) *What are deemed " facts " or " circumstances " capable of materiality ·—*

a thing, or a past or present event, 13

receipt of information, news, intelligence, rumours, &c, whether afterwards found to be true or false, 13, 14

mental states, opinions, expectations, apprehensions, existing in fact, whether well-founded or not, 14, 15

the making of an agreement, whether valid or not, 15, 16

(B) *Materiality —*

any fact, in order to have, must be of a nature to affect the judgment of a normal person in determining whether to enter into the proposed transaction on the precise terms proposed, 16

[64]

MEMORIAL,

of enrolment of deed, what knowledge of contents of deed is presumed from, 41

of enrolment of previous grant, raises a presumption of knowledge against grantee from Crown of a later inconsistent grant, and renders the latter the subject of revocation, 520

MENTAL,

state or condition is a "fact," which may be material to be disclosed, 14, 15

disease, when to be disclosed in negotiation for contract to marry, and when not, 114, 115

disease, to be disclosed in negotiation for contract of life insurance, if existing and permanent, but not if past, and cured, 72, 73

infirmity of servient party, and advantage taken thereof by dominant party, constitute circumstances from which a particular relation of influence may be presumed, 390—397

MEMORY,

want of, as affecting proof of ignorance of party complaining, 20, 167

knowledge of party charged, 161

MERCANTILE   *See* COMMERCIAL

METAPHOR,

"trustee by," in Lord Westbury's phrase, is under same duties of disclosure as any other trustee, 279, 280

promoter of company may be regarded as trustee by, 288, 289

dominant party, in relations of influence constituted by the particular circumstances, may be regarded as parent or guardian of servient party, by, 390

supposed "duties," when only duties by way of, and not in strict contemplation of law, e.g.—

so-called "duty" of diligence and inquiry, 191—194, 565, 566

mortgagee to mortgagor, 311

use and abuse of, in jurisprudence, 570, 571

MIND   *See* MENTAL

MINE,

duty of disclosure as to existence of, under surface, or exhaustion of, or other facts relating to, in cases of sale or purchase of land, as follows —

none arising out of mere relation of vendor and purchaser of land, 139, 140

but where relation of confidence exists between the vendor and purchaser, duty arises, 140, 277, 278

though no duty originally, supervening circumstances in the course of the negotiation may create one, 122, 123

exhaustion of, when a bar to rescission, 202

MINIMUM SUBSCRIPTION,

on which company will proceed to allotment, amount of, to be stated in prospectus, 478

non-disclosure of amount of, in prospectus, involves liability to damages, and (indirectly) other liabilities, 503, 505—507

MINORITY,

of shareholders in company, rights of against majority using their voting power oppressively to prevent illegal or fraudulent acts being judicially investigated, 356, 357

in sense of nonage   *See* INFANCY

MISCONDUCT,

of person whose fidelity is guaranteed, duty of employer to disclose to surety, 91—93

INDEX.

MISCONDUCT—*continued.*

of one whose credit or account only is guaranteed, no obligation on creditor or bank to disclose to surety, 90, 91

what, must be disclosed between persons negotiating for marriage engagement, 114

intended, when to be disclosed in negotiation for deed of separation, 119

need not be disclosed in any negotiation or relation to which no fiduciary duty attaches at all, 142

proof of personal, on the part of the party charged, may affect—
the question of whether interest shall be ordered to be paid, and the rate thereof, if ordered, 323, 342, 343, 346
discretionary relief, 143, 144
the measure of value or damage, 144, 323
the incidence or amount of costs, 144, 323, 425, 545—551

director of company who can prove absence of, is excused from statutory liability for going to allotment without having received the amount of " the minimum subscription " fixed by the memorandum, and named in prospectus, 505

of inquiry, pursuant to writ of *ad quod damnum*, destroys presumption which would otherwise arise of the Crown's knowledge of certain material facts, 521

MISFEASANCE,

statutory remedy, which liquidator is not bound to resort to, if he chooses to bring action against misfeasant, or settle his name on list of contributories, 351, 352, 541

procedure, is by summons in the High Court, and motion in any other, supported by affidavit, and may be resorted to in all three species of winding up, but where liquidation is voluntary, an order must be made on the application of the liquidator, or a contributory, or creditor, 542

means and includes an actionable breach of trust, or wrongful act in the nature thereof, causing loss to the company, 542

does not include any breach of duty which is not actionable, or which is only misfeasance at large (*e g* negligence), or which occasions no loss to the company, but only to the applicant individually, 542

no new rights or liabilities created by the statutory provisions as to, but only new and more convenient remedy, 542

procedure, persons entitled to resort to, are official receiver, liquidator, and (if in a position to prove that he has an interest in the application, but not otherwise) a contributory, or a creditor, 541, 542

persons who may be liable for, are promoter, past or present director (*de facto*, or *de jure*), liquidator, or " officer " of the company (which term, for this purpose, means a person holding an office constituted by the memorandum or articles of the company, or by statute, *de jure*, and not *de facto* merely), 542—544

illustrations of positions which do, and which do not, respectively, constitute a person an " officer of the company," liable, as such, to be proceeded against for, 543, 544

representative of deceased person alleged to have been guilty of, is not liable to proceedings in, but estate of person against whom, in his lifetime, an order has been made, may in certain circumstances be accountable, 351 note (*o*), 544

non-disclosure, when alleged as constituting the, must be proved by the applicant, 544

personal fraud not a necessary element in, 544

grounds of alleged, must be stated in summons or affidavit, 544

relief and remedy in cases of, 544

claims in, assignable and saleable, 544

not subject of set-off, but may be of release, 544

INDEX.

OBLIGATION,

generally *See* DUTY.

"cautionary," Scots term for contract of suretyship, 618, note (*b*)

OCCUPATION,

of land by third person, puts purchaser on inquiry as to nature and terms of, as against tenant or occupier, but not as against vendor, 44, 45

where land not under, no duty of inquiry as to last occupier, 45

OCCURRENCE *See* EVENT

OFFENSIVE PROCEEDINGS *See* RELIEF

OFFER,

by party charged, before, or at, trial, has no effect on relief unless everything offered to which party complaining is declared by the Court to be entitled, 337, 451, 452,—

but may affect damages in prospectus cases, 504

costs in all cases, 547, 548

effect of, on costs, when made either by expectant or dealer in "expectant" cases, 550, 551

receipt, and refusal by party charged of, to purchase reversion, &c , or, on the other hand, non-receipt by him of any, after endeavouring to obtain, is material evidence on the question of value, 463

to public of shares or debentures, when a prospectus for the purposes of statutory law as to omission therefrom, 473, 474. *And see* PROSPECTUS

amount received by company on any previous, of shares or debentures to the public, required by statute to be disclosed in prospectus, 478

OFFICER,

of company, actual knowledge of, when imputed to company, 32, 355

common, of two companies, when either company is affected by knowledge of, 33

of Court, when subject to same duties of disclosure and good faith, in sales by direction of Court, as other vendors, 221, 222

effect of articles of association providing for vacation of office by director or other, of company, 333

succeeding, when duty of disclosure to, as well as to the existing holder of the office, 354

duty of good faith specially incumbent on solicitor, as an, of the Court, 378, 512

who is deemed an, of a company, for purposes of misfeasance proceedings, 543, 544

concealment from judicial *See* JUDGMENT

of State *See* CROWN

OFFICIAL RECEIVER

may be an applicant in misfeasance proceedings, 542

OFFICIOUS,

and improper question, no duty to answer at all, or (in some cases) to answer truthfully, 134

intervention of self constituted adviser or manager in the affairs of the servient party may raise presumption of influence, 392, 393

OMISSION

of duty of disclosure, or good faith *See* DUTY

of matters required by statute to be stated in prospectus, consequences of *See* PROSPECTUS.

ONEROUS,

and unusual covenants in head lease, &c., duty of disclosure of, in negotiation for contract of sale of land, 81, 82 *And see* VENDOR (A)

INDEX.

INDEX.

ORDER,

of Court, duties of disclosure in sales by, 221, 222, 510, 511

forms of, made by way of relief against non-disclosure, 209—211, 456, 457

obtained by concealment from tribunal, 509—517

for " test action," when made, 530

exceptional, as to costs, when, 545, 546   *And see* Costs.

receiving, when secretly favoured creditor is refused, 528, 529

of local authorities, affecting title to land sold, must be disclosed by vendor to purchaser, 82

ORDINARY,

intelligence and education, any person of, is a normal person, whose judgment is the test in determining materiality, 16, 88—90

course of business, presumptive knowledge of dealings and practices in, 24—27

no presumptive knowledge by person dealing in, as to defects of title in negotiable instruments, 245, 246

contracts made in, exempt from statutory duty of disclosure in prospectus, 481

course of management, director of company is under no duty to impart knowledge obtained in, to any individual shareholder, and still less to a stranger, 140, 141, 308, 356

course of events, deterioration of property in, is no bar to rescission, 203

ORIGINAL,

debt, when unfavoured creditor is entitled to sue for, and to disregard composition arrangement with insolvent debtor, on discovery of secret bargain with favoured creditor, 529

lease, duty to disclose unusual and onerous covenants of, in negotiations for contract of sub-lease or assignment, 81

policy, when duty of assured to disclose unusual terms of, in negotiation for contract of marine reinsurance, 67

vendor, when promoter, must disclose to company price at which he bought the property from the,—

as part of common law duty, 291

in prospectus, pursuant to statutory duty, 479, 480

OVERDRAFT, duty of disclosure in negotiation for guarantee of, 90, 91

OVERDUE,

ship, duty to disclose facts indicating, 64

negotiable instrument, indorsee of, takes subject to equities, 245, 246

OVER-INSURANCE, OVER-VALUATION,

facts indicating, when to be disclosed by assured to underwriters in negotiation for marine insurance, 66

PAR,

when value of shares taken at, ordered to be paid to company by delinquent director, 345, 346

PARENTAL RELATION,

is the relation between parent and child, just emerging from infancy, or dependent upon parent for home, and livelihood, of whatever age, and includes the quasi parental relation between guardian and ward, and between any person, whether parent or not, who is *in loco parentis* and the person under his guardian. or protection, 372, 373

is one of the ' suspected " relations of influence, 369

INDEX.

PARENTAL RELATION—*continued.*

the same three presumptions made against the dominant party in, as in any other relation of influence, 372. *And see* INFLUENCE

by what evidence on the part of the dominant party two of the above presumptions may be rebutted in a case of, accordingly as the transaction is a gift or a contract, 372, 373, 376. *And see* INFLUENCE

where presumption in favour of family arrangements negatives the presumptions against the validity of a transaction during the existence of the, and what is a family arrangement for this purpose, 374, 375, 448, 449. *And see* FAMILY ARRANGEMENT

one who, with knowledge of the existence of a, between two persons, procures or leaves the parent to influence the child to pay or guarantee debt due from parent to himself, is subject to the same duties as the parent, 376

where a dominant party in a relation of influence constituted by the particular circumstances may be regarded as constructively standing in a, towards the servient party, 389, 390

in a mercantile sense, between promoter and company, 288, 280

PARITY *See* EQUALITY

PARLIAMENT,

company incorporated by, not subject to statutory liability for omissions in prospectus, 475

generally. *See* STATUTORY.

PARTIAL,

disclosure is no disclosure at all, 7—11

knowledge, alleged affirmation with only, is ineffective as an answer to a case of non-disclosure, 186, 187

rescission of transaction, when granted, and when not, 206, 339, 454, 455

repeal of Crown grant, when, and when not, 518, 519

relief, in marine insurance cases by " excepting out of the policy,' doctrine of, is now exploded, 218, 219

PARTICULAR,

titles, or rights, no presumptive knowledge of law as to, 23

' circumstances and conditions of the case," relation of influence constituted by *See* CIRCUMSTANCES AND CONDITIONS, &c

PARTICULARS,

of sale, waiver of right to complain of omissions in. *See* WAIVER.

not the proper place for a condition of waiver, 181

what, required by statute to be disclosed in prospectus of company, 477—484 *And see* PROSPECTUS

in pleadings, what must be given, 534—536

when discovery will be ordered to be given by party charged before party complaining is required to give, 535—537

generally, what must be given in discharge of duty of disclosure *See* EXACT

PARTIES,

what, may assert right to relief for non-disclosure and breaches of fiduciary duty, in cases of—

negotiations for contracts *uberrimæ fidei*, 239—242

relations of confidence, 353—357

influence, 464

bargains with " expectants, ' 404, 405

prospectuses of companies, 485, 486

obtaining judgments, 515, 516

grants from Crown or State, 518

composition arrangements with creditors, 526—531

misfeasance, 541, 542

[77]

INDEX.

PRACTICE (IN THE SENSE OF MERCANTILE USAGE),
evidence as to, admissible on question of materiality, 18, 227—229
presumptive knowledge of established, and honest, but none of unusual, novel, uncertain, or dishonest, 24—27
generally. *See* CUSTOM.

PRACTICE (IN SENSE OF LEGAL PROCEDURE),
certain rules of, in non-disclosure cases, 538—540

PRECISE. *See* EXACT.

PRE-CONTRACT,
of marriage, term formerly used to express a contract to marry, as distinguished from contract of marriage, 116, note (z)

PREDOMINANCE. *See* INFLUENCE.

PRELIMINARY EXPENSES,
required by statute to be disclosed in prospectus of a company, 480

PREMIUM,
(i) *in marine insurance cases* —
every fact likely to affect the judgment of the underwriter in determining whether to agree to the proposed rate of, may be material, 16, note (m)

(ii) *in insurance cases other than marine* —
is returnable to the assured, as a condition of rescission, unless it is otherwise provided by the contract, 203—205
is not returnable on rescission, if the contract is illegal, and either both parties had guilty knowledge, or both were in innocent ignorance, of the illegality, but is returnable where the assured in good faith relied upon the insurer's fraudulent misrepresentation of its legality, 205
is recoverable, or not recoverable, by the assured, as money had and received, under the same conditions as above stated, 212, 213
effect of extension of time for payment of, on duty of disclosure, 163, 164

PRESCRIBED, by statute. *See* STATUTORY.

PRESENT. *See* GIFT.

PRESSURE,
use of, to secure unfair advantage, over person in distress, is one of the circumstances from which a particular relation of influence will be presumed, 397
erroneously supposed at one time to be impliedly incidental to the position of a mortgagee in relation to the mortgagor, 415—417
exerted on debtor by favoured creditor in composition arrangement with creditors, how relieved against, 527

PRESUMPTIONS (IN LAW),
of knowledge. *See* KNOWLEDGE (B).
as to holdership and possession "in due course," 245—248
of existence, operation on the transaction, and undue use, of influence by the dominant party, 363—365. *And see* INFLUENCE.
as to influence, how rebuttable. *See* INFLUENCE.
of King's ignorance of previous inconsistent grant, and of subject's knowledge thereof, 519—521
of King's knowledge of previous inconsistent grant of market or charter of incorporation where there was an inquiry pursuant to writ of *ad quod damnum*, unless misconducted, 521

PRESUMPTIVE,
" knowledge," use of expression in this work justified, 370
" fraud,' expression criticized, 557—561
knowledge, erroneous views as to necessity of establishing fraud and negligence, and misuse of those terms and conceptions, in cases of, 561—566

[81]

INDEX.

PROOF,

in the sense of evidence. *See* EVIDENCE.

in the sense of claim in insolvency, when party complaining has a right of, 314, 351, 352 *And see* INSOLVENCY.

in printer's sense, prospectus in, when not subject to the statutory law relating to disclosure in prospectuses, 476, 477

PROPERTY,

for purposes of legal presumptions of knowledge, includes real and personal, and any right or interest in, whether in possession or not, and a debt or chose in action, 48, 49

various presumptions of knowledge as to title of, and condition of, 39—51

statutory presumptions (by reason of registration) of knowledge of title to, 52—55

duties of disclosure on vendor in negotiation for sale and purchase of *See* VENDOR (A)

purchaser, in the like *See* PURCHASER

specific, assignment or devise of, carries with it the right to avoid, 241, 242

consisting of specific fund which can be earmarked and traced, assignment of, carries with it the same right, 242, 356

private right of, in knowledge, skill, and experience of agent, &c., is one of the grounds on which rules as to disclosure in confidence relations are founded, 277, 278

rules as to disclosure of, and otherwise relating to, price of, or previously given for, in transactions of sale and purchase. *See* PRICE.

option of party complaining, in relation of confidence, to take the, for which the party charged is accountable, or to rescind the transaction, 341, 342

the like option of party complaining to take the actual, or its value, 344—346

family settlement or division of, arrangements for, when exempt from ordinary rules of disclosure. *See* FAMILY ARRANGEMENT.

what is, and what is not, deemed an expectation of, for the purposes of the rules relating to bargains with "expectants," 404—406

"expectant" not deemed emancipated, so as to constitute a confirmation by him of the transaction valid, until the, in reversion or expectation, falls into possession, 412

rules as to disclosure and knowledge of facts relating to value of the, and as to giving, or not taking more than, full value, for the *See* VALUE

sold to company, what contracts and facts relating to, are required by statute to be disclosed in prospectus *See* PROSPECTUS

restoration of, in misfeasance cases, 544

PROPOSAL,

in life insurance contracts. *See* LIFE AND HEALTH INSURANCE

for transaction, right of party complaining to reject, in the first instance, or when asked to confirm it, must be explained to him, 274, 329, 436, 437, 447

to waive, must be shown to have been accepted, 181

generally *See* OFFER.

PROPRIETY OF THE TRANSACTION,

burden on party charged to establish the, in relations of confidence, in order to rebut presumption of abuse of confidence, 329, 330

is shown, in relations of confidence, by proof of full disclosure, disinterested advice against himself, or (preferably) the advice of an independent third person, and (though probably this is not an indispensable *probandum*, if the other elements are proved) the giving of fair value, 273, 274

illustrations of proof of, in cases of trustee, and of agent, 280—285, 295—298

burden on dominant party to establish the, in relations of influence, in order to rebut presumption that influence was undue, 365, 366, 431, 432

is question of fact, 461

INDEX.

QUESTIONS OF LAW AND FACT—*continued.*

(D) *in the statutory action for non-disclosure in the prospectus of a company, as to the following* -

whether alleged prospectus answers to the statutory definition, 474

whether issued to the public or not, 474

by or on behalf of the defendant or not, 487, 488

materiality of omitted fact or contract, 491

whether alleged omitted contract amounted in law to a contract, or not, 492

whether such contract was entered into, or not, 493

whether plaintiff had knowledge of the undisclosed fact or contract, or not, 499

" honest mistake of fact " on part of defendant, 500, 501

QUIESCENCE,

amounting to affirmation of transaction impeached, but not otherwise, is a good affirmative plea to a case of non disclosure, 194

RATE,

of interest *See* INTEREST (IN THE FINANCIAL SENSE)

of commission payable for underwriting, or the amount, required by statute to be disclosed in prospectus, 480

RATIONAL *See* REASONABLE.

REAL,

intention, proof of, however produced, enough to sustain will, 414

necessary, but insufficient of itself, to sustain an impeached transaction in relations of influence, 414, 432, 433

affirmation not established by proof that the intention of the party complaining was actual and, unless complete emancipation and knowledge be also shown, 334, 335, 447, 448

contract, material to ascertain what was the, in case of alleged statutory non-disclosure of material contract in prospectus, 493

property, and chattels. *See* LAND

value *See* VALUE.

purchaser, or vendor, non-disclosure of identity of, in dealings between parties standing to one another in relation of confidence *See* IDENTITY

REASONABLE,

person, judgment of, test of materiality, 16

inquiries and inspections, presumptive knowledge of facts and documents discoverable by, 38—48

dominant party must establish that the impeached transaction was, in relations of influence, and, particularly if the transaction was with an " expectant," 391, 411, 431, 432

explanation of, or excuse for, non-delivery or non-production of title deeds absolves the party from further inquiry, and negatives the presumption of knowledge which otherwise would be made, 39—44

offer of either party, effect of, on costs, 547, 548, 550, 551

REBATE,

when presumptive knowledge of custom of agent to receive, and when not, 26

agent or partner must not receive, or stipulate for, from third person without disclosure to, or knowledge (actual or presumptive) of, the principal, or firm, 299—302

RELATION,

duty of party charged to disclose all facts indicating an alteration in the, existing between the parties, 278

no presumptive knowledge of facts which change the entire character of the, in which the parties stand to one another, 26

between parties negotiating for contracts *uberrimæ fidei*. *See* NEGOTIATION FOR CONTRACTS UBERRIMÆ FIDEI.

of confidence. *See* CONFIDENCE.

of influence *See* INFLUENCE

existence of, must always be proved, by the party seeking relief, whatever the relation alleged may be, *e g* —

relation between parties negotiating for a contract *uberrimæ fidei*, 151

relation of confidence, 314—317

influence, 418, 419

statutory relation in respect of omissions from prospectuses, 490, 491

in cases where judgment obtained by concealment from Court, 513

in cases where grant obtained by concealment from Crown or State, 519

in cases of composition arrangements with creditors, 530

what kinds of, give rise to no duty of disclosure *See* ACTIONABLE

when, and how, presumptions arising from proof of the existence of the, may be rebutted *See* AFFIRMATIVE ANSWERS

effect of the co-existence of two kinds of, 328, 396, 397

questions of law and fact as to the, in cases of confidence, or of influence. *See* QUESTIONS OF LAW AND FACT (B), (C)

in determining the exact nature of the, where the question is of importance, regard is had to the substance and reality of the, rather than to its description and form *See* SUBSTANCE.

RELEASE,

in negotiation for a specific, disclosure must be made of every fact material to the particular subject-matter, 96, 97

where a general, is negotiated for, disclosure must be made of the general nature and class of claims contemplated as the subject thereof, 97

above rules as to, are applied to " catching conditions of sale," and " tricky " waiver clauses in prospectuses of companies, 97

in determining whether a particular transaction negotiated for is a, or a compromise, the Court regards the substance, and not the form, 100

of original debt in composition arrangement remains valid, notwithstanding a condition that, if terms of arrangement not complied with, it shall be void, where the condition is itself void by reason of the non-disclosure of a special bargain with a particular favoured creditor, 528, 529

misfeasance claim may be the subject of, under the same conditions of validity as any other, 544

RELEVANT. *See* MATERIAL

RELIEF,

available for non-disclosure, and other breaches of duty, in—

(A) *Negotiations for Contracts Uberrimæ Fidei* ·

(i) rescission, 197—212. *And see* RESCISSION.

(ii) money had and received, 212, 213. *And see* MONEY HAD AND RECEIVED

(iii) summons under Vendor and Purchaser Act, 220, 221. *And see* VENDOR AND PURCHASER ACT

(iv) discharge of purchaser on motion to the Court, in case of sale by its direction, 221, 222

(v) defence, or answer, to proceedings for enforcement of the impeached transaction, 214—217. *And see* DEFENSIVE PROCEEDINGS.

(vi) damages, if, but not unless, the non-disclosure involved fraudulent misrepresentation, or was characterized by fraud, 121, 128, 129, 133, 134, 196, 224, 225

"*RES IPSA LOQUITUR,*"

in certain cases of materiality, 228

where the mere entering into a contract of insurance establishes the fact of non-disclosure, 157

where undervalue is so gross as, *per se,* to indicate fraud, 284, 312

in cases where the nature of the transaction reveals impropriety on the face of it, and abuse of influence, 307, 308

in case of a bargain with an expectant, so outrageous in its terms as, of itself, to constitute it unconscionable, 408

RESALE,

vendor-promoter must disclose the profit he is making on the, to the company of the property it is to acquire, 201

price paid, or agreed to be paid, to the dominant party for property on, is evidence against him of its value, 463

RESCISSION,

when party complaining is entitled to, on the ground of non-disclosure or kindred breaches of duty. *See* RELIEF

right of election between, and adherence to the contract, or other forms of relief. *See* ELECTION, RELIEF, and VOIDABLE.

right to, may be waived. *See* WAIVER.

can only be granted (whether for non-disclosure, or any other cause) under the following conditions —

1. there must be a subsisting and concluded contract, which is valid until avoided, and not one which is already void for illegality, or otherwise, or one which, though a contract, is something more (*e g* marriage), 199—201

2. the transaction to be rescinded must be executory on one side or the other, and not completed by conveyance, or otherwise fully executed on both sides, except where fraud, or difference in substance, &c, 201, 202

3. the party complaining must be in a position to make specific restoration of all property *in specie* (if any) which he has received under the transaction impeached, unless the destruction or alteration in character of such property is attributable to the party charged, 202—205

4. the rights of third parties honestly acquired on the faith of the subsistence and validity of the transaction must not be affected, 205, 206

5. the transaction must be set aside *in toto,* or not at all, except in the case of severable covenants, characters, or parties, 206, 339, 454, 455

may be granted either on a claim, or a counterclaim, 207

when prefaced by a declaration, 207, 208

all documents containing, or recording, or (in any case where a completed contract is subject to the relief) purporting to complete, the transaction are the subject of, in contemplation of law, and certain classes of instrument may further be ordered to be delivered up for physical, 208, 209

judgment for, is accompanied by all necessary orders and directions for repayment, redelivery, reconveyance. so as to effect complete mutual *restitutio ad integrum,* and for indemnity against expenses incurred under, but not expenses " arising out of," the impeached contract, and (in proper cases) expenses of investigating title, and for accounts, inquiries, and (in certain kinds of case) for injunction, 209—212

RESETTLEMENT,

of family estates, arrangements for *See* FAMILY ARRANGEMENT.

RESTORATION, RESTITUTION,

mutual, *in specie,* a condition of rescission, 202, 203, 209, 210

of property or money by misfeasant, is one of the forms of relief in misfeasance proceedings, 544

RESTRICTIONS, RESTRICTIVE COVENANTS,

in head lease, &c., duty to disclose in negotiations for sub-lease, or assignment of lease, if unusual, but not, if usual, 80, 81

when presumptive knowledge of, and when not, 40—43

RESULT,

damages in prospectus cases must be shown to have been the natural, of the statutory non-disclosure, 406, 407

validity of compromise not affected by the, of subsequent litigation showing that supposed rights the subject of the surrender never existed, 108

value of property, how far question, whether fair or not, is affected by the, of subsequent sales or dealings, 463

probable, to party complaining of avoiding transaction, is immaterial to his right to avoid, 195, 323—326, 426

RETAINER,

formal, of dominant party, not necessary to establish existence of a professional relation of influence, 419, 430

RETICENCE   *See* SILENCE.

RETRANSFER, of property, in judgments for rescission, 202, 203, 209, 210

REVERSION,

of expectant, unconscionable bargains with respect to.   *See* EXPECTANT.

statutory modification of law as to sales of, 403, 404

rules for ascertaining value of, 463

REVIEW, procedure by bill of, obsolete, 516

REVOCATION,

of proposed transaction, party charged must explain to party complaining his right of—

in relations of confidence, 329

influence, 436, 437

the like duty when the party complaining is invited, or is proposing, to confirm the transaction,—

in relations of confidence, 335

influence, 447

of Crown grants for non-disclosure, 518, 519

RIGHTS,

particular, as distinguished from general principles of law, no presumptive knowledge of, 23

of way, to be disclosed in negotiation for sale of land, 80

in property, included in " property," for the purposes of statutory rules as to presumptive knowledge, 48, 49

declaration of, when made as part of judgment for rescission, 207, 208

non-recognition of, under impeached transaction, must be pleaded in defence of party complaining who sets up non-disclosure, 217, 536

of party complaining, including his right to reject, and, when made, revoke the transaction, must be fully explained to him by the party charged—

(i) when the transaction is proposed, in—

relations of confidence, 329

influence, 436, 437

(ii) when the party complaining is invited, or is proposing, to affirm or confirm the transaction, in—

relations of confidence, 335

influence, 447

offer to concede or surrender, effect of, on relief and costs.   *See* OFFER

creation of new, by statute, 467, 468

INDEX.

RIGHTS—*continued*

no new, created by enactment as to misfeasance, 542

of voting attached to special classes of shares, required by statute to be disclosed in prospectus, 484

various remedies for the enforcement of, in respect of non-disclosure and breaches of cognate duties *See* RELIEF, REMEDIES.

in sense of title to property. *See* TITLE

who may enforce, and who liable to enforcement of. *See* PARTIES.

surrender of, by way of compromise. *See* COMPROMISE.

waiver. *See* WAIVER.

of third persons. *See* THIRD PERSONS.

joint. *See* JOINT.

several. *See* SEVERAL.

as correlative to duties. *See* DUTY.

RIGHTEOUSNESS,

of the transaction, must be affirmatively established by the party charged, to rebut legal presumptions of abuse of confidence or influence. *See* PROPRIETY OF THE TRANSACTION.

RISK,

in marine insurances. *See* MARINE INSURANCE

in life and health insurances *See* LIFE AND HEALTH INSURANCE.

in fire, &c , insurances. *See* FIRE INSURANCE

fact material to inducement, though not to the, may be a fact material to be disclosed, 16, 17

effect of express contract to buy at all risks, 177—179

nothing is material to be disclosed of the existence of which the party complaining is presumed to take the. *See* KNOWLEDGE (B), (C)

no answer to claim to rescind a transaction that party charged took the, of loss, when entering into it, 195, 325, 426

ROMAN LAW, as to non-disclosure, *bona fides,* and *dolus,* 601—616

RULES,

general, of the *corpus juris,* presumptive knowledge of, 23

of equity, ignorance of, is no defence to an established claim to relief as the ground of non-disclosure, &c., 170—172, 321—323, 424, 425

principle and reason of, rather than the rule itself, is to be regarded *See* SUBSTANCE.

of pleading and discovery, in cases of non-disclosure, 534—538

of practice, in the like cases, 538—540

RUMOUR,

existence of, is a " fact," which may be material to be disclosed, 13, 14

when duty to disclose existence and nature of, and when not, 65

SACERDOTAL RELATION,

is a recognized relation of influence, 382, 383

species of, viz. relations between priest, confessor, convent, monastic order, sisterhood, preacher, &c., of any denomination, on the one side, and penitent, disciple, nun, monk, novice, postulant, &c., on the other, 384, 385

special features in the influence presumed from, 382, 383

variety of modes in which the influence springing from, may be exerted, 382

subject to the same three presumptions of influence, affirmative answers, and relief, or any other relation of influence, 385, 386, as to which presumptions, answers, and relief, *see* INFLUENCE

attitude of the lay community towards, 585, 586

Roman law as to, 608

[97]

INDEX.

SPECIFIC PERFORMANCE,
  in a discretionary form of relief, not *ex debito justitiæ*, and the grant or refusal thereof, and the conditions of either, are affected by the conduct of the parties, 144
  non disclosure is defence to action for, 214
  the burden of proof on party complaining who resists, is greater than on one who is resisting claim to rescission, 215, 216

STANNARIES, jurisdiction, Courts exercising, 533, note (*b*)

STATE (IN SENSE OF GOVERNMENT),
  duty of disclosure in case of grants obtained from, 517—521
  regulations and orders of foreign, when duty to disclose, and presumptive knowledge of, and when not, 26, 65

STATE (IN SENSE OF CONDITION). *See* CONDITION (IN SENSE OF STATE)

STATE OF MIND. *See* MENTAL.

STATEMENT,
  when non-disclosure is an implied, 6
  false *See* MISREPRESENTATION

STATEMENT OF CLAIM *See* PLEADING.

STATUS,
  of marriage *See* MARRIAGE (B).
  of infancy, coverture, &c, no duty to disclose, 142

STATUTORY,
  provisions affecting the law of non-disclosure, classified, 467, 468
  relief, general rules as to, 501—503
  law as to prospectuses *See* PROSPECTUS.
  presumptions of knowledge, 46, 48—53
  periods of limitation *See* LIMITATION
  rules as to " the holder in due course " of a negotiable instrument, 245, 246
  codification of laws as to disclosure, &c , in partnership, 306, note (*c*)
  expressions used in certain enactments considered—
    " utmost good faith," 1, 2
    " actual fraud," 54
    " honest mistake," 500, 501, 566, 567
    " void," 198, 199
  repeal of usury laws, effect of, 403
  modification of the law as to sales of reversions, 403, 404, 409, 410
  remedies, in cases of misfeasance, 544
  procedure, under Vendor and Purchaser Act, 220, 221
  " meeting " of company, 505
  jurisdiction, courts exercising, 533, 534

STOCK EXCHANGE,
  mercantile clerk, secretly gambling in differences on, liable to dismissal, 301

STOCKBROKER,
  who, in closing his client's account, secretly buys back the shares sold at an advantage to himself is liable to his client for non disclosure, 302

SUBAGENT,
  when knowledge of, is imputed to the ultimate principal, 31
  who acts for one whom he knows to be agent of the party complaining and under a fiduciary duty to him may subject himself to the same fiduciary duty to such party, 301, 357, 358

SUBJECTION. *See* INFLUENCE

INDEX.

SUBLEASE,
duty of disclosure in negotiating for, 81
included in " purchase," for purposes of the statutory law relating to disclosure
in prospectuses, 479, 480

SUBORDINATION. *See* INFLUENCE.

SUBPURCHASER,
meaning of, for the purpose of the statutory law as to disclosure of sale and
purchase transactions in prospectuses, 479, 480

SUBSCRIPTION,
of each underwriter to a marine policy of insurance is a distinct contract, 239—
241
for shares or debentures on the faith of a prospectus omitting matters required
by statute to be disclosed therein. *See* PROSPECTUS.
" the minimum," on which it is intended to go to allotment, must be disclosed
in prospectus of a company. *See* MINIMUM SUBSCRIPTION

SUBSEQUENT,
offer of shares by company for subscription, in case of, certain facts as to
previous offers are required to be disclosed in prospectus, 478
to incorporation of company, issue of prospectus, may be subject to statutory
duty of disclosure, 487
shareholders in company, or holders of an office, &c , when duty of disclosure
is owed to, as well as to existing holders. *See* FUTURE.
events. *See* SUPERVENING EVENTS

SUBSERVIENCE *See* INFLUENCE.

SUBSTANCE,
illustrations of regard paid to, rather than to mere forms or names, in determining—
whether a contract is *uberrimæ fidei*, or not, 60, 61
transaction is one of suretyship, or of insurance, 87, 88
a compromise or a release, 100
whether a " warranty " so called, is also in the nature of a condition, in
life insurance cases, 145
whether a relation is one of confidence, or not, 306, 307
influence, 369—372
whether the parties are within the relation of solicitor and client, or not,
378, 379, 419
what is an " expectancy," 404, 405
whether property is in expectation, or in possession, 406
a transaction is a contract, or a gift, 420—422
what constitutes a third person " independent " of the influence, in cases
of " influence," 442, 443
of property the subject of the contract, difference between, and the substance
of what is tendered, defeats plea of
waiver, 183, 184
like difference in answer to objection
of " completed contract," 201, 202
alteration in, when bar to rescission,
202, 203

SUBUNDERWRITING,
of shares, commission paid for, is not required by the statute to be disclosed
in prospectus, 480

SUCCESSOR,
in office, when a duty of disclosure to, as well as to the existing holder, 354

[103]

INDEX.

SUMMARY,

    procedure and relief, under the Vendor and Purchaser Act, 220, 221

                in misfeasance cases, 540—544

                in cases of sales by order of the Court, 221, 222

    jurisdiction, court of, is authorized by statute to decide certain life insurance cases involving non disclosure, 531

SUMMONS,

    under the Vendor and Purchaser Act, 220, 221

    misfeasance, 540—544

    under O 14, affidavit in answer to, alleging fraud, must state the facts with same particularity and precision as is required in a pleading, 535

SUPERIOR LEASE, when duty to disclose unusual restrictions in, 81

SUPERIORITY, SUPREMACY. *See* INFLUENCE.

SUPERVENING EVENTS,

    may impose a duty of disclosure, though none existed in the first instance, 123—130

    showing invalidity of claims surrendered on a compromise cannot invalidate the compromise, 108

    value of reversion not to be judged by, 463

    when party charged succeeds by reason only of, he may be deprived of costs, 547

SUPERVISION OF COURT,

    winding up of company under, statutory misfeasance procedure may be applied in, 541

SUPPRESSION. *See* CONCEALMENT

SURETYSHIP,

    contract of, whether strictly *uberrimæ fidei* or not, is within the principle and reason of the rule which requires disclosure to be made in negotiations for certain transactions which presuppose superior knowledge on one side, and trust on the other, 85—87

    whether duty exists in any particular case of alleged, and whether the transaction is one of, or of insurance, or of both combined (as *e g.* a " guarantee policy "), is a question of substance, 87, 88

    rule of disclosure in cases of, is the same as in others, but is necessarily applied to a more restricted area, 88, 89

    in cases of, the test is whether the undisclosed fact was, or was not, such as might naturally be expected as an element in the particular kind of guarantee which formed the subject of the negotiation, 89, 90

    non-disclosure in negotiations for, is sometimes described as implied misrepresentation, 90

    three types of, involving difference in the kind of facts to be disclosed in negotiation, viz —

        (i) *financial* where there is no duty to disclose embarrassments of the person whose credit is guaranteed, for the surety must know that this is the very reason for his being applied to, nor his misconduct or dishonesty, but an agreement, as distinct from a mere intention, to apply the cash resulting from the guarantee in discharge of an old debt must be disclosed, 90, 91

        (ii) *fidelity* where past dishonesty or misconduct, or even suspicion thereof, is material to be disclosed, but not mere irregularity, without suspicion of dishonesty, 91—93

        (iii) *guarantee of the due performance of a particular contractual obligation,* where the question of what must be disclosed depends on the exact nature of the obligation in question, 93—95

[104]

SURETYSHIP—*continued.*

duty of disclosure in negotiation comes to an end on the conclusion of the contract of, any duty still remaining (as in the case of continuing guarantees) being purely contractual, and not fiduciary, 95, 96

when an implied obligation of, is imposed on a defendant solicitor in an action for non-disclosure, &c., by an order of the Court that he do pay the plaintiff's costs if his co defendant client fails to do so, 549

liability of one who induces or leaves the dominant party in a relation of influence to obtain a contract of, from the servient party guaranteeing payment of the dominant party's debt to himself, 376, 398

when in a contract of, procured as above stated, the delay of the surety in taking proceedings may be accounted for by a reasonable belief that the dominant party has discharged the debt, 450

where an insolvent and compounding debtor procures a third person to enter into a secret contract of, with a particular creditor, whereby such person guarantees the debtor's original, or composition, debt, the transaction may be relieved against, 525, 526

SURGEON. *See* MEDICAL ATTENDANT, and MEDICAL RELATION.

"SUSPECTED" RELATIONS OF INFLUENCE,

what are, 369—372

ethical views as to, 584—588

SUSPENSE,

of relation of confidence, or influence, at the time of the impeached transaction, is a good answer, 327, 328, 428—431

SUSPICION,

mere, of *mala fides* in disposition of goods not enough to destroy title of pledgee, 51

mere, will not defeat right to rely on a registered title, 53

of illegal gaming, duty on assured to disclose facts giving rise to, in negotiations for marine insurance, 66

of dishonesty of person whose fidelity is guaranteed, facts giving rise to, need not be disclosed in negotiation for financial guarantee, but must be disclosed in negotiation for fidelity guarantee, 91—93

mere, of facts giving the party complaining a right to avoid the transaction, not enough to support a plea of affirmation, 186, 187

delay of party charged in giving explanation when such as to give rise to, on the part of the party complaining may affect the former's costs, though he escapes liability, 546, 547

"SUSTAINING THE TRANSACTION." *See* PROPRIETY OF THE TRANSACTION

TACIT. *See* SILENCE.

TAXATION OF COSTS,

relief given against solicitor on, in case of abuse of influence, 459

TECHNICAL,

"fraud," criticism of term, 557—559

in sense of formal. *See* FORMAL.

TEMPTATION,

and tendency, to evil conduct, rather than actual dishonesty in the particular case, is the foundation of the equitable rules as to disclosure and good faith, as applied to—

relations of confidence generally, 275—277

in particular, the relation between promoter and company, 290, 292
director and company, 302—304

relations of influence generally, 368, 369

in particular, the relation between solicitor and client, 377, 378

the sacerdotal relation, 382, 383

INDEX.

[109]

INDEX.

INDEX.

INDEX.

INDEX.

INDEX.

THE END

PRINTED BY WILLIAM CLOWES AND SONS, LIMITED, LONDON AND BECCLES.

CPSIA information can be obtained at www.ICGtesting.com
Printed in the USA
BVOW10s1724121113

336108BV00007B/367/P